Native American
Periodicals and Newspapers
1828–1982

Native American Periodicals and Newspapers 1828–1982

Bibliography, Publishing Record, and Holdings

Edited by
JAMES P. DANKY

Compiled by
MAUREEN E. HADY

Ann Bowles
Research Assistant

In association with the
State Historical Society of Wisconsin

Foreword by
Vine Deloria, Jr.

Greenwood Press
Westport, Connecticut • London, England

Library of Congress Cataloging in Publication Data

Main entry under title:

Native American periodicals and newspapers, 1828–1982.

"In association with the State Historical Society of
Wisconsin."
 Bibliography: p.
 Includes indexes.
 1. Indians of North America—Periodicals—Bibliography—
Union lists. 2. Indian periodicals—Bibliography—Union
lists. 3. Indian newspapers—Bibliography—Union lists.
4. Catalogs, Union—United States. I. Danky, James
Philip, 1947–   . II. Hady, Maureen E., 1952–
III. State Historical Society of Wisconsin.
Z1209.2.U5N37 1984 [E77] 016.973'0497'005   83-22579
ISBN 0-313-23773-5 (lib. bdg.)

Library of Congress Catalog Card Number: 83-22579
ISBN: 0-313-23773-5

First published in 1984

Greenwood Press
A division of Congressional Information Service, Inc.
88 Post Road West, Westport, Connecticut 06881

Printed in the United States of America

10 9 8 7 6 5 4 3 2 1

Alternative Cataloging in Publication Data

Danky, James P., 1947- editor.
 Native American periodicals and newspapers, 1828-1982:
bibliography, publishing record, and holdings. Edited by James P.
Danky. Compiled by Maureen E. Hady. Ann Bowles Research Assistant.
Westport, Connecticut, Greenwood Press, in association with the State
Historical Society of Wisconsin, 1984, copyright 1984.

 1. Native American newspapers—Bibliography—Union lists.
2. Native American periodicals—Bibliography—Union lists.
I. Wisconsin. State Historical Society. II. Hady, Maureen E.,
compiler. III. Bowles, Ann. IV. Title.
 051.016 or 970.105'016

For Lyman Copeland Draper
who first collected
Native American Periodicals and Newspapers
for the State Historical Society of Wisconsin

Contents

Illustrations

Foreword

During the sixties and early seventies whenever Indians would gather
together at conferences, the discussion would inevitably turn to the
question of gaining access to information concerning programs, funding, and
eligibility requirements. Time after time an elder would rise and in
stirring tones denounce the conspiracy that prevented Indian people in
reservation communities from finding out how things worked and where the
resources were. And time after time anxious federal bureaucrats, worried
that their programs might sink for a lack of clients, would pace the floor
attempting to devise some means whereby news of their services could be
broadcast to the people most in need.

Out of this concern came a variety of tribal newspapers and
newsletters, generally funded by federal agencies, which sought to fill this
identified need. With little training in journalistic arts, the editors of
many such newsletters simply reprinted federal press releases and copied
articles from non-Indian newspapers or from the more affluent and
informative Indian newsletters of the next reservation. Indeed, Akwasasne
Notes, that great newspaper published by the people at St. Regis Mohawk
reservation on the Canadian border, began its existence and prospered for
many years by simply rearranging articles that had previously been published
elsewhere and reproducing them in a continuous format under nationalistic
headlines. Eventually, from this perceived need of Indians, the American
Indian Press Association was formed, and for a few years it produced a
variety of good articles on events, personalities, and policies in our
nation's capital.

Sometime during the late sixties several universities began to collect
copies of the extant Indian newspapers with the idea of establishing a
national Indian archives for use by future scholars. Many of the
universities that had entered the field of Indian newspapers so
energetically suddenly and silently faded from the scene. Whether these
institutions continue to add to their collections or have moved on to other
fields now that interest in American Indians has waned remains to be seen.
Some Indian organizations also attempted to bring together a collection of
Indian newsletters and newspapers, but the storage demands for maintaining
such an archive were impossibly large; and, lacking adequate funds for
microfilming, many Indian groups gave up their efforts to become the center
for future Indian and non-Indian scholarly studies. Likewise, many
universities simply transferred their Indian newspapers to microfilm and
stopped collecting any more. Consequently, there are few places in the
United States where one can find a collection sufficiently large to be
useful to the student of contemporary Indian affairs.

In the midst of this confusion and reduction in interest, we have now
discovered the rather extensive holdings and bibliography of the State
Historical Society of Wisconsin, an institution that had been hiding its
talents under something of a bushel and has now emerged with a comprehensive
bibliography of Indian newsletters and newspapers. This collection does
more than bring together copies of contemporary newsletters produced during
the last two decades. Indeed, its collection goes back to the very earliest
newspapers of the Five Civilized Tribes and locates in a very precise manner
almost every newsletter or newspaper printed since Indians adopted the white
man's way of communication.

When I was asked to write an introduction to this collection I
balked. I did not know the extent of the lists the Historical Society had
compiled, and I was certain that this effort would be another ill-prepared
and incomplete listing--the kind that is done so often today in the name
of communication and information. There are so many bibliographies of
Indian books, articles, and reports out today that are incomplete,
inadequately prepared, and speak only to the uninformed that I was
hesitant about looking at yet another effort to bring sense and order to
this field.

On looking over the extensive listing of newsletters and newspapers
prepared by the people at Wisconsin, however, two things caught my eye.
First, this collection is amazingly complete in its listing of newspapers
produced by people in the northern part of this hemisphere. There have
been, and are today, dozens of newsletters produced by people in Alaska,
and when one thinks of the tremendous difficulty in communication and
transportation and the sparsity of educational facilities available to
people of the Arctic regions, to discover a multitude of rather regularly
published newspapers in that region of the continent is an amazing
revelation. One begins to see how and why the Alaska Natives could get
themselves organized and do such a superb job of lobbying their land
claims bill through Congress in 1971. There must not have been any
villages up there that did not have access to specific and precise
information regarding the various proposals for settlement of their claims.

The second feature I noticed was the presence of some newsletters
published by organizations that lasted only a few months--another brave
effort by Indians to communicate, which circumstances were to doom to
obscurity. I have a good collection of obscure newsletters myself which I
have studiously preserved over several changes of residence because I
realized that I might never again have access to these kinds of
publications. In checking the lists prepared by the State Historical
Society of Wisconsin, I have discovered that they have located copies of
every one of the newsletters I was so zealously hoarding against a rainy
day. This identification of obscure publications is good news indeed
because it is a characteristic of these newsletters that they contain
articles of historical importance. In their enthusiasm to communicate
with their constituents, many Indian organizations did not bother to
publish federal press releases; instead, they featured articles by
founding members of the group that articulated well the concerns of
Indians in establishing the group. Thus we have in such publications a
good indication of the issues and concerns motivating Indian people in
obscure places and at unexpected times during this century.

A good deal more might be said about this collection. The compilers
have gone to considerable effort to list the various editors of newspapers
during the course of the publication's existence. This information makes
it possible for scholars studying the role and activity of some Indians in
this century to pinpoint more precisely the role that those people played
in Indian organizations. Additionally, we are given the number of copies
that each organization actually published, making it considerably easier
to be certain that the serious researcher has covered all existing issues.
One of the most annoying aspects of research into contemporary Indian
affairs is that of searching for certain issues of a newspaper

that one <u>assumes</u> must have been published, only to discover after months
of intense searching that the editors took a vacation after volume 6,
issue number 2, and did not resume publication of the newsletter until
volume 7, which then, because of the burst of activity, had twelve
numbers, after which the newspaper again lapsed to two issues.

In surveying the incredible list of Indian newspapers and newsletters
that have been produced by Indian people during this century, one can only
conclude that it has not been access to news that has been the deficiency.
Rather it has been the interpretation of the information that has been
sadly lacking. Indians seem to know what's happening. However, they seem
to be badly handicapped in interpreting what events, policies, and
personalities really mean in their lives. If this bibliography helps us
to move from the constant demand for information to the more important
task of producing a generation of people who can <u>interpret the meaning</u> of
events for their people, we will have made a very great stride toward
determining our own futures.

Thus it is my hope, as I am certain it is the hope of the State
Historical Society of Wisconsin, that the generation of Indian students
now attending high school and college will make maximum use of this
bibliography of Indian newspapers. If they can see their own
contributions as building on an already solid tradition of communication,
we may well be able to transcend some of the perennial problems that
plague us. At least part of the difficulty every generation of Indians
encounters is the sense that no previous generation of Indians has ever
faced the problems facing that group of people. Establishing clearly the
precedents that have led us to the future is the first task in escaping
the physical and conceptual barricades that have prevented us from solving
present problems. This bibliography can be inestimable assistance to us
in helping to take that next crucial step in awareness and perception.

      Vine Deloria, Jr.
      <u>Tucson, Arizona</u>

Introduction

The development of the Native American press in North America over the last one hundred and fifty years is consistent with patterns of the general-interest press and with those of other special-interest groups. Such publications are designed to perform two functions: to communicate within a group and to communicate the views of a group to those outside of it. A few Native American publications have succeeded in doing both, for example, The Cherokee Advocate and Akwesasne Notes; but the vast majority have focused on one to the exclusion of the other. The concerns of a specific group of Native Americans such as is found on a reservation or in a particular urban area are voiced through publications such as Oneida, Lac Courte Oreilles Journal, Smoke Signals, or The Phoenix Redskin.

The need for an independent voice to communicate with the dominant white society seems clear from the perspective of today, but it was even more important in the nineteenth century. Frank Luther Mott in his History of American Magazines (5 vols., Harvard University Press, 1958-1968) makes slight mention of the Native American periodical press in this massive standard source. References to Native Americans are few and concentrate on the views of whites. While this is a distressing omission, it is consistent with the author's coverage of blacks and Hispanics. In his discussion of American periodicals prior to the Civil War, Mott notes such contributions as Byron's poem, "Traits of the Indian," which was published in The Analectic Magazine edited by Washington Irving between 1813 and 1814. The Western Review and Miscellaneous Magazine, A Monthly Publication, Devoted to Literature and Science, which was edited by William Gibbes Hunt in Lexington, Kentucky from 1819 to 1821, was noted by Mott for an interesting series on "Indian antiquities which was highly regarded by contemporaries." Of even more interest to the Review's readers, however, were stories of battles between whites and Native Americans that were gathered widely by the enterprising editor. These "Heroic and Sanguinary Conflicts with the Indians" were all written by whites, many of whom had been participants.

The Society of Friends sponsored many periodicals in the nineteenth century, including The Friend, which has been continuously published since October 13, 1827; and the conservative benevolence of such early editors as Robert Smith led to articles on Indian education and related themes. The Friends' Review (1847-1894) detailed the work of the Quakers in the West and their concern for Native Americans. The Massachusetts Quarterly Review (1847-1850) was shorter-lived; but through such well-known editors as Ralph Waldo Emerson and Theodore Parker, it provided a forum for "the better minds of the age to express their best thoughts." Among these contributions was Wendell Phillips's "The Massachusetts Indians." William Lloyd Garrison's famous abolitionist paper The Liberator (1831-1865) was instrumental in mobilizing opposition to slavery but did not extend such editorial sympathy to the cause of the Native American.

Not surprisingly, publications such as Army and Navy Journal (1863-1921) devoted space to coverage of the wars against Native Americans, especially Custer's campaign. However, even the most popular of periodicals contained articles on the West and its settlement. The Overland Monthly began publication three years after the Civil War and

continued until 1935. In its pages readers around the United States
received much of their information concerning California and the West.
Articles included General O. O. Howard's account of the Indian Wars and
tales of pioneer history including encounters with Native Americans. "The
Indian Question" was frequently discussed in the pages of the Nation
(1865-) and Harper's Weekly. Both Harper's (1857-1976) and Leslie's
Illustrated (1855-1922) featured many illustrations of whites and Native
Americans in battle. By 1899, following the Battle of Wounded Knee and
the passage of the Dawes Act of 1887, which had ceded tribal lands to
individual owners, Henry L. Dawes could answer a resounding "No" to the
question posed by his article in the Atlantic, "Have We Failed With the
Indians?" These later publications all expressed a feeling of natural
inevitability concerning the demise of the Native American similar to the
fate of the buffalo. As Harper's concluded, "The Indians were,
unfortunately, located on the Great Highway of the West."

     A partial corrective to such attitudes were those articulated by the
popular novelist Helen Hunt Jackson through Ramona (1884) and A Century of
Dishonor (1888). Her efforts at promoting reform in the treatment of
Native Americans by whites were a beginning. Kate Field's Washington
(1890-1895), subtitled "A National Independent Weekly Review," which was
published in both Chicago and Washington, DC, was a highly opinionated
journal whose purview included justice for Native Americans. Council Fire
(1878-1889), published in both Washington, DC, and Philadelphia and edited
by A. B. Meacham and T.A. and M.C. Bland, was a specific voice for Native
American rights in this period.

     For historians of journalism, the minority press in the United States
offers convenient benchmarks. For the black press there is Freedom's
Journal edited by Samuel E. Cornish and John B. Russwurm, which was first
published in New York City on March 16, 1827. El Misisipi, the first
Spanish-language newpaper published in what is today the United States,
was actually bilingual. Based on the only two extant issues edited by
William H. Johnson, it was probably first published in New Orleans in
September 1808. The style and content of each of these "firsts" is
different, but such similarities as being produced in an urban seaport
that supported other newspapers should be noted. The beginning of The
Cherokee Phoenix and Indians' Advocate is distinct from the other firsts
mentioned because of its rural location and use of a nonroman alphabet.
The Cherokee Phoenix was first published on February 21, 1828, in New
Echota, Georgia, located in the northwest part of that state near
present-day Calhoun. Like El Misisipi, The Cherokee Phoenix was a
bilingual paper with articles in both English and Cherokee using the
eighty-six-character alphabet developed by Sequoyah.

     Newspapers have a greater effect on public opinion than do
periodicals because of their immediacy. However, they lack the
opportunity for reflection and cannot delay reacting to events because
deadlines have to be met. The periodical press is more oriented toward
features than rapidly developing news items. That is, the articles in a
periodical can investigate a topic to a depth that is less common in
newspapers. Thus newspapers have been the more important voice in
formulating the opinion of the white community concerning Native
Americans. Studies of Native American-white relations abound, including
many that have relied on the press for their evidence. However, the very

breadth of the subject and the vast amount of evidence have appeared as
barriers to both scholars and lay people interested in the subject.
Pagans in Our Midst (1982?) by Andre Lopez is a recent compendium of
newspaper accounts of Native Americans published in local white
newspapers. Drawn from six newspapers published in small communities of
western New York and southern Ontario (communities including Salamanca,
Malone, Massena, and Cornwall), with additional material from two Syracuse
newspapers, this selection of edited reprints is a detailed condemnation
of the triumph of white racism over the peoples of the Six Nations. Lopez
suggests that the history of the Six Nations is a microcosm of Indian
culture as presented by journalists of the day. The Seneca and Mohawk
peoples' interaction with white culture between 1885 and 1910 is shown
through the reprinted articles that rarely offer the Native American point
of view. Perhaps M. A. Wadsworth, writing in the Cattaragus Republican in
1888, would agree with Lopez about the area tribes serving as a microcosm.
In the February 24 issue Wadsworth noted:

>   I have lived for 25 years past, with unimportant
> exceptions, in towns adjoining or near either the Cattaragus
> or Allegany reservations, and am fully as well prepared to
> speak upon the subject as anyone that has preceded me in this
> discussion. Allegany and Cattaraugus Indians are not unlike
> those of several other tribes whose customs and conditions I
> have had an opportunity to observe.
>   As a rule they are devoid of integrity, lazy and
> shiftless, and Pagan and Christian, ignorant and educated, men
> and women, without honor and virtue.

The characterization of the white newspaper presented in Pagans in
Our Midst is a thesis that historians of journalism and others can
continue to investigate and debate. However, the decline of the
Native American population and culture during the eighteenth,
nineteenth, and twentieth centuries must be taken as evidence while
the press provides the stimulus and justification.

This review of white writings on Native Americans in the
nineteenth and early twentieth centuries and of scholarly perception
of those writings is necessary to an understanding of the development
of Native American publications designed for both internal and
external communication. For it is difficult to believe that a
significant presentation of Native American views was possible through
white writers or white publications. Further, by 1900 there was
already a rich tradition of the Native American press more than
seventy years old. In 1978 when the Native American press celebrated
its 150th anniversary, the greatest number of Native American
periodicals and newspapers to be published at any time was currently
available. From a single title published by Elias Boudinot in
Georgia, in 1828, The Cherokee Phoenix and Indians' Advocate, today
there are hundreds of Native American publications published in nearly
every state and province in North America.

In the parable of the keys a man is seen crawling around on the
sidewalk under a street lamp. A passerby asks him what he is doing
and the man on the ground says, "I'm looking for my car keys." The

passerby asks him where he thinks he lost, them and the crawler points
back down the darkened street and says, "Over there, by my car." The
passerby is puzzled by this response and only further confused when
the first man adds by way of explanation, "But this is where the light
is."

In a serious sense this can be seen as an analogy of the
relationship between bibliographic work and and scholarly analysis.
While the former does not always, or sometimes cannot, precede the
latter, it nevertheless does seem true that when an important,
high-quality bibliography is published it often can produce profound
results as evidenced in the scholarly monographs that follow. This
process is reciprocal. Scholars investigating a narrow area can
provide the bibliographer with new information about the area as well
as challenging them to produce ever more useful works, works that
encompass more than the scholar's particular topic.

There is no necessary relationship between bibliographers and
their works and the books and articles of analysis produced by
scholars. However, this relationship is an area worthy of discussion
and research by librarians and others, particularly in an era of
emphasis on publishing for librarians. In a positive sense it seems
that a bibliography, especially a detailed directory-like work such as
this one, provides more opportunity for the scholar doing synthesis.
Critics could fault such discussions by noting that a scholar might
not care about the totality of a subject field. A cynical critic
could note that a scholar might feel that no one, or virtually no one,
knows much about the field and that additional examples are not really
important. It still seems that a bibliography ought to proceed, ought
to form the foundation, of analysis. Otherwise, one surely has the
proverbial cart before the proverbial horse. Without an existing,
high quality bibliography scholars are left with a random sampling of
materials and a greater chance of a flawed sampling.

A bibliography is the humus on the forest floor. It is a crucial
element, fundamental to the creation of a synthesis. The one
exception might be the scholar working to create a synthetic account
in an area that is so limited and uncharted that no works are
available to guide, and that in this process a bibliography is
created. This is a rare occurrence. Far more common is the situation
where a scholar needs a bibliography that does not exist. The
necessity for a bibliography increases in proportion to the amount of
appropriate materials, especially when the available items are too
voluminous for one individual to examine. This is the point at which
a bibliography can play an important role. Perhaps this portion of
the introduction should be aimed at grantors, private foundations and
the government; for they should consider funding bibliographic work in
an area prior to funding scholarship by those who need the
bibliographies. The efficiency of this method seems obvious.

This bibliography had its origins in discussions among staff
members in the Newpapers and Periodicals Unit of the State Historical
Society of Wisconsin Library. During the 1970s and 1980s the Unit had
produced various bibliographies and union lists of periodical
literature, including Undergrounds (1974), Asian American Periodicals

and Newspapers (1979), and Women's Periodicals and Newspapers (1982).
Each publication attempted to create a more comprehensive and detailed
description of titles while also attempting to include a wider range
of libraries.

Native American Periodicals and Newspapers was created with funds
provided by the Wisconsin Department of Public Instruction's Division
for Library Services. The Unit applied for a grant of $52,214 under
the Library Services and Construction Act, Title III, which provided
the money to hire staff. James Danky, the Society's Newspapers and
Periodicals Librarian, served as project director and hired Maureen
Hady as project librarian and Ann Bowles as research assistant. In
addition, valuable assistance was provided by Barry Noonan and Cliff
Bass, especially in creating an automated system. The grant period
was originally October 1981 through September 1982, though a one month
extension was later granted.

The project, "Native Americans: Library Resources in Wisconsin,"
comprised three elements in addition to the compilation of a
bibliography of periodicals and newspapers. On April 22 and 23, 1982,
the State Historical Society of Wisconsin, along with the Library
School and the School of Journalism and Mass Communications of the
University of Wisconsin-Madison, sponsored a conference on the Native
American Press in Wisconsin and the nation. The conference drew
people from as distant as Wyoming and provided an opportunity for
editors and scholars to exchange ideas. The proceedings were
published by the University of Wisconsin-Madison Library School and
include a complete, edited account of the two days. "Framed with two
papers on Native American discourse, the conference transcripts
include others on journalism and journalists from Georgia to Alaska,
and from the early 19th century to the present" (Minnesota History,
Spring 1983). Practicing journalists, especially from the mainstream
press, were urged by the Columbia Journalism Review (May/June 1983) to
spend an hour with the proceedings as a way to "getting the
professional peace pipe started."

A series of workshops for librarians and archivists was held in
Milwaukee and Wausau in the spring of 1982 to familiarize people with
Native American materials. In addition to providing an account of the
conference and bibliographic work, the staff of "Native Americans:
Library Resources in Wisconsin" offered descriptions of the Society's
monographic and government publication holdings and a presentation of
the creation of the index to Wisconsin Native American publications.
Several speakers talked about archives, from an account of the
Winnebago tribal archives to descriptions of Wisconsin and national
Native American tribal archives training programs. The work of public
libraries and the Native American community was described by staff
members from Milwaukee Public Library and the Division for Library
Services. The workshops acquainted librarians and others with the
richness of human and published resources about Native Americans in
Wisconsin, information that they can use at their own institutions.

The third element was the creation of a name index to Native
American Peroidicals published in Wisconsin. Barry Christopher
Noonan, who has been responsible for the automation of the index to

the Wisconsin Magazine of History and the motivating force behind the
1905 Wisconsin State Census Index, determined the parameters to be
indexed and created the design for the computer. Ann Bowles did much
of the indexing of the Wisconsin titles drawn from the bibliographic
work done by Maureen Hady. This effort resulted in the Index to
Wisconsin Native American Periodicals, 1897-1981 (which was published
in microfiche by Greenwood Press). The Index contains over 44,000
entries drawn from a close examination of thirty-one periodical
titles. While the bulk of the titles indexed date from the period
1960-1981, Oneida and Anishinabwe Enamiad extend the work back into
the nineteenth century. The Index is the largest name index to Native
American periodicals in existence and should prove invaluable to
historians, genealogists, sociologists, and lawyers.

The present work, Native American Periodicals and Newspapers,
1828-1982, is a guide to the holdings and locations of 1,164
periodical and newspaper titles by and about Native Americans.
Information included in this work was gained through the examination
of every issue of every title by the project librarian, Maureen Hady,
or through the good offices of colleagues in libraries all over North
America. It includes older titles that have long since ceased
publication as well as those still being published. The scope of the
guide is broad, covering literary, political, and historical journals
as well as general newspapers and feature magazines. This guide is
the most extensive ever compiled, and its titles represent many phases
of Native American thought and action, from the religious and
educational press of the early nineteenth century to contemporary
publications of the current Native American movements. The intention
was to create a primary bibliography, not a secondary one. It is not
intended to be an historical account but rather a description of those
titles still in existence. Thus, works that make use of sources
beyond the issues themselves may offer information that is different
from that indicated here. The guide was prepared in order to assist
faculty and students who find it difficult to do research in this
area, as well as for Native Americans who are actively seeking their
past. We hope that the publication will facilitate the use of such
collections by scholars and others so that the Native American press
can be more fully understood, the ultimate aim being that Native
American concerns and views become an integral part of all discourse.

Methodologically, the bibliography was developed from a detailed
description of the periodical and newspaper holdings of the State
Historical Society of Wisconsin's Library. Since 1974, the Newspapers
and Periodicals Unit has been keeping a monthly list of new titles
added to its collection. This provided the basis from which Hady
created a list of Native American titles acquired since 1974. From
this list of titles, the public catalogs were searched for additional
holdings. Beyond this, microfilm of manuscript collections in the
Society and other repositories were examined for periodical and
newspaper issues and those were described. Included were the papers
of John Collier, Carlos Montezuma, Veda Stone, the Indian Rights
Association, and others. During the course of the yearlong project,
Clearwater Publishing of New York contacted the Unit about including
the Society's holdings as part of their Native American periodicals
microfiche and film project. By agreeing to contribute missing issues

and unique titles, the Society received a gratis copy of the entire
series, all of which is described in this bibliography.

For each title in the bibliography held by the Society, other
libraries in Wisconsin, the Newberry, and the National Library of
Canada, all issues have been examined. As for other reporting
institutions, they completed extensive work forms which were checked
as thoroughly as possible. Only through this labor-intensive approach
could a complete list of editors, title changes, and so forth be
obtained. In addition, during the grant period, we attempted to send
a copy of the completed citation to the editor of each currently
published title for review. At this time, we also requested that they
select a favorite or representative cover from their publication and
give us permission to use it as an illustration for this volume. The
cooperation of the Native American editors was most valuable and
served to remind us of the importance of the audience for this work
beyond that of academia. Of the 1,164 titles included in this work
823, or 71 percent, are held by the Society. The second largest
collection we identified, at Princeton University, has 304, or 26
percent. Thus, the preeminence of the Society's collection greatly
facilitated the work.

The cooperation of librarians in Madison and in every state in the
United States and each Canadian province was essential to this
compilation. Several librarians provided exemplary service that far
exceeded the boundaries of the ordinary. These include Mrs. C. F.
Gutch, Historical Committee, United Church of Christ of South Dakota;
Edith Ostrowsky, New York Public Library; Minnie Paugh, Montana State
University; Eugene D. Decker, Kansas State Historical Society; Carol
Ruppe, Arizona State University; Nancy Myers, University of South
Dakota; Daryl Morrison, University of Oklahoma; Ruth M. Christensen,
Southwest Museum Library; Marvin E. Pollard, Jr., Navajo Community
College; Phyllis DeMuth, Alaska Historical Library; David Farmer,
University of Tulsa; Joyce Ann Tracy, American Antiquarian Society;
Sedelta Verble, OHOYO Resource Center; Annette Bradley, Laurentian
University; Robin Minion, Boreal Institute for Northern Studies; Laura
Neame, Fraser Valley College; Lindsay Moir, Glenbow-Alberta Institute;
Diane Rudzevicius, Department of Indian Affairs and Northern
Development Library; Alfred Fisher, Sandra Burrows, and P. M.
Matheson, National Library of Canada; and David A. Hales, University
of Alaska at Fairbanks. Local librarians who were familiar with our
bibliographic projects continued to offer their support. Especially
helpful in this compilation were Bill Bunce, Kohler Art Library; Sally
Davis, Library School; Jane Doyle, College Library; Thurston Davini,
Social Work Library; Jo Ann Carr, School of Education IMC; William
Ebbott, Law Library; Marcia Griskovich, Criminal Justice Center;
Lenore Coral, Music Library; Janice Beaudin, Winnebago Research
Project. Other cooperative librarians throughout Wisconsin include
Gail Brown, Milwaukee Public Library; Nancy O. Lurie and Patricia
Laughlin, Milwaukee Public Museum; Edie Bjorkland and Louise Diodato,
University of Wisconsin-Milwaukee; Wilber Stolt and Stanley Mallach,
University of Wisconsin-Milwaukee Area Research Center; Phil Bantin
and Mark Thiel, Marquette University; Barbara Baruth, University of
Wisconsin-Kenosha-Parkside; Leslie Polk, Journalism Department,
University of Wisconsin-Eau Claire; Rick Peiffer, Eau Claire Area

Research Center; Dorothy Hanrich, Green Bay Area Research Center; Jennifer Tillis, University of Wisconsin-Green Bay; Richard Glazier, University of Wisconsin-Green Bay, Native American Studies Department; Ramona Koch and Mary Jane Herber, Brown County Library; Arthur M. Fish, Stevens Point Area Research Center; Al Barrows, University of Wisconsin-Stevens Point; Mary Alice Tsosie, University of Wisconsin-Stevens Point Native American Center; and Nadine Hindsley, Wisconsin Indian Resource Council, Stevens Point. The large number of holdings as well as the identification of some particularly obscure local publications could not have been done without the great number of librarians who surveyed their respective institutions and replied. Space does not allow the naming of each of the hundreds of people and institutions throughout the United States and Canada who have contributed their time and good will to this project.

In addition to those named above, Daniel F. Littlefield and James W. Parins provided assistance in identifying and locating titles while doing research for their historical guide to the Native American press (American Indian and Alaska Native Newspapers and Periodicals, Greenwood Press, 1984). Many materials were exchanged during the course of the project, but, beyond that, we reaped the benefits of both their scholarship and professionalism.

Sanford Berman, Head Cataloger of the Hennepin County Library in Edina, Minnesota, and author of The Joy of Cataloging (Phoenix, Oryx Press, 1981), reviewed the subject terms and provided the alternative cataloging in publication information. His support and companionship were invaluable just as they were when he performed similar tasks for our previous bibliographies on Asian American, Hispanic American, and Women's periodicals.

As we plan to update this bibliography and union list periodically, we would appreciate comments or suggestions for additional information or titles. Please submit them to James P. Danky, Newspapers and Periodicals Librarian, State Historical Society of Wisconsin, 816 State Street, Madison, Wisconsin 53706, telephone (608) 262-9584.

How to Use the Bibliography

The arrangement of this union list is alphabetical.
An explanation of the standard entry format follows.

[1]27   [2]Akwesasne Notes. [3]1969. [4]6 times a year. [5]$8. for
individuals and institutions. [6]John Mohawk, editor, Akwesasne
Notes, Rooseveltown, NY 13683. [7](518) 358-9531. [8]ISSN
0002-3949. [9]LC sn78-4955. [10]OCLC 1478885, 2257108,
[11]RLIN COSG19541287-S, UTUL1522-S, [12]Last issue 32 pages,
[13]Height 36 cm. [14]Line drawings, photographs. [15]Indexed in:
Alternative Press Index (1969-). [16]Available in microform: McA
(1969-); McP (1969-1973); UnM (1969-); WHi (1969-); Y (1969-).
[17]Published by Mohawk Nation. [18]Frequency varies: monthly,
Apr, 1969-Aug, 1972; [19]Previous editors: Jerry Gambill
(Rarichokwats), Apr, 1969-Oct, 1970; Rarichokwats and
Ateronhiatakon, Jan, 1971;... Some issues contain Longhouse News
(the official publication of the Mohawk Nation at Kanawake).
[20]Subject focus: rights, legislation, politics, socio-economic
conditions, education, health, women's rights, culture, religion,
poetry, ecology, ethnocide, Third World Folk peoples.

[21]WHi	[v.1, n.?]– April, 1969–	Microforms
WEU	[v.3, n.8–v.8, n.9] [Autumn, 1971–Summer, 1971]	Journalism Lab
Az	v.4, n.3–v.12, n.4; 1972–Autumn, 1980	Periodicals
ICN	Current issues	CHAI
CaOONL	v.3– 1970–	Periodicals

[22]Other holding institutions: ARU (AFU), [Amerind Foundation,
Inc., Dragoon, AZ], AzFU (AZN), AzTeS (AZS), CBaS (CBA), CChiS
(CCH),

1. Entry number.
2. Title (most recent title in the case of publications with various
   titles).
3. Year(s) publication began and/or ceased.
4. Frequency (most recent frequency in the case of publications with
   varying schedules).
5. Subscription rates for individuals and institutions (currently
   published titles only).
6. Current editor and editorial address.
7. Telephone number.

8. International Standard Serials Number (ISSN).
9. Library of Congress catalog card number.
10. OCLC, Inc. control number (cataloging record).
11. RLIN control number (cataloging record).
12. Number of pages in last issue and/or volume examined.
13. Height of last issue examined.
14. Indication if the title contains any of the following: line drawings, photographs, commercial advertising, and if any of these are in color.
15. Indication of where the title is indexed and for what period. (See list of "Indexes Included in this Compilation" following.)
16. Indication if the title is availble in microform and for what period. (See "Sources for the Purchase of Microfilm" following for interpretation of codes.)
17. Publisher(s).
18. Variations in title, place of publication, and/or frequency.
19. Previous editors.
20. Subject focus.
21. Library holding the title, volumes and issues and/or dates held, location within library.
    Wisconsin libraries are listed first, followed by other U.S. libraries and then Canadian libraries. (See "Libraries Included in this Compilation" following for interpretation of codes.)
22. Other holding institutions, National Union Catalogue symbol (OCLC participant symbol).

An indication of language or languages (other than English) is also included.

The main alphabetical listing, which contains all of the title variants, is followed by indexes to subjects, editors, publishing organizations, a geographical index arranged alphabetically by state and city, then by title, a catchword and subtitle index, and a chronological index.

Indexes Included in This Compilation

Abstracts in Anthropology. Farmingdale, New York: Baywood Publishing
Co., Inc.

Abstracts of Health Care Management Studies. Ann Arbor, Michigan:
Health Administration Press for the Cooperative Information Center
for Health Care Management Studies, The University of Michigan.

Alternative Press Index. Baltimore, Maryland: Alternative Press
Center.

America: History and Life. Santa Barbara, California: American
Bibliographical Center-Clio Press.

Book Review Index. Detroit Michigan: Gale Research Co.

Current Index to Journals in Education (CIJE). New York, New York:
CCM Information Sciences.

Educational Administration Abstracts. Columbus, Ohio: University
Council for Educational Administration.

Education Index. Bronx, New York: H.W. Wilson Co.

Index to Literature on the American Indian. San Francisco,
California: The Indian Historian Press, Inc.

Index to Periodical Articles By and About Negros. Boston, Massachusetts:
G.K. Hall.

Index to Wisconsin Native American Periodicals. Westport,
Connecticut: Greenwood Press in association with the State
Historical Society of Wisconsin (Microfiche, 1984).

MLA International Bibliography. New York, New York: Modern Language
Association of America.

Public Affairs Information Service Bulletin. New York, New York:
Public Affairs Information Service, Inc.

Psychological Abstracts. Lancaster, Pennsylvania: American
Psychological Abstracts.

RADAR (Repertoire Analytique d'Articles de Revues du Quebec).
Montreal, Quebec: Bibliotheque Nationale du Quebec.

Social Work Research & Abstracts. New York, New York: National
Association of Social Workers.

Sources for the Purchase of Microfilm

AkUF   Elmer E. Rasmuson Library
U of Alaska-Fairbanks
Fairbanks, AK 99701

BHP   Brookhaven Press
Division of Northern
   Micrographics
2004 Kramer St.,
P.O. Box 1653
La Crosse, WI 54601

BNN   British Library
(Newspaper Library)
Colindale Ave.
London, NW9 5HE England

CanLA   Canadian Library Assn.
151 Sparks Street
Ottawa, Ontario, K1P 5E3
Canada

CPC   Clearwater Publishing Co.
1995 Broadway, Room 400
New York, N.Y. 10023

DLC   Library of Congress
Photoduplication Service
Dept. C, 10 First St. SE
Washington, D.C. 20540

LM   Library Microfilms
737 Loma Verde Ave.
Palo Alto, CA 94303

McA   Microfilming Corp.
   of America
21 Harristown Rd.
Glen Rock, N.J. 07452

McL   McLaren Micropublishing
   Limited
P.O. Box 972, Station F
Toronto, Ontario, M4Y 2N9
Canada

McP   Bell & Howell
Micro Photo Division
P.O. Box 774
Wooster, OH 44691

MCR   Microfilm Recording Co.
102 Rivalda Rd.
Weston, Ontario, M9M 2M8
Canada

MML   Micromedia Ltd.
144 Front St. West
Toronto, Ontario, M5J 2L7
Canada

MRP   Micropublishers
   International
99 Madison Ave.,
17th floor
New York, N.Y. 10016

NN   New York Public Library
Photographic Service
Room 101,
5th Ave. & 42nd St.
New York, N.Y. 10018

OkHi   Oklahoma Historical
   Society
Division of Library
Resources
Historical Bldg.
2100 North Lincoln Blvd.
Oklahoma City, OK 73105

RM   Readex Microprint Corp.
101 5th Ave.
New York, N.Y. 10003

SBC   Historical Commission
Southern Baptist
   Convention
127 Ninth Ave. North
Nashville, TN 37234

SOC   Canadian Microfilming Co.
468 rue Saint-Jean,
Suite 10
Montreal, Quebec, H2Y 2SI
Canada

U   Perpetual Storage, Inc.
3322 South 300 East
Salt Lake City, UT 84115

UnM   University Microfilms
        International
        300 N. Zeeb Rd.
        Ann Arbor, MI 48106

WaU   University of Washington
        Libraries
        Curator of Manuscripts
        Seattle, WA 98105

WHi   State Historical Society
        of Wisconsin
        Library
        816 State St.
        Madison, WI 53706

WHi-A   State Historical Society
        of Wisconsin
        Archives Division
        816 State St.
        Madison, WI 53706

WSH   William S. Hein & Co.
        Hein Building,
        1285 Main St.
        Buffalo, N.Y. 14209

Y   Kraus Microforms
        Rte. 100
        Millwood, N.Y. 10546

Libraries Included in This Compilation

Wisconsin Libraries

WHi   State Historical Society of Wisconsin, Madison

WEU	University of Wisconsin-Eau Claire
WGr	Brown County Library, Green Bay
WGrU	University of Wisconsin-Green Bay
WIRC	Wisconsin Indian Resource Council, Stevens Point
WKenU	University of Wisconsin-Parkside, Kenosha
WM	Milwaukee Public Library, Milwaukee
WMaPI-RL	Reference and Loan, Madison
WMM	Marquette University, Milwaukee
WMMus	Milwaukee Public Museum Library, Milwaukee
WMSC	Mount Senario College, Ladysmith
WMUW	University of Wisconsin-Milwaukee
WNC	Northland College, Ashland
WOsh	Oshkosh Public Library, Oshkosh
WOshU	University of Wisconsin-Oshkosh
WRfC	University of Wisconsin-River Falls
WU	University of Wisconsin-Madison
WU/Coll	University of Wisconsin-Madison, College Library
WU-L	University of Wisconsin-Madison, Law School
WU-LS	University of Wisconsin-Madison, Library School
WUSP	University of Wisconsin-Stevens Point

Other United States Libraries

AkAML	Anchorage Municipal Libraries, Anchorage, AK
AkBC	Alaska Bible College, Glenallen, AK
AkHi	Alaska Historical Library, Juneau, AK
AkUF	Elmer Rasmuson Library, University of Alaska, Fairbanks, AK
Az	State Department of Library and Archives, Phoenix, AZ
AzAIBI	American Indian Bible Institute, Phoenix, AZ
AzFM	Museum of Northern Arizona, Flagstaff, AZ
AzHC	Arizona Heritage Center, Tucson, AZ
AzHM	Heard Museum, Phoenix, AZ
AzNCC	Navajo Community College, Tsaile, AZ
AzPa	City of Page Public Library, Page, AZ
AzPh	Phoenix Public Library, Phoenix, AZ
AzT	Tucson Public Library, Tucson, AZ
AzTeS	Arizona State University, Tempe, AZ
AzU	The University of Arizona, Tucson, AZ
CAz	Azuza City Library, Azuza, CA
CBri	Mono County Free Library, Bridgeport, CA
CCarm	Ralph Chandler Harrison Memorial Library, Carmel, CA
CL	Los Angeles Public Library, Los Angeles, CA
CLSM	Southwest Museum Library, Los Angeles, CA

CoCF   Colorado Springs Fine Arts Center, Colorado Spring, CO
CoKIM   Koshere Indian Museum Library, La Junta, CO
CRSSU   Sonoma State University, Rohnert Park, CA
CSmarP   Palomar College, San Marcos, CA
CtY-B   Yale University, Beinecke Library, New Haven, CT
CU-A   University of California-Davis, Davis, CA
CU-B   University of California-Berkeley-Bancroft Library,
           Berkeley, CA
IaHi   Iowa State Historical Society, Iowa City, IA
IC   Chicago Public Library, Chicago, IL
ICN   Newberry Library, Chicago, IL
IdB   Boise Public Library, Boise, ID
IdHi   Idaho Historical Society Library, Boise, ID
IdU   University of Idaho, Moscow, ID
KHi   Kansas State Historical Society, Topeka, KS
KU   University of Kansas-Lawrence, KS
L   Louisiana State Library, Baton Rouge, LA
LARC   Amistad Research Center, New Orleans, LA
Me   Maine State Library, Augusta, ME
MeUC   Unity College, Unity, ME
MHP   Peabody Museum, Harvard University, Cambridge, MA
Mi   Michigan State Library-Lansing, MI
MiU   University of Michigan, Ann Arbor, MI
MnBemT   Bemidji State University, Bemidji, MN
MnKRL   Kitchigami Regional Library, Pine River, MN
MoHi   State Historical Society of Missouri, Columbia, MO
MoS   St. Louis Public Library, MO
MoSHi   Missouri Historical Society, St. Louis, MO
MtBBCC   Blackfeet Community College, Browning, MT
MtBC   Montana State University, Bozeman, MT
MtGrCE   College of Great Falls Library, Great Falls, MT
MtHi   Montana Historical Society Library, Helena, MT
MtLD   Dull Knife Memorial College, Lame Deer, MT
MWA   American Antiquarian Society, Worcester, MA
N   New York State Library, Albany, NY
NbJAM   Joslyn Art Museum, Omaha, NE
NbU   University of Nebraska, Lincoln, NE
NCBE   National Clearinghouse for Bilingual Education, Rosslyn, VA
NcMhC   Mars Hills College, Mars Hills, NC
NcP   Pembroke State University, Pembroke, NC
NdFySR   Standing Rock Community College, Fort Yates, ND
NdMinS   Minot State College, Minot, ND
NHu   Huntington Public Library, New York, NY
NjMonM   The Montclair Art Museum, Montclair, NJ
NjNM   Newark Museum, Newark, NJ
NjP   Princeton University, Princeton, NJ
NmF   Farmington Public Library, Farmington, NM
NmScW   Western New Mexico University, Silver City, NM
NN   New York Public Library, New York, NY
NOneoU   Hartwick College, Oneonta, NY
NPotU   State University of New York College at Potsdam, Potsdam, NY
NvLV   Dickinson Library, University of Nevada, Las Vegas, NV
NvWNCC   Western Nevada Community College, Carson City, NV
OCHP   Cincinnati Historical Society, Cincinnati, OH
OClWHi   Western Reserve Historical Society, Cleveland, OH
OCU   University of Cincinnati, Cincinnati, OH

OkHi   Oklahoma Historical Society, Oklahoma City, OK
OkPAC   Philbrook Art Center, Tulsa, OK
OkSa   Sapulpa Public Library, Sapulpa, OK
OkT   Tulsa City County Library, Tulsa, OK
OkTahN   Northeastern State University, Tahlequah, OK
OkTG   Thomas Gilcrease Institute of American History and Art,
            Tulsa, OK
OkTU   University of Tulsa-McFarlin Library, Tulsa, OK
OkU   University of Oklahoma, Western History Collection,
            Norman, OK
Or   Oregon State Library, Salem, OR
OrHi   Oregon Historical Society, Portland, OR
OrJM   Southern Oregon Historical Society, Jacksonville Museum,
            Jacksonville, OR
OrU   University of Oregon, Eugene, OR
PCarlH   Cumberland County Historical Society, Carlisle, PA
PCCe   Cedar Crest College, Allentown, PA
PP   Free Library of Philadelphia, Philadelphia, PA
PPT   Temple University, Philadelphia, PA
SdHRC   State of South Dakota, Historical Resource Center,
            Pierre, SD
SdSifA   Center for Western Studies, Augustana College,
            Sioux Falls, SD
SdU   University of South Dakota, Vermillion, SD
SdYC   Yankton College, Yankton, SD
TxU   University of Texas at Austin, Austin, TX
UHi   Utah State Historical Society, Salt Lake City, UT
UPB   Brigham Young University, Provo, UT
USUSC   Southern Utah State College, Cedar City, UT
Wa   Washington State Library, Olympia, WA
WaOE   Evergreen State College, Olympia, WA
WaO-L   Washington State Law Library, Olympia, WA
WaS   Seattle Public Library, Seattle, WA
WaU   University of Washington, Seattle, WA
WyCWC   Central Wyoming College, Riverton, WY
WyU   University of Wyoming, Laramie, WY

Canadian Libraries

CaACG   Glenbow Museum Library, Calgary, Alberta
CaAEU   University of Alberta-Boreal Institute for Northern Studies,
            Edmonton, Alberta
CaBAbF   Fraser Valley College, Abbotsford, British Columbia
CaBViP   Provincial Archives of British Columbia, Victoria,
            British Columbia
CaMWU   The University of Manitoba, Winnipeg, Manitoba
CaNBFU   University of New Brunswick, Harriet Irving Library,
            Fredrickton, New Brunswick
CaNfSM   Memorial University of Newfoundland, St. Johns,
            Newfoundland
CaOAFN   Assembly of First Nations, Ottawa, Ontario
CaOAUC   Algoma University College, Sault Ste. Marie, Ontario

The American Indian Baptist Voice

Volume XXVIII   January-February 1982   Number 1

First Indian Baptist Phoenix Receives Building

The First Indian Baptist Church of Phoenix, Arizona, under the leadership of Rev. and Mrs. Victor Kaneubbe as missionaries, has moved into another and more adequate building. A non-Indian church in Phoenix disbanded and turned its building over to First Indian.

On Oct. 25, 1981 a joint service was held and the pastor of the disbanding church turned the keys of the buildings over to Rev. Kaneubbe. The service was both joyful and sad, but all were glad that the building would continue to be used for reaching the lost.

On November 1, the first Indian Baptist Church moved into the buildings. The Sanctuary seats 250, and First Indian church expects to soon grow to fill it.

Mississippi Choctaws

Stewardship and Evangelism are being emphasized by the chairmen in the Mississippi Choctaw Association. Rev. Dalton Haggan, Missionary, Stewardship Chairman, has urged the churches to have a tithers' commitment day. The first Sunday in January was suggested.

Rev. Clay Gibson, Evangelism Chairman and able Native minister, has recommended that January 10, be Witness commitment day.

Mattie Ann Thompson, Associational Youth Director, will lead the Youth Council in planning future Youth Activities at a meeting in January.

Rhodes is Director of IHS

A Kiowa Indian graduate of the University of Oklahoma Medical School has been appointed Director of Indian Health Service. Dr. Everett Rhodes, a native of Lawton, Okla., will assume his duties in Washington, D.C. February 1, 1982.

Dr. Rhodes succeeds Dr. Emery Johnson who has been Director since 1969.

Building in Billings

Rev. and Mrs. Jack Coward, Catalytic missionaries in Montana continue to see exciting things happen. Recently a building in Billings was purchased. It will be used for Indians, Spanish, and Asian.

The Cowards work, not only with the Indians but also with other Ethnic groups. And as rapidly as practical develop and encourage Native leadership to go forward in the work. they were recently surprised to find that 300 Laotians had moved into Billings.

Whitakers to Establish Church

Rev. and Mrs. Paul Whitaker of Tulsa, Okla. recently became General Missionaries with the Indians in the Tulsa Area. Previously they had served with the Indians in western Oklahoma and more recently with the Bowen Indian chapel in Tulsa.

The Whitakers hope to establish ten new churches in the near future. They are getting acquainted with the people and the area with their Good Times Wagon and their Mobile Chapel. The Mobile Chapel seats sixty and serves as a meeting place and classroom. the Good Times Wagon has a basketball backstop and a puppet stage.

NCAI Officers

Officers elected at the National Congress of American Indians meeting in Anchorage, Alaska in October 1981 include:

President—Joseph DeLaCruz, a Quinault Indian from Washington state.

Vice-President—Ralph L. Eluska, Anchorage, Alaska.

Treasurer—Hollis Stabler, an Omaha Indian, Macy, Neb.

Secretary—Ella Mae Horse, Oklahoma Cherokee, now in Washington, D.C.

2. Cover page, January-February 1982, courtesy of *The American Indian Baptist Voice*.

AMERICAN INDIAN EDUCATION NEWSLETTER
Wisconsin Department of Public Instruction
Barbara Thompson, Ph.D., State Superintendent
125 South Webster Street
Madison, WI 53702

Editor: Roger R. Philbrick, Supervisor
American Indian Education Program

Vol. 3, No. 1,
Fall, 1980

AMERICAN INDIAN TRIBAL HISTORIES –

Communication by any group or race of peoples has meant the destruction or survival of that culture. Since the beginning of time man and his cultures have come and gone. Today, of world cultures, the respective American Indian tribes rank among the oldest known. We all know something of the great flood which covered the earth and the great ice ages covering Europe, Asia, North America, etc. The American Indian speaks of the flood, the ice age and man's relationship to all the things animate and inaminate in his history.

Passing down understandings and values, by word of mouth through oral histories, has been used the world over. Present-day courts in the United States have accepted oral histories as expert testimony. Other examples of oral histories are the story of the people of the Island of Crete and of course the lost city of Atlantis. Scientists have proven the Cretan existence and the shifting of the ocean floor under Europe is an accepted fact. However, the respective stories of the American Indian tribes and their beginnings have yet to be known and sometimes accepted in today's public educational systems.

If one were to visit Germany, one would see that the histories of the American Indians of North America are taught in every school and the libraries are stocked with American Indian resource materials. Yet, there are still public schools in the United States who refer to the American Indian as heathens and savages. I am continually asked if American Indians still live in teepees and wear feathers, etc. To think that year one is when Columbus discovered America is a recognition of the American Indian as a non-people. Yet to see the American Indian foods, government, use of the land, etc., indicates that the American Indian was a very old, well cultured, civilized and scientific race of people comprising the most diverse, and yet human, cultures known to man. Why didn't one tribe rise up and conquer the other tribes? I would say that respect for his fellow-man, and his surroundings, was a practiced belief.

The citizens of this great United States deserve to know about people who practiced what they preached. Let's teach facts in our public schools and respect for one another. I have always maintained that the American Indian's concern for the future generations of peoples would transcend many cultures' concerns with the possibility of using up the natural resources of the earth. The idea of preserving what we have must be maintained if life as we know it is to survive. I would not say that knowing about the American Indian is going to be man's survival, but utilizing the philosophies, the understandings and values of the American Indian will contribute to man's survival.

Roger Philbrick

3. Cover page, Fall 1980, of *American Indian Education Newsletter*, courtesy of the State of Wisconsin, American Indian Education Program.

NEWSLETTER

AMERICAN INDIAN LAW

W. Paguro

AMERICAN INDIAN LAW CENTER, INC.

1117 STANFORD, N.E.   P.O. BOX 4456 – STATION A   ALBUQUERQUE, NEW MEXICO 87196

Volume: 15

Number: 1

Date: Jan.-Feb., 1982

In This Issue:

4. Cover of *American Indian Law Newsletter*, January-February 1982, courtesy of the American Indian Law Center, Inc.

ANNOUNCEMENTS

Native American Rights Fund

Indian Water Rights, Issue for the '80s

Indian water rights will undoubtedly be the major Indian rights issue in the 1980s. Nearly every tribe in the western United States if fighting to protect its water rights, either through litigation or negotiations. Even though it has been legally established since 1908 that Indians have special reserved water rights, these rights are still continually being ignored by state and private water users, with the consequences that tribal water resources are being threatened, are being illegally appropriated, or have already been completely diverted. This will continue until tribal water claims are protected by litigation or negotiated settlements.

Indian treaties which established reservations seldom mentioned and never defined Indian water rights. However, in writing for the U.S. Supreme Court in 1908 in a case in which non-Indian water users were asserting that the establishment of the Ft. Belknap Indian reservation in Montana carried with it no special water rights for the tribe, Justice McKenna stated:

> "The lands (of the reservation) were arid, and without irrigation, were practically valueless. And yet, it is contended (that) the means of irrigation were deliberately given up by the Indians . . . Did they reduce the area of their occupation and give up the waters which made (the reservation) valuable or adequate? . . . That the government did reserve (water rights for the tribe) we have decided, and for a use that would be necessarily continued through years . . . it would be extreme to

believe that within a year (of establishing the reservation) Congress destroyed the (water rights) and took from the Indians the consideration of their grant (of aboriginal lands) leaving them a barren waste . . . took from them the means of continuing their old habits, yet did not leave them the power to change to new ones."

With this decision, *Winters v. United States,* the U.S. Supreme Court laid down a basic tenet of Indian law — that with the establishment of an Indian reservation was an implied reservation of sufficient water to enable the Indians to live on these lands which were drastically reduced in size from the aboriginal lands that they were ceding in treaties with the United States, and to which they were being forcibly relocated. The *Winters* case, or *Winters Doctrine,* lay virtually dormant until 1963 when the Supreme Court once again addressed the issue of Indian water rights in *Arizona v. California.*

Arizona v. California was a suit to litigate the waters of the lower Colorado River among the states of Arizona, California, Nevada, the federal government and five southwestern tribes. In its decision, the Supreme Court not only reaffirmed the *Winters Doctrine,* but ruled that Indian reservations were entitled to sufficient water to irrigate all "practicably irrigable acreage" on reservations. The *Arizona* decision caused an uproar among the western states and land owners which continues today. There is little surprise that the 1908 *Winters* decision caused little notice for so long a time. Most western tribes, small in number and size,

The Native American Rights Fund is a non-profit, Indian-controlled organization supported by private foundations and companies, federal agencies, Indian tribes, individual donors and other sources. NARF works exclusively for Indian rights by providing legal representation in such major areas as tribal sovereignty and self-determination cases, tribal resources, and the preservation of tribal existence and Native American cultures. Requests for assistance should be directed to Jeanne Whiteing, Deputy Director. NARF requests expenses and attorney fees from those clients with ability to pay.

Contents

5. Cover page of *Announcements*, December 1981, courtesy of Native American Rights Fund.

The Blue Cloud Quarterly
Vol. 27, No. 4

TENTH ANNIVERSARY OF POETRY

6. Cover of *The Blue Cloud Quarterly*, December 1981, courtesy of the Benedictine Monks of Blue Cloud Abbey.

INTERRACIAL BOOKS FOR CHILDREN

BULLETIN

VOLUME 9, NUMBER 7, 1978 ISSN 0146-5562

Raising Children in a Racist Society:
Reflections of a Native American Parent at Thanksgiving

7. Cover of *Interracial Books for Children Bulletin*, 1978, courtesy of The Council on Interracial Books for Children, Inc.

Canadian Journal of Native Education

VOLUME 9   FALL 1981   NUMBER 1

CONTENTS

UNIVERSITY OF ALBERTA

8. Cover of *Canadian Journal of Native Education*, Fall 1981, courtesy of the *Canadian Journal of Native Education*.

PABLO, MONTANA 59855
ISSN: 0528-8592

MONTANA — BIG SKY COUNTRY

CHAR-KOOSTA

Chief Charlo

Chief Koostatah

NEWSPAPER OF THE SALISH, PEND d'OREILLE AND KOOTENAI TRIBES
OF THE FLATHEAD INDIAN RESERVATION, WESTERN MONTANA

| VOLUME 10 NUMBER 24 | NEW MOON OF THE BITTERROOT | MAY 1, 1982 |

Tribes and county to regulate shoreline use

Lake County's three commissioners recently agreed to work with the Tribes to enact Tribal Ordinance 64-A, the controversial Shoreline Protection act.

William A. Burley, Don Corrigan and Harold Fitzner will serve for one year on the Tribal Shoreline Protection Board with Tribal councilmen Joe Felsman (committee chairman), Jim Steele, E.W. Morigeau and Al Hewankorn.

The board's purpose is seen in slightly different lights, depending upon to whom you talk. Executive Secretary Fred Houle, Jr., says the seven-member board will be "developing administrative procedures" for fulfilling 64-A. Jim Steele says, "The intent behind forming a Shoreline Protection Board, as I see it, is to study some of the existing regulations designed and implemented by the county and to utilize them, along with the Tribes' ordinances, in order to reach a happy medium that would be equally beneficial towards protecting both Indian and non-Indians possessing lakefront property. After all, we both (the Tribes and the county) have some very competent and valuable human resources from which to draw, to assist us in our mutual endeavors."

County Commissioner Burley, in a story in Polson's weekly newspaper, says the board's objective will be to devise a compromise between the Tribes' and the county's regulations, fair and palatable to all.

The county's agreement to be a part of the Tribal board came about through the latest development in the Namen case. The Ninth Circuit Court of Appeals ruled January 11 that the Tribes can regulate structures built into or bordering Flathead Lake's southern portion. The ruling gave the Tribes some measure of authority over non-Indians.

(Continued on page 2)

McDonald throws hat in state political ring

Joe McDonald filed last month as a candidate for Montana's House of Representatives' District 25.

The 49-year-old Tribal resident of Ronan is president of the Salish Kootenai College in Pablo. His career to date has included many other positions in the field of education: He has been a teacher and athletic coach in Ronan and Hamilton, and at the University of Montana and the Northern Montana College; and a principal and assistant superintendent of Ronan schools. Earlier this year, he earned a doctorate in college administration from the University of Montana.

McDonald, a former two-term Tribal councilman, is running on the Democratic ticket.

INSIDE THIS ISSUE:

9. Cover page of *Char-Koosta*, May 1982, courtesy of the Tribal Council of the Confederated Salish and Kootenai Tribes of the Flathead Reservation in Montana.

THE CHEROKEE VOICE

PO BOX 507
CHEROKEE, NORTH CAROLINA 28719

A Brighter Day Ahead

The quarterly newsletter of the CHEROKEE CHILDREN'S HOME

VOL. 2 ᎠᏂᏣᎳᎩ ᏧᏂᎲᎱ ᏭᏂᎾᎩᏍᎢ MARCH 1982

OUR CHILD CARE TEAM

The Cherokee Children's Home, for the first time in many months, has a complete team of permanent and relief houseparents. After many months of recruitment and selection, the best people are now on the job. You may ask yourself, "just what is the job of a houseparent"? Each set of houseparents have responsibility for the everyday "goings on" at their cottage. They must be ready to be a doctor, social worker, spiritual leader, friend, disciplinarian, playmate, and most important Mother & Father. It is a very demanding job with 24 hour days sometimes filled with stress and frustration. But, many more days are filled with love and caring. Rewards like a hug around the neck from a child who has never shown affection, or a quiet talk with a child about a matter only a mother or father would talk about. That's what makes this job rewarding. These rewards don't show up on their paycheck or their evaluation sheet, but they do in their hearts. That's what a houseparent's job is all about, giving and receiving love from another human being. The Children's Home is proud to have on its team the following people: left to right, Rena Wachacha, Warren Faurie, Helen Lambert, J.C. Wachacha, John Dills, Connie Faurie, Earl Davis, and Lynn Smith. Not present for the picture are Glen & Wilma Davis, Jack & Tootsie Gloyne, Deb & Gil Jackson, Tom & Vangie Stephens, Joletta Crowe, and Dr. Joel Milner. These dedicated people represent over 15 years of child care service.

NUMBERS ADD UP TO CHILDREN

Numbers are important in all of our lives. The number in your bank account, the number of years in your life, the number of years left on your mortage and the number of children presently at the Children's Home. At press time, we are providing care for 18 children. In Burgess Cottage there are 7 boys, ages 7-18. In Ponting Cottage there are 7 girls, ages 10-16. In Jackson Cottage there are 4 children ages 9-17. All of these children attend school, go to church, and participate in activities such as skating, caving, etc. For many of these children numbers in their lives are the number of years until they are 18, the number of days until the next date, the number of minutes until their favorite T.V. program comes on, or the number of days since they found love and warmth. Yes, numbers are important, only if they add up to people.

VALENTINES DAY BENEFIT

The Cherokee Benefit Dance Committee sponsored a Valentines Day Dance on February 12th at the Boundary Tree Motel for the benefit of the Cherokee Children's Home. The Committee Members: Mary Ann Widenhouse, Freeman Owle, Jean Gentry, Patsy Jones, Mary Wachacha, Peggy Jenks & Heather O'Brian. Together and with the help of many businesses and individuals, over $800 was raised for the Children's Home. Pictured presenting the $800 to Stan Bienick are left to right; Mary Ann Widenhouse, Freeman Owle, and Jean Gentry.

10. Cover page of *The Cherokee Voice*, March 1982, courtesy of the Cherokee Children's Home.

The Chickasaw Times

VOL. XI No. 1   January-February, 1982

Chickasaw delegates visit funding agencies

Chickasaw delegates discuss the upcoming trip to Washinton, D.C. to discuss budget cuts with agencies that fund Indian programs. Pictured (left to right) are: Harold Hensley, Gov. Overton James, Lt. Gov. Bill Anoatubby and Robert Stephens.

Reagan administration to cut Indian programs

The Reagan administration is proposing a cut in Indian health funds that will terminate the jobs of 358 community health specialists in Oklahoma for fiscal year 1983.

"It will be devastating to tribal health programs," said John O'Connor, of the National Indian Health Board in Denver.

To be eliminated is the Community Health Representative (CHR) program, for which $28.8 million will be spent nationally this year.

The program supports Indian health efforts in rural areas where paramedics, nutritionists, and emergency medical technicians are employed.

According to "informal information" on the budget breakdown, the jobs of 358 community health representatives will be wiped out in Oklahoma, according to John Davis, director of the Indian Health Service

in Oklahoma.

The budget for that activity during the current fiscal year is $4.3 million in Oklahoma, but was eliminated from the proposed budget that was sent to Congress recently for the 1983 fiscal year.

Also trimmed is the Indian Health Manpower program, through which scholarships are given to Indians studying medicine, nursing and other health professions.

Although the community health representatives are being phased out in the new budget, it actually provides an increase overall for Indian health services, according to Davis.

The increase nationally is from $600 million to $613 million which includes: $529.6 million for clinical services; $25.7 million for preventive

See "Budget Cuts"
Page 9

A delegation representing the Inter-Tribal Council of the Five Civilized Tribes visited Washington, D.C. Feb. 22-25 to meet with congressional delegates and agencies that fund Indian programs.

Seven people were on hand to represent the Chickasaw Nation, including Governor Overton James, Lt. Gov. Bill Anoatubby, Pat Woods, Administrative Officer, and Lynn Gibson from the Headquarters, Robert Stephens, Chairperson of the Tribal Council and Harold Hensley, Tribal Council member. Claudell Overton, Housing, was also in attendance.

The Principal Chiefs of the Choctaw, Cherokee, Seminole and Creek were also in attendance with their own delegation.

The Five Tribes delegation met with several congressional representatives. They spoke to each about Federal funding cutbacks, about elimination of the community health representative (CHR) program, the Indian housing program, and the

reorganization of the Bureau of Indian Affairs.

They met with John Fritz, Deputy Assistant Secretary of Interior, (Operations) for Indian Affairs, about the reorganization of the Bureau of Indian Affairs (BIA). Fritz said the merging of the offices would probably move the two Area Offices to Oklahoma City. He has directed the BIA Area Directors to talk to tribal leaders and report their views concerning the reorganization.

The group also met with Dr. Everett R. Rhoades, new Director of Indian Health Services, to express their concerns over the elimination of the CHR program and other problems within the agency.

Gov. James stressed to all congressional leaders and agencies that he could understand Indian Tribes taking their fair share of funding cutbacks but he could not understand the reasons behind the complete elimination of programs demonstrated to fill such critical needs of the Indian people.

Chickasaw Nation HQ
Box 1548 Ada, OK 74820

NON-PROFIT
Bulk Mailing
Paid
Permit No. 15
Ada, OK 74820

11. Cover page of *The Chackasaw Times*, January-February 1982, courtesy of The Chickasaw Nation Headquarters.

Chief Circle

Vol. 2, No. 2   1980

My name is Glenn Lonetree and I'm a 16-year-old American Indian. I belong to the Winnebago, Comanche and Kiowa tribes, but still more important, I am a Christian.

I received Christ as my personal Savior at the age of eight under the ministry of Brother Tom Claus during a revival. All my life I had gone to church and heard about Jesus and the great things He had done, but it took Brother Claus to bring the message to me that God sent His only begotten Son, Jesus Christ, to die for me and you so we could have eternal life.

I live in Indiahoma, Oklahoma, where I'm a sophomore in high school. My favorite sports are basketball and baseball, and I'm an active member in our school Future Farmer of America chapter, showing livestock in area and state competition.

My hobbies are horseback riding and rodeos. I participate in high school rodeos in which I compete in bullriding and bareback

12. Cover of *Chief Circle*, 1980, courtesy of the Christian Hope Indian Eskimo Fellowship.

NON-PROFIT ORG.
U.S. POSTAGE
PAID
MINNEAPOLIS, MN
PERMIT NO.3626

JUNE, 1981

THE CIRCLE

Vol 2, No. 6   ". . . news from an American Indian perspective."

News of the Twin Cities American Indian Community

Brenda Beaulieu, Director of the Minneapolis American Indian Center Education Department sits at her office desk.

Urban Indian Education Program Axed

by Sandra King

"I should be thinking about our graduation ceremonies, not worrying over this," Brenda Beaulieu, Director, Education Dept. MAIC, shakes her head, frowning. Her curls bounce. She pays them no heed. "You know," she says, "last year MAIC Adult Basic Education had 85 graduates. And the total metropolitan area only produced about 90!"

In fact, in the last four years, MAIC Adult Basic Education (ABE) has produced about 300 Indian graduates. It would seem the ABE program is a success, giving new hope and vitality to many Indian people. But it has been axed.

It was partly a matter of timing. Monies for ABE are granted in a three year cycle. This year, when the U.S. Department of Education in Washington, D.C. considered grant applications, it gave first consideration to those programs that were still within their three year limit.

MAIC's education program was just ending it's three year cycle. So it's grant application was considered a new one. There were 61 new grant applications. Only eleven were funded. The grant for the Center's education program was not among those eleven.

What is being lost? Adult Basic Education

Three years ago fifty-eight people graduated from this program. Half of them went on to higher education.

Indian students always seem to end up here in spite of all the other ABE centers in the area.

Life Coping Skills

The life coping skills class has sponsored such things as a mini tax workshop, Red Cross workshops, depression workshops, classes in how to fill out job applications and how to write a resume.

Cultural Classes

Classes have included, Ojibwe language, Religion, Philosophy and History. Speakers have been brought in, such as Chuck Ross who delivered five lectures on the Origins of the Red Man.

It had been planned to have an elder teaching arts and crafts sometime in the future.

What is being done?

Brenda Beaulieu and her education staff have 90 days to act to appeal the Indian Education Department's decision. They are working hard at just that. But they are finding obstacles in their way.

The grant applications were reviewed in Washington by a committee of three. Those three people were one federal employee and two representatives of the Indian communty. Which Indian community was not specified. Also, the names of the three individuals are being withheld citing their right to privacy as the reason.

In the review of the Center's education grant application there are inconsistencies. Sometimes a point in the application was called good by one reviewer, no good by another. Sometimes the same person would contradict his own opinion in one point by giving a different answer on the next point.

So Beaulieu and her staff are not pinning their hopes on just the appeal. They are looking to other sources for funding; the State of Minnesota, the Continuing Community Education Program and corporations and foundations.

On June 26th, 1981, in the gymnasium of the Minneapolis American Indian Center, 50 or more Indian people will graduate from Adult Basic Education. There will be an honor song for them, and a pipe ceremony.

The tribal chairmen from the seven reservations in Minnesota have been invited. Two of the chairmen, Arthur Gahbow, Mille Lacs and William Houle, Grand Portage, have already accepted.

It should be quite an event, that 1981 graduation ceremony.

It is hoped 1982 will be the same.

INSIDE:

- **Riley Housely Dehoused**
- **Big Horn River**
- **Shoshone Land Rights**

13. Cover page of *The Circle*, June 1981, courtesy of the Minneapolis American Indian Center.

The DAKOTA SUN

ISSUE 135   15 CENTS   MARCH 18, 1982

Solen on alert because of Cannon Ball River's rising water

Sioux County Sheriff Miles Utter announced this week it's quite possible that the Cannon Ball River may rise above its banks and flood the community of Solen.

Utter said residents of Solen have been notified of the existing danger.

"Several residents of Solen near the banks of the Cannon Ball River have already vacated their home," said Utter.

According to the Sioux County Sheriff, the water level is rising because of an ice jam at the mouth of the Oahe River where the Cannon Ball River meets.

"I've never quite seen it this bad before," he said.

The Cannon Ball River's water level, he said, is being watched closely around the clock by the workers from the North Dakota State Highway Department and by some of the Solen residents.

In closing, he said residents from the community of Cannon Ball are not in any serious danger at the present time.

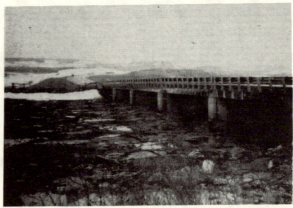

This is a view of the Cannon Ball River looking North from the South end of the Cannon Ball bridge. The severe ice jam under the bridge is presently causing flooding problems up river in the Solen and Breien areas.

Standing Rock Agency missing $200,000 from 1982 budget

It was discovered this week by officials from the Standing Rock Sioux Tribe (SRST) and the Standing Rock Agency that approximately $200,000 is missing from the total budget appropriated to the Standing Rock Agency for fiscal year 1982.

The finding has raised the eyebrows of Standing Rock Agency Superintendent Lionel Chase The Bear and SRST administrative heads Joseph Keepseagle and Robert McLaughlin as they have searched vigorously this week to explain how the baffling situation occurred.

The missing monies is the result of Public Law 93-638

Capacity Building Grant Monies being zeroed out of the fiscal year 1982 budget.

The error was spotted initially by Robert McLaughlin, special assistant to the Tribal Chairman and an expert with the 638 grant monies, earlier this week, said Keepseagle, when McLaughlin was reviewing the Agency's figures for this year.

The Agency Superinten-

(continued on page 12)

UTETC cut by 30 percent and forced to reduce services

The United Tribes Educational Technical Center (UTETC) has begun to reduce services to students this week due to a projected 30 percent reduction in its base operating budget.

Impacted by the reduction will be some 170 adult Indian vocational education students and 100 children. Sixty-eight staff have begun a four day work week in areas of instruction, counseling, and placement, administration, early childhood care, transportation, cafeteria and other campus support services. This is a 20 percent reduction in full time

equivalent personnel directly serving students. Continued reductions will be in supplies materials and equipment.

Despite U.S. Congressional action to provide a maximum of $1.5 million to $1.3 million for school operations this year, the Bureau of Indian Affairs has indicated a reduced level of $927,200 for fiscal year 1982. This amounts to 30 percent less than $1.3 million for UTETC operations during the past fiscal year (October 1, 1980 - September 30, 1981). Since 1979 UTETC has experienced a reduction from $1.5 million or a 39 per-

cent loss for school services.

While reductions are taking place, efforts at UTETC are to continue complete services. UTETC has continued support from North Dakota Tribes and from the surrounding community. Senators Quentin Burdick and Mark Andrews, and U.S. Representative Byron Dorgan have spearheaded discussions with the Department of the Interior for funds to continue basic services at UTETC.

UTETC, over 12 years old, was founded in 1969 by North Dakota Tribes to train and develop Indian persons for pro-

ductive lives and employment. It has traditionally served tribes from a 15 state area and some 39 tribes and graduated more than 1,350 students and provided short term training to over 2,000 Indian persons. Most of these individuals were either not served or poorly served by existing educational systems. It is the only Indian post-secondary institution designed to provide full family and individual educational services.

Meanwhile UTETC continues to seek full recognition by the North Central Association of Colleges and Schools,

and is preparing for a visit for full accreditation by an evaluation team in April. The vocational school has been a candidate with North Central since July 1978. It also has a state certified early childhood center and a state accredited elementary school on campus.

UTETC is owned and operated by the five tribes in the state. These are the Sisseton-Wahpeton Sioux Tribe, Turtle Mountain Band of Chippewa, Devils Lake Sioux Tribe, Three Affiliated Tribes of Ft. Berthold, and the Standing Rock Sioux Tribe.

14. Cover page of *The Dakota Sun*, March 1982, courtesy of Standing Rock Community College.

FEATHERS, by Kevin Red Star, Crow Indian artist. Collage of paper, pencil, ink, crayon and oils on illustration board. From the collection of the Indian Arts and Crafts Board, U. S. Department of the Interior. Photo courtesy Indian Arts and Crafts Board.

15. Cover of first issue of *The Exchange*, May 1976, courtesy of the Native American-Philanthropic News Service, Phelps-Stokes Fund.

IllUMINATIONS

VISIONS, VOICES IN INDIAN EDUCATION

REGIONAL NEWSLETTER

Native American Research Institute
Norman, Oklahoma 73069

Vol. 2, No. 3

March, 1982

NIEA OVERVIEW ON INDIAN EDUCATION

The National Indian Education Association (NIEA) presented several critical issues concerning the future of Indian education to participants at the January 26-29, 1982 Indian Education Convocation in Washington, D.C. The issues were presented as an "Overview: Critical Issues In Indian Education." The following has been excerpted from this overview paper.

"The primary issue concerning the education of American Indians which has been raised by the Reagan administration's efforts to reduce and curtail federal spending seemingly revolves around the question of who is responsible for educational services to American Indians. Is Indian education a federal responsibility or not?

"Indian Tribes which are members of the National Congress of American Indians, the oldest Indian organization in this country, have taken the position that education is a trust responsibility of the U.S. Federal Government.

"What Tribes have seen of the FY'82 budget cuts in Indian Education and the impact these cuts are having on Indian education services, and what can already be projected about the FY'82 budgets for Indian education lead to an inescapable conclusion: The federal government is retreating from its solemn commitments and responsibilities to provide quality services in education to American Indians and Alaskan Natives."

The NIEA 'overview' was separated into nine major issues and excerpts have been taken as follows:

BLOCK GRANTS

"Two new laws, the Omnibus Budget Reconciliation Act of 1981 and the Education Consolidation & Improvement Act block grant program will give control over

some 30 consolidated programs to the states and local officials. There is reason to doubt that a fair share of dollars for block grant programs will actually filter down to the Tribes and their Education Departments.

A 1980 report from the Education Commission of the States (ECES) entitled: *Indian Education - Problems in Need of Resolution* found that in five states which had a large Indian population that Indian education was a low priority for those states' legislatures."

If Congress were to amend the language of the Consol-
Continued on page 2

CENTER V EVALUATION MODULE INTERIM REPORT

Center V developed the idea of an evaluation module as a vehicle for effectively impacting procedures of evaluating Indian education projects in the Region V area. Past study indicated that the Title IV-Part A projects were not presenting complete evaluations of their projects because Title IV staff were not familiar with educational evaluation standards and procedures. Therefore Center V, in cooperation with the College of Education University of Oklahoma proposed that a formal structure of educational training be planned, pilot tested and, if proven effective, implemented as a method of alleviating standards and procedures problems.

Center V organized and implemented a module at the University of Oklahoma. Module emphasis is on educational evaluation theory, definitions, models and procedures. The module included guest lecturers, hands-on learning experiences and research. Participants were required to attend every session in order to obtain certification. Continued on page 3

16. Cover page of *Illuminations*, Center V Newsletter, March 1982, courtesy of the Native American Research Institute.

INDIAN ✠ HIGHWAYS

No. 183, March, 1982   Cook Christian Training School, Tempe, Arizona

17. Cover of *Indian Highways*, March 1982, courtesy of Cook Christian Training School. Amérindiennes au Québec.

INDIAN RECORD

VOL. 45, No. 2   SPRING 1982

Respect and promotion
of
Social Justice
Human Rights
Cultural Values

All photos in this article by Helen Norrie

Students in the Eagle's Circle at Winnipeg's Rossbrook House concentrate on maths.

Winnipeg schools offer alternative education for native children

by Helen Norrie

Last Christmas the students in room 14 at Hugh John MacDonald School cooked a complete turkey dinner, decorated a Christmas tree, purchased gifts for each other, and then invited the principal, Mr. Fred Taylor, to have dinner with them. This was all part of the *Falcon's Nest* program at the school. This program provides an alternative education situation for students of junior high age. The Falcon's Nest is only one of several special programs which are available in Winnipeg for students who have difficulty in adjusting to regular classroom situations.

"We concentrate on four R's, not three," principal Fred Taylor told me, "the fourth is respect — respect for themselves and for their culture." Sixteen of the eighteen students in the senior Falcon's Nest program are of native Indian origin, and this year they are all boys.

"There is a good feeling among the students in the program," their enthusiastic teacher, Heather Hunter, remarked. "The students have a strong sense of group identity and are very supportive of each other."

In the morning the class concentrates on learning basic skills: reading, writing, speaking and maths; in the afternoon they study native culture, take part in field trips, do arts and crafts. Woodworking, photography, cooking and art are offered to the students who travel to Aberdeen School for these classes.

Problems which may lead to a student being recommended for this program include chronic absenteeism or lateness, or failure to achieve acceptable academic or social standards in the regular classroom. Students appear to respond to the less formal, more individualized atmosphere of the Falcon's Nest, where Mrs. Cassie Einarrson, a native teaching aid, and Kathy McKay assist Heather Hunt in room 14. A second class of younger students under teacher Brian Marks carries on a similar alternative program in room 8.

(see: Alternative p. 18)

Teacher achieves creative writing among natives

First of a 3-part series

by Maara Haas

In the area of creative writing (the art of expressing thoughts and feelings in words on paper to shape a written literature) the creative ability of native people is more than equal to that of white and diversified students found in Manitoba schools, city, rural and northern.

Literary findings drawn from Churchill, Lynn Lake, Thompson, the Pas, Winnipeg, Kenora, Flin Flon, Leaf Rapids and Oxford House, substantiate this fact, contrary to myths pretending otherwise.

A common myth supports the theory that Indians are strictly oral: "Native people can *tell* a story but their aptitude, their level of creativity does not extend to the written word nor to *writing* stories."

Another myth perpetuates the image of the stereotyped, wooden TV Indian who expresses himself in sign language or is able to communicate on the barest level of intelligence, typically expressed in six words: "Ugh! White man speak with forked tongue!"

Socially contrived images born of prejudice, a lack of information, are

(see: Creative writing p. 20)

CONTENTS

18. Cover page of the *Indian Record*, Spring 1982, courtesy of the Oblate Fathers.

Indian youth.
June 1981

19. Cover of *Indian Youth*, June 1981, courtesy of the Institute for Career and Vocational Training.

20. Cover of *Inuvialuit*, Summer 1981, courtesy of the Committee for Original Peoples Entitlement.

A monthly newsletter
published by C.O.P.E.

DECEMBER 1981   Price: 50¢

RCMP RECRUITING FOR SPECIAL CONSTABLES

The RCMP is currently recruiting for Native Special Constables to serve in settlements and hamlets in the Western Arctic. There are ten positions open for Special Constable in communities from Fort Smith to Tuktoyaktuk. Recruiting personnel have recently made visits to Inuvik, Fort McPherson, Arctic Red, Aklavik, Fort Good Hope, and Tuk to tell settlement and hamlet councils about the program. The work of Special Constables is basically the same as that of regular members of the Force and includes a wide variety of community-related duties as well as investigations.

Qualifications and Training

To become a Special Constable, a person must:
- Be a resident of the N.W.T. and Canadian citizen.

- Be between 19 and 50 years of age.

- Be in good physical condition.

- Have a valid driver's license.

- Have a grade 10 education, although education up to lower grades will be considered.

- Have a knowledge of the language and customs of native communities.

- Have a good character, although previous criminal offenses do not necessarily stop a person from becoming a Special Constable.

Both men and women may apply to become Special Constables.

Special Constables receive hospital, medical, and dental care, uniforms and equipment, annual paid holidays, group life insurance, and a pension based on years of service. The salary of a Special Constable starts at $19,353 a year plus isolated post allowance.

A person becomes a Special Constable as soon as he or she is accepted into the Special Constable program. Training begins in the home community and continues there for several months. At some time after that training, a constable takes a 13-week course at the RCMP Academy in Regina, Saskatchewan. This is followed by a posting back to the home community, where on-the-job training continues.

Posting and Position

For the most part, Special Constables live and work in their homes areas, although they may be posted to other areas depending on their own wishes and on the needs of the RCMP.

This Issue

21. Cover page of the monthly newsletter *Atta*, December 1981, courtesy of the Committee for Original Peoples Entitlement.

19e Jaargang no. 2
maart / april 1982

22. Cover of *De Kiva*, April 1982, courtesy of J. Heyink.

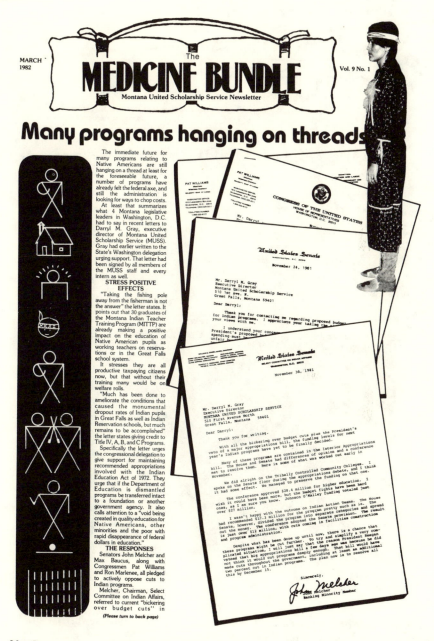

23. Cover page of *The Medicine Bundle*, March 1982, courtesy of the Montana United Scholarship Service.

No. 9
Winter, 1981

Center for the History of the American Indian | The Newberry Library
Editors: Herbert T. Hoover
David R. Miller

COOPERATIVE UNDERSTANDING

This Center is "a national research and education forum," wrote Emeritus Director Francis Jennings in the 1980 issue of *Meeting Ground*, whose "past is merely an introduction to its future." Since its establishment in 1972 (with a matching grant from the National Endowment for the Humanities), its principal goals have been the improvement of competence among men and women who teach the history of Indian-white relations and Indian culture; the publication and distribution of bibliographies on Indian-white contact history and cultural studies; and the distribution of materials to encourage better understanding between Indians and non-Indians, as well as to stimulate the study of Native American legacies. Now in its ninth year (operating with a third NEH grant), the work of the Center has not changed appreciably, as Mr. Jennings suggested. Its purposes remain the improvement of teaching through the operation of summer institute programs, and the assignment of fellowships; the completion of a bibliographical series in progress, plus the preparation of additional issues to keep subscribers informed about the

best publications on Indian history year after year; and the dissemination of information for use in classroom instruction and scholarship.

Important materials produced by projects in the Center will be available for distribution during the next year. A *Documentary History of the Iroquois* will be issued in microform by Research Publications, Inc., together with a printed guide from Syracuse University Press. An *Atlas of Great Lakes Indian History* will be published by the University of Oklahoma Press. The Center will distribute five occasional papers on request, and release several curriculum units for secondary school and community college teachers.

In the future, activities designed to improve teaching, to produce bibliographies for laymen as well as scholars, and to supply published materials on Indian-white relations and Indian culture will continue unabated. But in addition to these efforts, the Center will make greater effort to engender improvements in historiography.

Work on federal Indian policy and Indian-white rela-

Irene Spry, Ottawa University, and Jeanne Oyawin Eder, University of North Dakota, conversing during a break between sessions at the Metis Conference, September 3–5.

1

24. Cover page of *Meeting Ground*, Winter 1981, courtesy of The Newberry Library Center for the History of the American Indian.

25. Cover of *Mission*, Winter 1981, courtesy of the Sisters of the Blessed Sacrament.

QUARTERLY

Vol. 1, No. 2   Spring 1981

IN THIS ISSUE

AGE-INTEGRATED PROGRAMS: BRINGING THE GENERATIONS TOGETHER

26. Cover of *Quarterly*, Spring 1981, courtesy of the National Indian Council on Aging, Inc.

The Native HAWAIIAN

Vol. VI No. 3   To Tell the Story of the Hawai'i People So That All May Come to Know the People of Aloha   February, 1982

KUMULIPO, MANA'O KI'E KI'E

by Gard Kealoha

ASST. PROF. RUBELLITE KAWENA JOHNSON

The publication of *The Kumulipo - Hawaiian Hymn of Creation, Volume I* by UH Assistant Professor Rubellite K. Johnson is of profound importance to the Hawaiian community. The *Kumulipo* is part of Hawai'i's sacred oral literature. Hawaiians isolated from other civilizations and without a written language created an astonishing account of the origin of the universe. As far as Johnson is concerned this achievement places the *Kumulipo* on par with the world's great sacred literature and manifests the Hawaiian intellect as one that is just as rigorous in the great minds of other civilizations.

The *Kumulipo* is also a genealogy and records an account of the conception and embryonic development of a chief in the womb.

Johnson characterized the work as a crowning triumph of Hawaiian intellectual thought and paid homage to a culture that perceived an evolutionary creation of the cosmos as extraordinarily gifted.

Her new translation and interpretation is a result of over 25 years of hard work and diligent scholarship and is already stirring interest in academic circles. A native Hawaiian, Johnson was born on Kauai, attended public schools there and received a B.A. from the University of Hawai'i. She won a fellowship to attend Indiana University where she studied with outstanding anthropologists. She also worked at the Bishop Museum where she took oral histories from kupuna and helped work on the Pukui-Elbert Hawaiian dictionary.

Volume I contains two cantos. There are 14 more that will be published later in a four volume series. The book is handsomely bound, designed and illustrated with first rate photographs. Copies at $3.35 each may be ordered directly from Topgallant or purchased at the Honolulu Bookshops.

Frances and John Dominis Holt of Topgallant Publishing Co. Ltd. and the Hawai'i Cultural Research Foundation played a leading role in underwriting and supporting the completion of the *Kumulipo* material.

"The *Kumulipo*," asserts Johnson, "is really all about love. Today's surge in the reaffirmation of Hawaiian cultural values is predicated interestingly, on the deep spiritual regard and love for the land and sea. The *Kumulipo* affirms in a momentous way, our spiritual roots and is a work that has taken on a new importance for us to rediscover and use.

Other significant publications by Johnson include Na Inoa Hoku, a compendium of Hawaiian star names, Ka Nupepa Ku'okoa, a collection of translations for a leading Hawaiian newspaper and Kukini Alu Bono, translations of articles on history, culture and political debate from Hawaiian language newspapers during 1834 - 1948. All may be obtained from Topgallant Publishing Co., Ltd.

ALU LIKE Wins VISTA Grant

Alu Like has been awarded a VISTA grant enabling the placement of 10 VISTA workers at its five island centers to address the problems of literacy and drugs with Hawaiian youth. VISTA stands for Volunteers In Service To America and is a federal program addressing urgent needs. Alu Like's proposal earned the first ranking at both the local and regional levels. The selection and training process for the VISTA positions are already underway. VISTA provides full year volunteers at the request of community based groups to work on clearly defined tasks which lead to the mobilization of the community's ability to solve its own problems. In addition Alu Like's constituencies must actively participate in the development and implementation of the program.

Alarming statistics on Hawaiian youth absent from school, below average scores made on the Standard Achievement tests earned by an extraordinarily large percentage of Hawaiian youth and the large number of Hawaiian youth participating in federally funded substance abuse programs led to Alu Like's recognition and action taken in addressing these urgent concerns.

THE NATIVE HAWAIIAN
ALU LIKE INFORMATION OFFICE
2828 Paa Street, Suite 3035
Honolulu, HI 96819

Juliette May Fraser Cited

Juliette May Fraser recently celebrated her 95th birthday. The internationally known artist was recognized by Alu Like for her sensitive portrayal of the Hawai'i people in her many works. A koa framed certificate of appreciation was given to her by Board President Pilani Desha. We are happy to share our recognition with The Native Hawaiian readers.

Palapala Ho 'omaika'i

We aloha you, Juliette May Fraser, kaha ki'i o Hawai'i, incomparable artist of Hawai'i nei.

You are indeed, a mea makamae, a living treasure, to cherish and hold.

You have devoted a lifetime of labor and love in portraying the dignity and pride of the Hawai'i people.

You have captured the enduring verities and intrinsic grace of a people and their regard for the beauty of a beloved aina.

We palama you, Juliette May Fraser, for recording in a more permanent way with your extraordinary talents, the underlying meanings of a special people with their unique ways of looking at life.

We mahalo you, Juliette May Fraser, for your devotion and love for Hawai'i nei expressed in the countless ways of your creative genius and we bless you for the aloha you so freely share with us.

May the beauty of our islands and our people continue to sustain you in all that you do.

Aloha a nui loa, aloha pāha, aloha nō!

27. Cover page of *The Native Hawaiian*, February 1982, courtesy of the Alu Like Information Office.

NATIVE SELF-SUFFICIENCY

Woman: The Center of the Wheel of Life

Woman is the foundation on which
nations are built
She is the Heart of her nation
If that Heart is weak the people are weak
If her Heart is strong and her mind is clear
then the nation is strong and knows its purpose

The Woman is the center of everything.

Art Solomon, Ojibway Elder

Photo: Ron Botler

The Pomo Basketweavers - strong hearts, clear minds.   L-R Laura Somersal, Myrtle Hurtado, ?, Elsie Allen, Lucy Smith, Josephine Wright, Mabel MacKay, JoAnne Dempsey, Damien Dempsey.

WOMEN

THE YOUTH PROJECT
P.O. BOX 10
FORESTVILLE, CALIFORNIA 95436

address correction requested
forwarding and return postage guaranteed

28. Cover of *Native Self-Sufficiency*, September 1981, courtesy of the Tribal Sovereignty Program under the auspices of The Youth Program.

Volume 1, Issue 3 — February 1982

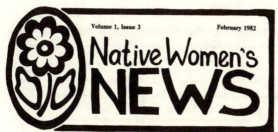

Native Women's NEWS

Native Women's Association of the N.W.T., Box 2321, Yellowknife, N.W.T.
5201 Franklin Avenue — Phone: 873-5509

One of the many popular events of the Yellowknife Home Management Program is the monthly luncheon. Helping themselves to this delicious Dene-Chinese style dinner are: Mary Blackduck, Lorraine Doctor and Richard Nerysoo. One of the Home Management staff, Vitaline Lafferty is busy looking for extra forks or chopsticks ... while Greta Baetz enjoys the ever popular bannock of Vitaline Lafferty.

National Nutrition Month - March

This year's National Nutrition Month across Canada is in March and in the N.W.T. the emphasis will be put on wholesome snack food.

The theme "Good Food Anytime" and the caribou logo has been chosen especially for the Northwest Territories to remind people that anytime food is chosen it should be done wisely.

This is also to encourage the use of traditional foods as much as possible since these sources are recognized as nutritious foods. The specific objectives are to "encourage residents of the N.W.T." to: identify the criteria of nutritious snacks which are: 1. wholesome foods, 2. foods low in sugar, 3. foods low in fat, and know examples of nutritious snacks.

Nutrition Month Resource Kit has been sent out to all the schools, nursing stations and health centres in the N.W.T. The kit includes the following: Nutrition Information, Nutrition Education Activities, Nutrition Education Material and Evaluation Sheets.

The information and comments received from the people will help to set guidelines to improve nutrition education and services in the N.W.T.

National Nutrition Month was initiated by the Canadian Dietetic Association and it was started last year as a "Nutrition Week." There is a committee in every province dealing with Nutrition Month and here in the N.W.T. it is the Nutrition Liaison Committee. The N.W.T. committee consists of the following: Department of Education, Department of Health, Health and Welfare Canada, Native Women's Association of N.W.T., and Hudson's Bay Company.

Lise Picard, the Regional Nutritionist from Health and Welfare Canada, and Marjorie Schurman, Nutritionist for The Bay Company in Winnipeg, have been designated to coordinate the Nutrition Month activity.

The Territorial and Federal Governments work jointly to promote nutrition — good health in the N.W.T.

According to Ms. Picard, "Nutrition is what you should be eating to maintain your body's health in terms of good foods."

Good health for you and your family is a feeling of total well-being, physical, psychological and emotional. Nutrition plays an important part in good health because it affects your skin, teeth, eyes, hair and overall appearance, as well as your personality, behavior, working potential and general look on life.

Although eating habits, both good and bad, are formed early in life, it's never too late to begin following the path to good nutrition.

Ms. Picard has been here since September 1981 and is acting as Nutrition Resource person for the Territories.

Nutrition education in the North is carried out by many people including all nursing stations, community health representatives, home economic teachers, primary school teachers, home management educators, The Hudson's Bay Nutritionist, N.W.T. Health Promotion, etc.

Ms. Picard's role includes being aware of these nutrition activities and coordinating some of them.

Nutrition is promoted through

pamphlets, posters and hopefully through workshops, radio and T.V. advertisements in the future.

She said "the whole N.W.T. population is taken into consideration when talking about nutrition, but we try to operate more by age groups, concentrating especially with the young women, since they are a big

Continued on Page 2

Dene Art Resource Centre

Boost to Native Art Scene

As busy as they are the Native Women's Association has begun yet another venture.

With the establishment of the Dene Art Resource Centre (DARC) early this year, Linda Cardinal and Tessa Macintosh began working out of a small office at the Native Women's Association in Yellowknife.

The purpose of DARC is to assist Dene artists and provide resources for the development of art in the Mackenzie Valley.

Ms. Macintosh says that DARC was set up in response to requests by a number of Native artists and also as a result of the desire of the NWA to develop arts and crafts.

"The crafts have done well in the past few years but the development of fine art has lagged far behind. Our purpose is to change that; to encourage and develop fine art."

The two women are undertaking programs to assist artists in the production of their art. This involves arranging both formal and informal educational experiences, organizing feasible print-making projects, applying for grants and providing raw materials.

Ms. Cardinal has already begun the process of setting up an art supply depot. Supplies will be made available to Native artists at wholesales prices.

Artists with established Northern reputations, as well as those who show serious potential will be encouraged to use the expertise and resources available at DARC.

"It's our business to search out shows, tours, patrons, grants and generally market and promote the artists work," says Ms. Cardinal.

Promotion activities include the production of artists profiles and arranging media publicity.

Presently there is a healthy, if somewhat limited art market in the North. It will be advantageous to expand that market and establish the artists' reputations on national and international levels.

PETT Project

When the Native Women's Association started out five years ago, its primary purpose was and still is, to motivate education and training for women in order to improve the quality of life in the N.W.T. They have live up to their expectation in the following areas: Arts and Crafts Program; Home Management Programs; monthly newsletter and Dene Art Resource Centre (DARC), and now PETT (Pre-employment, Employer and Trades Training) Project. This three-year project will open its door to students on March 29th at the NWA's Training Centre in Yellowknife.

The NWA Training Co-ordinator, Donna Laing has been very busy scheduling the different phases (there will be three phases a year), deciding what skills need to be developed and then finding the best people to help trainees develop their skills, knowledge and especially self-confidence.

She is also responsible for the on-going and final evaluation of the training project.

Her final responsibility will be training a new training co-ordinator

NWA Training Co-ordinator, Donna Laing

who will be responsible for carrying out the training project in 1983 in Inuvik.

The first phase is a pre-employment orientation course for women who are perhaps just looking for a job for the first time. It's also for women who would like to get a better job but

Continued on Page 2

29. Cover page of *Native Women's News*, February 1982, courtesy of the Native Women's Association of the N.W.T.

NAVAJO AREA NEWSLETTER

| Volume 11 Number 5 | Window Rock, Arizona | January, 1982 |

Della McCabe of Chinle, secretary to Supt. Thomas H. Begay, served a two-week detail in the area director's office following the retirement of Jessie LaFave on Jan. 8. Daughter of the late John D. Wallace Sr., a tribal council-man, she attended schools at Gallup, Ft. Sill, Okla., and St. Michaels. (See story inside on retirement of Mrs. LaFave and Harry Dohm).

BOB "T" TO ALBUQUERQUE

Robert Tsiosdia, a civil engineer who had served for the past eight months on detail at the Office of Reservation Programs, has transfer-red to Albuquerque. He has moved into the Albuquerque Area's Branch of Facility Management. Tsiosdia, of Laguna, came here from Albuquerque two years ago.

'Takeover' Talk Creates Furor And A Rebuttal

Navajo Tribal Chairman Peter Mac-Donald has expressed dissatisfaction with the speed at which contracting is being done in the Navajo Area and has proposed contracting of "certain functions" under Public Law 93-638.

He did not specify which functions he wanted to contract in his letter of Dec. 17, 1981 to Secretary of the Interior James G. Watt. But Carl Shaw, special assistant for public affairs in the office of Assistant Secretary Ken Smith, told the *Gallup Independent* that MacDonald wanted to takeover all of the programs presently being operated by the Bureau of Indian Affairs.

MacDonald charged in his letter that Navajo Area had obstructed the contracting process rather than expediting it; that the ones the tribe had to negotiate with were directly affected by the contracting process and did not want to contract themselves out of their jobs.

He proposed that the tribe open negotiations to contract directly with the Washington office, bypassing the area office, and he designated Caleb Roanhorse and Dr. Edgar S. Cahn as the tribal representatives.

The Interior Department's letter of transmittal carried the handwritten notation from Watt: "Let's do it with enthusiasm--pronto - JWatt." This was directed to Roy Sampsel, deputy assistant secretary for Indian affairs.

MacDonald said in his letter that the Bureau's contract-out procedures "have been a source of real dissatisfaction to the Navajo tribe and to other tribes. It is time to break new ground.

"As you are well aware," he said, "contracting out has, in the past, proceeded at a snail's pace. It takes years. Contracting out has been limited to agreements hammered out painfully,

Continued on Page 2

Matilda Sutton moved into the area director's office on a 30-day detail following Della McCabe's detail.

Tillie is a graduate of Navajo Methodist Mission at Farmington and Arizona State College, now Northern Arizona University, at Flagstaff where she received a bachelor of science degree in commercial sciences.

She is known as "the girl who made Mr. Udall famous" -- Stewart Udall, that is, the former Secretary of Interior, She worked in his office for three years in Washington, D.C., when he was a congressman from Arizona.

She also served for three years as secretary to the late Paul Jones when he was chairman of the Navajo Tribal Council and for the past 18 years she has been secretary/steno in the Navajo Area Branch of Land Operations and has seen several branch chiefs come and go, all of whom she has given her best advice and service.

People never refer to her by the pretty name of Matilda unless they are mad at her. She is always Tillie.

30. Cover page of *Navajo Area Newsletter*, January 1982, courtesy of Navajo Area, Bureau of Indian Affairs.

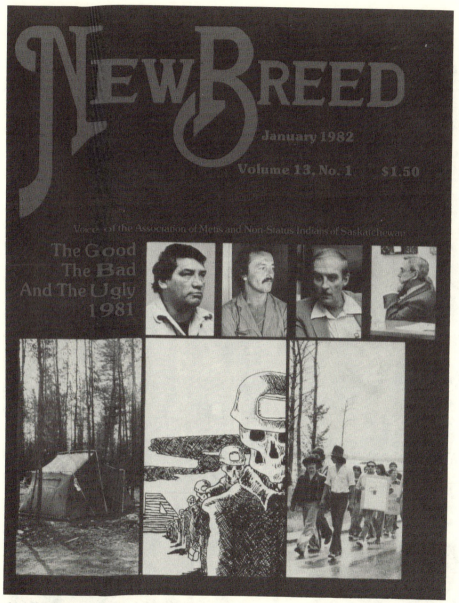

31. Cover of *New Breed*, January 1982, courtesy of the Association of Metis and Non-Status Indians of Saskatchewan.

Number 12

A Bulletin for American
Indian-Alaska Native Women

OH YO

April, 1982

Published Quarterly by
OHOYO Resource Center

Ancient Eastern Land Claims Law Introduced

Despite strong opposition from national Indian organizations, legislation has been introduced in Congress that would categorically deny recovery of Indian lands in South Carolina and New York.

"The Ancient Indian Land Claims Settlement Act of 1981" was introduced in the House (H.R. 5494) by Gary Lee and in the Senate (S. 2084) by Alfonse D'Amato, both Republicans from New York with strong support from Sen. Strom Thurmond (R-S.C.). The bills, if passed "would retroactively legalize the taking of lands once owned by the tribes of the eastern seaboard by states, municipalities and private individuals," and would substitute only a monetary reward for the extinguishment of Indian water, hunting and fishing rights on Indian claimed land now owned by non-Indians. Indian Law Resource Center, Native American Rights Fund and National Tribal Chairman's Association have expressed outrage at the intent of the bills which have been referred to House Committee on Interior and Insular Affairs and the Senate Select Committee on Indian Affairs.

FY '83 Recommendations: More Indian Budget Cuts

American Indian programs will continue to bear deep budget reductions if fiscal year 1983 recommendations recently released by the Reagan Administration are approved by Congress in upcoming months.

Most Indian programs funded through departments of Health and Human Services: Indian Health Service (IHS), Interior: Bureau of Indian Affairs (BIA), Education (ED), Housing and Urban Development (HUD) and Labor (DOL) will experience significant across-the-board funding reductions. The following represents a partial listing of programs slated for reduction or total elimination and serve as examples of services that would be lost should Congress approve Administration recommendations:

• IHS Community Health Representatives program would be eliminated completely.

• IHS Urban Health program would be totally wiped out eliminating health care to countless urban Indians who do not live on or near a reservation.

• IHS Manpower Program would be phased out, and monies would only be available to those applicants completing degree studies previously funded by IHS - no new applicants would be accepted for the program designed to address the severe shortage of Indian health professionals in Indian service.

(Con't. on page 3)

June 23-26
Ohoyo Regional Women's Conference Set for Seattle

The 3rd Annual Ohoyo Educational Equity Awareness conference will be held in Seattle, Wash., at the Daybreak Star Indian Cultural Center and will include sessions at the nearby Tulalip Reservation June 23-26.

Ada Deer (Menominee), distinguished political activist, will serve as Ohoyo program chairperson and Dr. Lee Piper (Eastern Cherokee), chairperson for the United Indians of All Tribes Foundation and the Daybreak Star Center, will serve as onsight coordinator for the regional event.

A number of distinguished Indian women will be assisting Dr. Piper with local arrangements: Jackie Delahunt, Carolyn Attneave, Linda Jones, Nancy Butterfield, Kay Rhoades, Mary Williams, Mary Hillaire and Jeri Eaglestaff.

The conference will follow the theme of leadership development for Indian women and will include sessions on educational equity awareness spotlighting Dr. Leslie Wolfe, national director of the Women's Educational Equity Act program of Washington, D.C.

Ohoyo will repeat campaign strategizing sessions which were well-received at last year's conference in Tahlequah, Okla., led by campaign technique expert Rosalie Whelan, executive director of the National Women's Education Fund.

The agenda will begin with a welcoming reception Wednesday night, June 23 at the Edgewater Inn located along the banks of Puget Sound in downtown Seattle scheduled to serve as headquarters for conference hotel space and registration.

A pre-registration form is included on page 7 for readers interested in receiving further details about the conference agenda once speakers and topics are finalized.

Sessions will be held at Daybreak Star Cultural Center and at the Tulalip Reservation Thursday through Saturday with participants departing on Sunday, June 27. An evening at the Daybreak Star Dinner Theatre which includes a program of Indian entertainment and a feast of baked salmon is planned for the conference.

The conference will provide Ohoyo an opportunity to honor area women tribal leaders who are past and present chairpersons of tribal governments.

Meal tickets and the dinner theatre tickets will be on sale during registration though participants are urged to purchase theatre tickets early as seating will be limited.

For further details about the conference, contact Sedelta Verble, Ohoyo Resource Center, 817-692-3841. For housing information, contact Dr. Lee Piper, Director of Minority Affairs, Highline Community College, Community College District 9, Midway, WA 98031; (206) 878-3710.

Ada Deer   Lee Piper

April 23 Deadline
Women's Educational Equity Act Program Accepting New Proposals for Fiscal Year 1983 Grant Awards

Proposals are being accepted by the Women's Educational Equity Act (WEEA) program in application for new 1982-83 grants until April 23.

It is not known what level of appropriations will be available for WEEA in fiscal year 1982, however, Education Department Secretary T. H. Bell has authorized the program to advertise for new applicants. Should monies be available for new grants, applicants would be notified about awards in August.

Of the monies that are appropriated for WEEA, 30 percent have been earmarked to fund model projects on educational equity for racial and ethnic minority women and girls. Another 30 percent has been set aside to fund model projects on Title IX Compliance, 15 percent for model projects on educational equity for disabled girls and women, 10 percent to influence leaders in educational policy and administration and 15 percent to fund model projects to eliminate persistent barriers to educational equity for women.

Application forms and program information packages are available from WEEA, U.S. Department of Education, (FOB 6 - Room 2030), 400 Maryland Ave., S.W. Washington, D.C. 20202-4104; (202) 245-8840.

1

34. Cover page of *Ohoyo*, April 1982, courtesy of the Ohoyo Resource Center.

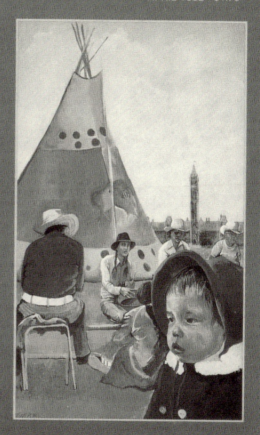

ONTARIO
INDIAN

VOL. 5 NO. 4   APRIL 1982 $1.75

A Peek
Under the Shell
of the Turtle

WA-WA-TA
Native
Communications
Society

Fiction by
BASIL
JOHNSTON

Aboriginal
Dance Theatre

35. Cover of *Ontario Indian*, April 1982, courtesy of the Union of Ontario Indians.

36. cover of *Padres' Trail*, Fall 1981, courtesy of the Franciscan Friars of the Province of St. John the Baptist.

the QUARTERLY of the SOUTHWESTERN ASSOCIATION on INDIAN AFFAIRS

VOLUME 16   FALL 1981   NUMBER 3

37. Cover of *The Quarterly of the Southwestern Association on Indian Affairs*, Fall 1981, courtesy of the Southwestern Association on Indian Affairs.

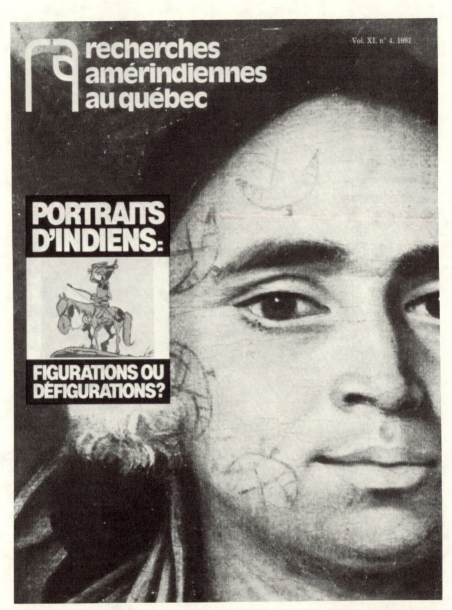

Vol. XI, n° 4, 1981

recherches amérindiennes au québec

PORTRAITS D'INDIENS:

FIGURATIONS OU DÉFIGURATIONS?

38. Cover of *Recherches Amérindiennes au Québec*, 1981, courtesy of Recherches Amérindiennes au Québec.

VOLUME 1 NUMBER 1   SEPTEMBER, 1980

THE REDLINER

Brantley Blue Memorial

September 26, 1980, the Lumbees will hold a memorial for
Brantley Blue in historic Old Main at
Pembroke State University, Pembroke, North Carolina.
A portrait of Brantly Blue will be unveiled to hang
permanently in the Indian Museum.
Brantley Blue was a friend to all Indian people and an advocate
for the rights of Eastern Indian peoples not living on federal reservations.
Brantley was the first Indian to serve on the
U.S. Indian Claims Commission. He constantly challenged
with his question "What have you done for your people today."

Contributions for this Memorial Portrait may be sent to:
Kenneth R. Maynor, Executive Director
Lumbee Regional Development Association, Inc.
P.O. Box 68, Pembroke, NC 28372

39. Cover page of *The Redliner*, September 1980, courtesy of Lumbee Regional Development Association, Inc., Indian Information Project.

UNITED INDIAN DEVELOPMENT ASSOCIATION

REPORTER

Volume XII, No. 2   "The Voice of American Indian Business"   February/March, 1982

Rincon Indian Reservation Market in its beautiful Valley setting. Inset: Berkeley Calac, Manager.

Tribal Market Reality For Rincon

By Welda Toler Johnson

Pauma Valley - The Rincon Market is truly a tribal endeavor. Built with a Housing and Urban Development block grant and tribal funds, the market is strictly Indian owned, operated and administered.

"It's owned by the tribe," says Berkeley Calac, manager, in response to questions concerning the progress of the market, which is located on Highway S-6, 16 miles northeast of Escondido. "All the profits will be turned back to the tribe. Everything is administered through the central tribal office, and everything that can be done there, is.

"The store is really the effort of a whole bunch of people," he noted. As manager, Mr. Calac came to the position after 18 years' experience with area Safeway stores, where he fulfilled a wide variety of positions. He was involved in operating and managing Safeway stores in Escondido, Encinitas, Solana Beach, Carlsbad, Vista and Fallbrook before opening the Rincon Market.

Mr. Calac credits the United Indian Development Association with helping the tribe formulate plans for the building and for gaining access to government funds.

"UIDA put all the management plans together for us," he adds. "UIDA helped us quite a bit... they were still in contact with us, even after the store was established."

Even though governmental funds are being minimized, Mr. Calac foresees a bright future for the tribal market. "The market is a way of show-
☐ Please Turn to Page 2, Col. 1

California's First Economic Development Workshops Set For March

By Bill Miller

The United Indian Development Association (UIDA), a California business and economic development organization, in association with the State Office of Local Economic Development, the Bureau of Indian Affairs, the Inter-tribal Council of California, California Tribal Chairmen's Association, California Indian Manpower Consortium and the Assembly of California Indian Women, will conduct two-day Tribal Enterprise Development Workshops for tribal council and board members, tribal business managers and tribal planners. The purpose of the workshop is to assist California tribes to:

(1) Strengthen their self-sufficiency through Tribal Enterprise Development.

(2) Analyze unique Tribal Enterprise Development problems and identify their solutions.

(3) Use basic methods and techniques for successfully developing, financing and managing tribal ventures.

(4) More effectively perform feasibility studies, management and operating plans.
☐ Please Turn to Page 3, Col. 1

40. Cover page of *United Indian Development Association Reporter*, February/March 1982, courtesy of the United Indian Development Association.

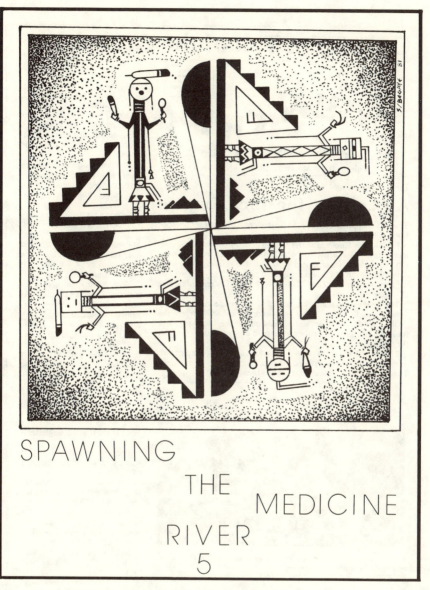

41. Cover of *Spawning the Medicine River*, Winter 1980/81, courtesy of Bureau of Indian Affairs, Institute of American Indian Arts.

Only Ruins Tell of the Great Inca

BULK RATE
U.S. Postage Paid
Rising Wolf
Missoula, MT 59801
Permit #530

the SUN CHILD

Volume II   March 31, 1980   Number 13

The Spanish Brought

An End To the Inca Empire

The first encounter between the Spanish and the Inca set the tone for the Spanish conquest.

Bartolomeo Ruiz was with the man called **Pizarro.** Ruiz' ship met an Inca balsa raft. There were 20 Inca men and women on the raft. Their cargo was estimated at 36 tons. The raft was under sail.,

For no reason, the Spanish captured the raft. They threw 11 of the Inca into the sea. They left four on board. The remaining five they took with them.

The Spanish invasion was preceded by pestilence—probably Spanish smallpox—and civil war among the Incas. When the Spanish landed, they ambushed Atahualpa, the Inca king, and took him hostage. After they were paid a huge ransom for him they strangled Atahualpa.

This set-off a war that lasted 40 years. In the end, the Spanish were victorious. They stripped the Inca Empire of its great riches. They tried to smash the civilization the Incas built.

By their costumes these people are identified as Guaymi. The Guaymi are people of what is now called Panama. (See *The Sun Child*, **March 10, 1980**.) This group is waiting for a ceremony to begin.

Part III

The West Coast of South America is a true land of mystery. Here civilizations have bloomed and died. Not even their true names remain. These civilizations rose and perished thousands of years before the first European arrived.

In this area countless millions have lived. In this dry country their mummies remain. Why did the peoples choose this particular place?

Some chose the high country 12-thousand feet above sea level. It is desolate and forbidding. Millions more chose the dry and hot, rainless coast. It is even more desolate than the high Andes Mountain.

These people had high civilizations. They had running water and in-door bathroom facilities a thousand years before the Europeans. But these American Indian societies are gone. Only the graves and vast ruins remain in the land that was to become the great empire of the people called the Inca.

Tiahuanaco

Tiahuanaco is the most puzzling city of the Inca lands. Its name means The Place Of Those Who Were. It was a magnificent city.

The ruins of this city are just inside what today is the country of Bolivia. This huge city was built 15-thousand feet above sea level. It is a few miles from the shores of Lake **Titacaca.**

Tiahuanaco is the most mysterious city in the Americas. It is probably the oldest city also, though only ruins remain.

The temples of Tiahuanaco were huge. Its buildings were very big.

continued on page 2

42. Cover page of *The Sun Child*, March 1980, courtesy of Harold E. Gray, Publisher.

Talking Leaf

.50

Vol. 44 No. 4 June/July 1979

Book Review—
Hanta Yo
Exposed!

People—

NM's "Junior Miss"
from Zia Pueblo

Jay Silverheels—

20 years after the
Lone Ranger

Published by
INDIAN CENTER, INC.
1127 W. WASHINGTON BLVD.
LOS ANGELES, CA

Non-Profit Org.
U.S. Postage Paid
Los Angeles, Calif.
Permit No. 32500

43. Cover page of *Talking Leaf*, June/July 1979, courtesy of Indian Centers, Inc.

SOUTH EASTERN MICHIGAN INDIANS
· INCORPORATED ·

November 81

TALKING
Peace Pipe

44. Cover of *The Talking Peace Pipe*, November 1981, courtesy of South Eastern Michigan Indians, Inc.

UNITED TRIBES NEWS

Bulk Mail
U.S. Postage Paid
Nonprofit Org.
Permit No. 12
Grafton, ND 58237

"An Enterprise of Communication"

| Vol. 7 No. 3 | Copyright 1982, UTETC Bismarck, N.D. | March/April 1982 |

BIA CUTS UTETC FUNDS 30 PERCENT

Bismarck, North Dakota · The United Tribes Educational Technical Center (UTETC) has begun to reduce services to students here March 15, 1982, due to a projected 30 percent reduction in its base operating budget.

Impacted by the reduction will be some 170 adult Indian vocational education students and 100 children. Sixty-eight staff have begun a four-day work week in areas of instruction, counseling, and placement, administration, early childhood care, transportation, cafeteria, and other campus support services. This is a 20 percent reduction in full-time equivalent personnel directly serving students. Continued reductions will be in supplies, materials, and equipment.

Despite U.S. Congressional action to provide a maximum of $1.5 million for school operations this year, the Bureau of Indian Affairs has indicated a reduced level of $927,200 for fiscal year 1982. This amounts to 30 percent less than $1.3 million for UTETC operations during the past fiscal year (October 1, 1980 - September 30, 1981). Since 1979, UTETC has experienced a reduction from $1.5 million or a 39 percent loss for school services.

While reductions are taking place, efforts at UTETC are to continue complete services. UTETC has continued support from North Dakota Tribes and from the surrounding community. Senators Quentin Burdick and Mark Andrews, and U.S. Representative Byron Dorgan have

spearheaded discussions with the Department of the Interior for funds to continue basic services at UTETC.

UTETC, over 12 years old, was founded in 1969 by North Dakota Tribes to train and develop Indian persons for productive lives and employment. It has traditionally served tribes from a 15 state area and some 39 tribes and graduated more than 1,350 students and provided short-term training to over 2,000 Indian persons. Most of these individuals were either not served or poorly served by existing educational systems. It is the only Indian post-secondary institution designed to provide full family and individual educational services.

Meanwhile, UTETC continues to seek full recognition by the North

Central Association of Colleges and Schools, and is preparing for a visit for full accreditation by an evaluation team in April. The vocational school has been a candidate with North Central since July, 1978. It also has a state certified early childhood center and a state accredited elementary school on campus.

The United Tribes Educational Technical Center is owned and operated by the five tribes in the state. These are the Sisseton-Wahpeton Sioux Tribe, Turtle Mountain Band of Chippewa, Devils Lake Sioux Tribe, Three Affiliated Tribes of Fort Berthold, and the Standing Rock Sioux Tribe.

UTETC RECEIVES BUSH FOUNDATION AWARD

Bismarck, North Dakota · On Tuesday, February 16, 1982, the Bush Foundation Board of Directors adopted a resolution to award the United Tribes Educational Technical Center a $75,000 grant to help support construction and renovation costs for a community service building.

In September, 1981, UTETC received a $421,800 grant from the Economic Development Administration (EDA) for a "multipurpose community service building and renovation of the existing recreation building." Because the cost of the new building exceeded the amount received from EDA it was necessary for UTETC to solicit matching funds from private funding sources.

The Bush Foundation, established by Mr. and Mrs. Archibald Granville Bush of St. Paul, Minnesota, was incorporated in 1953 to encourage and promote charitable scientific, literary and education efforts. The Foundation has concentrated activity in the areas of education, humanities and arts, community and social welfare, and health. Geographically, the Foundation's grants are made principally in Minnesota, North Dakota, South Dakota, and some in the Chicago area.

Construction of the new community service building is expected to get underway in April.

CONFERENCE TO BE HELD

Denver, Colorado · The American Indian Higher Education Consortium of Denver, Colorado, representing eighteen tribally-controlled community colleges, is having its First Annual American Indian/Alaskan Native Higher Education Conference. The conference, with the theme, "A Vision Quest for Indian Self-Determination Through Higher Education" will be held at the Rushmore Plaza Civic Center in Rapid City, South Dakota from April 4th through April 7th, 1982.

The conference will emphasize various aspects of higher education as it relates to American Indians. The major topics, such as legislation, institutional accreditation of Indian

Continued on Page 9.

ON THE INSIDE

45. Cover page of *United Tribes News*, March/April 1982, courtesy of United Tribes Educational Technical Center.

The University of South Dakota Bulletin   February 1982   News Report 90 (Issn 0042-0069)

THE INSTITUTE OF INDIAN STUDIES

►► WARRIORS ◄◄

The Sioux have established themselves as the most traditional nation of Indians in North America. This image concerns not only their regalia, tipis, songs and dances but also their reputation as a nation of warriors. This high reputation as warriors continued through America's recent campaigns in Europe, Korea and Viet Nam. Ceremonies have always had a strong military flavor, particularly the Scalp dance and the Sun dance. Service men returning from war are still highly honored by the tribe.

A man's status in the tribe was primarily determined by his success as a warrior and a hunter. The typical warrior was also a hunter. He went to war as a volunteer. Each man made his own weapons consisting of a bow and arrow, spear, shield, knife and club. He carried his personal war medicine and a supply of dried meat.

The acquisition of horses made warfare more mobile. The shield was reduced to half size and the bow shortened. There was more man-to-man combat and casualties increased.

The most common type of military operation was the raid to steal horses. Led by an experienced warrior, this was a small war party of volunteers. Sometimes boys in their middle teens were permitted to participate and learn

the art of war. War parties always sent scouts ahead to locate the enemy camp and to observe the terrain and avenues of approach. The war party moved at night and attacked at dawn.

It was a higher honor to take a weapon from a live enemy, or to kill him in hand-to-hand fighting, than to take the scalp of a dead warrior. On the other hand, American Indians took a dim view of cowards in battle. Some fainthearted were punished with death. Others were forced to dress and live as women no matter how long they lived.

The Dakota or Sioux were usually at war with the Crow, Hidatsa, Ponca, Arikara, Mandan and the Woodland Winnebago, even though they were somewhat related and all spoke variations of the Siouan language. When all the Sioux nation resided in the western Great Lakes area, the principal enemies were the Chippewa, (Ojibwa) and the Cree who spoke an Algonquian language.

During the early reservation period the real enemy became the U.S. Cavalry to those who refused to leave their hunting grounds for reservation life. The war of 1866-68, called the Red Cloud War, resulted in a clear victory for the Sioux. They also won a number of famous battles including those at Fort Phil Kearney, Fetterman Massacre and the Little Big Horn. ◄◄

46. Cover page of *University of South Dakota Bulletin*, February 1982, courtesy of the Institute of Indian Studies.

utah navajo
Baa Hane'

Winter 1981-82   Vol. 8 No. 2

UNDC Celebrates Ten-Year Anniversary

Host David John interviews UNDC Executive Director Tully Lameman and Board Chairman Robert Billie during taping session of "Voice of the Navajo."

In its tenth year of operation, the Utah Navajo Development Council (UNDC) has marked that milestone with a variety of activities that have included open houses, displays, a banquet and TV appearances. A "ten-year committee" worked with the UNDC Administration to plan the activities that started in September.

UNDC has worked with Utah Navajos to develop programs in Community Services, Education, Health and Natural Resources. A pictorial display depicting the programs was set up at the Navajo Nation Fair in Window Rock, AZ and again at the Northern Tribal Fair in Shiprock, NM. The information display was attended by UNDC employees who reported a large turnout at each location. This display was accompanied by video presentations and publications that illustrate UNDC programs.

The same display format was used locally at Red Mesa, Mexican Hat and the Off-Reservation Chapter in Blanding. In addition, the feature-length movie "Windwalker" was shown. According to UNDC Communications Specialist Stan Byrd, the open houses drew an average crowd of about 150 people at each location. "We were gratified to have the open houses well attended. We received enough positive comments from Chapter officials to justify our efforts to bring the open houses to local communities. Next year we hope to bring the same activities to each Chapter location," said Byrd.

The ten-year anniversary also was the subject discussed on "The Voice of the Navajo", a television show aired over a Farmington, NM channel that reaches a large segment of the Navajo population in the four-corners area. UNDC Executive Director Tully Lameman, and Board Chairman Robert Billie appeared on the show with host David John. During the half-hour segment, the UNDC guests discussed the programs and objectives of the UNDC organization. An additional "Voice of the Navajo" segment has been scheduled for UNDC sometime in March.

To culminate the ten-year activities, a banquet was held in Blanding to recognize the accomplishments of

Continued on page two

Published by the Utah Navajo Development Council

47. Cover page of *The Utah Navajo Baa Hane*, Winter 1981-82, courtesy of the Utah Navajo Development Council.

Wabanaki Alliance

Published with the support of the Penobscot Nation and Diocesan Human Relations Services, Inc.

40¢

March 1982

Non-profit Organization
Postage Paid
Permit No. 14
Orono, Maine

New school seen by 1984

INDIAN ISLAND — An expansive new school for Penobscot pupils could open its doors as early as Sept. 1, 1984, the tribal council has been told.

The proposed $3.5 million school complex would extend the present kindergarten (levels one and two) through sixth grade, to include all of junior high school. In most cases, students leave the reservation to attend nearby Old Town schools, and this practice would continue, following graduation from the K-9 school.

Probably the most important aspect of the proposed school is space. Currently, some 100 pupils are crowded into a building originally designed for about half that number of students. Gov. Timothy Love told the council and school board that this situation "impacts on the education" of the children. Love quoted a U.S.

Bureau of Indian Affairs (BIA) official as stating the Island school has the "worst conditions I've seen anywhere."

The design and construction of a 32,000 square foot school — twice the size of the tribal Community Building — hinges on funding by the BIA.

In a recent dramatic turnaround, the possibility of a new school rose from "almost nil to very high priority with the BIA. Two BIA officials from Albuquerque, N.M., visited the Island for a first meeting: Frank Latta, in charge of school facilities, and architect Jerry Gasparich. They viewed the site, and met with school committee chairman Kenneth Paul and members, school principal Sr. Helen McKeough, and Maine Indian Education superintendent Edward DiCenso.

(Continued on page 4)

Priest recalled from reservation

INDIAN TOWNSHIP — The Rev. Joseph Laughlin, a Jesuit priest at the Passamaquoddy reservation the past five years, has been ordered to leave by his Jesuit superiors in Boston.

According to reliable sources, Father Laughlin, or "Father Joe" as he preferred to be called, was recalled after considerable pressure was brought by persons objecting to his presence on the reservation. Father Joe was wholly identified with the Charismatic movement, and his Passamaquoddy following consisted of people drawn to that radical version of Catholicism.

Other parishioners at Indian Township were less than enthusiastic about Father Joe's unconventional ways. Objections included numerous reports that the priest was seldom at the rectory. He reportedly made many trips to Boston and elsewhere, and had connections with Charismatics in Brockton, Mass.

Father Joe left Indian Township in December 1981, but not before he had complained bitterly to some people about his treatment by the Roman Catholic Diocese of Portland. The Jesuits, or Society of Jesus, is under contract to the Diocese to provide priests to the reservation. A spokesman for the Diocese said Father Joe's complaints were groundless. The spokesman noted that respect for the Church's presence on the reservation had deteriorated in recent years, and the convent, housing the Sisters of Mercy, had been broken into.

Filling in on a part time basis at Indian Township is the Rev. Normand Carpentier of Woodland. He will continue as temporary administrator for St. Ann's Parish at Indian Township for an indefinite period. The Diocese of Portland is responsible for a successor to Father Laughlin, but plans were uncertain at press time. Father Laughlin succeeded the Rev. Raymond Picard, also a Jesuit.

PUPILS at old Indian Island Elementary School — at right — board school bus at end of day. Note fence and cramped yard.

Penobscots air complaints

INDIAN ISLAND — An unofficial group of residents here, calling themselves "concerned citizens," has held several meetings to discuss problems they are having with current tribal administration.

Last month, the group aired their complaints to Thomas Howard, a representative for U.S. Sen. William S. Cohen. Howard said all he would do is listen; he would not get involved in internal tribal matters, he said.

In general, group members say they are not getting a fair shake in terms of services and benefits, from tribal government. Also, some residents have said they

do not trust the government to handle the proceeds of the land claims settlement, and that tribal officials have been secretive about it.

Peter Hamilton, an organizer but not a spokesman for the group, said one of his objections to the administration is that, "they were supposed to have an audit every two years here, but they've never had one."

Further, he stated, "I get social security. All I get from them up there is $65 per month. I can use that for oil or food. Before, I got oil and food. I've run out of oil twice this winter. These people got no oil."

(Continued on back page)

Feelings mixed on land claims

ORONO — A recent Wabanaki Alliance reader survey reveals Indians have differing views on the $81.5 million settlement of Penobscot-Passamaquoddy land claims. Opinions weren't wishy-washy, however.

"It's a start, use it wisely," said one reader. Another reader wrote that "the people's opinions and questions were ignored and totally tossed out . . . we gave up more than what money can ever buy."

In 1980, President Carter signed a Congressionally-approved negotiated accord ending a decade of litigation and struggle by the sister tribes to assert a sovereign right to the return of aboriginal lands. The settlement provided a permanent $27 million trust, plus $54.5

million to buy land — up to 300,000 acres — for the Penobscots and Passamaquoddys.

Thus far, Penobscots have purchased some 140,000 acres; Passamaquoddys have bought closer to 30,000 acres, including some blueberry barrens. In general, Penobscots have bought more non-trust, taxable acreage, while the Passamaquoddy Tribe has acquired designated "trust land," that is tax-exempt.

Individual members of the tribes will probably net about $1,000 per person, per year, in interest earned on the trust fund.

Unfortunately for the survey, less than a dozen readers responded.

The first question asked if the reader was "personally satisfied with the Maine Indian land claims settlement act."

A New Haven, Ct., reader checked "no," and added, "I think the tribe accepted under pressure, and advice of legal advisors." The reader said "yes" to a question of whether the settlement changed his/her life, and the reader said the newspaper itself is satisfactory, although it should publish more letters to the editor, a pen pal column, and "more news of social life on the reservation."

Settlement saves home

A reader who identified herself, Jean Watson of Milford, Mich., said the settlement "gives a good economic base to our

tribe. We didn't have one before." Further, she wrote, "it provides jobs and extra income."

Watson said the settlement is changing her life; moreover, "it provided needed income to supplement social security (and) enabled us to stay in our home and pay the high taxes."

Watson praised the paper, saying it "provides news of the family and a beloved picture of my grandfather, Peter Ranco."

Noel Tomer, Jr., of Fitchburg, Mass., said he is happy with the settlement, and that it has changed his life, explaining: "The payments helped me catch up on my

(Continued on page 5)

48. Cover page of *Wabanaki Alliance*, March 1982, courtesy of Wabanaki Alliance.

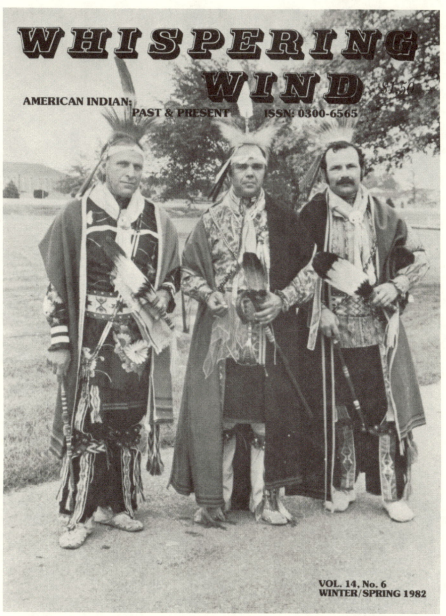

WHISPERING WIND

AMERICAN INDIAN:
PAST & PRESENT   ISSN: 0300-6565

$1.50

VOL. 14, No. 6
WINTER/SPRING 1982

49. Cover of *Whispering Wind*, Winter/Spring 1982, courtesy of Louisiana Indian Hobbyist Association, Inc.

Native American
Periodicals and Newspapers
1828–1982

Alphabetical Listing of Titles

ABC (Americans Before Columbus). 1963. Irregular. ABC (Americans
Before Columbus), 201 Hermosa, N.E., Albuquerque, NM 87108. (505)
266-7966. ISSN 0066-121x. OCLC 1480995. RLIN CUDG1246-S,
OHCP1480995-S. Last issue 8 pages. Line drawings, photographs.
Available in microform: WHi-A, Veda Stone Papers, (1963-1972), McP
(1971-1972). Published by the National Indian Youth Council. Editors:
Gerald T. Wilkinson and Anna Martin, Jan-July, 1971; Gerald T.
Wilkinson and Simon J. Ortiz, Aug, 1971-June, 1972. Subject focus:
Council news, rights, law.

WHi	(n.s.)v.3, n.1-v.14 (i.e. 4), n.2; Jan, 1971-Dec, 1974	Microforms
WHi	v.1, n.1, v.2, n.4; Oct, 1963, Dec, 1964	Pam 75-2763
WEU	(n.s.)v.2, n.3, v.3, n.2-3; Dec, 1970, Aug/Oct-Nov 4, 1971	Journalism Lab
WEU ARC	v.1, n.2-(n.s.)v.4, n.2; Dec, 1963-July/Nov, 1972	Micro 11
WMMus	(n.s.)v.3, n.1, v.8, n.1-2; Jan/July, 1971, Dec, 1979-Feb, 1980	Anthro Section
WMUW	(n.s.) [v.2, n.3-v.7, n.6] [Dec, 1970-Sept, 1977]	(SPL) E/75/A47x
WU Coll	Current issues	Ethnic Collection
AzNCC	(n.s.)v.1- Oct, 1969-	Indian File
CNoSU	(n.s.)v.3, n.1-2, v.4 Jan-Oct, 1971, 1972	Periodicals
CU-A	(n.s.)v.1- 1969-	E/77/A1/A1

IC	(n.s.)v.8, n.1- Dec,1979-	Periodicals
KU	v.1- 1969-	Kansas Collection
NjP	[v.1, n.1-(n.s.)v.7, n.8] [Oct, 1963-Oct, 1978]	Periodicals
OkTU	(n.s.)v.7, n.9- Jan, 1978-	Rare Book Room
OkU	[v.2, n.3-(n.s.)v.4, n.2] [July 27, 1964-Nov, 1972]	WHC
PPT	(n.s.)[v.2, n.2-v.7, n.9], v.8, n.1- [Apr, 1970-Nov, 1978], Dec, 1979-	Contemporary Culture

Other holding institutions: CLU (CLU), CU-UC (UCU), DI (UDI),
[Univeristy of Minnesota Union List, Minneapolis, MN] (MUL), NmScW,
NmU-L (NML), [Standing Rock Community College Library, Fort Yates, ND],
[Pittsburgh Regional Library Center Union List, Pittsburgh, PA], UU
(UUM).

2 ABE/GED Newsletter. 1975-?// Monthly? Last issue 4 pages, height 28
cm. Line drawings. Published by Yankton Sioux Tribe, Marty, SD.
Subject focus: adult and continuing education.

WUSP	v.6, n.1; Oct, 1980	Native American Center

3 ACE Newsletter. 1980? Monthly, irregular. ACE Newsletter, P.O. Box
99253, Seattle, WA 98199. Last issue 8 pages, height 28 cm. Line
drawings, photographs. Published by United Indians of All Tribes,
Adult and Career Education Program. Subject focus: adult and
continuing education.

ICN	Current issues	CHAI

4 AIC Newspaper. 1978? Monthly. AIC Newspaper, 1314 Munger Blvd.,
Dallas, TX 75206. (214) 826-8856. Last issue 4 pages, height 36 cm.
Line drawings, photographs. Published by American Indian Center.
Community newsletter.

WHi	n.46-49, 52-53; Jan-June, July-Aug, 1980	Microfilm

A.I.C.H., American Indian Community House, Inc. New York, NY

   see A.I.C.H. Newsletter. New York, NY

5 A.I.C.H. Newsletter. 1972. Irregular. A.I.C.H. Newsletter, 842
  Broadway, 8th Floor, New York, NY 10003. (212) 598-4845. Last issue
  10 pages, height 28 cm. Line drawings. Available in microform: WHi
  (1977-). Published by American Indian Community House, Inc. Title
  varies: A.I.C.H. American Indian Community House, Inc., June, 1979-Mar
  1980. Previous editors: Yvonne Funaro and Anthony Y. Hunter, Oct,
  1979; Yvonne Funaro, Pete Dyer and Anthony Y. Hunter, Nov/Dec, 1979;
  Yvonne Funaro and Anthony Y. Hunter, Jan, 1980. Subject focus:
  legislation, politics, poetry.

  WHi   [v.6, n.1-v.7, n.3], v.8, n.3-   Microforms
               [Jan/Feb, 1977-Apr, 1978], Feb, 1979-

  WMUW   v.6, n.1-8;   (SPL)
               Jan/Feb-Aug, 1977   E/75/A43x

  NjP   [v.1, n.2-v.3, n.4]   Periodicals
               [Aug/Sept, 1972-May/June, 1975]

  Other holding institutions: IC (CGP).

6 AICHA Newsletter. 1974. Unknown. Christine Porzucek, editor, AICHA
  Newsletter, Doyon Building, 201 First Ave., Fairbanks, AK 99701-9990.
  Last issue 40 pages, height 28 cm. Line drawings. Published by
  Association of Interior Community Health Aides, Tanana Chiefs Health
  Authority. Subject focus: health care.

  WHi   v.9, n.1-   Circulation
                                                           Spring, 1982-

7 AID, American Indian Development. 1968-?//. Unknown. Last issue 8
  pages. Photographs. Available in microform: WHi-A, Veda Stone Papers,
  (1968). Published by 13th Annual Workshop on Indian Affairs, Denver,
  CO. Editor: Ramona Suetopka. Workshop report.

  WHI   n.1;   Microforms
               July 15, 1968

  WEU   n.1;   Micro 11
  ARC   July 15, 1968

8 A.I.S.A. Newsletter. 1970-?//. Unknown. OCLC 1480011. RLIN
  OHCP1480011-S. Last issue 18 pages. Line drawings. Available in
  microform: WHI-A, Veda Stone Papers, (1971-1973). Published by

American Indian Student Association, Minneapolis, MN. Title varies:
American Indian Student Association Newsletter, Nov, 1971. School
newsletter. Subject focus: education, students.

WHi	Winter, 1981	Pam Cataloging
WHi	Nov, 1971, Nov?, 1972, May, Sept?, 1973	Microforms
WEU ARC	Nov, 1971, Nov?, 1972, May, Sept?, 1973	Micro 11
OkU	May, 1971	WHC

Other holding institutions: [University of Minnesota Union List,
Minneapolis, MN] (MUL).

9 ALISA News. 1975?-1976?//. Unknown. Last issue 4 pages, height 43
cm. Photographs. Published by American Indian Law Students
Association, University of Minnesota, St. Paul, MN. Editor: Joel
Thompson. School newsletter. Subject focus: law, law students,
organization news.

WUSP	Dec, 1975-Jan, 1976	Native American Center

ANCSA: Native Claims Settlement Act. Anchorage, AK

    see Conveyance News. Anchorage, AK

ANCSA News. Anchorage, AK

    see Conveyance News. Anchorage, AK

10 Aang Angagin Aang Angaginas. 1977. 4 times a year. Kathy R. Carter,
editor, Aang Angagin Aang Angaginas, 1689 C St., Anchorage, AK 99501.
(907) 276-2700. Last issue 20 pages, height 28 cm. Line drawings,
photographs. Published by Aleutian/Pribilof Islands Association, Inc.
and Aleutian Housing Authority. Title varies: Ang Wakun. Previous
editor: Carol Phillips. Community newsletter.

WHi	v.7, n.7– Sept, 1982–	Circulation
AkUF	v.3, n.2– 1979–	E/99/A34/A2

11 <u>A'Atomone</u>. 1972-1973//. Semi-monthly. Last issue 24 pages. height 37
   cm. Line drawings, photographs, commercial advertising. Published by
   St. Labre Teacher's Corps., Ashland, MT. Editor: Aaron A. Stansberry.
   School newsletter. Subject focus: school news, reservation problems.
   Superceded by A'tome.

   AzNCC   v.2, n.?-8;   Indian File
                  Oct 19-Dec 14, 1973

   MtBC   v.2, n.1-8;   E/78/M9/A62
                  Sept 7-Dec 14, 1973

12 <u>About Arts and Crafts</u>. 1977-1982//. 3 times a year. ISSN 0706-0203.
   LC ce79-70330, cf79-70330. OCLC 4632200, 4632199. Last issue 40
   pages, height 28 cm. Line drawings, photographs. Published by
   Canadian Eskimo Arts Council, Department of Indian Affairs and Northern
   Development, Ottawa, Ontario, Canada. Previous editors: Virginia Watt;
   Marie Rutledge. Subject focus: Inuit art and artists. English/French
   and English/Inuit editions.

   WHi   v.1, n.1-v.5, n.1;   R71-21
                  Winter, 1977-Spring, 1982

   CaACG   v.3, v.4, n.1;   Periodicals
                  Winter-Spring, 1979, 1980

   CaAEU   v.1, n.1-v.4, n.1;   Boreal
                  Winter, 1977-1980   Institute

   CaOOP   v.1, n.1-   E/99/E7C3
                  Winter, 1977-   A12

   Other holding institutions: CaOONL (NLC).

13 <u>Absalokaa News</u>. 1981//. Unknown. Last issue 6 pages, height 43 cm.
   Line drawings, photographs. Crow Agency, MT. Editor: Kitty Belle
   Deernose. Community newsletter. Subject focus: Crow people, culture.

   MtBC   v.1, n.1;   Periodicals
                  Oct 8, 1981

14 <u>Absaraka</u>. 1968-1969//? Irregular. Last issue 16 pages. Line
   drawings, photographs. Crow Agency, MT. Editors: Floyd Realbird and
   Eloise Whitebear Pease. Subject focus: Crow people, culture.

   MtBC   Feb, Mar, June, 1968; Feb, 1969   E/99/C92/A25

   NjP   June 10, 1968, Oct 20, Dec 19, 1969   Periodicals

15 Achimowin. 1972-1982//. Irregular. ISSN 0382-4586. LC cn76-301128.
OCLC 2297480. RLIN DCLCCN76301128-S, OHCP2297480-S. Last issue 16
pages. Line drawings. Available in microform: WHi (1974-1982).
Published by Sagitawa Friendship Centre, Peace River, Alberta, Canada.
Editor: Eleanor Brass. Community newsletter.

WHi   Fall, 1974-May, 1982   Microforms

CaACG   [1976-1979], 1981-1982   Periodicals

Other holding institutions: CaOONL (NLC).

16 Achimowin. 1973-1975//. Weekly. ISSN 0316-6155, 0705-839x. LC
cn75-31366, cn78-31300. OCLC 4249974, 2247627, 2247570. RLIN
DCLCCN7531366-S, DCLCCN7831300-S, OHCP4249974. Last issue 10 pages,
height 28 cm. Line drawings, photographs. Thompson, Manitoba, Canada.
Title varies: Bayline Weekly, Sept 9-Nov 14, 1974; Achimowin Weekly,
Nov 28, 1974-June 26, 1975. Place of Publication varies: Wabowen,
Manitoba, Canada, Sept 9, 1974-June 19, 1975. Editors: Archie Nabess,
Sept 9, 1974-Mar 27, 1975; Marilyn Giza, Apr 3-June 9, 1975; Jo Anne
Curry, June 26, 1975; Aubrey Gueboche, Aug 25-Dec 23, 1975. Community
newsletter. Subject focus: Manitoba Native people.

CaOONL   [v.2, n.91-v.3, n.31]   B/35/5
           [Oct 3, 1974-Dec 23, 1975]

17 Achimowin. 1974-1977//. Bi-weekly. Last issue 4 pages. Photographs.
Published by James Smith Reserve, Kinistino, Saskatchewan, Canada.
Community newsletter.

CaAEU   [v.1, n.1-v.3, n.21]   Boreal
           [Sept, 1974-July, 1977]   Institute

Achimowin Weekly. Wabowen, Manitoba, Canada

   see Achimowin. Thompson, Manitoba, Canada

18 Action News: "Fort Berthold's Community Newsletter". 1971. Biweekly.
$7. for individuals and institutions. P.O. Box 607, New Town, ND
58763. (701) 627-3626. OCLC 6194247. Last issue 6 pages, height 42
cm. Line drawings, photographs, commercial advertising. Available in
microform: WHi (1974-1975, 1979, 1981-). Published by Three Affiliated
Tribes Community Action Program. Community newsletter. Subject focus:
Mandan, Hidatsa and Ankara people.

WHi   [v.4, n.45-v.5, n.37]   Microforms
             v.9, n.11; v.10, n.13, 22, v.11, n.9-
             [Aug 23, 1974-June 20, 1975], June 1, 1979,
             June 20, Oct 24, 1980, Apr 24, 1981-

WMUW   [v.4, n.45-v.5, n.37]   (SPL)
             [Aug 23, 1974-June 20, 1975]   E/75/A32x

OkTU   v.8, n.21, v.9, n.3-   Rare Book
             Apr, 1978, Feb, 1979-   Room

Other holding institutions: [Standing Rock Community College Library,
Fort Yates, ND].

19 Adahooniligii. 1945-?//. Monthly. OCLC 5589414. RLIN NJPG1777-S.
Last issue 15 pages. Photographs. Available in microform: RM
(1953-1957). Published by United States Indian School, Window Rock,
Arizona. Previous editors: Leon Wall, Feb 1, 1953-Apr 1, 1956; Edward
Mays, May 1, 1956-May/June 1957. Community newsletter. Subject focus:
Navajo people. In Navajo, 50%.

WHi   v.9, n.4-v.14, n.8;   Microforms
             Feb 1, 1953-May/June, 1957

AzFM   v.8-v.14;   570.6/B952
             1952-1957

AzU   [v.2, n.1-v.14, n.8]   I9791/N31
             [Nov,1946-May/June, 1957]   A234

NjP   [v.4, n.5-v.12, n.9]   Periodicals
             [Mar 1, 1949-July, 1956]

NmG   v.4-v.14, n.8;   Periodicals
             Nov 1, 1949-May/June, 1957

Other holding institutions: CLSM, TxU (IXA).

20 Affairs. 1982. Unknown. Affairs, Department of Indian and Northern
Affairs, Vancouver, British Columbia, Canada. (604) 666-1316. Last
issue 8 pages, height 28 cm. Line drawings, photographs. Subject
focus: governmental relations, industry, land claims, legislation.

WHi   v.1, n.1-   Circulation
             Spring?, 1982-

21 Agenutemagen. 1971. Monthly. Agenutemagen, 35 Dedham St.,
Fredericton, New Brunswick, Canada. (506) 472-6281. Last issue 12
pages, last volume 140 pages, height 41 cm. Line drawings,
photographs, commercial advertising. Available in microform: McA

(1974-). Published by The Union of New Brunswick Indians. Editor:
Vincent Knockwood, Jan-Nov 1974. Newspaper.

WHi	v.3, n.3- Jan, 1974-	Microforms
WEU	v.3, n.3-v.4, n.1; Jan-Nov, 1974	Microfilm
NjP	[v.2, n.6-v.8, n.1] [Apr, 1973-Mar, 1979]	Periodicals
CaAEU	v.7, n.1-4; Aug-Dec, 1978	Boreal Institute
CaMBFU	v.1, n.1- Nov, 1971-	Archives
CaOONL	v.1, n.1, v.3- Nov, 1971, 1973-	Newspaper Section
CaOPeT	v.1, n.1- Nov, 1971-	Microfilm
CaSSIC	[v.1, n.1-v.3, n.12], v.13,n.1- [Nov, 1971-1974], 1982-	Periodicals

22 Ah Chi Mo Win. 1973-?// Monthly. Last issue 12 pages, height 28 cm.
Line drawings, photographs. Available in microform: WHi (1973-1974).
Rocky Boy Reservation, Box Elder, MT. Community newsletter. Subject
focus: Chippewa Cree people.

WHi	v.1, n.1, 4; 1973, June, 1974	Microforms
WMUW	v.1, n.1, 4; 1973, June, 1974	(SPL) E/75/A334x
MtHi	v.1, n.2-4; 1973-1974	Z/970.105 Ah21

23 The Ahkimal Awawtom. 1927-1931?//. Monthly. OCLC 8395339. Last
issue 8 pages. Line drawings, photographs. Available in microform:
CPC (1927-1931). Published by Presbyterian Indian Mission of the Gila
Indian Reservation, Sacaton, AZ. Editors: Rev. Dirk Lay and George
Walker. Subject focus: Presbyterian Church, missions, Pima, Papago and
Maricopa peoples.

WHi	[v.1, n.1-v.3, n.5] [May, 1927-Apr, 1931]	Microforms

NN   [v.1, n.1-v.3, n.5]   Microforms
            [May, 1927-Apr, 1931]

Other holding institutions: PPiU (PIT).

24 Ahtahkakoops Indian Day School Birch Barks. 1955?-?//. Unknown. Last
   issue 12 pages, height 22 cm. Line drawings. Sandy Lake Reserve,
   Ontario, Canada. Editor: Willard Ahenakew. School newsletter.

   CaACG   v.6, n.4;   Periodicals
               June, 1960

25 Ajungnagimmat Magazine.. 1976. Irregular. Mary Tutsuitok, editor,
   Arjungnagimmat Magazine, Eskimo Point, Northwest Territories, Canada
   XOC 0E0. ISSN 0707-2961, 0710-8397. LC cn79-30307, cn82-30452. OCLC
   4678018, 8555914. RLIN DCLCCN7930307-S, OHCP4678018-S. Photographs.
   Published by Inuit Cultural Institute. Title varies: Ajurnarmat,
   Winter, 1976-1979; Arjungnagimmat, Summer, 1980-Winter, 1981. Previous
   editors: Anthony Scullion, 1976-1979; Jim Shirley, Summer, 1980-Winter,
   1981. Subject focus: Inuit people and culture. In Inuit, 50%.

   CaACG   1977-   Periodicals

   CaAEU   Winter, 1976/1977-Special Editon, 1979   Boreal
                                                         Institute

   CaOONL   Winter, 1976/1977-   Periodicals

   CaOPeT   1977-1978   Serials
                                                         Dept.

   Other holding institutions: CaNfSM.

   Ajurnarmat. Eskimo Point, Northwest Territories, Canada

        see Ajungnagimmat Magazine. Eskimo Point, Northwest Territories,
            Canada

26 Aki Ko Wan News Letter. 1981. Unknown. Aki Ko Wan Newsletter, P.O.
   Box 819, Browning, MT 59417. (406) 338-5411. Last issue 4 pages,
   height 28 cm. Line drawings. Published by Blackfeet Women's Resource
   Center. Subject focus: women's rights.

   WHi   n.3;   Microforms
               Apr, 1981

   MtBBCC   n.1-2;   Periodicals
               Feb-Mar, 1981

27 Akwesasne Notes. 1969. 6 times a year. $8. for individuals and
   institutions. John Mohawk, editor, Akwesasne Notes, Rooseveltown, NY
   13683. (518) 358-9531. ISSN 0002-3949. LC sn78-4955. OCLC 1478885,
   2257108, 4249373, 4320392, 5652152. RLIN COSG19541287-S, UTUL1522-S,
   CSUP00291924, MIUG15607-S, NIUG15604-S, NJRG2826-S, OHCP4249373-S,
   OHCP1478884-S, NYPG754034482-S. Last issue 32 pages, height 36 cm.
   Line drawings, photographs. Indexed in: Alternative Press Index
   (1969-). Available in microform: McP (1969-1973); McA (1969-); UnM
   (1969-); WHi (1969-); WHi-A, Veda Stone Papers, (1969-1977); Y (1969-).
   Published by Mohawk Nation. Frequency varies: Monthly, Apr, 1969-Aug,
   1972; 8 times a year, Jan-Aug, 1973, 7 times a year, Early Spring-Early
   Autumn, 1974. Previous editors: Jerry Gambill (Rarichokwats), Apr,
   1969-Oct, 1970; Rarichokwats and Ateronhiatakon, Jan, 1971;
   Rarichokwats, Ateronhiatakon and Anonsowenrate, Mar, 1971;
   Rarichokwats, Apr, 1971-Aug, 1973? Some issues contain Longhouse News
   (the official publication of the Mohawk Nation at Kanawake). Subject
   focus: rights, legislation, politics, socio-economic conditions,
   education, health, women's rights, culture, religion, poetry, ecology,
   ethnocide, Third World Folk peoples.

WHi	[v.1, n.?]- Apr, 1969-	Microforms
WEU	[v.3, n.8-v.8, n.9] [Autumn, 1971-Summer, 1971]	Journalism Lab
WEU	v.1, n.1- Jan, 1969-	Microforms
WEU ARC	[v.1, n.5-v.3, n.8] [May, 1969-Autumn, 1977]	Micro 11
Wken-U	v.1, n.1- Jan, 1969-	Microfilm
WM	v.3, n.1- Oct/Nov, 1971-	Periodicals
WM	Current issues	Forest Home Branch
WMaPI-RL	v.9, n.4- Sept, 1972-	Periodicals
WMM	Current 2 years	Law
WMMus	v.1, n.9- Oct, 1969-	Anthro Section
WMSC	v.3, n.2- Mar, 1971-	Periodicals
WMUW	v.3, n.3- Apr, 1971-	(SPL) E/75/A38x

WMUW	v.1, n.5-v.11, n.5; May, 1970-?, 1979	Microfilm
WOsh	v.2, n.3-v.12, n.3; June, 1970-Summer, 1980	Periodicals
WU Coll	Current issues	Ethnic Collection
WU-L	Current issues	Periodicals Section
WUSP	v.9, n.1- Feb, 1972-	Microfilm
AkAML	Current year	Periodicals
Az	v.4, n.3-v.12, n.4; 1972-Autumn, 1980	Periodicals
AzFM	v.3- 1971-	570.6/M628a
AzHM	v.3, n.1-v.4, n.6; 1971-1972	Periodicals
AzNCC	v.1, n.2- Feb, 1969-	Indian File
AzPh	Current year	Periodicals
CL	v.1, n.2- Feb, 1969-	Periodicals
CLSM	v.1, n.9-v.12, n.3; Oct, 1969-Summer, 1980	Periodicals
CnoSU	[v.1, n.4-v.5, n.5] [Apr, 1969-Aug, 1973]	Periodicals
CRSSU	v.4- 1972-	Periodicals
CSmarP	[v.8-v.12] [1976-1980]	Stacks
CU-A	v.2- 1970-	E/77/A1/A5
IdB	v.5, n.4, 6, v.6- July, Oct, 1973, 1974-	Periodicals
IC	v.1, n.2-v.11, v.13- Feb, 1969-Dec, 1979, Mar, 1981-	Periodicals
ICN	Current issues	CHAI

KU	v.1, n.1– Jan, 1969–	Kansas Collection
LARC	v.6– 1974–	Periodicals
Mi	v.11, n.1–v.12, n.3? Feb, 1979–Aug, 1980	Periodicals
MnBemT	v.1– 1969–	Periodicals
MoS	v.1, n.1– Jan, 1969–	Periodicals
MoSHi	v.1, n.5; May, 1969	970.1/Ak89
NbU	v.1, n.5– May, 1969–	E/75/A4
NjP	[v.1, n.?–v.11, n.1] [Dec, 1968–Feb, 1979]	Periodicals
NmG	v.1, n.10–v.9, n.1; Nov, 1969–Spring, 1977	Periodicals
NmScW	v.1–v.3, v.5– 1969–1971, 1973–	Periodicals
N	[v.3, n.1–v.9, n.1] [Jan/Feb, 1971–Apr, 1977]	J970.5/ fA315
NN	v.1, n.5, 9; May, Oct, 1969	MA/FM
NN	v.1, n.1– Jan, 1969–	Microforms
NPotU	v.2– 1970–	E/99/M8A38
NOneoU	v.9, n.2– 1977–	Periodicals
NdMinS	v.10– 1978–	Periodicals
OCHP	v.1, n.1–v.10; Jan, 1969–1978	FLM/180
OCU	Current year	Periodicals
OkSa	[v.11–v.12], v.13– [1979–1980], 1981–	Periodicals

OkT	Current issues	Periodicals
OkTahN	v.1– 1969–	Microforms
OkTU	v.1, n.2– Feb, 1969–	970.305 M697
OkU	v.1, n.1– Jan, 1969–	WHC
OrU	v.2, n.5–6, v.4, n.2– Sept–Oct, 1970, Spring, 1972–	Periodicals
PCCe	v.1– 1969–	Microforms
PP	v.1–v.12; 1969–1981	Microfilm
PPT	[v.1, n.5–v.11, n.5], v.12, n.4– [May, 1969–Winter, 1979], Autumn, 1980–	Contemporary Culture
USUSC	[v.10, n.1–v.12, n.2] [Spring, 1978–May, 1980]	Special Collections
WaS	v.4– 1972–	History Dept.
WaU	v.3, n.6– 1971–	Soc Wk E/75/A38
WyCWC	v.1, n.?–v.7, n.5, v.12– Apr, 1970–Winter, 1975, 1980–	Periodicals
WyU	v.1– 1969–	E/75/A45
CaACG	[v.1, n.7–v.2, n.6], v.3,n.1– [July, 1969–Oct, 1970], Mar, 1971–	Periodicals
CaAEU	v.1– 1969–	Boreal Institute
CaMWU	[v.1], v.2– [1969], 1970–	Microfilm
CaNBFU	[v.1, n.?]– Apr, 1969–	Microforms
CaOAUC	v.5– 1973–	Periodicals
CaOONL	v.3– 1970–	Periodicals

CaOPeT   v.2-   Microfilm
            Apr, 1970-

CaOSuL   v.1-   Periodicals
            1970-

CaOSuU   v.6-v.12   Periodicals
            1974-1981

CaSSIC   v.1, n.2-   Periodicals
            Feb, 1969-

CaYW   v.4-v.7, v.10-v.12;   Periodicals
            1972-1975, 1978-1980

Other holding institutions: ARU (AFU), [Amerind Foundation, Inc.,
Dragoon, AZ], AzFU (AZN), AzTeS (AZS), CBaS (CBA), CChiS (CCH), CLobS
(CLO), CLU (CLU), CLSU (CSL), CU-UC (UCU), COU-A (COA), COFS (COF), CtW
(WLU), DeU (DLM), FU (FUG), GA (GAP), [Coe College, Cedar Rapids, IA]
(IOW), IaWavU (IOW), [Indiana Union List of Serials, Indianapolis, IN]
(ILS), KBB (KKB), KSteC (KKQ), MBSi (SCL), MBU (BOS), MChB (BXM), MH-P
(HLS), MWelC (WEL), MdBJ (JHE), MdStm (MDS), [Unity College Library,
Unity, ME], MiDU (EYU), MiDW (EYW), MiEM (EEM), MiHM (EZT), MiKC (EXK),
MiLC (EEL), MiU-Labadie (EYM), MiMtpT (EZC), MiRochOU (EYR), MnCC
(MCO), [Hennepin County Library, Edina, MN], [University of Minnesota
Union List, Minneapolis, MN] (MUL), MoWgT/MoWgW (ELW), [Western Nevada
Community College, Carson City, NV], NcU (NOC), NdU (UND), NbKS (KRS),
NhB (DRB), [Central New York Library Resources Council, Syracuse, NY]
(SRR), [Jefferson Community College Library, Watertown, NY] (VND),
[Monroe Community College-L.V. Good Library, Rochester, NY] (VQT), NAlf
(YAH), NAlU (NAM), NBrockU (XBM), NBu (VHB), NBuC (YBM), NCaS (XLM),
NCorniCC (ZDG), NCortU (YCM), [New York State Union List, Albany, NY]
(NYS), NFQC (XQM) NGcA (VJA), NGH (ZEM), NII (XIM), NOwU (ZOW), NPurU
(ZPM), NR (YQR), NRU (RRR), NSufR (VVR), NSyU (SYV), [Rochester
Institute of Technology-Wallace Memorial Library, Rochester, NY] (RUE),
[Western New York Library Resources Council, Buffalo, NY] (VZX),
[Standing Rock Community College Library, Fort Yates, ND], OAkU (AKR),
(CIN), ODaTS (UTS), OKentU (KSU), OY (YMM), OYU (YNG), [Raymond Walters
General and Technical Library, Blue Ash, OH] (ORW), Ok (OKD), OkAdE
(ECO), [Bacone College, Muskogee, OK], [University of Science and Arts
of Oklahoma, Chickasha, OK] (OUV), OrU-Special Collections, PBm (BMC),
PHC (CVH), [Pittsburgh Regional Library Center-Union List, Pittsburgh,
PA] (QPR), PPiCC (HHC), PPiPT (PKT), PPiU (PIT), PSC-P (PSP), RPB
(RBN), [AMIGOS Union List of Serials, Dallas, TX] (IUC), TxDa (IGA),
TxFTC (ICU), TxLT (ILU), TxNacS (TXK), TxU (IXA), ViRCU (VRC), WAChenE
(WEA), [WGrU-Native American Studies Dept.], [Arrowhead Library System-
Janesville Public Library, Janesville, WI] (WIJ), Shawano City-County
Library, Shawano, WI], [University of Wisconsin-Stevens Point, Native
American Center, Stevens Point, WI], [Wisconsin Indian Resource
Council, Stevens Point, WI].

28 Alabama Indian Advocate. 1981. Monthly. Jennie Dees, editor, Alabama
   Indian Advocate, Perry Hill Office Park, Suite 211, 2815 Interstate
   Ct., Montgomery, AL 36109. (205) 832-3829. Last issue 8 pages, height

28 cm. Line drawings, photographs. Published by Alabama Indian
Affairs Commission. Subject focus: Alabama Native people, legislation,
health, social services.

WHi   v.1, n.1-5;   Microforms
           May-Nov/Dec, 1981

ICN   Current issues   CHAI

Other holding institutions: [Dull Knife Memorial College, Lame Deer,
MT].

29 Ke Alahou. 1975-1980//. Bi-monthly. OCLC 8254302. Last issue 8
pages, height 43 cm. Line drawings, photographs, commmercial
advertising. Available in microform: WHi (1975-1980). Published by
Ahahui Oihana, Honolulu, HI. Frequency varies: monthly, Aug, 1975-Apr,
1980. Subject focus: Hawaiian culture, legends, education. In
Hawaiian, 50%.

WHi   Aug, 1975-Dec, 1980   Microforms

Other holding institutions: HU (HUH).

30 The Alaska Fisherman. 1923-?//. Monthly. Last issue 12 pages. Line
drawings, commerical advertising. Available in microform: WHi-A,
Papers of Carlos Montezuma, (1925). Published by Alaska Native
Brotherhood, Ketchikan, AK. Editor: William Paul. Subject focus:
Alaska Native people, acculturation.

WHi   v.2, n.6;   Microforms
           Apr, 1925

AkHi   [v.1-v.10]   Microforms
           [May, 1923-Sept, 1932]

31 Alaska Jesuit Missions. 1960?-1965?//. Irregular. Last issue 2
pages, height 34 cm. Line drawings. Portland, OR. Place of
publication varies: Seattle, WA, Feb?-Apr, 1960. Editor: Rev. Paul C.
O'Connor. Subject focus: missions, Catholic Church.

WMM   [Feb, 1960-Mar, 1965]   Special
                                                Collections

32 Alaska Native Association of Oregon [Newsletter]. 1974?//. Unknown.
Last issue 4 pages. Available in microform: AkUF (1974). Portland,
OR. Subject focus: 13th Regional Corporation, Native corporations,
health, local news.

WHi   Oct?, 1974   Microforms

AkUF   Oct?, 1974   Microfiche

33 Alaska Native Management Report. 1972-1978//. Bi-weekly. Line
   drawings. Published by Alaska Native Foundation, Anchorage, AK.
   Subject focus: village corporations, shareholders.

   AkUF   v.1, n.1-v,7. n.11;   E/78/A3/A42
              1972-June 15, 1978

   AkAML   v.4, n.9-v.7, n.11;   Periodicals
              June, 1975-June 15, 1978

34 The Alaska Native Times. 1976-1981//. Bimonthly. LC sc82-2005. OCLC
   709427. RLIN DCLCSC822005-S. Last issue 8 pages, last volume 100
   pages, height 45 cm. Line drawings, photographs, commercial
   advertising. Available in microform: WHi (1979-1981). Published by
   The 13th Regional Corporation Seattle, WA. Frequency varies: monthly,
   Jan, 1979-Dec, 1980. Editor: Gray Warriner, Mar, 1979-Jan/Feb, 1981.
   Subject focus: culture, socio-economic conditions, book and movie
   reviews.

   WHi   v.5, n.1-v.9, n.4;   Microforms
              Jan, 1979-Oct/Nov, 1981

   AkUF   [v.1, n.1-v.9, n.2]   E/78/A3/A425
              [1976-June/July, 1981]

   WaU   v.7, n.5-v.9, n.4;   E/78/A3/A45
              May, 1980-Oct/Nov, 1981

   Albuquerque Area Education Profile. Albuquerque, NM

       see Education Profile. Albuquerque, NM

35 The Albuquerque Indian. 1905-1906?//. Monthly. OCLC 5290339,
   8395323. RLIN CUBU13618106-S. Last issue 18 pages. Line drawings,
   photographs, commercial advertising. Available in microform: CPC
   (1905-1906). Published by Albuquerque Indian School, Albuquerque, NM.
   Editor: James K. Allen. School newsletter.

   WHi   v.1, n.1-12;   Microforms
              June, 1905-May, 1906

   Other holding institutions: NmU (IQU), PPiU (PIT).

Alcatraz, Indians of All Tribes. San Francisco, CA

   see Indians of All Tribes. San Francisco, CA

Aleut Corporation [Newsletter]. Anchorage, AK

   see Aleutian Current. Anchorage, AK

36 Aleutian Current. 1973. Monthly. Aleutian Current, 2550 Denali St.
   #900, Anchorage, AK 99503. (907) 274-1506. Line drawings,
   photographs. Published by Aleut Corporation. Title varies: Aleut
   Corporation [Newsletter], Feb 1, 1973-Feb, 1974. Frequency varies:
   bi-monthly, Mar/Apr-Sept/Oct, 1974; irregular, May-Dec, 1975.
   Corporate news.

   WHi   v.1, n.1-v.3, n.3;   Microforms
                Feb 1, 1973-Dec, 1975

   AkUF   v.1, n.1-   AK-129
                Feb 1, 1973-

37 Algoma Missionary News and Shingwauk Journal. 1877-1932//. Monthly.
   Last issue 48 pages. Available in microform: McL (1877-1880).
   Published by Diocese of Algoma, Sault Ste. Marie, Ontario, Canada.
   Subject focus: Catholic Church, missions.

   WHi   v.1, n.1-v.3, n.6;   Microforms
                July 1, 1877-June 1, 1880

   CaOONL   v.1, n.1-15;   Microfilm
                July 1, 1877-Sept, 1878

   CaOPeT   v.1, n.1-15, v.2, n.4, v.3, n.6;   Microfilm
                July 1, 1877-Sept, 1878,
                Apr 1, 1879, June 1, 1890

38 Alkali Speaks. 1981?//? Monthly. Last issue 30 pages, height 28 cm.
   Line drawings. Alkali Lake, British Columbia, Canada. Community
   newsletter.

   CaOAFN   Feb-Nov, 1981   Periodicals

The Alliance/L'Alliance. Hull, Quebec, Canada

   see The Alliance Journal/Le Journal Alliance. Hull, Quebec, Canada

39 <u>The Alliance Journal/Le Journal Alliance</u>. 1974. Irregular. The
   Alliance Journal/ Le Journal Alliance, 21, rue Brodeur, Hull, Quebec,
   Canada J8Y 2P6. (819) 770-7763. ISSN 0319-275x. LC ce75-34946. OCLC
   2442258, 2442459. RLIN DCLCCE7534946-S, OHCP2442258-S. Height 37 cm.
   Photographs, commercial advertising. Published by Laurentian Alliance
   of Metis & Non-Status Indians/Alliance laurentienne des Metis & Indiens
   sans statut. Title varies: The Alliance/L'Alliance, Feb, 1974-Mar/Apr,
   1975. Place of Publication varies: Val D'or, Quebec, Canada, Oct,
   1978-?, 1980. Subject focus: Metis people, Quebec Native people. In
   French, 50%.

CaAEU	v.5, n.10/11– Oct/Nov, 1978–	Boreal Institute
CaOAFN	v.8, n.1– Jan, 1981–	Periodicals
CaOONL	v.1, n.1– Feb, 1974–	Newspaper Section

40 <u>Alligator Times</u>. 1972. Monthly. Alligator Times, Seminole
   Communications, 6333 Forest St. Hollywood, FL 333024. OCLC 6169117.
   Last issue 4 pages. Line drawings, photographs. Available in
   microform: WHi (1977-1979); McP (1972-1973). Published by Seminole
   Tribe of Florida. Editor: Polly Osceola, May, 1972-Jan, 1973; Moses
   Jumper, Jr., Sept/Oct, 1977-Aug, 1978; Wanda Bowers, Dec, 1978-Apr/May,
   1979. Community newsletter. Subject focus: Seminole people of Florida.

WHi	v.1, n.2– May, 1972–	Microforms
WEU	v.1, n.11–v.2, n.4 June/July–Aug/Sept, 1975	Journalism Lab
WMUW	[v.3, n.6–v.5, n.2] [Sept/Oct, 1977–Apr/May, 1979]	(SPL) E/75/A42x
AzNCC	v.3, n.6– Sept/Oct, 1977–	Indian File
CNoSU	[v.1, n.2–10] [May, 1972–Jan, 1973]	Periodicals
NjP	v.1, n.1–v.3, n.6; Sept 13, 1968–Sept, 1977	Periodicals
OkU	v.1, n.2–10; May, 1972–Jan, 1973	WHC

   Other holding institutions: NmScW.

41 <u>Amedian</u>. 1973-1981?//. Bi-monthly. Last issue 20 pages, last volume
108 pages, height 28 cm. Line drawings, photographs, commercial
advertising. Published by German American Indian Group/Deutcher-
Indianischer Kreis, Stuttgart, West Germany. Editor: Dr. Axel
Schuze-Thulin. Subject focus: history, culture, arts and crafts,
socio-economic conditions, book reviews. In German, 100%.

ICN	v.4, n.6-v.8, n.2; Dec, 1976-Apr, 1980	CHAI
CaACG	[v.5, n.3/4-v.9, n.1] [June, 1977-Feb, 1981]	Periodicals

Other holding institutions: OkU

42 <u>American Aborigine</u>. 1959-?//. Unknown. Last issue 30 pages.
Available in microform: WHI-A, Veda Stone Papers, (1961). Published by
National Indian Youth Council, Gallup, NM. Editor: Herbert C.
Blatchford. Subject focus: organization news, history.

WHi	v.3, n.1; ?, 1961	Microforms
WEU ARC	v.3, n.1; ?, 1961	Micro 11
NmG	(n.s.?)v.1, n.1-4; 1962-1965	Periodicals

43 <u>The American Indian</u>. 1964?-1974//. Monthly, irregular. Last issue 8
pages, last volume 96 pages. Line drawings, photographs, commercial
advertising. Available in microform: WHi (1973-1974). Published by
American Indian Center, San Francisco, CA. Editor: Dolores Smith, Dec
1964-May 1968. Community newsletter. Subject focus: center news,
consumer and employment information.

WHi	Mar, 1964-Feb, 1965, Jan-Apr, 1967-Feb, May, 1968	Pam 76-840
WHi	(n.s.)v.2, n.25-28; Sept/Oct, 1973-Apr, 1974	Microforms
AzNCC	(n.s.)v.1-v.2, n.28; Sept/Oct, 1972-Apr, 1974	Indian File
NjP	[no nos.-(n.s.)v. 2, n.27] [Apr, 1964-Mar, 1974]	Periodicals
SdU	[v.5, n.1-v.6, n.1] [Jan, 1968-Jan/Feb, 1969]	Periodicals

Other holding institutions: MH-P (HLS).

44 American Indian: organized tribe's medium of expression.   1939-?//.
Quarterly. OCLC 1480002. Height 28 cm. Line drawings. Published by
North Central Publishing Co., St. Paul, MN. Editor: W.B. Pettit.
Subject focus: rights, culture.

TxU   n.1, 3;   970.05/Am351
             June, Dec, 1939

Other holding institutions: [University of Minnesota Union List,
Minneapolis, MN] (MUL), OAkU (AKR).

45 The American Indian. 1943-1959//. Semi-annual. LC 49-33497. OCLC
1480001. RLIN OHCP1480001-S. Last issue 48 pages, last volume 96
pages, height 19 cm. Published by Association on American Indian
Affairs, Inc., New York, NY. Frequency varies: quarterly, Nov
1943-Summer 1953; annual, Spring 1954-Spring 1955. Previous editors:
Carl Carmer, Nov 1943-Spring 1950; Alexander Lesser, Fall 1950-Winter
1958/59. Subject focus: history, culture, acculturation.

WHi   v.1, n.1-v.8, n.2;   E/77/A495
             Nov, 1943-Winter, 1958/59

WMM   [v.4, n.3-v.5, n.2]   Special
             [?, 1948-Spring, 1955]   Collections

AzFM   v.1, n.1-v.8, n.2;   570.6/A512a
             Nov, 1943-Winter, 1958/59

AzNCC   v.2-v.6;   Indian File
             Spring, 1952-Winter, 1956

AzU   v.1, n.1-v.8, n.2;   Periodicals
             Nov, 1943-Winter, 1958/59

CL   v.1, n.1-v.8, n.2;   Periodicals
             Nov, 1943-Winter, 1958/59

CLSM   v.1, n.1-v.8, n.2;   Periodicals
             Nov, 1943-Winter, 1958/59

ICN   v.1, n.1-v.8, n.2;   Ayer 2/A527
             Nov, 1943-Winter, 1958/59

MoS   v.1-v.8;   Periodicals
             1943-1958/59

NjP   [v.1, n.1-v.8, n.2]   Periodicals
             [Nov, 1943-Winter, 1958/59]

NHu   v.1, n.1-v.8, n.2;   Periodicals
             Nov, 1943-Winter, 1958/59

N   v.1, n.1-v.8, n.2;   C970.1/A511
             Nov, 1943-Winter, 1958/59

NN	v.1, n.1-v.8, n.2; Nov, 1943-Winter, 1958/59	HBA
OkTahN	v.7-v.8; 1958-1959	Spec. Coll. E/77/R495
OkU	v.3, n.2-v.8, n.2; Spring, 1946-Winter, 1958/1959	WHC
OrU	v.1, n.1-v.8, n.2; Nov, 1943-Winter, 1958/59	Periodicals
TxU	[v.1-v.8] [1943-1958/59]	970.105/Am35
UPB	[v.1, n.1-v.8, n.2] [Nov, 1943-Winter, 1958/59]	970.105/AM35IN
Wa	v.1-v.3, v.6; 1944-1946, 1951-1953	Periodcals

Other holding institutions: AzFU (AZN), CLU (CLU), CU-UC (UCU), [Emory
University Pittsburgh Theological Library, Atlanta, GA] (EMT), [Indiana
Union List of Serials, Indianapolis, IN] (ILS), InU (IUL), MH-P (HLS),
MiU (EYM), MNS (SNN), [University of Minnesota Union List, Minneapolis,
MN] (MUL), MoU (MUU), NRM (VXR), OCe (CLE), [Pittsburgh Regional
Library Center-Union List, Pittsburgh, PA] (QPR), PPi (CPL).

46 The American Indian. 1926-1931//. Monthly. OCLC 1480003. RLIN
CSUP00380301-S, OHCP1480003-S. Last issue 18 pages, height 36 cm.
Line drawings, photographs, commercial advertising. Available in
microform: CPC (1926-1931); NN (1926-1931). Tulsa, OK. Editor: Lee F.
Harkins. Subject focus: history, legends, fiction, poetry.

WHi	v.1, n.1-v.5, n.4; Oct, 1926-Mar, 1931	E/77/A492 Rare Books
WHi	v.1, n.1-v.5, n.3; Oct, 1926-Jan, 1931	Microforms
WMUW	v.1, n.1-v.5, n.4; Oct, 1926-Mar, 1931	E/77/A4x/ 1970
CL	v.1, n.1-v.5, n.4; Oct, 1926-Mar, 1931	Periodicals
CU-A	v.1, n.1-v.5, n.4; Oct, 1926-Mar, 1931	E/77/A1/A54
CtY-B	v.1, n.1-v.5, n.3; Oct, 1926-Jan, 1931	1972/Folio S1
IC	v.1, n.1-v.5, n.4; Oct, 1926-Mar, 1931	Periodicals

ICN	v.1, n.1–v.5, n.4; Oct, 1926–Mar, 1931	Ayer 1/A508
KU	v.1, n.1–v.5, n.4; Oct, 1926–Mar, 1931	Kansas Collection
MoSHi	v.1, n.1–v.5, n.3; Oct, 1926–Jan, 1931	970.1/Am35
NjP	v.2, n.7, 11, v.3, n.3; Apr, Aug, Dec,1 928	Periodicals
N	v.1, n.1–v.5, n.4; Oct, 1926–Mar, 1931	C970.1/qA51
NHu	v.1, n.1–v.5, n.4; Oct, 1926–Mar, 1931	Periodicals
NN	v.1, n.1–v.5, n.3; Oct, 1926–Jan, 1931	HBA
NN	v.1, n.1–v.5, n.3; Oct, 1926–Jan, 1931	Microforms
NdMinS	v.1, n.1–v.5, n.4; Oct, 1926–Mar, 1931	E/75/A54/1970
OkSa	v.1, n.1–v.3; Oct, 1926–1929	Periodicals
OkT	v.1, n.1–v.5, n.4; Oct, 1926–Mar, 1931	Periodicals
OkTU	v.1, n.1–v.5, n.4; Oct, 1926–Mar, 1931	Rare Book Room
OkU	v.1, n.1–v.5, n.4; Oct, 1926–Mar, 1931	WHC
OrU	v.1, n.1–v.5, n.4; Oct, 1926–Mar, 1931	Periodicals
SdU	v.1–4, v.5; 1927–1930, 1931	Stacks
Wa	v.1–v.5; 1926–1931	Periodicals
WyU	v.1, n.1–v.5, n.4; Oct, 1926–Mar, 1931	E/77/A492
CaACG	v.1, n.1–v.5, n.4; Oct, 1926–Mar, 1931	Periodicals

Other holding institutions: Aru (AFU), AzTeS (AZS), DI (UDI), GASU
(GSU), MBU (BOS), MH-P (HLS), MiU (EYM), [University of Minnesota Union

List, Minneapolis, MN] (MUL), [Central New York Library Resources
Council, Syracuse, NY] (SRR), OAkU (AKR), Ok (OKD), OKTD (OKT), OkEdT
(OKX), [Pittsburgh Regional Library System-Union List, Pittsburgh, PA]
(QPR), TxcLT (ILU), TxArU (IUA), TxU (IXA), [AMIGOS Union List of
Serials, Dallas, TX] (IUC).

American Indian Advocate. Independence, MO

   see Indian Teepee. Wheeling, WV

47 American Indian & Alaskan Native Census Report. 1981//. Unknown.
Last issue 6 pages, height 28 cm. Published by American Indian Census
& Statistical Data Project, Tulsa, OK. Editor: Bob Block. Subject
focus: socio-economic conditions, community development, population,
census, statistics.

   WHi   v.1;   Pam 82-552
               Sept, 1981

48 American Indian Art Magazine. 1975. Quarterly. $16. for individuals
and institutions. Roanne P. Goldfein, editor, American Indian Art
Magazine, 7314 E. Osborn Drive, Scottsdale, AZ 85251. (602) 994-5445.
ISSN 0362-2630. LC 76-643141. OCLC 2288031, 4343382, 7599739,
7599750. RLIN UTBG82-S1719, MIUG23552-S, OHCP4343382-S. Subject
focus: arts and crafts, art history, art exhibits and reviews,
auctions, books.

   WHi   v.1, n.1-   E/98/A7/A43
               Autumn, 1975-

   WGrU   Current issues   Native American
                                                       Studies Dept.

   WM   v.2, n.4-   Periodicals
               Autumn, 1977-

   WMMus   v.1, n.1-   572.7/7/A35
               Autumn, 1975-

   WMUW   v.1, n.1-   E/98/A7/A43
               Autumn, 1975-

   WRfC   v.1, n.1-   Periodicals
               Autumn, 1975-

   AkAML   Current two years   Periodicals

   AzFM   v.1, n.1-   570.6/A512ai
               Autumn, 1975-

AzHC	v.1, n.1- Autumn, 1975-	Periodicals
AzNCC	v.1, n.1- Autumn, 1975-	Indian File
AzPa	v.4, n.3- Summer, 1979-	Periodicals
AzPh	v.1, n.1- Autumn, 1975-	Periodicals
CL	v.1, n.2- Spring, 1976-	Periodicals
CSmarP	[v.1-v.4], v.5- [1975-1979], 1980-	Stacks
CU-A	v.1, n.1- Autumn, 1975-	E/98/A7/A45
CoCF	v.2- 1977-	Periodicals
IC	v.6, n.2- Spring, 1981-	Periodicals
ICN	v.1,n.1- Autumn, 1975-	Ayer 5/S95
MtBBCC	v.6- May, 1981-	Periodicals
MtGrCE	v.2- 1977-	Periodicals
MoHi	v.2, n.4- Autumm, 1977-	970.1/Am35a
MoSHi	v.2, n.3- May, 1977-	970.1/Am35
NbJAM	v.3, n.4- Autumn, 1978-	Periodicals
NbU	v.2- 1977-	E/98/A7A43
NjMonM	v.1, n.1- Autumn, 1975-	Periodicals
NjNM	v.1, n.1- Autumn, 1975-	Periodicals
NmG	v.1, n.1- Autumn, 1975-	Periodicals

NmScW	v.5– 1980–	Periodicals
NN	v.1, n.1– Autumn, 1975–	HBA 77-139
NcP	v.6. n.2; Feb, 1981	Periodicals
NdMinS	v.6, n.1– 1980–	Periodicals
OkPAC	v.1, n.1– Nov, 1975–	Periodicals
OkTahN	v.5– 1979–	Spec. Coll. E/98/A7/A43
OkTU	v.4, n.1– Winter, 1978–	Rare Book Room
OkU	v.1, n.1– Autumn, 1975–	WHC
Wa	v.3, n.2– 1978–	Periodicals
WaS	v.3– 1978–	Art Dept.
WaU	v.1, n.1– Autumn, 1975	Art E/98/A435
CaACG	v.1, n.1– Autumn, 1975–	Periodicals
CaMWU	v.3/4– 1977/1978–	700/A512/Ind Ar
CaOPeT	v.1, n.1– Autumn, 1975–	E98/E7A43
CaOSuU	v.1, n.1– Autumn, 1975–	Periodicals
CaSSIC	v.4, n.3– 1979–	Periodicals

Other holding institutions: [Amerind Foundation, Inc., Dragoon, AZ],
AzFU (AZN), AzTeS (AZS), AzT (AZT), CSdS (CDS), CLobS (CLO), CLSM, CLU
(CLU), CLCM (CNH), CU-S (CUS), [Pathfinder Regional Library Service
System, Montrose, CA] (DMP), CtY (YUS), DLC (DLC), DI (UDI), DeU (DLM),
FJUNF (FNP), FMFIL (FXG), GU (GUA), IGleD (IBI), IuIMu (IMO), InTI
(ISU), InIU (IUP), KSteC (KKQ), KMK (KKS), MBAt (BAT), MiD (EYP), MiU
(EYM), MnDuU (MND), MnU (MNU), MnM (MPI), [University of Minnesota
Union List, Minneapolis, MN] (MUL), MoS (SVP), NcRS (NRC), NdU (UND),

NhD (DRB), [Central New York Library Resources Council, Syracuse, NY]
(SRR), NSyU (SYB), NRM (VXR), NIFL (VYG), NBrockU (XBM), NA1fC (YDM),
NGH (ZEM), OAkU (AKR), [Bacone College, Muskogee, OK], Ok (OKD), OkOk
(OKE), OkU (OKU), [Pittsburgh Regional Library Center-Union List,
Pittsburgh, PA] (QPR), PPT (TEU), TMSC (TWS), TxR (IFA), [AMIGOS Union
List of Serials, Dallas, TX] (IUC), VtU (VTU), [Arrowhead Library
System-Janesville Public Library, Janesville, WI] (WIJ).

49 The American Indian Baptist Voice. 1955. Bi-monthly. B. Frank
   Belvin, editor, The American Indian Baptist Voice, 1724 East Ninth St.,
   Okmulgee, OK 74447. (918) 756-5567. OCLC 5130724. Last issue 4
   pages, last volume 24 pages, height 22 cm. Subject focus: Baptist
   Church, education, law.

   WHi   v.19, n.1-   Circulation
                Jan/Feb, 1973-

   AzNCC   v.23-   Indian File
                Nov, 1977-

   NjP   [v.1, n.1-v.24, n.2]   Periodicals
                [Jan/Feb, 1955-Mar/Apr, 1978]

   OkTU   v.24, n.2-   Rare Book
                Mar/Apr, 1978-   Room

   OkU   v.13-v.16;   WHC
                July, 1967-July, 1970

   Other holding institutions: [American Baptist Historical Society
   Library, Rochester, NY] (RXP).

50 American Indian Basketry Magazine. 1979. Irregular. $15./2 years for
   individuals and institutions. John M. Gogol, editor, American Indian
   Basketry Magazine, P.O. Box 66124, Portland, OR 97266. (503) 771-8540.
   LC 81-649293. OCLC 5767675, 8008285. RLIN DCLC81649293-S,
   NYPG814071368-S, DCLC81649294-S. Last issue 34 pages, height 28 cm.
   Line drawings, photographs, commerical advertising. Subject focus:
   basketry.

   WHi   v.1, n.1-   Circulation
                May?, 1979-

   WMMus   v.1, n.1-   572.7035/
                May?, 1979-   Am35

   WU   Current issues   Ethnic
   Coll   Collection

   CL   v.1, n.1-   Periodicals
                May?, 1979-

CoCF	v.1, n.1– May?, 1979–	Periodicals
NN	v.1, n.3– Oct 15, 1980–	Periodicals
OkPAC	v.1, n.1– May?, 1979–	Periodicals
OrHi	v.1, n.1– May?, 1979–	Periodicals
OrJM	v.1, n.1– May?, 1979–	Periodicals
Wa	v.1– 1979–	Periodicals
WaU	v.1– 1979–	E/98/B3A55
CaACG	v.1– 1979–	Periodicals
CaAEU	v.1– 1979–	Boreal Institute

Other holding institutions: CLSM, DLC (DLC), DSI (SMI).

51 American Indian Bilingual Education Center Newsletter. 1979.
Irregular. Free to individuals and institutions. Louis Baca, editor,
American Indian Bilingual Education Center Newsletter, University of
New Mexico, College of Education, Albuquerque, NM 87131. (505)
277-3763. Last issue 12 pages, height 28 cm. Photographs. Subject
focus: bilingual education and teaching (local). Supercedes Southwest
Bilingual Education Training Resource Center Newsletter.

NCBE	v.1–v.2; 1979–1980	Periodicals

52 American Indian Bulletin. 1929–?//. Monthly. Last issue 4 pages,
height 48 cm. Line drawings, photographs. Pipestone, MN. Editor:
James Irving. Newspaper. Subject focus: national news.

WMM	v.1, n.4; Apr, 1929	Special Collections

53 The American Indian: Captive or Citizen. 1927–?//. Unknown. OCLC
1480004. RLIN CUBU13636959, OHCP1480004, NYPG734166336-S. Last issue
4 pages, height 26 cm. Peoria, IL. Title varies: Our Captives or

"Wards"-The American Indian, Nov 1927–Apr, 1928. Place of publication
varies: New York, NY, Nov, 1927–Apr, 1928. Editor: Joseph W. Latimer.
Subject focus: rights, legislation, citizenship.

WHi   n.1–2, 8;   F809//LA
           Nov 1927–Apr, 1928, May, 1932   Cutter

Other holding institutions: [Minnesota Union List of Serials,
Minneapolis, MN] (MUL), NN (NYP).

54 American Indian Center News. 1955–?//. Monthly. Last issue 6 pages.
   Line drawings, photographs. Available in microform: WHI–A, Veda Stone
   Papers, (1961–1963). Chicago, IL. Community newsletter.

   WHi   v.7, n.1–3, v.8, n.3–4, v.9, n.1;   Microforms
              Oct 25–Dec, 1961, May 31–Aug, 1962,
              Feb 23, 1963

   WEU   v.7, n.1–3, v.8, n.3–4, v.9, n.1;   Micro 11
   ARC   Oct 25–Dec, 1961, May 31–Aug, 1962,
              Feb 23, 1963

   Other holding institutions: IC (CGP), ICN (IBV).

   American Indian Crafts and Culture Magazine. Tulsa, OK

       see Indian America. Tulsa, OK

55 American Indian Cultural Center Newsletter. 1970–1974?//. Quarterly.
   Last issue 30 pages, height 28 cm. Line drawings. Available in
   microform: WHI–A, Veda Stone Papers, (1971, 1972). Los Angeles, CA.
   Subject focus: center, area and national news.

   WHi   v.5, n.1/2–3;   Pam 76–2298
              Winter/Spring–Fall 1974

   WHi   v 2 n.7, v.3, n.5, v.4, n.2;   Microforms
              Aug 1971, ?, Mar, 1972

   WEU   v 2 n.7, v.3, n.5, v.4, n.2;   Micro 11
   ARC   Aug 1971, ?, Mar, 1972

   AzNCC   v.2–v.5;   Indian File
              June, 1971–June, 1974

   NjP   [v.1, n.2–v.5, n.3]   Periodicals
              [Sept, 1970–Fall, 1974]

   OrU   v.1–v.4;   Periodicals
              1970–1974

56 <u>American Indian Culture and Research Journal</u>. 1974. Quarterly. $6.
   for individuals and institutions. James R. Young, editor, American
   Indian Culture and Research Journal, 3220 Campbell Hall, University of
   California, 405 Highland Ave., Los Angeles, CA 90024. (213) 825-7315.
   ISSN 0161-6463. LC 78-643481. OCLC 1781938. RLIN CGTT318-S,
   DCLC78643481-S, CSUP101298-S, CUDG123-S, IAUG1111-S, MIUG1787-S,
   OHCP1781938-S. Last issue 124 pages, last volume 380 pages, height 23
   cm. Line drawings, photographs, commercial advertising. Available in
   microform: UM (1974-); WHI-A, Veda Stone Papers, (1974, 1975).
   Published by American Indian Studies Center. Previous editor: Kogee
   Thomas, 1974-1976. Subject focus: arts and crafts, culture, book
   reviews.

WHi	v.1, n.1– Spring, 1974–	E/75/A52
WEU	v.1, n.2, 4–v.2, n.3; Sept, Nov, 1974–Mar, 1975	Journalism Lab
WM	Current issues	Forest Home Branch
WMUW	v.1, n.1– Spring, 1974–	E/75/A4x
WRfC	v.3– Fall, 1978–	Periodicals
WMSC	v.1, n.2– Sept, 1974–	Periodicals
WUSP	v.1, n.1– Spring, 1974–	Periodicals
AzNCC	v.1, n.1– Spring, 1974–	Indian File
CL	v.1, n.1– Spring, 1974–	Periodicals
CSmarC	v.1– 1974–	Stacks
CU–A	v.1, n.1– Spring, 1974–	E/75/A5124
CoCF	v.1, v.3; 1974, 1976	Periodicals
IC	v.4– Oct, 1980–	Periodicals
IaHi	v.2–v.4; 1977-1980	E/75/A5124

KU	v.1, n.1– Spring, 1974–	Kansas Collection
LARC	v.1, n.1– Spring, 1974–	Periodicals
MtBBCC	v.5; July, 1981	Periodicals
MtGrCE	v.4– 1980–	Periodicals
NbU	v.1, n.1– Spring, 1974–	E/75/A5124
OkTahN	v.2– 1977–	Spec. Coll E/75/A5124
OkTU	v.1, n.1– Spring, 1974–	Rare Book Room
OkU	v.1, n.1– Spring, 1974–	WHC
OrU	v.1, n.1– Spring, 1974–	Periodicals
PPT	v.1– 1974–	Stacks
UPB	v.1–5; 1974–1981	970.105/AM35J
Wa	v.1– 1974–	Periodicals
WaOE	v.1– 1974–	Periodicals
WaU	v.1– 1974–	E/75/A497
WyCWC	[v.1–v.4] [1974–1980]	Periodicals
WyU	v.1– 1974–	E/77/A495x
CaOONL	v.1, n.1– Spring, 1974–	Periodicals
CaOPeT	v.1– 1974–	E75/A5124
CaOSuU	v.1–v.5 1974–1981	Periodicals

Other holding institutions: [Alabama Supreme Court and State Law
Library, Montgomery, AL] (ALS), ArU (AFU), AzTeS (AZS), CLobS (CLO),
CLU (CLU), CU-I (CUI), [Pepperdine University, Malibu, CA] (CPE),
[Pepperdine University Law Library, Malibu, CA] (CPF), COU-DA (COA),
CtY (YUS), DWG, (DWG), DC (DLC), FTS (FHM), GEU (EMU), GU (GEU), HU
(HUH), ICN (IBV), InLP (IPL), KSteC (KKQ), MBU (BOS), MNS (SNN), MdBJ
(JHE), MiEM (EEM), MiMtpt (EZC), MiU (EYM), MnU (MNU), [University of
Minnesota Union List, Minneapolis, MN] (MUL), MoU (MUU), [Washington
University Law Library, St. Louis, MO] (WUL), NeRS (NRS), NdU (UND),
[Creighton University Law Library, Omaha, NE] (CLL), NhD (DRB), NmLcU
(IRU), NmU-L (NML), NA1U (NAM), NOneoU, NRU, (RRR), NSyU (SYB), NSbSU
(YSM), OCU (CIN), [Ohio Historical Society, Columbus, OH] (OHT), OYU
(YNG), [Bacone College, Muskogee, OK], OkOk (OKE), OkS (OKS), [AMIGOS
Union List of Serials, Dallas TX] (IUC), TxCM (TXA), TxDa (IGA), ViRCU
(VRC).

57 <u>American Indian Culture Center Journal</u>. 1970-1973//. Quarterly. OCLC
1480006. Last issue 32 pages, last volume 56 pages, height 17 cm. Line
drawings, photographs. Available in microform: WHI-A, Veda Stone
Papers, (1970). Published by American Indian Cultural
Center-University of California at Los Angeles, Los Angeles, CA.
Previous editors: Alan Parker, Winter, 1971-Fall/Winter, 1971/1972;
Alan Parker and Virginia B. Morgan, Fall, 1972; Virginia B. Morgan,
Winter, 1973; Kogee Thomas, Fall, 1973. Subject focus: legislation,
politics, education, culture, history, poetry.

WHi	v.2, n.1-v.4, n.2; Winter, 1971-Fall, 1973	E/75/A5
WHi	v.1, n.4-5; Mar-May, 1970	Microforms
WEU ARC	v.1, n.4-5; Mar-May, 1970	Micro 11
WU-L	v.4, n.1-4; Spring-Winter, 1973	Periodicals Section
CL	v.2, n.1-v.4, n.2; Winter, 1971-Fall, 1973	Periodicals
CaOONL	v.3-v.4; 1971/1972-1973	Periodicals

Other holding institutions: [Alabama Supreme Court and State Law
Library, Montgomery, AL] (ALS), ArU (AFU), AzTeS (AZS), CLobS (CLO),
CU-I (CUI), InLP (IPL), MBU (BOS), [University of Minnesota Union List,
Minneapolis, MN] (MUL), [Creighton University Law Library, Omaha, NE]
(CLL), [New York State Union List, Albany, NY] (NYS), NRU (RRR), TxEU
(TXU), WaU (WaU).

American Indian Culture Research Center Newsletter. Marvin, SD

    see Blue Cloud Mission. Marvin, SD

58 American Indian Digest. 1957?//. Unknown. Last issue 4 pages, height
28 cm. Photographs. Published by Bulova Watch Co., Washington, DC.
Subject focus: acculturation.

WMM   May, 1957   Special
                                                  Collections

59 American Indian Education Newsletter. 1978-1981//. Irregular. OCLC
7844176, 4300605. Last issue 58 pages, last volume 124 pages, height
28 cm. Line drawings. Personal names indexed in: Index to Wisconsin
Native American Periodicals (1978-1981). Published by Wisconsin
Department of Public Instruction, Madison, WI. Title Varies: Indian
Education Newsletter, Jan, 1978-Summer, 1979. Previous editors: Leslie
Garrard and Helene Lincoln, Jan-Spring, 1978; Leslie Garrard, Summer,
1979; Roger R. Philbrick, Fall, 1980-Spring, 1981. Subject focus:
education, educational legislation, curriculum development.

WHi   v.1, n.1-v.3, n.2;   WI/Ed//4/2:
           Jan, 1978-Spring, 1981   I5/1978-

60 American Indian Fellowship Association. 1982? Unknown. American
Indian Fellowship Association, 2 E. Second St., Duluth, MN 55802. Last
issue 5 pages, height 28 cm. Line drawings. Community newsletter.

WHi   Sept-Nov, 1980, July, 1982-   Circulation

61 American Indian Health Care Association. 1978. Bi-monthly. American
Indian Health Care Association, 1925 Nicollet Ave., Minneapolis, MN
55403. Last issue 6 pages, height 28 cm. Subject focus: health care.

WHi   v.3, n.5-6;   Microforms
           July-Sept, 1980

62 American Indian Higher Education Consortium Newsletter. 1974.
Monthly. Geri Mills, editor, American Indian Higher Education
Consortium Newsletter, 1582 S. Parker Rd., Suite 204, Denver, CO 80231.
(303) 750-1883. Last issue 6 pages, height 28 cm. Line drawings,
photographs. Subject focus: higher education, adult and continuing
education, educational legislation.

WHi   [v.3, n.1-7], (n.s.)v.2, n.1-   Circulation
           [Sept/Oct, 1975-Jan, 1977], Nov, 1981-

AzNCC   v.1, n.1-   Indian File
             Spring, 1974-

MtBBCC   (n.s.)v.2, n.1-   Periodicals
             Nov, 1981-

NjP   [v.1, n.2-Spec. Ed.]   Periodicals
             [Summer, 1974-Winter, 1978]

Other holding institutions: [Dull Knife Memorial College, Lame Deer,
MT].

American Indian Hobbyist. Alton, IL

    see American Indian Tradition. Alton, IL

63 American Indian Horizon. 1962-1966?//?. Monthly. ISSN 0517-2268.
OCLC 4041715. RLIN OHCP4041715-S. Last issue 4 pages, height 28 cm.
Line drawings, photographs, commercial advertising. Available in
microform: WHI-A, Veda Stone Papers, (1963, 1964). Published by
American Indian Horizon Publishing Company, New York, NY. Editor:
Henri Ben-Ami. Subject focus: rights, legislation, culture.

WHi   [v.1, n.1-v.3, n.4]   Pam 76-851
             [Oct, 1962-Dec, 1964]

WHi   v.2, n.2, v.3, n.6;   Microforms
             Oct, 1963, Spring, 1966

WEU   v.2, n.2, v.3, n.6;   Micro 11
ARC   Oct, 1963, Spring, 1966

NjP   [v.1, n.8-v.3,n.2]   Periodicals
             [Apr, 1963-Oct, 1964]

OkU   [v.1, n.1-v.3, n.4]   WHC
             [Oct, 1962-Dec, 1964]

Other holding institutions: [University of Minnesota Union List,
Minneapolis, MN] (MUL), OrU-Special Collections.

64 American Indian Index. 1953-1968//. 8 times a year. ISSN 0569-5244.
LC 72-8243, sc80-1163. OCLC 2257321, 8392471. RLIN DCLCSC801163-S,
CSUP00380702-S, CUBG37068908-S, MIUG281162-S. Last issue 10 pages.
Available in microform: CPC (1953-1968). River Grove, IL. Index.

WHi   n.1-148;   Z/1209/A4
             1953-Nov, 1968

WHi	n.1–148; 1953–Nov, 1968	Microforms
ICN	[n.1–148] [1953–Nov, 1968]	Ayer 290 A51/1953
N	n.1–148; 1953–Nov, 1968	J970.1016/ qA514
SdU	n.1–148; 1953–Nov, 1968	Microfilm
CaMWU	n.101–148; 1963–1968	Z/1209/A5
CaOONL	n.1–n.148; 1953–Nov, 1968	Periodicals
CaOPeT	n.1–n.148; 1953–Nov, 1968	Microfiche

Other holding institutions: CLU (CLU), CU–UC (UCU), [U.S. Information Agency, Washington, DC] (USI), ILfC (IAK), IWW (ICW), LU (LUU), Me (MEA), MiEM (EEM), MiYEM (EYE), [University of Minnesota Union List, Minneapolis, MN] (MUL), NmU (IQU), [New York State Union List, Albany, NY] (NYS), NR (YQR), NWM (YWM), OAkU (AKR), OKentU (KSU), PBL (LYU), P (PHA), PPiU (PIT), TxDa (IGA).

65 American Indian Journal. 1975. Monthly. $35. for individuals and institutions. Kate Winslow, editor, American Indian Journal, 927 15th Street, N.W., Suite 200, Washington, DC 20005. (202) 638-2287. ISSN 0145-7993. LC 76-640032. OCLC 2256009. RLIN MABL81-S13, DCLC76640032-S, CUDL1641-S, CUBG12765168-S, CTYG2256009-S, CSCX240-S. Last issue 28 pages, height 28 cm. Line drawings. Available in microform: UM (1975–). Published by Institute for the Development of Indian Law, Inc. Previous editors: John Tiger, Oct, 1975; Loretta Lehman, Nov, 1975–July, 1976; Jenna Whitehead, Aug–Sept, 1976; Douglas Basinger, Oct, 1976–Oct, 1978; Nathan Stoltzfus, Nov, 1978–Oct, 1979. Subject focus: legislation, law, legal history.

WHi	v.1, n.1– Oct, 1975–	KF/8201/A3/ A4
WMM	v.1, n.1– Oct, 1975–	Law
WMUW	v.1, n.1– Oct, 1975–	K/1/M4x
WU Coll	Current issues	Ethnic Collection
WU–L	v.1, n.1– Oct, 1975–	Periodicals Section

WUSP	[v.1, n.1-v.4, n.1] [Oct, 1975-Jan, 1978]	Periodicals
AzNCC	v.1, n.1- Oct, 1975-	Indian File
CL	v.1, n.1- Oct, 1975-	Periodicals
CSmarP	[v.1-v.6], v.7- [1975-1980], 1981-	Stacks
IC	v.7, n.1- Jan, 1981-	Periodicals
ICN	Current issues	CHAI
Mi	v.1, n.1- Oct, 1975-	Periodicals
MtBBCC	v.7; Jan-Apr, 1981	Periodicals
NjP	[v.1, n.1-v.4, n.8] [Oct, 1975-Aug, 1978]	Periodicals
N	v.1, n.1- Oct, 1975-	J301.4519707/ qA512
NOneoC	v.6,n.8- 1980-	Periodicals
OkTahN	v.3- 1977-	Periodicals
OkTU	v.1, n.1- Oct, 1975-	Rare Book Room
OkU	v.1, n.1, v.6, n.11- Oct, 1975, Nov, 1980-	WHC
OrU	v.1, n.1- Oct, 1975-	Periodicals
SdU	v.1- 1975-	Law Library
Wa	v.1- 1975-	Periodicals
CaMWU	v.1- 1975-	K/1/M466
CaOAFN	v.2, n.5, v.4, n.10; May, 1976, Oct, 1978	Periodicals

CaOSuU   v.5-v.7   Periodicals
            1979-1981

CaSS1C   v.1, n.1-   Periodicals
            Oct, 1975-

Other holding institutions: [Alabama Supreme Court and State Law
Library, Montgomery, AL] (ALS), ArU (AFU), AzFU (AZN), AzU (AZU), CLU
(CLU), [Pepperdine University Law Library, Malibu, CA] (CPF), CtY
(YUS), [Congressional Research Service, Washington, DC] (CRS), DLC
(DLC), DSI (SMI), DI (UDI), FMU-L (FML), FTaSU-L (FSL), FU (FUG), HU
(HUH), ICD-L (IBC), ICarbS-L (SOL), InU (IUL), InTV (IVZ), LNL-L (LLT),
MChB (BXM), MH (HUL), MiEM (EEM), MiMtpT (EZC), MiU-L (EYM),
[University of Minnesota Union List, Minneapolis, MN] (MUL), [St. Louis
University Law Library, St. Louis, MO] (SLU), [Washington University
Law Library, St. Louis, MO] (WUL), NcWsW (EWL), NbU (LDL), NmU-L (NML),
[New York State Union List, Albany, NY] (NYS), [Central New York
Library Resources Council, Syracuse, NY] (SRR), NCaS (XLM), NA1LS
(YZA), NNepaSU (ZLM), [University of Akron Law Library, Akron OH]
(AKL), OC1U-L (LMC), OTU-L (UTL), OYU (YNG), [Bacone College, Muskogee,
OK], Ok (OKD), OkOkU-L (OKY), OkT (TUL), P (PHA), PPiU (PIT), PPiU-L
(PLA), [AMIGOS Union List of Serials, Dallas, TX] (IUC), [Southern
Methodist University Law Library, Dallas, TX] (IUF), UOW (UUO), ViBlbv
(VPI), ViW-L (VWL).

66 American Indian Journal. 1928?//. Quarterly. Last issue 80 pages,
    height 28 cm. Line drawings, photographs, commerical advertising.
    Billings, MT. Editor: Bob Pettit. Subject focus: history, culture.

    MtHi   ?, 1928   Z/970.105/Am37j

67 American Indian Law Newsletter. 1968. Bi-monthly. $20. for
    individuals and institutions; $15. for Native Americans and Native
    American organizations. Nancy M. Tuthill, editor, Ameican Indian Law
    Newsletter, 1117 Stanford, N.E., P.O. Box 4456-Station A, Albuquerque,
    NM 87196. (505) 277-5462. OCLC 1480008. RLIN UTUL0211-S, CUDL2930-S,
    CSUP00380805-S, OHCP1480008-S. Last issue 9 pages, last volume 54
    pages, height 28 cm. Available in microform: McA (1968-); CPC
    (1968-1978). Published by American Indian Law Center, Inc. Frequency
    varies: bi-weekly, May, 1968-Dec, 1979. Previous editors: Joseph D.
    Sabatini, May-June 7, 1968; Helen S. Carter, June 14-20, 1968; Joseph
    D. Sabatini, June 28, 1968-Dec 27, 1972; Toby F. Grossman, Feb 9,
    1973-June, 1974; Earl J. Waits, Feb-May/June, 1980; T. Parker Sando,
    July/Aug, 1980. Subject focus: legislation, congressional monitoring.

    WHi   v.1, n.1-   Microforms
               May, 1968-

    WEU   v.3, n.20-22;   Journalism
               Dec 15, 1970-Jan 9,1971   Lab

WGrU	v.4, n.10– May?, 1971–	Periodicals
WMUW	v.5, n.9– June?, 1972–	KF/200/A415x
WU–L	v.1, n.1– May, 1968–	Periodicals Section
AzNCC	v.6– Jan, 1973–	Indian File
CL	v.5, n.9– June?, 1972–	Periodicals
ICN	Current issues	CHAI
MtBBCC	v.13; July–Dec, 1980	Periodicals
NbU	v.1,n.1– May, 1968–	Law
NvWNCC	v.1, n.1–v.5; May, 1968–Dec, 1972	Microfilm
NjP	[v.1, n.1–v.11, n.15] [May, 1968–Aug, 1978]	Periodicals
NN	v.1, n.1–v.9; May., 1968–Sept, 1976	Microforms
NcP	v.13– 1980–	Periodicals
OkTahN	v.10– 1977–	Peroidicals
OkTU	v.11, n.6/7– Apr, 1978–	Rare Book Room
OkU	v.1, n.1– Mar, 1968–	WHC
SdU	v.1–v.9; 1968–1976	Microfilm
Wa	v.1– 1968–	Law Library
WyCWC	v.5, n.1–v.8, n.24; May, 1968–Jan, 1975	Periodicals
WyU	v.5– 1968–	Law Library

CaMWU   v.1-v.9;   Law
             1968-1976

CaOAFN   v.3, n.20, v.4, n.13-14;   Periodicals
             Dec 15, 1970, July 1-Aug 1, 1971

CaOPeT   v.8-   Microfilm
             1976-

CaSSIC   v.1-   Periodicals
             1968-

Other holding institutions: AzU (AZU), CLSM, CLU (CLU), [Congressional
Research Service, Washington, DC] (CRS), DHU (DHU), DGU-L (GUL), DI
(UDI), FMU-L (FML), FU-L (FUB), ICD-L (IBC), [Indiana Union List of
Serials, Indianapolis, IN] (ILS), MiDW (EYW), MiU-L (EYM), [University
of Minnesota Union List, Minneapolis, MN] (MUL), [St. Louis University
Law Library] (SLU), NmLcU (IRU), NmLvH (NMH), NbuUL (SBL), [Central New
York Library Resources Council, Syracuse, NY] (SRR), OTU-L (UTL), ONcM
(MSC), OkOkU-L (OKY), PPiU (PIT), PPiU-L (PLA), TU-L (UTL), [AMIGOS
Union List of Serials, Dallas, TX] (IUC), TxEU (TXU).

68 <u>American Indian Law Review</u>. 1973. Semi-annual. $7.50 for individuals
   and institutions. Sharon E. Claassen, editor, American Indian Law
   Review. Room 335, College of Law, 300 Timberdell Road, Norman, OK
   73019. (405) 325-2840. ISSN 0094-002x. LC 74-643419. OCLC 1793421.
   RLIN NJRL82-S46, CACL82-S92, NYPG20972857-S, UTUL0212-S,
   DCLC74643419-S, CUDL225-S, CSUP07165602-S, OHCP1793421-S,
   NYPG794295963-S. Last issue 184 pages, last volume 448 pages, height
   23 cm. Published by College of Law, University of Oklahoma. Previous
   editors: Robert A. Fairbanks, Winter, 1973; Terrill V. Landrum,
   Summer-Winter, 1974; John Gamino, Winter-Summer, 1975; John C. Dill,
   Winter, 1976; Bonnie J. Schomp, Summer, 1976; Joe D. Dillsaver, Winter,
   1977; Robert L. Johnston, Summer, 1977-Winter, 1978; Louis D. Persons
   II, Summer, 1978. Subject focus: law, rights, land claims, water
   rights, BIA, tribal government.

WGrU   v.6, n.1-   Periodicals
             Winter, 1978-

WM   v.2, n.1-   Periodicals
             Summer, 1974-

WMM   v.1, n.1-   Law
             Winter, 1973-

WOshU   v.1, n.1-   Periodicals
             Winter, 1973-

WU   Current issues   Ethnic
Coll   Collection

WU-L   v.1, n.1-   Periodicals
             Winter, 1973-   Section

AzNCC	v.2- Winter, 1974-	Indian File
IC	v.7, n.1- Apr, 1979-	Periodicals
Mi	v.1, n.1- Winter, 1973-	Law Library
MnBemT	v.1- 1974-	Periodicals
NbU	v.1, n.1- Winter, 1973-	Law
N	v.1, n.1- Winter, 1973-	Law/Per
NN	v.1, n.1- Winter, 1973-	HBA 79-449
OkTahN	v.1- 1973-	Law Library
OkTU	v.1- 1973-	Rare Book Room
OkU	v.1- 1973-	WHC
SdU	v.1- 1973-	Law Library
Wa	v.1- 1973-	Law Library
WaU	v.1- 1973-	Law Library
WyCWC	v.2, n.1-v.7, n.2; Summer, 1974-1980	Periodicals
CaMWU	v.1- 1973-	Law K/1/M469

Other holding institutions: [Alabama Supreme Court and State Law
Library, Miontgomery, AL] (ALS), ArU (AFU), AzFU (AZN), CLU (CLU),
CLavC (CLV), [Pepperdine University Law Library, Malibu, CA] (CPF), Ct
(CZL), [Congressional Research Service, Washington, DC] (CRS), DLC
(DLC), DSI (SMI), DI (UDI), [Delaware Law School of Widener College,
Wilmington, DE] (DLA), FTaSU-L (FSL), FU-L (FUB), FGULS (FUL), ICD-L
(IBC), ICN (IBV), ICI-K (ILK), ICarbS-L (SOL), [Indiana Union List of
Serials, Indianapolis, IN] (ILS), InTV (IVZ), LNL-L (LLT), LNT-L (LRL),
MiEM (EEM), MiKW (EXW), MiDW (EYW), MiMtpT (EZC), MiU-L (EYM), MnSAG
(MAG), MnMCC (MCO), [University of Minnesota Union List, Minneapolis,
MN] (MUL), MoU (MUU), [St. Louis University Law Library, St. Louis, MO]
(SLU), MT-L (MTS), NcWsW (EWL), [Creighton University Law Library,

Omaha, NE] (LDL), NhD (DRB), NmU-L (NML), [New York State Union List,
Albany, NY] (NYS), NRU (RRR), NNYU (YYP), NA1LS (YZA), [University of
Akron Law Library, Akron, OH] (AKL), OC1U-L (LMC), [University of
Dayton Law Library, Dayton, OH] (ODL), [University of Cincinnati Marx
Law Library, Cincinnati, OH] (OML), OTU-L (UTL), [Bacone College,
Muskogee, OK], OkLC (OKC), Ok (OKD), OkTOR (OKO), OkS (OKS), OkokU-L
(OKY), [Dickinson School of Law-Sheely Lee Law Library, Carlisle, PA]
(DKL), P (PHA), PPiU-L (PLA), TU-L (TLK), [AMIGOS Union List of
Serials, Dallas, TX] (IUC), [Southern Methodist University Law Library,
Dallas, TX] (IUF), TxEU (TXU), ViW-L (VWL), ViW (VWM).

69 American Indian Libraries Newsletter. 1976. 3 times a year. $5. for
individuals, $7. for institutions, $12. international. Dr. Cheryl
Metoyer-Duran, editor, American Indian Libraries Newsletter, Office for
Library Outreach Services, P.O. Box 111, Liberty Corner, NJ 07938.
(312) 944-6780. ISSN 0193-8207. LC sc79-3386, 82-644014. OCLC
3633821. RLIN DCLC82644014-S, CUDG82-S34, CUBG1276002X-S, OHCP3633821.
Last issue 4 pages, last volume 22 pages, height 28 cm. Photographs.
Available in microform: UM (1976-). Published by ALA OLOS Committee on
Library Service for Native American People. Place of publication
varies: Chicago, IL, Fall, 1976-1981. Subject focus: libraries,
library education.

WM	Current issues	Forest Home Branch
WM	Current 5 years	Periodicals
WMaPI-RL	v.1, n.1– Fall, 1976–	Periodicals
WMSC	v.1, n.1–v.4, n.1; Fall, 1976-1979	Periodicals
WU Lib S	v.1, n.1– Fall, 1976–	Periodicals Section
AzHM	v.1, n.1– Fall, 1976–	Periodicals
AzNCC	v.1, n.1– Fall, 1976–	Indian File
AzPh	v.1, n.1– Fall, 1976–	Periodicals
IC	v.1, n.1– Fall, 1976–	Periodicals
ICN	Current issues	CHAI
L	v.2– 1977–	Periodicals

MnKRL	v.1, n.1– Fall, 1976–	Periodicals
MtBBCC	v.1, n.1– Fall, 1976–	Periodicals
NjP	[v.1, n.1–v.3, n.3] [Fall, 1976–Spring, 1979]	Periodicals
N	v.1, n.1– Fall, 1976–	J027.63 A512
NPotU	v.1, n.1– Fall, 1976–	E/97.8/A6
OkTU	v.1, n.1– Fall, 1976–	Rare Book Room
OkU	v.1, n.1– Fall, 1976–	WHC
CaOAFN	v.5, n.2–3/4; Winter-Spring/Summer, 1981	Periodicals
CaOONL	v.1, n.1– Fall, 1976	Periodicals

Other holding institutions: [Alabama Public Library Service,
Montgomery, AL] (ASL), AzU (AZU), CLU (CLU), CU-UC (UCU), COU-DA (COA),
COD (DPL), DI (DI), GEU (EMU), IDEKN (JNA), I (SPI), IU (UIU), In
(ISL), MchB (BXM), MiDW (EYW), [University of Minnesota Union List,
Minneapolis, MN] (MUL), MoU (MUU), NmLcU (IRU), NA1U (NAM), [New York
State Union List, Albany, NY] (NYS), NBP (VZQ), NGenoU (YGM), OKentU
(KSU), Ok (OKD), [Northwestern Oklahoma State University Library, Alva,
OK] (OKT), PPD (DXU), PPiU (PIT), PCLS (REC), ScU (SUC), TxDN (INT),
TxArU (IUA), [AMIGOS Union List of Serials, Dallas TX], (IUC), TxDW
(IWU), WaU (WAU).

70 <u>American Indian Life</u>. 1925–1936//. Quarterly. OCLC 1480009. RLIN
CSUP00380908-S, CUBU13623400-S, OHCP1480009-S. Last issue 8 pages,
height 28 cm. Line Drawings, photographs. Available in microform:
McA, John Collier Papers (1925–1935). Published by American Indian
Defense Association, Inc., Washington, DC. Place of publication
varies: San Francisco, CA, June, 1925–May, 1929. Subject focus:
legislation, BIA.

WHi	n. 26; Mar, 1935	F801//+AM Cutter
WHi	n.1–26; June, 1925–Mar, 1935	Microforms J. Collier Papers

WMM	[n.14-21] [May, 1929-Jan, 1933]	Special Collections
WUSP	n.1-26; June, 1925-Mar, 1935	Microfilm J. Collier Papers
AzNCC	July, 1931	Indian File
CL	n.1-27; June, 1925-Apr, 1936	Periodicals
NjP	[n.1-26] [June, 1925-Mar, 1935]	Periodicals
NN	[n.10-27] Oct/Nov, 1927-Apr, 1937]	HBA+
OkU	n.1-27; June, 1925-Apr, 1936	WHC
OrU	n.14-16, 18; May 29-July 30, 31, 1929	Periodicals
WyU	n.1-26; June, 1925-Mar, 1935	Microfilm

Other holding institutions: [University of Minnesota Union List,
Minneapolis, MN] (MUL).

American Indian Life. Custer, SD

   see Indian Life. Custer, SD

71 American Indian Magazine. 1913-1920//. Quarterly. LC 15-7546. OCLC
1780015. RLIN CUBG12825992-S, MIUG051267-S, MIUG051265-S4,
OHCP1780015-S. Last issue 44 pages, last volume 186 pages, height 29
cm. Line drawings, photographs, commercial advertising. Available in
microform: CPC (1913-1920). Published by The Society of American
Indians, Washington, DC. Title varies: The Quarterly Journal of the
Society of American Indians, Apr 15, 1913-Oct/Dec, 1915. Editors:
Arthur C. Parker, Jan/Apr, 1913-Summer, 1918; Gertrude Bonner, Autumn,
1918-Fall, 1919. Subject focus: acculturation, education, law,
biographies, book reviews.

WHi	v.1, n.1-v.7, n.4; Apr 15, 1913-Aug,1920	F801/856/Q Cutter
WHi	v.1, n.1-v.7, n.4; Apr 15, 1913-Aug,1920	Microforms

WMM	[v.2, n.1-v.4, n.4] [Jan/Mar, 1914-Oct/Dec, 1916]	Special Collections
CLSM	v.1, n.1-v.7, n.4; Apr 15, 1913-Aug, 1920	Periodicals
IaHi	v.1, n.1-v.7, n.4; Apr 15, 1913-Aug, 1920	E/77/A5
IC	v.1, n.1-v.7, n.4; Apr 15, 1913-Aug, 1920	Periodicals
ICN	v.1, n.1-v.7, n.4; Apr 15, 1913-Aug, 1920	Ayer 1/A515
MWA	v.4; 1916	Periodicals
MoSHi	[v.1, n.2-v.7, n.4] [1913-1920]	970.1/Am34
MoHi	[v.1], v.2-v.7, n.2 [1913], 1914-Summer, 1919	Periodicals
NjP	v.4, n.1, v.5, n.4; Jan/Mar, 1916, Winter, 1917	Periodicals
N	[v.1, n.1-v.7, n.4] [Apr 15, 1913-Aug,1920]	C970.1/S67
NHu	v.1, n.1-v.7, n.4; Apr 15, 1913-Aug, 1920	Periodicals
NN	v.1, n.1-v.7, n.4; Apr 15, 1913-Aug, 1920	HBA
OCHP	v.1, n.1-v.7; Apr, 15, 1913-1920	970.05/ AM35
OC1WHi	v.7, n.1-3; 1920	Periodicals
OkU	[v.1, n.2-v.7, n.2] [May, 1914-Summer, 1919]	WHC
PP	v.1-v.3; 1913-1915	970.1/So13q
PP	v.4-v.7; 1916-1920	Microfilm
SdU	v.1, n.1-v.7, n.4; Apr 15, 1913-Aug,1920	Microfilm
TxU	[v.1, n.1-v.7, n.3] [Apr 15, 1913-1920]	970.106 Am351

UPB   v.4;   970.105/AM35M
           1916

CaOPeT   v.1-v.7;   Microfiche
           1913-1920

Other holding institutions: CoD (DPL), MH-P (HLS), [University of
Minnesota Union List, Minneapolis, MN] (MUL), MoU (MUU), NRM (VXR).

72 <u>American Indian Movement</u>. 1972?-?//. Unknown. Last issue 24 pages.
   Line drawings. Available in microform: WHI-A, Veda Stone Papers,
   (1972). Milwaukee, WI. Community newsletter. Subject focus:
   education, social services.

   WHi   Feb, 1972   Microforms

   WEU   Feb, 1972   Micro 11
   ARC

73 <u>American Indian National Bank Newsletter</u>. 1974-?//. Monthly. Last
   issue 4 pages, height 28 cm. Photographs. Available in microform: WHi
   (1974). Washington, DC. Subject focus: banking, economics.

   WHi   n.2;   Microforms
               Apr, 1974

74 <u>American Indian News</u>. 1968-?//?. Monthly. ISSN 0300-7278. LC
   sc77-414. OCLC 1334428. RLIN DCLC77414-S, OHCP1334428-S. Last issue
   2 pages, height 28 cm. Line drawings. Available in microform: CPC
   (1968-1973). Published by Indian League of the Americas, New York, NY.
   Title varies: Indian Life Newsletter, Mar-Sept, 1968; ILOTAN, Nov,
   1968-Sept, 1970. Subject focus: organization news and programs.

   WHi   v.1, n.19-v.3, n.48   Microforms
               Nov, 1968-June, 1973

   WEU   [v.2, n.7-v.3, n.23]   Journalism
               [June/July, 1969-Jan, 1971]   Lab

   AzNCC   v.2-v.3, n.48;   Indian File
               Mar, 1971-June, 1973

   CU-A   v.2, n.15-v.3, n.4, 43-48;   E/77/A1/A55
               Mar, 1970-Oct, 1972, Jan-June, 1973

   NjP   [v.1, n.19-v.3, n.48]   Periodicals
               [Nov, 1968-June, 1973]

   NHu   [v.1, n.19-v.3, n.1]   Periodicals
               [Nov 1968-1969]

NN	v.1, n.19-v.3, n.48 Nov, 1968-June, 1973	Microforms
PPT	[v.3, n.29-42] [Oct, 1971-Dec, 1972]	Contemporary Culture
SdU	v.1, n.27, 32; 1968	Richardson Archives
CaAEU	v.3, n.23-48 Jan, 1971-June, 1973	Boreal Institute
CaOPeT	[v.1, n.19-v.3, n.48] [Nov, 1968-June, 1973]	Microfiche

Other holding institutions: DLC (NSD), DI (UDI), MH-P (TOX), OrU-Special Collections.

75 American Indian Policy Review Commission Newsletter. 1976?//.
Unknown. Last issue 6 pages, height 35 cm. Photographs. Available in microform: WHi (1976). Washington, DC. Subject focus: governmental relations, legislation, rights.

WHi	May, 1976	Microforms
NjP	Apr, May, 1976	Periodicals

76 American Indian Press Association News Service. 1974-1975//.
Irregular. OCLC 4022192. Last issue 4 pages, height 28 cm. Available in microform: CPC (229 issues). Published by American Indian Press Association, Washington, DC. Subject focus: politics, law.

WHi	May 27, 1974-Sept 29, 1975	E/75/A54
WHi	[Sept, 1972-June, 1975]	Microforms
WMUW	[Sept, 1972-June, 1975]	(SPL) E/77/A63x
AzNCC	1971-Oct, 1975	Indian File
CL	1971-1972	Periodicals
SdU	May 27, 1974-Sept 29, 1975	Microfilm

Other holding institutions: [University of Minnesota Union List, Minneapolis, MN] (MUL), NHu.

77 American Indian Program Field Bulletin. 1964-?//. Unknown. Last issue 6 pages, height 28 cm. Photographs. Available in microform: WHi

(1964). Published by Save the Children Foundation and Community
Development Foundation, Albuquerque, NM. Subject focus: health,
education, social services.

WHi	v.1, n.3; July, 1964	Microforms

78 <u>American Indian Quarterly</u>. 1974. Quarterly. $15. for individuals,
   $20. for institutions. William Turnbull, editor, American Indian
   Quarterly, NAS, 3415 Dwinnelle Hall, Berkeley, CA 94720. (415)
   642-6717. ISSN 0095-182x. LC 74-647596. OCLC 1795987. RLIN
   PAUG81-S141, DCLC74647596-S, CSUP04421310-S, CUDG2139-S, MIUG0210-S,
   NHDG143-S,CUPG2846-S, CTYG1795987-S, CUBU2314-S, OHCP1795987-S,
   CSUG1838261-S. Last issue 120 pages, last volume 414 pages, height 21
   cm. Line drawings, commercial advertising. Indexed in: Abstracts in
   Anthropology (1977, 1978, 1982); America: History and Life (1975-); MLA
   International Bibliography (1975-); Book Review Index (1975-).
   Published by the Southwestern American Indian Society. Place of
   publication varies: Hurst, TX, Spring, 1974-Aug, 1979. Subject focus:
   culture, history, literature, socio-economic conditions, book reviews,
   bibliographic citations.

WHi	v. 1, n. 1- Spring, 1974-	Circulation
WMUW	v., n.1- Spring, 1974-	E/75/A547
WUSP	v.1, n.1-v.5, n.2; Spring, 1974-May, 1979	Periodicals
AzFM	v.2- 1975-	570.6/ A512aq
AzHC	v. 1, n. 1-v.5; Spring, 1974-Summer, 1979	Periodicals
AzNCC	v.1, n.1-v.4; Spring, 1974-Feb, 1978	Indian File
CL	v.1, n.1- Spring, 1974-	Periodicals
CSmarP	[v.1-v.5]- [1974-1979]-	Stacks
CoCF	v.1, n.1- Spring, 1974-	E/75/A547
ICN	v.1, n.1- Spring, 1974-	Ayer E/75/ A547
LARC	v.1, n.1- Spring, 1974-	Periodicals

NbU	v.3- 1977-	E/75/A547
NPotU	v.1, n.1- Spring, 1974-	E/75/A55
NOneoC	[v.1,n.1-v.5, n.2] [Spring, 1974-May, 1979]	Periodicals
OkTahN	v.1, n.1- Spring, 1974-	E/75/A547
OkTU	v.1, n.1- Spring, 1974-	Rare Book Room
OkU	v.1, n.2- Summer, 1974-	WHC
OrHi	v.1, n.1-v.4; Spring, 1974-1978	Periodicals
OrU	v.1, n.1- Spring, 1974-	Periodicals
SdU	v.1, n.1- Spring, 1974-	Stacks
TxU	v.1, v.3- 1974/1975, 1977-	E/77/A2474
UPB	v.1, n.1- Spring, 1974-	970.105/AM35IQ
WaU	v.1, n.1- Spring, 1974-	E/75/A547
WyCWC	v.5, n.2-4; 1979	Periodicals
WyU	v.1- 1974-	E/75/A547
CaACG	v.1, n.1- Spring, 1974-	Periodicals
CaOPeT	v.1- 1974-	E/75/A547
CaOONL	v.3- 1977-	Periodicals

Other holding institutions: AzFU (AZN), AzTeS (AZS), CSdS (CDS), CArcHt
(CHU), CLSM, CLU (CLU), CLCM (CNH), [Pepperdine University, Malibu, CA]
(CPE), [University of Redlands, Redlands, CA] (CUR), COU-DA (COA), CtY
(YUS), DLC (DLC) (NSD), FTS (FHM), GEU (EMO), GU (GUA), INS (IAI), ICL
(IAL), IMgU (IAP), InLP (IPL), InTI (ISU), KSteC (KKQ), KyU (KUK),

MWalB (MBB), MiU (EYM), MiDW (EYW), MiMtpt (EZC), MnU (MNU),
[University of Minnesota Union List, Minneapolis, MN] (MUL), MoU (MUU),
NcGU (NGU), NdU (UND), NmU-L (NML), NIC (COO), [New York State Union
List, Albany, NY] (NYS), NRU (RRR), [Central New York Library Resources
Council, Syracuse, NY] (SRR), NSyU (SYB), NNRH (VVQ), NFQC (XQM), NGH
(ZEM), NPurU (ZPM), OAkU (AKR), OTU (TOL), OkAdE (ECO), OkS OKS), PBL
(LYU), PPiU (PIT), RPB (RBN), TNJ (TJC), TxFTIC (ICU), InElk (IEA), TxF
(IFA), TxLT (ILU), TxDN (INT), TxDaM (ISM), TxU-Da (ITD), TxArU (IUA),
TxSW (IWU), TxWicM (TMI), UOW (UUO), ViBlBv (VPI).

79 American Indian Society of Washington. 1967. Monthly. $5. for
   individuals and institutions. American Indian Society of Washington,
   519 5th Street, S.E., Washington, DC 20003. (202) 547-0125. Last
   issue 4 pages, last volume 48 pages, height 28 cm. Line drawings.
   Available in microform: WHi (1976, 1977, 1979, 1980-). Editor: Vern
   Halley, May, 1979-Apr, 1980. Subject focus: society meeting minutes,
   calendar.

   WHi   v.10, n.4, 12, v.11, n.6, v.13, n.5,   Microforms
                v.14, n.3-
                Apr, Dec, 1976, June, 1977, May, 1979
                Mar, 1980-

   WMUW   v.10, n.4, 12, v.11, n.6;   (SPL)
                Apr, Dec, 1976, June, 1977   E/75/A44x

   NHu   [v.7, n.7-v.10, n.2]   Periodicals
                [1973-1976]

80 American Indian Student Association Newsletter. 1982? Monthly.
   Ruthie Outlaw, editor, American Indian Student Association Newsletter,
   18111 Nordhoff St., SS 218, Northridge, CA 91330. (213) 885-3504.
   Last issue 10 pages, height 28 cm. Line drawings. Published by
   American Indian Student Association, California State University,
   Northridge. College newsletter.

   WHi   Apr?, 1982-   Circulation

   American Indian Student Association Newsletter.
           Minneapolis, MN

      see A.I.S.A. Newsletter. Minneapolis, MN

   American Indian Teepee. Independence, MO

      see Indian Teepee. Wheeling, WV

81 The American Indian Times. 1974-?//. Unknown. Last issue 32 pages,
    height 28 cm. Line drawings, photographs, commercial advertising.
    Published by American Indian Agency, Hollywood, CA. Editor: Sandy
    Sirkus. Subject focus: health, education, employment, social services.

    WMM   v.1, n.1;   Special
                Summer/Fall, 1974   Collections

82 The American Indian Times: Special Bicentennial Edition. 1976//. 48
    pages, height 28 cm. Line drawings, photographs. Published by
    American Indian Times Agency, Los Angeles, CA. Editor: Susan Weyl.
    Subject focus: culture, health, education, employment information.

    WHi   ?, 1976   Pam 76-5044

83 American Indian Tradition. 1954-1963//. Bimonthly. ISSN 0517-2284.
    LC 66-7789. OCLC 2250778, 2250779. Line drawings, photographs,
    commercial advertising. Publsihed by Society of American Indian
    Tradition, Alton, IL. Title varies: American Indian Hobbyist, Sept,
    1954-Oct, 1960. Editor: Richard R. McAllister. Subject focus: arts
    and crafts.

    WHi   v.6, n.5/6-v.9, n.1;   Museum
                Jan/Feb, 1960-Apr, 1963

    CoKIM   v.1-v.6;   Periodicals
                1955-1960

    NN   v.1-v.7;   HBA
                Sept, 1954-Oct, 1960

    OkPAC   [v.1, n.2-v.8, n.5]   Periodicals
                [1954-1962]

    OkU   v.5, n.9/10-v.9, n.1;   WHC
                Spring, 1959-Apr, 1963

    CaACG   [v.3, n.9-v.8]   Periodicals
                [May, 1957-1962]

    CaOPeT   v.1-v.6, n.3/4;   Microfilm
                1954-Nov/Dec, 1959

    Other holding institutions: CLSM, DSI (SMI), MiDW (EYW), NRM (VXR).

84 American Indian Treasures Inc., Newsletter. 1977-1980//? Unknown.
    Last issue 2 pages, height 28 cm. Line drawings. Guilderland, NY.
    Editor: Lillian Samuelson. Subject focus: art exhibits.

CaACG   v.4, n.4;   Periodicals
           Nov, 1980

Americans Before Columbus. Albuquerque, NM

   see ABC (Americans Before Columbus). Albuquerque, NM

85 Amerind News. 1974?//. Quarterly. Last issue 22 pages, height 28 cm.
Line drawings. Published by Amerind Club, Sandstone, MN. Editor:
Larry Propotnik. Prison newsletter. Includes poetry.

WMM   Apr, 1974   Special
                                                 Collections

86 The Amerindian. 1952-1976//. Bi-monthly. ISSN 0003-164x. LC
63-27398. OCLC 1481011. RLIN DCLC6327398-S, MIUG81-S228,
CSUP00471409-S, CUBG10084605-S, OHCP1481011-S, NYPG754196220-S. Last
issue 12 pages, height 28 cm. Photographs, commercial advertising.
Available in microform: McP (1952-1973); McA (1952-1974); CPC
(1952-1974). Published by American Indian Review, Inc., Chicago, IL.
Editor: Marion E. Gridley. Subject focus: economics, politics,
achievements, culture.

WHi   v.1, n.1.-v.23, n.1;   Microforms
           Sept, 1952-Oct, 1974

WHi   v.1, n.1-v.16, n.6, v.22, n.1-v.23, n.1;   E/77/A57
           Sept, 1952-July/Aug, 1968,
           Sept/Oct, 1973-Sept/Oct, 1974

WEU   v.19, n.3 v.22, n.2-3;   Journalism
           Jan/Feb 1971, Nov/Dec, 1973-Jan/Feb 1974   Lab

WEU   v.12, n.4-v.22, n.2;   Micro 11
ARC   Mar 1964-Dec 1973

WGrU   v.19, n.6-v.23, n.1;   Periodicals
           July/Aug, 1971-Sept/Oct, 1974

WM   v.1, n.1-v.23, n.1;   Periodicals
           Sept, 1952-Sept/Oct, 1974

WMM   v.1, n.1.-v.23, n.1;   MFL G-114
           Sept, 1952-Oct, 1974

WMM   [v.1, n.1-v.22, n.4]   Special
           [Sept, 1952-Mar/Apr, 1974]   Collections

WMSC   v.19, n.4-v.23, n.1;   Periodicals
           Mar/Apr, 1971-Sept/Oct, 1974

AzFM	v.1, n.1-v.23, n.1; Sept, 1952-Sept/Oct, 1974	570.6/A5123
AzNCC	v.1-v.23; 1952-1974	Indian File
CL	v.1, n.3-v.23, n.1; Jan, 1962-Sept/Oct, 1974	Periodicals
CLSM	v.1, n.1.-v.23, n.1; Sept, 1952-Oct, 1974	Periodicals
CNoSU	v.1-v.21; 1952-1973	Microfilm
CU-A	v.1, n.1-v.23, n.1; Sept, 1952-Sept/Oct, 1974	E/77/A1/A57
IC	v.14, n.1-v.23, n.1; Sept, 1965-Sept/Oct, 1974	Periodicals
ICN	v.1, n.1-v.23. n.1; Sept, 1952-Sept/Oct, 1974	Ayer 1/A530
MnBemT	v.1, n.1.-v.23, n.1; Sept, 1952-Oct, 1974	Periodicals
NjP	[v.1, n.1-v.24, n.3] [Sept, 1952-June, 1976]	Periodicals
NmG	v.1, n.1.-v.23, n.1; Sept, 1952-Oct, 1974	Periodicals
NmScW	v.1-v.22; 1952-1973	Periodicals
N	v.1, n.1-v.23. n.1; Sept, 1952-Sept/Oct, 1974	C970.105/ qA518
NN	v.1, n.1-v.23. n.1; Sept, 1952-Sept/Oct, 1974	HBA
NPotU	v.19-v.23,n.1; 1970-Sept/Oct, 1974	E/77/A57
OkPAC	[v.6, n.5-v.15, n.5] [1957-1966]	Periodicals
OkTU	[v.1, n.1-v.9, n.6] [Sept, 1952-?, 1961]	Rare book Room
OkU	v.1, n.1-v.23, n.1; Sept, 1952-Oct, 1974	WHC
OrU	v.21, n.3-v.23, n.1; Jan/Feb, 1973-Sept/Oct, 1974	Periodicals

WHi   v.1, n.1-5 [i.e. 4]   Pam 76-114
           Apr-July, 1918

WHi   v.1, n.1;   Microforms
           Apr, 1918

Other holding institutions: [University of Minnesota Union List,
Minneapolis, MN] (MUL).

91 Anishinabe Giigidowin/Nishnabe Gigdowen. 1976-1982?//. Unknown. Last
    issue 10 pages. Photographs. Available in microform: WHi-A, Veda Stone
    Papers, (1977). Published by Indian Studies Program, Bemidji State
    University, Bemidji, MN. Subject focus: bilingual education and
    teaching, Potawatomi people. In Potawatomi, 10%.

    WHi   v.2, n.3;   Microforms
               Mar, 15, 1977

    WEU   v.2, n.3;   Micro 11
    ARC   Mar, 15, 1977

    NCBE   v.3-   Periodicals
               1978-

    Other holding institutions: ICN (IBV), MnBemT, WM (GZD), [Saskatchewan
    Indian Cultural College, Saskatoon, Saskatchewan].

92 Aniskay-Achemowin: Grand Council Treaty No. 9 Newsletter. 1977-?//.
    Unknown. Last issue 16 pages, height 28 cm. Line drawings,
    photographs. Published by Ojibway Cree Culture Centre, Timmins,
    Ontario, Canada. Editor: Gerry Martin. Center newsletter. Subject
    focus: Cree people.

    CaOORD   v.1, n.1;   Periodicals
               Winter, 1977

    CaOPeT   v.1, n.1-5, 8;   Periodicals
               Feb-Fall, 1977, June, 1978

93 Annals of the Catholic Indian Missions of America. 1877-1881?//.
    Semi-annual. Last issue 32 pages, height 23 cm. Line drawings.
    Published by Bureau of Catholic Missions, Washington, DC. Subject
    focus: Catholic Church, missions, temperance.

    WHi   v.1, n.1-v.2, n.2;   E/98/B65
               Jan, 1877-July, 1878   Rare Books

    WHi   v.2, n.4;   F805/C36
               June, 1881   Cutter

CLSM   v.2, n.2-4;   Periodicals
            July, 1878-June, 1881

94 <u>Annoosch</u>. 1972?-1976?//. Bi-weekly. ISSN 0318-5761. LC cn76-319220.
   OCLC 1691161. Last issue 4 pages, height 28 cm. Line drawings.
   photographs. Norway House, Manitoba, Canada. Frequency varies:
   irregular, June, 1972-Nov 13, 1974; weekly, Nov 26, 1974-Mar 25, 1976.
   Editors: Ida Moore, Dec 1973-Apr 5, 1974; Arlene Robertson, Oct 17,
   1974-July 30, 1976. Community newsletter.

   CaOONL   [v.2, n.1-v.4, n.1]   K-11-2
               [June 1, 1973-July 30, 1976]

95 <u>Announcements</u>. 1972. Quarterly. Donation. Oran LaPointe, editor,
   Announcements, 1506 Broadway, Boulder CO 80302. (303) 447-8760. ISSN
   0197-2073. LC sc79-6038. OCLC 5104414. CSUP82-S3308, UTUL257-S,
   DCLCSC796038-S, CUDL0996-S, CSUP08400301-S, OHCP5104414-S,
   CSUG10945598-S, CGGL6479243-S, CSUL5355753-S. Last issue 16 pages,
   last volume 48 pages, height 28 cm. Line drawings, photographs.
   Available in microform: McA (1972-1977); McP (1972-1974). Published by
   Native American Rights Fund. Frequency varies: monthly, June-Dec,
   1972; bi-monthly, Jan, 1973-Apr/June, 1975. Previous editors: Joan L.
   Carpenter, Mar/Sept-June, 1977; Lorraine P. Edmo, Aug, 1977-Aug, 1979.
   Subject focus: rights, legislation.

   WHi   v.1, n.1-v.4, n.3/4; v.6, n.?, v.7, n.1-   Microforms
               June, 1972-Dec, 1977, Fall, 1980,
               May, 1981-

   WMM   v.2, n.3-v.3, n.2;   Special
               Oct/Dec, 1973-Apr/June, 1974   Collections

   WMUW   v.5, n.1;   (SPL)
               Winter, 1979   E/75/N33x

   WU   Current issues   Ethnic
   Coll   Collection

   WU-L   v.2, n.1-   Periodicals
               Jan/Feb, 1973-   Section

   ICN   Current issues   CHAI

   LARC   v.7-   Periodicals
               1981-

   NjP   [v.1, n.1-v.5, n.1]   Periodicals
               [June, 1972-Winter, 1979]

   OkTU   v.1, n.1-   Rare Book
               June, 1972-   Room

OkU   [v.1, n.1-v.7, n.2;   WHC
           [June, 1972-Sept, 1981]

CaOPeT   v.1-v.4;   Microfilm
           1972-1977

Other holding institutions: AzTes-L (AZC), CLU (CLU), CSfH (CUH),
COU-DA, COA), DI (UDI), FTaSU-L, (FSL), IaDmD-L (IWD), IC (CGP), ICD-L
(IBC), ICarbS-L (SOL), IU (UIU), MiEM (EEM), MnSH-L (MHL), MnU-L (MLL),
[University of Minnesota Union List, Minneapolis, MN] (MUL), [Western
Nevada Community College, Carson City, NV], UdU-L (UNE), NmScW, NmU-L
(NML), NBiSU (BNG), NIC (COO), [New York State Union List, Albany, NY]
(NYS), NBuUL (SBL), Ok (OKD), OkU-L (OKL), OkOkU-L (OKY), OrPL-L (ONS).

96 Anpao The Daybreak. 1878-1937//. Monthly. RLIN CUBU13639195-S. Last
   issue 4 pages. Line drawings, photographs. Published by The
   Protestant Episcopal Church, Mission, SD. Previous editors: Rev. J. W.
   Cook; W. J. Cleveland; William T. Selwyn; Rev. Edward Ashley; Rev. P.
   C. Bruger; Rev. H. H. Whipple; William M. Robertson; Rev. Paul H.
   Barbour; Rev. C. C. Rouillard. Subject focus: missions, Episcopal
   Church. In Dakota, 80%.

NN   v.3, n.3, v.6, n.6   Rare Book
           Mar, 1880, May, 1887   Division

SdSifA   [1878-1937]   Archives

97 Apache Drumbeat. 1963-?//. Monthly. Last issue 8 pages. Line
   drawings, photographs. Available in microform: WHi-A, Veda Stone
   Papers, (1965). Published by San Carlos Tribal Council, San Carlos,
   AZ. Community newsletter. Subject focus: Apache people.

WHi   n.34;   Microforms
           Jan, 1965

WEU   n.34;   Micro 11
ARC   Jan, 1965

AzU   [n.8-40]   I9791/A6
           [Oct, 1962-Dec, 1967]   A63

NjP   n.15, 17, 19, 40;   Periodicals
           May, July, Sept, 1963, Dec 15, 1967

OkU   n.37-40;   WHC
           Sept-Dec 15, 1967

Other holding institutions: MH-P (HLS).

98 <u>Apache Lutheran</u>. 1923?-1981?//. Monthly. OCLC 1777408. RLIN
OHCP1777408-S. Last issue 8 pages, height 23 cm. Line drawings,
photographs. Whiteriver, AZ. Title varies: Apache Scout, 1927-1953.
Editor: Alf M. Uplegger. Subject focus: missions, Lutheran Church.

WIRC   [v.35, n.4-v.46, n.9]   216 COPS
              [Apr, 1957-Oct, 1968]

AzHC   v.5-v.31, v.35-v.59?;   Perodicals
              1927-Aug, 1953, Jan, 1957-Nov, 1981

Other holding institutions: [Universtiy of Minnesota Union List,
Minneapolis, MN] (MUL).

99 <u>Apache Newsletter</u>. 1952-1956?//. Monthly. Last issue 6 pages. Line
drawings, photographs. Available in microform: McA, John Collier
Papers (1952-1956). Published by San Carlos Indian Reservation, San
Carlos, AZ. Title varies: San Carlos Newsletter, Feb, 1952-Jan, 1953.
Community newsletter. Subject focus: Apache people, agriculture.

WHi   [v.1, n.2-v.4, n.9]   Microforms
              [Feb, 1952-Mar/Apr/May, 1956]   J. Collier
                                                           Papers

WUSP   [v.1, n.2-v.4, n.9]   Microfilm
              [Feb, 1952-Mar/Apr/May, 1956]   J. Collier
                                                           Papers

AzTeS   v.1-v.4   XRSC 3.7
              1952-1956   N/38/2

AzU   v.1-v.4, n.9;   I9791/A6
              1952-Mar/Apr/May, 1956   S19

<u>Apache Scout</u>. Whiteriver, AZ

    see <u>Apache Lutheran</u>. Whiteriver, AZ

100 <u>Apache Sunrise: Voice of the San Carlos Indian Tribe</u>. 1973-1975//.
Bi-monthly. Last issue 12 pages, last volume 54 pages, height 42 cm.
Photographs, commerical advertising. Published by Apache Sunrise
Association, San Carlos, AZ. Editor: Fernando Machukay. Community
newsletter. Subject focus: Apache people. Superceded by Da' Anii/The
Truth.

AzHC   v.1, n.1-6;   Periodicals
              Oct 1, 1973-Jan 1, 1975

101 <u>Aq-ua-chamine/Menominee Talking</u>. 1974-1976//. Monthly. OCLC 4022153.
Last issue 6 pages, last volume 96 pages. Line drawings. Personal
names indexed in: Index to Wisconsin Native American Periodicals
(1974-1976). Available in microform: WHi (1974-1976); WHi-A, Veda
Stone Papers, (1975). Published by Menominee Restoration Committee,
Keshena, WI. Editors: Arlin Pamanet, Sept 15, 1974; Al Fowler, Mar
20-June 20, 1975. Subject focus: committee news, land claims,
legislation, social services, Menominee people.

WHi	[v.1, n.1]-v.3, n.3; Sept 15, 1974-June 30, 1976	Microforms
WEU ARC	v.2, n.3, 6, 11; Mar 20, May 31, Oct, 20, 1975	Micro 11
WMUW	[v.1, n.2-v.2, n.3]; [Oct 10, 1974-Mar 20, 1975]	(SPL) E/75/A63x
NjP	[v.1, n.1-v.3, n.3] [Sept 15, 1974-June 30,1976]	Periodicals

Other holding institutions: [University of Minnesota Union List,
Minneapolis, MN] (MUL).

<u>Arctic Coastal Zone Management Newsletter</u>. Anchorage, AK

   see <u>The Arctic Policy Review</u>. Anchorage, AK

102 <u>Arctic News</u>. 1948?. Irregular. Arctic News, 1055 Avenue Rd.,
Toronto, Ontario, Canada M5N 2C8. ISSN 0518-3839. LC cn76-300363.
OCLC 1639135, 8444338. RLIN DCLCCN76300363-S, OHCP1639135-S. Last
issue 16 pages. Line drawings, photographs. Available in microform:
CPC (1948-1976). Published by Diocese of the Arctic. Subject focus:
Catholic Church, Arctic peoples. Preceded by four separately titled
articles: "Twilight," "Arctic Advance," "Fort George," and "Fog, Ice
and Sunshine."

WHi	Oct, 1949-Fall, 1976	Microforms
WHi	Fall, 1974-	Circulation
NjP	[1941-Fall, 1978]	Periodicals
NN	Oct, 1949-Fall, 1976	Microforms
SdU	Oct, 1949-Fall, 1976	Microfilm
CaAEU	1941-1976	Boreal Institute
CaOONL	1959-	Periodicals

CaOPeT   [1941-1976]   Microfiche

Other holding institutions: [University of Minnesota Union List,
Minneapolis, MN] (MUL), NhD (DRB), PPiU (PIT).

103 <u>The Arctic Policy Review</u>. 1977. Irregular. Arctic Policy Review,
North Slope Borough, Anchorage Liaison Office, 3201 C St., #602,
Anchorage, AK 99503. (907) 276-4374. RLIN COSG81-S66, NYPG2262-S.
Last issue 24 pages, height 28 cm. Line drawings, photographs. Title
varies: Arctic Coastal Zone Management Newsletter, Jan, 1977-July,
1981. Subject focus: Native Alaskan people, culture, history, industry.

WHi   n.1-   Circulation
          Jan, 1977-

ICN   Current issues   CHAI

CaAEU   n.1-   Boreal
          Jan, 1977-   Institute

CaOAFN   n.26-   Periodicals
          Feb, 1980-

104 <u>Arctic Village Echoes</u>. 1970?//. Unknown. Line drawings. Arctic
Village, AK. Community newsletter.

AkUF   Jan, 1970   AK 319

105 <u>Arizona Indian Monthly</u>. 1968-1981//. Monthly. ISSN 0196-6987. LC
sn80-8617. OCLC 0873858, 4822519, 8073927. RLIN AZPG1621-S. Last
issue 28 pages, height 41 cm. Line drawings, photographs, commercial
advertising. Available in microform: WHi (1979-1980). Published by
Indian Development District of Arizona, Phoenix, AZ. Title varies:
Indian Arizona News, Sept, 1979-Apr, 1980; Arizona Indian Now,
July-Nov, 1980. Editor: Janice Brunson, Sept, 1979-Sept, 1980.
Subject focus: Arizona people, culture, health, biographies.

WHi   [v.2, n.5-v.4, n.12]   Microforms
          [Sept, 1979-Apr, 1981]

AzFM   v.1-   570.6/I39az
          1978-

AzHC   v.2, n.5-v.3, n.?;   Periodicals
          Sept, 1979-June, 1980

AzHM   [v.1, n.6-v.3, n.2]   Periodicals
          [1978-1980]

AzNCC	v.3; Dec, 1980-May, 1981	Indian File
AzT	v.1, n.1-v.4, n.12; May, 1978-Apr, 1981	Periodicals
AzTeS	[v.1-v.3] [1978-1980]	XR 2.3 I52
AzU	[v.1, n.1-v.4, n.12] [May, 1978-Apr, 1981]	I9791/I5
OkTU	v.1, n.4-v.4, n.10; Aug, 1978-Feb, 1981	Rare Book Room

Other holding institutions: AzPh, KSteC (KKQ).

Arizona Indian Now. Phoenix, AZ

   see Arizona Indian Monthly. Phoenix, AZ

Arjurnangimmat. Eskimo Point, Northwest Territories, Canada

   see Ajurnangimmat Magazine. Eskimo Point, Northwest Territories,
        Canada.

106 Arrow. 1959-?//. Unknown. Last issue 8 pages, height 31 cm. Line
drawings, photographs. Published by Arrow, Inc., Washington, DC.
Subject focus: rights, legislation, organization news.

| WHi | v.1, n.1;
July, 1959 | Pam 76-903 |

107 The Arrow. 1950? Monthly during school year. The Arrow, Labre Indian
School, Ashland, MT 59003. (406) 784-2347. Last issue 8 pages, height
28 cm. Line drawings. Published by Labre High School. School
newsletter. Subject focus: school news and activities.

| WHi | v.26, n.5, v.28, n.4, 6-
May 24, 1979, Dec, 1980, Jan, 1981- | Circulation |
| WMM | [v.6, n.1-4]
[Nov 7, 1955-May 25, 1956] | Special
Collections |

The Arrow. Tahlequah, OK

    see The Tahlequah Arrow. Tahlequah, OK

The Arrow. Carlisle, PA

    see Carlisle Arrow and Redman. Carlisle, PA

108 The Arrow-Telephone. 1894-?//. Weekly. Last issue 8 pages. Line drawings, commercial advertising. Available in microform: OkHi (1894). Tahlequah, OK. Editors: Waddie Hudson and J.H. Dick. Newspaper.

| WHi | v.1, n.4, 8, 10-11; | Microforms |
| | Oct 2, Nov 2, 23-30, 1894 | |

| OkHi | v.1, n.4, 8, 10-11; | Microforms |
| | Oct 2, Nov 2, 23-30, 1894 | |

109 Arrows to Freedom. 1972-?//. Monthly. Last issue 30 pages, height 28 cm. Line drawings. Published by Alberta Native Brotherhood of Indian and Metis, Drumheller, Alberta, Canada. Editor: Joe Holy Whiteman. Prison newsletter. Includes poetry.

| CaACG | v.1, n.5, 9-10; | Periodicals |
| | Sept, 1972, Jan-Feb, 1973 | |

110 Arts & Culture of the North. 1976. Quarterly. Sandra Barz, editor, Arts & Culture of the North, Box 1333, Gracie Square Station, New York, NY 10028. ISSN 0275-6927. LC sn81-693, sn81-3115, sn81-39055. OCLC 4772459. RLIN CTYG18207804-S, DCLCSC813115-S. Last issue 28 pages, height 28 cm. Line drawings, photographs, commercial advertising. Subject focus: Inuit art, artists, biographies, art reviews, art auctions.

| WHi | v.1, n.1- | E/99/E7/A78 |
| | Nov, 1976- | |

| CaACG | v.1, n.1-v.5, n.4; | Periodicals |
| | Nov, 1976-Winter, 1981 | |

| CaAEU | v.1, n.1-v.5, n.4; | Boreal |
| | Nov, 1976-Winter, 1981 | Institute |

Other holding institutions: DSI (SMI), MiRochoU (EYR), CaOONL (NLC), [Pittsburgh Regional Library Center-Union List, Pittsburgh, PA] (QPR), WaU (WAU).

111 <u>Assistance Expenditures for Needy Indians</u>. 1972?-1978//. Quarterly.
    OCLC 6769204. Last issue 1 page, last volume 6 pages, height 30 cm.
    Published by Iowa Department of Social Services, Des Moines, IA.
    Subject focus: social services, statistics.

    IaHi   [Apr, 1972-Dec, 1978]   E/78/I6/A88

112 <u>Association of American Indian and Alaska Native Social Workers, Inc.</u>
    <u>Newsletter</u>. 1979-?//. Unknown. Last issue 10 pages, height 28 cm.
    Line drawings. Madison, WI. Editor: Dr. Ron Lewis. Subject focus:
    social services, family, women.

    WUSP   Spring, 1979   Native American
                                                           Center

113 <u>Association of American Indian Physicians</u>. 1974-?// Last issue 4
    pages, height 28 cm. Photographs. Available in microform: WHi (1977).
    Oklahoma City, OK. Subject focus: medical education, health care,
    legislation.

    WHi   v.4, n.1;   Microforms
              July. 1977

    WMUW   v.4, n.1;   (SPL)
              July. 1977   E/75/A75x

    MtBBCC   (n.s.)v.2   Periodicals
              Mar., 1981

114 <u>Athapaskan Quarterly</u>. 1979. Quarterly. $2. for individuals and
    institutions. Dave Henry, editor, Athapaskan Quarterly, Box 21, Old
    Pinchbeck, R. R. #1, Williams Lake, British Columbia, Canada V2G 2P1.
    Last issue 7 pages, last volume 34 pages, height 28 cm. Subject focus:
    Athapaskan linguistics.

    CaACG   v.1, n.1-4;   Periodicals
              Nov, 1979-Dec, 1980

    <u>Atoka Chahta Kallo</u>. Atoka, OK

       see <u>Atoka Choctaw Champion</u>. Atoka, OK

115 <u>Atoka Choctaw Champion</u>. 1898-?//. Weekly. Last issue 8 pages. Line
    drawings, commercial advertising. Atoka, OK. Available in microform:
    OkHi (1898). Title varies: Atoka Chahta Kallo, July 15-29, 1898.
    Editor: William J. Grant. Newspaper. Subject focus: Choctaw people.
    In Choctaw, 50%. Also described in: Foreman, Carolyn Thomas. <u>Oklahoma</u>
    <u>Imprints, 1835-1907</u>. Norman: University of Oklahoma Press, 1936.

WHi   v.1, n.25-30;
             July 15-Aug 19, 1898   Microforms

OkHi   v.1, n.25-30;
             July 15-Aug 19, 1898   Microforms

116 <u>Atoka Independent</u>. 1877-1878//. Weekly. Last issue 8 pages. Line
    drawings, commercial advertising. Atoka, OK. Available in microform:
    OkHi (1877-1878). Editor: W. J. Hemby. Newspaper. Also described in:
    Foreman, Carolyn Thomas. <u>Oklahoma Imprints, 1835-1907</u>. Norman:
    University of Oklahoma Press, 1936.

WHi   [v.1, n.1-v.2, n.2]
             [July 27, 1877-Aug 30, 1878]   Microforms

OkHi   [v.1, n.1-v.2, n.2]
             [July 27, 1877-Aug 30, 1878]   Microforms

    <u>Atoka Independent</u>. 1886. Atoka, OK

        see <u>The Indian Chieftain</u>. Atoka, OK

117 <u>Atoka Record</u>. 1912-?//. Weekly. Last issue 8 pages. Line drawings,
    photographs, commercial advertising. Available in microform: OkHi
    (1912). Atoka, OK. Editors: A.R. Bowen, Apr 5-26, 1912; J.R. Cole,
    May 3-June 7, 1912. Newspaper.

WHi   v.1, n.3-12;
             Apr 5-June 7, 1912   Microforms

OkHi   v.1, n.3-12;
             Apr 5-June 7, 1912   Microforms

118 <u>A'tome/Northern Cheyenne Press</u>. 1974-1975?//. Bi-weekly. OCLC
    6168804. Last issue 12 pages, height 39 cm. Line drawings,
    photographs, commercial advertising. Lame Deer, MT. Editor: Beverley
    Geary, Feb 14, 1974-Mar 27, 1975; James King, Apr 10, 1975. Community
    newsletter. Subject focus: Cheyenne people. Supercedes A'atomone;
    superceded by Tsistsistas Press.

WHi   v.1, n.1-v.2, n.3;
             Feb 14-Apr 10, 1975   Microforms

WMUW   [v.1, n.1-v.2, n.2];
             [Feb 14, 1974-Mar 27, 1975]   (SPL)
                                                     E/75/A82x

AzNCC   v.1, n.1-v.2, n.3;
             Feb 14-Apr 10, 1975   Indian File

MtBC   [v.1, n.1-v.2, n.3]   E/78/M9/A622
            [Feb 14, 1974-Apr, 1975]

NjP   [v.1, n.3-v.2, n.5]   Periodicals
            [Mar 14, 1974-July 17, 1975]

119 Atta. 1981. Monthly. Last issue 4 pages, height 28 cm. Published by
    C.O.P.E. (Committee for Original Peoples Entitlement), Inuvik,
    Northwest Territories, Canada. Editor: Larry Osgood. Subject focus:
    Inuvialuit people, education, health, socio-economic, political
    conditions. Superceded by Akana.

    WHi   July/Aug, 1981-Oct, 1982   Circulation

    CaAEU   1981-1982   Boreal
                                                        Institute

    CaYW   Winter, 1981-Oct, 1982   Periodicals

120 Attan-Akamik. 1969-1972//. Irregular. Last issue 6 pages, height 36
    cm. Line drawings, photographs. Published by Powhatan Press, Davis,
    CA. Title varies: Tsen-Akamak, Aug? 1969-Aug? 1970. Editors: Jack D.
    Forbes and Roy Crazy Horse, July?-Oct, 1978. Subject focus:
    Powhatan-Renapoak people, history, culture.

    WHi   v.1, n.1-4, v.2, n.1-2;   Pam 74-129
              Aug? 1969-Mar 16, 1972, July?-Oct, 1978

    WEU   v.1, n.1-2;   Journalism
              Aug? 1969-Aug? 1970   Lab

    NjP   v.1, n.1-5;   Peridicals
              Aug? 1969-1972

    OkTU   [v.1, n.1-5]   Rare Book
              [Aug? 1969-May, 1972]   Room

    WHi   v.1, n.1-4;   WHC
              Aug? 1969-Mar 16, 1972

    Other holding institutions: ICN (IBV).

121 Atuaqnik: The Newspaper of Northern Quebec. 1979-1980//? Irregular.
    ISSN 0708-5990. LC cn79-31308. OCLC 5375500. RLIN DCLCCN7931308-S,
    OHCP5375500-S. Last issue 20 pages, height 44 cm. Line drawings,
    photographs. Published by Taqralik/Atuagrik Publications, Kuujjuaq
    (Fort Chimo), Quebec, Canada. Editor: Alec C. Gordon. Newspaper.
    Subject focus: Inuit people. In Inuit, 50%.

    CaAEU   v.1, n.1-?;   Boreal
              Jan, 1979-June/July, 1980   Institute

CaOONL   v.1, n.1-?;   Newspaper
            Jan, 1979-June/July, 1980   Section

122 Au-Authm Action News. 1978?. Monthly. Janell M. Sixkiller, editor,
     Au-Authm Action News, Route 1 Box 215, Scottsdale, AZ 85256. (602)
     949-7234 ext. 361. OCLC 6169360. RLIN AZPG3016-S. Last issue 16
     pages, height 36 cm. Line drawings, photographs. Available in
     microform: WHi (1978-1979, 1981-). Published by Salt River
     Pima-Maricopa Indian Community. Previous editors: Jackie Thomas, Oct
     22, 1979-Sept 22, 1980; Teresa Leonard, Oct 20-Nov 21, 1980.
     Newspaper. Subject focus: Pima and Maricopa people, health, employment
     information.

     WHi   Apr, 1978-Aug, Oct 22-Nov 30, 1979,   Microforms
                Jan 21, 1981-

     WMUW   Apr, 1978-Aug, 1979   (SPL)
                                                            E/75/A88x

     AzNCC   1974-Aug, 1977   Indian File

     AzTeS   1979-   XRSR 3.3/A81

     OkTU   Mar 24, 1980-   970.305
                                                            P644

     Other holding institutions: [American Indian Bible Institute, Phoenix,
     AZ], CaOONL (NLC).

123 Awo-Talm Ah-Pa-Tac. 1935-1942//. Monthly. Last issue 6 pages, height
     26 cm. Line drawings. Sells, AZ. Editor: Alden W. Jones. Subject
     focus: Papago people.

     AzU   v.1-v.8, n.2;   I9791/P21/
                Jan 15, 1935-Mar, 1942   A96

     B.A.I.C. Smoke Signals. Baltimore, MD

        see Smoke Signals Newsletter. Baltimore, MD

124 BCNWS Newsletter. 1981? Bi-monthly. BCNWS Newsletter, 116 Seymour
     St., Kamloops, British Columbia, Canada V2C 2E1. Last issue 12 pages,
     height 28 cm. Line drawings, photographs. Published by British
     Columbia Native Women's Society. Subject focus: women's rights,
     organization news.

     CaOAFN   May/June, 1981, Jan/Feb, 1982-   Periodicals

125 BIA Education Research Bulletin. 1973-1979//. Irregular. Last issue
    36 pages. ISSN 0147-4391. LC 77-649625. OCLC 2568290, 8398844. RLIN
    UTBG81-S282, DCLC77649625, OHCP2568290-S. Line drawings, photographs.
    Indexed in: Index to Literature on the American Indian (1973).
    Available in microforms: CPC (1973-1977). Published by Division of
    Evaluation & Program Review Branch of Reseach for Teachers and
    Educators Who are Dedicated to Improving Indian Education, Wahington,
    DC. Editor: Eugene Leitka, Sept, 1974-May, 1973. Subject focus:
    education, curriculum development.

    WHi   v.1, n.1-v.5, n.2;   Microforms
                  Jan, 1973-May, 1977

    AzNCC   v.1-v.7;   Indian File
                  1973-Aug, 1979

    NjP   [v.1, n.2-v.7, n.1]   Periodicals
                  [May, 1973-Jan, 1979]

    SdU   v.1, n.1-v.5, n.2;   Microfilm
                  Jan, 1973-May, 1977

    CaOPeT   v.1, n.1-v.5, n.2;   Microfiche
                  Jan, 1973-May, 1977

    Other holding institutions: DLC (DLC), DI (UDI), MiEM (EEM), NmU (IQU),
    PP (PLF), [U.S. Government Printing Office-Serials, Alexandria, VA]
    (GPA), DGPO (GPO), ICN (IBV).

126 The Baconian. 1898-?//. 3 times a month. Last issue 24 pages.
    Photographs, commercial advertising. Available in microform: WHi-A,
    Papers of Carlos Montezuma, (1903). Published by Indian University,
    Bacon, OK. Editor: Laura Edwards. School newsletter.

    WHi   v.6, n.3;   Microforms
                  May, 1903

127 Banknotes. 1979//. Unknown. Last issue 4 pages, height 28 cm. Line
    drawings, photographs. Available in microform: WHi (1979). Published
    by American Indian National Bank, Washington, DC. Subject focus:
    banking, economics.

    WHi   v.1, n.1-2;   Microforms
                  June 1-Sept 30, 1979

    Banks Land Letter. Sachs Harbour, Northwest Territories, Canada

        see Bankslander/Sachs Echo. Sachs Harbour,
                Northwest Territories, Canada

128 <u>Bankslander/Sachs Echo</u>. 1968-1970//. Monthly. Last issue 4 pages, height 35 cm. Line drawings. Sachs Harbour, Northwest Territories, Canada. Title varies: Banks Land Letter, Aug, 1968-Feb, 1969. Editor: Father L. Lemer. Community newsletter.

CaAEU   n.1-25;   Boreal
           Aug, 1968-Nov, 1970   Institute

<u>Bayline Weekly</u>. Wabowen, Manitoba, Canada

   see <u>Achimowin</u>. Thompson, Manitoba, Canada

<u>Bear</u>. Fort Wingate, NM

   see <u>Shush/Bear</u>. Fort Wingate, NM

129 <u>Bear Facts Newsletter</u>. 1973. Irregular. Bear Facts Newsletter, 3415 Dwinelle Hall, N.A.S. Student Services, University of California, Berkeley, CA 94720. (415) 642-0245. Last issue 8 pages. Line drawings. Available in microform: McA (1973-). Published by Native American Studies Department, University of California-Berkeley. Previous editor: Ruth A. Hopper, Dec 1976. Subject focus: education, politics, culture, socio-economic conditions.

WHi   Mar 29, 1973-   Microforms

CaOPeT   Apr, 1973-   Periodicals

130 <u>Bear Hills Native Voice</u>. 1970?-?//. Monthly. Last issue 8 pages, height 44 cm. Line drawings, photographs, commercial advertising. Published by Four Bands Enterprise, Hobbema, Alberta, Canada. Editors: Alfred Saddleback, Dec 1971-June, 1972; Jack Art, Dec 1, 1977. Newspaper.

NjP   (n.s.)v.1, n.1, 5;   Periodicals
           Aug 1, Sept/Oct, 1977

CaOONL   v. 2, n.4-8, (n.s.)v.2, n.21;   Newspaper
           Dec, 1971-June, 1972, Dec 1, 1977   Section

CaACG   [(n.s.)v.1, n.20-v.4, n.45]   Periodicals
           [Oct 15, 1977-July 17, 1980]

131 <u>Bear Talk</u>. 1977? Monthly. Bear Talk, 3239 Christy Way, Saginaw, MI 48603. (517) 792-4610. Last issue 8 pages, height 28 cm. Line drawings. Published by Saginaw Inter-Tribal Indian Center. Community

newsletter. Subject focus: health, social services, employment
information.

Circulation

WHi   v.2, n.6-
            Nov, 1981-

Periodicals

Mi   v.1?-
            1977-

132 Bells of Saint Ann. 1938-?//. Bi-monthly. Last issue 4 pages, height
    28 cm. Line drawings, photographs. Publshed by St. Ann's Indian
    Mission, Belcourt, ND. Editors: Hildebrand Elliott, July/Aug,
    1959-Jan/Feb, 1965; Rev. Roger Dieckhaus, May/June-July/Aug, 1968.
    Subject focus: missions, Catholic Church.

                                                    Special
WMM   [v.22, n.4-v.31, n.4]   Collections
            [July/Aug, 1959-July/Aug, 1968]

                                                    Periodicals
NjP   [v.31, n.1-v.33, n.7]
            [Jan/Feb, 1968-Jan/Feb, 1970]

133 The Bells of Saint Marys. 1956-?//. Irregular. Last issue 8 pages,
    height 28 cm. Line drawings. Published by St. Mary's High School, St.
    Mary's, AK. School newsletter.

                                                    Special
WMM   [v.1, n.3-v.4, n.2]   Collections
            [Jan1959-Oct, 1959]

134 Bering Straits Agluktuk. 1973. Monthly. Bering Straits Agluktuk,
    P.O. Box 1008, Nome, AK 99762. OCLC 6189133. Last issue 8 pages,
    height 44 cm. Line drawings, photographs. Available in microform: WHi
    (1975-1976); AkUF (1973-1975). Published by Bering Straits Native
    Corp. Community newsletter. Subject focus: corporation news, housing,
    land claims.

                                                    Microforms
WHi   v.1, n.5-v.3, n.5;
            July, 1973-Feb, 1976

                                                    Circulation
WHi   Aug, 1982-

                                                    (SPE)
WMUW   v.3, n.3-5;   E/75/B47x
            Nov, 1975-Feb, 1976

                                                    AK-News
AkUF   [v.1, n.5-v.4, n.3]
            [1973-1977]

135 Big Cove News Letter. 1975?//. Unknown. Last issue 18 pages, height
    28 cm. Line drawings. Rexton, New Brunswick, Canada. Editor: Carol

Coguen. Community newsletter.

WHi   n.19;   Microforms
           June 11, 1976

136 The Birney Arrow. 1959?-1971?//. Weekly. Last issue 6 pages.
    Available in microform: McA (1959-1971). Birney, MT. Place of
    publication varies: Busby, MT, May 21, 1970. Editor: Donald
    Hollowbeast. Feb 27, 1959-Aug 18, 1970? Community newsletter. Subject
    focus: governmental policies.

    WHi   Feb 27, 1959-Aug 18,   Microforms
               1970

    WEU   Aug 18, 1970, Jan 23,   Journalism
               Mar 8, Apr 15, 1971   Lab

    NjP   [Oct 4, 1962-Apr 5,   Periodicals
               1971]

    OkU   Feb 27, 1959-Aug 18,   WHC
               1970

    UPB   [Aug, 1960-Dec 16, 1968]   970.105/B538

    Other holding institutions: NvWNCC.

137 Bishinik. 1978-1981//. Monthly. Last issue 12 pages, height 39 cm.
    Line drawings, photographs. Published by the Choctaw Nation of
    Oklahoma, Durant, OK. Editors: Len F. Green, July 1, 1978-Mar, 1981.
    Jon Bonds, Apr-Aug/Sept, 1981. Subject focus: Choctaw Nation of
    Oklahoma news, poetry.

    WHi   v.1, n.2-v.4, n.2;   Microforms
               July 1, 1978-Oct, 1981

    OkU   [v.2, n.1-v.4, n.2]   WHC
               [1979-1981]

    Other holding institutions: [Bacone College, Muskogee, OK].

138 Black Eagle News. 1971-1972?//. Irregular. Last issue 12 pages.
    Line drawings, photographs. Available in microform: WHi (1971-1972).
    Published by Treaty Indians of the Columbia, Inc., Cooks, WA. Editor:
    Terry Black Eagle. Subject focus: politics, legislation, culture,
    history.

    WHi   [July, 1971-Jan, 1972]   Microforms

139 Black Hills Paha Sapa Report. 1979. Irregular. $5. for individuals
    and institutions. Evelyn Lifsey, editor, Black Hills Paha Sapa Report,
    P.O. Box 2508, Rapid City, SD 57709. (605) 342-5127. Last issue 8
    pages, last volume 76 pages, height 37 cm. Line drawings, photographs,
    commercial advertising. Published by Black Hills Alliance. Newspaper.
    Subject focus: land claims, environmental protection, rights.

    WHi   v.1, n.1, 4-   Circulation
                 July, 1979, Feb, 1980-

    SdU   v.1, n.1, 4-   South
                 July, 1979, Feb, 1980-   Dakota Room

    Other holding institutions: IC (CGP), [Standing Rock Community College
    Library, Fort Yates, ND], University of Wisconsin Stevens Point-Native
    American Center, Stevens Point, WI].

    Black Hills State College, Spearfish, South Dakota,
              Center of Indian Studies

      see Center of Indian Studies. Spearfish, SD

140 Blackfeet Journal. 1969-?//? Monthly. ISSN 0523-7297. OCLC 2504872.
    OHCP2504872-S. Last issue 9 pages, height 28 cm. Line drawings.
    Browning, MT. Community newsletter. Subject focus: Blackfeet people.

    MtBC   n.1-23;   E/78/M9/B55
                 Jan22, 1969-Feb 12, 1970

141 Blackfeet Tribal News. 1982. Monthly. Blackfeet Tribal News, P.O.
    Box 830, Browning, MT 59417. (406) 338-7521. Last issue 12 pages,
    height 41 cm. Line drawings, photographs, commercial advertising.
    Published by Blackfeet Media Department. Community newsletter.
    Subject focus: Blackfeet people.

    WHi   v.1, n.8-   Circulation
                 Aug 26, 1982-

    MtBBCC   v.1, n.1-   Periodicals
                 Mar, 1982-

142 Blackfoot News. 1977?-1978//? Irregular. Last issue 13 pages, height
    36 cm. Line drawings. Gleichen, Alberta, Canada. Editor: Lesley
    Stimson. Community newsletter. Subject focus: Blackfoot people.

    CaACG   Sept, 1977-?, 1978   Periodicals

143 Blue Cloud Missions. 1969. Quarterly. Blue Cloud Missions, Blue Cloud
    Abbey, Marvin, SD 57251. (605) 432-5528. Last issue 4 pages. Line
    drawings, photographs. Available in microform: McA (1969-), WHi-A,
    Veda Stone Papers, (1971, 1972). Published by American Indian Culture
    Research Center. Title varies: Tekawitha Conference Newsletter, Sept,
    1969-Winter, 1970; American Indian Culture Research Center Newsletter,
    Mar-Aug, 1970; Blue Cloud News, Sept, 1970-Jan, 1973. Frequency
    varies: Monthly, Sept, 1969-Jan, 1973. Subject focus: Catholic Church,
    culture, history, governmental policies.

WHi	v.1, n.1-v.3, n.5, v.7, n.1-4, v.10, n.1- Sept, 1969-Jan, 1973, Jan/Mar-Oct/Dec,1978 Jan/Mar, 1981-	Microforms
WEU ARC	v.1, n.3, v.2, n.4, 6, v.3, n.1; Apr, Dec, 1971, Feb, Sept, 1972	Micro 11
WMM	[v.2, n.1-v.5, n.3] [Sept, 1971-Jan, 1973]	Special Collections
AzNCC	v.9- July, 1980-	Indian File
ICN	Current issues	CHAI
NjP	[v.1, n.1-v.8, n.2] [Sept, 1969-Apr/May/June, 1979]	Periodicals
OkU	v.1, n.1-v.3, n.4; Sept, 1969-Dec, 1972	WHC
WyCWC	v.3, n.5; Jan, 1973	Periodicals
CaOPeT	v.1, n.1- Sept, 1969-	Microfilm

Other holding institutions: [Western Nevada Community College, Carson
City, NV].

Blue Cloud News. Marvin, SD

    see Blue Cloud Missions. Marvin, SD

144 Blue Cloud Quarterly. 1955. Quarterly. Blue Cloud Quarterly, Blue
    Cloud Abbey, Marvin, SD 57251. (605) 432-5528. ISSN 0006-5064. LC
    78-645161. OCLC 1536599, 4470389. RLIN RIBG82-S273, DCLC78645161-S,
    NHDG2520-S, CUBU13688261-S, OHCP1536599-S, NYPG754816644-S. Last issue
    17 pages. Line drawings, photographs. Available in microform: McA
    (1969-). Published by Benedictine Missionary Monks, Blue Cloud Abbey.
    Subject focus: poetry, fiction, legends.

WHi	v.14, n.1– Sept, 1969–	Microforms
WEU	[v.14, n.3–v.17, n.4]; [Summer? 1970–Fall, 1973]	Journalism Lab
WMM	[v.5, n.2–v.21, n.4] [Spring, 1958–?, 1975]	Special Collections
WU	v.13, n.1– ?, 1968–	Rare Books Room
AzNCC	v.24–v.26; 1978–1980	Periodicals
CL	v.14, n.3– ?, 1969–	Periodicals
KU	v.1– 1955–	Kansas Collection
NjP	[v.11, n.1–v.25] [[1965–1979]	Periodicals
OkTU	v.19, n.1– Feb?, 1973–	Rare Book Room
OkU	v.11, n.2– June, 1965–	WHC
SdU	v.18– 1972–	South Dakota Room
TxU	[v.19, n.1–v.27, n.1] [1972–1980]	E/77/B484
WyCWC	v.19, n.1–v.20, n.4; 1973–1974	Periodicals
CaOAFN	v.27, n.1– Spring, 1981–	Periodicals
CaOPeT	v.12– 1966–	Microfilm

Other holding institutions: ArU (AFU), AzU (AZU), CLU (CLU), COFS (COF), DLC (DLC), IaDuU (IOV), MiEM (EEM), MnU (MNU), [University of Minnesota Union List, Minneapolis, MN] (MUL), [Western Nevada Community College, Carson City, NV], NdU (UND), NbU (LDL), NmLcU (IRU).

145 <u>Board In Brief</u>. 1981. Quarterly. Board in Brief, 125 S. Webster Street, Box 7841, Madison, WI 53707. (608) 267-9232. Last issue 2 pages, height 36 cm. Personal names indexed in: Index to Wisconsin Native American Periodicals (1981). Published by American Indian

Language and Culture Board, Wisconsin Department of Public Instruction.
Subject focus: Board news.

WHi   v.1, n.1-   Circulation
           Sept, 1981-

146 Boreal. 1974-1978//. Quarterly. ISSN 0315-8144. LC ce79-39065.
    OCLC 2287752, 2287799. Last issue 104 pages, height 20 cm. Line
    drawings, commercial advertising. Available in microform: (MML 1974-).
    Published by University College of Hearst, Hearst, Ontario, Canada.
    Subject focus: history, arts and crafts, culture, graphics, poetry. In
    French, 30%, some issues articles in Cree.

    CaOAFN   n.2-11/12;   Periodicals
               ?, 1975-Sept, 1978

    CaOORD   n.1-11/12;   Periodicals
               Summer, 1974-Sept, 1978

    Other holding institutions: [University of Minnesota Union List,
    Minneapolis, MN] (MUL), CaOONL (NLC).

    The Branding Iron. Atoka, OK

       see Indian Champion. Atoka, OK

147 Bristol Bay Native Corporation News. 1972. Irregular. Bristol Bay
    Native Corporation News, P.O. Box 220, Anchorage, AK 99510. (907)
    278-3602. Last issue 6 pages, height 28 cm. Line drawings, commercial
    advertising. Available in microform: AkUF (1972-1974). Place of
    publication varies: Dillingham AK, Aug? 1972-May, 1974. Frequency
    varies: bi-weekly, Aug?-Dec 5, 1972. Subject focus: corporate and
    shareholder news, land claims.

    WHi   Mar/Apr, 1982-   Circulation

    WHi   [v.1, n.1]-v.3, n.4;   Microforms
               Aug?, 1972-May, 1974

    AkUF   [v.1, n.1]-v.3, n.4;   Microfiche
               Aug?, 1972-May, 1974

148 Brothers of Time. 1981?//? Unknown. Last issue 34 pages, height 28
    cm. Line drawings. Published by Millhaven Institution Native
    Brotherhood, Bath, Ontario, Canada. Editor: Kenneth Manitowabi.
    Prison newsletter. Subject focus: culture, religion, arts and crafts,
    fiction, poetry, socio-economic conditions, and politics.

CaOAFN   Winter?, 1981   Periodicals

149 <u>Brotherton Messenger</u>. 1981. Bi-monthly. Mark Baldwin, editor,
    Brotherton Messenger, 802 E. Court St., Janesville, WI 53543. (608)
    754-5903. Last issue 16 pages, height 28 cm. Line drawings. Personal
    names indexed in: Index to Wisconsin Native American Periodicals
    (1981). Subject focus: Brotherton people, history, culture, genealogy.

    WHi   v.1-   Circulation
               Nov, 1981-

    ICN   Current issues   CHAI

150 <u>Browning Sentinel</u>. 1969-1970?//?. Monthly. Last issue 4 pages, height
    43 cm. Photographs, commercial advertising. Published by National
    Association of Blackfeet Indians, Browning, MT. Subject focus:
    Blackfeet people, association news.

    MtBC   v.1, n.1-v.2, n.9;   E/78/M9/B75
               Nov, 1969-Oct, 1970

    NjP   [v.1, n.1-v.2, n.9]   Periodicals
               [Nov, 1969-Oct, 1970]

151 <u>The Buckskin</u>. 1970-1971?//. Irregular. OCLC 3252923, 8398177. RLIN
    OHCP3252923-S. Last issue 40 pages. Available in microform: CPC
    (1970-1971). Eufaula, OK. Editor: B. B. Scott. Community newsletter.

    WHi   (n.s.)n.1-6;   Microforms
               Jan, 1970-July, 1971

    NjP   (n.s.)n.1-9, (n.s.)n.1-6;   Periodicals
               Jan-Oct, 1970, Jan-
               July, 1971

    OkU   n.12-(n.s.)n.6   WHC
               Sept, 1967-July, 1971

    CaOPeT   (n.s.)n.1-6;   Microfilm
               Jan, 1970-July, 1971

    Other holding institutions: CU-UC (UCU), PPiU (PIT).

152 <u>Buffalo Grass</u>. 1975-1980?//. Monthly. OCLC 6161377. Last issue 18
    pages, height 28 cm. Line drawings. Available in microform: WHi
    (1975). Published by Qua Qui Corp., Missoula, MT. Subject focus:
    center news, health, social services.

        WHi   Jan, Apr?, 1975, Sept, 1980   Microforms

        WMUW   Jan, Apr?, 1975   (SPL)
                                                              E/75/B83x

153 The Bugle. 1962-?//. Quarterly. OCLC 4270098. RLIN OHCP4270098-S.
    Last issue 8 pages. Line drawings, photographs. Available in
    microform: WHi-A, Veda Stone Papers, (1966-1972). Published by St.
    Mary's Episcopal School for Indian Girls, Springfield, SD. School
    newsletter. Subject focus: school events, alumni news.

        WHi   [v.10, n.1-v.11, n.4];   Microforms
                   [Mar, 1966-Dec, 1972]

        WEU   [v.10, n.1-v.11, n.4];   Micro 11
        ARC   [Mar, 1966-Dec, 1972]

        NjP   [v.4, n.3-v.18, n.3]   Periodicals
                   [June, 1960-June, 1979]

    Other holding institutions: [University of Minnesota Union List,
    Minneapolis, MN] (MUL), OrU-Special Collections.

    Bulletin. Washington, DC

        see Sentinel Bulletin. Washington, DC

154 Bulletin: Mount Tolman. 1979-1981//. Monthly. Last issue 4 pages,
    height 28 cm. Photographs. Available in microform: WHi (1981).
    Published by The Colville Confederated Tribes and AMAX, Inc., Spokane,
    WA. Subject focus: environment, Mount Tolman mining project.

        WHi   v.3, n.4;   Microforms
                   July, 1981

155 Bureau of Catholic Indian Missions Newsletter. 1977. Irregular.
    Monsignor Paul A. Lenz, editor, Bureau of Catholic Indian Missions
    newsletter, 2021 H Street, Washington, DC 20006. (202) 331-8542. Last
    issue 4 pages, last volume 106 pages, height 28 cm. Photographs.
    Previous editor: Darla Fera, Jan-June, 1978. Subject focus: missions,
    Catholic Church.

        WHi   v.1, n.1-6, 9-   Circulation
                   Dec, 1977-June, Sept/Oct, 1978-

156 Bureaucracy A La Mode. 1924-1925//. Unknown. RLIN CUBU13646813-S.
    Last issue 6 pages, height 28 cm. Line drawings, photographs.
    Available in microform: CPC (1924-1925). New York, NY. Editor: Joseph
    W. Latimer. Subject focus: legislation, law.

    WHi   n.2-11;   F809//+BU
               Apr 15, 1924-Dec, 1925   Cutter

    NjP   n.3, 5, 7;   Periodicals
               June 25, Nov 27, 1924, Mar 20, 1925

157 CAIM News. 1973-?//. Quarterly. OCLC 6194244. Last issue 6 pages,
    height 28 cm. Line drawings, photographs. Available in microform: WHi
    (1974). Published by Council for American Indian Ministry of the
    United Church of Christ, Bismarck, ND. Subject focus: missions, United
    Church of Christ.

    WHi   v.2, n.2;   Microforms
               Apr/May/June, 1974

    WMUW   v.2, n.2;   (SPL)
               Apr/May/June, 1974   E/75/U5x

    C.A.S.N.P. Bulletin. Toronto, Ontario, Canada

        see Canadian Association in Support of Native Peoples Bulletin.
            Toronto, Ontario, Canada

158 The CERT Report. 1979. Semi-monthly. $22. for individuals and
    non-profit institutions, $57. for profit-making institutions. Richard
    V. La Course, editor, The CERT Report, 1140 Connecticut Ave., N.W.,
    Suite 310, Washington, DC 20036. (202) 887-9155. ISSN 0197-3126. LC
    sc79-4354. OCLC 5131933. RLIN COSG19771797-S, COSG82-S155,
    DCLCSC794354-S, OHCP5121933-S. Last issue 16 pages, height 28 cm.
    Line drawings, photographs. Published by Council of Energy Resource
    Tribes. Subject focus: natural resource management, economic
    development, energy resources, law.

    WHi   v.4, n.4-   Circulation
               Mar 23, 1982-

    ICN   Current issues   CHAI

    MtBBCC   v.4-   Periodicals
               May, 1982-

    CaOAFN   v.2, n.13-   Periodicals
               July, 1980-

Other holding institutions: AzU (AZU), [Congressional Research Service, Washington, DC] (CRS), DI (UDI).

159 CHW Newsletter. 1982? Unknown. $6. for individuals and institutions. CHW Newsletter, 1615 Broadway, Oakland, CA 94612. Last issue 2 pages, height 28 cm. Published by Community Health Workers, California Indian Health Council, Inc. Subject focus: health care, community health resources.

WHi   May, 1982–   Circulation

160 CICSB Newsletter. 1972–?//. Monthly, irregular. Last issue 12 pages, height 28 cm. Line drawings, photographs. Available in microform: CPC (1972-1976). Published by Coalition of Indian Controlled School Boards, Inc., Denver, CO.   Subject focus: education, educational legislation, Native American Studies, funding, statistics, teaching, curriculum development, employment information, book reviews.

WHi   [Apr. 15, 1972-Sept/Oct, 1976]   Microforms

WMM   [Oct 31, 1972, June 14,   Special
           Nov, 1974, Apr, 1975   Collections

NjP   [Apr, 1972-Feb, 1979]   Periodicals

SdU   1973-1976   Microfilm

161 CIE Bilingual Education Service Center Newsletter. 1980//. Unknown. Last issue 6 pages, height 28 cm. Photographs. Published by Arizona State University, Tempe, AZ. Editor: Barbara A. Robbins. Subject focus: education, bilingual education and teaching. Superceded by Center for Indian Education Newsletter.

NCBE   v.1;   Periodicals
           1980

162 CIMC Newsletter. 1979-1980. Irregular. Last issue 6 pages, height 28 cm. Photographs. Available in microform: WHi (1979-1980). Published by California Indian Manpower Consortium, Inc., Employment and Training Program, Sacramento, CA. Editor, Daniel Ortiz. Subject focus: employment information and vocational training programs.

WHi   [v.1-v.8]   Microforms
           [Oct, 1979-Dec., 1980]

163 <u>CIRA Newsletter</u>. 1973. Irregular. Wanda Hillard, editor, CIRA
Newsletter, P.O. Drawer 4-N, 2525 C St., Anchorage, AK 99509. (907)
274-8638. Line drawings, photographs. Available in microform: AkUF
(1973-1979). Published by Cook Inlet Region, Inc. Corporate
newsletter. Supercedes Cook Inlet Region, Inc. [Newsletter].

WHi   [v.1, n.1-v.2, n.1]   Microforms
              July, 1973-Jan, 1976]

AkUF   v.1, n.1-v.5, n.10;   E/99/T185/C2
              July, 1973-1979

164 <u>CRESS-Notes</u>. 1966. Semi-annual. Amelita Hill, editor, CRESS-Notes,
Box 3AP, New Mexico State University, Las Cruces, NM 88003. (505)
646-2623. Last issue 6 pages, height 28 cm. Available in microform:
McA (1966-); WHi-A, Veda Stone Papers, (1969). Published by ERIC
Clearinghouse on Rural Education and Small Schools. Title varies:
Retriever, Fall-May, 1968. ERIC/CRESS News Letter, Fall? 1968-Fall,
1973. Previous editors: Ginny Chenowith, Winter, 1971-Spring, 1972;
Laurie Keaton, Summer, 1972; Denise M. DeValle, Fall, 1972-Fall, 1973.
Subject focus: teaching, rural education, curriculum development.

WHi   v.1, n.1-v.8, n.3;   Microforms
              Fall, 1966-Fall, 1973

WEU   v.4, n.3;   Micro 11
ARC   Fall, 1969

WU   Current issues   Ethnic
Coll   Collection

AzNCC   v.13-   Indian File
              Fall, 1979-

NjP   [v.3, n.2-v.8, n.3]   Periodicals
              [Dec, 1968-Fall, 1973]

OkU   v.1, n.1-v.7;   WHC
              Fall, 1966-Winter, 1972

CaOPeT   v.1-v.8, n.3;   Microfilm
              1966-Fall, 1973

Other holding institutions: [Western Nevada Community College, Carson
City, NV], [University of Wisconsin-Stevens Point-Native American
Center, Stevens Point, WI]

165 <u>CRITFC News</u>. 1977. Monthly. Laura Berg and Elizabeth Smith, editors,
CRITFC News, 8383 N.E. Sandy Blvd., Portland, OR 97220. Last issue 6
pages, height 28 cm. Photographs. Title varies: Columbia River
Inter-Tribal Fish Commission Monthly News, Aug/Dec, 1980-Jan/Feb/Mar,

1981. Subject focus: fishing industry, environmental protection, ecology.

WHi   v.2, n.1, v.4, n.1, v.5, n.2-   Circulation
           Feb, 1975, Jan/Feb/Mar, 1981,
           Apr/May/June, 1982-

MtBBCC   v.3;   Periodicals
           Aug-Dec, 1980

166 CUIHC Newsletter. 1974? Unknown. CUIHC Newsletter, 1615 Broadway,
     Oakland, CA 94612. Last issue 2 pages, height 28 cm. Published by
     California Urban Indian Health Council, Inc. Subject focus: health,
     health care.

WHi   Jan, 1981-   Circulation

CLSM   Apr, 1974-May, 1976   Periodicals

Le Cakabee: Ulu News.

   see Ulu News.

Calgary Indian Friendship Centre. Calgary, Alberta, Canada

   see Elbow Drums. Calgary, Alberta, Canada

167 Calgary Indian Newsletter. 1965-?//. Unknown. Last issue 3 pages,
     height 28 cm. Published by Calgary Indian Services Committee, Calgary
     Alberta, Canada. Subject focus: urban community, social services.

CaACG   v.1, n.1;   Periodicals
           Apr, 1965

168 California Indian Herald. 1923-1924?//. Monthly. OCLC 8398187. RLIN
     CSUP01069007-S, CUBU13655139-S. Last issue 16 pages. Line drawings,
     photographs. Available in microform: CPC (1923-1924). Published by
     Indian Board of Cooperation, San Francisco, CA. Editors: George
     Wharton James, Jan-Dec, 1923; Frederick G. Collett, Jan-Dec, 1924.
     Subject focus: rights, legislation, California people.

WHi   v.1, n.1-v.2, n.8;   Microforms
           Jan, 1923-Aug, 1924

NN   v.1, n.1-v.2, n.8;   Microforms
           Jan, 1923-Aug, 1924

Other holding institutions: PPiU (PIT).

169 <u>California Indian Legal Services Newsletter</u>. 1968-1980//. 3 times a
    year. OCLC 1552550. RLIN OHCP1552550-S. Last issue 16 pages.
    Available in microform: McP (1971-1972); WHi (1979, 1980). Published
    by California Indian Legal Services, Berkeley, CA. Subject focus:
    rights, legal aid.

    WHi   v.4, n.1-v.5, n.4, v.9, n.1, v.10, n.1;   Microforms
               Feb 11, 1971-Dec 25, 1972, Dec, 1979,
               July, 1980

    WEU   v.2, n.7-v.4, n.1   Journalism
               Oct 9, 1969-Feb 11, 1971   Lab

    AzNCC   v.4-v.8;   Indian File
               Dec, 1971-Oct, 1976

    CNoSU   [v.4, n.1-v.5, n.4]   Microfilm
               [Feb 11, 1971-Dec 25, 1972]

    NjP   [v.2, n.1-v.8, n.3]   Periodicals
               [Mar 4, 1969-July 19, 1976]

    OkU   [v.4, n.1-v.10, n.1]   WHC
               Feb 11, 1971-July, 1980]

    Other holding institutions: CLSM, CLU (CLU), [University of Minnesota
    Union List, Minneapolis, MN] (MUL), NmScW.

170 <u>California Indian News</u>. 1935-1940?//. Irregular. Last issue 19
    pages, Last volume 220 pages, height 24 cm. Line drawings,
    photographs. Published by Yangna Council, California Indian Rights
    Association, Los Angeles, CA. Editors: Allan Gardner; Stella Von
    Bulow. Subject focus: law, rights, California people.

    CL   [v.1, n.1-v.6, n.2]   Periodicals
               [Apr, 1935-July, 1940]

    Other holding institutions: CLSM.

171 <u>California League for American Indians [Newsletter]</u>. 1958?-1962?//.
    Irregular. Last issue 4 pages, height 28 cm. Line drawings. San
    Francisco, CA. Subject focus: legislation, organization news.

    CLSM   1959-1962   Periodicals

172 <u>California Newsdrum</u>. 1978?//. Monthly. Last issue 8 pages, height 39
cm. Line drawings, photographs, commercial advertising. Published by
San Francisco American Indian Center, San Francisco, CA. Editor:
Frances Vinia Snyder. Subject focus: urban community.

WHi   Feb, 1978   Pam 81-1467

WMUW   Feb, 1978   (SPL)
                                                E/75/C34x

Calista News Bulletin. Anchorage, AK

   see Calisten Erinii. Anchorage, AK

173 <u>Calisten Erinii</u>. 1972-1975?//. Bi-monthly. Last issue 4 pages.
Photographs. Available in microform: AkUF (1972-1975). Published by
Calista Corporation, Anchorage, AK. Title varies: Calista News
Bulletin, Jan 16-Dec, 1974. Frequency varies: weekly, Dec 15,
1972-June 29, 1973. Corporation newsletter. Subject focus:
environment, land claims, fishing rights, local news.

WHi   [v.1, n.3-v.3, n.3]   Microforms
           [Dec 15, 1972-Dec, 1975]

AkUF   [v.1, n.3-v.3, n.3]   Microfiche
           [Dec 15, 1972-Dec, 1975]

174 <u>Calumet</u>. 1860//. Unknown. Last issue 32 pages, height 24 cm. Line
drawings. New York, NY. Editor: John Beeson. Subject focus:
acculturation, history. Photostat.

WHi   v.1, n.1;   Pam 82-2254
           Feb, 1860

ICN   v.1, n.1;   Graff 555
           Feb, 1860

N   v.1, n.1;   C970.1/C16
           Feb, 1860

175 <u>The Calumet</u>. 1913?-1958?//. Quarterly. Last issue 20 pages. Line
drawings, photographs. Published by Marquette League, New York, NY.
Editors: Bernard A. Cullen, Aug, 1943-Feb, 1958; Lawrence J. Cahill,
Summer-Winter, 1958. Subject focus: missions, Catholic Church,
education.

WHi   [v.41, n.1-v.46, n.4]   Microforms
           [Feb, 1954-Winter, 1958]

WMM   [v.1-v.46, n.4]   Special
           [Apr, 1913-Winter, 1958]   Collections

NjP   v.30, n.4;   Periodicals
           Nov, 1943

NN   [v.41, n.1-v.46, n.4]   Microforms
           [Feb, 1954-Winter, 1958]

176 Calumet. 1968-1972?//. Irregular. Last issue 16 pages. Line
    drawings, photographs. Available in microform: MCR (1968-1972).
    Published by Union of Ontario Indians, Toronto, Ontario, Canada.
    Editor: Helen Domenchuk. Subject focus: rights, law, land claims,
    education.

    NjP   v.1;   Periodicals
               Apr-May, 1971

    AzNCC   v.1;   Indian File
               May, 1969

    CaMWU   v.1, n.1-v.2, n.2;   Microfilm
               Sept 30, 1968-Feb, 1972

    CaOONL   v.1, n.1-v.2, n.2;   Newspaper
               Sept 30, 1968-Feb, 1972   Section

Camp Crier. Harlem, MT

    see Fort Belknap Camp Crier. Harlem, MT

177 The Camsell Arrow. 1947-1969//. Irregular. Last issue 92 pages,
    height 28 cm. Line drawings, photographs. Published by Charles
    Camsell Indian Hospital, Edmonton, Alberta, Canada. Editor: Madge La
    P. Grantham. Hospital newsletter.

    CaOONL   v.4, n.5, v.9, n.5-v.11, n.1;   K-10-1
               Jan/Feb, 1952, Jan/Feb, 1956-
               Mar/Apr/May, 1957

    CaOPeT   v.1-v.22;   Microfilm
               1947-1969

178 Canadian Association in Support of the Native Peoples Bulletin.
    1960-1978//?. Irregular. ISSN 0019-4727, 0319-2938. LC cn77-318483.
    OCLC 1837974, 1838028, 1838141, 6181458, 6181556, 6186032. RLIN
    UTBG82-S1204. Last issue 46 pages. Line drawings, photographs.
    Available in microform: CPC (1960-1972). Published by Indian-Eskimo

Association of Canada, Toronto, Ontario. Title varies: Indian-Eskimo
Association of Canada Bulletin, May, 1964-July?, 1972; C.A.S.N.P.
Bulletin, Oct, 1972-July, 1974. Editors: C.D. Rouillard, May,
1960-May/June, 1966; Edith Fowke, Oct, 1966-Mar, 1970; G. Allan MacKay,
May, 1970-Apr, 1972; Gerda Kaegi, July, 1972; R.C. Freeman, Oct, 1972;
Joan Hoople, Apr, 1974-Oct, 1975; Collin Gibbons, Dec, 1975-Dec, 1976;
William Caves, Sept, 1977; Ted Jackson, Oct, 1977; Sylvia Maracle,
Fall, 1978. Subject focus: Canadian people, governmental relations,
non-reservation problems. Some articles in French.

WHi	v.1, n.1-v.18, n.4; Mar, 1960-Fall, 1978	Microforms
WGrU	[v.12, n.6-v.16, n.4] [?, 1971-Dec, 1975]	Periodicals
WMUW	[v.1, n.1-v.18, n.4]; [Mar, 1960-Fall, 1978]	E/78/C2I53x
AzNCC	v.14-v.18; 1973-1978	Indian File
CL	v.11-v.18, n.1; Oct, 1970-Sept, 1977	Periodicals
NjP	[v.1, n.1-v.15, n.2] [Mar, 1960-July, 1974]	Periodicals
SdU	v.5, n.1-v.10, n.1; 1964-1971	Stacks
WaU	v.13, n.4-v.18, n.4; Oct, 1972-Fall, 1978	970.4105/C168U
WaU	v.15, n.3-v.18, n.4; Dec, 1974-Fall, 1978	E/78/C2C35
CaACG	v.1, n.1-v.13, n.4; Mar, 1960-Oct, 1972	Periodicals
CaAEU	v.1, n.1-v.18, n.4; Mar, 1960-Fall, 1978	Boreal Institute
CaBViP	v.1, n.1-v.18? Mar, 1960-1978	NW/970.1 I39i
CaMWU	[v.1-18] [1960-1977]	970/C16 As Sub
CaOAFN	[v.9,n.4-v.18, n.4] [Nov, 1968-Fall, 1978]	Periodicals
CaOONL	v.1, n.1-2, [v.2-v.5], v.6-v.18; 1960, [1961-1964], 1965-1978	Periodicals

CaOOP	v.1, n.1-v.18, n.4;	E/78/C2/E53
	Mar, 1960-Fall, 1978	

CaOPeT   v.1-v.18;   Microfilm
          1960-1978

CaSSIC   v.14, n.1-v.18;   Periodicals
          1973-1978

Other holding institutions: CLU (CLU), CtY (YUS), DI (UDI), [University
of Minnesota Union List, Minneapolis, MN] (MUL), NhD (DRB).

179 Canadian Association in Support of the Native Peoples Newsletter.
    1974-1978//. Bi-monthly. ISSN 0319-7514. OCLC 2442969. Last issue 2
    pages, height 36 cm. Ottawa, Ontario, Canada. Subject focus:
    association news, rights, Canadian people.

WHi   n.2-3, 15, 18-19;   Cataloging
          Dec, 1974-Feb, 1975, Nov/Dec, 1977,
          July-Oct, 1978

CaOAFN   [n.2-19]   Periodicals
          [Dec, 1974-Oct, 1978]

CaOONL   [n.2-19]   Periodicals
          [Dec, 1974-Oct, 1978]

CaOOP   n.1-19;   E/78/C2/I53
          Sept, 1974-Oct, 1978]

Other holding institutions: CLU (CLU).

180 The Canadian Indian. 1890-1891//. Monthly. ISSN 0382-9456. LC
    cn76-308762. OCLC 1553115. RLIN DCLCCN76308762-S, CUBU12667593-S,
    OHCP1553115-S. Last issue 32 pages, last volume 356 pages, height 24
    cm. Line drawings, commercial advertising. Available in microform:
    WHi (1890-1891); McL (1890-1891). Published by Canadian Indian
    Research Society, Owen Sound, Ontario. Editors: Rev. E. F. Wilson and
    H. B. Small. Supercedes Our Forest Children. Subject focus: missions,
    education, history, legends.

WHi   v.1, n.1-12;   E/75/C3
          Oct, 1890-Sept, 1891

WHi   v.1, n.1-12;   Microforms
          Oct, 1890-Sept, 1891

ICN   v.1, n.1-12;   Ayer 1/C2
          Oct, 1890-Sept, 1891

OkU   v.1, n.1-12;   WHC
          Oct, 1890-Sept, 1891

CaMWU   v.1, n.1-12;   Microfilm
               Oct, 1890-Sept, 1891

CaOONL   v.1, n.1-12;   Periodicals
               Oct, 1890-Sept, 1891

CaOPeT   v.1, n.1-12;   Microfilm
               Oct, 1890-Sept, 1891

Other holding institutions: [University of Minnesota Union List,
Minneapolis, MN] (MUL), NN (NYP).

181 Canadian Indian Artcrafts. 1974-1979//?. Quarterly. ISSN 0315-9604.
    LC cn75-30581. OCLC 2247345. Last issue 12 pages, height 40 cm. Line
    drawings, photographs, commercial advertising. Available in microform:
    WHi (1975-1979). Published by National Indian Arts and Crafts Advisory
    Corp., Ottawa, Ontario. Editor: Madeline Risser. Subject focus: arts
    and crafts.

    WHi   v.1, n.4-v.5, n.1;   Microforms
                  Aug, 1975-1979

    CaACG   v.1, n.1-v.5, n.1;   Periodicals
                  Aug, 1974-1979

    CaAEU   v.1, n.4-v.5, n.1;   Boreal
                  Aug, 1975-1979   Institute

    CaOSuU   v.1-v.5   Periodicals
                  1974-1979

    Other holding institutions: DSI (SMI), CaOONL (NLC).

182 Canadian Indians and Eskimos of Today. 1965-?//. Irregular. ISSN
    0576-5390, 0576-5382. LC cn77-318867. OCLC 3318635, 3318675. Last
    issue 4 pages, height 28 cm. Photographs. Published by the
    Indian-Eskimo Association of Canada, Toronto, Ontario, Canada. Title
    varies: Canadian Indians of Today, Feb-Apr, 1965. Subject focus:
    Inuit, Canadian people.

    WHi   n.[1]-5;   Pam 2478
                  Feb, 1965-Sept, 1966

    AzNCC   n.[1]-5;   Indian File
                  Feb, 1965-Sept, 1966

    CaACG   n.2-4;   Periodicals
                  Apr, 1965-May, 1966

    CaAEU   n.[1]-5;   Boreal
                  Feb, 1965-Sept, 1966   Institute

CaOOP   n.2-4;   Periodicals
           Apr, 1965-May, 1966

Other holding institutions: [University of Minnesota Union List,
Minneapolis, MN] (MUL), CaOONL (NLC).

Canadian Indians of Today. Toronto, Ontario, Canada

    see Canadian Indians and Eskimos of Today. Toronto, Ontario, Canada

183 Canadian Journal of Native Education. 1973. Quarterly. $3. for
    individuals and institutions. Dr. R. J. Carney and Dr. A. M. Decore,
    editors, Canadian Journal of Native Education, 5-109 Education North,
    University of Alberta, Edmonton, Alberta, Canada T6G 2G5. (403)
    432-3751. ISSN 0318-8647, 0710-1481. LC cn76-319937, cn81-31402.
    OCLC 2030025, 7748558, 8185769. RLIN NYPG82-S8802, DCLCCN8131402-S,
    NYPG804179441-S. Last issue 24 pages, height 21 cm. Published by
    Intercultural Education Program, University of Alberta. Title varies:
    Indian-ed., ?, 1973-Summer, 1980. Previous editor: Allen Berger, [v.1,
    n.1], 1973-[v.1, n.4], 1974. Subject focus: education, teaching,
    ethnic studies, book reviews.

    WMUW   v.7, n.3-   E/97/I5x
               1977-

    WU   v.1, n.1-   AP/I38/E24
               1973

    WUSP   v.1, n.1-   Periodicals
               1973-

    AzNCC   v.8, n.1-   Indian File
               Fall, 1980-

    CaACG   v.8, n.1-   Periodicals
               Fall, 1980-

    CaAEU   v.1, n.1-   Boreal
               1973-   Institute

    CaOONL   v.1, n.1-   Periodicals
               1973

    CaOPeT   v.1-   E97/I32
               1973-

Other holding institutions: CLU (CLU), InTI (ISU), MiYEM (EYE), MiDW
(EYW), MnU (MNU), [University of Minnesota Union List, Minneapolis, MN]
(MUL), [University of Wisconsin-Stevens Point, Stevens Point, WI] (WIS).

184 Canadian Journal of Native Studies. 1981. Semi-annual. $16. for
    individuals; $25. for libraries; $30. for institutions. Samuel W.
    Corrigan, editor, Canadian Journal of Native Studies, 1229 Lorne Ave.,
    Brandon, Manitoba, Canada R7A 0V3. (204) 727-1725. OCLC 8137717.
    Height 23 cm. Subject focus: Native American studies, book reviews.

    WHi   v.2, n.1-   Circulation
                1982-

    CaACG   v.1, n.1-   Periodicals
                1981-

    CaAEU   v.1, n.1-   Boreal
                1981-   Institute

    CaOONL   v.1, n.1-   Periodicals
                1981-

    CaOPeT   v.1-   E77/C35
                1981-

    Other holding institutions: CU-Riv (CRU), ICN (IBV), MH (HUL), MH-P
    (TOZ), NdU (UND).

    Canadian Native Friendship Centre.   Edmonton, Alberta, Canada

        see Edmonton Native News.   Edmonton, Alberta, Canada

185 Canadian Native Law Reporter. 1979. Quarterly. $30. for individuals
    and institutions. Martha Morgan, editor, Canadian Native Law Reporter,
    410 Cumberland Ave. North, Saskatoon, Saskatchewan, Canada S7N 1M6.
    ISSN 0225-2279. Last issue 164 pages, height 28 cm. Published by
    University of Saskatchewan Native Law Centre. Subject focus: legal
    cases, legislation, law.

    WU-L   n.1-   Periodicals
                1981-

    CaOONL   n.1-   Periodicals
                1979-

    CaOSuU   n.1-   Periodicals
                1979-

    Other holding institutions: ArU (AFU), AzU (AZU), CLU (CLU), FTaSU-L
    (FSL), ICU-L (IBC), IU (UIU), Ku-L (KFL), LU-L (LUL), MnU-L (MLL),
    [UNiversity of Minnesota Union List, Minneapolis, MN] (MUL), [St. Louis
    University Law Library, St. Louis, MO] (SLU), NcDL (NDL), NmU-L (NML),
    NIC (COO), [New York Union List of Serials, Albany, NY] (NYS), OkU-L
    (OKL), OrPL-L, (ONS), TxU (TXQ), ViU-1 (VAL).

186 Canadian Native News Service: Canada's Weekly Update on Indian, Metis
    and Inuit Affairs. 1977-1978//? Weekly. ISSN 0703-170x. LC
    cn78-39043. OCLC 3827668. RLIN DCLCCN7839043-S, OHCP3827668-S.
    Height 28 cm. Ottawa, Ontario, Canada. Editor: Barbara Laurie.
    Newspaper.

    CaAEU   [v.1, n.1-v.2, n.31]   Boreal
               [June, 1977-Aug, 1978]   Institute

    CaOAFN   v.1-v.2;   Periodicals
               Dec, 1977-1978

    Other holding institutions: DLC (DLC), CaOONL (NLC).

187 Canadian Native Prints, Ltd., Newsletter. 1980? Unknown. Last issue
    4 pages, height 28 cm. Photographs. Vancouver, British Columbia,
    Canada. Subject focus: art exhibits, prints and print-makers.

    CaACG   Dec, 1980, June, Nov, 1981   Periodicals

188 Capitol City Report. 1982? Unknown. Capitol City Report, 4010 N.
    Lincoln Blvd., Oklahoma City, OK 73105. OCLC 7768775. Last issue 10
    pages, height 28 cm. Line drawings, photographs. Published by
    Oklahoma Indian Affairs Commission. Subject focus: legislation,
    health, education.

    ICN   Current issues   CHAI

    Other holding institutions: Ok (OKD).

189 Carcajou Wolverine. 1972-?//. Unknown. Last issue 8 pages, height 44
    cm. Line drawings, photographs. Available in microform: SOC (1972-).
    Published by Indians of Quebec Association, Huron Village, Quebec,
    Canada. Editor: David Monture. Newspaper. Subject focus: Quebec
    Native people. In Cree, 30%; in French, 30%.

    CaOONL   v.1, n.1-2;   Newspaper
               June?-July?, 1972   Section

190 Caribou. 1981. Monthly. Caribou, P.O. Box 375, St. Georges,
    Newfoundland, Canada, A0N 1Z0. (709) 647-3733. Last issue 8 pages,
    height 44 cm. Line drawings, photographs, commercial advertising.
    Published by Newfoundland Federation of Indians. Subject focus:
    legislation, rights, provincial and national news, Micmac people.

    WHi   v.2, n.8-   Circulation
               Aug 31, 1982-

CaOAFN   v.1, n.2-   Periodicals
           Jan 21, 1981-

Other holding institutions: CaNfSM.

191 Caribou News. 1981. Bi-monthly. $19.95 for individuals and
    institutions. Caribou News, Suite 100, 196 Bronson Ave., Ottawa,
    Ontario, Canada K1R 6H4. (613) 233-6252. Line drawings, photographs.
    Published by Nortext Information Design, Ltd. Subject focus:
    preservation of Beverly and Kaminuriat herds. Some articles in Inuit,
    Chipewyan, Cree.

    CaAEU   v.1, n.1-   Boreal
               May, 1981-   Institute

    CaOAFN   v.1, n.1-   Periodicals
               May, 1981-

    Carlisle Arrow. Carlisle, PA

        see Carlisle Arrow and Redman. Carlisle, PA

192 Carlisle Arrow and Redman. 1904-1918//. Weekly during school year.
    Last issue 8 pages. Available in microform: WHi-A, Papers of Carlos
    Montezuma, (1916); CPC (1904-1908). Published by Carlisle Indian
    Schools, Carlisle, PA. Title varies: The Arrow, Aug 25, 1904-June 19,
    1908; The Carlisle Arrow, Sept 11, 1908-Sept 28, 1917. School
    newsletter. Subject focus: school events, conferences.

    WHi   v.1, n.1-v.4, n.42, v.13, n.8;   Microforms
               Sept 8, 1904-June, 19, 1908, Oct 27, 1916

    WHi   v.9, n.1-v.4, n.42;   F8095/+C28
               Sept 28, 1912-Oct 5, 1917   Cutter

    MoSHi   v.9-v.11;   970.1/C194
               Sept 5, 1913-Sept 17, 1915

    NHu   [v.1, n.3-v.4, n.42]   Periodicals
               [1904-1908]

    PCarlH   [v.1-v.14]   I/Per/Red4
               [Aug 25, 1904-1913]

    Other holding institutions: CLSM.

193 Carolina Indian Voice. 1973. Weekly. $12. for individuals and
    institutions. The Carolina Indian Voice, P.O. Box 1075, Pembroke, NC

28372. (919) 521-2826. OCLC 6168850, 8131402. Last issue 8 pages,
height 58 cm. Line drawings, photographs, commerical advertising.
Available in microform: WHi (1979-). Published by Lumbee Publishing
Co., Inc. Newspaper. Subject focus: North Carolina Native people.

WHi   v.7, n.21, 36-   Microforms
           May 24, Aug 30, 1979-

AzNCC   v.5-   Indian File
           Oct 20, 1977-

NcP   v.1-   Periodicals
           1973-

194 Carrier Sekani Tribal Council Newsletter. 1982. Unknown. M. Wallace,
    editor, Carrier Sekani Tribal Council Newsletter, 1274 5th Ave., Prince
    George, British Columbia, Canada V2L 3L2. (604) 562-6279. Last issue
    16 pages, height 28 cm. Line drawings, photographs. Community
    newsletter. Subject focus: Carrier and Sekani people, governmental
    relations.

    CaOAFN   v.1, n.2-   Periodicals
               June, 1982-

195 Catholic Indian Herald. 1932-1948?//. Monthly. OCLC 8269724,
    8269788. Last issue 4 pages, height 30 cm. Line drawings,
    photographs. Published by St. Paul's Catholic Indian Mission, Marty,
    SD. Title varies: Sina Sapa Wocekine Taenanpaha/The Catholic Sioux
    Herald, Jan 15, 1931-Nov 15, 1939. Subject focus: missions, Catholic
    Church, Sioux people. In Dakota, 50-100%.

    WMM   [v.1, n.1-v.14, n.22]   Special
               [Jan 15, 1932-Dec 15, 1939]   Collections

    SdU   [v.14-22]   Periodicals
               [Feb, 1, 1940-July 15, 1948]

    Other holding institutions: InND (IND).

    The Catholic Sioux Herald. Marty, SD

        see The Catholic Indian Herald. Marty, SD

196 The Catholic Voice in Navajoland. 1971-?//. Irregular. Last issue 4
    pages, height 28 cm. Line drawings, photographs. Published by St.
    Michaels Mission, St. Michaels, AZ. Subject focus: Catholic Church,
    Navajo people.

WMM   v.1, n.3, 5, 7;   Special
             Summer, 1971, Winter, Summmer, 1972   Collections

NmG   v.1, n.2-v.3;   Periodicals
             Spring, 1972-Winter, 1974

Centre d'Amitie Autochtone de Montreal. Montreal, Quebec, Canada

     see Native American Friendship Centre of Montreal/Centre d'Amitie
         Autochtone de Montreal. Montreal, Quebec, Canada

197 Center of Indian Studies. 1979?-1982//. Monthly. Last issue 16
    pages, height 28 cm. Line drawings. Spearfish, SD. Title varies:
    Black Hills State College, Spearfish, South Dakota, Center of Indian
    Studies, Jan, 1979-July, 1980. Subject focus: research, teacher
    education, educational and teaching opportunities.

    WHi   Jan, 1979-June, 1982   Microforms

    Ceremonial Magazine. Gallup, NM

       see Indian Life. Gallup, NM

198 Chahta Anumpa/The Choctaw Times. 1968-1971?//. Monthly. ISSN
    0577-5043. OCLC 3022513. RLIN OHCP3022513-S. Last issue 4 pages,
    last volume 52 pages. Line drawings, photographs. Available in
    microform: WHi (1968-1971). Published by Southeastern Indian
    Antiquities Survey, Nashville, TN. Editor: Bob Ferguson. Subject
    focus: archaeology, history, Choctaw people, national and local news.

    WHi   v.1, n.1-v,2, n.7;   Microforms
                 Apr/May, 1968-May, 1971

    WEU   v.1, n.12-v.2, n.7;   Journalism
                 May/June, 1969-May, 1971   Lab

    WEU   v.1, n.1-v.2, n.6;   Microforms
                 Apr/May, 1968-Dec?, 1969

    AzNCC   v.1, n.1-v,2, n.7;   Indian File
                 Apr/May, 1968-May, 1971

    CL   v.1, n.1-v,2, n.7;   Periodicals
                 Apr/May, 1968-May, 1971

    NjP   v.1, n.1-v.2, n.7;   Periodicals
                 Apr/May, 1968-May, 1971

KU	v.1–v.2 1968–1971	Kansas Collection
OkU	[v.1, n.6–v.2, n.7] [Nov, 1968–May, 1971]	WHC
WaU	v.2, n.7; May, 1971	Periodicals

Other holding institutions: CU-UC (UCU), MH-P (HLS), [University of Minnesota Union List] (MUL), OAU (OUN), OkTahN.

199 <u>Char-Koosta</u>. 1956. Semi-monthly. $15. for individuals and institutions. Clair Krebsbach, editor, Char-Koosta, P.O. Box 278, Pablo, MT 59855. (406) 675-4790. ISSN 0528-8592. LC sn79-7540, sn79-7539. OCLC 5420430, 2539761. RLIN OHCP5420430-S, OHCP2539761-S. Last issue 28 pages, last volume 500 pages, height 28 cm. Line drawings, photographs, commercial advertising. Published by Tribal Council of the Confederated Salish and Kootenai Tribes. Place of publication varies: Dixon, MT, Apr 28, 1972–Jan 15, 1979. Previous editors: Germaine White, Apr 28–Sept 15, 1972; Ralph Ducharme, Dec 1, 1972; Sharon Orr and Ralph Ducharme, Dec 15, 1972–Jan 1, 1973; Sharon Orr, Jan 15–Nov 15, 1973; Lonny Desimone, Aug 15, 1975–Apr 15, 1977; Lonny Schmach, May 1–Sept 1, 1977; Ardyth Deadrick, Nov 15, 1977–Feb 1, 1980. Newspaper. Subject focus: Salish, Pend d'Oreille and Kootenai peoples, national, area and reservation news. Suspended publication, 1961–1971.

WHi	(n.s.)v.2, n.1– Apr 28, 1972–	E/75/C5
WMUW	[(n.s.)v.3, n.19–v.6, n.2]; [Feb 1, 1974–Feb 15, 1977]	(SPL) E/75/C45x
AzNCC	(n.s.)v.4– Dec, 1975	Indian File
MtBBCC	(n.s.)v.10; Aug, 1980–Nov, 1981	Periodicals
MtBC	v.1, n.1– 1956–	E/99/S2/C43
MtGrCE	Current issues	Periodicals
UPB	[v.2, n.7–v.4, n.10] [1958–1960]	970.48605/C37

Other holding institutions: [Standing Rock Community College Library, Fort Yates, ND], OKTU (OKT), OrU-Special Collections.

200 <u>Chemawa American</u>. 1900?-1981//. Quarterly. Chemawa Indian School,
Salem OR 97305. OCLC 6221091. Last issue 10 pages, last volume 34
pages, height 28 cm. Line drawings, photographs. Available in
microform: WHi (1952-1981); CPC (1926-1938, 1969-1976). Place of
publication varies: Chemawa, OR, Sept 22, 1926-Nov., 24, 1972.
Frequency varies: weekly, Sept 22, 1926-Sept 23, 1931; bi-weekly, Oct
7, 1931-Apr 11, 1935; tri-weekly, Dec 10, 1937-Mar 18, 1938; monthly
Sept 15-Dec 15, 1955. Previous editors: Mildred Quaempts, Nov, 1971;
Ronni Wesley, Jan-Mar 23, 1972; Nancy Barnes, Nov 24-Feb 8, 1972; Nancy
Barnes, Paul Kotongan and Lynn Miller, Mar 23, 1973; Eleanor
Carltikoff, Oct 12, 1973-May 8, 1974; Bonnie James and Marti Moses,
Sept 30, 1974. School newsletter.

WHi	v.28, n.1- Sept 22, 1926-	Microforms
WMUW	v.74, n.1-5; Oct, 1977-May, 1978	(SPL) E/75/C48x
AzNCC	v.70-v.77, n.4] May, 1973-May, 1981]	Indian File
NjP	[v.64, n.3-v.74, n.5] [Mar, 1968-May, 1978]	Periodicals
NN	[v.28, n.1-v.72, n.9] [Sept 22, 1926-July 23, 1976]	Microforms
OkTU	[v.62], v.72, n.9-v.81, n.4; [1965], July, 1976-May, 1981	Rare Book Room
OrHi	v.58-v.77, n.4; 1961-May, 1981	Periodicals

201 <u>Chemawa Magazine</u>. 1917-1918?//. Weekly. Last issue 32 pages, height
24 cm. Line drawings, photographs. Published by Salem Indian Training
School, Chemawa, OR. School newsletter.

Or	Jan, Apr, 1917, July, 1918	Periodicals

202 <u>Chemehuevi Newsletter</u>. 1968-?//?. Bi-monthly. RLIN CUBU1447-S. Last
issue 24 pages, height 28 cm. Line drawings. Available in microform:
CPC (1968-1973). Los Angeles, CA. Editor: Georgia Culp, June/July-
Oct/Nov, 1971. Subject focus: Chemehuevi people, culture,
socio-economic conditions, education.

WHi	[v.1, n.1?]-v.6, n.2; Aug, 1968-May/June, 1973	Microforms
WEU	v.4, n.5, 8; June/July, Oct/Nov, 1971	Journalism Lab

AzNCC   v.4-6;   Indian File
           Oct, 1971-Jan, 1973

NjP   [v.1, n.1-v.6]   Periodicals
           [Aug, 1968-Apr/June, 1973]

NN   [v.1, n.1?]-v.6, n.2;   Microforms
           Aug, 1968-May/June, 1973

PPT   v.4, n.7, v.5, n.1-4;   Contemporary
           Sept, 1971, Jan-Apr, 1972   Culture

203 The Cherokee Advocate. 1844-1906//. Weekly. Last issue 4 pages.
    Photographs, commercial advertising. Available in microform: DLC
    (1870-1871, 1881-1897); OkHi (1845-1906). Published by Cherokee
    Nation, Tahlequah, OK. Editors: William P. Ross, May 1, 1845-Dec 9,
    1848; Daniel Hicks Ross, June 5, 1848; William P. Ross, Aug 14, 1848;
    James Shepherd Vann, Jan 15, 1849; W. P. Boudinot, June 18, 1870-Oct
    18, 1873; John Lynch Adair, Nov 29, 1873-Jan 30, 1875; Boudinot, Mar 1,
    1876-June 27, 1877; George Washington Johnson, Dec 15, 1877-Nov 12,
    1879; Elias C. Boudinot, Jr., Nov 26, 1879-Nov 16, 1881; D. H. Ross,
    Nov 15, 1881-Nov 13, 1885; E. C. Boudinot, Jr., Dec 4, 1885-Oct 12,
    1887; Ridge Paschal, Jan 4, 1888; W. P. Boudinot, Aug 6, 1890-Apr 29,
    1891; H. M. Adair, Nov 18, 1891-Nov 18, 1893; George O. Butler, Nov 25,
    1893-July 10, 1895; Waddie Hudson, Feb 29, 1896-Oct 30, 1897; J. R.
    Sequichie, Dec 11, 1897-Nov 11, 1898; William T. Leoser, Mar 3,
    1900-Nov 16, 1901; G. O. Butler, Nov 23, 1901-Nov 7, 1903; W. J.
    Melton, Nov 21, 1903-Mar 3, 1906. Newspaper. Subject focus: Cherokee
    people. In Cherokee, 50%. Suspended publication Sept 28, 1853-Apr,
    1870. Also described in: Foreman, Carolyn Thomas. Oklahoma Imprints,
    1835-1907. Norman: University of Oklahoma Press, 1936.

    WHi   [v.1, n.32-v.5, n.?],   Microforms
               (n.s.) [v.1, n.10-v.5, n. 36],
               (n.s.) [v.1, n.1-v.30, n.3]
               [May 1, 1845-Jan 15, 1849],
               [June 18, 1870-Jan 30, 1875]
               [Mar 1, 1876-Mar 3, 1906]

    MWA   [v.1, n.1-v.10?, n.?],   Periodicals
               (n.s.)v.1, n.34?-36?
               [Sept 26, 1844-Sept 28, 1853],
               Oct 21-Nov 5, 1876

    NjP   (n.s.)v.1, n.1-v.2, n.5;   Periodicals
               Mar 1, 1876-Apr 11, 1877

    N   [v.1, n.35-48], (n.s.)v.12, n.25;   Vault
               [May 22-Sept 8, 1845], Nov 23, 1887

    NN   [v.1, n.27-v.9, n.15]   Rare Book
               [Mar 27, 1845-Aug 13, 1853]   Division

OkHi   [v.1, n.32-v.5, n.?]   Microforms
            (n.s.) [v.1, n.10-v.5, n. 36]
            (n.s.) [v. 1, n.1-v.30, n.3]
            [May 1, 1845-Jan 15, 1849]
            [June 18, 1870-Jan 30, 1875]
            [Mar 1, 1876-Mar 3, 1906]

OkTahN   v.1-(n.s.)v.30   Microfilm
            Sept, 1844-Mar 5, 1906

OkTG   [v.2-(n.s.)v.29]   Periodicals
            [Mar 20, 1845-Feb 18, 1905]

OkU   v.1, n.1-v.10,   WHC
            (n.s.)v.1, n.1-v.26;
            Sept 27, 1844-Sept 28, 1853,
            Mar 1, 1876-Nov, 1902

204 <u>Cherokee Advocate</u>. 1977. Semi-annual. $5. for individuals and
    institutions. S.G. Long, editor, Cherokee Advocate, P.O. Box 948,
    Tahlequah, OK 74464. (918) 456-0671. OCLC 6168829. Last issue 12
    pages, last volume 192 pages, height 39 cm. Line drawings,
    photographs, commercial advertising. Published by Cherokee Nation of
    Oklahoma. Frequency varies: monthly, Feb, 1977-Nov, 1981. Previous
    editors: Helen Bennett, Feb-Apr, 1977; Irene Gilbert, May-Nov, 1977;
    Jeff P. McLemore, Dec, 1977-Jan, 1980; Dan Garber, Feb, 1980-June,
    1981; Pat Frank, July-Nov, 1981. Newspaper. Subject focus: Cherokee
    people, education, culture, history, sports.

WHi   v.1, n.1-   Circulation
            Feb, 1977-

WEU   v.1, n.1;   Journalism
            Feb, 1977   Lab

WMUW   [v.1, n.1-v.3, n.6];   (SPL)
            [Feb, 1977-July, 1979]   E/75/C52x

AzNCC   v.1, n.2-   Indian File
            Mar, 1977-

CL   v.4, n.2-   Periodicals
            Mar, 1980-

CRSSU   v.4-   Periodicals
            1980-

CU-A   v.1, n.1-   E/77/A1/C42
            Feb, 1977-

OkTahn   v.1, n.1-   Periodicals
            Feb, 1977-

OkTU	v.2, n.2– Mar, 1978–	970.305 C522Ca
OkU	v.1, n.1– Feb, 1977–	WHC

Other holding institutions: [Standing Rock Community College Library, Fort Yates, ND], [Bacone College, Muskogee, OK], TxDa (IGA), [AMIGOS Union List of Serials, Dallas, TX] (IUC).

205 Cherokee Boys Club, Inc., Newsletter. 1966. Quarterly. Cherokee Boys Club, Inc., Newsletter, Box 507, Cherokee, NC 28719. (704) 497-9101. OCLC 6194252. Last issue 4 pages, last volume 16 pages, height 28 cm. Photographs. Available in microform: McA (1974-). Frequency varies: irregular Jan, 1974-Dec, 1978. Organization newsletter. Subject focus: Cherokee children.

WHi	v.9, n.6– Jan, 1974–	Microforms
WEU	v.6, n.4–v.9, n.5; Nov, 1970–Nov/Dec, 1973	Microforms
WMUW	[v.11, n.3–12]; [Oct, 1976–July, 1977]	(SPL) E/75/C523x
AzNCC	v.9– Dec, 1974–	Indian File
ICN	Current issues	CHAI
NjP	[v.7, n.8–v.10, n.10] [July, 1972–May, 1976]	Periodicals
OkU	v.17– Spring, 1982–	WHC
CaOPeT	v.9, n.6–v.11, n.5, v.14, n.1– Jan, 1974–Nov/Dec, 1976, Spring, 1979	Microfilm

206 Cherokee Examiner. 1969-?//. Unknown. OCLC 1554057, 7401849. RLIN CSUP01210300-S, CUBG1549570X-S, CUBU12671083-S, OHCP1554057-S. Last issue 40 pages, height 28 cm. Line drawings, photographs. Available in microform: McP (1969). Published by Rabid, South Pasadena, CA. Editor: N. Magowan. Subject focus: rights, culture, history, education, poetry, biographies.

WHi	n.1–5; Jan–?, 1969	Pam 72-3055
WHi	n.2, 4; 1969	Microforms

WEU	n.4; 1969	Journalism Lab
WKenU	n.2, 4; Jan, ?, 1969	Microfilm
WMUW	n.2, 4; 1969	MF/AN104
CL	n.2, 4; 1969	Periodicals
KU	n.1-5; Jan-?, 1969	Kansas Collection
N	n.2, 4; 1969	MA/FM
PPT	n.1-5; 1969	Contemporary Culture

Other holding institutions: MiU-Labadie (EYM), [University of Minnesota Union List, Minneapolis, MN] (MUL), NFQC (XQM), NSbSU (YSM), OAkU (AKR), OKentU (KSU), WMUW (GZN).

207 The Cherokee Messenger. 1844-1846//. Irregular. OCLC 1040826, 8188188. Last issue 16 pages, height 24 cm. Line drawings. Published by Baptist Mission Press, Breadtown, OK. Available in microform: OkHi (1844-1846). Editor: Rev. Evan Jones. Subject focus: Bible, Baptist Church, Cherokee people, Cherokee language. In Cherokee, 85-90%.

WHi	v.1, n.1-12; Aug, 1844-May, 1846	F8097/C52M Cutter Rare Books
WHi	v.1, n.1-12; Aug, 1844-May, 1846	Microforms
OkHi	v.1, n.1-12; Aug, 1844-May, 1846	Microforms
OkTahN	v.1, n.1-12; Aug, 1844-May, 1846	Microforms
OkU	v.1, n.1-12; Aug, 1844-May, 1846	WHC

Other holding institutions: DeU (DLM), GU (GUA), MoU (MUU), OOxM (MIA). Also described in: Foreman, Carolyn Thomas. Oklahoma Imprints, 1835-1907. Norman: University of Oklahoma Press, 1936.

208 Cherokee Nation News. 1967-1977//. Weekly. ISSN 0009-322x. OCLC
    3080081. RLIN OHCP3080081-S. Last issue 6 pages. Photographs,
    commercial advertising. Published by Cherokee Nation of Oklahoma,
    Tahlequah, OK. Title varies: Cherokee Nation Newsletter, Aug 24,
    1967-Feb 22, 1968. Frequency varies: irregular, Aug 24, 1967-Feb 22,
    1968. Editors: Ralph F. Keen, Mar, 7, 1968-Feb 4, 1969; Anna
    Kilpatrick, Feb 11, 1969-Mar 18, 1970; Sue Thompson, Apr 21, 1970-June
    21. 1974. Newspaper. Subject focus: Cherokee people.

WHi	n.67/2-v.10, n.52; Aug 24, 1967-Jan 3, 1977	Microforms
WEU	v.7, n. 13, 15-16, v.9, n.50, v.10, n.52 Mar 29, Apr 12-19, 1974, Dec 10, 1976, Jan 7, 1977	Journalism Lab
WMUW	[v.8, n.15-v.10, n.27] [Apr, 1975-July, 1977]	(SPL) E/75/C525x
AzNCC	v.3-v.10; Feb, 1971-Jan, 1977	Indian File
CU-A	v.6, n.9-v.10; 1973-1977	E/77/A1/C44
NjP	[v.2, n.1-v.3,n.25] [Jan 7, 1969-June 23, 1970]	Periodicals
OkTahN	1968-1974, 1975-1976	Microfilm E/71/C577
OkU	[v.1, n.1-v.9, n.52] [1968-1976]	WHC

Other holding institutions:CU-UC (UCU).

Cherokee Nation Newsletter. Tahlequah, OK

    see Cherokee Nation News. Tahlequah, OK

209 The Cherokee One Feather. 1968. Weekly. $18. for individuals and
    institutions. Richard Welch, editor, The Cherokee One Feather, P.O.
    Box 501, Cherokee, NC 28719. (704) 497-5513. OCLC 1554058. RLIN
    OHCP1554058-S. Last issue 8 pages, last volume 400 pages, height 38
    cm. Line drawings, photographs, commercial advertising. Available in
    microform: McP (1971-1973); McA (1969-). Published by Cherokee Tribal
    Council of the Eastern Band of Cherokee Indians. Previous editors:
    Alvin Smith, Tom Bradley, and Calvin Lossiah, Feb 12-May 14, 1969; Gwen
    Owl, May 21, 1969-Oct 30, 1974; Reuben Teesatuskie, Dec 11, 1974-Sept
    14, 1977. Newspaper. Subject focus: Cherokee people, Tribal council
    news, local and national news.

WHi	v.2, n.7–	Microforms
	Feb 12, 1969–	
WEU	[v.4, n.7–v.10, n.8]	Journalism
	[Feb 17, 1971–Feb 23, 1977]	Lab
WMWU	v.9, n.39;	(SPL)
	Sept, 29, 1976	E/75/C526x
AzNCC	v.6–	Indian File
	1973–	
CNoSU	[v.4, n.1–v.6, n.47]	Microfilm
	[Jan, 1971–Dec 5, 1973]	
KU	v.1–	Kansas
	1968–	Collection
NjP	[v.1, n.2–v.12, n.24]	Periodicals
	[Jan 21, 1968–June 20, 1979]	
OkTahN	v.12–	Periodicals
	1979–	
OkTU	v.11, n.1–	Rare Book
	Jan, 1978–	room
OkU	[v.2, n.7–v.6], v.12, n.49–	WHC
	[Feb 12, 1969–Dec 5, 1973], 1979–	
WyCWC	v.6, n.1–v.8, n.51;	Periodicals
	1973–1975	
CaOPeT	v.2–	Microfilm
	Feb, 1969–	

Other holding institutions: CLU (CLU), CU-UC (UCU), KSteC (KKQ),
[University of Minnesota Union List, Minneapolis, MN] (MUL), [Western
Nevada Community College, Carson City, NV], NmScW.

210 <u>Cherokee Orphan Asylum Press</u>. 1880?–1881?//. Weekly. Last issue 4
pages, height 20 cm. Cherokee Nation, OK. Available in microform:
OkHi (1841). Editors: William Cobb and Lizzie Stinson, June 9–Aug 11,
1881; W.A. Duncan, Nov 4–17, 1881. School newsletter. Also described
in: Foreman, Carolyn Thomas. <u>Oklahoma Imprints, 1835–1907</u>. Norman:
University of Oklahoma Press, 1936.

WHi	v.2, n.1–1, 4;	F8096/C52//
	Nov 4–10, 17, 1881	CH Cutter
WHi	v.1, n.5, 36;	Microforms
	June 9, Aug 11, 1881	
OkHi	v.1, n.5, 36;	Microforms
	June 9, Aug 11, 1881	

Cherokee Phoenix. New Echota, GA

see Cherokee Phoenix and Indians' Advocate. New Echota, GA

211 Cherokee Phoenix and Indians' Advocate. 1828-1834//. Weekly. RLIN
AZPG0832-S. Last issue 4 pages, height 54 cm. Available in microform:
BNN (1828-1834). New Echota, GA. Title varies: Cherokee Phoenix, Feb
21, 1828-Feb 4, 1829. Editor: Elias Boudinot, Feb 21, 1828-Aug 11,
1832; Elijah Hicks, Sept 8, 1832-MAy 21, 1834. Newspaper. Subject
focus: Cherokee people. In Cherokee, 30%.

WHi	v.1, n.1-v.5, n.52; Feb 21, 1828-May 31, 1834	Microforms
ICN	v.1, n.1-v.5, n.52; Feb 21, 1828-May 31, 1834	Ayer Film 1/C45
ICN	v.1, n.1-v.5, n.52; Feb 21, 1828-May 31, 1834	Ayer 1/C45
MWA	v.1, n.1-v.5, n.52; Feb 21, 1828-May 31, 1834	Periodicals
NjP	v.1, n.1-v.5, n.52; Feb 21, 1828-May 31, 1834	Periodicals
N	[v.1, n.1-v.5, n.18] [Feb 21, 1828-1833]	Microforms
NN	[v.1, n.15-v.5, n.38] [June 4, 1828-Feb 8, 1834]	Rare Book Division
OkTahN	v.1, n.1-v.5, n.52; Feb 21, 1828-May 31, 1834	Microfilm
OkU	v.1, n.1-v.5, n.52; Feb 21, 1828-May 31, 1834	WHC

212 Cherokee Rose Buds. 1854-?//. Irregular. Last issue 8 pages.
Published by Female Seminary of the Cherokee Nation, Tahlequah, OK.
Available in microform: OkHi (1855). Editors: Catherine Gunter and
Nancy E. Hicks. School newsletter. Subject focus: Cherokee children,
school news, temperance, fiction, poetry. In Cherokee, 10%. Also
described in: Foreman, Carolyn Thomas, Oklahoma Imprints, 1835-1907,
University of Oklahoma Press, Norman OK, 1936.

WHi	v.1, n.2, v.2, n.1; Aug 2, 1854, Aug, 1, 1855	Microforms

OkHi   v.1, n.2, v.2, n.1;   Microforms
            Aug 2, 1854, Aug, 1, 1855

Cherokee Telephone. Tahlequah, OK

    see The Telephone. Tahlequah, OK

213 The Cherokee Times. 1955-?//. Weekly. ISSN 0045-6551. OCLC
47357533. RLIN OHCP4737533-S. Last issue 8 pages, height 28 cm.
Commercial advertising. Available in microform: WHi (1965). Cherokee,
NC. Editor: Sarah Beck. Community newsletter. Subject focus:
Cherokee people, legends, fiction.

    WHi   v.10, n.13;
               Jan 9, 1965   Microforms

    WEU   v.15, n.8;
               Mar 14, 1970   Journalism
                                           Lab

    NjP   v.13, n.3;
               Nov 11, 1967   Periodicals

    OkU   v.13, n.3;
               Nov, 11, 1967   WHC

    UPB   [v.5, n.16-v.16, n.2]
               [1096-1972]   970.45605/C424

Other holding institutions: CLU (CLU), CU-UC (UCU), OrU-Special
Collections.

214 The Cherokee Voice. 1981. Quarterly. Stan Bienick, editor, P.O. Box
507, Cherokee, NC 28719. (704) 497-9101. Last issue 2 pages, height
36 cm. Photographs. Published by Cherokee Children's Home. Subject
focus: Cherokee children, organization news, family services.

    WHi   v.1, n.1-
               Dec, 1981-   Circulation

215 Cherokee Voices. 1976-1981//. Monthly. Height 38 cm. Line drawings,
photographs. Published by Communications Center of the Cherokee Nation
of Oklahoma, Tahlequah, OK. Editor: Wes Studie. Newspaper. Subject
focus: Cherokee people.

    OkTahN   v.1, n.1-v.6;
               1976-Mar, 1981   Periodicals

216 Cheyenne & Arapaho Bulletin. 1971-1980//. Monthly. Last issue 16
    pages. Line drawings, photographs. Available in microform: WHi
    (1978-1980). Published by Cheyenne-Arapaho Tribal Office, Concho, OK.
    Frequency varies: irregular, Jan/Feb-Aug/Sept, 1978. Agency
    newsletter. Subject focus: Cheyenne people, Arapaho people.

    WHi   v.8, n.7-10, 16, v.10, n.1/2, 12-   Microforms
                  v.11, n.1, (n.s)v.1, n.1;
                  Feb, Apr-May/June, 1977, Jan/Feb,
                  Aug/Sept, 1978, Aug, 1979-Jan/Feb,
                  July, 1980

    WMUW   v.8, n.7, 9-10;   (SPL)
                  Feb, Apr-May/June, 1977   E/75/C527x

    AzNCC   v.6-v.8, n.1;   Indian File
                  1973-Jan, 1975

    NjP   [v.2, n.3-v.8, n.1]   Periodicals
                  [Jan, 1968-Jan, 1975]

    OkU   [v.2, n.3-v.8, n.1]   WHC
                  [Jan, 1968-Jan, 1975]

217 Cheyenne Transporter. 1879-1886?//. Semi-monthly. Last issue 8
    pages. Line drawings, commercial advertising. Published by Cheyenne
    and Arapaho Agency, Darlington, OK. Available in microform: OkHi
    (1880-1886). Editors: W. A. Eaton, Aug 25, 1880-Apr 25, 1882; George
    W. Maffet and Lafe Merritt, May 10, 1882-Aug 12, 1886. Newspaper.
    Subject focus: Cheyenne people, Arapaho people. Also described in:
    Foreman, Carolyn Thomas. Oklahoma Imprints, 1835-1907. Norman:
    University of Oklahoma Press, 1936.

    WHi   v.2, n.1-v.7, n.21;   Microforms
                  Aug 25, 1880-Aug 12, 1886

    OkHi   v.2, n.1-v.7, n.21;   Microforms
                  Aug 25, 1880-Aug 12, 1886

218 Chicago Warrior. 1972-?//. Irregular. Last issue 14 pages. Line
    drawings. Published by American Indian Center, Chicago, IL. Subject
    focus: urban community, center news and activities. Supercedes The
    Warrior.

    WMUW   v.5, n.4-v.7, n.1;   (SPL)
                  Oct/Nov/Dec, 1976-Jan/Feb/Mar, 1978   E/75/C53x

    The Chickasaw Newsletter. Ada, OK

       see The Chickasaw Times. Ada, OK

219 The Chickasaw Times. 1972. Bi-monthly. Pat Woods, editor, The
   Chickasaw Times, Box 1548, Ada, OK 74820. (405) 436-2603. OCLC
   6188883. Last issue 12 pages, last volume 168 pages, height 36 cm.
   Photographs, commercial advertising. Published by Chickasaw Nation.
   Title varies: Chickasaw Tribal Newsletter, Jan, 1972; The Chickasaw
   Newsletter, Apr/May/June, 1972-Jan/Feb/Mar, 1974; The Newsletter of the
   Chickasaws, Apr/May/June, 1974-Oct/Nov/Dec, 1975. Frequency varies:
   irregular, Jan, 1972-Jan/Feb/ Mar, 1974; quarterly, Apr/May/June, 1974-
   Oct/Nov/Dec, 1979. Previous editors: Micah P. Smith, Jan/Feb/Mar,
   1976-July/Aug/Sept, 1979; J. Y. Tomlinson, Jr., May/June, 1980-Mar/Apr,
   1981. Newspaper. Subject forcus: Chickasaw people.

   WHi   v.1, n.1-
                Jan, 1972-   Circulation

   OkU   v.1, n.1-
                Jan, 1972-   WHC

   Other holding institutions: [Pioneer Multi-County Public Library,
   Norman, OK] (OKM).

   Chickasaw Tribal Newsletter. Ada, OK

      see The Chickasaw Times. Ada, OK

220 Chief Circle. 1979. Irregular. Chief Circle, P.O. Box 2600, Orange,
   CA 92669. (714) 997-3920. Last issue 6 pages, height 28 cm. Line
   drawings, photographs. Published by Christian Hope Indian Eskimo
   Fellowship (CHIEF). Subject focus: Christian religion, missions.

   WHi   v.3, n.1-
                Mar, 1981-   Circulation

221 Chief Seattle Club. 1972-?//. Unknown. Last issue 1 page, height 28
   cm. Seattle, WA. Editor: Rev. Raymond L. Talbott. Organization
   newsletter.

   WMM   Jan 10, Nov 1, 1972
                                                     Special
                                                     Collections

222 The Chieftain. 1957-?//. Unknown. Last issue 8 pages, height 28 cm.
   Line drawings. Published by St. Mary's High School, Omak, WA. School
   newsletter. Subject focus: Catholic Church.

   WMM   v.1, n.1, 3-5;
                Nov, 1957, Feb-May 22, 1958   Special
                                                     Collections

223 <u>Children of the Prairie</u>. 1935?-1964?//. Quarterly. Last issue 4
pages, height 25 cm. Line drawings, photographs. Published by St.
Joseph's Indian School, Chamberlain, SD. Editor: Father George.
Subject focus: missions, Catholic Church.

    WMM   v.27, n.6-v.31, n.6], (n.s.)v.1, n.1-4;   Special
                 [July/Aug, 1959-July/Aug, 1963],   Collections
                 Jan/Feb/Mar-Oct/Nov/Dec, 1964

    NjP   v.4, n.1;   Periodicals
                 Sept, 1938

224 <u>Children of the Raven Gallery, Newsletter</u>. 1981?//? Unknown. Last
issue 4 pages, height 28 cm. Photographs. Vancouver, British
Columbia, Canada. Gallery newsletter. Subject focus: arts and crafts.

    CaACG   Mar, Nov, 1981   Periodicals

<u>Chilocco Farmer and Stock Grower</u>. Chilocco, OK

    see <u>Indian School Journal</u>. Chilocco, OK

225 <u>Chin Lee Informant</u>. 1936-?//. Irregular. Last issue 28 pages, height
28 cm. Line drawings. Published by Chin-Lee Boarding School, Chinle,
AZ. School newsletter.

    CLSM   v.1, n.3-v.3, n.3;   Periodicals
                May, 1936-May, 1937

226 <u>Chippewa Flowage Bulletin</u>. 1971//. Unknown. Last issue 4 pages,
height 58 cm. Line drawings, photographs. Published by Save the
Chippewa Flowage Alliance, Hayward, WI. Personal names indexed in:
Index to Wisconsin Native American Periodicals (1971). Subject focus:
environment, ecology, land claims.

    WHi   ?, 1971   Pam 81-870

    WEU   ?, 1971   Journalism
                                              Lab

227 <u>Choctaw Community News</u>. 1970. Monthly. Edward John, editor, Choctaw
Community News, Route 7, Box 21, Philadelphia, MS 39350. (601)
656-5251. OCLC 3974836. RLIN OHCP3974836-S. Last issue 16 pages,
height 28 cm. Photographs. Available in microform: McA (1969-).
Published by Mississippi Band of Choctaw Indians. Previous editors:
Robert Benn, Dec 5, 1969-Jan 26, 1973; Connie J. Adams, Feb 23-Aug,

1973; Sara Rand, Sept 14, 1973-Oct 31, 1974; Ben Harrison, Feb-Dec 20, 1974; Julie Smith, Mar 15-Aug 24, 1979. Community newsletter. Subject focus: Choctaw people.

WHi	v.1, n.1- Dec 5, 1969-	Microforms
WEU	v.2, n.3-4; Feb 12-Mar 12, 1971	Journalism Lab
WMUW	v.6, n.6; Apr, 14, 1975	(SPL) E/75/C54x
WUSP	Current year only	Periodicals
AzNCC	v.5- Jan, 1974-	Indian File
CU-A	v.4, n.9- Sept 14, 1973-	E/77/A1/C5
ICN	Current issues	CHAI
KU	v.1, n.1- Dec 5, 1969-	Kansas Collection
NjP	[v.1, n.1-v.10, n.6] [Dec 5, 1969-June 18, 1979]	Periodicals
NcP	[v.8-v.9] [1977-1978]	Periodicals
OkU	v.1, n.1- Dec 5, 1969-	WHC
CaOPeT	v.1, n.1- Dec 5, 1969-	Microfilm

Other holding institutions: CU-UC (UCU), COU-DA (COA), DSI (SMI), IC (CGP), [University of Minnesota Union List, Minneapolis, MN] (MUL), [Western Nevada Community College, Carson City, NV], NmU (IZU), [Bacone College, Muskogee, OK], [WGrU-Native American Studies Dept.].

228 <u>Choctaw Intelligencer</u>. 1850-1852//. Weekly. Last issue 4 pages. Commercial advertising. Doaksville, OK. Available in microform: OkHi (1851). Editors: L. D. Alsobrook and Rev. J. E. Dwight. Newspaper. Subject focus: Choctaw people. In Choctaw, 50%. Also described in: Foreman, Carolyn Thomas, <u>Oklahoma Imprints, 1835-1907</u>, Norman: University of Oklahoma Press, 1936.

WHi	v.2, n.15; Oct 15, 1851	Microforms

OkHi   v.2, n.15;   Microforms
            Oct 15, 1851

OkTahN   v.2, n.15;   Microforms
            Oct 15, 1851

229 Choctaw News. 1878?-?//. Daily. Last issue 2 pages, height 24 cm.
    Chata-Tamaha, OK. Community newsletter. Subject focus: Choctaw people.

    OkTG   [v.1, n.3-28]   Periodicals
                [Oct 10-Nov 8, 1878]

    The Choctaw Times. Nashville, TN

        see Chahta Anumpa/The Choctaw Times. Nashville, TN

230 Choggiung Limited [Newsletter]. 1975?//. Irregular. Last issue 2
    pages. Available in microform: AkUF (1975). Dillingham, AK.
    Corporation newsletter. Subject focus: stockholders, land claims,
    Alaska Native Claims Settlement Act.

    WHi   v.1, n.1-3;   Microforms
                Sept-Dec, 1975

    AkUF   v.1, n.1-3;   Microfiche
                Sept-Dec, 1975

231 The Christian Indian. 1968?-1979//. Bi-monthly. OCLC 6039265. Last
    issue 16 pages, height 28 cm. Line drawings, photographs, commercial
    advertising. Available in microform: WHi (1978-1979). Published by
    Alliance Indian Publications, Wheaton, IL. Editor: George McPeek.
    Subject focus: Christian religion, Church news.

    WHi   Jan, 1978-Oct, 1979;   Microforms

    WMUW   Sept/Oct, 1976-Sept/Oct, 1979   (SPL)
                                                    E/75/I45x

    AkBC   July/Aug, 1978-Sept/Oct, 1979   Periodicals

    NmG   Feb, 1968-Sept/Oct, 1979   Periodicals

232 Chronicles of the North American Savages. 1835//. Monthly. OCLC
    1554538, 4354248. RLIN MIUG82-S5334, NYPG774318298-S, CSUP01257705-S,
    OHCP4354248-S, OHCP1554538-S. Last issue 25 pages, last volume 79
    pages, height 28 cm. Published by T. H. Shreve, Cincinnati, OH.

Editor: Isaac Galland. Subject focus: ethnology, Chippewa language, Chippewa, Sauk, Fox and Musquakie peoples.

ICN	v.1, n.1; May, 1835	Graff 1487
IaHi	v.1, n.1-5; May-Sept, 1835	Periodicals
N	v.1, n.1-5; May-Sept, 1835	MA/FM
OrU	v.1, n.1-5; May-Sept, 1835	Periodicals

Other holding institutions: [Ambassador College, Pasadena, CA] (ACL), MiEM (EEM), MiDW (EYW), [University of Minnesota Union List, Minneapolis, MN] (MUL), MoU (MUU), McWsW (EWF), [New York State Union List, Albany, NY] (NYS), [Central New York Library Resources Council, Syracuse, NY] (SRR), [Ogdensburg Public Library, Ogdensburg, NY] (VNE), NOneoU (ZBM), OKentU (KSU), OkU (OKU), TxDN (INT), TxArU (IUA), [AMIGOS Union List of Serials, Dallas, TX] (IUC).

233 Chugach Natives Newsletter. 1973. Quarterly. Lois Sandborn, Editor, Chugach Native Newsletter, 903 W. Northern Lights Blvd., Anchorage, AK 99503. (907) 276-1080. Last issue 12 pages, height 28 cm. Line drawings. Available in microform: AkUF (1973-1975). Subject focus: land claims, community development, natural resources, environment.

WHi	[v.1, n.10-v.3, n.5] [June, 1973-Nov, 1975]	Microforms
WHi	v.9, n.2- June, 1982-	Circulation
AkUF	[v.1, n.10-v.3, n.5] [June, 1973-Nov, 1975]	Microforms

234 The Circle. 1976. Irregular. $3. for individuals and institutions. The Circle, 105 Huntington Ave., Jamaica Plain, MA 02130. (617) 232-0343. OCLC 6189111. Last issue 12 pages, height 34 cm. Line drawings, photographs, commercial advertising. Published by Boston Indian Council. Previous editors: Louise Erdich, Sept-Oct/Nov, 1979; Louise Erdich and Suzanne Govan, Winter, 1979-Summer, 1980. Jackie Dean and Suzannne Govan, Fall, 1980. Subject focus: Council news, urban community, health, poetry.

| WHi | v.1, n.3-
June, 1976- | Circulation |
| AzNCC | v.2-
July, 1977- | Indian File |

WMUW   v.2, n.2-3;   (SPL)
            May-Aug, 1977   E/75/C55x

MtBBCC   v.3;   Periodicals
            June/Aug, 1980

Other holding institutions: MChB (BXM).

235 The Circle. 1979. Monthly. Antony Stately, editor, The Circle, 1530
    E. Franklin Ave., Minneapolis, MN 55404. (612) 874-0713. OCLC
    3175584. RLIN OHCP3175584-S. Last issue 16 pages, last volume 172
    pages, height 41 cm. Line drawings, photographs, commercial
    advertising. Published by Minneapolis American Indian Center.
    Previous editors: Marcia McEachron, Sept-Dec, 1979; Jim Lenfestey, Feb,
    1980 Lori Mollenhoff, Mar, 1980-Mar, 1981; Antony Stately, Apr, 1981;
    Sandra King, May-Dec, 1981. Newspaper. Subject focus: urban
    community, poetry, fiction, graphics.

WHi   [no nos.]; v.1, n.1-   Circulation
            [Aug, 1979-Feb, 1980]; Mar, 1980-

WM   [no nos.]; v.1, n.1-   Forest Home
            [Aug, 1979-Feb, 1980]; Mar, 1980-   Branch

ICN   Current issues   CHAI

Other holding institutions: [Hennepin County Library, Edina, MN],
[University of Minnesota Union List, Minneapolis, MN] (MUL) [University
of Wisconsin-Stevens Point-Native American Center, Stevens Point, WI],
[Wisconsin Indian Resource Council, Stevens Point, WI].

236 City Smoke Signals. 1968?. Irregular. $4. for individuals and
    institutions. City Smoke Signals, 304 Pearl St., Sioux City, IA 51101.
    (712) 258-6439. Last issue 26 pages, height 28 cm. Line drawings,
    photographs. Available in microform: CPC (1968-1969). Published by
    Sioux City American Indian Center. Frequency varies: monthly, Aug,
    1970-Feb, 1974. Previous editors: Claire Brown, Feb-July, 1968; Linda
    St. Cyr, Sept-Oct, 1968; Ernest Ricehill and Fay Whitebeaver, Dec,
    1968; John Buehlmann, Mar-Sept, 1970; Fay Whitebeaver, Oct, 1970; Reva
    Barta, Nov, 1970-June, 1972; Joyce Miera and Richard Two Elk, Oct-Nov,
    1972; Joyce Miera and Elaine Harlan, Jan, 1973; Susan Barta, June-Nov,
    1973. Subject focus: Center programs and services.

WHi   [Feb, 1968-June, 1969]   Microforms

WHi   Aug, 1970-   Circulation

WEU   July? 1969, Dec, 1970-Jan, 1971   Journalism
                                                    Lab

AzNCC   Feb, 1969-   Indian File

NjP   [Feb, 1968-May, 1979]   Periodicals

SdU   Feb, 1968-Feb, 1979   Microfilm

237 The Clary Institute. 1980-1981//. Semi-monthly. ISSN 0197-9396. LC
    sn80-11886. OCLC 6163528. Last issue 24 pages, height 28 cm.
    Available in microform: WHi (1979-1981). Washington, DC. Subject
    focus: local and national news, economic development, education,
    employment, social services, housing.

    WHi   [v.1, n.1]-v.3, n.8;   Microforms
               July 9, 1979-Apr 30, 1981

    WUSP   [v.2, n.1-v.3, n.9]   Native American
               [July, 1980-May, 1981]   Center

    Other holding institutions: [Congressional Research Service,
    Washington, DC] (CRS).

238 Cleveland American Indian Center Newsletter. 1982//? Monthly. Last
    issue 8 pages, height 28 cm. Line drawings. Cleveland, OH. Center
    newsletter. Subject focus: urban community.

    WHi   Aug, 1982   Pam-Cataloging

239 Clinicians Letter. 1981? Unknown. $10. for individuals and
    institutions. Clinicians Letter, 1615 Broadway, Oakland, CA 94612.
    Last issue 6 pages, height 28 cm. Published by California Urban Indian
    Health Council, Inc. Subject focus: health care, community health
    resources.

    WHi   Feb, 1982-   Circulation

240 Cochiti Lake Sun. 1968-1981//. Irregular. Last issue 8 pages, height
    41 cm. Photographs. Cochiti Lake, NM. Editor: Bill Penn. Community
    newsletter.

    WHi   v.14, n.1-2;   Pam
               Mar-Oct, 1981-   Cataloging

    NjP   Spec. Ed., v.1, n.1;   Periodcials
               Jan, Fall, 1970

241 The Coeur d'Alene Teepee. 1937-1940?//. Irregular. Last issue 12
    pages, last volume 96 pages, height 28 cm. Line drawings. Published

by Sacred Heart Mission, Coeur d'Alene Indian Reservation, De Smet, ID.
Subject focus: missions, Christian religion, fiction, poetry. Reprint
of originals--Su Harms, editor, Serento Press, Plummer ID, 1980.

WHi   v.1, n.1-v.3, n.21;   Circulation
               Nov, 1937-Nov, 1940

IdHi   v.1, n.1-v.3, n.21;   Periodicals
               Nov, 1937-Nov, 1940

242 Co-Ever News. 1967?//. Unknown. Last issue 4 pages, height 28 cm.
    Photographs. Published by Cooperatives Everywhere, Ottawa, Ontario,
    Canada. Editor: P.A. Moran. Subject focus: cooperatives.

    CaACG   n.5;   Periodicals
               Autumn, 1967

    Columbia River Inter-Tribal Fish Commission Monthly News. Portland, OR

        see CRITFC News. Portland, OR

243 Committee on Native American Struggles. 1977. Quarterly. $5. for
    individuals and institutions. Committee on Native American Struggles,
    P. O. Box 6401, Albuquerque, NM 87197. (505) 988-3021. Last issue 24
    pages, height 28 cm. Line drawings. Published by National Lawyers
    Guild. Subject focus: legislation, energy resources, rights,
    sovereignty.

    WHi   v.5, n.1-   Circulation
               Winter, 1981-

244 Communique. 1980. Irregular. Communique, 1760 Regent St., Sudbury,
    Ontario, Canada P3C 3Z8. Last issue 2 pages, height 28 cm. Line
    drawings. Published by the Department of Indian Affairs and Northern
    Development. Subject focus: rights, housing, social services,
    governmental programs.

    CaOSuU   n.1-   Periodicals
               1980-

245 Community School News. 1975//. Unknown. Last issue 10 pages, height
    28 cm. Line drawings, photographs. Keshena?, WI. Personal names
    indexed in: Index to Wisconsin Native American Periodicals (1975).
    School newsletter.

    WHi   Jan?, Mar?, 1975   Pam 75-2702

246 <u>Common Sense</u>. 1978. Bi-weekly. $7. for individuals and institutions.
Andrea Kelsey, editor, Common Sense, P.O. Box 218, Hoopa, CA 95546.
Last issue 12 pages, height 39 cm. Line drawings, photographs,
commercial advertising. Published by Hoopa Valley Indian Reservation.
Community newsletter. Subject focus: local and national news.

WHi	v.3, n.24, v.4, n.21; Dec 22, 1980, Dec 28, 1981	Microforms
MtBBCC	v.3-v.4; Aug, 1980-Mar, 1981	Periodicals

247 <u>The Concerned Indian</u>. 1970-?//. Monthly? Last issue 8 pages, height
43 cm. Line drawings, photographs. Phoenix, AZ. Subject focus: urban
community.

WUSP	Sept, 1974	Native American Center

248 <u>Confederated Umatilla Journal</u>. 1975-1982//. Monthly. OCLC 6168895.
Last issue 12 pages, height 42 cm. Line drawings, photographs,
commercial advertising. Availble in microform: WHi (1976-1979).
Pendleton, OR. Editors: Richard La Course, July, 1976; Deanna Hansell,
Jan/Feb, 1977-Apr, 1978; John Barkley, May, 1978-July, 1979.
Newspaper. Subject focus: Cayuse, Umatilla and Walla Walla peoples.

WHi	[v.1, n.7-v.4, n.6] [July, 1976-July, 1979]	Microforms
WMUW	[v.1, n.7-v.4, n.6] [July, 1976-July, 1979]	(SPL) E/75/C66x
AzNCC	v.1-v.6; Dec, 1975-July, 1981	Indian File
ICN	Current issues	CHAI
MnBemT	[v.1-v.2], v.3- [1975-1977], 1978-	Periodicals
NjP	[v.2, n.7-v.4,n.4] [July, 1977-May, 1979]	Periodicals
Or	v.1-v.7; Dec, 1975-June, 1982	Periodicals
OrHi	v.1-v.3, n.2; 1975-Feb, 1978	Periodicals

Other holding institutions: [University of Minnesota Union List,

Minneapolis, MN] (MUL), [Standing Rock Community College Library, Fort
Yates, ND].

249 Conveyance News. 1978. Irregular. Free to individuals and
institutions. Marnie Isaacs, editor, Conveyance News, 701 C St., Box
13, Anchorage, AK 99513. (907) 271-5060. OCLC 7995906. Last issue 4
pages, height 28 cm. Line drawings, photographs. Published by Bureau
of Land Management. Title varies: ANCSA: Alaska Native Claims
Settlement Act, Nov, 1978-Jan, 1979; ANCSA News, Feb-June, 1982.
Frequency varies: monthly, Nov, 1978-May, 1979. Subject focus: Alaska
Native Claims Settlement Act.

WHi   [v.1, n.10-v.4, n.8], v.5, n.1-   Circulation
           [Nov, 1978-Nov/Dec, 1981], Feb, 1982-

CaAEU   v.1, n.1-v.4, n.4;   Boreal
           Nov, 1978-May, 1981   Institute

Other holding institutions: CrivLM (UEC), DI (UDI).

250 Cook Inlet Region, Inc. [Newsletter]. 1972.// Irregular. Last issue
5 pages. Anchorage? AK. Available in microform: AkUF (1972).
Corporation newsletter. Superceded by CIRA Newsletter.

WHi   Feb?-June 30, 1972   Microforms

AkUF   [Feb?-June, 1972   Microfiche

251 Co-op North. 1979. Irregular. Co-op North, Box 2039, Yellowknife,
Northwest Territories. Editorial address: P.O. Box 250, Ashton,
Ontario, Canada K0A 1B0. (613) 233-6252. Line drawings, photographs.
Published by Arctic Co-operatives, Ltd. Subject focus: cooperatives,
Inuit people. Some articles in Inuit.

CaAEU   v.1, n.4-   Boreal
           Mar, 1980-   Institute

252 The Council. 1976. Monthly. Judy Reynolds, editor, The Council,
Doyon Building, 201 First Ave., Fairbanks, AK 99701. Last issue 12
pages, height 44 cm. Line drawings, photographs. Published by Tanana
Chiefs Conference, Inc. Previous editor: Yvonne Mozee, Oct/Nov,
1980-Sept, 1981; Ray Kent, Oct, 1981. Subject focus: corporate news.

WHi   v.1, n.1-   Circulation
          Mar, 1976-

AkUF   v.1, n.1-   E/99/A86/T37
          Mar, 1976-

Council Fire. Washington, DC

   see The Council Fire and Arbitrator. Washington, DC

253 Council Fire. 1977-1980//. Irregular. Last issue 12 pages, height 40
    cm. RLIN OHCP2442972-S. Line drawings, photographs, commercial
    advertising. Available in microform: WHi (1977-1980). Published by
    Grand Council Treaty N. 3, Kenora, Ontario, Canada. Community
    newsletter.

    WHi   [v.1, n.2-v.3, n.4]   Microforms
               [July 29, 1977-Apr, 1980]

254 The Council Fire and Arbitrator. 1878-1889?//. Monthly. LC ca07-656.
    OCLC 3147938. Last issue 16 pages, Last volume 120 pages. Commercial
    advertising. Available in microform: BHP (1878-1885). Washington, DC.
    Title varies: Council Fire, Jan, 1878-Dec, 1881. Place of publication
    varies: Philadelphia, PA, Jan-Mar, 1878. Editors: A. B. Meacham, Jan,
    1878-Dec, 1881; T. A. Bland and M. C. Bland, Mar, 1882-July, 1885.
    Subject focus: rights, law.

    WHi   v.1, n.1-v.8, n.7;   Microforms
               Jan, 1878-July, 1885

    WMM   v.1, n.1-v.8, n.7;   MFL P-268
               Jan, 1878-July, 1885

    CLSM   v.4-v.8;   Periodicals
               1881-1885

    NN   v.1-v.12;   ZAN-H254
               1878-1889

    OC1WHi   v.1-v.4;   Peridicals
               1878-1881

    OkTU   v.1-v.7;   Rare Book
               1878-1884   Room

    OrU   v.1-v.12;   Periodicals
               1878-1889

    UPB   v.1-v.12;   970.105/C832
               1878-1889

    Other holding institutions: [University of Minnesota Union List,
    Minneapolis, MN] (MUL), PHC (HVC).

255 Council Fires. 1977-1981//. Monthly. Last issue 4 pages, height 41
    cm. Line drawings, photographs, commercial advertising. Available in

microform: WHi (1980-1981). Published by CDA Tribal Council, Plummer
ID. Editor: Su Harms, July, 1980-Apr, 1981. Community newsletter.
Subject focus: Coeur d'Alene people.

WHi	v.4, n.9-v.5, n.2; July, 1980-Apr, 1981	Microforms
WM	Current issues	Forest Home Branch
OkTU	v.3, n.3-v.5, n.3; Jan, 1979-Sept, 1981	970.305 S628C
IdHi	v.4, n.1-v.5, n.3; Nov, 1979-Sept, 1981	Periodicals

256 Coyote. 1970-?//?. Irregular. OCLC 4020436. RLIN OHCP4020436-S.
Last issue 12 pages, height 38 cm. Line drawings, photographs.
Available in microform: WHi (1970-1971). Published by Powhatan Press,
Davis, CA. School newsletter. Subject focus: student news, politics,
rights, governmental relations, education, poetry.

WHi	v.1, n.1-v.2, n.2; Spring, 1970-May? 1971	Microforms
WEU	v.1, n.1-v.2, [n.4]; Spring, 1970-Dec, 1971	Journalism Lab
AzNCC	v.2; Spring-Fall, 1971	Indian File
AzU	v.1, n.1, v.2, n.1; Spring, 1970-1971	I9791/C881
CU-A	v.1, n.1-v.2? Spring, 1970-1971?	E/77/A1/C6
NjP	v.1, n.1-v.2, n.2; Spring, 1970-May? 1971	Periodicals
WaU	v.2, n.1; 1971	Periodicals
PPT	v.1, n.1-v.2, n.2; Spring, 1970-May? 1971	Contemporary Culture

Other holding institutions: CU-UC (UCU), OKTU (OKT).

Coyote News. Warm Springs, OR

   see Spilyay Tymoo: Coyote News. Warm Springs, OR

257 <u>Coyoti Prints</u>. 1975. Irregular. $5. for individuals and
institutions. Agness Jack, editor, Coyoti Prints, Box 257, 150 Mile
House, British Columbia, Canada VOK 2G0. (604) 296-3344. ISSN
0700-902x. LC cn77-31326. OCLC 3304233. RLIN DCLCCN7731326-S,
OHCP3304233-S. Published by Caribou Indian Education Training Centre.
Community newsletter.

WHi	v.9– July, 1982–	Circulation
CaAEU	v.3, n.? 9, v.4, n.1– Spec. Ed., Sept, 1976, Jan, 1977–	Boreal Institute
CaOAFN	v.8– June, 1981–	Periodicals
CaOONL	v.1– 1975–	Periodicals
CaOPeT	[v.3–v.6], v.7– [1976-1979], 1980–	E78/B9C6

258 <u>Crazy Horse News</u>. 1974-1981//. Irregular. OCLC 4346564. Last issue
8 pages, height 44 cm. Line drawings, photographs, commercial
advertising. Available in microform: WHi (1974-1976, 1980-1981).
Manderson, SD. Place of publication varies: Rapid City, SD, Mar 22-May
10, 1974. Editor: Aaron G. DeSersa, Sr., Mar 22, 1974-Sept 10, 1976.
Subject focus: Oglala Sioux people, rights, legislation, land claims.

WHi	v.1, n.28–v.3, n.4, [no nos.] Mar 22, 1974-Sept 10, 1976, Dec, 1980-July, 1981	Microforms
WEU	v.2, n.4; Aug 16, 1974	Journalism Lab
WMM	v.2, n.7; Mar, 1975	Special Collections
AzNCC	v.1– Apr, 1973–	Indian File
KU	v.1– Mar, 1973?–	Kansas Collection
SdU	v.1–v.6, n.1; 1973-Jan, 1978	South Dakota Room

Other holding institutions: [Standing Rock Community College Library,
Fort Yates, ND].

259 <u>Cree Ajemoon</u>. 1982. 8 times a year. $12. for individuals and
institutions. Cree Ajemoon, Rupert House, James Bay, Quebec, Canada
JOM 1RO. Last issue 32 pages, height 28 cm. Line drawings,
photographs. Published by Cree Way Centre. Subject focus: Cree people
and language. In Cree, 50%.

CaOAFN   v.1, n.1-   Periodicals
           1982-

260 <u>Cree Review</u>. 1939?-1979//. Bimonthly. Last issue 16 pages, height 26
cm. Line drawings, photographs. Published by Oblate Fathers, Lac La
Biche, Alberta, Canada. Place of publication varies: Hobbema; Saddle
Lake; Edmonton; Le Goff. Frequency varies: monthly, Oct, 1939-Jan,
1963; 9 times a year, Sept, 1963-?, 1978. Editors: Rev. P. Calais; Fr.
Romeo Levert; Marcell Landry; Rev. V. LeCalvez. Subject focus:
missions, Catholic Church. In Cree, 100%.

CaACG   [Oct, 1939-Sept/Oct, 1979]   Periodicals

261 <u>Cree Way News</u>. 1981?//. Irregular. Last issue 16 pages, height 36
cm. Line drawings, photographs. Published by Cree Way Centre, James
Bay. Quebec, Canada. Organization newsletter. Subject focus: Cree
people, Cree language. In Cree, 30-50%. Superceded by Cree Ajemoon?

CaOAFN   Fall?, 1981   Periodicals

262 <u>Cree Witness</u>. 1959?-1978?//. 6 times a year. Last issue 15 pages,
height 23 cm. Line drawings, photographs. Published by Northern
Canada Evangelical Mission, Prince Albert, Saskatchewan, Canada.
Frequency varies: monthly; 9 times a year. Editors: Lorena Goossen;
Billy Jackson and John Unger; Judy Matteson. Subject focus: missions,
Christian religion, Cree people. Some articles in Cree.

CaACG   [Feb, 1961-Jan/Feb, 1978]   Periodicals

263 <u>Creek Nation Advocate</u>. 1980//. Unknown. Last issue 8 pages, height
38 cm. Line drawings, photographs. Tulsa, OK. Subject focus: Creek
people, monitoring tribal government.

WHi   v.1, n.1;   Tem Pam 39
          July 16, 1980

264 <u>The Cross and the Calumet</u>. 1962-1970?//. Irregular. Last issue 4
pages. Photographs. Available in microform: CPC (1962-1970).
Published by Committee on American Indian Work, Episcopal Diocese of

Chicago, Chicago, IL. Editor: Rev. Father Peter J. Powell. Subject
focus: Episcopal Church.

WHi	[Dec, 1962-Winter, 1970]	Microforms
WEU ARC	1965-Winter, 1970	Micro 11
AzNCC	Spring, 1970	Indian File
NjP	[Dec, 1962-Spring, 1970]	Periodicals
NN	[Dec, 1962-Winter, 1970]	Microforms
OkU	[Dec, 1962-Winter, 1967]	WHC
CaOPeT	[Dec, 1962-Winter, 1970]	Microfilm

Other holding institutions: OrU-Special Collections.

265 <u>Crown Dancer</u>. 1976-1980//. Bi-monthly. Last issue 8 pages, last
volume 160 pages, height 38. Photographs, commercial advertising.
Published by San Carlos Apache Tribe, San Carlos, AZ. Editors: Anna
Cadue, May 6-Nov 11, 1977; Kathryn Astor, Jan 6-Mar 3, 1978; Velma
Swift, Mar 17, 1978-May 11, 1979; Velma Cassa, May 25-Aug 10, 1979;
Austin Titla, Aug 24, 1979-Oct 24, 1980. Community newsletter.
Subject focus: Apache people.

Az	[v.1, n.27-v.2, n.20] [May 6, 1977-Oct 24, 1980]	Periodicals
AzHC	[v.1-v.2] [1976-1980]	Periodicals

Other holding institutions: AzTeS.

266 <u>The Crusader</u>. 1979-?//. Monthly. Last issue 4 pages, height 28 cm.
Line drawings. Published by Red Cloud Indian School, Pine Ridge, SD.
School newsletter. Supercedes Red Cloud News.

WMM	v.1, n.2-3; Apr 26-May 21, 1979	Special Collections

267 <u>Cultural Education Centre News</u>. 1982? Unknown. Mike Michell, editor,
Cultural Education Centre News, R.R. no. 3, Cornwall Island, Ontario,
Canada K6H 5R7. Last issue 32 pages, height 44 cm. Line drawings,
photographs. Published by North American Indian Travelling College for
the National Committee. Subject focus: education, culture.

CaOAFN	June, 1982-	Periodicals

DNA in Action. Window Rock, AZ

   see DNA Newsletter. Window Rock, AZ

268 DNA Newsletter. 1968. Monthly. DNA Newsletter, Window Rock, AZ
86515. (602) 871-4151. OCLC 7209895. Last issue 10 pages. Line
drawings, photographs. Available in microform: McA (1968-); CPC
(1968-1975). Published by DNA, Inc. (Dinebeiina Nahiilna Be Agaditahe,
Inc.) Title varies: Law in Action, Aug 27, 1968-Sept 30, 1969; DNA in
Action, Oct 31, 1969-Mar, 1973. Subject focus: Navajo people, law, DNA
activities.

WHi	v.1, n.1- Aug 27, 1968-	Microforms
AzNCC	v.5- Oct, 1973-	Indian File
CLSM	v.1, n.1-v.3, n.8; Aug 27, 1968-July 2, 1971	Periodicals
ICN	Current issues	CHAI
NjP	[v.1, n.1-v.8, n.1] [Aug 27, 1968-Mar, 1975]	Periodicals
OkTU	v.9, n.4- Aug?, 1976-	Rare Book Room
OkU	v.1, n.1-v.5; Aug 27, 1968-Dec, 1972	WHC
CaOPeT	v.1, n.1-v.2, n.2; Aug 27, 1968-Sept, 1969	Microfilm

Other holding institutions: AzFU (AZN), [Western Nevada Community
College, Carson City, NV].

269 DNAU Newsletter. 1978-1981//. Monthly. Last issue 20 pages, last
volume 248 pages, height 22 cm. Line drawings, commercial advertising.
Available in microform: WHi (1979-1981). Published by Denver Native
Americans United, Inc., Denver, CO. Title varies: Denver Native
Americans United, Jan, Apr-May, Oct-Nov, 1979. Editors: Renae Bogh,
Jan, 1979; Donald M. Hickman, Feb, 1979; Tom Teegarden, Mar-Aug, 1979;
Sam Gardipe, Sept-Aug, 1980; Milton Nelson, Sept, 1980-Jan, 1981.
Community newsletter. Subject focus: social services, education.

WHi	v.2, n.1-v.4, n.1; Jan, 1979-Jan, 1981	Microforms
MtBBCC	v.3-v.4, n.1; Sept, 1980-Jan, 1981	Periodicals

Other holding institutions: IC (CGP).

270 Da' Anii/The Truth: Voice of the San Carlos Apache Tribe. 1975-?//.
Irregular. Last issue 4 pages, last volume 12 pages, height 42 cm.
Photographs, commercial advertising. Published by Native American
Program, San Carlos, AZ. Editor: Fernando Machukay. Community
newsletter. Subject focus: Apache people. Supercedes Apache Sunrise.

    AzHC   v.1, n.2-7;   Periodicals
                July 17, 1975-Apr, 1976

271 The Daily Bulletin. 1980//. Daily. Published by The Annual
Convention of the National Congress of American Indians, Spokane, WA.
Editor: Mark Trahant. Convention report.

    WHi   n.1-4;   Pam
                Oct 27-29, 1980   Cataloging

272 Daily Indian Chieftain. 1891-?//. Daily. Last issue 4 pages. Line
drawings, photographs, commercial advertising. Vinita, OK. Available
in microform: OkHi (1912-1913). Editor: D. M. Marrs. Newspaper. Also
described in: Foreman, Carolyn Thomas, Oklahoma Imprints, 1835-1907,
University of Oklahoma Press, Norman, OK, 1936.

    WHi   v.1, n.1-3, v.14, n.13-235;   Microforms
                Sept 23-25, 1891, May 11, 1912-
                Jan 31, 1913

    OkHi   v.1, n.1-3, v.14, n.13-235;   Microforms
                Sept 23-25, 1891, May 11, 1912-
                Jan 31, 1913

273 Daily Indian Journal. 1876-?//. Daily. Last issue 4 pages.
Commercial advertising. Available in microform: OkHi (1876).
Muskogee, OK. Editors: W. P. Ross and M. P. Roberts. Newspaper.
Subject focus: Creek, Cherokee and Choctaw peoples. In Choctaw 30%, in
Creek 30%.

    WHi   n.3 [extra edition]   Microforms
                Oct 19, 1876

    NjP   n.3 [extra edition]   Microfilm
                Oct 19, 1876

    OkHi   n.3 [extra edition]   Microfilm
                Oct 19, 1876

OkTG   n.2-3 [extra edition]   Periodicals
          Oct 18-19, 1876

274 The Daily Indian Youth. 1981//. Daily. Last issue 2 pages, height 36
    cm. Photographs. Arlington, WV. Editors: Mark Trahant and Daliah
    Preacher. Billy Mills National Indian Youth Conference reports.

    WHi   v.1, n.1-6;   Pam 82-1359
              Aug 8/9-15, 1981   Oversize

275 The Daily Telephone. 1888-?//. Daily. Last issue 8 pages. Line
    drawings, commercial advertising. Available in microform: OkHi (1889).
    Tahlequah, OK. Newspaper.

    WHi   v.2,n.19;   Microforms
              Nov 30, 1889

    OkHi   v.2,n.19;   Microforms
              Nov 30, 1889

The Dakota Friend. St. Paul, MN

    see Dakota Tawaxitku Kin/The Dakota Friend. St. Paul, MN

276 Dakota Indian Parish News Letter. 1939-?//. Irregular. Last issue 2
    pages, last volume 25 pages, height 28 cm. Published by Dakota Indian
    Parish of the Congregational Christian Church (United Church of
    Christ), Eagle Butte, SD. Editor: Rudolf Hertz. Subject focus: United
    Church of Christ, Dakota people.

    LARC   [v.1, n.4-v.3, n.10]   Periodicals
              [Dec, 1939-June, 1942]

277 Dakota Ojibway Tribal Council. 1974?-1981?//. Irregular. Last issue
    8 pages, height 44 cm. Line drawings, photographs. Brandon, Manitoba,
    Canada. Community newsletter. Subject focus: Dakota and Ojibwa
    peoples.

    CaOAFN   v.8, n.1-5;   Periodicals
              Dec/Jan-Sept, 1981

278 The Dakota Sun. 1977. Weekly. $10. for individuals and institutions.
    Al Bruno, editor, The Dakota Sun, P.O. Box 483, Fort Yates, ND 58538.
    (701) 854-3425. ISSN 0194-9691. LC sn79-628. OCLC

5163230. RLIN OHCP5163203-S. Last issue 12 pages, height 43 cm. Line
drawings, photographs, commercial advertising. Published by Standing
Rock Community College. Previous editors: Bill Grueskin, May 24, 1979;
Dan Mills, Aug 16, 1979-Apr 24, 1980. Community newsletter. Subject
focus: Dakota people.

WHi	n.10, n.92, 104- Oct 27, 1977, May 24, Aug 16, 1979-	Circulation
AzNCC	Sept 8, 1977-	Indian File
OkTU	n.64- Nov 9, 1978-	Rare Book Room

Other holding institutions: KSteC (KKQ), [Standing Rock Community
College Library, Fort Yates, ND].

279 Dakota Tawaxitku Kin/The Dakota Friend. 1850-1852//. Monthly. LC
    31-22881. OCLC 1644692. RLIN OHCP1644692-S. Last issue 4 pages,
    height 42 cm. Line drawings. Published by Dakota Mission, St. Paul,
    MN. Editor: G. H. Pond. Subject focus: missions, Dakota people. In
    Dakota, 50%.

| MWA | v.2, n.1, 3, 8;
Jan 1, Mar, Aug, 1852 | Periodicals |

Other holding institutions: [University of Minnesota Union List,
Minneapolis, MN] (MUL).

280 Dallas Inter-Tribal Center Newsletter. 1980? Monthly. Dallas
    Inter-Tribal Center Newsletter, 209 E. Jefferson, Dallas, TX 75203.
    Last issue 8 pages, height 22 cm. Line drawings. Previous editors:
    Wayne Holdine, June-Aug, 1980; Bernice Johnson, Sept, 1980-Nov, 1981.
    Community newsletter. Subject focus: health and employment information.

| WHi | May, 1980-Nov, 1981 | Microforms |

281 Daybreak Star; The Herb of Understanding. 1975. Monthly. OCLC
    7833924. RLIN DCLCSC821121-S. Last issue 24 pages, height 28 cm.
    Line drawings, photographs. Published by United Indians of All Tribes
    Foundation and the National Indian Lutheran Board, Seattle, WA.
    Editors: Karen Forsyth, Oct, 1981-Mar, 1982; Kathryn Oneita, Apr, 1982.
    Subject focus: Lutheran Church, children's periodicals, legends,
    crafts, book reviews, grade school audience.

| WHi | v.7, n.1-n.7;
Oct, 1981-Apr, 1982 | Microforms |

NjP   v.3, n.2;   Periodicals
             Nov, 1977

WaU   v.6-   E/75/D38
             Oct, 1980-

Other holding institutions: IC (CGP), ICN (IBV), WM (GZD).

282 De-Bah-Ji-Mon. 1978-1981//. Irregular. Last issue 8 pages, height 39
    cm. Line drawings, photographs, commercial advertising. Available in
    microform: WHi (1979-1981). Published by Leech Lake RBC, Cass Lake,
    MN. Editors: Pauline Brunette, Apr-July/Aug, 1979; Anne Humphrey,
    Nov, 1979-Oct, 1980; Helen Blue, Jan-Sept, 1981. Community newsletter.

WHi   v.2, n.19-v.3, n.5[i.e.7]   Microforms
             Apr, 1979-Dec, 1981

MnBemT   [v.2-v.3, n.6]   Periodicals
             [1979-Sept, 1981]

Deh Ha Neh. Fort Defiance, AZ

    see ONEO Bahane. Fort Defiance, AZ

Democratic Leader. Tahlequah, OK

    see Tahlequah Leader. Tahlequah, OK

283 Dene Express. 1970?-1977//. Bi-weekly. Commercial advertising. Fort
    Good Hope, Northwest Territories. Title varies: Hare Express, Jan,
    1972-Dec, 1974. Editor: Sister B. Matte. Community newsletter.

CaAEU   v.2, n.1-v.6, n.8;   Boreal
             Jan, 1973-May, 1977   Institute

284 Dene Nation Newsletter. 1980. Irregular. Marie-Helene
    Laraque-Paulette, editor, Dene Nation Newsletter, Box 2338,
    Yellowknife, Northwest Territory, Canada XOE 1HO. (403) 873-4081.
    Last issue 12 pages, last volume 24 pages, height 44 cm. Line
    drawings, photographs. Published by Dene Nations Communications
    Department. Subject focus: Dene people, education, law, land claims.

WHi   v.1, n.1-   Circulation
             June, 1980-

AkUF   v.2, n.1–   Periodicals
              Jan/Feb, 1981–

AzNCC   v.1, n.1-2; v.2–   Indian File
              June-July, 1980, July, 1981–

CaACG   v.1, n.1, v.2, n.1–   Periodicals
              June, 1980, Jan/Feb,
              1981–

CaAEU   v.1, n.1–   Boreal
              June, 1980–   Institute

CaOAFN   v.2, n.1–   Periodicals
              Jan/Feb, 1981–

CaOSuU   v.2;   Periodicals
              1981

285 Dene Supporter. 1977?//. Unknown. Last issue 10 pages, height 28 cm.
Line drawings. Cold Lake, Alberta, Canada. Community newsletter.
Chipewyan people.

CaACG   n.2;   Periodicals
              ?, 1977

286 Denosa. 1975. Bi-monthly. Free to individuals and institutions.
Gill Gracie, editor, Denosa, Box 500, La Ronge, Saskatchewan, Canada
S0J 1L0. (306) 425-4246. LC cn75-81529. OCLC 2593361. RLIN
DCLCCN7581529-S, OHCP2593361-S. Height 28 cm. Photographs. Published
by Department of Northern Saskatchewan. Previous editors: Tim Myers;
Valerie Harlton. Department Newsletter.

WHi   v.7, n.3–   Circulation
              June, 1981–

CaAEU   v.1, n.1–   Boreal
              Jan, 1975–   Institute

Other holding institutions: CaOONL (NLC).

Denver Native Americans United. Denver, CO

    see DNAU Newsletter. Denver, CO

Detroit Indian Center. Detriot, MI

    see Native SUN. Detroit, MI

287 Dialogue. 1973-1976//. Monthly, irregular. Last issue 28 pages,
    height 28 cm. Published by Indian and Eskimo Affairs Program. Ottawa,
    Ontario, Canada. Subject focus: govenmental relations, health,
    education, social services. In French, 50%.

    CaOORD   [v.1,n.1-v.3, n.1]   Periodicals
               [Dec, 1973-?, 1976]

288 Dialogue North. 1973-1979//. Irregular. ISSN 0226-4897. LC
    ce80-71674, cf80-71674. OCLC 4360550, 7314212. Last issue 36 pages,
    height 28 cm. Photographs. Published by Department of Indian Affairs
    and Northern Development, Yellowknife, Northwest Territories, Canada.
    Subject focus: Northwest Territories Native people, natural resource
    development, mineral, oil, gas exploration. In Inuit, 50%.

    CaOORD   Feb, 1973-Spring? 1979   Periodicals

    Other holding institutions, CaOONL (NLC).

    Dimensions. Willowdale, Ontario, Canada

        see Special Editions. Willowdale, Ontario, Canada.

289 Dine Baa-hani. 1969-1973?//. Monthly. OCLC 2260384, 4364973,
    7410776. RLIN CSUP04275706-S. Last issue 12 pages. Line drawings,
    photographs, commercial advertising. Indexed in: Alternative Press
    Index (1971). Available in microform: McP (1969-1970); CPC
    (1969-1972). Published by Navajo Nation, Fort Defiance, AZ. Editors:
    Leonard B. Jimson, Dec 13, 1969; Orville McKinley, May-Sept, 1970;
    Howard Leonard, Nov-Mar 17, 1971. Subject focus: Navajo people,
    culture, socio-economic conditions.

    WHi   v.1, n.1-v.4, n.3;   Microforms
               Sept, 1969-Dec, 1972

    WEU   [v.1, n.4-v.3, n.10];   Journalism
               [Dec 13, 1969-Mar 30,   Lab
               1972

    WMUW   v.2, n.4-v.4, n.4;   MF/AN014
               Dec, 1970-Dec, 1973

    AzFM   v.1-v.3;   570.6/D58
               1969-1971

    AzU   [v.1, n.4-v.4, n.3]   I9791/N31
               [Dec 13, 1969-Dec, 1972]   D582

    CNoSU   [v.1, n.1-v.2, n.4]   Microfilm
               Sept, 1969-Dec, 1970]

CU-A   v.1, n.1-v.4, n.4;   E/77/A1/D5
            Sept, 1969-July, 1973

KU   v.1, n.1-v.4;   Kansas
            Sept 10, 1969-1973   Collection

NjP   v.1, n.1-v.4, n.3;   Periodicals
            Aug 27, 1968-Dec 24, 1972

NmG   v.2, n.1-v.3, n.15;   Periodicals
            Apr 22, 1971-July 31, 1972

N   v.2, n.3-v.4, n.4;   MA/FM
            Nov, 1970-July, 1973

OkU   v.1, n.1-v.2;   WHC
            Sept, 1969-Dec, 1970

PPT   [v.1, n.5-v.4, n.4]   Contemporary
            [Feb, 1970-July, 1973]   Culture

Other holding institutions: CU-UC (UCU), MH-P (HLS), MiU-Labadie (EYM),
[University of Minnesota Union List, Minneapolis, MN] (MUL), NmScW, NmU
(IQU), NFQC (XQM), NSbSU (YSM), OKentU (KSU), PPiU (KSU).

Dine' Biolta Baahane. Rough Rock, AZ

    see The Rough Rock News/Dine' Biolta Baahane. Rough Rock, AZ

290 Directory of Field and Central Offices, Bureau of Indian Affairs.
    1953-1967?//. Quarterly. OCLC 1153241. RLIN OHCP1553241-S. Last
    issue 8 pages. Available in microform: RM (1953-1967). Published by
    Bureau of Indian Affairs, Washington, DC. Subject focus: government
    agencies.

    WHi   Jan 1, 1953-May 15, 1967   Microforms

    Other holding institutions: DI (UDI).

291 Done: Northwest Territories Indian Brotherhood Newsletter. 1971-?//.
    Monthly. Last issue 9 pages. Line drawings, photographs. Available
    in microform: MML (1971). Yellowknife, Northwest Territories, Canada.
    Subject focus: Northwest Territories people. Superceded by Brotherhood
    Report.

    CaOPeT   v.1, n.1-2;   Periodicals
               Feb-Mar, 1971

Doyon, Limited Newsletter.   Fairbanks, AK

   see Doyon Newsletter.   Fairbanks, AK

292 Doyon Newsletter. 1972. Monthly. Margaret Bauman, editor, 201 First
Ave., Fairbanks, AK 99701. Last issue 4 pages, height 44 cm.
Photographs. Available in microforms: AkUF (1972-1975); WHi (1972-).
Published by Doyon Ltd. Title varies: Tanana Chiefs Conference
Newsletter, Dec, 1972-Mar, 1973; Doyon, Limited Newsletter, Apr,
1973-Dec, 1975. Subject focus: corporate news.

   WHi   v.1, n.1-   Circulation
             Dec, 1972-

293 Drum Beat. 1971-?//. Quarterly. Last issue 44 pages, height 27 cm.
Line drawings, photographs. Published by American Indian Cultural
Group, Leavenworth, KS. Editors: Rudy M. Homan and T. J. Graven.
Prison newsletter. Subject focus: fiction, poetry, interviews.

   WHi   v.1, n.3;   Pam 74-3731
             Fall, 1972

   AkUF   v.2, n.1-v.3, n.3;   Microfiche
             Dec, 1972-Nov, 1975

   NjP   v.1, n.3;   Periodicals
             Fall, 1972

   CaOPeT   v.1, n.1-3;   Microfilm
             Oct, 1971-Fall, 1972

   Other holding institutions: MH-P (HLS).

Drumbeat.   Portola Valley, CA

   see Screaming Eagle.   Portola Valley, CA

294 Drumbeat. 1964-?//. Monthly. OCLC 6221097. Last issue 32 pages,
height 28 cm. Line drawings, photographs, commercial advertising.
Available in microform: WHi (1965). Tulsa, OK. Editor: J. W. West.
Community newsletter.

   WHi   v.1, n.5, 8;   Microforms
             Feb, June, 1965

   WMUW   v.1, n.5, 8;   (SPL)
             Feb, June, 1965   E/75/D77x

NN   v.1, n.1-v.3;   HBA
            Oct, 1964-Oct, 1966

OkTahN   v.1-v.6?   Spec. Coll.
            1964-1973?   E/77/D85

OkTU   v.1, n.1-v.6, n.5;   Rare Book
            Oct, 1964-Jan, 1973   Room

295 Drumbeat. 1981//. Irregular. Last issue 8 pages, height 22 cm. Line
    drawings. Published by Crow Creek High School, Stephan, SD. High
    School newsletter.

WHi   v.1, n.2-4;   Pam
            Sept 28-Nov 13, 1981   Cataloging

296 Drumbeats. 1966-1974?//. Monthly during school year. OCLC 5698642.
    RLIN OHCP5698642-S. Last issue 14 pages. Photographs. Available in
    microform: WHi (1973). Published by Institute of American Indian Arts
    High School, Santa Fe, NM. Editors: Shirley Naganashe and Hilda
    Tsethlika, Jan 26-May 25, 1973. High School newsletter.

WHi   v.6, n.5-8;   Microforms
            Jan 26-May 25, 1973

NjP   [v.2, n.2-v.7, n.2]   Periodicals
            [Dec 18, 1968-1974?]

Other holding institutions: CU-UC (UCU).

297 Drums. 1971-1975//. Irregular. OCLC 4614146, 6194229. Last issue 7
    pages. Line drawings. Available in microform: McP (1971-1972); CPC
    (1972-1975). Published by Menominee Tribe, Drums, Inc., Keshena, WI.
    Subject focus: business and corporate news, Menominee Tribal
    stockholders, Menominee people.

WHi   v.1, n.1-v.4, n.1;   Microforms
            Mar, 1971-Mar 1, 1975

WEU   v.3, n.2-5;   Journalism
            Jan 15-Apr 1, 1974   Lab

WEU   v.1, n.3-5, v.2, n.14, v.3, n.4;   Micro 11
ARC   Sept-Oct 16, 1972, Aug 24, 1973,
            Mar 15, 1974

WMUW   [v.1, n.3-v.4, n.1]   (SPL)
            [Sept, 1972-Mar 1, 1975]   E/75/D78x

NjP   [v.1, n.6-v.3, n.8]   Periodicals
           [Nov 10, 1972-July 31, 1974]

OkU   v.1, n.1-v.2;   WHC
           Mar, 1971-June 14, 1972

CaOPeT   [v.1, n.1-v.4, n.1]   Microfiche
           [Mar, 1971-Mar 1, 1975]

Other holding institutions: NmScW.

298 Dsuq' Wub' Siatsub/The Suquamish News. 1978-1981//. Monthly. Last
    issue 8 pages, last volume 44 pages, height 39 cm. Line drawings,
    photographs. Available in microform: WHi (1979-1981). Suquamish, WA.
    Frequency varies: bi-monthly, June/July, 1979-Dec/Jan, 1980. Community
    newsletter. Subject focus: Suquamish people.

    WHi   v.2, n.10-v.4, n.12;   Microforms
               June/July, 1979-Sept, 1981

299 Dxw Hiide: "The Spirit Who Brings Abundance in Fish and Game". 1979?
    Irregular. Dxw Hiide, 814 NE 40th ?St., Seattle, WA 98105. Last issue
    6 pages, height 28 cm. Line drawings. Published by National Coalition
    to Support Indian Treaties. Subject focus: legislation, treaty
    enforcement, land claims.

    WHi   Feb, 1979-Aug, 1980, Mar/Apr, 1982-   Microforms

    ERIC/CRESS Newsletter. Las Cruces, NM

       see CRESS Notes. Las Cruces, NM

    Eadle Keatah Toh. Carlisle, PA

       see The Red Man and Helper. Carlisle, PA

300 The Eagle Views. 1968. Monthly. R. Runicki and J. Grezlik, editors,
    The Eagle Views, Brigham City, UT 84302. (801) 734-2071. Last issue 4
    pages, height 28 cm. Line drawings, photographs. Published by
    Intermountain Inter-Tribal School. School newsletter.

    WHi   v.15, n.5-   Circulation
               Dec 14, 1981-

    AzNCC   v.7-   Indian File
               Feb, 1973-

301 Eagle Wing Press. 1981? Monthly. $5. for individuals and
    institutions. Eagle Wing Press, P.O. Box 117, Meriden, CT 06450.
    (203) 238-4009. Last issue 24 pages, height 39 cm. Line drawings,
    photographs, commerical advertising. Published by American Indians for
    Development. Subject focus: rights, legislation, social services,
    community development, health, local and national news, history,
    culture.

    WHi   Nov/Dec, 1981-   Circulation

    ICN   Current issues   CHAI

    Other holding institutions: [American Indian Bible Institute, Phoenix,
    AZ], [Standing Rock Community College Library, Fort Yates, ND].

    The Eagle's Cry. Oraibi, AZ

       see Qua Toqti/The Eagle's Cry. Oraibi, OR

302 Eagle's Eye. 1970. Ten times a year. $5. for individuals and
    institutions. Marie Robbins, editor, Eagle's Eye, 360A Brimhall
    Building, Brigham Young University, Provo, UT 84602. (901) 378-4129.
    ISSN 0046-0915. OCLC 1914273. RLIN CSUP01532819-S, MIUG13130-S,
    OHCP1914273-S, CSUG1973908-S. Last issue 8 pages, last volume 80
    pages, height 41 cm. Line drawings, photographs. Available in
    microform: CPC (1970-1979). Published by Indian Education Department,
    Brigham Young University. Previous editor: Ron Schlinske, Dec,
    1970-Mar, 1971; Edward Allebes, Apr, 1971; Shirleen Billy, Oct,
    1971-Apr/May, 1972; Glenna Jenks, Sept 29, 1972-Apr, 1973; Amelia
    Clark, Mar-Dec, 1975; Chris Lowery, Jan-Oct, 1976; Ramona Nez, Nov-Dec,
    1976; Wanda Manning, Oct-Dec, 1977; Sandra K. Lucas, Jan-May, 1978;
    Wanda Manning, June, 1978; Larry Shurz, Sept, 1978-Mar, 1979; Wanda
    Manning and Vickie Manning, May/June-July/Aug, 1979; Wanda Manning,
    Oct, 1979-Summer, 1980; Tami Lyons, Sept, 1980-Jan, 1981; Tami Lyons
    and Marie Robbins, Feb-Apr, 1981. College newsletter.

    WHi   v.1, n.1-   Microforms
                Dec, 1970-

    WMUW   [no nos.]   (SPL)
                [Nov, 1977-May/June, 1979]   E/75/E2x

    AzNCC   v.1-   Indian File
                1970-

    AzU   [v.1-v.11]   I9791/E11
                [1970-1979]

    CU-A   v.1-v.4, [no nos.]   E/77/A1/E4
                1970-1974, 1975-Apr, 1975

IdU	[v.1-v.13, n.10]	Superfolio
	[1970-Dec, 1981]	E/75/E2
KU	v.1-	Kansas
	Dec, 1970-	Collection
MtBBCC	v.9-v.13;	Periodicals
	Nov, 1977-Jan, 1981	
NjP	[v.1, n.1-v.11, n.4]	Periodicals
	[Dec, 1970-Apr, 1979]	
OkU	v.1, n.1-	WHC
	Dec, 1970-	
OrU	[no nos.]	Periodicals
	Nov, 1975	
UHi	v.1, n.1-	Periodicals
	Dec, 1970-	
UPB	[v.1, n.3-v.14, n.7]	970.105/EA33
	[1971-1981]	
USUSC	[no nos.-v.11, n.4]	Special
	[Jan, 1970-Apr, 1979]	Collections

Other holding institutions: CLU (CLU), CtY (YUS), DLC (NSD), [Indiana Union List of Serials, Indianapolis, IN] (ILS), (KMK (KKS), KWiU (KSW), OKentU (KSU), [Bacone College, Muskogee, OK].

303 Early American: Newsletter of the California Indian Education Association. 1968. Irregular. $6. for individuals and institutions. Kay Black, editor, Early American, P.O. Box 4095, Modesto, CA 95352. (207) 571-6575. ISSN 0012-8139. OCLC 1567177. Last issue 4 pages, last volume 40 pages, height 36 cm. Line drawings. Available in microform: CPC (1968-1979). Subject focus: educational legislation, educational opportunities.

WHi	v.1, n.1-	Circulation
	Jan, 1968-	
WEU	v.3, n.1-6;	Journalism
	Jan-Nov/Dec, 1970	Lab
WEU	v.11, n.1-	Periodical
	Jan, 1978-	Stacks
CL	v.10, n.1-	Periodicals
	Winter, 1977-	
AzNCC	v.2-	Indian File
	1969-	

CLSM	v.3, n.6, v.4, n.2-3; Dec, 1970, 1971	Periodicals
CRSSU	v.2- 1969-	Periodicals
CSmarP	[v.3-10], v.11- [1970-1977], 1978-	Stacks
CU-A	v.1- July, 1968-	E/97/A1/E36
CU-B	v.1, n.1- Jan, 1968-	Periodicals
ICN	Current issues	CHAI
NjP	[v.1, n.4-v.10, n.1] [Summer, 1968-Winter, 1977]	Periodicals
NHu	[v.3, n.1-v.11, n.4] [1970-1978]	Periodicals
NN	v.1, n.1-v.9; Jan, 1968-Winter, 1976	Microforms
NcP	v.13, n.5-v.14; 1980-1981	Periodicals
OkTU	v.9, n.4- Mar, 1976-	Rare Book Room
OkU	v.1, n.1- Jan, 1968-	WHC
OrU	v.6- 1973-	Periodicals
PPT	[v.5-v.9, n.5], v.10, n.1- [Dec, 1972-Dec, 1977], Winter, 1978/79-	Contemporary Culture

Other holding institutions: CLobS (CLO), CLU (CLU), IC (CGP),
MiU-Labadie (EYM), [University of Minnesota Union List, Minneapolis,
MN] (MUL), OkU (OKU), OrU-Special Collections.

304 <u>Earth Song</u>. 1981? 8 times a year. Hansley Hadley, editor, Earth
    Song, Room 501 Student Center, Southern Utah State College, Cedar City,
    UT 84720. (801) 586-1111. Last issue 4 pages, height 38 cm. Line
    drawings, photographs, commercial advertising. Published by Southern
    Utah State College Multi-cultural Center. College newsletter. Subject
    focus: Navajo and Paiute people.

USUSC	Feb, 1981-	Periodicals

East River Echo. Washington, DC

    see West River Times/East River Echo. Washington, DC

305 Eastern Arctic Star. 1970?-1972//. Weekly. Last issue 14 pages,
    height 36 cm. Line drawings, commerical advertising. Frobisher Bay,
    Northwest Territories, Canada. Editor: R.E. Jackson. Community
    newsletter.

    CaOONL   v.1, n.1, 25-v.2, n.18;   Newspaper
               Mar 2, 1970, Sept 7, 1970-Jan 17, 1972   Section

306 Eastern Navajo News. 1935?//. Unknown. Last issue 15 pages, height
    27 cm. Line drawings. Subject focus: Navajo people, 24 organized
    Chapters on the Eastern Navajo Jurisdiction.

    CLSM   Mar, 1935   Periodicals

307 Edmonton Native News. 1963? Monthly. Canadian Indian Friendship
    Centre, 10176-117th St., Edmonton, Alberta, Canada T5K 1X3. (403)
    482-7632. ISSN 0046-1296, 0382-7534. LC cn76-301333, cn76-308843.
    OCLC 2325968, 2322328. RLIN DCLCCN76308843-S, OHCP2325968-S. Last
    issue 8 pages, height 28 cm. Line drawings. Title varies: Canadian
    Native Friendship Centre, Sept-Nov, 1970. Subject focus: urban
    community, centre news.

    WHi   Jan, 1973-   Circulation

    NjP   [Oct, 1972-May, 1978]   Periodicals

    CaAEU   June, 1972-Mar, 1974   Boreal
                                                    Institute

    CaOONL   Sept, 1970-Mar, 1971   Periodicals

    CaOPeT   1972-   Periodicals

308 Education Dialogue. 1971?-?//. Unknown. Last issue 8 pages, height
    27 cm. Line drawings, photographs. Published by Bureau of Indian
    Affairs, Haskell Junior College, Lawrence, KS. Subject focus:
    education, Bureau of Indian Affairs.

    WHi   Mar, 1972   Microforms

    AzNCC   Oct, 1971-May, 1975   Indian File

    CLSM   [Oct, 1971-Mar/Apr, 1980]   Periodicals

309 <u>Education Indienne</u>. 1971-1973//. Irregular. Last issue 16 pages,
    height 28 cm. Photographs. Published by Department of Indian Affairs
    and Northern Development, Ottawa, Ontario, Canada. Subject focus:
    education. In French, 100%.

       CaOORD   [v.3, n.1-5]   Periodicals
                 [?, 1972-June, 1973]

310 <u>Education Journal</u>. 1972-1975//. Ten times a year. ISSN 0090-0958.
    LC 73-640527. OCLC 1784690 RLIN DCLC73640527-S, CUDL1978-S,
    CSUP0715270X-S, OHCP1784690-S, OHCP1775284-S. Last issue 20 pages,
    height 28 cm. Line drawings, photographs. Published by Institute for
    the Development of Indian Law, Inc., Washington, DC. Frequency varies:
    monthly, Dec 28, 1972-Mar, 1973. Editors: Kirke Kickingbird, Dec 28,
    1972-June/July, 1973. Subject focus: education, educational
    opportunities.

       WHi   [v.1, n.5-v.2, n.9]   K/9/N73
                 [Dec 28, 1972-1975]

       IaHi   v.1-v.2;   E/97/E4/I55
                 1972-1973

       NjP   [v.1, n.1-v.2, n.9]   Periodicals
                 [Aug 28, 1972-1975]

       N   [v.1, n.1-v.2, n.9]   J371.975/qI59
                 [1972-1975]

    Other holding institutions: CLobS (CLO), DLC (DLC), DI (UDI), MiMtpT
    (EZC), [University of Minnesota Union List, Minneapolis, MN] (MUL), N
    (NYG), [New York State Union List, Albany, NY] (NYS), OkU (OKL).

311 <u>Education Profile</u>. 1971. 3 times a year. Louis T. Baker, editor,
    Education Profile, Box 8327, Albuquerque, NM 87198. (505) 766-3160.
    OCLC 3471414, 7259113. Last issue 8 pages. Line drawings,
    photographs. Available in microform: McA (1974-). Published by Bureau
    of Indian Affairs, Albuquerque, NM. Title varies: Albuquerque Area
    Education Profile, Mar, 1974- Oct/Dec, 1975. Frequency varies:
    bi-monthly, Mar-Dec, 1974; quarterly, Jan/Feb, 1975-Oct/Dec, 1979.
    Previous editor: Wayne A. Winterton Nov, 1974-Jan/Mar, 1979; Wayne A.
    Winterton and Louis T. Baker, Apr/June, 1979. Subject focus: education.

       WHi   v.4, n.4-   Microforms
                 Mar, 1974-

       WEU   v.1, n.1-v.4, n.3;   Microforms
                 Feb, 1971-Jan, 1974

       AzNCC   v.4-   Indian File
                 Mar, 1974-

NjP   [v.1, n.1-v.9, n.2]   Periodicals
           [Feb, 1971-Jan/Mar, 1978]

UPB   [v.5, n.15-v.11, n.1]   970.48905/UN3P
           [1974-1981]

CaOPeT   v.1, n.1-   Microfilm
           Feb, 1971-

Other holding institutions: COU-DA (COA), KEmt (KKR), NmU (IQU), [U.S.
Government Printing Office-Serials, Alexandria, VA] (GPA).

312 Educational Opportunity Center. 1981?-1982//. Irregular. Last issue
    3 pages, height 28 cm. Oneida, WI. Subject focus: educational
    opportunities in Wisconsin.

WHi   Feb?-July, 1982   Pam 82-572

WUSP   May, 1981-July, 1982   Native American
                                                      Center

313 Elbow Drums. 1966?-1981//. Monthly. OCLC 6244831, 6245069. Last
    issue 12 pages, height 28 cm. Line drawings. Available in microform:
    McA (1971-1978); WHi (1969-1981). Published by Calgary Indian
    Friendship Centre, Calgary, Alberta, Canada. Title varies: Calgary
    Indian Friendship Centre, May, 1976-Jan, 1977. Frequency varies:
    irregular, Apr, 1970-July, 1979. Editors: Roy Littlechief, Apr, 1970;
    Pat Burnett, Apr, 1977-Dec, 1978; Wanda First Rider, and Jo-Anne Dan,
    Feb-July, 1979; Nick Ternette, Aug, 1979-Jan, 1981. Subject focus:
    urban community, centre news.

WHi   Jan, 1969-Jan, 1981   Microforms

NjP   [Apr, 1972-May, 1978]   Periodicals

OkU   July/Aug, 1971-Sept/Oct, 1979   WHC

WyCWC   Jan, 1973-Jan, 1975   Periodicals

CaACG   [1966-1979]   Periodicals

CaMWU   [May, 1976-Jan, 1978]   971/E375/Dr

CaOONL   1968-1969, 1974-1979   Periodicals

CaOPeT   Nov, 1971-Jan, 1981   Periodicals

Other holding institutions: MiEM (EEM) [Western Nevada Community
College, Carson City, NV], [University of Wisconsin Stevens
Point-Native American Center, Stevens Point, WI].

314 <u>Emergency Response International Network Bulletin</u>. 1981. Irregular.
Emergency Response International Network Bulletin, c/o Akwesasne,
Mohawk Nation, via Rooseveltown, NY 13683. (518) 358-9531. Last issue
2 pages, height 28 cm. Subject focus: aboriginal rights.

    CaOAFN   Aug 12, 1981-   Periodicals

315 <u>The Eskimo</u>. 1916-1947//. Quarterly. Last issue 8 pages, height 23
cm. Published by United States Bureau of Education, Eugene, OR. Place
of publication varies: Nome, AK, Sept, 1916-Dec, 1918; Seattle, WA,
Feb, 1936-Oct, 1940. Frequency varies: monthly, Sept, 1916-Dec., 1918.
Editors: Dyfed Evans, Sept, 1916-June, 1917; Arthur Shields, July,
1917-June, 1917; Dyfed Evans, July/Aug, 1918; Arthur Shields, Dec,
1918; C.L. Lewis, Apr, 1936-July, 1947. Suspended publication,
1919-1935. Subject focus: culture, legends.

    WHi   [v.1, n.7-v.2, n.14?]   F945//ES
               [Mar, 1917-Dec, 1918]   Cutter

    WHi   [v.1, n.1-v.2, n.10]   Microforms
               [v.3, n.1-v.14, n.3]
               [Sept, 1916-July/Aug, 1918],
               [Apr, 1936-July, 1947]

    AkHi   [v.1, n.1-v.2, n.10],   Periodicals
               [v.3, n.1-v.14, n.3]
               [Sept, 1916-July/Aug, 1918],
               [Apr, 1936-July, 1947]

    AkUF   v.1, n.1-?   Periodicals
               Sept, 1916-Aug, 1917

316 <u>Eskimo</u>. 1944. Semi-annual. $1. for individuals and institutions.
Guy Mary-Rousseliere, editor, Eskimo, P.O. Box 10, Churchill, Manitoba,
Canada ROB OEO. (204) 675-2568. ISSN 0318-7551. LC cn76-319818.
OCLC 6870182, 2006883, 2006693. RLIN DCLCCN76319818-S, DCLCCN76319817,
OHCP2006883-S, OHCP2006693-S. Last issue 32 pages, height 23 cm. Line
drawings, photographs. Available in microform: McA (1974-). Published
by Diocese of Churchill-Hudson Bay. Frequency varies: quarterly, May,
1946-Summer, 1968. Subject focus: missions, Christian religion, Inuit
culture and heritage.

    WHi   (n.s.)n.6-   Microforms
               Fall/Winter, 1973-

    WEU   (n.s.)n.6-7;   Microforms
               Fall/Winter, 1973-Spring/Summer, 1974

    WMM   [v.3-(n.s.)n.2]   Special
               [May, 1946-Autumn/Winter, 1971]   Collections

WMUW	[(n.s.)n.6-17] [Fall/Winter, 1973-Spring/Summer, 1979]	(SPL) E/99/E7E7x
NjP	[v.9-(n.s.)n.16] [Mar, 1956-Fall/Winter, 1978/1979]	Periodicals
CaACG	v.3- 1946-	Periodicals
CaAEU	v.1- 1944-	Boreal Institute
CaOONL	v.17- 1961-	Periodicals
CaOOP	n.71-84, (n.s.)n.1- 1966-1970, 1971-	E/99/E7/E84
CaOPeT	v.69?-v.84, (n.s.)n.1- 1964-1970, 1971-	E99/E7E685

Other holding institutions: AzFU (AZN), InFwCT (ITC), MWalB (MBB).

317 <u>Etudes/Inuit/Studies</u>. 1977. Semi-annual. $8. for students; $14. for individuals; $20 for institutions. Etudes/Inuit/Studies, Departement d'anthropologie, Universite Laval, Quebec, Canada G1K 7P4. (418) 656-2320. ISSN 0701-1008. LC ce78-30259, cf78-30259, 80-640922. OCLC 3979926. RLIN DCLCCF7830259-S, DCLC80640922-S, OHCP3979926-S. Height 23 cm. Indexed in: RADAR. Published by Inuksiutiit Katimajiit Association. Subject focus: anthropology, Inuit people. In French, 50%.

CaAEU	v.1, n.1- 1977-	Boreal Institute
CaMWU	v.1- 1977-	970/E855/In
CaOONL	v.1- 1977-	Periodicals

Other holding institutions: AzTeS (AZS), AzU (AZU), CLU (CLU), DLC (DLC), DSI (SMI), IU (UIU), KyU (KUK), [University of Minnesota Union List, Minneapolis, MN] (MUL), NbU (LDL), NBiSU (BNG), NIC (COO), [New York State Union List, Albany, NY] (NYS), NNU (ZYU), WyU (WYU), CaNfSM.

318 <u>The Exchange</u>. 1976. Irregular. $20. for individuals and institutions. Rose Robinson, editor, The Exchange, 1029 Vermont Ave., N. W., Washington, DC 20005. (202) 638-7066. OCLC 5158140. Last issue 22 pages, height 28 cm. Line drawings, photographs. Published by Native American Philanthropic News Service, Phelps-Stokes Fund.

Subject focus: politics, economics, legislation, philanthropic
activities, culture, book reviews.

WHi	v.1, n.1– May, 1976–	Circulation
WM	Current issues	Forest Home Branch
WMUW	v.1, n.2– Jan/Mar, 1977–	Periodicals
AzNCC	v.2– Spring, 1978–	Indian File
NbU	v.1– 1977–	E.99/E7E88x
OkTU	v.1, n.1– May, 1976–	Rare Book Room
CaACG	v.2, n.3– Winter, 1978/1979–	Periodicals

Other holding institutions: Ok (OKD), [Wisconsin Indian Resource
Council, Stevens Point, WI].

319 Eyak Corporation Newsletter. 1975?//. Unknown. Last issue 10 pages.
Photographs. Available in microform: AkUF (1975). Cordova, AK.
Subject focus: corporate news, shareholders, land claims, Alaska Native
Claims Settlement Act.

WHi	v.1, n.102; July–Nov, 1975	Microforms
AkUF	v.1, n.102; July–Nov, 1975	Microforms

320 Eyanpaha. 1946?-1973?//. Unknown. Last issue 7 pages, height 28 cm.
Line drawings. Published by Red Cloud Indian School, Holy Rosary
Mission, Pine Ridge, SD. Editor: Mona Yocu. High school newsletter.

WMM	v.28, n.2; Dec 17, 1973	Special Collections

Eyapaha. Rosebud, SD

   see Rosebud Sioux Herald (Eyapaha). Rosebud, SD

321 The Eyapaha, American Indian Center Newsletter. 1978? Monthly.
    Shelly Schomer, editor, The Eyapaha, American Indian Center Newsletter,
    4656 Gravois, St. Louis, MO 63116. (314) 353-4517. Last issue 12
    pages, height 28 cm. Commercial advertising. Previous editors: Ralph
    Donaldson, Mar-June, 1981; Richard Jordan July-Aug, 1981. Subject
    focus: history, culture, center news, poetry.

    WHi   Mar, 1981-   Circulation

    ICN   Current issues   CHAI

    MoSHi   Sept, 1981-   Periodicals

    Other holding institutions: [American Indian Bible Institute, Phoenix,
    AZ].

322 E'yanpaha Reservation News. 1976-1980//. Weekly. Last issue 8 pages.
    Line drawings, photographs. Available in microform: WHi (1979-1980).
    Published by Devils Lake Sioux Tribe, Fort Totten, ND. Editor: Myra
    Pearson, June/July, 1979-Dec 15, 1980. Community newsletter. Subject
    focus: Dakota people, history, health.

    WHi   v.4, n.6/7-v.5, n.36;   Microforms
               June/July, 1979-Dec 15, 1980

    WMUW   [v.2, n.5-v.4, n.15]   (SPL)
               [Apr, 1978-Sept, 1979]   E/75/E87x

    MtBBCC   v.5;   Periodicals
               Aug-Dec., 1980

    Other holding institions: [Standing Rock Community College Library,
    Fort Yates, ND].

323 FCNL Indian Report. 1977. Irregular. FCNL Indian Report, 245 Second
    St., N. E., Washington, DC 20002. (202) 547-6000. Last issue 10
    pages, height 28 cm. Line drawings. Published by Friends Committee on
    National Legislation. Subject focus: legislation, sovereignty,
    administrative reform, health, education, housing.

    WHi   v.1, n.1-   Circulation
               June 22, 1977-

324 FIRE!: Forwarding Indian Responsibility in Education. 1967-?//.
    Unknown. Last issue 16 pages, height 28 cm. Line drawings,
    photographs, some in color. Published by Bureau of Indian Affairs, San
    Fernando, CA. Editor: N. S. Foy, May-Aug, 1967. Subject focus:
    education, bi-cultural teaching.

WHi   v.1, n.1-2;   Pam 68-2308
             May-Aug, 1967

325 FIS Newsletter. 1967-1974?//. Quarterly. Last issue 8 pages. Line
    drawings, photographs. Available in microform: McA (1967-1974); WHi-A,
    Veda Stone Papers, (1971, 1972, 1973). Published by Flandreau Indian
    School, Flandreau, SD. School newsletter.

    WHi   v.1, n.1-v.9, n.2;   Microforms
                 Apr, 1967-Dec 24, 1974

    WEU   v.2, n.3-4. v.3, n.3-4, v.5, n.2-3; Journalism
                 Apr 1-June 3, 1968, Mar 29-June 6, 1969, Lab
                 Dec 26, 1970-Mar 29, 1971

    WEU   v.5, n.4, v.7, n.1-2, 4, v.8, n.8;   Micro 11
    ARC   June 12, 1971, Nov 13-Dec 26, 1972,
                 May 30, 1973, June 3, 1974

    NjP   [v.3, n.1-v.10, n.1]   Periodicals
                 [Jan, 1971-Mar, 1973]

    OkU   v.1, n.1-v.7;   WHC
                 Apr, 1967-Dec, 1972

    WyCWC   v.7, n.3-v.9, n.2;   Periodicals
                 Apr 3, 1973-Dec 24, 1974

    CaOPeT   v.1, n.1-v.9, n.2;   Microfilm
                 Apr, 1967-Dec 24, 1974

    Other holding institutions: [Western Nevada Community College, Carson
    City, NV], [University of Wisconsin-Stevens Point-Native American
    Center, Stevens Point, WI]

326 The First American. 1952?-?//. Irregular. Last issue 4 pages, height
    28 cm. Herndon, VA. Editor: A.L. Tandy Jemison. Subject focus:
    rights, legislation.

    WMM   v.2, n.1;   Special
                 Sept 21, 1953   Collections

327 The First Citizen. 1969-1972?//. Monthly. Last issue 6 pages. Line
    drawings, photographs, commercial advertising. Available in microform:
    WHi (1969-1972). Vancouver, British Columbia, Canada. Frequency
    varies: bi-monthly, Nov, 1969-Apr, 1970. Editor: Fred Favel, June,
    1970-July, 1972. Community newsletter. Subject focus: rights,
    legislation, history.

WHi	n.1-19; Nov, 1969-[July?], 1972	Microforms
NjP	n.1-19; Nov, 1969-[July?], 1972	Periodicals
CaACG	1970-1972	Periodicals
CaOONL	1970-1972	Periodicals
CaOOP	n.1-19; Nov, 1969-[July?], 1972	E/78/C3/F57

328 First Citizen. 1981. Irregular. $5. for individuals and institutions. Glen Wasicuna, editor, First Citizen, 274 Garry St., Winnipeg, Manitoba, Canada R3C 1H3. (204) 944-8245. Last issue 8 pages, height 44 cm. Line drawings, photographs. Published by Four Nation Confederacy. Previous editor: John Cuthand, May, 1981. Subject focus: rights, legislation, land claims.

WHi	Dec., 1982-	Circulation
CaOAFN	v.1, n.1- May, 1981-	Periodicals

329 The First People. 1974-1975?//. Irregular. Last issue 8 pages. Line drawings. Published by American Friends Service Committee, Pacific Southwest Region, American Indian Affairs, Pasadena, CA. Subject focus: rights, legislation, land claims.

CLSM	v.1, n.?, 7; July, 1974, Mar/Apr, 1975	Periodicals

Five Feathers News. Lompoc, CA

see Tribe of Five Feathers News. Lompoc, CA

330 Five Tribes Journal. 1975-?//? Bi-monthly. OCLC 4161856. Last issue 44 pages, height 27 cm. Photographs. Published by Five Civilized Tribes Foundation, Muskogee, OK. Editor: Janey Hendrix. Subject focus: Five Civilized Tribes.

OkTahN	v.1; Feb-June, 1975	Periodicals

Other holding institutions: Ok (OKD).

331 <u>The Flandreau Spirit</u>. 1971. Irregular. The Flandreau Spirit,
    Flandreau Indian School, Flandreau, SD 57028. (605) 997-2451. OCLC
    6169139. Last issue 2 pages. Photographs. Available in microform:
    McA (1971-). School newsletter.

WHi	v.1, n.1- Sept 24, 1971-	Microforms
WMUW	v.11, n.13-v.12, n.26; Jan 27, 1978-May 4, 1979	(SPL) E/75/F53x
WUSP	Current year only	Periodicals
AzNCC	v.3- Apr, 1973-	Indian File
OkTU	v.11, n.24- Apr 14, 1978-	Rare Book Room
OkU	v.1, n.1-v.2; Sept 24, 1971-Dec, 1972	WHC
WyCWC	[v.2, n.6-v.9,n.12] [1972-1976]	Periodicals
CaOPeT	v.1, n.1- Sept 24, 1971-	Microfilm

Other holding institutions: [University of Minnesota Union List,
Minneapolis, MN] (MUL), [Western Nevada Community College, Carson City,
NV].

332 <u>Focus: Indian Education</u>. 1970-1974//. Monthly. OCLC 1757775. RLIN
    OHCP1757775-S. Last issue 12 pages. Line Drawings, photographs.
    Available in microform: McP (1971-1972); WHi-A, Veda Stone Papers,
    (1971-1972). Published by Minnesota State Indian Education Department,
    St. Paul, MN. Editors: Marie A. McLaughlin, Apr-June, 1971; Rosemary
    Christiansen, Sept 30, 1971-Dec, 1972. Subject focus: education,
    educational opportunities.

WHi	v.2, n.3-v.3, n.10; Apr, 1971-Dec, 1972	Microforms
WEU ARC	[v.2, n.2-v.3, n.5] [Feb, 1971-May 31, 1972]	Micro 11
CNoSU	v.2, n.3-v.3, n.10; Apr, 1971-May 31, 1972	Microfilm
MnBemT	v.1-v.4, n.2; 1970-Feb, 1974	Periodicals
OkU	v.2, n.3-v.10; Apr, 1971-Dec, 1972	WHC

Other holding institutions: [University of Minnesota Union List,
Minneapolis, MN] (MUL).

333 <u>Forgotten People/Peuple Oublic</u>. 1972-1981//. Irregular. ISSN
    0315-4459. LC cn82-30098, cn82-300993, cf76-30963, ce76-30963. OCLC
    2578795, 2578776, 4116713, 5966892, 8469778, 8469786. RLIN
    DCLCCN8230099-S, DCLCCN8230098-S, DCLCCF7630963-S, DCLCCE7630963-S,
    OHCP2578795-S, OHCP2578776. Last issue 16 pages, last volume 188
    pages, height, 39 cm. Line drawings, photographs. Available in
    microform: WHi (1972-1981). Published by Native Council of Canada,
    Ottawa, Ontario, Canada. Editors: Marianne Dettmers, Summer,
    1972-July, 1973; Ruth Daily, Aug-Dec, 1973; Lena Friesen, Mar-June,
    1974; Cap Williams, July/Aug-Sept, 1974; Fern Perron, Dec, 1976-July,
    1977; Bob Gairns, Sept/Oct-Nov/Dec, 1977; A. G. Ruffo, Sept, 1978-June,
    1981. Subject focus: legislation, rights of Metis and non-status
    people. In French, 10%.

WHi	v.1, n.1-v.8, n.2; Summer, 1972-June, 1981	Microforms
NjP	v.1, n.1; Summer, 1972	Periodicals
CaACG	v.6, n.5/6-v.8; May/June, 1977-Feb, 1981	Periodicals
CaAEU	v.2, n.6-v.8, n.2 1973-June, 1981	Boreal Institute
CaBAbF	v.5-v.8 Apr, 1976-Mar, 1981	Periodicals
CaMWU	v.1-v.8, n.2 1972-June, 1981	970/F7637/Pe
CaOAFN	v.8, n.1-2; ?-June, 1981	Periodicals
CaOONL	v.1, n.1-v.8, n.2 Summer, 1972-June, 1981	Periodicals
CaOOP	v.1, n.1-v.8, n.2 Summer, 1972-June, 1981	LC/1041/M35
CaOPeT	v.1, n.1-v.8, n.2; Summer, 1972-June, 19811	Microfilm
CaOSuL	v.3-v.8; 1972-1981	Periodicals
CaOSuU	v.6-v.8; 1977-1981	Periodicals

Other holding institutions: [University of Minnesota Union List,
Minneapolis, MN] (MUL).

334 <u>Fort Apache Scout</u>. 1962-1981//. Bi-weekly. OCLC 4414186. RLIN
AZPG0112-S. Last issue 16 pages, last volume 416 pages, height 45 cm.
Line drawings, photographs, commercial advertising. available in
microform: WHi (1964, 1970-); WHi-A, Veda Stone Papers, (1969).
Published by White Mountain Apache Tribe, Whiteriver, AZ. Frequency
varies: monthly, Apr, 1964-Jan 4, 1977. Previous editors: Dale L.
Slocum, Sept, 1971-Mar, 1976; Bill Hess, May, 1976-Apr 27, 1979; Max
Evans, May 11, 1979-July, 25, 1980; Judith A. Miketta, Aug 8, 1980-Oct
30, 1981. Community newsletter. Subject focus: Apache people.

WHi	v.2, n.12, v.8, n.29; v.9, n.9-v.20, n.12;	Microforms
	Apr, 1964, Oct, 1969, Sept, 1970-	
	Oct 30, 1981	
WEU	[v.9, n.2-v.10, n.4]	Journalism
	[Feb, 1970-Apr, 1971]	Lab
WEU	v.8, n.29;	Micro 11
ARC	Oct, 1969	
AzHM	[v.9, n.2-12]	Periodicals
	[1970	
AzNCC	v.8-	Indian File
	Nov, 1969-	
AzT	v.9, n.10-	Periodicals
	Oct, 1970-	
AzTeS	v.16-	XRFA 1.3/N38
	1977-	
Az	v.1, n.1-	Periodicals
	June 6, 1962-	
AzU	[v.1, n.1-v.17]	I9791/A6/F7
	[June 6, 1962-1978]	
CL	v.9, n.2-	Periodicals
	Feb, 1970-	
CU-A	v.1, n.4-	E/77/A1/F6
	Apr, 1971-	
NjP	[v.4, n.2-v.15, n.3]	Periodicals
	[Aug, 1965-Dec, 1976]	
OkU	v.1, n.1-	WHC
	June 6, 1962-	
PPT	v.9, n.5-v.10, n.4, n.11;	Contemporary
	May, 1970-Apr, Nov, 1971	Culture
UPB	v.2, n.1-	970.49105/F776
	1963-	

WaU   [v.11, n.3-v.12, n.12]   Periodicals
           [Mar, 1972-Dec, 1973]

CaOPeT   v.11-   Periodicals
           1972-

Other holding institutions: [American Indian Bible Institute, Phoenix,
AZ], CtY (YUS), MH-P (HLS), [University of Minnesota Union List,
Minneapolis, MN] (MUL), [Bacone College, Muskogee, OK], CaOONL (NLC).

335 Fort Belknap Camp Crier. 1971-1981//. Weekly. OCLC 6168751. Last
    issue 8 pages, height 39 cm. Line drawings, photographs, commercial
    advertising. Available in microform: CPC (1971-1976). Published by
    Fort Belknap Agency, Harlem, MT. Title varies: Camp Crier, July 30,
    1971-Dec 19, 1975. Editors: Sarah KillEagle, July 30, 1971-Feb 15,
    1974; Rebecca King, Feb 22-Aug 30, 1974; Angie Shawl, Sept 20, 1974-May
    21, 1981. Community newsletter.

    WHi   v.3, n.30-v.7, n.53; v.10, n.21,   Microforms
               v.11, n.12-v.12, n.20;
               July, 1971-Dec 30, 1976, May 31, 1979,
               Mar 27, 1980-May 21, 1981

    WMUW   [no nos.-v.10, n.37];   (SPL)
               [Mar 30, 1973-Sept 6, 1979   E/75/F67x

    AzNCC   v.4-   Indian File
               Sept, 1972-

    MtBBCC   v.11-v.12;   Periodicals
               Mar, 1980-Mar, 1981

    MtBC   v.1, n.1-v.2, n.42; [v.7-v.10]   E/78/M9/F67
               Sept 19, 1969-Aug 16, 1970, [1976-1979]

    NjP   [v.3, n.30-v.10, n.23]   Periodicals
               [July 30, 1971-June 14, 1979]

    NN   v.3, n.30-v.7, n.53;   Microforms
               July, 1971-Dec 30, 1976

    Other holding institutions: KSteC (KKQ).

336 Fort Berthold Agency News Bulletin. 1951-1968?//. Bi-weekly. Last
    issue 26 pages. Line drawings. Available in microform: McA (John
    Collier Papers). Elbowoods, ND. Community newsletter. Subject focus:
    law, relocation, education.

    WHi   v.2, n.34, v.4, n.5   Microforms
               Oct 15, 1951, May 18, 1953   J. Collier Papers

WUSP   v.2, n.34, v.4, n.5   Microforms
              Oct 15, 1951, May 18, 1953   J. Collier Papers

NjP   [v.2, n.1-v.19]   Periodicals
              [Jan 3, 1951-Jan, 1968]

Other holding institutions: [Standing Rock Community College Library,
Fort Yates, ND].

337 Fort Gibson Post. 1897-1920//. Weekly. Last issue 8 pages. Line
    drawings, commercial advertising. Published by the Post Publishing
    Company, Muskogee, OK. Available in microform: OkHi (1897-1904).
    Editors: James S. Holden and Will T. Canup, Sept 30-Nov 4, 1897; Will
    T. Canup, Jan 13-May 7, 1898; James S. Holden, Nov 3, 1898. Newspaper.
    Also described in: Foreman, Carolyn Thomas. Oklahoma Imprints,
    1835-1907. Norman: University of Oklahoma Press, 1936.

    WHi   [v.8, n.2-v.12, n.25]   Microforms
                  [Sept 30, 1897-Dec 1, 1904]

    OkHi   [v.8, n.2-v.12, n.25]   Microforms
                  [Sept 30, 1897-Dec 1, 1904]

338 Fort Yuma Newsletter. 1972?//?. Unknown. Last issue 14 pages, height
    28 cm. Line drawings. Available in microform: WHi (1975). Yuma, AZ.
    Community newsletter.

    WHi   Nov 17, 1975   Microforms

    WMUW   Nov 17, 1975   (SPL)
                                                           E/75/F68x

    NjP   [May 19, 1972-Apr 15, 1974]   Periodicals

339 Foster's Indian Record and Historical Data. 1876-1877//. Irregular.
    LC 02-14406. OCLC 4402184. Last issue 4 pages, height 52 cm.
    Washington, DC. Editor: Thomas Foster. Subject focus: history,
    statistics, census, languages, culture, Iowa, Winnebago, Arapaho
    peoples.

    ICN   n.1-3;   Ayer 1/F7
                  Nov 30, 1876-Mar 1, 1877

    Other holding institutions: CtHC (TYC).

340 4-H News. 1981? Irregular. 4-H News, Division of Extension and
    Community Relations, University of Saskatchewan, Saskatoon,
    Saskatchewan, Canada S7N 0W0. Last issue 6 pages, height 28 cm. Line

drawings, photographs. Published by Indian 4-H Program. Organization newsletter.

WHi   Nov, 1980-   Circulation

CaOAFN   Jan, 1981-   Periodicals

341 Four Directions. 1977-1979?//. Quarterly. Last issue 16 pages, height 39 cm. Line drawings, photographs. Published by Native American Studies, University of New Mexico, Albuquerque, NM. Editor: Millie Arviso. College newsletter. Subject focus: local and national news.

AzNCC   v.1-   Indian File
           Mar, 1977-

ICN   v.3, n.1;   CHAI
           Apr, 1979

MtBBCC   v.3;   Periodicals
           Dec, 1979

NjP   [v.1, n.7-v.2, n.3]   Periodicals
           [Sept, 1977-Spring, 1978]

Four Lakes Indian Council Newsletter. Madison, WI

    see Four Lakes News. Madison, WI

342 Four Lakes News. 1977. Monthly. Four Lakes News, Room 27 A, 1601 N. Sherman Ave., Madison, WI 53704. (608) 241-1607. Last issue 8 pages, height 28 cm. Line drawings. Available in microform: WHi (1977-). Published by Four Lakes Indian Council. Title varies: Four Lakes Indian Council Newsletter, Nov, 1977-May, 1978. Community newsletter.

WHi   n.2-   Microforms
           Nov, 1977-

WM   Current issues   Forest Home
                                               Branch

Other holding institutions: [WGrU-Native American Studies Dept.], [University of Wisconsin-Stevens Point-Native American Center, Stevens Point, WI], [Wisconsin Indian Resource Council, Stevens Point, WI.]

343 Four Winds. 1980. Quarterly. $22. for individuals and institutions. Charles J. Lohrmann, editor, Four Winds, 703 W. Ninth, P.O. Box 156, Austin, TX 78767. (512) 472-7701. ISSN 0274-9300. LC 82-641733,

sn80-1981. OCLC 6697852. RLIN DCLC82641733-S. Last issue 88 pages,
height 28 cm. Line drawings, photographs, some in color, commerical
advertising. Published by Hundred Arrows Press. Subject focus:
history, arts and crafts, art exhibits, book reviews, fiction.

WHi	v.1, n.4– Autumn, 1980–	Circulation
NmG	v.1– Summer, 1981–	Periodicals
OkPAC	v.1, n.5– Winter, 1981–	Periodicals
OkU	v.1, n.1– Winter, 1980–	WHC

Other holding institutions: CoD (DPL), DLC (DLC), MH (HLS, HUL),
[Bacone College, Muskogee, OK], Ok (OKD), OKTU (OKT), TxSvT (TTS), TxAu
(TXG), TxU (TXQ).

344 <u>Four Winds</u>. 1977–?//?. Unknown. OCLC 6221085. Last issue 30 pages,
height 28 cm. Line drawings. Available in microform: WHi (1977).
Published by Confederated Indian Tribes Council, Washington State
Penetentiary, Walla Walla, WA. Editor: Reggie Acquin. Prison
newsletter.

WHi	July, 1977	Microforms
WMUW	July, 1977	(SPL) E/75/F7x
CoCF	Winter, 1981	Periodicals
OkTU	Winter, 1981	Rare Book Room

345 <u>The Franciscan Missions of the Southwest</u>. 1913-1922//. Annual. OCLC
7163419. RLIN NYBG82-SO, CUBG12785714-S. Last issue 58 pages, height
25 cm. Line drawings, photographs, commercial advertising. Published
by Franciscan Fathers, St. Michaels, AZ. Subject focus: missions,
Catholic Church.

WHi	n.1-9 1913-1921	F805/C36F Cutter
CLSM	n.1-10? 1913-1922	Periodicals

Other holding institutions: AzFU (AZN).

346 <u>From the Pipe</u>. 1980-1981//? Quarterly. Last issue 36 pages, height
36 cm. Line drawings, photographs. Published by Institute for the
Development of Indian Government, Prince Albert, Saskatchewan, Canada.
Editors: Keith A. Jamieson, ?, 1980; Beth Cuthand, Spring, 1981.
Subject focus: tribal governments, rights, legislation, social services.

    CaOAFN   v.1, n.1-2;   Periodicals
                  ?, 1980-Spring, 1981

347 <u>G.V.I.A. Indian Grapevine</u>. 1981. Bi-monthly. G.V.I.A. Indian
Grapevine, G-3500 Flushing Rd, Suite 400, P.O. Box 4146, Flint, MI
48504. (313) 239-6621. Last issue 12 pages, height 28 cm. Line
drawings. Published by Genesee Indian Center. Subject focus: urban
community, center news and programs, arts and crafts.

    WHi   Dec, 1981-   Circulation

    Mi   Jan/Feb, 1982-   Periodicals

348 <u>Ganado Today</u>. 1975-?//?. Quarterly. OCLC 6169146. Last issue 4
pages, height 40 cm. Line drawings, photographs. Available in
microform: WHi (1976, 1977). Published by College of Ganado, Ganado,
AZ. School newsletter. Subject focus: Navajo people, education,
graphics, poetry.

    WHi   v.1, n.2, v.2, n.3;   Microforms
                Winter, 1976, Winter, 1977

    WMUW   v.1, n.2, v.2, n.3;   (SPL)
                Winter, 1976, Winter, 1977   E/75/G36x

349 <u>Ged' Za-dump</u>. 1955-?//? Unknown. Last issue 4 pages, height 33 cm.
Published by Shoshone-Bannock Tribes, Inc., Fort Hall, ID. Editor:
Joseph Thorpe, Jr. Community newsletter. Subject focus: Shoshone and
Bannock people.

    WMM   [no nos.]   Special
                Aug 1, 1955-June 2, 1956   Collections

    IdHi   v.2, n.1;   Periodicals
                July 12, 1963

    NjP   [no nos.], [v.1, n.1-v.5, n.79]   Periodicals
                [Aug 11, 1955-Feb, 1957],
                [July 30, 1962-Jan 3, 1968]

350 <u>Gigmanag, (Our People)</u>. 1976. Monthly. $3. for individuals and
Institutions. Gigmanag, P.O. Box 2170, 129 Kent St., Charlottetown,

Prince Edward Island, Canada C1A 8B9. ISSN 0226-6202. LC cn80-30855.
OCLC 6472467. Last issue 12 pages, height 44 cm. Line drawings,
photographs, commercial advertising. Published by Native Council of
Prince Edward Island. Title varies: No Name News, Jan., 1976.
Community newsletter.

| WHi | v.1, n.1– | Microforms |
| | Jan, 1976– | |

| CaOAFN | v.6, n.3; | Periodicals |
| | Mar, 1981 | |

Other holding institutions: CaOONL (NLC).

351 Gila River News. 1964-?//. Monthly. Last issue 14 pages, height 39
cm. Line drawings. Available in microform: WHi (1964-1965). Sacaton,
AZ. Editor, Alexander Lewis, Sr. Community newsletter. Subject
focus: Pima people.

| WHi | v.1, n.6-7; | Microforms |
| | Dec, 1964-Jan, 1965 | |

| NjP | v.8, n.3; | Periodicals |
| | Sept, 1970 | |

352 The Glacier. 1885?-1888?//. Unknown. Last issue 2 pages, height 28
cm. Published by Tlinkit Training Academy, Fort Wrangel, AK. School
newsletter. Subject focus: Tlinkit people, history, culture, school
news. Photostat.

| WHi | v.1, n.9; | Microforms |
| | Aug, 1886 | |

353 Goinsiday: Telling the News. 1972-1975//. Monthly, irregular. Line
drawings, photographs. Available in microform: (1972-1975). Published
by Northwest Territories Department of Information, Yellowknife,
Northwest Territories, Canada. Editor: Raymond Sonfrere. Community
newsletter. Superceded by the Interpreter.

| WHi | [v.1, n.1-v.4, n.3] | Microforms |
| | [Aug, 1972-Mar, 1975] | |

| CaAEU | [v.1, n.4-v.4, n.3] | Boreal |
| | [Dec, 1972-Mar, 1975] | Institute |

| CaACG | [v.2, n.6-v.4, n.3] | Periodicals |
| | [July, 1973-Mar, 1975] | |

354 <u>Great Lakes Agency News</u>. 1964-1967//. Quarterly. Last issue 4 pages,
    height 29 cm. Photographs. Personal names indexed in: Index to
    Wisconsin Native American Periodicals (1964-1967). Available in
    microform: WHi-A, Veda Stone Papers, (1964-1967). Published by Great
    Lakes Agency, Bureau of Indian Affairs, Ashland, WI. Editors: Frank R.
    Brady, June 30, 1964-Jan 30, 1965; Delmar Armstrong, June 30-Dec, 1965;
    Harold L. LaRoche, Mar 31, 1966-Mar 31, 1967. Subject focus:
    government programs.

WHi   v.1, n.1-v.3, n.2;   I20.994:
             June 30, 1964-Mar 31, 1967

WHi   [v.1, n.1-v.3, n.2]   Microforms
             [June 30, 1964-Mar 31, 1967]

WEU   [v.1, n.1-v.3, n.2]   Micro 11
ARC   [June 30, 1964-Mar 31, 1967]

NjP   [v.1, n.1-v.3, n.2]   Periodicals
             [June 30, 1964-Mar 31, 1967]

355 <u>Great Lakes Indian Community Voice</u>. 1967-1975//. Semi-monthly. OCLC
    4434027. Last issue 4 pages. Photographs. Available in microform:
    DLC (1968-1975); WHi-A, Veda Stone Papers, (1964-1967). Published by
    Great Lakes Inter-Tribal Council, Inc., Menominee, MI. Editor: Betty
    J. Richie, May 10, 1971-Feb, 1972. Community newsletter.

WHi   v.1, n.1-v.5, n.5;   Microforms
             Mar, 13, 1967-Aug/Sept, 1975

WEU   v.1, n.37, v.2, n.2-5, v.4, n.5;   Journalism
             May 10, Nov 15, 1971-Feb 21, 1972,   Lab
             Jan, 1974

WEU   [v.1, n.1-v.4, n.6]   Micro 11
ARC   [Mar 13, 1967-Feb, 1974]

WMMus   [v.1, n.39-v.5, n.5]   Anthro
             [July 26, 1971-Aug/Sept, 1975]   Section

WMUW   [v.1, n.36-v.5, n.5]   (SPL)
             [Apr 9, 1971-Aug/Sept, 1975]   E/75/G73x

CU-A   v.4, n.4-5;   E/77/A1/V6
             Dec, 1973-1975

NjP   [v.1, n.1-v.5, n.5]   Periodicals
             [Mar, 13, 1967-Aug/Sept, 1975]

356 <u>Great Lakes Indian Press</u>. 1981//. Unknown. Last issue 4 pages,
    height 28 cm. Photographs. Published by University of Wisconsin-Eau
    Claire, Eau Claire, WI. Personal names indexed in: Index to Wisconsin

Native American Periodicals (1981). Subject focus: journalism, Native American press.

WHi   n.1;   Pam 81-869
            May 26-29, 1981

357 Greater Lowell Indian Cultural Association. 1977? Irregular. Onkwe Tase (Edward J. Guillemette), editor, Greater Lowell Indian Association, 551 Textile Ave., Dracut, MA 01826. (617) 957-4714. Last issue 8 pages, height 28 cm. Line drawings, photographs. Subject focus: history, culture, land claims, poetry.

WHi   [Feb, 1977-Dec, 1980], Mar, 1981-   Circulation

CaOAFN   Feb-May, 1981   Periodicals

358 Green Arrow. 1980?// Irregular. Last issue 10 pages, height 28 cm. Line drawings. Published by Indian Education Office, Freedom, WI. School newsletter.

WHi   v.5, n.6;   Pam
            Apr/May, 1982   Cataloging

Other holding institutions: [WGrU Native American Studies Dept.], [Wisconsin Indian Resource Council, Stevens Point, WI].

359 Guts and Tripe. 1969-?//?. Unknown. Last issue 20 pages, height 28 cm. Line drawings. Available in microform: WHi (1969-1972); WHi-A, Veda Stone Papers, (1970). Published by Coalition of American Indian Citizens, Denver, CO. Subject focus: rights, education, satire.

WHi   v.1, n.1-3;   Microforms
            Dec, 1969-May?, 1972

WEU   v.1, n.1-2;   Journalism
            Dec? 1969-Jan? 1970   Lab

WEU   v.1, n.2;   Micro 11
ARC   Jan? 1970

PPT   v.1, n.2;   Contemporary
            Jan?, 1970   Culture

360 The Hallaquah. 1879-?//. Monthly. Last issue 8 pages, height 15 cm. Wyandotte Mission, Grand River, OK. Editors: Ida Johnson; Lula Walker; Arizona Jackson. Subject focus: missions, Christian religion.

KU   v.1, n.2, 4/5;   Kansas
            Jan, Mar/Apr, 1880   Collection

361 Halne'ii of the San Juan Mission. 1966-?//. Irregular. Last issue 2
    pages, height 28 cm. Farmington, NM. Subject focus: Navajo people,
    missions, Christian religion.

    WHi   Dec, 1969, Nov, ?, 1970, Oct, 1971   Pam 72-2898

    WEU   Nov, 1966-Fall, 1973   Microfilm

    NjP   Nov, 1967, 1970   Periodicals

362 Han Zaadlitl'er/We Live by the River. 1982. Monthly. C. Mark
    Fuerstenau, editor, P.O. Box 00309, Nenana, AK 99760. (907) 832-5594.
    Last issue 4 pages, height 28 cm. Line drawings, photographs.
    Published by Yukon-Koyukuk School District. Previous editor: Mary
    Erickson, Mar/Apr, 1982. Subject focus: education, curriculum
    development, teacher education.

    WHi   v.1, n.5-   Circulation
                Mar/Apr, 1982-

    Hare Express. Fort Good Hope, Northwest Territories, Canada

        see Dene Express. Fort Good Hope, Northwest Territories, Canada

363 Ha-Shilth-Sa. 1974. Irregular. Ha-Shilth-Sa, P.O. Box 1383, Port
    Alberni, British Columbia, Canada V9Y 7M1. Last issue 16 pages, height
    44 cm. Published by Nuu-Chah-Nulth Tribal Council. Frequency varies:
    bi-monthly, Mar 9-Nov 10, 1978. Previous editors: Jan Broadland, Aug
    30, 1974-Sept 14, 1976; Charlotte Rampanen, Nov 29, 1976-May 26, 1977.
    Community newsletter.

    WHi   v.9, n.6-   Circulation
                Sept 16, 1982-

    CaOONL   v.1, n.4-14, v.2, n.4-   Newspaper
                Mar 29-Dec 13, 1974, Apr 14, 1975-   Section

364 Haskell Alumni Association Newsletter. 1978//. Unknown. OCLC
    6745193. Last issue 4 pages. Photographs. Available in microform:
    WHi (1978). Published by Haskell Indian Junior College, Lawrence, KS.
    College newsletter.

    WHi   v.1, n.1-2;   Microforms
                Mar 28-Aug, 1978

AzNCC   v.1, n.1;
           Mar 28, 1978   Indian File

365 Hawaii Council of American Indians, Inc. [Newsletter]. 1979? Monthly.
    Hawaii Council of American Indians, Inc., 3260 Ualena St., Honolulu, HI
    96819. (808) 833-4581. Last issue 4 pages, height 35 cm. Commerical
    advertising. Published by American Indian Center. Subject focus:
    urban community, center news.

    ICN   Current issues
                                                       CHAI

    MtBBCC   Aug, 1980-Jan, 1981
                                                       Periodicals

366 Health Newsletter. 1979. Unknown. Health Newsletter, Paiute
    Professional Center, Tusu and Westline Sts., P.O. Box 1296, Bishop, CA
    93514. Last issue 7 pages, height 36 cm. Line drawings. Published by
    Toiyabe Indian Health Project. Subject focus: health, nutrition,
    physical fitness.

    WHi   v.3, n.5-
               Nov/Dec, 1981-   Circulation

    Heart of America Indian Center Newsletter. Kansas City, MO

        see Inter-Tribal Tribune. Kansas City, MO

367 The Herald. 1895-?//. Weekly. Last issue 12 pages. Line drawings,
    commercial advertising. Miami, OK. Available in microform: OkHi
    (1902). Editor: V.C. Yantis. Newspaper. Also described in: Foreman,
    Carolyn Thomas, Oklahoma Imprints, 1835-1907, University of Oklahoma
    Press, Norman, OK, 1936.

    WHi   v.8, n.7;
               Jan 3, 1902   Microforms

    OkHi   v.8, n.7;
               Jan 3, 1902   Microforms

368 Hi Line Indian Alliance. 1975-1980//. Irregular. Last issue 4 pages,
    height 36 cm. Line drawings. Available in microform: WHi (1979-1980).
    Havre, MT. Subject focus: employment training opportunities, health.

    WHi   Apr 25-June 1, 1975
               [June? 1979-July, 1980]   Microforms

WMUW   Apr 25-June 1, 1975   (SPL)
                                                          E/75/H54x

369 Highlights. National Tribal Chairmen's Association. 1976-1977?//.
    Monthly. OCLC 6188850. Last issue 12 pages, height 28 cm.
    Photographs. Available in microform: WHi (1977). Washington, DC.
    Subject focus: organization news.

                                                         Microforms
    WHi   May, 1977
                                                         E/75/N3x
    WMM   July/Aug, 1977
                                                         (SPL)
    WMUW   May, 1977   E/75/N3x

    NjP   Dec, 1976, May-Nov/Dec, 1977   Periodicals

370 Ho Chunk Wazee ja chee rla. 1962-?//. Unknown. Last issue 10 pages.
    Available in microform: WHi-A, Veda Stone Papers, (1962). Published by
    Wisconsin Winnebago Business Committee, Madison? WI. Subject focus:
    Winnebago people, organization, rights.

                                                         Microforms
    WHi   v.1, n.1;
               Apr, 1962
                                                         Micro 11
    WEU   v.1, n.1;
    ARC   Apr, 1962

371 Holy Rosary Mission News Page. 1927?-?//. Irregular. Last issue 1
    page, height 28 cm. Pine Ridge, SD. Subject focus: Catholic Church,
    missions, Oglala Sioux people.

                                                         Special
    WMM   [Jan, 1927-Sept, 1930]   Collections

372 Home Mission Monthly. 1885-1924//. Monthly. OCLC 1590828, 1716919.
    RLIN MIUG82-S3299, CSUP04658802-S, OHCP1590828-S. Last issue 28 pages.
    Photographs. Available in microform: WHi-A, Papers of Carlos
    Montezuma, (1920). Published by Woman's Board of Home Missions of the
    Presbyterian Church, New York, NY. Subject focus: missions,
    Presbyterian Church, education.

                                                         Microforms
    WHi   v.34, n.4;
               Feb, 1920

    Other holding institutions: [Indiana Union List of Serials,
    Indianapolis, IN] (ILS), MBTI (BTI), MiMtpT (EZC), [University of
    Minnesota Union List, Minneapolis, MN] (MUL). NNUT (VYN), OWoC (WOO),

PPi (CPL), PCarlD (DKC), [Pittsburgh Regional Library Center,
Pittsburgh, PA] (QPR).

373 Honga. 1978. Monthly, irregular. Honga, 613 S. 16th St., Omaha, NE
68102. (402) 344-0111. Last issue 4 pages, height 28 cm. Line
drawings. Published by American Indian Center of Omaha. Subject
focus: urban community, center news.

WHi	[v.3, n.8-v.5, n.4] [Aug, 1980-Apr, 1982]	Microforms
AzNCC	v.3, n.4- Apr, 1980-	Indian File
ICN	Current issues	CHAI
MtBBCC	v.3; Sept-Dec, 1980	Periodicals

374 Hopi Action News. 1966-1978?//. Weekly. OCLC 8392345. Last issue 14
pages. Line drawings, photographs. Available in microform: CPC
(1966-1968). Keams Canyon, AZ. Community newsletter. Subject focus:
Hopi people.

WHi	[v.1, n.1-v.2, n.7] [July 22, 1966-Oct 25, 1968]	Microforms
AzFM	v.1-? 1966-?	570.6/H79a
AzU	[v.1, n.1-v.2, n.15] [July 22, 1966-1968]	I9791/H7/H8
NjP	[v.1, n.1-v.13] [July 22, 1966-Apr 27, 1978]	Periodicals
NN	[v.1, n.1-v.2, n.7] [July 22, 1966-Oct 25, 1968]	Microforms
OkU	[v.6-v.8] [Nov 2, 1972-June 6, 1974]	WHC
PPT	v.5; Oct 7, 1971	Contemporary Culture

Other holding institutions: PPiU (PIT).

375 Hopi Tribal News. 1979-1980//. Bi-weekly. Last issue 6 pages, height
28 cm. Line drawings, photographs. Oraibi, AZ. Editors: Amos Poocha,

Nov, 1978–Feb, 1980; Nadine Polacca, Mar–Oct, 1980. Subject focus:
Hopi people, culture, social services.

WHi	v.2, n.21-22, 24-42; Nov–Dec, 1979, Jan–Oct, 1980	Pam Cataloging
Az	[v.2, n.21–v.3, n.25] [Nov, 1979-1980]	Periodicals
AzTeS	v.2; 1980	XRHO 1.3/N38
NjP	v.1, n.1–v.2, n.10; July, 1978–June, 1979	Periodicals

376 <u>How Ni Kan</u>. 1979. Irregular. How Ni Kan, Route 5, Box 151, Shawnee,
OK 74801. Last issue 8 pages, height 36 cm. Line drawings,
photographs. Published by Citizens Band of Potawatomi Indians of
Oklahoma. Community newsletter. Subject focus: Potawatomi people.

ICN	Current issues	CHAI

377 <u>Humming Arrows</u>. 1974–?//. Unknown. Last issue 8 pages, height 28 cm.
Line drawings, photographs. Available in microform: WHi (1976).
Published by Native American Program, Stanford University, Stanford,
CA. Editor: Rencie Eteeyan. College newsletter. Includes poetry.

WHi	v.3, n.7; May, 1976	Microforms
AzNCC	v.4– Mar, 1977–	Indian File

378 <u>The Hunter Newsletter</u>. 1970. Quarterly. The Hunter Newsletter, P.O.
Box 7, Deer Lodge, MT 59722. OCLC 6161360. Last issue 22 pages. Line
drawings, photographs, commercial advertising. Available in microform:
McP (1970-1972). Published by North American Indian League of the
Montana State Prison. Editors: Cloyce Little Light, Jan 17, 1971; Levi
Campbell, Feb–May, 1971; Alex LaFontaine, Aug–Sept, 1971; Cloyce Little
Light, Oct–Dec, 1971; Levi Campbell and Dewey Stone, Jan, 1972; Levi
Campbell, Apr, 1972; Cloyce Little Light, Sept–Dec, 1972; K. C.
Strandburg, Dec, 1977. Prison newsletter. Subject focus: prison
conditions, socio-economic conditions, politics, culture, sports.

WHi	Dec, 1971–Dec, 1972, Summer, 1982–	Microforms
WMUW	Dec, 1977–Mar, 1978	(SPL) E/75/H87x
AzNCC	1971–Mar, 1978	Indian File

CNoSU   Jan, 1972-1972   Microfilm

NjP   Jan-Feb/Mar, 1978   Periodicals

OkU   [Jan, 1971-Dec, 1972]   WHC

PPT   Aug, 1971-Nov/Dec, 1972,   Contemporary
           Apr-May/June, 1973   Culture

Other holding institutions: [University of Minnesota Union List,
Minneapolis, MN] (MUL), NmScW.

379 ICI Newsletter. 1978? Quarterly. ICI Newsletter, Eskimo Point,
    Northwest Territories, Canada XOC 0E0. Last issue 11 pages, height 28
    cm. Published by Inuit Cultural Institute. Subject focus: Inuit
    culture, linguistics. Some articles in Inuit.

    CaACG   v.1, n.3, v.2, n.1, v.3, n.1;   Periodicals
               Winter, 1978, Winter, 1979, Winter, 1980

    CaNfSM   v.3;   Periodicals
               1980

    CaOONL   v.1, n.3, v.2, n.1, v.3, n.1;   Periodicals
               Winter, 1978, Winter, 1979, Winter, 1980

    CaOPeT   Current year   Periodicals

380 IEC [Newsletter]. 1973-?//. Irregular. Available in microform: McA
    (1973). Published by Indian Educational Club of William Head
    Institution, Metchosin, British Columbia, Canada. Editor: Bob
    Hinchcliffe. Prison newsletter.

    CaOPeT   May, 1973   Periodicals

381 IERC Bulletin. 1973-1978?//. Irregular. Last issue 10 pages. OCLC
    2568312, 8479229. RLIN OHCP2568312-S. Line drawings. Available in
    microform: CPC (1973-1978). Published by Indian Education Resources
    Center, Albuquerque, NM. Subject focus: education, curriculum
    development.

    WHi   [v.1, n.1-v.6, n.8]   Microforms
               [Apr, 1973-Aug, 1978]

    NjP   [v.1, n.1-v.6, n.10]   Periodicals
               [Apr, 1973-Oct, 1978]

    SdU   v.1, n.1-v.6, n.8;   Microfilm
               Apr, 1973-Aug, 1978

Other holding institutions: DI (UDI), NmU (IQU), PP (PLF), PPiU (PIT), [U.S. Government Printing Office-Serials, Alexandria, VA] (GPA).

ILOTAN. New York, NY

    see American Indian News. New York, NY

382 IMBO Echoes to Peace and Freedom. 1980?// Unknown. ISSN 0703-6795. LC cn77-33378. OCLC 3436740. Last issue 16 pages, height 28 cm. Line drawings. Published by Indian and Metis Brotherhood Organization, Winnipeg, Manitoba, Canada. Editor: V. Pelletier. Subject focus: culture, poetry.

    CaOAFN   v.2;   Periodicals
              Feb, 1981

    CaOONL   2 issues, no dates   Periodicals

383 INDURBANCOM-Indians in the Urban Community. 1964-?//. Unknown. Last issue 6 pages, height 28 cm. Available in microform: WHi (1964). Published by Indian-Eskimo Association of Canada, Toronto, Ontario, Canada. Editor: Dennis O'Neill. Subject focus: urban community, center news.

    WHi   v.1, n.1;   Microforms
              Feb, 1964

384 ITC News. 1976?-1980//. Irregular. ISSN 0702-8938. LC cn77-33523. OCLC 3519955. RLIN DCLCCN7733523-S, OHCP3519955-S. Last issue 20 pages, height 28 cm. Line drawings. Available in microform: WHi (1976-1980). Published by Inuit Tapirisat of Canada. Ottawa, Ontario, Canada. Community newsletter. Subject focus: Inuit people. In Inuit, 50%.

    WHi   Aug/Sept, 1976-Sept, 1980   Microforms

    AzNCC   Apr, 1978-1979   Indian File

    CaACG   Aug/Sept, 1976-July, 1980   Periodicals

    CaAEU   Aug/Sept, 1976-Sept, 1980   Boreal
                                                 Institute

    CaOAFN   [May-Nov, 1979]   Periodicals

    CaOONL   June, 1976-July, 1980   Periodicals

385 <u>Iapi Oaye</u>. 1871-1939?//. Monthly. OCLC 1644510. RLIN OHCP1644510-S.
Last issue 4 pages, last volume 48 pages, height 41 cm. Line drawings.
Published by Dakota Mission, Santee Agency, NE. Available in
microform: CPC (1871-1939). Title varies: Iapi Oaye/The Word Carrier,
May, 1871-Dec, 1883. Place of publication varies: Greenwood, SD, May,
1871-Dec, 1976. Frequency varies: weekly, Oct 15, 1936-June 23, 1937.
Editors: John P. Williamson, May, 1871-June, 1872; Stephen R. Riggs and
John P. Williamson, Jan, 1873-Dec, 1876; Stephen R. Riggs and Alfred
L. Riggs, Jan, 1877-Sept, 1993; Alfred L. Riggs, Oct-Dec, 1883; John P.
Williamson, Apr, 1884-Dec, 1886; John P. Williamson and Alfred Riggs,
Jan-Dec, 1887; Alfred L. Riggs, Jan, 1888-Dec, 1915; Frederick B.
Riggs, Jan, 1925-Aug/Sept, 1933; Rudolf Hertz, Oct, 1933-Aug/Sept,
1936; Millard M. Fowler, Oct 15, 1936-Aug, 1937; Robert Brown and F.
Philip Frazier, Sept, 1937-Sept, 1938; Rudolf Hertz, Oct, 1938-Jan,
1939. Subject focus: Dakota people, missions, Christian religion. In
Dakota, 75-100%. The Word Carrier, English edition published 1884-1937.

WHi	v.1, n.1-v.6, n.12; May, 1871-Dec, 1877	F805/"ZI11
WHi	[v.1, n.1-v.68, n.5] [May, 1871-Jan, 1939]	Microforms
WMM	v.62, n.5; May, 1933	Special Collections
ICN	[v.1, n1-v.68, n.7] [May, 1871-Mar, 1939]	Ayer 1/I2
MWA	[v.1-43] [1871-1914]	Periodicals
NjP	[v.1, n.10-v.7, n.7] [Apr, 1872-July, 1878]	Periodicals
NHu	[v.1, n1-v.68, n.7] [May, 1871-Mar, 1939]	Periodicals
NN	[v.1, n.2-v.16, n.12] [June, 1871-Dec, 1887]	Rare Book Division
OkTG	[v.3-v.10] [Jan, 1873-Jan, 1880]	Periodicals
SdHRC	v.1, n.1-v.59, n.10; May, 1871-1930	Periodicals
SdU	v.24-v.25, v.28, v.30-v.43, v.64; 1895-1896, 1899, 1901-1914, 1935	South Dakota Room
SdU	v.1, n.1-v.68, n.7; May, 1871-Mar, 1939	Microfilm
SdYC	v.1, n.1-v.68, n.7; May, 1871-Mar, 1939	Microfilm

SdYC   [v.1-v.59]   Bound
            [1871-1930]

Other holding institutions: CtHT (TYC), [Universtiy of Minnesota Union
List, Minneapolis, MN] (MUL), WaU (WAU).

386 **Ideas/Idees**. 1973-1976?//. Quarterly. LC ce77-70611. OCLC 3227505,
    1099646, 3227510. RLIN OHCP1099646-S, DCLCCF7770611-S,
    DCLCCE7770611-S, OHCP3227510-S, OHCP3227505-S. Last issue 16 pages,
    last volume 68 pages, height 28 cm. Photographs. Ottawa, Ontario,
    Canada. Editors: W. A. Lewis, June, 1973-July, 1974; Lois A. Wraight,
    Autumn, 1974-Spring, 1976. Subject focus: business, community
    development. In French, 50%.

WHi   v.1, n.2-v.4, n.1   Microforms
            June, 1973-Spring, 1976

NjP   v.2, n.1;   Periodicals
            Mar, 1974

CaACG   v.3, n.4;   Periodicals
            1975

CaOONL   v.1, n.1-v.4, n.1;   Gov. Docs.
            1973-Spring, 1976

CaOOP   v.1, n.1-v.4, n.1;   E/78/C2/A17
            1973-Spring, 1976

Other holding institutions: DI (UDI), NSyU (SYB), PPiU (PIT).

Idees. Ottawa, Ontario, Canada

    see **Ideas/Idees**. Ottawa, Ontario, Canada

387 **Igalaaq: A Window on the World of Inuit**. 1978. Monthly. $11. for
    individuals and institutions. Harry Hill, editor, Igalaaq, Suite 100,
    196 Bronson Ave., Ottawa, Ontario, Canada K1R 6H4. (613) 233-6252.
    ISSN 0707-7459. LC cn79-30446. OCLC 4747039. RLIN NYPG82-S1547,
    DCLCCN7930446-S, OHCP4747039-S. Height 41 cm. Line drawings,
    photographs, commerical advertising. Published by Nortext Information
    Design, Ltd. Place of publication varies: Stittsville, Ontario,
    Canada. Previous editors: Michael Roberts; Rita Novalinga. Subject
    focus: Inuit people, vocational training and education. In Inuit, 50%.

WHi   v.4, n.3-   Circulation
            Jan, 1982-

CaACG   v.2, n.2-   Periodicals
            Dec, 1979-

CaAEU	v.1, n.1– Nov, 1978–	Boreal Institute
CaOONL	v.1, n.1; Nov, 1978	Periodicals
CaOPeT	v.4, n.7– May, 1982–	E99/E7I32

388 Illuminations, Visions, Voices in Indian Education Regional Newsletter.
1981-1982//. Monthly. Last issue 4 pages, height 28 cm. Published by
Native American Research Institute, Norman, OK. Editor: Margo
Kickingbird. Frequency varies: irregular, Feb–Dec, 1981. Subject
focus: education, curriculum development.

| WHi | v.1, n.1–v.2, n.6;
Feb, 1981–July, 1982 | Microforms |

Other Holding institutions: [University of Wisconsin–Stevens Point,
Native American Center, Stevens Point, WI]

389 The Indian. 1921-?//. Unknown. Last issue 20 pages. Commercial
advertising. Available in microform: WHi-A, Papers of Carlos
Montezuma, (1922). Published by Mission Indian Federation, Riverside,
CA. Subject focus: missions, Christian religion, legends, governmental
relations, poetry.

| WHi | Mar–Oct, 1922 | Microforms |
| CLSM | 1922–1934 | Periodicals |

390 The Indian. 1969-?//. Monthly. Last issue 6 pages, height 41 cm.
Line drawings, photographs. Published by American Indian Leadership
Council, Rapid City, SD. Editors: Birgil Kills Straight and Frank
LaPointe, June 26, 1969–Aug 6, 1970. Newspaper.

WEU	[v.1, n.3–v.2, n.3] [June 26, 1969–Aug 6, 1970]	Journalism Lab
WMM	v.1, n.8; Nov 20, 1969	Special Collections
AzNCC	[v.1, n.1–b.2, n.3] [May 15, 1969–Aug 6, 1970]	Indian File
NjP	[v.1, n.1–v.2, n.3] [May 15, 1969–Aug 6, 1970]	Periodicals

SdHRC   [v.1, n.1-v.2, n.3]   Periodicals
           [May 15, 1969-Aug 6, 1970]

391 Indian. 1969?//. Quarterly. Last issue 14 pages. Available in
    microform: McA (1969). Published by Indian Educational Club of William
    Head Institution, Metchosin, British Columbia, Canada. Editor: Kenzie
    Basil. Prison newsletter. Continued by IEC [Newsletter]?

    CaOPeT   Sept., 1969   Periodicals

392 The Indian: Devoted to the Interests of the Aborigines of North
    America. 1885-1886?//. Bi-weekly. Last issue 6 pages, last volume 262
    pages. Line drawings, commercial advertising. Available in microform:
    McL (1885-1886). Published by Indian Publishing Company, Hagersville,
    Ontario, Canada. Frequency varies: monthly, Dec 30, 1885-Oct 20, 1886.
    Editors: Kah-ke-wa-quo-na-by (Dr. P.E. Jones) Dec 30, 1885-Nov 24,
    1886; S. T. Wright, Dec. 1-29, 1886. Newspaper. Subject focus:
    acculturation. Some articles in Ojibwa.

    WHi   v.1, n.1-24;   E/75/"I5
               Dec 30, 1885-Dec 29,1886

    WHi   v.1, n.1-24;   Microforms
               Dec 30, 1885-Dec 29, 1886

    ICN   v.1, n.1-24;   Ayer 1/I39
               Dec 30, 1885-Dec 29, 1886

    CaMWU   v.1, n.1-24;   Microfilm
               Dec 30, 1885-Dec 29, 1886

    CaOONL   v.1, n.1-24;   Microforms
               Dec 30, 1885-Dec 29, 1886

393 Indian Advisory Committee Newsletter. 1965?-1968//. Semi-annual.
    Last issue 25 pages, height 28 cm. Line drawings. Published by
    British Columbia Indian Advisory Committee, Victoria, British Columbia,
    Canada. Subject focus: education, health, social services.

    CaOORD   v.1, n.5-v.2, n.5;   Periodicals
               Oct, 1965-Feb, 1968

394 Indian Advocate. 1846-1855?//. Monthly. Last issue 4 pages, height 45
    cm. Published by Board of Indian Missions, American Indian Mission
    Association, Louisville, KY. Frequency varies: bi-monthly, May, 1846.
    Editors: Rev. Isaac McCoy, May, 1846; Rev. Sidney Dyer, Mar, 1952.
    Subject focus: missions, Christian religion.

MWA   v.1, n.3, v.6, n.9;   Periodicals
             May, 1846, Mar, 1852

395 The Indian Advocate. 1832//. Quarterly. Last issue 24 pages, height
    18 cm. Published by Association for Diffusing Information on the
    Subject of Indian Rights, Albany, NY. Subject focus: Cherokee removal.

    WHi   n.1;   Pam
                 Feb, 1832   Cataloging

    CtY-B   n.1;   Zc12/806tr
                 Feb, 1832

    MWA   n.1;   Periodicals
                 Feb, 1832

    N   n.1;   AI/439.28
                 Feb, 1832

396 The Indian Advocate. 1891-1894?//. Monthly. Height 29 cm. Line
    drawings, commercial advertising. Published by Albany Indian
    Association, Albany, NY. Editor: Mrs. W. Winslow Crannell. Subject
    focus: acculturation, culture, Christian religion.

    WHi   [v.1, n.1-v.4, n.8]   Microforms
                 [Apr, 1891-Nov, 1894]

    MWA   v.4, n.2;   Periodicals
                 May, 1894

    NN   [v.1, n.1-v.4, n.8]   KSD+
                 [Apr, 1891-Nov, 1894]

397 Indian Advocate. 1889-1910//. Irregular. OCLC 8490225. Height 23
    cm. Line drawings, photographs. Published by Benedictine Fathers of
    the Sacred Heart Mission, Sacred Heart, OK. Subject focus: Catholic
    religion, missions.

    CtY-B   v.16;   Zc13/M6/In3
                 Jan, 1904

    NjP   v.13, n.2;   Periodicals
                 Feb, 1901

    OkU   v.1-v.21;   WHC
                 1889-1910

    Other holding institutions: InND (IND).

398 Indian Affairs. 1933. Irregular. $3. for individuals and
institutions. Steven Unger, editor, Indian Affairs, 432 Park Ave.
South, New York, NY 10016. (212) 689-8720. ISSN 0046-8967. LC
sc77-526. OCLC 1681425, 7722407. RLIN OHCP1681425-S, DCLCSC77526-S,
CUDL0513-S, CSUP02192913-S, CUBG16448303-S, PAUG1614-S, NYPG1030-S.
Last issue 8 pages, height 28 cm. Photographs. Available in
microform: McP (1949-1973); UnM (1949-); WHi-A, Veda Stone Papers,
(1956-1972). Published by Association on American Indian Affairs, Inc.
Previous editors: Oliver LaFarac, Jan, 1938; La Vern Madigan, Mon.,
1958-Feb, 1960; Samuel Birnkrant, Apr, 1960-May, 1961; Phyllis
Brociner, July, 1961-Dec, 1962; Lenie Correll, June, 1963-Dec, 1964;
Mary Gloyne Byler, Mar, 1965-Fall/Winter, 1979. Subject focus: law,
litigation, case histories.

WHi	v.1, n.2- Oct, 1933-	Microforms
WEU ARC	(n.s.) [n.15-83] [Mar, 1956-May, 1972]	Micro 11
WGrU	Current two years	Periodicals
WM	Current issues	Forest Home Branch
WMM	(n.s.)n.1- May 16, 1949-	E/77/I55x
WMM	(n.s.) [n.4-74] [Sept 5, 1950-June/July, 1969]	Special Collections
WMUW	(n.s.)n.54- Feb, 1964-	(SPL) E/77/I414
WU Coll	Current issues	Ethnic Collection
AzFM	1957-	570.6/A512i
AzNCC	May, 1949-1979	Indian File
AzT	Current issues	Periodicals
CL	(n.s.)n.2- 1949-	Periodicals
CNoSU	(n.s.)n.77- 1970-	Periodicals
CU-A	(n.s.)n.83- May, 1972-	E/77/I48
IdU	(n.s.)n.76- Oct/Dec, 1969-	E/75/I45

IC	(n.s.)n.1–	Periodicals
	May 16, 1949–	
ICN	Current issues	CHAI
MoS	(n.s.)n.1–	Periodicals
	May 16, 1949–	
MtHi	(n.s.) [n.5–90], 93–	Z/970.105
	[1952–1975], 1977–	Af26
NbU	(n.s.)1957–	E/75/A5131
NjP	[v.2, n.1–(n.s.)n.98]	Periodicals
	[Dec, 1934–Fall/Winter, 1978/1979]	
N	(n.s.)n.1–93;	J970.5/
	May 16, 1949–Mar, 1977	qI396af
N	(n.s.)1975–	MA/FM
NHu	(n.s.)n.1–	Periodicals
	May 16, 1949–	
NN	(n.s.)n.1–93;	HBA
	May 16, 1949–Mar, 1977	
NdMinS	(n.s.)n.53–	Periodicals
	1963–	
OkTU	(n.s.)n.93–	Rare Book
	1977–	Room
OkU	(n.s.)n.1–	WHC
	May 16, 1949–	
OrU	(n.s.)n.29–	Periodicals
	Dec, 1958–	
PP	(n.s.)1949–1950, 1952–1971	Microfilm
SdU	(n.s.)1955–1969;	South
		Dakota Room
TxU	(n.s.)n.37, 40, 52;	E/77/15/HRC
	June, 1960, Feb, 1961, Aug, 1963	
CaOAFN	[(n.s.)n.86–102]	Periodicals
	[Mar/Apr, 1975–Mar, 1981]	
CaOPeT	(n.s.)n.74–	E75/I48
	1969–	

Other holding institutions: AzTeS (AZS). CLU (CLU), [Congressional
Research Service, Washington, DC] (CRS), FMU (FQG), FOV (FVC), GStG
(GPM), InLP (IPL), MBU (BOS), MH-P (HLS), MiU-Labadie (EYM),

[University of Minnesota Union List, Minneapolis, MN] (MUL), MoS
(SVP),NcAU (NIM), NeWsN (NZG), NhD (DRB), NmLcU (IRU), NmScW, NIC
(COO), [New York State Union List, Albany, NY] (NYS), NSbSU (YSM), OC1W
(CWR), OY (YMM), OkU (OKL), PKuS (KZS), OrU-Special Collections, PMilS
(MVS), PP (PLF), UPB, WaS, WaU (WAU).

399 Indian Affairs. 1964?-1971//. Irregular. OCLC 1752824, 4380079.
     RLIN OHCP1752824-S, CSUP02193000-S, NYPG814024395-S. Last issue 82
     pages, height 20 cm. Published by Institute of American Indian
     Studies, Brigham Young University, Provo, UT. Subject focus:
     sociology, anthropology.

     CU-A   v.5;   Periodicals
               1971

     AzFM   v.4-?   570.6/P969i
               1970-?

     Other holding institutions: ArU (AFU), CLU (CLU), [University of
     Minnesota Union List, Minneapolis, MN] (MUL).

400 Indian Affairs Bureau Press. 1956?-1968//. Irregular. LC sn82-5029.
     OCLC 2153843. RLIN OHCP1145623-S, OHCP2153843-S. Last issue 2 pages.
     Available in microform: RM (1956-1968). Published by Bureau of Indian
     Affairs, Washington, DC. Subject focus: governmental relations, land
     claims, law.

     WHi   [1956-Jan 22, 1968]   Microforms

     Other holding institutions: I (SPI).

401 Indian Affairs in California. 1957-1972//. Quarterly. OCLC 1681210.
     RLIN OHCP1681210-S, CUBU1546-S. Last issue 6 pages, height 28 cm.
     Line drawings, photographs. Published by California League for
     American Indians, Sacramento, CA. Editor: J. O. Chandler, June,
     1968-Dec, 1970. Community newsletter.

     WEU   June, 1968-De., 1970   Journalism
                                                 Lab

     AzNCC   Mar, 1971-Apr, 1972   Indian File

     NjP   Sept, 1967-June, 1970, Mar-Sept, 1971   Periodicals

     Other holding institutions: CLU (CLU) CU-UC (UCU), [University of
     Minnesota Union List, Minneapolis, MN] (MUL).

402 Indian Alcohol Times. 1981? Monthly. $10. for individuals and
    institutions. Indian Alcohol Times, 1615 Broadway, Oakland, CA 94612.
    Last issue 4 pages, height 28 cm. Published by California Urban Indian
    Health Council, Inc. Subject focus: alcoholism, treatment programs.

    WHi   v.1, n.5-   Circulation
                 May, 1982-

403 Indian America. 1967-1976//. Quarterly. ISSN 0044-7714, 0099-0361.
    LC 70-665814, 75-645511. OCLC 1480005, 2242480, 2387528. RLIN
    DCLC75645511-S, OHCP2242480-S, NYPG794272218-S. Last issue 28 pages,
    last volume 132 pages, height 26 cm. Line drawings, photographs,
    commercial advertising. Published by Indian Development Foundation,
    Tulsa, OK. Title varies: Singing Wire, Jan, 1967-June, 1970; American
    Indian Crafts and Culture Magazine, Sept, 1970-June, 1974. Frequency
    varies: 10 times a year, Jan, 1967-June, 1974. Editor: Tyrone Stewart.
    Subject focus: arts and crafts, culture, politics, rights.

    WHi   v.1, n.1-v.9, n.3;   E/98/C9/A44
                 Jan, 1967-Spring, 1976

    WEU   [v.4, n.7-v.7, n.6]   Journalism
                 [Sept, 1970-June. 1973]   Lab

    WEU   v.5, n.5-v.8, n.6;   Periodicals
                 June, 1971-June, 1974

    WMUW   V.8, n.6-v.9, n.3;   (SPL)
                 June, 1974-Spring, 1976   E/98/C9844

    WUSP   v.5, n.9-v.9, n.3;   Periodicals
                 Oct, 1971-Spring, 1976

    AzFM   [v.4-v.9]   570.6/T92a
                 1970-1976

    AzNCC   v.8;   Indian File
                 Winter, 1974

    AzT   v.7, n.3-v.9, n.3;   Periodicals
                 Mar, 1973-Spring, 1976

    CL   v.3, n.5-v.9, n.3;   Periodicals
                 May, 1969-Spring, 1976

    CLSM   v.1-v.3;   Periodicals
                 1967-1969

    CSmarP   [v.4-v.9]   Stacks
                 [1970-1976]

    CU-A   v.5, v.7-v.9. n.3;   E/77/A1/
                 1971, 1973-Spring, 1976   A545

CoKIM	v.1–v.7; 1967–1974	Periodicals
IdU	v.8, n.7–v.9, n.3; Winter, 1974–Spring, 1976	E/75/A42
IC	v.5, n.1–v.9, n.3; Jan, 1971–Spring, 1976	Periodicals
LARC	v.4–v.9; 1970–1976	Periodicals
MnBemT	[v.5–v.9] [1971–1976]	Periodicals
MoSHi	v.6, n.10–v.7, n.2; 1972–1973	970.1/Am34c
NjMonM	v.5–v.6, n.6; June, 1971–1972	Periodicals
NjP	[v.1, n.5–v.9, n.2] [May, 1967–Spring, 1976]	Periodicals
NHu	[v.1, n.5–v.9, n.3] [May, 1967–Spring, 1976]	Periodicals
NN	v.1, n.1–v.9, n.3; Feb, 1967–Spring, 1976	HBA 79–517
OkT	[v.5, n.7–v.9, n.2] [Sept, 1971–Winter, 1976]	Periodicals
OkTahN	v.6–v.8, n.6; 1972–1974	Spec. Coll.
OkTU	[v.1, n.5–v.9, n.3] [May, 1967–Spring, 1976]	Rare Book Room
OkU	v.5, n.6–v.9, n.3; June, 1971–Spring, 1976	WHC
OrU	v.7, n.6–v.9, n.3; June, 1973–Spring, 1976	Periodicals
Wa	v.5, n.6– June, 1971–	Periodicals
WaU	v.9, n.1–3; 1975–Spring, 1976	E/98/C9A442
CaACG	[v.3, n.4–v.9, n.3] [1969–Spring, 1976]	Periodicals
CaAEU	v.5, n.1–v.8, n.5; June, 1971–1974	Boreal Institute

CaOPeT   [v.3-v.9]   E98/C9A44
          [1969-1976]

Other holding institutions: AzFU (AZN), CChiS (CCH), CLobS (CLO),
[Pepperdine University, Malibu, CA] (CPE), CtY (YUS), DLC (DLC, NSD),
DI (UDI), GU (GUA), KPT (KFP), KSteC (KKQ), MdBJ (JHE), MiL (EEP), MiDW
(EYW), MnU (MNU), [Univeristy of Minnesota Union List, Minneapolis, MN]
(MUL), NIC (COO), [New York State Union List of Serials, Albany, NY]
(NYS), [Central New York Library Resources Council, Syracuse, NY]
(SRR), NBu (VHB), PPiU (PIT), [Pittsburgh Regional Library Center-Union
List, Pittsburg, PA] (QPR), PNC (QNC), ScU (SUC), TU (TKN), TCollsM
(TMS), [University of Wisconsin-Stevens Point-Native American Center,
Stevens Point, WI].

404 Indian American Folklore Group Newsletter. 1977//? Monthly. OCLC
    6221093. Last issue 6 pages, height 28 cm. Line drawings. Available
    in microform: WHi (1977). Stillwater, MN. Editor: W. Waukazo.
    Community newsletter.

    WHi   May, 1977   Microforms

    WMUW   May, 1977   (SPL)
                                                          E/75/I43x

405 Indian and Inuit Newsclippings. 1977? Weekly. Indian and Inuit
    Newsclippings, 1760 Regent St., Sudbury, Ontario, Canada P3E 3Z8.
    (416) 966-5544. Last issue 10 pages, height 28 cm. Line drawings,
    photographs. Published by Regional Information Services, Indian and
    Inuit Affairs. Reprints of articles in establishment papers.

    CaOSuU   May, 1977-   Periodicals

406 Indian and Inuit Supporter. 1979. Irregular. $10. for individuals,
    $5. for the unemployed. Indian and Inuit Supporter, P.O. Box 582,
    Station C, St. John's, Newfoundland, Canada A1C 5K8. (709) 753-2208.
    Last issue 36 pages, last volume 50 pages, height 21 cm. Line
    drawings. Published by Indian and Inuit Support Group of Newfoundland
    and Labrador. Subject focus: history, governmental relations, local
    and regional news.

    CaNfSM   v.1, n.1-   Periodicals
              May, 1979-

407 Indian Archives. 1968-1975?//. Irregular. OCLC 4567645. Last issue
    18 pages. Line drawings. Available in microform: WHi (1973?-1975).
    Published by Antelope Indian Circle, Susanville, CA. Prison
    newsletter. Subject focus: culture, legends, history, socio-economic
    conditions.

WHi	Jan, 1973?-Summer, 1975	Microforms
WEU	Jan/Feb-Mar/Apr, 1971, Mar, 1972	Journalism Lab
AzNCC	Summer, 1975	Indian File
NjP	[May, 1968-Dec, 1973]	Periodicals
OkU	1972-Summer, 1975	WHC
UPB	1970-1972	970.105/IN2AR

Indian Arizona News. Phoenix, AZ

   see Arizona Indian Now. Phoenix, AZ

Indian Arrow. Fort Gibson, OK

   see Tahlequah Arrow. Tahlequah, OK

408 Indian Brotherhood News. 1961-1965//. Quarterly. Last issue 10
pages, height 28 cm. Line drawings, photographs, commercial
advertising. Kamloops. British Columbia, Canada. Frequency varies:
monthly, June-Oct, 1961; bi-monthly, Jan/Feb, 1962-May, 1964. Editors:
George Manuel, June-July, 1973; Benjamin R. Paul, Jan/Feb, 1962-Summer,
1965. Community newsletter.

| CaACG | [v.1, n.1-v.3]
[June, 1961-May, 1964] | Periodicals |
| CaOORD | [v.1, n.1-v.4, n.2]
[June, 1961-Summer, 1965] | Periodicals |

409 The Indian Bulletin. 1888-1899?//. Quarterly. Last issue 4 pages.
Line drawings, photographs. Available in microform: NN (1892-1899).
Published by Connecticut Indian Association, Hartford, CT. Subject
focus: acculturation, education.

| WHi | [v.4, n.14-v.13, n.38]
[June 1892-Feb, 1899] | Microforms |
| NN | v.4, n.14, v.12, n.35-36, v.13, n.37-38;
June, 1892, Apr-Dec, 1898, Feb, 1899 | HBA |

410 <u>Indian Center</u>. 1964?//. Monthly. Last issue 14 pages, height 28 cm.
Line drawings. Published by American Indian Council, Inc., San
Francisco, CA. Subject focus: urban community, council news.

WHi   Aug, 1964   Pam 76-981

<u>Indian Center News</u>. Sacramento, CA

    see <u>Sacramento Indian Center News</u>. Sacramento, CA

411 <u>Indian Center News</u>. 1960-?//. Monthly. ISSN 0445-7188. OCLC
5057528. RLIN OHCP5057528-S. Last issue 4 pages, height 36 cm. Line
drawings. Published by American Indian Women's Service League,
Seattle, WA. Editor: Jean Halliday, Jan 5, 1966. Subject focus: urban
community, center news.

WHi   v.5, n.5;   Pam 76-5830
             Jan 5, 1966

NjP   [v.5, n.28-(n.s.)v.1, n.2]   Periodicals
             [Sept 10, 1966-May, 1979]

OkU   [v.3, n.15-v.9]   WHC
             [Jan, 1964-1971]

SdU   [v.6-v.8]   South
             [1967-1969]   Dakota Room

Wa   v.5-v.9;   NW
             1965-1970

WaU   v.3, n.11-v.9, n.9;   970.1/IC
             1963-1971

Other holding institutions: CLU (CLU), [University of Minnesota Union
List, MN] (MUL), UPB.

412 <u>Indian Center of San Jose Newsletter</u>. 1976? Unknown. Indian Center
of San Jose Newsletter, 3485 East Hills Dr., San Jose, CA 95127. (408)
259-9722. Last issue 10 pages, height 28 cm. Line drawings. Subject
focus: urban community, center news.

WHi   v.7, n.8-   Circulation
             Aug?, 1982-

413 <u>Indian Center of Topeka Newsletter</u>. 1975// Monthly. OCLC 6189026.
Last issue 8 pages, height 38 cm. Line drawings. Available in

microform: WHi (1975). Topeka, KS. Subject focus: urban community,
center news. Superceded by Nish Nau Bah?

| WHi | Apr-June, 1975 | Microforms |
| WMUW | Apr-June, 1975 | (SPL) E/75/I44x |

414 Indian Champion. 1884-?//. Weekly. Last issue 8 pages. Line
drawings, commercial advertising. Atoka, OK. Available in microform:
OkHi (1885). Title varies: The Branding Iron, Feb 23-Mar 15, 1884.
Editors ors: Renfrew M. Roberts, Feb 23, 1884-Feb 21, 1885, H. F.
O'Beirne, Mar 4-Nov 7, 1885. Newspaper. Subject focus: Choctaw
people. In Choctaw, 5%. Also described in: Foreman, Carolyn Thomas,
Oklahoma Imprints, 1835-1907. Norman: University of Oklahoma Press,
1936.

WHi	[v.1, n.1-v.2, n.36] [Feb 23, 1884-Nov 7, 1885]	Microforms
ICN	v.2, n.24-32, 34-38; Aug 15-Oct 10, 24-Nov 28, 1885	Ayer 1.I391
NN	v.1-v.2; Nov 1, 1884-Feb 7, 1885	Rare Book
OkHi	[v.1, n.47-v.2, n.36] [Jan 10-Nov 7, 1885]	Microforms
OkTG	[v.1-v.2] [Oct 25, 1884-May 16, 1885]	Periodicals

415 Indian Chieftain. 1882-?//. Weekly. Last issue 4 pages. Line
drawings, commercial advertising. Published by Chieftain Publishing
Co., Vinita, OK. Available in microform: OkHi (1882-1895). Editors:
Gus Ivey, Sept 29, 1882; Robert L. Owens and William Hollingsworth, Jan
19-June 7, 1883; Robert L. Owens and J. L. Sweesy, June 15-Sept 7,
1883; William P. Ross and J. W. Scroggs, Sept 14, 1883-Apr 7, 1884; S.
J. Thompson and M. E. Milford, July 3, 1884-Dec 17, 1885; John Adair,
Dec 24, 1885-Oct 17, 1889; M. E. Milford, Oct 24-Jan 30, 1890; Harvey
W. C. Shelton, Feb 6-Oct 23, 1890; D. M. Marrs, May 14, 1891-June 27,
1895. Newspaper. Also described in: Foreman, Carolyn Thomas.
Oklahoma Imprints, 1835-1907. Norman: University of Oklahoma Press,
1936.

WHi	[v.1, n.2-v.13, n.43] [Sept 29, 1882-June 27, 1895]	Microforms
KHi	v.1-v.20; June 15, 1883-Dec 11, 1902	Periodicals
OkHi	[v.1, n.2-v.13, n.43] [Sept 29, 1882-June 27, 1895]	Microforms

OkU   [v.4-v.19]   WHC
             [1885-1901]

416 Indian Child Advocate. 1981//. Unknown. Last issue 8 pages, Line
    drawings, photographs. Available in microform: WHi (1981). Published
    by Indian Child and Family Resource Center in cooperation with the Los
    Angeles Indian Centers, Inc., Los Angeles, CA. Editor: Colleen Keane.
    Subject focus: children, Indian Child Welfare Act, adoption, law,
    education, family.

    WHi   n.1;   Microforms
                 Feb, 1981

417 The Indian Citizen. 1886-?//. Weekly. Last issue 8 pages. Line
    drawings, commercial advertising. Atoka, OK. Available in microform:
    OkHi (1886-1907). Title varies: Atoka Independent, June 5, 1886-May
    19, 1889. Editors: H.F. O'Beirne and D. J. Folsom, June 5, 1886-May
    19, 1888; Butler S. Smiser and James S. Standley, Mar 2, 1889-July 14,
    1892; Butler S. Smiser, James S. Standley and Norma E. Smiser, July 21,
    1892-Oct 3, 1893; Butler S. Smiser and Norma E. Smiser, Oct 10,
    1893-Apr 13, 1899; Norma E. Smiser, Apr 20, 1899-Mar 23, 1905; Paul B.
    Smith, Apr 20, 1905-Sept 26, 1907. Newspaper. Also described in:
    Foreman, Carolyn Thomas. Oklahoma Imprints, 1835-1907. Norman:
    University of Oklahoma Press, 1936.

    WHi   [v.1-v.22, n.20]   Microforms
                 [June 5, 1886-Sept 26, 1907]

    OkHi   [v.1-v.22, n.20]   Microforms
                 [June 5, 1886-Sept 26, 1907]

418 Indian Community Action Project. 1966?-?//. Weekly. Last issue 1
    page. Available in microform: WHi-A, Veda Stone Papers, (1971).
    Published by Bemidji State University, Bemidji, MN. Subject focus:
    education, career opportunities.

    WHi   [Apr 11, 1969-July 2, 1971]   Microforms

    WEU   [Apr 11, 1969-July 2, 1971]   Micro 11
    ARC

    AzNCC   Feb-June, 1970   Indian File

    SdU   1966-1967   South
                                                             Dakota Room

419 Indian Council Talk. 1963-1969//. Irregular. Last issue 6 pages,
    last volume 28 pages, height 28 cm. Line drawings. Personal names

indexed in: Index to Wisconsin Native American Periodicals (1963-1969).
Available in microform: WHi-A, Veda Stone Papers, (1963-1969).
Published by Wisconsin Indian Youth Council, Eau Claire, WI. Title
varies: Wisconsin Indian Youth Council Newsletter, Jan 14, 1963-Aug,
1969. Subject focus: education, young adults.

WHi   [v.1, n.1-v.7, n.1]   Pam 68-172
             [Jan 14, 1963-Dec, 1969]

WEU   [v.1, n.1]-v.7, n.1]   Micro 11
ARC   Jan 14, 1963-Dec, 1969

NjP   [v.5, n.1-v.6]   Periodicals
             [Dec 15, 1966-Apr, 1969]

The Indian Craftsman. Carlisle, PA

   see The Red Man. Carlisle, PA

420 The Indian Crusader. 1969?. Quarterly. The Indian Crusader, 4009
     Halldale Ave., Los Angeles, CA 90062. (213) 299-1810. OCLC 6188862.
     Last issue 4 pages, last volume 16 pages, height 28 cm. Line drawings,
     photographs. Available in microform: CPC (1969-1976). Published by
     American Indian Liberation Crusade. Subject focus: Christian religion.

     WHi   [Sept/Oct, 1969-   Microforms
                  May/June, 1976]

     WHi   Jan-Dec, 1972, Apr/June, 1973,   Circulation
                  Jan/Mar, 1975-

     WMUW   [Jan/Mar, 1975-Oct/Dec, 1977]   (SPL)
                                                      E/75/I46x

     NjP   Sept/Oct, 1969-June, 1973,   Periodicals
                  Jan-Feb, Mar, 1978

421 Indian Culture Group. 1970?-?// Unknown. Last issue 26 pages, height
     22 cm. Line drawings. Bismarck, ND. Prison newsletter. Includes
     fiction, poetry.

     ICN   Nov?, 1979   CHAI

     NjP   May, 1970   Periodicals

422 Indian Culture Newsletter. 1977?-?//. Quarterly. OCLC 6415399. Last
     issue 8 pages, height 22 cm. Line drawings. Pulbished by Kansas State
     Penitentiary, Lansing, KS. Editors: Francis F. Wishteyah, Jr., and

Gary W. Metzger. Prison newsletter. Subject focus: arts and crafts, graphics, poetry.

WMUW   Dec, 1977/Jan, 1978   (SPE)
                                                          E/75/I48x

423 Indian Echo. 1973?//. Quarterly. Last issue 22 pages, height 28 cm.
Line drawings. Published by Indian and Metis Educational Club, New
Westminster, British Columbia, Canada. Editor: G. Paul. Prison
newsletter. Includes poetry.

CaOONL   Sept, 1973   H-46-2

Indian Ed. Edmonton, Alberta, Canada

    see Canadian Journal of Native Education. Edmonton, Alberta, Canada

424 Indian Education. 1936-1966//. Semi-monthly. OCLC 1644533. RLIN
OHCP1644533-S, CSUP011326-S, CUBG50016507-S. Last issue 8 pages,
height 19 cm. Line drawings, photographs. Published by Bureau of
Indian Affairs, Branch of Education, Washington, DC. Editors: Willard
W. Beatty, Sept 15, 1936-Feb 15, 1950; Hildegard Thompson, Jan 15,
1953-Nov 15, 1965; L. Madison Coombs, Dec 1, 1965-May 15, 1966.
Subject focus: education, anthropology, agriculture, book reviews.

WHi   n.1-191;   F8095/U58I
          Sept 15, 1936-Feb 15, 1950   Cutter

WHi   n.232-435;   Microforms
          Jan 15, 1953-May 15, 1966

AzNCC   1963-1966   Indian File

AzU   n.1-n.435;   Periodicals
          Sept 15, 1936-May 15, 1966

CL   n.2-441;   Periodicals
          Oct, 1936-1966

CLSM   n.1-441;   Periodicals
          Sept 15, 1936-1966

NjP   [n.1-v.24, n.360]   Periodicals
          [Sept 15, 1936-May 15, 1961]

NmG   n.286-300;   Periodicals
          Sept 15, 1956-Dec 1, 1961

N   n.1-433;   C301.975/I39ed
          Sept 15, 1936-May, 1966

OkPAC   [n.188-239]   Periodicals
           Dec 15, 1949-May 1, 1953

OkU   n.1-433;   WHC
           Sept 15, 1936-May, 1966

SdU   v.1-v.29;   Gov. Docs.
           1936-1966

Other holding institutions: AzFU (AZN), CChiS (CCH), DI (UDI), MiU
(EYM), MWelC (WEL), MnCS (MNJ), [University of Minnesota Union List,
Minneapolis, MN] (MUL), [Central New York Library Resources Council,
Syracuse, NY] (SRR). OAkU (AKR), OkAdE (ECO).

425 Indian Education. 1971. Irregular. Indian Education, 1115 2nd Ave.,
    South, Lower Level, Minneapolis, MN 55403. (701) 255-3285. OCLC
    6188755. Last issue 16 pages, height 28 cm. Line drawings,
    photographs. Available in microform: WHi (1971-1978); WHi-A, Veda
    Stone Papers, (1971, 1972, 1974). Published by National Indian
    Education Association. Title varies: News Line, Jan, 1976; National
    Indian Education Association, Feb-Oct, 1971. Subject focus: education,
    educational legislation.

WHi   [v.1, n.1-v.8, n.2]   Microforms
           [Feb, 1971-Mar, 1978]

WU   v.8, n.2, v.12, n.1-   Periodicals
           Mar, 1978, June, 1981-   Room

WEU   v.1, n.1, ?, v.3, n.1, v.4, n.2;   Micro 11
ARC   Feb, Oct, 1971, Sept, 1972, Oct, 1974

WMUW   v.7, n.4-10;   (SPL)
           ?, 1977   E/97/I53x

AzNCC   v.2-v.5;   Indian File
           Sept, 1972-May, 1975

NjP   [v.3, n.1-v.4, n.2]   Periodicals
           [Sept, 1972-Oct, 1974]

NPotU   Current 5 years   E/97/I54

NdMinS   v.5, n.1-3;   Periodicals
           1975

OkU   v.10, n.2-3, v.12, n.1;   WHC
           Sept-Oct, 1979, June, 1981

SdU   v.4, n.1-v.8, n.2;   Stacks
           1974-Mar, 1978

Other holding institutions: AzFU (AZN), CLSM, DI (UDI), IC (CGP), NmScW.

426 Indian Education. 1976? Bi-monthly. Indian Education, 1350 Teakwood,
    Coos Bay, OR 97420. (503) 269-1611. Last issue 2 pages, height 36 cm.
    Line drawings, photographs. Published by Coos County Educational
    Service District with the Willow River Indian Benevolent Association.
    Subject focus: education, (local).

    WHi   Sept/Oct, 1978   Microforms

    CLSM   Sept, 1976-   Periodicals

427 Indian Education. 1970?-1973?//. Irregular. Last issue 36 pages,
    last volume 56 pages, height 28 cm. Photographs. Published by
    Department of Indian Affairs and Northern Development, Ottawa, Ontario,
    Canada. Subject focus: education.

    CaACG   [v.1, n.2-v.3, n.3]   Periodicals
               [Fall, 1970-1973]

    Indian Education Newsletter. Madison, WI

        see American Indian Education Newsletter. Madison, WI

    Indian Education Newsletter. Medford, OR

        see Indian Student Services [Newsletter]. Medford, OR

428 Indian Education Newsletter. 1970-1975?//. Irregular. Last issue 14
    pages. ISSN 0318-000x. LC cn76-319938. OCLC 2030340. RLIN
    DCLCCN76319938-S, OHCP2030340-S. Line drawings. Available in
    microform: CPC (1970-1975). Published by Indian Education Resources
    Center, University of British Columbia, Vancouver, British Columbia,
    Canada. Subject focus: education, curriculum development.

    WHi   v.1, n.1-v.5, n.3/4;   Microforms
               Oct 23, 1970-Feb, 1975

    SdU   v.1, n.1-v.5, n.3/4;   Microfilm
               Oct 23, 1970-Feb, 1975

    CaACG   [v.1, n.1-v.5, n.3/4]   Periodicals
               [Oct 23, 1970-Feb, 1975]

    CaAEU   v.1, n.1-v.5, n.3/4;   Boreal
               Oct 23, 1970-Feb, 1975   Institute

    CaOONL   v.1, n.1-v.5, n.3/4;   Periodicals
               Oct 23, 1970-Feb, 1975

OPeT   v.1, n.1-v.5, n.3/4;   Microfiche
            Oct 23, 1970-Feb, 1975

429 Indian Education Record of Oklahoma. 1975. Irregular. Indian
    Education Record of Oklahoma, 716 S. Troost, Tulsa, OK 74120. (918)
    584-7221. OCLC 6194262. Height 28 cm. Line drawings, photographs.
    Published by Tulsa Indian Youth Council. Subject focus: educational
    programs.

    OkTU   v.1, n.1-   Rare Book
                Sept, 1975-   Room

    Other holding institutions: [Bacone College, Muskogee, OK].

430 The Indian Educator. 1978. Monthly during school year. $10. for
    individuals and institutions. The Indian Educator, c/o UIATF, 619 2nd
    Ave. #210, Seattle, WA 98104. (206) 325-0854. Last issue 12 pages,
    height 28 cm. Line drawings, photographs. Available in microform: WHi
    (1978). Published by United Indians of All Tribes Federation. Editor:
    Bruce Van Brocklin, Apr? 1979. Subject focus: adult and continuing
    education, teaching.

    WHi   v.1, n.3;   Microforms
                Apr?, 1978

    WU   v.2, n.3-   Periodicals
                Dec?, 1979-   Room

    WM   Current issues   Forest Home
                                                     Branch

    ICN   Current issues   CHAI

    Wa   v.1, n.3-   Periodicals
                Apr?, 1978-

    WaS   v.4-   Education
                1981-   Dept.

    Other holding institutions: [Dull Knife Memorial College, Lame Deer,
    MT].

    Indian-Eskimo Association of Canada Bulletin. Toronto, Ontario, Canada

        see Canadian Association in Support of Native Peoples Bulletin.
            Toronto, Ontario, Canada

431 <u>Indian Eskimo Friendship Centre Newsletter</u>. 1982? Bi-monthly.
Indian Eskimo Friendship Centre Newsletter, 66 Elm St. West, Sudbury,
Ontario, Canada P3C 1T5. Last issue 18 pages, height 28 cm. Line
drawings. Subject focus: urban community, health, social services,
employment information.

WHi   Oct/Nov, 1982–   Circulation

432 <u>Indian Family Defense</u>. 1974-1979//. Irregular. OCLC 1780927. RLIN
CTYG1780927-S, OHCP1780927-S, CLCL10472428-S. Last issue 12 pages.
Photographs. Available in microform: WHi (1974-1979). Published by
Association on American Indian Affairs, Inc, New York, NY. Editor:
Mary Gloyne Byler. Subject focus: child welfare, legislation.

WHi	v.1, n.1-11; Winter, 1974-Feb, 1979	Microforms
WMUW	v.1, n,1-11; Winter, 1974-Feb, 1979	(SPL) E/75/I53x
WU Soc Wk	v.1, n.1-10; Winter, 1974-June, 1978	Periodicals Section
AzFM	v.1, n.1-11; Winter, 1974-Feb, 1979	570.6/ A512if
AzNCC	v.1, n.3-11; Summer, 1974-Feb, 1979	Indian File
NjP	v.1, n.1-2, 11; Winter-Summer, 1974, Feb, 1979	Periodicals
NN	v.1, n.1-11; Winter, 1974-Feb, 1979	Periodicals
MtHi	n.8-11; Nov, 1977-Feb, 1979	Z/970.105 F21
OkTU	v.1, n.9-11; Feb, 1978-Feb, 1979	Rare Book Room

Other holding institutions: CLU (CLU), CU-UC (UCU), COFS (COF), CtY
(YUS), [Congressional Research Service, Washington, DC] (CRS), DI
(UDI), IC (CGP), MiEM (EEM), MnU-L (MLL), [University of Minnesota
Union List, Minneapolis, MN] (MUL), NbU (LDL), NmLcU (IRU), NIC,
(COO), [Western New York Library Resources Council, Buffalo, NY]
(VZX), OkOkU-L (OKY). TxArU (IUA), WM (GZD).

433 <u>Indian Forerunner</u>. 1972-1974//. Irregular. Last issue 6 pages.
Line drawings, photographs, commercial advertising. Available in
microform: McA (1972-1974). Published by Eight Northern Indian

Pueblos Council, San Juan Pueblo, NM. Community newsletter. Subject focus: Pueblo people. Editor: Juan Diego Aquino.

WHi	v.1, n.1-v.3; Feb, 1972-Fall, 1974	Microforms
WEU	v.1, n.1-v.2, n.8; Feb, 1972-Fall?, 1973	Microforms
AzNCC	v.3; 1974	Indian File
NjP	[v.1, n.1-v.3] [Feb, 1972-Fall, 1974]	Periodicals
OkU	v.1, n.1-v.3; Feb, 1972-Fall, 1974	WHC
CaOPeT	v.3; Jan-Fall, 1974	Microfilm

434 The Indian Helper. 1885-1900//. Weekly. Last issue 4 pages. Photographs. Available in microform: WHi-A, Papers of Carlos Montezuma, (1899-1900). Published by Indian Industrial School, Carlisle, PA. School newsletter.

WHi	[v.15, n.3-35]; [Nov 10, 1899-June 29, 1900]	Microforms
NjP	v.1, n.1-v.15, n.36; Aug 14, 1885-July 6, 1900	Periodicals
NN	v.7-v.12, n.52, v.13, n.20; Sept, 1891-Oct, 1897, Mar, 1898	SSR
PCarlH	[v.1, n.10-v.15, n.32] [1885-1900]	I/Per/Red2

435 The Indian Herald. 1875-?//. Monthly. Last issue 4 pages. Line drawings, commercial advertising. Pawhuska, OK. Available in microform: OkHi (1875, 1876, 1877). Editor: W. McKay Dougan. Newspaper. Also described in: Foreman, Carolyn Thomas. Oklahoma Imprints, 1835-1907. Norman: University of Oklahoma Press, 1936.

WHi	v.1, n.2, 8, v.2, n.16, 44; Feb, 1875, Jan 29, June 20, 1876, Jan 27, 1877	Microforms
OkHi	v.1, n.2, 8, v.2, n.16, 44; Feb, 1875, Jan 29, June 20, 1876, Jan 27, 1877	Microforms

436 Indian Highways. 1945. Irregular. Indian Highways, 708 S. Linden
Ave., Tempe, AZ 85281. (602) 968-9354. Last issue 4 pages. Line
drawings, photographs. Available in microform: McA (1945-); WHi-A,
Veda Stone Papers, (1965-1972). Published by Cook Christian Training
School. Place of publication varies: Phoenix, AZ, June, 1945-July,
1965. Previous editors: Rev. George Walker, Feb, 1956-Jan, 1966;
George W. Smart, June, 1966-July, 1967; Raymond G. Baines, July-Dec,
1969; Lemuel F. Ignacio, Mar, 1970-July, 1971; Sidney H. Byrd, Oct,
1971-Mar, 1976. Subject focus: Christian religion, education.

WHi	n.1– June, 1945–	Microforms
WEU ARC	[n.97-141] [Mar, 1965-June, 1972]	Micro 11
AzHC	May, 1979-Oct, 1981	Periodicals
AzNCC	June, 1972–	Indian File
ICN	Current issues	CHAI
NjP	[n.42-166] [Apr, 1956-Mar, 1978]	Periodicals
OkTU	n.162– Mar, 1977–	Rare Book Room
OkU	[n.1-n.?] [June, 1945-1972]	WHC
CaOPeT	n.1– June, 1945–	Microfilm

Other holding institutions: [Western Nevada Community College, Carson
City, NV].

The Indian Historian. San Francisco, CA

see Wassaja, The Indian Historian. San Francisco, CA

437 Indian Journal. 1876-1972//?. Weekly. Last issue 8 pages. Line
drawings, photographs, commercial advertising. Eufaula, OK.
Available in microform: OkHi (1894-1898). Place of publication
varies: Muskogee, OK, June 1-Dec 18, 1876, Oct 3, 1878-Mar 23, 1887.
Editors: William P. Ross, June 1-July 13, 1876; William P. Ross and M.
P. Roberts, Aug 10, 1876-Apr 26, 1877; M. P. Roberts, May 3, 1877-Dec
28, 1882; W. L. Squires and R. M. Roberts, Jan 4-25, 1883; R.M.
Roberts, Feb 1, 1883-Apr 29, 1887; Leo E. Bennett, May 5, 1887-Jan 5,
1888; S. B. Callahan, Jan 12-June 28, 1888; Albert A. Wortham and G.W.
Grayson, Jan 3, 1889-Jan 9, 1890; Albert A. Wortham, Jan 12-Aug. 21,
1890; I.W. Singleton, Jan 29, 1891-Oct 27, 1892; K. W. Whitmore, Feb

15, 1894-Aug 26, 1895; Mary E. Rule, Dec 21, 1972. Newspaper.
Subject focus: law, governmental relations.

WHi   [v.1, n.4-v.23, n.34], v.97, n.7;   Microforms
             [July 1, 1877-July 6, 1895], Dec 21, 1972

NjP   [v.1, n.4-v.94, n.38]   Periodicals
             [June 1, 1877-May 7, 1970]

OkHi   [v.1, n.4-v.23, n.34], v.97, n.7;   Microforms
             [July 1, 1877-July 6, 1895], Dec 21, 1972

OkTG   [v.1-v.4, v.69]   Periodicals
             [June 1, 1876-Apr 17, 1879, Aug 22, 1946]

438 Indian Law Reporter. 1974. Monthly. $225. for individuals and
    Institutions. Barbara Fritzmeyer, editor, Indian Law Reporter, 319
    MacArthur Blvd., Oakland, CA 94610. (415) 834-9333. ISSN 0097-1154.
    LC 74-648433. OCLC 1796534. RLIN MABL82-S94, DCLC74648433-S,
    CUDL1245-S, CSUP07176909-S, OHCP1796534-S, OHCP1779764-S. Last issue
    88 pages, last volume 1056 pages, height 28 cm. Available in
    microform: WSH (1974-1978). Published by American Indian Lawyer
    Training Program. Place of publication varies: Washington, DC, Jan,
    1974-?, 1979. Previous editors: Alan Parker, Jan-May, 1974; Alice
    Riehl, June-Sept, 1974; Kaye Armstrong, Nov, 1974-Nov, 1977; Maryann
    Lunderman, Dec, 1977-May, 1978; Kaye Armstrong, June, 1978-Dec, 1979;
    Carrie Small, Jan, 1980-May, 1981. Subject focus: law, court and
    administrative decisions, litigation reports.

WMUW   v.1, n.1-   REF/K/I38x
             Jan, 1974-

WU-L   v.1, n.1-   Periodicals
             Jan, 1974-   Section

WUSP   v.6, n.1-   Gov't Docs
             Jan, 1979-   Section

AzNCC   v.2-   Indian File
             Oct, 1975-

NjP   [v.1, n.2-v.6, n.4]   Periodicals
             [Feb, 1974-Apr, 1979]

N   v.1-   Law
             1974-

NHu   [v.3, n.12-v.5, n.12]   Periodicals
             [Dec, 1976-Dec, 1978]

SdU   v.2-   Law Library
             1975-

Wa   v.1-   Law
              1974-

CaOAFN   v.1, n.1-v.2, n.10;   Periodicals
              Jan, 1974-Oct, 1975

Other holding institutions: ArU (AFU), ArLUA-L (ALR), AzFU (AZN),
CChiS (CCH), CArcHT (CHU), CLobS (CLO), CLU (CLU), [Colorado Union
Catalog, Denver Public Library, Denver, CO] (CLF), [Denver Law
Librarians Group, Denver CO] (COY), DLC (DLC), [General Accounting
Office, Washington, DC] (GAO), DGW-L (GWL), DUSC (LAW), FMU-L (FML),
FTaSU-L (FSL), FU-L (FUB), ICarbS-L (SOL), InTV (IVZ), MiEM (EEM),
MiU-L (EYM), MnSAG (MAG), MnSH-L (MHL), [Univeristy of Minnesota Union
List, Minneapolis, MN] (MUL), MsU-L (MUW), MT-L (MTS), UdU-L (UNE),
NbU (LDL), NhD (DRB), NmU-L (NML), [New York State Union List, Albany,
NY] (NYS), NNJJ (VVJ), NNYU (YYP), NA1LS (YZA), [University of Akron
Law Library, Akron, OH] ((AKL), [University of Cincinnati, Marx Law
Library, Cincinnati, OH] (OML), OTU-L (UTL), OkU-L (OKL), OkOkU-L
(OKY), OrPL-L (ONS), PPiU-L (PLA), [AMIGOS Union List of Serials,
Dallas, TX] (IUC), [Southern Methodist University Law Library, Dallas,
TX] (IUF), TxU (TXQ), ULA (UUS), [WGrU-Native American Studies Dept.].

439 The Indian Leader. 1897. Bi-weekly during school year. $1. for
    individuals and institutions. June Adams, editor, The Indian Leader,
    Haskell Indian Junior College, Lawrence, KS 66044. (913) 841-2000,
    ext. 243. ISSN 0364-8028. LC ca06-1655. OCLC 1752948. RLIN
    NYPG774141217-S, OHCP1752948-S, DCLCCA061655-S. Last issue 4 pages,
    Last volume 52 pages, height 44 cm. Line drawings, photographs.
    Available in microform: WHi-A, Veda Stone Papers, (1977); BHP
    (1914-1973). Published by Haskell Indian Junior College. Frequency
    varies: weekly during school year, Sept, 1914-May 12, 1939. Previous
    editors: J. R. Wise, Sept, 1914-Apr 20, 1917; H. B. Peairs, Apr 27,
    1917-Dec 29, 1922; Mitchell Bush, Sept 25, 1953-May 14, 1954; Albert
    Brewer, Oct 27, 1954-Apr 8, 1955; Mildred Sittingbull, Sept 30-Dec 14,
    1955; Edward Haag, Oct 12-Nov 23, 1956; Doris Fields, Nov 22-Jan 10,
    1957; Oran LaPointe, Jan 24-Feb 28, 1958; Wynona Brokenboulder, Mar
    14-May 9, 1958; Joanne Kitchkom, Oct 10-Dec 12, 1958; Theresa Bird,
    Mar 27-Apr 10, 1959; Dixie Whitetree, Oct 23-Nov, 1959; Gerald
    Jackson, Jan 8-Mar 11, 1960; Joy Spicer, Mar 25-May 13, 1960; Jane
    Wade, Oct 14-Nov 11, 1960; Rose Marie Powell, Nov 25, 1960-May 12,
    1961; Florence Albert, Oct 27-Dec 8, 1961; Judy Hammons, Oct 26-Dec
    14, 1962; Lena Washington, Jan 12-May 11, 1962; Gloria Holden, Jan
    11-May 10, 1963; Lillie Hulbutta, Oct 23-Dec 11, 1964; Jackie Wopate,
    Jan 8, 1963-May 13, 1966; Lucinda Rios, Nov 17, 1967-May 3, 1968;
    Eloise Willow, Sept 20-May 16, 1969; William Howell, Sept 14, 1973-Feb
    22, 1974; Fain Haumpo, Jr., Apr 25, 1975; Charles Nestell, May 14,
    1975-Jan 30, 1976; Kim Black, Feb 10, 1978-Mar 14, 1980; Cindy
    Conklin, Mar 28-Dec 12, 1980. College newsletter.

WHi   v.18, n.3-   Microforms
              Sept, 1914-

WEU   v.80, n.10;   Micro 11
ARC   Mar 4, 1977

WMM	v.21, n.12, v.26, n.26; Nov 23, 1917, Mar 23, 1923	Special Collections
WMUW	[v.78, n.9-v.82, n.15]; [Jan 31, 1975-May 16, 1979]	(SPL) E/75/I54x
AzHC	v.34-v.60; Sept, 1930-May, 1956	Periodicals
AzNCC	v.75-v.84; 1972-Apr 3, 1981	Indian File
ICN	Current issues	CHAI
KHi	v.1, n.1- Mar 6, 1897-	Periodicals
NjP	[v.75, n.1-v.82, n.15] [Sept 17, 1971-May 16, 1979]	Periodicals
N	v.28, n.3-v.53, n.15; Sept 12, 1924-May 12, 1940	C371.975/ qI39
OkTU	v.81, n.8-v.85, n.7; Jan, 1978-Mar, 1982	Rare Book Room
OkU	[v.17, n.21-v.76, n.8] [Jan, 1914-May, 1973]	WHC
CaOPeT	[v.42-v.82], v.83- [1937-1979], 1980-	E97/H43

Other holding institutions: CLobS (CLO), DLC (DLC), ICNE (IAO),
[University of Minnesota Union List, Minneapolis, MN] (MUL), [Standing
Rock Community College Library, Fort Yates, ND], OkAdE (ECO), PP
(PLF), [U. S. Government Printing Office-Serials, Alexandria, VA]
(GPA).

440 <u>Indian Liahona</u>. 1963-?//?. Bi-monthly. ISSN 0445-7838. OCLC
4538285. RLIN OHCP4538285-S. Last issue 32 pages, height 28 cm.
Line drawings, photographs. Published by Church of Jesus Christ of
the Latter Day Saints, Salt Lake City, UT. Subject focus: Mormon
Church.

WEU	v.7, n,4-v.8, n.2; July/Aug, 1970-Mar/Apr, 1971	Journalism Lab
NjP	[v.1-v.7] [Summer, 1963-Dec, 1970]	Periodicals
OkU	v.4, n.3-v.8, n.3; June, 1967-June, 1971	WHC

SdU   v.5-v.6;   South
             1967-1968   Dakota Room

Other holding institutions: [University of Minnesota, Minneapolis, MN]
(MUL).

441 <u>Indian Life</u>. 1966-1979?//. Irregular. LC sc82-4102. OCLC 4899838,
    6169188. RLIN DCLCSC824102-S. Last issue 8 pages. Line drawings,
    photographs, commercial advertising. Available in microform: WHi
    (1973-1979); WHi-A, Veda Stone Papers, (1973, 1974). Published by
    Christian Hope Indian Eskimo Fellowship (CHIEF), West Sedonia, AZ.
    Place of publication varies: Rapid City, SD, Mar, 1973-May/June, 1976;
    Orange, CA, July/Aug, 1976-Summer, 1978. Subject focus: missions,
    Christian religion.

    WHi   v.6, n.5-v.13, n.6;   Microforms
                 Mar?, 1973-Feb?, 1979

    WEU   v.6, n.4, v.8, n.4;   Micro 11
    ARC   Feb?, 1973, ?, 1974

    WMM   v.9, n.2;   Special
                 Jan?, 1975   Collections

    WMUW   v.6, n.3, v.11, n.2;   (SPL)
                 1972, Mar/Apr, 1977   E/75/I55x

    AzNCC   v.11-v.13, n.6;   Indian File
                 1977-Feb?, 1979

    CL   v.11, n.1-v.13, n.6;   Periodicals
                 Jan/Feb, 1977-Feb?, 1979

    MnBemT   [v.10-v.11], v.12-v.13, n.6;   Periodicals
                 [1976-1977], 1978-Feb?, 1979

    NjP   [v.7, n.5-v.11, n.2]   Periodicals
                 [1973-Mar/Apr, 1977]

    PPT   v.10, n.5-6;   Contemporary
                 Sept/Nov-Dec, 1976   Culture

    Other holding institutions: [University of Minnesota Union List,
    Minneapolis, MN] (MUL), NmG.

442 <u>Indian Life</u>. 1912?-1960?//. Annual. ISSN 0098-7948, 0364-1201. LC
    75-641568, 75-641788. OCLC 2240546, 2744938. RLIN DCLC75641788-S,
    CUBU12790941-S, OCHP2744938. Last issue 50 pages. Line drawings,
    photographs. Available in microform: McA (1954-1961). Published by
    Inter-Tribal Indian Ceremonial Association, Gallup, NM. Title varies:
    Ceremonial Magazine, Aug, 1954-Aug, 1958. Editor: Edward S. Merry.
    Subject focus: ceremonial arts, crafts, culture, legends.

WHi	Aug, 1954-Aug, 1961	Microforms
AzFM	1940-1960	570.6/G175i1
MoSHi	1955, 1960	970.1/In2L
NjP	Aug, 1961	Periodicals
NmG	Aug, 1939-Aug, 1961	Periodicals
OkPAC	1957, 1959-1961	Periodicals
OkU	[Aug, 1954-June, 1973]	WHC
CaOPeT	Aug, 1954-Aug, 1961	Microfilm

Other holding institutions: DLC (DLC) MH-P (HLS), [Western Nevada
Community College, Carson City, NV], NmPE (IPU), NmLcU (IRU), Ok
(OKD), WaU (WAU), [Wisconsin Indian Resource Council, Stevens Point,
WI].

443 Indian Life. 1966-1974?//. Irregular. Published by American Indian
Mission, Inc., Custer, SD. Title varies: American Indian Life,
1968?-1970. Editor: R.L. Gowan. Subject focus: missions, Christian
religion.

SdHRC	v.3, n.1-v.7, n.6; 1968-1974	Periodicals

444 Indian Life Magazine. 1979. Bi-monthly. $3. for individuals and
institutions. George McPeek, editor, P.O. Box 3765, Station B,
Winnipeg, Manitoba, Canada R2W 3R6 (204) 338-0311. ISSN 0226-9317.
OCLC 6169243. RLIN NJPG2463-S. Last issue 16 pages, last volume 96
pages, height 28 cm. Line drawings, photographs, some in color,
commercial advertising. Published by Intertribal Christian
Communication Ministries International. Subject focus: Christian
religion, culture.

WHi	v.1, n.1- Nov/Dec, 1979-	Circulation
WMUW	v.1, n.1- Nov/Dec, 1979-	(SPL) E/75/I57x
AkBC	v.1, n.1- Nov/Dec, 1979-	Periodicals
OkU	v.1,n.1- Nov/Dec, 1979-	WHC

Indian Life Newsletter. New York, NY

   see American Indian News. New York, NY

445 Indian Magazine. 1967-1970//. Monthly. Last issue 2 pages, height 36 cm. Available in microform: WHi (1967-1970). Published by Canadian Broadcasting Corporation, Toronto, Ontario, Canada. Place of Publication varies: Montreal, Quebec, Canada, Sept 23, 1967-Mar 29, 1969. Frequency varies: weekly, Sept 23, 1967-Mar 29, 1969. Subject focus: national news. Broadcast reprints.

WHi	[Sept 23, 1967-Mar 29, 1969]	Microforms
NjP	[Oct 19, 1968-Sept, 1970]	Periodicals
CaACG	[Aug, 1967-Mar, 1970]	Periodicals
CaOORD	[Dec 16, 1967-Aug, 1970]	Periodicals
CaOPeT	Jan-Sept, 1970	Microfilm

446 Indian Mailman. 1962?-?// Monthly. ISSN 0455-7862. OCLC 2397878. RLIN OHCP2397878-S. Last issue 3 pages, height 39 cm. Available in microform: WHi (1964). Published by the Arizona Indian Association, Phoenix, AZ. Community newsletter.

WHi	Oct/Nov, 1964	Microforms
NjP	[Oct, 1962-Dec, 1967]	Periodicals
UPB	[Feb, 1964-Dec, 1970	970.49105/IN2

Other holding institutions: DI (UDI).

447 Indian Mission. ?//. Unknown. Last issue 4 pages, height 24 cm. Line drawings. Published by Immaculate Heart of Mary Indian School, Dunseith, ND. Subject focus: missions, education, Catholic Church, Chippewa people.

WMM	v.1, n.1; [no date]	Special Collections

448 The Indian Missionary. 1884-1891?//. Monthly. Last issue 9 pages. Commercial advertising. Atoka, OK. Available in microform: OkHi (1884-1891); SBC (1884-1891). Place of publication varies: McAlester, OK, Sept, 1884-Apr, 1886; South Canadian, OK, May-Nov, 1886. Previous editors: W.P. Blake and A. Frank Ross, Sept-Dec, 1884; A. Frank Ross, Jan-Mar, 1885; W. P. Blake, July, 1885; A. Frank Ross, Aug-Sept, 1885;

Daniel Rogers, Oct, 1885–Nov, 1886; J. S. Murrow, Dec, 1886–Sept, 1891. Subject focus: missions, Baptist Church. Some columns in Choctaw, Chickasaw and Seminole. Also described in: Foreman, Carolyn Thomas. Oklahoma Imprints, 1835–1907. Norman: University of Oklahoma Press, 1936.

WHi   v.1, n.1–v.7, n.9;   Microforms
           Sept, 1884–Sept, 1891

OkHi   v.1, n.1–v.7, n.9;   Microforms
           Sept, 1884–Sept, 1891

OkTG   v.3, n.12, v.4, n.5;   Periodicals
           Dec, 1886, May, 1887

OkU   v.1, n.1–v.7, n.9;   WHC
           Sept, 1884–Sept, 1891

Indian Missionary Record. Lebret, Saskatchewan, Canada

   see Indian Record. Winnipeg, Manitoba, Canada

449 The Indian Nation. 1975?//. Unknown. Last issue 28 pages, height 44 cm. Line drawings, photographs. Chase, British Columbia, Canada. Editor: Ken Dennis. Subject focus: rights, sovereignty.

   CaOAFN   Oct, 1975   Periodicals

450 Indian Nations of the Eastern United States. 1982. Monthly. $30. for individuals and institutions. Bobby Jerry Locklear, editor, Indians of the Eastern United States, P.O. Box 37, Maxton, NC 28364. Last issue 33 pages, height 28 cm. Line drawings. Published by BJL Publications. Subject focus: genealogy.

   NcP   v.1, n.1–   Periodicals
             Apr, 1982–

451 Indian Natural Resources. 1977–1980//. Irregular. OCLC 5159860. Last issue 8 pages, height 28 cm. Photographs. Available in microform: WHi (1977–1980). Published by Association on American Indian Affairs, Inc., New York, NY. Frequency varies: quarterly, May–Dec, 1977. Editors: Mary Gloyne Byler, May, 1977–Feb, 1979; Steven Unger, Dec, 1980. Subject focus: ecology, land claims, governmental relations.

   WHi   n.1–6;   Microforms
             May, 1977–Dec, 1980

WMUW	n.1; May, 1977	(SPL) E/75/I58x
WUSP	n.6; Dec, 1980	Periodicals
AzNCC	n.?-6; Jan, 1978-Dec, 1980	Indian File
OkTU	n.3-6; Dec, 1977-Dec, 1980	330.017497 I39
OkU	n.6; Dec, 1980	WHC

Other holding institutions: AzU (AZU), DI (UDI). IC (CGP), MoUst (UMS), NmLcU (IRU), TxArU (IUA), WM (GZD).

452 <u>Indian News</u>. 1961-?//. Monthly. RLIN MIUG82-S6995. Last issue 17 pages. Available in microform: WHi-A, Veda Stone Papers, (1961-1962, 1963). Published by New Mexico Commission on Indian Affairs, Santa Fe, NM. Subject focus: legislation, land claims.

WHi	Nov, 1961-June, 1962, Jan-Mar, June, Dec,1963	Microforms
WEU ARC	Nov, 1961-June, 1962, Jan-Mar, June, Dec,1963	Micro 11
NjP	Nov, 1961-Mar, 1964	Periodicals
OkU	Jan, 1962-Mar, 1964	WHC
SdU	1966-1969	South Dakota Room

Other holding institutions: MH-P (HLS), MiU (EYM).

453 <u>Indian News/Nouvelles Indiennes</u>. 1954-1982//. Monthly. ISSN 0019-6029. LC cn77-70313. OCLC 1697242. RLIN NYPG814229541-S, OHCP1697242-S, DCLCCN7770313-S, DCLCCF7770313-S, DCLCCE7770313-S, CUBG30991705-S, OHCP4249539-S. Last issue 16 pages, last volume 180 pages, height 44 cm. Line drawings, photographs. Available in microform: WHi (1966-1982); WHi-A, Veda Stone Papers (1968-1970); MML (1954-). Published by Indian and Inuit Affairs Program, Ottawa, Ontario, Canada. Frequency varies: quarterly, Apr, 1966-Dec, 1967. Previous editors: Keith R. Miller, Aug, 1967-Oct, 1969; David Monture, Nov, 1969-June, 1971; Theresa Nahanee, July, 1971-Dec, 1973; Howard Bernard, Jan, 1974-June, 1982. Newspaper. In French, 50%.

| WHi | v.9, n.1-v.23, n.3;
Apr, 1966-June, 1982 | Microforms |

WEU ARC	v.11, n.3-7, v.12, n.8-10 Oct, 1968-Mar, Nov, 1969-Jan, 1970	Micro 11
WGrU	v.14, n.1-v.20, n.4; Apr, 1971-Aug, 1979	R31-10/
AkUF	[v.17, n.9-v.23, n.3] [1976-June., 1982]	E/78/C2/I58
AzNCC	v.13-v.23, n.3; May, 1970-June, 1982	Indian File
CL	v.13, n.8-v.23, n.3; Nov, 1970-June, 1982	Periodicals
NjP	[v.1, n.3-v.20, n.1] [Apr, 1955-May, 1979]	Periodicals
OkTU	v.17, n.12-v.23, n.3; Dec?, 1976-June, 1982	Rare Book Room
OkU	[v.4, n.1-v.22, n.11] [1959-1980]	WHC
WaU	[Special edition] June 25, 1969	Periodicals
CaACG	v.1, n.1-v.23, n.3; Aug, 1954-June, 1982	Periodicals
CaAEU	v.1-v.23, n.3; 1954-June, 1982	Boreal Institute
CaBAbF	v.15-v.23,n.3; Oct, 1974-June, 1982	Periodicals
CaNBFU	v.1-v.23, n.3; 1954-June, 1982	Gov Docs
CaOAFN	v.21, n.10-v.23, n.3; Jan, 1981-June, 1982	Periodicals
CaOAUC	v.10-v.23, n.3; 1967-June, 1982	Periodicals
CaOONL	v.1-v.23, n.3; Aug, 1954-June, 1982	Periodicals
CaOOP	v.1-v.23, n.3; Aug, 1954-June, 1982	E/78/C2/A15
CaOPeT	v.1-v.23, n.3; Aug, 1954-June, 1982	Periodicals
CaOSuU	[v.20-v.23] [1979-1982]	Periodicals

CaYW   [v.14, n.?–v.22, n.7]   Periodicals
            [June, 1971–1982]

Other holding institutions: CU–UC (UCU), DeU (DLM), [University of
Minnesota Union List, Minneapolis, MN] (MUL), NhD (DRB), NSyU (SYB),
NCaS (XLM), NGenoU (YGM), NOneoU (ZBM), NPotU (ZQM), OkU (OKU), PPiU
(PIT), TxU (IXA), WM (GZD), WGrU (GZW).

454 Indian News Clips. 1971–1978?//. Irregular. Last issue 48 pages,
    height 28 cm. Photographs. Published by Bureau of Indian Affairs,
    Washington, DC. Reprints of articles on Native Americans from
    establishment papers.

    CaOAFN   [v.6, n.21–v.8, n.17]   Periodicals
                [May 22, 1976–Aug 19, 1978]

455 Indian News Notes. 1977? Unknown. Indian News Notes, Bureau of
    Indian Affairs, Office of Public Information, Washington, DC 20240.
    (202) 343-7445. Last issue 4 pages, height 28 cm. Subject focus:
    Bureau staff news, rights, law, land claims.

    WHi   Summer?, 1982–   Circulation

    SdU   [Feb 1, 1978–June 27, 1979]   Periodicals

456 Indian Newsletter. 1968–?//. Monthly? Last issue 8 pages, height 28
    cm. Line drawings, photographs. Published by Access–Pala, Pala, CA.
    Subject focus: urban community news.

    WEU   Oct, 1970–Sept, 1972   Jouralism
                                                         Lab

    CSmarP   1970–1972   Stacks

457 Indian Notes. 1924–1934//. Quarterly. ISSN 0196-3015. LC 24–11173,
    sc79–3927. OCLC 1604815, 2449085. RLIN DCLCSC793927-S,
    CUBG49302103-S, CUBU12854219-S, OHCP2449085-S, OHCP1604815-S. Last
    issue 172 pages, last volume 581 pages, height 18 cm. Line drawings,
    photographs. Available in microform: BHP (1924–1930). Published by
    Museum of the American Indian, Heye Foundation, New York, NY.
    Frequency varies: irregular, June–Oct, 1924. Subject focus:
    anthropology, archaeology, art, ethnology.

    WHi   v.1, n.1–v.7, n.4;   PW83/
                Jan, 1924–Oct, 1930   8M98IN

    WMM   [v.2, n.2–v.7, n.4]   Special
                [Apr, 1925–Oct, 1930]   Collections

WMMus	v.1, n.1-v.11, n.1/2; Jan, 1924-Jan/Feb, 1934	572.07/ M972n
AzFM	v.1-v.6; 1924-1929	570.6/H61i
AzNCC	v.1-v.5, 1924-1928	Indian File
IaHi	v.2, n.2-v.7, n.4; Apr, 1925-Oct, 1930	E/51/I35
MtHi	v.6. n.1-v.7, n.4; 1929-Oct, 1930	Z/970.105 In2m
NjP	v.1, n.1-v.7, n.4; Jan, 1924-Oct, 1930	Periodicals
N	v.1-v.11, n.1/2; 1925-Jan/Feb, 1934	J970.1/ N54b
OkU	v.1, n.1-v.7; Jan., 1924-Dec., 1930	WHC
CaACG	[v.1, n.1-v.7, n.4] [Jan, 1924-Oct, 1930]	Periodicals

Other holding institutions: ArU (AFU), [Amerind Foundation, Inc.,
Dragoon, AZ], AzFU (AZN), AzTes (AZS), DeU (DLM), FTaSU (FDA), FOFT
(FTU), ICL (IAL), [Indiana Union List of Serials, Indianapolis, IN]
(ILS), MWC (CKM), MiEM (EEM), MiMtpT (EXC), MnSH-L (MHS), [University
of Minnesota Union List, Minneapolis, MN] (MUL), NmU (IQU), [New York
State Union List, Albany, NY] (NYS), NDFM (VZE), NSbSU (YSM), OAKU
(AKR), OAK (APL), OCl (CLE), OClw (CWR), OKentU (KSU), [Pittsburgh
Regional Library Center Union List, Pittsburgh, PA] (QPR), [AMIGOS
Union List of Serials, Dallas, TX] (IUC), TxLT (ILU), TxU (IXA).

458 Indian Observer. 1911-?//. Monthly. Last issue 4 pages. Available
im microform: WHi-A, Papers of Carlos Montezuma, (1911). Washington,
DC. Subject focus: rights, legislation.

| WHi | v.1,n.1;
Jan, 1911 | Microforms |

459 Indian Orphan. 1903?-?//. Monthly. Height 32 cm. Photographs.
Published by Murrow Indian Orphans' Home, Atoka, OK. Editor: J.S.
Murrow. School newsletter.

| OkTG | [no nos.], v.7, n.1, 3, 8, 15;
June, 1903, Mar 1, June 1,
Oct 1, Nov 1, 1908 | Periodicals |

460 Indian Outlook. 1923-1931?//. Monthly, irregular. Height 32 cm.
Line drawings, photographs. Published by American Indian Institute,
Wichita, KS. Editor: H.R. Cloud. Subject focus: education.

    CtY-B   [v.1, n.1-v.9, n.1]
               [Nov 1, 1923-1931]   Zc13/E3/+In2

461 Indian Outlook. 1960-1963?//. Irregular. ISSN 0384-1901. LC
cn76-302203. OCLC 2534234. Last issue 6 pages, height 28 cm. Line
drawings, photographs. Published by Federation of Saskatchewan
Indians, Regina, Saskatchewan, Canada. Community newsletter. Subject
focus: Saskatchewan Native people.

    CaOONL   v.1, n.1-3, ?;
              May, 1960-June, 1961, May, 1963   B-338-5

462 Indian Pride. 1979-?//. Monthly. Last issue 18 pages, height 43 cm.
Line drawings, photographs. Published by Robeson County Board of
Education, Lumberton, NC. Community newsletter. Subject focus:
education, educational opportunities.

    WUSP   May, 1980   Native American
                                                  Center

463 Indian Programs. 1969-1980//. Irregular. ISSN 0572-4112. OCLC
4153830. OHCP4153830-S. Last issue 8 pages, height 28 cm. Line
drawings, photographs. Published by University of Arizona, Tucson,
AZ. Previous editor: Stanley Throssell, May, 1975-Summer, 1976.
Subject focus: Native American studies, curriculum development.

    WHi   v.1, n.1-v.3, n.1;
           Spring, 1969-Spring. 1980   E/97/I4

    WMUW   v.2, n.9;
           Summer, 1977   (SPL)
                                                  E/75/I62x

    AzFM   v.1, n.1-v.3, n.1;
           Spring, 1969-Spring. 1980   570.6/I39p

    AzNCC   v.1-v.2, n.9;
           June, 1975-Summer, 1977   Indian File

    NjP   [v.1, n.1-v.2, n.10]
           [Spring, 1969-Spring, 1979]   Periodicals

    OkTU   [v.2, n.3-9]
           [Spring, 1972-Summer, 1977]   Rare Book
                                                    Room

    OkU   [v.1, n.1-v.2, n.3]
           [Spring, 1969-Summer, 1972]   WHC

CaOPeT   v.1-2. v.5-   Periodicals
           1960-1970, 1975-

Other holding institutions: [University of Minnesota Union List,
Minneapolis, MN] (MUL).

464 The Indian Progress. 1963-1967//. Unknown. OCLC 1752971.
    OHCP1752971-S. Last issue 8 pages, height 28 cm. Line drawings,
    photographs. Available in microform: WHi-A, Veda Stone Papers, (1961,
    1962-1965). Published by Workshop on American Indian Affairs,
    Boulder, CO. Editors: Jerri Chitwood and Hattie Thundercloud, July
    8-Aug 3, 1960; Clyde Warrior and Bernadine Eschief, July 10, 1961-Mar
    30, 1962; Maria Elena Olguin, July 18-24, 1963; Tom Cochnauer, June
    18, 1964; Clara Anderson, July 15, 1965, LaVonna A. Weller, July 25,
    1966. Subject focus: workshops, rights, law.

    WHi   July 18-24, 1963, June 18, 1964,   Pam 76-833
              July 15, 1965, July 25, 1966-July, 1967

    WHi   July 10, 1961, Mar 30, 1962-July 15, 1965 Microforms

    WEU   July 10, 1961, Mar 30, 1962-July 15, 1965 Micro 11
    ARC

    WMM   July 8, 1960-Mar 30, 1962   Special
                                                         Collection

    NjP   July 24, 1963, July 15,1965,   Periodicals
              July 25, 1966

    OkU   June, 1963. July,1964, July, 1965   WHC

    Other holding institutions: [Indiana Union List of Serials,
    Indianapolis, IN] (ILS), [University of Minnesota Union List,
    Minneapolis, MN] (MUL).

465 Indian Progress. 1955?. 3 times a year. $2. for individuals and
    institutions. Sterrett L. Nash, editor, Indian Progress, 612 Plum
    St., Box 161, Frankton, IN 46044. (317) 754-7977. ISSN 0046-9041.
    Last issue 4 pages, last volume 12 pages, height 32 cm. Line
    drawings, photographs. Published by Associated Committee of Friends
    on Indian Affairs. Place of publication varies: Noblesville, IN,
    June, 1971-June, 1977. Previous editors: Sterret L. Nash and Grace K.
    Nash, Feb, 1979-Feb, 1980. Subject focus: association news, programs.

    WHi   June, 1971-   Circulation

    WEU   [Oct, 1969-June, 1970]   Journalism
                                                         Lab

    WGrU   Current year   Periodicals

AzNCC   Feb, 1978–
                                            Indian File

OkTU   Oct, 1976–
                                            Rare Book
                                            Room

UPB   [1959–Feb,] June, 1982–
                                            970.105IN2P

466 The Indian Progress. 1966?–?//. Unknown. Last issue 8 pages. Line
    drawings, photographs. Available in microform: WHi–A, Veda Stone
    Papers, (1967). Published by American Indian Development, Inc.,
    Albuquerque, NM. Subject focus: rights, legislation, culture, poetry.

    WHi   n.13;
               July, 1967   Microforms

    WEU   n.13;
    ARC   July, 1967   Micro 11

467 Indian Progress. 1875–?//. Weekly. Height 60 cm. Commerical
    advertising. Published by Progress Publishing Company, Muskogee, OK.
    Newspaper.

    OkTG   v.1, n.1;
               Oct 22, 1875   Periodicals

468 Indian Pueblo Legal Services Newsletter. 1979–?//. Unknown. Last
    issue 4 pages, height 40 cm. Line drawings, photographs. Laguna, NM.
    Subject focus: legal aid.

    WHi   v.1, n.1;
               July/Aug, 1979   Microforms

469 Indian Record. 1966. Bi–monthly. Indian Record, Department of the
    Interior, 1951 Constitution Ave, N. W., Washington, DC 20245. (202)
    343–7445. ISSN 0537–2488. OCLC 1589991. RLIN CSUP041973–S,
    CUBG05757–S, OHCP1589991–S. Last issue 8 pages, height 28 cm.
    Photographs. Available in microform: WHi–A, Veda Stone Papers, (1967,
    1968, 1969–1971). Published by Bureau of Indian Affairs. Frequency
    varies: monthly, Mar, 1967–Nov, 1970. Subject focus: Bureau of Indian
    Affairs activities and programs.

    WHi   Mar, 1967, Sept, 1968,
               Feb, 1969–Aug/Sept, 1971   Microforms

    WHi   Aug, 1970–Jan/Feb, 1972
                                            I20.55: 1970–72

    WEU   Oct, 1969–
                                            Microforms

WEU	Mar, 1967, Sept, 1968,	Micro 11
ARC	Feb, 1969-Aug/Sept, 1971	
WMUW	[Oct, 1969-July, 1978]	(SPL)
		E/75/I63x
WOshU	1968-1974	Periodicals
AzNCC	June, 1978-	Indian File
CL	Aug, 1970-Jan/Feb, 1972	Periodicals
ICN	Current issues	CHAI
LARC	Aug, 1970-Jan/Feb, 1972	Periodicals
MtHi	[Mar, 1968-July, 1978]	Z/970.105/R245
NjP	[Dec, 1966-June. 1978]	Periodicals
NmG	June, 1968, Jan, 1969, July, 1970	Periodicals
NPotU	1970-1971	E/77/I5
NdMinS	Mar, 1970-Sept, 1975	Periodicals
OrU	[Mar, 1968-Jan/Feb, 1972]	Periodicals
SdU	Dec, 1966-Feb, 1972	Gov. Docs.

Other holding institutions: DI (UDI), [Indiana Union List of Serials, Indianapolis, IN] (ILS), MiU (EYM), [University of Minnesota Union List, Minneapolis, MN] (MUL), OKTU (OKT), PPiU (PIT), [University of Wisconsin-Stevens Point-Native American Center, Stevens Point, WI].

470 Indian Record. 1886-1887?//. Monthly. Last issue 4 pages, photographs. Published by Presbytery of the Indian Territory, Muskogee, OK. Subject focus: missions, Presbyterian Church, politics.

WHi	v.1, n.2-9;	Microforms
	June, 1886-Mar, 1887	
NjP	v.1, n.2-9;	Microfilm
	June, 1886-Mar, 1887	

471 Indian Record. 1938. Quarterly. $4. for individuals and institutions. Rev. Gontran Laviolette, editor, Indian Record, 1301 Wellington Crescent, Winnipeg, Manitoba, Canada R3N 0A9. (204) 489-9593. ISSN 0019-6282. LC 76-319940. OCLC 2030416. RLIN DCLCCN76319940-S, NYPG152-S, OHCP2030416. Last issue 24 pages, height 28 cm. Line drawings, photographs, commercial advertising. Available in microform: McA (1973-); CPC (1964-1978); MML (1938-). Published by

Oblate Fathers. Title varies: The Indian Missionary Record, Mar,
1946-Dec, 1956. Place of publication varies: Lebret, Saskatchewan,
Canada, Mar, 1946-July/Aug, 1947; St. Boniface, Manitoba, Canada, Dec,
1947-Oct, 1951; Ottawa, Ontario, Canada, Jan, 1952-Dec, 1956.
Frequency varies: bi-monthly, Jan, 1974-Nov/Dec, 1977. Subject focus:
missions, Catholic Church.

WHi	[v. 27, n.5-v.32, n.4/5], v.36, n.1/2- [May, 1964-Apr/May, 1969], Jan/Feb, 1973-	Microforms
WMM	[v.9, n.3-v.35, n.3/4] [Mar, 1946-May/June, 1972]	Special Collections
AzNCC	1979-	Indian File
CU-A	v.34, n.3/4- May?, 1971-	E/77/A1.I532
NjP	[v.27, n.5-v.41,n.12] [May, 1964-Jan/Apr, 1977]	Periodicals
NcJ	v.43- 1980-	Periodicals
OkU	v.26, n.1- Jan/Feb, 1963-	WHC
UBP	v.26, n.4- 1963-	970.4105/IN3
CaACG	[v.8-v.19], v.20, n.1- [Jan, 1945-May, 1956], Jan, 1957-	Periodicals
CaAEU	v.1- 1938-	Boreal Institute
CaMWU	v.27-v.32; 1964-1969	Microfiche
CaMWU	v.33-v.38; 1970-1975	970/I392/Re
CaNBFU	v.43- 1980-	E/75/I74
CaOAFN	v.44, n.3- Summer, 1981-	Periodicals
CaOONL	[v.1-v.38], v.39- [1938-1975], 1976-	Periodicals
CaOPeT	v.17, v.19, [v.30-38], v.40- 1954, 1946, [1967-1975, 1977-	Microfilm

Other holding institutions: CChiS (CCH), CLU (CLU), CU-UC (UCU),
[University of Minnesota Union List, Minneapolis, MN] (MUL), CaBViP.

472 Indian Record Bulletin. 1970?-?//. Bi-weekly. Last issue 2 pages.
Available in microform: WHi-A, Veda Stone Papers, (1970-1971).
Washington, DC. Subject focus: education, Native American press.

WHi   Dec 16, 1970-Jan 12, 1971   Microforms

WEU   Dec 16, 1970-Jan 12, 1971   Micro 11
ARC

473 Indian Relic Trader. 1981. Quarterly. $7. for individuals and
institutions. James L. Green and James E. Weidmer, editors, Indian
Relic Trader, Box 13044 Whitehall, OH 43213. (614) 237-8834. Last
issue 16 pages, height 39 cm. Line drawings, photographs, commercial
advertising. Subject focus: relics.

WHi   v.2, n.2;   Pam
           Spring, 1982   Cataloging

The Indian Reporter: The Newspaper of the Southern California Indian.
        Hemet, CA

    see Your Indian Reporter. Hemet, CA

474 Indian Reserve Forest Survey Report. 1963-1969?//. Unknown.
Published by Forest Management Institute, Ottawa, Ontario, Canada.
Subject focus: reservations, forestry, forestry surveys.

WaU   n.1-15, 17-29;   SD13/A28
           1963-1969

475 Indian School Bulletin. 1947?-?//. 5 times a year. Last issue 6
pages, height 35 cm. Line drawings, photographs. Published by Indian
Affairs Branch, Education Divison, Ottawa, Ontario, Canada. Subject
focus: elementary education.

CaACG   v.10, n.3;   Periodicals
           Jan, 1956

476 Indian School Journal. 1901-1980//. Bi-monthly during school year.
ISSN 0364-7056. LC cau06-1219, sc78-2038. OCLC 1589965, 2371409.
RLIN DCLCSC782038-S, OHCP2371409-S, OHCP1589965-S. Last issue 8
pages, height 28 cm. Line drawings, photographs. Available in
microform: CPC (1901-1979). Published by Chilocco Indian School,
Chilocco, OK. Title varies: Chilocco Farmer and Stock Grower
(supercedes The Chilocco Beacon), Mar, 1902-Apr 15, 1904. Frequency
varies: monthly, Mar, 1902-Jan, 1921; weekly, Oct, 1952-Sept, 1968.

Editors: S. M. McCowan, Feb-Dec, 1905; Edgar A. Allen, Sept, 1912-Jan, 1918; Oscar H. Lipps, Apr 1918-June, 1919; Clyde M. Blair, Dec, 1919-Apr, 1926; L.E. Correll, Nov, 1926-Mar 31, 1956; W. Keith Kelly, Apr 7, 1956-Oct 8, 1961; Leon Wall, Oct 19, 1962-Mar 28, 1969; Daniel Sohmount, Sept 26, 1969-May 12, 1970; Ralph Bahe, Oct 9-Dec 4, 1970; Caroline Jenkins, Dec 8, 1970; Jimmy Baker, Sept 27, 1975-June 3, 1977; Patty Leemhuis, Feb 9-May 4, 1979; Patti He Crow and Patty Leemhuis, Sept 7, 1979-Jan 29, 1980. School newsletter.

WHi	v.52, n.1-v.79, n.11; Oct 4, 1952-Apr 25, 1980	Microforms
WHi	[v.5, n.2-v.22, n.19] [Jan, 1905-Jan, 1923]	F801/7I38 Cutter
AzHC	v.30-v.41; 1931-1942	Periodicals
AzNCC	v.61-v.79; 1962-June, 1980	Indian File
NHu	[v.9, n.12-v.77, n.8] [1909-1978]	Periodicals
MoSHi	v.4, n.1, 4, 74; Nov, 1903, Feb, Oct, 1904	OK/05/C439
NN	[v.4-v.41] [1904-1942]	SSR
OkTU	[v.4, n.57-v.22, n.3] [May, 1904-1922]	Rare Book Room
OkU	[v.4, n.4-v.72, n.24] [Feb, 1904-May, 1973]	WHC
CaOPeT	v.2, n.5-v.76, n.11; Mar, 1902-June, 1977	Microfiche

Other holding institutions: AzTeS (AZS), CLSM, DI (UDI), [University of Minnesota Union List, Minneapolis, MN] (MUL), NmLvH (NMH), Ok (OKD), PP (PLF), [U.S. Government Printing Office-Serials, Alexandria, VA] (GPA).

477 Indian Scout. 1915-1918?//. 10 times a year. Last issue 16 pages. Photographs, commercial advertising. Available in microform: WHi (1915-1918). Published by U. S. Indian School, Shawnee, OK. School newsletter. Subject focus: career opportunities, poetry.

WHi	v.1, n.2-v.4, n.7; Feb, 1915-Apr/May, 1918	Microforms
WHi	v.1, n.2-v.4, n.7; Feb, 1915-Apr/May, 1918	F8095/S531 Cutter

OkU   [v.1-v.4]   WHC
           [1915-1918]

478 Indian Scrapbook. 1965-1967//. Quarterly. ISSN 0537-2496. OCLC
    3417083. RLIN OHCP3417083-S, NYPG784394012-S. Last issue 18 pages,
    height 22 cm. Line drawings. Editor: Frederick Goshe. Subject
    focus: history, culture, stereotypes.

    WU   Autumn, 1965-Winter, 1966/1967   Rare Books

    Other holding institutions: [University of Minnesota Union List,
    Minneapolis, MN] (MUL).

479 The Indian Sentinel. 1902-1962//. Quarterly. ISSN 0276-0169. LC
    sf80-556. OCLC 1752978, 5886361, 7240158, 7240172. RLIN
    OHCP1752978-S, DCLCSF80556-S, DCLC362510-S, CUBU12840361-S,
    CUBU1284035X-S. Last issue 21 pages, last volume 82 pages, height 23
    cm. Line drawings, photographs, commercial advertising. Available in
    microform: CPC (1916-1962). Published by Bureau of Catholic Missions,
    Washington, DC. Frequency varies: annual, 1902/1903-1916; Monthly,
    June, 1936-Dec, 1956; bi-monthly, Jan/Feb, 1957-July/Aug, 1960.
    Subject focus: missions, Catholic Church. German edition entitled Die
    Indianer Wache.

    WHi   [no nos.]-v.40, n.4;   Microforms
               1902/1903-Winter, 1962

    WHi   [no nos.]-v.40, n.4;   F805/C36/I
               1902/1903-Winter, 1962   Cutter

    WMM   [no nos.]-v.40, n.4;   Special
               1902/1903-Winter, 1962   Collections

    AzNCC   v.8-v.13;   Indian File
               Spring, 1928-Spring, 1933

    MtHi   [v.1, n.4-v.40, n.4]   Z/970.105
               [1917-1962]   In2s

    NjP   v.1, n.1, v.23, n.8,   Periodicals
               v.26, n.7, v.27, n.2;
               July, 1916, Oct, 1943,
               Sept, 1946, Feb, 1947

    N   [no nos.]   C970.6/
               1902-1915   I388

    NHu   [no nos.]-v.40, n.4;   Periodicals
               1902/1903-Winter, 1962

    MoSHi   [v.1], v.3-v.13, [v.14]   970.7/In2
               [1917], 1919-1933, [1934]

OkU   [no nos.]-v.10;   WHC
           1902/1903-1931

SdU   v.4-v.40;   Microfilm
           1920-1962

Other holding institutions: CLSM, DLC (DLC), DI (UDI), [Indiana Union
List of Serials, Indianapolis, IN] (ILS), MBTI (BTI), MiGrC (EXC),
[University of Minnesota Union List, Minneapolis, MN] (MUL), OAkU
(AKR), OKTU (OKT).

480 Indian Sentinel. 1890-?// Weekly. Last issue 8 pages. Line
    drawings, commercial advertising. Tahlequah, OK. Available in
    microform: OkHi (1891, 1900). Editors: William A. Thompson, Oct
    21-Dec 16, 1891; W. J. Cunningham, May 9, 1895; J.T. Parks, Jan 7,
    1898-May 12, 1900; J. W. Patton and F. P. Sheilds, May 19-June 29,
    1900. Newspaper. Also described in: Foreman, Carolyn Thomas.
    Oklahoma Imprints, 1835-1907. Norman: University of Oklahoma, 1936.

    WHi   [v.2, n.28, 36, v.11, n.1]   Microforms
               Oct 21, Dec 16, 1891, June 29, 1900

    OkHi   [v.2, n.28, 36, v.11, n.1]   Microforms
               Oct 21, Dec 16, 1891, June 29, 1900

481 The Indian Speaking Leaf; Red Man's Journal. 1938-1949//. Irregular.
    Last issue 14 pages, height 28 cm. Line drawings. Published by
    Indian Association of America and Mayan Temple of MU, Newark, NJ.
    Place of publication varies: Kirkwood, MO, 1938. Editor: Barnabas
    S'Hiuhushu. Subject focus: culture, arts and crafts, spiritualism.

    CL   v.1, n.1-v.12, n.60;   Periodicals
               Jan, 1938-Feb, 1949

    NjP   v.4, n.18-b.12, n.60;   Periodcials
               Jan/Feb, 1941-Jan/Feb, 1949

    NN   v.1, n.1-v.12, n.60;   HBA
               Jan, 1938-Jan/Feb, 1949

482 Indian Student Services [Newsletter]. 1978?-1982//. Irregular. Last
    issue 10 pages, last volume, 18 pages, height 36 cm. Line drawings.
    Published by Jackson County Education Services District, Medford, OR.
    Title varies: Indian Education Newsletter, Aug, 1978-June, 1980.
    Subject focus: education, Jackson County schools, school news, poetry.

    OrHi   Aug, 1978-June, 1982   Periodicals

483 Indian Talk: The Native American's Magazine. 1973-1975?//. Monthly.
RLIN MIUG21938-S. Last issue 32 pages, height 22 cm. Line drawings,
commerical advertising. Published by Indian Talk, Inc., Grand Rapids,
MI. Title varies: Indian Talk in Southern Michigan, Nov, 1973-May,
1974. Editor: Shirley Francis. Subject focus: rights, Michigan
Native people.

MiU-B	[v.1, n.9-v.2, n.10]	Periodicals
	[July, 1974-Aug, 1975]	
MiU	v.1, n.4-8, 10	Labadie
	Feb-June, Aug, 1974	Collection
Mi	v.1, n.1-v.2, n.12;	Periodicals
	Nov, 1973-Oct, 1975	

Indian Talk in Southern Michigan. Grand Rapids, MI

    see Indian Talk: The Native American Magazine. Grand Rapids, MI

484 Indian Teepee. 1920-1928//. 5 times a year. OCLC 1586675. RLIN
OHCP1586675-S. Last issue 8 pages, last volume 40 pages. Line
drawings, photographs, commercial advertising. Available in
microform: WHi (1922-1928); WHi-A, Papers of Carlos Montezuma,
(1920-1922). Published by American Indian Association, Wheeling, WV.
Title varies: American Indian Teepee, Spring-Winter, 1921; American
Indian Advocate, Summer/Fall-Winter, 1922. Place of publication
varies: Independence, MO, Spring, 1921-Sept, 1927. Frequency varies:
quarterly, Spring, 1921-Spring?, 1925. Editors: Rev. Red Fox, [v.3,
n.1], 1922; Chief Strong Wolf, Summer, 1924-Winter, 1925; Francis
Valle Boyce (Running Bear), Nov, 1927-May/June, 1928. Subject focus:
rights, legislation, citizenship, history.

WHi	v.2, n.1-v.3, n.4, v.6, n.2-v.10, n.3;	Microforms
	Spring, 1921-Winter, 1922,	
	Summer, 1924-May/June, 1928	
CLSM	v.1-v.6;	Periodicals
	1920-1924	
NN	v.6-v.10;	HBA
	1925-1928	
Wa	v.1, n.1-3;	NW
	1920	

Other holding institutions: [University of Minnesota Union List,
Minneapolis, MN] (MUL).

485 <u>Indian Time</u>. 1976. Irregular. Larry Jones, editor, Indian Time, P.O. Box 27228, Raleigh, NC 27611. (919) 733-5998. OCLC 7181265. Last issue 6 pages, last volume 30 pages, height 28 cm. Line drawings, photographs. Published by North Carolina Commission of Indian Affairs. Subject focus: North Carolina Native people, state programs and policies.

WHi	v.5, n.2; Nov, 1980	Microforms
NcP	v.4, n.4- Feb, 1980-	Periodicals

Other holding institutions: Nc (NCS).

486 <u>Indian Time</u>. 1950-1959?//. Quarterly. ISSN 0442-7467. OCLC 2251425. Last issue 32 pages, height 28 cm. Line drawings. Published by Pan-American Indian League, Vancouver, British Columbia, Canada. Frequency varies: monthly, Nov, 1950-Apr, 1951; quarterly, May, 1951-May, 1952; bi-monthly, June-Sept, 1952. Editor: Eloise White Street Harries. Community newsletter.

MiU	v.[1], n.1-v.3, n.4; Nov, 1950-[1958]	Labadie Collection
NjP	v.2, n.15; Winter, 1955	Periodicals
OkU	v.[1], n.1-v.3, n.6; Nov, 1950-Spring, 1959	WHC
CaACG	[v.[1], n.1-v.3, n.6] Nov, 1950-Spring, 1959]	Periodicals
CaOONL	[v.1-v.3] [1950-1958]	Periodicals

Other holding institutions: [University of Minnesota Union List, Minneapolis, MN] (MUL).

487 <u>Indian Times</u>. 1960?. Monthly. $5. for individuals and institutions. Z. Susanne Aikmann, editor, P.O. Box 4131, Santa Fe Station, Denver, CO 80204. (303) 922-5880. OCLC 2385166. RLIN COSG81-S36, OHCP2385166-S. Last issue 4 pages, height 28 cm. Line drawings, photographs, commercial advertising. Available in microform: WHi-A, Veda Stone Papers, (1969-1970). Published by White Buffalo Indian Council, Inc. Previous editors: Rachel Ashley, Jan, 1965; Charles Trimble, May, 1969-June, 1970; Juanda Henderson, Sept, 1970. Community newsletter.

WHi	[v.6, n.1-v.21, n.3], (n.s.)v.1, n.1- [Jan, 1965-May/June, 1980], May 15, 1981-	Circulation

WEU   [v.9, n.4-v.10, n.3];   Micro 11
ARC   [May, 1969-Nov, 1970]

AzHM   (n.s.)v.1, n.2, 4;   Periodicals
           1981

AzNCC   v.9-13;   Indian File
           Oct, 1969-June, 1973

MtBBCC   (n.s.)v.1-   Periodicals
           Nov, 1981-

NjP   v.1, n.1-v.10;   Periodicals
           Oct, 1960-Sept, 1970

NN   v.7, n.4-v.10;   HBA
           1966-1970

OkTU   v.19, n.1;   Rare Book
           Jan/Feb, 1978   Room

PPT   v.13, n.10, v.18, n.3-v.21, n.6/7;   Contemporary
           Dec, 1972, Mar, 1977-Aug/Sept, 1980   Culture

SdU   v.4-v.7;   South
           1963-1966

Other holding institutions: DI (UDI), OrU-Special Collections.

488 The Indian Trader. 1970. Monthly. Hubert Guy, editor, The Indian
     Trader, Box 404, La Mesa, CA 92041. (505) 863-3838. ISSN 0046-9076.
     LC sn78-510. OCLC 4112458. RLIN MIUG20825943-S, OHCP4112458-S. Last
     issue 48 pages. Line drawings, photographs, commercial advertising.
     Available on Microfilm: McA (1970-). Published by Indian Trader
     Enterprises. Billings, MT. Place of publication varies: La Mesa, CA,
     Sept, 1970-Jan, 1976; Gallup, NM, Feb, 1976-Jan, 1978; Billings, MT,
     Feb, 1978-Dec?, 1980. Frequency varies: 6 times a year, Sept,
     1970-Nov, 1975. Previous editors: Hubert Guy, Sept, 1970-Jan, 1976;
     Jo Smith, July, 1976-Jan, 1980; Jerry Kammer, Feb-June, 1980; Bill
     Donovan, July-Dec, 1981. Subject focus: arts and crafts,
     merchandising.

     WHi   v.1, n.1-   Microforms
                Sept, 1970-

     WEU   v.1, n.1-2, v.2, n.1;   Journalism
                Sept-Dec, 1970, Feb, 1971   Lab

     WMM   v.7, n.6;   Special
                June, 1976   Collections

     AzFM   v.1-v.2;   570.6/L22t
                1970-1971

AzHC	v.2, n.1– Feb, 1971–	Periodicals
AzPh	Current year only	Periodicals
AzNCC	v.1, n.1– Sept, 1970–	Indian File
AzT	v.7, n.3– Mar, 1976–	Periodicals
CBri	v.7–v.12; 1976–1981	Periodicals
CCarm	v.11– 1980–	Periodicals
CL	v.1, n.1– Sept, 1970–	Periodicals
CSmarP	[v.11], v.12– [1980], 1981–	Stacks
CoKIM	Current issues	Periodicals
LARC	v.11– 1980–	Periodicals
MtBC	v.10; 1979	Periodicals
MtHi	[v.2, n.4–v.9, n.11], v.10, n.1– [1971–1978], 1979–	Z/970.105/T675
NbJAM	v.11, n.9– Sept, 1980–	Periodicals
NjP	[v.1, n.1–v.8, n.8] [Sept, 1970–July, 1979]	Periodicals
NmG	v.7, n.2– Feb, 1976–	Periodicals
NcP	v.12– 1981–	Periodicals
OkPAC	v.5, n.6, v.8, n.1– Nov, 1974, Jan, 1977–	Periodicals
OkTU	v.9, n.12– Dec, 1978–	Rare Book Room
OkU	v.1, n.2–v.7, n.7], v.9, n.2– [Sept, 1970–1976] 1978–	WHC

OrHi   v.1, n.1-v.5, n.6;   Periodicals
            Sept, 1970-Nov, 1974

WaU   v.12, n.7-   E/98/I5/I55
            July, 1981-

WyCWC   v.6, v.13-   Periodicals
            1974, 1982-

CaACG   v.9, n.7-   Periodicals
            July, 1978-

CaOPeT   v.1-   Microfilm
            1970-

Other holding institutions: CLobS (CLO), CLSM, DI (UDI), [University
of Minnesota Union List, Minneapolis, MN] (MUL), [Western Nevada
Community College, Carson City, NV], WaU (WAU), [Wisconsin Indian
Resource Council, Stevens Point, WI].

489 Indian Travel Newsletter. 1972-1980//. Quarterly. OCLC 6188857.
    Last issue 8 pages. Photographs. Available in microform: McA
    (1972-1980). Published by Discover America Travel Organization and
    American Indian Travel Commission, Washington, DC. Subject focus:
    tourism.

WHi   v.3, n.1-v.9, n.6;   Microforms
            Spring, 1974-Dec, 1980

WMUW   [v.4, n.3-v.7, n.2]   (SPL)
            [Winter, 1975-Spring, 1977]   E/75/I64x

AzNCC   v.1-v.3, n.1;   Indian File
            May, 1972-Spring, 1974

CaOPeT   v.3, n.1-v.9, n.6;   Microfilm
            Spring, 1974-Dec, 1980

Other holding institutions: [Amerind Foundation, Inc., Dragoon, AZ],
CLSM, ICN (IBV).

490 Indian Truth. 1924. Bi-monthly. $15. for individuals and
    institutions. Marg Emery and Ann Laquer, editors, Indian Truth, 1505
    Race St., Philadelphia, PA 19102. (215) 563-8349. ISSN 0019-6452.
    LC 28-13971. OCLC 1587868, 6296525, 7214629, 7722413. RLIN
    CSUP16547-S, CSUP04695409-S, CSUP02203807-S, CUBG16585208-S,
    MIUG13436-S, OHCP1587868-S, CSUL8520550-S, NYPG784197646-S. Last
    issue 16 pages, height 23 cm. Line drawings, photographs. Available
    in microform: CPC (1924-1973); Y (1924-1979). Published by Indian
    Rights Association. Frequency varies: irregular, Feb, 1924-Oct, 1973.
    Previous editors: M. K. Sniffen, Feb, 1924-June, 1939; Lawrence E.
    Lindley, Oct, 1939-Feb, 1943; Charles E. Faris, Mar, 1943-May/June,

1944; Jonathan M. Steere, Oct/Nov, 1944-Apr/June, 1958; Lawrence E.
Lindley, July/Oct, 1958-Dec, 1966; Armin L. Saeger, Jr., Spring,
1968-Jan, 1969; Theodore B. Hetzel, Feb, 1969-Jan, 1977; Elaine P.
Lariviere, Apr, 1977-June, 1978; Jeanne E. Baumann, Sept, 1978-Oct,
1979; Ann T. Laquer, Dec, 1979-Sept, 1980. Subject focus: rights,
legal, political, judicial news, tribal self-determination, book
reviews.

WHi	n.1-v.43, n.6; Feb, 1924-Dec, 1966	E/77/I44
WHi	n.1- Feb, 1924-	Microforms
WEU	v.47, n.1-3, v.48, n.1; Feb-Sept, 1970, Jan, 1971	Journalism Lab
WEU ARC	[v.38, n.1-v.48, n.2]; [June, 1961-Apr, 1971]	Micro 11
WM	Current issues	Forest Home Branch
WM	Current 5 years	Periodicals
WMM	[n.1-208] [Feb, 1924-June, 1972]	Special Collections
WMUW	n.215-217; Apr, 1976-Apr, 1977	(SPL) E/75/I65x
AzFM	v.10- 1933-	570.6/I39i
AzNCC	1925-	Indian File
CL	n.1- Feb, 1924-	Periodicals
CNoSU	[n.1-n.211] [1924-Oct, 1973]	Microfilm
CRSSU	n.223- Dec, 1978-	Periodicals
CU-A	v.48- 1971-	E/77/A1/I54
IC	v.58, n.2- Feb, 1981-	Periodicals
ICN	Current issues	CHAI
IaHi	n.1-v.48 1924-1971	E/77/I44

IdU	v.48; n.207-227; 1971, Mar, 1972-Aug, 1979	E/75/I56
KU	n.1- Feb, 1924-	Kansas Collection
Mi	n.1- Feb, 1924-	Periodicals
MnBemT	n.1-215; Feb, 1924-Apr, 1976	J970.5/I396
MoSHi	[n.1-v.48], n.207-223; [Feb, 1924-1971], Mar, 1972-Dec, 1978	970.7/In2i
MtHi	[v.1, n.1-n.223] [Feb, 1924-Dec, 1978]	Z/970.105 In2t
NjP	n.1-215; Feb, 1924-Apr, 1976	Periodicals
NmScW	n.1-v.48; Feb, 1924-1971	Periodicals
N	n.1-223; Feb, 1924-Dec, 1978	J970.5/I396
NHu	[n.1-v.48], n.216- [Feb, 1924-1971], 1977-	Periodicals
NN	n.1-v.45, n.219; Feb, 1924-Oct, 1977	HBA
NcP	n.237- 1981-	Periodicals
OCPH	n.1- Feb, 1924-	970.35/In2
OkTU	n.223- Dec, 1978-	Rare Book Room
OkU	n.1- Feb, 1924-	WHC
PP	n.1-211; Feb, 1924-Oct, 1973	Microfiche
PPT	n.207-222, 224-227, 230- Mar, 1972-Sept, 1978, Feb-Aug, 1979, Feb, 1980-	Contemporary Culture
SdU	[v.43, n.2-v.47, n.1] [July, 1967-Feb, 1970]	South Dakota Room

UPB	v.35, n.3– 1958–	970.105/IN2
WaU	n.1– Feb, 1924–	E/75/0534
CaAEU	v.38, n.1– June, 1961–	Boreal Institute
CaOAFN	n.237– Feb, 1981–	Periodicals
CaOPeT	n.1–211; Feb, 1924–Oct, 1973	Microfiche
CaSSIC	n.1–n.211; Feb, 1924–Oct, 1973	Microfiche

Other holding institutions: ArU (AFU), AzFU (AZN), AzTeS (AZS), CLSM, CLU (CLU), CU-UC (UCU), CtHT (TYC), CtY (YUS), DI (UDI), I (SPI), [Indiana Union List of Serials, Indianapolis, IN] (ILS), MMeT (TFW), MdBJ (JHE), MiU-Labadie (EYM), [University of Minnesota Union List, Minneapolis, MN] (MUL), NdU (UND), NbU (LDL), NhD (DRB), NmScW, NIC (COO), [New York State Union List, Albany, NY] (NYS), [Central New York Library Resources Council, Syracuse, NY] (SRR), NBu (VHB), [Western New York Library Resources Council, Buffalo, NY] (VZX), NCH (YHM), NR (YQR), NSbSU (YSM), OAkU (AKR), [Ohio Historical Society, Columbus, OH] (OHT), [Bacone College, Muskogee, OK], OrU-Special Collections, PPi (CPL), PSC-Hi (PSH), [Pittsburgh Regional Library Center Union List, Pittsburg, PA] (QPR), TxLT (ILU), [AMIGOS Union List of Serials, Dallas, TX] (IUC), Vi (VIC), WaS.

491 Indian Viewpoint. 1973–1975?//. Monthly. OCLC 1779769. RLIN OHCP1779769-S. Last issue 8 pages, height 44 cm. Line drawings, photographs. Duluth, MN. Available in microform: WHi (1974–1975). Community newsletter. Subject focus: local, state and national news, education, poetry.

WHi	[v.1, n.2–v.3, n.5] [Nov, 1973–June, 1975]	Microforms
WMUW	[v.2, n.2–v.3, n.5] [Feb, 1974–June, 1975]	(SPL) E/75/I66x
AzNCC	v.1–v.3, n.5; Oct, 1973–Aug, 1975	Indian File
MnHi	v.2, n.12; Dec, 1974	Periodicals
OkU	[v.1, n.1–v.3, n.6] [1973–1975]	WHC

Other holding institutions: [University of Minnesota Union List, Minneapolis, MN] (MUL).

492 Indian Views. 1958//. Unknown. Height 22 cm. Line drawings, photographs. Published by League of North American Indians, Los Angeles, CA. Subject focus: rights, legislation, reprints of articles from other newspapers.

    CLSM   [no no.], n.1-2;   Periodicals
              Mar/June-?, 1958

493 Indian Voice. 1971-1973?//. Monthly. ISSN 0091-102x. LC 73-643209. OCLC 1786483. RLIN DCLC73643209-S, CSUP02203911-S, CUBG11483106-S, OHCP1786482-S, NYPG744635977-S. Last issue 50 pages. Line drawings, photographs, commercial advertising. Available in microform: McA (1971-1973), McP (1971-1972). Published by Native American Publishing Company, Santa Clara, CA. Editors: Fern Williams, Feb, 1971-June, 1972; Fern Eastman, July-Sept, 1972. Subject focus: history, culture, poetry.

    WHi   v.1, n.1-v.3, n.4;   Microforms
              Feb, 1971-July, 1973

    AzNCC   v.1, n.1-v.2;   Microforms
              Feb, 1971-Sept, 1972

    AzU   v.1, n.2?-v.3, n.2;   Periodicals
              Mar, 1971-Apr, 1973

    CNoSU   [v.1, n.1-v.3, n.5]   Microfilm
              [Feb, 1971-Aug/Sept, 1973

    CU-A   v.2-v.3;   E/75/I5
              1972-1973

    IdU   v.3, n.1-4;   E/75/I6
              Mar-July, 1973

    NjP   [v.1, n.2-v.3, n.1]   Periodicals
              [Mar, 1971-Mar, 1973]

    OkU   v.1, n.1-v.2;   WHC
              Feb, 1971-Sept, 1972

Other holding institutions: AzFU (AZN), DLC (DLC), [University of Minnesota Union List, Minneapolis, MN] (MUL), [Western Nevada Community College, Carson City, NV], NmScW, OkAdE (ECO).

494 Indian Voice. 1981?. Unknown. Indian Voice, Bureau of Indian Affairs, Albuquerque, NM 87184. (505) 766-3275. Last issue 1 page,

height 28 cm. Published by Southwestern Indian Polytechnic Institute.
School newsletter.

WHi   Nov, 1981–   Circulation

495 Indian Voice. 1971. Monthly. $6. for individuals and institutions.
    Robert S. Johnson, editor, Indian Voice, 520 Pacific Ave., Box 578,
    Sumner, WA 98390. (206) 593-2894. OCLC 6169393. Last issue 8 pages,
    last volume 96 pages, height 45 cm. Line drawings, photographs,
    commercial advertising. Available in microform: McP (1971-1972).
    Community newsletter.

WHi   v.1, n.7–   Microforms
           Nov, 1971–

WM   Current issues   Forest Home
                                                           Branch

WMUW   [v.1, n.1–v.8, n.12]   (SPL)
           [May 1, 1971–Dec, 1978]   E/75/I67x

AzNCC   v.2–   Indian File
           1972–

CNoSU   [v.1, n.7–v.2]   Microfilm
           [Nov, 1971–1972]

NjP   [v.1, n.1–v.9, n.6]   Periodicals
           [May 1, 1971–June, 1979]

OkU   v.1, n.7–v.2, v.10, n.1–   WHC
           Nov, 1971–Oct, 1972, Jan, 1980–

Wa   v.1–   Periodicals
           1971–

WaOE   v.2–   Periodicals
           1972

CaBAbF   v.5–   Periodicals
           Mar, 1975–

Other holding institutions: CLSM, NmScW, WaU (WAU).

496 The Indian Voice. 1969. Monthly. $6. (Canada), $6.50 (U.S.) for
    individuals and institutions. Donna Doss, editor, The Indian Voice,
    102-423 W. Broadway, Vancouver, British Columbia, Canada V5Y 1R4.
    (604) 876-0944. ISSN 0073-6732. LC cn76-319654. OCLC 1928562. RLIN
    DCLCCN76319654-S, OCHP1928562-S. Last issue 16 pages, last volume 130
    pages, height 43 cm. Line drawings, photographs, commercial
    advertising. Available in microform: McA (1974-). Published by

British Columbia Indian Homemakers Association. Newspaper. Subject
focus: law, rights, politics.

WHi	v.6, n.3– Mar, 1974–	Circulation
WMUW	v.9, n.7; July, 1977	(SPE) E?75/I68x
AzNCC	v.2– Mar, 1970–	Indian File
NjP	v.9, n.7; July, 1977	Periodicals
NcP	v.2–v.3, v.13– 1970–1971, 1981–	Periodicals
OkTU	v.10, n.12– Dec, 1978–	Rare Book Room
OkU	v.11, n.11– Nov, 1979–	WHC
UPB	[v.1, n.3–v.8, n.7] [1969–1976]	970.4105/IN23V
WaU	v.3, n.3; Apr/May, 1971	Periodicals
WyCWC	v.3, n.1–4, v.7, n.2–12; 1971, 1975	Periodicals
CaAEU	v.3, n.1– 1971–	Boreal Institute
CaBAbF	v.9– May, 1977–	Periodicals
CaOAFN	v.13, n.1– Jan, 1981–	Periodicals
CaOONL	v.1, n.3–v.12; Dec, 1969–Nov, 1980	Newspaper Section
CaOOP	v.9– 1977–	E/78/B9/I53
CaOPeT	[v.6], v.9–v.10; [1974], 1977–1978	Microfilm
CaYW	v.6–v.7, v.10–v.13; 1974–1975, 1978–1981	Periodicals

497 <u>Indian Voices</u>. 1963-1978//. Irregular. ISSN 0537-2674. LC
    77-644062. OCLC 2379184. RLIN DCLC77644062-S, CSUP02204009-S,
    CUBG16582-S, OHCP2379184-S. Last issue 32 pages, height 28 cm.
    Photographs. Available in microform: CPC (1963-1968). Published by
    University of Chicago, Chicago, IL. Editor: Robert K. Thomas. Subject
    focus: rights, legislation, young adults, biographies.

WHi	[Apr 1, 1963-Winter, 1968]	Pam 75-2796
WHi	[Apr 1, 1963-Winter, 1968]	Microforms
WEU	[June, 1963-Winter, 1968]	Journalism Lab
WEU ARC	[Apr 1, 1963-Winter, 1968]	Micro 11
WMM	Sept-Oct, 1963	Special Collections
AzFM	1963-1968	570.6/C53i
AzU	[Dec, 1962-Winter, 1968]	I9791/I139
NjP	Apr, 1963-Winter, 1968	Periodicals
NHu	Apr 1, 1963-Winter, 1968	Periodicals
NN	[Apr 1, 1963-Winter, 1968]	HBA
OkPAC	Oct, 1963, Apr-Aug, 1965, June, Aug, 1966	Periodicals
SdU	1963-1966	South Dakota Room
UPB	1963-1966	970.105/IN2V
CaACG	Apr, 1964-Dec, 1977/Jan, 1978	Periodicals
CaOPeT	[Apr 1, 1963-Winter, 1968]	Microfiche

Other holding institutions: [Amerind Foundation, Inc., Dragoon, AZ],
DLC (DLC), DI (UDI), MH-P (HLS), [University of Minnesota Union List,
Minneapolis, MN] (MUL).

498 <u>The Indian War Drum</u>. 1946-?//. Monthly. Last issue 27 pages, height
    29 cm. Line drawings. Published by Laurel Hill Indian Reservation,
    Three Mile Harbor, Long Island, NY. Community newsletter.

NN	v.1, n.7-9; Oct-Dec, 1946	HBA

499 <u>Indian Word</u>. 1971-1975//. Unknown. Height 28 cm. Line drawings.
Published by Minnesota Indian Affairs Commission, St. Paul, MN.
Subject focus: rights, legislation.

MnHi   [v.1, n.3-v.2, n.8]   Periodicals
              [1971-1974/1975]

500 <u>Indian World</u>. 1978-1981//?. Monthly. Line drawings, photographs.
Published by Union of British Columbia Indian Chiefs, Vancouver,
British Columbia, Canada. Title varies: UBCIC News, Spring-Dec, 1978.
Editors: Beth Cutland; Darrell Ned. Subject focus: politics,
socio-economic conditions.

CaAEU   v.2, n.6-v.4, n.2;   Boreal
              Sept, 1979-May/June, 1981   Institute

CaOAFN   v.3, n.9-v.4, n.3;   Periodicals
              Jan-Fall, 1981

CaOSuU   v.3, n.10-v.4, n.3;   Periodicals
              Feb?-Fall, 1981

CaSICC   v.1;   Periodicals
              Spring-Dec, 1978

501 <u>Indian Youth</u>. 1978. Quarterly. Mark Trahant, editor, Indian Youth,
1725 K St. N. W., Suite 811, Washington DC 20006. (800) 421-1054.
Last issue 30 pages, height 28 cm. Line drawings, photographs, some
in color, commercial advertising. Published by Institute for Career
and Vocational Training. Subject focus: young adults, education,
biographies.

WHi   v.2, n.1, v.3, n.1-   Circulation
              July, 1980, Dec, 1980-

WM   Current issues   Forest Home
                                                          Branch

MtBBCC   v.2-   Periodicals
              July, 1980-

Other holding institutions: [Standing Rock Community College Library,
Fort Yates, ND], [Wisconsin Indian Resource Council, Stevens Point,
WI].

502 <u>Indianer Heute</u>. 1973//? Unknown. Last issue 30 pages, height 22 cm.
Line drawings. Published by Arbeitsgruppe fur Nordamericanische
Indianer, Dusseldorf, West Germany. In German, 100%. Subject focus:
culture, history.

WHi   n.1;   Pam 74-6076
           Jan, 1973

503 <u>Die Indianer Wache</u>. 1903-1918//. Quarterly. Published by Bureau of
    Catholic Missions, Washington, DC. Frequency varies: annual,
    1902/1903-1916. Subject focus: Catholic Church, missions. In German,
    100%. English edition entitled Indian Sentinel.

    WMM   1903-1918   Special
                                                      Collections

504 <u>Indianland-New Life News</u>. 1982? Unknown. $3. for individuals and
    institutions. Duane Hammond, editor, Indianland-New Life News, Box
    455, McDermitt, NV 89421. Last issue 8 pages, height 22 cm. Subject
    focus: Christian religion.

    AzAIBI   Current issues   Periodicals

505 <u>Indians at Work</u>. 1933-1945//. Semi-monthly. LC 35-17595. OCLC
    2657944. RLIN CSUP011192-S, CUBG33427008-S, CUBG2455-S,
    OHCP2657944-S. Last issue 36 pages, height 27 cm. Line drawings,
    photographs. Available in microform: BHP (1933-1945); CPC
    (1933-1945). Published by U. S. Department of the Interior, Office of
    Indian Affairs, Washington, DC. Subject focus: emergency conservation
    work programs.

    WHi   v.1, n.1-v.8, n.12, v.13, n.1;   I20.22: 1-8, 13
               Aug, 1933-Aug, 1941, May/June, 1945

    WHi   v.1, n.1-v.13, n.1;   Microforms
               Aug, 1933-May/June, 1945

    WMM   [v.1, n.1-v.13, n.1]   Special
               [Aug, 1933-May/June, 1945]   Collections

    AzFM   v.1, n.1-v.13, n.1;   Microforms
               Aug, 1933-May/June, 1945

    AzHC   v.1, n.1-v.13, n.1;   Periodicals
               Aug, 1933-May/June, 1945

    CL   v.1, n.1-v.13;   Periodicals
               Aug, 1933-Nov, 1945

    CLSM   v.1-v.13, n.1;   Periodicals
               1933-May/June, 1945

    IaHi   v.1, n.1-v.13, n.1   E/98/I5/U7
               Aug, 1933-May/June, 1945

| MtHi | [v.8, n.11–v.9, n.8] | Z/970.105 |
| | [1941–1942] | In24w |

| NjP | [v.1, n.3–v. 13, n.1] | Periodicals |
| | [Sept 15, 1933–May/June, 1945] | |

| N | v.1, n.1–v.13, n.1; | C970.1/qI39w |
| | Aug, 1933–May/June, 1945 | |

| NHu | [v.1, n.1–v.13, n.1] | Periodicals |
| | [Aug, 1933–May/June, 1945] | |

| NN | v.1, n.1–v.13; | HBB |
| | Aug, 1933–Nov, 1945 | |

| OkTahN | [v.2–v.4]. v.6–v.12; | Spec. Coll. |
| | [1934–1937], 1938–1945 | |

| OkU | v.1, n.1–v.12; | WHC |
| | Aug, 1933–1945 | |

| CaACG | [v.4–v.9] | Periodicals |
| | [Sept 1, 1936–Dec, 1942] | |

Other holding institutions: ArU (AFU), AzU (AZU), CLobS (CLO), MiGrC (EXC), MiU (EYM), [Central New York Library Resouces Council, Syracuse, NY] (SRR), OkAdE (ECO), SdU (USD).

506 The Indian's Friend. 1888–1957//. Bi-monthly. OCLC 1753048, 5206941. RLIN MIUG82-S6172, OHCP1753048-S, CSUP04695604-S, CUBG12836606-S, CTYG5206941-S, OHCP5206941-S. Last issue 8 pages, last volume 48 pages. Line drawings, commercial advertising. Available in microform: CPC (1888–1951); DLC (1888–1940); Y (1888–1951). Published by National Indian Association. Place of publication varies: Philadelphia, PA, Mar 1888–Jan, 1902; New Haven, CT, Feb, 1902–Jan, 1907. Frequency varies: monthly, Mar, 1888–July, 1915. Editors: Marie E. Ives Humphrey, Jan, 1902–Dec, 1906. T. C. Marshall, Feb, 1907–Dec, 1914; John W. Clark, Jan, 1915–Mar, 1927. Subject focus: organization news, legislation, Christian religion.

| WHi | v.1, n.1–v.52, n.1; | Microforms |
| | Mar, 1888–Jan, 1940 | |

| WHi | v.17, n.1–v.50, n.6; | F805/ZN27/I |
| | Sept, 1904–Nov, 1938 | Cutter |

| AzNCC | v.51–v.57; | Indian File |
| | Oct, 1939–June, 1945 | |

| CL | v.27–v.63, n.2; | Periodicals |
| | Oct, 1914–June, 1951 | |

| ICN | v.1, n.1–v.63, n.2; | Microfilm |
| | Mar, 1888–June, 1951 | 318 |

KU	v.1-v.69; 1888-1957	Kansas Collection
NjP	[v.55, n.4-v.56, n.6] [July, 1943-Nov, 1944]	Periodicals
N	[v.3. n.3-v.46, n.5] [Nov, 1890-Sept, 1934]	C970.1/qI399
N	v.1, n.1-v.63, n.2; Mar, 1888-June, 1951	MA/FM
NHu	v.1-v.69; 1888-1957	Periodicals
NN	v.1, n.1-v.63, n.2; Mar, 1888-June, 1951	ZAN-H404
OkU	v.25, n.1-v.34, n.6; Oct, 1912-July, 1922	WHC
OrU	v.17. n.1-v.46, n.5; Sept, 1904-Sept, 1934	Periodicals
PP	v.1-v.63, n.2; Mar, 1888-June, 1951	Microfilm
SdU	v.33-v.45; 1921-1933	Stacks

Other holding institutions: AzTeS (AZS), CtY (YUS), MiU (EYM),
[University of Minnesota Union List, Minneapolis, MN] (MUL), NNG
(VXM), OkS (OKS), PP (PLF).

507 Indians Illustrated. 1967-?//. Monthly, irregular. OCLC 4894571.
Last issue 22 pages, height 29 cm. Photographs, commercial
advertising. Available in microform: WHi (1967-1968). Published by
Talking Leaves, Inc., Buena Park, CA. Place of publication varies:
Huntington Park, CA, Feb, 1967; Los Angeles, CA, Apr-Sept, 1967.
Editors: Bill Barnett, Feb-Apr, 1967; Francis Allen, May, 1967; Bryan
V. King, Sept, 1967; Francis Allen, June-July, 1968. Subject focus;
culture, history, education, governmental relations.

WHi	v.1, n.1-6; Feb, 1967-June, 1968	Microforms
WMM	v.1, n.2; Apr, 1967	Special Collections
OkU	v.1, n.1-?; Feb, 1967-Nov, 1968	WHC

Other holding institutions: [University of Minnesota Union List,
Minneapolis, MN] (MUL).

508 Indians of All Tribes Newsletter. 1970//. Monthly. Last issue 16
    pages, height 22 cm. Line drawings, photographs, some in color.
    Alcatraz Island, San Francisco, CA. Title varies: Alcatraz, Indians
    of All Tribes. Editor: Peter Blue Cloud. Subject focus: rights, land
    claims, Alcatraz occupation.

CU-A	n.1-4; Jan-Apr, 1970	Periodicals
KU	n.1-4; Jan-Apr, 1970	Kansas Collection
MiU	v.1, n.2 Feb, 1970	Labadie Collection
NjP	[n.1-4] [Jan-Apr, 1970]	Periodicals

509 Indians of Quebec/Indiens du Quebec. 1977-1982//. Irregular. ISSN
    0228-0841. LC ce80-31318. OCLC 6859078. RLIN DCLCCF8031318-S,
    DCLCCE8031318-S. Last issue 28 pages, last volume 144 pages, height
    39 cm. Line drawings, photographs, commercial advertising. Published
    by Confederation of Indians of Quebec, Caughnawaga (Kahnawake),
    Quebec, Canada. Title varies: Indians of Quebec News/Nouvelles des
    Indiens de Quebec, July, 1977. Editors: Joe Curotte, July-Sept, 1977;
    Mark Montour, Mar-Aug?, 1978; Peter Dione, Jan, 1979-July, 1982.
    Subject focus: rights, politics, law. In French, 50%.

WHi	v.1, n.1?-v.5, n.3; July, 1977-July, 1982	Microforms
WMUW	v.4, n.5-v.5, n.3; 1980-July, 1982	(SPL) E/78/Q315x
CaAEU	v.4, n.5-v.5, n.3; 1980-July, 1982	Boreal Institute
CaNBFU	v.4-v.5, n.3; 1980-July, 1982	E/78/Q3152
CaOAFN	v.4, n.7-v.5, n.3; 1981-July, 1982	Periodicals
CaOONL	v.1, n.1?-v.5, n.3; July, 1977-July, 1982	Newspaper Section
CaOPeT	v.4-v.5, n.3; 1980-July, 1982	Periodicals

Indians of Quebec News/Nouvelles des Indiens. Caughnawaga, Quebec,
        Canada

see <u>Indians of Quebec/Indiens du Quebec</u>. Caughnawaga, Quebec,
Canada

<u>Indiens du Quebec</u>. Caughnawaga, Quebec, Canada

see <u>Indians of Quebec/Indiens du Quebec</u>. Caughnawaga, Quebec,
Canada

510 <u>Indigena</u>. 1974-1978?//. Iregular. OCLC 4367817, 4173100, 2694648.
RLIN MIUG82-S6049, CSUP0803980X-S, CTYG4173100-S, OHCP4173100-S,
OHCP2694648-S, CSUG2174812-S, NYPG784392791-S. Last issue 32 pages.
Line drawings, photographs. Available in microform: WHi (1978).
Berkeley, CA. Subject focus: political, economic and legal status of
Native peoples in the U. S., Canada, the Caribbean and Latin America.
In Spanish, 50%.

WHi	v.2, n.2, v.3, n.1, v.4, n.1; Fall, 1976, Summer, 1977, Summer, 1978	Microforms
WEU	v.2, n.2; Fall, 1976	Journalism Lab
WKenU	v.1, n.4; Apr, 1975	Microforms
WMMus	v.2, n.1-v.4, n.1; Summer, 1976-Summer, 1978	Anthro Section
WMUW	v.1, n.4; Apr, 1975	MF/AN014
AzNCC	v.1-v.4, n.1; Sumer, 1974-Summer, 1978	Indian File
CU-A	v.1, n.2-v.4, n.1; Summer, 1974-Summer, 1978	E/77/A1/I6
NjP	[v.1, n.1-v.4, n.1] [Summer, 1974-Summer, 1978]	Periodicals
N	v.1, n.4; Apr, 1975	MA/FM
PPT	v.1, n.4; Apr, 1975	Contemporary Culture

Other holding institutions: AzTeS (AZS), COU-DA (COA), InU (IUL), CtY
(YUS), OAKU (AKR), MiU-Labadie (EYM), [Minnesota Union List of
Serials, Minneapolis, MN] (MUL), NSbSU (YSM), OKentU (KSU),
OrU-Special Collections, PPiU (PIT), TxU (IXA).

511 <u>Indodem</u>. 1972-?//. Monthly. Last issue 8 pages. Line drawings.
Available in microform: WHi-A, Veda Stone Papers, (1973). Published
by Indian Studies Department, College of St. Scholastica, Duluth, MN.
Editor: Jennifer Wakanabo. Subject focus: education, culture, poetry.

WHi   v.2, n.1;   Microforms
             Jan, 1973

WEU   v.2, n.1;   Micro 11
ARC   Jan, 1973

512 <u>Informant</u>. 1980?-1982//. Monthly. Last issue 4 pages, height 28 cm.
Available in microform: WHi (1981-1982). Published by Institute of
Indian Studies, University of South Dakota, Vermillion, SD. College
newsletter. Subject focus: school, local and national news.

WHi   [n.17-28]   Microforms
             [May, 1981-June, 1982]

513 <u>Information Letter</u>. 1955-1958//. Irregular. Last issue 4 pages,
height 29 cm. Available in microform: McA (1955-1958). Published by
National Congress of American Indians, Washington, DC. Subject focus:
law, legislation.

WHi   v.1, n.1-v.4, n.3;   Microforms
             Mar, 1955-July 31, 1958

Other holding institutions: NN (NYP), WaU (WAU).

514 <u>Institute of Alaska Native Arts, Inc.: The Newsletter of Native Arts</u>.
1976? Unknown. Jan Steinbright, editor, The Newsletter of Native
Arts, P.O. box 80583, Fairbanks, AK 99708-0583. (907) 479-8473. Last
issue 8 pages, height 28 cm. Line drawings, photographs. Subject
focus: visual, performing, literary arts.

WHi   Oct/Nov, 1981-   Circulation

515 <u>Integrated Education</u>. 1963. Bi-monthly. $15. for individuals; $18.
for institutions. Meyer Weinberg, editor, Integrated education, Room
2220, University Library, University of Massachusetts, Amherst, MA
01003. (413) 545-0327. ISSN 0020-4862. LC 76-1531. OCLC 1753326.
RLIN CSUP81-S1523, CLCG71283579-S, OHCP1753326-S, DCLC761531-S,
CSUP02276513-S, CUBG10589909-S, MIUG1289-S, NYGP784505045-S,
NYPG764761548-S. Last issue 172 pages, last volume 552 pages, height
28 cm. Line drawings, photographs. Indexed in: Education Index
(1969-), Current Index to Journals in Education (1971-), Educational
Administration Abstracts, Index to Periodicals By and About Negroes

(1963-1970), Public Affairs Information Service. Subject focus:
educational equality, bibliography.

WU IMC	v.13, n.2– Mar/Apr, 1975–	Periodicals Section
WM	v.16, n.1– Jan/Feb, 1978–	Periodicals
WKenU	[v.1, n.1–v.15, n.6]v.16, n.1– 1963-Nov/Dec, 1977], Jan/Feb, 1978–	Microfilm

Other holding institutions: AU (ALM), ArU (AFU), ArAt (AKH), ArRuA
(AKP), AzFU (AZN), AzTeS (AZS), CChiS (CCH), [California State
University, Dominguez Hills, Carson, CA] (CDH), CFIS (CFI),
[Pepperdine University, Malibu, CA] (CPE), CsjU (CSJ), COU-DA (COA),
COFS (COF), [Bibliographic Center for Research, Denver, CO] (TPS),
CtY-D (YUS), [Congressional Research Service, Washington, DC] (CRS),
DHU (DHU), DLC (DLC), DeU (DLM), FBoU (FGM), FJUNF (FNP), FU (FUG),
FMFIL (FXG), FMFIU (FXN), GEU (EMU), GASU (GSU), GCarrWG (GWC), ICI
(IAH), ICL (IAL), ICRC (IAR), ICSX (ICS), IDeKN (JNA), InMuB (IBS),
InWhC (ICC), InRE (IEC), InE (IEP), InICC (III), [Indiana Union List,
Indianapolis, IN] (ILS), InHamP (IPC), InLP (IPL), InES (ISE), InTI
(ISU), InEU (IUE), InIU (IUP), KLindB (KFB), KPT (KFP), KSteC (KKQ),
LU-S (LUS), MBU (BOS), [Boston STate College Library, Boston, MA]
(BST), M (MAS), MBNU (NED), MNS ((SNN), MdBJ (JHE), MdStm (MDS), MiAdc
(EEA), MiLC (EEL), MiEM (EEM), MiGrc (EXC), MiYEM (EYE), MiDu (EYU),
MiDW (EYW), MiMtpT (EZC), MnAH (MHA), MnStjos (MNF), [University of
Minnesota Union List, Minneapolis, MN] (MUL), MoWgT/MoWgW (ELW), NcGU
(NGU), NcEUcE (NPE), NcRs (NRC), NbU (LDL), NhD (DRB), NhPIS (PSM),
NmLcU (IRU), NmLvH (NMH), NIC (COO), N (NYG), [New York State Union
List, Albany, NY] (NYS), NRU (RRR), [Central New York Library
Resources Council, Syracuse, NY] (SRR), NSyU (SYB), NSbSU-H (VZB),
NDFM (VZE), [Western New York Library Resources Council, Buffalo, NY]
(VZX), NII (XIM), NCaS (XLM), NFQC (XQM), NGenoU (YGM), NCH (YHM), NR
(YQR), NSbSU (YSM), NOneoU (ZXBM), NNepaSU (ZLM), NPotU (ZQM) NNR
(ZXC), OAkU (AKR), OBgU (BGU), OC1U (CSU), OC1W (CWR), OKentU (KSU), O
(OHI), OU (OSU), OAU (OUN), OTU (TOL), ODaTs (UTS), OkAdE (ECO), Ok
(OKD), OkS (OKS), OkU (OKU), OkEP (OKZ), PBm (BMC), PU (PAU), PPiU
(PIT), PP (PLF), [Pittsburgh Regional Library Center-Union List,
Pittsburgh, PA] (QPR), PCW (UWC), ScU (SUC), INJ (TJC), TN (TNN),
TMurS (TXM), TxFTC (ICU), TxComS (IEA), TxF (IFA), TxDa (IGA), TxLT
(ILU), TxDN (INT), TxDaM (ISM), TxU-Da (ITD), [AMIGOS Union List of
Serials, Dallas, TX] (IUC), TxDW (IWU), TxU (IXA), TxHU-D (THD),
TxWicM (TMI), TxSvT (TTS), TxFTW (TWC), TxCM (TXA), TxNacSD (TXK),
ViNO (VOD), WaU (WAU), WMaPI-RL (GZR).

516 Inter-Com. 1980. Irregular. Beatrice Chevalier, editor, Inter-Com,
    4550 Hermitage St., Chicago, IL 60640. (312) 728-1662. Last issue 16
    pages, height 28 cm. Photographs. Published by Indian Community
    Inter-Agency Communication, Native American Education Service.
    Subject focus: education.

WHi   v.2, n.1-   Circulation
            Sept, 1982-

ICN   n.5-10;   CHAI
            Jan-Oct, 1981

517 Intercom. 1958-1971//. Irregular. Last issue 34 pages, last volume
    86 pages, height 28 cm. Line drawings, photographs. Published by
    Department of Indian Affairs and Northern Development, Ottawa,
    Ontario, Canada. Editors: Mona C. Ricks, Aug, 1968-Apr, 1970; Sharon
    Doyle, Nov, 1970-Jan/Feb, 1971. Subject focus: environment, natural
    resources, community development, culture. In French, 50%.

WHi   v.11, n.3-v.14, n.1;   R12-1/
            Aug, 1968-Jan/Feb, 1971

WaU   v.11, n.3-v.14, n.1;   HC117/N48/I55
            Aug, 1968-Jan/Feb, 1971

CaOOP   v.11-v.14,n.1;   HC/113.5/A15
            1968-Jan/Feb, 1971

518 The Interpreter. 1975-?//?. Monthly. LC cn79-70608. OCLC 4678197.
    Last issue 16 pages, height 46 cm. Line drawings, photographs.
    Available in microform: WHi (1977). Yellowknife, Northwest
    Territories, Canada. Editor: Chris Aylott. Community newsletter. In
    Inuit, 50%.

WHi   v.3, n.3;   Microforms
            Mar, 1977

WMUW   v.3, n.3;   (SPL)
            Mar, 1977   E/75/I72x

Other holding institutions: CaOONL (NLC).

519 Interracial Books for Children Bulletin. 1966. 8 times a year. $10.
    for individuals; $15. for institutions. Bradford Chambers, editor,
    Interracial Books for Children Bulletin, 1841 Broadway, New York, NY
    10023. (212) 757-5339. ISSN 0146-5562. LC sc77-815, 78-648204.
    OCLC 2972338. RLIN UTBG21810273-S, DCLC78648207-S, UTBG2240-S,
    DCLCSC77815-S, CSUP212511-S, MIUG08166-S, OHCP2972338-S. Last issue
    40 pages, height 28 cm. Line drawings, photographs. Indexed in:
    Alternative Press Index (1981-); Education Index (1977-). Available in
    microform: UM (1976-). Published by Council on Interracial Books for
    Children. Subject focus: minority culture, multicultural education,
    curriculum development, book reviews, bibliography, women's issues,
    racism, sexism and bias in children's materials, children's literature.

WU IMC	v.6, n.1– Winter?, 1975–	Periodicals Section
WU Lib Sc	v.2, n.3– Summer, 1969–	Periodicals Section
WU	v.2, n.1/2– Spring/Summer, 1968–	AP/+I61694/ +B727
WM	v.5, n.7/8– Fall, 1975–	CYC
WMUW	v.1, n.2– 1967–	CCM/Z1037/ A1/I78x
WGrU	v.6, n.3–v.11; Summer, 1972-1980	Periodicals

Other holding institutions: ABAU (ABC), AU (ALM), CLobS (CLO), CLU (CLU), COU-DA (COA), COD (DPL), CoDU (DVP), [St. Joseph's College, West Hartford, CT] (STJ), DLC (DLC), FBoU (FGM), FOFT (FTU), FMFIL (FXG), FMFIU (FXN), GAuA (GJG), HU (HUH), IaCfT (NIU), IChurE (IAD), INS (IAI), ICRC (IAR), I (SPI), InE (IEP), InLP (IPL), InU (IUL), InIU (IUP), InTV (IVC), KyU (KUK), LU (LUU), [Boston State College Library, Boston, MA] (BST), MWC (CKM), MBSi (SCL), MdU (UMC), MiAdC (EEA), MiLC (EEL), MiEM (EEM), Mi (EEX), MiDU (EYU), MiDW (EYW), MiSW (EZW), MnStcls (MST), [University of Minnesota Union List, Minneapolis, MN] (MUL), MnSRC (RCL), NcD (NDD), NcGU (NGU), NcCU (NKM), NcEUcE (NPE), NmU (IQU), N (NYG), [New York State Union List, Albany, NY] (NYS), NBP (VZQ), [Western New York Library Resources Council, Buffalo, NY] (VZX), NFQC (XQM), NGenoU (YGM), NR (YQR), NOneoU (ZBM), NPotU (ZQM), NNR (ZXC),OAkU (AKR), OC1U (CSU), OKentU (KSU), O (OHI), OU (OSU), ODaWU (WSU), OKTU (OKT), OkEP (OKZ), [Northwestern Oklahoma State University Library, Alva, OK] (OUF), [Pittsburgh Regional Library Center-Union List, Pittsburgh, PA] (QPR), PPST (SJD), Sc (DSC), TNJ (TJC), TCU (TUC), TxComS (IEA), TxDa (IGA), TxLT (ILU), TxDN (INT), [AMIGOS Union List of Serials, Dallas, TX] (IUC), TxDW (IWU), TxU (IXA), TxWicM (TMI), TxFTW (TWC), TxCM (TXA), TxAu (TXG), TxSmS (TXI),ViU (VA@), ViPetS (VSC), WMenU (GZS), [Arrowhead Library System, Janesville Public Library, Janesville, WI] (WIJ).

520 Intertribal Friendship House Newsletter. 1981//. Monthly. Last issue 6 pages, height 22 cm. Line drawings, photographs. Oakland, CA. Subject focus: urban community, organization news.

WHi	v.1, n.3-6; July-Dec, 1981	Pam Cataloging

Other holding institutions: IC (CGP).

521 Inter-Tribal Tribune. 1975. Monthly. Inter-Tribal Tribune, 1340 E. Admiral Blvd., Kansas City, MO 64106-1590. (816) 421-7608. OCLC

6161399. Last issue 8 pages, last volume 48 pages, height 28 cm.
Line drawings, commercial advertising. Available in microform: WHi
(1975-). Published by Heart of America Indian Center. Title varies:
Heart of America Indian Center Newsletter, Aug, 1975-Apr, 1980.
Subject focus: urban, center news.

WHi   [v.2, n.5?-v.6, n.5], v.6, n.7-   Circulation
             [May, 1975-May,] July, 1980-

WEU   v.4, n.2-3;   Journalism
             Feb-Mar, 1977   Lab

WMUW   [v.2, n.7-v.6, n.9]   (SPL)
             [Aug, 1975-Feb, 1976]   E/75/H42x

522 Inter-Tribal Voice. 1982. Bi-monthly. Tony Arkeketa, editor,
    Inter-Tribal Voice, 1740 W. 41st St., Tulsa, OK 74107. (918)
    446-8432. Last issue 8 pages, height 39 cm. Line drawings,
    photographs. Published by Native American Coalition of Tulsa, Inc.
    Subject focus: urban community, local and national news.

    WHi   v.1, n.1-   Circulation
                 Sept, 1982-

    Inuit Cultural Institute Newsletter. Eskimo Point, Northwest
              Territories, Canada

       see ICI Newsletter. Eskimo Point, Northwest Territories, Canada

    Inuit Monthly. Ottawa, Ontario, Canada

       see Inuit Today. Ottawa, Ontario, Canada

523 Inuit North. 1979-1980//? Unknown. ISSN 0709-843x. LC cn80-30283.
    OCLC 6136588. Last issue 71 pages, height 28 cm. Line drawings,
    photographs. Published by Nortext and A. Barry Roberts Consultants,
    Ottawa, Ontario, Canada. Subject focus: Inuit people, politics.

    CaACG   July, 1979, Jan, 1980   Periodicals

524 Inuit Today. 1971. 6 times a year. $10. for individuals; $25. for
    institutions. Alootook Ipellic, editor, Inuit Today, 176 Gloucester
    St., 4th Floor, Ottawa, Ontario, Canada K2P 0A6. (613) 238-8181.
    ISSN 0318-5354, 0318-5346. LC cn75-34636. OCLC 2442086. RLIN
    DCLCCN7534636-S, OHCP2442086-S. Last issue 60 pages, height 28 cm.
    Line drawings, photographs, commercial advertising. Published by

Inuit Tapirisat of Canada. Title varies: Inuit Monthly, Feb,
1974-Feb, 1975. Frequency varies: monthly, Feb, 1974-Dec, 1977.
Previous editors: Jennifer Farris, Feb-Sept, 1974; Luci Marquand, Oct,
1974-Sept, 1975; Seemee Nookiguak, Oct, 1975; Leah d'Argencourt,
Nov/Dec, 1975-July/Dec, 1978. Subject focus: politics, history,
legends, biographies, poetry. In Inuktitut, 50%.

WHi	v.3, n.2– Feb, 1974–	E/99/E7/I58
AkU	v.4, n.3– Mar, 1975–	E/78/C2/I7
AzNCC	v.7– 1978–	Indian File
NjP	[v.1, n.1-v.8] [Dec., 1971-June, 1979]	Periodicals
CaACG	v.4, n.7– 1975–	Periodicals
CaAEU	v.2, n.5– 1973–	Boreal Institute
CaMWU	[v.4-v.5] [1975-1976]	Microfilm
CaOAUC	v.1-v.9; 1972-1980	Periodicals
CaOONL	v.1– 1971–	Periodicals
CaOPeT	v.1– 1971–	E99/E7I58

Other holding institutions: VtU (VTU), CaNfSM.

Inukshuk. Frobisher Bay, Northwest Territories, Canada

   see Nunatsiaq News. Frobisher Bay, Northwest Territories, Canada

Inuktitun. Ottawa, Ontario, Canada

   see Inuktitut. Ottawa, Ontario, Canada

525 Inuktitut. 1959. Irregular. Inuktitut, Ottawa, Ontario, Canada K1A
    0H4. (819) 997-9660. ISSN 0020-9872. LC cn79-310994. OCLC 2007217,
    4146119. RLIN DCLCCN79310994-S, CUBG30991201-S, OHCP4145119-S. Last

issue 92 pages. Line drawings, photographs. Available in microform:
McA (1959-). Published by the Social and Cultural Development
Division of the Northern Branch of the Department of Indian Affairs
and Northern Development. Title varies: Inuttutuut/Inuktitun, May,
1959-1977. Subject focus: culture, history, cultural and linguistic
development, education, language, circumpolar relations. In
Inuktitut, 30%; in French, 30%.

WHi	May, 1959-	Microforms
WGrU	July, 1981-	R/71/11
CoCF	1978-	Periodicals
NjP	[1959-Summer, 1970]	Periodicals
OkU	May, 1959-Spring, 1972	WHC
WyCWC	Spring/Summer, 1974-Winter, 1975	Periodicals
CaACG	Spring, 1977-	Periodicals
CaAEU	1967-	Boreal Institute
CaOOP	Nov, 1959-	E/99/E7/I58
CaOPeT	May, 1959-	Microfilm

Other holding institutions: ArU (AFU), [University of Minnesota Union
List, Minneapolis, MN] (MUL), NhB (DRB), [Western Nevada Community
College, Carson City, NV].

526 Inummarit. 1972-1977?//. 3 times a year. ISSN 0382-8085. LC
cn76-32208. OCLC 3193490. RLIN DCLCCN7632208-S, OHCP3193490-S,
NYPG764402132-S. Last issue 6 pages. Line drawings, photographs.
Available in microform: WHi (1972-1976). Published by Inummarit
Cultural Association, Igloolik, Northwest Territories, Canada.
Frequency varies: quarterly, 1972. Subject focus: education. In
Inuit, 50%.

WHi	v.1, n.1-v.3, n.1; Mar, 1972-1976	Microforms
CaACG	v.1, n.1-v.3, n.1; Mar, 1972-1976	Periodicals
CaAEU	v.1-v.4; 1972-1977	Boreal Institute
CaMWU	v.1-v.3; 1972-1974	970/I6186

CaOONL   v.1–v.3;
            1972–1976   Periodicals

CaOPeT   v.1, n.1–v.4?
            Mar, 1972–1977?   E99/E7I62

Inuttutuut/Inuktitun. Ottawa, Ontario, Canada

    see Inuktitut. Ottawa Ontario, Canada

527 Inuvialuit. 1975. Quarterly. $6. for individuals and institutions. Larry Osgood, editor, Inuvialuit, P.O. Box 2000, Inuvik, Northwest Territories, Canada X0E 0T0. (403) 979-3510. ISSN 0383-204x. LC cn77-30250. OCLC 3209835. RLIN DCLCCN7730250-S, OHCP3209835-S. Last issue 24 pages, height 28 cm. Line drawings, photographs. Published by Committee for Original Peoples entitlement (C.O.P.E.). Frequency varies: bi-monthly, ?, 1978. Previous editor: Susan Shewan, ?, 1978. Subject focus: culture, history. Some Inuit.

WHi   ?, 1978, Spring, 1981–   Circulation

CaACG   n.6–
           Winter, 1976–   Periodicals

CaAEU   n.3–
           1976–   Boreal
                                   Institute

CaMWU   v.2–v.4, v.6–v.8;
           1975–1977, 1978–1979   970/I6198

CaOONL   v.2–
           Sept, 1972–   Periodicals

528 Iowa Indian. 1976?–?//. Bi-monthly. OCLC 6188838. Last issue 10 pages, height 28 cm. Line drawings, photographs. Available in microform: WHi (1976-1977). Sioux City, IA. Community newsletter.

WHi   Sept/Oct, 1976–July/Aug, 1977   Microforms

WMUW   Sept/Oct, 1976–July/Aug, 1977   (SPL)
                                        E/75/I76x

529 Ne Jaguhnigoagesgwathah/The Mental Elevator. 1842-1850?//. Irregular. Last issue 12 pages, height 20 cm. Line drawings. Cattaraugus Reservation, NY. Subject focus: Seneca people, missions. In Seneca, 75-100%.

WHi   v.1, n.2-19;   F8097/S47M
            Dec 28, 1841-Apr 15, 1950   Rare Books

530 <u>Jibkenyan</u>. 1979. Bi-weekly. Jibkenyan, R.R. 3, Wallaceburg,
    Ontario, Canada N8A 4K9. Last issue 18 pages, height 28 cm. Line
    drawings. Published by Walpole Island Council. Community newsletter.
    Subject focus: Ojibwa and Chippewa peoples.

                                                 Periodicals
    CaOAFN   v.3, n.28-
                Jan 5, 1981-

531 <u>Jicarilla Chieftain</u>. 1961. Bi-weekly. Mary F. Polanco, editor,
    Jicarilla Chieftan, Bank and Post Office Complex, Dulce, NM 87528.
    (505) 759-3242. ISSN 0021-695x. LC sn78-623. OCLC 4073951. RLIN
    OHCP4073951-S. Last issue 8 pages, height 38 cm. Line drawings,
    photographs, commercial advertising. Available in microform: McP
    (1970-1973). Published by Jicarilla Apache Tribe. Previous editors:
    Beatrice Kemm, July 27, 1970; Jolene Velarde, Aug 24-Dec 28, 1970;
    Rudolfo Velarde, Feb 22, 1971-July 22, 1974; Dolores Velarde, Aug 19,
    1974-Apr 14, 1975; Travis Chavez, Apr 28, 1975-Mar 15, 1976.
    Community newsletter. Subject focus: Jicarilla Apache people, book
    and movie reviews.

    WHi   v.10, n.15-   Microforms
                July 27, 1970-

    WEU   v.11, n.5-6;   Journalism
                Mar 8-22, 1971   Lab

    WMUW   v.17, n.4;   (SPL)
                July 18, 1977   E/75/J5x

    AzNCC   v.14-   Indian File
                1974-

    NjP   [v.7, n.26-v.16, n.3]   Periodicals
                [Jan 1, 1968-Feb 16, 1976]

    NHu   [v.10, n.24-v.18, n.25]   Periodicals
                [Nov 30, 1970-1978]

    OkU   [v.10, n.24-v.21, n.15]   WHC
                [Nov 30, 1970-1981]

    CaOPeT   v.12-   Periodicals
                1972-

    Other holding institutions: [University of Minnesota Union List,
    Minneapolis, MN] (MUL), NmScW, NmU (IQU), [Wheelwright Museum, Santa
    Fe, NM], [Standing Rock Community College Library, Fort Yates, ND].

532 <u>Journal of American Indian Education</u>. 1961. 3 times a year. $6.50
for individuals and institutions. George A. Gill, editor, Journal of
Amercian Indian Education. College of Education, Arizona State
University, Tempe, AZ 85281. (602)965-6292. ISSN 0021-8731. LC
sf77-156. OCLC 1604081, 3916092, 4785967. RLIN NYPG814176954-S,
DCLCSF77156-S, CSUP02470007-S, CUBG2502730X-S, CTYG4785967-S,
OHCP4785967-S, OHCP3916092-S, OHCP1604081-S. Last issue 32 pages,
last volume 96 pages, height 23 cm. Line drawings, photographs.
Indexed: Index to Literature on the American Indian (1970-1972).
Available in microform: WHi-A, Veda Stone Papers, (1965). Published
by Center for Indian Education, Arizona State University. Previous
editors: Robert A. Roessel, Jr. and Bruce S. Meador, June, 1961-Oct,
1966; George A. Gill and Bruce Meador, Jan-May, 1967. Subject focus:
education, curriculum development.

WHi	v.1, n.1- June, 1961-	E/97/J55
WHi	v.12, n.2-v.17, n.1; Jan, 1973-Oct, 1978	Microforms
WEU	v.1, n.1- June, 1961-	Microforms
WEU ARC	v.4, n.2; Jan, 1965	Micro 11
WU IMC	v.16, n.2- Jan, 1977-	Periodicals Section
WU Coll	Current issues	Ethnic Collection
WM	Current issues	Forest Home Branch
WMUW	v.3, n.1- June?, 1963-	E/97/J68x
WGrU	v.11, n.1- June, 1971-	Microfilm
WGrU	v.1, n.1-v.13, n.2; June, 1961-Jan, 1974	Periodicals
WUSP	v.11, n.1- Jan, 1971-	Periodicals
WMSC	v.11, n.2- Oct, 1971-	Periodicals
AzFM	v.1- 1961-	570.6/T28i
AzHC	v.1; June, 1961-Jan, 1962	Periodicals

AzPh	v.6-v.9, v.12- 1966-1970, 1972-	Periodicals
AzNCC	v.3- May, 1963-	Indian File
AzT	v.19, n.1- May, 1979-	Periodicals
AzU	v.1, n.1- June, 1961-	Periodicals
CL	v.14- Oct, 1974-	Periodicals
CNoSU	v.1, n.1- June, 1961-	Periodicals
CRSSU	v.1, n.1- June, 1961-	Microfilm
CSmarP	[v.9-v.21]- [1969-1981]-	Stacks
CU-A	[v.1-v.7], v.8- [1961-1968], 1968-	E/97/A1/J65
IdU	[v.1, n.1-v.2, n.1], v.3- [1961-1963], 1964-	E/97/S1/J67
IC	v.1, n.1- June, 1961-	Periodicals
LARC	v.8-v.18; 1968-1979	Periodicals
MnBemT	v.1, n.1- June, 1961-	Periodicals
MtBBCC	v.20- Jan, 1981-	Periodicals
MtGrCE	v.14- 1974-	Periodicals
NbU	v.1, n.1- June, 1961-	E/97/J6
NjP	[v.1, n.1-v.9, n.1] [June, 1961-Oct, 1969]	Periodicals
NmG	v.1, n.1- June, 1961-	Periodicals
NmScW	v.12- 1973-	Periodicals

N	v.1, n.1– June, 1961–	J371.97/J86
N	v.15, n.1– May, 1976–	MA/FM
NN	v.1, n.1–v.16; June, 1961–May, 1977	HBA
NPotU	v.2– Oct, 1962–	E/97/J6
NcP	v.5– 1965–	Periodicals
NdMinS	v.11– 1971–	Periodicals
OkTahN	v.1– 1961–	E/77/J6
OkU	v.1, n.1– June, 1961–	WHC
SdU	v.1–v.13, v.15– 1961–1973, 1975–	Stacks
WaS	v.11– 1971–	Education Dept.
WaU	v.4, n.1– 1964–	371.075/JO
WyCWC	v.8, n.1–v.16, n.3; 1968–1977	Periodicals
CaMWU	v.1–v.3, v.14–v.16; 1961–1964, 1974–1977	370/J826/Ai
CaNFBU	v.1– 1961–	E/97/J66
CaOPeT	v.1– 1961–	Microfilm
CaSSIC	v.1, n.1–v.13, n.3; June, 1961–1974	Microfiche

Other holding institutions: AU (ALM), ArU (AFU), AzFu (AZN), AzTeS
(AZS), CChiS (CCH), CLobS (CLO), CLSM, CLU (CLU), WeharU (HRM), CtY
(YUS), [Congressional Research Service, Washington, DC] (CRS), DLC
(DLC), FBoU (FGM), GAuA (GJG), ICL (IAL), InMuB (IBS), [Indiana Union
List of Serials, Indianapolis, IN] (ILS), InLP (IPL), InU (IUL), KMK
(KKS), KPT (KFP), KyRE (KEU), KyU (KUK), LGra (LGS), MBU (BOS),
[Boston State College Library, Boston, MA] (BST), MNS (SNN), MdBJ
(JHE), MiEM (EEM), MiYEM (EYE), MiU (EYM), MiDW (EYW), MiMtpT (EZC),

MnHi (MHS), [University of Minnesota Union List, Minneapolis, MN]
(MUL), NcEUcE (NPE), NcRs (NRC), NbU (LDL), NhPls (PSM), NmLcU (IRU),
NmLvH (NMH), NIC (COO), [New York State Union List, Albany,NY] (NYS),
NRU (RRR), [Central New York Library Resources Council, Syracuse, NY]
(SRR), NSyU (SYB), NBu (VHB), NPV (VXM), [Western New York Library
Resources Council, Buffalo, NY] (VZX), NFQC (XQM), NAlf (YAH), NSbSU
(YSM), NUtSU (YTM), NOneoU (ZBM), NNepaSU (ZLM), OAkU (AKR), OBgU
(BGU), OKentU (KSU), OAU (OUN), [State Library of Ohio Catalog Center,
Columbus, OH] (SLC), OTU (TOL), OYU (YNG), OkAdE, (ECO), [Bacone
College, Muskogee, OK], OkLC (OKC), OkOk (OKE), OkS (OKS), OKTU (OKT),
[Northwestern Oklahoma State University Library, Alva OK] (OUF),
[University of Science and Arts of Oklahoma Library, Chickasha, OK]
(OUV), PU (PAU), PPiU (PIT), PPiPP (PTP), [Pittsburgh Regional Library
Center Union List, Pittsburgh, PA] (QPR), PNwC (WFN), TNJ (TJC), TMurS
(TXM), INElk (IEA), TxDa (IGA), TxLT (ILU), TxArU (IUA), [AMIGOS Union
List of Serials, Dallas, TX] (IUC), TxDW (IWU), TxU (IXA), TxCM (TXA),
TxHU (TXH), WaU (WAU), WMaPI-RL (GZR), WGrU (GZW), [University of
Wisconsin-Stevens Point, Stevens Point, WI] (WIS).

533 The Journal of American Indian Family Research. 1980. Quarterly.
$12 for individuals and institutions. Larry Watson, editor, The
Journal of American Indian Family Research, P.O. Box 687, Lawton, OK
73502. (405) 353-2624. OCLC 7805403. Last issue 50 pages, last
volume 198 pages, height 28 cm. Line drawings, commercial
advertising. Published by Histree. Subject focus: genealogy, family
history.

WHi   Jan, 1980-   Circulation

Mi   Jan, 1980-   Periodicals

Other holding institutions: ICN (IBV).

534 Journal of Cherokee Studies. 1976. Quarterly. $10. for individuals
and institutions. Duane King, editor, Journal of Cherokee Studies,
Museum Complex, P.O. Box 770-A, Cherokee, NC 28719. (704) 497-3481.
ISSN 0146-2962. LC 77-648853. OCLC 2690846. RLIN DCLC77648853-S,
CSUP20512-S, CUBG12774741-S, MIUG1968-S, CTYG2690846-S, OHCP2690846-S,
CSUG7455658-S. Last issue 54 pages. Line drawings, photographs.
Published by Museum of the Cherokee Indian and The Cherokee Historical
Association. Subject focus: scholarly articles on Cherokee history
and culture.

WHi   v.1, n.1-   E/99/C5/J68
           Summer, 1976-

WUSP   v.1, n.1-   Periodicals
           Summer, 1976-

CL   v.1, n.1-   Periodicals
           Summer, 1976-

CRSSU   v.5-   Periodicals
           1980-

ICN   Current issues   CHAI

NHu   [v.1, n.1-v.3, n.2]   Periodicals
           [Summer, 1976-1978]

NcMhC   v.1-   Periodicals
           1976-

OkTahN   v.1, n.1-   Special
           Summer, 1976-   Collections

OkTU   v.1, n.1-   Rare Book
           Summer, 1976-   Room

OkU   v.4, n.2-   WHC
           Spring, 1979-

Other holding institutions: AAP (AAA), AU (ALM), CtY (YUS), DLC (DLC),
FU (FUG), GEU (EMU), GASU (GSU), GU (GUA). MBU (BOS), MH-P (HLS), MiU
(EYM), [University of Minnesota Union List, Minneapolis, MN] (MUL),
NcGU (NGU), NcAU (NIM), NcRS (NRC), [Bacone College, Muskogee, OK],
OkAdE (ECO), PPiU (PIT), TNJ (TJC), [University of Wisconsin-Stevens
Point, Stevens Point, WI] (WIS).

535 Journal of the Wisconsin Indian Research Institute. 1965-1978//.
    Semi-annual. ISSN 0300-6581. LC 65-64757. OCLC 1770029. RLIN
    DCLC6564757-S, CUDL0325-S, NJPG1717-S, MIUG13853-S, PAUG0737-S,
    OHCP1770029-S. Last issue 85 pages, last volume 184 pages, height 28
    cm. Line drawings. Available in microform: WHi-A, Veda Stone Papers,
    (1965). Published by Department of Anthropology, University of
    Northern Colorado, Greeley, CO. Place of publication varies: Oshkosh,
    WI, Mar-Oct, 1965. Editor, George E. Fay. Subject focus: Menominee,
    Chippewa and Oneida peoples, history, anthropology.

WHi   v.1, n.1-v.5, n.2;   E/78/W8/W84
           Mar, 1965-June, 1978

WEU   v.1, n.1-v.5, n.2;   Periodical
           Mar, 1965-June, 1978   Stacks

WEU   v.1, n.1-2;   Micro 11
ARC   Mar-Oct, 1965

WGrU   v.2, n.1-v.4, n.2;   Periodicals
           June, 1966-June, 1968

WKenU   v.1, n.1-v.4, n.2;   Periodicals
           Mar, 1965-June?, 1968

WMMus   v.1, n.1-v.5, n.2;   970.1/775/W753
           Mar, 1965-June, 1978

WMUW	v.1, n.1–v.5, n.2; Mar, 1965–June, 1978	E/77/W47x
WOshU	v.1, n.1–v.5, n.2; Mar, 1965–June, 1978	Periodicals
WUSP	v.1, n.1–v.4, n.2; Mar, 1965–June?, 1968	E/78/W8/W86
CLSM	v.1, n.1–v.5, n.2; Mar, 1965–June, 1978	Periodicals
IC	v.1, n.1–v.4, n.2; Mar, 1965–June?, 1968	Periodicals
IaHi	v.1, n.1–v.3, n.1; Mar, 1965–1967	E/78/W8/W86
MnBemT	v.1, n.1–v.5, n.2; Mar, 1965–June, 1978	Periodicals
NjP	v.1, n.1–v.2, n.2; Mar, 1965–Dec, 1966	Periodicals
N	v.1, n.1–v.5, n.1; Mar, 1965–Mar, 1970	Periodicals
NN	v.1, n.1–v.5; Mar, 1965–Mar, 1970	HBB
NPotU	v.1, n.1–v.5, n.2; Mar, 1965–June, 1978	E/78/W8/W86
OkU	v.1, n.1–v.5, n.2; Mar, 1965–June, 1978	WHC
UPB	v.1, n.1–v.5, n.2; Mar, 1965–June, 1978	970.105/W753

Other holding institutions: [Amerind Foundation, Inc., Dragoon, AZ],
AzTeS (AZS), DLC (DLC), DeU (DLM), ICL (IAL), IRA (ICY), [Indiana
Union List of Serials, Indianapolis, IN] (ILS), InU (IUL), KMK (KKS),
KWiU (KSW), MiEM (EEM), MiBatW (EEW), MiU (EYM), [University of
Minnesota Union List, Minneapolis, MN] (MUL), NmU (IQU), NFQC (XQM),
NSbSU (YSM), PPiU (PIT), [Pittsburgh Regional Library Center Union
List, Pittsburgh, PA] (QPR), RPB (RBN), TNJ (TJC), [AMIGOS Union List,
Dallas, TX], (IUC), WE (GZF), WGr (GZG) WMaPI-RL (GZR), WLac (GZX),
[Arrowhead Library System-Janesville Public Library, Janesville, WI
(WIJ), WMa (WIM), WRac (WIR).

536 Kainai News. 1968. Bi-weekly. $9.50 for individuals and
institutions. Jackie Red Crow, editor, Kainai News, Box 120,
Standoff, Alberta, Canada T0L 1Y0. (403) 737-3784. ISSN 0047-3081.
LC cn76-310348. OCLC 2049497. Last issue 24 pages, last volume 570

Pages, height 44 cm. Line drawings, photographs, commerical
advertising. Available in microform: WHi (1971-); MML (1968-).
Published by Indian News Medica. Place of publication varies:
Cardston, Alberta, Mar 15, 1971-Apr 25, 1973. Previous editor: Caen
Bly, Mar 31, 1971-July 1, 1980. Newspaper. Subject focus: Blood
Tribal Council news, Blackfoot people.

WHi	v.4, n.3-v.6, n.3, v.7, n.9- Mar 15, 1971-Apr 25, 1973, Aug 19, 1974-	Microforms
WMUW	v.9, n.14; Aug 6, 1976	(SPL) E75/K33x
AzNCC	v.1- 1968-	Microfilm
CLSM	v.11, n.19; Oct 1, 1978	Periodicals
MtBBCC	v.11-v.14; Oct, 1978-May, 1981	Periodicals
NjP	[v.1. n.3-v.12, n.5] [Apr 15, 1968-Mar 1, 1979]	Periodicals
OkU	[v.5, n.16-v.12, n.2] [1972-1979]	WHC
WaU	[v.5, n.1-v.6, n.17] [1972-1973]	Periodicals
CaACG	v.1- 1968-	Periodicals
CaAEU	v.1- 1968-	Boreal Institute
CaMWU	[v.2-v.5], v.9; [1970-1973], 1976	970/K1227/Ne
CaOAFN	v.14?, n.1-24; Jan-Dec, 1981	Periodicals
CaOONL	[v.1, n.4-10], 12- [May 15-Nov 15, 1968], Jan 21, 1969-	Newspaper Section
CaOPeT	v.1- 1968-	Microfilm
CaOSuU	v.11-v.14; 1978-1981	Periodicals

Other holding institutions: CLU (CLU), KSteC (KKQ), [University of
Minnesota Union List, Minneapolis, MN] (MUL), [Standing Rock Community
College Library, Fort Yates, ND].

Kali Wisaks. Oneida, WI

   see Kalihwi Saks. Oneida, WI

537 Kalihwi Saks. 1971-1982//. Bi-Weekly. OCLC 6188799. Last issue 8
pages, last volume 410 pages, height 36 cm. Line drawings, commercial
advertising. Personal names indexed in: Index to Wisconsin Native
American Periodicals (1974-1981). Available in microform: WHi
(1974-1982). Oneida, WI. Title varies: Kali' Wisaks, Sept 9,
1974-Aug 3, 1979. Previous editors: Betty T. Ritchie, Sept 9, 1974-Mar
4, 1977; Paul A. Skenandore, Mar 18, 1977-Aug 15, 1980; Rick Wheelock,
Aug 29, 1981-Aug 14, 1981; Melanie M. Ellis, Aug 28-Sept 23, 1981;
Loretta Webster, Nov 6, 1981; Melanie M. Ellis, Nov 20, 1981-Mar 26,
1982. Community newsletter. Subject focus: Oneida people, culture,
poetry.

WHi   v.4, n.5-v.8, n.6;   Microforms
            Sept 9, 1974-Mar, 1982

WMUW   v.6, n.6-v.8, n.6;   (SPL)
            Mar 14, 1980-Mar, 1982   E/75/K35x

Other holding institutions: [WGrU-Native American Studies Dept.],
[University of Wisconsin-Stevens Point-Native American Center, Stevens
Point, WI], [Wisconsin Indian Resource Council, Stevens Point, WI].

538 Kalikaq Yugnek. 1974-1978//. Semi-annual. OCLC 6211685. Last issue
106 pages, last volume 168 pages, height 28 cm. Line drawings,
photographs. Published by Bethel Regional High School, Bethel, AK.
Subject focus: Inuit people, culture, includes fiction. (Youth
emphasis).

WHi   v.1, n.2-v.4, n.2;   E/99/E7/K2
            Spring, 1975-Spring, 1978

539 Kalumet. 1952-1974//. Bi-monthly. Last issue 24 pages, last volume
334 pages, height 21 cm. Line drawings, photographs, some in color,
commercial advertising. Published by Mitteilungorgan der IFI
Interessengemeinschaft fur Indianerkunde, Karlsruhe, West Germany.
Subject focus: culture, arts, crafts. In German, 100%.

TxU   [v.14-v.22, n.7]   970.105/K127
            [1965-1974]

540 Kamloops Wawa. 1892-?//. Unknown. OCLC 1587781. RLIN
CUBU12805282-S, OHCP1587781-S. Last issue 94 pages, height 20 cm.
Photographs, commercial advertising. Kamloops, British Columbia,
Canada. Subject focus: missions, Christian religion. In Chinook, 50%.

WHi   v.10, n.3;   F805//KA
           Sept, 1901   Cutter

CaOONL   [v.4-v.7]   BR1 K3
           [1895-1898]

Other holding institutions: [University of Minnesota Union List, Minneapolis, MN] (MUL), OKTU (OKT).

541 Kanatha. 1974-1977//. Irregular. Last issue 46 pages, height 28 cm. Line drawings, photographs. Published by Centre Socio-Culturel Amerinden, Village Huron, Ouebec, Canada. Editor: Georges Sioui. Subject focus: rights, education, poetry. In French, 50-80%.

WHi   v.1, n.3-v.3, n.1, v.4, n.1;   E/78/Q3/K2
           Apr, 1974-May, 1976, May? 1977

CaOAFN   v.4, n.1;   Periodicals
           May, 1977

CaOONL   v.1, n.3-v.3, n.1, v.4, n.1;   Periodicals
           Apr, 1974-May, 1976, May? 1977

CaOPeT   v.1-v.3, n.1;   Periodicals
            1974-May, 1976

542 Kanawake News. 1964-1975?//. Quarterly. ISSN 0453-1922. LC cn76-309055. OCLC 2454750. Last issue 32 pages, height 28 cm. Line drawings, photographs. Caughnawaga, Quebec, Canada. Frequency varies: monthly, May, 1977-June, 1966. Editors: Alice Marquis, Apr-Oct, 1965; Eilean Marquis, Spring, 1971-July, 1975. Community newsletter. Subject focus: Caughnawaga people.

CaOONL   [May, 1964-July, 1975]   K-117-4

Other holding institutions: NjP.

543 Kariwenhawi Newsletter. 1971. Monthly. St. Regis Mohawk Reservation, Hogansburg, NY 13655. (518) 358-2240. Last issue 8 pages, height 36 cm. Line drawings. Published by Akwesasne Library/Cultural Center. Community newsletter.

WHi   v.11, n.4-   Circulation
           Feb 28, 1982-

544 Kee-Ne-Goh: Winnipeg Native Student Newsletter. 1980?//. Monthly. Last issue 4 pages, height 28 cm. Winnipeg, Manitoba, Canada.

Editors: Doris Fontaine, Aug, 1980; Janet Assineboine, Sept, 1980.
School newsletter.

CaOAFN   v.1, n.2-3;   Periodicals
            Aug-Sept, 1980

545 Keetoowah Speaker. 1963-1965?//. Unknown. Last issue 4 pages,
    height 28 cm. Line drawings, photographs. Available in microform:
    WHi (1965). Tahlequah, OK. Community newsletter. Subject focus:
    Cherokee people.

WHi   Jan, 1965   Microforms

UPB   Oct, 1963-Aug, 1965   970.105/K258

Other holding institutions: OkU.

546 Keewatin Echo. 1967-1975//. Monthly. Height 45 cm. Line drawings,
    photographs. Published by Adult Education, Department of Indian and
    Northern Affairs, Churchill, Manitoba, Canada. Place of publication
    varies: Eskimo Point, Northwest Territories, Canada, Oct, 1967-Jan,
    1971. Editors: Tagak Curley; Mark Kalluak. Community newsletter.
    Subject focus: Inuit people. Some articles in Inuit.

CaAEU   n.36-77;   Boreal
            Apr, 1971-Jan, 1975   Institute

CaACG   n.48-77;   Periodicals
            May, 1972-Jan, 1975

547 Kenomadiwin News. 1968?-1972?//. Irregular. Last issue 8 pages.
    Line drawings, photographs, commerical advertising. Available in
    microform: MCR (1968-1972). Thunder Bay, Ontario, Canada. Place of
    publication varies: Port Arthur, Ontario, Canada, Oct 15, 1968-Oct 15,
    1969. Editors: William E. Sault, Mar 1-Aug. 15, 1969; Harlem Olsen,
    Sept 15, 1969; Naz Therreault, Oct 15, 1969-May 30, 1970; Elizabeth
    Morriseau, June 30, 1970-Dec 17, 1971; Elizabeth Pelletier, Feb
    15-Mar. 31, 1972; Val Chapman, Apr 30, 1972. Newspaper.

WHi   v.1-v.2, n.20;   Microforms
            Oct 15, 1968-June 30, 1972

AzNCC   v.1-v.2;   Indian File
            Mar, 1971-Apr, 1972

NjP   [v.1, n.4-v.2, n.20]   Periodicals
            [Feb 1, 1969-June 30, 1972]

CaACG   v.1, n.1-v.2, n.20;   Periodicals
            June, 1971-June, 1972

CaMWU   v.1-v.2, n.20;   Periodicals
             Oct 15, 1968-June 30, 1972

CaOONL   v.1-v.2, n.20;   Newspaper
             Oct 15, 1968-June 30, 1972   Section

CaOPeT   [1969-1972]   Periodicals

548 Kil-Kaas-Git. 1973-1977//. 3 times during school year. OCLC
    3692529. Line drawings, photographs, some in color. Published by
    Craig Schools, Craig, AK. Frequency varies: 4 times during school
    year, 1973-1975?. School newsletter. Subject focus: Haida and
    Tlinget people.

    AkUF   [v.1, n.1-v.6, n.2]   AK-47
                 [1973-1977]

    Other holding institutions: CtY (YUS).

549 Kinatuinamot Ilengajuk. 1972. Weekly. Amos Dicker, editor,
    Kinatuinamot Ilengajuk, Nain, Labrador, Newfoundland, Canada. (709)
    922-2973. Last issue 8 pages, height 36 cm. Published by Labrador
    Inuit Association. Community newsletter. Subject focus: Inuit
    people. Some articles in Inuit.

    WHi   v.5, n.47-   Circulation
                 June 11, 1982-

    CaAEU   [v.2, n.12-v.5, n.13], v.5, n.19-   Boreal
                 [Jan, 1978-Aug, 1981], Oct, 1981-   Institute

    CaNfSM   v.1-   Periodicals
                 1972-

550 Kinzua Planning Newsletter. 1961-1965//. Irregular. Last issue 4
    pages, height 28 cm. Line drawings. Available in microform: CPC
    (1961-1965). Published by Seneca Nation of Indians, Salamanca, NY.
    Editors: Jack Preston, Oct 11-31, 1961; Walt Taylor, May 16, 1962-Feb
    27, 1963; Merrill Bowen, Mar 23, 1963-Oct, 1965. Subject focus:
    Seneca people, land claims, treaty rights, housing, legislation.

    WHi   v.1, n.1-v.3, n.9;   Microforms
                 Oct 11, 1961-Oct, 1965

    WHi   v.1, n.1-v.3, n.7;   Pam 76-836
                 Oct, 11, 1961-Mar, 1965

    NjP   [v.1, n.2-v.3, n.9]   Periodicals
                 [Oct 31, 1961-Oct, 1965]

551 Kiowa Indian News. 1974. Monthly. $10. for individuals and
institutions. Kiowa Indian News, P.O. Box 361, Carnegie, OK 73015.
(405) 654-2300. Last issue 8 pages, height 37 cm. Line drawings,
photographs, commercial advertising. Available in microform: WHi
(1979-). Title varies: Kiowa Tribal Newsletter, Mar, 1975-Sept, 1976.
Previous editors: A. Aunko, Oct, 1975-Mar, 1977; Rudy Bantista, May,
1979-Feb, 1981; Charles Kauben, June-Nov, 1981. Newspaper. Subject
focus: Kiowa people.

WHi   v.6, n.8-   Microforms
             May, 1979-

MtBBCC   v.7-v.8;   Periodicals
             Sept, 1980-Feb, 1981

OkTU   v.5, n.11-   Rare Book
             Aug, 1978-   Room

Other holding institutions: [Bacone College, Muskogee, OK].

Kiowa Tribal Newsletter. Carnegie, OK

   see Kiowa Indian News. Carnegie, OK

552 De Kiva. 1964. Bi-monthly. De Kiva, Ixialaan 8, 2121TA, Bennebroek,
Netherlands. ISSN 0453-9753. OCLC 5504267. Last issue 16 pages,
last volume 116 pages, height 22 cm. Line drawings, photographs.
Subject focus: general articles on Native Americans, book reviews. In
Dutch, 100%.

WHi   v.2, n.6, v.3, n.4, v.4, n.2-   E/75/K58
             Nov/Dec, 1965, July/Aug, 1966,
             Mar/Apr, 1967-

Klah' Che' Min/Squaxin Island Newsletter. Shelton, WA

   see Klah' Che' Min News. Shelton, WA

553 Klah' Che' Min News. 1977-1982//. Monthly. Last issue 8 pages,
height 36 cm. Line drawings, photographs, commercial advertising.
Published by Squaxin Island Tribe, Shelton, WA. Title varies: Klah'
Che' Min/Squaxin Island Newsletter, July, 1979-May, 1981. Previous
editor: Marian Carpenter, July, 1979-May, 1981; Nancy Butterfield,
June, 1981-June, 1982. Community newsletter.

WHi   v.3, n.6-v.4, n.5;   Microforms
             July, 1979-June, 1982

554 <u>Klallam Newsletter</u>. 1973-1975?//. Monthly? OCLC 6221114. Last
    issue 8 pages, height 28 cm. Available in microform: WHi (1973,
    1975). Little Boston, WA. Community newsletter.

    WHi   Mar 16, 1973, Mar, 1975   Microforms

    WMUW   Mar 16, 1973, Mar, 1975   (SPL)
                                                             E/75/K4x

555 <u>Koniag Inc., Newsletter</u>. 1972-1973//. Monthly. Last issue 8 pages.
    Line drawings. Available in microform: AkUF (1972-1973). Kodiak, AK.
    Subject focus: corporate news, shareholders, land claims, Alaska
    Native Claims Settlement Act.

    WHi   v.1, n.1-3;   Microforms
                 Nov, 1972-Jan, 1973

    AkUF   v.1, n.1-3;   Microfiche
                 Nov, 1972-Jan, 1973

556 <u>Koniag Islander</u>. 1972-1975?//? Semi-monthly. Last issue 28 pages.
    Line drawings, photographs. Available in microform: AkUF (1972-1975).
    Kodiak, AK. Editors: Karl Armstrong and Dolores Padilla. Subject
    focus: corporate, local and national news, shareholders, Alaska Native
    Claims Settlement Act.

    WHi   v.1, n.1-v.3, n.6;   Microforms
                 Nov 30, 1972-Aug, 1975

    AkUF   v.1, n.1-v.3, n.6;   Microfiche
                 Nov 30, 1972-Aug, 1975

557 <u>Kootznoowoo Incorporated Newsletter</u>. 1975?//. Unknown. Last issue 6
    pages. Line drawings. Available in microform: AkUF (1975). Angoon,
    AK. Corporation newsletter. Subject focus: corporate board news.

    WHi   v.1, n.1;   Microforms
                 Mar, 1975

    AkUF   v.1, n.1;   Microfiche
                 Mar, 1975

558 <u>LIHA News</u>. 1976? Semi-annual. Cindy Dow, editor, LIHA News,
    Laconia, NH 03246. (603) 524-2031. Last issue 6 pages, height 28 cm.
    Published by Laconia Indian Historical Association. Organization
    newsletter. Subject focus: history, culture.

    WHi   v.4, n.1-   Circulation
                 Sept/Nov, 1979

LCO Journal American. Hayward, WI

   see Lac Courte Oreilles Journal. Hayward, WI

559 Labrador Resources Advisory Council Newsletter. 1977. Irregular.
    Labrador Resources Advisory Council Newsletter, P.O. Box 430, Happy
    Valley, Labrador, Newfoundland, Canada A2V 2K7. Last issue 10 pages,
    Last volume 70 pages, height 28 cm. Line drawings, photographs.
    Subject focus: housing, energy resources, wildlife, Beaufort Sea. In
    Inuit, 20%.

    CaNfSM   Aug, 1977–   Periodicals

560 Lac Courte Oreilles Journal. 1977. Monthly. $7. for individuals;
    $10. for institutions. Paul DeMain, editor, Lac Courte Oreilles
    Journal, Route 2, Hayward, WI 54843. (715) 634-8072/8175. Last issue
    12 pages, height 45 cm. Line drawings, photographs, commercial
    advertising. Personal names indexed in: Index to Wisconsin Native
    American Periodicals (1980-1981). Available in microform: WHi-A, Veda
    Stone Papers, (1977). Published by LCO Graphic Arts, Inc. Frequency
    varies: bi-monthly, Aug, 1977-Fall, 1978. Community newsletter.
    Subject focus: Lac Courte Oreilles Chippewa people, Great Lakes area
    news.

    WHi   v.1, n.1–   Microforms
              Aug, 1977–

    WEU   v.1, n.3;   Micro 11
    ARC   Dec, 1977

    WM   Current issues only   Forest Home
                                                            Branch

    WMSC   v.4, n.2–   Periodicals
              Feb, 1981–

    AzNCC   v.1–   Indian File
              1977–

    Other holding institutions: [University of Wisconsin-Stevens
    Point-Native American Center, Stevens Point, WI], [Wisconsin Indian
    Resource Council, Stevens Point, WI].

561 Lac du Flambeau Public School Newsletter. 1979?//. Unknown. Last
    issue 10 pages, height 28 cm. Line drawings. Published by Title VII,
    ESAA Project, Lac du Flambeau, WI. School newsletter. Subject focus:
    Lac du Flambeau Chippewa people.

    WUSP   May–Nov 28, 1979   Native American
                                                           Center

562 <u>Lac du Flambeau Tribal Update</u>. 1982. Monthly. Steve St. Germaine,
    editor, Lac du Flambeau Tribal Update, Box 67, Lac du Flambeau, WI
    54538. (715) 488-3303, est. 249. Last issue 12 pages, height 28 cm.
    Line drawings, photographs, commercial advertising. Community
    newsletter. Subject focus: Lac du Flambeau Band of Chippewas.

    WHi   n.1-   Circulation
                May 27, 1982-

563 <u>Lakota Eyapaha</u>. 1977-1981//. Irregular. Last issue 48 pages, last
    volume 144 pages, height 37 cm. Line drawings, photographs.
    Published by Oglala Sioux Community College, Pine Ridge, SD. Subject
    focus: Olgala Sioux people, education, politics, social services, book
    reviews, fiction, poetry.

    WHi   v.1, n.1-v.5, n.2;   Microforms
                Apr, 1977-Feb, 1981

    AzNCC   v.1, n.2-   Indian File
                May, 1977-

    MnBemT   [v.2], v.3-v.5, n.2;   Periodicals
                [1977], 1978-Feb, 1981

    MtBBCC   [v.2-v.5]   Periodicals
                [June, 1978-Feb, 1981]

    CaOAFN   v.5, n.1;   Periodicals
                Feb, 1981

    Other holding institutions: ICN (IBV), [Standing Rock Community
    College Library, Fort Yates, ND].

564 <u>Lakota Oyate-Ki</u>. 1973?-1979//. Irregular. OCLC 6221102. Last issue
    50 pages, height 28. Line drawings, photographs. Published by Lakota
    Indian Club, Oregon State Penetentiary, Salem OR. Editors: Peter B.
    Launer, Winter, 1973-Summer, 1974; Ray Eagle Pipe, Winter,
    1974-Summer, 1975, Colin Hockings, Winter, 1975-Summer, 1979. Prison
    newsletter. Subject focus: Dakota people, culture, fiction, poetry.

    WHi   Winter, 1973-Summer, 1979   Microforms

    WMUW   Winter, 1977;   (SPL)
                                                    E/75/L34x

    NjP   [Sept?, 1970-Winter, 1976]   Periodicals

565 <u>Language in American Indian Education</u>. 1971-1972?//. Semi-annual.
    ISSN 0196-5328. LC sc79-5228. OCLC 1586707. Last issue 112 pages,
    height 28 cm. Line drawings. Published for the Bureau of Indian

Affairs by the University of Utah, Salt Lake City, UT. Editor:
William R. Slager. Subject focus: bilingual teaching and education.

CaOAFN   Spring-Winter, 1972   Periodicals

Other holding institutions: CLU (CLU), DI (UDI), [University of
Minnesota Union List, Minneapolis, MN] (MUL), OkAdE (ECO), PPT (TEU).

Language of the Bears. Fort Wingate, NM

  see Shush Da Bizaad/Language of the Bears. Fort Wingate, NM

Law in Action. Window Rock, AZ

  see DNA Newsletter. Window Rock, AZ

566 League of Nations Pan-Am Indians. 1935-?//?. Quarterly. Last issue
    4 pages, height 28 cm. Johnstown, PA. League newsletter.

    WEU   May, 1970   Journalism
                                                     Lab

567 Legal Information Service. 1979. 5 times a year. $10. for
    individuals and institutions. Legal Information Service, 410
    Cumberland Ave. North, Saskatoon, Saskatchewan, Canada S7N 1M6. ISSN
    0225-2287. LC cn80-30231. OCLC 6054512. Last issue 24 pages, height
    28 cm. Published by University of Saskatchewan Native Law Centre.
    Subject focus: legislation, law.

    WU-L   v3-   Periodicals
              1981-

    CaOSuU   v.1-   Periodicals
              1979

    Other holding institutions: CLU (CLU), CSdU-L (KLL), FTaSU-L (FSL),
    Ku-L (KFL), MnSH-L (MHL), MnU-L (MLL), NHemH-1 (ZHL), OkU-L (OKL),
    CaOONL (NLC).

568 Legal Notes. 1981? Unknown. $6. for individuals and institutions.
    Legal Notes, 1615 Broadway, Oakland, CA 94612. Last issue 2 pages,
    height 28 cm. Published by California Urban Indian Health Council,
    Inc. Subject focus: legal aid.

    WHi   Feb, 1982-   Circulation

569 <u>Legislative Review</u>. 1971-1975//. Monthly. ISSN 0300-7677. LC
    sc79-3519. OCLC 1775586. RLIN DCLCSC793519-S, CUDL1836-S,
    OHCP1775586-S. Last issue 8 pages, height 28 cm. Line drawings,
    photographs. Available on microfim: McP (1971-1972); WHi (1972-1975);
    WHi-A, Veda Stone Papers, (1971). Published by Institute for the
    Development of Indian Law, Inc., Washington, DC. Previous editors:
    Kirke Kickingbird, John Tiger and Kathy McKee, Nov, 1972; Kirke
    Kickingbird and John Tiger, [v.2, n.12]; Kirke Kickingbird and Leigh
    Price, [v.3, n.2-3]; Kirke Kickingbird, Leigh Price and Curtis Berkey,
    [v.3, n.4]; Leigh Price and Curtis Berkey, [v.3, n.5-v.3, n.10].
    Subject focus: legislation, governmental relations. Superceded by
    American Indian Journal.

    WHi   v.1, n.1-v.3, n.11;   Microforms
               [Sept], 1971-1975

    WEU   v.1, n.1, 4;   Micro 11
    ARC   Aug, Dec, 1971

    WMUW   [v.1, n.3-11]   K/12/E34x
               [Nov, 1971-1978]

    AzNCC   v.1, n.1-v.3, n.10;   Microfilm
               Aug, 1971-1978

    NjP   [v.1, n.2-v.3, n.11]   Periodicals
               [Oct, 1971-1978

    Other holding institutions: [Indiana Union List of Serials,
    Indianapolis, IN] (ILS), [University of Minnesota Union List,
    Minneapolis, MN] (MUL), NmScW, NCaS (XLM), OKU (OKL).

570 <u>Lend a Hand</u>. 1886?-1891?//. Monthly. OCLC 7239849. Last issue 72
    pages, last volume 291 pages, height 23 cm. Commecial advertising.
    Boston MA. Editor: Edward Everett Hall. Subject focus: charities,
    Apache people.

    CLSM   [v.2, n.6-v.6, n.4]   Periodicals
               [1887-1891]

    Other holding institutions: DLC (DLC), GASU (GSU), [Indiana Union List
    of Serials, Indianapolis, IN] (ILS), MH-AH (BHA), MBU (BOS), MBTI
    (BTI), Mi (EEX), [University of Minnesota Union List, Minneapolis, MN]
    (MUL), NbU (LDL), NA1U (NAM), OAkU (AKR), OC1 (CLE), OC1W (CWR), OO
    (OBE), OAU (OUN), OWoC (WOO), MoSW (WTU), PPi (CPL), PP (PLF),
    [Pittsburgh Regional Library Center Union List, Pittsburgh, PA] (QPR),
    TxWicM (TMI), ViU (VA@).

571 <u>Letan Wankatakiya</u>. 1969. 2 times a summer. Ann Freier and Barry
    Zephier, editors, Letan Wankatakiya, Room 26, Dakota Hall, University
    of South Dakota, Vermillion, SD 57609. (605) 677-5308. Last issue 4
    pages, height 44 cm. Line drawings, photographs. Frequency varies: 3
    times a summer, Aug 12, 1970-Aug 9, 1973. Previous editors: Tina Opp

and Brenda Dupris, Aug 12, 1970; Jim Watters, July 22, 1972; Wayne Bad
Wound and Joyce Owen, July 4, 1973; Kathy Campbell and Lynelle
Whitebull, June 25–July 30, 1979. Subject focus: Project Upward
Bound, education, career opportunities.

WHi	[v.3, n.2–v.11, n.2], v.13, n.1– [July 22, 1971–July 30, 1979], July 31, 1981–	Circulation
WEU	v.1, n.3, v.2, n.2–3; July 8, 21–Aug 12, 1970	Journalism Lab
NjP	[v.1, n.1–v.4, n.3] [July 8, 1969–Aug 8, 1972]	Periodicals

572 The Lightbulb. 1967–1968//. Irregular. Last issue 8 pages. Line
drawings. Available in microform: MCR (1967–1968). Port Arthur,
Ontario, Canada. Community newsletter.

WHi	v.1, n.1–?; Dec, 1967–May, 1968	Microforms
CaMWU	v.1, n.1–?; Dec, 1967–May, 1968	Periodicals
CaOONL	v.1, n.1–?; Dec, 1967–May, 1968	Newspaper Section

573 The Lily of the Mohawks. 1938?–?//. Quarterly. Last issue 8 pages,
height 28 cm. Line drawings, photographs. Published by Tekakwitha
League, Clarence Center, NY. Place of publication varies: New York,
NY, Jan, 1960–May, 1961; Auriesville, NY, July, 1961–Spring, 1967.
Subject focus: Catholic Church.

WMM	[v.23, n.4–v.36, n.2] [Jan, 1960–Fall, 1972]	Special Collections

574 The Link. 1945?//. Unknown. Last issue 8 pages, height 23 cm. Line
drawings, photographs. Published by Oblate Fathers of the Hudson Bay
Vicariate, Churchill, Manitoba, Canada. Subject focus: missions,
Catholic Church, Inuit people.

WMM	May, Oct, 1945	Special Collections

575 Linkages for Indian Child Welfare Programs. 1981. Unknown. Nancy
Gale, editor, Linkages for Indian Child Welfare Programs, 1000
Connecticut Ave., NW, #401, Washington, DC 20036. Last issue 12

pages, height 28 cm. Line drawings, photographs. Published by
National American Indian Court Judges Association. Previous editor:
Gwendolyn D. Packard, June/July-Oct, 1981. Subject Focus: child
welfare, social services, education, legislation.

WHi	v.1, n.1– Apr, 1981–	Circulation
CaOAFN	v.1, n.2–3; June/July-Oct, 1981	Periodicals

576 **Listen**. 1966. Monthly. $2. for individuals and institutions.
Listen, 24826 Colorado Rd., Cortez, CO 81321. Last issue 8 pages,
last volume 17 pages, height 22 cm. Line drawings. Published by
Navajo Gospel Crusade. Subject focus: Christian religion.

WHi	v.10, n.8– Apr, 1975–	Circulation
AzAIBI	Current issues	Periodicals

577 **The Listening Post**. 1968?–1971//. Monthly. ISSN 0709-2199. LC
cn79-72751. OCLC 5377783. Last issue 20 pages, height 36 cm. Line
drawings, photographs. Published by Baffin Region Adult Education
Office, Frobisher Bay, Northwest Territories, Canada. Editors: Elija
Erkloo, Oct, 1968-Dec, 1969; Joanasie Salomonie, June, 1970-Sept,
1971. Community newsletter. Subject focus: education. In Inuit, 50%.

CaACG	n.?, 19; Feb, 1970, Apr, 1971	Periodicals
CaOORD	[n.5–21] [Oct, 1968-Sept, 1971]	Periodicals

Other holding institutions: CaOONL (NLC).

578 **The Literary Voyager; or Muzzeniegun**. 1826–1827//. Irregular. LC
62-15112. OCLC 420989. Last issue 6 pages, height 23 cm. Sault Ste.
Marie, MI. Editor: Henry Rowe Schoolcraft. Subject focus: culture,
legends, biographies. Reprint: edited with an introduction by Philip
P. Mason, Michigan State University Press, 1962.

WHi	n.1–15; Dec, 1826-Apr 11, 1827	E/77/S405
WKenU	n.1–15; Dec, 1826-Apr 11, 1827	E/77/S405
WM	n.1–15; Dec, 1826-Apr 11, 1827	970.1/S371

WMM	n.1-15; Dec, 1826-Apr 11, 1827	E/77/S405
WU	n.1-15; Dec, 1826-Apr 11, 1827	E/77/S405
ICN	n.1-15; Dec, 1826-Apr 11, 1827	Ayer 1/S37/1962
MiU-B	n.1-15; Dec, 1826-Apr 11, 1827	EP/101/S372/L776
MoHi	n.1-15; Dec, 1826-Apr 11, 1827	970.105/Sch65
N	n.1-15; Dec, 1826-Apr 11, 1827	970.105/S372
TxU	n.1-15; Dec, 1826-Apr 11, 1827	E/75/S36/1974

Other holding institutions: ArU (AFU), ArAT (AKH), CAzPC (CAP), CBaS
(CBA), [California State University-Dominguez Hills, Carson, CA]
(CHD), CLS (CLA), CNoS (CNO), CPomCP (CPO), [California State College,
San Bernardio, CA] (CSB), FBoU (FGM), FTS (FHM), FJUNF (FNP), FMFIU
(FXG), ICNE (IAO), IMacoW (IAZ), ICarbS (SOI), InTI (ISU), InU (IUL),
KyRE (KEU), [Suffolk University, Boston, MA] (SUF), MdU-BC (MUB), MiLC
(EEL), MiAlbc (EXA), MiYem (EYE), MiRochoU (EYR), MiMarqS (EZP), MiSW
(EZW), MnBems (MNB), MnMan (MNM), MnStcls (MST), NdFq/MnMohs/MnMohC
(TRI), NcCuw (NMW), NjUPM (NJM), NBwU (BUF), NA1U (NAM), NEE (VXE),
NONEOH (VZH), NnM (YAM), NP1aU (YPM), NSbSU (YSM), NOwU (ZOW), NPurU
(ZPM), NPotU (ZQM), NNU (ZYU), OC1 (CLE), OC1U (CSU), OKentU (KSU),
OCo (OCO), OAdN (ONU), OAU (OUN), OTU (TOL), ODaWU (WSU), OYU (YNG),
OkTOR (OKO), PManM (MAN), PU (PAU), SdB (SDB), TNJ (TJC), TM (TMN),
TNTU (TUN), TxCM (TXA), ViLxW (VLW).

579 The Little Bronzed Angel. 1924-1978//. Bi-monthly. ISSN 0024-5011.
LC sc79-4938. OCLC 4981444, 5255849. RLIN DCLCSC794938-S,
OHCP5255849-S. Last issue 5 pages. Photographs. Available in
microform: McA (1974-1978); CPC (1954-1974). Published by St. Pauls
Catholic Indian Mission, Marty, SD. Editor: Sylvester Eisenman, Jan
1935-Dec, 1943. Subject focus: Sioux people, Catholic Church,
missions.

WHi	[v.30. n.2-v.54, n.5] [Feb, 1954-Sept/Dec, 1978]	Microforms
WEU	v.46, n.6-v.47, n.2; Sept, 1970-Feb, 1971	Journalism Lab
WMM	[v.11, n.1-v.48, n.9] [Jan, 1935-Dec, 1972]	Special

AzNCC	v.53-v.54; Oct, 1977-Jan, 1978	Indian File
NjP	[v.30, n.2-v.54, n.5] [Feb, 1954-Sept/Dec, 1978]	Periodicals
SdU	v.1-v.48; June 1, 1924-May, 1972	Microfilm
WyCWC	v.51, n.1-6; 1975	Periodicals
CaOPeT	v.50-v.54; 1974-1978	Microfilm

Other holding institutions: [University of Minnesota Union List, Minneapolis, MN] (MUL).

580 Little Sioux. 1957?. Bi-monthly. Little Sioux, St. Francis, SD 57572. (605) 747-2828. Last issue 4 pages, height 28 cm. Line drawings, photographs. Available in microform: McA (1976-). Published by St. Francis Indian Mission. Previous editors: Richard G. Pates, Aug/Sept, 1959-June/July, 1963; Richard T. Jones, Aug/Sept, 1963-Apr/May, 1969; Bernard Fagan, June/July, 1969. School Newsletter. Subject focus: Catholic Church, missions, education, Dakota people.

WHi	[v.19, n.2-v.22, n.4], v.23, n.3- [Spring, 1976-May, 1979], Mar, 1980-	Microforms
WEU	v.13, n.5-v.14, n.4; Apr/May, 1970-Feb/Mar, 1971	Journalism Lab
WMM	[v.1, n.1-v.22, n.3] [1957-Jan, 1979]	Special Collections
NjP	[v.2, n.3-v.19, n.2] [1959-Spring, 1976]	Periodicals
OkTU	v.20, n.1-v.22, n.4; Jan, 1977-May, 1979	Rare Book Room
CaOPeT	v.18, n.3-v.19, n.2; Spring, 1975-Spring, 1976	Microfilm

581 The Log. 1960?-1974//? Irregular. Last issue 8 pages. Line drawings, photographs. Available in microform: CPC (1965-1974). Published by Columbia Coast Mission, Victoria, British Columbia, Canada. Place of publication varies: Vancouver Island, British Columbia, Autumn, 1965. Editors: Cecil Fitzgerald, Autumn, 1965; I.P. Baird, Christmans, 1965; J.W. Forth and D.S. Mitchell, Summer, 1966-Summer, 1968; Canon Hywell Jones and D.S. Mitchell, Fall, 1968;

D.S. Mitchell, Christmas, 1968-Fall, 1974. Subject focus: missions,
Anglican Church.

WHi   Autumn, 1965-Fall, 1974   Microforms

NjP   Autumn, 1965-Fall, 1974   Periodicals

Loma-Tu-A-We. Hotevilla, AZ

   see Lomati'awi. Hotevilla, AZ

582 Lomati'awi. 1980? Unknown. Lomatt'awi, Box 48, Hotevilla, AZ 86030.
    (602) 734-2462. Last issue 12 pages, height 28 cm. Line drawings,
    photographs. Published by Hotevilla Bacavci Community School. Title
    varies: Loma-Tu-A-We, Nov/Dec, 1980-Feb, 1981. School newsletter.

    WHi   n.11, 17-21, 31-   Circulation
               Nov/Dec, 1980, Feb-Nov, 1981, Aug, 1982-

    AzHM   n.18-19, 22-   Periodicals
               1981, 1982-

583 The Longest Walk. 1978//. Irregular. Last issue 4 pages, height 28
    cm. Line drawings. Published by D Q University, Davis, CA. Subject
    focus: organization news for Washington DC walk/demonstration.

    WHi   v.1, n.1, 4-8;   Pam 81-1466
               Feb, Mar 22-May 22, 1978

    NjP   v.1, n.3-4;   Periodcials
               Mar 15-22, 1978

584 Luchip Spearhead. 1968-1977//. Semi-annual. ISSN 0362-8981. OCLC
    2142294. RLIN CGTT82-S75, OHCP2142294. Last issue 18 pages, height
    28 cm. Line drawings, photographs. Available in microform: WHi, Veda
    Stone Papers, (1968). Published by Lutheran Church and Indian People,
    Sioux Falls, SD. Subject focus: missions, Lutheran Church, social
    services.

    WHi   v.1, n.1-2, [v.4, n.3-v.10, n.1];   Microforms
               Jan-June, 1968, [Dec, 1971-June, 1977]

    WEU   v.1, n.1-2;   Micro 11
    ARC   Jan-June, 1968

    WMUW   v.9, n.1, v.10, n.1;   (SPL)
               Jan, 1976, June, 1977   E/75/L82x

Other holding institutions: DLC (NSD), MH-AH (BHA), MBTI (BTI),
[Wisconsin Indian Resource Council, Stevens Point, WI].

585 Lumbee Nation Times. 1979. Unknown. Princess Silver Star Reed,
     editor, Lumbee Nation Times, P.O. Box 512, Fall River Mills, CA 96028.
     (916) 336-6701. Last issue 8 pages, height 39 cm. Line drawings,
     photographs. Community newsletter. Subject focus: local and national
     news, Lumbee people.

     ICN   Current issues   CHAI

586 Lummi Indian Review. 1970-?//. Unknown. Last issue 4 pages, height
     44 cm. Photographs. Available in microform: WHi (1972). Published
     by Lummi Indian Tribal Enterprise, Marietta and Seattle, WA.
     Community newsletter. Subject focus: Lummi people, community
     development.

     WHi   v.2, n.1;   Microforms
                Oct, 1972

     CaOPeT   v.1, v.2, n.1;   Microfilm
                Sept, 1970, Oct, 1972

587 Lummi Squol Quol. 1973-1981//. Bi-weekly. Last issue 4 pages,
     height 28 cm. Line drawings, photographs, commmercial advertising.
     Available in microform: WHi (1973-1981). Published by Lummi Indian
     Tribe, Bellington, WA. Title varies: Squol Quol: Lummi Indian News,
     Nov/Dec, 1973. Place of publication varies: Marietta, WA, Nov/Dec,
     1973-June 11, 1976. Frequency varies: weekly, Feb 21, 1975-Apr 8,
     1977. Editors: William Jones, Nov/Dec, 1973-Aug 26, 1977; Josie
     Jones, Nov 29, 1977-Sept 26, 1980; Pete Merton, Jr., Oct 24, 1980-June
     5, 1981; Theresa Mike, June 19-Nov, 1981. Community newsletter.
     Subject focus: Lummi people.

     WHi   v.1, n.1, v.3, n.7-v.6, n.26,   Microforms
                v.7, n.7-v.9, n.20;
                Nov/Dec, 1973, Feb 21, 1975-Dec 8, 1978,
                Jan 11, 1980-Nov, 1981

     AzNCC   v.5-v.9, n.20;   Indian File
                Oct 28, 1977-Nov, 1981

     NjP   [v.1, n.1-v.6, n.7]   Periodicals
                [Nov/Dec, 1973-Apr 16, 1978]

     OrU   [v.1, n.1-v.18]   Periodicals
                [Nov/Dec, 1973-1980]

     Wa   v.1, v.3-   NW
                1973, 1975-

WaU   v.3-   E/99/L95L9
             1975-

CaOPeT   v.1, n.1-   Microfilm
             Nov/Dec, 1973-

588 <u>MCIA Newsletter</u>. 1980. Unknown. MCIA Newsletter, 2525 Riva Rd.,
    Annapolis, MD 21401. Last issue 4 pages, height 28 cm. Published by
    Maryland Commission on Indian Affairs. Title varies: The Newsletter,
    Jan/Apr-May/Aug, 1980. Subject focus: Maryland Native people,
    business, health and education information.

    WHi   v.1, n.1-   Circulation
                 Jan/Apr, 1980-

589 <u>MGS Newsletter</u>. 1977. Irregular. MGS Newsletter, E 1658 Central,
    Spokane, WA 99207. Last issue 6 pages, height 28 cm. Published by
    Metis Genealogical Society. Subject focus: genealogy, Metis people.

    WHi   v.2, n.3-   Circulation
                 Apr, 1978-

<u>Mah No Men ee Kay Gee Zes</u>. White Earth, MN

    see <u>White Earth Reservation Newsletter</u>. White Earth, MN

590 <u>Mah'Piya Luta Oyakapi</u>. 1976?//. Weekly. Last issue 2 pages, height
    28 cm. Published by Red Cloud Indian School, Pine Ridge, SD. Editor:
    Elaine Steele. High school newsletter.

    WMM   v.1, n.1-2, 5;   Special
                 Sept 25-Oct 1, 22, 1976   Collections

591 <u>Mahpiya Luta Tawowapi Wicohan</u>. 1974?//. Unknown. Last issue 6
    pages, height 22 cm. Line drawings. Published by Red Cloud Indian
    School, Pine Ridge, SD. Elementary school newsletter.

    WMM   n.1-3;   Special
                 Nov 1, 1974-Jan 27, 1975   Collections

592 <u>Mahpiya Luta Woyaka</u>. 1979. Irregular. Mahpiya Luta Woyaja, Red
    Cloud Indian School, Pine Ridge, SD 57770. Last issue 18 pages,
    height 28 cm. Line drawings, photographs. School newsletter.

WMM   v.1, n.1-v.2, n.5, v.3, n.4;   Special
           Sept?, 1979-May 15, Dec, 1981   Collections

593 <u>Maine Indian Newsletter</u>. 1966-1972?//. Quarterly. Last issue 20
    pages. Available in microform: WHi (1971-1972); McP (1971). Old
    Town, ME. Editor: Eugenia T. Thompson, May-Winter, 1971. Subject
    focus: Penobscot people, history, culture, politics, socio-economic
    conditions.

    WHi   v.4, n.1-v.5, n.5;   Microforms
               Jan?, 1971-Winter, 1972

    WMUW   v.4, n.1-v.5, n.5;   (SPL)
               Jan?, 1971-Winter, 1972   E/78/M2M3x

    AzNCC   v.4-v.5;   Microfilm
               Summer, 1971-Winter, 1972

    CNoSU   v.4, n.2-5;   Microfilm
               May-Winter, 1971

    Me   v.1-v.2, v.4-v.5, n.5;   Periodicals
               1966-June, 1969, 1971-Winter, 1972

    OkU   [v.4]   WHC
               May-Summer/Winter, 1971

    Other holding institutions: MH-P (HLS), NmScW.

594 <u>Makah Viewer</u>. 1977//? Monthly. Last issue 8 pages, height 32 cm.
    Line drawings, photographs, commercial advertising. Available in
    microform: WHi (1977). Published by Makah Tribal Council, Neah Bay,
    WA. Editor: Verna R. Bunn. Community newsletter. Subject focus:
    Makah people.

    WHi   v.1, n.1-2;   Microforms
               Mar 16-Apr 8, 1977

    WMUW   v.1, n.1-2;   (SPL)
               Mar 16-Apr 8, 1977   E/75/M34x

595 <u>Mal-I-Mic News</u>. 1973. Monthly. $5.50 for individuals and
    institutions. Jennifer Sappier, editor, Mal-I-Mic News, 390 King St.,
    Suite 2, Frederickton, New Brunswick, Canada E3B 1E3. ISSN 0229-012x,
    0382-7291. LC cn76-32056, cn81-30382. OCLC 2850242, 7970384. Last
    issue 16 pages, height 44 cm. Line drawings, photographs. Published
    by New Brunswick Association of Metis and Non-Status Indians.
    Community newsletter. Subject focus: Metis and Non-Status people.

WHi   v.10, n.1–   Circulation
           Jan, 1982–

CaOAFN   v.9, n.1–   Periodicals
           Jan, 1981–

Other holding institutions: CaOONL (NLC).

596 <u>Malki Museum Newsletter</u>. 1973?-1978//? Bi-monthly. Last issue 2
    pages, height 36 cm. Morongo Indian Reservation, Banning, CA.
    Subject focus: art exhibits, art publications.

    CL   Dec, 1973/Jan, 1974–June/July/Aug, 1978   Periodicals

    CLSM   Dec, 1975–   Periodicals

597 <u>Management Memo</u>. 1982? Quarterly. $10. for individuals and
    institutions. Management Memo, 1615 Broadway, Suite 210, Oakland, CA
    94612. Last issue 6 pages, height 28 cm. Published by California
    Urban Indian Health Council, Inc. Organization newsletter.

    WHi   June, 1982–   Circulation

598 <u>Manataba Messenger</u>. 1980-1982//. Monthly. OCLC 7323714. RLIN
    UTGB1236-S. Last issue 12 pages, last volume 350 pages, height 41 cm.
    Line drawings, photographs, commercial advertising. Available in
    microform: WHi (1980-1982). Published by Colorado River Indian
    Tribes, Parker, AZ. Frequency varies: weekly, Sept 12, 1980-Dec,
    1981. Previous editors: Richard V. La Course, Sept 12, 1980-Apr 24,
    1981; Joan M. Travis, Apr 31, 1981-May, 1982. Newspaper.

    WHi   v.1, n.1–v.1 [i.e. 3], n.5;   Microforms
             Sept 12, 1980–June, 1982

    Az   v.1, n.1–v.1 [i.e. 3], n.5;   Periodicals
             Sept 12, 1980–June, 1982

    AzHM   [v.1, n.11–v.2, n.15]   Periodicals
             [1980-1981]

    AzNCC   v.2-3;   Indian File
             1981-1982

    AzT   v.1, n.3;   Periodicals
             Apr, 1982

    AzTeS   v.1–v.3;   Periodicals
             1980-1982

    Other holding institutions: AzU (AZU).

Manipogo News. Toutes Aides, Manitoba, Canada

   see Manipogo News and Porcupine Notes. Toutes Aides, Manitoba,
      Canada

599 Manipogo News and Porcupine Points. 1973-1979//. Weekly. ISSN
0316-7585. OCLC 4731498. Last issue 8 pages. Line drawings,
photographs, commercial advertising. Available in microform: WHi
(1976-1978). Published by Porcupine and Manipogo Information Centres,
Toutes Aides, Manitoba, Canada. Title varies: Manipogo News, June 17,
1976-Jan, 1977. Community newsletter.

WHi   v.4, n.7-v.5, n.29;   Microforms
          June 17, 1976-Mar 9, 1978

600 Manitoba. 1871-1900//. Weekly. Commercial Advertising. Available
in microform: CanLA: (1871-1900). Published by Le Manitoba, St.
Boniface, Manitoba, Canada. Title varies: Metis, May 27, 1871-Sept
29, 1881. Newspaper. Subject focus: Metis people. In French, 100%.

CaOPeT   v.1, n.1-v.30, n.6;   Periodicals
          May 27, 1871-Dec 26, 1900

601 Manitoba Indian News. 1971-1972//. Monthly, irregular. Last issue
10 pages, height 42 cm. Photographs. Published by Manitoba Indian
Brotherhood, Winnipeg, Manitoba, Canada. Editor: Lena Friesen.
Newspaper. Subject focus: Manitoba Native people.

CaACG   v.1, n.1-v.2, n.5;   Periodicals
          Mar, 1971-June/July, 1972

CaOPeT   v.1, n.1-v.2, n.5;   Periodicals
          Mar, 1971-June/July, 1972

602 Manitoba Metis Federation News. 1972-1974//. Irregular. RLIN
DCLCCN7830095-S. Last issue 16 pages, height 43 cm. Line drawings,
photographs, commercial advertising. Winnipeg, Manitoba, Canada.
Editors: Stan Fulham, June, 1973; John P. Burelle, Oct, 1973-Sept,
1974. subject focus: Manitoba Metis people, education, women's
rights, history, poetry. Superceded by Le Metis.

CaMWU   v.1;   970/M3146/
          1974   Me Fen

CaOONL   [v.1, n.4-14]   Newspaper
          [Nov, 1972-Sept, 1974]   Section

603 Many Smokes: Metis Earth Awareness Magazine. 1966. 3 times a year.
$4. for individuals and institutions. Wabun, editor, Many Smokes,
P.O. Box 9167, Spokane, WA 99209. (509) 489-6170. ISSN 0025-2670.
LC sc79-4431. OCLC 1756670. RLIN NYPG774215872-S, OHCP1756670-S,
DCLCSC794431-S, CUBG10597-S, CUBU229-S. Last issue 40 pages, last
volume 120 pages, height 28 cm. Line drawings, photographs,
commercial advertising. Available in microform: McP (1966-1973); McA
(1973-); CPC (1962-1979). Published by The Bear Tribe Medicine
Society. Place of publication varies: Reno, NV, Winter, 1966-Winter,
1974; Klamanth Falls, OR, Spring, 1974-Summer, 1975. Frequency
varies: quarterly, Winter, 1966-Spring/Summer, 1980; semi-annual,
Fall, 1980-Winter, 1981. Previous editor: Sun Bear, Fall,
1966-Spring, 1973. Subject focus: ecology, Native American medicine,
tribal news, poetry, graphics, book reviews.

WHi	v.1, n.1– Winter, 1966–	E/77/M2
WHi	v.1, n.1–v.13, n.1; Winter, 1966-Spring/Summer, 1979	Microforms
WEU	v.7, n.2; Summer, 1973	Journalism Lab
WM	Current issues	Forest Home Branch
WMUW	v.11, n.2; Summer, 1977	(SPL) E/75/M36x
WRfC	v.4– Spring, 1970–	Periodicals
AzNCC	v.7– Winter, 1973–	Indian File
CL	v.6, n.2– Summer, 1972–	Periodicals
CLSM	[v.1, n.4–v.3, n.3] [1966-1968]	Periodicals
CNoSU	[v.1–v.7] [1966-Fall, 1973]	Microfilm
CRSSU	v.5– 1970–	Periodicals
CU-A	v.1, n.1–v.5, n.3, v.6– Winter, 1969-Summer, 1970, Spring, 1972–	E/77/A1/M3
CU-E	v.1, n.1– Winter, 1966–	Periodicals
IdU	v.1, n.4, v.2– 1966, 1967–	E/75/M3

ICN	Current issues	CHAI
MnBemT	[v.2], v.3– [1967], 1968–	Periodicals
MoSHi	[v.2, n.4–v.7, n.3] [1967–1973]	Nev/05/M319
MtBBCC	v.14; Apr–Aug, 1980	Periodicals
NjP	v.2, n.12; Dec, 1967	Periodicals
NN	v.1, n.1–v.11; Spring, 1966–Winter, 1978	HBB
OkTU	v.13, n.1– Spring/Summer, 1979–	Rare Book Room
OkU	v.1, n.1–v.7; Spring, 1966–Fall, 1973	WHC
OrU	v.12, n.2– Summer, 1978–	Periodicals
PPT	[v.1, n.4–v.12, n.2] [Autumn, 1966–Summer, 1978]	Contemporary Culture
SdU	v.1–v.3; 1966–1968	South Dakota Room
TxU	v.11, n.1; 1977	E/77/M35/HRC
WaU	v.9, n.3– Fall, 1975–	E/75/M33
WyCWC	v.10, n.4– 1977–	Periodicals
CaOPeT	v.1– 1966–	Microfilm

Other holding institutions: AzTes (AZS), CChiS (CCH), CLobS (CLO), CLU
(CLU), CtY (YUS), MH-P (HLS), MiEM (EEM), MiKW (EXW), MiU (EYW),
MiU-Labadie (EYM), [University of Minnesota Union LIst, Minneapolis,
Mn] (MUL), [Western Nevada Community College, Carson City, NV], NmScW,
TxLT (ILU), WaChenE (WEA).

604 <u>Masenayegun</u>. 1980. Unknown. Harvey Knight, editor, Masenayegun, 465
Alexander Ave., Winnipeg, Manitoba, Canada R3A 0N7. Last issue 12
pages, height 44 cm. Line drawings, photographs. Published by

Winnipeg Friendship Centre. Subject focus: urban community, centre news.

CaACG	v.1, n.1– Aug, 1980–	Periodicals
CaOAFN	v.1, n.5– Jan, 1981–	Periodicals

605 The Masterkey for Indian Lore and History. 1927. Bi-monthly. $5.
for individuals and institutions. Bruce Bryan, editor, The Masterkey
for Indian Lore and History, Highland Park, Los Angeles, CA 90042.
(213) 221-2163. ISSN 0025-5084. LC 29-9308. OCLC 1606224, 4624777.
RLIN DCLC299308-S, MIUG10840-S, PAUG118-S, CUPG2849-S, CUBU3016-S,
OHCP4624777-S, OHCP1606224-S. Last issue 34 pages, last volume 164
pages, height 19 cm. Line drawings, photographs. Indexed: Index to
Literature on the American Indian (1970, 1971, 1973). Available in
microform: BHP (1927-1976). Published by Southwest Museum. Frequency
varies: irregular, Feb, 1928-Feb, 1931. Subject focus: anthropology,
archaeology, museum news, book reviews.

WHi	v.1, n.7– Feb, 1928–	E/51/M42
WHi	v.1, n.1–v.50, n.4; May, 1927–Oct/Dec, 1976	Microforms
WMMus	v.1, n.1– May, 1927–	507/S98/M
WMUW	v.5, n.2– July/Aug, 1931–	E/51/M42
AzFM	v.1– 1927–	570.6/S72m
AzNCC	v.2– 1928–	Indian File
AzT	v.23, n.2– Apr/June, 1979–	Periodicals
CU-A	v.1, n.7, v.2, n.3– Feb, Sept, 1928–	E/51/M42x
CSmarP	[v.25–v.40], v.41– [1951–1966], 1967–	Stacks
CoCF	v.4– 1931–	Periodicals
NbU	v.3– 1930–	913.78/M39

NmG	v.9, n.1-v.23, n.4; Jan, 1935-July, 1949	Periodicals
N	v.1, n.7, v.2, n.3, v.41, n.3; Feb, Sept/Oct, 1928, July/Sept, 1967	J970.479/M423
OkU	v.1, n.5- Nov/Dec, 1927-	WHC
TxU	v.1, n.1- May, 1927-	R/77/M35/HRC
WaU	v.1, n.7- Feb, 1928-	913.78MA
CaACG	[v.4, n.1-v.18, n.3], v.24- [1930-1944], 1950-	Periodicals
CaMWU	v.42- 1968-	970/M3937

Other holding institutions: ArU (AFU), ArLUA (AKU), [Amerind
Foundation, Inc., Draggon, AZ], AzTeS (AZS), CFS (CFS), CLU (CLU),
CLCM (CNH), CChiS (CCH), CCmS (CSM), COU-DA (COA), CtY (YUS), DLC
(DLC), FMU (FQG), FTaSU (FDA), GU (GUA), InU (IUL), KyU (KUK),
[University of Minnesota Union List, Minneapolis, MN] (MUL), MoS
(SVP), MoStcL (MOQ), MsU (MUM), NcGU (NGU), NmLcU (IRU), NmLvH (NMH),
NA1U (NAM), NIC (COO), [New York State Union List, Albany, NY] (NYS),
NRM (VXR), NBrockU (XBM), NSbSU (YSM), NOneoU (ZBM), NNepaSU (ZLM),
OKentU (KSU), [Ohio Historical Society, Columbus, OH] (OHT), OU (OSU),
OkTU (OKT), PPiU (PIT), TU (TKN), TxCM (TXA), TxDN (INT), TxDaM (ISM),
TxU-Da (ITD), [AMIGOS Union List of Serials, Dallas, TX] (IUC).

606 Mauneluk Association Newsletter. 1976//. Unknown. Last issue 6
pages, height 28 cm. Line drawings, photographs. Available in
microform: WHi (1976). Kotzebue, AK. Subject focus: community
development, social services.

WHi	Mar, 1976	Microforms

607 Mauneluk Report. 1977-1980//. Monthly. Last issue 9 pages, height
44 cm. Line drawings, photographs. Available in microform: WHi
(1977-1980). Published by Mauneluk Association, Kotzebue, AK.
Editors: R.W. Frampton, May, 1977-June/July, 1978; John David
Christensen, Dec, 1978-Jan, 1979; Judith V. Diamondstone, Feb, 1979;
John David Christensen, Mar, 1979-July, 1980. Subject focus: culture,
self-determination, community development.

WHi	v.1, n.1-v.4, n.6; May, 1977-July, 1980	Microforms

AkUF   [v.2, n.1-v.4, n.6]   AK-Per 2345
            [1978-July, 1980]

608 The Medicine Bundle. 1974. Irregular. The Medicine Bundle, 510
    First Ave., N., Great Falls, MT 59401. (406) 761-8471. Last issue 8
    pages, last volume 64 pages, height 41 cm. Line drawings,
    photographs. Published by Montana United Scholarship Service.
    Frequency varies: monthly, Sept 6, 1974-May, 1977. Subject focus:
    education, career opportunities.

    WHi   v.1, n.1-   Circulation
                Sept 6, 1974-

    MtBBCC   [v.3-v.8]   Periodicals
                [Jan, 1977-Apr, 1981]

    CaACG   [v.7-v.9]   Periodicals
                [Spring, 1980-Mar, 1982]

    Other holding institutions: [Standing Rock Community College Library,
    Fort Yates, ND].

609 The Medicine Pouch. 1980-1981?// Quarterly. Last issue 6 pages,
    height 28 cm. Line drawings, photographs. Published by American
    Indian Scouting Outreach, Boy Scouts of America, Dallas, TX. Place of
    Publication varies: Dayton, NJ, Spring, 1980-Winter, 1981. Subject
    focus: scouting outreach program, organization news.

    WHi   Spring-Summer, 1981   Microforms

    Other holding institutions: ICN (IBV).

610 Medium Rare. 1973-1974//. Bi-monthly? Last issue 6 pages.
    Published by AIPA News Bureau, Washington, DC. Subject focus:
    American Indian Press Association news.

    WHi   v.2, n.5-6;   Pam 75-3088
                July/Aug-Sept/Dec, 1974

    AzNCC   v.1-v.2;   Indian File
                Feb, 1973-1974

    NHu   [v.1, n.3-v.2, n.6]   Periodicals
                [Apr, 1973-Nov, 1974]

    Other holding institutions: OrU-Special Collections.

611 <u>Meeting Ground</u>. 1973. Annual. Herbert T. Hoover and David R.
Miller, editors, Meeting Ground, 60 W. Walton St., Chicago, IL 60610.
(312) 943-9090. OCLC 7501910. RLIN NJPG1216-S. Last issue 20 pages,
height 28 cm. Photographs. Published by Newberry Library Center for
the History of the American Indian. Previous editors: Martin Zanger
and Joseph Narum, Summer, 1976; William Swaggerty, Winter, 1978.
Subject focus: Native American studies, curriculum development,
history, culture, research.

WHi	v.1, n.1– Spring, 1973–	Circulation
WM	v.2, n.1– Spring, 1975–	Periodicals
AzNCC	v.2, n.1– Spring, 1975–	Indian File
MtBBCC	v.6; Winter, 1980	Periodicals
NjP	v.1, n.1; Spring, 1973	Periodicals
OkTU	v.1, n.2– Fall, 1974–	Rare Book Room

Other holding institutions: IC (CGP), PPiU (PIT), [University of
Wisconsin-Stevens Point-Native American Center, Stevens Point, WI].

612 <u>Menominee Indian Adult Educational Program Informational Bulletin</u>.
1957-?//. Monthly. Last issue 6 pages. Available in microform:
WHi-A, Veda Stone Papers, (1958). Keshena, WI. Subject focus:
Menominee people, adult and continuing education, community
development.

| WHi | v.1, n.3, 6;
Jan 15, Apr 10, 1958 | Microforms |
| WEU
ARC | v.1, n.3, 6;
Jan 15, Apr 10, 1958 | Micro 11 |

613 <u>Menominee News</u>. 1954-1965?//. Irregular. Last issue 13 pages. Line
drawings. Personal names indexed in: Index to Wisconsin Native
American Periodicals (1954-1965). Available in microform: WHi
(1954-1965); WHi-A, Veda Stone Papers, (1958, 1959, 1961). Published
by Menominee Enterprises, Inc., Keshena, WI. Subject focus: Menominee
people, organization news, governmental relations.

| WHi | Oct 29, 1954-Sept 24,
1965 | Microforms |

WEU   Aug 20, Sept 29, Oct 28, Nov-Dec 15, 1958, Micro 11
ARC   Mar 4, 1959, Apr 26, 1961

614 Menominee Prints. 1966-1970//. Semi-monthly. Last issue 9 pages.
    Personal names indexed in: Index to Wisconsin Native American
    Periodicals. Available in microform: WHi (1966-1970). Published by
    Community Action Program, Keshena, WI. Title varies: Moccasin Tracks,
    Mar 21, 1966. Frequency varies: monthly, Mar 21, 1961; bi-monthly,
    May 23, 1966; semi-monthly, Jan 27-Oct 17, 1966; monthly, Nov 14,
    1966-Mar 27, 1967; semi-monthly, Apr 17, 1967-Jan 1, 1968; monthly,
    Jan 15-July 29, 1968; semi-monthly, Aug 12-26, 1968; monthly, Sept
    23-Nov 11, 1968. Editors: Mabel Brown, Sept 23-Nov 25, 1968; Karen
    Menore, Dec 30, 1968-Jan 10, 1969; Loredana Dixon, Jan 31-Mar 17,
    1969; Evelyn T. Kaquatosh, Mar 31, 1969-Oct 26, 1970. Community
    newsletter. Subject focus: Menominee people.

WHi   v.1, n.1-v.5;   Microforms
           Mar 21, 1966-Oct 26, 1970

WEU   [v.1, n.8-v.5, n.25]   Micro 11
ARC   [Aug 15, 1966-July 20, 1970]

WUSP   [v.1, n.5-v.5, n.24]   ARC
           [June 6, 1966-June 1, 1970]

Other holding institutions: MH-P (HLS).

Menominee Talking. Keshena, WI

    see Aq-ua-chamine/Menominee Talking. Keshena, WI

615 Menominee Tribal News. 1976. Monthly. $5. for individuals; $10. for
    institutions. Laurie Ann Fish, editor, Menominee Tribal News, P.O.
    Box 397, Keshena, WI 54135. (715) 799-3629. OCLC 6188781. Last
    issue 20 pages, last volume 200 pages, height 41 cm. Line drawings,
    photographs, commercial advertising. Personal names indexed in: Index
    to Wisconsin Native American Periodicals (1976-1981). Available in
    microform: WHi-A, Veda Stone Papers, (1976, 1977). Community
    newsletter. Subject focus: Menominee people, history, legislation,
    education.

WHi   v.1, n.1-   Circulation
           Oct, 1976-

WU   Current issues only   Ethnic
Coll   Collection

WEU   v.1, n.2, v.2, n.2, 4, 6;   Micro 11
ARC   Nov, 1976, Feb, Apr, June, 1977

WMMus	v.1, n.1– Oct, 1976–	Anthro Section
WM	Current issues only	Forest Home Branch
WMUW	v.1, n.3– Dec, 1976–	(SPL) E/75/M46x
WGrU	v.2, n.1–v.3, n.4; Jan, 1977–Apr, 1978	Special Collections
NjP	v.4, n.1–6; Jan–June, 1979	Periodicals

Other holding institutions: [University of Wisconsin–Stevens Point–Native American Center, Stevens Point, WI], [Wisconsin Indian Resources Council, Stevens Point, WI].

The Mental Elevator. Cattaraugas Reservation, NY

   see Ne Jaguhnigoagesgwathah/ The Mental Elevator. Cattaraugas
       Reservation, NY

616 The Messenger. 1967–?//. Irregular. Last issue 28 pages, height 28 cm. Line drawings. Published by Indian Educational Club of William Head Institution, Metchosin, British Columbia, Canada. Editors: M. Walkus and J. Cornell, July, 1971; J. Cornell, Dec, 1971. Prison newsletter. Includes poetry.

WHi	July, Dec, 1971	Pam 2321
CaOONL	Sept, 1967, Sept, 1969, May, 1970, Feb, 1971, Mar, 1972	Periodicals
CaOPeT	May, 1970–Mar, 1972	Microfilm

617 Messenger (Tasutit). 1966–1970//. Bi-weekly. Last issue 6 pages. Line drawings. Available in microform: McA (1966–1970). Eskimo Point, Northwest Territories, Canada. Community newsletter. Subject focus: Inuit people. In Inuit, 100%.

NjP	Nov 1, 1969	Periodicals
OkU	[1966–1970]	WHC
WyCWC	[Aug 2, 1966–July 1, 1970]	Periodicals
CaOPeT	Aug, 1966–Fall, 1972	Microfilm

Other holding institutions: [Western Nevada Community College, Carson City, NV].

618 Messenger of the Holy Childhood. 1896?-1912//. Monthly. Last issue 32 pages, last volume 320 pages, height 22 cm. Photographs. Published by The Franciscan Fathers of the Holy Childhood Indian School, Harbor Springs, MI. Subject focus: missions, Catholic Church, Chippewa and Ottawa people. Chippewa edition titled Anishinabe Enamiad.

WMM   v.9, n.5-v.16, n.10;   Special
             July, 1904-Dec, 1912   Collections

619 Meta Tantay Newsletter. 1982?// Unknown. Last issue 8 pages, height 28 cm. Line drawings. Published by Amerine Enterprises, Carlin, NV. Subject focus: environment, culture, health. Superceded by Voice of Thunder.

WHi   n.3;   Pam
             Fall? 1982   Cataloging

Metis. St. Boniface, Manitoba, Canada

    see Manitoba. St. Boniface, Manitoba, Canada

620 Le Metis. 1974?-1978//. Irregular. ISSN 0703-5438. LC cn77-33680. OCLC 5785076. RLIN DCLCCN7733680-S, OHCP5785076-S. Line drawings, photographs, commerical advertising. Published by Manitoba Metis Federation, Winnipeg, Manitoba, Canada. Editors: Doug Marshall; John Burelle; Barbara Bruce; Marcel McIvor. Subject focus: Metis people.

CaACG   [v.1, n.6-v.7, n.12]   Periodicals
             [Apr, 1975-Mar, 1978]

CaAEU   [v.1, n.12-v.7, n.12]   Boreal
             [July/Aug, 1974-Mar, 1978]   Institute

CaMWU   [v.1-v.6]   970/M3164/
             [Nov, 1974-Dec, 1977]   Me Fen

Other holding institutions: CaOONL (NLC).

621 The Metis. 1980?//. Monthly. Last issue 12 pages, height 44 cm. Photographs. Published by Metis Association of the Northwest Territories, Yellowknife, Northwest Territories, Canada. Editor: Joe

Mercredi. Community newsletter. Subject focus: Metis people.
Superceded by Metis Newsletter.

WHi   July/Aug, 1980   Microforms

622 Metis Newsletter. 1980. Monthly. Bren Kolson, editor, Metis
    Newsletter, P.O. Box 1375, Yellowknife, Northwest Territories, Canada
    X1A 2P1. (403) 873-3505. Last issue 8 pages, height 43 cm. Line
    drawings, photographs. Published by Metis Association of the
    Northwest Territories. Subject focus: Metis people, rights, land
    claims, culture.

    WHi   v.1, n.8-   Circulation
                May, 1981-

    AkU   [v.1, n.4-15], 20-   Periodicals
                [1980-1981], 1982-

    ICN   Current issues   CHAI

    CaACG   v.1, n.3-   Periodicals
                Oct, 1980-

    CaAEU   v.1, n.4-   Boreal
                Jan, 1981-   Institute

    CaOAFN   v.1, n.17-   Periodicals
                Feb 15, 1982-

623 The Metlakahtlan. 1888-?//. Irregular. Last issue 4 pages, height
    22 cm. Metlakahtlan, AK. Subject focus: missions, education,
    Christian religion, history, culture, Tsimshean and Haida people.

    WHi   v.1, n.1-7;   Microforms
                Nov, 1888-Mar, 1891

624 Miccosukee Clans Crier. 1979. Monthly. Miccosukee Clans Crier, P.O.
    Box 440021 Tamiami Station, Miami, FL 33144. (305) 223-8380. Last
    issue 4 pages, height 44 cm. Line drawings, photographs. Published
    by Miccosukee Tribe of Indians of Florida. Community newsletter.
    Subject focus: Miccosukee people.

    WHi   v.2, n.3-   Circulation
                Dec, 1982-

625 Michigan Indian. 1975-1980//. Irregular. OCLC 6188791. Last issue
    40 pages, height 28 cm. Line drawings. Available in microform: WHi
    (1975-1980). Published by Michigan Commission on Indian Affairs,

Lansing, MI. Editor: Lorraine Jowett. Subject focus: state and
national news, art, education, employment information.

WHi	July/Aug, 1975-May, 1980	Microforms
WMUW	July/Aug, 1975-May, 1980	(SPL) E/75/M52x
AzNCC	Oct, 1977-May, 1980	Indian File
Mi	[?, 1974-May, 1980]	State Doc AD/I39 50/
NjP	May/June, 1975	Periodicals

Other holding institutions: MiDW (EYW).

626 <u>Micmac News</u>. 1971. Bi-weekly. $5. for individuals and institutions.
Vivian Basque, editor, Micmac News, P.O. Box 344, Sydney, Nova Scotia,
Canada B1P 6H2. (902) 539-0045. Last issue 24 pages, last volume 288
pages, height 38 cm. Line drawings, photographs, commmercial
advertising. Available in microform: WHi (1973-). Frequency varies:
monthly, Mar, 1974-Dec, 1980. Previous editors: Roy Gould, May,
1974-Oct, 1975; Russell Marshall, Jan, 1976-Apr, 1977; Joan Johnson,
May, 1977-June, 1980. Community newsletter. Subject focus: local and
provincial news, politics.

WHi	v.4, n.3- Mar, 1973-	Microforms
AzNCC	v.4- May, 1973-	Indian File
NjP	[v.1, n.2-v.8, n.6] [Jan, 1971-June, 1979]	Periodicals
OkU	v.8, n.12- Dec, 1979-	WHC
CaAEU	v.7, n.1- 1978-	Boreal Institute
CaNBFU	[v.2-v.3], v.4- [1972-1973], 1974-	Archives
CaOAFN	v.10, n.1- Jan, 1981-	Periodicals
CaOONL	v.1, n.2- Feb, 1971-	Periodicals
CaOPeT	[v.3-v.7], v.8- [1973-1977], 1978-	Periodicals

Other holding institutions: CaNfSM.

627 The Midnight Sun. 1969?-1974//. Weekly. Last issue 20 pages, height
36 cm. Line drawings. Igloolik, Northwest Territories, Canada.
Community newsletter. Subject focus: Inuit people. In Inuit, 50%.

WHi	[Apr 20, 1973-Apr, 1974]	Pam Cataloging
NjP	[Mar 30, 1973-Apr, 1974]	Periodicals
CaACG	Nov 10, 1972-Apr, 1974	Periodicals
CaOONL	[1969-1974]	Newspaper Section
CaOPeT	Mar, 1973-Apr, 1974	Microfilm

628 Milwaukee Indian News. 1976-1981//. Irregular. OCLC 6207411. Last
issue 8 pages, height 41 cm. Line drawings, photographs, commerical
advertising. Available in microform: WHi (1976-1981). Milwaukee, WI.
Editors: Fred Muskovitch and Karen Skenadore. Subject focus: urban
community news.

WHi	July, 1976-July, 1981	Microforms
WMMus	July, 1976-July, 1981	Anthro Section
WMUW	[July, 1976-Apr, 1977]	(SPL) E/75/M54x
WM	Feb, 1980-July, 1981	Periodicals
NjP	Sept, 1977	Periodicals

Other holding institutions: [University of Wisconsin-Stevens
Point-Native American Center, Stevens Point, WI], [Wisconsin Indian
Resources Council, Stevens Point, WI].

629 Ministikok. 1968?-1974?//. Monthly. ISSN 0300-3876. LC
cn77-318932. OCLC 1423835. Last issue 24 pages. Line drawings.
Moose Factory, Ontario, Canada. Editors: Ed Stevens, Sept-Nov, 1968;
Lorraine Hall and Edith Smith, Sept, 1974. Community newsletter.
Subject focus: Cree people.

CaACG	v.1, n.?; Jan 1, 1968	Periodicals

CaOONL   v.1, n.8-10, (n.s.)v.1, n.6;   Newspaper
          Sept-Nov, 1968, Sept, 1974   Section

CaOPeT   v.5?-(n.s.)v.1?   Periodicals
          1972-1974?

630 The Minnesota Chippewa Tribal Newsletter. 1974//. Unknown. Height
    28 cm. Cass Lake, MN. Editor: Tod LeGarde. Community newsletter.
    Subject focus: Chippewa people.

MnHi   v.1, n.1;   Periodicals
          June, 1974

631 Mission. 1934. Quarterly. $3. for individuals and institutions.
    Sister M. Franceline Malone, editor, Mission, 1663 Bristol Pike,
    Bensalem, PA 19020. (215) 638-9244. Last issue 18 pages, height 23
    cm. Line drawings, photographs. Available in microform: McA (1974-);
    WHi (1970-1973). Published by Sisters of the Blessed Sacrament.
    Title varies: News Bulletin of Mission Fields at Home, Autumn,
    1934-Jan/Feb, 1939. Frequency varies: bi-monthly, Jan/Feb,
    1935-July/Sept, 1977. Previous editor: Sister M. Maurice, May/June,
    1974-Fall, 1978. Subject focus: missions, Catholic Church.
    Supercedes Mission Fields at Home.

WHi   v.1, n.1-   Microforms
          Autumn, 1934-

WMM   [v.1, n.1-v.5, n.7], v.44, n.2;   Special
          [Autumn, 1934-Nov/Dec, 1939],   Collections
          Apr/May/June, 1976

AzNNC   v.42;   Microfilm
          Feb-Dec, 1974

NjP   [v.24, n.2-v,.47, n.1]   Periodicals
          [Apr, 1957-Spring, 1979]

CaOPeT   v.42-   Microfilm
          1974-

632 Mission Bells. 1940?-1972?//. Every six weeks. Last issue 8 pages,
    height 35 cm. Line drawings. Personal names indexed in: Index to
    Wisconsin Native American Periodicals (1965-1969). Published by
    Mission High School, Hays, MT. Editors: William Talks Different, May
    22, 1959; Helen Quincy, Oct 16, 1959-May 20, 1960; Mary S. Jones, Nov
    23, 1960-Apr 14, 1961; Phyllis Werk, Oct 13, 1961; Sharon Quincey, Oct
    11, 1963-Apr 17, 1964; Veronica White Cow, Oct 9, 1964-Apr 9, 1965;
    Oscar Morin, Apr 7, 1967; Patricia Walker, Apr 10-May 24, 1968; Kathy
    Hawley, Oct 6, 1968; James Shambo, Apr 7, 1971; Robert Fox, Oct 9,

1971–May 26, 1972; Lucille Stiffarm, Nov 17, 1972. High school
newsletter. Subject focus: school news, Catholic Church.

| WMM | [v.6, n.3–v.34, n.2] | Special |
| | [Jan 20, 1950–Nov 17, 1972] | Collections |

633 <u>The Mission Bells</u>. 1965?–?//. Irregular. Last issue 2 pages. Line
drawings. Available in microform: WHi–A, Veda Stone Papers,
(1965–1969). Published by The Winnebago Indian Mission Church, United
Church of Christ, Black River Falls, WI. Editor: J. W. Grether.
Subject focus: missions, United Church of Christ.

| WHi | [Feb, 1965–Dec, 1969] | Microforms |
| WEU ARC | [Feb, 1965–Dec, 1969] | Micro 11 |

634 <u>Mission Fields at Home</u>. 1928–1934// Monthly. Last issue 14 pages,
last volume 174 pages, height 28 cm. Line drawings, photographs.
Available in microform: WHi (1928–1934). Published by Sisters of The
Blessed Sacrament, Cornwell Heights, PA. Subject focus: missions,
Catholic Church. Superceded by Mission.

WHi	[v.1, n.1–v.6, n.12]	Microforms
	[Oct, 1928–Sept, 1934]	
WMM	[v.1, n.1–v.6, n.12]	Special
	[Oct, 1928–Sept, 1934]	Collections

635 <u>The Mission Indian</u>. 1895?–?//. Unknown. Last issue 10 pages, height
30 cm. Line drawings, photographs. Published by St. Boniface's
Industrial School, Banning, CA. School newsletter. Subject focus:
missions, Catholic Church, school news.

WMM	v.8, n.1;	Special
	July, 1906	Collections
CLSM	v.5, n.1–8;	Periodicals
	Oct 15, 1899–Feb 1, 1900	

636 <u>Mittark: Mashpee Wampanoag Newsletter</u>. 1978. Irregular. Mittark,
Box 1048, Mashpee, MA 02649. Last issue 4 pages, height 28 cm. Line
drawings. Available in microform: WHi (1978–1981). Community
newsletter. Subject focus: Mashpee Wampanoag people.

| WHi | v.1, n.1–v.4, n.5, v.5, n.3– | Microforms |
| | 1978–Mar, 1981, Oct, 1982– | |

637 <u>Moccasin News</u>. 1960?//. Unknown. Last issue 36 pages, height 28 cm.
Line drawings. Published by Ermineskin Indian School, Hobbema,
Alberta, Canada. School newsletter. Subject focus: Cree people.

   CaACG   June, 1960   Periodicals

638 <u>Moccasin Telegraph</u>. 1978. Monthly. Moccasin Telegraph, 5th Floor,
55 St. Clair Ave., E., Toronto, Ontario, Canada M4T 2P8. Last issue 6
pages, height 46 cm. Line drawings, photographs. Published by
Department of Indian Affairs and Northern Development. Staff
newsletter.

   CaOAFN   v.4, n.1-   Periodicals
              Jan, 1981-

   <u>Moccasin Tracks</u>. Keshena, WI

      see <u>Menominee Prints</u>. Keshena, WI

639 <u>Moccasin Tracks</u>. 1976. 10 times a year. $6. for individuals and
institutions. Jerry Smith, editor, Moccasin Tracks, 7812 Jennifer
Circle, La Palma, CA 90623. ISSN 0199-3747. LC sn79-7856. OCLC
5820012. Last issue 16 pages, height 28 cm. Line drawings,
photographs, commercial advertising. Published by California Indian
Hobbyist Association. Subject focus: arts and crafts, culture.

   WHi   v.7, n.7, 9-   Circulation
              Mar, May, 1982-

   OkU   v.5, n.8-   WHC
              Apr, 1979-

640 <u>Moccasin Trails</u>. 1975-?//. Unknown. OCLC 6221123. Last issue 8
pages, height 28 cm. Line drawings, photographs. Personal names
indexed in: Index to Wisconsin Native American Periodicals
(1975-1976). Available in microform: WHi (1975-1976). Lac du
Flambeau, WI. School newsletter.

   WHi   v.1, n.6-7;   Microforms
              June 17, 1975-Apr 14, 1976

   WMUW   v.1, n.6-7;   (SPL)
              June 17, 1975-Apr 14, 1976   E/75/M62x

641 <u>Mod-Nu-Set</u>. 1978//. Unknown. Last issue 86 pages, height 28 cm.
Line drawings, photographs, some in color, commercial advertising.

Published by Lyle Thomson and Mod-Nu-Adventures, Calgary Alberta, Canada. Subject focus: history, culture, socio-economic conditions, housing, Blackfeet and Blood people.

| CaACG | v.1, n.1;
Sept, 1978 | Periodicals |

642 Montana Inter-Tribal Policy Board Minutes. 1968?-1970//. Irregular. Last issue 26 pages. Available in microform: CPC (1968-1970). Helena, MT. Place of publication varies: Great Falls, MT, July 19, 1968. Meeting minutes.

WHi	[July 29, 1968-July 7/8, 1970]	Microforms
NjP	July 29, 1968-July 7/8, 1970	Periodicals
NN	Dec, 1968-July, 1970	HBA+ 74-468

Monthly Mailout. Stevens Point, WI

see Wisconsin Indian Resource Council Monthly Mailout. Stevens Point, WI

643 Moose Call. 1963?-1970?//. Unknown. OCLC 1606630. Last issue 3 pages, height 35 cm. Published by Prince Albert Indian and Metis Service Council, Prince Albert, Saskatchewan, Canada. Community newsletter.

| UPB | [1966-1970] | 970.41242/M789 |
| CaACG | May 30, 1963 | Periodicals |

Other holding institutions: CLU (CLU), CU-UC (UCU), [University of Minnesota Union List, Minneapolis, MN] (MUL).

Morley News and Bulletin. Morley, Alberta, Canada

see Stoney News and Bulletin. Morley, Alberta, Canada

The Morning Star. Carlisle, PA.

see Red Man and Helper. Carlisle, PA

644 The Morning Star People. 1965. Quarterly. $1. for individuals and
    institutions. Rev. Wally Balduck, editor, The Morning Star People,
    St. Labre Indian School, Ashland, MT 59004. (406) 784-6152. ISSN
    0047-8121. LC sn78-5519. OCLC 3858528. RLIN NYPG81-S653,
    OHCP3858528-S. Last issue 6 pages, last volume 24 pages, height 23
    cm. Line drawings, photographs. Available in microform: McA (1973-);
    WHi (1972-1973). Previous editor: Rev. Emmett Hoffman, Mar, 1972-Mar,
    1977. School newsletter. Subject focus: Catholic Church, financial
    reports.

    WHi   v.9, n.1-   Microforms
                 Mar, 1972-

    WEU   v.9, n.2;   Journalism
                 June, 1972   Lab

    WMM   v.13, n.4, v.17, n.2;   Special
                 Dec, 1976, June, 1980   Collections

    CLSM   [v.2, n.4-v.5, n.3]   Periodicals
                 [Dec, 1966-1969]

    IdU   v.8-v.12, v.13, n.3-   E/75/M6
                 1971-1975, Sept, 1976-

    NjP   [v.1, n.1-v.12, n.3]   Periodicals
                 [Feb, 1965-Sept, 1975]

    OkTU   v.15, n.1-   Rare Book
                 Mar, 1978-   Room

    OkU   v.1, n.1-v.9; v.16, n.4-   WHC
                 [Feb, 1965-Dec, 1972], Dec, 1979-

    CaOPeT   v.1, n.1-   Microfilm
                 Feb, 1965-

    Other holding institutions: KMK (KKS), [University of Minnesota Union
    List, Minneapolis, MN] (MUL), [Western Nevada Community College,
    Carson City, NV].

645 The Morning Sun. 1893-?//. Daily. Last issue 4 pages. Line
    drawings, commercial advertising. Tahlequah, OK. Available in
    microform: OkHi (1893). Editor: Jonathan L. Springston. Newspaper.
    Subject focus: Cherokee people. In Cherokee, 15%.

    WHi   v.1, n.1, 3, 14;   Microforms
                 Nov 6, 8, 21, 1893

646 Muckleshoot Smoke Signals. 1980? Monthly, irregular. Muckleshoot
    Smoke Signals, 39015 172nd Ave., S.E., Auburn, WA 98002. Last issue
    16 pages, height 28 cm. Line drawings. Community newsletter.

Subject focus: environment, legislation, social services, poetry,
Muckleshoot people.

WHi   Sept, 1982-   Circulation

ICN   Current issues   CHAI

647 Mukluks Hemcunga: "Indian Talk". 1973. Irregular. $2. for
    individuals and institutions. Bob Bojorcas, editor, Mukluks Hemcunga,
    O.F.A., P.O. Box 1257, Klamath Falls, OR 97601. Last issue 20 pages,
    last volume 36 pages, height 39 cm. Line drawings, photographs,
    commercial advertising. Available in microform: WHi (1973-1981).
    Editors: Cindy Sargeant, Oct/Nov, 1974-May, 1975. Cindy McWilliams,
    Jan/Feb, 1976-Oct, 1979. Subject focus: politics, social services,
    health, education, poetry, (includes reprints from other newsletters).

    WHi   v.1, n.2, 4-   Microforms
               July/Aug, Oct/Nov, 1973-

    Or   v.1-v.13, n.1;   Periodicals
               1973-June/July, 1981

648 Museum Notes. 1981. Unknown. Museum Notes, Box 158, Schoharie, NY
    12157. Last issue 10 pages, height 28 cm. Photographs. Published by
    Schoharie Museum of the Iroquois Indian. Subject focus: Iroquois
    people, art, archaeology, museum exhibits.

    ICN   Current issues   CHAI

649 Muskeg Moccasingraph. 1963. Bi-monthly. Jay Jennings, editor,
    Muskeg Moccasingraph, Box 98, Thompson, Manitoba, Canada R8N 1M9.
    Last issue 16 pages, last volume 96 pages, height 22 cm. Line
    drawings, photographs. Published by Continental Mission, Inc.
    Subject focus: missions, Christian religion, Cree people. Some
    articles in Cree.

    CaACG   v.17, n.2-   Periodicals
               MAr/Apr, 1979-

650 Muskogee Daily Phoenix. 1901-?//. Daily. Last issue 8 pages. Line
    drawings, photographs, commercial advertising. Available in microform:
    OkHi (1901). Muskogee, OK. Newspaper.

    WHi   v.1, n.45;   Microforms
               Oct 4, 1901

    OkHi   v.1, n.45;   Microforms
               Oct 4, 1901

651 Muskogee Nation News. 1973. Monthly. $6. for individuals and
    institutions. Tommy Cummings, editor, Muscogee Nation News, P.O. Box
    580, Okmulgee, OK 74447. (918) 756-8700. Last issue 8 pages, last
    volume 94 pages, height 36 cm. Line drawings, photographs. Previous
    editors: Jerry Wilson, Nov, 1975; David King, June-Nov, 1979; Helen
    Bennett, Dec, 1979-Jan, 1980; Elias R. Haikey. Feb-July, 1980.
    Community newsletter.

    WHi   v.7, n.6-   Circulation
                 June, 1979-

    WEU   v.2, n.11;   Journalism
                 Nov, 1975   Lab

    Other holding institutions: [Bacone College, Muskogee, OK].

652 Muskogee Phoenix. 1888-?// Weekly. Last issue 12 pages. Line
    drawings, commercial advertising. Published by Phoenix Printing Co.,
    Muskogee, OK. Available in microform: OkHi (1894-1905). Frequency
    varies: semi-weekly, Sept 19, 1894-Apr 17, 1895. Editors: Frank C.
    Hubbard, Dec 31, 1891-Feb 9, 1893; I.W. Singleton, June 1, 1893-Feb 6,
    1895; F. C. Hubbard, Aug 6, 1896-June 7, 1897; M. R. Moore, Jan 3,
    1901-Jan 23, 1902; Clarence B. Douglas, Aug 25, 1904-June 7, 1905.
    Newspaper.

    WHi   [v.4, n.46-v.18, n.14]   Microforms
                 [Dec 31, 1891-June 7, 1905], Feb 16, 1963

    OkHi   [v.4, n.46-v.18, n.14]   Microforms
                 [Dec 31, 1891-June 7, 1905]

653 Muskogee Times. 1897-?//. Weekly. Line drawings, photographs,
    commercial advertising. Published by Times Publishing Co., Muskogee,
    OK. Newspaper.

    WHi   v.1, n.45;   Microforms
                 Nov 25, 1897

    KU   v.1, n.45;   Kansas
                 Nov 25, 1897   Collection

654 Mustang News. 1973?-1982//. Unknown. Last issue 6 pages, height 58
    cm. Line drawings, photographs. Published by Little Wound School,
    Pine Ridge Reservation, Kyle, SD. Editors: S. Langly; Bill Lone Hill.
    School newsletter.

    CLSM   v.4, n.1, 4;   Periodicals
                 Sept/Oct, 1976, Jan/Feb, 1977

    MtBBCC   May, 1981-Jan, 1982   Periodicals

Muzzeniegun. Sault Sainte Marie, MI

    see The Literary Voyager; or Muzeniegun. Sault Sainte Marie, MI

655 NAC News. 1971?//. Weekly. Last issue 4 pages. Available in
microform: WHi-A, Veda Stone Papers, (1971). Published by Native
American Church, Wittenberg Chapter, Eland, WI. Subject focus: Church
news, Christian religion.

WHi	Jan 13-27, Mar 3-June 30, 1971	Microforms
WEU ARC	Jan 13-27, Mar 3-June 30, 1971	Micro 11

NACA Newsletter. Flagstaff, AZ

    see Voice in the Pines. Flagstaff, AZ

656 NACIE Newsletter. 1981?-1982// Unknown. Last issue 4 pages, height
28 cm. Published by National Advisory Council on Indian Education,
Washington, DC. Subject focus: education, educational legislation.

WHi	May, 12, 1982	Pam-Cataloging
MtBBCC	July, 1981	Periodicals

657 NAD Advocate. 1973-?//. Monthly. Last issue 9 pages, height 28 cm.
Line drawings. Available in microform: WHi (1973). Published by
Native American Students at Dartmouth College, Hanover, NH. College
newsletter.

WHi	v.1, n.1; Dec, 1973	Microforms

658 NAD Winds. 1977?//. Unknown. Last issue 8 pages, height 42 cm.
Line drawings, photographs. Available in microform: WHi (1977).
Published by Native American Students at Dartmouth College, Hanover,
NH. Editor: Tim Craig. College newsletter. Subject focus: local and
national news.

WHi	Winter?, 1977	Microforms

659 NAES Rule. 1979. Irregular. NAES Rule, 4550 N. Hermitage, Chicago,
IL 60640. Last issue 10 pages, height 28 cm. Line drawings.

Available in microform: WHi (1979-). Published by Native American
Educational Services. Subject focus: education, curriculum
development, bibliography.

WHi   [n.10-22], n. 26-   Microfilm
           [Apr 19, 1979-Apr 1, 1981], Sept, 1982-

IC   [n.10-22];   Periodicals
           [Apr 19, 1979-Apr 1, 1981]

ICN   Current issues   CHAI

660 NAFC News Magazine. 1973-1981?//. Irregular. OCLC 8407005. Last
    issue 14 pages. Line drawings, photographs. Available in microform:
    CPC (1973-1975). Published by National Association of Friendship
    Centres, Ottawa, Ontario, Canada. Place of publication varies:
    Vancouver, British Columbia, Jan-Mar/Apr, 1973. Editors: Angie
    Dennis, Jan-Mar/Apr, 1973; Betsy Beardy, Nov-Dec, 1973; Ameshia McKay,
    Mar-Apr, 1974; Gloria Wright, Oct, 1974-June, 1975. Organization
    newsletter.

WHi   v.1, n.1-v.3, n.3;   Microforms
           Jan, 1973-June, 1975

NjP   [v.1, n.1-v.3. n.3]   Periodicals
           [Jan, 1973-June, 1975]

CaOAFN   [no nos.]   Periodicals
           Oct, 1980-Feb, 1981

Other holding institutions: PPiU (PIT).

661 NANA Regional Corp. Newsletter. 1973. Monthly. Sarah Scanlan,
    editor, NANA Regional Corp. Newsletter, Box 49, Kotzebue, AK 99752.
    (907) 442-3262. Line drawings, photographs. Available in microform:
    AkUF (1973-1976). Subject focus: corporate and community news.

WHi   [v.1, n.1-v.2, n.10]   Microforms
           [July?, 1973-Dec, 1975/Jan, 1976]

WHi   (n.s.)v.7, n.4-   Circulation
           May, 1982-

AkUF   v.1, n.1-   HD/2798/
           July?, 1973-   A4/N2

662 NARP Newsletter. 1968-?//. Irregular. Last issue 12 pages, height 28
    cm. Line drawings, photographs. Published by Native Alliance for Red

Power, Vancouver, British Columbia, Canada. Editor: Ray Bobb. Subject
focus: radical politics, law, rights.

WHi	n.3-5; Jan/Feb, 1969-Feb/Mar, 1970	Pam 72-298
AzNCC	n.5; Feb/Mar, 1970	Indian File
CU-A	n.5; Feb/Mar, 1970	E/77/A1/N32
NjP	n.5; Feb/Mar, 1970	Periodicals

663 NAS News. 1974. Irregular. NAS News, Northland College, Ashland, WI
54806. (715) 682-4531. OCLC 8081767. Last issue 4 pages, height 28
cm. Line drawings, photographs. Title varies: Northland Native
American News, Nov, 1974-Mar, 1979. School newsletter.

| WHi | v.3, n.1-
Jan, 1977- | Circulation |
| WNC | v.1, n.1-
Nov, 1974- | Periodicals |

Other holding institutions: [Wisconsin Indian Resource Council,
Stevens Point, WI].

NASC News. St. Paul, MN

   see Native American Solidarity Committee. St. Paul, MN

664 NAS-NW Newsletter. 1970-1972?//. Unknown. Last issue 8 pages,
height 28 cm. Line drawings, photographs. Available in microform:
WHi (1971-1972). Published by Native American Scholars-Northwest,
Moscow, ID. Subject focus: education, Native American studies.

| WHi | n.3-4;
Sept, 1971-Fall, 1972 | Microforms |

665 NCAI Sentinel. 1941? Irregular. $10. for individuals and
institutions. NCAI Sentinel, 202 E St., NE, Washington, DC 20002.
(202) 546-1168. OCLC 8376386. Last issue 14 pages, height 28 cm.
Line drawings. Published by National Congress of American Indians.
Subject focus: legislation, rights, culture, organization news.

WHi   [v.37, n.3/4-v.39, n.27], v.42, n.5-   Circulation
           [Mar/Apr, 1981-Jan/Feb], May, 1982-

MtBBCC   v.37   Periodicals
           Mar-Apr, 1981

NCAI Sentinel Bulletin. Washington, DC

   see Sentinel Bulletin. Washington, DC

666 NCIC Bulletin. 1957-?//. Unknown. Last issue 4 pages, height 28 cm.
    Published by National Commission on the Indian Canadian of the
    Canadian Association for Adult Education, Toronto, Ontario, Canada.
    Subject focus: urban community.

    CaACG   Apr, 1957   Periodicals

    CaOONL   May, Nov, 1958   Periodicals

667 NCIO News. 1970-1972//. Irregular. OCLC 1768547. RLIN CUBG81-S912,
    NYPG720190848-S. Last issue 12 pages. Photographs. Available in
    microform: McA (1970-1972); CPC (1970-1972). Published by National
    Council on Indian Opportunity, Washington, DC. Subject focus:
    government policies and programs.

    WHi   v.1, n.1-v.3, n.1;   Microforms
               Dec, 1970-Sept, 1972

    WEU   v.1, n.3, 5, v.2, n.1-4;   Y/3.1N/2/919
               Feb, May, July/Sept, 1971-Jan/May, 1972

    WEU   v.1, n.1-5, v.2, n.2, v.3, n.1;   Micro 11
    ARC   Dec, 1970-May, Oct/Nov, 1971, Sept, 1972

    WMM   [v.1, n.5-v.3, n.1]   Special
               [May, 1971-Sept, 1972]   Collections

    AzNCC   v.1-v.3;   Microfilm
               1971-May, 1972

    NjP   v.1, n.1-v.3, n.1;   Periodicals
               Dec, 1970-Sept, 1972

    OkU   v.1, n.1-v.3, n.1;   WHC
               Dec, 1970-Sept, 1972

    OrU   v.1, n.1-v.3, n.1;   Periodicals
               Dec, 1970-Sept, 1972

    CaOPeT   v.1, n.1-v.3;   Microfilm
               Dec, 1970-Dec, 1972

Other holding institutions: MiU (EYM), [University of Minnesota Union
List, Minneapolis, MN] (MUL), [Western Nevada Community College,
Carson City, NV], OKentU (KSU), OrU-Special Collections.

668 NCIW News. 1970-1973//. Irregular. Last issue 6 pages. Line
    drawings, photographs. Available in microform: WHi-A, Veda Stone
    Papers, (1970-1973). Published by National Commission on Indian Work
    of the Episcopal Church, New York, NY. Editor, Howard Meredith, Mar,
    1972. Subject focus: missions, Episcopal Church, education.

    WHi   [v.1, n.2-v.3, n.1]   Microforms
                 [June, 1970-Feb, 1973]

    WEU   [v.1, n.2-v.3, n.1]   Micro 11
    ARC   [June, 1970-Feb, 1973]

    NjP   [v.1, n.1-(n.s)v.2, n.3]   Periodicals
                 [May, 1970-July, 1974]

    OkU   [v.1, n.5-(n.s.)v.2, n.3]   WHC
                 [Sept, 1970-July, 1974]

    Other holding institutions: OrU-Special Collections.

669 NDP Native Network. 1980? Unknown. Jim Manly and Terry Sargeant,
    editors, NDP Native Network, Room 748, House of Commons, Ottawa,
    Ontario, Canada K1A 0A6. Last issue 4 pages, height 35 cm. Line
    drawings. Subject focus: News Democratic Party, politics.

    CaACG   Dec?, 1980-   Periodicals

670 NIBIS (Native Indian Brotherhood Information Service). 1971-1973?//.
    Weekly. Last issue 22 pages, height 35 cm. Line drawings,
    photographs. Ottawa, Ontario, Canada. Reprints of articles on Native
    people from establishment presses.

    CaOONL   [v.1, n.1-v.3, n.20]   J-10-1
              [Oct?, 1971-May 16, 1973]

671 NICOA News. 1977-1980//. Quarterly. Last issue 16 pages, height 28
    cm. Line drawings, photographs. Available in microform: WHi
    (1977-1980). Published by National Indian Council on Aging,
    Albuquerque, NM. Editors: Juana P. Lyon, May, 1978; Larry Curley,
    Fall, 1979-Fall, 1980. Subject focus: resources and social services
    for the elderly.

    WHi   v.1, n.1-v.4, n.3;   Microforms
                 Apr, 1977-Fall, 1980

AzNCC   v.2–v.4;   Indian File
           1978–1980

IC   v.4, n.1–3;   Periodicals
           Spring–Fall, 1980

672 <u>NICOA Quarterly</u>. 1981. Quarterly. Peggy Ross, editor, NICOA
    Quarterly, P.O. Box 2088, Albuquerque, NM 87103. (505) 766–2276.
    Last issue 14 pages, height 28 cm. Line drawings, photographs.
    Published by National Indian Council on Aging, Inc. Subject focus:
    resources and social services for the elderly.

    WHi   v.1, n.1–   Circulation
              Winter, 1981–

    WU   v.1, n.1–   Social Work
              Winter, 1981–

    IC   v.1, n.1–   Periodicals
              Winter, 1981–

673 <u>NICOA Update</u>. 1980. Monthly. Peggy Ross, editor, NICOA Update, P.O.
    Box 2088, Albuquerque, NM 87103. (505) 766–2276. Last issue 4 pages,
    height 28 cm. Line drawings, photographs. Published by National
    Indian Council on Aging, Inc. Subject focus: aging, politics,
    economics.

    WHi   v.1, n.1–   Circulation
              Nov, 1980–

    WU   v.1, n.1–   Social Work
              Nov, 1980–

674 <u>NIHB Health Reporter</u>. 1980. Bi–monthly. John P. O'Connor, editor,
    NIHB Health Reporter, 1602 S. Parker Rd., Suite 200, Denver, CO 80231.
    OCLC 7962444. Last issue 20 pages, height 28 cm. Line drawings,
    photographs. Published by National Indian Health Board. Frequency
    varies: monthly, Sept, 1981. Subject focus: health care.

    WHi   v.2, n.15–   Circulation
              Sept, 1981–

    Other holding Institutions: COU-DA (COA).

675 <u>NITRC News</u>. 1970?//. Unknown. Last issue 5 pages, height 28 cm.
    Available in microform: WHi (1970). Published by National Indian
    Training and Research Center, Tempe, AZ. Subject focus: community
    development, health, education.

WHi   Oct, 1970   Microforms

676 El Nahutzen. 1978-1979?//. Semi-annual. LC sn78-2141, 79-644841.
    OCLC 4252977. Last issue 30 pages, height 24 cm. Line drawings.
    Iowa City, IA. Editors: Lowell Jaeger, Fall? 1978; Lowell Jaeger,
    Hector Perez, Andres Rodriguez and Jeffery Valadez, Spring, 1979.
    Subject focus: Hispanic and Native American poetry.

    WU   v.1, n.1-2;   Rare Book
               Fall? 1978-Spring? 1979   Room

    AzNCC   v.1;   Indian File
               1979

    IaHi   v.1, n.1-2;   PS/591/M49/
               Fall? 1978-Spring? 1979   N3

    Other holding institutions: DLC (DLC), IaHi (IOQ).

677 Nainemiok. 1955-?//. Unknown. Height 31 cm. Published by the
    Moravian Church, Labrador, New Foundland, Canada. Editor: Rev. Dr.
    F.W. Peacock. Subject focus: Moravian Church, Inuit people. In
    Inuit, 100%.

    CaNfSM   n.1;   Periodicals
               Nov, 1955

678 The Nambe Dragon. 1933-1934?//. Monthly. Last issue 4 pages. Line
    drawings. Available in microform: McA (John Collier Papers).
    Published by Nambe Day School, Nambe, NM. School newsletter.

    WHi   v.1, n.2-7;   Microforms
               Nov, 1933-Apr 30, 1934   J. Collier
                                                        Papers

    WUSP   v.1, n.2-7;   Microfilm
               Nov, 1933-Apr 30, 1934   J. Collier
                                                        Papers

679 N'Amerind Friendship Centre Newsletter. 1982? Monthly. N'Amerind
    Friendship Centre Newsletter, 260 Colborne St., London, Ontario,
    Canada N6B 2S6. (519) 672-0131. Last issue 14 pages, height 28 cm.
    Line drawings. Title varies: N'Amerind News, Mar, 1982. Center
    newsletter. Subject focus: urban community, centre news.

    WHi   Mar, 1982-   Circulation

N'Amerind News. London, Ontario, Canada

   see N'Amerind Friendship Centre Newsletter. London, Ontario, Canada

680 Nana. 1960-1964//. Quarterly. Last issue 32 pages, height 22 cm.
    Line drawings. Published by Oblate Missions of the Canadian Arctic,
    Cambridge Bay, Northwest Territories, Canada. Community newsletter.
    Subject focus: Inuit people, missions, Catholic Church. In Inuit, 15%.

    CaOORD   n.1-15;   Periodicals
               Summer, 1960-Summer, 1964

    CaOPeT   n.7-10;   E99/E7N85
               Winter, 1962-Jan, 1963

681 Nanih Waiya. 1973-1978//. Quarterly. ISSN 0148-6047. LC sc77-373.
    OCLC 2627933. RLIN DCLCSCX77373-S, MIUG21212-S, OHCP2627933-S. Last
    issue 42 pages, last volume 82 pages, height 26 cm. Line drawings,
    photographs. Published by Choctaw Student Press, Philadelphia, MS.
    Subject focus: Choctaw culture and history.

    WHi   v.1, n.1-v.5, n.3/4;   E/99/C8/N35
               Fall, 1973-Spring/Summer, 1978

    Other holding institutions: CtY (YUS), LNU (LNU), MiU (EYM).

682 Napi News. 1969? Monthly. Napi News, P.O. Box 657, Pincher Creek,
    Alberta, Canada TOK 1W0. ISSN 0701-1911. LC cn77-32249. OCLC
    3409301. Last issue 13 pages, hieght 29 cm. Line drawings,
    photographs. Published by Napi Friendship Association. Frequency
    varies: bi-monthly, Apr/May-Nov/Dec, 1973. Previous editors: Reggie
    Newkirk; John Fletcher. Community newsletter. Subject focus: Peigan
    people.

    CaACG   [Dec, 1969-Nov, 1981], Jan, 1982-   Periodicals

    Other holding institutions: CaOONL (NLC).

683 Narragansett Dawn. 1935-1936?//. Monthly. Last issue 16 pages, last
    volume 294 pages, height 23 cm. Commercial advertising. Available in
    microform: CPC (1935-1936). Oakland, RI. Editor: Princess Red Wing.
    Subject focus: Narragansett people, Christian religion, culture,
    acculturation, poetry.

    WHi   v.1, n.1-v.2, n.6;   F8096/N23/N
               May, 1935-Oct, 1936   Cutter

CLSM	v.1, n.1–v.2, n.6; May, 1935–Oct, 1936	Periodicals
NjP	v.2, n.6; Oct, 1936	Periodicals
NHu	v.1, n.1–v.2, n.6; May, 1935–Oct, 1936	Periodicals
NN	v.1, n.1–v.2, n.6; May, 1935–Oct, 1936	HBA

Other holding institutions: MH-P (HLS).

684 National Association on Indian Affairs Bulletin. 1923-1937//.
   Irregular. OCLC 4291027, 8448443, 8447467. Last issue 6 pages. Line
   drawings, photographs. Available in microform: CPC (1924?-1937).
   Published by Eastern Association on Indian Affairs (1923-1931), New
   York, NY. Subject focus: culture, health, history.

WHi	n.3-26; Nov, 1924–Feb, 1937	Microforms
WMM	[n.4-22] [1924–Mar, 1931]	Special Collections
NjP	n.3-22, 26; Nov 24, 1924–Mar, 1931, Feb, 1937	Periodicals
NN	n.3-26; Nov, 1924–Feb, 1937	HBA
SdU	n.3-26; Nov, 1924–Feb, 1937	Microfilm
TxU	n.25; Nov, 1936	E/77/N3/HRC
CaOPeT	n.3-n.26; Nov, 1924–Feb, 1937	Microfilm

Other holding institutions: NmPE (IPU), NmU (IQX), PPiU (PIT).

685 National Congress of American Indians Bulletin. 1947-1972//.
   Monthly. OCLC 7557738. Last issue 6 pages. Line drawings,
   photographs. Available in microform: McP (1947-1972); WHi-A, Veda
   Stone Papers, (1972). Washington, DC. Frequency varies: irregular,
   Oct, 1957-Dec, 1958. Editors: Ruth M. Bronson, Mar, 1947-Feb, 1950;
   John Rainer, Mar, 1950-May, 1951; Ruth M. Bronson, June, 1951-Apr,
   1952; Frank George, May, 1952-June, 1953; Helen Peterson, Nov,
   1953-May, 1961; Tom Edwards, Apr-July, 1972; John Tiger, Nov-Dec,

1972. Subject focus: organization news, rights, politics,
legislation, governmental relations.

WHi	v.1, n.1-v.28, n.4; Feb, 1947-Dec, 1972	Microforms
WEU ARC	v.28, n.2-3; Apr-June/July, 1972	Micro 11
CNoSU	v.1, n.1-v.28, n.4; Feb, 1947-Dec, 1972	Microfilm
NjP	[v.3, n.?-v.28, n.3] [Feb, 1949-July/Aug, 1972]	Periodicals
OkU	v.1, n.1-v.28, n.4; Feb, 1947-Dec, 1972	WHC

Other holding institutions: IU (UIU), [Western Nevada Community
College, Carson City, NV], NmScW.

686 National Congress of American Indians Newsletter. 1945?-1948//.
Irregular. Last issue 7 pages. Photographs. Available in microform:
McP (1945-1947). Washington, DC. Subject focus: organization news,
rights, politics, legislation.

WHi	[July, 1945-Aug, 1948]	Microforms
CNoSU	Apr, Oct, 1947	Periodicals
NjP	Oct, 1947	Periodicals
NHu	Apr, Oct, 1947	Periodicals
OkU	[July, 1945-Aug, 1948]	Microforms

Other holding institutions: NmScW.

687 National Congress of American Indians Sentinel Bulletin. 1956-1973//
Irregular. Last issue 4 pages. Line drawings, photographs,
commercial advertising. Available in microform: McP (1963-1973);
WHi-A, Veda Stone Papers, (1964-1973). Washington, DC. Editors:
Robert Burnette, Jan-May, 1963; Vine Deloria, Jr., Feb-Summer, 1965.
Subject focus: legislation, rights, culture, organization news.

WHi	v.8, n.1-v.29, n.2; June, 1963-Aug, 1973	Microforms
WEU ARC	[v.9, n.1-v.15, n.1] [Feb/Mar, 1964-Winter, 1970]	Micro 11

CNoSU   [v.8, n.10-v.29, n.2]   Microfilm
             [June, 1963-Aug, 1973]

NjP   [v.8, n.2-v.15, n.1]   Periodicals
             [Feb/Mar, 1963-Winter, 1973]

OkU   v.8, n.10-v.29, n.2;   WHC
             June, 1963-Aug, 1973

UPB   v.12, n.4-v.27;   970.105/N213
             1967-1971

CaACG   v.5, n.1-2;   Periodicals
             Feb 1-Mar, 1959

688 National Excerpts. 1916?-?//. Unknown. Last issue 2 pages, height
    43 cm. Published by Board of National Missions of the Presbyterian
    Church, New York, NY. Subject focus: missions, Presbyterian Church.

WMM   v.23, n.1;   Special
             Apr, 1938   Collections

689 National Fellowship of Indian Workers. Newsletter. 1936-1964?//.
    Quarterly. OCLC 6507096. Last issue 12 pages, height 31 cm.
    Available in microform: WHi-A, Veda Stone Papers, (1966-1967, 1969).
    Published by Division of Home Missions, National Council of Churches,
    New York, NY. Place of publication varies: Philadelphia, PA,
    1936-Apr, 1937; Lawrence, KS, Spring, 1947-Spring, 1959. Editor: E.
    Russell Carter, Fall/Winter, 1954-Fall, 1964. Subject focus:
    Christian religion, missions.

WHi   n.2-81;   F805/"ZN24/
             1936-Fall, 1964   N5 Cutter

WHi   n.82-84, 88;   Microforms
             Summer, 1966-Summer, 1967, Winter, 1969

WEU   n.82-84, 88;   Micro 11
ARC   Summer, 1966-Summer, 1967, Winter, 1969

WMM   [n.2-88]   Special
             [1936-Winter, 1969]   Collections

NjP   n.23-25, 71, 84;   Periodicals
             Feb-Oct, 1944, Spring, 1959, Summer, 1967

Other holding institutions: MBTI (BTI).

690 The National Indian. 1977-1980//. Irregular. ISSN 0702-8857. LC
    cn77-33518. OCLC 3453071. RLIN DCLCCN7733518-S, OHCP3453071-S.

Height 28 cm. Line drawings, photographs. Published by National
Indian Brotherhood, Ottawa, Ontario, Canada. Editors: Karen Isaac;
Bruce Spence. Subject focus: Canadian people.

CaACG	v.1, n.1-v.3, n.6; Jan, 1977-Nov, 1980	Periodicals
CaAEU	[v.1, n.1-v.3, n.6] [Jan, 1977-Nov, 1980]	Boreal Institute
CaOAFN	[v.1, n.1-v.3, n.6] [Jan 28, 1977-Nov, 1980] ≻	Periodicals
CaOONL	v.1, n.1-v.3, n.6; Jan, 1977-Nov, 1980	Periodicals
CaOOP	v.1, n.1-v.3, n.6; Jan, 1977-Nov, 1980	Periodicals
CaOORD	[v.1, n.1-v.3, n.6] [Jan, 1977-Nov, 1980]	Periodicals
CaOPeT	v.1-v.3? 1977-1980?	Periodicals

National Indian Education Association. Minneapolis, MN

   see Indian Education. Minneapolis, MN

691 National Urban Health Center Newsletter. 1980. Unknown. National
Urban Health Center Newsletter, 245 E. 6th St., Suite 818, St. Paul,
MN 55101. (612) 293-0233. Last issue 6 pages, height 28 cm.
Photographs. Published by American Indian Health Care Association.
Subject focus: health, health care.

WHi	v.2, n.1 Spring, 1981	Circulation

692 Nations: The Native American Magazine. 1981//. Monthly. Last issue
44 pages, height 28 cm. Line drawings, photographs, commercial
advertising. Published by Nations Communications, Inc., Seattle, WA.
Editor: Duane F. Warren. Subject focus: politics, history, economics,
education.

WHi	v.1, n.1-3; [July]-Oct, 1981	Pam 81-2016
IdB	v.1, n.1-3; [July]-Oct, 1981	Periodicals

MtBBCC   v.1, n.1-2;   Periodicals
            [July]-Aug, 1981

OrHi   v.1, n.1-3;   Periodicals
            [July]-Oct, 1981

WaU   v.1, n.1-3;   E/75/N38
            [July]-Oct, 1981

Other holding institutions: ICN (IBV), WM (GZD).

693 Nations' Ensign. 1980. Monthly. $15. for individuals and
    institutions. Stella Calahasen, editor, Nations' Ensign, 1110 Markum
    Place, 10234-124th St., Edmonton, Alberta, Canada T5N 1P9. Last issue
    32 pages, height 44 cm. Line drawings, photographs, some in color,
    commercial advertising. Published by Alberta Society for the
    Preservation of Indian Identity. Title varies: Native Ensign, Spet,
    1980-Aug?, 1981. Subject focus: rights, law, land claims, culture.

    WHi   v.1, n.1-   Circulation
                Sept, 1980-

    MtBBCC   v.1;   Periodicals
                Oct, 1980

    CaOAFN   v.2, n.6-   Periodicals
                June, 1982-

The Native American. Phoenix, AZ

    see   The Redskin. Phoenix, AZ

694 The Native American. 1975-1977?// Bi-monthly. OCLC 3454117. Last
    issue 12 pages, height 28 cm. Line drawings, photographs. Published
    by U.S. Department of Health Education and Welfare, Office of Native
    American Programs, Washington, DC. Editor: Harold Eidlin, Oct-Dec,
    1975. Subject focus: education, history, rights, legislation,
    culture. Incorporated in Human Development News, Feb, 1980-Dec, 1981.

    WHi   [Oct, 1975-May/June, 1977]   Pam 81-1653

    AzNCC   Dec, 1975-Apr, 1977   Indian File

    NjP   [Nov, 1976-Apr, 1977]   Periodicals

    Other holding institutions: OKTU (OKT), PP (PLF), [U.S. Government
    Printing Office-Serials, Alexandria, VA] (GPA).

695 <u>Native American Advocate</u>. 1972//. Monthly. RLIN MIUG291037-S. Last
issue 4 pages, height 28 cm. Published by University of Michigan
Native American Student Association, University of Michigan, Ann
Arbor, MI. School newsletter.

MiU	v.1, n.1; Nov, 1972	Labadie Collection

696 <u>Native American Arts</u>. 1968-?//. Unknown. LC 75-600781. OCLC
1142764, 1759471. RLIN OHCP1142764-S, CSUP181988-S, CUBG03584-S,
OHCP1759471-S. Last issue 88 pages. Line drawings, photographs.
Available in microform: McP (1968-1969); WHi-A, Veda Stone Papers,
(1968). Published by Indian Arts and Crafts Board, U. S. Interior
Department, Washington, DC. Subject focus: arts-education,
arts-promotion. Supercedes Smoke Signals.

WHi	n.1-2 1968-1969	Microforms
WEU ARC	n.1; 1968	Micro 11
CNoSU	n.1-2 1968-1969	Microfilm
NjP	n.1-2; 1968-1969	Periodicals
OkU	n.1-2 1968-1969	WHC
WaU	n.2 1969	E/98/A7N36
CaACG	n.1-2; 1968-1969	Periodicals

Other holding institutions: ArU (AFU), CLS (CLS), [California State
College-San Bernardino, San Bernardino, CA] (CSB), DI (UDI), DeU
(DLM), ICSU (IAA), ICRC (IAR), InWhC (ICC), [Indiana Union List of
Serials, Indianapolis, IN] (ILS), InLP (ILP), KSteC (KKO), MiLC (EEL),
MiKC (EXK), MiU (EYM), MnNS (MNO), [University of Minnesota Union
List, Minneapolis, MN] (MUL), NdBV (BPL), NhD (DRB), NmScW, NCortU
(YCM), TxU (IXA).

697 <u>Native American Coalition of Tulsa, Newsletter</u>. 1980? Unknown.
Native American Coalition of Tulsa, 6539 E. 31st St., Tulsa, OK 74145.
(918) 663-7843. Last issue 8 pages, height 28 cm. Organization
newsletter. Subject focus: urban community.

WHi	June, 1980	Microforms

698 <u>Native American Cultural Center</u> [Newsletter]. 1981? Monthly. Native
American Cultural Center, P.O. Box 272, Rochester, NY 14601. (716)
442-2337. Last issue 4 pages, height 28 cm. Line drawings.
Community newsletter. Subject focus: health, social services,
employment information.

WHi   Oct-Dec, 1981   Microforms

699 <u>Native American Free University</u>. 1971?//. Unknown. Last issue 28
pages, height 36 cm. Yelm, WA. Editors: Janet and Laura McCloud.
Subject focus: legislation, rights, draft resistance, prison reform.

WHi   1971 [1 no.]   Pam 72-1718

WEU   1971 [3 nos.]   Journalism
                                                               Lab

Other holding institutions: NjP.

700 <u>Native American News</u>. 1973-?//. Unknown. Last issue 7 pages, height
28 cm. Line drawings. Published by Native American Summer Institute,
San Marcos, CA. School newsletter.

WEU   v.1, n.1;   Jounalism
           July, 1973   Lab

701 <u>Native American Review</u>. 1971?//. Unknown. Last issue 2 pages.
Available in microform: WHi-A, Veda Stone Papers, (1971). Stevens
Point?, WI. Editors: Gayle Hansen and Laurene Soulier. Subject
focus: law, rights, land claims, (includes reprints of articles from
other Native American newsletters).

WHi   July 9, 1971   Microforms

WEU   July 9, 1971   Micro 11
ARC

702 <u>Native American Scholar</u>. 1971?-?//. Bi-monthly. Last issue 8 pages.
Line drawings, photographs. Available in microform: WHi (1972);
WHi-A, Veda Stone Papers, (1971, 1972). Published by Higher Education
Program, BIA, Albuquerque, NM. Subject focus: education, scholarship
information, BIA.

WHi   Oct, 1971, Jan-Nov, 1972   Microforms

WEU   Oct, 1971, Jan, Nov, 1972   Micro 11
ARC

NjP	Apr, Aug, Nov, 1972	Periodicals
OkU	Jan-Nov, 1972	WHC
OrHi	1972	Periodicals
WaU	Jan, 1972	Periodicals

703 <u>Native American Solidarity Committee Newsletter</u>. 1976-1979?//.
Monthly. OCLC 4731720. Last issue 8 pages. Line drawings,
photographs. Personal names indexed in: Index to Wisconsin Native
American Periodicals (1977). Available in microform: WHi (1976-1977).
San Francisco, CA. Subject focus: rights, politics.

WHi	v.1, n.2-v.2, n.1; Mar, 1976-Feb, 1977	Microforms
CaOAFN	v.4, n.1; Spring, 1979	Periodicals

704 <u>Native American Solidarity Committee</u>. 1976-1979//. Irregular. OCLC
6395979, 6396045, 6396063. Last issue 16 pages. Line drawings,
photographs. Available in microform: WHi (1976-1979). St. Paul, MN.
Title varies: NASC News, Feb-Mar, 1976; Spirit of the People, Apr,
1976-June, 1977. Subject focus: rights, politics.

WHi	v.1, n.2-v.4, n.1; Feb, 1976-Spring, 1979	Microforms
WMUW	v.1, n.5-v.2, n.2; Mar, 1976-June, 1977	(SPL) E/75/S74x
WHi	v.4, n.1; Spring, 1979	Indian File

Other holding institutions: MiEM (EEM), [University of Minnesota Union
List, Minneapolis, MN] (MUL).

705 <u>Native American Solidarity Committee, Madison Chapter News</u>. 1977//.
Unknown. Last issue 4 pages, height 28 cm. Line drawings. Madison,
WI. Subject focus: rights, politics.

WHi	Mar, 1977	Pam Cataloging

706 <u>Native American Student Union Newsletter</u>. 1971?//. Monthly. Last
issue 20 pages, height 36 cm. Available in microform: WHi (1971).
Published by University of California, Berkeley, CA. College

newsletter. Subject focus: politics, education, curriculum
development, bibliography.

WHi   July?, 1971   Microforms

Other holding institutions: NjP.

707 Native American Theological Association [Newsletter]. 1980.
Semi-annual. Native American Theological Association, Minnesota
Church Center, Room 310, 122 W. Franklin Ave., Minneapolis, MN 55404.
(612) 870-3685. Last issue 4 pages, height 28 cm. Photographs.
Subject focus: Protestant Churches, biographies, religious education.

WHi   v.1-   Circulation
           1980-

708 Native Arts/West. 1980-1981//. Monthly. ISSN 0274-791x. LC
sn80-1513. OCLC 6600365. RLIN NYPG20488181-S, NYPG814024179-S. Last
issue 32 pages, height 36 cm. Line drawings, photographs, some in
color, commercial advertising. Available in microform: WHi
(1980-1981). Billings, MT. Editor: Kenneth R. Canfield. Subject
focus: arts and crafts.

WHi	v.1, n.1-10; July, 1980-Apr, 1981	Microforms
WMSC	v.1, n.1-10; July, 1980-Apr, 1981	Periodicals
AzPh	[v.1] [1980-1981]	Periodicals
AzNCC	v.1, n.1-10; July, 1980-Apr, 1981	Periodicals
AzT	v.1, n.1-10; July, 1980-Apr, 1981	Periodicals
CLSM	v.1, n.1-10; July, 1980-Apr, 1981	Periodicals
CoCF	v.1, n.1-10; July, 1980-Apr, 1981	Periodicals
MtBBCC	v.1, n.5-7; Nov, 1980-Jan, 1981	Periodicals
OkPAC	v.1, n.3-10; Sept, 1980-Apr, 1981	Periodicals
OkTU	v.1, n.1-10; July, 1980-Apr, 1981	709.701 N278

OkU   v.1, n.1-10;   WHC
           July, 1980-Apr, 1981

CaACG   [v.1, n.1-10]   Periodicals
           [July, 1980-Apr, 1981]

Other holding institutions: CoD (DPL), DSI (SMI), ICN (IBV),
[University of Minnesota Union List, Minneapolis, MN] (MUL), NvLV, Ok
(OKD).

Native Brotherhood Newscall. Prince Albert, Saskatchewan, Canada

    see Newscall Newsletter. Prince Albert, Saskatchewan, Canada

709 The Native California Indian Newsletter. 1978-1981//. Monthly. OCLC
    7411866. RLIN CUBL240-S, CSUP301208-S, CUBG12778527-S, CCSD7087624-S,
    CLCL6674747-S. Last issue 4 pages, height 36 cm. Published by
    Governor's Office of Planning and Research, Sacramento, CA. Frequency
    varies: quarterly, Feb-July, 1978, irregular, Feb-Aug, 1979. Editor:
    Claudia Buckner, Feb, 1978-Sept, 1981. Subject focus: legislation,
    rights.

    WHi   vl, n.1-v.3, n.3;   Circulation
               Feb, 1978-Sept, 1981

    CCarm   v.2, n.1-v.3, n.2;   Periodicals
               Dec, 1979-Aug, 1980

    CL   vl, n.2-v.3, n.3;   Periodicals
               July, 1978-Sept, 1981

    OkU   v.3, n.1-3;   WHC
               July-Sept, 1981

    Other holding institutions: CLU (CLU), [WGrU-Native American Studies
    Dept.].

710 Native Counseling Service of Alberta. 1976. 10 times a year.
    Marlene Benson, editor, Native Counseling Service of Alberta,
    Commonwealth Building, 9912-106 St., Edmonton, Alberta, Canada T5K
    1C5. Last issue 8 pages, height 35 cm. Line drawings, photographs.
    Previous editors: George Lafleur; K. Purves; Lena Fraser.
    Organization newsletter. Subject focus: law, legal aid.

    CaACG   v.1, n.1-   Periodicals
               ?, 1976-

Native Ensign. Edmonton, Alberta, Canada.

see Nations' Ensign. Edmonton, Alberta, Canada.

711 Native Friendship Center of Montreal, Inc./Centre d'Amitie Autochtone de Montreal. [Newsletter]. 1982? Monthly. Native Friendship Center of Montreal, 3730 Cote des Neiges, Montreal, Quebec, Canada H3H 1V6. (514) 937-5338. Last issue 6 pages, height 36 cm. Line drawings. Center newsletter. Subject focus: urban community, center news.

WHi   Sept., 1982-

                                                    Circulation

712 The Native Gem. 1974-?//. Monthly. Last issue 12 pages, height 37 cm. Line drawings, photographs. Published by Idaho Inter-Tribal Policy Board, Inc., Boise, ID. Subject focus: Nez Perce, Coeur d' Alene, Kootenai, Shoshone, Bannock and Paiute people.

IdHi   v.1, n.1-4;
         Feb-May/June. 1974   Periodicals

713 The Native Hawaiian. 1977. Monthly. $6. for individuals and institutions. Gard Kealoha, editor, The Native Hawaiian, 2828 Paa St., Suite 3035, Honolulu, HI 96819. (808) 833-5871. Last issue 8 pages, height 41 cm. Line drawings, photographs, commercial advertising. Published by Alu Like Information Office. Newspaper. Subject focus: law, culture.

WHi   v.5, n.1-
         Dec, 1980-   Circulation

714 The Native Nevadan. 1964. Monthly. $10. for individuals and institutions. Arline Fisher, editor, The Native Nevadan, 650 S. Rock Blvd., Building 11, Reno, NV 89502. (702) 786-3128. ISSN 0028-0534. OCLC 1638994. RLIN OHCP1638994-S, UTBL11480270-S. Last issue 12 pages. Line drawings, photographs, commercial advertising. Available in microform: McP (1971-1972); CPC (1965-1976). Published by Sparks Publishing Company. Previous editors: Edward Johnson, May-Sept 17, 1965; Ralph Keen, Oct 22, 1965-June 27, 1966; Edith Hunter, July 25, 1966-Sept 29, 1967; Sun Bear, Dec 29, 1967-June, 1968; Carol Wright, Apr-Dec, 1971; Bob Shaw, Jan, 1972-June/July, 1974; Elmer D. Miller, Nov 22, 1974-Nov 3, 1978. Newspaper.

WHi   v.2, n.3-v.11, n.12, v.17, n.9-
         May, 1965-Aug, 1976, Nov 9, 1980-   Microforms

WMUW   [v.10, n.7-v.16, n.5];
         [Mar 20, 1975-July 6, 1979]   (SPL)
                                                    E/75/N36x

AzNCC	v.6– 1971–	Indian File
CNoSU	[v.7, n.8–v.8, n.11], v.19– [Jan, 1978–Dec, 1972], 1982–	Periodicals
CRSSU	v.7– 1971–	Periodicals
CU-A	v.6, n.4–? Sept, 1969–?	E/77/A1/N35
ICN	Current issues	CHAI
NjP	[v.2, n.3–v.16, n.4] [May, 1965–June 1, 1979]	Periodicals
NHu	[v.8, n.6–v.11, n.6] [Nov, 1971–Nov, 1976]	Periodicals
NN	v.2, n.3–v.14, n.12 May, 1965–Feb, 1978	Microforms
OkTU	v.15, n.9– Nov 3, 1978–	Rare Book Room
OkU	[v.7–8] [Jan, 1971–Dec, 1972]	WHC
PPT	v.7, n.6, v.8, n.5, v.10, n.7/8; Nov, 1970, Sept, 1971, Apr 22, 1975	Contemporary Culture

Other holding institutions: CLU (CLU), CU-UC (UCU), KSteC (KKQ), MH-P (HLS), [University of Minnesota Union List, Minneapolis, MN] (MUL), NmScW, [Standing Rock Community College Library, Fort Yates, ND], [Bacone College, Muskogee, OK], OrU-Special Collections.

715 <u>Native News and BIA Bulletin</u>. 1959–1977//. Bi-monthly. ISSN 0300-6255. OCLC 1451934, 6189126. Last issue 12 pages. Photographs. Available in microform: McA (1974–1976); WHi (1972–1976); AkUF (1959–1976). Published by Bureau of Indian Affairs, Juneau, AK. Subject focus: BIA projects, Alaska Native people.

WHi	v.9, n.7–v.13, n.5/6; Sept/Dec, 1972–Nov/Dec, 1976	Microforms
WMUW	v.12. n.6; Nov/Dec, 1975	(SPL) E/75/N37x
AkUF	v.1–v.13; 1959–1976	Ak-39
AzNCC	v.8–v.13; 1971–1976	Indian File

OkU	v.8-v.13, n.5/6; 1971-Nov/Dec, 1976	WHC
WyCWC	v.12, n.1-6; 1976	Periodicals
CaAEU	v.9, n.3-v.13, n.5/6; 1972-Nov/Dec, 1976	Boreal Institute
CaOPeT	v.11, n.1-v.13, n.5/6; Jan/Feb, 1974-Nov/Dec, 1976	Microfilm

Other holding institutions: DLC (NSD), University of Minnesota Union List, Minneapolis, MN] (MUL).

716 <u>Native People</u>. 1968. Weekly. $15. for individuals and institutions. Laurent Roy, editor, Native People, 9311 60th Ave., S., Edmonton, Alberta, Canada T6E 0C2. (403) 437-0580. ISSN 0047-9144. LC cn76-300047. OCLC 2076456. RLIN DCLCCN76300047-S, OHCP2076456-S. Available in microform: McA (1973-); WHi (1969-1974); UM (1969-). Published by Alberta Native Communications Society. Frequency varies: monthly, May, 1969-Feb, 1972. Previous editors: Doug Cuthand, May, 1969-July, 1971; Bill Lafferty, Aug-Dec, 1971; George LaFleur, Jan, 1972-Aug 30, 1974; David Anderson, Dec 24, 1976-June 23, 1977; Cecil Nepoose, July 15, 1977-Feb 10, 1978; Laurent Roy, Feb 17-Dec 29, 1978; Bert Crowfoot, Jan 28-May 23, 1980; Margie Lockhart, June 6-20, 1980; Erica Denhoff, June 27-Sept 26, 1980; Tim Buttle, Nov 3, 1980-Nov 6, 1981. Newspaper. Early issues contain some Cree.

WHi	v.1, n.11- May, 1969-	Microforms
AkUF	v.12, n.49- 1979-	AK-News
AzNCC	v.3- Jan, 1970-	Indian File
CU-A	v.3- May, 1970-	E/77/A1/N36
NjP	[v.1, n.1-v.7, n.45] [July, 1968-Nov 8, 1974]	Periodicals
WaU	[v.4, n.8-v.7, n.5] [Mar 2, 1972-Jan 18, 1974]	Periodicals
WyCWC	v.6, n.1-v.9, n.2; 1973-1975	Periodicals
CaACG	v.1, n.1- Apr, 1969-	Periodicals

CaAEU	v.9– 1976–	Boreal Institute
CaBAbF	v.8– June, 1975–	Periodicals
CaMWU	[v.3–v.7], v.8– [1971–1974], 1975–	970/N2137 Peo
CaNBFU	v.8–v.9, v.11– 1975–1976, 1978–	E/78/A34N33
CaOAFN	v.14, n.1– Jan 2, 1981–	Periodicals
CaOONL	v.1, n.12– June, 1969–	Periodicals
CaOOP	v.1– 1968–	E/78/C2/N385
CaOPeT	v.6– 1973–	Microfilm
CaOStM	v.9– Apr, 1976–	Periodicals
CaOSuU	v.14– 1981–	Periodicals

Other holding institutions: MiEM (EEM), [University of Minnesota Union List, Minneapolis, MN] (MUL), MsU (MUM), [Standing Rock Community College Library, Fort Yates, ND].

717 <u>Native People</u>. 1972?//. Irregular. Last issue 23 pages. Available in microform: McA (1972). Published by William Head Institution, Metchosin, British Columbia, Canada. Editor: Bob Hinchcliffe. Prison newsletter.

                                                        Periodicals
CaOPeT   Aug 31, 1972

718 <u>The Native Perspective</u>. 1975–1978//. 10 times a year. ISSN 0381-7717. LC cn77-30393. OCLC 3213256, 6860693. RLIN NYPG814088806-S, DCLCCN7730393-S, NJpg224-S, OHCP3213256-S. Last issue 12 pages, last volume 122 pages. Line drawings, photographs, commercial advertising. Available in microform: WHi (1975–1978); MML (1976–1979). Published by National Association of Friendship Centres, Ottawa, Ontario, Canada. Editors: Cliff Gazee and Carmen Maracle, Oct, 1975–Apr, 1976; Lucille Bell, May–June/July, 1976; Del C. Anaquod, Aug, 1976; Cliff Gazee, Sept–Dec, 1976; Melissa Lazore and Carmen Maracle, Jan/Feb–Mar, 1977; Cliff Gazee May, 1977–Oct, 1978. Subject focus: provincial and national news.

WHi	v.1, n.2-v.3, n.2; Oct, 1975-Sept, 1978	Microforms
WMUW	v.1, n.2-v.3, n.2; Oct, 1975-Sept, 1978	E/78/C2N38x
AkUF	v.1-v.3, n.1; 1975-1978	E/75/C2/N33
AzNCC	v.1, n.1-v.3; Aug, 1975-1978	Indian File
NjP	[v.1, n.4-v.3, n.2] Mar, 1976-Sept, 1978]	Periodicals
CaACG	v.1, n.5-v.3, n.2; Apr, 1976-Sept, 1978	Periodicals
CaAEU	v.1, n.1-v.3, n.2; Aug, 1975-Sept, 1978	Boreal Institute
CaMWU	v.1-v.3, n.2; 1975-Sept, 1978	971/N2137 Per
CaNBFU	v.1, n.1-v.3, n.2; Aug, 1975-Sept, 1978	970.105/ N2781
CaOAFN	v.1, n.1-v.2, n.5; Aug, 1975-July/Aug, 1977	Periodicals
CaOOP	v.1, n.2-v.3, n.2; Oct, 1975-Sept, 1978	E/78/C2/N386
CaOONL	v.1, n.1-v.3, n.2; Aug, 1975-Sept, 1978	Periodicals
CaOPeT	v.2, n.1-v.3, n.1; 1976-1978	Periodicals
CaOStM	v.1, n.5-v.2, n.10; Apr, 1976-1978	Periodicals
CaOSuL	v.1-v.3; 1975-1978	Periodicals

Other holding institutions: DI (UDI), [University of Minnesota Union
List, Minneapolis, MN] (MUL), NhD (DRB).

719 <u>Native Press</u>. 1971. Bi-weekly. $12. for individuals and
institutions. Dan Mandin, editor, Native Press, Box 1919,
Yellowknife, Northwest Territories, Canada X0E 1H0. (403) 873-2661.
OCLC 4773351. Last issue 20 pages, Last volume 500 pages, height 44
cm. Line drawings, photographs, commercial advertising. Available in
microform: WHi (1973-); MML (1971-1974). Published by Native

Communications Society of the Western Northwest Territories. Previous
editors: Tony Buggins, Feb 26, 1975-June 1, 1976; Tapwe Chretien, June
28-Aug 20, 1976; Bob L'Hirondelle, Oct 15, 1976-July 22, 1977; Tony
Buggins, Aug 19-Sept 30, 1977; Rene Lemothe, Nov 10, 1977; Willy
Anderson, May 12-Dec 8, 1978; Bren Kolson, Dec 22, 1978-Apr 18, 1980;
Walter Brown, May 2-June 27, 1980; Nancy Heron and Bob Rupert, July
25-Aug 21, 1980; Nancy Heron, Sept 5-Nov 17, 1980; Jane Lewington, Dec
18, 1980-Jan 16, 1981; Jane Lewington and Cheeko Desjarlais, Feb
13-Mar 27, 1981; Jane Lewington, Apr 10-June 5, 1981; Jane Lewington
and Dan Mandin, June 19, 1981. Newspaper. Subject focus: provincial
and national news.

WHi	Nov 1, 1973-	Microforms
AkUF	1978-	AK-News
AzNCC	1971-	Microfilm
MnBemT	[1973-1977], 1978-	Periodicals
NjP	[June 24, 1972-Jan 13, 1978]	Periodicals
CaACG	May 22, 1971-	Periodicals
CaAEU	1971-	Boreal Institute
CaOAFN	Jan 16, 1981-	Periodicals
CaOONL	June 11, 1971-	Newspaper Section
CaOPeT	1971-	Microfilm
CaSSIC	1970-1974	Microfilm

Other holding institutions: [WGrU-Native American Studies Dept.],
CaNfSM.

Native Profile. St. Paul, MN

   see Smoke Signals. St. Paul, MN

720 Native Self-Sufficiency. 1978. 4-5 times a year. $6. for
individuals; $15. for institutions. Paula Hammett, editor, Native
Self-Sufficiency, P.O. Box 10, Forestville, CA 95436. (707) 887-1550.
ISSN 0196-4240. LC sn79-18675. OCLC 5815530. RLIN OHCP5815530-S.
Last issue 16 pages, last volume 48 pages, height 45 cm. Line
drawings, photographs. Indexed in: Alternative Press Index (1981-).
Published by Tribal Sovereignty Program. Place of publication varies:
Guerneville, CA, Apr, 1978-Oct, 1979. Previous editors: Paula Hammett
and Daniel Bomberry, June-Aug, 1978. Subject

focus: economic self-reliance, alternative energy and technologies, community development.

WHi   v.1, n.1-   Circulation
             Apr, 1978-

CSmarP   [v.2-v.4]-   Stacks
             [1979-1981]-

CaOAFN   v.4, n.1-   Periodicals
             Jan, 1981-

Other holding institutions: CLU (CLU), [Standing Rock Community College Library, Fort Yates, ND], [University of Wisconsin-Stevens Point-Native American Center, Stevens Point, WI], [Wisconsin Indian Resource Council, Stevens Point, WI].

721 <u>Native Sisterhood</u>. 1969. Irregular. Irene Slaferek, editor, Native Sisterhood, P.O. Box 515, Kingston, Ontario, Canada K7X 4W7. ISSN 0703-9190. LC cn78-30179. OCLC 73951264. Last issue 46 pages, height 28 cm. Line drawings, some in color. Prison newsletter. Includes poetry.

CaOPeT   1975-   Periodicals

CaOONL   May, 1976-Dec, 1978   Periodicals

Other holding institutions: [University of Minnesota Union List, Minneapolis, MN] (MUL).

722 <u>Native Sons</u>. 1975-1981//? Unknown. Last issue 12 pages, height 28 cm. Line drawings. Guelph, Ontario, Canada. Prison newsletter. Includes poetry.

CaOAFN   Mar, 1981   Periodicals

723 <u>Native Sun</u>. 1971. Monthly. Simone Wheat, editor, Native Sun, 360 John R, Detroit, MI 48226. (313) 963-1729. Last issue 10 pages, height 28 cm. Line drawings. Published by North American Indian Association. Title varies: North American Indian Association of Detroit Newsletter, Dec, 1974-Jan, 1976; Detroit Indian Center, Feb-Oct, 1976. Previous editors: Carol Coulon, Oct? 1978-Dec, 1979; Theresa Wix, Jan-Dec, 1980; Valerie Beavers, Jan/Feb-Mar, 1981; Marla Cornelius, Apr, 1981; Valerie Beavers, May-June, 1981. Subject focus: urban community, association news.

WHi   v.8, n.10, v.9, n.1-   Circulation
             Oct, 1978, Jan, 1979-

MiU-B   [v.4, n.12-v.9, n.11]   Periodicals
           [Dec, 1974-Nov, 1979]

Other holding institutions: Mi (EEX).

Native Times. Toronto, Ontario, Canada

    see Toronto Native Times. Toronto, Ontario, Canada.

724 Native Voice. 1946. Irregular. $5. for individuals and
    institutions. Jim White, editor, Native Voice, 517 Ford Building, 193
    Hastings St., Vancouver, British Columbia, Canada V6A 1N7. (604)
    685-2255. ISSN 0028-0542. LC cn76-319833. OCLC 2010156. RLIN
    NYPG81-S434, DCLCCN76319833-S, OHCP2010156-S. Last issue 12 pages,
    height 43 cm. Line drawings, photographs, commercial advertising.
    Available in microform: WHi (1972-); MML (1946-). Published by Native
    Brotherhood of British Columbia. Previous editors: G. R. Williams,
    Nov/Dec, 1972-Mar, 1973; Kristina Reclama, Apr, 1973-Apr, 1974; Diana
    Reclama, July, 1974-July/Aug, 1977; Robert Joseph, Oct, 1977-May,
    1978; Christine D. Oliver, Sept, 1978-Aug, 1979. Subject focus: land
    claims, fishing rights, area news.

    WHi   (n.s)v.2, n.11-   Microforms
               Nov/Dec, 1972-

    AkUF   (n.s.)v.9, n.8-   AK-News
               1979-

    AzNCC   (n.s)v.1-   Indian File
               1971-

    ICN   Current issues   CHAI

    KU   (n.s)v.1-   Kansas
               1971-   Collection

    NjP   [v.17, n.3-(n.s.)v.9, n.4]   Periodicals
               [Mar, 1963-Apr/May, 1979]

    OkTU   (n.s)v.8, n.4-   Rare Book
               Oct/Nov, 1978-   Room

    UPB   17, n.10-   970.41105/N213
               1963-

    CaACG   v.1, n.1-v.22, n.8, (n.s.)v.1, n.3-   Periodicals
               Dec, 1946-Nov, 1968, Jan, 1971-

    CaAEU   (n.s)v.8, n.3-   Boreal
               1978-   Institute

CaBAbF	(n.s)v.4– Dec, 1974–	Periodicals
CaBViP	v.1, n.1– Dec, 1946–	Microfilm D–4
CaBViP	(n.s)v.9, n.1– Dec/1978/Jan, 1979–	NW/970.1/N285
CaMWU	(n.s)[v.4–v.10], v.11– [1974–1980], 1981–	970/N2135/Voi
CaOAFN	(n.s)v.10, n.5– Sept, 1981–	Periodicals
CaOONL	v.1, n.1– Dec, 1946–	Newspaper Section
CaOOP	(n.s)v.8– 1978–	Periodicals
CaOPeT	v.1, n.1– Dec, 1946–	Microfilm

Other holding institutions: WaU (WAU).

725 <u>Native Women's News</u>. 1981. Monthly. Marie Blackduck, editor, Native
Women's News, Box 2321, Yellowknife, Northwest Territories, Canada X0E
1H0. (403) 873-5509. Last issue 4 pages, height 43 cm. Line
drawings, photographs. Published by Native Women's Association of the
Northwest Territories. Subject focus: education and training for
women, arts and crafts, legends.

WHi	v.1, n.1– Dec, 1981–	Circulation
AkUF	v.1, n.3– 1982–	AK-News
CaACG	v.1, n.1– Dec, 1981–	Periodicals

<u>Native Youth</u>. Regina, Saskatchewan, Canada

    see <u>Native Youth Movement</u>. Regina, Saskatchewan, Canada

726 <u>Native Youth Movement</u>. 1971-1973//. Bi-monthly. Last issue 8 pages.
Line drawings, photographs. Available in microform: WHi (1972-1973).
Regina, Saskatchewan, Canada. Title varies: Native Youth, Aug 13,
1971; Native Youth News, Aug/Sept-Dec, 1972; Native

Youth, Jan/Feb, 1973. Subject focus: politics, education, social services, poetry, young adults.

WHi	Apr, Aug/Sept, 1972-Mar/Apr, 1973	Microforms
NjP	Aug 13, 1971, Aug/Sept, 1972- Jan/Feb, 1973	Periodicals
CaACG	Feb-Dec, 1972	Periodicals
CaOONL	Aug 13, 1971-May/June, 1973	H-3-3

Native Youth News. Regina, Saskatchewan, Canada

see Native Youth Movement. Regina, Saskatchewan, Canada

727 Natotawin. 1976?-1978//. Unknown. Last issue 24 pages, height 28 cm. Line drawings, photographs, commercial advertising. Beauval, Saskatchewan, Canada. Editor: Simon Paul. Community newsletter.

| CaSiCc | Aug 15, 1976-Aug 15, 1978 | Periodicals |

728 Navajo and Hopi Indian Relocation Commission Program Update and Report. 1977. Monthly. Navajo and Hopi Indian Relocation Commission Program Update and Report, 2717 N. Steven Blvd., Building A, Flagstaff, AZ 86001. Last issue 8 pages, last volume 64 pages, height 28 cm. Line drawings. Subject focus: Navajo and Hopi people, relocation, commission news.

| NmG | Aug, 1977 | Periodicals |

729 Navajo Area Newsletter. 1972. 9 times a year. Dick Hardwick, editor, Navajo Area Newsletter, Window Rock, AZ 86515. (602) 871-5128. ISSN 0193-4503. LC sc79-367. OCLC 1759529, 4644567. RLIN DCLCSC793671-S, OHCP4644567-S. Last issue 6 pages. Line drawings, photographs. Available in microform: McA (1974-). Published by Education Division, Navajo Area, Bureau of Indian Affairs. Title varies: Navajo Education Newsletter, Feb, 1974-May, 1977. Frequency varies: monthly, Feb, 1974-May, 1977. Subject focus: Navajo people, education.

| WHi | [v.1, n.8-v.3, n.3], 5-
[May, 1972-Oct], Dec, 1973- | Microforms |
| WMUW | [v.1, n.8-v.8, n.5]
[May, 1972-Jan, 1979] | (SPL)
E/75/N382x |

AzNCC   v.6-v.9;   Indian File
           Feb, 1977-

CaOPeT   v.3, n.6-   Microfilm
           Feb, 1974-

Other holding institutions: KSteC (KKQ), [University of Minnesota
Union List, Minneapolis, MN]

730 <u>Navajo Community College Newsletter</u>. 1969-1973//. Monthly. OCLC
    7296136. Last issue 8 pages. Photographs. Available in microform:
    McA (1973); CPC (1969-1973). Many Farms, AZ. Editors: Broderick H.
    Johnson, Aug, 1969-Feb, 1971; Becky Minter, Mar-Dec, 1971; Ken
    Neundorf, May, 1972-May, 1973. School newsletter.

    WHi   [v.1, n.1-v.5, n.3]   Microforms
               [Aug, 1969-May, 1973]

    WEU   v.2, n.6-7;   Micro 11
    ARC   June-July/Aug, 1970

    AzNCC   v.1, n.1-v.5, n.3;   Indian File
               Aug 15, 1969-Mar, 1973

    NjP   [v.1, n.1-v.5, n.3]   Periodicals
               [Aug 15, 1969-May, 1973]

    OkU   [v.1, n.1-v.5, n.3]   WHC
               [Aug 15, 1969-May, 1973]

    WyCWC   v.1, n.1-v.4, n.9, v.5, n.1-3;   Periodicals
               Aug, 1969-Dec, 1972, 1973

    CaOPeT   [v.1, n.1-v.5, n.3]   Microfilm
               [Aug, 1969-May, 1973]

    Other holding institutions: AzFU (AZN), [Western Nevada Community
    College, Carson City, NV].

731 <u>Navajo Education</u>. 1971-1975//. Monthly. OCLC 4751312. Last issue 8
    pages. Photographs. Available in microform: WHi (1973-1974).
    Published by Dine Bi Olta Association, Ganado, AZ. Subject focus:
    Navajo people, education, politics.

    WHi   v.2, n.4-7;   Microforms
               Dec, 1973-May, 1974

    AzNCC   v.2-v.3;   Indian File
               Sept, 1973-Feb, 1975

    NjP   v.2, n.4-7, ?;   Periodicals
               Dec, 1973-May, Nov, 1974

Navajo Education Newsletter. Window Rock, AZ

   see Navajo Area Newsletter. Window Rock, AZ

732 Navajo Missionary Newsletter. 1968?-?//. Irregular. Last issue 4
pages, height 28 cm. Photographs. Published by St. Michaels Mission,
St. Michaels, AZ. Subject focus: Catholic Church, missions,
education, book reviews, Navajo people.

WMM   v.1, n.3-v.4, n.1;   Special
             Winter, 1969-?, 1972   Collections

733 Navajo Nation CETA Newsletter. 1979-1980//? Monthly. OCLC 5794343.
Last issue 12 pages, height 28 cm. Line drawings, photographs.
Published by Navajo Division of Labor, Window Rock, AZ. Editor:
Tazbah McCullah. Subject focus: Navajo people, CETA programs.

AzU   Feb, Apr, 1979   I9791/N31/N3152

AzNCC   Feb, 1979-June, 1980   Indian File

734 Navajo Nation Education Review. 1976-1978?//. Monthly. OCLC
7903991. Last issue 8 pages, height 28 cm. Line drawings,
photographs. Published by Navajo Division of Education, Window Rock,
AZ. Subject focus: education, Navajo people.

AzU   v.1, n.1-v.3, n.8;   I9791/N31/N3155
          Jan, 1976-1978

AzNCC   v.1-v.3;   Indian File
          Apr, 1976-June, 1978

Other holding institutions: NmPE (IQU).

735 The Navajo Service News. 1936-1937?//. Monthly. OCLC 4993888,
8419440. Last issue 40 pages. Line drawings. Available in
microform: CPC (1936-1937). Window Rock, AZ. Frequency varies:
semi-monthly, May 1-Oct 15, 1936. Editors: Dom May, May 1-Oct 15,
1936, G. Straus, Nov 15, 1936-Oct 15, 1937. Community newsletter.
Subject focus: Navajo people.

WHi   v.1, n.1-v.2, n.11?   Microforms
          May 1, 1936-Oct 15, 1937

AzHM   v.1;   Periodicals
          1936

AzU   [v.1, n.1-v.2, n.11]   I9791/N31
          [May 1, 1936-Oct 15, 1937]   N312

Other holding institutions: AzFM, CLSM, NmU (IQU), PPiU (PIT).

736 <u>Navajo Times</u>. 1959. Weekly. $25. for individuals and institutions.
Eugene Foster, editor, Navajo Times, P.O. Box 310, Window Rock, AZ
86515. (505) 722-4306. ISSN 0470-5106. OCLC 1606465, 7608917.
UTBG81-S260, CSUP02161912-S, MIUG10724-S, MIUG10725-S, OHCP1606465-S,
CSUG5233321-S. Last issue 16 pages. Line drawings, photographs,
commercial advertising. Available in microform: McP (1968-1973); WHi
(1964, 1967-). Previous editors: Marshall Tome, Aug 13, 1964; Jack
Luttrell, Feb 23, 1967; Dick Hardwick, Jan 4, 1968-Mar 25, 1971;
Chester A. MacRorie, Apr 1, 1971-Dec, 1973. Newspaper. Subject
focus: Navajo people, politics, law, socio-economic conditions, and
education news.

WHi	v.5, n.33; v.8, n.8- Aug 13, 1964, Feb 23, 1967-	Microforms
WEU	[v.11, n.37-v.16, n.37] [Sept 10, 1970-Sept 11, 1975]	Jounalism Lab
WEU	v.9, n.1-50; Jan 4-Dec, 1968	Microforms
WM	Current issues	Forest Home Branch
WMM	v.1, n.2; Dec, 1959	Special Collections
WMMus	[v.16, n.50-v.21, n.2] [Dec 16, 1975-Apr 12, 1979]	Anthro Section
WMUW	v.17, n.8- Apr 29, 1976-	(SPL) E/75/N387x
WU Coll	Current issues	Ethnic Collection
Az	v.1- Aug 4, 1960-	Periodicals
AzHM	v.13-v.14, v.22- 1972-1973, 1980-	Periodicals
AzPh	v.8-v.17, 1967-1976; Current year	Periodicals
AzNCC	v.1, n.1- Nov, 1959-	Microfilm

AzT	v.19, n.14– Apr 6, 1978–	Periodicals
AzU	v.1– Aug 4, 1960–	I9791/N31 N314
CL	v.10, n.49– Dec, 1969–	Periodicals
CLSM	v.7– 1966–	Periodicals
CNoSU	[v.9–v.13, n.49] [Jan, 1968–Dec 6, 1973]	Microfilm
CRSSU	v.15– 1974–	Periodicals
CSmarP	Current 6 months	Stacks
CU–A	v.10, n.31– Aug 7, 1969–	E/77/A1/N37
KU	v.1– 1959–	Kansas Collection
MnBemT	[v.17–v.18], v.19– [1976–1977], 1978–	Periodicals
NjP	[v.2, n.24–v.21, n.12] [July 5, 1961–June 21, 1979]	Periodicals
NmF	Current year	Periodicals
NmG	v.1– Aug 4, 1960–	Periodicals
NmScW	v.17– 1976–	Periodicals
NcP	v.22– Dec, 1980–	Periodicals
OkTU	v.19, n.1– Jan 4, 1978–	Rare Book Room
OkU	v.3, n.4– 1962–	WHC
UHi	v.5–v.6; 1964–1965	Periodicals
USUSC	v.10– June 4, 1970–	Special Collections

CaOPeT   [v.13-v.18], v.19-   Periodicals
          [1972-1977], 1978-

Other holding institutions: AzTeS, [American Indian Bible Institute,
Phoenix, AZ], COU-DA (COA), [Congressional Research Service,
Washington, DC] (CRS), [Indiana Union List of Serials, Indianapolis,
IN] (ILS), KSteC (KKQ), MH-P (HLS), MiU (EYM), [University of
Minnesota Union List, Minneapolis, MN] (MUL), NhD (DRB), [Wheelwright
Museum, Santa Fe, NM], [Standing Rock Community College Library, Fort
Yates, ND], [Bacone College, Muskogee, OK], OrU-Special Collections,
PC1vU (URS), WaU (WAU).

737 Ne We Kawg Ge Ged Newsletter. 1978-?//. Monthly? Last issue 10
pages, Height 39 cm. Line drawings. St. Croix, WI. Community
newsletter.

    WUSP   Dec, 1978
                                                      Native American
                                                      Center

738 The Nebraska Indian Commission Newsletter. 1976. Irregular. Janna
Ashley, editor, The Nebraska Indian Commission Newsletter, 301
Centennial Mall, S., P.O. Box 94914, Lincoln, NE 68509. (402)
471-2757. Last issue 6 pages, last volume 24 pages, height 28 cm.
Line drawings. Frequency varies: bi-monthly, Aug-Nov, 1980. Previous
editor: Lisa Skoog, Aug-Nov, 1980. Subject focus: legislation, social
services, governmental relations.

    WHi   v.5, n.1-
             Aug, 1980-   Circulation

739 Neh-Muh News. 1979?//. Monthly. Last issue 8 pages, height 28 cm.
Line drawings. Published by Walker River Paiute Tribe, Schurz, NV.
Community newsletter. Subject focus: Paiute people.

    WHi   v.1, n.5, 9;
             June 8, Oct 5, 1979   Tem Pam 115

740 Nesika. 1972-1977//. Monthly. OCLC 4751212. RLIN NJPG1819-S. Last
issue 20 pages, height 43 cm. Line drawings, photographs, commercial
advertising. Available in microform: WHi (1972-1977). Published by
Union of British Columbia Indian Chiefs, Vancouver, British Columbia,
Canada. Editors: Lou Demerais, Dec, 1972-Sept, 1973; Perlas Sabino,
Oct, 1973-July, 1974; Ken Iwamura, Aug-Nov, 1974; G. McKevitt,
Jan-Mar, 1975. Subject focus: politics, culture, education,
provincial news.

    WHi   v.1, n.3-[v.3, n.27]
             Dec, 1972-Summer/Early Fall, 1977   Microforms

NjP   [v.1, n.1-v.3, n.27]   Periodcials
           [Sept, 1972-Summer/Early Fall, 1977]

CaACG   v.1, n.2-[v.3, n.27]   Periodicals
           Oct, 1972-Summer/Early Fall, 1977

CaAEU   v.1, n.1-[v.3, n.27];   Microforms
           Sept, 1972-Summer/Early Fall, 1977

CaOONL   v.1, n.1-[v.3, n.27];   Newspaper
           Sept, 1972-Summer/Early Fall, 1977   Section

Other holding institutions: WaU (WAU).

741 <u>Neskainlith News</u>. 1982? Monthly. Dianne Anthony, editor,
    Neskainlith News, P.O. Box 608, Chase, British Columbia, Canada V0E
    1M0. Last issue 16 pages, height 36 cm. Title varies: Neskonlith,
    Dec, 1981. Community newsletter. Subject focus: Neskainlith people.

    WHi   Dec, 1981-   Circulation

    CaOAFN   Mar/Apr, 1982-   Periodicals

<u>Neskonlith News</u>. Chase, British Columbia, Canada

    see <u>Neskainlith News</u>. Chase, British Columbia, Canada

<u>New Breed</u>. Regina, Saskachewan, Canada

    see <u>New Breed Journal</u>. Regina, Saskachewan, Canada

742 <u>New Breed Journal</u>. 1969. 10 times a year. $10. for individuals and
    institutions. Joan Beatty, editor, New Breed Journal, Suite 301, 2505
    11th Ave., Regina, Saskachewan S4P 0K6. (306) 525-9501. OCLC
    4751189. RLIN NYPG794357941-S. Last issue 32 pages, last volume 400
    pages, height 44 cm. Line drawings, photographs, commercial
    advertising. Available in microform: CPC (1970-1979). Published by
    Metis Association of Saskatchewan. Title varies: New Breed, Sept,
    1970-May/June, 1982. Previous editors: Brian Dagdick, Feb-July/Aug,
    1973; Brian Dagdick and Linda Finlayson, Sept/Oct., 1973-Jan, 1974;
    Linda Finlayson, Sept-Nov, 1974; Wayne McKenzie, Dec, 1974; Clifford
    Bunnie, Feb/Mar, 1975-Dec, 1977; John Cuthand, July, 1979-Jan, 1980;
    Liz Nicholls, Oct-Nov, 1980. Subject focus: Metis people, law,
    biographies, legends, provincial and national news, book reviews.
    Some issues contain some Cree.

    WHi   v.1, n.9, v.2, n.1-   Microforms
               Sept, 1970, Jan, 1971-

ICN	Current issues	CHAI
NjP	[v.1, n.9-v.10] [Sept, 1970-Mar/Apr, 1979]	Periodicals
CaACG	v.1, n.1- Nov, 1969-	Periodicals
CaAEU	v.5- Sept, 1974-	Boreal Institute
CaMWU	v.8- 1977-	970/N42/Bre
CaOAFN	v.12, n.1- Jan, 1981-	Periodicals
CaOONL	v.1- June 1, 1970-	Newspaper Section
CaOOP	v.3- 1973-	E/75/N48
CaOPeT	[v.2-v.8], v.9- [1971-1977], 1978-	E78/S2N4
CaOSuU	v.11- 1980-	Periodicals

743 <u>New Breed News</u>. 1970-1976//. Irregular. Last issue 18 pages. Line drawings. Available in microform: McA (1974-1976); CPC (1970-1975). Published by North American Indian League of Idaho, Boise, ID. Editors: Roger J. Boy, Jan/Feb-Apr, 1974; Ray Ainsworth, Feb, 1975; John S. Daley, Aug, 1975; John Faulkner, Feb?-Nov?, 1976. Prison newsletter. Subject focus: culture, law, poetry.

WHi	June? 1974-Nov?, 1976	Microforms
AzNCC	Jan/Apr, 1974	Microfilm
IdHi	May-June, 1970	Periodcials
NjP	[1970-Apr, 1972]	Periodicals
CaOPeT	June? 1974-Nov?, 1976	Microfilm

744 <u>The New Cherokee Advocate</u>. 1950-1953?//. Tri-weekly. Last issue 8 pages, last volume 42 pages, height 58 cm. Line drawings, photographs, commercial advertising. Tahlequah, OK. Editor: Watie Pettit. Newspaper. Subject focus: Cherokee people.

OkTG   [v.1, n.2-v.2, n.3]   Periodicals
            [Apr 26-Oct 30, 1950]

New Mexico Office of Indian Affairs Newsletter. Santa Fe, NM

    see The Source. Santa Fe, NM

745 The New Nation. 1972-1982//. Monthly. OCLC 6169125, 8092097. Last
    issue 16 pages, height 41 cm. Line drawings, photographs, commercial
    advertising. Available in microform: WHi (1974-1982). Thompson,
    Manitoba, Canada. Community newsletter.

    WHi   v.2, n.13-v.11, n.10;   Microforms
                Feb, 1974-Feb, 1982

    WMUW   v.6, n.5/6-7;   (SPL)
                May/June-July/Aug, 1977   E/75/N44x

    NjP   [v.2, n.7-v.9, n.9]   Periodicals
                [July, 1973-Sept, 1977]

    CaACG   v.1, n.1-v.11, n.10;   Periodicals
                June, 1972-Feb, 1982

    CaAEU   v.7, n.1-v.11, n.10;   Boreal
                1978-Feb, 1982   Institute

    CaMWU   v.6-v.7;   970/N42/Na
                1977-1978

    CaOAFN   v.10, n.1-v.11, n.10;   Periodicals
                Jan, 1981-Feb, 1982

    CaOONL   [v.1-v.11, n.10]   Newspaper
                [July, 1972-Feb, 1982]   Section

    CaOSuL   v.1-v.11, n.10;   Periodicals
                1972-Feb, 1982

746 New News. 1967-1969?//. Monthly. Last issue 14 pages, height 36 cm.
    Line drawings. Churchill, Manitoba, Canada. Editor: Tagak Curley.
    Community newsletter. Subject focus: Keewatin Region people.

    CaOORD   [n.5-14]   Periodicals
                [Feb 20, 1968-Jan 27, 1969]

747 New River Times. 1971. Irregular. $5. for individuals and
    institutions. Billie Ashcrast, editor, New River Times, 310 1/2 First

Ave., Fairbanks, AK 99701. (907) 452-1648. Last issue 8 pages, last volume 116 pages, height 44 cm. Published by Johnson O'Malley Program. Title varies: River Times, 1971-1977. Previous editors: Sharyn Tolle, Jan, 1979-Mar, 1980; Sue Gamache, Apr, 1980-May, 1981; Robert Polasky, Nov-Dec, 1981. Subject focus: Alaska Native people, history, culture, education.

WHi	v.10, n.5, 7-10, v.11, n.1- Jan, Mar-June, Sept, 1979-	Circulation
AkUF	v.1, n.1- 1971-	AK-News

News. Milwaukee, WI

    see Zoar's Weekly Information. Milwaukee, WI

News. Sacramento Indian Center. Sacramento, CA

    see Sacramento Indian Center, News. Sacramento, CA

748 News Around the Wheel. 1958-?//. Unknown. Last issue 8 pages, height 26 cm. Line drawings, photographs. Published by Copper Valley School, Glenallen, AK. Editor: Judy Ashby. High school newsletter. Subject focus: Catholic Church.

WMM	v.2, n.3; May 7, 1959	Special Collections

News Bulletin. Washington, DC

    see Sentinel Bulletin. Washington, DC

News Bulletin of Mission Fields at Home. Bensalem, PA

    see Mission. Bensalem, PA

749 News Drum. 1980-1981//. Irregular. Last issue 8 pages, height 37 cm. Line drawings, photographs. Published by Community Action for the Urbanized American Indian, Inc., San Francisco American Indian Center, San Francisco, CA. Editor: John C. Slater. Subject focus: urban community, center news.

WHi   Apr?. 1980-July, 1981   Pam-Cataloging

Other holding institutions: IC (CGP).

750 News from...Foundation of North American Indian Culture. 1964-?//.
    Unknown. Last issue 4 pages, height 28 cm. Bismarck, ND. Subject
    focus: foundation news.

    WHi   v.1, n.6;   Pam 76-983
               May 22, 1964

751 News from MAAIC. 1971. Irregular. News from MAAIC, 605 N. Seneca,
    Wichita, KS 67203. (316) 262-5221. Last issue 6 pages, height 36 cm.
    Line drawings. Published by Mid-America All-Indian Center. Subject
    focus: organization news, health center news, museum news, social
    services, poetry.

    WHi   v.9, n.6-   Circulation
               June, 1979-

    OkU   [v.2, n.2-v.9, n.1]   WHC
               [Feb, 1974-Jan, 1979]

    Other holding institutions: IC (CGP).

752 News from MONAC. 1976. Irregular. Colleen Brandon, editor, News
    from MONAC, P.O. Box 3044 T.A., Spokane, WA 99220. (509) 326-4550.
    Last issue 4 pages, height 28 cm. Line drawings, photographs.
    Published by Museum of Native American Cultures, Pacific Northwest
    Indian Center. Museum newsletter. Previous editor: Carolyn Granner.
    Subject focus: art, culture, museum exhibits.

    WHi   v.3, n,14-   Circulation
               Oct, 1980-

    CLSM   v.3, n.9-   Periodicals
               Feb, 1980-

    MtHi   [v.1, n.1-v.4, n.5], v.5, n.1-   Z/970.105
               [June, 1976-1981], Jan, 1982-   N39

    CaACG   v.3, n.13;   Periodicals
               June, 1980

    News Letter, Sinte Gleska College Center.

        see Sinte Gleska College Center, News Letter.

<u>News Line</u>. Minneapolis, MN

   see <u>Indian Education</u>. Minneapolis, MN

753 <u>Newscall Newsletter</u>. 1968. Irregular. Newscall Newsletter, P.O. Box
160, Prince Albert, Saskatchewan, Canada S6V 5R6. ISSN 0225-1248,
0700-690x. LC cn80-302002, cn80-39025. OCLC 2790539, 6136420,
76136420. RLIN DCLCCN8039025-S. Last issue 60 pages, height 28 cm.
Line drawings. Published by Native Brotherhood of Indian and Metis.
Title varies: Native Brotherhood Newscall, July, 1968-Winter, 1976.
Editors: Cal H. Smoker, July, 1968; Fred Stevenson, Spring, 1969; Ray
Delorme, ?, 1970, A. Skead, ?, 1970, Reaford Bom, Sept?, 1974; Allen
Stone Child, Feb, 1975; Merve Akan, Apr, 1975; Anthony M. Cote,
Winter, 1976. Prison newsletter.

NjP	Aug 30, 1971, May 8, 1972	Periodicals
CaACG	[1968-1975]	Periodicals
CaOPeT	1978-	Periodicals
CaOONL	July?, 1968-Winter, 1976	K-111-2
CaOPeT	[1972-1976]	E75/M388

<u>The Newsletter</u>. Annapolis, MD

   see <u>MCIA Newsletter</u>. Annapolis, MD

<u>Newsletter-Canadian Association in Support of the Native Peoples</u>.
      Ottawa, Ontario, Canada

   see <u>Canadian Association in Support of the Native Peoples
      Newsletter</u>. Ottawa, Ontario, Canada

754 <u>Newsletter in Higher Education</u>. 1970?-?//. Monthly? Last issue 14
pages. Available in microform: WHi-A, Veda Stone Papers, (1971).
Published by Bureau of Indian Affairs, Albuquerque, NM. Subject
focus: education, educational opportunities.

WHi	n.12; Mar, 1971	Microforms
WEU ARC	n.12; Mar, 1971	Micro 11

Newsletter-Indian American Folklore Group. Stillwater, MN

    see Indian American Folklore Group Newsletter. Stillwater, MN

755 Newsletter of the American Indian/Alaska Native Nurses Association.
1972?-1981//?. Unknown. Last issue 12 pages, height 28 cm.
Photographs. Norman, OK. Subject focus: nursing.

    CaOAFN   v.6, n.4, v.10, n.1;   Periodicals
                  Mar/Apr, 1978, Jan/Feb, 1981

Other holding institutions: OrU-Special Collections.

756 Newsletter of the American Indian Ethnohistoric Conference.
1956-1963//. Semi-annual. ISSN 0569-5236. OCLC 1480007. RLIN
CUBG04618-S, OHCP1480007-S. Last issue 19 pages, height 28 cm.
Available in microform: WHi (1956-1963). Columbus, OH. Editors:
Richard C. Knopf, Jan, 1957-Fall, 1961; Erminie Wheeler-Voegelin, Jan,
1962-Nov, 1963. Subject focus: conference reports.

    WHi   v.1, n.1-v.7, n.2;   Microforms
               Jan, 1956-Nov, 1963

    WEU   [v.1, n.1-v.7, n.1];   Jounalism
               [Jan, 1956-Jan, 1963   Lab

    OkU   v.1, n.1-v.7, n.2;   WHC
               Jan, 1956-Nov, 1963

    OrHi   v.1, n.1-v.7, n.2;   Periodicals
               Jan, 1956-Nov, 1963

    TxU   v.1, n.1-v.7, n.1;   E/51/A823
               Jan, 1956-Jan, 1963

    WaU   v.1, n.1-v.7, n.1;   E/76/A43
               Jan, 1956-Jan, 1963

Other holding institutions: [Indiana Union List of Serials,
Indianapolis, IN] (ILS), InU (IUL), MiDW (EYW), [University of
Minnesota Union List, Minneapolis, MN] (MUL), NmU (IQU), PPiU (PIT),
Vi (VIC).

The Newsletter of the Chickasaws. Ada, OK

    see The Chickasaw Times. Ada, OK

757 <u>Newsletter of the National Center for American Indian and Alaska Native
Mental Health Research and Development</u>. 1977-1978?//. Quarterly.
Last issue 6 pages, height 28 cm. Photographs. Available in
microform: WHi (1978). Portland, OR. Editor: S. Sheoships. Subject
focus: mental health.

    WHi   v.2, n.2;   Microforms
                     Spring, 1978

758 <u>Newsletter of the Wisconsin Indians Research Institute</u>. 1965//.
Monthly during school year. RLIN NJPG0329-S, PAUG0739-S. Last issue
20 pages, height 28 cm. Available in microform: WHi-A, Veda Stone
Papers, (1965). Oshkosh, WI. Editor: George E. Fay. Subject focus:
legislation, socio-economic conditions.

    WHi   v.1, n.1-4;   E/78/W8/W86
                     Sept-Dec, 1965

    WEU   v.1, n.1-2;   Periodical
                     Sept-Dec, 1965   Stacks

    WEU   v.1, n.1-2;   Micro 11
    ARC   Sept-Dec, 1965

    UPB   v.1, n.1-4;   970.105/W753
                     Sept-Dec, 1965

<u>Newsletter, Southwestern Association on Indian Affairs</u>. Santa Fe, NM

    see <u>Southwestern Association on Indian Affairs Newsletter</u>.
        Santa Fe, NM

759 <u>Nez Perce</u>. 1914-?//. Semi-monthly. Last issue 4 pages, height 28 cm.
Lapwai, ID. Community newsletter. Photostat.

    WHi   v.2, n.3;   Microfilm
                     July 1, 1915

    IdHi   v.2, n.3;   Periodicals
                     July 1, 1915

<u>Ni Ma Me Kwa Zoo Min</u>. Cass Lake, MN

    see <u>Speaking of Ourselves</u>. Cass Lake, MN

760 <u>Niagi News</u>. 1969?-1974?//. Irregular. Last issue 5 pages. Available in microform: McA (1974); McP (1972). Published by National Indian Assistant Group, Inc., National City, CA. Community newsletter.

WHi	July/Aug, 1972, Dec, 1973-Aug/Sept, 1974	Microforms
WEU	Jan?, 1969-Dec, 1973	Microforms
AzNCC	Dec, 1973-Aug/Sept, 1974	Microfilm
CNoSU	July/Aug, 1972	Microfilm
NjP	June/July-July/Aug, 1972	Periodicals
OkU	July/Aug, 1972	WHC
CaOPeT	Dec, 1973-Sept, 1974	Microfilm

Other holding institutions: NmScW.

761 <u>Nicola Indian</u>. 1978-1982//. Irregular. ISSN 0228-2194. LC cn80-31404. OCLC 6859986. Line drawings, photographs, commercial advertising. Published by Nicola Valley Indian Administration, Merritt, British Columbia, Canada. Editors: Vernita Bob; Lynne Jorgesen. Community newsletter.

CaOAFN	v.3, n.1-v.4; Jan, 1981-Apr 1, 1982	Periodicals

Other holding institutions: CaOONL (NLC).

<u>19 Pueblos News</u>. Albuquerque, NM

see <u>Pueblo News</u>. Albuquerque, NM

762 <u>Nish Nah Bah</u>. 1975?. Irregular. Nish Nah Bah, 915 N. Western, North Topeka, KS 66608. (913) 233-5531. Last issue 8 pages, height 44 cm. Line drawings, photographs, commercial advertising. North Topeka, KS. Subject focus: urban community, center news. Supercedes Indian Center of Topeka Newsletter?

WHi	Mar, May, 1979-	Circulation
WMUW	July, 1975-July, 1979	(SPL) E/75/N56x
CaACG	[1978-1979]	Periodicals

Other holding institution: IC (CGP).

Nishnabe Gigdowen/Anishnabe Giigidowin. Bemidji, MN

  see Anishinabe Giigidowin. Bemidji, MN

763 Nishnawbe Muzinigun. 1977?-?//. Bi-monthly. OCLC 6188804, 6188828.
Last issue 10 pages, height 28 cm. Line drawings. Available in
microform: WHi (1978). Published by Ann Arbor Indian Center, WANT,
(Women of American Native Tribes), Inc., Ann Arbor, MI. Title varies:
WANT Newsletter, Aug, 1977. Editor: Victoria Garner. Subject focus:
women, child rearing, legislation, rights, poetry.

WHi	Mar-Sept, 1978	Microforms
WMUW	Mar-Sept, 1978	(SPL) E/75/N57x
MiU-B	Aug, 1977, Jan-Sept, 1978	Periodicals

764 Nishnawbe News. 1971. Quarterly. $6.50 for individuals and
institutions. Victoria Johndrow, editor, Nishnawbe News, 4 Lee Hall,
Northern Michigan University, Marquette, MI. 49855. (906) 227-2241.
OCLC 1639260. RLIN CSUP03267209-S, MIUG211117-S, OHCP1639260-S. Last
issue 8 pages, height 58 cm. Line drawings, photographs. Available
in microform: McA (1971-); McP (1971-1972); WHi-A, Veda Stone Papers,
(1971-1973). Published by Native American Students of Northern
Michigan University. Frequency varies: monthly, July, 1971-Spring,
1976. Previous editors: Michael J. Wright, July, 1971-Fall, 1973;
Marlene T. Gauther, Nov, 1973-Oct, 1974; Nancy Hatch and Carol Bailey,
Mar-Winter, 1977; Nancy Hatch, Nov, 1977-May, 1978; Wendy Corp,
Spring, 1979; John Hatch, June, 1979-Spring, 1980; Jeff Dickinson,
Summer-Winter, 1980; H. James St. Arnold, Spring-Fall, 1981.
Newspaper. Subject focus: Great Lakes area, history, movie and book
reviews.

WHi	v.1, n.1- July, 1971-	Microforms
WEU	v.3, n.9, v.4, n.2; Summer, 1975, Summer, 1976	Jounalism Lab
WEU ARC	[v.1, n.1-v.2, n.10/11] [July, 1971-Nov, 1973]	Micro 11
WM	Current issues	Forest Home Branch
WM	Current 5 years	Periodicals
WMUW	v.2, n.10/11- Nov, 1973-	(SPL) E/75/N58x

WOsh	v.1, n.1– July, 1971–	Periodicals
AzNCC	v.1, n.1– July, 1971–	Microfilm
CNoSU	v.1, n.1–v.2, n.4; July, 1971–Summer, 1972	Microfilm
IC	v.2, n.1– Apr, 1973–	Periodicals
ICN	Current issues	CHAI
MiU-B	v.1, n.1– July, 1971–	Periodicals
Mi	v.1, n.1– July, 1971–	Microfilm
MnBemT	v.2– 1973–	Periodicals
MtBBCC	v.8; Oct., 1980	Periodicals
NjP	[v.1, n.2–v.7, n.1] [Aug, 1971–June, 1979]	Periodicals
OkTU	v.6, n.4– Fall, 1978–	Rare Book Room
OkU	v.1, n.1–v.2?; July, 1971–Dec, 1972	WHC
CaOAFN	v.8, n.2– Spring, 1981–	Periodicals
CaOSuL	v.2– 1973–	Periodicals
CaOSuU	v.7– 1979–	Periodicals

Other holding institutions: [Congressional Research Service,
Washington, DC] (CRS), [Indiana Union List of Serials, Indianapolis,
IN] (ILS), InLP (IPL), KSteC (KKQ), MiLC (EEL), MiHM (EZT),
MiU-Labadie (EYM), [University of Minnesota Union List, Minneapolis,
MN] (MUL), [Western Nevada Community College, Carson City, NV], NmScW,
[Standing Rock Community College Library, Fort Yates, ND], OKentU
(KSU), OAU (OUN), PPiU (PIT), WFon (WIF), [University of
Wisconsin-Stevens Point-Native American Center, Stevens Point, WI],
[Wisconsin Indian Resource Council, Stevens Point, WI].

Nord. Ottawa, Ontario, Canada

see North/Nord. Ottawa, Ontario, Canada

765 The North American Indian. 1980. Quarterly. $6. for individuals and institutions. John J. Rochfort and Edward G. Buie, editors, The North American Indian, 2370 Esplanade, Chico, CA 95926. (916) 345-2629. Last issue 7 pages, height 28 cm. Line drawings, photographs, commercial advertising. Subject focus: arts and crafts, fiction.

WHi	v.1, n.1– Fall, 1980–	Circulation
AzHM	v.1, n.1– Fall, 1980–	Periodicals
CLSM	v.1, n.1– Fall, 1980–	Periodicals

North American Indian Association of Detroit Newsletter. Detroit, MI

see Native Sun. Detriot, MI

766 North/Nord. 1954. Quarterly. $1450 (Canada) $17.40 (U.S) for individuals and institutions. Jacqueline April, editor, North/Nord, Publishing Centre, Supply and Services Canada, 270 Albert St., Ottawa, Ontario, Canada K1A 0S9. (819) 997-0011. ISSN 0029-2362. OCLC 1036103. RLIN MIUG13330-S, NYPG804114774-S, DCLCCN76308827-S, DCLCCF7671335-S, DCLCCE7671335-S, CUBG30991304-S, OHCP2443661-S, OHCP1760500-S. Last issue 72 pages, height 28 cm. Line drawings, photographs, some in color. Indexed in: Index to Literature on the American Indian (1970-1972). Published by Department of Indian Affairs and Northern Development. Title varies: Northern Affairs Bulletin, Jan/Feb-May/June, 1960; North, July/Oct, 1960-May/June, 1971. Frequency varies: bi-monthly, Jan/Feb, 1960-Oct, 1978. Previous editors: M. Gillen, Jan/Feb, 1960-July/Aug, 1962; Harry Howith, Sept/Oct, 1962-Mar/Apr, 1965; Diane Armstrong, May/June, 1965-May/June, 1968; Helen Burgess, July/Aug, 1968-Nov/Dec, 1969; Jane Pequegnat, Jan/Feb, 1970-July/Aug, 1971; Michele Tetu, Sept/Oct, 1971-May/June, 1972; Sharon Doyle, July/Aug, 1972-July/Aug, 1973; Martha Haluszka, Sept/Oct, 1973; Robert Shannon, Nov/Dec, 1973-Summer, 1979; Evan Brown, Fall, 1979-Winter/Spring, 1981; Robert Shannon, Winter, 1982. Subject focus: Inuit people, culture, history. In French, 50%.

| WHi | v.7, n.1–
Jan/Feb, 1960– | R71/10//7-24 |
| WGrU | v.12, n.1–
Jan, 1965– | R71/10//7 |

WMUW	v.9, n.6– Nov/Dec, 1962–	F1060/A1N6
WU Coll	Current issues	Ethnic Collection
IC	v.26, n.1– Spring, 1979–	Periodicals
CaBAbF	v.23– May, 1976–	Periodicals
CaOAFN	v.28, n.2– Summer, 1981–	Periodicals
CaOONL	v.2– 1955–	Gov. Docs.
CaOOP	[v.6], v.7– [1959], 1960–	E/5600/N67
CaOPeT	v.8– 1961–	E5900/N67

Other holding institutions: NbU (LDL), NhD (DRB), PPiU (PIT), WaU (WAU).

Northern Affairs Bulletin. Ottawa, Ontario, Canada

   see North/Nord. Ottawa, Ontario, Canada

767 Northern Breed. 1976?-1978//. Monthly. ISSN 0703-8364. LC
cn77-22595. OCLC 3520250. Last issue 28 pages, height 28 cm.
Photographs, commerical advertising. Yellowknife, Northwest
Territories, Canada. Community newsletter.

   CaSICC   Dec, 1976-Mar, 1978   Periodicals

   Other holding institutions: CaOONL (NLC).

768 Northern Breezes. 1960?-?//. Unknown. Last issue 8 pages, height 36
cm. Line drawings. Published by Holy Cross Mission, Holy Cross, AK.
school newsletter. Subject focus: Catholic Church.

   WMM   Oct?, 1960   Special
                                                    Collections

Northern Cheyenne Press. Lame Deer, MT

see A'Tome/Northern Cheyenne Press. Lame Deer, MT

769 The Northern Light, A Journal of the Missions in Alaska.
    1893-1903?//. Quarterly. RLIN CUBU13729688-S. Last issue 4 pages,
    height 23 cm. Photographs, commercial advertising. Fort Wrangel, AK.
    Place of publication varies: Brooklyn, NY. Editor: Dr. Clarence
    Thwing. Subject focus: missions, Presbyterian Church.

    MWA   n.5;   Periodicals
               June, 1894

770 Northern Lights. 1932-1972//. Quarterly. Last issue 4 pages. Line
    drawings, photographs. Available in microform: McA (1932-1972).
    Published by The Little Flower Indian Mission School, Marvin, ND.
    Place of publication varies: St. Michael, ND, Apr, 1932-Mar/Apr, 1971.
    Frequency varies: bi-monthly, Apr, 1932-Oct, 1938; monthly, Dec,
    1938-Sept, 1955. Editors: Damian Preshe, Apr, 1932-Sept, 1933;
    Ambrose Mattingley and Damian Preshe, Nov, 1933-Aug, 1934; Edward
    Berheide and Damian Preshe, Nov, 1934-Dec 31, 1936. Subject focus:
    Catholic Church, missions.

    WHi   v.1, n.1-v.18, n.1;   Microforms
               Apr, 1932-Feb, 1972

    WEU   v.16, n.4-v.17, n.2;   Journalism
               July/Aug, 1970-Mar/Apr, 1971   Lab

    WMM   [v.2, n.1-v.17, n.6]   Special
               [Feb, 1933-Nov/Dec, 1971]   Collections

    NjP   [v.3,n.6-v.15, n.1]   Periodicals
               [May/June, 1957-Jan/Feb, 1970]

    OkU   [v.1, n.1-v.18, n.1]   WHC
               [Apr, 1932-Feb, 1972]

    CaOPeT   [v.1, n.1-v.18, n.1]   Microfilm
               [Apr, 1932-Feb, 1972]

    Other holding institutions: [Western Nevada Community College, Carson
    City, NV], [University of Wisconsin-Stevens Point-Native American
    Center, Stevens Point, WI].

771 Northern Lights. 1966-1978//?. Monthly. ISSN 0380-5468. LC
    cn76-3000090. OCLC 2084146. RLIN OHCP2085146-S. Last issue 8 pages,
    height 28 cm. Line drawings, commerical advertising. Berens River,
    Manitoba, Canada. Editor: Walter Green. Feb, 1967-June, 1975.
    Community newsletter.

    CaOONL   [Feb, 1967-Dec, 1978]   K-109-1

772 <u>Northern Pueblos Agency News Digest</u>. 1975-?//? Monthly. OCLC
    6168910. Last issue 4 pages, height 28 cm. Available in microform:
    WHi (1975). Published by Bureau of Indian Affairs, Northern Pueblos
    Agency, Santa Fe, NM. Subject focus: Eight Northern Pueblos,
    education, social services.

    WHi   v.1, n.14-15;   Microforms
                 Jan-Feb, 1975

    WMUW   v.1, n.14-15;   (SPL)
                 Jan-Feb, 1975   E/75/N6x

773 <u>The Northian</u>. 1964. Semi-annual. The Northian, Saskatoon,
    Saskatchewan, Canada S7N 0W0. (306) 343-3139. ISSN 0029-3253. LC
    cn76-300095. OCLC 2084651. RLIN DCLCCN76300095-S, OHCP2084651-S,
    NYPG804144789-S. Last issue 44 pages. Line drawings, photographs.
    Indexed in: Index to Literature on the American Indian (1970-1971).
    Available in microform: MML (1964-); McA (1974-). Published by
    Society for Indian and Northern Education. Frequency varies:
    quarterly, Winter, 1974-Fall, 1975. Previous editors: Tim Jones,
    Winter, 1974-Spring, 1978; Del M. Koenig and S. Rose Marcuzzi,
    Summer-Autumn, 1978. Subject focus: multicultural education,
    community development.

    WHi   v.10, n.1-   Microforms
                 Winter, 1974-

    WHi   v.6, n.1-v.8, n.4;   E/97/N6
                 Jan, 1969-Mar, 1972

    WEU   v.10, n.1-2;   Microforms
                 Winter-Spring, 1974

    AzNCC   v.4-v.13;   Indian File
                 Apr, 1968-Summer, 1978

    NjP   v.5, n.1;   Periodicals
                 Winter, 1969

    CaACG   v.4, n.2-v.13, n.3;   Periodicals
                 Spring, 1967-Autumn, 1978

    CaAEU   v.1, n.1-v.13, n.3;   Boreal
                 1964-1978   Institute

    CaMWU   v.6-v.12, n.3;   Education
                 1969-1976

    CaOONL   v.1-   Periodicals
                 1964-

    CaOOP   v.1-   E/97/C3N67
                 1964-

CaOPeT   v.1-   Microfilm
            1964-

Other holding institutions: CLU (CLU), [University of Minnesota Union
List, Minneapolis, MN] (MUL).

774 The Northian Newsletter. 1961-1975//. Quarterly. ISSN 0050-712x.
    RLIN DCLCCN7939061-S, DCLCCN76300096-S, OHCP2084718-S,
    NYPG744734167-S. Last issue 25 pages. Photographs. Available in
    microform: McA (1974-1975). Published by Society for Indian and
    Northern Education, Saskatoon, Saskatchewan, Canada. Subject focus:
    multicultural education, community development.

    WHi   n.38-43;   Microforms
                Jan, 1974-Sept/Nov, 1975

    WHi   n.9-27/28;   E/97/N65
                Oct, 1969-Nov/Dec, 1971

    WEU   n.38-41;   Microforms
                Jan-Dec, 1974

    AzNCC   n.?-43;   Microfilm
                Mar, 1971-Sept/Nov, 1975

    NjP   [n.?-43]   Periodicals
                [Fall/Winter, 1972-Sept/Nov, 1975]

    CaACG   n.7-44;   Periodicals
                1969-1975

    CaAEU   n.1-44;   Boreal
                1964-1975   Institute

    CaOONL   n.8-   Periodicals
                1968-

    CaOOP   n.8-43;   E/97/C3/N68
                Nov, 1968-Sept/Nov, 1975

    CaOPeT   n.?, 38-43;   Microforms
                Jan, 1971-Fall, 1973,
                Jan, 1974-Sept/Nov, 1975

Northland Native American News. Ashland, WI

    see NAS News. Ashland, WI

775 Northwest Arctic Nuna. 1980. Irregular. John David Christensen and
    Bunny Schaeffer, editors, Northwest Arctic Nuna, P.O. Box 256,

Kotzebue, AK 99725.   (907) 442-3311.   Last issue 12 pages, height 44
cm.   Line drawings, photographs, commercial advertising.   Available in
microform: WHi (1980-).   Published by Maniilaq Association.   Subject
focus: cultural self-determination, Alaska Native peoples, community
development.   Supercedes Mauneluk Report.

WHi   v.1, n.1-   Microforms
             Oct, 1980-

AkUF   v.1, n.1-   AK Per 2345
             Oct, 1980-

776 Northwest Indian Fisheries Commission News.   1975.   Irregular.
    Northwest Indian Fisheries Commission News, 2625 Parkmont Lane, S. W.,
    Olympia, WA 98502.   (206) 352-8030.   OCLC 5713929, 5718232, 6155376,
    6221119.   Title varies: Northwest Indian Fisheries Commission
    Newsletter, Nov 12, 1975-Sept, 1978.   Subject focus: fishing rights
    and regulations, legislation.

WHi   v.1, n.2-   Circulation
             June 19, 1975-

OrHi   v.4, n.4-   Periodicals
             Aug, 1978-

WaU   v.1, n.5-   E/78/W3N676
             Sept, 1975-

CaOAFN   v.7, n.1;   Periodicals
             Mar, 1981

Other holding institutions: CLSM.

777 Northwest Indian News.   1971.   Monthly. $5. for individuals and
    institutions.   Ella Aquino, editor, Northwest Indian News, P.O. Box
    4322, Pioneer Square Station, Seattle, WA 98104.   (206) 624-8700.
    ISSN 0146-1877.   LC sc77-1292.   OCLC 2868613.   RLIN DCLCSC771292-S,
    OHCP2868613-S.   Last issue 8 pages.   Line drawings, photographs,
    commercial advertising.   Available in microform: McA (1974-), McP
    (1971-1972).   Published by Seattle Indian Center and American Indian
    Women's Service League.   Subject focus: urban community, center news.

WHi   v1, n.1-v.2, n.6, 11, v.3, n.6-   Microforms
             Jan, 1971-Dec, 1972, May, 1973, Jan, 1974-

WEU   v.3, n.6-v.4, n.8;   Microforms
             Jan-Dec, 1974

WMUW   v.4, n.10-v.5, n.2;   (SPL)
             Feb-June, 1975   E/75/N67x

AkUF	v.9-v.10; Dec, 1979-Nov, 1980	AK-news
AzNCC	v.3-v.11; 1974-Mar, 1980	Indian File
CU-A	[v.1-v.3], v.4- [June 1971-July, 1974], Aug, 1974-	E/75/N6
NjP	[v.1, n.3-v.9, n.5; [June, 1971-May/June, 1979]	Periodicals
OrHi	v.10-v.11; 1979-1980	Periodicals
Wa	v.1- 1972-	NW
OkTU	v.7, n.7-v.[10], n.4; Feb, 1978-Mar, 1980	Rare Book Room
UPB	v.1-v.10; Nov, 1971-Nov, 1980	970.47905/N819
OkU	[v.1, n.1-v.10, n.9] [Jan, 1971-1980]	WHC
CaOPeT	[v.1-v.7], v.10- [1971-1978], 1980-	Microfilm

Other holding institutions: CLU (CLU), KSteC (KKQ), [University of
Minnesota Union List, Minneapolis, MN] (MUL), NmScW, NmU-L (NML),
[Standing Rock Community College Library, Fort Yates, ND], WaU (WAU)
WaChenE (WEA).

778 <u>Northwest Indian Times</u>. 1969-1972//. Irregular. OCLC 1760699. RLIN
OHCP1760699-S. Last issue 16 pages. Line drawings, photographs.
Available in microform: McP (1971-1972); McA (1969-1972). Published
by Spokane, Coeur d'Alene and Kalispel Tribes, Spokane, WA. Community
newsletter. Subject focus: Coeur d'Alene and Kalispel people.

WHi	v.1, n.1-v.4, n.1; Feb 7, 1969-Mar, 1972	Microforms
WEU	v.3, n.1; July/Aug, 1971	Journalism Lab
AzNCC	v.2-v.3; 1970-Nov, 1971	Indian File
CU-A	[v.1-v.4] [1969-1972]	E/77/A1/N6

NjP   [v.2, n.5-v.4, n.1]   Periodicals
           [June 30, 1970-Mar, 1972]

OkU   v.1, n.1-v.4, n.1;   WHC
           Feb 7, 1969-Mar, 1972

Wa   v.1-v.4;   NW
           1969-1972

WaU   v.1, n.1-v.4, n.1;   E/78/N77/N6
           Feb 7, 1969-Mar, 1972

CaOPeT   v.1, n.1-v.4, n.1;   Microfilm
           Feb 7, 1969-Mar, 1972

Other holding instituions: [University of Minnesota Union List,
Minneapolis, MN] (MUL), [Western Nevada Community College, Carson
City, NV], NmScW, WaChenE (WEA).

779 Northwest Languages Newsletter. 1979. 3 times a year. $2.50 for
    individuals and institutions. Yvonne M. Hebert, editor, Northwest
    Languages Newsletter, Department of Linguistics, University of British
    Columbia, Vancouver, British Columbia, Canada V6T 1W5. (604)
    228-4256. Last issue 9 pages, height 35 cm. Subject focus:
    linguistics, Native language instruction.

    NCBE   v.1-   Periodicals
               1979-

780 Northwest Moccasin Trails. 1970-1971?//. Bi-monthly. Last issue 4
    pages, height 28 cm. Photographs. Published by Northwest Indian
    Bible School, Alberton, MT. Editor: Robert W. Pelton. School
    newsletter.

    CaACG   v.2, n.1-3;   Periodicals
               Jan/Feb-May/June, 1971

781 Northwest Native American News. 1973?//. Unknown. Line drawings,
    photographs. Published by Native American Rehabilitation Association,
    Portland, OR. Organization newsletter.

    WaU   v.1, n.1;   Periodicals
               Dec?, 1973

    Nouvelles des Indiens de Quebec. Caughnawaga, Quebec, Canada

        see Indians of Quebec/Indiens du Quebec. Caughnawaga, Quebec,
            Canada

Nouvelles Indiens. Ottawa, Ontario, Canada

    see Indian News. Ottawa, Ontario, Canada

782 Nugguam. 1971?-?//. Irregular. OCLC 6221110. Last issue 10 pages,
    height 28 cm. Line drawings. Available in microform: WHi
    (1977-1978). Published by Quinault Tribe, Taholah, WA. Community
    newsletter. Subject focus: Quinault people.

WHi	July, 1977-Mar, 1978	Microforms
WMUW	July, 1977-Mar, 1978	(SPE)
		E/75/N83x

783 Nuna: Magazine for Eskimos. 1960-1964?//. Quarterly. Last issue 30
    pages, last volume 120 pages, height 23 cm. Line drawings. Published
    by Oblate Missionaries of the Canadian Arctic, Cambridge Bay,
    Northwest Territories, Canada. Subject focus; Inuit people, local and
    national news, fiction.

CaACG	[n.1-15] [Summer, 1960-Summer, 1964]	Periodicals
CaOONL	n.10; Jan, 1963	Periodicals

784 Nunatsiaq News. 1973. Weekly. $22. for individuals and
    institutions. Monica Connolly, editor, Nunatsiaq news, Box 8,
    Frobisher Bay, Northwest Territories, Canada X0A 0H0. (819) 979-5357.
    ISSN 0702-7015, 0702-7923. LC cn77-32366. OCLC 3409689. RLIN
    DCLCCN7732366-S, OHCP3409689-S. Last issue 36, last volume 210,
    height 28 cm. Line drawings, commercial advertising. Available in
    microform: WHi (1973-). Title varies: Inukshuk, Mar 16, 1973-June 3,
    1976. Previous editors: Ann Hansen, Apr 6-20, 1973; Nedra Greenaway,
    Apr 27, 1973-June 4, 1975. Community newsletter. Subject focus:
    Inuit people. In Inuit, 50%.

WHi	v.1, n.4- Mar 16, 1973-	Microforms
AzNCC	v.5- Nov 3, 1977-	Indian File
CaACG	[v.2, n.40-v.7, n.33], v.9, n.2- [Nov 6, 1974-1979], Mar 13, 1981-	Periodicals
CaOONL	v.1, n.1- Feb 9, 1973-	Newspaper Section

Other holding institutions: [University of Minnesota Union List, Minneapolis, MN] (MUL).

785 <u>OIE Office of Indian Education Newsletter</u>. 1976?-1981//. Irregular. Last issue 8 pages, height 28 cm. Line drawings. Published by Department of Education, Washington, DC. Subject Focus: curriculum development.

WHi   Dec, 1977-Jan, 1981   Pam
                                                        Cataloging

AzNCC   1980-   Indian File

Other holding institutions: WM (GZD), [Wisconsin Indian Resource Council, Stevens Point, WI].

786 <u>OIO News</u>. 1982. Quarterly. Iola Hayden, editor, OIO News, 555 Constitution Ave., Norman, OK 73069. (405) 329-3737. Last issue 6 pages, height 28 cm. Line drawings, photographs. Published by Oklahomans for Indian Opportunity. Subject focus: self-determination, employment opportunities. Supercedes OIO Journal.

WHi   Jan/Feb/Mar, 1982-   Circulation

OkU   Jan/Feb/Mar, 1982-   WHC

787 <u>OIO Newsletter</u>. 1969?-1979//. Monthly. OCLC 1589489. RLIN OHCP1589489-S. Last issue 4 pages. Photographs. Available in microform: McP (1971-1972). Published by Oklahomans for Indian Opportunity, Norman OK. Community newsletter. Subject focus: self-determination, employment opportunities. Superceded by OIO Journal.

WHi   Jan, 25, 1971-June, 1972,   Microforms
           Feb, 1973-Nov/Dec, 1979

AzNCC   Feb, 1976-Aug, 1980   Indian File

NjP   [July, 1971-May.June, 1979]   Periodicals

OkTU   Aug, 1969-Dec, 1979   Rare Book
                                                        Room

OkU   Jan, 1971-June, 1972   WHC

Other holding institutions: (University of Minnesota Union List, Minneapolis, MN] (MUL), NmScW.

788 <u>OIO Journal</u>. 1980-1981//. 3 times a year. RLIN UTBL1413-S. Last
    issue 14 pages, last volume 50 pages, height 28 cm. Line drawings,
    photographs. Published by Oklahomans for Indian Opportunity, Norman,
    OK. Subject focus: self-determination, employment opportunities.
    Supercedes OIO Newsletter; superceded by OIO News.

    WHi   v.1, n.1-?;   Circulation
                Apr, 1980-Fall, 1981

    OkU   v.1, n.1-?;   WHC
                Apr, 1980-Fall, 1981

789 <u>OKC Camp Crier</u>. 1976. Monthly. $5. for individuals and
    institutions. Tonekei, editor, OKC Camp Crier, 2830 S. Robinson,
    Oklahoma City, OK 73109. (405) 232-2512. OCLC 6189139. Last issue 12
    pages, height 37 cm. Line drawings, photographs. Published by Native
    American Center, American Indian Training and Employment Program and
    The Indian Health Project of Oklahoma City. Community newsletter.
    Subject focus: local and national news, health, education, poetry.

    WHi   v.4, n.2-   Circulation
                Feb, 1979-

    WMUW   [v.3, n.11-v.4, n.4];   (SPL)
                [Aug, 1977-Apr, 1979]   E/75/04x

    AzNCC   v.5-   Indian File
                Mar, 1980-

    MtBBCC   v.5;   Periodicals
                Aug,. 1980

790 <u>OMNSIAT: Ontario Metis and Non Status Indian Association Telegraph</u>.
    1981. Unknown. Last issue 18 pages, height 28 cm. Line drawings.
    Willowdale, Ontario, Canada. Subject focus: rights, legislation.

    WHi   v.1, n.2-   Circulation
                Dec, 1981-

791 <u>ONAS Newsletter</u>. 1969-?//. Unknown. Last issue 6 pages.
    Photographs. Available in microform: WHi (1969); WHi-A, Veda Stone
    Papers, (1969). Published by Organization of Native American
    Students, Concord, NH. Editor: Vance Good Iron. Subject focus:
    education, educational opportunities, legislation.

    WHi   v.1, n.1, 3;   Microforms
                Jan, July, 1969

    WEU   v.1, n.3;   Micro 11
    ARC   July, 1969

```
AzNCC      v.2;                                          Indian File
           Mar, 1970
```

Other holding institutions: OrU-Special Collections.

792 ONEO Bahane. 1972. Monthly. ONEO Bahane, Box 589, Fort Defiance, AZ
    86504. RLIN CUBU82-S55. Last issue 4 pages, height 28 cm. Line
    drawings, photographs. Available in microform: McA (1972-).
    Published by Office of Navajo Economic Opportunity, DEH-HA-NEH. Title
    varies: Deh-Ha-Neh, Oct, 1972-Jan, 1973; Office of Navajo Economic
    Opportunity, Feb, 1973-May, 1976. Community newsletter. Subject
    focus: Navajo people, organization news.

```
WHi        v.1, n.1-                                     Microforms
           Oct, 1972-

AzNCC      v.1, n.1-v.7;                                 Indian File
           Oct, 1972-1980

NjP        [v.1, n.1-v.4, n.1]                           Periodicals
           [Oct, 1972-Spring, 1977]

OkU        [v.1, n.1-v.4, n.1]                           WHC
           [Oct, 1972-Spring, 1977]

CaOPeT     v.1, n.1-                                     Microfilm
           Oct, 1972-
```


793 O He Yoh Noh, Allegany Indian Reservation Newsletter. 1967?. Weekly.
    $12. for individuals and institutions. O He Yoh Noh, Allegany Indian
    Reservation Newsletter, Museum Annex, Salamanca, NY 14779. Last issue
    4 pages, height 28 cm. Line drawings. Available in microform: CPC
    (1970-1976). Editor: Shirley Vanatta. July 9, 1970-Jan 24, 1973.
    Community newsletter.

```
WHi        [Jan 14, 1970-May 29,], Aug 15, 1976-        Microforms

NjP        [May, 1967-June 26, 1979]                     Periodicals
```


Office of Navajo Economic Opportunity. Fort Defiance, AZ

    see ONEO Bahane. Fort Defiance, AZ

794 Official Newsletter. 1979? Monthly. Marlene Johnson, editor,
    Official Newsletter, P.O. Box 231, Salamanca, NY 14779. Last issue 12

pages, height 28 cm. Line drawings, photographs. Published by Seneca
Nation of Indians. Subject focus: Seneca people, Tribal Council,
health, education, museum news.

WHi   Mar, June, 1979   Microforms

795 Official Rumors. 1963?-?//. Irregular. Last issue 5 pages, height 37
     cm. Line drawings. Published by Northern Cheyenne Agency, Lame Deer,
     MT. Community newsletter. Subject focus: Cheyenne people.

     MtHi   v.8, n.31, 43-44;   Z/970.105/Of2
                  Oct 19, 1970, Mar 19, 29, 1971

796 Oglala Lakota. 1970-?//. Irregular. Last issue 12 pages, height 37
     cm. Line drawings, photographs. Published by Pine Ridge Reservation,
     Pine Ridge, SD. Editor: Birgil L. Kills Straight. Community
     newsletter. Subject focus: Oglala Sioux people, legislation.

     WEU   v.1, n.3-5;   Journalism
                  Dec, 11, 1970-Feb 15, 1971   Lab

797 Oglala Light. 1900?-?//. Irregular. OCLC 4178192. RLIN
     OHCP4178192-S. Last issue 12 pages, height 28 cm. Line drawings.
     Published by Oglala Community School, Pine Ridge, SD. School
     newsletter. Subject focus: Oglala Sioux people.

     WMM   v.13, n.2, v.20, n.6-7, 20;   Special
                  Feb, 1912, Mar-Apr, June, 1919   Collections

     ICN   [no nos.]   Ayer 1/035
                  Dec, 1913, Mar, 1915, Mar-Apr, 1917

     SdHRC   [v.2, n.10-v.21, n.1]   Periodicals
                  [1902-1919]

     SdSifA   [v.4, n.3-v.21, n.6]   Archives
                  [June 4, 1903-Feb 15, 1920]

     Other holding institutions: [University of Minnesota Union List,
     Minneapolis, MN] (MUL).

798 Oglala War Cry. 1970-?//. Bi-monthly. Last issue 6 pages. Line
     drawings, photographs, commercial advertising. Available in
     microform: McP (1971). Pine Ridge, SD. Community newsletter.
     Subject focus: Dakota people.

     WHi   v.1, n.18-22;   Microforms
                  Jan 25-Mar 22, 1971

KU   v.1-?   Kansas
          1970-1971   Collection

NjP   [v.1, n.14-23]   Periodicals
          [Nov 30, 1970-May, 10, 1971]

OkU   v.1, n.18-22;   WHC
          Jan 25-Mar 22, 1971

Other holding institutions: NmScW.

799 Ohoyo. 1979. Quarterly. Sedelta Verble, editor, Ohoyo, 2301
    Midwestern Pkwy., Suite 214, Wichita Falls, TX 76308. (817) 692-3841.
    Last issue 8 pages, height 28 cm. Photographs. Published by Ohoyo
    Resource Center. Subject focus: women's rights, education, economics.

WHi   n.1, 1-   Circulation
          July, 1979-

WM   Current issues   Forest Home
                                                   Branch

ICN   Current issues   CHAI

Other holding institutions: IC (CGP), [University of Wisconsin-Stevens
Point-Native American Center, Stevens Point, WI], [Wisconsin Indian
Resource Council, Stevens Point, WI].

800 Oklahoma Indian School Magazine. 1932-1933//. Monthly during school
    year. Last issue 30 pages, height 26 cm. Line drawings, photographs.
    Chilocco, OK. School newsletters. Published at various Oklahoma
    Boarding Schools.

OkTU   v.1, n.1-v.2, n.5;   Rare Books
          Mar, 1932-May, 1933

OkU   v.1, n.1-v.2, n.5;   WHC
          Mar, 1932-May, 1933

801 Okolakiciye Wakan Wotanin Wowapi. 1970?-1979?//. Irregular. OCLC
    8416549. Last issue 4 pages. Line drawings. Available in microform:
    CPC (1970-1971). Published by Rosebud Mission of the Episcopal Church,
    Mission, SD. Subject focus: missions, Episcopal Church, Rosebud Sioux
    people.

WHi   Feb, 1970-Feb?, 1971   Microforms

NjP   Jan, 1970-Apr, 1974]   Periodicals

Other holding institutions: PPiU (PIT).

802 <u>Okuruk</u>. 1969-1976//. Bi-monthly. ISSN 0380-6014. LC cn76-300115.
OCLC 2086887. Last issue 8 pages, last volume 48 pages, height 43 cm.
Published by Petroleum Industry Committee on the Employment of
Northern Residents, Calgary, Alberta, Canada. Subject focus: natural
resource development, employment information.

CaACG v.1, n.1-v.7, n.6;   Periodicals
      Dec, 1969-Oct, 1976

Other holding institutions: CaOONL (NLC).

803 <u>Omaha Community Council News</u>. 1959?-?//. Unknown. Last issue 8
pages, height 35 cm. Line drawings, photographs. Macy, NE.
Community newsletter. Subject focus: Omaha people.

WMM   v.1, n.11/12;   Special
      Aug/Sept, 1959   Collections

804 <u>On the Areas: Metis Rehabilitation Newsletter</u>. 1958-1959?//.
Monthly. Last issue 2 pages, last volume 21 pages, height 28 cm.
Published by Metis Rehabilitation Branch, Department of Public
Welfare, Ottawa, Ontario, Canada. Frequency varies: monthly,
Jan-June, 1958; bi-monthly, July/Aug-Nov/Dec, 1958. Subject focus:
Metis people, social services.

CaACG v.1, n.1-v.2, n.1, 5;   Periodicals
      Jan, 1958-Jan, Oct/Nov/Dec, 1959

805 <u>Oneida</u>. 1897?-1906?//. Unknown. Last issue 20 pages, height 24 cm.
Line drawings, photographs. Personal names indexed in: Index to
Wisconsin Native American Periodicals (1897-1906). Published by
Hobart Church, Oneida, WI. Subject focus: missions, Christian
religion.

WHi   Dec?. 1897-?, 1906   F8096//+058/0
                 Cutter

806 <u>Onkweonwe</u>. 1900-?//. Bi-weekly. Last issue 4 pages, height 36 cm.
Ottawa, Ontario, Canada. Community newsletter. Subject focus:
Iroquis people. In Iroquis, 100%.

CaOONL v.1, n.1;   Newspaper
      Oct 25, 1900   Section

807 <u>Ontario Indian</u>. 1978. Monthly. $17. for individuals and
    institutions. Juanite Rennie, editor, Ontario Indian, 27 Queen St.,
    East, Toronto, Ontario, Canada M5C 1R5. (416) 366-3527. ISSN
    0707-3143. LC cn79-30313. OCLC 4635222. RLIN UTBG81-S316,
    DCLCCN7930313-S, NJRX154-S, OHCP4635222-S. Last issue 42 pages, last
    volume 540 pages, height 28 cm. Line drawings, photographs, some in
    color, commercial advertising. Published by Union of Ontario Indians.
    Previous editor: Dennis Martel, Jan, 1980-Mar, 1982. Subject focus:
    rights, legislation, local and national news, health, tribal councils,
    book reviews.

WHi	v.3, n.1– Jan, 1980–	Circulation
WM	Current issues	Forest Home Branch
WMUW	v.3, n.8– Aug, 1980–	E/78/05057x
ICN	Current issues	CHAI
CaACG	v.3, n.8– Aug, 1980–	Periodicals
CaAEU	v.3, n.1– Jan, 1980–	Boreal Institute
CaOAFN	Current issues	Periodicals
CaOAUC	v.3, n.10– Oct, 1980–	Periodicals
CaOONL	v.1, n.1– Sept, 1978–	Periodicals
CaOOP	v.1, n.1– Sept, 1978–	Periodicals
CaOPeT	[v.1–v.2], v.3– [1978–1979], 1980–	E78/05057
CaOSuL	v.2– 1979–	Periodicals
CaOSuU	v.1– 1978–	Periodicals

Other holding institutions: MH (HLS, HUL), MnSAG (MAG), NBwU (BUF),
NmU-L (NML) OkU (OKL), TxU (TXQ), [WGrU-Native American Studies
Dept.], [Wisconsin Indian Resource Council, Stevens Point, WI].

808 <u>Ontario Native Examiner</u>. 1972?//. Monthly. ISSN 0316-7623. LC
    cn75-32015. OCLC 2247891. Last issue 8 pages, height 43 cm. Line

drawings, photographs, commercial advertising. Published by Communications Division of the Union of Ontario Indians, Toronto, Ontario, Canada. Newspaper.

NjP   v.1, n.1;   Periodicals
         Feb, 1972

CaOONL v.1, n.4;   Newspaper
         May/June, 1972   Section

809 Ontario Native Experience. 1973-1976//. Monthly. ISSN 0380-1519. LC cn76-320001. OCLC 2040823. RLIN DCLCCN76320001-S, OHCP2040823-S. Last issue 8 pages, last volume 96 pages. Line drawings, photographs, commercial advertising. Available in microform: WHi (1973-1976). Published by Ontario Federation of Indian Friendship Centres, Toronto, Ontario, Canada. Editors: Susan Daybutch and Patricia Leslie, Dec, 1974; Sylvia Maracle, Oct, 1975-Aug, 1976. Subject focus: organization news, local and national news, education.

WHi   v.1, n.4-v.3, n.11;   Microforms
         Nov, 1973-Aug, 1976

CaAEU   v.2, n.1-v.3, n.11;
         1974-Aug, 1976   Boreal
                                     Institute

CaOONL v.1-
         1973-   Periodicals

810 Open Span Newsletter Highlites. 1980?//? Bi-monthly. Last issue 5 pages, height 28 cm. Line drawings. Published by Open Span School, Pine Ridge, SD. Elementary school newsletter.

WMM   v.1, n.1;   Special
         Apr 3, 1980   Collections

811 Oracle. 1975-1979?//. Unknown. ISSN 1709-1389. LC cn75-73267. OCLC 2248887. RLIN DCLCCN7573267-S, DCLCCN7573263-S. Last issue 4 pages. Line drawings, photographs. Published by Department of Indian Affairs and Northern Development, National Museums of Canada, Ottawa, Ontario, Canada. Subject focus: culture, arts and crafts.

WHi   n.1-32;   R34-2/1-32
         ?, 1979

Other holding institutions: CaOONL (NLC).

812 Order of the Indian Wars, Journal. 1980. Quarterly. $15. for individuals and institutions. Jerry L. Russell, editor, Order of the

Indian Wars, Journal, P.O. Box 7401, Little Rock, AK 72217. OCLC
7700099. Last issue 46 pages, height 22 cm. Subject focus: history,
military history.

WHi   v.1, n.1   Microforms
             Winter, 1980

Other holding institutions: ArU (AFU).

813 Oregon Indian Education Association Newsletter. 1981? Unknown. Jim
    Thornton and Dean Azule, editors, Oregon Indian Education Association
    Newsletter, 2528 Lady Bug Ct., Salem, OR 97303. Last issue 6 pages,
    height 39 cm. Subject focus: education, law, curriculum development.

WHi   Spring-May, 1981   Microforms

    The Oregonian. Boston, MA

       see The Oregonian and Indian's Advocate. Boston, MA

814 The Oregonian and Indian's Advocate. 1838-?//. Monthly. LC 5-2267.
    OCLC 1124182. Last issue 32 pages, height 24 cm. Published by
    Committee of the Oregon Provisional Emigration Society, Boston, MA.
    Title varies: The Oregonian, Oct-Nov, 1838. Subject focus: missions,
    Christian religion, culture, territorial explorations.

WHi   v.1, n.1-[11];   F/871/075
             Oct, 1838-Aug, 1839   Cutter
                                                         Rare Books

CtY-B   v.1, n.1-[11];   Zc74/Or4
             Oct, 1838-Aug, 1839

ICN   v.1, n.1-[11];   Graff 3127
             Oct, 1838-Aug, 1839

NjP   v.1, n.1-[11];   Periodicals
             Oct, 1838-Aug, 1839

OrU   v.1, n.1-[11];   Rare Books
             Oct, 1838-Aug, 1839

Other holding institutions: AzTeS (AZS), DeU (DLM), OOxM (MIA), TxFTC
(ICU), UU (UUM).

815 The Osage Journal. 1898-?//. Weekly. Last issue 8 pages. Line
    drawings, commerical advertising. Published by Osage Publishing Co.,
    Pawhuska, OK. Editors: W. C. Bridwell, Jan 3-Mar 28, 1901; Charles B.

Peters, Apr 11, 1901-Jan 16, 1902; William Murdock, and R. F. Timmons, Jan 23-Apr 3, 1902; R. F. Timmons, Apr 10-Oct 9, 1902; Charles B. Peters, Oct 16, 1902-July 30, 1903. Newspaper. Subject focus: Osage people.

WHi	[v.4, n.4-v.7, n.4]	Microforms
	[Jan 3, 1901-July 8, 1905]	

816 Osage Nation News. 1977. Irregular. Janet Kennett, editor, Osage Nation News, P.O. Box 147, Pawhuska, OK 74056. (918) 287-2495. OCLC 6189018. Last issue 8 pages, last volume, 24 pages, height 39 cm. Line drawings, photographs. Available in microform: WHi (1978, 1979-). Community newsletter. Subject focus: Osage people.

WHi	v.2, n.3; v.3, n.3-	Circulation
	June, 1978, Sept, 1979-	
WMUW	v.2, n.3;	(SPL)
	June, 1978	E/75/082x

817 Oshkaabewis. 1974-1980?//? Unknown. OCLC 2253709. Last issue 8 pages, height 39 cm. Line drawings, photographs. Available in microform: WHi (1976/77). Published by Bemidji State University, Bemidji, MN. Title varies: Oshkabewis, Sept, 1974-Jan/Feb, 1978. Editor: Kent Smith. School newsletter. Subject focus: education, poetry.

WHi	Winter, 1976/77, Spring, 1980	Microforms
WMUW	Winter, 1976/77	(SPL)
		E/75/084x
MnBemT	1974-	Periodicals
MnHi	[Sept, 1974-Spring, 1980]	Periodicals
NjP	Winter, 1977-1978	Periodicals

Other holding institutions: MnDuU (MND), [University of Minnesota Union List, Minneapolis, MN] (MUL).

Oshkabewis. Bemidji, MN

   see Oshkaabewis. Bemidji, MN

Our Captives or "Wards"-The American Indian. Peoria, IL

   see The American Indian: Captive or Citizen. Peoria, IL

818 <u>Our Forest Children</u>. 1887-1890//. Monthly. OCLC 2434515. RLIN
    DCLCCN76301842-S, OHCP2434515-S. Last issue 16 pages, last volume 256
    pages, height 24 cm. Line drawings, commercial advertising. Sault
    Ste. Marie, Ontario, Canada. Editor: Rev. E. F. Wilson. Subject
    focus: culture, education, Christian religion.

    WHi   v.3, n.30-v.4, n.6;   F8095/W74
                 June, 1889-Sept, 1890   Cutter

    ICN   v.1-v.4, n.6;   Ayer 1/09
                 Feb, 1887-Sept, 1890

    CaOONL   v.3-v.4;   P-57
                 1889-1890

    CaOPeT   v.3, n.30-v.4, n.6;   Microfilm
                 June, 1889-Sept, 1890

    Other holding institutions: MnHi (MHS).

819 <u>Our Monthly</u>. 1872-?//. Monthly. Last issue 4 pages, height 31 cm.
    Tullahassee, OK. Community newsletter. Subject focus: Creek people.
    In Creek, 85-90%.

    WHi   v.4, n.7;   F8097/C92/0
                 July, 1875   Cutter
                                                           Rare Books

820 <u>Our Native Land</u>. 1970-1974?//. Monthly. Last issue 2 pages, height
    36 cm. Available in microform: McA (1972-1974). Published by
    Canadian Broadcasting Corporation, Societe Radio Canada, Winnipeg,
    Manitoba, Canada. Community newsletter.

    WHi   Nov, 1972-Feb, 1973   Pam 74-329

    WHi   May-Dec, 1974   Microforms

    WEU   May-Dec, 1974   Microforms

    AzNCC   May-Dec, 1974   Microfilm

    NjP   [Oct, 1970-May, 1974]   Periodicals

    OkU   [Aug, 1972-Feb, 1975]   WHC

    CaOPeT   Oct, 1970-Dec, 1973, May-Dec, 1974   Microfilm

821 <u>Outlook</u>. 1967?//. Monthly. Last issue 7 pages. Available in
    microform: WHi-A, Veda Stone Papers, (1967). Published by Federation

of Saskatchewan Indians, Regina, Saskatchewan, Canada. Community
newsletter.

WHi	Sept, 1967	Microforms
WEU ARC	Sept, 1967	Micro 11
NjP	Nov, 1967	Periodicals

822 O-Wai-Ya-Wa Newsletter. 1973-1977?//. Unknown. Last issue 10 pages,
    height 28 cm. Line drawings. Available in microform: WHi (1973,
    1974). Chicago, IL. Elementary school newsletter.

WHi	Aug?, 1973, Mar, 1974	Microforms
NjP	Nov, 1974, Feb, 1975, Dec, 1977	Periodicals

823 O'yaka Native Americans Newsletter. 1976-?//. Bi-weekly during
    school year. Last issue 6 pages, height 28 cm. Line drawings.
    Available in microform: WHi (1977). Published by Office of Indian
    Studies, University of North Dakota, Grand Forks, ND. College
    newsletter.

WHi	v.2, n.1-2; Oct 12-26. 1977	Microforms
AzNCC	v.3; Mar, 1978-?	Indian File

824 Oyate-Anishinabe News. 1982? Unknown. Lynda Yellow Bird-Ament,
    editor, Oyate-Anishinabe News, 104 Jones Hall, 27 Pleasant S.E.,
    Minneapolis, MN 55455. (612) 376-4829. Last issue 16 pages, height
    28 cm. Line drawings, photographs. Published by American Indian
    Student Cultural Center, University of Minnesota. College newsletter.
    Subject focus: local and national news, rights, legislation, health,
    women's rights, poetry.

ICN	Current issues	CHAI

825 Pacific Northwest Indian Center News. 1969-?//. Unknown. Last issue
    4 pages, height 31 cm. Photographs. Published by Friends of Indian
    Center, Spokane, WA. Subject focus: urban community, center news.

CaACG	v.1, n.1; Feb, 1969	Periodicals

826 The Padre's Trail. 1937. Quarterly. $2. for individuals and
    institutions.   John Mittelstadt, editor, The Padre's Trail, St.
    Michaels, AZ 86511. (602) 871-4171. ISSN 0030-9222. LC sn77-5155.
    OCLC 4101719, 7618602. RLIN OHCP4101719-S, NYPG754363047-S. Last
    issue 20 pages. Line drawings, photographs. Available in microform:
    McA (1938-). Published by Franciscan Fathers. Title varies:
    Traveling the Padre's Trail, Sept, 1938-Sept, 1945. Frequency varies:
    monthly, Sept, 1938-Jan, 1975. Editors: Martan Rademaker, Feb/Mar,
    1975-June/July. 1978. Subject focus: missions, Catholic Church,
    Navajo people.

    WHi   [v.1, n.1]-   Microforms
               Sept, 1938-

    WEU   v.33, n.3-8;   Journalism
               Nov, 1970-Apr, 1971   Lab

    WMM   [v.2, n.?-v.38, n.3]   Special
               [May, 1939-Dec, 1977/Jan, 1976]   Collections

    AzNCC   v.35-   Microfilm
               1973-

    NjP   [v.1, n.1-v.32]   Periodicals
               [Sept, 1938-Jan, 1970]

    NN   v.9?-v.33;   HBA
               Jan, 1946-July, 1971

    NmG   v.30-   Periodicals
               June, 1968-

    SdU   v.35, n.4?-v.38;   Microfilm
               Jan, 1973-Jan, 1975

    CaOPeT   v.35, n.4?-   Microfilm
               Jan, 1973-

    Other holding institutions: AzFU (AZN), CLU (CLU), [University of
    Minnesota Union List, Minneapolis, MN] (MUL), [Western Nevada
    Community College, Carson City, NV], OKTU (OKT).

827 The Paiute Indian Tribe of Utah Newsletter. 1980. Monthly. Celeste
    Denton, editor, 600 North 100 East, Cedar City, UT 84720. (801)
    586-1111. Last issue 5 pages, height 28 cm. Line drawings.
    Community newsletter. Subject focus: Paiute people.

    USUSC   Sept 17, 1980-   Periodicals

828 Papago Bulletin. 1964-1965?//? Monthly. Last issue 8 pages, height
    28 cm. Line drawings, photographs, commercial advertising. Published

by Papago Federal Credit Union, Sells, AZ. Editor: Carl Mattias.
Community newsletter. Subject focus: Papago people.

AzU   v.1, n.1-v.2, n.9;   I9791/P21/
            Mar, 1964-Dec, 1965   P2128

829 Papago Indian News. 1954-1968?//. Monthly. Last issue 13 pages,
     last volume 156 pages, height 36 cm. Line drawings, commercial
     advertising. Published by Papago Indian Agency, Sells, AZ. Community
     newsletter. Subject focus: Papago people.

     AzHC   v.8-v.15;   Periodicals
                 Dec, 1962-Feb, 1967

     AzU   v.1, n.1-v.16?;   I9791/P21/
                 May, 1954-May, 1968   P212

     CLSM   v.7, n.6;   Periodicals
                 Oct, 1960

     NN   [v.5, n.2-v.15, n.12]   HBA
                 [July, 1958-Apr, 1968]

830 The Papago News. 1973//? Monthly. Last issue 8 pages, height 44 cm.
     Line drawings, photographs, Commercial advertising. Sells, Az.
     Community newsletter. Subject focus: Papago people.

     AzU   v.1, n.1;   I9791/P21/
                 Sept, 1973   P2128

831 Papago Newsletter. 1953-1954//. Monthly. Last issue 10 pages,
     height 27 cm. Published by Papago Indian Agency, Sells, AZ.
     Community newsletter. Subject focus: Papago people.

     AzU   v.1, n.1-4;   I9791/P21/
                 Dec, 1953-June, 1954   P213

832 The Papago Runner. 1977. Monthly. $7. for individuals and
     institutions. Stanley G. Throssell, editor, The Papago Runner, P.O.
     Box 773, Sells, AZ 85634. (602) 383-2221. OCLC 6513983. AZPG3017-S.
     Last issue 8 pages. Last volume 90 pages, height 44 cm. Line
     drawings, photographs, commercial advertising. Community newsletter.
     Subject focus: Papago people.

     WHi   v.3, n.6, 9-   Circulation
                 Apr 25, July 12, 1979-

Az   [v.3, n.10–v.5, n.9], v.6, n.1–   Periodicals
          [1979–1981], 1982–

AzT   Current two months   Periodicals

AzTeS   v.3–   XRP 1.3/R85
          1979–

AzU   v.1, n.1–   I9791/P21
          Sept, 1976–   P215

MtBBCC   v.4;   Periodicals
          Aug–Oct, 1980

Other holding institutions: [U.S. Dept. of the Interior, Western
Archaeological Center, Tuscon, AZ] (UDZ).

833 The Papoose. 1902–1903?//. Monthly. OCLC 8419422. RLIN
    CUBG1283676x–S. Last issue 30 pages. Line drawings, photographs.
    Available in microform: CPC (1902–1903). Published by Hyde Exploring
    Expedition, New York, NY. Editor: Thomas F. Barnes. Subject focus:
    ethnology, arts and crafts, archaeology.

    WHi   v.1, n.1–9;   Microforms
              Dec, 1902–Aug, 1903

    Other holding institutions: PPiU (PIT).

834 The Pathfinder. 1981? Unknown. Barbara Dickerson, editor, The
    Pathfinder, 5908 Columbia Pike, Falls Church, VA 22041. Last issue 4
    pages, height 28 cm. Line drawings, photographs. Published by
    American Indian Heritage Foundation. Title varies: Walk In Beauty,
    Fall–Dec, 1981. Previous editor: Rob Huberman, Fall, 1981. Subject
    focus: Christian religion.

    WHi   Fall, 1981–   Circulation

835 Pa–zo–o'. 1979. Semi–annual. Pat Lyons, editor, Pa–zo–o', P.O. Box
    1296, Bishop, CA 93514. (714) 873–8461. Last issue 14 pages, height
    28 cm. Line drawings, photographs. Published by Toiyabe Indian
    Health Project. Frequency varies: quarterly, Summer?, 1979–Summer?,
    1981. Subject focus: health, safety, aging, nutrition, gardening.

    WHi   v.1, n.3–   Circulation
              Summer?, 1979–

836 The Pee Posh News. 1965–1967?// Unknown. Last issue 8 pages, height
    28 cm. Line drawings, photographs. Available in microform: WHi

(1966, 1967). Laveen, AZ. Community newsletter. Subject focus: Maricopa people.

WHi	v. 2, n.20, ?; Sept 9, 1966, Feb 17, 1967	Microforms

837 The Pemmican Journal. 1981. Quarterly. $10. for individuals and institutions. Corinne Courchene, editor, The Pemmican Journal, 34 Carlton St., Winnipeg, Manitoba, Canada R3C 1N9. (204) 942-0926. ISSN 0710-3670. LC cn82-30355. OCLC 8499616. Last issue 4 pages, height 28 cm. Line drawings, photographs, commercial advertising. Published by Pemmican Publications, Inc. Previous editors: Dorine Thomas, Autumn, 1981; Jim Compton, Winter, 1981-Spring, 1982. Subject focus: history, photography, culture, poetry, book reviews, Metis people.

WHi	Autumn, 1981-	Circulation
CaACG	Autumn, 1981-	Periodicals
CaOONL	Autumn, 1981-	Periodicals
CaOPeT	Autumn, 1981-	E78/C2P36

838 People and progress. 1974-1976//? Quarterly. Last issue 17 pages. Line drawings, photographs. Available in microform: AkUF (1974-1976). Published by Sealaska Corporation, Juneau, AK. Subject focus: corporate and financial news.

WHi	Oct/Nov, 1974-Apr/June, 1976	Microforms
AkUF	Oct/Nov, 1974-Apr/June, 1976	Microfiche

839 Petaubun, Peep of Day. 1861-1866?//. Monthly. Last issue 4 pages. Available in microform: Microfilm Recording Co., (1862). Subject focus: missions, Christian religion. In Chippewa, 80-100%.

CaMWU	v.2, n.2, 7; Mar, Aug, 1862	Microfilm
CaOONL	v.2, n.2. 7; Mar, Aug, 1862	Newspaper

Peuple Oublic. Ottawa, Ontario, Canada.

see Forgotten People/Peuple Oublic. Ottawa, Ontario, Canada

840 <u>Phoenix Indian Center</u>. 1977. Monthly. Phoenix Indian Center, 3302
    N. 7th. St., Phoenix, AZ 85014-5481. (602) 279-4116. Last issue 6
    pages, height 28 cm. Line drawings, photographs. Subject focus:
    urban community, center news.

    WHi   v.6, n.2-   Circulation
               May, 1982-

    Other holding institutions: [Phoenix Indian Center, Phoenix, AZ].

    <u>The Phoenix Redskin</u>. Phoenix, AZ

       see <u>The Redskin</u>. Phoenix, AZ

841 <u>Piegan Storyteller</u>. 1976. Quarterly. $7.50 for individuals and
    institutions. David C. Andrews, editor, The Piegan Storyteller, Box
    53, Andes, NY 13731. ISSN 0195-5799. LC 79-644191. OCLC 3370212.
    Last issue 24 pages, height 28 cm. Line drawings, photographs.
    Available in microform: WHi (1976-). Published by James Willard
    Schulz Society. Subject focus: history, culture, legends.

    WHi   v.1, n.1-   Microforms
               Jan, 1976-

    CaACG   v.1, n.1-   Periodicals
               Jan, 1976-

    Other holding institutions: DLC (DLC), [University of Minnesota Union
    List, Minneapolis, MN] (MUL).

842 <u>Pierre Indian Learning Center</u>. 1978?-?//. Unknown. OCLC 6221125.
    Last issue 20 pages, height 28 cm. Line drawings. Pierre, SD.
    School newsletter.

    WMUW   Jan, 1978   (SPL)
                                                      E/75/P54x

843 <u>The Pima/Maricopa Echo</u>. 1971. Monthly.   The Pima-Maricopa Echo,
    P.O. Box 185, Sacaton, AZ 85247. Last issue 8 pages, last volume 96
    pages, height 37 cm. Line drawings, photographs. Community
    newsletter. Subject focus: Pima and Maricopa people.

    WHi   v.3, n.8, v.4. n.16-v.9, n,10/11; n.1-   Microforms
               Nov, 1973, June, 1976-Oct/Nov, 1981,
               May/June, 1982-

    WMUW   v.6, n.?;   (SPL)
               Apr, 1978   E/75/P55x

Az   [v.1, n.3-v.9, n.10/11], n.1-   Periodicals
            [May, 1971-Oct/Nov, 1981], May, 1982-

AzNCC   v.1, n.8-   Indian File
            Dec, 1972-

AzTeS   v.4-v.9;   XRG 1.3/N38
            1976-1981

NHu   v.1, n.8-v.3, n.8   Periodicals
            Dec, 1972-Jan, 1976

Other holding institutions: [Bacone College, Muskogee, OK].

844 Pine Ridge Village News. 1976?//. Unknown. Last issue 4 pages,
    height 28 cm. Pine Ridge, SD. Community newsletter.

    WMM   Aug, 1976   Special
                                                         Collections

845 Pipeline. 1970-1975?//. Irregular. Last issue 4 pages, height 28
    cm. Photographs. Published by Department of Housing and Urban
    Development and Indian Nations Council of Governments, Tulsa, OK.
    Subject focus: social services, housing.

    OkTU   v.1, n.1-v.11, n.4;   Rare Book
                Dec, 1970-Mar, 1975

846 Point Arrow. 1969?-?//. Weekly. Last issue 8 pages. Line drawings,
    photographs. Available in microform: WHi-A, Veda Stone Papers, (1970,
    1971). Published by Upward Bound, University of Wisconsin-Stevens
    Point, Stevens Point, WI. Editors: Gail Rave and Elmer Tutor, Summer,
    1969; Gail Rave, July 1-25, 1970; Rita Cleveland, July 29, 1971; Nancy
    Cook, Aug 5?, 1971. Subject focus: organization news, education,
    history, culture, poetry.

    WHi   Summer, 1969, July 1-25,   Microforms
                1970, July 29-Aug 5?, 1971

    WEU   Summer, 1969, July 1-25,   Micro 11
    ARC   1970, July 29-Aug 5?, 1971

847 Powhatan Newsletter. 1981. Bi-monthly. Powhatan Newsletter, Box
    323A, Route 70 RD 1, Medford, NJ 08055. (609) 654-1300. Last issue 4
    pages, height 28 cm. Line drawings. Community newsletter. Subject
    focus: Powhatan Renape people.

WHi   v.1, n.3-   Circulation
           Oct?, 1981-

848 Powwow Trails. 1964-1970?//. Monthly. ISSN 0048-5055. LC
    79-640014. OCLC 4525414. RLIN DCLC79640014-S, CUBG10952500-S,
    OHCP4525414-S, NYPG764225263-S. Last issue 20 pages. Line drawings,
    photographs, commercial advertising. Available in microform: McA
    (1964-1970). South Plainfield, NJ. Place of publication varies:
    Somerset, NJ, Apr, 1964-Feb, 1967. Editors: William K. Powers, Apr,
    1964-Feb, 1967; Lawrence E. Morgan, Apr, 1967. Subject focus:
    culture, arts and crafts, ceremonies, book reviews.

    WHi   v.1, n.1-v.7, n.1;   Microforms
               Apr, 1964-Apr, 1970

    AzFM   v.1-v.6;   570.6/P88p
               1964-1969

    AzFM   v.1-v.7;   Periodicals
               1964-1970

    NjP   [v.1, n.6-v.5, n.10]   Periodicals
               [Nov, 1964-Mar, 1969

    NN   v.1, n.1-v.6, n.4;   HBA
               Apr, 1964-Sept, 1969

    OkU   v.1, n.1-v.7, n.1;   WHC
               Apr, 1964-Apr, 1970

    Other holding institutions: DLC (DLC), [University of Minnesota Union
    List, Minneapolis, MN] (MUL), [Western Nevada Community College,
    Carson City, NV].

849 Prairie Call. 1961?-?//. Irregular. Last issue 16 pages, height 28
    cm. Line drawings. Published by Indian and Metis Friendship Centre,
    Winnipeg, Manitoba, Canada. Editors: Norma Sluman, June/July, 1964;
    A.J. Favel, Aug/Sept/Oct, 1964; Norma Sluman and A.J. Favel, Nov/Dec,
    1964; Norma Sluman and Marie Baker, Jan, 1965; Norma Sluman, Mar/Apr,
    1965; Marie Baker, May/June, 1965; Dorothy Roy, June, 1966; Don Smith
    and Darlene Moar, July, 1966; Louise La Fremiere and Ken Young,
    Aug-Nov, 1966; Louise La Fremiere, Jan-Oct, 1967. Subject focus:
    urban community, centre news.

    NjP   v.8;   Periodicals
               Mar, 1968

    CaACG   [v.3, n.1-v.8]   Periodicals
               [1963-Mar, 1968]

    CaOORD   [v.3-v.8]   Periodicals
               [Mar 24, 1963-Mar, 1968]

Private Property. Sacramento, CA

   see The Stealing of California. Sacramento, CA

850 Project Media Bulletin. 1973?-1978?//. Unknown. Last issue 10
    pages, height 22 cm. Line drawings. Available in microfilm: WHi
    (1973-1978). Published by National Indian Education Association,
    Minneapolis, MN. Editor: Naomi Lyons, June, 1978. Subject focus:
    Native American studies, bibliography, library services.

    WHi   Nov, 1973-Feb, 1974, June, 1978   Microforms

    OkU   Mar, 1977   WHC

851 Project North Newsletter. 1975. Monthly, irregular. Project North
    Newsletter, 80 Sackville St, Toronto, Ontario, Canada M5A 3E5. Last
    issue 8 pages, height 44 cm. Photographs. Subject focus: Christian
    Churches, poetry.

    CaOSuU   v.5-   Periodicals
               1980-

852 Pueblo Horizons. 1977. Unknown. Jeff Gardner, editor, Pueblo
    Horizons, 2401 Twelfth St. NW, Albuquerque, NM 87102. (505) 843-7270.
    Last issue 4 pages, height 28 cm. Line drawings. Published by
    Friends of the Indian Pueblo Culture Center, Inc. Subject focus:
    Pueblo people, center news, culture.

    WHi   [v.5, n.4-12], v.6, n.3-   Circulation
               [June, 1981-Feb], May, 1982-

    AzHM   v.3-   Periodicals
               1979-

853 Pueblo News. 1973. Monthly. $5. for individuals and institutions.
    Stan Zuni, editor, Pueblo News, P.O. Box 6507, Albuquerque, NM 87197.
    (505) 247-0371. OCLC 3602781. Last issue 16 pages, last volume 160
    pages, height 40 cm. Line drawings, photographs, commercial
    advertising. Available in microform: WHi (1976, 1979-). Published by
    All Indian Pueblo Council, Inc. Title Varies: 19 Pueblos News,
    Aug-Sept, 1976. Previous editor: Michael J. Hartranft, June,
    1979-Feb, 1982. Subject focus: rights, legislation, council reports,
    government programs, Taos, Santa Ana, Laguna, Tesuque, Sandia,
    Pojoaque, San Juan, Cochiti, Zuni, Jemez, San Felipe, Isleta. Picuris,
    Nambe, Acoma, Lia, Santo Domingo, Santa Clara and San Ildefonso
    Pueblos.

WHi	v.4, n.8-9, v.7, n.6, 11- Aug-Sept, 1976, June, Nov, 1979-	Microforms
WMUW	v.4, n.8-9; Aug-Sept, 1976	(SPL) E/75/N53x
AzHM	v.10, n.4-5, 7- Apr-May, July, 1982-	Periodicals
AzNCC	v.3- Mar, 1974-	Indian File
CL	v.8, n.5- May, 1980-	Periodicals
ICN	Current issues	CHAI
NmG	v.6, n.4- Apr, 1978-	Periodicals
NmScW	Current month	Periodicals
OkTU	v.6, n.11- Nov, 1978-	Rare Book Room

Other holding institutions: AzFM, DSI (SMI), KsteC (KKQ), NmU (IQR), NmLcU (IRU), [Bacone College, Muskogee, OK].

QDNR&ED Newsletter. Taholah, WA

    see Quinault Resources. Taholah, WA

854 Qua' Toqti/The Eagle's Cry. 1973. Weekly. $17. for individuals and institutions. Abbott Sekaquaptewa, editor, Qua' Toqti/The Eagle's Cry, P.O. Box 266, Oraibi, AZ 86039. (602) 734-2425. OCLC 4930195. Last issue 6 pages, height 57 cm. Line drawings, photographs, commercial advertising. Available in microform: WHi (1974-). Community newsletter. Subject focus: Hopi people.

WHi	v.1, n.35- Mar 21, 1974-	Microforms
WMUW	[v.1, n.44-v.3, n.49]; [May, 1974-July, 1976]	(SPL) E/75/Q3x
Az	v.1, n.1- July 19, 1973-	Periodicals
AzFM	v.1- 1974-	570.6/Q1

AzHM	v.5, n.4– 1979–	Periodicals
AzNCC	v.1– 1974–	Indian File
AzPh	Current year only	Periodicals
AzU	[v.1–v.5, n.36] [1973–Mar, 1980]	I9791/H7/E11
MnBemT	[v.3], v.4?– [1976–1977], 1978–	Periodicals
NjP	[v.1, n.1–v.4, n.36] [July 19, 1973–Apr 12, 1979]	Periodicals
NmScW	v.1–v.4; 1974–1977	Periodicals
OkTU	v.4, n.123– Jan 11, 1977–	Rare Book Room
USUSC	[v.3–v.5] [Apr 3, 1975–Mar 26, 1981]	Special Collections

Other holding institutions: [University of Minnesota Union List,
Minneapolis, MN] (MUL).

855 Quarter Moon. 1980–1981//. Quarterly. Last issue 4 pages, height 28
cm. Line drawings, photographs. Available in microform: WHi
(1980–1981). Published by Daybreak Star Press, Seattle, WA. Subject
focus: arts and crafts, games, children's periodicals

WHi	v.1, n.1–4; Fall, 1980–Summer, 1981	Microforms

The Quarterly Journal of the Society of American Indians.
            Washington, DC

  see American Indian Magazine. Washington, DC

856 Quarterly of the Southwestern Association on Indian Affairs. 1964.
Quarterly. John R. Bott, editor, Quarterly of the Southwestern
Association on Indian Affairs, P.O. Box 1964, Santa Fe, NM 87501.
(505) 983–5220. OCLC 5663052. Last issue 16 pages, last volume 56
pages, height 22 cm. Line drawings, photographs. Subject focus: arts
and crafts, culture, education, organization news.

WHi	v.14, n.1– Spring, 1979–	Circulation
AzFM	v.1–v.6, v.8– 1964–1969, 1971–	570.6/S23q
AzNCC	v.8– Summer, 1977–	Indian File
AzU	[v.1, n.1–v.12, n.2] [1964–1977]	I9791/S728
CLSM	[v.1, n.1–v.10, n.3], v.11– [1964–1975], 1976–	Periodicals
NHu	[v.3, n.1–v.13, n.4] [1966–1978]	Periodicals
NmG	v.6–v.7? Sept, 1970–Mar, 1972	Periodicals
OkTU	v.14, n.2– Summer, 1979–	Rare Book Room

Other holding institutions: AzFU (AZN).

857 Quin 'A Month 'A. 1972. Irregular. Quin 'A Month 'A, Box 300, Route
1, Bowler, WI 54416. (715) 793-4270. Last issue 24 pages, last
volume 54 pages, height 28 cm. Line drawings. Personal names indexed
in: Index to Wisconsin Native American Periodicals (1972–1981).
Available in microform: WHi (1972–). Published by Stockbridge-Munsee
Library Museum. Subject focus: library and museum news, Stockbridge,
Munsee people.

WHi	v.1, n.1– Apr, 1972–	Microforms
WMUW	v.6, n.4?–v.9, n.1; June, 1977–Mar, 1980	(SPL) E/75/Q5x
NjP	[v.1, n.1–v.8, n.2] [Apr, 1972–July, 1979]	Periodicals

858 Quinault Resources. 1978. Monthly. Jacqueline Storm, editor
Quinault Resources, Box 189, Taholah, WA 98587. (206) 276-8211. OCLC
6082816, 7136894. Last issue 28 pages, height 28 cm. Line drawings,
photographs. Published by Quinault Department of Natural Resources
and Economic Development. Title varies: QDNR&ED Newsletter, Dec,
1980–Feb, 1982. Subject focus: environment, ecology, forestry,
fishing industry, community development.

WHi	v.3, n.11, v.4, n.4, 7– Dec, 1980, June, Oct/Dec, 1981–	Circulation
IdU	v.5, n.2; Mar/Apr, 1982	E/99/Q6/A2
ICN	Current issues	CHAI

Other holding institutions: WAChenE (WEA), WaS.

859 <u>The Race of Sorrows</u>. 1956-1971?//. Quarterly. Last issue 4 pages, height 28 cm. Photographs. Published by St. Labre Indian Mission, Ashland, MT. Editor: Father Emmett. Subject focus: missions, Catholic Church, Northern Cheyenne people, book reviews.

WHi	v.17, n.4; Dec, 1971	Pam 72-3056
WEU	[v.15, n.4–v.17, n.1]; [Dec, 1969–Mar, 1971]	Journalism Lab
WMM	[v.4, n.2–v.17, n.2] [June, 1959–June, 1971]	Special Collections
NjP	[v.2, n.1–v.15, n.4] Jan, 1957–Dec, 1969]	Periodicals
OkU	[v.1, n.1–v.17, n.4] [Oct, 1956–Dec, 1971]	WHC
WyCWC	[v.1, n.1–v.17, n.4] [Oct, 1956–Dec, 1971]	Periodicals
CaOPeT	v.1–v.17; 1956-1971	Microfilm

Other holding institutions: [Western Nevada Community College, Carson City, NV].

860 <u>Rainbow People</u>. 1971//. Irregular. OCLC 1642322. RLIN OHCP1642322-S, CSUP05067807-S. Last issue 16 pages. Line drawings, photographs. Available in microform: WHi (1971). John Day, OR. Community newsletter. Includes reprints of articles from other Native American newsletters.

| WHi | v.1, n.1-5;
Jan-May, 1971 | Microforms |
| WEU | v.1, n.1-4
Jan-Apr, 1971 | Journalism
Lab |

AzNCC   v.1, n.1-4   Indian File
           Jan-Apr, 1971   Lab

CL   v.1, n.1-5;   Periodicals
           Jan-May, 1971

CU-A   v.1, n.1-5;   E/A1/R2
           Jan-May, 1971

PPT   v.1, n.1-5;   Contemporary
           Jan-May., 1971   Culture

Other holding institutions: MiU (EYM), [University of Minnesota Union
List, Minneapolis, MN] (MUL), PPiU (PIT).

861 Ramona Days. 1887-1888//. Quarterly. OCLC 1717564. RLIN
    OHCP1717564-S. Last issue 38 pages, height 23 cm. Line drawings,
    photographs. Published by Indian Department, University of New
    Mexico, Santa Fe, NM. Editor: Rev. Horatio O. Ladd. Subject focus:
    New Mexico Native people.

MWA   v.1, n.4-v.2, n.3;   Periodicals
           Jan-Oct, 1888

OkU   v.2, n.1;   WHC
           Apr, 1888

Other holding institutions: [Minnesota Union List of Serials,
Minneapolis, MN] (MUL), NmPE (IPU).

862 Rankin Times. 1973-1976?//. Weekly. ISSN 0702-746x. LC cn77-32321.
    OCLC 3409551. Last issue 20 pages, height 36 cm. Line drawings,
    commerical advertising. Rankin Inlet, Northwest Territories, Canada.
    Community newsletter. Subject focus: Inuit people. In Inuit, 50%.

CaOONL   [Oct 5, 1973-Mar 22, 1976]   Newspaper
                                               Section

863 The Raven Speaks. 1968-1972?//. Monthly. RLIN NYPG804580620-S.
    Last issue 4 pages, last volume 48 pages. Line drawings. Available
    in microform: WHi-A, Veda Stone Papers, (1970-1972). Published by
    Raven Hail, Dallas, TX. Subject focus: history, legends, culture,
    Christian religion, Cherokee people. Some issues contain some
    Cherokee.

WHi   v.1, n.1-v.4, n.12;   Pam 73-1415
           Apr 7, 1968-Mar 7, 1972

WHi	[v.2, n.8-v.4, n.12]; [Nov 7, 1970-Mar 7, 1972]	Microforms
WEU	v.1, n.1-v.4, n.12; Apr 7, 1968-Mar 7, 1972	Journalism Lab
WEU ARC	[v.2, n.8-v.4, n.12] [Nov 7, 1970-Mar 7, 1972]	Micro 11
AzNCC	v.2-v.4, n.12; Apr, 1969-Mar 7, 1972	Indian File
NjP	v.1, n.1-v.4, n.12; Apr 7, 1968-Mar 7, 1972	Periodicals
NN	v.1, n.1-v.4,n.12; Apr 7, 1968-Mar 7, 1972	HBA 80-739
OkU	v.1, n.1-v.4, n.12; Apr 7, 1968-Mar 7, 1972	WHC
CaOPeT	v.1, n.1-v.4, n.12; Apr 7, 1968-Mar 7, 1972	Microfilm

864 <u>Rawhide Press</u>. 1958. Monthly. Mary L. Wynne, editor, Rawhide Press,
Box 393, Wallpinit, WA 99040. (509) 258-7320. ISSN 0300-6328. OCLC
1333059, 6169107. RLIN OHCP1333059-S. Last issue 16 pages. Line
drawings, photographs. Available in microform: McA (1958-).
Published by Spokane Tribal Council. Frequency varies: irregular,
Apr, 1958-Feb, 1972. Previous editors: Barbara Reutlinger, June,
1972-Nov, 1977; Bob May, Dec, 1977-Aug, 1978; Barbara Reutlinger, Dec,
1978-Nov, 1981. Community newsletter.

WHi	[v.1, n.1]- Apr, 1958-	Microforms
WMUW	[v.5, n.3-v.8, n.3] [July, 1974-Feb, 1977]	(SPL) E/75/R32x
AzNCC	v.8- Nov, 1977-	Indian File
IdU	[v.8, n.10-v.11, n.8], n.10- [Sept 16, 1977-July], Sept, 1980-	Folio E/75/S7
NjP	[v.3, n.4-v.10, n.8] [July, 1972-July, 1979]	Periodicals
OkTU	v.10, n.2- Jan, 1979-	Rare Book Room
WHi	[v.1, n.1-v.9, n.3] [Apr, 1958-June, 1978]	WHC

Wa   v.3, n.4-   NW
            July, 1972-

CaOPeT   v.3, n.10-   Microfilm
            Jan, 1973-

Other holding institutions: DLC (NSD), [University of Minnesota Union
List, Minneapolis, MN] (MUL), [Western Nevada Community College,
Carson City, NV], WaChenE (WEA).

865 Re-America (Restore America). 1939-?//. Irregular. OCLC 6578133.
    Last issue 14 pages, height 28 cm. Line drawings, photographs,
    commercial advertising. Minneapolis, MN. Editor: IKTOmi. Subject
    focus: satire.

WHi   n.1-5;   F801/7R288
            Autumn, 1939-Summer?, 1940   Cutter

ICN   n.1-6;   Ayer/1/R288
            Autumn, 1939-Fall, 1941

Other holding institutions: MnHi (MHS).

866 Recherches Amerindiennes au Quebec. 1971. 4 times a year. $17. for
    individuals, $24. for institutions, $14.50 for students. Recherches
    Amerindiennes au Quebec, 4050 Rue Berri, Montreal, Quebec, Canada H2L
    4H3. (514) 849-9704. ISSN 0318-4137. LC cn75-34413. cn76-308875.
    OCLC 1869167, 2442005. RLIN DCLCCN7534413-S, DCLCCN76308875-S,
    CSUP27409-S, OHCP2442005-S, OHCP1869167-S, CSUG9411925-S. Last issue
    80 pages, last volume 378 pages, height 28 cm. Line drawings,
    photographs. Subject focus: art, culture, anthropology, history. In
    French, 100%, (with English abstracts).

WHi   v.1, n.1-   E/78/Q3/R4
            1971-

Wau   v.4, n.2-   E/78/S63S642
            Apr, 1974-

CaAEU   v.1, n.1-   Boreal
            1971-   Institute

CaMWU   v.1, n.4/5-   970/R2434/Am
            1971-

CaOONL   v.1-   Periodicals
            1971-

CaOOP   v.1-   E/78/Q3/R42
            1971-

CaOPeT   v.1, n.1-   E77/R4
           1971-

Other holding institutions: AzTeS (AZS), InU (IUL), MH (HUL), MiMtpT
(EZC), [University of Minnesota Union List, Minneapolis, MN] (MUL),
NcU (NOC), NhD (DRB), NIC (COO), [New york State Union List, Albany,
NY] (NYS), OKTU (OKT).

867 Recontre. 1979. Quarterly. Free to individuals and institutions.
    Marcel Gilbert, editor, SAGMAI 875, Grand-Allee est, Quebec (City),
    Quebec, Canada G1R 4Y8. (418) 643-3166. ISSN 0709-9487. LC
    cn80-80545. OCLC 6174003. Height 30 cm. Line drawings, photographs,
    some in color. Published by Gouvernement du Quebec, Ministere du
    Conseil executif. Subject focus: Amerindian and Inuit peoples. In
    French, 100%.

    CaAEU   v.1, n.1-   Boreal
               Oct, 1979-   Institute

    Other holding institutions: CaOONL (NLC).

868 Red Alert. 1977? Unknown. La Donna Harris, editor, Red Alert, 600
    2nd St., NW, Suite 808, Albuquerque, NM 87102. Last issue 37 pages,
    height 28 cm. Published by Americans for Indian Opportunity. Subject
    focus: politics, environment, health, natural resource development.

    AzHM   1980-   Periodicals

    AzNCC   Dec 21, 1977-   Indian File

    ICN   Current issues   CHAI

869 Red Cliff Newsletter. 1974?. Monthly. $2.50 for individuals and
    institutions. Red Cliff Newsletter, P.O. Box 529, Bayfield, WI
    54814-0529. (715) 779-5805. OCLC 6221130. Last issue 16 pages, last
    volume 196 pages, height 28 cm. Personal names indexed in: Index to
    Wisconsin Native American Periodicals (1974-1977, 1979-1981).
    Available in microform: WHi (1974-1977, 1979-). Community newsletter.
    Subject focus: Chippewa people.

    WHi   [Sept, 1974-Apr?, 1977], Sept, 1979-   Microforms

    WMUW   [Sept, 1974-Apr?, 1977]   (SPL)
                                                                E/75/R37x

    Other holding institutions: [University of Wisconsin-Stevens
    Point-Native American Center, Stevens Point, WI].

870 Red Cloud Country. 1963. Quarterly. $3. for individuals and
    institutions. Red Cloud Country, Pine Ridge, SD 57770. (604)
    867-5491. ISSN 0300-6344. LC sn78-4276, sc79-3808. OCLC 1329873.
    RLIN DCLCSC793808-S, OHCP1329873-S. Last issue 4 pages, last volume
    16 pages, height 28 cm. Photographs. Available in microform: McA
    (1973-). Published by Red Cloud Indian School, Holy Rosary Mission.
    School newsletter. Subject focus: Oglala Sioux people.

    WHi   v.10, n.1-   Microforms
                 Jan, 1973-

    WEU   v.7, n.1-v.8, n.1;   Journalism
                 Jan/Feb/Mar, 1970-Jan/Feb/Mar, 1971   Lab

    WMM   [v.1, n.1-v.13, n.1]   Special
                 [Spring, 1964-Jan/Feb/Mar, 1976]   Collections

    WMUW   v.14, n.3-4;   (SPL)
                 July/Aug/Sept-Oct/Nov/Dec, 1977   E/75/R38x

    NjP   [v.1, n.1-v.16, n.2]   Periodicals
                 [Spring, 1964-Apr/May/June, 1979]

    OkU   v.1-v.9;   WHC
                 Nov, 1963-Dec, 1972

    SdU   v.1-v.9;   Microfilm
                 Nov, 1963-Dec, 1972

    CaOPeT   v.1-   Microfilm
                 1963-

    Other holding institutions: DLC (NSD), [University of Minnesota Union
    List, Minneapolis, MN] (MUL), [Western Nevada Community College,
    Carson City, NV].

871 Red Cloud News. 1979?//. Irregular. Last issue 2 pages, height 28
    cm. Published by Red Cloud Indian School, Pine Ridge, SD. High
    school newsletter.

    WMM   v.1, n.1;   Special
                 Apr 19, 1979   Collections

872 Red Current: American Journalism Quarterly. 1978-?//. Quarterly.
    Last issue 20 pages, height 45 cm. Line drawings, photographs,
    commercial advertising. Toppenish, WA. Subject focus: journalism,
    legislation, creative writing.

    WHi   v.1, n.1;   Pam
                 Spring, 1978   Cataloging

| WEU | v.1, n.1;
Spring, 1978 | Journalism
Lab |
| AzNCC | v.1, n.1;
Spring, 1978 | Indian File |

873 The Red Horizon. 1971-?// Unknown. Last issue 4 pages, height 28
cm. Line drawings. Published by Haskell Indian Junior College,
Lawrence, KS. Editor: Gary White. College newsletter.

| KU | v.1, n.1-2;
Jan?-Feb 7, 1971 | Kansas
Collection |

874 Red Lake Reservation News. 1966-1969?//. Unknown. Last issue 5
pages. Available in microform: WHi-A, Veda Stone Papers, (1966).
Published by Red Lake Band of Chippewa Indians Tribal Council, Red
Lake, MN. Community newsletter. Subject focus: Chippewa people.

WHi	v.1, n.12; Oct 28, 1966	Microforms
WEU ARC	v.1, n.12; Oct 28, 1966	Micro 11
AzNCC	v.2-v.7; Dec, 1967-July, 1972	Indian File
MnBemT	v.1-v.3 1966-1969	Periodicals

875 Red Letter. 1974. Monthly. $5. for individuals and institutions.
Red Letter, 4546 N. Hermitage, Chicago, IL 60640. (312) 728-1477.
OCLC 6169144. Last issue 4 pages, height 39 cm. Line drawings,
photographs. Available in microform: WHi (1976-1979, 1981-).
Published by Native American Committee, Inc. Previous editor: Dorene
Porter, Apr-Dec, 1976. Subject focus: urban community, center news.

WHi	[v.1, n.1-v.4, n.3], v.6, n.5, 8- [Apr, 1976-July/Aug, 1979], July, Dec, 1981-	Microforms
WM	Current issues	Forest Home Branch
WMUW	[v.1, n.1-v.4, n.3] [Apr, 1976-July/Aug, 1979]	(SPL) E/75/R43x
AzNCC	v.51- Spring, 1979-	Indian File

IC	v.5, n.1– Mar, 1980–	Periodicals
ICN	Current issues	CHAI
NjP	[no nos.]–v.4 [Aug, 1974–May, 1979]	Periodicals
CaOAFN	v.6, n.6; Aug/Sept, 1981	Periodicals

876 <u>The Red Man</u>. 1909–1917//. 10 times a year. LC 11–24446. OCLC
1640454, 4839674, 5274749, 5275324. RLIN CUBG12818021–S,
CTYG5274749–S, OHCP5274749–S, OHCP4839662–S, OHCP1640454–S. Last
volume 268 pages. Line drawings, photographs. Available in
microform: DLC (1909–1917) Published by U. S. Indian School,
Carlisle, PA. Title varies: The Indian Craftsman, Feb, 1909–Jan,
1910. Editor: M. Friedman, Feb, 1909–Jan, 1914. Subject focus:
re-education, cultural assimilation.

WHi	v.1, n.1–v.9, n.7; Feb, 1909–May/June, 1917	Microforms
WHi	v.4, n.1–v.9, n.7; Sept, 1911–May/June, 1917	E/97/C284
WMM	v.1, n.1–v.9, n.?; Feb, 1909–Oct, 1917	E/976/C2/R3
WMUW	v.1, n.1–v.9, n.7; Feb, 1909–May/June, 1917	MF/E014
WUSP	v.1, n.1–v.9, n.7; Feb, 1909–May/June, 1917	Microfilm
AzNCC	v.1–v.9; 1909–1917	Periodicals
CU–A	v.1–v.9; 1909–1917	E/97.6/C2/ R3
ICN	v.4–v.9; 1911–1917	Ayer 1/R4
OClWHi	[v.2–3] [1910–1911]	Periodicals
MnBemT	v.1–v.9; 1909–1917	Periodicals
MoS	v.1–v.9; Feb, 1909–Oct, 1917	Periodicals

MoSHi   v.4, n.1-v.9, n.6   970.1/R245
            Sept, 1911-1917

N   v.1, n.1-v.9, n.7;   C371.975
            Feb, 1909-May/June, 1917   R31

NN   v.1-v.9;   HBA
            Feb, 1909-Oct, 1917

NPotU   v.1, n.1-v.9;   E/97.6/C2P3
            Feb, 1909-Oct, 1917

NOoneU   v.1, n.1-v.9, n.7;   Microfilm
            Feb, 1909-May/June, 1917

NdMinS   v.1-v.9;   E/97.6/C2/R3
            1909-1917   1971

OCHP   v.5, 7-9;   970.1/R245
            1912-1917

OkU   v.1, n.1-v.9, n.7;   WHC
            Feb, 1909-May/June, 1917

OrU   v.1, n.1-v.6;   Periodicals
            Feb, 1909-June, 1914

PCarlH   v.1, n.1-v.9, n.7;   I/Per/Red4
            Feb, 1909-May/June, 1917

SdU   v.1-v.9;   South
            1909-1917   Dakota Room

Other holding institutions: COU-DA (COA), CtY (YUS), CoD (DPL),
[Indiana Union List of Serials, Indianapolis, IN] (ILS), InU (IUL),
MH-P (HLS), MiKW (EXW), MiDW (EYW), [University of Minnesota Union
list, Minneapolis, MN] (MUL), NcGU (NGU), [New York State Union List,
Albany, NY] (NYS), NFQC (XQM), NSbSU (YSM), NR (YQR), OAkU (AKR), PPi
(CPL), [Pittsburgh Reginal Library Center Union List, Pittsburgh, PA]
(QPR), ScRhW (SWW), [AMIGOS Union List of Serials, Dallas,TX] (IUC).

877 The Red Man and Helper. 1880-1904//. Weekly. Last issue Line
     drawings, photographs. Available in microform: WHi-A, Papers of
     Carlos Montezuma, (1898-1900); OkHi (1884-1885). Published by Indian
     Industrial School, Carlisle, PA. Title varies: Eadle Keatah Toh, Apr,
     1880-Mar, 1882; Morning Star, Apr, 1882-Dec, 1887; The Red Man, Jan
     1888-June, 1900. School newsletter. Frequency varies: monthly, Apr,
     1880-Mar, 1900. Subject focus: education, school news.

     WHi   v.4, n.9, v.5, n.6, v.15, n.2,   Microforms
                 v.16, n.1-2, 23;
                 Apr, 1884, Jan, 1885, Oct/Nov, 1898,
                 Apr-May, Nov 23, 1900

ICN	v.1, n.4-v.2, n.7; July, 1880-Feb, 1882	Ayer Collection
NHu	[v.3, n.3-v.18, n.52] [Nov, 1883-July, 1903]	Periodicals
NN	v.1, n.2-v.19; Mar, 1880-July, 1904	HBA+
OkHi	v.4, n.9, v.5, n.6; Apr, 1884, Jan, 1885	Microforms
PCarlH	[v.1, n.3-v.19] [June, 1880-July, 1904]	I/Per/Red

878 <u>Red Messenger</u>. 1971-?//. Unknown. Last issue 6 pages. Personal names indexed in: Index to Wisconsin Native American Periodicals. Available in microform: WHi-A, Veda Stone Papers, (1971). Published by Wisconsin Indian Youth Council, University of Wisconsin-River Falls, River Falls, WI. School newsletter.

WHi	n.1; Nov 15, 1971	Microforms
WEU ARC	n.1; Nov 15, 1971	Micro 11

879 <u>The Red Messenger News and Notes</u>. 1973-?//. Monthly? Last issue 8 pages. Line drawings. Personal names indexed in: Index to Wisconsin Native American Periodicals. Available in microform: WHi-A, Veda Stone Papers, (1973, 1974). Published by Native American Council, University of Wisconsin-River Falls, River Falls, WI. School newsletter.

WHi	v.1, n.1-2, v.2, n.1; June 28-July 20, 1973, Mar 7, 1974	Microforms
WEU ARC	v.1, n.1-2, v.2, n.1; June 28-July 20, 1973, Mar 7, 1974	Micro 11

880 <u>The Red Times</u>. 1976-1981//. Monthly. OCLC 6169384, 7818713. Last issue 16 pages, height 40 cm. Line drawings, photographs, commercial advertising. Available in microform: WHi (1976-1981). Published by Johnson O'Malley Indian Education Program, New Laguna, NM. Frequency varies: bi-weekly, Dec 10, 1976-Dec 1, 1980. Editors: Caty Stetson, Frank Romero and Louis Abeita, Sept 9-23, 1977; Frank Romero and Louis Abeita, Oct 7-Dec 2, 1977; Frank Romero, Dec 16, 1977-Dec 15, 1978; Linda Day, Jan 26-Feb 23, 1979; Patricia Weatherman, Mar 23-May 1, 1979; Tracy Wright, May 11, 1979-Aug 22, 1980; Meg Desmond, Sept,

1980-Sept 1, 1981. Community newsletter. Subject focus: Acoma and
Laguna Pueblos, includes poetry.

WHi	v.1, n.2-v.7, n.12; Dec 10, 1976-Sept 1, 1981	Microforms
WMUW	[v.1, n.2-v.2, n.12] [Dec 10, 1976-Dec, 1977]	(SPL) E/75/R42x
AzHM	v.1, n.10-v.7; 1976-1981	Periodicals
NjP	[v.2, n.8-v.3, n.23] [Nov 4, 1977-May 25, 1979]	Periodicals

881 Redlake Benedictine. 1955-1959?//. Quarterly. Last issue 6 pages,
height 22 cm. Line drawings, photographs. Published by St. Mary's
Mission, Red Lake, MN. Editor: Rev. Allan Fruth. Subject focus:
missions, Catholic Church, education, Chippewa people.

WMM	[v.1, n.1-v.5, n.14] [Spring, 1955-Dec, 1959]	Special Collections

882 Redlake Neighborhood Center Newsletter. 1969-1981//. Irregular.
Last issue 12 pages, height 36 cm. Line drawings. Available in
microform: WHi (1981). Published by Red Lake Band of Chippewa Indians
Tribal Council, Red Lake, MN. Comununity newsletter. Subject focus:
Chippewa people.

WHi	Jan 30-July 3, 1981	Microforms
AzNNC	1968-July 3, 1981	Indian File
MnBemT	[1974-1977], 1979-July 3, 1981	Periodicals

883 The Redliner. 1980. Monthly? The Redliner, 3902 Executive Ave.,
John Tyler Bldg., Alexandria, VA 22305. (202) 543-3302. Last issue 4
pages, height 28 cm. Published by Indian Information Project. Place
of publication varies: Washington, DC, Sept., 1980. Subject focus:
Native Americans in Eastern States, education, health, labor.

WHi	v.1, n.1- Sept, 1980-	Circulation
AzNCC	v.1, n.1- Sept, 1980-	Indian File
ICN	Current issues	CHAI

Other holding institutions: IC (CGP).

884 The Redskin. 1900. Weekly during school year. The Redskin, P.O. Box
    7188, Phoenix, AZ 85011. (602) 241-2104. OCLC 1779247, 8208328,
    8416749, 8416768. RLIN CUBU1294709X-S, OHCP1779247-S, DCLCSC822107-S.
    Last issue 10 pages, height 26 cm. Line drawings, photographs,
    commercial advertising. Available in microform: DLC (1900-1923); CPC
    (1900-1947). Published by Phoenix Indian School. Title varies: The
    Native American, Jan, 1900-June 6, 1931; The Phoenix Redskin, Aug,
    1931-May 12, 1967. Editors: John B. Brown, Mar 8, 1924-June 6, 1931;
    Letitia Kirk, Sept 26, 1931-June 4, 1932; Juan Carlos, Oct 15,
    1932-May 13, 1933; Clarence Norris, Nov 4, 1933; Adam Hall, Oct 13,
    1934-June, 1936; Bert Walker, Sept 22, 1936-May 11, 1937; Willetto
    Antonio, Oct 1, 1937-May 15, 1938; Thurman Spangle, Dec 31, 1939-June
    1, 1940. School newsletter. Subject focus: education, legislation.

WHi	v.5, n.14-45 Apr 9-Dec, 24, 1904	E/75/N4
WHi	[v.1, n.1-v.66, n.15], v.80, n.2- [Jan, 1900-Oct 24, 1947], Dec 15, 1980-	Microforms
AzHC	v.30-v.43; Jan, 1930-May, 1943	Periodicals
AzNCC	v.69- 1970-	Indian File
CLSM	[v.1, n.14-v.61, n.5] [1900-1961]	Periodicals
ICN	[v.17-v.27] [Jan 8, 1916-1927]	Ayer Collection
NHu	[v.22, n.7-v.31, n.12] [Mar, 1921-June, 1931]	Periodicals
NN	v.3-v.51, n.16; Sept, 1902-May, 1953	SSR
SdU	v.1, n.1-v.31; Jan, 1900-June 16, 1931	Microforms
CaOPeT	[v.1-v.31, n.12] [1900-June, 1931]	Periodicals

Other holding institutions: AzTeS (AZS), CLU (CLU), [University of
Minnesota Union List, Minneapolis, MN] (MUL), PPiU (PIT).

885 The Redskin. 1966-1979//. Quarterly. ISSN 0034-2157. LC sc76-37,
    80-649887. OCLC 1869147. RLIN DCLC80649887-S, CUBG10997908-S.
    MIUG03195-S, OHCP1869147-S. Last issue 40 pages, last volume 160
    pages, height 27 cm. Line drawings, photographs. Published by
    Genuine Indian Relic Society, Inc., Memphis, TN. Place of publication
    varies: East St. Louis, IL, July, 1966-Jan, 1968; Memphis, TN, Jan,

1969–July, 1972; St. Louis, MO, Oct, 1972–Apr, 1977; Angola, IN, July, 1974–July, 1977; Franklin, IN, Oct, 1977–Jan, 1978. Editors: Gary R. LaDassor, July, 1966; Jack Berner, Apr, 1969–Oct, 1971; Gary LaDassor, Jan, 1972–Oct, 1977; John Baldwin, Jan, 1978–Oct?. 1979. Subject focus: artifacts and relics, archaeology.

WHi	v.1, n.1–v.14, n.4;	E/77/R42
	July, 1966–Oct?, 1979	
MoHi	v.1–v.11;	970.1/R249
	1966–1976	
OkU	v.1, n.1–v.8, n.4;	WHC
	July, 1966–Oct, 1973	

Other holding institutions: DLC (DLC), InMuB (IBS), [Indiana Union List of Serials, Indianapolis, IN] (ILS), In (ISL), MiU (EYM), [University of Minnesota Union List, Minneapolis, MN] (MUL), NIC (COO), [New York State Union List of Serials, Albany, NY] (NYS), WaU (WAU), WvHfp (UDH).

886 Redskin News. 1977–1978?//. Irregular. OCLC 6169377. Last issue 12 pages, height 36 cm. Line drawings, photographs. Available in microform: WHi (1977–1978). Published by Phoenix Indian High School, Phoenix, AZ. School newsletter.

WHi	n.1–7;	Microforms
	Sept?. 1977–Jan 13, 1978	
WMUW	n.1–7;	(SPL)
	Sept?. 1977–Jan 13, 1978	E/75/R44x

887 The Renegade. 1969?–1972?//. Unknown. Last issue 8 pages. Line drawings, photographs. Available in microform: WHi (1971, 1972). Published by Survival of the American Indian Association, Tacoma, WA. Editor: Hank Adams. Subject focus: rights, fishing rights, Washington Native people.

WHi	June, 1971, June, 1972	Microforms
WEU	June?, 1970, June, 1972	Journalism Lab
AzNCC	May, 1969, June, 1971	Indian File
CU-A	May, 1969–June, 1972	E/77/A1/R45
KU	May, 1969–June, 1972	Kansas Collection
NjP	May, 1969–June, 1972	Periodicals

WaU   June, 1972   Periodicals

CaOPeT   May, 1969-June, 1972   Microfilm

Other holding institutions: MiU-Labadie (EYM).

888 The Reno Talking Leaf. 1979. Monthly. Carla Molino and Rachel Shaw,
    editors, The Reno Talking Leaf, 916 E. 6th St., Reno, NV 89512. Last
    issue 4 pages, height 22 cm. Line drawings. Published by Nevada
    Urban Indians, Inc. Previous editors: Carla Molino and Amanda Astor,
    Jan 7-May 7, 1982; Susan Numan, June 7, 1982. Subject focus: urban
    community, organization news.

    WHi   v.4, n.1-   Circulation
               Jan 7, 1982-

889 Report on Indian Legislation. 1964?-1972//. 10 times a year. Last
    issue 6 pages. Available in microform: WHi (1971-1972). Published by
    Friends Committee on National Legislation, Washington, DC. Subject
    focus: legislation, Congressional monitoring.

    WHi   n.35-44;   Microforms
               Nov/Dec, 1971-Nov, 1972.

    WMM   n.1-33;   Special
               Feb 20, 1964-July/Aug, 1968   Collections

    AzFM   1971-1972   570.6/W311

    AzNCC   n.35;   Indian File
               Nov/Dec, 1971

    IdU   n.36-n.44;   E/75/R4
               Jan-Nov, 1972

    NjP   n.1-44;   Periodicals
               Feb 20, 1964-Nov, 1972

    OkU   n.35;   WHC
               Nov/Dec, 1971

    PPT   [n.35-44]   Contemporary
               [Nov/Dec, 1971-Nov, 1972]   Culture

890 Reporter: American Indian News and Affairs. 1982. Unknown. Tony
    Arkeketa, edtior, Reporter: American Indian News and Affairs, P.O. Box
    2646, Tulsa, OK 74107-2646. (918) 446-8432. Last issue 10 pages,
    height 28 cm. Line drawings, photographs. Published by Native
    American Coalition of Tulsa, Inc. Subject focus: local and national
    news.

WHi   v.1, n.2-   Circulation
             Aug, 1982-

891 <u>Research and Data Report</u>. 1978//. Irregular. Last issue 12 pages,
    height 28 cm. Line drawings. Published by American Indian Higher
    Education Consortium, Denver, CO. Subject focus: community colleges,
    consortia, resource sharing, educational planning, educational
    legislation.

    WHi   v.1, n.1;   Microforms
                 June, 1978

892 <u>Research Review</u>. 1967-1975//. Quarterly. RLIN CUBU11992815-S,
    NYPG744878212-S. Last issue 28 pages, height 23 cm. Line drawings,
    photographs. Published by Little Big Horn Association, Seattle, WA.
    Editors: R. L. Nelson, Spring, 1973; Bruce R. Leddic, Summer-Fall,
    1973; Tom E. Bookwalter, Winter-Fall, 1974; John F. McCormack,
    Winter-Summer, 1975. Subject focus: history, Battle of the Little Big
    Horn.

    WHi   v.7, n.1-v.9, n.2;   E/83.876/L6
                 Spring, 1973-Summer, 1975

893 <u>Resolutions of District Councils</u>. 1971?-1978//? Irregular. OCLC
    8487386. Last issue 10 pages. Available in microform: CPC
    (1971-1978). Crownpoint, NM. Subject focus: Navajo people.

    WHi   May 1, 1971-Jan 5, 1978   Microforms

    NjP   Oct 9, 1971-Jan 5, 1978   Microforms

    Other holding institutions: PPiU (PIT).

894 <u>Restmor</u>. 1931?//. Monthly. Last issue 17 pages, height 28 cm. Line
    drawings, photographs. Published by Shawnee Indian Sanitorium,
    Shawnee, OK. Institution newsletter.

    WMM   v.4, n.9;   Special
                 Sept, 1934   Collections

    <u>Retriever</u>. Las Cruces, NM

       see <u>CRESS-Notes</u>. Las Cruces, NM

895 <u>Rising Sun</u>. 1977-1979?//. Unknown. Last issue 8 pages, height 39
    cm. Line drawings. Published by United American Indians of the
    Delaware Valley, Philadelphia, PA. Community newsletter.

    WHi   v.3, n.5;   Microforms
                 July, 1979

896 <u>River Times</u>. 1971-1975?//. Monthly. Last issue 8 pages. Line
    drawings, photographs, commercial advertising. Available in
    microform: McP (1971-1972). Published by Fairbanks Native Community
    Center, Fairbanks, AK. Subject focus: urban community, center news.

    WHi   v.1, n.1-v.2, n.4;   Microforms
                 Sept 27, 1971-Dec, 1972

    AkHi   v.1, n.4-v.2, n.4;   Periodicals
                 Jan-Dec, 1972

    AkUF   v.1, n.1-v.2, n.4;   Periodicals
                 Sept 27, 1971-Dec, 1972

    CNoSU   v.1, n.1-v.2, n.4;   Microfilm
                 Sept 27, 1971-Dec, 1972

    NjP   v.2, n.7, v.4, n.5;   Periodicals
                 Mar/Apr, 1973, June/July, 1975

    OkU   v.1, n.1-v.2, n.4;   WHC
                 Sept 27, 1971-Dec, 1972

    Other holding institutions: NmScW, [University of Wisconsin-Stevens
    Point-Native American Center, Stevens Point, WI].

897 <u>River Tribes Review</u>. 1971-1972//. Quarterly. Last issue 16 pages.
    Line drawings, photographs, commercial advertising. Available in
    microform: WHi (1971-1972). Published by the Five River Tribes,
    Parker, AZ. Editor: Bill Brennan. Subject focus: inter-tribal news,
    education, business, agriculture, community development.

    WHi   v.1, n.1-v.2, n.2;   Microforms
                 Spring, 1971-Summer, 1972

898 <u>Rocky Boy's Native Voice</u>. 1978. Weekly. Last issue 8 pages, height
    41 cm. Line drawings, photographs. Available in microform: WHi
    (1979-1982). Published by Rocky Boy Health Board, Box Elder, MT.
    Editors: William Denny, Jr., Aug 29-Oct 31, 1979; Gilbert Belgarde,
    Nov 7, 1979-July 30, 1982. Community newsletter. Subject focus:
    Chippewa Cree people.

WHi   v.1, n.83, 92-v.2, n.94;   Microforms
           June 6, Aug 29, 1979-July 30, 1982

MtBBCC   v.2;   Periodicals
           Mar, 1980-Jan, 1981

899 The Roadrunner. 1978. Unknown. Rosilda Manuel, editor, The
     Roadrunner, Star Rt. 1, Box 92, Sells, AZ 85634. Published by San
     Simon High School, Papago Agency. Elementary school newsletter.

WHi   v.4, n.10;   Microforms
           Oct 7, 1981

900 Rosebud Sioux Herald (Eyapaha). 1964-1971//. Weekly. OCLC 1764534.
     RLIN OHCP1764534-S. Last issue 12 pages, height 25 cm. Line
     drawings, photographs, commercial advertising. Available in
     microform: McP (1970-1971); CPC (1963-1969). Rosebud, SD. Editor:
     Frank LaPointe. Community newsletter. Subject focus: Dakota (Rosebud
     Sioux) people. Some issues contain supplement: Voices for Unity.

WHi   v.7, n.47-v.8, n.43;   E/77/R6
           July 6, 1970-June 7, 1971

WHi   [v.1, n.1-v/6. n.14], v.8, n.1-43;   Microforms
           [Aug 5, 1963-Feb 24, 1969]
           Aug 17, 1970-June 7, 1971

WEU   v.7, n.2-5, v.8, n.21-28;   Journalism
           Aug 25-Sept 15, 1969, Jan 4-Feb 22, 1971 Lab

WMM   [v.3, n.1-v.8, n.43]   Special
           [Nov 15, 1965-June 7, 1971]   Collections

CNoSU   v.8;   Microfilm
           1970-1971

NjP   [v.1, n.1-v.7, n.25], n.27-   Periodicals
           Aug 5, 1973-Feb 2,] 16, 1970-

NN   [v.2, n.4-v.7, n.36]   HBA
           [Sept 28, 1964-Apr 20, 1970]

SdU   v.1, n.1-v.8, n.33;   Microfilm
           Aug 5, 1963-Mar 29, 1971

WaU   v.8, n.30;   Periodicals
           Mar 8, 1971

Other holding institutions: [University of Minnesota Union List,
Minneapolis, MN] (MUL), NmScW, OrU-Special Collections.

901 Rosebud Teepee Talk. 1959-1968?//. Monthly. OCLC 4274715, 8448417.
RLIN OHCP4274715-S. Last issue 12 pages. Line drawings. Available
in microform: CPC (1959-1968). Rosebud Agency, SD. School
newsletter. Subject focus: education, social services, Dakota
(Rosebud Sioux) people.

WHi	[Dec, 1959-May, 1968]	Microforms
WMM	Nov, 1967	Special Collections
NjP	[Dec, 1959-May, 1968]	Periodicals
NN	[Dec, 1959-May, 1968]	Microforms
SdHRC	[July, 1961-Feb, 1968]	Periodicals
SdU	[May, 1962-Apr, 1968]	South Dakota Room
SdU	[Dec, 1959-May, 1968]	Microfilm

Other holding institutions: [University of Minnesota Union List,
Minneapolis, MN] (MUL), PPiU (PIT).

902 The Rough Rock News/Dine Biolta Baahane. 1966. Irregular. $5. for
individuals and institutions. Beverly BySura Njaa, editor, The Rough
Rock News/Dine Biolta Baahane, Rough Rock, AZ 86503. (602) 728-3311.
OCLC 6169386. Last issue 4 pages, height 40 cm. Photographs,
commercial advertising. Available in microform: McA (1973-); WHi-A,
Veda Stone Papers, (1969). Published by Rough Rock Demonstration
School. Place of publication varies: Chinle, AZ Jan 17, 1973-Jan 21,
1977. Previous editors: Gary Galluzzo, Jan 17-May 30, 1973; Arlene
Bowman, Oct 3, 1973; Ken Neundorf, Dec 1973; Margaret Dunlap, Mar
4-June 3, 1974; Jeanne Willetto, Sept 16, 1974-Dec, 1976. Community
and school newsletter. Subject focus: Navajo people.

WHi	v.4, n.10, v.8, n.10- Nov 6, 1969, Jan 17, 1973-	Microforms
WEU	v.6, n.7-12; Dec 9, 1970-Mar 3, 1971	Journalism Lab
WEU	v.1, n.1-v.8, n.9; July 14, 1966-Dec 13, 1972	Microfilm
WEU ARC	v.4, n.10; Nov 6, 1969	Micro 11
WMUW	v.12, n.1-10; Sept 10, 1976-Jan 8, 1977	(SPL) E/75/R68x
Az	[v.6, n.13-v.15, n.1] [1970-June, 1980]	Periodicals

ICN	Current issues	CHAI
NjP	[v.1, n.14-v.14, n.7] [Jan 12, 1967-May 15, 1979]	Periodicals
NHu	[v.8, n.5-v.14, n.5] [Mar, 1972-Jan, 1979]	Periodicals
OkTU	[v.5, n.10-v.6, n.15/16] v.14, n.4-v.15, n.1; June, 1970-May, 1971, Dec 19, 1978-June, 1980	Rare Book Room
SdU	v.8-v.9; Jan, 1973-Dec, 1974	Microfilm
CaOPeT	v.8, n.10- Jan 17, 1973-	Microfilm

Other holding institutions: [University of Wisconsin-Stevens
Point-Native American Center, Stevens Point, WI].

903 Round the Campfire. 1929-1930?//. Monthly. Last issue 4 pages,
    height 28 cm. Line drawings. Published by Convent of Mary
    Immaculate, De Smet, ID. School newsletter. Subject focus: Catholic
    Church.

WMM	v.1, n.1-5; Sept, 1929-Jan, 1930	Special Collections

904 The Roundup. 1977. Irregular. $15. for individuals and
    institutions. The Roundup, 1029 Vermont Ave., N. W., Suite 1100,
    Washington, DC 20005. (202) 638-7066. OCLC 7743066. Last issue 16
    pages, height 28 cm. Published by Native American Philanthropic News
    Service (NAPNS) of the American Indian Program, the Phelp-Stokes Fund.
    Subject focus: consortia, resource referrals in education, employment,
    social services, philanthropic activities.

WHi	v.1, n.1- Jan, 1977-	Circulation
AzNCC	v.2- Aug, 1978	Indian File
OkTU	v.2, n.1- Jan, 1978-	001.4405/R859
OkU	v.3, n.6- Apr, 1980-	WHC

CaACG   [v.2, n.5-v.3, n.3], v.4, n.3-   Periodicals
           [Mar, 1979-1980], Dec, 1981-

Other holding institutions: [Amerind Foundation, Inc., Draggon, AZ],
Ok (OKD), [Wisconsin Indian Resource Council, Stevens Point, WI]

SJC Today. Sitka, AK

   see Today: Sheldon Jackson College. Sitka, AK

Sachs Echo. Sachs Harbour, Northwest Territories, Canada

      see Bankslander/Sachs Echo. Sachs Harbour, Northwest Territories,
          Canada

905 Sacramento Indian Center, News.   1979-1981//. Monthly. OCLC
    5530352. RLIN NJPG1736-S. Last issue 6 pages, height 36 cm. Line
    drawings, photographs, commerical advertising. Sacramento, CA. Title
    varies: Indian Center News, Apr-Oct, 1979. Editor: Jean Thatcher,
    Mar/Apr, 1980-Nov, 1981. Subject focus: urban community, center news.

    WHi   v.1, n.1-v.2, n.6;   Microforms
               Apr, 1979-Nov, 1980

    MtBBCC   v.2, n.5;   Periodicals
               Sept., 1980

    Other holding institutions: NmU-L (NML), [Standing Rock Community
    College Library, Fort Yates, ND].

906 The Sagkeeng News. 1963-1977?//. Irregular. Last issue 8 pages.
    Line drawings, photographs. Available in microform: WHi (1973-1977).
    Fort Alexander, Manitoba, Canada. Community newsletter.

    WHi   v.1, n.2-20   Microforms
               Sept, 1973-Apr, 1977

    CaOONL   [no nos.]   Newspaper
               Nov 1, 1963, Oct 30, 1964,   Section
               Apr 18, 1969, July, 1973

907 St. Christopher's Mission to the Navajo Newsletter. 1953?-1977//.
    Quarterly. OCLC 8416629. Last issue 8 pages. Line drawings,
    photographs. Available in microform: CPC (1964-1977). Bluff, UT.
    Subject focus: Episcopal Church, missions, Navajo people.

WHi	[Winter, 1964-Summer, 1977]	Microforms
CLSM	[Fall, 1966-Lent, 1968]	Periodicals
NjP	[Winter, 1964-Summer, 1977]	Periodicals
UHi	1953-1977	Periodicals

Other holding institutions: OrU-Special Collections, PPiU (PIT).

908 St. Francis News. 1976//. Monthly. Last issue 16 pages, height 44 cm. Line drawings, photographs. St. Francis, SD. Editor: Charlie Archambault. Community newsletter. Subject focus: Catholic Church.

WMM	v.1, n.1-3; July-Sept, 1976	Special Collections

St. Paul American Indian Center. [Newsletter] St. Paul, MN

see Smoke Signals. St. Paul, MN

909 Salt River Awathm Awawhan. 1963-1967?//. Monthly. Last issue 14 pages, height 39 cm. Line drawings. Available in microform: WHi (1963-1967). Published by The Salt River Pima-Maricopa Reservation, Scottsdale, AZ. Editors: Alfretta Antone, June, 1965-Feb, 1966; Anna M. Shaw, June, 1966-Sept, 1967. Community newsletter. Subject focus: Pima and Maricopa people.

WHi	[Dec, 1963-Sept, 1967]	Microforms
NjP	Aug, 1967	Periodicals

910 The Salt River Pima-Maricopa Bulletin. 1958-1960?//. Irregular. Last issue 14 pages, height 28 cm. Available in microform: WHi (1959-1960). Published by Salt River Pima-Maricopa Reservation, Scottsdale, AZ. Editors: Leroy Lewis Smith and Claire G. Seota, Dec, 1959-Mar, 1960. Community newsletter. Subject focus: Pima and Maricopa people.

WHi	v.2, n.5-v.3, n.3; Aug, 1959-Mar, 1960	Microforms

San Carlos Newsletter. San Carlos, AZ

see Apache Newsletter. San Carlos, AZ

Sand and Sun. Fort Wingate, NM

   see Shush Da Bizaad/Language of the Bears. Fort Wingate, NM

911 The Saponi. 1982? Monthly. The Saponi, 102 Indian Dr.,
    Fayetteville, NC 28301. Last issue 4 pages, height 41 cm. Line
    drawings, photographs. Published by Cumberland County Association for
    Indian People. Community newsletter. Subject focus: social services,
    educational opportunities.

    WHi   Sept, 1982-   Circulation

912 Saskatchewan Indian. 1970. Monthly. $12. for individuals and
    institutions. Kenny Loon, editor, Saskatchewan Indian, P.O. Box 3085,
    Saskatoon, Saskatchewan, Canada S7K 3S9. (306) 244-1146. ISSN
    0048-9204. LC cn79-310922. OCLC 1606150, 5270820. RLIN
    DCLCCN79310922-S, OHCP1606150-S, NYPG794417444-S. Last issue 56
    pages, last volume 400 pages, height 28 cm. Line drawings,
    photographs, commercial advertising. Available in microform: WHi
    (1971-). Published by Federation of Saskatchewan Indians. Frequency
    varies: bi-weekly, Jan 15-Oct 30, 1975. Previous editors: Doug
    Cuthand, July/Aug, 1971-Apr, 1973; Richard Scott, May, 1973-Nov, 1974;
    Lucille Bell, Dec, 1974-Oct 30, 1975; Doug Cuthand, Dec, 1975-Jan,
    1977; Geoff White, Feb-Sept, 1977; Peter Harrington, Oct, 1977-June,
    1978; Miguel V. Calderon, Aug, 1978; Louise Cuthand, Oct/Nov 1978-Oct,
    1979; Rod Andrews, Feb/Mar-Aug, 1980. Subject focus: national and
    provincial news, poetry, book reviews.

    WHi   v.2, n.2-   Microforms
               Feb, 1971-

    WM   Current issues   Forest Home
                                                    Branch

    AzNCC   v.2, n.2-   Indian File
               Feb, 1971-

    NjP   [v.2, n.4-v.9, n.6]   Periodicals
               [Apr, 1971-June, 1979]

    OkTU   v.8, n.12-   Rare Book
               Dec, 1978-   Room

    OkU   v.2, n.1-   WHC
               Jan. 1971-

    CaACG   v.2, n.4-   Periodicals
               Apr, 1971-

    CaAEU   v.2, n.2-   Boreal
               Feb, 1971-   Institute

CaMWU   v.4-v.8;   970/S2525/
           1974-1978   In

CaOAFN   Current issues   Periodicals

CaOONL   v.1-   Periodicals
           1970-

CaOOP   v.2, n.4-   Periodicals
           Apr, 1971-

CaOPeT   v.1-   Microfilm
           1970-

CaSSIC   v.3, n.1-   Microfilm
           Jan, 1972-

Other holding institutions: CLU (CLU).

913 <u>Saskatchewan Native Library Service Newsletter</u>. 1981. Unknown. $10.
    for individuals and institutions. Saskatchewan Native Library Service
    Newsletter, c/o Native Law Centre, University of Saskatchewan, 410
    Cumberland Ave., N., Saskatoon, Saskatchewan, Canada S7N 1M6. (306)
    343-4273. ISSN 0229-9496. LC cn81-31173. OCLC 8294985. RLIN
    DCLCCN8131173-S. Last issue 12 pages, height 28 cm. Subject focus:
    bibliography, book reviews, curriculum development.

    WHi   v.1, n.1-   Circulation
               Feb, 1981-

    Other holding institutions: CaOONL (NLC).

914 <u>School News</u>. 1880-1883//. Monthly. OCLC 8327347. Last issue 4
    pages, last volume 48 pages, height 20 cm. Published by Indian
    Industrial School, Carlisle Barracks, PA. Editors: Samuel Townsend,
    June, 1880-June, 1881; Charles Kihega, July, 1881-May, 1883. School
    newsletter.

    ICN   [v.1, n.1-v.3, n.7]   Ayer 398/
               [June, 1880-Dec, 1882]   C2/S3

    PCarlH   [v.1, n.1-v.3, n.12]   Periodicals
               [June, 1880-Mar, 1883]

    Other holding institutions: CtHT (TYC).

915 <u>The Scout</u>. 1966?-1982//. Unknown. ISSN 0380-8971. LC cn76-300551.
    OCLC 2142778. RLIN OHCP2142778-S. Last issue 12 pages, height 28 cm.
    Line drawings. Published by Indian-Metis Friendship Centre,

Brandon, Manitoba, Canada. Editor: Linda Boys. Subject focus: urban
community, centre news.

WHi   Dec, 1981, Mar, 1982   Pam
                                                         Cataloging

NjP   Jan?-Nov, 1966   Periodicals

CaMWU   [Nov, 1973-July, 1977]   Dafoe Per
                                                         970/S4327

Other holding institutions: CaOONL (NLC).

916 Screaming Eagle. 1978-1981//. Bi-monthly. Last issue 24 pages,
    height 36 cm. Line drawings, photographs, commercial advertising.
    Portola Valley, CA. Editor: Loti Hutchinson. Title varies: Drumbeat,
    May?, 1980. Community newsletter.

    WHi   v.3, n.2-5;   Pam
               May?, 1980-Apr, 1981   Cataloging

    Other holding institutions: ICN (IBV).

917 Sealaska Shareholder. 1976. Monthly. Ross V. Soboleff, editor,
    Sealaska Shareholder, 1 Sealaska Plaza, Suite 400, Juneau, AK 99801.
    (907) 586-1512. Last issue 12 pages, height 39 cm. Photographs, some
    in color. Published by Sealaska Corporation. Subject focus: Fishing
    and timber industries, corporate and regional news.

    WHi   v.7, n.3-   Circulation
               Mar, 1982-

    AkUF   v.2-   HD/2798
               Mar, 1977-   A4/S44

918 Seminole Bilingual Education Project Newsletter. 1972-1978?//.
    Irregular. OCLC 8416656. Last issue 6 pages. Line drawings.
    Available in microform: CPC (1972-1978). Published by Eastern Central
    State College, Ada, OK. Subject focus: bilingual education and
    teaching, Seminole language and culture.

    WHi   [Aug, 1972-May, 1978]   Microforms

    NjP   [Feb? 1973-Dec, 1977]   Periodicals

    SdU   [Aug, 1972-1976]   Microfilm

    Other holding institutions: PPiU (PIT).

919 The Seneca Nation Newsletter. 1961-1968?//. Unknown. Last issue 10
pages, height 28 cm. Line drawings. Salamanca, NY. Editor: Merrill
W. Bowen. Community newsletter. Subject focus: Seneca people.

WHi   v.4, n.1;   Pam 76-899
            Jan, 1966

NjP   v.1, n.1-v.6, n.2;   Periodicals
            Oct 11, 1961-June, 1968

920 The Sentinel. 1968-1977//. Irregular. OCLC 1759145. RLIN
NYPG81-S418, OHCP1759145-S. Last issue 42 pages, height 29 cm. Line
drawings, photographs. Published by National Congress of American
Indians, Washington, DC. Title varies: NCAI Sentinel, Spring,
1968-Winter, 1969. Editors: Vine Deloria, Jr. and John Belinda, Fall,
1968; John Belinda, Winter/Spring, 1969-Winter, 1970. Subject focus:
rights, politics, legislation, governmental relations.

WHi   Fall, 1968-Winter, 1971   E/75/S4

AzNCC   Spring, 1970-Winter, 1972   Indian File

MnBemT   [1970-1972]   Periodicals

NjP   [July, 1970-Summer, 1977]   Periodicals

NN   Spring-Dec, 1970, Winter, 1972   HBA

Other holding institutions: [University of Minnesota Union List,
Minneapolis, MN] (MUL).

921 The Sentinel Bulletin. 1947-1973//. Irregular. ISSN 0047-8784.
OCLC 1759144, 7556906. RLIN MIUG28222-S. Last issue 4 pages, height
28 cm. Line drawings, photographs. Available in microform: McA
(1947-1973); McP (1947-1973); WHi-A, Veda Stone Papers, (1971).
Published by National Congress of American Indians, Washington, DC.
Title varies: Bulletin, 1947. 1972; Washington Bulletin, 1948-1952;
News Bulletin, 1952-1954; NCAI Bulletin, 1955-1961; NCAI Sentinel
Bulletin, 1962-1967, Apr-Oct, 1971; NCAI Sentinel, 1969-1970;
Sentinel, Winter, 1971. Editors: Robert Burnette, Jan-May, 1963; Vine
Deloria, Jr., Feb-Summer, 1965. Subject focus: legislation,
organization news.

WHi   v.1, n.1-v.29, n.2;   Microforms
            Feb, 1947-July/Aug, 1973

WHi   [v.27, n.4-9]   Pam 72-35
            Apr-Sept/Oct, 1971

WEU   [v.27, n.4, 6]   Micro 11
ARC   Apr, June, 1971

Other holding institutions: ArU (AFU), IU (UIU), MH-P (HLS),
[University of Minnesota Union List, Minneapolis, MN] (MUL), NN (NYP).

922 Sequoyah Memorial. 1855-?//. Weekly. Last issue 4 pages. Published
by Male Seminary of the Cherokee Nation, Tahlequah, OK. Available in
microform: OkHi (1855-1856). Editors: R. J. Ross, J. F. Thompson and
Albert Barnes. School newsletter. Subject focus: Cherokee people.
In Cherokee, 50%. Also described in: Foreman, Carolyn Thomas.
Oklahoma Imprints, 1835-1907. Norman: University of Oklahoma Press,
1936.

WHi   Aug 2, 1855, July 31, 1856   Microforms

923 Setaneoei. 1887?-1934?//. Monthly. Last issue 4 pages, height 25
cm. Line drawings, photographs. Restigouche, Quebec, Canada.
Subject focus: Catholic Church, Micmac people. In Micmac, 50-80%.

WMM   [n.269-v.2, n.34]   Special
             [Sept 1909-Oct, 1934]   Collections

Shannon County News. Pine Ridge, SD

    see Shannon County News and Eyapaha Wakokipe'shi. Pine Ridge, SD

924 Shannon County News and Eyapapa Wakokipe'shi. 1940?-1974//. Weekly.
Last issue 12 pages. Line drawings, photographs, commercial
advertising. Available in microform: WHi (1973-1974). Pine Ridge,
SD. Title varies: Shannon County News. Mar 2, 1973-Feb 15, 1974.
Editor: Aaron Desersa, Mar 2, 1973. Community newsletter. Subject
focus: Oglala people.

WHi   v.34, n.1-v.35, n.17;   Microforms
             Mar 2, 1973-July 5, 1974

WEU   v.32, n.9-13;   Journalism
             Apr 9-May 7, 1971   Lab

AzNCC   v.32-v.34;   Indian File
             Apr, 1971-Dec, 1973

NjP   [v.26, n.27-37]   Periodicals
             [Aug 1-Oct 10, 1963]

Other holding institutions: OrU-Special Collections.

925 <u>Shareholder News</u>. 1981. Unknown. Shareholder News, P.O. Box 116,
    Angoon, AK 99820. (907) 788-3553. Last issue 20 pages, height 28 cm.
    Line drawings, photographs. Published by Kootznoowoo, Inc.
    Corporation newsletter. Subject focus: timber and fishing industries,
    land claims, community development, history, culture, tourism.

    WHi   v.1, n.1-   Circulation
                Oct, 1981-

    <u>Sheldon Jackson College Today</u>. Sitka, AK

        see <u>Today: Sheldon Jackson College</u>. Sitka, AK

926 <u>Shenabe Quai</u>. 1979?-1981//. Irregular. Last issue 8 pages, height
    28 cm. Line drawings, photographs. Available in microform: WHi
    (1979-1981). Published by North American Indian Women's Council on
    Chemical Dependency, Turtle Lake, WI. Subject focus: alcoholism, drug
    abuse.

    WHi   Feb, 1979-Apr, 1981   Microforms

    Other holding institutions: WM (GZD), [University of Wisconsin-Stevens
    Point-Native American Center, Stevens Point, WI].

927 <u>Shenandoah</u>. 1974? Irregular. Paul A. Skenandore, editor,
    Shenandoah, P.O. Box 266, Oneida, WI 54155. Last issue 22 pages,
    height 28 cm. Community newsletter.

    WHi   v.7, n.10-   Circulation
                Jan, 1981-

    ICN   Current issues   CHAI

    Other holding institutions: [Wisconsin Indian Resource Council,
    Stevens Point, WI]

928 <u>The Sherman Bulletin</u>. 1907?-?//. Bi-weekly. Last issue 4 pages,
    last volume 68 pages, height 31 cm. Line drawings, photographs.
    Published by Sherman Institute, Riverside, CA. Frequency varies:
    Weekly, May 20, 1912-Jan 30, 1920. School newsletter.

    CLSM   [v.6, n.12-v.55]   Periodicals
                [May 20, 1912-May, 1963]

929 <u>Sho-Ban News</u>. 1970. Weekly. Daliah Uribe, editor, Sho-Ban News,
    P.O. Box 427, Fort Hall, ID 83203. (208) 237-3673. ISSN 0197-7954.

LC sc79-4264. OCLC 4574547. RLIN DCLCSC794264-S, OHCP4574547-S.
Last issue 4 pages. Line drawings, photographs, commercial
advertising. Available in microform: McP (1970-1971). Fort Hall, ID.
Editors: Lorraine Edmo, Oct 22, 1970-May 28, 1971; Mark N. Trahant,
Apr, 1971-Sept 12, 1972; Andy DeLosAngeles, Aug 15-Sept 5, 1979;
Daliah Preacher, Oct 17, 1979-Dec 2, 1981. Community newsletter.
Subject focus: Shoshone and Bannock people.

WHi	v.1, n.1-6; v.3, n.4- Oct 22, 1970-May 28, 1971, Jan 3, 1973-	Microforms
WMUW	[v.1, n.5-v.2, n.13; [Apr 1971-Sept 12, 1972]	(SPL) E/75/S55x
IdB	Current issue only	Periodicals
IdHi	(n.s.)v.1, n.1- Dec 11, 1976-	Periodicals
IdP	Current issues	Periodicals
IdU	[(n.s.)v.1, n.15-v.5]- [Sept 16, 1977-Nov 12, 1980]-	Folio E/75/S5
MtBCC	(n.s.)v.4- Mar, 1980-	Periodicals
OkTU	(n.s.)v.2, n.8/9, June, Aug, 1978, [spec. ed.]	Rare Book Room
OkU	v.1; Dec, 1970-Mar 4, 1971	WHC

Other holding institutions: DI (UDI), [Sho-Ban Library, Fort Hall,
ID], [University of Minnesota Union List, Minneapolis, MN] (MUL),
NmScW.

930 The Shoshone-Bannock Tribes Educational Newsletter. 1975-?//.
    Irregular. Last issue 6 pages, height 28 cm. Line drawings,
    photographs. Published by The Shoshone-Bannock Tribal Education
    Department, Fort Hall, ID. Subject focus: education, educational
    opportunities, Shoshone and Bannock people.

IdHi	v.1, n.1-12; Dec 1, 1975-Nov 1, 1976	Periodicals

931 Shush/Bear. 1968-1973?//. Weekly. Last issue 22 pages, Last volume
    28 pages, height 22 cm. Line drawings. Published by Wingate High
    School, Fort Wingate, NM. High school newsletter.

NmG	v.3, n.5-v.5,n.32; Oct 9, 1979-May 4, 1973	Periodicals

932 Shush Da Bizaad/Language of the Bears. 1970-1972?//. Monthly. Last
     issue 20 pages, last volume 41 pages, height 23 cm. Line drawings.
     Published by Language Arts Dept., Wingate High School, Fort Wingate,
     NM. Title varies: Sand and Sun, Sept-Oct, 1970. Subject focus:
     poetry, drama.

     NmG   Sept, 1970-Mar, 1972   Periodicals

933 Si Wong Geh. 1974?. Weekly. Mary Snow, editor, Si Wong Geh, Box 93,
     Irving, NY 14081. (716) 532-4900. Last issue 8 pages. Line
     drawings, commercial advertising. Available in microform: McA
     (1974-); CPC (1971-1976). Published by Cattaraugus Indian
     Reservation. Community newsletter.

     WHi   [Feb 24, 1971-Feb 16,] Mar 8, 1972-   Microforms

     WEU   Jan 9-May, July-Dec 18, 1974   Microfilm

     AzNCC   1974   Microfilm

     NjP   [Oct 18, 1972-June 20, 1979]   Periodicals

     OkU   Nov 9, 1972   WHC

     SdU   1975   Microfilm

     CaOPeT   Apr, 1973-   Microfilm

934 Sina Sapa Taeyapaha. 1923-1924//. Monthly. Last issue 4 pages,
     height 39 cm. Line drawings, photographs, commercial advertising.
     Fort Yates, ND. Editor: Benjamin White. Subject focus: missions,
     Catholic Church, Dakota people. In Dakota, 100%. Photostat.

     WHi   v.1, n.1-3/4;   Pam
                Dec 15, 1923-Mar, 1924   Cataloging

     WMM   v.1, n.2;   Special
                Jan 15, 1924   Collections

935 Sina Sapa Wocenkine Taenanpaha. 1893-1921?//. Monthly. Last issue 4
     pages, height 44 cm. Published by St. Michael's Mission, Fort Totten,
     ND. Editor: Jerome Hunt. Subject focus: missions, Catholic Church,
     Dakota (Sioux) people. In Dakota, 100%.

     WMM   [v.2, n.4-v.26, n.2]   Special
                [May, 1893-Nov 15, 1921]   Collections

Sina Sapa Wocenkine Taenanpaha/The Catholic Sioux Herald.
          Marty, SD

   see Catholic Indian Herald. Marty, SD

Singing Wire. Tulsa, OK

   see Indian America. Tulsa, OK

936 Sinte Gleska College Center, News Letter. 1973?//. Monthly. Last
    issue 8 pages, height 28 cm. Line drawings, photographs. Available
    in microform: WHi (1976). Rosebud, SD. School newsletter.

    WHi   Nov, 1976   Microforms

    AzNCC   1973-Apr, 1974   Indian File

937 Sinte Gleska College News. 1974. Bi-monthly. Charlie Garriott,
    editor, Sinte Gleska College News, Library-Media Center, Box 107,
    Mission, SD 57555. Last issue 20 pages, height 39 cm. Line drawings,
    photographs. Previous editor: Rose Cordier-Beauvais, June, 1979-Jan,
    1980. Subject focus: local and national news, health, environment,
    Dakota people, children's literature.

    WHi   [no nos.], v.1, n.1-   Microforms
               Jan-Feb, Oct,, 1978-

    WU   Current issues   Ethnic
    Coll   Collection

    AzNCC   v.1, n.1-   Indian File
               Oct, 1978-

    ICN   Current issues   CHAI

    MtBBCC   v.1-   Periodicals
               Sept, 1979-

    SdHRC   [no nos.]   Periodicals
               Feb/Mar/Apr, 1977-Dec, 1978

    SdU   1974-1977   South
                                                     Dakota Room

    CaOAFN   Current issues   Periodicals

    Other holding institutions: IC (CGP), MH-P (HLS), [Standing Rock
    Community College Library, Fort Yates, ND], [Bacone College, Muskogee,
    OK], [WGrU-Native American Studies Dept.]

938 <u>Siouan and Caddoan Linguistics</u>. 1978?-1980//? Irregular. Last issue 22 pages, height 28 cm. Published by University of Colorado, Boulder, CO. Subject focus: linguistics, bibliography, book reviews.

WUSP   Mar, 1980   Native American
                                                            Center

Other holding institutions: ICN (IBV).

939 <u>Sioux Chieftain</u>. 1933?-?//. Bi-monthly. Last issue 8 pages, height 28 cm. Line drawings. Published by St. Francis Mission High School, St. Francis, SD. Frequency varies: monthly, June, 1936. Editor: J. Eagle Dog, June, 1936. School newsletter. Subject focus: Catholic Church.

WMM   [v.3, n.2-(n.s.)v.1, n.8]   Special
            [Nov, 1935-Apr, 1968]   Collection

940 <u>Sioux Journal</u>. 1966-?//. Unknown. Last issue 6 pages, height 31 cm. Photographs. Published by Cheyenne River Reservation, Eagle Butte, SD. Editors: Lila Robertson and Carole Clown. Community newsletter. Subject focus: Cheyenne people.

WMM   v.1, n.1;   Special
            Apr 8, 1966   Collections

NjP   v.1, n.4;
            Dec 9, 1966   Periodicals

941 <u>Sioux Messenger</u>. 1971?-?//. Monthly. OCLC 6221100. Last issue 6 pages, height 28 cm. Line drawings, photographs, commercial advertising. Available in microform: WHi (1973, 1974). Published by Yankton Sioux Tribe, Wagner, SD. Editors: Harold McBride and Herbert Hare. Community newsletter. Subject focus: Yankton Sioux people.

WHi   v.3, n.34, v.6, n.5-6;   Microforms
            Sept, 1973, July, 1974

WMUW   v.3, n.34, v.6, n.5;   (SPL)
            Sept, 1973, July-Aug, 1974   E/75/S56x

942 <u>Sioux News letter</u>. 1969-?//?. Monthly. Last issue 3 pages, height 36 cm. Eagle Butte, SD. Community newsletter. Subject focus: Sioux people.

WEU   Jan 20-Mar 31, 1971   Journalism
                                                            Lab

943 <u>Sioux San Sun</u>. 1965-?//?. Monthly. Last issue 8 pages, height 28
cm. Line drawings. Available in microform: CPC (1967-1973).
Published by Sioux Sanitorium, Rapid City, SD. Previous editors:
Carolyn Emery, Dec, 1965; Sarah Lee Limpy, Feb, 1967; Geraldine Kieth,
May, 1967; Vivian Archambeau, June, 1967; Laverne Yellow Hawk, July,
1967; Cathy Edwards, Dec, 1967; Darlene Ghost, Jan-May, 1968; Lois
Quigley, June-July, 1968; Ione Red Cloud, Aug-Dec, 1968; Jessie High
Pipe, Jan, 1969; Henrietta Harte, June-Aug, 1969; Lois Quiroz, Jan,
1970; Delma Blackburn, Feb, 1970; Jason Black Tomahawk, Mar, 1970;
Delma Blackburn, Apr, 1970; Lydia Roach, May, 1970; Delma Blackburn,
June, 1970; Veronica Chase In Sight, July/Aug, 1970; Delores Irving,
Sept, 1970; Mary Iron Rope, Oct, 1970; Inez One Star, Nov, 1970;
Joseph Traversie, Dec, 1970-Jan, 1971; Robert Bluebeard, Feb, 1971;
Lynn Salway, Mar, 1971; Delores Irving, Sept, 1971; Lynn Salway, Oct,
1971-May, 1972; Vincent LeBeau, June, 1972; Gaylene Roach, Sept-Oct,
1972; Victoria Yellow Boy, Jan, 1973. Subject focus: institution
news, fiction, poetry, Sioux people.

WHi	[June, 1968-Jan, 1973]	Microforms
WEU	[Dec, 1965-Mar, 1971]	Journalism Lab
AzNCC	Oct, 1971-Jan, 1973	Indian File
NjP	[June, 1967-Jan, 1973]	Periodicals
NN	[June, 1968-Jan, 1973]	Microforms
SdU	June, 1967-Jan, 1973	Microfilm

944 <u>Siwinowe Kesibwi</u>. 1835-1844//. Irregular. Last issue 2 pages,
height 25 cm. Published by Baptist Mission Press, Shawanoe, KS.
Editor: Johnston Lykins. Subject focus: Baptist Church, Shawnee
people. In Shawnee, 100%. Photostat. Also decribed in McMurtrie,
Douglas C. "The Shawnee Sun," <u>Kansas Historical Quarterly</u>, 9 (1933)
pp.339-342.

| WHi | Nov, 1841; | Pam Cataloging |

945 <u>The Six Nations</u>. 1926-1930?//. Quarterly. OCLC 8419511. Last issue
16 pages. Line drawings, photographs. Available in microform: CPC
(1926-1930). Published by Society for the Propagation of Indian
Welfare in New York State, Irving, NY. Place of publication varies:
Lawtons, NY, Nov, 1926-Apr, 1928. Editors: William B. Newell, Nov,
1926-July, 1928; Rev. W. David Owl, Jan-Apr., 1929. Subject focus:
rights, legislation, education, health, New York Native people.

| WHi | v.1, n.1-v.4, n.1; Nov, 1926-June, 1930 | Microforms |

NN   v.1, n.1-v.3, n.2;   HBA
            Nov, 1926-Apr, 1929

SdU   v.1, n.1-v.4, n.1   Microfilm
            Nov, 1926-June, 1930

Other holding institutions; PPiU (PIT).

946 S'Klallam News. 1979?. Irregular. S'klallam News, P.O. Box 280,
    Kingston, WA 98346. (206) 297-2646. Last issue 12 pages, height 28
    cm. Line drawings, photographs. Published by Port Gamble Klallam
    Tribe. Community newsletter. Subject focus: Klallam people.

    WHi   May, 1979, May 16, 1980-   Circulation

947 Skoekoi Dak Chick Pan. 1932?-1942?//. Monthly. Last issue 10 pages,
    height 28 cm. Line drawings. Sacaton, AZ. Community newsletter.
    Subject focus: Pima people.

    AzHC   v.4, n.12-v.12, n.1;   Periodicals
                June 15, 1935-Jan, 1942

948 Skopabish Smoke Signals. 1982? Monthly. Skopabish Smoke Signals,
    39015 372nd Ave., S.E., Auburn, WA 98002. Last issue 8 pages, height
    37 cm. Photographs. Published by Muckleshoot Adult Basic
    Education/CETA Career Awareness Program. Subject focus: adult and
    continuing education, career planning.

    ICN   Current issues   CHAI

949 Smog Signals. 1970-1972?//. Monthly. OCLC 6221396. Last issue 10
    pages. Line drawings. Available in microform: WHi-A, Veda Stone
    Papers, (1970-1972). Published by American Indian Information and
    Action Group, Milwaukee, WI. Editors: Walter Funmaker, June-Aug,
    1970; Louis Wynos, May, 1971; Michael Conners, Dec 1, 1971. Community
    newsletter.

    WHi   [v.1, n.2-v.3, n.3];   Microforms
                [Jan, 1970-June, 1972]

    WEU   [v.1, n.2-v.3, n.3];   Micro 11
    ARC   [Jan, 1970-June, 1972]

    WMUW   v.1, n.2;   (SPL)
                Jan, 1970   E/75/S62x

    NjP   v.1, n.9?;   Periodicals
                Oct, 1970

950 <u>The Smoke Signal of the Federated Indians of California</u>. 1942-1977?//.
Bi-monthly. OCLC 5388748, 5467993. RLIN CUBU15269206-S. Last issue
10 pages. Available in microform: McP (1971-1972). Sacramento, CA.
Frequency varies: quarterly, May-Oct, 1971. Subject focus: local and
national news, legislation, education, educational opportunities.

WHi	v.30, n.1-v.31, n.6; Jan, 1971-Dec, 1972	Microforms
WHi	v.23, n.1, 4; Jan/Feb/Mar, Nov/Dec, 1964	Pam 76-1167
WEU	v.29, n.3-v.30, n.1; May/July, 1970-Jan/Feb, 1971	Journalism Lab
WMUW	v.31, n.4; Apr/May, 1972	(SPE) E/75/S65x
AzNCC	v.30- May, 1971-	Indian File
CNoSU	[v.30-v.31] [1971-1972]	Microfilm
CU-A	v.31-v.36, n.3; Jan/Feb, 1972-1977	E/77/A1/S54
CU-B	v.34-v.36 1975-1977	Periodicals
NjP	[v.21, n.3-v.28, n.3] [Oct, 1962-Apr, 1969]	Periodicals
OkU	v.30, n.1-v.31, n.5; Jan, 1971-Sept, 1972	WHC
UPB	[v.22, n.3-v.36, n.2] [[1963-1977]	970.49405/SM75

Other holding institutions: CLU (CLU), NmScW.

951 <u>Smoke Signals</u>. 1956-?//. Monthly. ISSN 0560-3439. LC sn79-8711.
OCLC 5459773. RLIN AZPG82-S55, OHCP5459773-S. Last issue 20 pages,
height 28 cm. Line drawings. Available in microform: CPC (1956-1979).
Published by Colorado River Indian Tribes, Parker, AZ. Editors: Dean
C. Welsh, July 15, 1967-June 15, 1974; Daphne Peck, Jan 15, 1975-Jan
15, 1976. Community newsletter. Superceded by Manataba Messenger.

WHi	v.1, n.1-v.24. n.12; July 4, 1956-July, 1979	Microforms

WEU	v.15, n.4, 9, v.20, n.1-3; Oct, 1970, Mar 15, 1971, July 15,-Sept 15, 1975	Journalism Lab
WEU ARC	v.6, n.6 Jan, 18, 1963	Micro 11
WMUW	v.20, n.9-10; Mar 15-Apr 15, 1976	(SPL) E/75/S66s
AzNCC	v.14; Mar, 1969	Indian File
AzTeS	[v.11-v.22] [1967-1978]	XRCL 1.3/M15
AzT	v.23, n.7-v.25, n.11; Jan, 1979-June, 1980	Periodicals
CLSM	[v.11-v.22] [Jan, 1967-1978]	Periodicals
NjP	[v.1, n.1-v.24, n.12] [July 4., 1956-July, 1979]	Periodicals
UPB	[1965-1980]	970.49105/SM75

Other holding institutions: [Congressional Research Service, Washington, DC] (CRS), MH-P (HLS), [University of Minnesota Union List, Minneapolis, MN] (MUL), OrU-Special Collections.

952 <u>Smoke Signals</u>. 1970?-1974?//. Monthly. ISSN 0049-0784. OCLC 8423141. Last issue 16 pages. Line drawings, photographs, commercial advertising. Available in microform: CPC (1970-1974). Published by United American Indians of Santa Clara Valley, Santa Clara, CA. Place of publication varies: San Jose, CA, May, 1970-Jan, 1971. Editors: Fern Williams, May-Dec, 1970; Frank Garcia, Nov, 1971-June, 1974. Community newsletter. Subject focus: urban and reservation news.

WHi	[May, 1970-June, 1974]	Microforms
AzNCC	Feb-Sept, 1973	Indian File
NjP	[May, 1970-Mar, 1974]	Periodicals

Other holding institutions: PPiU (PIT).

953 <u>Smoke Signals</u>. 1959-1968?//. 3 times a year. ISSN 0583-659x. OCLC 1765660. RLIN CUBG10894925-S, CUBU10895012-S, OHCP1765660-S. Last issue 44 pages, height 29 cm. Line drawings, photographs. Available in microform: McP (1951-1968). Published by Indian Arts and Crafts

Board, United States Department of Interior, Washington, DC. Subject
focus: arts and crafts, artists.

WHi	n.1-54 Nov, 1951-Spring, 1968	Microforms
WHi	n.49-n.54; Summer, 1966-Spring, 1968	I1.84/2:49-54
AzNCC	n.?-n.54; Summer, 1965-Spring, 1968	Indian File
CLSM	n.1-54; Nov, 1951-Spring, 1968	Periodicals
CNoSU	n.1-54; Nov, 1951-Spring, 1968	Microfilm
NjP	n.33-44, 54; Feb, 1960-Spring, 1965, Spring, 1968	Periodicals
OkPAC	[n.2-54] [Feb, 1952-Spring, 1968]	Periodicals
OkU	n.1-54 Nov, 1951-Spring, 1968	WHC
OrU	n.50-54; Fall/Winter, 1966-Spring, 1968	Periodicals
UPB	[n.1-54] [Nov, 1951-Spring, 1968]	970.105/SM75

Other holding institutions: MiEM (EEM), [University of Minnesota Union
List, Minneapolis, MN] (MUL), NmScW, TxU-Da (ITD).

954 **Smoke Signals**. 1978? Monthly. Smoke Signals, 211 S. Broadway,
Baltimore, MD 21231. (301) 675-3535. Last issue 12 pages, height 28
cm. Line drawings. Available in microform: WHi (1979-). Published
by Baltimore American Indian Center. Title varies: B.A.I.C Smoke
Signals, Oct, 1980-Mar/Apr, 1981. Subject focus: urban community,
center news, social services.

WHi	Jan, 1979-Mar/Apr, 1981, Mar, 1982-	Microforms
OkTU	Aug 1, 1978-Mar/Apr, 1981	Rare Book Room

Other holding institutions: IC (CGP).

955 **Smoke Signals**. 1970? Irregular. Smoke Signals, 1001 Payne Ave., St.
Paul, MN 55101. (612) 776-8592. RLIN OHCP1605067-S. Last issue 10

pages, height 28 cm. Line drawings. Available in microform: WHi-A,
Veda Stone Papers, (1970). Published by St. Paul American Indian
Center. Title varies: Native Profile, Apr-Dec, 1980/Jan,1981.
Community newsletter. Subject focus: Catholic Church, center news.

WHi	July?, 1970	Microforms
WHi	July/Aug, 1979–	Pam 80-1133
WEU ARC	July?, 1970	Micro 11

956 <u>Smoke Signals</u>. 1982. Unknown. Smoke Signals, Box C, Lame Deer, MT
59043. (406) 477-6387. Last issue 8 pages, height 28 cm. Line
drawings, photographs. Published by Northern Cheyenne Follow Through
Resource Center and Demonstration Site. Subject focus: education
programs, center news.

WHi	v.1, n.2– May, 1982–	Circulation

957 <u>Smoke Signals</u>. 1949-1961//. Bi-monthly. OCLC 2450586. Last issue
16 pages, last volume 96 pages, height 24 cm. Line drawings,
photographs, commercial advertising. Published by Indian Association
of America, Inc., Newark, NJ. Editor: Delores M. Becker. Subject
focus: culture, legends, legislation, book reviews.

WHi	v.1, n.1–v.13, n.6; May/June, 1949–Nov/Dec, 1961	F801/8I3 Cutter
CLSM	[v,4, n.3–v.13, n.6] [1952–Nov/Dec, 1961]	Periodicals
NjMonM	v.8–v.11; 1956–1959	Periodicals
NjP	[v.1, n.1–v.8, n.6] [May/June, 1949–Nov/Dec, 1956]	Periodicals
NHu	v.1, n.1–v.13, n.6; May/June, 1949–Nov/Dec, 1961	Periodicals
NN	v.1, n.1–v.13, n.6; May/June, 1949–Nov/Dec, 1961	HBA
OC1WHi	v.2, n.4; July/Aug, 1950	Periodicals
OkTU	v.11, n.3–v.12, n.1; May.June, 1959–Jan/Feb, 1961	Rare Book Room

Other holding institutions: [Pittsburgh Regional Library Center Union
List, Pittsburgh, PA] (QPR), PCLS (REC).

958 Smoke Signals. 1954-?//. Unknown. Last issue 6 pages, height 28 cm.
    Photographs. Published by St. Francis Mission, St. Francis, SD.
    Mission newsletter. Subject focus: school news, Catholic Church.

    WMM   v.1, n.2;   Special
               Nov 12, 1954   Collections

959 Smoke Signals. 1970-?//. Irregular. Last issue 6 pages. Line
    drawings. Available in microform: WHi-A, Veda Stone Papers, (1974).
    Odanah, WI. Community newsletter.

    WHi   [Aug 11, 1971-June, 1974]   Microforms

    WEU   [Aug 11, 1971-June, 1974]   Micro 11
    ARC

960 Smoke Signals from Bacone College. 1965. 2 times a year. $3. for
    individuals and institutions. Dottie Witter, editor, Smoke Signals
    from Bacone College, Bacone College, Muskogee, OK 74401. (918)
    683-4581, ext. 279. OCLC 6194249. Last issue 16 pages, last volume
    68 pages, height 28 cm. Line drawings, photographs. Available in
    microform: WHi (1977-). Previous editor: Sandy Wagner, Spring,
    1978-Summer, 1979. School newsletter.

    WHi   n.29-   Microforms
               Spring, 1977-

    WM   Current issues   Forest Home
                                                      Branch

    WMUW   n.29-38;   (SPL)
               Spring, 1977-Summer, 1978   E/75/S67x

    NjP   ?, n.6-7;   Periodicals
               Spring, July, 1970-
               Jan, 1971

    OkU   [no nos.-n.12]   WHC
               [Summer, 1965-Winter, 1972]

    Other holding institutions: [Blackfeet Community College, Browning, MT]

961 Smoke Signals from Intermountain Indian School. 1950-?//. Irregular.
    Last issue 6 pages, last volume 38 pages, height 32 cm.

Line drawings, photographs. Brigham City, UT. School newsletter.
Subject focus: education, school news.

CLSM	v.2, n.1-v.5, n.3; Oct 26, 1951-Dec 30, 1955	Periodicals

962 <u>Smoke Signals, News and Views</u>. 1969//. Unknown. Last issue 6 pages,
height 28 cm. Photographs. Available in microform: WHi (1969).
Published by All American Indian Days, Sheridan, WY. Subject focus:
arts and crafts, artists, pagent news.

WHi	July?, 1969	Microfilm

963 <u>Smoke Signs/Fire Flames</u>. 1969-?//. Monthly. Last issue 8 pages,
height 22 cm. Line drawings, photographs. Available in microform:
CPC (1969-1970). New York, NY. Editor: Spiritu Siboney (Joe
Casanova), Jan, 1969-Dec, 1970. Subject focus: radical politics,
(reprints of articles from other newspapers).

WHi	v.1, n.1-v.2, n.12; Jan, 1969-Dec, 1970	Microforms
WEU	[v.1, n.1-12] [Jan-Dec, 1969]	Journalism Lab
AzNCC	v.1, n.1-v.2, n.12; Jan, 1969-Dec, 1970	Indian File
NjP	v.1, n.1-v.2, n.12; Jan, 1969-Dec, 1970	Periodicals
NHu	v.1, n.1-v.2, n.12; Jan, 1969-Dec, 1970	Periodicals
PPT	[v.1, n.4-v.2, n.7/8] [July, 1969-July/Aug, 1970]	Contemporary Culture

Other holding institutions: OrU-Special Collections.

964 <u>Smoke Talk</u>. 1971-1973?//. Last issue 16 pages. Line drawings,
photographs. Available in microform: McP (1971-1972). Published by
U. S. Department of Justice, Steilacoom, WA. Editors: Niva Henshaw,
Sept 17-Dec 10, 1971; Vic Fourstar, Jan 7, 1972; Vic Fourstar and
Peter Johnson, Jan 28-Apr 7, 1972; Vic Fourstar, June 9, June 23,
1972; Percy "Bucky" Comes Last, July-Dec, 1972. Subject focus:
culture, religion, socio-economic conditions, politics.

WHi	v.1, n.11-v.2, n.14; Sept 17, 1971-Dec, 1972	Microforms

AzNCC   v.1-v.2, n.9;   Indian File
            Oct, 1971-Aug, 1972

CNoSU   v.1, n.11-v.2, n.14;   Microfilm
            Sept 17, 1971-Dec, 1972

NjP   [v.2, n.9-v.3, n.2]   Periodicals
            [Aug, 1972-Feb, 1973]

OkU   v.1, n.11-v.2, n.14;   WHC
            Sept 17, 1971-Dec, 1972

Other holding institutions: NmScW.

965 Sota Eya Ye Yapa. 1970-1978?//. Bi-weekly. OCLC 6189093. Last
     issue 4 pages. Line drawings. Available in microform: WHi (1973);
     CPC (1970-1973). Published by Sisseton-Wahpeton Sioux Tribe of the
     Lake Traverse Reservation, Sisseton, SD. Editor: Sandra Roberts, Dec
     16, 1971-Sept 21, 1972; Silas Ortley, Mar 22-Aug 23, 1973. Community
     newsletter, supplement to Sisseton Courier.

     WHi   [v.1, n.1?]-33;   Microforms
                 Feb 1970-Aug 23, 1973

     WEU   [no numbers]   Journalism
                 Jan-Mar, 1971   Lab

     WMUW   [v.2, n.8-19]   (SPL)
                 [July 28, 1977-June 29, 1978]   E/75/S68x

     AzNCC   Nov/Dec, 1971   Indian File

     NjP   [v.1, n.1?]-33;   Periodicals
                 [Feb, 1970-Aug 23, 1973]

     Other holding institutions: [Standing Rock Community College Library,
     Fort Yates, ND].

966 The Source. 1980. Monthly, irregular. The Source, Room 130, Bataan
     Memorial Bldg., Santa Fe, NM 87503. (505) 827-2762. OCLC 7744991.
     Last issue 7 pages, height 36 cm. Line drawings. Published by New
     Mexico Office of Indian Affairs. Title varies: New Mexico Office of
     Indian Affairs Newsletter, Mar, 1980-Apr, 1981. Subject focus: local
     and state news, legislation.

     WHi   v.1, n.1-   Circulation
                 Mar, 1980-

     Other holding institutions: NmLcU (IRU).

967 <u>South Piegan Drum/Estukimatisis</u>. 1979. Monthly. $5. for individuals
    and institutions. Jean McDonald, editor, South Piegan Drum, Central
    Ave., E, Highway 2, Browning, MT 59417. (406) 338-4881. Last issue
    16 pages. height 41 cm. Line drawings, photographs, commercial
    advertising. Published by Blackfeet Tribal Council, Department of
    Blackfeet Multi-Media. Community newsletter. Subject focus: local
    and national news, Blackfeet people.

    MtBBCC   v.1, n.1-10;   Periodicals
                Jan-Nov, 1979

    MtHi   v.1, n.1-11;   Z/970.105
                Jan-Dec, 1979   So87p

968 <u>Southern Cheyenne & Arapaho Nation News</u>. 1980-1981//. Monthly. Last
    issue 8 pages, height 38 cm. Line drawings, photographs, commercial
    advertising. Available in microform: WHi (1980-1981). Concho, OK.
    Editors: Francis Hamilton, Sept, 1980; Michelle Hoffman, Nov, 1980,
    Valerie White, Dec, 1980. Community newsletter. Subject focus:
    Cheyenne and Arapaho people, poetry.

    WHi   v.1, n.1-7;   Microforms
                July, 1980-May, 1981

    OkU   v.1, n.5-7;   WHC
                Jan-May, 1981

969 <u>Southern Indian Co-operative News</u>. 1968?// Last issue 4 pages,
    height 36 cm. Photographs. Calgary, Alberta, Canada. Editor: T.
    Douglas Irwin. Subject focus: cooperatives of southern Alberta.

    CaACG   Feb 27, Apr 9, 1968   Periodicals

970 <u>Southern Indian Studies</u>. 1949-1976//?. Annual. ISSN 0085-6525. LC
    58-37269. OCLC 1766191. RLIN CUBG49673403-S, MIUG15963-S,
    OHCP1766191-S. Last issue 30 pages. Line drawings, photographs.
    Available in microform: McA (1949-1973) CPC (1950-1973). Published by
    Archaeological Society of North Carolina and the Research Laboratories
    of Anthropology and Archaeology, Chapel Hill, NC. Frequency varies:
    semi-annual, Apr, 1949-Oct, 1950. Editor: Joffee L. Coe, Apr,
    1949-Oct, 1958. Subject focus: archaeology, anthropology, history.

    WHi   v.1, n.1-v.28;   PWA83S/7S727
                Apr, 1949-Oct, 1976   Cutter

    WHi   v.1, n.1-v.28;   Microforms
                Apr, 1949-Oct, 1976

    OkTU   v.20-v.26;   Indian File
                Oct, 1968-Oct, 1974

CLSM	v.1, n.1-v.28; Apr, 1949-Oct, 1976	Periodicals
CU-A	v.1, n.1-v.28; Apr, 1949-Oct, 1976	E/78/S65/S6
ICN	v.1, n.1-v.28; Apr, 1949-Oct, 1976	Ayer 1/S722 1949
NjP	[v.1, n.2-v.26] [Oct, 1949-Oct, 1974]	Periodicals
NcMhC	v.1- 1949-	Periodicals
OkTU	v.25-v.26; Oct, 1973-Oct, 1974	Rare Book
OkU	v.1-v.21; 1949-1969	WHC
UPB	[v.1-v.29] [1949-1977]	970.105/SC88
CaOPeT	v.1-v.23, v.26- 1949-1971, 1974-	E78/S55S6

Other holding institutions: AAP (AAA), ArU (AFU), [Amerind Foundation, Ind., Dragoon, AZ], AzTeS (AZS), CLU (CLU), GASU (GSU), InMuB (IBS), [Indiana Union list of Serials, Indianapolis, IN] (ILS), InU (IUL), MiEM (EEM), MnHi (MHS), [University of Minnesota Union List, Minneapolis, MN] (MUL), [Western Nevada Community College, Carson City, NV], NcDaD (NNM), NSbSU (YSM), OC1W (CWR), PU (PAU), [Pittsburgh Regional Library Center Union List, Pittsburgh, PA] (QPR), ScU (SUC), TNJ (TJC), TxU (IXA), Vi (VIC), ViW (VWM).

971 Southern Plains Inter-Tribal Center. 1980. Monthly. Southern Plains Inter-Tribal Center, 124 N.E. Rogers Ln., Lawton, OK 73501. (405) 353-4604. Last issue 4 pages, height 40 cm. Line drawings. Center newsletter.

| WHi | v.1, n.2-3, v.2, n.1-5;
July-Sept, 1980, Apr-Sept, 1981 | Microforms |

972 The Southern Ute Drum. 1968. Bi-weekly. $4. for individuals and institutions. The Southern Ute Drum, Ignacio, CO 81137. (303) 563-4525. ISSN 0587-0674. OCLC 1773546. RLIN OCHP1773546-S. Last issue 12 pages. Photographs, commercial advertising. Available in microform: McP (1971-1972); WHi (1968-). Previous editors: James Jefferson, Mar 26, 1971-Jan 14, 1972; John E. Baker, Sr., Jan 28-Feb 25, 1972; Eddie Box, Sr., Mar 10, 1972-Sept 6, 1974; Tom Longhurst, Sept 20, 1974-Oct 1, 1976; Jeanne W. Englert, Oct 29, 1976-Nov 23,

1977; James Jefferson, Feb 17, 1978-Dec 21, 1979. Community
newsletter. Subject focus: Ute people.

WHi	v.1, n.1– Aug, 1968–	Microforms
WEU	v.2, n.18–v.3, n.3; Jan 1-June 4, 1971	Journalism Lab
WMUW	[v.7. n.1–v.9, n.13] [Jan 10, 1975-July 7, 1977]	(SPL) E/75/S7x
AzNCC	v.2– 1969–	Indian File
CNoSU	[v.2–v.4] [1971-Dec 20, 1972]	Microfilm
NjP	[v.1–v.9, n.24] [Dec 23, 1968-Dec 8, 1977]	Periodicals
OkU	[v.2–v.4] [Jan 1, 1971-Dec 29, 1972]	WHC

Other holding institutions: KSteC (KKQ), [University of Minnesota
Union List, Minneapolis, MN] (MUL), NmScW.

973 Southwest Bilingual Education Training Resource Center Newsletter.
1977-1978//. Quarterly. Last issue 8 pages, height 28 cm.
Photographs. Published by University of New Mexico, College of
Education, Albuquerque, NM. Subject focus: bilingual education and
teaching (local). Superceded by American Indian Bilingual Education
Center Newsletter.

| NCBE | v.1, n.2-6
1977-1978 | Periodicals |

974 Southwestern Association on Indian Affairs Newsletter. 1958?//.
Unknown. Last issue 6 pages. Available in microform: WHi-A, Veda
Stone Papers, (1958). Santa Fe, NM. Subject focus: education,
educational opportunities.

| WHi | Jan, 1958 | Microforms |
| WEU
ARC | Jan, 1958 | Micro 11 |

975 Spawning the Medicine River. 1979. 3 times a year. $6. for
individuals and institutions. Phillip Foss, Jr., editor, College of
Santa Fe Campus, St. Michaels Dr., Santa Fe, NM 87501-9990. (505)

988-6295. RLIN NHDG82-S77. Last issue 60 pages, height 28 cm. Line
drawings. Published by Bureau of Indian Affairs-Institute of American
Indian Arts. Subject focus: graphics, fiction, poetry.

WU	n.7– Fall, 1981–	Rare Book Room
AzNCC	n.?– Fall, 1980–	Indian File
AzHM	n.8– 1982–	Periodicals

976 The Speaking Leaves. 1971-1975//. Irregular. OCLC 5050589. Last
issue 26 pages. Line drawings, photographs. Available in microform:
McP (1971-1972); WHi (1973-1975). Published by American Indian
Cultural Group-California Penal System, Vacaville, CA. Editors:
Joseph Reynolds, Apr, 1971; Frank Bliss, May-June, 1971; Anthony D.
Esposito, July-Aug, 1971; Harry Schader, Nov-Dec, 1971; Frederick
Dillon, Mar-Apr, 1972; Gene Lamoreau, Sept, 1972-Jan, 1973; Richard G.
Hone, Feb-May, 1973; Melvin R. Parra, July, 1973-Feb, 1975; Warren
Conrad, Mar-May, 1975; Robert Martinez, Aug-Oct, 1975; Ernest J.
Sherwood, Nov-Dec, 1975. Prison newsletter.

WHi	v.1, n.4–v.2, n.12; Apr, 1971–Dec, 1975	Microforms
CNoSU	v.1, n.4–?; Apr, 1971–1972	Microfilm
NjP	v.1, n.1; Jan, 1971	Periodicals
NHu	[v.1–v.2] [Oct, 1972–Nov, 1975]	Periodicals

Other holding institutions: NmScW.

977 Speaking of Ourselves. 1974. Monthly. Betty Blue, editor, Speaking
of Ourselves, Box 217, Cass lake, MN 56633. (218) 335-2252. OCLC
6188897, 6188912. Last issue 8 pages, last volume 120 pages, height
39 cm. Line drawings, photographs, commercial advertising. Available
in microform: WHi (1975-1977, 1978-). Published by Minnesota Chippewa
Tribe. Title varies: Ni Ma Mi Kwa Zoo Min, Dec?, 1974-Oct, 1977.
Community newsletter. Subject focus: Chippewa people. Includes
separately paged and numbered reservation news sections: The News,
no-dah-mo-win (Bois Fort Reservation); Anishinabe dee-bah- gee-mo-win
(White Earth Reservation); Mi-se-as-ka-e-ka-nink (Mille Lacs
Reservation); Ba-bash-ki-mini-ti-gog (Fond du Lac Reservation) Kitchi
Onigaming, Bimadisiwin (Grand Portage Reservation).

WHi   [v. 1, n.8-v.3, n.11], v.4, n.1-   Circulation
           [Apr, 1975-Oct, 1977], Jan, 1978-

WMUW   [v. 1, n.8-v.3, n.11], v.4, n.1-   (SPL)
           [Apr, 1975-Oct, 1977], Jan, 1978-   E/75/N5x

MnBemT   v.1-   Periodicals
           1974-

MnHi   v.1, n. 3-   Periodicals
           Dec, 1974-

MtBBCC   [v.6-v.7]   Periodicals
           [Aug, 1980-Feb, 1981]

Other holding institutions: IC (CGP), [University of Wisconsin-Stevens
Point-Native American Center, Stevens Point, WI]. [Wisconsin Indian
Resource Council, Stevens Point, WI].

978 Special Editions. 1973-1981//. 6 times a year. ISSN 0139-8304,
    0139-8340. Last issue 60 pages, height 28 cm. Line drawings,
    photographs, some in color, commercial advertising. Published by
    Ontario Metis and Non-Status Indian Association, Willowdale, Ontario,
    Canada. Title varies: Dimensions, Jan, 1974-July, 1980. Frequency
    varies: quarterly, Jan 1974; bi-monthly, June, 1974-Jan/Feb, 1975;
    Monthly, May 1975-June/July, 1979. Editors: Mina H. Caunce, Jan,
    1974-July, 1980; Marty Dunn, June/July, 1980-Sept/Oct, 1981. Subject
    focus: rights, culture, Metis and Non-Status people.

WHi   [v.2, n.1-v.9, n.5]   Bindery
           [Jan, 1974-Sept/Oct, 1981]

CaAEU   v.6, n.1-v.9, n.4;   Boreal
           1978-1981   Institute

CaOAFN   v.9, n.2?-5;   Periodicals
           Apr-Sept/Oct, 1981

CaOONL   v.1, n.1-6;   Periodicals
           1973

979 Spilyay Tymoo: Coyote News. 1976. Bi-weekly. $6. for individuals
    and institutions. Sid Miller, editor, Spilyay Tymoo: Coyote News,
    P.O. Box 735, Warm Springs, OR 97761. (503) 553-1644. OCLC 6168822,
    6573994. Last issue 12 pages, last volume 320 pages, height 42 cm.
    Line drawings, photographs. Available in microform: WHi (1977-).
    Published by Confederated Tribes of the Warm Springs Reservation of
    Oregon. Community newsletter.

WHi   v.2, n.5-   Microforms
           Mar 4, 1977-

WM   Current issues   Forest Home
                                                                Branch

WMUW   [v.1, n.5-v.3, n.5]   (SPL)
            [Mar 19, 1976-Mar 10, 1978]   E/75/S72x

MtBBCC   v.5;   Periodicals
            Aug-Dec, 1980

OrHi   v.4, n.12-   Periodicals
            June, 1979-

Spirit of the People. ST. Paul, MN

   see Native American Solidarity Committee. St. Paul, MN

980 Spiritual Light. 1943?//. Quarterly. OCLC 1608182. Last issue 10
     pages, height 28 cm. Published by United Church Board of Home
     Missions, Norway House, Manitoba, Canada. Editor: Rev. F.G. Stevens.
     Subject focus: missions, Christian religion, Cree people. In Cree,
     100%.

     CaACG   Spring, Fall, 1943   Periodicals

     Other holding institutions: [University of Minnesota Union List,
     Minneapolis, MN] (MUL).

Squol Quol: Lummi Indian News. Billington, WA

   see Lummi Squol Quol. Billington, WA

981 Standing Rock Star. 1971-?//?. Bi-weekly. Last issue 6 pages,
     height 25 cm. Standing Rock Sioux Reservation, ND. Community
     newsletter. Subject focus: Dakota (Standing Rock Sioux) people.

     WEU   v.1, n.2-7;   Journalism
                Jan 18-Mar 29, 1971   Lab

     NjP   v.2, n.16-19;   Periodicals
                Nov 6-Dec 18, 1972

     Other holding institutions: [Standing Rock Community College Library,
     Fort Yates, ND], OrU-Special Collections.

982 The Stealing of California. 1976-1979//. Quarterly. OCLC 5071861.
     RLIN NYPG774180524-S, CUBU12748328-S. Last issue 12 pages. Line

drawings. Available in microform: WHi (1976). Published by Native
American Training Associates Institute, Inc., Sacramento, CA. Title
varies: Private Property, California Indian Land, June, 1976. Subject
focus: history, education, religion, culture, politics.

WHi	v.1, n.1-2; June-Dec, 1976	Microforms
CL	v.2, n.1 Winter, 1978/79	Periodicals
CLSM	v.1, n.1-v.2, n.1 June, 1976-Winter, 1978/79	Periodicals

Other holding institutions: DSI (SMI).

983 <u>Sto:Lo Nation News</u>. 1976? Monthly. Cathy Hall, editor, Sto:Lo
Nation News, Box 370, Sardis, British Columbia, Canada. VOX 140.
Last issue 8 pages, height 28 cm. Line drawings, photographs.
Published by Coqualeetza Education Training Centre. Subject focus:
education.

WHi	v.7, n.68, 71- Jan, Apr/May, 1982-	Circulation
CAOAFN	v.7, n.70- Feb?, 1982-	Periodicals

984 <u>Stoney Country</u>. 1972-1975?//. Irregular. Last issue 28 pages,
height 28 cm. Photographs. Published by Stoney Cultural Education
Program, Morley, Alberta, Canada. Community newsletter. Subject
focus: education, Stoney people.

CaACG	Dec, 1972-Dec, 1975	Periodicals

985 <u>Stoney Echo</u>. 1981. Monthly. Walt Chomyn, editor, Stoney Tribal
Administration Office, Morley, Alberta, Canada T0L 1N0. (403)
881-3770/3993. Last issue 24 pages, height 44 cm. Line drawings,
photographs, commercial advertising. Published by Stoney Tribal
Administration. Newspaper. Subject focus: Stoney people, Bearspaw,
Chiniquay and Wesley bands.

CaACG	v.1, n.4-5; Sept-Oct., 1981	Periodicals
CaOPeT	v.1, n.1- Apr, 1981-	Periodicals

986 <u>Stoney News</u>. 1977-1978?//. Bi-weekly. Last issue 8 pages, height 28
    cm. Line drawings, photographs. Published by Stoney Tribal Council,
    Morley, Alberta, Canada. Community newsletter. Subject focus: Stoney
    people.

    CaACG   [n.1-8]   Periodicals
             [Nov 23, 1977-Apr 28, 1978]

987 <u>Stoney News and Bulletin</u>. 1974-1976?//. Bi-weekly. Last issue 3
    pages, height 28 cm. Photographs. Morley, Alberta, Canada. Title
    varies: Morley News and Bulletin, Oct 25, 1974-May 23, 1975. Editors:
    Ernest Wesley; Dave Sweeney. Community newsletter. Subject focus:
    Stoney people.

    CaACG   [n.1-26]   Periodicals
             [Oct 25, 1974-Apr 9, 1976]

988 <u>Studies in Native American Literature Newsletter</u>. 1977. Quarterly.
    Studies in Native American Literature Newsletter, 602 Philosophy Hall,
    Columbia University, New York, NY 10027. OCLC 8275170. Last issue 16
    pages, height 22 cm. Subject focus: literature, bibliography, book
    and movie reviews.

    WHi   v.4, n.4;   Microforms
             Autumn, 1980

    AzNCC   v.6-   Indian File
             Winter, 1982-

    ICN   Current issues   CHAI

    OkU   v.1, n.1-   WHC
             Mar, 1977-

    Other holding institutions: MH (HUL), MH-P (TOZ).

989 <u>The Sun Child</u>. 1979-1981//. Weekly during school year. ISSN
    0198-5914. LC sn80-11927. OCLC 6190504. Last issue 4 pages, height
    28 cm. Line drawings, photographs. Missoula, MT. Editors: Patrica
    Scott, Oct 1, 1979-Sept 22, 1980; Charles Courchene, Sept 29, 1980-May
    4, 1981. School newsletter. Subject focus: culture, history, art.

    WHi   v.2, n.1-v.3, n.18;   Circulation
             Sept 24, 1979-May 4, 1981

    WMM   v.2, n.21;   Special
             Oct 6, 1980   Collections

    AzNCC   v.2-v.3, n.18;   Indian File
             Dec, 1980-May 4, 1981

MtBBCC   v.3;   Periodicals
           Jan-May, 1981

CaACG   [v.1, n.1-v.3, n.18]   Periodicals
           [Sept 24, 1979-May 4, 1981]

990 Sun Dance Echo. 1964-1966//. Monthly. Last issue 16 pages, height
    36 cm. Line drawings, photographs, commercial advertising. Published
    by Blood Reserve, Cardston, Alberta, Canada. Community newsletter.
    Subject focus: Blood people.

    CaACG   v.1, n.3-v.3, n.2;   Periodicals
               Apr, 1964-Mar, 1966

    CaOORD   [v.1, n.2-v.3, n.2]   Periodicals
               [Mar, 1964-Mar, 1966]

991 Sun Tracks. 1971-1980//?. Annual. ISSN 0300-788x. LC sn80-11499,
    80-643320. OCLC 1335401, 8487523. RLIN RIBG82-S620, NYPG19572832-S,
    NYPG82-S71, DCLC80643320-S, CSUP102437-S, NHDG232-S, OHCP1335401-S.
    Last issue 240 pages. Line drawings, photographs. Available in
    microform: CPC (1971-1980). Tucson, AZ Frequency varies: quarterly,
    June, 1971-Spring, 1972; semi-annual, Fall, 1975-Spring, 1977.
    Subject focus: fiction, poetry, graphics, photography.

    WHi   v.1, n.1-v.6;   Microforms
               June, 1971-1980

    AzFM   v.1, n.1-v.6;   570.6/T88s
               June, 1971-1980

    AzNCCU   v.1, n.1-v.6;   Indian File
               June, 1971-1980

    AzT   v.1, n.1-v.6;   Periodicals
               June, 1971-1980

    AzU   v.1, n.1-v.6;   I979/S95
               June, 1971-1980

    CL   v.1, n.2-3, v.3-v.6;   Periodicals
               Fall, 1971-Spring, 1972, Fall, 1975-1980

    CLSM   v.1, n.1;   Periodicals
               June, 1971

    NjP   [v.1, n.2-v.4]   Periodicals
               [Fall, 1971-1978]

    NN   v.1, n.1-v.6;   JFM 82-1
               June, 1971-1980

OkU   v.1, n.1–v.6;   WHC
           June, 1971–1980

WaS   v.1, n.1–v.6;   Literature
           June, 1971–1980   Dept.

Other holding institutions: AzTeS (AZS), CLU (CLU), CTurS (CTU), CXv
(SXP), DLC (DLC), ICN (IBV), MWelC (WEL), [Dull Knife Memorial
Library, Lame Deer, MT], NdU (UND), NmU (IQU), NPotU (ZQM), PPiU
(PIT), SdU (USD), TU (TKN), UU (UUM), WyU (WYU).

992 Sundevil Roundup. 1976–1979//. Irregular. Last issue 12 pages.
    Line drawings, photographs. Available in microform: WHi (1979).
    Published by Rough Rock Community High School, Rough Rock, AZ.
    Editor: Abbie Willetto. School newsletter.

WHi   v.3, n.3, v.4, n.2, 5;   Microforms
           Mar 16, 1978, Mar 6, July 6, 1979

AzNCC   v.2–v.4;   Indian File
           Oct, 1977–July, 1979

NjP   v.3, n.3;   Periodicals
           Mar 16, 1978

OkTU   v.4, n.2, 5;   Rare Book
           Mar 6, July 6, 1979   Room

CaOPeT   v.2, n.3–v.3, n.2;   Microfilm
           Feb, 1977–1978

The Suquamish News. Suquamish, WA

    see Dsuq' Wab' Siatsub/The Suquamish News. Suquamish, WA

993 The Swift Arrow. 1961–1964?//. Monthly. Last issue 10 pages.
    Personal names indexed in: Index to Wisconsin Native American
    Periodicals (1964). Available in microform: WHi–A, Veda Stone Papers,
    (1964). Published by First English Lutheran Church, Wisconsin Rapids,
    WI. Subject focus: Lutheran Church, local news.

WHi   v.4, n.6, 9–10;   Microforms
           June, Sept–Oct, 1964

WEU   v.4, n.6, 9–10;   Micro 11
ARC   June, Sept–Oct, 1964

994 T.A. Newsletter. 1976? Monthly. Free to individuals and
    institutions. Colleen E. Ned, editor, T.A. Newsletter, P.O. Box
    99253, Seattle, WA 98199. (206) 285-4425. Last issue 8 pages, height
    28 cm. Published by United Indians of All Tribes, Resource and
    Evaluation Center 3. Subject focus: education.

    NCBE   v.2, n.16-   Periodicals
                1978-

995 TC Newsletter. 1967-?//. Irregular. Last issue 4 pages. Line
    drawings. Available in microform: WHi-A, Veda Stone Papers, (1967,
    1968). Published by University of Minnesota Training Center for
    Community Programs, Minneapolis, MN. Subject focus: social services
    for minorities, programs for area Native Americans.

    WHi   n.3, 7-8, 12;   Microforms
                May, Oct-Nov, 1967, Apr/May, 1968

    WEU   n.3, 7-8, 12;   Micro 11
    ARC   May, Oct-Nov, 1967, Apr/May, 1968

996 Tacoma Indian News. 1977-1982//. Monthly. OCLC 6189081. Last issue
    8 pages, last volume 96 pages, height 44 cm. Line drawings,
    photographs, commercial advertising. Tacoma, WA. Editors: Kai Silva,
    Sept 23, 1976-Mar 30, 1979; Donna Matheson, May 31, 1979-Mar 28, 1980;
    Riva Red Swallow, June 27-Nov 7, 1980, Sandra Susanna Griffith, Dec 1,
    1980-Feb, 1982; Dennis Gustafson, May, 1982. Community newsletter.
    Subject focus: local and national news.

    WHi   v.1, n.1-v.6, n.5;   Microforms
                Sept 23, 1976-May, 1982

    WMUW   v.1, n.1;   (SPE)
                Sept 23, 1976   E/75/T32x

    MtBBCC   v.5;   Periodicals
                June-Aug, 1981

    NjP   [v.1, n.5-v.3, n.1]   Periodicals
                [Jan 13, 1977-Nov 20, 1978]

    OkTU   v.2, n.9-v.6, n.5;   Rare Book
                July, 1978-May, 1982   Room

    Other holding institutions: ICN (IBV), [Standing Rock Community
    College Library, Fort Yates, ND].

997 The Tahlequah Arrow. 1888-1920//. Weekly. Last issue 8 pages. Line
    drawings, commercial advertising. Tahlequah, OK. Available in
    microform: OkHi (1888-1897). Title varies: Indian Arrow, Feb 24,

1888–July 7, 1894; The Arrow, Jan 25, 1895–Sept 12, 1896. Place of
Publication varies: Vinita, OK, Feb 24, 1888; Fort Gibson, OK, Apr 12,
1888–Aug 15, 1889. Editors: William P. Ross, Feb 24, 1888–Aug 15,
1889; John T. Drew, Aug 23, 1890; James W. Duncan, Feb 23, 1893;
Waddie Hudson, Nov 21, 1903. Newspaper. Also decribed in: Foreman,
Carolyn Thomas. Oklahoma Imprints, 1835–1907. Norman: University of
Oklahoma Press, 1936.

WHi	[v.1, n.3–v.11, n.2] [Feb 24, 1888–Sept 18, 1897]	Microforms
OkHi	[v.1, n.3–v.11, n.2] [Feb 24, 1888–Sept 18, 1897]	Microforms
MWA	[v. 11, n.53–v.17, n.52] [Sept 10, 1898–Sept 3, 1904]	Periodicals

998 Tahlequah Courier. 1893–?//. Weekly. Last issue 4 pages. Line
    drawings, commercial advertising. Tahlequah, OK. Available in
    microform: OkHi (1893). Editor: John L. Adair, Sr. Newspaper.
    Supercedes Indian Sentinel. Also described in: Foreman, Carolyn
    Thomas. Oklahoma Imprints, 1835–1907. Norman: University of Oklahoma
    Press, 1936.

| WHi | v.1, n.13, 17, 22;
Sept 19, Oct 17, Dec 13, 1893 | Microforms |
| OkHi | v.1, n.13, 17, 22;
Sept 19, Oct 17, Dec 13, 1893 | Microforms |

999 Tahlequah Leader. 1904–?//. Weekly. Last issue 6 pages. Line
    drawings, commercial advertising. Tahlequah, OK. Available in
    microform: OkHi (1904). Editor: Stewart B. Stone. Newspaper. Also
    described in: Foreman, Carolyn Thomas. Oklahoma Imprints, 1835–1907.
    Norman: University of Oklahoma Press, 1936.

| WHi | v.1, n.6, 14;
Aug 5, Sept 30, 1904 | Microforms |
| OkHi | v.1, n.6, 14;
Aug 5, Sept 30, 1904 | Microforms |

1000 Tahlequah Leader. 1921–?//. Weekly. Last issue 4 pages. Line
     drawings, commercial advertising. Available in microform: OkHi
     (1921–1923). Tahlequah, OK. Title varies: Democratic Leader, May 26,
     1921–Oct 19, 1922. Editors: George P. Hardy and J. H. Ragland, May
     26, 1921–Feb 9, 1922; George P. Hardy and William Condon, Mar 2–Oct
     12, 1922; O. E. Butler, Oct 19, 1922–Feb 5, 1923. Newspaper. Also
     described in: Foreman, Carolyn Thomas. Oklahoma Imprints, 1835–1907.
     Norman: University of Oklahoma Press, 1936.

WHi   v.1, n.1-v.2, n.40;   Microforms
             May 26, 1921-Feb 15, 1923

The Tahlequah Telephone. Tahlequah, OK

    see The Telephone. Tahlequah, OK

1001 Talking Leaf. 1935. Monthly. Adrian Lewis, editor, Talking Leaf,
     1111 W. Washington Blvd., Los Angeles, CA 90015. (213) 747-9521.
     ISSN 0300-6247. LC sn80-3058. OCLC 1342763. RLIN NYPG764839593-S,
     OHCP1342763-S. Last issue 16 pages, last volume 144 pages, height 38
     cm. Line drawings, photographs, commercial advertising. Available in
     microform: McA (1974-); McP (1972). Published by The Indian Centers,
     Inc. Previous editors: Sandra Osawa, Jan, 1972-June, 1973; Ellis R.
     Haikey, July, 1973-Jan, 1981; Dorothy Reese, Feb, 1981-Mar 15, 1982.
     Community newsletter. Subject focus: local and national news,
     education, career opportunities, poetry.

        WHi   v.37. n.1-   Microforms
                   Mar, 1972-

        WEU   v.37, n.1-v.38, n.6;   Microfilm
                   Mar, 1972-Nov, 1973

        WMUW   [v.41, n.5-v.43, n.7]   (SPL)
                   [May, 1976-Oct, 1978]   E/75/T34x

        AzNCC   v.38-   Microfilm
                   1973-

        CLSM   v.17?;   Periodicals
                   May, 1951-

        CL   v.33-   Periodicals
                   1968-

        MnBemT   [v.41-v.42], v.43-   Periodicals
                   [1976-1977], 1978-

        MtBBCC   [v.45-v.46]   Periodicals
                   [Aug, 1980-Jan, 1981]

        NjP   v.31?-v.44, n.3]   Periodicals
                   [Oct/Nov, 1966-Apr/May, 1979]

        OkU   v.37, v.41, n.11-   WHC
                   Jan/Feb-Oct/Nov, 1972, Nov, 1976-

        SdU   v.41;   Microfilm
                   1976

        CaOAFN   Current issues   Periodicals

CaOPeT   v.38, n.7-   Microfilm
           Jan/Feb, 1974-

Other holding institutions: AzU (AZU), CLobS (CLO), CLU (CLU), KSteU
(KKQ), MH-P (HLS), [University of Minnesota Union List, Minneapolis,
MN] (MUL), NmScW, [Standing Rock Community College Library, Fort
Yates, ND], Ok (OKD).

1002 Talking Leaves. 1972-1978?//. Irregular. Last issue 18 pages,
     height 28 cm. Line drawings. Chicago, IL. Community newsletter.
     Subject focus: urban community, poetry, fiction.

     ICN   [v.6, n.2-v.7, n.1]   CHAI
                [May/June, 1977-Oct, 1978]

1003 Talking Leaves. 1963?//. Monthly. Last issue 20 pages, height 28
     cm. Line drawings, photographs. Published by Skiatook News,
     Skiatook, OK. Subject focus: history, art, culture, Oklahoma Native
     people.

     OkU   v.1, n.1, 3;   WHC
                June, Aug, 1963

     CaACG   v.1, n.2;   Periodicals
                July, 1963

1004 Talking Leaves. 1971-1974//. Unknown. ISSN 0384-1782, 0384-1790.
     LC cn77-030674, cn77-03675. OCLC 3258426. Last issue 18 pages,
     height 28 cm. Line drawings. Published by Native Brotherhood of the
     Joyceville Institution, Kingston, Ontario, Canada. Editors: Robert
     (Sarge) O'Connor, Dec?, 1973, Al Sinobert, Mar, 1974. Penal
     Newletter. Includes fiction, poetry, legends.

     CaOONL   Dec?, 1973, Mar, 1974   Periodicals

1005 Talking Peace Pipe. 1975. Monthly. Talking Peace Pipe, 8830 E. 10
     Mile Rd., P.O. Box 861, Warren, MI 48090-0861. (313) 756-1350. Last
     issue 16 pages, height 28 cm. Line drawings. Published by
     Southeastern Michigan Indians. Community newsletter.

     WHi   Jan, 1982-   Circulation

     WM   Current issues   Forest Home
                                                          Branch

     MiU-B   Mar, 1980-   Periodicals

     Other holding institutions: [WGrU-Native American Studies Dept.].

1006 <u>Talks and Thoughts of the Hampton Indian Students</u>. 1886-?//.
     Unknown. Last issue 4 pages, height 21 cm. Published by Hampton
     Institute, Hampton, VA. Editors: Walter Battice, Samuel De Fond,
     Margaret La Flesche. School newsletter. Subject focus: acculturation.

     WHi   v.2, n.2;   Pam 76-1314
                Apr, 1887

     NN   n.6-21;   HBA
                June, 1891-July, 1907

     <u>Tanana Chiefs Conference Newsletter</u>. Fairbanks, AK

         see <u>Doyon Newsletter</u>. Fairbanks, AK

1007 <u>Tapwe</u>. 1980?. Weekly. $15. Canada; $20. United States for
     individuals and institutions. Vicky Latour, editor, Tapwe, Box 130,
     Hay River, Northwest Territories, Canada X0E 0R0. Last issue 12
     pages, height 43 cm. Photographs, commerical advertising. Subject
     focus: national, provincial and local news.

     CaSiCC   Current issues   Periodicals

1008 <u>Taqralik</u>. 1974. 10 Times a year. $10. for individuals; $20. for
     institutions. Andre Girard, editor, Taqralik, P.O. Box 179, Kuujjuaq
     (Fort Chimo), Quebec, Canada J0M 1C0. (819) 964-2925. ISSN
     0319-1311. LC cn75-34723. OCLC 2442114. RLIN OHCP2442114-S. Last
     issue 56 pages, height 28 cm. Line drawings, photographs, commercial
     advertising. Published by Makivik Information Department. Frequency
     varies: monthly, Apr-June, 1977. Previous editor: Alec C. Gordon,
     Apr-June, 1977. Subject focus: culture, language preservation,
     hunting and trapping rights, politics, local and regional news, Inuit
     people. In Inuit, 30%; in French, 30%.

     WHi   v.2, n.9-10; [no nos.]   Circulation
                Apr-June, 1977, Dec, 1980-

     CaAEU   May, 1974-Oct, 1978   Boreal
                                                               Institute

     CaMWU   [v.1-v.3]   971/T1695
                [1974-1978]

     Other holding institutions: CaOONL (NLC).

     <u>Tasutit</u>. Eskimo Point, Northwest Territories, Canada

see <u>The Messenger (Tasutit)</u>. Eskimo Point, Northwest Territories,
Canada

1009 <u>Tawow</u>. 1970-1980//. Quarterly. ISSN 0039-9930. LC cn72-13706,
     cn77-70312, cn79-72809. OCLC 1247055, 3219254, 5385751. RLIN
     DCLCCN7972809-S, SCLCCN7770312-S, DCLCCN7213706-S, MIUG270-S,
     AZPG134-S, OHCP5385751-S, OHCP3219254-S, NYPG744524605-S. Published
     by Department of Indian and Northern Affairs, Ottawa, Ontario, Canada.
     Editors: Jean Goodwill, [v.1, n.1-v.2, n.2]; Sheila Erickson,]v.2,
     n.3]; Mary E. Jamieson,]v.3, n.1-v.4, n.4]; Tom Hill, [v.5, n.1-v.6,
     n.1]; Georges Sioui, [v.6, n.2-v.7, n.1]. Subject focus: culture.
     Some issues contain articles in French.

WHi	v.1, n.1-v.7. n,1; Spring, 1970-1980	R31-11
WGrU	v.1, n.2-v.7, n.1; 1970-1980	R31-11
AzNCC	v.1, n.2-v.7, n.1; Summer, 1970-1980	Indian File
CL	v.1, n.3-v.4, n.3; Autumn, 1970-Autumn, 1974	Periodicals
NjP	v.1, n.1-3; Spring-Autumn, 1970	Periodicals
N	v.1, n.1-v.6. n,1; Spring, 1970-1978	J970.41/ qT234
NPotU	v.1, n.1-v.6. n,1; Spring, 1970-1978	E/78/C2T3
OkU	v.1, n.3-v.4, n.3; Autumn, 1970-Autumn, 1974	WHC
CaACG	v.1, n.1-v.7, n.1; Spring, 1970-1980	Periodicals
CaAEU	v.1, n.1-v.7. n,1; Spring, 1970-1980	Boreal Institute
CaMWU	v.1-v.7, n.1; Spring, 1970-1980	970/T1985
CaNBFU	v.1, n.1-v.7. n,1; Spring, 1970-1980	Gov Docs
CaOdPL	v.2-v.4; Spring, 1971-Fall, 1976	Periodicals
CaOONL	v.1, n.1-v.7. n,1; Spring, 1970-1980	Gov Docs

CaOOP   v.1, n.1-v.7. n,1;   E78/C2T38
             Spring, 1970-1980

CaOPeT   v.1, n.1-v.7. n,1;   E78/C2T3
             Spring, 1970-1980

CaOSuU   v.5-v.7;   Periodicals
             1977-1980

CaYW   [v.1-v.6]   Periodicals
             [1970-1979]

Other holding institutions: CLSU (CSL), DI (UDI), MiU (EYM),
[University of Minnesota Union List, Minneapolis, MN] (MUL), NdU
(UND), NhD (DRB) NIC (COO), [New York State Union List of Serials,
Albany, NY] (NYS), [Central New York Library Resources Council,
Syracuse, NY] (SYB).

1010 Techqua Ikachi; Land and Life. 1975. Unknown. Techqua Ikachi: Land
     and Life, Box 174, Hotevilla, AZ 86030. OCLC 5543502. Last issue 4
     pages, height 28 cm. Line drawings, photographs. Subject focus: Hopi
     people, culture.

     WHi   n.9, 19-   Circulation
                 Nov/Dec, 1976, Nov, 1981-

     AzU   n.1-   I9791/H7/T255
                 Aug, 1975-

     CL   n.8-14;   Periodicals
                 Aug/Sept, 1976-Nov/Dec, 1978

     CLSM   n.2-13;   Periodicals
                 Oct, 1975-July/Aug, 1978

     NmG   n.1-?;   Periodicals
                 Aug, 1975-June, 1980

     Other holding institutions: AzU (AZU), CLU (CLU).

1011 The Teepee Book. 1915-1916//. Unknown. LC 20-15179. OCLC 2256292,
     5385722. RLIN OHCP5385722-S. Last issue 20 pages, height 20 cm.
     Line drawings, photographs, commercial advertising. Sheridan, WY.
     Subject focus: legends, history, poetry.

     WHi   v.1, n.2;   F804//CR
                 Feb, 1915   Cutter

     CLSM   v.1-v.2;   Periodicals
                 1915-1916

| ICN | v.1, n.2;
Feb, 1915 | Ayer 4/A1990 |

| OC1WHi | v.1-v.2;
1915-1916 | Periodicals |

| OkTU | v.1-v.2;
1915-1916 | Rare Book
Room |

| OkU | v.1-v.2;
1915-1916 | WHC |

| SdU | v.2;
1916 | South
Dakota Room |

Other holding institutions: CChiS (CCH), CU-SB (CUT), DeU (DLM),
[University of Minnesota Union List, Minneapolis, MN] (MUL), NIC
(COO), NN (NYP), [New York State Union List, Albany, NY] (NYS), OCo
(OCO), [U. S. Army Military History Institute, Carlisle, PA] (MHR),
SdsiPA (SDA), TxCM (TXA).

1012 Teepee Smoke. 1933-?//. Quarterly. Last issue 4 pages. Line
     drawings, photographs. Available in microform: WHi-A, Veda Stone
     Papers, (1965, 1967). Published by Lutheran Indian Mission, Box
     Elder, MT. Subject focus: missions, Lutheran Church.

| WHi | v.33, n.4, v.35, n.3;
Nov, 1965, Dec, 1967 | Microforms |

| WEU
ARC | v.33, n.4, v.35, n.3;
Nov, 1965, Dec, 1967 | Micro 11 |

1013 Teepee Tidings. 1946?//. Unknown. Last issue 12 pages, height 28
     cm. Line drawings. Published by Indian School Administration,
     M.S.C.C., Ottawa, Ontario, Canada. Subject focus: Anglican Church,
     education.

| CaACG | n.3;
Nov, 1946 | Periodicals |

1014 Tekawennake. 1968. Irregular. Roberta Greene, editor, Tekawennake,
     P.O. Box 1506, Brantford, Ontario, Canada N3T 5V6. (519) 753-5531.
     ISSN 0300-3159, 0319-1338. LC cn75-34826, cn79-310899. OCLC 1445615,
     2442179. RLIN DCLCCN79310899-S, OHCP1445615-S, OHCP2442179-S. Last
     issue 20 pages, height 28 cm. Line drawings, photographs. Available
     in microform: McA (1974-). Published by Woodland Indian Cultural
     Educational Centre. Previous editors: Carolyn Beaver, Jan 9, 1974-Nov
     7, 1980; Amos Key, Jan 6-May 6, 1981. Community newsletter. Subject
     focus: Reserves of Walpole Island, Oneida, New Credit, Gibson, Six
     Nations, Tyendinaga, St. Regis and Moravian.

WHi	Jan 9, 1974-	Microforms
WHi	Aug, 1975-Feb, 1976	Pam 76-1449
WEU	Jan 9-Dec 18, 1974	Microfilm
AzNCC	1974-	Indian File
NjP	[June 1, 1968-Feb 22, 1977]	Periodicals
SdU	Jan, 1975-Dec, 1976	Microfilm
CaAEU	1980-	Boreal Institute
CaOAFN	Current issues	Periodicals
CaOONL	Feb/Mar, 1968-Jan 25, 1978	A 218-4
CaOPeT	1973-	Microfilm
CaOSuU	1971-	Periodicals

Other holding institutions: DLC (NSD), [[Minnesota Union List of Serials, Minneapolis, MN] (MUL).

Tekawitha Conference Newsletter. Marvin, SD

    see Blue Cloud Missions. Marvin, SD

1015 The Telephone. 1887-?//. Weekly. Last issue 8 pages. Line drawings, photographs. Tahlequah, OK. Available in microform: OkHi (1895). Title varies: The Tahlequah Telephone, June 10, 1887-Feb 3, 1888; The Cherokee Telephone, July 3, 1890-Dec 7, 1893. Editors: B. H. Stone, June 10-Oct 1, 1887; Mrs. B. H. Stone, Oct 28, 1887-Feb 3, 1888; Harvey W. Courtland, Feb 22, 1888-Jan 15, 1890; Augustus E. Ivey, Feb 5, 1890-Dec 7, 1893; J. H. Dick, Oct 2, 1894-Jan 18, 1895; Jno L Adair, Jr., Mar 1-June 14, 1895. Newspaper. Also described in Foreman, Carolyn Thomas. Oklahoma Imprints, 1835-1907. Norman: University of Oklahoma Press, 1936.

    WHi   [v.1, n.1-v.8, n.24]   Microforms
             [June 10, 1887-June 14, 1895]

    OkHi   [v.1, n.1-v.8, n.24]   Microforms
             [June 10, 1887-June 14, 1895]

1016 The Telling Stone. 1968-1969?//. Bi-monthly. ISSN 0703-4296. LC cn77-309725. OCLC 3435529. Last issue 28 pages, height 28 cm. Line drawings. Published by Vancouver Indian Centre, Vancouver, British

Columbia, Canada. Frequency varies: monthly, Feb-Dec, 1968. Editor:
June Johnson. Subject focus: urban community, centre news.

CaBViP   1968-Nov, 1969   NW/970.1/T276

CaOONL   [Feb, 1968-July, 1969]   H-13-6

CaOORD   Feb, 1968-June, 1969   Periodicals

1017 The Teocentli. 1926-1944//. Irregular. RLIN CUBG49817607-S. Last
     issue 16 pages. Available in microform: WHi (1926-1944). Published
     by University of Michigan, Ann Arbor, MI. Subject focus: archaeology,
     anthropology.

     WHi   n.1-28;   Microforms
                May, 1926-Dec, 1944

     Other holding institutions: [Amerind Foundation, Inc., Dragoon, AZ].

1018 Tepatshimuwin. 1976. 10 times a year. $12.50 for individuals and
     institutions. Ghislain Picard, editor, 80, Bou. Bastien, Village
     Huron, Quebec, Canada G0A 4V0. (418) 842-0277. Last issue 24 pages,
     height 28 cm. Line drawings, photographs. Published by Conseil
     Attikamek-Montangnais. Subject focus: rights, legislation, Attikamek
     and Montangnais people. In French 30%; in Attakamek 30%; in
     Montangnais, 30%.

     WHi   [v.3, n.6-v.6, n.1], v.7, n.1-   Circulation
                [Nov, 1978-May, 1981], Jan, 1982-

1019 Tewaterehwarenia'tha. 1978. Quarterly. Tewaterehwarenia'tha, Box
     750, Kahnawake, Quebec, Canada J0L 1B0. (514) 638-0880. Last issue
     24 pages, height 22 cm. Line drawings. Published by Kanien' Kehaka
     Taotitiohkwa Cultural Center. Subject focus: Mohawk language,
     culture, history, Mohawks of Caughnawaga.

     WHi   v.1, n.1, v.4, n.1-   Circulation
                May, 1978, Mar, 1982-

     CaOAFN   Current issues   Periodicals

1020 Theata. 1973. Annual. $5.50 for individuals and institutions.
     Theata, University of Alaska, Fairbanks, AK 99701. (907) 474-7181.
     OCLC 4098330. Last issue 60 pages, height 28 cm. Line drawings,
     photographs. Published by Cross-cultural Communications Department.
     Subject focus: history, culture, customs, arts of Native Alaskan
     peoples: Tlingit, Haida, Inuit (Eskimo), Athabascan. Tsimpshian and
     Aleut.

WHi   v.1-   Circulation
           Spring, 1973-

Other holding institutions: AzFU (AZN), CLS (CLA).

1021 The Thlinget. 1908-?//. Monthly. Last issue 4 pages, last volume 48
     pages, height 28 cm. Line drawings, photographs, commercial
     advertising. Published by Sitka Training School, Sitka, AK.
     Community newsletter. Subject focus: Alaskan Native peoples.

     WHi   [v.2, n.2-v.4, n.10]   F8096/T62/T
                [Sept, 1909-May, 1912]

     AkHi   [v.1, n.1-v.4, n.11]   Microforms
                [Aug, 1908-June, 1912]

     AkUF   [v.1, n.1-v.4, n.11]   Microforms
                [Aug, 1908-June, 1912]

1022 Three Tribes Herald. 1959. Quarterly. Three Tribes Herald, New
     Town, SD 58770. OCLC 6758831. Last issue 6 pages. Line drawings,
     photographs. Available in microform: McA (1975-); CPC (1960-1979).
     Published by Fort Berthold Council of Congregational Churches. School
     newsletter. Subject focus: Congragational Church.

     WHi   [v.2, n.1-v.12, 3], v.16, n.1-   Microforms
                [Jan/Feb, 1960-Sept, 1970], Jan/Mar, 1975-

     LARC   [v.12, n.1-v.23, n.3]   Periodicals
                [Jan, 1970-Dec, 1981]

     NjP   [v.2, n.1-v.12, n.3]   Periodicals
                [Jan/Feb, 1960-Sept, 1970]

     SdU   v.16, n.1-v.17;   Microfilm
                Jan, 1975-Dec, 1976

     CaOPeT   [v.16-v.17], v.19-   Microfilm
                [1975-1976], 1978-

     Other holding institutions: [University of Minnesota Union List,
     Minneapolis, MN] (MUL), NdU (UND).

1023 Thunderbird. 1944-?//. Irregular. Last issue 4 pages, height 28 cm.
     Line drawings, photographs. Published by St. John's Indian School,
     Komathe, AZ. School newsletter. Subject focus: Catholic Church.

     WMM   [v.1, n.1-v.26, n.2]   Special
                [Oct, 1944-Apr, 1972]   Collections

1024 Thunderbird. 1949-1955//. Irregular. Last issue 16 pages, height 30
     cm. Line drawings, photographs, commerical advertising. North
     Vancouver, British Columbia, Canada. Editor: Andy Paull. Subject
     focus: rights, law.

       CaACG   Apr-May, 1951, May 15, 1952,   Periodicals
                  May, 1954, Sept, Dec, 1955

       CaBViP   1949-1955?   NWp/970.1/T535

       CaOORD   [June 1, 1949-Dec, 1955]   Periodicals

1025 Thunderbird. 1964?-1965?//. Monthly. Last issue 12 pages, height 43
     cm. Photographs, commercial advertising. Ottawa, Ontario, Canada.
     Editor: Thomas Peltier. Subject focus: poltics, rights,
     socio-economic conditions.

       CaACG   v.1, n.10, v.2, n.1;   Periodicals
                  June, Sept, 1965

1026 Thunderbird. 1963?//. Monthly. Last issue 12 pages, height 28 cm.
     Line drawings. Published by North American Indian Club of Toronto,
     Toronto, Ontairo, Canada. Editor: Isaac Beaulieu, Apr-Dec, 1963.
     Subject focus: urban community, club news.

       CaACG   v.1, n.3;   Periodicals
                  June, 1963

       CaOORD   v.1, n.1-6;   Periodicals
                  Apr-Dec, 1963

1027 Thunderbird Quill. 1961-1971//. Monthly. Last issue 8 pages, height
     28 cm. Line drawings, photographs. Published by Manitoba Regional
     Affairs Branch, Winnipeg, Manitoba, Canada. Community newsletter.

       NjP   v.1, n.1-v.3, n.2;   Periodicals
                  June, 1969-July/Aug, 1971

       OkU   v.1, n.1-v.3, n.2;   WHC
                  June, 1969-July/Aug, 1971

       CaOORD   v.1, n.1-v.3, n.2;   Periodicals
                  June, 1969-July/Aug, 1972

       CaOPeT   v.1, n.1-v.2;   Microfilm
                  June, 1969-Aug, 1971

     Other holding institutions: [Western Nevada Community College, Carson
     City, NV].

1028 <u>Thunderer</u>. 1966. Irregular. Donald Keeter, editor, Thunderer, 10020
     N. 15th Ave., Phoenix, AZ 85021. (602) 944-3335. Last issue 8 pages,
     height 22 cm. Published by American Indian Bible Institute. Subject
     focus: Christian religion, institute news.

       WHi   v.14, n.4, v.16, n.3-   Circulation
                     May, 1979, Spring, 1981-

       Other holding institutions: [American Indian Bible Institute, Phoenix,
       AZ].

1029 <u>Ti swawwi? itst</u>. 1982? Unknown. Ti swawwi? itst, Route 5, Box 432,
     Shelton, WA 98584. Last issue 4 pages, height 45 cm. Line drawings.
     Published by Skokomish Tribal Office. Community newsletter. Subject
     focus: Skokomish people.

       WHi   Sept 14, 1982-   Circulation

1030 <u>Tipachimowin</u>. 1955-1974//. Quarterly. ISSN 0382-0556. LC
     cn76-301111. OCLC 2292915. Last issue 20 pages, height 22 cm. Line
     drawings. Published by Missionary Oblates of Mary Immaculate,
     Moosonee, Ontario, Canada. Subject focus: Cree and Ojibwa people. In
     Cree, 80%.

       CaOONL   n.1-20, v.9-v.11;   Periodicals
                     Jan, 1955-Aug, 1959, 1972-1974

       CaOPeT   n.1-20;   Periodicals
                     Jan, 1955-Aug, 1959

1031 <u>Title I Newsletter</u>. 1972?//. Monthly. Last issue 2 pages, height 28
     cm. Published by St. Francis Indian School, St. Francis, SD. School
     newsletter. Subject focus: Catholic Church.

       WMM   v.3, n.4, 6, 8;   Special
                     Dec 31, 1974, Feb 28, Apr 28, 1975   Collections

1032 <u>The Tiyospaye Network Voice</u>. 1977? Unknown. Marjorie Weeks, editor,
     The Tiyospaye Network Voice, University of South Dakota, Vermillion,
     SD 57069. Last issue 12 pages, height 28 cm. Line drawings,
     photographs. Published by Institute of Indian Studies. Organization
     newsletter. Includes poetry.

       WHi   Summer?, 1981-   Microforms

1033 <u>Tlingit & Haida Tribal News</u>. 1980. Monthly. Judson Cranston,
     editor, Tlingit & Haida Tribal News, One Sealaska Plaza, Suite 200,
     Juneau, AK 99801. (907) 586-1432. Last issue 12 pages, height 28 cm.
     Line drawings, photographs. Community newsletter. Subject focus:
     Tlingit and Haida people.

     WHi   v.2, n.6-   Microforms
                Apr 21, 1981-

1034 <u>Today: Sheldon Jackson College</u>. 1914? Quarterly. Jari Roloff,
     editor, Today: Sheldon Jackson College, P.O. Box 479, Sitka, AK 99835.
     (907) 747-5220. Last issue 4 pages, last volume 20 pages, height 42
     cm. Line drawings, photographs. Available in microform: WHi (1971-).
     Published by Board of National Missions of the Presbyterian Church.
     Title varies: Verstovian, May-Dec, 1971; SJC Today, Jan,
     1972-Apr/June, 1979; Sheldon Jackson College Today, July/Aug/Sept,
     1979-July/Aug/Sept, 1981. Previous editors: Darryl A. Sczepanski,
     Oct/Nov/Dec, 1973-Apr/May/June, 1975; Mary T. Steil, July/Aug/Sept,
     1975; Edwin Scholz, Jan/Feb/Mar, 1976; Jon R. Nyberg, July/Aug/Sept,
     1976-July/Aug/Sept, 1978; Cathy Hanson, Oct/Nov/Dec, 1978-Jan/Feb/Mar,
     1979; Marlys Burnett, Apr/May/June, 1979-Apr/June, 1980; Maxwell V.
     Perrow, July/Aug/Sept, 1980-Apr/May/June, 1981. College newsletter.

     WHi   v.50, n.4-   Microforms
                May, 1971-

     AkHi   v.1, n.1-   Periodicals
                Oct, 1914-

     AkUF   [v.13?-v.40]   Periodicals
                [1934-1961]

     NjP   [v.1, n.1-v.59, n.2]   Periodicals
                [Oct, 1914-Apr/May/June, 1979]

1035 <u>The Tom Tom</u>. 1966-?//. Unknown. Last issue 10 pages, height 36 cm.
     Line drawings. Published by Holy Rosary Mission, Pine Ridge, SD.
     High school newsletter. Subject focus: Catholic Church.

     WMM   v.1, n.4, v.3, n.4;   Special
                May, 1966, May 17, 1968   Collections

1036 <u>The Tom-Tom</u>. 1935-1947?//. Irregular. Last issue 24 pages, height
     21 cm. Line drawings, photographs. Published by Holy Rosary Mission,
     Pine Ridge, SD. Editors: F. Martinez, May, 1935; C. Nelson, Nov,
     1931-June, 1938; Walter Lee, Oct, 1938-May, 1939; Orvillo Cuny,
     Autumn, 1940; Lyle Clifford, Fall, 1941-May, 1942; David Crazy
     Thunder, Autumn, 1942-May, 1943; Leo Vocu, May, 1944; Dennis Compos,

Dec, 1944-May, 1945; Leo Vocu, Oct, 1946-Mar, 1947; Marvin Tuttle, Apr-May, 1947. High school newsletter.

| WMM | v.1, n.4-v.11, n.8; | Special |
| | May, 1935-May, 1947 | Collections |

1037 Tonawanda Community News. 1964?//. Unknown. Last issue 8 pages, height 39 cm. Line drawings. Available in microform: WHi (1964). Akron, NY. Community newsletter.

| WHi | June, 1964 | Microforms |

1038 Toronto Native Times. 1968-1981//. Monthly. OCLC 7055378. Last issue 20 pages. Line drawings, photographs. Available in microform: WHi (1972-1979). Published by Canadian Indian Centre of Toronto, Toronto, Ontario, Canada. Title varies: Native Times, Jan, 1972-Feb, 1973. Editor: Dan Longboat. Subject focus: urban community, centre news.

WHi	[Jan, 1972]-Dec, 1978, Jan, 1979	Microforms
NjP	[Mar, 1969-Jan, 1979]	Periodicals
CaAEU	1971-1981	Boreal Institute
CaOAFN	1979-1981	Periodicals
CaOONL	1968-1981	Newspaper Section
CaOPeT	[1973-1981]	Microfilm
CaOSuU	1976, 1979;	Periodicals

1039 Tosan. 1971-1978?//. Quarterly. Last issue 24 pages. Line drawings, photographs, commercial advertising. Available in microform: McA (1972-1978). Published by Shawnee Nation-United Remnant Band (U.R.B.), Xenia, OH. Place of publication varies: Indianapolis, IN, Winter, 1972-Fall, 1974. Editors: Jerry L. Pope, Winter, 1972-Fall, 1974; Tukemas (Hawk at Setting Sun), Mar, 1975-Sept, 1978. Subject focus: inter-tribal news, law, politics, culture, Shawnee people.

WHi	v.2, n.5-v.5;	Microforms
	Winter, 1972-Sept, 1978	
WMM	v.4, n.2;	Special
	Mar 20, 1975	Collections

NjP   [v.1, n.4–v.5, n.2]   Periodicals
           [Aug 22, 1971–Mar 20, 1975]

OkU   [v.1–v.4, n.5]   WHC
           [Feb, 1971–Dec, 1976]

SdU   v.1–v.4, v.5;   Microforms
           Feb, 1971–Fall, 1974, Mar, 1975

CaOPeT   v.1–v.5?   Microfilm
           1971–1978?

Other holding institutions: [Western Nevada Community College, Carson
City, NV].

1040 Totem Newsletter. 1967–1969?//. Monthly. Last issue 16 pages,
     height 28 cm. Winnipeg, Manitoba, Canada. Subject focus: urban
     community, local news.

     CaOORD   [Aug, 1967–Mar, 1969]   Periodicals

1041 The Totem Speaks. 1953?//. Unknown. Last issue 12 pages, height 31
     cm. Photographs, commerical advertising. Vancouver, British
     Columbia, Canada. Editor: Andy Paull. Newspaper.

     CaACG   Dec, 1953   Periodicals

1042 Trail. 1962?–?//. Monthly. Last issue 6 pages. Line drawings.
     Available in microform: WHi–A, Veda Stone Papers, (1962–1965).
     Minneapolis, MN. Subject focus: urban community, local news.

     WHi   [Nov, 1962–Nov, 1965]   Microforms

     WEU   [Nov, 1962–Nov, 1965]   Micro 11
     ARC

1043 Trail Blazer. 1973–1976?//? Irregular. Last issue 4 pages. Line
     drawings, photographs. Available in microform: AkUF (1973–1976).
     Published by Cook Inlet Native Association, Anchorage, AK. Community
     newsletter. Subject focus: education and employment information.

     WHi   [no no.], v.1, n.1–10;   Microforms
               May, 1973, Mar?, 1975–Feb, 1976

     AkUF   [no no.], v.1, n.1–10;   Microfiche
               May, 1973, Mar?, 1975–Feb, 1976

Travelling the Padre's Trail. St. Michaels, AZ

   see The Padre's Trail. St. Michaels, SD

1044 Treaty Council news. 1977-?//. Monthly. Last issue 4 pages, height
28 cm. Line drawings, photographs. Published by International Indian
Treaty Council, San Francisco, CA. Subject focus: rights, treaties,
sovereignty recognition, land claims.

WHi	v.1, n.11; Feb, 1978	Pam 81-1468
AzNCC	v.1-v.2 Apr, 1977-Aug, 1978	Indian File
NN	[v.1, n.2-v.2, n.2] [1977-1978]	Periodicals

Other holding institutions: ICN (IBV).

Tree of Peace. Yellowknife, Northwest Territories, Canada

   see Tsigondi/Tree of Peace. Yellowknife, Northwest Territories,
       Canada

1045 Tribal Court Reporter. 1979-1980//. Quarterly. ISSN 1217-4272. LC
80-644834. OCLC 5021049. RLIN NYCL82-S73, CLCL82-S57, UTBL080-S,
DCLC80644834-S, CSUP052495-S, CSUL2317-S, OHCP5021049-S. Last issue
68 pages, looseleaf, height 23 cm. Published by American Indian
Lawyer Training Program, Oakland, CA. Editor: Carrie Small, Mar,
1979-Dec, 1980. Subject focus: court decisions, tribal courts, law
and analysis.

WU-L	v.1, n.1-v.2, n.4; Mar, 1979-Dec, 1980	KF/8220/A515
WaO-L	v.1-v.2, n.4; 1979-Dec, 1980	Periodicals

Other holding institutions: ArLUA-L (ALR), CLU (CLU), CU-SB (CUI), DLC
(DLC), DI (UDI), IU-L (FUB), ICarbS-L (SOL), IU (UIU), MnSWM 9WMM),
MsU-L (MUW), MT-L (MTS), NmU-L (NML), NIC (COO), NBuU-L (SBL), OTU-L
(UTL), IkU-L (OKL), IKOKU-L (OKY), OrPL-L (ONS), [Williamette
University College of Law, Salem , OR] (OWT). SdU-L (USE), TxU (TXQ),
ViU-L (VAL).

1046 Tribal Indian News. 1971-1973?//. Monthly. Last issue 4 pages,
height 43 cm. Line drawings. London, Ontario, Canada. Editor:

Robert A. Antone. Subject focus: rights, politics.

WHi   v.3, n.1-2;   Pam 74-6510
           Feb-Mar, 1973

AzNCC   v.1-v.2;   Indian File
           Apr, 1971-Sept, 1972

NjP   v.2, n.6-v.3, n.2;   Periodicals
           Jan-Mar, 1973

CaOONL   v.2, n.1, v.3, n.1;   Newspaper
           Jan, 1972, Feb, 1973   Section

1047 Tribal Office Newsletter. 1978?. $10. for institutions. Tribal
      Office Reporter, Route 1, Bowler, WI 54416. (715) 793-4111. Last
      issue 4 pages, height 28 cm. Line drawings. Personal names indexed
      in: Index to Wisconsin Native American Periodicals (1980-1981).
      Published by Stockbridge-Munsee Community. Community newsletter.
      Subject focus: Stockbridge and Munsee people.

      WHi   v.3, n.6-   Circulation
                 May 14, 1980-

1048 Tribal People's Survival. 1979. Unknown. John Redhouse, editor,
      Tribal People's Survival, P.O. Box 7082, Albuquerque, NM 87104. (505)
      265-1509. Last issue 8 pages, height 40 cm. Line drawings,
      photographs. Published by American Indian Environmental Council.
      Subject focus: environment, ecology, water rights, land claims,
      legislation, culture.

      WHi   v.2 n.1-   Circulation
                 Apr, 1980-

      ICN   Current issues   CHAI

1049 Tribal Spokesman. 1969-1977//. Monthly. ISSN 0041-2643. OCLC
      5472196, 5575932. Last issue 4 pages. Line drawings, photographs,
      commercial advertising. Available in microform: McP (1971-1972); WHi
      (1973-1977); LM (1968-). Published by Inter-Tribal Council of
      California, Sacramento, CA. Editors: Tanna Beebe, Jan 29-Mar 10,
      1971; Alice Echo-Hawk, Apr 15-June, 1971; Barbara Garcia, Oct,
      1971-Apr, 1972; David M. Vallo, May-July, 1972; Darlene Brown, Sept,
      1972-May, 1977. Community newsletter. Subject focus: legislation,
      education, poetry.

      WHi   v.3, n.1-v.9, n.1   Microforms
                 Jan 29, 1971-May, 1977

WEU	[v.2, n.1-v.3, n.3] [July,1970-Mar 10, 1971]	Journalism Lab
AzNCC	v.3-v.4; 1971-Jan, 1972	Microfilm
CL	v.3, n.9-v.7, n.3; Nov, 1971-June, 1975	Periodicals
IdU	v.1-v.7, n.5; 1969-Sept/Oct, 1975	Superfolio
NjP	[v.1, n.4-v.7, n.5] [Mar, 1969-Sept/Nov, 1975]	Periodicals
OkU	v.3-v.4; Jan 29, 1971-Dec, 1972	WHC

Other holding institutions: CLU (CLU), [University of Minnesota,
Minneapolis, MN] (MUL), NmScW, [WGrU-Native American Studies Dept.].

1050 Tribal Tribune. 1961. Monthly. $5. for individuals and
institutions. Sheila L. Wilder, editor, Tribal Tribune, P.O. Box 150,
Nespelem, WA 99155. (509) 634-4711. OCLC 6168837. Last issue 24
pages, last volume 240 pages, height 44 cm. Line drawings,
photographs, commercial advertising. Available in microform: WHi
(1973-1974, 1975-). Published by Coville Confederated Tribes.
Previous editors: Ronald G. Warren, Jan 17-Feb 15, 1975; Charlene
Belgarde, Nov 4, 1976-Dec 29, 1977; Roger Jack, Jan 26, 1978-Apr 26,
1979; Ray Gonzales, July 26, 1979-Apr 24, 1980. Community newsletter.
Subject focus: Coville people.

WHi	v.13, n.1-v.15, n. 10, (n.s.)v.1, n.3- Feb 6, 1973-Dec, 1974, Mar 27, 1975-	Microforms
WHi	(n.s.)v.1, n.1-2; Dec 23, 1974-Feb 15, 1975	Pam 76-841
WMUW	[(n.s.)v.1, n.6-v.5, n.7] [June 12, 1975-July 26, 1979]	(SPE) E/75/T73x
AzNCC	(n.s.)v.3- Oct, 1977-	Indian File
NjP	[v.2, n.3-(n.s.)v.5, n.1] [Mar, 1961-June 29, 1979]	Periodicals
OkTU	(n.s.)v.5, n.1- Jan, 1979-	Rare Book Room
OrHi	v.3, n.2-v.15, n.5; (n.s.)v.1, n.4- Feb, 1962-June, 1974, Apr, 1975-	Periodicals

Wa	v.12-v.15; 1972-1974	NW

WaU	(n.s.)v.1- 1975-	E/78/W3T73

Other holding institutions: OKTU (OKT), [University of
Wisconsin-Stevens Point-Native American Center, Stevens Point, WI].

1051 <u>Tribe of Five Feathers News</u>. 1971-1978?//. Monthly. OCLC 7084462,
7084487. Last issue 18 pages, height 28 cm. Line drawings.
Available in microform: CPC (1971-1978). Lompoc, CA. Title varies:
Five Feathers News, Jan, 1971-Sept, 1974. Community newsletter.
Subject focus: local and national news, fiction, poetry.

WHi	v.1, n.1-? Jan, 1971-Aug, 1978	Microforms

NjP	[v.1, n.1-?] [Jan, 1971-July 28, 1978]	Periodicals

OkTU	v.1, n.1-4; Feb-Aug, 1975	Rare Book Room

1052 <u>Tribes Alert</u>. 1971//? Unknown. Last issue 4 pages, height 28 cm.
Published by American Indian Historical Society, San Francisco, CA.
Community newsletter.

CL	n.1; Sept, 1971	Periodicals

1053 <u>Tri-State ICAP Newsletter</u>. 1971?//. Weekly. Last issue 1 page.
Available in microform: WHi-A, Veda Stone Papers, (1971). Published
by Indian Community Action Project, Inc., Cass Lake, MN. Community
newsletter. Subject focus: rights, government programs.

WHi	[Aug 13-Oct 25, 1971]	Microforms

WEU ARC	[Aug 13-Oct 25, 1971]	Micro 11

1054 <u>The Trumpet Call</u>. 1945-?//. Monthly. Last issue 4 pages, height 28
cm. Line drawings, photographs. Published by St. Augustine's Indian
Mission School, Winnebago, NE. Editor: Monsignor Frank J. Hulsman.
Subject focus: missions, Catholic Church, education.

WEU	v.26, n.2-7; Oct, 1970-Mar, 1971	Journalism Lab

WMM   [v.11, n.5-v.12, n.10]   Special
             [Jan, 1956-June, 1957]   Collections

The Truth: Voice of the San Carlos Apache Tribe. San Carlos, AZ

   see Da' Anii/The Truth: Voice of the San Carlos Apache Tribe.
       San Carlos, AZ

1055 Tsa' Aszi'. 1973. Quarterly. $9. for individuals and institutions.
     Delbert Henio, editor, Tsa' Aszi', C.P.O. Box 12, Pine Hall, NM 87321.
     (505) 783-5503. LC 81-642964. OCLC 4588873. RLIN DCLC81642964-S,
     CUBU17959305-S. Last issue 64 pages, height 28 cm. Line drawings,
     photographs. Available in microform: CPC (1974-1978). Published by
     Pine Hill High School Students. Editors: Kee Lee and Alvin Rafealito,
     Summer, 1977-Summer/Fall, 1978; Bill T. Cohoe, Delbert Henio and
     Annette Lorenzo, Spring, 1980. School newsletter. Subject focus:
     Navajo people, culture, poetry.

     WHi   v.1, n.2?-v.3. n.3;   Microforms
                  Apr, 1974-Spring, 1978

     WHi   v.3, n.3-   Circulation
                  Spring, 1978-

     WMUW   v.1, n.3-v. 2, n.3;   (SPL)
                  Spring/Summer, 1976-Spring, 1977   E/75/T82x

     AzNCC   v.1-   Indian File
                  Apr, 1973-
     AzU   v.1, n.1-   I9791/N31
                  1973-   T877

     CL   v.3, n.3-   Periodicals
                  Spring, 1978-

     CU-B   v.1-   Periodicals
                  1973-

     ICN   Current issues   CHAI

     NjP   [v.1, n.1-v.3, n.3]   Periodicals
                  [1973-Spring, 1978]

     NHu   [v.1, n.4-v.3, n.3]   Periodicals
                  [1974-Spring, 1978]

     NmU   v.1, n.1-   Periodicals
                  1973-

     USUSC   [v.1-v.4]   Special
                  [Fall, 1974-1979]   Collections

Other holding institutions: DLC (DLC), IU (UIU) MiU (EYM).

Tsen-Akamak. Davis, CA

    see Attan-Akamik. Davis, CA

1056 Tsigonde: Tree of Peace. 1971-1972?//. Monthly. ISSN 0381-9647,
     0381-9655. LC cn76-300333, cn76-300332. OCLC 2222705, 2222658. Last
     issue 18 pages, height 34 cm. Line drawings, photographs.
     Yellowknife, Northwest Territories, Canada. Title varies: Ttsigoinda,
     Oct, 1971-May, 1972. Editors: Paul Andrews, Oct, 1971-Apr, 1972; Mark
     Scott, May, 1972. Community newsletter.

     CaOONL   v.1, n.11-v.2, n.6;   D/205/5
                 Oct, 1971-June, 1972

1057 Tsistsistas Press. 1976-1980?//. Irregular. OCLC 6168784. Last
     issue 28 pages, height 36 cm. Line drawings, photographs, commercial
     advertising. Available in microform: WHi (1976-1979). Lame Deer, MT.
     Editor: Bertha Medicine Bull, July-Sept, 1976. Community newsletter.
     Subject focus: Northern Cheyenne people.

     WHi   [v.1, n.1-v.4, n.6]   Microforms
                 [July, 1976-June, 1979]

     WMUW   [v.1, n.1-v.4, n.6]   (SPL)
                 [July, 1976-June, 1979]   E/75/T83x

     AzNCC   v.2-v.4, n.7]   Microforms
                 Mar, 1977-July, 1979]

     MtBBCC   v.7;   Periodicals
                 Aug, 1980

     MtBC   v.2-v.4;   Periodicals
                 Feb, 1977-Dec, 1979

     NjP   ?, v.4, n.4;   Periodicals
                 Aug, 1978, Feb, 1979

     Other holding institutions: ICN (IBV), [Standing Rock Community
     College Library, Fort Yates, ND].

Ttsigoinda/Tree of Peace. Yellowknife, Northwest Territories, Canada

    see Tsigonde/Tree of Peace. Yellowknife, Northwest Territories,
        Canada

1058 Tukisiviksal. 1972-1975//. Monthly, irregular. Last issue 12 pages, height 28 cm. Line drawings, photographs. Published by Department of Information, Government of the Northwest Territories, Yellowknife, Northwest Territories, Canada. Subject focus: governmental relations, social services, education and employment information.

    CaACG   [v.1, n.5-v.3, n.11]   Periodicals
              [June, 1971-Dec, 1973]

    CaOORD   [v.1, n.1-v.5,n.3]   Periodicals
              [Feb, 1971-Mar, 1975]

1059 Tulalip Bulletin. 1916-1919?//. Monthly. Last issue 4 pages. Line drawings, photographs. Available in microform: WaU (1916-1919). Published by Tulalip Indian Agency, Tulalip, WA. Subject focus: news of Tulalip, Swinomish, Port Madison and Lummi reservations, school and health news.

    WHi   v.1, n.1-v.4, n.4;   Microforms
              Apr, 1916-July, 1919

    WaU   v.1, n.1-v.4, n.4;   970.3/TU
              Apr, 1916-July, 1919

1060 Tulalip See-Yaht-Sub. 1979?-1980//. Irregular. Last issue 4 pages, height 45 cm. Line drawings, photographs. Tulalip, WA. Editor: Brenda Stewart. Community newsletter.

    WHi   June 18, 1979-June, 1980   Microforms

1061 Tulsa Indian News. 1974. Monthly. M.A. Anquoe, editor, Tulsa Indian News, 1240 E. Fifth Place, Room 11, Tulsa, OK 74120. (918) 587-7119. Last issue 12 pages, height 36 cm. Photographs. Published by Tulsa Indian Media Association. Subject focus: urban community, association news.

    OkPAC   [v.3-v.8]   Periodicals
             [Apr, 1976-Oct, 1981]

    OkTU   v.2, n.11-   Rare Book
             Jan, 1975-   Room

    OkU   [v.1, n.16]-   WHC
             [1974]-

Other holding institutions: [Standing Rock Community College Library, Fort Yates, ND].

1062 <u>Tumbleweed Connection</u>. 1975?-?//? Monthly. OCLC 6169336. Last
     issue 4 pages, height 28 cm. Line drawings, photographs. Available
     in microform: WHi (1975, 1976). Published by The College of Ganado,
     Ganado, AZ. College newsletter.

     WHi   Dec 18, 1975, Jan, 29, Dec, 1976   Microforms

     WMUW   Dec 18, 1975, Jan, 29, Dec, 1976   (SPL)
                                                               E/75/T85x

1063 <u>Tundra Times</u>. 1962. Weekly. Thomas Richards, Jr., editor, Tundra
     Times, 639 I St., Anchorage, AK 99501. (907) 279-0012. ISSN
     0049-4801. LC 77-640436. OCLC 2712152, 4850080. RLIN
     DCLC77640436-S, CSUP00056406-S, OHCP2712152-S, CSUG23415509-S,
     NYPG794344160-S. Available in microform: McA (1962-); McP
     (1970-1973); CPC (1962-1976); AkUF (1965-). Published by Eskimo,
     Indian, Aleut Publishing Co. Previous editors: Howard Rock, Oct 1,
     1962-Feb 18, 1976; Thomas Richards, Feb 25, 1976-Apr 16, 1980.
     Subject focus: national and local news, Alaska Native people,
     education, legislation, politics.

     WHi   v.1, n.1-   Microforms
                  Oct 1, 1962-

     WEU   v.8, n.16-22, v.10, n.3, v.11, n.4-7   Journalism
                  Jan 27-Mar 10, 1971, Jan 17, 1973,   Lab
                  Jan 23-Feb 13, 1974

     WMUW   [v.12, n.9-v.13, n.36]   (SPE)
                  [Mar, 1975-1976]   E/75/T68x

     AkAML   Current three months   Periodicals

     AkBC   v.17, n.10-   Periodicals
                  Mar 5, 1980-

     AkHi   v.1, n.1-   Microforms
                  Oct 1, 1962-

     AkUF   v.1, n.1-   Microforms
                  Oct 1, 1962-

     AzNCC   v.1, n.1-   Microfilm
                  Oct 1, 1962-

     CL   v.9, n.17-   Periodicals
                  1972-

     CNoSU   [v.7-v.10]   Microfilm
                  [Sept, 1970-Nov 28, 1973]

     CU-A   v.7, n.241-   E/99/E7/T9
                  Jan 2, 1970-

NjP	[v.1, n.1–v.16, n.23] [Oct 1, 1962–June 6, 1979]	Periodicals
NN	v.1–v.10; 1962–1973	Newspaper Collection
OkTU	v.14, n.1– Jan, 1977–	Rare Book Room
OkU	v.1, n.1– Oct 1, 1962–	WHC
SdU	v.10–v.13; Jan, 1973–Dec, 1976	Microfilm
UPB	[v.1, n.12–v.7, n.282] [1963–1970]	970.49805/T834
CaAEU	v.1, n.1– Oct 1, 1962–	Boreal Institute
CaOPeT	v.1, n.1– Oct 1, 1962–	Microfilm

Other holding institutions: CLU (CLU), [Congressional Research
Service, Washington, DC] (CRS), DLC (DLC), DeU (DLM), [University of
Minnesota Union List, Minneapolis, MN] (MUL), [Western Nevada
Community College, Carson City, NV], NhU (DRB), NmScW, OrU–Special
Collections, WaU (WAU).

1064 The Turning Tide. 1963–?//. Unknown. Last issue 10 pages, height 36
cm. Line drawings. Available in microform: WHi (1965). Lillooet,
British Columbia, Canada. Editor: Paul E. Orth. Subject focus:
rights, legislation.

WHi	n.8; July, 1965	Microforms
NjP	n.1?–2, 8; July–Oct, 1962, July, 1965	Periodicals

1065 Turtle. 1979. Quarterly. $3. for individuals and institutions.
Turtle, 25 Rainbow Mall, Niagra Falls, NY 14303. (716) 284–2427.
Last issue 16 pages, last volume 40 pages, height 43 cm. Line
drawings, photographs. Published by Native American Center for the
Living Arts, Inc. Subject focus: arts and crafts, culture, center
news.

WHi	v.1, n.1– Spring, 1979–	Circulation

AzHM   v.2, n.1-   Periodicals
            1980-

ICN   Current issues   CHAI

MtBBCC   v.2;   Periodicals
            Jan, 1980-Jan, 1981

NbJAM   v.1, n.4-v.3, n.2;   Periodicals
            Winter, 1980-Summer, 1981

CaACG   [v.1, n.1-v.2, n.3]   Periodicals
            [Spring, 1979-Fall, 1980]

CaOSuU   v.2-v.3;   Periodicals
            1980-1981

Other holding institutions: IC (CGP), [WGrU-Native American Studies
Dept.].

1066 Turtle Mountain Echo. 1973-1975?//. Bi-weekly. Last issue 8 pages,
     height 43 cm. Line drawings, photographs, commercial advertising.
     Available in microform: WHi (1973-1975). Belcourt, ND. Editors:
     Valerie Sullivan, Sept 7, 1973-Jan 18, 1974; Jane Hjeldness, Oct 24,
     1974; Jane Hjeldness and Gail Svendahl, Nov 20, 1974-Feb 12, 1975;
     Jane Hjeldness, Feb 26-Mar 26, 1975; Sammy Azure, May 7-21, 1975.
     Community newsletter. Subject focus: Turtle Mountain Band of
     Chippewas.

     WHi   [v.1, n.4-v.2, n.15]   Microforms
                [Sept 7, 1973-May 21, 1975]

     WMUW   [v.1, n.4-v.2, n.15]   (SPL)
                [Sept 7, 1973-May 21, 1975]   E/75/T87x

1067 Turtle Mountain Echo II. 1979. Bi-weekly. Last issue 10 pages,
     height 58 cm. Line drawings, photographs, commercial advertising.
     Belcourt, ND. Editor: Leslie W. Peltier. Community newsletter.

     WHi   v.2, n.2-v.3, n.12;   Microforms
                Feb 6, 1980-Aug 4, 1981

     Other holding institutions: [Standing Rock Community College Library,
     Fort Yates, ND].

1068 Turtle Talk. 1982? Unknown. Turtle Talk, 45 Lexington, N.W., Grand
     Rapids, MI 49504. Last issue 10 pages, height 28 cm. Line drawings.
     Published by Grand Rapids Inter-Tribal Council. Subject focus: urban
     community, health, education, fishing rights.

WHi   Oct, 1982–   Circulation

1069 Tushkahomman, The Red Warrior. 1935-1936//. Semi-monthly. OCLC
     8468545. Last issue 4 pages, height 56 cm. Line drawings,
     photographs, commercial advertising. Available in microform: CPC
     (1935-1936). Stroud, OK. Frequency varies: weekly, 1935. Newspaper.

     WHi   v.1, n.1-v.2, n.10;   Microforms
                Mar 5, 1935-June 25, 1936

     OkTU   v.1, n.1-v.2, n.10;   Rare Book
                Mar 5, 1935-June 25, 1936   Room

     Other holding institutions: PPiU (PIT).

1070 Twin Cities Indian News. 1964-?//. Irregular. OCLC 2254323. Last
     issue 4 pages. Line drawings, photographs. Available in microform:
     WHi-A, Veda Stone Papers, (1964-1966). Published by Community Health
     and Welfare Council of Hennepin County and Bureau of Indian Affairs
     Area Office, Minneapolis, MN. Editor: Mrs. Glenn Speidel. Subject
     focus: rights, law, social services.

     WHi   v.1, n.1-v.2;   Microforms
                Aug, 1964-June, 1966

     WEU   v.1, n.1-v.2;   Micro 11
     ARC   Aug, 1964-June, 1966

     Other holding institutions: [University of Minnesota Union List,
     Minneapolis, MN] (MUL).

1071 Twin Territories; The Indian Magazine. 1898-1904?//. Monthly.
     Height 26 cm. Photographs, commercial advertising. Muskogee, OK.
     Community newsletter.

     NN   [v.4-v.5]   HBA
                [July, 1902-July, 1903]

     OkTU   [v.4, n.3-v.6,n.4]   Rare Book
                [Mar, 1902-May, 1904]   Room

     TxU   v.4,;   970.05/T923
                Nov, 1902

1072 Tyonek 1991 Newsletter. 1975//? Monthly. Last issue 4 pages.
     Available in microform: AkUF (1975). Anchorage, AK. Subject focus:
     corporate news.

| WHi | n.1-2;
Aug-Sept, 1975 | Microforms |
| AkUF | n.1-2;
Aug-Sept, 1975 | Microfiche |

UBCIC News. Vancouver, British Columbia, Canada

    see Indian World. Vancouver, British Columbia, Canada

1073 UIDA Reporter. 1971. 8 times a year. S.L.A. Stallings, editor, UIDA
Reporter, 1514 Wilshire Blvd., Los Angeles, CA 90017. (213) 483-1460.
Last issue 4 pages, last volume 40 pages, height 28 cm. Photographs,
commercial advertising. Available in microform: McA (1974-); CPC
(1972-1979). Published by United Indian Development Association.
Frequency varies: monthly, Jan, 1974-Dec, 1975. Previous editor: Bob
Moses, Apr, 1977-Mar, 1978. Subject focus: business and economic news.

WHi	[v.2, n,7-v.4, n.11], v.5, n.1- [July, 1972-Nov, 1974], Jan, 1975-	Circulation
WHi	v.2, n.6- June, 1972-	Microforms
WEU	v.6, n.7-v.7, n.1; Aug, 1976-Feb, 1977	Journalism Lab
WEU ARC	v.2, n.4; Apr, 1972	Micro 11
AzNCC	v.4; 1974	Microfilm
CLSM	[v.1, n.3-v.4, n.11], v.5- [Sept, 1971-1974], 1975-	Periodicals
NjP	[v.2, n.6-v.9, n.5] [June, 1972-May, 1979]	Periodicals
CaOPeT	v.2, n.6- Jan, 1973-	Microfilm

Other holding institutions: IC (CGP), [WGrU-Native American Studies
Dept.].

1074 UIPA News. 1976-1980//? Monthly. OCLC 6188843. Last issue 24
pages, height 28 cm. Line drawings, photographs. Available in
microform: WHi (1978). United Indian Planners Association,

Washington, DC. Editor: Kristina Mast. Subject focus: community
development.

WHi   v.3, n.3;   Microforms
           Mar, 1978

WMUW   v.3, n.3;   (SPL)
           Mar, 1978   E/75/U4x

WIRC   [v.2-v.5, n.2]   216 COPS
           [Nov, 1977-July, 1980]

Other holding institutions: IC (CGP).

1075 USET Calumet. 1978. Bimonthly. Gloria Wilson, editor, USET Calumet,
     1101 Kermit Dr., Suite 800, Nashville, TN 37217. (615) 361-8700.
     Last issue 20 pages, height 28 cm. Line drawings, photographs.
     Published by United South and Eastern Tribes, Inc. Subject focus:
     legislation, housing, health, women's rights, land claims.

     WHi   Sept/Oct, 1982-   Circulation

     ICN   Current issues   CHAI

1076 Ulu News. 1970? Daily during Arctic Winter Games held every 2 years.
     (907) 456-6661. ISSN 0702-1909. LC cn77-309341. OCLC 3440298. RLIN
     DCLCCN77309341-S, OHCP3440298-S. Height 43 cm. Photographs. Title
     varies: Le Cakabee: Ulu News, 1976. Place of publication varies:
     Yellowknife, Northwest Territories, 1970; Whitehorse, Yukon, 1972;
     Anchorage, AK, 1974; Shefferville, Quebec, 1976; Hay River, Northwest
     Territories, 1978; Whitehorse, Yukon, 1980; Fairbanks, AK, 1982.
     Subject focus: Arctic Winter Games.

     AkHi   v.2?   Periodicals
               Mar 3-10, 1974

     CaAEU   v.1, n.1-   Boreal
               1972-   Institute

     Other holding institutions: CaOONL (NLC).

1077 Unalakleet Native Corporation [Newsletter]. 1974-1975//? Monthly.
     Last issue 5 pages. Available in microform: AkUF (1974-1975).
     Unalakleet, AK. Subject focus: corporate news, shareholders, local
     news, land claims, housing.

     WHi   v.1, n.1-v.2, n.5;   Microforms
               Jan, 1974-Dec, 1975

AkUF   v.1, n.1-v.2, n.5;   Microfiche
          Jan, 1974-Dec, 1975

1078 <u>United Amerindian Center, Inc. Newsletter</u>. 1982? Unknown. United
     Amerindian Center, Inc. Newsletter, 401 9th St., Green Bay, WI 54304.
     (414) 437-2161. Last issue 12 pages, height 28 cm. Line drawings.
     Subject focus: urban community, center news.

     WHi   May, 1982-   Circulation

1079 <u>United Methodist Reporter Advocate Edition</u>. 1973. Weekly. $10. for
     individuals and institutions. Spurgeon M. Dunnam III, editor, United
     Methodist Reporter Advocate Edition, P.O. Box 221076, Dallas, TX
     75222. (214) 630-6495. OCLC 8083718. Last issue 4 pages, height 58
     cm. Line drawings, photographs, commercial advertising. Available in
     microform: WHi (1977-). Published by The Oklahoma Indian Missionary
     Conference, The United Methodist Church. Subject focus: missions,
     Methodist Church, local and national Church news.

     WHi   v.5, n.32-   Microforms
              July 22, 1977-

1080 <u>United National Indian Tribal Youth</u>. 1982? Unknown. United National
     Indian Tribal Youth, P.O. Box 25042, Oklahoma City, OK 73125. (405)
     524-2031. Last issue 8 pages, height 37 cm. Line drawings,
     photographs. Subject focus: young adults.

     WHi   Fall, 1980, Spring, 1982-   Microforms

1081 <u>United Scholarship Service News</u>. 1966-1969?//. Irregular. Last
     issue 8 pages. Line drawings, photographs. Available in microform:
     WHi (1968-1969); WHi-A, Veda Stone Papers, (1968-1969). Denver, CO.
     Subject focus: educational and scholarship information.

     WHi   v.1, n.2-6;   Microforms
              Feb, 1968-Nov, 1969

     WEU   v.1, n.2-3, 5-6;   Micro 11
     ARC   Feb, 1968-Feb, July-Nov, 1969

     WMM   [no nos.]   Special
              Jan 15, 1966   Collections

     AzNCC   June, 1974-1976   Indian File

     NjP   v.1, n.3;   Periodicals
              Feb, 1969

Other holding institutions: OrU-Special Collections.

1082 United Sioux Tribes Newsletter. 1975-?//. Monthly. OCLC 6221127.
     Last issue 9 pages, height 28 cm. Line drawings. Available in
     microform: WHi (1975). Published by United Sioux Tribes of South
     Dakota Development Corp., Pierre, SD. Community newsletter. Subject
     focus: Yankton, Cheyenne, Crow Creek, Flandreau, Pine Ridge, Lower
     Brule, Rosebud, Sisseton and Standing Rock Sioux.

     WHi   Winter?, Spring, 1975   Microforms

     WMUW   Winter?, Spring, 1975   (SPL)
                                                              E/75/U57x

1083 United States Indian Service Bulletin. 1909-1927//. Irregular. OCLC
     6069050, 6464704. 6464694. Last issue 6 pages, height 23 cm.
     Published by United States Office of Indian Affairs, Washington, DC.
     Subject focus: acculturation, economics.

     WHi   n.1-3;   F809//BU
                Dec 31, 1909-Jan 16, 1911   Cutter

     WMM   [n.6-20]   Special
                [1920-1922]   Collections

     IaHi   n.1-23;   E/93/U582
                Dec 31, 1909-1927

     NjP   n.3;   Periodicals
                Jan 16, 1911

     Other holding institutions: COFS (COF), Tx (IXA).

1084 United Tribes News. 1974. Monthly. $7. for individuals and
     institutions. United Tribes News, 3315 S. Airport Rd., Bismarck, ND
     58501. (701) 255-3285. OCLC 2252659. Last issue 16 pages, height 42
     cm. Line drawings, photographs, commercial advertising. Available in
     microform: WHi (1974-1977, 1981-). Published by Office of Public
     Information, United Tribes Educational Technical Center. Previous
     editor: Sheri BearKing, July-Oct, 1981. Subject focus: national and
     state news. history, culture, education, health, poetry.

     WHi   [v.1, n.1-v.3, n.6], v.6, n.1-   Microforms
                [Sept, 1974-July, 1977], Feb, 1981-

     WMM   v.3, n.1;   Special
                Oct, 1976   Collections

     WMUW   [v.1, n.1-v.3, n.6]   (SPL)
                [Sept, 1974-July, 1977]   E/75/U58x

AzNCC	v.2– Sept, 1975–	Indian File

MtBBCC	v.6, n.1– Feb, 1981–	Periodicals

NdMinS	v.5– 1980–	Periodicals

Other holding institutions: DI (UDI), [University of Minnesota Union List, Minneapolis, MN] (MUL), [Standing Rock Community College Library, Fort Yates, ND].

1085 University of South Dakota Bulletin. 1956. Quarterly. T. Emogene Paulson, editor, University of South Dakota Bulletin, University of South Dakota, Vermillion, SD 57069. (605) 677-5209. ISSN 0042-0069. LC sc78-5748. OCLC 3954875. RLIN OHCP3954875-S. Last issue 4 pages, height 28 cm. Line drawings, photographs. Available in microform: McA (1975–); CPC (1956-1981). Published by Institute of Indian Studies. Frequency varies: 7 times a year, Feb, 1975-Nov, 1978. Previous editors: Robert L. Hall, Jan 15, 1959-Aug 1, 1961; Jay Brandon, Aug, 1962-Feb, 1963; James Howard and Ira H. Grinnell, Nov, 1963; James Howard, Ira H. Grinnell and B. Anthony Luscombe, Feb, 1964; James Howard and B. Anthony Luscombe, Aug, 1964-May, 1966; Carroll M. Mickey, Aug, 1966-May, 1967; Lloyd R. Moses, Aug 1967-Aug, 1974; Webster Two Hawk, Nov, 1974-Nov, 1976. Subject focus: education, Sioux people.

WHi	n.2– Mar 15, 1956–	Microforms

WEU ARC	series 63, n.5, series 64, n.28; Feb, 1963, Feb, 1964	Micro 11

WMM	[series 63, n.28–series 75, n.7] [Nov, 1963-Nov, 1975]	Special Collections

WU Coll	Current issues	Ethnic Collection

NjP	[n.1-79] [Dec 15, 1955-May, 1979]	Periodicals

NHu	n.2– 1956–	Periodicals

NN	n.2-67; Mar 15, 1956-May, 1976	Microforms

OkTU	n.61– Nov, 1974–	Rare Book Room

OkU	n.1– Dec, 1955–	WHC

SdHRC   Series 63, n.5-   Periodicals
               Feb, 1963-

SdU   n.1-68?;   Microfilm
               Dec, 1955-Nov, 1976

Other holding institutions: [Navajo Community College, Tsaile, AZ],
[Congressional Research Service, Washington, DC] (CRS), [Western
Nevada Community College, Carson City, NV], NdU (UND)

1086 Unyter. 1971?//. Unknown. Last issue 8 pages, height 44 cm. Line
     drawings. Published by United Native Youth Council, Edmonton,
     Alberta, Canada. Organization newsletter. Includes fiction, history,
     poetry.

     CaACG   Nov, 1971, Apr, 1972   Periodicals

     CaOONL   June?, 1972   E/98/U5
                                                            Folio

1087 Update. 1982?. Irregular. Roger Warner and Cathy Buburuz, editor,
     Update, Woodbine Building, 2332 11th Ave., Regina, Saskatchewan,
     Canada S4P 2G7. (306) 359-6429. Last issue 32 pages, height 44 cm.
     Line drawings, photographs. Published by Department of Indian Affairs
     and Northern Development-Saskatchewan Region. Subject focus:
     Saskatchewan Native people, land claims, rights, education,
     governmental relations.

     WHi   v.2, n.7-   Circulation
                   Sept, 1980-

1088 Uqualugaanich Newsletter. 1973. Unknown. Uqualugaanich Newsletter,
     313 E St., Suite 5, Anchorage, AK 99501. (907) 276-1552. Last issue
     8 pages, height 28 cm. Line drawings, photographs. Available in
     microform: AkUF (1973-1975). Published by Arctic Slope Regional Corp.
     Subject focus: corporate news.

     WHi   v.1, n.1-v.3, n.2, (n.s.)v.2, n.1, 3-   Microforms
                   Oct, 1973-Feb 28, 1975, Spring, Oct, 1981-

     AkUF   v.1, n.1-v.4, n.5;   AK-856
                   Oct, 1973-1976

1089 Utah Navajo Baa Hane'. 1975. Irregular. Utah Navajo Baa Hane',
     Blanding, UT 84511. (801) 678-2285. Last issue 12 pages, last volume
     18 pages, height 28 cm. Photographs. Published by Utah Navajo
     Development Council. Community newsletter. Subject focus: Navajo
     people.

WHi   v.2, n.7-   Circulation
            Oct, 1976-

AzNCC   v.4;   Indian File
            June-July, 1978

1090 The Ute Bulletin. 1961. Monthly. $3.50 for individuals and
     institutions. Maxine Natchee, editor, The Ute Bulletin, P.O. Box 190,
     Fort Duchesne, UT. (801) 722-5141. ISSN 0300-6806. OCLC 1354325.
     OHCP1354325-S. Last issue 4 pages, last volume 140 pages, height 39
     cm. Line drawings, photographs. Available in microform: McA (1972-);
     WHi-A, Veda Stone Papers, (1961-1964). Subject focus: local and
     national news, education, economics, politics, Ute people.

     WHi   [v.1, n.9-v.4, n.2], v.8, n.1-   Microforms
                 [July 8, 1961-Sept 12, 1964], Jan 31, 1972-

     WEU   [v.1, n.9-v.3, n.12]   Micro 11
     ARC   [July 8, 1961-Mar 21, 1964]

     WMUW   v.12, n.2;   (SPL)
                 June 22, 1977   E/75/U83x

     AzNCC   v.13-   Indian File
                 1978-

     CNoSU   v.8;   Microfilm
                 1972

     NjP   v.3, n.7, 10, v.8, n.8;   Periodicals
                 Aug 17, Dec 7, 1963, Oct 6, 1972

     OkTU   v.13, n.1, v.14, n.2-   Rare Book
                 Jan, 1978, June 7, 1979-   Room

     OkU   v.8, n.1-?, v.16, n.1-   WHC
                 Jan 31-Dec, 1972, 1981-

     Other holding institutions: DLC (DLC), [University of Minnesota Union
     List, Minneapolis, MN] (MUL), NmScW, [Standing Rock Community College
     Library, Fort Yates, ND], OrU-Special Collections.

1091 The Valley Roundup. 1973?-1978?//. Monthly. OCLC 6168927. Last
     issue 16 pages. Line drawings, commercial advertising. Available in
     microform: WHi (1973-1974, 1978). Published by Journalism Department,
     Owyhee High School, Owyhee, NV. Editor: Marthayn Manning. Community
     newsletter. Subject focus: Shoshone and Paiute people.

     WHi   Apr, 1973-Apr/May,   Microforms
                 1974, Feb-May, 1978

WMUW   Feb-May, 1978   (SPL)
                                                            E/75/V34x

NjP   Nov, 1972, 1973   Periodicals

Verstovian. Sitka, AK

   see Today: Sheldon Jackson College. Sitka, AK

1092 Vie Indienne. 1962-1970?//. Quarterly. Last issue 8 pages. height
     32 cm. Photographs. Published by Procure des Missions Oblates de
     Mary Immaculee, Montreal, Quebec, Canada. Subject focus: missions,
     Catholic Church. In French, 100%.

     CaOORD   [v.2, n.22-v.4, n.21]   Periodicals
               [Mar, 1964-May, 1970]

1093 Village Newsletter. 1980//? Monthly. Line drawings. Published by
     Copper River Native Association, Inc., Copper Center, AK. Editor:
     Sheila Logsdon. Community newsletter.

     AkUF   July-Aug, 1980   AK Per 2257

1094 The Vindicator. 1875-?//. Weekly. Last issue 4 pages. Line
     drawings, commercial advertising. Atoka, OK. Available in microform:
     OkHi (1875-1876). Editors: J.L. Caldwell and J.H. Moore, Mar 27,
     1875-Aug 2, 1876; J.H. Moore, Aug 9-Dec 20, 1876. Newspaper. Subject
     focus: Choctaw and Chickasaw people. In Choctaw, 2%. Also described
     in: Foreman, Carolyn Thomas, Oklahoma Imprints, 1835-1907, University
     of Oklahoma Press, Norman, OK, 1936.

     WHi   v.1, n.1-v.2, n.40;   Microforms
               Mar 27, 1875-Dec 20, 1876

     OkHi   v.1, n.2-v.2, n.40;   Microforms
               Mar 27, 1875-Dec 20, 1876

1095 The Vindicator. 1872-?//. Weekly. Last issue 8 pages. Line
     drawings, commercial advertising. New Boggy, OK. Available in
     microform: OkHi (1872-1873). Editors: J.H. Moore and E.A. Kline, Mar
     16-Dec 21, 1872; T.R. Heiston, May 17-Aug 27, 1873. Newspaper.
     Subject focus: Choctaw and Chickasaw people. Also described in:
     Foreman, Carolyn Thomas, Oklahoma Imprints, 1835-1907, University of
     Oklahoma Press, Norman, OK, 1936.

WHi   [v.1, n.2-v.2, n.11]   Microforms
           [Mar 16, 1872-Aug 27, 1873]

OkHi   [v.1, n.2-v.2, n.11]   Microforms
           [Mar 16, 1872-Aug 27, 1873]

1096 <u>Vision on the Wind</u>. 1973? Monthly. Vision on the Wind, 3045 Park
     Ave., S., Minneapolis, MN 55407. (612) 827-1795. OCLC 6188776. Last
     issue 22 pages, height 28 cm. Line drawings, photographs. Published
     by Division of Indian Work, Greater Minneapolis Council of Churches.
     Title varies: Wig-I-Wam, May, 1979-Sept, 1981. Subject focus: young
     adults, rights, council reports, reprints of articles from other
     Native American newsletters.

     WHi   May, 1979-   Circulation

     WMUW   Feb, 1980-   (SPL)
                                                         E/75/W53x

     MnHi   Feb, 1979-   Periodicals

     NHu   [1973-1975]   Periodicals

1097 <u>Voice in the Pines</u>. 1973. Bimonthly. Voice in the Pines, 15 N. San
     Francisco St., P.O. Box 572, Flagstaff, AZ 86002. Last issue 7 pages,
     height 28 cm. Line drawings, photographs. Published by Native
     Americans for Community Action, Flagstaff Indian Center. Title
     varies: NACA Newsletter, Nov, 1980-Jan, 1981. Frequency varies:
     monthly, Nov, 1980-Jan, 1981. Subject focus: culture, social
     services, employment information.

     WHi   v.9, n.3-6, 9-11;   Microforms
               Nov, 1980-Feb/Mar, June/July-Oct/Nov, 1981

     AzNCC   v.9-   Indian File
               May, 1981-

1098 <u>The Voice of Brotherhood</u>. 1954-1975?//. Monthly. ISSN 0300-6913.
     LC sn79-6335. OCLC 1357627. RLIN OHCP1357627-S. Last issue 6 pages,
     height 45 cm. Line drawings, photographs, commercial advertising.
     Available in microform: WHi (1959-1974). Juneau, AK. Editors: C. E.
     Peck, July, 1959-Sept, 1972. Charlotte Siberly, July, 1973; Raymond
     Peck, Mar/Apr, 1974. Subject focus: Alaskan Native people, culture,
     law.

     WHi   [v.5, n.7-v.22, n.3]   Microforms
               [July, 1959-Mar/Apr, 1974]

     WEU   v.23, n.3;   Journalism
               June/July, 1975   Lab

WMUW	[v.5, n.7-v.22, n.3]	(SPE)
	[July, 1959-Mar/Apr, 1974]	E/75/V64x
AkHi	v.1, n.1?-v.24?	Microforms
	Dec, 1954-1976?	
AkUF	v.1, n.1?-v.24?	Microforms
	Dec, 1954-1976?	
AzNCC	v.21-v.24;	Indian File
	Aug, 1971-May, 1976	
NjP	[v.1, n.11-v.22, n.3]	Periodicals
	[Nov, 1955-Apr, 1974]	
UPB	[v.9, n.10-v.18, n.9]	970.49805/V087
	[1963-1970]	

Other holding Institutions: CLU (CLU), CU-UC (UCU), DLC (DLC, NSD).

1099 Voice of Menominee Youth. 1974//. Unknown. Last issue 8 pages,
height 28 cm. Line drawings, photographs. Personal names indexed in:
Index to Wisconsin Native American Periodicals (1974). Keshena?, WI.
Editor: Janice Menore. School newsletter. Subject focus: Menominee
children.

WHi	v.1, n.2;	Pam 75-923
	Jan, 1974	

1100 Voice of Red Cloud. 1975?-1980?//? Irregular. Last issue 49 pages,
height 28 cm. Line drawings. Published by Red Cloud Indian School,
Holy Rosary Mission, Pine Ridge, SD. School newsletter. Subject
focus: Catholic Church, fiction, poetry, essays.

WMM	Spring, 1975-Spring, 1980	Special
		Collections

WANT Newsletter. Ann Arbor, MI

   see   Nishnawbe Muzinigun. Ann Arbor, MI

1101 WIDC Newsletter. 1976-?//. Unknown. Last issue 6 pages.
Photographs. Personal names indexed in: Index to Wisconsin Native
American Periodicals (1976). Available in microform: WHi-A, Veda
Stone Papers, (1976). Published by Wisconsin Indian Development
Corp., Schofield, WI. Subject focus: housing, community development.

WHi   v.1, n.1;   Microforms
            Jan 1, 1976

WEU   v.1, n.1;   Micro 11
ARC   Jan 1, 1976

1102 WNASA Newsletter. 1972-?//. Unknown. Last issue 15 pages.
      Available in microform: WHi-A, Veda Stone Papers, (1972). Published
      by Wisconsin Native American Student Association, Eau Claire, WI.
      Subject focus: education, organization news.

      WHi   v.1, n.1;   Microforms
                  May 1, 1972

      WEU   v.1, n.1;   Micro 11
      ARC   May 1, 1972

1103 Wabanaki Alliance. 1977. Monthly. $5. for individuals, $10. for
      institutions. Steven Cartwright, editor, Wabanaki Alliance, 95 Main
      St., Orono, ME 04473. (207) 866-4903. OCLC 6169098. Last issue 8
      pages, last volume 96 pages, height 43 cm. Line drawings,
      photographs, commercial advertising. Subject focus: inter-tribal
      news, land claims, social services.

      WHi   [v.1, n.3-v.3, n.4], v.3, n.6-   Circualtion
                  [Sept, 1977-Apr], June, 1979-

      WMUW   [v.1, n.5-v.3, n.7]   (SPL)
                  [Dec, 1977-July, 1979]   E/75/W24x

      AzNCC   v.1, n.4-   Indian File
                  Oct, 1977-

      ICN   Current issues   CHAI

      CaOAFN   Current issues   Periodicals

      Other holding institutions: Me (MEA), [Unity College Library, Unity,
      ME].

1104 Wahbung Ogi Chi Daw/Tomorrow's Leader. 1981. Monthly. Wahbung Ogi
      chi daw, 292 Walnut St., St. Paul, MN 55102. (612) 292-1861. Last
      issue 28 pages, height 22 cm. Line drawings, photographs. Published
      by Red School House Materials Development Project. Subject focus:
      education-basic skills, Ojibwa language and culture. Subject focus:
      young adults.

      WHi   v.1, n.1-   Circulation
                  Dec, 1981-

1105 <u>Wahpeton Highlights</u>. 1953-1979//? Irregular. OCLC 8433316. Last
     issue 26 pages. Line drawings. Available in microform: CPC
     (1953-1979). Published by Wahpeton Indian School, Wapheton, ND.
     Elementary school newsletter.

    WHi   [v.1, n.1-v.37, n.1]   Microforms
              [Feb 13, 1953-Jan, 1979]

    NjP   [v.1, n.1-v.37. n.1]   Periodicals
              [Feb 13, 1953-Jan, 1979]

    SdU   v.1-v.34;   Microfilm
              1953-1976

    Other holding institutions: PPiU (PIT).

    <u>Walk in Beauty</u>. Falls Church, VA

       see <u>The Pathfinder</u>. Falls Church, VA

1106 <u>Walker River Paiute Tribe News Notes</u>. 1977-1978?//. Monthly. OCLC
     6168952. Last issue 4 pages, height 28 cm. Available in microform:
     WHi (1978). Schurz, NV. Community newsletter. Subject focus: Paiute
     people.

    WHi   v.2, n.2;   Microfforms
              Feb, 1978

    WMUW   v.2, n.2;   (SPE)
              Feb, 1978   E/75/W27x

1107 <u>Wampum</u>. 1940-?//. Quarterly. Last issue 12 pages, height 28 cm.
     Published by United Church Indian Missionaries Association of Western
     Ontario, Muncey, Ontario, Canada. Editor: Rev. E. E. M. Jobbin.
     Subject focus: missions, Christian religion.

    WHi   v.4, n.3;   F805//+WA
              July, 1943   Cutter

    NjP   [v.5, n.3-v.7, n.3]   Periodicals
              [july, 1944-July, 1946]

1108 <u>Wanbli Hoton News</u>. 1977?//? Unknown. Last issue 4 pages, height 37
     cm. Line drawings, photographs. Published by Red Cloud Indian
     School, Pine Ridge, SD. School newsletter.

    WMM   Oct?-Nov 21, 1977   Special
                                        Collections

1109 <u>Wanbli Sapa</u>. 1973?-?//. Bi-monthly. Last issue 4 pages, height 28
cm. Line drawings, photographs. Published by St. Francis Mission,
St. Francis, SD. Community newsletter. Subject focus: area Catholic
Churches.

WMM   [v.2, n.1-v.5, n.3]   Special
             [Feb, 1974-Dec, 1976]   Collections

1110 <u>War Cry</u>. 1975-?//? Unknown. OCLC 6189088. Last issue 8 pages,
height 43 cm. Line drawings. Available in microform: WHi (1975).
Fort Thompson, SD. Community newsletter. Subject focus: Sioux people.

WHi   v.1, n.2;   Microforms
             Apr 5, 1975

WMUW   v.1, n.2;   (SPL)
             Apr 5, 1975   E/75/W32x

1111 <u>War Cry</u>. 1966-?//. Unknown. Last issue 4 pages, height 44 cm. Line
drawings, photographs. Published by Office of Economic Development,
Pine Ridge, SD. Community newsletter.

WMM   v.3, n.2;   Special
             June 28, 1968   Collections

1112 <u>Warm Springs</u>. 1972-1976//. Quarterly. Last issue 4 pages, last
volume 16 pages, height 28 cm. Photographs. Published by the
Confederated Tribes of the Warm Springs Reservation of Oregon, Warm
Springs, OR. Community newsletter.

OrHi   v.3-v.4, n.1;   Periodicals
             1975-Jan, 1976

1113 <u>Warpath</u>. 1968-1977//. Irregular. OCLC 1589213. RLIN
CSUP06753115-S, OHCP1589213-S. Last issue 16 pages. Line drawings,
photographs. Available in microform: CPC (1968-1973). Published by
United Native Americans, San Francisco, CA. Editor: Lehman L.
Brightman, Apr, 1971-May, 1973. Subject focus: national and local
news, history, rights, legislation.

WHi   v.1, n.2-v.4, n.10;   Microforms
             Fall, 1968-May, 1973

WEU   [v.1, n.2-v.4, n.6]   Journalism
             [Fall, 1968-?, 1969]   lab

WEU   v.1, n.4;   Micro 11
ARC   Fall, 1969

WMUW	[v.7, n.8-17] [Dec 15, 1976-May 15, 1977]	(SPL) E/75/W36x
AzNCC	v.1, v.2; 1969, 1970	Indian File
CL	[v.2, n.1-v.4, n.10] [Spring, 1970-May, 1973]	Periodicals
CU-A	v.1-v.4, n.10; Summer, 1968-May, 1973	E/77/A1/A36
LARC	v.1, v.2; 1968, 1969	Periodicals
NjP	[v.1, n.2-v.2, n.1] [Fall, 1968-Spring, 1970]	Periodicals
OkTU	[v.1, n.2-v.4, n.10] [Fall, 1968-May, 1973]	Rare Book Room
OkU	[v.1, n.2-v.4, n.9] [Fall, 1968-1973]	WHC
PPT	v.2, n.3-4, v.4, n.6-10; 1970-May, 1973	Contemporary Culture
SdU	v.1, n.2-v.3; Fall., 1968-Dec, 1972	Microfilm
WaU	v.4, n.10; May, 1973	Periodicals
CaOPeT	v.1-2; 1968-1972	Microfilm

Other holding institutions: ICN (IBV), MiU-Labadie (EYM), [University
of Minnesota Union List, Minneapolis, MN] (MUL), [Western Nevada
Community College, Carson City, NV], OrU-Special Collections.

1114 The Warrior. 1956?-1972//. Monthly. RLIN NYPG734245752-S. Last
     issue 14 pages, last volume 120 pages. Line drawings. Available in
     microform: WHi (1970-1972); WHi-A, Veda Stone Papers, (1963, 1964,
     1965). Published by American Indian Center, Chicago, IL. Editors:
     Rose M. Mandan and Edith Jones, May-Sept, 1964; Patti Hill, May,
     1971-Oct, 1972. Subject focus: urban community, center news.

WHi	[v.9, n.3-v.17, n.7] [Dec, 1963-Oct, 1972]	Microforms
WEU	[v.15, n.3-v.16, n.6] [Apr, 1970-July, 1971]	Journalism Lab

```
WEU        v.9, n.3, v.10, n.1-5, 7, v.11, n.1        Micro 11
ARC        Dec, 1963, Feb-May, Aug, 1964, Mar 20, 1965

WMM        [v.10, n.3-8]                              Special
           [Mar-Sept, 1964                           Collections

AzNCC      v.14-v.17, n.7;                            Indian File
           June, 1969-Oct, 1972

NjP        [v.5, n.3-v.17, n.8]                       Periodicals
           [Oct 20, 1959-Nov, 1972]

NN         v.12, n.1-v.15, n.3;                       HBA
           Feb, 1967-Apr, 1970

OkU        v.12, n.6-v.15, n.4;                       WHC
           Sept, 1967-Oct, 1970

UPB        [v.6, n.3-v.16, n.6]                       970.105/C432
           [1960-1971]
```

1115 Warrior Echo. 1968?-?//. Irregular. Last issue 4 pages, height 28
cm. Photographs. Published by St. Francis Alumni Association, St.
Francis, SD. Alumni newsletter.

```
WMM        v.3, n.1; (n.s.)v.1, n.2, v.2, n.1;        Special
           May? 1970, May, 1971, Dec, 1975           Collections
```

1116 The War-Whoop. 1916//. Semi-monthly. Last issue 4 pages. Available
in microform: WHi-A, Papers of Carlos Montezuma, (1916). Lawrence,
KS. Editor: Phillip Gordon. Subject focus: rights, Catholic Church.

```
WHi        n.1;                                       Microforms
           Jan, 1916
```

1117 Wasah Mabin: Looking Beyond. 1977-1979?// Bi-monthly. Last issue 4
pages, height 28-38 cm. Published by A Bridge Between Two Worlds
(Title IV, Indian Education Act Project), Lansing, MI. Subject focus:
education.

```
MiU-B      [Nov, 1977-Apr, 1979]                      Periodicals
```

Washington Bulletin. Washington, DC

   see Sentinel Bulletin. Washington, DC

1118 <u>Wassaja</u>. 1916-1922//. Monthly. Last issue 4 pages, height 23 cm.
     Line drawings. Available on microfilm: WHi-A, Papers Of Carlos
     Montezuma, (1916-1922). Washington, DC. Editor: Carlos Montezuma.
     Subject focus: rights, self-determination, legislation, criticism of
     government bureaus.

WHi	v.1, n.3-v.9, n.21; June, 1916-Nov, 1922	Microforms
WHi	v.1, n.1-2, 4, v.2, n.2; Apr-May, July, 1916, May, 1917	F801//WA Cutter
WMM	v.1, n.7; Oct, 1916	Special Collections
ICN	v.1, n.1-12; Apr, 1916-Mar, 1917	Ayer 1/W27
OCHP	v.1, n.1-12; Apr, 1916-Mar, 1917	Harding Libr/455
MoSHi	[v.4, n.8-v.8, n.21] [1919-1922]	970.1/W282

1119 <u>Wassaja</u>. 1973-1979//. 8 times a year. ISSN 0160-287x. LC sc78-746.
     OCLC 1773249, 6811640. RLIN DCLCSC78746-S, CSUP07695202-S,
     CSUP04064203-S, MIUG277-S, OHCP1773249-S, NYPG784407489-S. Last issue
     20 pages, last volume 120 pages. Line drawings, photographs,
     commercial advertising. Indexed in: Index to Literature on the
     American Indian (1970-1973). Available in microform: McA (1974-1979);
     WHi-A, Veda Stone Papers, (1973-1977); Y (1973-). Published by
     American Indian Historical Society, San Francisco, CA. Frequency
     varies: monthly, Jan, 1973-May, 1977. Editors: Rupert Costo and
     Jeanette Henry. Subject focus: culture, history, legislation,
     education. Merged with the Indian Historian to form Wassaja, The
     Indian Historian.

WHi	[v.1, n.1-v.7, n.6/7] [Jan, 1973-Oct/Nov, 1979]	Microforms
WEU	[v.1, n.8-v.5, n.4] [Nov, 1973-Apr, 1977]	Journalism Lab
WEU	[v.1, n.1-v.7, n.6/7] [Jan, 1973-Oct/Nov, 1979]	Microforms
WEU ARC	[v.1, n.3-v.5, n.5] Apr/May, 1973-May, 1977]	Micro 11
WKenU	v.1, n.1-v.2, n.5; Jan, 1973-Aug, 1974	Microfilm
WM	v.1, n.1-v.7, n.4; Jan, 1973-May, 1979	Periodicals

WMaP-RL	[v.1, n.1-v.7, n.6/7] [Jan, 1973-Oct/Nov, 1979]	Periodicals
WMM	v.1, n.1-v.7, n.6/7; Jan, 1973-Oct/Nov, 1979	E/75/W3x
WMM	[v.1, n.5-v.3, n.6] [July, 1973-July, 1975]	Special Collections
WMMus	v.1, n.2-v.5, n.2; Feb/Mar, 1973-Feb, 1977	Anthro Section
WMUW	[v.1, n.1-v.7, n.6/7] [Jan, 1973-Oct/Nov, 1979]	Microforms
WMSC	v.1, n.1-v.7, n.4; Jan, 1973-May, 1979	Periodicals
WOsh	v.1, n.1-v.2, n.5; Jan, 1973-Aug, 1974	Periodicals
WUSP	v.1, n.1-v.7, n.6/7; Jan, 1973-Oct/Nov, 1979	Periodicals
AzFM	v.1, n.1-v.7, n.6/7 Jan, 1973-Oct/Nov, 1979	570.6/W321
AzHC	v.7; 1979	Periodicals
AzHm	v.6, n.1-v.7; 1978-1979	Periodicals
AzNCC	v.1, n.1-v.7, n.6/7; Jan, 1973-Oct/Nov, 1979	Indian File
AzT	v.1, n.3-v.7, n.6/7; Apr/May, 1973-Oct/Nov, 1979	Periodicals
CL	v.1, n.1-v.7, n.6/7; Jan, 1973-Oct/Nov, 1979	Periodicals
CLSM	v.1-v.7; 1964-1979	Periodicals
CNoSU	[v.1, n.1-v.7, n.6/7] [Jan, 1973-Oct/Nov, 1979]	Microfiche
CSmarP	v.1-v.7; 1973-1979	Stacks
CU-A	v.1, n.1-v.7, n.6/7 Jan, 1977-Oct/Nov, 1979	E/77/A1/W37
IdU	[v.1-v.7, n.6/7] [1973-Oct/Nov, 1979]	E/75/W3

IC	v.3, n.11-v.5, n.2; Nov/Dec, 1975-Feb, 1977	Periodicals
KU	v.1, n.1-v.7, n.6/7 Jan, 1977-Oct/Nov, 1979	Kansas Collection
LARC	v.1, n.1-v.7, n.6/7; Jan, 1973-Oct/Nov, 1979	Periodicals
MnBemT	v.1, n.1-v.7, n.6/7; Jan, 1973-Oct/Nov, 1979	Periodicals
MoHi	v.3-v.5; 1975-1977	970.1/In23
MoSHi	v.3, n.9-11, v.4, n.1-12, v.5, n.1; [1975-1977]	970.1/W282
NbU	[v.1-v.5] [1973-1977]	E/75/W34
NjP	[v.1, n.1-v.7, n.4] [Jan, 1973-May, 1979]	Periodicals
NmG	v.1, n.1-v.7, n.6/7; Jan, 1973-Oct/Nov, 1979	Periodicals
N	[v.1, n.7-v.2, n.10] [Oct, 1977-Dec, 1974]	MA/FM
NN	[v.1, n.1-v.7, n.6/7] [Jan, 1973-Oct/Nov, 1979]	XLB-42
NPotU	v.1-v.7; 1973-1979	E/75/W3
OClWHi	[v.1-v.7] [1973-1979]	Periodicals
OkTU	[v.1, n.1-v.7, n.6/7] [Jan, 1973-Oct/Nov, 1979]	Rare Book Room
OkU	[v.1, n.1-v.7, n.6/7] [Jan, 1973-Oct/Nov, 1979]	WHC
OrHi	v.1, n.1-v.7, n.6/7; Jan, 1973-Oct/Nov, 1979	Periodicals
PPT	[v.1, n.1-v.v, n.7] [Jan, 1973-July, 1976]	Contemporary Culture
SdU	[v.1, n.1-v.7, n.6/7] [Jan, 1973-Oct/Nov, 1979]	South Dakota Room
TxU	[v.1-v.7] [1973-1979]	E/77/W3239

UPB   [v.1, n.5-v.7, n.4]   970.105/W282
           [1973-1979]

CaOPeT   v.1, n.1-v.6;   Microfilm
           Jan, 1973-1978

Other holding institutions: ArU (AFU), [Amerind Foundation, Dragoon,
AZ], AzFU 9AZN), AzTeS (AZS), AzU (AZU), CChiS (SSH), CPFT (CFT),
CArcHT (CHU), CLU (CLU), CSUuP (CPS), CU-Riv (CRU), COU-DA (COA), COFS
(COF), CoDU (DVP). DSI (SMI), DI (UDI), DeU (DLM), [Flagler College,
St. Augustine, FL] (FFC), IDeKN (JNA), [Indiana Union List of Serials,
Indianapolis, IN] (ILS), In (ISL), InU (IUL), KSteC (KKQ), LNU (LNU),
MWelC (WEL), MeB (BBH), MiEM (EEM), MiGrC (EXC), MiKC (EXK),
MiU-Labadie (EYM), MiDW (EYW), MnHi (MHS), MnManS (MNM), [Hennepin
County Library, Edina, MN], [University of Minnesota Union List,
Minneapolis, MN] (MUL), NdU (UND), NhD (DRB), NIC (COO), [Central New
York Library Resouces Council, Syracuse, NY] (SRR), NSyU (SYB), NbU
(VHB), [Western new York Library Resources Council, Buffalo, NY]
(VZX), NBrockU (XBM), NCaS (XLM), NFQC (XQM), NR (YQR), NSbSU (YSM),
[Standing Rock Community College Library, Fort Yates, ND], OAkU (AKR),
OKentU (KSU), OOxM (MIA), [Ohio Historical Society, Columbus, OH]
(OHT), OYU (YNG), OkAdE (ECO), Ok (OKD), OrU-Special Collections, PPiU
(PIT), ScU (SUC), TU (TKN), T (TNS), TxDN (INT), TxDaM-P (ISB), TxArU
(IUA), [AMIGOS Union List of Serials, Dallas, TX] (IUC), VtU (VTU),
WaU (WAU), [Arrowhead Library System, Janesville, WI] (WIJ), [Shawano
City-County Library, Shawano, WI], [University of Wisconsin-Stevens
Point-Native American Center, Stevens Point, WI], [Wisconsin Indian
Resource Council, Stevens Point, WI], WyU (WYU).

1120 Wassaja, The Indian Historian. 1964-1980//. Quarterly. ISSN
     0199-9052, 0019-4840. OCLC 1752881, 6275206. RLIN IAUL82-S111,
     CUDG82-S176, DCLC649495-S, OHCP02195227-S, DCLC80648957-S,
     CSUP2195227-S, NHDG0614-S, NJRG2911-S, NJRG2811-S, AZPG253-S,
     AZPG252-S, AZPG251-S, CTYG1852-S, MDJG083-S, MDJG082-S,
     CUBU10053633-S. Last issue 54 pages, last volume 232 pages, height 28
     cm. Line drawings. Indexed in: Current Index to Journals in
     Education (1980); Social Work Research and Abstracts (1980); United
     States Political Science Documents. Available in microform: McA
     (1974-1980); WHi-A, Veda Stone Papers, (1969-1973); Y (1967-1979).
     Published by American Indian Historical Society, San Francisco, CA.
     Title varies: The Indian Historian, Oct, 1964-Dec, 1979. Editors:
     Jeanette Henry, Jan, 1966-Dec, 1979; Rupert Costo and Jeanette Henry,
     Mar-Nov, 1980. Subject focus: history, culture, law, linguistics,
     education.

     WHi   v.1, n.1-(n.s.)v.13, n.4;   E/75/A513
                Oct, 1964-Nov, 1980

     WHi   (n.s.)v.7, n.1-v.13, n.4;   Microforms
                Winter, 1974-Nov, 1980

     WEU   (n.s.)v.1, n.1-v.13, n.4;   Microfilm
                Dec, 1967-Dec, 1980

WEU ARC	(n.s.) [v.2, n.s.n.1-v.6, n.4] [Spring, 1969-Fall, 1973]	Micro 11
WGr	(n.s.)v.8, n.2-v.13, n.4; Spring, 1975-Nov, 1980	HLSS
WGrU	v.1, n.1(n.s.)-v.13, n.4; Dec, 1967-Nov, 1980	Periodicals
WKenU	(n.s.)v.10, n.1-v.13, n.4; Winter, 1977-Nov, 1980	Periodicals
WM	(n.s.)v.11, n.1-v.13, n.4; Winter, 1978-Nov, 1980	Periodicals
WMaPI-RL	(n.s.)v.13, n.1-3; Mar-Sept, 1980	Periodicals
WMM	v.1, n.1-(n.s.)v.13, n.4; Oct, 1964-Nov, 1980	E/75/A513
WMM	(n.s.)v.3, n.4; Fall, 1970	Special Collections
WMMus	[v.1, n.1-12], (n.s.)v.4, n.1-v.13, n.4; [Oct, 1964-Dec, 1965] Jan/Feb, 1967-Nov, 1980	970.1/In2
WMUW	v.1, n.2-(n.s.)v.13, n.4; Nov, 1964-Nov, 1980	E/77/I53x
WNC	(n.s.)v.8-v.12; 1975-1979	Periodicals
WRfC	(n.s.)v.3-v.13, n.4; Winter, 1970-Nov, 1980	Periodicals
WUSP	(n.s.)v.2, n.1-v.13, n.4; Spring, 1969-Nov, 1980	Periodicals
WMSC	(n.s.)v.2, n.1-v.13, n.4; Spring, 1969-Nov, 1980	Periodicals
AkBC	(n.s.)v.6,n.1-v.13, n.4 Winter, 1973-Nov, 1980	Periodicals
AzHC	(n.s.)v.1-v.9; Spring, 1967-Fall, 1976	Periodicals
AzNCC	(n.s.)v.1-v.13, n.4; Spring, 1967-Nov, 1980	Indian File

AzPh	v.1-(n.s.)v.12; 1966-1980	Periodicals
AzT	(n.s.)v.4, n.4-v.13, n.4; Winter, 1971-Nov, 1980	Periodicals
AzU	(n.s.)v.13, n.1-4; Mar-Nov, 1980	I1979/W315
CAz	[v.8, n.1-v.13, n.4] [Spring, 1975-Nov, 1980	Periodicals
CL	v.3, n.5-(n.s.)v.13, n.4; May, 1966-Nov, 1980	Periodicals
CLSM	(n.s.)v.13; 1980	Periodicals
CNoSU	(n.s.) [v.1-v.12] [1968-1979]	Periodicals
CSmarP	(n.s.) [v.1-v.13] [1968-1980]	Stacks
CU-A	(n.s.)v.1, n.1-v.13, n.4; Dec, 1967-Nov, 1980	E/77/A1/I5
CoCF	(n.s.)v.1, n.1-v.11, n.2; Dec, 1967-Spring, 1978	Periodicals
CoKIM	(n.s.)v.1-v.6; 1968-1973	Periodicals
IdU	(n.s.)v.1-v.12; 1967-1979	E/75/I5
IC	(n.s.)v.2, n.1-v.13, n.4; Spring, 1969-Nov, 1980	Periodicals
ICN	(n.s.)v.1, n.1-v.13, n.4; Dec, 1967-Nov, 1980	Ayer 1 I3945
KU	(n.s.)v.1, n.1-v.12, n.4; Dec, 1967-Fall, 1979	Kansas Collection
LARC	(n.s.)v.3-v.4, v.6, v.8, v.13; 1969-1970, 1972, 1974, 1980	Periodicals
MWA	(n.s.)v.1-v.2 1967-1969	Periodicals
Mi	(n.s.)v.1, n.1-v.13, n.4; Dec, 1967-Nov, 1980	Periodicals

MnBemT	v.1, n.1-(n.s.)v.13, n.4; Oct, 1964-Nov, 1980	E/75/A513
MoHi	(n.s.)v.10-v.13; 1977-1980	970.1/In23
MoS	(n.s.)v.6-v.12; 1973-1979	Periodicals
NbU	v.1, n.1-(n.s.)v.13, n.4; Oct, 1964-Nov, 1980	E/75/W37
NjP	(n.s.)[v.1, n.1-v.5, n.4] [Dec, 1967-Winter, 1972]	Periodicals
NmG	(n.s.)v.1, n.1-v.12; Dec, 1967-Summer, 1979	Periodicals
NmScW	(n.s.)[v.1-v.13] [1967-1980]	Periodicals
N	(n.s.)[v.1, n.1-v.3, n.3], v.4, n.1; [Dec, 1967-Winter, 1969], Spring, 1971	J970.105 qI39
NN	v.1, n.1-(n.s.)v.13, n.4; Oct, 1964-Nov, 1980	HBA 80-540
NPotU	(n.s.)v.1-v.13; 1968-1980	E/78/W37
NcP	(n.s.)v.11-v.17, v.20-v.23; 1969-1974, 1977-1980	Periodicals
OCHP	(n.s.)v.6, n.1, v.8, n.1-v.13, n.4; Winter, 1973, Winter, 1975-Nov, 1980	970.05/In2
OkT	(n.s.)[v.3, n.7-v.1, n.2] [Aug/Sept, 1966-Spring, 1968]	Periodicals
OkTU	v.1, n.1-(n.s.)v.13, n.4; Dec, 1964-Nov, 1980	Rare Book Room
OkTahN	v.1, n.1-(n.s.)v.13, n.4; Oct, 1964-Nov, 1980	E/75/W37
OkU	v.2, n.1-(n.s.)v.13, n.4; Jan, 1965-Nov, 1980	WHC
OrHi	(n.s.)v.1, n.1-v.13, n.4; Dec, 1967-Nov, 1980	Periodicals
OrU	(n.s.)v.1, n.1-v.13, n.4; Dec, 1967-Nov, 1980	Periodicals
PP	(n.s.)v.1-v.12; 1967-1979	970.1/In25h

SdU	v.3-(n.s.)v.12, v.13; 1966-1979, 1980	Stacks
TxU	v.1, n.1-(n.s.)v.13; Oct, 1964-1980	E/75/A513
UPB	[v.3, n.1-(n.s.)v.13, n.4] [1966-Nov, 1980]	970.105/IN2H
WaU	(n.s.)v.1, n.1-v.13, n.4; Dec, 1967-Nov, 1980	E/75/A5132
WyCWC	(n.s.)v.4, n.1-v.13, n.3; Spring, 1971-Sept, 1981	Periodicals
CaNBFU	(n.s.)v.3-v.13, n.4; 1970-Nov, 1980	E/75/W3
CaOPeT	(n.s.)[v.1, n.1-v.13, n.4] [Dec, 1967-Nov, 1980]	Microfilm
CaOSuL	(n.s.)v.13; 1980	Periodicals
CaOSuU	(n.s.)v.12-v.13; 1979-1980	Periodicals
CaSSIC	(n.s.)v.1, n.1-v.5, n.4; Dec, 1967-Winter, 1972	Microfiche

Other holding institutions: AU (ALM), [Alabama Public Library
Service, Montgomery, AL] (ASL), ArU (AFU), ArStC (ASU), [Amerind
Foundation, Inc., Dragoon, AZ], AzFU (AZN), AzTeS (AZS), [U. S. Dept.
of the Interior, Western Archaeological Center, Tuscon, AZ] (UDZ),
CChiS (CCH), CLO (CCO), [California State University, Dominguez Hills,
Carson, CA] CU (CUY), (CDH), CSdS (CDS), CFS (CFS), CLobS (CLO), CPFT
(CFT), CArcHT (CHU), CLS (CLA), CLavC (CLV), CNoS (CNO), CLCM (CNH),
CSUuP (CPS), CU-Riv (CRU), CsjU (CSJ), CCmS (CSM), CSfI (CUF), CU-S
(CUS), COU-DA (COA),COFS (COF), COD (DPL), CoDU (DVP), CtW (WLU) CtY
(YUS), [Congressional Research Service, Washington, DC] (CRS), DLC
(DLC), DSI (SMI), DI (UDI), DeU (DLM), [Flagler College, St.
Augustine, FL] (FFC), FL (FGM), FTS (FHM), FJF (FJN), FJK (FJS), FOFT
(FTU), GEU (EMU), GAuA (GJG), GASU (GSU), GU (GUA), GVaS (GYG), HU
(HUH), IaDL (IOH), IaDuU (IOV), IaWavU (IOW), IaCfT NIU), ICharE
(IAD), INS (IAI), ICL (IAL), ICRC (IAR) IRA (ICY), IDeKN (JNA), IU
(UIU), InMuB (IBS), InE (IEP), InGo (IGC), [Indiana Union List of
Serials, Indianapolis, IN] (ILS), InND (IND), InLP (IPL), In (ISL),
InUpt (ITU), InU (IUL), KHayF (KFH), KPT (KFP), KSteC (KKQ), KWiU
(KSW), KyRE (KEU), KyU (KUK), LGra (LGS), LNU (LNU), LU (LUU), MBU
(BOS), [Boston State College Library, Boston, MA] (BST), MAH (HAM),
MH-ED (HMG), MH (HUL), MH-P (HLS), MWalB (MBB), MShM (MTH), MBNU
(MTH), MNS (SNN), MWelC (WEL), MdBJ (JHE), MdStm (MDS), [Frostburg
State College Library, Frostburg, MD] (MFS), UMC (MdU), MiGrC (EXC),
MiKC (EXK), MiKW (EXW), MiYEM (EYE), MiU-Labadie (EYM), MiDW (EYW),
MiMtpT (EZC), MnMCC (MCO), MnHi (MHS), MnDuU (MND), MnManS (MNM),
MnStcls (MST), [Hennepin County Library, Edina, MN], [Universtiy of

Minnesota Union List, Minneapolis, MN] (MUL), MnSRC (RCL), MoWat/MoWgW
(ELW), [Central Missouri State University, Warrensburg, MO] (MCW), MoU
(MUU), MoKU (UMK), MsU (MUM), [Dull Knife Memorial Library, Lame Deer,
MT], NcGrE (ERE), NcGU (NGU), NcU (NOC), NcRS (NRC), NdU (UND), NbKS
(KRS), NbOU (NBU), NmLcU (IRU), NmLvH (NMH), NmU-L (NML), NBwu (BUF),
NIC (COO), [New York State Union List of Serials, Albany, NY] (NYS),
NA1U (NAM), NRU (RRR), [Central New York Library Resources Council,
Syracuse, NY] (SRR), NSyU (SYB), NGcA (VJA), NSufR (VVR), NReonSL
(VVS), NPV (VXW), [Western New York Library Resources Council,
Buffalo, NY] (VZX), NBrockU (XBM), NFredU (XFM), NII (XIM), NCaS
(XLM), NFQC (XQM), NBuC (YBM), NGenoU (YGM), NCH (YHM), NOsU (YOM), NR
(YQR), NSbSU (YSM), NOneoU (ZBM), NGH (ZEM), NNepaSU (ZLM), NPurU
(ZPM), OAkU (AKR), OCU (CIN), OC1U (CSU), OC1W (CWR), OKentU (KSU),
OOxM (MIA), OO (OBE), O (OHI), [Ohio Historical Society, Columbus, OH]
(OHT), OAU (OUN), OTU (TOL), ODaUW (WSU), OY (YMM), OYU (YNG), [Bacone
College, Muskogee, OK], OkAdE (ECO), OkShB (OKB), OkLC (OKC), Ok
(OKD), PCalS (CSC), PPD (DXU), PHC (HVC), PEL (LAF), PManM (MAN), P
(PHA), PPiU (PIT), PP (PLF), PPiC (PMC), [Pittsburgh Regional Library
Center-Union List, Pittsburgh, PA] (QPR), PSt (UPM), PC1vU (URS), ScU
(SUC), SdB (SDB), TNJ (TJC), TU (TKN), TCo11M (TMS), T (TNS), TMSC
(TWS), TMurS (TXM), TxF (IFA), TxDa (IGA), TxLT (ILU), TxD1V (INT),
TxArU (IUA), [AMIGOS Union List of Serials, Dallas, TX] (IUC), TxPR
(RCE), TxWicM (TMI), TxCM (TXA), TxAU (TXG), TxNacS (TXK), ViNO (VOD),
ViBlbr (VPI), ViRUC (VRC), VtU (VTU), WaS, WFon (WIF), [WGrU-Native
American Studies Dept.], [Arrowhead Library System, Janesville Public
Library, Janesville, WI] (WIJ), [University of Wisconsin-Stevens
Point-Native American Center, Stevens Point, WI], [Wisconsin Indian
Resource Council, Stevens Point, WI], WyU (WYU).

1121 Wawatay News: Voice of the North. 1974. Monthly. $8. for
individuals; $10. for institutions. Kathy Chisel, editor, Wawatay
News: Voice of the North, P.O. Box 1180, Sioux Lookout, Ontario,
Canada POV 2TO. (807) 737-2951. ISSN 0703-9387. LC cn78-30169.
OCLC 3951241. RLIN DCLCCN7830169-S, OHCP3951241-S. Last issue 12
pages, height 59 cm. Line drawings, photographs, commercial
advertising. Published by Wa-Wa-Ta Native Communication Society.
Newspaper. Subject focus: Cree people. In Cree, 50%.

WHi	v.7, n.1- Nov, 1980-	Circulation
CaAEU	v.4, n.3- 1978-	Boreal Institute
CaOAFN	Current issues	Periodicals
CaOONL	[v.1, n.13-v.3, n.13] [Aug, 1975-Nov, 1977]	Newspaper Section
CaOSuU	v.3- 1977-	Periodicals

1122 We Cooperate. 1967-1970?//. Irregular. Last issue 8 pages, height
     28 cm. Line drawings. Published by Cooperative Union of Canada,
     Ottawa, Ontario, Canada. Editor: J.T. Phalen. Subject focus:
     cooperatives, business, Arctic region, Inuit people. In Inuit, 50%.

     CaOORD   n.1-6;   Periodicals
               Spring, 1967-Spring, 1970

     We Live by the River. Nanana, AK

        see Han Zaadlitl'ee/We Live by the River. Nanana, AK

     We Sa Ma Dong. Hayward, WI

        see We Sam I Dong. Stone Lake, WI

     We Sa Mi Dong. Hayward, WI

        see We Sam I Dong. Stone Lake, WI

1123 We Sam I Dong. 1968?-1970?//. Irregular. Last issue 8 pages. Line
     drawings. Available in microform: WHi-A, Veda Stone Papers (1969,
     1970). Published by Lac Courte Oreilles Band of Chippewa Indians,
     Stone Lake, WI. Title varies: We Sa Mi Dong, May-Sept, 1969; We Sa Ma
     Dong, Feb-Mar, 1970. Place of publication varies: Hayward, WI, May,
     1969-Apr, 1970. Editor: Peter Larson. Community newsletter. Subject
     focus: Lac Courte Oreilles Band of Chippewas.

     WHi   n.18-19, 22, 26-31;   Microforms
               May-June, Sept, 1969, Feb-July, 1970

     WEU   n.18-19, 22, 26-31;   Micro 11
     ARC   May-June, Sept, 1969, Feb-July, 1970

1124 The Weekly Capital. 1889-?// Weekly. Last issue 4 pages. Line
     drawings, commercial advertising. Available in microform: OkHi
     (1896). Tahlequah, OK. Editor: S. E. Dick. Newspaper.

     WHi   v.8, n.49, v.9, n.1;   Microforms
               Jan 10, Feb 14, 1896

     OkHi   v.8, n.49, v.9, n.1;   Microfilm
               Jan 10, Feb 14, 1896

1125 <u>Weewish Tree</u>. 1972-1980?//. 7 times a year. ISSN 0049-7088. LC
     72-621634/AC. OCLC 1586328. RLIN DCLC72621634-S, MIUG0118-S,
     CUBU10053657-S, OHCP1586328-S, NYPG734338470-S. Last issue 32 pages,
     height 22 cm. Line drawings, photographs. Indexed in: Current Index
     to Journals in Education (1972-1980); Index to Literature on the
     American Indian (1971-1973). Published by American Indian Historical
     Society, San Francisco, CA. Subject focus: children, fiction, poetry,
     culture.

     WMSC   v.1, n.1-v.8, n.6;   Periodicals
                 Nov, 1971-Nov/Dec, 1980

     AzNCC   v.2-v.8, n.6;   Indian File
                 1972-Nov/Dec, 1980

     CL   v.1, n.1-v.8, n.5;   Periodicals
                 Nov, 1971-Oct, 1980

     CLSM   v.1, n.1-v.8, n.5;   Periodicals
                 Nov, 1971-Oct, 1980

     MnBemT   v.1, n.1-v.8, n.6;   Periodicals
                 Nov, 1971-Nov/Dec, 1980

     NjP   [v.1, n.1-v.7, n.7]   Periodicals
                 [Nov, 1971-Sept, 1979]

     NN   v.1, n.1-4;   HBA
                 Nov, 1971-Fall, 1972   73-2722

     OkTU   v.1, n.1-v.8, n.6;   Rare Book
                 Nov, 1971-Nov/Dec, 1980   Room

     OkU   v.1, n.1;   WHC
                 Nov, 1971

     OrHi   v.1-v.6;   Periodicals
                 1971-1978

     SdU   v.4-v.8;   Stacks
                 1976-1970

     CaOORD   v.2, n.3-v.3, n.3;   Periodicals
                 Nov, 1973-Nov/Dec, 1974

     Other holding institutions: AzU (AZU), COU-DA (COA), DLC (DLC), DSI
     (SMI), DI (UDI), FJ (JPL), [Indiana Union List of Serials,
     Indianapolis, IN] (ILS), [Boston State College Library, Boston, MA]
     (BST), Mi (EEX), MiDW (EYW), MiMpT (EZC), [Minnesota Union List of
     Serials, Minneapolis, MN] (MUL), NmLcU (IRU), NBu (VHB), [Western New
     York Library Resources Council, Buffalo, NY] (VZX), NCortU (YCM),
     NOneoU (ZBM), [Bacone College, Muskogee, OK], Ok (OKD), [Pittsburgh
     Regional Library Center Union List, Pittsburg, PA], (QPR), PPSJ (SJD),
     TxComS (IEA), TxDa (IGA), TxLT (ILU), [AMIGOS Union List of Serials,
     Dallas, TX] (IUC), Radford College Library, Radford, VA] (VRA), WFon
     (WIF), [Davis & Elkins College, Elkins, WV] (WVD).

1126 West River Times/East River Echo. 1976-?//. Unknown. Last issue 8
     pages, height 28 cm. Line drawings, photographs. Available in
     microform: WHi (1976). Published by Native American Solidarity
     Committee, Washington, DC. Subject focus: rights, politics,
     legislation, sovereignty, land claims.

     WHi   v.1, n.4;   Microforms
                May, 1976

1127 Western Shoshone Sacred Land Association. 1981? Unknown. Dagmar
     Thorpe, editor, Western Shoshone Sacred Land Association, P.O. Box
     1522, Elko, NV 89801. (702) 738-3992. Last issue 24 pages, height 39
     cm. Line drawings, photographs. Subject focus: land claims,
     environment, culture, Shoshone people.

     WHi   Spring, 1981-   Microforms

1128 Whispering Wind Magazine. 1967. Monthly. Jack B. Heriard, editor,
     Whispering Wind Magazine, 8009 Wales St., New Orleans, LA 70126.
     (504) 241-5866. ISSN 0300-6565. LC sn78-4239, 81-640191. OCLC
     1355769. RLIN DCLC81640191, OHCP1355769-S. Last issue 24 pages.
     Line drawings, photographs, commercial advertising. Available in
     microform: McA (1973-). Published by Louisiana Indian Hobbyist
     Association, Inc. Subject focus: culture, arts and crafts, music and
     dance, history.

     WHi   v.6, n.4-   Microforms
                Jan, 1973-

     AzNCC   v.6-   Indian File
                1973-

     ICN   Current issues   CHAI

     MnBemT   v.6-   Periodicals
                1973-

     NjP   [v.1, n.2-v.12, n.2]   Periodicals
                [Nov, 1967-Dec, 1978]

     NcP   [v.8-v.11], v.12-   Periodicals
                [1974-1977], 1978-

     OkTahN   v.7, n.8   E/75/W46
                1974-

     OkTU   v.11, n.3, 6-   Rare Book
                Feb, Aug, 1978-   Room

     OkU   v.1, n.1-   WHC
                Oct, 1967-

SdU   v.4-v.9;   Microfilm
             Oct, 1971-Dec, 1976

CaOPeT   v.4-   Microfilm
             1971-

Other holding institutions: DLC (DLC) GU (GUA), KSteC (KKQ), [Western
Nevada Community College, Carson City, NV], [Bacone College, Muskogee,
OK], TxArU (IUA), [AMIGOS Union List of Serials, Dallas, TX] (IUC).

1129 White Cloud Journal of American Indian/Alaska Native Mental Health.
     1978. Irregular. $15. for individuals and institutions. Robert A.
     Ryan, editor, White Cloud Journal of American Indian/Alaskan Native
     Mental Health, National Center for American Indian Mental Health
     Research, Allied Health Science, Vermillion, SD 57069. (605) 677-5298.
     ISSN 0190-2482. LC 81-640063, sc79-4537, sn79-1852. OCLC 4648615.
     RLIN NYCG82-S469, NYCG23451696-S, CSUG23451696-S, DCLC81640063-S,
     CSUP282120-S, CUBG13723039-S, NJPG182-S, OHCP4648615-S, CSUG7733488-S,
     NYPG794035002-S. Height 28 cm. Indexed in: Social Work Research and
     Abstracts (1981-1982); Psychological Abstracts; Abstracts of Health
     Care Management Studies; Current Index to Journals in Education. Place
     of publication varies: Portland, OR, Spring, 1978-?, 1979. Subject
     focus: mental health. Supercedes White Cloud Center Newsletter.

     ICN   Current issues   CHAI

     AzNCC   v.3-   Indian File
                  1982-

     NjP   v.1, n.1-2;   Periodicals
                  Spring-Fall, 1978

     NN   v.1, n.1-v.2, n.3;   Periodicals
                  Spring, 1978-1981

     OkTU   v.1, n.1-   Rare Book
                  Spring, 1978-   Room

     WaU   v.1-   Health S
                  Apr, 1979-

     CaAEU   v.1, n.1-   Boreal
                  Spring, 1978-   Institute

     Other holding institutions: AzTeS (AZS), AzU (AZU), CLU (CLU), DHU
     (DHU), DLC (DLC), MH (HUL), MH-P (TOZ), DNLM (NLM), [University of
     Minnesota Union List, Minneapolis, MN] (MUL), NmU (IQU), OKU-M (OKH),
     WMenU (GZS).

1130 White Earth Reservation Newsletter/Mah No Men Ee Kay Gee Zes.
     1977?-1978//. Monthly? OCLC 6168959. Last issue 4 pages, height 36

cm. Line drawings. Available in microform: WHi (1977-1978). White
Earth, MN. Community newsletter. Subject focus: Ojibwa people.

WHi   Aug, 1977-Oct?. 1978   Microforms

WMUW   Aug, 1977-Oct?. 1978   (SPL)
                                                        E/75/W44x

Wig-I-Wam. Minneapolis, MN

   see Vision on the Wind. Minneapolis, MN

1131 The Wiky Gazette. 1977-1982//. Bi-weekly. Last issue 12 pages,
     height 28 cm. Line drawings. Wikwemikong, Ontario, Canada. Community
     newsletter.

     WHi   v.6, n.11-v.7, n.3;   Pam
                July 7, 1982-Aug 24, 1982   Cataloging

1132 Win Awenen Nisitstam. 1979. Monthly. $7. for individuals and
     institutions. Susan Moore, editor, Win Awenen Nisitstam, 206 Greenough
     St., Sault Ste. Marie, MI 49783. (906) 635-0581. Last issue 16 pages,
     height 45 cm. Line drawings, photographs, commercial advertising.
     Community newsletter. Subject focus: Chippewa people, local and
     regional news.

     WHi   v.2, n.4, 6-   Circulation
                Sept/Oct, Dec, 1980-

1133 Wind River Journal. 1978. Weekly. $12. for indivduals and
     institutions. Joan Willow, editor, Wind River Journal, P.O. Box 157,
     Fort Washakie, WY 82514. (307) 332-3958. Last issue 8 pages, last
     volume 416 pages, height 39 cm. Line drawings, photographs, commercial
     advertising. Available in microform: WHi (1979-). Previous editors:
     June Stagner, June 15, 1979-Apr 16, 1980; David Perry, Apr 25, 1980-Jan
     16, 1981. Community newsletter. Subject focus: Shosone and Arapaho
     people.

     WHi   v.2, n.80-   Microforms
                June 22, 1979-

1134 The Wind River Rendezvous. 1971. Bi-monthly. $10. for individuals
     and institutions. The Wind River Rendezvous, P.O. Box 278, St.
     Stevens, WY 82524. (307) 856-6797. Last issue 12 pages, last volume
     80 pages, height 28 cm. Line drawings, photographs, some in color.

Published by St. Stevens Indian Mission Foundation. Subject focus:
Arapaho and Shohone people, reservation, area and foundation news.

| WHi | v.2, n.6– | Circulation |
| | Nov/Dec, 1972– | |

| WMM | [v.1, n.2–v.8, n.4] | Special |
| | [May/June, 1971–July/Aug, 1978] | Collections |

| OkTU | v.9, n.1– | Rare Book |
| | Jan/Feb, 1979– | Room |

| WyCWC | v.3, n.1– | Periodicals |
| | 1973– | |

Other holding institutions: NjP.

1135 Winnebago Indian News. 1972–1980?//. Weekly. OCLC 6992460. Last
issue 6 pages. Available in microform: McP (1972). Published by
Winnebago Tribe of Nebraska, Winnebago, NE. Community newsletter.
Subject focus: Winnebago people.

WHi	v.1, n.1–53, [v.7, n.37–46]	Microforms
	Jan 7–Dec 29, 1972, [Aug 24, 1979–	
	Feb 28, 1980]	

| CNoSU | v.1, n.1–53; | Microforms |
| | Jan 7–Dec 29, 1972 | |

| MtBBCC | v.8; | Periodicals |
| | Nov, 1980 | |

| OkTU | v.7, n.46–60; | Rare Book |
| | Feb–Nov, 1979 | Room |

| OkU | v.1, n.1–53; | WHC |
| | Jan 7–Dec 29, 1972 | |

Other holding institutions: ICN (IBV), NbU (LDL), NmScW, OKTU (OKT), WM
(GZD).

1136 Winnebago Research Center, Inc. Update. 1981. Irregular. Winnebago
Research Center, Inc. Update, 315 W. Gorham St., Madison, WI 53703.
(608) 256-4828. Last issue 6 pages, height 28 cm. Line drawings,
photographs. Personal names indexed in: Index to Wisconsin Native
American Periodicals (1981). Subject focus: Winnebago people, history,
archives.

| WHi | Fall, 1981– | Circulation |

1137 The Winner. 1980//. Unknown. Last issue 22 pages, height 28 cm.
     Line drawings. Published by Work Incentive Program, Browning, MT.
     Subject focus: Blackfeet people, vocational training and education,
     employment, program news.

     MtBBCC   Jan, 1980   Periodicals

1138 Wisconsin Indian Resource Council Monthly Mailout. 1975. Monthly.
     Monthly Mailout, 216 COPS Bldg., University of Wisconsin-Stevens Point,
     Stevens Point, WI 54481. (715) 346-2746. Last issue 18 pages, height
     28 cm. Line drawings. Available on Microfilm: WHi (1977-). Title
     varies: Wisconsin Indian Resource Council, Inc., Feb 1977-Sept, 1981.
     Frequency varies: irregular, Feb, 1977-Sept, 1981. Community
     newsletter. Subject focus: local, state and national news.

     WHi   Feb, 1977-   Circulation

     Other holding institutions: [Wisconsin Indian Resource Council, Stevens
     Point, WI].

     Wisconsin Indian Youth Council Newsletter. Eau Claire, WI

         see Indian Council Talk. Eau Claire, WI

1139 Wisconsin Inter-Tribal News. 1978-1979//. Monthly. OCLC 6188880.
     Last issue 16 pages. Line drawings, photographs. Available in
     microform: WHi (1978-1979). Published by Great Lakes Inter-Tribal
     Council, Inc., Odanah, WI. Editor: Walt Bresette. Subject focus:
     national and local news, Great Lakes area, land claims, education.

     WHi   v.1, n.1-?;   Microforms
                Sept, 1978-July, 1979

     WMMus   v.1, n.1-?;   Anthro
                Aug, 1978-July, 1979   Section

     WMUW   v.1, n.1-3;   L11/W4
                Aug-Oct, 1978

     Other holding institutions: [University of Wisconsin-Stevens
     Point-Native American Center, Stevens Point, WI], [Wisconsin Indian
     Resource Council, Stevens Point, WI],

1140 Wisconsin Tribal Women's News/Najinakwe. 1974-?//. Irregular. Last
     issue 8 pages. Line drawings. Available in microform: WHi-A, Veda
     Stone Papers, (1964, 1965). Published by Cooperative Extention
     Programs, University of Wisconsin-Extention, Madison, WI. Subject
     focus: women's rights, politics, day care.

WHi v.1, n.1, 4;   Microforms
    Oct, 1974, July, 1975

WEU v.1, n.1, 4;   Micro 11
ARC Oct, 1974, July, 1975

Other holding institutions: [University of Wisconsin Stevens
Point-Native American Center, Stevens Point, WI].

1141 Wisconsin Winnebago Newsletter. 1964-1965//. Irregular. Last issue 2
   pages, height 28 cm. Line drawings. Personal names indexed in: Index
   to Wisconsin Native American Periodicals (1964-1965). Wisconsin
   Winnebago Business Committee, Oshkosh, WI. Subject focus: Winnebago
   people, education, social services, land claims, committee news.

   WHi v.1, n.1-v.2, n.10;   Pam 68-185
      Nov 27, 1964-Nov 27, 1965

1142 Wisconsin Winnebago Newsbrief. 1979? Irregular. Wisconsin Winnebago
   Newsbrief, Route 1 Creamery Rd., Nekoosa, WI 54457. (715) 886-5050.
   Last issue 14 pages, height 28 cm. Published by Wisconsin Winnebago
   Business Committee. Subject focus: Winnebago people, education, social
   services, land claims, committee news. other holding institutions:
   [WGrU-Native American Studies Dept.], [Wisconsin Indian Resource
   Council, Stevens Point, WI].

   WHi Oct, 1979, May 15, 1982-   Circulation

   WUSP Current issues   Native American
                 Center

   WM Current issues   Forest Home
                 Branch

1143 Wo-Lda-Lda-Ka. 1975-?//. Unknown. OCLC 8313397. Last issue 10
   pages, height 28 cm. Published by Wisconsin Winnebago Business
   Committee, Stevens Point, WI. Subject focus: Winnebago people,
   education, health, social services, committee news.

   WHi v.1, n.6;   Pam 81-1469
      Oct, 1975

1144 Wood County Inter-Tribal Council Newsletter. 1965-?//. Monthly. Last
   issue 4 pages. Line drawings, photographs. Available in microform:
   WHi-A, Veda Stone Papers, (1965). Wisconsin Rapids, WI. Editor: Rita
   Nichols. Community newsletter.

WHi   v.1, n.1-2;   Microforms
           Mar 31-Apr, 1965

WEU   v.1, n.1-2;   Micro 11
ARC   Mar 31-Apr, 1965

NjP   v.1, n.1-2;   Periodicals
           Mar 31-Apr, 1965

1145 Wopeedah. 1952?-1976//. Bi-monthly. OCLC 6221088. Last issue 4
     pages. Photographs. Available in microform: McA (1974-1976); WHi
     (1973-1976). Published by Immaculate Conception Mission School,
     Stephan, SD. Subject focus: missions, Catholic Church.

     WHi   v.22, n.147-v.25, n.162;   Microforms
                Jan/Feb, 1974-July/Aug, 1976

     WEU   v.18, n.125-130;   Journalism
                May/June, 1970-Mar/Apr, 1971   Lab

     WMM   [v.7, n.47-v.21, n.141]   Special
                [Apr/May, 1957-Jan/Feb, 1973]   Collections

     WMUW   v.25, n.162;   (SPL)
                July/Aug, 1976   E/75/W66x

     AzNCC   v.23;   Microfilm
                1974

     NjP   [v.5, n.34-v.25, n.162]   Periodicals
                [Feb/Mar, 1955-July/Aug, 1976]

     SdU   v.25;   Microfilm
                Jan-July/Aug, 1976

     CaOPeT   v.22, n.147-v.25, n.162;   Microfilm
                1974-1976

1146 The Word Carrier. 1884-1939?//. Monthly. Last issue 4 pages, last
     volume 48 pages, height 41 cm. Line drawings. Published by Dakota
     Mission, Santee Agency, NE. Frequency varies: bi-monthly, June/July,
     1898-Sept/Oct, 1936. Editors: Alfred L. Riggs, Mar, 1884-July/Aug,
     1915; Frederick B. Riggs, Jan/Feb, 1925-May/June, 1933; Millard M.
     Fowler, Sept/Oct, 1936-Aug, 1937. Subject focus: Dakota people,
     missions, Christian religion. Iapi Oaye, the Dakota edition, published
     1871-1939.

     WHi   [v.1, n.1-v.66, n.7]   Circulation
                [Mar, 1884-Aug, 1937]

     SdHRC   v.1, n.1-v.4, n.12, v.17, n.1-v.59, n.7;   Periodicals
                Mar, 1884-1887, 1888-1930

SdU	v.24-v.64; 1895-1935	Stacks
SdYC	v.1, n.1-v.68, n.7; Mar, 1884-Mar, 1939	Microfilm

Wotanin Fort Peck Tribal Newspaper. Poplar, MT

    see Wotanin Wowapi. Poplar, MT

1147 Wotanin Wowawpi 1970. Bi-monthly. $10. for individuals and
institutions. Bonnie Clincher, editor, Wotanin Wowapi, Box 493,
Poplar, MT 59255. (406) 768-5241. OCLC 6189066. Last issue 12 pages,
last volume 280 pages, height 58 cm. Line drawings, photographs,
commercial advertising. Available in microform: McP (1971-1972); CPC
(1970-1976). Published by Fort Peck Tribal Executive Board. Title
varies: Wotanin Fort Peck Tribal Newspaper, Jan 4, 1971-Dec 12, 1972.
Frequency varies: weekly, May 11, 1970-Mar, 1982. Community newsletter.

WHi	v.1, n.1- Mar 16/19, 1970-	Microforms
WMUW	[v.1, n.5-v.10, n.13] [May 11, 1970-Nov, 1979]	(SPE) E/75/W67x
CNoSU	[v.2-v.3] [1971-1972]	Microfilm
IC	v.12- Aug 18, 1981-	Periodicals
ICN	Current issues	CHAI
MtBBCC	v.11-v.12; Mar, 1980-Mar, 1981	Periodicals
MtBC	v.2, n.8- Apr 19, 1971-	E/78/M9/W68
NjP	[v.1, n.1-v.10, n.11] [Mar 16/19, 1970-June 29, 1979]	Periodicals
OkU	v.2-3; Jan 4, 1971-Dec 12, 1972	WHC

Other holding institutions: NmScW, [Standing Rock Community College
Library, Fort Yates, ND].

1148 Wounded Knee District News Sheet. 1978?//. Monthly. Last issue 10

pages, height 28 cm. Line drawings. Wounded Knee, SD. Community
newsletter.

WMM   Sept 26, 1978   Special
                                                           Collections

1149 Wounded Knee Legal Defense/Offense Committee Newsletter. 1972-1975//.
     Irregular. OCLC 5699739. Last issue 4 pages. Line drawings.
     Available in microform: WHi (1973-1975). Place of publication varies:
     Sioux Falls, SD, Dec 5, 1973-Aug 6, 1974; Lincoln, NE, Sept 20-Oct 29,
     1974; Council Bluffs, IA, Jan-June, 1975. Subject focus: rights,
     legislation. politics, Wounded Knee rebellion.

     WHi   v.2, n.8-v.3, n.5   Microforms
                Dec 5, 1973-Sept/Oct, 1975

     NHu   [v.2, n.16-v.3, n.3]   Periodicals
                [Aug, 1974-June, 1975]

     Other holding institutions: [Standing Rock Community College Library,
     Fort Yates, ND], [University of Wisconsin Stevens Point-Native American
     Center, Stevens Point, WI].

1150 Wow. 1980//? Unknown. Last issue 28 pages, height 43 cm. Line
     drawings, photographs, commercial advertising. Published by United
     Tribes Educational Technical Center, Office of Public Information,
     Bismarck, ND. Editor: Shirley Bordeaux. Subject focus: children,
     puzzles, games, culture.

     WHi   v.1, n.1;   Microfilm
                Sept, 1980

1151 Wowapi: A Magazine Devoted to the Cause of the Indians. 1883//.
     Unknown. LC 30-12815. OCLC 6269995. Last issue 98 pages, height 27
     cm. Line drawings, commercial advertising. Available in microform:
     WHi (1883). Boston, MA. Subject focus: acculturation, poetry, fiction.

     WHi   Nov 7, 1883   Microforms

     CLSM   Nov 7, 1883   Periodicals

     Other holding institutions: CtHT (TYC).

1152 Woyakapi. 1968?-1972?//. Monthly. Last issue 5 pages, height 28 cm.
     Line drawings, photgraphs. Published by St. Francis High School, St.
     Francis, SD. Frequency varies: bi-weekly, Apr 21-Oct 27, 1969;
     bi-monthly, Dec 7, 1970; bi-weekly, May 27, 1971. Editors: Coke

Millard, Dec 7, 1970; Ed Schmidt, Jan 28, 1972. High school
newsletter. Subject focus: Catholic Church.

WMM	[v.1, n.3-v.4, n.13] [1968-May 16, 1972]	Special Collections
NjP	[v.1, n.4-v.3, n.8] [Nov 18, 1968-Jan 18, 1971]	Periodicals
SdU	v.1, n.4-12; Nov 18, 1968-Apr 20, 1970	Periodicals

1153 YMCA Bulletin. 1912-?//. Monthly. Last issue 4 pages, height 30 cm.
Photographs. Published by Haskell Institute, Lawrence, KS.
Organization newsletter.

WMM	[v.5, n.5-v.7, n.1/2] [Jan, 1916-Oct/Nov, 1917]	Special Collections

1154 Yakima Drum Beat. 1965. Bi-monthly. Yakima Drum Beat, Box 31,
Toppenish, WA 98948. Last issue 4 pages, height 28 cm. Line drawings,
photographs. Published by Yakima Indian Christian Mission. Subject
focus: Yakima people, missions, Christian religion.

WHi	v.15, n.6- Dec, 1979-	Circulation

1155 Yakima Nation Review. 1970. Bi-monthly. Yakima Nation Review, Box
386, Toppenish, WA 98948. (509) 865-2673. ISSN 0199-3046. LC
sn79-7779. OCLC 5084787. Last issue 6 pages. Line drawings,
photographs. Available in microform: McP (1971-1972). Frequency
varies: monthly, Feb, 1971-Nov, 1972. Subject focus: Yakima people,
politics, law, culture.

WHi	v.1, n.11- Jan 1, 1971-	Microforms
WEU	v.6, n.16-17, v.8, n.17, v.9, n.5; Jan 18-Feb 4, 1977, Apr 5, Aug 4, 1978	Journalism Lab
WMUW	[v.6, n.20-v.10, n.3] [Apr 29, 1977-July 16, 1979]	(SPL) E/75/Y3x
AzNCC	v.1-v.2; 1971-Nov, 1972	Microfilm
CNoSU	[v.1-v.3] [1971-1973]	Microfilm

MnBemT	[v.6-v.7], v.9- [1977-1978], 1978-	Periodicals
MtBBCC	v.11-v.12 June, 1980-Jan, 1981	Periodicals
NjP	[v.1, n.1-v.10, n.2] [May, 1970-June 30, 1979]	Periodicals
NHu	[v.2, n.11-v.4, n.17] [1973-Jan, 1976]	Periodicals
OkTU	v.9, n.11- Nov 24, 1978-	Rare Book Room
OkU	[v.2, n.6-v.3, n.28] [1971-1973]	WHC
Wa	v.1- 1970-	NW

Other holding institutions: [Congressional Research Service,
Washington, DC] (CRS), [University of Minnesota Union List,
Minneapolis, MN] (MUL), NmScW, WaU (WAU), [WGrU-Native American Studies
Dept.].

1156 Yakima Reservation News. 1966-1970//? Monthly. OCLC 8426503. Last
     issue 4 pages. Line drawings. Available in microform: CPC
     (1966-1970). Published by Yakima County Extension, Washington State
     Extension Service, Toppenish, WA. Subject focus: Yakima people,
     health, social services, education.

| WHi | Sept, 1966-July, 1970 | Microforms |
| NjP | Sept, 1966-Sept, 1970 | Periodicals |

Other holding institutions: OrU-Special Collections, PPiU (PIT).

1157 Yankton Sioux Messenger. 1980. Irregular. Yankton Sioux Messenger,
     Rt. 3, Wagner, SD 57380. Last issue 8 pages, height 44 cm. Line
     drawings, photographs, commercial advertising. Community newsletter.
     Subject focus: local and national news, Yankton Sioux people.

| WHi | v.2, n.3-6;
Apr-Nov, 1981 | Microforms |

1158 Young Native American. 1981. Monthly. $6. for individuals and
     institutions. John Figueroa, editor, Young Native American, Suite 131,
     World Trade Center, San Francisco, CA 94111. Last issue 8 pages,

height 36 cm. Line drawings, photographs. Subject focus: history, biographies, young adults.

| WHi | v.1, n.1– Oct, 1981– | Microforms |

1159 <u>Your Indian Reporter</u>. 1962–1971?//. Bi–monthly. Last issue 4 pages, height 28 cm. Line drawings. Hemet, CA. Title varies: Indian Reporter, Nov, 1963–May/June, 1969. Subject focus: bibliography, educational opportunities, local and regional news.

| CLSM | v.1, n.8–v.6, n.3, [no nos.] Nov, 1963–May/June, 1969, Feb, June/July, 1971, Feb, 1972 | Periodicals |
| SdU | v.4, n.5–v.6, n./2; Sept/Oct, 1967–Mar/Apr, 1969 | Periodicals |

1160 <u>Yukon Indian News</u>. 1974. Bi–weekly. $10. for individuals, $20 for institutions. Bobbi Smith, editor, Yukon Indian News, 22 Nisutlin Dr., Whitehorse, Yukon, Canada Y1A 3S5. ISSN 0382-7305. LC cn76-31946. OCLC 2740398. RLIN DCLCCN7631946-S, OHCP2740398-S. Published by Ye Sa To Communications Society. Community newsletter. Subject focus: rights, women's rights, education.

WHi	v.7, n.21-23, v.8, n.1– Nov 6–Dec 11, 1980, Jan 15, 1981–	Circulation
AkUF	v.7, n.5– 1980–	AK–News
AzNCC	v.5– Feb 15, 1978–	Indian File
NjP	[v.1, n.2–v.6, n.12] [July, 1974–June 21, 1979]	Periodicals
CaACG	v.3, n.22– Dec 17, 1976–	Periodicals
CaAEU	v.1, n.1– June, 1974–	Boreal Institute
CaYW	v.1, n.1– June, 1974–	Periodicals

Other holding institutions: CaOONL (NLC).

1161 <u>The Yukon Sun and the Yukon Weekly</u>. 1893-?//. Weekly. Last issue 8 pages, last volume 416 pages. Line drawings, photographs, commercial

advertising. Available in microform: OkHi (1902-1904). Yukon, OK.
Editors: William Albert Maxwell, Sept 5, 1902-Sept 9, 1904; Gordon
McComas, Sept 16-Dec 30, 1904. Newspaper. Also described in: Foreman,
Carolyn Thomas, Oklahoma Imprints, 1835-1907, University of Oklahoma
Press, Norman, OK, 1936.

WHi   v.10, n.36-v.13, n.1;   Microforms
             Sept 5, 1902-Dec 30, 1904

OkHi   v.10, n.36-v.13, n.1;   Microforms
             Sept 5, 1902-Dec 30, 1904

1162 Zoar's Weekly Information. 1980-1981//. Irregular. Milwaukee, WI.
      Last issue 14 pages, last volume 56 pages, height 28 cm. Personal
      names indexed in: Index to Wisconsin Native American Periodicals
      (1980-1981). Available in microform: WHi (1980-1981). Title varies:
      News, June?, 1980. Editor: Zoar Fulwilder. Community newsletter.
      Subject focus: urban community, culture, book reviews, education,
      puzzles.

      WHi   v.1, n.1-v.2, n.16;   Microforms
                   June?, 1980-Nov, 1981

      Other holding institutions: WM (GZD), [Wisconsin Indian Resource
      Council, Stevens Point, WI].

1163 Zuni Legal Aid Newsletter. 1971-1972//. Irregular. Last issue 6
      pages, height 36 cm. Published by Zuni Legal Aid and Defender Society,
      Zuni, NM. Subject focus: Zuni people, legal aid, law, litigation.

      WHi   v.1, n.3;   Pam
                   Jan 20, 1972   Cataloging

      NjP   v.2, n.1;   Periodicals
                   Apr 17, 1972

1164 Zuni Tribal Newsletter. 1967?-1976//?. Irregular. OCLC 6168939.
      Last issue 12 pages. Available in microform: McA (1974-1975). Zuni,
      NM. Frequency varies: bi-weekly, May 10-Oct 18, 1974. Community
      newsletter. Subject focus: Zuni people.

      WHi   v.8, n.15-v.9, n.8;   Microforms
                   Jan 25, 1974-May 23, 1975

      WMUW   v.10, n.6;   (SPL)
                   Apr 19, 1976   E/75/Z8x

      AzNCC   v.5-v.9, n.8;   Indian File
                   Feb, 1971-May 23, 1975

OkU   [v.8, n.11-v.9, n.8]   WHC
           [1973-May 23, 1975]

CaOPeT   v.8, n.15-v.9, n.8;   Microfilm
           Jan 25, 1974-May 23, 1975

Subject Index

Numbers refer to specific entries and not page numbers.

Choctaw language materials, 115, 228, 272, 414, 448, 1094

Choctaw people, 115, 137, 198, 227, 228, 229, 273, 414, 681

Christian Churches, 851
see also specific denominations, e.g. Baptist Church

Christian religion, 220, 231, 241, 262, 316, 360, 385, 389, 394, 396, 420, 436, 441, 443, 444, 504, 506, 540, 576, 623, 649, 655, 683, 689, 805, 814, 818, 834, 839, 863, 980, 1028, 1107, 1146, 1154
see also specific denominations, e.g. Baptist Church

Circumpolar relations, 525

Citizenship, 53, 484
see also Self-determination

Cochiti Pueblo
see Pueblo, Cochiti people

Coeur d'Alene people, 255

College newsletter, 80, 302, 304, 341, 364, 377, 439, 511, 512, 657, 658, 706, 823, 824, 873, 1034, 1062

Community colleges, 891

Community development, 47, 233, 301, 386, 517, 586, 606, 607, 612, 675, 720, 773, 774, 775, 858, 897, 925, 1074, 1101

Comprehensive Employment and Training Act
see CETA programs

Conferences, 192, 756

Congregational Church, 1022

Congressional monitoring, 67, 889

Conservation, 87

Consortia, 891, 904

Consumer information, 43, 87

Continuing education,
see adult and continuing education

Cooperatives, 87, 242, 251, 969, 1122

Corporate and shareholder news,
see Alaska Native corporations, Alaska Native Claims Settlement Act

Court decisions, 438, 1045
see also Law, Legal case histories, Legislation

Coville people, 1050

Crafts
see Arts and crafts

Creative writing, 872
see also Journalism, Literature

Cree language materials, 146, 189, 191, 259, 260, 261, 262, 649, 716, 742, 980, 1030, 1121

Cree people, 22, 92, 146, 189, 191, 259, 260, 261, 262, 629, 637, 649, 716, 742, 898, 980, 1030, 1121
see also Chippewa people, Ojibwa people

Creek language materials, 273, 819

Creek people, 263, 273, 819

Criticism of government bureaus, 1118

Crow Creek Sioux people
see Sioux, Crow Creek

Crow people, 13, 14

Cultural assimilation
see Acculturation

Cultural devlopment, 525

Cultural self-determination, 775

Culture, 13, 14, 27, 34, 41, 44,
45, 56, 57, 63, 66, 78, 82, 86,
103, 105, 120, 129, 138, 143,
146, 148, 149, 202, 204, 206,
267, 289, 301, 315, 318, 321,
352, 357, 375, 378, 382, 396,
403, 406, 407, 442, 444, 466,
478, 481, 493, 502, 507, 511,
517, 525, 527, 537, 538, 539,
558, 564, 578, 593, 607, 611,
619, 622, 623, 639, 641, 665,
683, 684, 587, 693, 694, 713,
740, 743, 747, 752, 766, 811,
814, 818, 837, 841, 846, 848,
852, 856, 863, 866, 925, 957,
964, 978, 982, 989, 1003, 1008,
1009, 1010, 1019, 1020, 1039,
1048, 1055, 1065, 1084, 1097,
1098, 1119, 1120, 1125, 1127,
1128, 1150, 1155, 1162

Curriculum development, 59, 125,
160, 164, 362, 381, 388, 428,
463, 519, 532, 611, 659, 706,
785, 813, 891, 913

DNA (Dinebeiina Nahiila Be
Agaditahe), 268

Dakota language materials, 96,
195, 279, 385, 934, 935

Dakota people, 276, 277, 278,
279, 322, 385, 580, 796, 797,
798, 870, 900, 901, 924, 934,
935, 937, 1085, 1110, 1146
see also Sioux

Dance, 1128

Day care, 1140

Dene people, 284

Departmemt of Indian Affairs and
Northern Development staff
news, 638

Dinebeiina Nahiila Be Agaditahe
see DNA

Draft resistance, 699

Drama, 514, 932

Drug abuse, 926
see also Alcoholism

Drums, Inc., corporate news, 297

Dutch language materials, 552

Ecology, 27, 165, 226, 451, 603,
858, 1048
see also Environment

Economic development, 158, 237

Economic opportunities
see Career opportunities,
Employment information

Economic self-reliance, 720
see also Self-determination,
Socio-economic conditons

Economics, 73, 86, 127, 318, 510,
673, 692, 799, 1073, 1083, 1090
see also Business, Alaska
Native Corporations,
Socio-economic conditons

Education and training for women,
725

Education, 8, 27, 29, 49, 57, 59,
71, 77, 81, 82, 88, 119, 125,
129, 160, 161, 164, 175, 176,
180, 183, 188, 202, 204, 206,
237, 257, 267, 269, 284, 287,
308, 309, 310, 311, 323, 324,
332, 336, 348, 359, 362, 372,
381, 388, 393, 409, 416, 418,
419, 424, 425, 426, 427, 428,
436, 446, 447, 460, 462, 472,
482, 491, 501, 507, 511, 516,
525, 526, 532, 541, 563, 571,
575, 577, 580, 602, 608, 615,
623, 647, 656, 659, 664, 668,
675, 692, 694, 696, 702, 706,
726, 729, 731, 732, 734, 736,
740, 747, 754, 772, 789, 791,
794, 799, 809, 813, 817, 818,
846, 856, 877, 881, 883, 884,
897, 901, 930, 945, 950, 961,
974, 982, 983, 984, 994, 1001,
1013, 1049, 1054, 1063, 1068,
1084, 1085, 1087, 1090, 1102,
1117, 1119, 1120, 1139, 1141,
1142, 1143, 1156, 1160, 1162

Editors Index

Numbers refer to specific entries and not page numbers.

Index of Publishers

Numbers refer to specific entries and not page numbers.

American Indian Leadership
  Council, 390
American Indian Liberation
  Crusade, 420
American Indian Mission
  Association, 394
American Indian Mission, Inc.,
  443
American Indian National Bank,
  127
American Indian Press
  Association, 76, 610
American Indian Scouting
  Outreach, Boy Scouts of
  America, 609
American Indian Student
  Association, Minneapolis, 8
American Indian Student
  Association, California State
  University, Northridge, 80
American Indian Student Cultural
  Center, University of
  Minnesota, 824
American Indian Studies Center,
  56
American Indian Times Agency, 82
American Indian Training and
  Employment Program, 789
American Indian Travel
  Commission, 489
American Indian Women's Service
  League, 411, 777
American Indians for Development,
  301
Americans for Indian Opportunity,
  868
Amerind Club, 85
Amerine Enterprises, 619
Ann Arbor Indian Center, Women of
  American Native Tribes, Inc.,
  763
Annual Convention of the National
  Congress of American Indians,
  The, 271
Antelope Indian Circle, 407
Apache Sunrise Association, 100
Arbeitsgruppe fur
  Nordamericanische Indianer,
  502
Archaeological Society of North
  Carolina, 970
Arctic Slope Regional Corp., 1088
Arizona Indian Association, 446
Arizona State University, 161,
  532
Arrow, Inc., 106

Associated Committee of Friends
  on Indian Affairs, 465
Association for Diffusing
  Information on the Subject of
  Indian Rights, 395
Association of Interior Community
  Health Aides, Tanana Chiefs
  Health Authority, 6
Association on American Indian
  Affairs, Inc. 45, 398, 432,
  451

BJL Publications, 450
Baffin Region Adult Education
  Office, 577
Baltimore American Indian Center,
  954
Baptist Mission Press, 207, 944
Bear Tribe Medicine Society, The,
  603
Bemidji State University, 418,
  817
Benedictine Fathers of the Sacred
  Heart Mission, 397
Benedictine Missionary Monks, 144
Bering Straits Native Corp., 134
Bethel Regional High School, 538
Black Hills Alliance, 139
Blackfeet Media Department, 141
Blackfeet Tribal Council,
  Department of Blackfeet
  Multi-Media, 967
Blackfeet Women's Resource
  Center, 26
Blood Reserve, 990
Board of Indian Missions,
  American Indian Mission
  Association, 394
Board of National Missions of the
  Presbyterian Church, 688, 1034
Boston Indian Council, 234
Boy Scouts of America, 609
Branch of Education, Bureau of
  Indian Affairs, 424
Bridge Between Two Worlds, A,
  1117
Brigham Young University, 302,
  399
British Columbia Indian Advisory
  Committee, 393
British Columbia Indian
  Homemakers Association, 496
British Columbia Native Women's
  Society, 124
Bulova Watch Co, 58

Geographic Index

Numbers refer to specific entries and not page numbers.

CALIFORNIA (continued)

  Portola Valley, 916
  Riverside, 389, 928
  Sacramento, 162, 401, 709, 905,
    950, 982, 1049
  San Fernando, 324
  San Francisco, 43, 70, 168,
    171, 172, 410, 508, 703,
    749, 1044, 1052, 1113, 1119,
    1120, 1125, 1158
  San Jose, 412, 952
  San Marcos, 700
  Santa Clara, 493, 952
  South Pasadena, 206
  Stanford, 377
  Susanville, 407
  Vacaville, 976

COLORADO

  Boulder, 95, 464, 938
  Cortez, 576
  Denver, 7, 62, 160, 269, 359,
    487, 674, 891, 1081
  Greeley, 535
  Ignacio, 972

CONNECTICUT

  Hartford, 409
  Meriden, 301
  New Haven, 506

DISTRICT OF COLUMBIA

  Washington, 58, 65, 70, 71, 73,
    75, 76, 79, 93, 106, 125,
    127, 155, 158, 237, 254,
    290, 310, 318, 323, 339,
    369, 400, 424, 438, 454,
    455, 458, 469, 472, 479,
    489, 501, 503, 505, 513,
    569, 575, 610, 656, 665,
    667, 685, 686, 687, 694,
    696, 785, 883, 889, 904,
    920, 921, 953, 1074, 1083,
    1118, 1126

FLORIDA

  Hollywood, 40
  Miami, 624

GEORGIA

  New Echota, 211

HAWAII

  Honolulu, 29, 365, 713

IDAHO

  Boise, 712, 743
  De Smet, 241, 903
  Fort Hall, 349, 929, 930
  Lapwai, 759
  Moscow, 664
  Plummer, 255

ILLINOIS

  Alton, 83
  Chicago, 54, 69, 86, 218, 264,
    497, 516, 611, 659, 822,
    875, 1002, 1114
  East St. Louis, 885
  Peoria, 53
  River Grove, 64
  Wheaton, 231

INDIANA

  Angola, 885
  Franklin, 885
  Frankton, 465
  Indianapolis, 1039
  Noblesville, 465

IOWA

  Council Bluffs, 1149
  Des Moines, 111
  Iowa City, 676
  Sioux City, 236, 528

KANSAS

  Lansing, 422
  Lawrence, 308, 364, 439, 689,
    873, 1116, 1153
  Leavenworth, 293
  North Topeka, 762
  Shawanoe, 944
  Topeka, 413
  Wichita, 460, 751

Catchword and Subtitle Index

Numbers refer to specific entries and not page numbers.

Action News, 122
Adult and Career Education
   Program Newsletter, 3
Advisory Committee Newsletter,
   393
Agluktuk, 134
Ajemoon, 259
Alaska Native and American Indian
   Mental Health Research and
   Development, 757
Alaska Native/American Indian
   Mental Health, 1129
Alaska Native Arts, 514
Alaska Native Nurses Association,
   755
Alaska Native Social Workers Inc.
   Newsletter, 112
Alaskan Native Census Report, 47
Alcohol Times, 402
All Tribes Newsletter, 508
Allegany Indian Reservation
   Newsletter, 792
Alumni Association Newsletter,
   364
American Folklore Group
   Newsletter, 404
American Indian/Alaska Native
   Nurses Association, 755
American Indian/Alaska Native
   Mental Health, 1129
American Indian and Alaska Native
   Mental Health Research and
   Development, 757
American Indian Center, 4
American Indian Center
   Newsletter, 321
American Indian Community House,
   Inc. Newsletter, 5
American Indian Development, 7
American Indian Education, 565
American Indian Ethnohistoric
   Conference, 756
American Indian Family Research,
   533
American Indian News and Affairs,
   890
American Indian Physicians, 113
American Journalism Quarterly,
   872

Americans Before Columbus, 1
Amerindian Center, Inc., 1078
Arapaho and Cheyenne Nation News,
   968
Arapaho Bulletin, 216
Arctic Star, 305
Artcrafts, 181
Association of Interior Community
   Health Aides, 6
Association on Indian Affairs,
   974
Atomone, 11
Awathm Awawhan, 909
Awawtom, 23

BIA Bulletin and Native News, 715
Baa Hane', 1089
Bacone College, 960
Baptist Voice, 49
Bear, 931
Benedictine, 881
Bilingual Education Service
   Center Newsletter, 161
Bilingual Education Training
   Resource Center, 973
Birch Barks, 24
Boys Club, Inc., Newsletter, 205
Brotherhood, 1098

CETA Newsletter, 733
Caddoan Linguistics, 938
California Indian Newsletter, 709
California Urban Indian Health
   Council, 166
Calumet and the Cross, 264
Camp Crier, 335, 789
Captive or Citizen, 53
Catholic Indian Missions
   Newsletter, 155
Catholic Indian Missions of
   America, 93
Center for Indian Education, 161
Cherokee Advocate, 744
Cheyenne and Arapaho Nation News,
   968
Chieftain, 531, 939
Chippewa Tribal Newsletter, 630

Chronological Index

Numbers refer to specific entries and not page numbers.

<u>1930-1939</u>: (continued)

200, 223, 225, 225, 241, 260,
276, 306, 315, 371, 385, 389,
398, 424, 437, 439, 442, 457,
460, 471, 476, 479, 481, 490,
505, 506, 566, 573, 579, 605,
631, 634, 652, 678, 683, 684,
688, 689, 735, 770, 797, 800,
826, 865, 884, 894, 903, 923,
928, 939, 945, 947, 1001, 1012,
1017, 1034, 1036, 1069, 1146

<u>1940-1949</u>:

19, 45, 98, 102, 123, 132, 170,
175, 176, 177, 195, 200, 223,
241, 260, 276, 315, 316, 320,
398, 424, 436, 437, 439, 442,
471, 475, 476, 479, 481, 490,
498, 505, 506, 566, 573, 574,
579, 605, 631, 632, 652, 665,
685, 686, 689, 724, 770, 797,
826, 865, 884, 921, 924, 928,
939, 947, 950, 957, 970, 980,
1001, 1012, 1013, 1017, 1023,
1024, 1034, 1036, 1054, 1107

<u>1950-1959</u>:

19, 24, 42, 45, 49, 54, 58, 64,
83, 86, 98, 99, 102, 106, 107,
132, 133, 136, 144, 171, 175,
176, 177, 199, 200, 213, 222,
223, 260, 262, 290, 316, 320,
326, 336, 349, 398, 400, 401,
424, 436, 437, 439, 442, 453,
465, 471, 475, 476, 479, 486,
490, 492, 506, 513, 517, 525,
539, 566, 573, 579, 580, 605,
612, 613, 631, 632, 652, 665,
666, 677, 685, 687, 689, 715,
724, 736, 744, 748, 756, 766,
770, 797, 803, 804, 826, 829,
831, 859, 864, 881, 884, 901,
907, 910, 921, 924, 928, 939,
950, 951, 953, 957, 958, 961,
970, 974, 1001, 1012, 1022,
1023, 1024, 1030, 1034, 1041,
1054, 1085, 1098, 1105, 1114,
1145

<u>1960-1969</u>:

1, 7, 14, 24, 27, 31, 42, 43,
49, 54, 63, 64, 67, 74, 77, 79,
83, 86, 87, 97, 98, 102, 105,
107, 120, 128, 132, 136, 140,
143, 144, 150, 153, 164, 167,
169, 171, 176, 177, 178, 182,
198, 199, 200, 202, 205, 206,
208, 209, 213, 218, 223, 231,
236, 240, 242, 260, 262, 264,
268, 289, 290, 294, 296, 300,
303, 307, 313, 316, 320, 324,
325, 327, 334, 336, 349, 351,
354, 355, 359, 361, 370, 374,
383, 390, 391, 393, 398, 399,
400, 401, 403, 407, 408, 410,
411, 418, 419, 420, 424, 436,
437, 439, 440, 441, 442, 443,
445, 446, 452, 453, 456, 461,
463, 464, 465, 466, 469, 471,
474, 476, 478, 479, 487, 490,
496, 497, 507, 515, 517, 519,
525, 531, 532, 535, 536, 539,
542, 545, 546, 547, 550, 552,
566, 571, 572, 573, 575, 576,
577, 579, 580, 581, 584, 593,
603, 605, 613, 614, 616, 617,
627, 629, 631, 632, 633, 637,
642, 643, 644, 649, 652, 662,
665, 680, 682, 685, 687, 689,
696, 714, 715, 716, 721, 724,
730, 732, 736, 742, 746, 750,
753, 756, 758, 760, 766, 768,
770, 771, 773, 774, 778, 783,
787, 791, 793, 795, 797, 802,
821, 825, 826, 828, 829, 836,
846, 848, 849, 856, 859, 863,
864, 870, 874, 882, 884, 885,
889, 892, 900, 901, 902, 906,
907, 909, 910, 919, 920, 921,
924, 928, 931, 939, 940, 942,
943, 950, 951, 953, 957, 960,
962, 963, 969, 970, 972, 990,
993, 995, 1001, 1003, 1012,
1014, 1016, 1022, 1023, 1025,
1026, 1027, 1028, 1030, 1034,
1035, 1037, 1038, 1040, 1042,
1049, 1050, 1054, 1063, 1064,
1070, 1081, 1085, 1090, 1092,
1098, 1105, 1111, 1113, 1114,
1115, 1120, 1122, 1123, 1128,
1141, 1144, 1145, 1152, 1154,
1156, 1159, 1164

1970-1979: (continued)

1045, 1046, 1047, 1048, 1049,
1050, 1051, 1052, 1053, 1054,
1055, 1056, 1057, 1058, 1060,
1061, 1062, 1063, 1065, 1066,
1067, 1072, 1073, 1074, 1075,
1076, 1077, 1079, 1082, 1084,
1085, 1086, 1088, 1089, 1090,
1091, 1092, 1096, 1097, 1098,
1099, 1100, 1101, 1102, 1103,
1105, 1106, 1108, 1109, 1110,
1112, 1113, 1114, 1115, 1117,
1119, 1120, 1121, 1122, 1123,
1125, 1126, 1128, 1129, 1130,
1131, 1132, 1133, 1134, 1135,
1138, 1139, 1140, 1142, 1143,
1145, 1147, 1148, 1149, 1152,
1154, 1155, 1156, 1159, 1160,
1163, 1164

1980-1982:

1, 2, 3, 4, 5, 6, 8, 10, 12, 13,
15, 18, 20, 21, 25, 26, 27, 28,
29, 34, 38, 39, 40, 41, 47, 48,
49, 50, 51, 56, 59, 60, 61, 62,
65, 67, 68, 69, 78, 79, 80, 84,
95, 98, 102, 103, 105, 107, 110,
113, 114, 119, 121, 122, 124,
129, 130, 131, 134, 137, 139,
141, 143, 144, 145, 147, 148,
149, 152, 154, 155, 158, 159,
161, 162, 163, 164, 165, 166,
169, 183, 184, 185, 187, 188,
190, 191, 193, 194, 197, 199,
200, 204, 205, 209, 214, 215,
216, 219, 220, 224, 227, 233,
234, 235, 236, 237, 238, 239,
240, 243, 244, 246, 248, 249,
251, 252, 253, 255, 257, 258,
259, 261, 263, 265, 267, 268,
269, 271, 274, 277, 278, 280,
281, 282, 284, 286, 292, 295,
298, 299, 300, 301, 302, 303,
304, 307, 311, 312, 313, 314,
316, 317, 318, 321, 322, 323,
328, 331, 333, 334, 335, 340,
342, 343, 344, 346, 347, 350,
356, 357, 358, 362, 363, 365,
366, 368, 373, 375, 376, 378,
379, 382, 384, 387, 388, 398,
402, 405, 406, 412, 416, 420,
425, 426, 429, 430, 431, 436,
438, 439, 444, 450, 451, 453,

1980-1982: (continued)

455, 463, 469, 471, 473, 476,
482, 485, 487, 488, 489, 490,
493, 494, 495, 496, 500, 501,
504, 509, 512, 514, 515, 516,
519, 520, 521, 522, 523, 524,
525, 527, 530, 531, 532, 533,
534, 536, 537, 543, 544, 549,
551, 552, 553, 558, 559, 560,
562, 563, 567, 568, 571, 575,
576, 580, 582, 585, 587, 588,
589, 592, 595, 597, 598, 603,
604, 605, 607, 608, 609, 611,
615, 619, 621, 622, 624, 625,
626, 628, 631, 636, 638, 639,
644, 646, 647, 648, 649, 651,
654, 656, 659, 660, 661, 663,
665, 669, 671, 672, 673, 674,
679, 682, 690, 691, 692, 693,
697, 698, 707, 708, 709, 710,
711, 713, 714, 716, 719, 720,
721, 722, 723, 724, 725, 728,
729, 736, 738, 741, 742, 745,
747, 749, 751, 752, 753, 755,
761, 762, 764, 765, 766, 773,
775, 776, 777, 779, 784, 785,
786, 788, 789, 790, 792, 793,
799, 807, 810, 812, 813, 816,
817, 824, 826, 827, 832, 834,
835, 837, 840, 841, 843, 847,
851, 852, 853, 854, 855, 856,
857, 858, 864, 866, 867, 868,
869, 870, 875, 880, 882, 883,
884, 888, 890, 898, 899, 902,
904, 905, 911, 912, 913, 915,
916, 917, 925, 926, 927, 929,
933, 937, 938, 946, 948, 954,
955, 956, 960, 966, 967, 968,
971, 972, 975, 977, 978, 979,
983, 985, 988, 989, 991, 994,
996, 1001, 1005, 1007, 1009,
1010, 1014, 1018, 1019, 1020,
1022, 1028, 1029, 1032, 1033,
1034, 1038, 1045, 1047, 1048,
1050, 1055, 1057, 1060, 1061,
1063, 1065, 1067, 1068, 1073,
1074, 1075, 1076, 1078, 1079,
1080, 1084, 1085, 1087, 1088,
1089, 1090, 1093, 1096, 1097,
1100, 1103, 1104, 1120, 1121,
1125, 1127, 1128, 1129, 1131,
1132, 1133, 1134, 1135, 1136,
1138, 1142, 1147, 1150, 1154,
1155, 1157, 1158, 1160, 1162

ABOUT THE CONTRIBUTORS

ANN L. BOWLES received her B.A. degree from Connecticut College and is currently working toward a M.A. in Library Science at the University of Wisconsin-Madison. A former schoolteacher, she is married and the mother of two children. Bowles is presently employed as a Research Assistant on the project "Native Americans: Library Resources in Wisconsin" at the State Historical Society of Wisconsin. Indexing Wisconsin Native American periodicals is one of her many duties.

JAMES P. DANKY is Newspapers and Periodicals Librarian at the State Historical Society of Wisconsin in Madison, and the author/compiler of many publications including *Women's Periodicals and Newspapers from the 18th Century to 1981* (G. K. Hall, 1982), *Women's History: Resources at the State Historical Society* (fourth edition revised, 1982), as well as union lists of newspapers and periodicals for Hispanic Americans, Blacks, and Asian Americans. Danky has served as Project Director for Native Americans: Library Services in Wisconsin, which produced this volume plus the *Index to Wisconsin Native American Periodicals, 1897–1981* with Barry Christopher Noonan, assisted by Ann L. Bowles (Microfiche, Greenwood Press, 1984), and *Native American Press in Wisconsin and the Nation* (University of Wisconsin-Madison Library School, 1982) with Maureen Hady.

MAUREEN E. HADY is Project Librarian, Native Americans: Library Resources in Wisconsin at the State Historical Society of Wisconsin. Hady received both a B.A. in English and a M.A. in Library Science from the University of Wisconsin-Madison. She is the co-compiler of *Women's Periodicals and Newspapers from the 18th Century to 1982* (G. K. Hall, 1982), *Black Periodicals and Newspapers: A Union List of Holdings in Libraries of the University of Wisconsin and the Library of the State Historical Society of Wisconsin,* second edition revised, 1979 (also available as ERIC Report E 192800), and *Asian American Periodicals and Newspapers: A Union List of Holdings in the Library of the State Historical Society of Wisconsin and the Libraries of the University of Wisconsin-Madison,* 1979 (also available as an ERIC Report, October 1982).

Engineering Psychology and Human Performance

THIRD EDITION

CHRISTOPHER D. WICKENS
University of Illinois at Champaign-Urbana

JUSTIN G. HOLLANDS
University of Idaho

Prentice Hall
Upper Saddle River, New Jersey 07458

Library of Congress Cataloging-in-Publication Data

Wickens, Christopher D.
  Engineering psychology and human performance/ Christopher D. Wickens, Justin G. Hollands. 3rd ed.
    p. cm.
  Includes bibliographical references and index.
  ISBN 0-321-04711-7
  1. Human engineering.   2. Human-machine systems.   3. Psychology, Industrial.
I. Hollands, Justin G.   II. Title
TA166.W53 1999   99-25476
620.8'2--dc21   CIP

Editor-in-Chief: Nancy Roberts
Executive Editor: Bill Webber
AVP/Director of Manufacturing and Production: Barbara Kittle
Senior Managing Editor: Bonnie Biller
Assistant Managing Editor: Mary Rottino
Assistant Editor: Jennifer Cohen
Manufacturing Manager: Nick Sklitsis
Prepress and Manufacturing Buyer: Lynn Pearlman
Full Service Production Manager: Eric Jorgensen
Project Coordination, Text Design, and Electronic Page Makeup: Electronic Publishing Services Inc.,
N.Y.C.

For permission to use copyrighted material, grateful acknowledgment is made to the copyright holders
cited throughout this book which are hereby made part of this copyright page.

This book was set in 10/12 Minion
The cover was printed by Phoenix Color Corp.

Copyright © 2000 by Prentice-Hall Inc.
Upper Saddle River, New Jersey 07458

ISBN 0-321-04711-7

11 12 13 14 15   HPC   13 12 11 10 09

Prentice-Hall International (UK) Limited, London
Prentice-Hall of Australia Pty. Limited, Sydney
Prentice-Hall Canada Inc., Toronto
Prentice-Hall Hispanoamericana, S.A., Mexico
Prentice-Hall of India Private Limited, New Delhi
Prentice-Hall of Japan, Inc., Tokyo
Pearson Education Asia Pte. Ltd., Singapore
Editoria Prentice-Hall do Brasil Ltda., Rio de Janeiro

PEARSON

Education

595026

**This book is not for sale or
distribution in the U.S.A. or Canada**

BRIEF CONTENTS

CONTENTS

PREFACE

This book was written, both the first and second editions, because of a perceived need to bridge the gap between the problems of system design and much of the excellent theoretical research in cognitive and experimental psychology and human performance. Many human-machine systems do not work as well as they could because they impose requirements on the human user that are incompatible with the way people attend, perceive, think, remember, decide, and act, that is, the way in which people perform or process information. Over the past five decades, tremendous strides have been made in understanding and modeling human information processing and human performance. Our goal is to show how these theoretical advances have been, or might be, applied to improving human-machine interactions.

Although engineers encountering system design problems may find some answers or guidelines either implicitly or explicitly stated in this book, it is not intended to be a handbook of human factors or engineering psychology. Many of the references in the text provide a more comprehensive tabulation of such guidelines. Instead, we have organized the book directly from the perspective of human information processing. The chapters generally correspond to the flow of information as it is processed by a human being—from the senses, through the brain, to action—and are less clearly organized from the perspective of different system components or engineering concerns, such as displays, illumination, controls, computers, and keyboards. Furthermore, although the following pages contain recommendations for certain system design principles, many of these are based only on laboratory research and theory; they have not been tested in real-world systems.

It is our firm belief that a solid grasp of theory will provide a strong base from which the specific principles of good human factors can be more readily derived. Our intended audience, therefore, is (1) the student in psychology, who will begin to recognize the relevance to many areas in the real-world applications of the theoretical principles of psychology that he or she may have encountered in other courses; (2) the engineering student, who, while learning to design and build systems with which humans interact, will come to appreciate not only the nature of human limitations—the essence of human factors—but also the theoretical principles of human performance and information processing underlying them; and (3) the actual practitioner in engineering psychology, human performance, and human factors engineering, who can understand the close cooperation that should exist between principles and theories of psychology and issues in system design.

The 13 chapters of the book span a wide range of human performance topics. Following the introduction in Chapter 1, in which engineering psychology is put into the broader framework of human factors and system design, Chapters 2 through 8 deal with perception, attention, cognition (both spatial and verbal), memory, learning, and decision making, emphasizing the potential applications of these areas of cognitive psychology. Chapters 9 through 12 cover the selection and execution of control actions, time-sharing, error, and stress, thereby addressing areas that are more traditionally associated with the engineering field. Finally, Chapter 13 is systems-oriented, discussing process control, complex systems and automation. This chapter shows how many of the principles explained in earlier chapters are pertinent to one specific application of rapidly growing importance.

Although the 13 chapters are interrelated (just as are the components of human information processing), we have constructed them in such a way that any chapter may be deleted from a course syllabus and still leave a coherent body. Thus, for example, a course on applied cognitive psychology might include Chapters 1 through 8, and another emphasizing more strictly engineering applications might include Chapters 1, 2, 4, 5, 6, 9, 10, 11, 12, and 13.

In addition to incorporating new experiments and studies where appropriate, we have made a number of changes in the third edition that set it apart from the second. First, most prominently, we have added a chapter, reflecting the growth of computer-based graphics systems, and their relevance for human performance issues in virtual environments and data visualization. Second, our chapters on decision making and automation and process control have been substantially rewritten, reflecting many of the changes in knowledge that our field has experienced since 1991 when the second edition was written. Third, throughout other chapters, substantial sections have been added describing important research developments in expertise, situation awareness, display integration, multimedia, the learning process and long term memory representation, planning and problem solving, voice control, and stress models.

In any project of this kind, one is indebted to numerous people for their assistance. For both of us the list includes several colleagues who have read and commented on various chapters, provided feedback on the second edition, and have stimulated our thinking. In addition to all acknowledgments in the first two editions (the text of which, of course, remains very much at the core of the current book), we would like to single out the extensive and helpful feedback on the second edition offered by Doug Gillan, Melody Carswell, Joe Goldberg, and Dan Fisk. We also thank countless students who, in one form or another, offered feedback regarding either good or bad elements of the second edition.

Christopher Wickens would like to acknowledge the contributions of faculty colleagues – in particular, Art Kramer and Gary Bradshaw who provided feedback on early drafts of chapters. He also acknowledges the contributions of four specific individuals who contributed to the development of his interest in engineering psychology: Delos Wickens, stimulated an early interest in experimental psychology; Dick Pew provided an introduction to academic research in engineering psychology and human performance;

Stan Roscoe pointed out the importance of good research applications to system design; and Emanuel Donchin continues to emphasize the importance of solid theoretical and empirical research. Also, it is impossible to do justice in crediting Karen Ayers' and Mary Welborn's contributions to this book. Without their hours of dedication at the word processor of a sometimes hostile computer, the project never would have succeeded. Chris's wife, Linda, was supportive during the hours of preparation for all three editions.

Justin Hollands also has many people to thank. Candace Schmidt tirelessly tracked down numerous references. The Psychology Department at the University of Idaho (especially Curt Braun, Brian Dyre, Sallie Gordon, Steve Meier, Philip Mohan, and Richard Reardon) provided useful comments and a supportive environment. Sharon McFadden at the Defence and Civil Institute of Environmental Medicine (Canada) provided time to put the finishing touches on the book. Lisa Fournier helped tackle the large literature on attention; Joel Warm did the same for vigilance; Stan Roscoe was helpful in providing valuable commentary on the history of the frequency-separated display. Justin also thanks his wife, Cindy, for her patience while this book was being written.

Christopher D. Wickens and Justin G. Hollands

Introduction to Engineering Psychology and Human Performance

The new driver of a van delivering perishable food in a city was seated in a cab that was equipped with some of the most advanced technology. An electronic console showed him a map indicating his location in the city and highlighting locations of destinations, which were color coded in terms of their priority. The map was also equipped with information on traffic buildups and a series of "zoom" options. A separate table below indicated the required time for each delivery.

As evening approached on this dreary winter day, wet snow fell, and the traffic on the southbound highway was heavy but moving fast. Looking down at the north-up map on his console, the driver tried to figure out his next destination and what direction to turn at the upcoming exit. The map was cluttered, hard to read, and upside down relative to his direction of travel, so he pressed what he thought was the "zoom in" button. Immediately, all the destinations on the map turned the same "high priority" color. He glanced back at the road to check the traffic and then went head down again, to try to figure out where he was and what he might have done to create the unexpected and unusual display. His memory of what he had read in the wordy instruction manual before he departed was fuzzy. Suddenly he noticed that the vehicle ahead of him had stopped. In a panic, he swerved into the left lane, only to hear the blast of a truck horn. Swinging his wheel rapidly to the far right, he avoided colliding with a stopped car in front but lost control on the berm, weaving crazily for a few seconds before flipping the van over and landing in the ditch. With his seatbelt on, he was only slightly injured, but the van was seriously damaged and the load of perishable food ruined. He cursed the map and his own stupidity for trying to fix the thing while driving, since the manual cautioned him to use the map's interactive features when the vehicle was stationary.

The story above, fictional but highly plausible, illustrates a breakdown in human performance. While some portion of the breakdown can be attributed to "human error" (Woods, Johannesen, Cook, & Sarter, 1994; Reason, 1990), it is equally evident that a substantial portion of blame for that error can be attributed to poor system design, one that imposed heavily on the driver's information-processing limits. We might well describe other "human errors" that can be better attributed to poor technology, whether these are related to misprogramming a VCR, setting the wrong time on an alarm clock, or more serious disasters such as airline crashes or nuclear power accidents. Several of these will be introduced as examples in later chapters. Indeed, the focus of this book is to describe the causes of such breakdowns in human performance and, by extension, to suggest ways in which the design of equipment and task environments can bypass the limitations of human performance and exploit its strengths.

ENGINEERING PSYCHOLOGY AND HUMAN FACTORS

Designing machines to accommodate the limits of the human user is the concern of the field called *human factors*. Meister (1989) defines human factors as "the study of how humans accomplish work-related tasks in the context of human-machine system operation, and how behavioral and nonbehavioral variables affect that accomplishment" (p. 2). The fundamental goal of human factors engineering is to reduce error, increase productivity, and enhance safety and comfort when the human interacts with a system. Human factors as a discipline involves the study of factors and development of tools that help to achieve these goals. The field is broader than this book, which is focused specifically on designing systems that accommodate the information-processing capabilities of the brain. Many principles that are important for designing machines that humans use, and that therefore belong in the province of human factors, are not related to the human capacity to process information. For example, designing an automobile in such a way that all controls can be reached easily and manipulated without muscle fatigue, and all displays are visible without straining the neck, is a human factors concern. This design problem, however, must respond to the physical properties and constraints of the driver's body, not the brain's information-processing capabilities. These problems are real and legitimate concerns, but they are not within the purview of this text.

A focus on the information-processing capacities of the human brain, then, is a key characteristic defining the scope and contents of this book. Study of the processes of the brain falls within the realm of psychology. It is the discipline of engineering psychology, specifically, that applies a psychological perspective to the problems of system design.

Among the notable features of engineering psychology as it has emerged as a discipline in the last four decades are its solid theoretical basis (Howell & Goldstein, 1971; Wickens & Kramer, 1985; Howell, 1993) and its close relation to the study of experimental psychology. Although engineering psychology is similar to both human factors and experimental psychology, its goals are nevertheless unique. The goal of experimental psychology is to uncover the laws of behavior through experiments. However, the design of these experiments is not constrained by a requirement to apply the laws. That is, it is not required that experiments generate immediately useful information. The goal of human factors, on the other hand, is to apply knowledge in designing systems that work, accommodating the limits of human performance *and* exploiting the advantages of the human operator in the process. Engineering psychology arises from the intersection of these two domains. "The aim of engineering psychology is not simply to compare two possible designs for a piece of equipment [which is the role of human factors], but to specify the capacities and limitations of the human [generate an experimental data base] from which the choice of a better design should be directly deducible" (Poulton, 1966, p.178). That is, although research topics in engineering psychology are selected because of applied needs, the research goes beyond specific one-time applications and has the broader objective of providing a usable theory of human performance.

It should be reemphasized that the decision to exclude certain areas of human factors from this book does not reflect a view that they are less important. In fact, much of the research in these areas is potentially more informative about actual design modifications and decisions than is research in human performance. The reader is referred to articles in journals such as *Applied Ergonomics, Ergonomics, Ergonomics and Design, Human Factors, Human Factors and Ergonomics in Manufacturing, International Journal of Cognitive Ergonomics,* and *Le Travaille Humain,* along with books by Bailey (1996), Boff and Lincoln (1988), Meister (1989), Salvendy (1997), Proctor and Van Zandt (1994), Sanders and McCormick (1993), and Wickens, Gordon, and Liu (1998) for more detailed treatments of these areas. This book is intended to complement, rather than supplement or replace, these treatments. However, the following section provides a brief overview of the nature of these broader human factors issues.

A Brief History

Motivation for the development of human factors and engineering psychology as disciplines has arisen from three general sources: practical needs, technological advancements, and linguistic developments. Before the birth of human factors, or ergonomics, in World War II, emphasis was placed on "designing the human to fit the machine." That is, the emphasis was on training. Experience in World War II, however, revealed a situation in which systems with well-trained operators weren't working. Airplanes were flying into the ground with no apparent mechanical failures; enemy contacts were missed on radar by highly motivated monitors. As a result, experimental psychologists from both sides of the Atlantic were brought in to analyze the operator-machine interface, to diagnose what was wrong, and to recommend solutions (Fitts & Jones, 1947; Mackworth, 1950). This represented the practical need underlying the origin of human factors engineering.

A second motivation has come from evolutionary trends in technology. With increased technological development in this century, systems have become increasingly complex, with more and more interrelated elements, forcing the designer to consider the distribution of tasks between human and machine. The advance of computer technology and automation has only enhanced the importance of these considerations (Landauer, 1995). This problem has led system designers to consider the analysis of human performance in different kinds of tasks. At the same time, with increased technology, the physical parameters of all systems have grown geometrically. For example, consider the increases in the maximum velocity of vehicles, progressing from the oxcart to the spacecraft; in the temperature range of energy systems, from fires to nuclear reactors; and in the physical size of vehicles, from wagons to supertankers and wide-bodied aircraft such as the Boeing 747. Particularly with regard to speed, this increase forces psychologists to analyze quite closely the operator's temporal limits of processing information. To the oxcart driver, a fraction of a second delay in responding to an environmental event will be of little consequence. To the pilot of a supersonic aircraft, however, a delay of the same magnitude may be critical in causing a collision.

Finally, an influence for the growth of human factors has come from the field of information theory and cybernetics that began to replace the stimulus-response language of behavioral psychology after World War II. Terms such as *feedback*, *channel capacity*, and *bandwidth* began to enter the descriptive language of human behavior. This new language enabled some aspects of human performance to be described in the same terms as the mechanical, electronic, or information systems with which the operator was interacting, which helped integrate humans and machines in system design and analysis.

Since its birth, the field of human factors has evolved from a discipline applied primarily to aviation and weapons systems, to one applied to a much broader range of products with which people interact, including such things as toys, telephones, medical devices, paper forms, power plants, and cars. People increasingly interact with computers, or with other devices like automatic teller machines or databases, through computer interfaces. Hence, the topic of *human-computer interaction* has evolved into a major focus of human factors (Shneiderman, 1992), just as the term "usability," typically applied to computer devices, has often replaced that of "good human factors" (Landauer, 1995).

Despite the evolution of products, the fundamental importance of designing for the strengths and limitations of the human user remains constant, because the fundamental characteristics of the human user have remained pretty much the same, as have the basic goals of human factors. In the following section, we elaborate somewhat on them and the process by which those goals are obtained.

The Process of Human Factors Engineering

In order to understand more clearly the contributions of engineering psychology, it is important to take a brief look at the larger overall process of applying human factors engineering to the development, design, and evaluation of a product, a process which is elaborated in Sanders and McCormick (1993) and Wickens, Gordon, and Liu (1998). As shown in Figure 1.1, this process is iterative one, involving repeated cycles of design and evaluation.

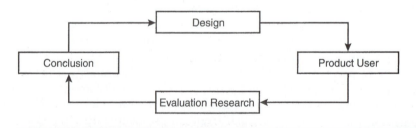

Figure 1.1   Product design and evaluation cycle.

Thus, design of a product is followed by its use; this use in turn can be subject to an evaluation of the success or failures, and conclusions drawn from this evaluation can then be employed to improve the original design. However, this description does not really indicate where the process starts, and a more elaborate model, detailing various possible start points in the cycle is shown in Figure 1.2.

This figure suggests that often the design process cycles or iterates through several "products" ($P_1 - P_4$ in the figure), each one becoming more refined, "realistic" (and ultimately more costly), until a final product is available to be used in the real world. For example, with the navigational system described in the story at the beginning of this chapter, the designer may have started by designing a simple electronic map (P_1), then carrying out an experimental evaluation to establish if the map should rotate or be fixed in a north-up orientation or how much text it should contain, or a variety of other features. Based on these results, modifications and improvements of the design would then generate a full display console, including the table of destinations and the selectable options for the user interface (P_2). Further evaluation of the console design would lead to further improvements, and an evaluation of this product (P_3) might take place within a driving simulator cab or an experimental field test of the final system on the road (P_4). Each opportunity to observe the product's use should be employed by the human factors engineer to extract "lessons learned" and provide subsequent input for redesign or refinement, a process that has great benefits for all involved (Landaur, 1995).

Figure 1.2 makes it clear that the cycle can be entered at any level, and that it need not proceed through the full sequence of iterations. For example, an existing product (P_4) that proves unsatisfactory might trigger the very first human factors analysis of its problems (evaluation research). Thus, a computer product developed with no human factors input may fail in the marketplace because it is too difficult for intended users to employ, or because a poorly positioned switch causes the product to be inadvertently turned off. The figure also shows that in the creation of a product, the designer need not go through the full cycle from P_1 to P_4 but can borrow directly from databases of other research results to apply principles to the design. For example, principles of color coding pertain to

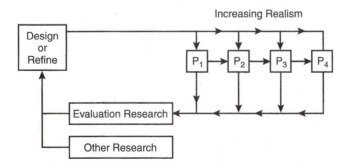

Figure 1.2   Iteration cycles of design and evaluation. P represents different phases of a product design.

the design of displays for drivers, computer users, and those who monitor large industrial systems. It is the responsibility of engineering psychologists to generate many of these principles through carefully controlled psychological research and then establish their relevance and applicability in the less controlled environment of real-world users.

In examining the evolution of systems, one finds that human factors input can occur through a variety of paths, as represented in Figure 1.2. However, two elements remain of critical importance for effective human factors: task analysis and the choice of appropriate research method.

Task Analysis   Prior to completing specifications for design of a product, the designer must understand the full range of tasks that a user performs with the product, so that design principles are chosen appropriately, and early evaluations of the product capture task demands. For example, will the driver in our story only use the electronic map while stopped, or will he use it while moving? Does the driver need to know characteristics of the client at each delivery spot, or only the client's location? There are many different task analysis methods (Kirwan & Ainsworth, 1992; Wickens, Gordon, & Liu, 1998; Seamster, Redding, & Kaempf, 1997). Some of these focus on the physical actions and goals required. For example, what sequence of switches are necessary to turn on a piece of equipment? Others focus on the cognitive mental operations, such as the amount of information the operator must hold in memory to understand an unexpected problem that develops, or the kinds of decisions that will be required. However, a feature of most useful task analyses is that they proceed *hierarchically*, starting with the top-level goals of the user (e.g., send an e-mail message), and then breaking these goals down into the more specific physical or cognitive actions necessary to obtain the goal. Often these mid-level steps can be broken down into still more detailed levels. For example, the step "identify the address" in sending an e-mail may itself spawn a series of subtasks (call up address list, scan list, identify name). If a designer were to use this book to design a particular system, then a task analysis might start by identifying which chapters were most relevant to the design task.

Choice of Research Method   Human factors research aims to discover "the truth" about the user's interaction with a system—not just one particular user, but a "generalized user," such that the principles or design guidelines identified will be appropriate for a broad class of users. To gain this truth, researchers can choose from an array of research methods. Some methods are more appropriate in some circumstances than others, some are less expensive, and some offer more reliable estimates of the truth. Seven research methods are described below and listed in Table 1.1. We briefly consider their strengths and weaknesses, which are shown across the columns in Table 1.1 (see Wickens, Gordon, & Liu, 1998, or Weimer, 1995, for more detail).

1. *Field studies* are generally evaluations of real users employing the system in question "in the field" (i.e., in operational circumstances). They may be based on videotapes of performance, recording of performance measures (e.g., keystrokes, vehicle motion), or user reports of their cognitive processes as the system is used. For example, we might videotape a series of users of ATM machines to find out what sorts of transactions they use, what ones they avoid, and when they make errors. We could augment this information by interviewing the users to understand the source of their confusion. This is the evaluation that would follow P_4 in Figure 1.2.

TABLE 1.1 Research Methodologies

	Cost of Methodology	Ease of Product Change	Ease of Control & Inference	Design Relevance of Conclusions
1. Field Studies	$$$		Lower	
2. Accident/Incident Reports		Hard	Lowest	High
3. Surveys	$		Medium	
4. Task Simulations	$$	Easier	Medium	
5. Laboratory Experiments	$		High	
6. Literature (research and handbooks)	$	Easy		Lower
7. Models (human simulations)	$			

2. *Accident and incident reports* are like field studies in that they involve real-world performance, but are different in that they focus exclusively on the cause of events when things went wrong (as in our story at the beginning of the chapter). These events may be catastrophic, leading to death, injury, or damage (accidents), or relatively minor (incidents). The aviation industry heavily relies on accident and incident analyses to help identify causes of human factors breakdowns.

Both field studies and accident or incident reports have limitations as research methodologies because the researcher typically does not have much control over the events and circumstances that lead to the performance observed. Without this control, it is often difficult to determine the specific cause of behavior, whether that behavior was appropriate or inappropriate. Accident reports are further limited because the number of accidents is (fortunately) small, and it is hard to draw statistically valid conclusions from small samples and, therefore, hard to draw valid inferences as to what is wrong.

3. *Surveys* of users can sample a larger number of real-world systems than is possible with incident and particularly (because of their small numbers) accident reports. These surveys can reveal users' attitudes toward the strengths and weaknesses of a particular system. However, such surveys will be limited if the sample of users is small or biased so that it is not representative of the typical user. Furthermore, what people like (i.e., preferences expressed on surveys) may not always correspond with what supports the best performance (Andre & Wickens, 1995). For example, people invariably like color displays. As we shall discuss in Chapter 3, however, color does not always help and can sometimes hurt performance.

4. *Task simulations* do not typically have the full complexity of real-world field testing, but they capture much of that complexity in environments that offer control over the events and circumstances in which performance is observed. For example, a driving simulator might capture many aspects of on-the-road driving, yet allow greater control of traffic and visibility, and hence provide an opportunity for evaluation across a range of these variables. In comparison with field studies, which might provide input into P_4 in Figure 1.2, simulations can provide input earlier (e.g., P_3).

5. *Laboratory experiments* are generally applied still earlier in the design cycle to identify and manipulate variables that are expected to influence performance with the system in question, while controlling (i.e., holding constant) other variables. This input might be at P_1 or P_2 in Figure 1.2. Such experiments can often generalize across a wide range of design applications. For example, the researcher may want to understand how the choice of color allows the user to focus attention on the colored element in the display and, hence, reduce the undesirable effects of clutter. Such knowledge could be applicable to design of displays across a wide range of systems, from the yellow pages in a phone book to an air traffic controller's display. However, it is important for the researcher to be sensitive to the degree to which the conditions in the laboratory, often highly controlled, might not fully generalize to the user conditions in "the world," where such control may be lacking.

6. *Literature and handbooks.* The previous five methodologies all require the researcher to collect and examine "raw data" from human users. Sometimes data have already been collected by others and are compiled in the research literature (other studies) or in design principles and standards that can be found in various human factors handbooks (e.g., Boff & Lincoln, 1988; Salvendy, 1997). As with the application of laboratory experiments, it is important that the context of the principle or standard is appropriate for the context of the current product. For example, the guidelines for the use of color in statistical charts will not be the same as the guidelines for color in warning display panels. Task analysis of the target product is quite important here.

7. *Models* represent a special case of the data provided by literature and handbooks. Whereas handbooks may be characterized by verbal statements of principles or design guidance, models are generally quantitative. They often take the form of mathematical equations, in which design parameters can be provided as input, and a measure of predicted user performance or preference is the model output (Wickens, Vincow, Schopper, & Lincoln, 1997). Other models are *computer simulations* of human performance activities (Meyer & Kieras, 1997; Tyler, Neukom, Logan, & Shively, 1998), in which a computer-simulated representation of the human operator, performing a task, generates an output (or set of outputs).

Moving progressively down the list of research methodologies shown in Table 1.1, five features help to define the tradeoffs regarding which methodology might be best for a given occasion. First, those toward the top tend to be more expensive to implement. It is more expensive to run a fully developed field study, with lots of observations, than it is to develop a laboratory experiment or compute the output from a model. Second, because methodologies toward the top of the list tend to be carried out when the product is farther along in the design cycle (P_3 and P_4 in Figure 1.2), it is more expensive to change the design if the methodology reveals the product to be deficient. Indeed, it may often be financially impossible to make changes in response to *substantial* human factors deficiencies revealed by product use in the real world, or in response to deficiencies revealed late in the design cycle on the basis of user surveys, incident, or accident reports. Third, it is easiest to exert experimental control on those methods towards the bottom of the list. The research environment is less complex, more constrained, and the researchers can thereby be more certain in inferring the factors that cause changes or differences in human performance.

Fourth, while cost, modification, and control features favor the methodologies toward the end of the list, the feature of **design relevance** favors those toward the beginning. Does the researcher have confidence that the results of the methodology will generalize to the product in question? Not surprisingly, the more realistic the circumstances of evaluation, the greater that confidence is. Given the strengths and weaknesses of the different methodologies, it is desirable to use several, rather than just one.

Performance Measurement

The first five methodologies presented in Table 1.1 all depend to some extent on extracting specific measures of performance or behavior from the user. Generally such measures can be associated with one of four categories of raw data:

1. Measures of speed or time: How fast can data be entered into a computer? How long does it take to estimate one's position on an electronic map?
2. Measures of accuracy or error: What is the probability of a correct data entry string on the computer? How much does a driver deviate from the center of the highway as she tries to use a cellular phone?
3. Measures of workload or capacity demands: How difficult, on a scale of 1–7, is it to use the product?
4. Measures of preference: Does the operator prefer the electronic map over a paper map, or use the rotating more than the fixed version of the former?

Which of these categories is chosen to evaluate system quality depends on the real-world task and user environment to which the results of the evaluation are generalized. For example, it is very appropriate to use a measure of speed (time) for design of an emergency shutdown switch because time is the most critical aspect of performance. However, a measure of accuracy would be more appropriate for the design of a device to assist a physician in reaching a diagnosis. We would prefer that the diagnosis be correct, even if it takes a little longer to reach. Measures of user preference are of greater value for consumer products where safety is not involved than for high-risk systems like vehicles or chemical plants, where performance accuracy (avoiding errors) becomes the most critical measure.

For many domains, it is possible to use various classes of raw performance measurements to create two sorts of derived measures. *Evaluative measures,* or the *figure of merit,* are measures that have a clearly defined "good" and "bad" endpoint and are of greatest use to the designer. For example, an evaluative measure of a data entry device might combine speed and accuracy into a single weighted index. According to such an index, a device that is both fast *and* accurate will be superior to one that is fast but not accurate, or is accurate but slower. An evaluative measure of a device to be used in a vehicle might also add a component indexing its visual workload or attention demands, such that it supports fast and accurate performance with low visual workload.

In contrast to evaluative measures, *strategic* measures do not necessarily have "good" and "bad" endpoints. Instead they characterize a particular style of behavior, whose appropriateness will depend on the circumstances. For example, a measure of the *speed-accuracy trade-*

off (Wickelgren, 1977; see Chapter 9), such as one expressed by the quantity: [accuracy + response time] or [accuracy − response rate], will take on high values for slow but accurate performance, and low values for fast but less accurate performance. Which style of performance is better clearly depends on the circumstances and the degree of penalty imposed by being late, versus the cost of errors in performance. If you have an absolute deadline for turning in a paper, after which you will receive a 0, it is better to meet the deadline (i.e., "fast"), even if the paper contains some errors. If you are given an unlimited extension, however, it is probably better to delay and make the paper as near perfect as possible. In the same way, performance with the emergency shutdown switch should have a greater weighting on speed, but performance with the physician's diagnostic aid should have a greater weighting on accuracy. Information about the strategies people use in task performance can often be obtained from verbal protocols

A MODEL OF HUMAN INFORMATION PROCESSING

Knowing the different dimensions of performance (e.g., speed and accuracy) that can be measured in different research environments (e.g., lab, field studies) can assist the human factors engineer in understanding how performance is changed by system design or environmental differences. But such knowledge is not always sufficient for the engineering psychologist, who is interested in *why* performance might be changed. For example, does a new interface for the radio control in a vehicle invite errors because a control cannot be touched without bumping another one, because the control is too sensitive, because the driver is confused about which way to turn the control to increase frequency, or because the driver cannot understand the icon showing what the control does? These distinctions between the different psychological and motor processes affected by design are of critical importance because, on the one hand, they link to basic psychological theory, and on the other hand, they can help identify different sorts of design solutions.

A model of human information processing stages, shown in Figure 1.3, provides a useful framework for analyzing the different psychological processes used in interacting with systems and for carrying out a task analysis, as well as a framework for the organization of the chapters that follow in this book.

Two overall properties of the model shown in the figure are immediately apparent. First, information processing is represented as a series of *stages*, whose function is to transform or carry out some other operation on the information. Second, the presence of the feedback loop shown at the bottom suggests that there is no fixed starting point in the sequence of processing operations. Processing may start by an environmental input at the left, or it may start by the operator's voluntary intention to act, initiated somewhere in the middle of the sequence. In the pages below, we provide an overview of each of these stages or processes; they will be described in greater detail in the chapters that follow.

Sensory Processing   Information and events in the environment must gain access to the brain. Thus, our driver in the story at the beginning of the chapter must see the stalled car or hear the truck horn before any response can be made to these events. Properties of both our visual and auditory receptors (as well as those of the other senses) have a tremendous impact on the quality of information that reaches the brain. For example, the low visual quality of the degraded viewing retarded the driver's ability to de-

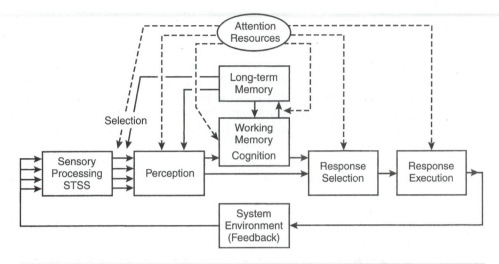

Figure 1.3   A model of human information processing stages.

tect the stalled car. Most of these properties of the peripheral sensory organs (e.g., the eye and ear) are not covered in this book, and the reader is referred to texts on perception (Coren, Ward, & Enis, 1999) or human factors (e.g., Sanders & McCormick, 1993; Proctor & Van Zandt, 1994; Wickens, Gordon, & Liu, 1998), or handbooks (e.g., Salvendy, 1997; Boff, Kaufman, & Thomas, 1986), for more detail on how the properties of the sensory receptors influence information processing. However, as shown in Figure 1.3, all sensory systems have an associated *short-term sensory store* (STSS) that resides within the brain. This is a temporary mechanism for prolonging the representation of the raw stimulus evidence for durations as short as around one half second (visual STSS), to as long as 2–4 seconds (auditory STSS). Thus, for example, if the dispatching device used by our driver was equipped with an auditory display of routing directions, the driver could continue to "hear" the command to initiate a particular maneuver (e.g., "prepare to exit right") for a few seconds after the synthetic voice had finished delivering the message. Hence, even if he was distracted at the moment of message delivery, he could still recover its contents for a few seconds after.

Perception   Sensory processing is necessary but not sufficient for effective human performance. Raw sensory data relayed to the brain (and perhaps preserved in a sensory store) must be interpreted, or given meaning, through the stage of *perception*. Thus, the horn heard by the driver is not just an intense sound but conveys the meaningful message "danger on the left." It is the role of perception to decode this meaning from the raw sensory data. Perceptual processing has two important features. First, it generally proceeds automatically and rapidly (requiring little attention). Second, it is driven both by sensory input (which we call *bottom-up processing*) and by inputs from long-term memory about what events are expected (which we call *top-down processing*).

The speed and relative automaticity of perception is what distinguishes it from the *cognitive* processes discussed below. Thus, when the driver reads the phrase "Display Error" printed on the CRT display, it is a perceptual operation. When, instead, he must infer that the system has an error because the table and the map depict conflicting information, the operation is a cognitive one, requiring more time and mental effort. Nevertheless, either operation ultimately signals the same information to the driver, that the system is not functioning correctly. Of course the distinction between perceptual and cognitive operations is not always clear-cut; the two represent endpoints on a continuum.

Perception is partially determined by an analysis of the stimulus or environmental input, relayed from the sensory receptors by the sensory or "lower" channels of neural information. Hence, this aspect of processing is often termed *bottom-up* perceptual processing. However, when sensory evidence is poor, perception may be driven heavily by our *expectations* based on past experience, an influence known as *top-down* processing (Rumelhart, 1977). This past experience is stored in long-term memory and, hence, is represented by the downward curved arrow from this box in Figure 1.3. Bottom-up and top-down processing usually work harmoniously together, supporting rapid and accurate perceptual work. However, sometimes unfamiliar circumstances remove the ability to use past experience, leading bottom-up processing to do nearly all the work. Alternatively, poor sensory quality sometimes forces the perceiver to use top-down expectancies. If such expectancies are wrong, perceptual errors can occur. Thus, the quality of bottom-up evidence regarding the road ahead was poor for the accident discussed at the beginning of the chapter. Our driver relied on his expectations (that traffic ahead on a freeway moves forward; Evans, 1991) to "perceive" the vehicle in front to be moving. In this case the perception was wrong, and the near collision resulted.

Sometimes perception involves the process of categorization of raw sensory evidence, as when the driver assigns the sound of the horn into the category "danger warning." However, as we move through the environment, our perception may also involve extracting information continuously about our self-motion or the motion of other objects in the environment (Gibson, 1979; Warren & Wertheim, 1991). Our driver was of course performing such an operation as he drove down the freeway, continuously sensing his speed and trajectory.

Cognition and Memory   As we noted above, the boundary between perception and cognition is sometimes blurred because both may provide similar implications for action. However, the important distinction is that cognitive operations generally require greater time, mental effort, or attention. This is because such cognitive operations as rehearsal, reasoning, or image transformation are carried out by using what is called *working memory* (Baddeley, 1986), a vulnerable, temporary store of activated information. Working memory would be involved in each of the following cognitive operations: when the driver mentally rotates the electronic north-up map because he is heading south; when he rehearses the name of an exit after glancing at the map; when he *plans* the optimal route through the city to minimize driving time and deliver the highest priority items first; when he attempts to *diagnose* the failure on the system. The key features of all of these operations is that they are conscious activities which transform or retain information, and that they are *resource limited* (Norman & Bobrow, 1975). That is, each is highly vulnerable to disruption when attentional resources are diverted to other mental activities.

Sometimes material that is rehearsed in working memory can get access to a memory system that is less vulnerable, and hence more permanent: *long-term memory*. For example, if the driver ever does diagnose the cause of the apparent error in the dispatch system, he will probably be better able to remember its cause the next time it has occurred. He has therefore *learned*. As we have discussed above, learning about the properties of information in an environment forms the basis for expectancies that drive top-down perceptual processing.

Response Selection and Execution   The understanding of a situation, achieved through perception and augmented by cognitive transformations, often triggers an action—the selection of a response. However, when he reached a decision on where to exit, after consulting the map, a good deal of cognition was required. When he swerved to the left after detecting the stopped car and to the right after hearing the horn, these responses involved little or no cognition.

The selection of a response or choice of an action is quite distinct from its *execution*, the latter requiring the coordination of the muscles for controlled motion, to assure that the chosen goal is correctly obtained. Thus, our driver correctly *selected* the action to swerve to the far right to avoid both the truck and the stalled car, but he *executed* the action poorly by overcorrecting, losing control, and ultimately flipping over the vehicle.

Feedback   The feedback loop at the bottom of the model indicates that actions are directly sensed by the human or, if those actions influence the system with which the human is interacting, will be observable sooner or later. The presence of the feedback loop has two implications. First, its presence emphasizes that the "flow" of information can be initiated at any point. Thus, a driver's decision to turn on the radio is not driven by a perceived environmental event, but rather by a cognitive motivation to obtain information or music. The feedback loop is important for establishing that the intended goal was achieved. Second, the feedback loop emphasizes that in many real-world tasks, such as driving, walking, or navigating through a computer information database, the flow of information is continuous; thus, it is just as appropriate to say that "action causes perception" as it is to say that perception causes action (Powers, 1973; Neisser, 1976).

A critical factor that influences the extent of this closed-loop interactivity is the *delay* of the system in responding to human actions. For steering vehicles, this delay is typically short. The driver immediately perceives the change caused by turning the wheel, and hence, special properties of closed-loop dynamic systems must be considered in examining human performance. However, for some actions like the driver's decision to follow the advice of the dispatcher system to take the back streets and avoid a traffic tie-up on the freeway, it may be several minutes before the implications of that decision are realized. Hence, human performance with the dispatcher system can be analyzed with less concern for the feedback loop. (Although the driver's learning *about* the reliability of system's advice will depend very much on this delayed loop).

Attention   A final property or component of the model is *attention*, represented by a supply of mental resources at the top of Figure 1.3. Many mental operations are not carried out automatically but require the selective application of these limited resources (Kahneman, 1973; Pashler, 1998). To the left of the figure, we see attention *selectively* allocated to channels of sensory material to process (*selective attention*). For visual information, this limited resource is foveal vision, which can be (through eye movements) directed to different channels in the environment. Like top-down perceptual processing, this scanning process is often driven by past experience—knowing where to look when. But this experience may also be the cause of errors. We saw that our driver chose to look downward at the console for too long, apparently trusting past experience that a stationary object would not be suddenly present in the lane ahead.

The selective application of limited attentional resources is much broader than its application to scanning. Indeed, when the operator has many tasks to perform—keeping the car in the lane, searching for the exit sign, and trying to plan the next route to take—he must select a strategy for *dividing* attention or allocating resources between these different tasks or mental operations (Gopher, 1993; Kahneman, 1973). When the total attention demand of these tasks is excessive, one task or the other must suffer. So, for example, if the driver becomes preoccupied with planning the future route, or diagnosing the cause of the system failure, he may still fail to detect the stalled vehicle, even if his eyes are looking forward.

CONCLUSION

The model that we have described for human information processing is not a computational one that can provide estimates, say, of the time required to perform certain tasks, or the error rates expected. Rather, it provides a general framework for analyzing human performance, as discussed in the remaining chapters of this book. The structure of the model suggests that its components can be studied and analyzed independently from others. Thus, for example, the limited capacity of working memory will have similar design implications, no matter whether the operator must take action on its contents using vocal commands, key presses, or continuous manipulations of a joystick. Indeed, in the following chapters we discuss more specific models of the individual processing components like visual search or manual control.

The model shown in Figure 1.3 provides a framework for organizing many of the chapters in this book. In Chapter 2, we discuss the more basic aspects of perception such as stimulus detection and classification. In Chapter 3, we consider the selective aspects of attention. Chapters 4, 5, and 6 address the more complex aspects of perception that are relevant to the design of displays. Chapter 7 addresses the role of cognition and memory and their relevance to learning and training. Chapters 8 and 9 address the selection of action. In Chapter 8, this selection is the deliberative process of decision making also heavily involving working memory. In Chapter 9, the selection represents more rapid actions. Chapter 10 addresses the coordination of response execution in manual control. The final chapters consider general topics that involve all processes in the model: attention and multiple task performance (Chapter 11), stress and error (Chapter 12), and automation and the control of complex systems (Chapter 13).

REFERENCES

Andre, A. D., & Wickens, C. D. (1995, October). When users want what's not best for them: A review of performance-preference dissociations. *Ergonomics in Design*, 10–13.

Baddeley, A. D. (1986). *Working memory*. Oxford, UK: Oxford University Press.

Bailey, R. W. (1996). *Human performance engineering:* (3d ed.). Upper Saddle River, NJ: Prentice Hall.

Boff, K. R., Kaufman, L., & Thomas, J. (Eds.). (1986). *Handbook of perception and human performance.* New York: Wiley.

Boff, K., & Lincoln, J. (Eds.). (1988). *Engineering data compendium.* Dayton, OH: Wright-Patterson AFB, Harry Armstrong Aerospace Medical Research Laboratory.

Coren, S., Ward, L. M. and Enns, J.T. (1999). *Sensation and Perception* (5th ed.). New York: Harcourt Brace.

Evans, L. (1991). *Traffic safety and the driver.* New York: Van Nostrand Reinhold.

Fitts, P. M., & Jones, R. E. (1947). *Analysis of factors contributing to 460 "pilot-error" experiences in operating aircraft controls* (AMC Memorandum Report TSEAA–694–12). Dayton, OH: Wright-Patterson AFB, Air Materiel Command.

Gibson, J. J. (1979). *The ecological approach to visual perception.* Boston: Houghton Mifflin.

Gopher, D. (1993). The skill of attentional control: Acquisition and execution of attention strategies. In D. E. Meyer & S. Kornblum (Eds.), *Attention and performance, 14* (pp. 299–322). Cambridge, MA: MIT Press.

Howell, W. C. (1993). Engineering psychology in a changing world. *Annual Review of Psychology, 44,* 231–263.

Howell, W. C., & Goldstein, I. L. (Eds.). (1971). *Engineering psychology: Current perspectives in research.* New York: Appleton-Century-Crofts.

Kahneman, D. (1973). *Attention and effort.* Englewood Cliffs, NJ: Prentice Hall.

Kirwan, B., & Ainsworth, L. K. (1992). *A guide to task analysis.* London: Taylor & Francis.

Landauer, T. (1995). *The trouble with computers.* Cambridge, MA: MIT Press.

Mackworth, N. (1950). Research on the measurement of human performance. Medical Research Council special report series, H. M. Stationery Office No. 268. (Reprinted in *Selected papers on human factors in the design and use of control systems,* W. Sinaiko, Ed., 1961, New York: Dover)

Meister, D. (1989). *Conceptual aspects of human factors.* Baltimore, MD: Johns Hopkins University Press.

Meyer, D. E., & Kieras, D. E. (1997). A computational theory of executive cognitive processes and multiple-task performance: Part 1. Basic mechanisms. *Psychological Review, 104*(1), 3–65.

Neisser, U. (1976). *Cognition and reality.* San Francisco: Freeman.

Norman, D., & Bobrow, D. (1975). On data-limited and resource-limited processing. *Cognitive Psychology, 7,* 44–60.

Pashler, H. (1998). *The psychology of attention.* Cambridge, MA: MIT Press.

Poulton, E. C. (1966). Engineering psychology. *Annual Review of Psychology, 17,* 177–200.

Powers, W. T. (1973). *Behavior: The control of perception.* New York: Aldine de Gruyter.

Proctor, R. W., & Van Zandt, T. (1994). *Human factors in simple and complex systems.* Needham Heights, MA: Allyn and Bacon.

Reason, J. (1990). *Human error.* New York: Cambridge University Press.

Rumelhart, D. (1977). *Human information processing.* New York: John Wiley.

Salvendy, G. (Ed.) (1997). *The handbook of human factors and ergonomics* (2d ed.). New York: Wiley.

Sanders, M. S., & McCormick, E. J. (1993). *Human factors in engineering and design.* New York: McGraw Hill.

Shneiderman, B. (1992). *Designing the user interface: Strategies for effective human-computer interaction* (2d ed.). Reading, MA: Addison-Wesley.

Seamster, T. L., Redding, R. E., & Kaempf, G. L. (1997). *Applied cognitive task analysis in aviation*. Brookfield, VT: Ashgate.

Tyler, S. W., Neukom, C., Logan, M., & Shively, J. (1998). The MIDAS human performance model. *Proceedings of the 42d annual meeting of the Human Factors & Ergonomics Society* (pp. 320–324). Santa Monica, CA: Human Factors Society.

Warren, R., & Wertheim, A. H. (Eds.). (1991). *Perception and control of self-motion*. Hillsdale, NJ: Lawrence Erlbaum.

Weimer, J. (Ed.). (1995). *Research techniques in human engineering*. Englewood Cliffs, NJ: Prentice Hall.

Wickelgren, A. (1977). Speed accuracy tradeoff and information processing dynamics. *Acta Psychologica, 41,* 67–85.

Wickens, C. D., Gordon, S., & Liu, Y. (1998). *An introduction to human factors engineering*. New York: Addison Wesley Longman, Inc.

Wickens, C. D., & Kramer, A. (1985). Engineering psychology. *Annual Review of Psychology, 36,* 307–348.

Wickens, C. D., Vincow, M. A., Schopper, A. W., & Lincoln, J. E. (1997). *Computational models of human performance in the design and layout of controls and displays* (CSERIAC SOAR Report 97–22). Dayton, OH: Wright-Patterson AFB, Crew System Ergonomics Information Analysis Center.

Woods, D. D., Johannesen, L. J., Cook, R. I., & Sarter, N. B. (1994). *Behind human error: Cognitive systems, computers, and hindsight* (CSERIAC SOAR Report 94–01). Dayton, OH: Wright-Patterson AFB, Crew System Ergonomics Information Analysis Center.

Signal Detection, Information Theory, and Absolute Judgment

OVERVIEW

Information processing in most systems begins with the detection of some environmental event. In a major catastrophe, the event is so noticeable that immediate detection is assured. The information-processing problems in these circumstances are those of recognition and diagnosis. However, there are many other circumstances in which detection itself represents a source of uncertainty or a potential bottleneck in performance because it is necessary to detect events that are near the threshold of perception. Will the security guard monitoring a bank of television pictures detect the abnormal movement on one of them? Will the radiologist detect the abnormal x-ray as it is scanned? Will the industrial inspector detect the flaw in the product? Will the van driver described in Chapter 1 be able to detect a vehicle in front of him in poor visibility conditions?

This chapter first will deal with the situation in which an observer classifies the world into one of two states: a signal is present or it is absent. The detection process is modeled within the framework of signal detection theory, and we show how the model can assist engineering psychologists in understanding the complexities of the detection process, in diagnosing what goes wrong when detection fails, and in recommending corrective solutions.

The process of detection may involve more than two states of categorization. It may, for example, require the human operator to choose between three or four levels of uncertainty about the presence of a signal or to detect more than one kind of signal. At this point, we introduce information theory, and then use it to describe the simplest form of multilevel categorization, the absolute judgment task. Finally, we consider the more complex multidimensional stimulus judgment. We again use a signal detection approach to account for performance in both multilevel and multidimensional categorization judgments.

SIGNAL DETECTION THEORY

The Signal Detection Paradigm

Signal detection theory is applicable in any situation in which there are two discrete *states of the world* (signal and noise) that cannot easily be discriminated. Signals must be detected by the human operator, and in the process two response categories are produced: Yes (I detect a signal) and no (I do not). This situation may describe activities such as the detection of a concealed weapon by an airport security guard, the detection of a contact on a radar scope (N. H. Mackworth, 1948), a malignant tumor on an x-ray plate by a radiologist (Parasuraman, 1985; Swets & Pickett, 1982), a malfunction of an abnormal system by a nuclear plant supervisor (Lees & Sayers, 1976), a critical event in air traffic control (Bisseret, 1981), typesetting errors by a proofreader (Anderson & Revelle, 1982), an untruthful statement from a polygraph (Szucko & Kleinmuntz, 1981), a crack on the body of an aircraft, or a communications signal from intelligent life in the bombardment of electromagnetic radiation from outer space (Blake & Baird, 1980).

The combination of two states of the world and two response categories produces the 2 x 2 matrix shown in Figure 2.1, generating four classes of joint events, labeled *hits*, *misses*, *false alarms*, and *correct rejections*. It is apparent that perfect performance is that in which no misses or false alarms occur. However, since the signals are not very intense in the typical signal detection task, misses and false alarms do occur, and so there are normally data in all four cells. In signal detection theory (SDT) these values are typically

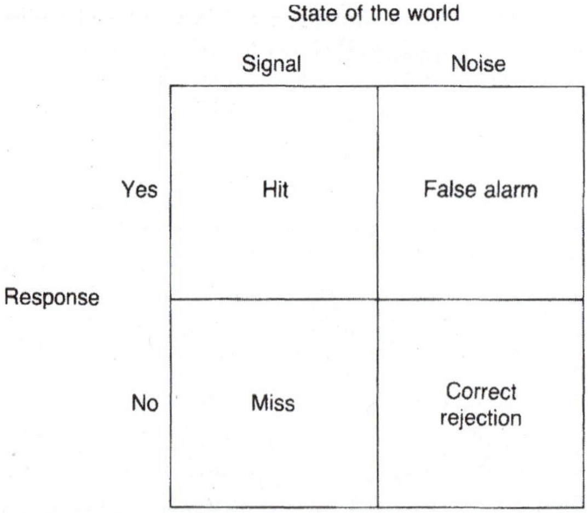

State of the world

	Signal	Noise
Yes	Hit	False alarm
No	Miss	Correct rejection

Response

Figure 2.1   The four outcomes of signal detection theory.

expressed as probabilities, by dividing the number of occurrences in a cell by the total number of occurrences in a column. Thus if 20 signals were presented, and there were 5 hits and 15 misses, we would write $P(\text{hit}) = 5/20 = 0.25$.

The SDT model (Green & Swets, 1966) assumes that there are two stages of information processing in the task of detection: (1) Sensory evidence is aggregated concerning the presence or absence of the signal, and (2) a decision is made about whether this evidence indicates a signal or not. According to the theory, external stimuli generate neural activity in the brain. Therefore, on the average there will be more sensory or neural evidence in the brain when a signal is present than when it is absent. This neural evidence, X, may be conceived as the rate of firing of neurons at a hypothetical "detection center." The rate increases with stimulus intensity. We refer to the quantity X as the *evidence variable*. Therefore, if there is enough neural activity, X exceeds a critical threshold X_C, and the operator decides "yes." If there is too little, the operator decides "no."

Because the amount of energy in the signal is typically low, the average amount of X generated by signals in the environment is not much greater than the average generated when no signals are present (noise). Furthermore, the quantity of X varies continuously even in the absence of a signal because of random variations in the environment and in the operator's own "baseline" level of neural firing (e.g., the neural "noise" in the sensory channels and the brain). This variation is shown in Figure 2.2. Therefore, even when no signal is present, X will sometimes exceed the criterion X_C as a result of random variations alone, and the operator will say "yes" (generating a false alarm at point A of Figure 2.2). Correspondingly, even with a signal present, the random level of activity may be low, causing X to be less than the criterion, and the operator will say "no" (generating a miss at point B of Figure 2.2). The smaller the difference in intensity between signals and noise, the greater these error probabilities become because the amount of variation in X resulting from randomness increases relative to the amount of energy in the signal. In Figure 2.2, the average level of X is increased slightly in the presence of a weak signal and greatly when a strong signal is presented.

For example, consider a person monitoring of a noisy radar screen. Somewhere in the midst of the random variations in stimulus intensity caused by reflections from clouds and rain, there is an extra increase in intensity that represents the presence of the signal—an aircraft. The amount of noise will not be constant over time but will fluctuate; sometimes it will be high, completely masking the stimulus, and sometimes low, allowing the plane to stand out. In this example, "noise" varies in the environment. Similarly, this random variation produced noise so that it was more difficult for him to observe relevant signals—vehicles in the road ahead. Suppose, instead, you were standing watch on a ship, searching the horizon on a dark night for a faint light. It becomes difficult to distinguish the flashes that might be real lights from those that are just "visual noise" in your own sensory system. In this case, the random noise is internal. Thus "noise" in signal detection theory is a combination of noise from external and internal sources. The van driver described in Chapter 1 was subject to inclement weather, which produced random variations in reflectances in sleet and spray.

The relations between the presence or absence of the signal, random variability of X, and X_C can be seen in Figure 2.3. The figure plots the probability of observing a specific value of X, given that a noise trial (left curve) or signal trial (right curve) in fact occurred. These data might have been tabulated (from the graph of the evidence variable

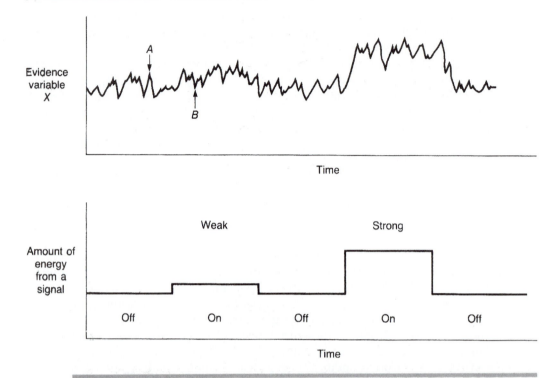

Figure 2.2   The change in the evidence variable X caused by a weak and a strong signal. Notice that with the weak signal, there can sometimes be less evidence when the signal is present (point *B*) than when the signal is absent (point *A*).

at the top of Figure 2.2) by counting the relative frequency of different X values during the intervals when the signal was off, creating the probability curve on the left of Figure 2.3, and making a separate count of the probability of different X values while the weak signal was on, generating the curve on the right of Figure 2.3. As the value of X increases, it is more likely to have been generated while a signal was present.

When the absolute probability that X was produced by the signal equals the probability that it was produced by only noise, the signal and noise curves intersect. The criterion value X_C chosen by the operator is shown by the vertical line. All X values to the right ($X > X_C$) will cause the operator to respond "yes." All to the left generate "no" responses. The different shaded areas represent the occurrences of hits, misses, false alarms, and correct rejections. Since the total area within each curve is one, the two shaded regions within each curve must sum to one. That is, $P(H) + P(M) = 1$ and $P(FA) + P(CR) = 1$.

Setting the Response Criterion: Optimality in SDT

In any signal detection task, observers may vary in their response bias. For example, they may be "liberal" or "risky": prone to saying yes, and therefore detecting most of the signals

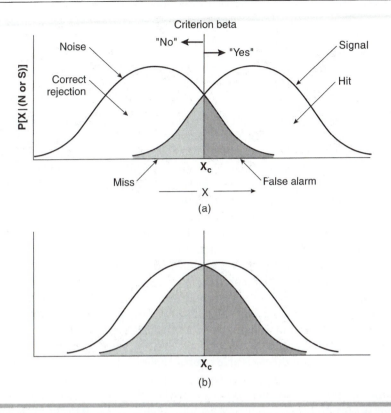

Figure 2.3   Hypothetical distributions underlying signal detection theory: (a) high sensitivity; (b) low sensitivity.

that occur but making many false alarms. Alternatively, they may be "conservative": saying no most times and making few false alarms but missing many of the signals.

Sometimes circumstances dictate whether a conservative or a risky strategy is best. For example, when the radiologist scans the x-ray of a patient who has been referred because of other symptoms of illness, it is better to be biased to say yes (i.e., "you have a tumor") than when examining the x-ray of a healthy patient, for whom there is no reason to suspect any malignancy (Swets & Pickett, 1982). Consider, on the other hand, the monitor of the power-generating station who has been cautioned repeatedly by the supervisor not to unnecessarily shut down a turbine, because of the resulting loss of revenue to the company. The operator will probably become conservative in monitoring the dials and meters for malfunction and may be prone to miss (or delay responding to) a malfunction when it does occur.

As can be seen in Figure 2.3, an operator's conservative or risky behavior is determined by placing the decision criterion X_C. If X_C is placed to the right, much evidence is required for it to be exceeded, and most responses will be "no" (conservative responding). If it is placed to the left, little evidence is required, most responses will be "yes," and the strategy is risky. An important variable that is positively correlated with X_C is beta, which is the ratio of neural activity produced by signal and noise at X_C:

$$\beta = \frac{P(X|S)}{P(X|N)} \tag{2.1}$$

This is the ratio of the height of the two curves in Figure 2.3, for a given level of X_C. Imagine shifting the value of X_C to the right. This will produce a beta value greater than one. When this occurs, there will be fewer yes responses: therefore, there will be fewer hits, but also fewer false alarms. Next imagine shifting X_C to the left. Now beta is less than one, and there will be more yes responses and more hits, but also more false alarms. Thus both beta and X_C define the *response bias* or *response criterion*.

More formally, the actual probability values for each of the cells in Figure 2.1 would be calculated from obtained data. These data would describe the areas under the two probability distribution functions of unit area shown in Figure 2.3, to the left and right of the criterion. Thus, for example, the probability of a hit, with the criterion shown, is the relative area under the "signal" curve (a signal was presented) to the right of the criterion (the subject said yes). One can determine by inspection that if the two distributions are of equal size and shape, then the setting of beta = 1 occurs where the two curves intersect as shown in Figure 2.3 and will provide data in which $P(H) = P(CR)$ and $P(M) = P(FA)$, that is, a truly "neutral" criterion setting.

Signal detection theory is able to prescribe exactly where the optimum beta should fall, given (1) the likelihood of observing a signal and (2) the costs and benefits (payoffs) of the four possible outcomes (Green & Swets, 1966; Swets & Pickett, 1982). We will first consider the influence of signal probability, then payoffs, on the optimal setting of beta, and finally, human performance in setting beta.

Signal Probability   First consider the situation in which signals occur just as often as they do not, and there is neither a different cost to the two bad outcomes nor a different benefit to the two good outcomes of Figure 2.1. In this case optimal performance minimizes the number of errors (misses and false alarms). Optimal performance will occur when X_C is placed at the intersection of the two curves in Figure 2.3: that is, when beta = 1. Any other placement, in the long run, would reduce the probability of being correct.

However, if a signal is more likely, the criterion should be lowered. For example, if traffic is busy on the freeway, increasing the likelihood of collision with another vehicle, our van driver should be more likely to apply the brakes than if the road ahead were empty. If the radiologist has other information to suggest that a patient is likely to have a malignant tumor, or the physician has received the patient on referral, the physician should be more likely to categorize an abnormality on the x-ray as a tumor than to ignore it as mere noise in the x-ray process. Conversely, if signal probability is reduced, beta should be adjusted conservatively. For example, suppose an inspector searching for defects in computer microchips is told that the current batch has a low estimated fault frequency, because the manufacturing equipment has just received maintenance. In this case, the inspector should be more conservative in searching for defects. Formally, this adjustment of the *optimal beta* in response to changes in signal and noise probability is represented by the prescription

$$\beta_{opt} = \frac{P(N)}{P(S)} \tag{2.2}$$

This quantity will be reduced (made riskier) as P(S) increases, thereby moving the value of X_C producing optimal beta to the left of Figure 2.3. If this setting is adhered to, performance will maximize the number of correct responses (hits and correct rejections). Note that the setting of optimal beta will not produce perfect performance. There will still be false alarms and misses as long as the two curves overlap. However, optimal beta is the best that can be expected for a given signal strength and a given level of sensitivity.

The formula for beta (Equation 2.1) and the formula for optimum beta (Equation 2.2) are sometimes confused. β_{opt} defines where beta *should* be set, and it is entirely determined by the ratio of the probability with which noise and signals occur in the environment. In contrast, where beta *is* set is determined by the observer and must be derived from empirical data.

Payoffs   The optimal setting of beta is also influenced by payoffs. In this case, *optimal* is no longer defined in terms of minimizing errors but is now maximizing the total expected financial gains (or minimizing expected losses). If it were important for signals never to be missed, the operator might be given high rewards for hits and high penalties for misses, leading to a low setting of beta. This payoff would be in effect for a quality control inspector who is admonished by the supervisor that severe costs in company profits (and the monitor's own paycheck) will result if faulty microchips pass through the inspection station. The monitor would therefore be more likely to discard good chips (a false alarm) in order to catch all the faulty ones. Conversely, in different circumstances, if false alarms are to be avoided, they should be heavily penalized. These costs and benefits can be translated into a prescription for the optimum setting of beta by expanding Equation 2.2 to

$$\beta_{opt} = \frac{P(N)}{P(S)} \times \frac{V(CR) + C(FA)}{V(H) + C(M)} \tag{2.3}$$

where V is the value of desirable events (hit, H, or correct rejection, CR), and C is the cost of undesirable events (miss, M, or false alarm, FA). An increase in denominator values will decrease the optimal beta and should lead to risky responding. Conversely, an increase in numerator values should lead to conservative responding. Notice also that the value and probability portions of the function combine independently. An event like the malfunction of a turbine may occur only very rarely, thereby raising the optimal beta; however, the cost of a miss in detecting it might be severe, and thus optimal beta should be set to a relatively low value.

Human Performance in Setting Beta   The actual value of beta that an operator uses can be computed from the number of hits and false alarms obtained from a series of detection trials. Therefore, we may ask how well people set their criteria in response to changes in payoffs and probabilities, relative to optimal beta. Humans do adjust beta as dictated by changes in these quantities. However, laboratory experiments have shown that beta is not adjusted as much as it should be. That is, subjects demonstrate a *sluggish beta*, as shown in Figure 2.4. They are less risky than they should be if the ideal beta is high, and less conservative than they should be if the ideal beta is low. As shown in Figure 2.4, the sluggishness is found to be more pronounced when beta is manipulated by probabilities than by payoffs (Green & Swets, 1966).

A number of explanations have been proposed to account for why beta is sluggish in response to probability manipulations. It may be a reflection of the operator's need to respond "creatively" by introducing the rare response more often than is optimal, since extreme values of beta dictate long strings of either yes (low beta) or no (high beta) responses. Another explanation may be that the operator misperceives probabilistic data. There is evidence that people tend to overestimate the probability of rare events and underestimate that of frequent events (Peterson & Beach, 1967; Sheridan & Ferrell, 1974). This behavior, to be discussed in more detail in Chapter 8, would produce the observed shift of beta toward unity.

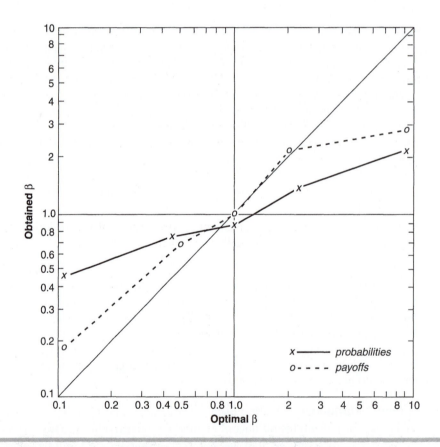

Figure 2.4   Relationship between obtained and optimal decision criteria.

The sluggish beta phenomenon can be demonstrated most clearly in the laboratory, where precise probabilities and values can be specified to the subjects. There is also evidence for sluggish beta in real-world environments. For example, Harris and Chaney (1969), who examined the performance of inspectors in a Kodak plant, reported that as the defect rate fell below about 5 percent, inspectors failed to lower beta accordingly. Bisseret (1981) applied signal detection theory to the air traffic controller's task of judging whether an impending conflict between two aircraft will (signal) or will not (noise) require a course correction. He found that controllers were more willing to detect a conflict (i.e., more likely to lower beta), and therefore command a correction, as the difficulty of the problem and therefore the uncertainty of the future increased. Bisseret also compared the performance of experts and trainees and found that experts used lower beta settings, being more willing to call for a correction. Bisseret suggested that trainees were more uncertain about how to carry out the correction and therefore more reluctant to take the action, and argued that a portion of training should be devoted to the issue of criterion placement.

In medicine, Lusted (1976) reported evidence that physicians adjust their response criterion in diagnosis according to how frequently the disease occurs in the population—essentially an estimate of P(signal)—but they adjust less than the optimal amount specified by the changing probabilities. However, the difficulty of specifying precisely the costs or benefits of all four of the joint events in medical diagnosis, as in air traffic control, makes it difficult to determine the exact level of optimal beta (as opposed to the direction of its change). How, for example, can the physician specify the precise cost of an undetected malignancy (Lusted, 1976), or the air traffic controller specify the costs of an undetected conflict that might produce a midair collision? The problems associated with specifying costs define the limits of applying signal detection theory to determine optimal response criteria.

Sensitivity

Signal detection theory has made an important conceptual and analytical distinction between the response bias parameters described above and the measure of the operator's *sensitivity*, the keenness or resolution of the detection mechanisms. We have seen that the operator may fail to detect a signal if response bias is conservative. Alternatively, the signal may be missed because the detection process is poor at discriminating signals from noise.

Sensitivity refers to the separation of noise and signal distributions along the X axis of Figure 2.3. If the separation is large (Figure 2.3a), sensitivity is high and a given value of X is quite likely to be generated by either S or N but not both. If the separation is small (Figure 2.3b), sensitivity is low. Since the curves represent neural activation, their separation could be reduced either by physical properties of the signal (e.g., a reduction in its intensity or salience) or by properties of the observer (e.g., a loss of hearing for an auditory detection task or a lack of training of a medical student for the task of detecting tumor patterns on an x-ray).

In the theory of signal detection, the sensitivity measure is called d' and corresponds to the separation of the means of two distributions in Figure 2.3, expressed in units of their standard deviations. For most situations d' varies between 0.5 and 2.0. Table of d' and beta values generated by different hit and false-alarm rates can be found in Swets, 1964.

Like bias, sensitivity also has an optimal value (which is not perfect). The computation of this optimal is more complex and is based on an ability to characterize precisely the statistical properties of the physical energy in signal and no-signal trials. Although this can be done in carefully controlled laboratory studies with acoustic signals and white-noise background, it is difficult to do in more complex environments. Nevertheless, data from auditory signal detection investigations suggest that the major cause for the departure results from the operator's poor *memory* for the precise physical characteristics of the signal. When memory aids are provided to remind the operator of what the signal looks or sounds like, d' approaches optimal levels. This point will be important when we consider the nature of vigilance tasks later in the chapter.

THE ROC CURVE
Theoretical Representation

All detection performance that has the same sensitivity is in some sense equivalent, regardless of bias. A graphic method of representation known as the *receiver operating characteristic* (ROC) is used to portray this equivalence of sensitivity across changing levels of bias. The ROC curve is useful for obtaining an understanding of the joint effects of sensitivity and response bias on the data from a signal detection analysis. In this section we will describe the ROC curve and note its relation to the 2 x 2 matrix of Figure 2.1 and the theoretical signal and noise curves of Figure 2.3.

Figure 2.1 presents the raw data that might be obtained from a signal detection theory (SDT) experiment. Of the four values, only two are critical. These are normally P(H) and P(FA), since P(M) and P(CR) are then completely specified as 1 − P(H) and 1 − P(FA), respectively. Figure 2.3 shows the theoretical representation of the neural mechanism within the brain that generated the matrix of Figure 2.1. As the criterion is set at different locations along the X axis of Figure 2.3, a different set of values will be generated in the matrix of Figure 2.1. Figure 2.5 also shows the ROC curve, which plots P(H) against P(FA) for different settings of the response criterion.

Each signal detection condition generates one point on the ROC. If the signal strength and the observer's sensitivity remain constant, changing beta from one condition to another (either through changing payoffs or varying signal probability) will produce a curved set of points. Points in the lower left of Figure 2.5 represent conservative responding; points in the upper right represent risky responding. When connected, these points make the ROC curve. Figure 2.5 shows the relationship among the raw data, the ROC curve, and the theoretical distributions, collected for three different beta values. One can see that sweeping the criterion placement from left (low beta or "risky" responding) to right (high beta or "conservative" responding) across the theoretical distributions produces progressively more "no" responses and moves points on the ROC curve from upper right to lower left.

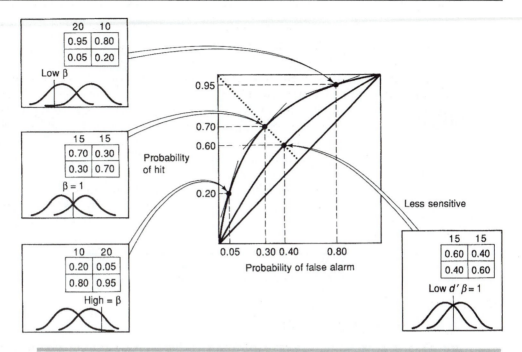

Figure 2.5   The ROC curve. The figure shows how three points on an ROC curve of high sensitivity relate to the raw data and underlying signal and noise curves. As beta is shifted at the right, the figure also shows one point of lower sensitivity.

It can be time-consuming to carry out the same signal detection experiment several times, each time changing only the response criterion by a different payoff or signal probability. A more efficient means of collecting data from several criterion sets is to have the subject provide a rating of confidence that a signal was present (Green & Swets, 1966). If three *confidence levels* are employed (e.g., "1" = confident that no signal was present, "2" = uncertain, and "3" = confident that a signal was present), the data may be analyzed twice in different ways, as shown in Table 2.1. During the first analysis, levels 1 and 2 would be considered a "no" response and level 3 a "yes" response. This classification corresponds to a conservative beta setting, since roughly two-thirds of the responses would be called "no." In the second analysis, level 1 would be considered a "no" response, and levels 2 and 3 would be considered a "yes" response. This classification corresponds to a risky beta setting. Thus, two beta settings are available from only one set of detection trials. Economy of data collection is realized because the subject is asked to convey more information on each trial.

Formally, the value of beta (the ratio of curve heights in Figure 2.3) at any given point along the ROC curve is equal to the slope of a tangent drawn to the curve at that point. This slope (and therefore beta) will be equal to 1 at points that fall along the negative diagonal (shown by the dotted line in Figure 2.5). If the hit and false-alarm values of these points are determined, we will find that $P(H) = 1 - P(FA)$, as can be seen for the two points on

TABLE 2.1 Analysis of Confidence Rating in Signal Detection Tasks [a]

Subject's Response	Stimulus Presented		How Responses Are Judged	
	Noise	Signal		
"1" = "No Signal"	4	2	No	No
"2" = "Uncertain"	3	2	No	Yes
"3" = "Signal"	1	4	Yes	Yes
Total No. Of Trials	8	8	↓	↓
			Conservative Criterion	Risky Criterion
			$P(FA) = \frac{1}{8}$	$P(FA) = \frac{4}{8}$
			$P(HIT) = \frac{4}{8}$	$P(HIT) = \frac{6}{8}$

[a] The table shows how data with three levels of confidence can be collapsed to derive two points on the ROC curve. Entries within the table indicate the number of times the subject gave the response on the left to the stimulus (signal or noise) presented.

the negative diagonal of Figure 2.5. Performance here is equivalent to performance at the point of intersection of the two distributions in Figure 2.3. Note also that points on the positive diagonal of Figure 2.5, running from lower left to upper right, represent chance performance: No matter how the criterion is set, $P(H)$ always equals $P(FA)$, and the signal cannot be discriminated at all from the noise. A representation of Figure 2.3 that gives rise to such chance performance would be one in which the signal and noise distributions were perfectly superimposed. Finally, points in the lower right region of the ROC space represent worse than chance performance. Here, the subject says "signal" when no signal is perceived and vice versa, implying that the subject is misinterpreting the task.

We will now discuss how the ROC curve represents sensitivity. Figure 2.5 shows that the ROC curve for a more sensitive observer is more bowed, being located closer to the upper left. Note that the ROC space in Figure 2.5 is plotted on a linear probability scale, and therefore shows a typically bowed curve. An alternative way of plotting the curve is to use z-scores (Figure 2.6). Constant units of distance along each axis represent constant numbers of standard scores of the normal distribution. This representation has the advantage that the bowed lines of Figure 2.5 now become straight lines parallel to the chance diagonal. For a given point, d' is then equal to $Z(H) - Z(FA)$, reflecting the number of standardized scores that the point lies to the upper left of the chance diagonal. A measure of response bias that correlates very closely with beta, and is easy to derive from Figure 2.6, is simply the z-score of the false-alarm probability for a particular point (Swets & Pickett, 1982).

Empirical Data

It is important to realize the distinction between the theoretical, idealized curves in Figures 2.3, 2.5, and 2.6 and the actual empirical data collected in a signal detection

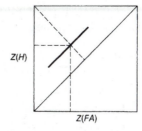

$Z(H)$

$Z(FA)$

Figure 2.6   The ROC curve on probability paper.

experiment or a field investigation of detection performance. The most obvious contrast is that the representations in Figures 2.5 and 2.6 are continuous, smooth curves, whereas empirical data would consist of a set of discrete points. More important, empirical results in which data are collected from a subject as the criterion is varied often provide points that do not fall precisely along a line of constant bowedness (Figure 2.5) or a 45-degree slope (Figure 2.6). Often the slope is slightly shallower. This situation arises because the distributions of noise and signal-plus-noise energy are not in fact precisely normal and of equal variance, as the idealized curves of Figure 2.3 portray, particularly if there is variability in the signal itself. This tilting of the ROC curve away from the ideal presents some difficulties for the use of d' as a measure of sensitivity. If d' is measured as the distance of the ROC curve of Figure 2.6 from the chance axis, and this distance varies as a function of the criterion setting, what is the appropriate setting for measuring d'? One approach is to measure the distance at unit beta arbitrarily (i.e., where the ROC curve intersects the negative diagonal). This measure is referred to as d_a and may be employed if data at two or more different beta settings are available so that a straight-line ROC can be constructed on the probability plot of Figure 2.6 (Green & Swets, 1966).

Although it is therefore desirable to generate two or more points on the ROC curve, there are some circumstances in which it may be impossible to do so, particularly when evaluating detection data in many real-world contexts. In such cases, the experimenter often cannot manipulate beta or use rating scales and must use the data available from only a single stimulus-response matrix. This does not always present a problem. Collection of a full set of ROC data may not be necessary if bias is minimal (Macmillan & Creelman, 1991). Nonetheless, if there are only one or two points in the ROC space and there is evidence for strong risky or conservative bias, another measure of sensitivity should be used.

Under these circumstances, the measure $P(A)$ or the area under the ROC curve is an alternative measure of sensitivity (Calderia, 1980; Craig, 1979; Green & Swets, 1966). The measure represents the area to the right and below the line segments connecting the lower left and upper right corners of the ROC space to the measured data point (Figure 2.7). Craig (1979) and Calderia (1980) have argued that the advantage of this measure is that it is "parameter free." That is, its value does not depend on any assumptions concerning the shape or form of the underlying signal and noise distributions. For this reason, it is a measure that may be usefully employed even if two or more points in the ROC space are available but do not fall along a 45-degree line. (This suggests that the data do not meet the equal variance assumptions.) The measure $P(A)$ may be calculated from the formula

$$P(A) = \frac{P(H) + [1 - P(FA)]}{2} \tag{2.4}$$

Alternative measures of bias also exist. For example, the measure C locates the criterion relative to the intersection of the two distributions. The intersection point is the zero point, and then distance from this criterion is measured in Z-units. Thus, $C = 0.5(Z(FA) + Z(H))$. Conservative biases produce positive C-values; risky biases produce negative values. Recent summaries of bias measures suggest that C is a better measure of bias than beta, because it is less sensitive to changes in d' (See, Warm, Dember, & Howe, 1997; Snodgrass & Corwin, 1988). Nonparametric measures of bias are also available, and are described in See et al. (1997).

The reader is referred to Calderia (1980), Green and Swets (1966), Macmillan and Creelman (1991), and Snodgrass and Corwin (1988) for further discussion of the relative merits of different sensitivity and bias measures.

APPLICATIONS OF SIGNAL DETECTION THEORY

Signal detection theory has had a large impact on experimental psychology, and its concepts are highly applicable to many problems of human factors as well. It has two general benefits: (1) It provides the ability to compare sensitivity and therefore the quality of performance between conditions or between operators that may differ in response bias. (2) By partitioning performance into bias and sensitivity components, it provides a diagnostic tool that recommends different corrective actions, depending on whether change in performance results from a loss of sensitivity or a shift in response bias.

The implications of the first benefit are clear. Suppose the performance of two operators or the hit rate obtained from two different pieces of inspection equipment are compared. If A has a higher hit rate but also a higher false-alarm rate than B, which is

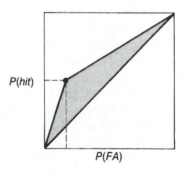

Figure 2.7   Example of the sensitivity measure P(A), the area under the ROC curve, derived from one point.

superior? Unless the explicit mechanism for separating sensitivity from bias is available, this comparison is impossible. Signal detection theory provides the mechanism.

The importance of the second benefit—the diagnostic value of signal detection theory—will be evident as we consider some actual examples of applications of signal detection theory to real-world tasks. In the many possible environments where the operator must detect an event and does so imperfectly, the existence of these errors presents a challenge for the engineering psychologist: Why do they occur, and what corrective actions can prevent them? Three areas of application (medical diagnosis, eyewitness testimony, and industrial inspection), will be considered, leading to a more extensive discussion of vigilance.

Medical Diagnosis

Medical diagnosis is a fruitful realm for the application of signal detection theory (Lusted, 1971, 1976; Parasuraman, 1985). Abnormalities (diseases, tumors) are either present in the patient or they are not, and the physician must decide "present" or "absent." Sensitivity is related to factors such as the salience of the abnormality or the number of converging symptoms, as well as the training of the physician to focus on relevant cues. Response bias, meanwhile, can be influenced by both signal probability and payoffs. In the former category, influences include the disease prevalence rate and whether the patient is examined in initial screening (probability of disease low, beta high) or referral (probability higher, beta lower). Lusted (1976) has argued that physicians' detections generally tend to be less responsive to variation in the disease prevalence rate than optimal. Parasuraman (1985) found that radiologist residents were not responsive enough to differences between screening and referral in changing beta. Both results illustrate the sluggish beta phenomenon.

Although payoffs may influence decisions, it is difficult to quantify consequences of hits (e.g., a detected malignancy leads to its surgical removal with associated hospital costs and possible consequences), false alarms (an unnecessary operation), and misses. Placing values on these events based on financial costs of surgery, malpractice suits, and the intangible costs of human life and suffering is clearly difficult. Yet there is little doubt that they influence the physician's detection rate. Lusted (1976) and Swets and Pickett (1982) have shown how diagnostic performance can be quantified with an ROC curve. In a thorough treatment, Swets and Pickett describe the appropriate methodology for using signal detection theory to examine performance in medical diagnosis.

Several investigations have examined the more restricted domain of tumor diagnosis by radiologists. Rhea, Potsdaid, and DeLuca (1979) have estimated the rate of omission in the detection of abnormalities to run between 20 and 40 percent. In comparing the detection performance of staff radiologists and residents, Parasuraman (1985), found differences in sensitivity (favoring the radiologists) and bias (radiologists showing a more conservative criterion).

Swennson, Hessel, and Herman (1977) examined the effect of directing the radiologist's attention to a particular area of an x-ray plate where an abnormality was likely to occur. They found that this increased the likelihood of the tumor's detection, but did so by reducing beta rather than increasing sensitivity. In related work, Swennson (1980) conducted an ROC analysis of the performance of radiologists searching for tumors in chest x-rays. Swennson found the counterintuitive result that examining the entire radiograph produced greater sensitivity than a control condition in which only one part of the radiograph was examined. Swennson proposed a model having two detection components. The first identifies likely candidate locations, and the second identifies tumors in those locations. By using different sensitivities in the two stages, Swennson's model accounted for the obtained results.

A signal-detection approach has been used to distinguish between the relative merits of two different imaging techniques for examining brain lesions: computerized tomography (CT) and radionuclide (RN) scans (Swets et al., 1979). A confidence level procedure was used such that the radiologists made judgments on a 5-point scale. Hit and false-alarm rates were computed from these data using the procedure described above. Plots of the ROC space showed that higher levels of sensitivity were evident with the CT method relative to the RN method, with little difference in terms of bias.

Schwartz, Dans, and Kinosian (1988) performed an ROC analysis on data from a study by Nishanian et al. (1987; see Swets, 1992). Nishinian et al. compared the accuracy for three diagnostic tests for HIV. The analysis showed that two of the tests produced nearly the same sensitivity value, higher than that produced by the third test. However, the two tests having greater sensitivity differed in terms of bias; one test was much more likely to make a false positive decision (a false alarm—that is, diagnosing someone with HIV when they did not have it) for a slight increase in the number of hits. Signal detection analysis of this type can be very important in helping physicians determine which diagnostic test to use in a given situation. For example, it may be appropriate to use the more liberal test (and run the increased risk of a false alarm) when other factors suggest that the patient is more likely to be HIV positive.

Recognition Memory and Eyewitness Testimony

The domain of recognition memory represents a somewhat different application of signal detection theory. Here the observer is not assessing whether or not a physical signal is present but rather decides whether or not a physical stimulus (the person or name to be recognized) was seen or heard at an earlier time.

One important application of signal detection theory to memory is found in the study of eyewitness testimony (e.g., Ellison & Buckhout, 1981; Wells, 1993; Wright & Davies, 1999). The witness to a crime may be asked to recognize or identify a suspect as the perpetrator. The four kinds of joint events in Figure 2.1 can readily be specified. The suspect examined by the witness either is (signal) or is not (noise) the same individual actually perceived at the scene of the crime. The witness in turn can either say "That's the one" (Y) or "No, it's not" (N).

In this case, the joint interests of criminal justice and protection of society are served by maintaining a high level of sensitivity while keeping beta neither too high (many misses, with criminals more likely to go free) nor too low (a high rate of false alarms, with an increased likelihood that innocent individuals will be prosecuted). Signal detection theory has been most directly applied to a witness's identification of suspects in police lineups (e.g., Ellison & Buckhout, 1981). In this case, the witness is shown a lineup of five or so individuals, one of whom is the suspect detained by the police, and the others are "foils." Hence, the lineup decision may be considered a two-stage process: Is the suspect in the lineup, and if so, which one is it?

Ellison and Buckhout (1981) have expressed concern that witnesses generally have a low response criterion in lineup identifications and will therefore often say yes to the first question. This bias would present no difficulty if their recognition memory was also accurate, enabling them to identify the suspect accurately. However, considerable research on staged crimes shows that visual recognition of brief events is notoriously poor (e.g., Loftus, 1979). Poor recognition memory coupled with the risky response bias allows those conducting the lineup to use techniques that will capitalize on witness bias to ensure a positive identification. These techniques include ensuring that the suspect is differently dressed, is seen in handcuffs by the witness before the lineup, or is quite different in appearance from the foils. In short, techniques are used that would lead even a person who had *not seen* the crime to select the suspect from the foils or would lead the witness to make a positive identification from a lineup that *did not contain the suspect* (Ellison & Buckhout, 1981; Wells & Bradfield, 1998). This process is not testing the sensitivity of recognition memory but is emphasizing response bias.

How could the bias in the lineup process be reduced? Ellison and Buckhout (1981) suggest a simple procedure: inform the witness that the suspect may not be in the lineup. As does reducing the probability of a signal, this procedure will drive beta upward toward a more optimal setting. Ellison and Buckhout further argue that people in the lineup should be equally similar to one another (such that a nonwitness would have an equal chance of picking any of them). Although greater similarity will reduce the hit rate slightly, it will reduce the false-alarm rate considerably more. The result will be a net increase in sensitivity.

Wells (1993) offers two approaches to improving the eyewitness sensitivity in the lineup situation. The first, called a *blank lineup control*, requires the witness to view two lineups, the first being a blank lineup containing no suspect, and the second being a lineup with the suspect. (The witness does not realize there is a second lineup while observing the first.) This is similar to the signal-absent trial in the signal detection situation. Wells (1984) found that those witnesses who do not make an identification with the blank lineup are more likely to make an accurate identification in the real lineup than witnesses who go directly to the real lineup. The second approach noted by Wells (1993) is called a *mock witness control*. Here, a lineup is shown to a set of people who were not witnesses, and who are given only limited information about the crime. If the mock witnesses identify the suspect at a rate greater than chance, then it suggests that something in the limited information is leading them to choose the suspect. Both approaches are akin to adding a control group to an experiment, which allows for comparison with the real situation (the experimental group).

Gonzales, Ellsworth, and Pembroke (1993) contrasted recognition memory performance in the lineup situation with recognition memory in the *showup*. A showup occurs when the witness is shown one suspect and is asked whether the suspect is the person who committed the crime. It is widely believed that the showup is biased towards saying "yes" (and thereby increasing false alarms) relative to the lineup. However, Gonzales et al. found that witnesses were more likely to say "yes" with a lineup than a showup, even when the suspect was absent, demonstrating a risky bias for the lineup. Gonzales et al. speculated that the initial process of finding a best match within the lineup may bias the witness to make an identification. Therefore, the result of the initial decision (the suspect is in the lineup) serves to lower the criterion for subsequent decisions (which one is the suspect). This would serve to increase both hits and false alarms, as observed.

A further danger is that eyewitnesses tend to become more certain of their judgment after being told they selected the suspect (Wells & Bradfield, 1998). In the United States, there is nothing to stop an investigator from telling an eyewitness that they selected the suspect from a lineup after the choice has been made. In the Wells and Bradfield study, subjects were shown a security video and then later asked to identify the gunman from a set of photographs. All subjects made identifications, although the actual gunman was not in the set. Following the identification, subjects were told whether or not they had iden-tified the suspect. If they were told that they had identified the suspect, they were later more certain that they had identified the gunman. However, since the gunman was not in the set, these were all false identifications. In signal detection terms, this is an increase in the false-alarm rate resulting from a reduction in beta. The problem is that eyewitnesses appear at trial convinced they have identified the criminal, and juries are in turn more eas-ily convinced by the eyewitness's testimony (Wells & Bradfield, 1998). For these reasons, researchers have recommended that investigators should not reveal any information about the outcome of the identification until a clear statement of confidence has been obtained from the eyewitness (Wells & Seelau, 1995).

Industrial Inspection

In many industries, there is a need to check on the quality of manufactured products or product parts. An industrial inspector might check on the quality of welds in an au-tomobile factory, for example. Since the inspector may not know the location of the flaw, industrial inspection often involves a *visual search* (to be discussed further in Chapter 3). For example, Swets (1992) examined technicians inspecting metal fatigue in airplanes. A large number of metal specimens, some with and some without flaws, were inspected using ultrasound and eddy-current methods. The performance of each technician was specified by a hit rate and false-alarm rate and plotted as a point in an ROC space. The ROC plot for the inspectors using the ultrasound showed the points randomly distributed above the positive diagonal. In contrast, the points in the eddy-current ROC space were more tightly clustered in the extreme upper left corner of the space. Thus, inspectors were better able to detect a flaw using the eddy-current method than the ultrasound method (greater sensitivity) and there was less variability in the criterion setting. Despite the large variability among observers, the general advantage of the eddy-current method was evident.

VIGILANCE

In the vigilance task an operator is required to detect signals over a long period of time (referred to as the *watch*), and the signals are intermittent, unpredictable, and infrequent. Examples include the radar monitor, who must observe infrequent contacts; the airport security inspector, who examines x-rayed carry-on luggage; the supervisory monitor of complex systems, who must detect the infrequent malfunctions of system components; and the quality control inspector, who examines a stream of products (sheet metal, circuit boards, microchips, fruit) to detect and remove defective or flawed items.

Two general conclusions emerge from the analysis of operators' performance in the vigilance situation. First, the steady-state level of vigilance performance is known as the *vigilance level*, and operators often show lower vigilance levels than desirable. Second, the vigilance level sometimes declines steeply during the first half hour or so of the watch. This phenomenon was initially noted in radar monitors during World War II (N. H. Mackworth, 1948), has been experimentally replicated numerous times, and has been observed in industrial inspectors (Harris & Chaney, 1969; Parasuraman, 1986). This decrease in vigilance level over time is known as the *vigilance decrement*.

Vigilance Paradigms

It is important to distinguish two classes of vigilance situations, or paradigms. The *free-response* paradigm is one in which a target event occurs at any time and nonevents are not defined. This is analogous to the task confronting the power plant monitor. In contrast, with the *inspection* paradigm, events occur at fairly regular intervals. A few of these events are targets (defects), but most are nontargets (normal items). This is the task faced by a circuit board inspector, for example. In the free-response paradigm, *event rate* is defined by the number of targets per unit time. In the inspection paradigm event rate is ambiguous because it may be defined either by the number of targets per unit time or (incorrectly) by the ratio of targets to total events (targets and nontargets). The latter measure (which we shall refer to as *target probability*) will stay constant even if the number of targets per unit time is increased—the result of speeding up a conveyor belt, for example. In typical industrial inspection tasks, event rate may be fairly high, but in other tasks such as that of the airport security inspector, it will be much lower.

It is also important to distinguish between a *successive* and a *simultaneous* vigilance paradigm. In a successive paradigm or task, observers must remember the target stimulus and compare successively presented stimulus configurations against the remembered representation. For example, an inspector might be asked to detect if the color of a garment is darker than usual. In a simultaneous paradigm, all the information needed to make the discrimination is present for each event. For example, each garment could be compared to a standard piece of fabric.

Finally, we should distinguish between *sensory* and *cognitive* paradigms (See, Howe, Warm, and Dember, 1995). In a sensory task, signals represent changes in auditory or visual intensity. In a cognitive task, like proofreading a final manuscript, symbolic or alphanumeric stimuli are used. Since cognitive stimuli such as letters or numbers are often familiar, some researchers claim this distinction is really between familiar or unfamiliar stimuli (e.g., Koelega, Brinkman, Hendriks, & Verbaten, 1989). Nonetheless, there appear to be important differences in the results obtained in the different paradigms (See et al., 1995), as described below.

Measuring Vigilance Performance

A large number of investigations of factors affecting the vigilance level and the vigilance decrement have been conducted over the last five decades with a myriad of experimental variables in various paradigms. An exhaustive listing of all of the experimental results of vigilance studies is beyond the scope of this chapter. Readers interested in more extensive treatments are referred to the following sources: Davies and Parasuraman (1982); Parasuraman (1986); See et al. (1995); Warm (1984); Warm and Dember (1998). Before summarizing the most important results, we will discuss how vigilance performance should be measured.

Specifying vigilance performance in terms of number of targets detected is analogous to gauging performance in a signal detection task using hit rate [P(H)]. Specifying the vigilance decrement this way is misleading because P(H) could decline through an increase in beta with no decline in sensitivity (i.e., P(FA) is also decreasing). Hence, vigilance performance is better understood by applying a signal detection approach.

Indeed, it has been shown repeatedly that the vigilance decrement can arise either as a result of a decrease in sensitivity (e.g., J. F. Mackworth & Taylor, 1963) or as a shift to a more conservative criterion (e.g., Broadbent & Gregory, 1965), depending on the task and experimental situation. Therefore, rather than trying to account for factors affecting the vigilance decrement, it is more informative to describe those factors that affect the *sensitivity decrements* or *beta increments* that underlie the vigilance decrement.

In inspection tasks, when nontarget events are clearly defined, a signal detection analysis is straightforward, since the false-alarm rate may be easily computed. In the free-response paradigm, however, when nontarget events are not well defined, further assumptions must be made to compute a false-alarm rate. In the laboratory, this is typically accomplished by defining an appropriate *response interval* after each signal within which a subject's response will be designated a hit. The remaining time during a watch is partitioned into a number of *false-alarm intervals*, equal in duration to the response intervals. P(FA) is simply the number of false alarms divided by the number of false-alarm intervals (Parasuraman, 1986; Watson & Nichols, 1976). Although beyond the scope of this treatment, there are caveats that should be considered when applying signal detection theory to vigilance phenomena, particularly when the false-alarm rates are low (Craig, 1977; Long & Waag, 1981).

Factors Affecting Sensitivity Level and Sensitivity Decrement

The following factors affect sensitivity in a vigilance task:

1. Sensitivity decreases, and the sensitivity decrement increases, as a target's *signal strength* is reduced, which occurs when the intensity or duration of a target is reduced or otherwise made more similar to nontarget events (J. F. Mackworth & Taylor, 1963; Teichner, 1974).
2. Sensitivity decreases when there is *uncertainty* about the time or location at which the target signal will appear. This uncertainty is particularly great if there are long intervals between signals (J. F. Mackworth & Taylor, 1963; Milosevic, 1974; Warm, Dember, Murphy, & Dittmar, 1992).
3. For inspection tasks, which have defined nontarget events, the sensitivity level decreases and the decrement increases when the *event rate* is increased (Baddeley & Colquhoun, 1969; See et al., 1995). Event rate is defined as the number of events per unit time; an example of increasing the event rate would be speeding up the conveyer belt in an inspection situation. Note that this keeps the ratio

of target to nontargets constant, and therefore event rate should not be confused with target probability, which affects bias (see below).

4. The sensitivity level is higher for *simultaneous* tasks than for *successive* tasks (Parasuraman, 1979). A sensitivity decrement occurs for successive tasks at high event rates but does not occur at low event rates, or for simultaneous tasks at either rate (Parasuraman, 1979).

5. The sensitivity decrement is eliminated when observers are highly practiced so that the task becomes *automatic*, rather than *controlled* (Fisk & Schneider, 1981; Fisk & Scerbo, 1987; see Chapters 6, 7, and 11 for detailed coverage of automaticity).

6. A *sensitivity increment* (i.e., improvement with time on watch) sometimes occurs in simultaneous paradigms with *cognitive* (familiar) but not *sensory* stimuli (See et al., 1995).

Factors Affecting Response Bias Level and Bias Increment

Changes in bias also occur, and the more salient results are as follows:

1. *Target probability* affects response bias, with higher probabilities decreasing beta, (more hits and false alarms) and lower probabilities increasing it (more misses and correct rejections) (Loeb & Binford, 1968; See et al., 1997; Williges, 1971), although sluggish beta is evident (Baddeley & Colquhoun, 1969). Note that a decrease in target probability can occur if nontarget events are more densely spaced between targets. Such changes in target probability are sometimes incorrectly referred to as event rate.

2. *Payoffs* affect response bias as in the signal detection task (e.g., Davenport, 1968; See et al., 1997), although the effect of payoffs is less consistent and less effective than manipulating probability (see Davies & Parasuraman, 1982). This stands in contrast to the relative effects of manipulating probability and payoffs in the signal detection task where signals are more common.

3. Increased beta values are evident when *signal strength* is reduced (Broadbent, 1971).

Theories of Vigilance

We present three theories used to explain vigilance performance and the influence of factors such as type of display, task type, or environmental stressors, and we will show how they suggest corrective improvements. The advantage of such theories is that they provide parsimonious ways to account for vigilance performance and thereby suggest techniques to improve it. The first theory accounts for sensitivity loss; the others account for criterion shifts. It may be possible to integrate the theories, as described below.

Sensitivity Loss: Fatigue and Sustained Demand Theory   In the earliest laboratory studies investigating vigilance (N. H. Mackworth, 1948), the subject monitored a clock hand that ticked at periodic intervals (nontarget events). Occasionally the hand underwent a "double tick" (target event), moving twice the angle of the nontarget events. In this paradigm, and many others that have employed visual signals, a sensitivity decrement usually occurs. To account for the decrement, Broadbent (1971) argued that the sustained attention necessary to fixate the clock hand or other visual signals continuously extracts a toll in fatigue. Indeed, sometimes the vigilance task is referred to as a *sustained attention* task (Parasuraman, 1979). Because of the resulting fatigue, the subject looks away or blinks more often as the watch progresses, and therefore signals are missed.

More recently, investigators have concluded that a vigilance task imposing a sustained load on working memory (e.g., having to recall what the target signal looks or sounds like, as in a successive task) will demand the continuous supply of processing resources (Deaton & Parasuraman, 1988; Parasuraman, 1979). Indeed ratings of mental workload (see Chapter 9) show that the workload of vigilance tasks is generally high (Warm, Dember, & Hancock, 1996). This mental demand may be as fatiguing as the sustained demand to keep one's eyes open and fixated, and here too the eventual toil of fatigue will lead to a loss in sensitivity. A further implication of the resource-demanding nature of vigilance tasks is their susceptibility to interference from concurrent tasks (to be discussed in Chapter 11).

One would expect, therefore, that situations demanding greater processing resources (e.g., when the target is difficult to detect, when there is uncertainty about where or when the target will occur, when the event rate is fast, when the observer has to remember what the target looks or sounds like, when the target is not familiar) should produce greater fatigue, leading to a lower vigilance level. For example, there is evidence that successive tasks are more strongly resource-limited than simultaneous tasks (Matthews, Davies, & Holley, 1993). One would also expect that the sustained demand of the task over time will be greater in these situations, leading to greater sensitivity decrements. Therefore, *sustained demand theory* proposes that sustained demand over time leads to the sensitivity decrement; and that factors demanding greater mental resources will lower sensitivity levels (Parasuraman, 1979; Matthews, Davies, & Holley, 1993). The finding that the sensitivity level is higher, and the sensitivity decrement eliminated, when observers detect the target automatically with little effort is also consistent with sustained demand theory, since a characteristic of automatic processing is that it produces little resource demand (Schneider & Shiffrin, 1977).

Criterion Shifts: Expectancy Theory   In many vigilance situations, the vigilance decrement is due not so much to a sensitivity decrement, but rather a bias increment. The sustained-demand theory described above cannot account for such increases, since sustained demand is postulated to decrease d', not increase beta. On the other hand, the *expectancy theory* proposed by Baker (1961) attributes the vigilance decrement to an upward adjustment of the response criterion in response to a reduction in the perceived frequency (and therefore expectancy) of target events. Assume that the subject sets beta on the basis of a subjective perception of signal frequency, $P_s(S)$. If a signal is missed for any reason, subjective probability $P_s(S)$ is reduced because the subject believes that one less signal occurred. This reduction in turn causes an upward adjustment of beta, which further increases the likelihood of a miss, and so on, in a "vicious circle" (Broadbent, 1971). Although this behavior could lead to an infinite beta and a negligible hit rate, in practice other factors will operate to level off the criterion at a stable but higher value.

When the signal probability is lowered, it should serve to decrease the expectation of the signal, and therefore increase beta. Payoffs may have similar effects. Since the vicious circle depends on signals being missed in the first place, it stands to reason that the kinds of variables that reduce sensitivity (short, low-intensity signals) should also increase the expectancy effect in vigilance, as noted above.

An alternative theoretical conception for the bias increment was proposed by Welford (1968). *Arousal theory* postulates that in a prolonged low-event environment, the "evidence variable" X (see Figure 2.3) shrinks while the criterion stays constant. This change is shown in Figure 2.8. The shrinking results from a decrease in neural activity (both signal and noise) with decreased arousal. This decreased arousal may be related to the sustained attentional demands of the vigilance task that affects sensitivity. An examination of Figure 2.8 reveals that such an effect will reduce both hit and false-alarm rates (a change in beta) while keeping the separation of the two distributions, as expressed in standard scores, at a constant level (a constant d').

The arousal view is consistent with some physiological findings (e.g., Dardano, 1962; McGrath, 1963; Milosevic, 1975). However, some recent studies with drugs that affect arousal have found changes in sensitivity, but not the changes in response bias predicted by arousal theory. For example, drugs like caffeine that increase arousal do not produce changes in response bias but increase sensitivity (Fine et al., 1994); drugs like antihistamine and oxazepam that decrease arousal do not affect response bias but decrease sensitivity (Fine et al. 1994; van Leeuwen et al., 1994). In addition, there

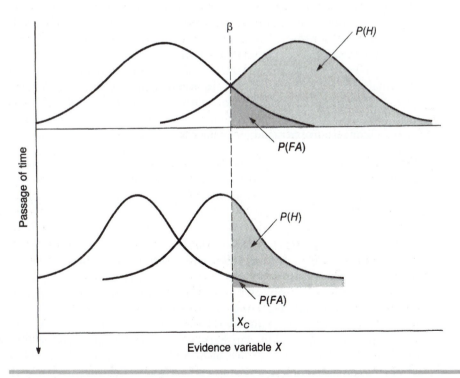

Figure 2.8 Welford's arousal theory of the vigilance decrement.

is good evidence that this theory is insufficient to explain all occurrences of criterion shifts. This evidence is provided by instances in which a manipulated variable that would be expected to influence the arousal level does not produce the expected effect on the criterion. For example, as we have seen, increasing the total event rate, while keeping the absolute target frequency constant (thereby decreasing the target/nontarget ratio), increases the decrement. Yet arousal theory should predict the opposite effect, since the more frequent nontarget events should increase arousal, not decrease it.

Nonetheless, arousal theory is parsimonious in that the same physiological mechanism—increased fatigue, decreased arousal—that accounts for the bias increment can also account for the sensitivity decrement. It is possible that arousal might interact with expectancy, with lowered arousal (greater fatigue) increasing the chance of a miss and lowering $P_s(S)$. Thus, the best general explanation might be that decreasing arousal (increasing fatigue) decreases sensitivity, increases beta, and also lowers the subjective probability of a signal, again increasing beta. Expectancy theory is necessary to properly account for the effects of probabilities and payoffs on the steady-state vigilance level, however.

Techniques to Combat the Loss of Vigilance

In many vigilance situations, vigilance performance reflects some combination of shifts in sensitivity and response bias. Very often d' and beta shifts are observed in a single vigil. It is also important to reemphasize that the theoretical mechanisms proposed to account for the vigilance decrement also account for differences between conditions or tasks that are not related to time. Although Teichner (1974) has pointed out that the vigilance decrement can be small (around 10 percent), corrective techniques that reduce the decrement will also improve the absolute level of performance. As Parasuraman (1986) noted, performance levels may be consistently lower than some minimum acceptable level of performance even if there is no decrement, which may be of concern to management. Like the theories of vigilance, these corrective techniques may be categorized into those that enhance sensitivity and those that shift the response criterion.

Increasing Sensitivity   We note the following techniques for improving sensitivity in a vigilance task.

(1) *Show target examples (reduce memory load).* A logical outgrowth of the sustained demand theory is that any technique aiding or enhancing the subject's memory of signal characteristics should reduce sensitivity decrements and preserve a higher overall level of sensitivity. Hence, the availability of a "standard" representation of the target should help. For example, Kelly (1955) reported a large increase in detection performance when quality control operators could look at television pictures of idealized target stimuli. Furthermore, a technique that helps reduce the bias increment caused by expectancy may also combat a loss in sensitivity. The introduction of false signals, as described in the next section, could improve sensitivity by refreshing memory.

A study by Childs (1976), which found that subjects perform better when monitoring for only one target than when monitoring for one of several, is also consistent with the importance of memory aids in vigilance. Childs also observed an improvement in performance when subjects were told specifically what the target stimuli were rather than what they were not. Schoenfeld and Scerbo (1997) found that the sensitivity decrement was less when searching for the presence of a feature in a visual display than when searching for its absence. The general recommendation is that inspectors should have access to visual representation of possible defectives rather than simply the representation of those that are normal.

(2) *Increase target salience.* Various artificial techniques of signal enhancement are closely related to the reduction in memory load. Available solutions capitalize on procedures that will differentially affect signals and nonsignals. For example, Luzzo and Drury (1980) developed a signal-enhancement technique known as "blinking." When successive events are similar to one another (e.g., wired circuit boards), detection of miswired boards can be facilitated by rapidly and alternately projecting an image of a single location of a known good prototype and the item to be inspected. If the latter is "normal," the image will be identical, fused, and continuous. If the item contains a malfunction (e.g., a gap in wiring), the gap location will blink on and off in a highly salient fashion as the displays are alternated.

A related signal-enhancement technique is to induce coherent motion into targets but not nontargets, thereby taking advantage of the human's high sensitivity to motion. For example, an operator scanning a radar display for a target blip among many similar nontargets encounters a very difficult detection problem. Scanlan (1975) has demonstrated that a radar target undergoes a coherent but slow motion whereas the noise properties are random. If successive radar frames are stored, recent frames can be replayed in fast time, forward and backward. Under these conditions, the target's coherent motion stands out improving detection performance.

An alternative approach is to transcribe the events to an alternate sensory modality. This technique takes advantage of the redundancy gain that occurs when a signal is presented in two modalities at once. Employing this technique, Colquhoun (1975), Doll and Hanna (1989), and Lewandowski and Kobus (1989) found that sonar monitors detected targets more accurately when the target was simultaneously displayed visually and auditorially than when either mode was employed by itself.

(3) *Vary event rate.* Sustained demand theory suggests that high event rates can produce larger losses in vigilance performance. As Saito (1972) showed in a study of bottle inspectors, a reduction of the event rate from 300 to under 200 bottles per minute markedly improved inspection efficiency. Allowing observers to control event rate is also effective: Scerbo, Greenwald, and Sawin (1993) showed that giving observers such control improves sensitivity and lowers the sensitivity decrement.

(4) *Train observers.* A technique closely related to the enhancement of signals through display manipulations is one that emphasizes operator training. Fisk and Schneider (1981) demonstrated that the magnitude of a sensitivity decrement could be greatly reduced by training subjects to respond consistently and repeatedly to the target elements. This technique of developing automatic processing of the stimulus (described further in Chapter 6) tends to make the target stimulus "jump out" of the train of events, just as one's own name is heard in a series of words. Fisk and Schneider note that the

critical stimuli must consistently appear as a target stimulus, and that the probability of target must be high during the training session.

Shift in Response Criterion   The following methods may be useful in shifting the criterion to an optimal level.

(1) *Instructions.* An unsatisfactory vigilance or inspection performance can occur because the operator's perceptions of the probability of signals or the costs of errors do not agree with reality. For example, in quality control, an inspector may believe that it is better to detect more defects and not worry about falsely rejecting good parts although it would be more cost-effective to maintain a higher criterion because the probability of a defective part is low. Simple instructions in industrial or company policy may adjust beta to an appropriate level. In airline security inspection, increased stress on the seriousness of misses (failing to detect a weapon smuggled through the inspection line) could cause a substantial decrease in the number of misses (but a corresponding increase in false alarms).

(2) *Knowledge of Results.* Less direct means can also adjust the response criterion to a more optimal level. For example, where possible, knowledge of results (*KR*) should be provided to allow an accurate estimation of the true $P(S)$ (N. H. Mackworth, 1950). It appears that *KR* is most effective in low-noise environments (Becker, Warm, Dember, & Hancock, 1995).

(3) *False Signals.* Baker (1961) and Wilkinson (1964) have argued that introducing false signals should keep beta low. False signals will raise the subjective $P_s(S)$ and might raise the arousal level as well. Furthermore, if the false signals refresh the operator's memory, the procedure should improve sensitivity and reduce the sensitivity decrement by reducing the sustained demand of the task, as discussed earlier. For example, as applied to the quality control inspector, a certain number of predefined defectives might be placed on the inspection line. These would be "tagged," so that if missed by the inspector, they would still be removed. Their presence in the inspection stream should guarantee a higher $P_s(S)$ and therefore a lower beta than would be otherwise observed. However, this technique should not be used if the actions that the operator would take after detection have undesirable consequences for an otherwise stable system. An extreme example would occur if false warnings were introduced into a chemical process control plant and these led the operator to shut down the plant unnecessarily.

(4) *Confidence levels.* Finally, allowing operators to report signal events with different confidence levels decreases the bias increment (Broadbent & Gregory, 1965; Rizy, 1972). If rather than classifying each event as target or nontarget, the operator can say "target," "uncertain," or "nontarget" (or a wider range of response options), beta should not increase as quickly since the observer would say "nontarget" less often, and the subjective perception of signal frequency, $P_s(S)$ should not decrease as quickly. The idea of a graded confidence in detection has important implications for the design of alarms (discussed in Chapter 13).

(5) *Other techniques.* Other techniques to combat the decrement have focused more directly on arousal and fatigue. Parasuraman (1986) noted that rest periods can have

beneficial effects. Presumably, rest periods serve to increase arousal, which as we have seen influences both sensitivity and response bias. Welford (1968) has argued persuasively that any event (such as a phone call, drugs, or noise) that will sustain or increase arousal should reduce the decrement or at least maintain beta at a more constant level. Using biofeedback techniques, Beatty, Greenberg, Deibler, and O'Hanlon (1974) have shown that operators trained to suppress theta waves (brain waves at 3–7 Hz, indicating low arousal) will also reduce the decrement.

Conclusions

Despite the plethora of vigilance experiments and the wealth of experimental data, the application of research results to real-world vigilance phenomena has not yet been extensive. This is somewhat surprising in light of the clear shortcomings in many inspection tasks, with miss rates sometimes as high as 30 to 40 percent (Craig, 1984; Parasuraman, Warm, & Dember, 1987). One reason the results of laboratory studies have not been more fully applied relates to the discrepancy between the fairly simple stimuli with known location and form employed in many laboratory tasks, and the more complex stimuli existing in the real world. The monitor of the nuclear power plant, for example, does not know precisely what configuration of warning indicators will signal the onset of an abnormal condition, but it is unlikely that it will be the appearance of a single near-threshold light in direct view. Some laboratory investigators have examined the effects of signal complexity and uncertainty (e.g., Adams, Humes, & Stenson, 1962; Childs, 1976; Howell, Johnston, & Goldstein, 1966). These studies are consistent in concluding that increased complexity or signal uncertainty will lower the absolute vigilance level. However, their conclusions concerning the influence of signal complexity and uncertainty on other vigilance effects (e.g., the size of the vigilance decrement), and therefore the generalizability of these effects to complex signal environments, have not been consistent.

A second possible reason laboratory results have not been fully exploited relates to the differences in motivation and signal frequency between laboratory data and real vigilance phenomena. In the laboratory, signal rates may range from one an hour to as high as three or four per minute—low enough to show decrements, and lower than fault frequencies found in many industrial inspection tasks, but far higher than rates observed in the performance of reliable aircraft, chemical plants, or automated systems, in which defects occur at intervals of weeks or months. This difference in signal frequency may well interact with differences in motivational factors between the subject in the laboratory, performing a well-defined task and responsible only for its performance, and the real-time system operator confronted with a number of other competing activities and a level of motivation potentially influenced by large costs and benefits. This motivation level may be either lower or far higher than those of the laboratory subjects, but it will probably not be the same.

These differences do not mean that the laboratory data should be discounted. The basic variables causing vigilance performance to improve or deteriorate that have been uncovered in the laboratory should still affect detection performance in the real world, although the effect may be attenuated or enhanced. Data have been collected in real or highly simulated environments: in process control (Crowe, Beare, Kozinsky, & Hass, 1983; Lees and Sayers, 1976), in maritime ship navigation monitoring (Schmidke, 1976), and in aviation (Molloy & Parasuraman, 1996; Ruffle-Smith, 1979), and many of the same vigilance phenomena occurring in the laboratory occur in the real world. For example, Pigeau, Angus, O'Neill, and Mack (1995) found a sensitivity decrement with NORAD operators detecting the presence of aircraft entering Canadian airspace. These results show that vigilance effects can occur in real-world situations. It should also be noted that there is increasing implementation of automation in many work environments, and since perfectly reliable automated systems have not yet been developed, the vigilance task is becoming more commonplace in many work domains in the form of monitoring an automated system (Parasuraman & Riley, 1997; see Chapter 13).

INFORMATION THEORY

The Quantification of Information

The discussion of signal detection theory was our first direct encounter with the human operator as a transmitter of information: An event (signal) occurs in the environment; the human perceives it and transmits this information to a response. Indeed, a considerable portion of human performance theory revolves around the concept of transmitting information. In any situation when the human operator either perceives changing environmental events or responds to events that have been perceived, the operator is encoding or transmitting information. The van driver in our Chapter 1 example must process visual signals from the in-vehicle map display, from traffic signs, from other vehicles, as well as process auditory signals (e.g., the truck horn). A fundamental issue in engineering psychology is how to quantify this flow of information so that different tasks confronting the human operator can be compared. Using information theory, we can measure task difficulty by determining the rate at which information is presented. We can also measure processing efficiency, using the amount of information an operator processes per unit of time. Information theory, therefore, provides metrics to compare human performance across a wide number of different tasks.

Information is potentially available in a stimulus any time there is some uncertainty about what the stimulus will be. How much information a stimulus delivers depends in part on the number of possible events that could occur in that context. If the same stimulus occurs on every trial, its occurrence conveys no information. If two stimuli (events) are equally likely, the amount of information conveyed by one of them when it occurs, expressed in *bits*, is simply equal to the base 2 logarithm of this number, for example, with two events, $\log_2 2 = 1$ bit. If there were four alternatives, the information conveyed by the occurrence of one of them would be $\log_2 4 = 2$ bits.

Formally, information is defined as the *reduction of uncertainty* (Shannon & Weaver, 1949). Before the occurrence of an event, you are less sure of the state of the world (you possess more uncertainty) than after. When the event occurs, it has conveyed information to you, unless it is entirely expected. The statement "Mexico declared war on the United States this morning" conveys quite a bit of information. Your knowledge and understanding of the world are probably quite different after hearing the statement than they were before. On the other hand, the statement "The sun rose this morning" conveys little information because you could anticipate the event before it occurred. Information theory formally quantifies the amount of information conveyed by a statement, stimulus, or event. This quantification is influenced by three variables:

1. The number of possible events that could occur, N

2. The probabilities of those events
3. The events' sequential constraints, or the context in which they occur.

We will now describe how each of these three variables influences the amount of information conveyed by an event.

Number of Events   Before the occurrence of an event (which conveys information), a person has a state of knowledge that is characterized by uncertainty about some aspect of the world. After the event, that uncertainty is normally less. The amount of uncertainty reduced by the event is defined to be the average minimum number of true-false questions that would have to be asked to reduce the uncertainty. For example, the information conveyed by the statement "Clinton won" after the 1996 election is 1 bit because the answer to one true-false question—"Did Clinton win?" (True) or "Did Dole win?" (False)—is sufficient to reduce the previous uncertainty. If, on the other hand, there were four major candidates, all running for office, two questions would have to be answered to eliminate uncertainty. In this case, one question might be "Was the winner from the liberal (or conservative) pair?" After this question was answered, a second question would be "Was the winner the more conservative (or liberal) member of the pair?" Thus, if you were simply told the winner, that statement would formally convey 2 bits of information. This question-asking procedure assumes that all alternatives are equally likely to occur. Formally, then, when all alternatives are equally likely, the information conveyed by an event H_s, in bits, can be expressed by the formula

$$H_s = \log_2 N \qquad (2.5)$$

where N is the number of equally likely alternatives.

Because information theory is based on the minimum number of questions and therefore arrives at a solution in a minimum time, it has a quality of optimal performance. It is this optimal aspect that makes the theory attractive in its applications to human performance.

Probability   Real-world events do not always occur with equal frequency or likelihood. If you lived in the Arizona desert, much more information would be conveyed by the statement "It is raining" than the statement "It is sunny." Your certainty of the state of the world is changed very little by knowing that it is sunny, but it is changed quite a bit (uncertainty is reduced) by hearing of the low-probability event of rain. In the example of the four election candidates, less information would be gained by learning that the favored candidate won than by learning that the Socialist Worker or Libertarian candidate won. The probabilistic element of information is quantified by making rare events convey more bits. This in turn is accomplished by revising Equation 2.5 for the information conveyed by event i to be

$$H_s = \log_2\left(\frac{1}{P_i}\right) \qquad (2.6)$$

where P_i is the probability of occurrence of event i. This formula increases H for low-probability events. Note that if N events are equally likely, each event will occur with probability $1/N$. In this case, Equations 2.5 and 2.6 are equivalent.

As noted, information theory is based on a prescription of optimal behavior. This optimum can be prescribed in terms of the order in which the true-false questions should be asked. If some events are more common or expected than others, we should ask the question about the common event first. In our four-candidate example, we will do the best (ask the minimum number of questions on the average) by first asking "Is the winner Clinton?" or "Is the winner Dole?" assuming that Clinton and Dole have the highest probability of winning. If instead the initial question was "Is the winner an independent?" or "Is the winner from one of the minor parties?" we have clearly "wasted" a question, since the answer is likely to be no, and our uncertainty would be reduced by only a small amount.

The information conveyed by a single event of known probability is given by Equation 2.6. However, psychologists are often more interested in measuring the *average* information conveyed by a series of events with differing probabilities that occur over time—for example, a series of warning lights on a panel or a series of communication commands. In this case the average information conveyed is computed as

$$H_{\text{ave}} = \sum_{i=1}^{n} P_i \left[\log_2 \left(\frac{1}{P_i} \right) \right] \tag{2.7}$$

In this formula, the quantity within the square brackets is the information per event as given in Equation 2.6. This value is now weighted by the probability of that event, and these weighted information values are summed across all events. Accordingly, frequent low-information events will contribute heavily to this average, whereas rare high-information events will not. If the events are equally likely, this formula will reduce to Equation 2.5.

An important characteristic of Equation 2.7 is that if the events are not equally likely, H_{ave} will be less than its value if the same events are equally probable. For example, consider four events, A, B, C, and D, with probabilities of 0.5, 0.25, 0.125, and 0.125. The computation of the average information conveyed by each event in a series of such events would proceed as follows:

Event	A	B	C	D
P_i	0.5	0.25	0.125	0.125
$\dfrac{1}{P_i}$	2	4	8	8
$\log_2 \dfrac{1}{P_i}$	1	2	3	3
$\sum P_i \left[\log_2 \dfrac{1}{P_i} \right] =$	0.5 +	0.5 +	0.375 +	0.375 = 1.75 bits

This value is less than $\log_2 4 = 2$ bits, which is the value derived from Equation 2.5 when the four events are equally likely. In short, low-probability events convey more information because they occur infrequently. However, the fact that low-probability events are infrequent causes their high-information content to contribute less to the average.

Sequential Constraints and Context   In the preceding discussion, probability has been used to reflect the long-term frequencies, or *steady-state* expectancies, of events will occur. However, there is a third contributor to information that reflects the short-term sequences of events, or their transient expectancies. A particular event may occur rarely in terms of its absolute frequency. However, given a particular *context*, it may be highly expected, and therefore its occurrence conveys very little information in that context. In the example of rainfall in Arizona, we saw that the absolute probability of rain is low. But if we heard that there was a large front moving eastward from California, our expectance of rain, given this information, would be higher. That is, information can be reduced by the context in which it appears. As another example, the letter *u* in the alphabet is not terribly common and therefore normally conveys quite a bit of information when it occurs; however, in the context of a preceding *q,* it is almost totally predictable and therefore its information content, given that context, is nearly 0 bits.

Contextual information is frequently provided by *sequential constraints* on a series of events. In the series of events ABABABABAB, for example, P(*A*) = P(*B*) = 0.5. Therefore, according to Equation 2.7, each event conveys 1 bit of information. But the next letter in the sequence is almost certainly an *A*. Therefore, the sequential constraints reduce the information the same way a change in event probabilities reduces information from the equiprobable case. Formally, the information provided by an event, given a context, may be computed in the same manner as in Equation 2.6, except that the absolute probability of the event P_i is now replaced by a *contingent* probability $P_i | X$ (the probability of event *i* given context *X*).

Redundancy   In summary, three variables influence the amount of information that a series of events can convey. The number of possible events, *N*, sets an upper bound on the maximum number of bits if all events are equally likely. Making event probabilities unequal and increasing sequential constraints both serve to reduce information from this maximum. The term *redundancy* formally defines this potential loss in information. Thus, for example, the English language is highly redundant because of two factors: All letters are not equiprobable (*e* vs. *x*), and sequential constraints such as those found in common digraphs like *qu, ed, th,* or *nt* reduce uncertainty.

Formally, the *percent redundancy* of a stimulus set is quantified by the formula

$$\% \text{ redundancy} = \left(1 - \frac{H_{\text{ave}}}{H_{\text{max}}}\right) \times 100 \tag{2.8}$$

where H_{ave} is the actual average information conveyed taking into account all three variables (approximately 1.5 bits per letters for the alphabet) and H_{max} is the maximum possible information that would be conveyed by the *N* alternatives if they were equally likely ($\log_2 26 = 4.7$ bits for the alphabet). Thus, the redundancy of the English language is $(1 - 1.5/4.7) \times 100 = 68$ percent. Wh-t th-s sug-est- is t-at ma-y of t-e le-ter- ar- not ne-ess-ry fo- com-reh-nsi-n. However, to stress a point that will be emphasized in Chapter 5, this does not negate the value of redundancy in many circumstances. We have seen already in our discussion of vigilance that redundancy gain can improve performance when perceptual judgments are difficult. At the end of this chapter, we will see its value in absolute judgment tasks.

Information Transmission of Discrete Signals

In much of human performance theory, investigators are concerned not only with how much information is *presented* to an operator but also with how much is *transmitted* from stimulus to response, the *channel capacity*, and how rapidly it is transmitted, the *bandwidth*. Using these concepts, the human being is sometimes represented as an information channel, an example of which is shown in Figure 2.9. Consider the typist typing up some handwritten comments. First, information is present in the stimuli (the handwritten letters). This value of stimulus information, H_S, can be computed by the procedures described, taking into account probabilities of different letters and their sequential constraints. Second, each response on the keyboard is an event, and so we can also compute response information, H_R, in the same manner. Finally, we ask if each letter on the page was appropriately typed on the keyboard. That is, was the information faithfully transmitted, H_T. If it was not, there are two types of mistakes: First, information in the stimulus could be lost, H_L, which would be the case if a certain letter was not typed. Second, letters may be typed that were not in the original text. This is referred to as *noise*. Figure 2.9a illustrates the relationship among these five information measures. Notice that it is theoretically possible to have a high value of both H_S and H_R but to have H_T equal to zero. This result would occur if the typist were totally ignoring the printed text, creating his or her own message. A schematic example is shown in Figure 2.9b.

We will now compute H_T in the context of a four-alternative stimulus-response reaction-time task rather than the more complex typing task. In this task, the subject is confronted by four possible events, any of which may appear with equal probability, and must make a corresponding response for each.

For the ideal information transmitter, $H_S = H_T = H_R$. In optimal performance of the reaction-time task, for example, each stimulus (conveying 2 bits of information if equiprobable) should be processed ($H_S = 2$ bits) and should trigger the appropriate response ($H_R = 2$ bits). As we saw, in information-transmitting systems, this ideal state is rarely obtained because of the occurrence of equivocation and noise.

The computation of H_T is performed by setting up a stimulus-response matrix, such as that shown in Figure 2.10, and converting the various numerical entries into three sets of probabilities: the probabilities of events, shown along the bottom row; the prob-

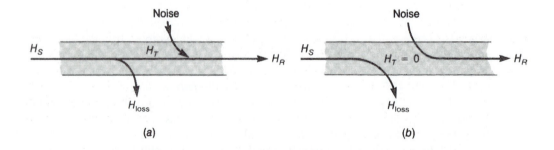

Figure 2.9   Information transmission and the channel concept: (*a*) information transmitted through the system; (*b*) no information transmitted.

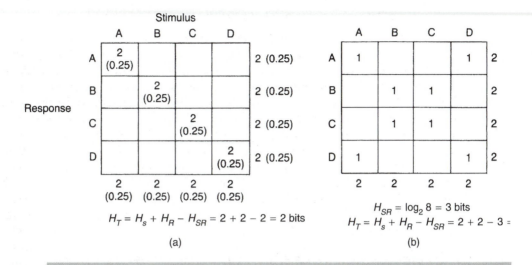

Figure 2.10   Two examples of the calculation of information transmission.

abilities of responses, shown along the right column; and the probabilities of a given stimulus-response pairing. These latter values are the probability that an entry will fall in each filled cell, where a cell is defined jointly by a particular stimulus and a particular response. In Figure 2.10a, there are four filled cells, with P = 0.25 for each entry. Each of these sets of probabilities can be independently converted into the information measures by Equation 2.7.

Once the quantities H_S, H_R, and H_{SR} are calculated, the formula

$$H_T = H_S + H_R - H_{SR} \tag{2.9}$$

allows us to compute the information transmitted. The rationale for the formula is as follows: The variable H_S establishes the maximum possible transmission for a given set of events and so contributes positively to the formula. Likewise, H_R contributes positively. However, to guard against situations such as that depicted in Figure 2.9b, in which events are not coherently paired with responses, H_{SR}, a measure of the dispersion or lack of organization within the matrix, is subtracted. If each stimulus generates consistently only one response (Figure 2.10a), the entries in the matrix should equal the entries in the rows and columns. In this case, $H_S = H_R = H_{SR}$, which means that by substituting the values in Equation 2.9, $H_S = H_T$. However, if there is greater dispersion within the matrix, there are more bits within H_{SR}. In Figure 2.10b, this is shown by eight equally probable stimulus-response pairs, or 3 bits of information in H_{SR}. Therefore, $H_{SR} > H_S$ and $H_T < H_S$. The relation between these quantities is shown in a Venn diagram in Figure 2.11.

Often the investigator may be interested in an information transmission *rate* expressed in bits/second rather than the quantity H_T expressed in bits. To find this rate, H_T is computed over a series of stimulus events, along with the average time for each transmission (i.e., the mean reaction time, RT). Then the ratio H_T/RT is taken to derive a measure of the

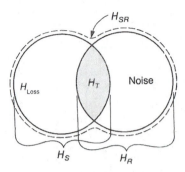

Figure 2.11   Information transmission represented in terms of Venn diagrams.

bandwidth of the communication system in bits/second. This is a useful metric because it represents processing efficiency by taking into account both speed and accuracy, and it allows comparison of efficiencies across tasks. For example, measures of processing efficiency can be obtained for typing or monitoring tasks, and the bandwidths can be compared.

Conclusion

In conclusion, it should be noted that information theory has its clear benefits —it provides a single combined measure of speed and accuracy that is generalizable across tasks—but it also has its limitations (see Wickens, 1984). In particular, H_T measures only whether responses are consistently associated with events, not whether they are *correctly* associated, and the measure does not take into account the magnitude of an error. Sometimes larger errors are more serious, such as when the stimulus and response scales lie along a continuum (e.g., driving a car on a windy road, tracking a moving target). Information theory can also be applied to such continuous tasks, and Wickens (1992) describes methods for doing this. However, an alternative is to use either a correlation coefficient or some measure of the integrated error across time, as discussed in Chapter 10. Further discussion of H_T and its relation to measures of d' and percentage correct can be found in Wickens (1984).

ABSOLUTE JUDGMENT

The human senses, although not perfect, are still relatively keen when contrasted with the detection resolution of machines. In this light, it is somewhat surprising that the limits of *absolute judgment*—in which an observer assigns a stimulus into one of multiple categories along a sensory dimension—are relatively severe. This is the task, for example, that confronts an inspector of wool quality who must categorize a given specimen into one of several quality levels; or our van driver who must interpret and recognize the color of a display symbol appearing on his map display. Our discussion of absolute judgment will first describe performance when stimuli vary on only a single physical dimension. We will then consider absolute judgment along two or more physical dimensions that are perceived simultaneously and discuss the implications of these findings to principles of display coding.

Single Dimensions

Experimental Results   For a typical absolute judgment experiment, a stimulus continuum (e.g., tone pitch, light intensity, or texture roughness) and a number of discrete levels of the continuum (e.g., four tones of different frequencies) are selected. These stimuli are then presented randomly to the subject one at a time, and the subject is asked to associate a different response to each one. For example, the four tones might be called A, B, C, and D. The extent to which each response matched the presented stimulus can then be assessed. When four discriminable stimuli (2 bits) are presented, transmission (H_T) is usually perfect—at 2 bits. Then the stimulus set is enlarged, and additional data are also collected with five, six, seven, and more discrete stimulus levels, and H_T is computed each time by using the procedures described in the preceding section. Typically, the results indicate that errors begin to be made when about five to six stimuli are used, and the error rate increases as the number of stimuli increase further. These results indicate that the larger stimulus sets have somehow saturated the subject's capacity to transmit information about the magnitude of the stimulus. We say the subject has a maximum *channel capacity*.

Graphically, these data can be represented in Figure 2.12, in which the actual information transmitted (H_T) is plotted as a function of the number of absolute judgment stimulus alternatives (expressed in informational terms as H_S). The 45-degree slope of the dashed line indicates perfect information transmission, and the "leveling" of the function takes place at the region in which errors began to occur (i.e., $H_T < H_S$) The level of the flat part or asymptote of the function indicates the channel capacity of the operator: somewhere between 2 and 3 bits. George Miller (1956), in a classic paper entitled "The Magical Number Seven Plus or Minus Two," noted the similarity of the asymptote level across a number of different absolute judgment functions with different

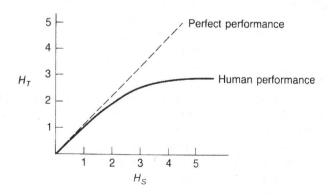

Figure 2.12   Typical human performance in absolute judgment tasks.

sensory continua. Miller concluded that the limits of absolute judgment at 7 ± 2 stimulus categories (2–3 bits) is fairly general. This limit does, however, vary somewhat from one stimulus continuum to another; it is less than 2 bits for saltiness of taste and about 3.4 bits for judgments of position on a line. Nonetheless, there are clear capacity limitations for the absolute judgment of sensory stimuli.

The level of the asymptote does not appear to reflect a basic limit in sensory resolution, for two reasons. First, the senses are extremely keen in their ability to make discriminations between two stimuli ("Are they the same or different?"). For example, the number of adjacent stimulus pairs that a human can accurately discriminate on the sensory continuum of tone pitch is roughly 1,800 (Mowbray & Gebhard, 1961). Second, Pollack (1952) has observed that the limits of absolute judgment are little affected by whether the stimuli are closely spaced on the physical continuum or widely dispersed. Conversely, sensory discrimination of stimuli is clearly affected by stimulus spacing. Hence, the limit is not sensory but is in the accuracy of the subject's memory for the representation of the four to eight different standards (Siegel & Siegel, 1972).

If, in fact, absolute judgment limitations are related to memory, there should be some association between this phenomenon and difference in learning or experience, since differences in memory are closely related to those of learning. It is noteworthy that sensory continua for which we demonstrate good absolute judgments are those for which such judgments in real-world experience occur relatively often. For example, judgments of position along a line (3.4 bits) are made in measurements on rulers, and judgments of angle (4.3 bits) are made in telling the time from analog clocks. High performance in absolute judgment also seems to be correlated with professional experience with a particular sensory continuum in industrial tasks (Welford, 1968) and is demonstrated by the noteworthy association of absolute pitch with skilled musicians (Carroll, 1975; Klein, Coles, & Donchin, 1984; Siegel & Siegel, 1972).

Many attempts to model performance in absolute judgment tasks are similar to signal detection theory (see Luce, 1994; Shiffrin & Nosofsky, 1994), extending it to situations where there are more than two stimulus possibilities. In these approaches, each stimulus is assumed to give rise to a distribution of "perceptual effects" along the unidimensional continuum, an approach initially developed by Torgerson (1958). The observer partitions the continuum into response regions using a set of decision criteria, instead of the one criterion used in the simple signal detection situation. If the variance of these distributions increased with the number of stimuli, it would be more difficult to absolutely identify each stimulus. That is, as the number of stimuli increases, sensitivity (our ability to accurately determine which stimulus we are perceiving) decreases. Such models (e.g., Braida et al., 1984; Luce, Green, and Weber, 1976) can account for edge effects as well: stimuli located in the middle of the range of presented stimuli are generally identified with poorer accuracy than those at extremes (Shiffrin & Nosofsky, 1994). The *edge effect* appears to be due to lowered sensitivity for stimuli in the middle of the range, and not simply response bias or factors related to fewer response choices at the extremes (Shiffrin & Nosofsky, 1994).

Applications   The conclusions drawn from research in absolute judgment are relevant to the performance of any task that requires operators to sort stimuli into levels along a physical continuum, particularly for industrial inspection tasks in which products must be sorted into various levels for pricing or marketing (e.g., fruit quality) or for different uses (e.g., steel or glass quality). The data from the absolute judgment paradigm indicate the kind of performance limits that can be anticipated and suggest the potential role of training. Edge effects suggest that inspection accuracy should be better for extreme stimuli. One potential method for improving performance would be to have different inspectors sort different levels of the dimension in question. This would lead to different extreme stimulus categories for each inspector, thereby creating more "edges" where absolute judgment performance is superior. The method remains untested, however.

Absolute judgment data are also relevant to *coding*, where the level of a stimulus dimension is assigned a particular meaning, and the operator must judge that meaning. For example, computer monitors can display a very large range of colors (e.g., 64,000 levels) and software designers are sometimes tempted to use the large available range to code variables. However, it is clear that people cannot correctly classify colors beyond about seven levels, so coding a variable in terms of color cannot be accurately processed by the user (see Chapter 3). In general, basic data on the number and conceptual categories that can be employed without error are relevant to the development of display codes.

Moses, Maisano, and Bersh (1979) have cautioned that a conceptual continuum should not be arbitrarily assigned to a physical dimension. They have argued that some conceptual continua have a more "natural" association or compatibility with some physical display dimensions than with others. The designers of codes should be wary of the potential deficiencies (decreased accuracy, increased latency) imposed by an arbitrary or incompatible assignment. For example, Moses, Maisano, and Bersh suggest that the representation of danger and unit size should be coded by the color and size of a displayed object, respectively, and not the reverse. (The issue of display compatibility will receive more discussion in Chapters 3, 4, and 5.)

Multidimensional Judgment

If our limits of absolute judgment are severe and can only be overcome by extensive training, how is it that we can recognize stimuli in the environment so readily? A major reason is that most of our recognition is based on the identification of some combination of two or more stimulus dimensions rather than levels along a single dimension. When a stimulus can vary on two (or more) dimensions at once, we make an important distinction between *orthogonal* and *correlated dimensions*. When dimensions of a stimulus are orthogonal, the level of the stimulus on one dimension can take on any value, independent of the other—for example, the weight and hair color of an individual. When dimensions are correlated, the level on one constrains the level on another—for example, height and weight, since tall people tend to weigh more than short ones.

Orthogonal Dimensions   The importance of multidimensional stimuli in increasing the total amount of information transmitted in absolute judgment has been repeatedly demonstrated (Garner, 1974). For instance, Egeth and Pachella (1969) demonstrated that subjects could correctly classify only 10 levels of dot position on a line (3.4 bits of information). However, when two lines were combined into a square, so that subjects classified the spatial position of a dot in the square, subjects could correctly classify 57 levels (5.8 bits). Note, however, that this improvement does not represent a perfect addition of channel capacity along the two dimensions. If processing along each dimension were independent and unaffected by the other, the predicted amount of information transmitted would be $3.4 + 3.4 = 6.8$ bits, or around 100 positions (10×10) in the square.

Egeth and Pachella's results suggest that there is some loss of information along each dimension resulting from the requirement to transmit information along the other.

Going beyond the two-dimensional case, Pollack and Ficks (1954) combined six dimensions of an auditory stimulus (e.g., loudness, pitch) orthogonally. As each successive dimension was added, subjects showed a continuous gain in total information transmitted but a loss of information transmitted per dimension. These relations are shown in Figure 2.13a, with seven bits the maximum capacity. The reason people with absolute pitch are superior to those without does not lie in greater discrimination along a single continuum. Rather, those with absolute pitch make their judgments along two dimensions: the pitch of the octave and the value of a note within the octave. They have created a multidimensional stimulus from a stimulus that others treat as unidimensional (Carroll, 1975; Shepard, 1982; Shiffrin & Nosofsky, 1994).

Correlated Dimensions   The previous discussion and the data shown in Figure 2.13a suggest that combining stimulus dimensions orthogonally leads to a loss in information transmitted. As noted, however, dimensions can be combined in a correlated or redundant fashion. For example, the position and color of an illuminated traffic light are redundant dimensions. When the top light is illuminated, it is always red. In this case, H_S, the information in the stimulus, is no longer the sum of H_S across dimensions since this sum is reduced by redundancy between levels on the two dimensions. If the correlation is 1, as with the traffic light, total H_S is just the H_S on any single dimension (since other dimensions are completely redundant). Thus, the maximum possible H_S for all dimensions in combination is less than its value would be in the orthogonal case. However, Eriksen and Hake (1955) found that by progressively combining more dimensions redundantly, the information loss ($H_S - H_T$) is much less for a given value of H_S than it is when they are combined orthogonally, and the information transmitted (H_T) is greater than it would be along any single dimension. As illustrated in Figure 2.13b, H_S represents a limit on

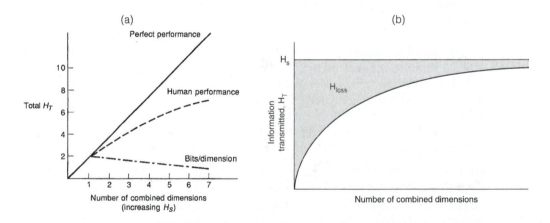

Figure 2.13   Human performance in absolute judgment of multidimensional auditory stimuli. (a) Orthogonal dimensions. As more dimensions are added, more total information is transmitted, but less information is transmitted per dimension. (b) Correlated dimensions. As more dimensions are added, the security of the channel improves, but H_S limits the amount of information that can be transmitted.

information transmitted with correlated dimensions, and as the number of redundant or correlated dimensions increases, H_T will approach that limit.

It should be noted that the value of the correlation between redundant dimensions can range from 0 to 1. Such correlation may result from natural variation in the stimulus material (e.g., height and weight of a person, or perhaps hue and brightness of a tomato). Alternatively, it may result from artificially imposed constraints by the designer, in which case the correlation is usually 1, indicating complete redundancy (e.g., color and location in traffic lights).

In summary, we can see that orthogonal and correlated dimensions accomplish two different objectives in absolute judgment of multidimensional stimuli. Orthogonal dimensions maximize H_T, the *efficiency* of the channel. Correlated dimensions minimize H_{loss}; that is, they maximize the *security* of the channel.

Dimensional Relations: Integral, Separable, and Configurable. Orthogonal or correlated dimensions refer to properties of the information conveyed by a multidimensional stimulus, and not the physical form of the stimulus. However, combining dimensions in multidimensional absolute judgment tasks has different effects, depending on the nature of the physical relationship between the two dimensions. In particular, Garner (1974) made the important distinction between an *integral* and a *separable* pair of physical dimensions. Separable dimensions are defined when the levels along each of the two dimensions can be specified without requiring the specification of the level along the other. For example, the length of the horizontal and vertical lines radiating from the dot in Figure 2.14a are two separable dimensions; each can be specified without specifying the other. For integral dimensions, this independence is impossible. The height and width of a single rectangle are integral because to display the height of a rectangle, the width must be specified; otherwise, it would not be a rectangle (Figure 2.14b). Correspondingly, the color and brightness of an object are integral dimensions. Color cannot be

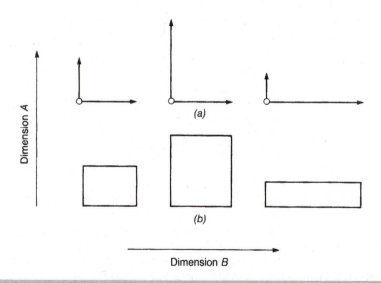

Figure 2.14   (*a*) Separable dimensions (height and width of a line segment); (*b*) integral dimensions (height and width of a rectangle). Dimension *A* is height; dimension *B* is width.

physically represented without some level of brightness. Hence, integral and separable pairs differ in the degree to which the two dimensions can be independently specified.

To reveal the different implications on human performance of integral versus separable dimensional pairs, experiments are performed in which subjects categorize different levels of one dimension for a set of stimuli. In the *one-dimensional control condition*, subjects would sort on one varying dimension while the other dimension is held constant. In the stimulus example in Figure 2.14b, they might sort the rectangles by height while the width remained constant. In the *orthogonal condition*, they sort on one varying dimension while ignoring variation in the other dimension. Thus, as in Figure 2.14b, they might sort rectangle heights as the rectangle widths vary, even though the width is irrelevant to their task and hence should be ignored. Finally, in the *correlated (redundant) condition*, the two dimensions are perfectly correlated. An example would be sorting rectangles whose height and width are perfectly correlated. Thus, the rectangles would all be of the same shape but would vary in size.

An experiment by Garner and Felfoldy (1970) revealed that sorting with integral dimensions (e.g., rectangles), helped performance in the correlated condition (relative to the control condition), but hurt performance in the orthogonal condition. In the context of our discussion in Chapter 3, we refer to the latter as a failure of focused attention. In contrast, when sorting with separable dimensions (the stimuli in Figure 2.14a), performance is little helped by redundancy and little hurt by the orthogonal variation of the irrelevant dimension. These differences between integral and separable dimensions are observed no matter whether performance is measured by accuracy (i.e., H_T), when several levels of each dimension are used, or by speed, when only two levels of each dimension are used and accuracy is nearly perfect. Table 2.2 lists examples of integral and separable pairs of dimensions, as determined by Garner's classification methodology.

For example, as Table 2.2 indicates, pitch and loudness have been shown to be integral dimensions (Grau & Kemler-Nelson, 1988; Melara & Marks, 1990). Thus, changes in the pitch of a warning signal will affect how loud it appears to be, and vice versa. In contrast, Dutta and Nairne (1993) found that spatial location and temporal order are separable dimensions: that is, when subjects had to remember which of two stimuli (a circle or square) occurred first, they were not affected by variation in the location (top-bottom) of the stimuli, and vice versa. This suggests that for dynamic data displays (e.g., in a dynamic map display, or on a radar screen), changing the location of a symbol or display element should not affect judgments concerning whether it appeared before or after another symbol. A radar monitor remembering the position of two aircraft each coded by a symbol on a radar screen should not be affected by differences in which one appeared on the radar screen first. It also suggests that differences in the time when two symbols appeared on the screen should not affect judgments of relative location of the two symbols. For example, a radar operator's judgment of which aircraft appeared first on the radar screen should not be affected by the relative location of the two aircraft.

Traditionally, only two levels of the irrelevant dimension have been tested in speeded classification. Using more than two levels allows an understanding of the relationship between the number of levels of the irrelevant dimensions on interference. It also allows us to examine the effects of the spacing of the levels (are the levels far apart, or close together) on interference. Melara and Mounts (1994) found that increased spacing on the irrelevant dimension increased interference in the orthogonal sort. They also found that increasing the number of levels reduced interference, a counterintuitive result. The

TABLE 2.2 Pairs of Integral and Seperable Dimensions

Integral Dimensions		*Separable Dimensions*	
height of rectangle	width of rectangle	height	width
lightness	color, saturation	size (area)	color, saturation
hue	color,saturation	size (area)	brightness
pitch	timbre	shape	color, saturation
pitch	loudness	shape (& letter shape)	color
		duration	location
		orientation (angle)	size
		spatial location	temporal order

result might be better understood by realizing that the levels of the unattended dimension become less distinct when there are more of them.

Problems for the Integral-Separable Distinction   Despite the general trends noted above, there are some problems with the integral-separable distinction. It is unclear exactly what makes dimensions integral or separable (Carswell & Wickens, 1990; Cheng & Pachella, 1984), and the two symptoms of integrality (redundancy gain and orthogonal cost) do not always co-occur. It appears that there is a continuum of integrality, with some dimensional pairs being clearly integral (hue and brightness), others somewhat so (height and width of a rectangle), others fairly separable (color and shape of a geometric figure), and others clearly separable (the height of two parallel bar graphs). There are also other methods for establishing whether dimensions are integral or separable (e.g., multidimensional scaling) and the results for all methods do not always produce the same result, because different methods are biased towards different outcomes (see Kemler-Nelson, 1993, for a discussion). The fact that the concept of integrality is not absolute, with two categories (integral and separable), but is rather defined along a continuum does not diminish its importance. However, it is also important to consider two qualifications to the general principles of separability and integrality.

The first qualification is that some combinations of dimensions are *asymmetric*. That is, variation in Dimension A affects Dimension B, but the reverse does not hold true. For example, Shechter and Hochstein (1992) found that variation in position or width of bar stimuli affected judgments of contrast, but judgments of position and width were not affected by variation in contrast. Hollands and Spence (1997) found similar relations between the overall size or scaling of a stacked bar graph and the size of the proportion shown within the graph. Variation in scaling affected perception of proportion, but the reverse did not hold true. Garner (1974) has noted similar results with other stimuli (e.g., pitch and phoneme). He noted that stimuli that combine in this asymmetric manner may have certain hierarchical properties, with one dimension being more fundamental than the other. For example, a phoneme must have a pitch, but pitch can exist as a dimension without any linguistic properties. Similar claims can be made for the dimensions examined by Hollands and Spence, and Shechter and Hochstein.

The second qualification—really an elaboration—concerns correlated dimensions, such as the rectangles of varying shape shown in Figure 2.14. When dimensions are separable, like the color and shape of a symbol, it matters little which level of one dimension is paired with which level of the other (e.g., whether the red symbol is a square and the blue symbol is a circle, or vice versa). For integral dimensions, however, the pairing often does make a difference. For example, when the height and width of rectangles are positively correlated, creating rectangles of constant shape and different size, performance is not as good as if the dimensions are negatively correlated, such as those shown in Figure 2.14, creating rectangles of different shapes (Lockhead & King, 1977; Weintraub, 1971). Pairs of dimensions for which the pairing of particular levels makes a difference are referred to as *configurable* (Carswell & Wickens, 1990; Pomerantz & Pristach, 1989) or *congruent* (Melara & Marks, 1990). Pomerantz (1981) has referred to the *emergent properties* that can be produced when configurable dimensions are combined. These emergent properties, or *emergent features*, like the shape and size of a rectangle, will have important implications for object displays (to be discussed in Chapter 3).

A Theoretical Understanding   General Recognition Theory (GRT), a model proposed by Ashby and coworkers (Ashby & Lee, 1991, Ashby & Maddox, 1994; Maddox & Ashby, 1996) has attempted to model the mechanisms that might lead to interference and facilitation in the speeded classification task. GRT is based on signal detection theory and generalizes the signal detection theory concepts to situations where stimuli vary on more than one physical dimension. Imagine that you are a food inspector examining tomatoes on two criteria: size and color saturation (a light red versus a deep, rich red). According to GRT, a particular stimulus generates a point in multidimensional space. A small, light-red tomato would occupy a point in a two-dimensional space, where the two dimensions are size and color saturation. Like signal detection theory, GRT assumes that repeated presentations of the same stimulus lead to different amounts of neural activity. Hence, the perceptual effect of a stimulus can be represented by a multivariate probability distribution, which has a three-dimensional, bell-like shape. Although this could be represented as a three-dimensional figure, it is simpler to draw as if viewed from above, as shown by each circle in Figure 2.15. The diameter of the circle represents the variability of the distribution. The circles in Figure 2.15 could represent 95 percent of the distribution, for example.

Different stimuli produce distributions in different locations, as shown in Figure 2.15a. For example, small, light-red tomatoes produce a distribution of neural activity in the bottom left of Figure 2.15a. Conversely, large, deep-red tomatoes produce a distribution in the upper right of the figure. Note that the vertical positions of the distributions (representing color saturation) are not affected by the level of size, and that the horizontal positions (representing size) are not affected by the level of color saturation. In this case, the dimensions are separable. In contrast, Figure 2.15b shows the integral dimensions of color saturation and lightness. We would expect, therefore, that variations in color saturation affect judgments of lightness, and vice versa. In the GRT model, the vertical position of the distributions (representing color saturation) is affected by the horizontal position (lightness). Varying one dimension affects the perceived level of the other.

In an orthogonal condition, subjects sort on one varying dimension while ignoring variation in the other dimension. Hence the inspector sorting fruits in terms of size and color saturation would maintain a mental representation like that shown in Figure

2.15a. Imagine that the inspector sets a criterion perpendicular to the dimension being judged and uses that criterion to classify the dimension into its levels. For example, in Figure 2.15a, the inspector could call everything to the left of the criterion small, and everything to the right large. The relatively large distance from the center of the distribution to the criterion will produce a quick decision, according to GRT. Note that this distance decreases in Figure 2.15b, where the inspector is now classifying lightness with color saturation varying and a longer sort should result.

An inspector examining the width of wooden pegs commonly shipped with furniture needing assembly, and who notices that the wider pegs are consistently longer, would be well served by attending to both varying dimensions, rather than continuing to sort strictly on width. Maddox and Ashby (1996) have shown that it is possible to obtain facilitation with correlated dimensions even if they are perceptually separable due to changes in decision criteria. In particular, if the inspector considers only one dimension while sorting (peg width), the decision criterion would be the vertical line shown in Figure 2.15c and errors would be likely. However, if the inspector considered both dimensions (peg width and height), the decision criterion would be the diagonal line shown in Figure 2.15c and errors would be likely. Notice how the diagonal orientation maximizes the distance from the line to the centers of the distributions, decreasing error relative to the vertical orientation. Thus, the GRT model explains why our inspector would be more accurate by considering the apparently irrelevant dimension.

This analysis may explain why dimensions that are normally separable can provide redundancy gain (Garner, 1974). For example, auditory and visual signals are clearly separable but offer redundancy gain in a vigilance task, as discussed earlier. In degraded sensory conditions when differences in one dimension, the other, or both are hard to perceive (i.e., the variability of the circles increases, as shown by the dotted circles in Figure 2.15c) it makes sense that the observer would seek to optimize the decision criterion used.

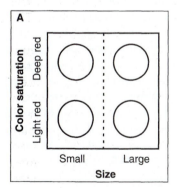
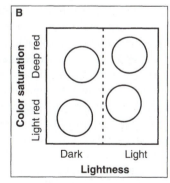
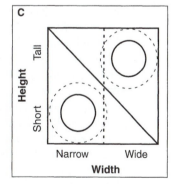

Figure 2.15   Multidimensional stimulus judgment. The size of the circle represents the variability in the perceived value along the dimension. (*a*) Separable dimensions. (*b*) Integral dimensions. Note that a diagonal criterion violates decisional separability. (*c*) A correlated sort. The observer will be faster and more accurate if using the diagonal criterion (violating decisional separability).

Summary   Before we discuss the practical implications of multidimensional absolute judgment, we will briefly summarize the concepts. The information conveyed by a set of stimuli may vary independently on several dimensions at once. If the human operator is asked to classify all of these dimensions, more total information can be transmitted than if stimuli vary on only one dimension, but the information transmitted per dimension will be less (H_{loss} will increase). This loss will increase as more dimensions are varied, although it will not be so great if the dimensions are separable rather than integral.

The information conveyed by stimulus dimensions may also be correlated, which produces a redundancy gain in the speed and accuracy of information transmission; the redundancy gain will be greatest when the dimensions are integral but may also be found with separable dimensions. Finally, stimulus dimensions may combine differently, sometimes configuring to make a new emergent property. If they do, the dimensions are said to be configurable, and performance will differ, depending on which levels of one dimension are paired with which levels of the other. Increasing the number of levels of the unattended dimension reduces interference; increasing the discriminability of levels increases it. The general recognition theory developed by Ashby and coworkers can be used to account for performance in classification tasks. Indeed, it suggests that sorting on correlated dimensions can be speeded by using a multidimensional classification, and it explains why facilitation is seen in a correlated classification task with separated dimensions when the dimensions are hard to perceive.

Implications of Multidimensional Absolute Judgment   As with single dimensions, the implications of multidimensional absolute judgment performance for engineering psychology may fall into two different classes, depending on the nature of the task. In the sorting task, the operator sorts natural stimuli over whose physical form the human factors designer has little control. This may be the industrial inspector who is sorting a manufactured product (e.g., a piece of sheet metal) into categories along some dimension (e.g., shininess). In this task, it is important to realize that the quality of sort will be less if the stimuli vary along some other dimension in addition to the relevant one for sorting and the two dimensions are integral. For example, a poorer sort should result if the inspector is sorting by hue and the sheet metal varies not only in its hue but also in its shininess or texture. Additionally, larger differences between two levels of the unattended dimension (e.g., very shiny vs. matte) will worsen the interference.

Consider however, the situation when levels of dimensions are used for coding purposes. Here, the operator is confronted by an artificial symbol, created on a display by the system designer, which is to be interpreted as representing levels on two or more information dimensions. The meteorologist, for example, will view a weather station symbol on the display. The symbol might represent levels on several ordered dimensions: temperature, humidity, altitude, wind speed, and direction. How should these dimensions be physically represented? Of course, one choice is to represent them digitally. Such a display is good for precise checking of a single-station reading. But if the stations are close together, a cluttered display results. In addition, it is not easy to take a rapid glance at a digitally coded display and visualize all of the stations with a temperature reading of greater than 20 degrees to form a global understanding of the temperature gradient across the map. The task would be much easier if temperature were coded by an analog variable like color saturation. (See also Chapters 3 and 4.)

Given that a choice has been made to code displays by continuous dimensions (rather than digitally), the results of studies in multidimensional absolute judgment become relevant. Is there a correlation between the displayed variables (e.g. higher altitudes are typically associated with colder temperatures)? If so, using integral dimensions should lead to an improvement in performance on each dimension. However, if the correlation is less than perfect (i.e., less than complete redundancy), the ability to read one dimension and ignore differences on the other will be hurt by using integral dimensions. However, interference effects should be minimized if levels of the unattended dimension are not too different, and this could be accomplished by decreasing the range of physical values assumed by a dimension of lesser importance (and therefore more likely to be irrelevant). Alternatively, with interactive computer displays, the range of physical values of each dimension could be user adjustable.

If it is critical to avoid information loss on any particular variable, or the conditions of viewing or hearing are degraded, then completely redundant display coding is the answer. The designer should use two physical dimensions to code changes in one of the represented quantities (e.g., use the height of a bar and its color to represent temperature). The redundancy gain will be greater if the dimensions are integral but will be realized even with separable dimensions. For example, Kopala (1979) found that Air Force pilots were better able to encode information concerning the level of threat of displayed targets when such information was presented redundantly by shape and color than when it was presented by either dimension alone. Traffic lights are also a good example of redundant coding: The position of the light is perfectly correlated with the color. So are auditory warning systems, in which the loudness of the horn will be correlated with its distinct pitch to indicate the seriousness of an alarm condition.

We consider the applied implications of configurable dimensions and emergent properties again in the next chapter.

TRANSITION

In this chapter, we have seen how people classify stimuli into two levels along one dimension, several levels along one dimension, and several levels along several dimensions. In our discussion of the first of these tasks, we saw that signal detection was characterized by the probabilistic element of decisions under uncertainty; this characteristic will be addressed in much more detail in Chapter 8 as we discuss more complex forms of decision making. In our treatment of multidimensional absolute judgment, we saw that more information could be transmitted as dimensions were combined, and indeed, most complex patterns that we encounter and classify in the world are multidimensional. We discuss these elements of pattern recognition in Chapter 6 and the integration of multiple redundant cues in decision making in Chapter 8. Finally, it is apparent that when human operators transmit information along all dimensions of a two-dimensional (or more) stimulus, they must divide attention between the dimensions. When they are asked to process one dimension and ignore changes on the others, they are focusing attention. These concepts of divided and focused attention will be considered in much more detail in the next chapter, where we will consider their broader relevance to the issue of attention to events and objects in the world as well as to the dimensions used in display design.

REFERENCES

Adams, J. A., Humes, J. M., & Stenson, H. H. (1962). Monitoring of complex visual displays III: Effects of repeated sessions on human vigilance. *Human Factors, 4,* 149–158.

Anderson, K. J., & Revelle, W. (1982). Impulsivity, caffeine, and proofreading: A test of the Easterbrook hypothesis. *Journal of Experimental Psychology: Human Perception and Performance, 8,* 614–624.

Ashby, F. G., & Lee, W. W. (1991). Predicting similarity and categorization from identification. *Journal of Experimental Psychology: General, 120,* 150–172.

Ashby, F. G., & Maddox, W. T. (1994). A response time theory of perceptual separability and perceptual integrality in speeded classification. *Journal of Mathematical Psychology, 33,* 423–466.

Baddeley, A. D., & Colquhoun, W. P. (1969). Signal probability and vigilance: A reappraisal of the "signal rate" effect. *British Journal of Psychology, 60,*169–178.

Baker, C. H. (1961). Maintaining the level of vigilance by means of knowledge of results about a secondary vigilance task. *Ergonomics, 4,* 311–316.

Beatty, J., Greenberg, A., Deibler, W. P., & O'Hanlon, J. P. (1974). Operator control of occipital theta rhythm affects performance in a radar monitoring task. *Science, 183,* 871–873.

Becker, A, B., Warm, J. S., Dember, W. N., & Hancock, P. A. (1995). Effects of jet engine noise and performance feedback on perceived workload in a monitoring task. *International Journal of Aviation Psychology, 5,* 49–62.

Bisseret, A. (1981). Application of signal detection theory to decision making in supervisory control. *Ergonomics, 24,* 81–94.

Blake, T., & Baird, J. C. (1980). Finding a needle in a haystack when you've never seen a needle: A human factors analysis of SET I. In G. Corrick, E. Hazeltine, & R. Durst (Eds.), *Proceedings of the 24th annual meeting of the Human Factors Society*. Santa Monica, CA: Human Factors Society.

Braida, L. D., Lim, J. S., Berliner, J. E., Durlach, N. I., Rabinowitz, W. M., & Purks, S. R. (1984). Intensity perception. XIII. Perceptual anchor model of context-coding. *Journal of the Acoustical Society of America, 76,* 722–731.

Broadbent, D. E. (1971). *Decision and stress*. New York: Academic Press.

Broadbent, D. E. & Gregory, M. (1965). Effects of noise and of signal rate upon vigilance as analyzed by means of decision theory. *Human Factors, 7,* 155–162.

Calderia, J. D. (1980). Parametric assumptions of some "nonparametric" measures of sensory efficiency. *Human Factors, 22,* 119–130.

Carroll, J. B. (1975). Speed and accuracy of absolute pitch judgments: Some latter-day results. *The L. L. Thurstone Psychometric Laboratory Research Bulletin*. Chapel Hill: University of North Carolina.

Carswell, C. M., & Wickens, C. D. (1990). The perceptual interaction of graphical attributes: Configurality, stimulus homogeneity, and object integration. *Perception & Psychophysics, 47,* 157–168.

Cheng, P. W., & Pachella, R. G. (1984). A psychophysical approach to dimensional separability. *Cognitive Psychology, 16,* 279–304.

Childs, J. M. (1976). Signal complexity, response complexity, and signal specification in vigilance. *Human Factors, 18,* 149–160.

Colquhoun, W. P. (1975). Evaluation of auditory, visual, and dual-mode displays for prolonged sonar monitoring in repeated sessions. *Human Factors, 17,* 425–437.

Craig, A. (1977). Broadbent and Gregory revisited: Vigilance and statistical decision. *Human Factors, 19,* 25–36.

Craig, A. (1978). Is the vigilance decrement simply a response adjustment towards probability matching? *Human Factors 20, 447–451.*

Craig, A. (1979). Nonparametric measures of sensory efficiency for sustained monitoring tasks. *Human Factors, 21,* 69–78.

Craig, A. (1984). Human engineering, the control of vigilance. In J. S. Warm (Ed.), *Sustained attention in human performance* (pp. 247–291). Chichester, UK: Wiley.

Crowe, D. S., Beare, A. N., Kozinsky, E. J., & Hass, P. M. (1983). *Criteria for safety-related nuclear power plant operator action* (NUREG/CR–3123 ORNL/TM–8626). Oak Ridge, TN: Oak Ridge National Laboratory.

Dardano, J. F. (1962). Relationships of intermittent noise, intersignal interval, and skin conductance to vigilance behavior. *Journal of Applied Psychology, 46,* 106–114.

Davenport, W. G. (1968). Auditory vigilance: The effects of costs and values of signals. *Australian Journal of Psychology, 20,* 213–218.

Davies, D. R., & Parasuraman, R. (1982). *The psychology of vigilance.* London: Academic Press.

Deaton, J. E., & Parasuraman, R. (1988). Effects of task demands and age on vigilance and subjective workload. *Proceedings of the 32d annual meeting of the Human Factors Society* (pp. 1458–1462). Santa Monica, CA: Human Factors Society.

Doll, T. J., & Hanna, T. E. (1989). Enhanced detection with bimodal sonar displays. *Human Factors, 31,* 539–550.

Dutta, A., & Nairne, J. S. (1993). The separability of space and time: Dimensional interaction in the memory trace. *Memory & Cognition, 21,* 440–448.

Egeth, H., & Pachella, R. (1969). Multidimensional stimulus identification. *Perception Psychophysics, 5,* 341–346.

Ellison, K. W., & Buckhout, R. (1981). *Psychology and criminal justice.* New York: Harper & Row.

Eriksen, C. W., & Hake, H. N. (1955). Absolute judgments as a function of stimulus range and number of stimulus and response categories. *Journal of Experimental Psychology, 49,* 323–332.

Fine, B. J., Kobrick, J. L., Lieberman, H. R., Marlowe, B., Riley, R. H., & Tharion, W. J. (1994). Effects of caffeine or diphenhydramine on visual vigilance. *Psychopharmacology, 114,* 233–238.

Fisk, A. D., & Scerbo, M. W. (1987). Automatic and control processing approach to interpreting vigilance performance: A review and reevaluation. *Human Factors, 29,* 653–660.

Fisk, A. D., & Schneider, W. (1981). Controlled and automatic processing during tasks requiring sustained attention. *Human Factors, 23,* 737–750.

Garner, W. R. (1974). *The processing of information and structure.* Hillsdale, NJ: Erlbaum.

Garner, W. R., & Felfoldy, G. L. (1970). Integrality of stimulus dimensions in various types of information processing. *Cognitive Psychology, 1,* 225–241.

Gonzalez, R., Ellsworth, P. C., & Pembroke, M. (1993). Response biases in lineups and showups. *Journal of Personality and Social Psychology, 64,* 525–537.

Grau, J. W., & Kemler-Nelson, D. G. (1988). The distinction between integral and separable dimensions: Evidence for the integrality of pitch and loudness. *Journal of Experimental Psychology: General, 117,* 347–370.

Green, D. M., & Swets, J. A. (1966). *Signal detection theory and psychophysics.* New York: Wiley. (Reprinted 1988, Los Altos, CA: Peninsula)

Harris, D. H., & Chaney, F. D. (1969). *Human factors in quality assurance.* New York: Wiley.

Hollands, J. G., & Spence, I. (1997). Integral and separable dimensions in graph reading. In *Proceedings of the Human Factors and Ergonomics Society 41st Annual Meeting* (pp. 1352–1356). Santa Monica, CA: Human Factors and Ergonomics Society.

Howell, W. C., Johnston, W. A., & Goldstein, I. L. (1966). Complex monitoring and its relation to the classical problem of vigilance. *Organizational Behavior & Human Performance, 1,* 129–150.

Jerison, M. L., Pickett, R. M., & Stenson, H. H. (1965). The elicited observing rate and decision process in vigilance. *Human Factors, 7,* 107–128.

Kelly, M. L. (1955). A study of industrial inspection by the method of paired comparisons. *Psychological Monographs, 69,* (394), 1–16.

Kemler-Nelson, D. G. (1993). Processing integral dimensions: The whole view. *Journal of Experimental Psychology: Human Perception and Performance, 19,* 11–5–1113.

Klein, M., Coles, M. G., & Donchin, E. (1984). People without absolute pitch process tones without producing a P300. *Science, 223,* 1306–1308.

Koelega, H. S., Brinkman, J. A., Hendriks, L., & Verbaten, M. N. (1989). Processing demands, effort, and individual differences in four different vigilance tasks. *Human Factors, 31,* 45–62.

Kopala, C. (1979). The use of color-coded symbols in a highly dense situation display. In C. Bensel (Ed.), *Proceedings of the 23d annual meeting of the Human Factors Society.* Santa Monica, CA: Human Factors Society.

Lees, F. P., & Sayers, B. (1976). The behavior of process monitors under emergency conditions. In T. Sheridan & G. Johannsen (Eds.), *Monitoring behavior and supervisory control.* New York: Plenum.

Lewandowski, L. J., & Kobus, D. A. (1989). Bimodal information processing in sonor performance. *Human Performance, 2,* 73–84.

Lockhead, G. R., & King, M. C. (1977). Classifying integral stimuli. *Journal of Experimental Psychology: Human Perception & Performance, 3,* 436–443.

Loeb, M., & Binford, J. R. (1968). Variation in performance on auditory and visual monitoring tasks as a function of signal and stimulus frequencies. *Perception & Psychophysics, 4,* 361–367.

Loftus, E. F. (1979). *Eyewitness testimony.* Cambridge, MA: Harvard University Press.

Long, C. M., & Waag, W. L. (1981). Limitations and practical applicability of d' and β as measures. *Human Factors, 23,* 283–290.

Luce, R. D. (1994). Thurstone and sensory scaling: Then and now. *Psychological Review, 101,* 271–277.

Luce, R. D., Green, D. M., & Weber, D. L. (1976). Attention bands in absolute identification. *Perception & Psychophysics, 20,* 49–54.

Lusted, L. B. (1971). Signal detectability and medical decision making. *Science, 171,* 1217–1219.

Lusted, L. B. (1976). Clinical decision making. In D. Dombal & J. Grevy (Eds.), *Decision making and medical care.* Amsterdam: North Holland.

Luzzo, J., & Drury, C. G. (1980). An evaluation of blink inspection. *Human Factors, 22,* 201–210.

Mackworth, J. F., & Taylor, M. M. (1963). The d' measure of signal detectability in vigilance-like situations. *Canadian Journal of Psychology, 17,* 302–325.

Mackworth, N. H. (1948). The breakdown of vigilance during prolonged visual search. *Quarterly Journal of Experimental Psychology, 1,* 5–61.

Mackworth, N. H. (1950). Research in the measurement of human performance (MRC Special Report Series No. 268). London: H.M. Stationery Office. (Reprinted in *Selected papers on human factors in the design and use of control systems,* W. Sinaiko, Ed., 1961, New York: Dover)

Macmillan, N. A., & Creelman, C. D. (1991). *Detection theory: A user's guide.* Cambridge, UK: Cambridge University Press.

Maddox, W. T., & Ashby, F. G. (1996). Perceptual separability, decisional separability, and the identification-speeded classification relationship. *Journal of Experimental Psychology: Human Perception and Performance, 22,* 795–817.

Matthews, G. (1996). Signal probability effects on high-workload vigilance tasks. *Psychonomic Bulletin and Review, 3,* 339–343.

Matthews, G., Davies, D. R., & Holley, P. J. (1993). Cognitive predictors of vigilance. *Human Factors, 35,* 3–24.

McGrath, J. J. (1963). Irrelevant stimulation and vigilance performance. In D. M. Buckner & J. J. McGrath (Eds.), *Vigilance: A symposium.* New York: McGraw-Hill.

Melara, R. D., & Marks, L. E. (1990). Interaction among auditory dimensions: Timbre, pitch, and loudness. *Perception & Psychophysics, 48,* 169–178.

Melara, R. D., & Mounts, J. R. W. (1994). Contextual influences on interactive processing: Effects of discriminability, quantity, and uncertainty. *Perception & Psychophysics, 56,* 73–90.

Miller, G. A. (1956). The magical number seven plus or minus two: Some limits on our capacity for processing information. *Psychological Review, 63,* 81–97.

Milosevic, S. (1974). Effect of time and space uncertainty on a vigilance task. *Perception & Psychophysics, 15,* 331–334.

Milosevic, S. (1975). Changes in detection measures and skin resistance during an auditory vigilance task. *Ergonomics, 18,* 1–18.

Molloy, R., & Parasuraman, R. (1996). Monitoring an automated system for a single failure: Vigilance and task complexity effects. *Human Factors, 38,* 311–322.

Moses, F. L., Maisano, R. E., & Bersh, P. (1979). Natural associations between symbols and military information. In C. Bensel (Ed.), *Proceedings of the 23d annual meeting of the Human Factors Society.* Santa Monica, CA: Human Factors Society.

Mowbray, G. H., & Gebhard, J. W. (1961). Man's senses vs. informational channels. In W. Sinaiko (Ed.), *Selected papers on human factors in the design and use of control systems.* New York: Dover.

Nishanian, P., Taylor, J. M. G., Korns, E., Detels, R., Saah, A., & Fahey, J. L. (1987). Significance of quantitative enzyme-liked immunosorbent assay (ELISA) results in evaluation of three ELISAs and Western blot tests for detection of antibodies to human immunodeficiency virus in a high-risk population. *Journal of the American Medical Association, 259,* 2574–2579.

Nolte, L. W,. & Jaarsman, D. (1967). More on the Detection of One of *M* Orthogonal Signals. *Journal of the Acoustical Society of America, 41,* 497–505.

Parasuraman, R. (1979). Memory load and event rate control sensitivity decrements in sustained attention. *Science, 205,* 925–927.

Parasuraman, R. (1985). Detection and identification of abnormalities in chest x-rays: Effects of reader skill, disease prevalence, and reporting standards. In R. E. Eberts & C. G. Eberts (Eds.), *Trends in ergonomics/human factors II* (pp. 59–66). Amsterdam: North-Holland.

Parasuraman, R. (1986). Vigilance, monitoring, and search. In K. Boff, L. Kaufman, & J. Thomas (Eds.), *Handbook of perception and human performance. Vol. 2: Cognitive processes and performance* (pp. 43.1–43.39). New York: Wiley.

Parasuraman, R., & Riley, V. (1997). Humans and automation: Use, misuse, disuse, abuse. *Human Factors, 39,* 230–253.

Parasuraman, R., Warm, J. S., & Dember, W. N. (1987). Vigilance: Taxonomy and utility. In L. S. Mark, J. S. Warm, & R. L. Huston (Eds.), *Ergonomics and human factors* (pp. 11–31). New York: Springer-Verlag.

Peterson, C. R., & Beach, L. R. (1967). Man as an intuitive statistician. *Psychological Bulletin, 68,* 29–46.

Pigeau, R. A., Angus, R. G., O'Neill, P., & Mack, I. (1995). Vigilance latencies to aircraft detection among NORAD surveillance operators. *Human Factors, 37,* 622–634.

Pollack, I. (1952). The information of elementary auditory displays. *Journal of the Acoustical Society of America, 24,* 745–749.

Pollack, I., & Ficks, L. (1954). The information of elementary multidimensional auditory displays. *Journal of the Acoustical Society of America, 26,* 155–158.

Pomerantz, J. R. (1981). Perceptual organization in information processing. In M. Kubovy & J. R. Pomerantz (Eds.), *Perceptual organization* (pp. 141–180). Hillsdale, NJ: Erlbaum.

Pomerantz, J. R., & Pristach, E. A. (1989). Emergent features, attention and perceptual glue in visual form perception. *Journal of Experimental Psychology: Human Perception & Performance, 15,* 635–649.

Pond, D. J. (1979). Colors for sizes: An applied approach. In C. Bensel (Ed.), *Proceedings of the 23d annual meeting of the Human Factors Society.* Santa Monica, CA: Human Factors Society.

Rhea, J. T., Potsdaid, M. S., & DeLuca, S. A. (1979). Errors of interpretation as elicited by a quality audit of an emergency facility. *Radiology, 132,* 277–280.

Rizy, E. F. (1972). *Effect of decision parameters on a detection/localization paradigm quantifying sonar operator performance* (Report No. R–1156). Washington, DC: Office of Naval Research Engineering Program.

Ruffle-Smith, H. P. (1979). *A simulator study of the interaction of pilot workload with errors, vigilance, and decision* (NASA Technical Memorandum 78482). Washington, DC: NASA Technical Information Office.

Saito, M. (1972). A study on bottle inspection speed-determination of appropriate work speed by means of electronystagmography. *Journal of Science of Labor, 48,* 395–400. (In Japanese, English summary)

Scanlan, L. A. (1975). Visual time compression: Spatial and temporal cues. *Human Factors, 17,* 337–345.

Scerbo, M. W., Greenwald, C. Q., & Sawin, D. A. (1993). The effects of subject-controlled pacing and task type on sustained attention and subjective workload. *Journal of General Psychology, 120,* 293–307.

Schmidke, I. I. (1976). Vigilance. In E. Simonson & P. C. Weiser (Eds.), *Psychological and physiological correlates of work and fatigue.* Springfield, MA: Thomas.

Schneider, W., & Shiffrin, R. M. (1977). Controlled and automatic human information processing II: Perceptual learning, automatic attending, and a general theory. *Psychological Review, 84,* 127–190.

Schoenfeld, V. S., & Scerbo, M. W. (1997). Search differences for the presence and absence of features in sustained attention. *Proceedings of the Human Factors and Ergonomics Society 41st Annual Meeting* (pp. 1288–1292). Santa Monica, CA: Human Factors and Ergonomics Society.

Schwartz, J. S., Dans, P. E., & Kinosian, B. P. (1988). Human immunodeficiency virus test evaluation, performance, and use: Proposals to make good tests better. *Journal of the American Medical Association, 259,* 2574–2579.

See, J. E., Howe, S. R., Warm, J. S., & Dember, W. N. (1995). Meta-analysis of the sensitivity decrement in vigilance. *Psychological Bulletin, 117,* 230–249.

See, J. E., Warm, J. S., Dember, W. N., Howe, S. R. (1997). Vigilance and signal detection theory: An empirical evaluation of five measures of response bias. *Human Factors, 39,* 14–29.

Shannon, C. E., & Weaver, W. (1949). *The mathematical theory of communications.* Urbana: University of Illinois Press.

Shechter, S., & Hochstein, S. (1992). Asymmetric interactions in the processing of the visual dimensions of position, width, and contrast of bar stimuli. *Perception, 21,* 297–312.

Shepard, R. N. (1982). Geometrical approximations to the structure of musical pitch. *Psychological Review, 89,* 305–333.

Sheridan, T. B., & Ferrell, W. A. (1974). *Man-machine systems: Information, control, and decision models of human performance.* Cambridge, MA: MIT Press.

Shiffrin, R. M., & Nosofsky, R. M. (1994). Seven plus or minus two: A commentary on capacity limitations. *Psychological Review, 101,* 357–361.

Siegel, J. A., & Siegel, W. (1972). Absolute judgment and paired associate learning: Kissing cousins or identical twins? *Psychological Review, 79,* 300–316.

Snodgrass, J. G., & Corwin, J. (1988). Pragmatics of measuring recognition memory: Applications to dementia and amnesia. *Journal of Experimental Psychology: General, 117,* 34–50.

Swennson, R. G. (1980). A two-stage detection model applied to skilled visual search by radiologists. *Perception & Psychophysics, 27,* 11–16.

Swennson, R. G., Hessel, S. J., & Herman, P. G. (1977). Omissions in radiology: Faulty search or stringent reporting criteria? *Radiology, 123,* 563–567.

Swets, J. A. (Ed.). (1964). *Signal detection and recognition by human observers: Contemporary readings.* New York: Wiley.

Swets, J. A. (1992). The science of choosing the right decision threshold in high-stake diagnostics. *American Psychologist, 47,* 522–532.

Swets, J. A., & Pickett, R. M. (1982). *The evaluation of diagnostic systems.* New York: Academic Press.

Swets, J. A., Pickett, R. M., Whitehead, S. F., Getty, D. J., Schnur, J. A., Swets, J. B., & Freeman, B. A. (1979). Assessment of diagnostic technologies. *Science, 205,* 753–759.

Szucko, J. J., & Kleinmuntz, B. (1981). Statistical vs. clinical lie detection. *American Psychologist, 36,* 488–496.

Teichner, W. (1974). The detection of a simple visual signal as a function of time of watch. *Human Factors, 16,* 339–353.

Torgerson, W. S. (1958). *Theory and method of scaling.* New York: Wiley.

van Leeuwen, T. H., Verbaten, M. N., Koelega, H. S., Camfferman, G., Van der Gugten, J., & Slangen, J. L. (1994). "Effects of oxazepam on performance and event-related brain protentials in vigilance tasks with static and dynamic stimuli." *Psychopharmacology, 116,* 499–507.

Warm, J. S. (Ed.). (1984). *Sustained attention in human performance.* Chichester: Wiley.

Warm, J. S., & Dember, W. N. (1998). Tests of a vigilance taxonomy. In R. R. Hoffman, M. F. Sherrick, & J. S. Warm (Eds.), *Viewing psychology as a whole: The integrative science of William N. Dember.* Washington, DC: American Psychological Association.

Warm, J. S., Dember, W. N., & Hancock, P. A. (1996). Vigilance and workload in automated systems. In R. Parasuraman & M. Mouloua (Eds.), *Automation and human performance: theory and applications* (pp. 183–200). Mahwah, NJ: Erlbaum.

Warm, J. S., Dember, W. N., Murphy, A. Z., & Dittmar, M. L. (1992). Sensing and decision-making components of the signal-regularity effect in vigilance performance. *Bulletin of the Psychonomic Society, 30,* 297–300.

Watson, D. S., & Nichols, T. L. (1976). Detectability of auditory signals presented without defined observation intervals. *Journal of Acoustical Society of America, 59,* 655–668.

Weintraub, D. J. (1971). Rectangle discriminability: Perceptual relativity and the law of pragnanz. *Journal of Experimental Psychology, 88,* 1–11.

Welford, A. T. (1968). *Fundamentals of skill.* London: Methuen.

Wells, G. L.(1984). The psychology of lineup identifications. *Journal of Applied Social Psychology, 14,* 89–103.

Wells, G. L. (1993). What do we know about eyewitness identification? *American Psychologist, 48,* 553–571.

Wells, G. L., & Bradfield, A. L. (1998). "Good, you identified the suspect": Feedback to eyewitnesses distorts their reports of the witnessing experience. *Journal of Applied Psychology, 83,* 360–376.

Wells, G. L., & Seelau, E. P. (1995). Eyewitness identification: Psychological research and legal policy on lineups. *Psychology, Public Policy, and Law, 1,* 765–791.

Wickens, C. D. (1984). *Engineering psychology and human performance.* Columbus, OH: Merrill.

Wickens, C. D. (1992). *Engineering psychology and human performance* (2d ed.). New York: HarperCollins.

Wickens, C. D., & Kessel, C. (1979). The effect of participatory mode and task workload on the detection of dynamic system failures. *IEEE Transactions on Systems, Man, and Cybernetics, 13,* 24–34.

Wickens, C. D., & Kessel, C. (1981). The Detection of Dynamic System Failures. In J. Rasmussen & W. Rouse (Eds.), *Human Detection and Diagnosis of System Failures.* New York: Plenum.

Wright, D. B., & Davies, G. M. (1999) Eyewitness Testimony In F. Durso (Ed.) *Handbook of Applied Cognition.* West Sussix, U.K.: John Wiley & Sons.

Williges, R. C. (1971). The role of payoffs and signal ratios on criterion changes during a monitoring task. *Human Factors, 13,* 261–267.

Wilkinson, R. T. (1964). Artificial "signals" as an aid to an inspection task. *Ergonomics, 7,* 63–72.

Attention in Perception and Display Space

OVERVIEW

The limitations of human attention represent one of the most formidable bottlenecks in human information processing. We can easily recall times when we failed to notice the words of a speaker because we were distracted or when we had so many tasks to perform that some were neglected. These intuitive examples of failures of attention may be described more formally in terms of three categories:

1. *Selective attention.* In some instances we select inappropriate aspects of the environment to process. For example, as we discuss in Chapter 8, decision makers sometimes select the cues that stand out rather than useful, diagnostic cues. The van driver described in Chapter 1 was so engrossed in reading the map display that he could not attend to the roadway ahead. We could say that his attention was too selective, in that important roadway information (the stalled car) was ignored until it was too late. Another dramatic example is provided by the behavior of the flight crew of an Eastern Airlines L–1011 flight that crashed in the Florida Everglades. Because they were preoccupied with a malfunction elsewhere in the cockpit, no one on the flight deck attended to the critical altimeter reading and to subsequent warnings that the plane was gradually descending to the ground (Wiener, 1977; see also Chapter 13). Here again, attention was too selective, a situation sometimes referred to as *cognitive tunneling*.

2. *Focused attention.* Occasionally we are unable to concentrate on one source of information in the environment; in spite of our desires to do so that is, we have a tendency to be distracted. The clerical worker transcribing a tape in a room filled with extraneous conversation encounters such a problem. So also does the translator who must ignore the feedback provided by his or her own voice

to concentrate solely on the incoming message. Another example is the process control room operator attempting to locate a critical item of information in the midst of a "busy" display consisting of many changing variables. The difference between failures of selective and focused attention is that in the former case there is an intentional but unwise choice to process nonoptimal environmental sources. In the latter case this processing of nonoptimal sources is "driven" by external environmental information despite the operator's efforts to shut it out (Yantis, 1993). Attention could not be focused on the appropriate stimulus source.

3. *Divided attention.* When problems of focused attention are encountered, some of our attention is inadvertently directed to stimuli or events we do not wish to process. When problems of divided attention are encountered, we are unable to divide our attention among stimuli or tasks, all of which we wish to process. Here we may again consider our van driver, who must scan the highway for road signs while maintaining control of the vehicle, or a fault diagnostician who must maintain several hypotheses in working memory while scanning the environment for diagnostic information and also entering this information into a recording device. Thus the limits of divided attention sometimes describe our limited ability to *time-share* performance of two or more concurrent tasks, and sometimes describe the limits in integrating multiple information sources.

Attention may be described by the metaphor of a searchlight (Wachtel, 1967). Two properties of the searchlight are relevant: its breadth and direction. The beam's breadth can be subdivided into two components: that which we want to process (focused attention), and that which we must process but do not want to (divided attention). The direction of the searchlight—how it knows when, what, and where in the environment to illuminate—describe the properties of selective attention. Each of these will be considered in detail as we consider examples of how operators search the complex stimulus world for critical information and how the information is processed once found.

The searchlight metaphor describes the various characteristics of attention with respect to perception, the topic of this chapter. Yet the concept of attention is relevant to a range of activities beyond perception. We can speak of dividing attention between two tasks no matter what stage of processing they require. The broader issue of divided attention as it relates to the time-sharing of activities will be the concern of Chapter 11, after we have discussed other stages of information processing. In this chapter we will present an overview of the experimental findings of selective, focused, and divided attention in perception and their relevance to display layout, addressing first those aspects of attention that are serial (e.g., visual scanning) before considering its parallel characteristics in vision and audition.

SELECTIVE ATTENTION
Visual Sampling

Our discussion of selective attention begins with the eye and with *visual sampling*, that is, when the operator seeks information and searches for targets. Although selective attention can occur without a change in direction of gaze (Egeth & Yantis, 1997), it is still the case that for much of the time, our gaze is driven by our need to attend. Thus we can learn a lot about selective attention by studying visual scanning behavior, a close analog to the attentional searchlight (Fisher, Monty, & Senders, 1981; Moray, 1986).

Before we describe models of visual sampling, it is important to understand a few basic characteristics of the eye fixation system. First, only a small region of the visual field perceives detail. This region, the *fovea*, is about 2 degrees of visual angle. To keep objects in foveal vision, to "look at" them, the eyeball exhibits two different kinds of movement. *Pursuit* movements occur when the eye follows a target moving across the visual field. As you follow the trajectory of a ball or a flying bird, your eyes will show pursuit movements of roughly constant velocity. *Saccadic* movements are discrete, jerky movements that jump from one stationary point in the visual field to the next. They can sometimes be superimposed on pursuit movements. If the velocity of the moving ball or flying bird is too fast for pursuit movement, a saccade will be used to "catch up" and bring the target back into foveal vision (Young & Stark, 1963).

The saccadic behavior used in visual sampling has two components: the saccade and the fixation. During the saccade, the visual system suppresses visual input (Chase & Kalil, 1972), and so display information can be properly processed only during fixation. The fixation is characterized by a *location* (the center of the fixation), a *useful field of view* (diameter around the central location from which information is extracted), and a *dwell time* (how long the eye remains at that location).

Visual sampling behavior has been studied in two somewhat different applied contexts. In what we shall refer to as the *supervisory control* context, the operator scans the display of a complex system under supervision—an aircraft cockpit, for example—and allocates attention through visual fixations to various instruments, as these represent sources of information. In the *target search* context, the operator scans a region of the visual world, looking for something at an unknown location: it may be a failure in a circuit board examined by a quality control inspector (see Chapter 2), a search and rescue mission for a downed aircraft, or a receiver suddenly breaking into the open on the football field. In the supervisory control context, the location of the target (or targets) is known, but in target search, the observer must find a target whose location and existence is unknown (Liu & Wickens, 1992). We will discuss each of these situations in turn.

Supervisory Control Sampling

Optimality of Selective Attention   In the aircraft cockpit or the process control console, many information sources must be sampled periodically. In these situations, engineering psychologists have studied how optimal performance is when the observer must select relevant stimuli at the appropriate times. As in our discussions of signal detection theory (Chapter 2), *optimal* was defined in terms of a behavior that will maximize expected value or minimize expected cost. For example, the van driver in Chapter 1 who continuously sampled the map display while ignoring the road ahead is not behaving optimally. If he sampled both the road and the map but never checked the fuel gauge, he is doing better but performance is still not optimal, for he is incurring the expected costs of missing an important event (running out of gas).

Engineering psychologists often divide the stimulus environment into *channels*, along which critical *events* may periodically occur. They assume that environmental sampling is guided by the expected cost that results when an event is missed. The probability of missing an event in turn is directly related to event frequency and uncertainty (discussed in the vigilance section of Chapter 2). Those events that occur often are more likely to be missed if the channels along which they occur are not sampled, and when the timing of events is uncertain regularly scheduled samples will become less effective. In addition, the probability of missing an event on a channel typically increases with the amount of time since the channel was last sampled. For example, the probability of speeding increases with the time that has passed since the driver last looked at the speedometer.

When optimum sampling is examined in the laboratory, the subject is typically presented with two or more channels of stimulus information, along which events may arrive at semipredictable rates. For example, a channel might be an instrument dial, with an "event" defined as the needle moving into a danger zone, as in Figure 3.1 (e.g., Senders, 1964). Six general conclusions of these studies are described below. Some of these conclusions are based on summaries by Moray (1981, 1986).

1. *Mental model guides sampling.* People appear to form a *mental model* of the statistical properties of events in the environment and use it to guide visual sampling. The mental model consists of a set of expectancies about how frequently and when events will occur on each channel, and about the correlation between events on pairs of channels. As expertise develops, the mental model becomes refined, and sampling changes accordingly (Bellenkes, Wickens, & Kramer, 1997). Because sampling strategies provide estimates of the operator's mental model, the patterns of fixations should help the system designer arrange information

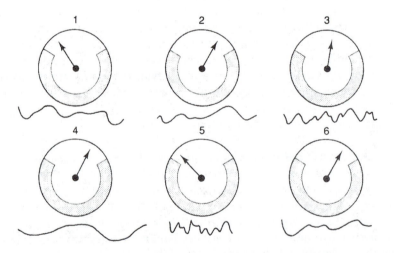

Figure 3.1   Display typical of those used for studying instrument scanning. Under each display is an example of the time-varying input the operator must sample to ensure that none of the needles moves into the danger zones.

displays so that optimal performance results. Dating from the pioneering work of Fitts, Jones, and Milton (1950), engineering psychologists have employed scanning data to configure displays according to two principles: Frequently sampled displays should be placed centrally, and pairs of displays that are often sampled sequentially should be located close together (Elkind, Card, Hochberg, & Huey, 1990; Wickens, Vincow, Schopper, & Lincoln, 1997).

2. *Adjustment to event rate—sluggish beta.* In line with the predictions of signal detection theory, people learn to sample channels with higher event rates more frequently and with lower rates less frequently. However, the sampling rate is not adjusted upward or downward with event frequency as much as it should be. This is similar to the sluggish beta phenomenon discussed in Chapter 2, in which observers were reluctant to adjust the response criterion in signal detection. To elaborate on this second point, some models (e.g., Carbonnell, Ward, & Senders, 1968) propose that the time between samples should be determined by two factors: the growth of uncertainty of the state of the unsampled channel (related to the event rate on that channel) and the cost of taking a sample. These factors trade off. Since sampling, or switching visual attention, has some subjective cost, people will not scan too rapidly across all channels of a dynamic instrument panel. Nor is there need for frequent sampling if channels change their state slowly (Channel 4 in Figure 3.1); hence, the operator's uncertainty about the state of the unsampled channel grows slowly. But eventually the operator's uncertainty will reach a high enough level so that it becomes worth the cost of a fixation to find out what is happening there (i.e., to "reset" uncertainty to zero). Carbonnell, Ward, and Senders found that their model accurately described the fixation patterns of pilots making an instrument landing.

3. *Sampling affected by arrangement.* Donk (1994) examined eye movements in observers monitoring several instruments and found that they were more likely to make horizontal scans than diagonal scans. Donk also found that operators were reluctant to make diagonal scans to view high event rate channels. Donk proposed that operators use simplifying rules and heuristics based on channel arrangement to decrease attentional demands, which lead to systematic biases in performance. Hence, understanding instrument scanning just in terms of channels and event rates cannot completely account for performance—the arrangement of the instruments matters.

4. *Memory imperfect; sampling imperfect.* Human memory is imperfect, and sampling reflects this fact. People tend to sample information sources more often than they would need to if they had perfect memory about the status of an information source when it was last sampled. This fact explains the "oversampling" of channels with low event rates described above. Also, people may forget to sample a particular display source entirely if there are many possible sources, as might well be the case for the monitor of a nuclear process control console. Such forgetfulness will be more likely if the channels are not physically represented by a display location but are stored in a computer and must be accessed for inspection on a display screen by a manual or vocal request. These limitations in memory suggest the usefulness of "sampling reminders" (Moray, 1981).

5. *Preview helps.* When people are given a *preview* of scheduled events that are likely to occur in the future, sampling and switching become somewhat more optimal. Now subjects' sampling can be guided by an "external model", the display of the previewed events. Thus the dispatcher or industrial scheduler can be helped by having a preview of anticipated demands on different resources (Sanderson, 1989; see also Chapter 13), just as the student is helped by having a preview of upcoming assignments in different courses. However, as the number of channels increases, people fail to take advantage of preview information, apparently because of the heavy load on working memory required to do so (Tulga & Sheridan, 1980). This may be why predictive displays for industrial scheduling have not always been useful (Sanderson, 1989).

6. *Processing strategies—cognitive tunneling.* Scanning behavior may reflect the operator's mental model of the environment, and therefore also reflect biases in the operator's strategy. In a study of a simulated process control plant, Moray and Rotenberg (1989), for example, used a scanning analysis to determine that operators engaged in cognitive tunneling on a failed system. When one system under supervision "failed", operators stopped examining the status of other systems as their diagnosis of the failed system was carried out. Moray and Rotenberg also used scanning measures to identify problems associated with delayed feedback. After making a control adjustment to one system, operators switch their visual attention to the indicator where feedback for that response is expected. Their fixation often stays locked on to that indicator until it eventually reflects the control input. This can represent a substantial waste of visual attention if the delay is long. Bellenkes, Wickens, and Kramer (1997) found similar results in the cockpit. They found that novice pilots performing high-workload maneuvers tended to focus on the most important instrument (the attitude directional indicator) and failed to carefully monitor other instruments, even though the information displayed on those instruments was also important for keeping the aircraft on the desired flight path. Wikman, Niemeinen, and Summala (1998) made a similar observation that novice drivers tended to dwell for significantly longer periods than experts as they scanned head down to tune a radio or dial a cellular phone.

Eye Movements in Target Search

When the operator is looking for an object in the environment, such as a flaw in a piece of sheet metal or the presence of survivors in aircraft wreckage on the ground, the visual scan pattern tends to be far less structured than in the supervisory/control task. As a consequence, scanning is less amenable to optimal modeling. Nevertheless, a number of characteristics of visual search have emerged.

Environmental Expectancies   Like supervisory/control scanning, target search is driven in part by cognitive factors related to the expectancy of where a target is likely to be found. These areas tend to be fixated first and most frequently. This characteristic of information-seeking and scanning behavior has been used to account for differences between novices and experts. In football, the expert quarterback will know where to look for the open receiver with the highest probability (Abernethy, 1988; Walker & Fisk, 1995). Kundel and LaFollette (1972) have studied differences in the way that novice and expert radiologists scan x-ray plates in search of a tumor. The expert examines first and most closely those areas in which tumors are most likely to appear; the novice tends to search the whole plate evenly.

The role of information in visual scanning has also been used to explain how we scan pictures (Yarbus, 1967). People tend to fixate most on areas containing the most information (e.g., faces, contours, and other areas of high visual detail). Furthermore, a scan path over the same picture will change, depending on what information the viewer is expected to extract (Yarbus, 1967).

Display Factors and Salience   Since visual search behavior is often internally driven by cognitive factors, there is no consistent pattern of display scanning (e.g., left-to-right or circular-clockwise) and no optimal scan pattern in search, beyond the fact that search should be guided by the expectancy of target location. Nevertheless, certain display factors tend to guide the allocation of visual attention.

Visual attention will be drawn to display items that are large, bright, colorful, and changing (e.g., blinking), a characteristic that can be exploited when locating visual warnings (see Chapter 13) but that may bias decision making (see Chapter 8). These salient items can be used to guide or direct visual attention, as discussed in more detail later in this chapter. An abrupt stimulus onset (e.g., a light turning on) also serves to attract attention, especially in the visual periphery (Remington, Johnston, & Yantis, 1992; Yantis & Jonides, 1984). Yantis and Hillstrom (1994) have collected evidence suggesting that this may be due to the visual system being extremely sensitive to new perceptual objects.

Visual search is also captured by the presence of unique stimuli, often called *singletons*. For example, Theeuwes (1992) found that subjects were slower in finding a target (a diamond among circles) when one of the distractors or nontargets was unique in color, (e.g., a green circle when all other circles were red). Thus, the presence of the unique features of the singleton slowed detection of other targets. However, singletons are less likely to capture attention when the target is defined in a more complex manner (Bacon & Egeth, 1994). Presumably, this is because when the targets are complex, the searcher does not have a "set" for simply defined targets like a singleton.

There is evidence also that search behavior is sometimes guided by physical location in the display. For example, Megaw and Richardson (1979) found that when subjects exhibited a systematic scan pattern in searching for targets, they tended to start at the upper left. This fact may reflect eye movement in reading. A search also tends to be most concentrated toward the center regions of the visual field, avoiding the edges of a display, a pattern that Parasuraman (1986) dubbed the *edge effect*. Also, as in supervisory/control sampling, scans tend to be made most frequently between adjacent elements on a display, and horizontal or vertical scans are more common than those along the diagonal.

These display-driven search tendencies are usually dominated by conceptually or knowledge-driven scan strategies (Levy-Schoen, 1981). However, it seems reasonable that a knowledge of these tendencies should be employed in designing multi-element displays to locate information of greatest importance (e.g., warning and hazard labels) in areas of greatest salience, an issue that we will return to in Chapter 8 in the discussion of the cues used for decision making.

Display-Driven and Conceptually Driven Processing   Display-driven and conceptually driven strategies commonly interact: Theeuwes and Godthelp (1995) noted that standardization of roadway and sign design helps drivers know when to expect certain events. Hence, the driver responds to the stimuli in the road environment (signs, signals, intersections, interchanges) and interprets these in terms of conceptual expectations (e.g., "I know that the distance signs are large and green and occur just after an interchange; to figure out how far I am from Springfield, I'll look for a large green sign after the next interchange"). It is also important to forecast the unexpected event, a technique called *positive guidance* (Dewar, 1993). For example, in North America, left exits off a freeway should be signed well in advance (Wickens, Gordon, & Liu, 1998). Creating an expectancy for the user and then making the display or stimulus salient can be an effective combination in driving the scanning behavior of an observer.

Search Coverage and the Useful Field of View   How much visual area is covered in each visual fixation? Although we can sometimes take in information from peripheral vision (see Chapter 4), resolution of fine visual detail requires the highest acuity region of the fovea, an angle of no more than about 2 degrees surrounding the center of fixation. Mackworth (1976) addressed this uncertainty by defining the "useful field of view" (UFOV) as a circular area around the fixation point from which information necessary for the task can be extracted. The size of a UFOV can be estimated from the minimum distance between successive fixations in a search task, on the assumption that two adjacent UFOVs touch but do not overlap. The data collected by Mackworth and others suggest that the size of the UFOV varies from 1 to 4 degrees of visual angle.

Several factors affect the UFOV. The size appears to be determined by the density of information and by the discriminability of the target from the background. Thus, looking for a dark flaw on a clear background in glass inspection will lead to a larger UFOV than scanning for a misaligned connection in a circuit board or microchip. Aging tends to lead to a restricted UFOV (Ball, Beard, Roenker, Miller, & Griggs, 1988; Scialfa, Kline, & Lyman, 1987). Scialfa et al. proposed that older adults take smaller perceptual samples from the visual scene and scan the samples more slowly than do young adults. However, training can enlarge the UFOV, and the benefits of training are equal across age groups (Ball et al., 1988). Reduction in UFOV has serious implications for tasks having visual search as a component, such as driving. Ball and Rebok (1994) found that vehicular crash frequency was greater for people having smaller UFOVs. Finally, the UFOV is sensitive to task demands in the foveal region (Williams, 1989). Williams found that as a foveal task becomes more difficult, information at the periphery of the UFOV is processed less well.

The size of the UFOV and the maximum rate with which different fixations can be made (2–4 per second) limit the amount of area that can be searched in a given time. However, even in the absence of time limits, it is apparent that humans do not search in exhaustive fashion, blanketing an entire area with UFOVs, and inevitably locating a target. Stager and Angus (1978) studied airborne search and rescue experts who searched photographs for crash sites; the searches covered only 53 percent of the available terrain, a fact that led to less than perfect performance. In addition, targets may be fixated within a UFOV and yet not detected (Abernethy, 1988; Kundel & Nodine, 1978; Stager & Angus, 1978), suggesting that potential targets are measured against some decision criterion (like beta in signal detection theory, Chapter 2) during the search process. The advantage of training described above may be due to optimizing the placement of the decision criterion.

Fixation Dwells   We have said little about how long the eye rests at a given fixation. Since the eye extracts information over time, one might think that long dwells should be associated with greater information pickup. Indeed, the attitude directional indicator found in the cockpit produces longer dwells (Bellenkes, Wickens, & Kramer, 1997; Harris & Christhilf, 1980) and is fixated on most frequently (Fitts, Jones, & Milton, 1950). This is presumably due to its high information content. Harris and Christhilf also found that pilots fixated longer on critical instruments (showing information necessary to control the aircraft) than on those requiring a mere check to assure that they were "in bounds." In target search, Kundel and Nodine (1978) distinguished between short *survey dwells*, used to establish those regions more likely to contain a target, and longer *examination dwells*, used to provide a detailed examination of the region for an embedded target.

In addition to scanning and sampling strategies, fixation dwells are also governed by the *difficulty* of information extraction. Thus, displays that are less legible or contain denser information will be fixated on longer (Mackworth, 1976). In normal reading, longer dwells are made on less familiar words and while reading more difficult text (McConkie, 1983; see Chapter 6). When examining pictures, people fixate longer on objects that are unusual and out of context (Friedman & Liebelt, 1981). As we saw in Chapter 2, low familiarity, low frequency, and out of context messages have higher information content, suggesting that dwell time has some relation to the information content of a display. In addition, expertise affects the difficulty of information extraction and, therefore, fixation dwell times. For example, Bellenkes, Wickens, and Kramer (1997) found that novice pilots dwell nearly twice as long on the information-rich attitude directional indicator as experts, requiring more time to extract the more difficult information. As noted above, Wikman, Niemeinen, and Summala (1998) found that novice drivers had longer head-down dwells than experts.

Conclusion   The discussion of visual scanning behavior yields two general conclusions. First, scanning tells us a good deal about the internal expectancies that drive selective attention. Second, the greatest usefulness of scanning research to engineering psychology is probably in the area of diagnostics. Frequently watched instruments can be seen as those that are most important to an operator's task. This fact may lead to design decisions to place these instruments in prominent locations or close together (e.g., Elkind, Card, Hochberg, & Huey, 1990; Wickens, Vincow, Schopper & Lincoln, 1997). Differences between novice and expert fixation patterns can indicate how the mental model or the search strategy of the novice departs from that of the expert, and display items that require long dwells may indicate nonoptimal formatting. We will revisit the topic of visual scanning in Chapter 6, where we examine visual fixations in reading, a task that is neither search nor supervisory control but is of great importance in design.

Visual Search Models

Visual scanning is of course heavily involved in visual search. However, there are other aspects of search that cannot be revealed by scanning, including such aspects as the uncertainty of target identification or differences in the physical makeup of targets (e.g., one-dimensional versus multidimensional). Furthermore, whereas scanning reveals details about the process of visual search, human factors engineers may often be interested in the *product* of that search: How long does it take to find a target? Or what is the probability that a target will be detected in a given period of time? Hence, engineering psychologists have been concerned with the development of visual search models that will allow these values to be predicted.

One such model was developed by Drury (1975, 1982) to predict the time it would take an industrial quality control inspector to detect a flaw in a product. Drury examined the inspection of sheet metal. The model has two stages. The first stage describes the target search and predicts that the probability of locating a target will increase with more search time. However, it will increase at a diminishing rate, as shown in Figure 3.2. This is not surprising, given that (1) a target may be fixated on more than once without being detected, and (2) search strategies do not usually cover the whole search field with UFOVs, even when adequate time is given. In a later "decision" stage, the operator uses the expectancy of flaws (the overall manufacturing quality) to set a decision criterion, as in signal detection theory (Chapter 2). If the expectancy of a flaw is high, the criterion will be set low.

The shape of the curve in Figure 3.2 has important implications for the designer of industrial inspection stations: There is an optimal amount of time that each product should be searched, given that one can specify a cost for inspection time (which increases linearly with longer time) and a cost for misses. If the operator searches for a longer time to achieve a higher detection rate, this leads to diminishing gains in inspection accuracy. Drury (1975, 1982) discusses how this optimal time could be established, given factors like the desired rate at which products should be inspected (often set by a manager), the probability of fault occurrence, and the desired overall level of inspection accuracy. Then industrial material to be inspected can be presented at a rate determined by the optimal time.

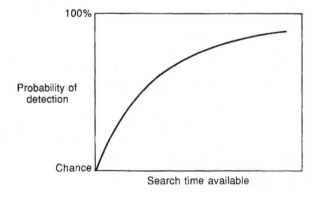

Figure 3.2   Probability of detection as a function of time available for search.

Source: Adapted from C. Drury, "Inspection of Sheet Metal: Model and Data," *Human Factors, 17* (1975). Reprinted with permission. Copyright 1975 by the Human Factors Society, Inc. All rights reserved.)

Another, more basic, approach has been to model the kinds of variables that affect search speed through a set of stimuli to locate a particular target. In these tasks, the operator searches through an array such as that shown in Figure 3.3 and might report:

1. the presence of a white X
2. the presence of a large T
3. the presence of a black target

Extensive research in this area reveals a number of general conclusions. First, in situations like Tasks 1 and 2, the number of elements to be searched has the dominant effect on search time (Drury & Clement, 1978; Treisman & Gelade, 1980). This is because the search is usually serial, as each item is inspected in turn. If there are more items, search times will increase. Many researchers have replicated this finding (e.g., Egeth & Dagenbach, 1991; Wolfe, Cave, & Franzel, 1989). The slope of the function for trials without the target reflects the average time required to scan each item in the array and is about 50 milliseconds per item for simple items like letters. The slope of the function for trials with the target is roughly half that of target-absent trials (e.g., Wolfe, Cave, & Franzel, 1989). This is what one would expect for a search that is *serial* and *self-terminating*. In a serial search, each item is inspected in turn. In a self-terminating search, the search stops when the target item is found. Thus, when a target is present it will be found, *on the average*, after about half of the items have been inspected.

Second, exceptions to the first conclusion regarding serial search occur when the target is defined by one level along one salient dimension (Treisman & Gelade, 1980). For example, performance of Task 3 above will be little affected by the number of items, since the target in Figure 3.3 is defined by a single level (black) of one dimension (color). It appears to "pop out" of the search field. That is, parallel search can occur when the target can be defined using a simple rule. Eye movements correlate with the performance data, showing greater search efficiency (fewer scans) for parallel than serial search (Williams, Reingold, Moscovitch, & Behrmann, 1997). Some visual search models (e.g., Treisman & Gelade, 1980; Wolfe, 1994) propose that parallel search of this type is *preattentive* (requiring few

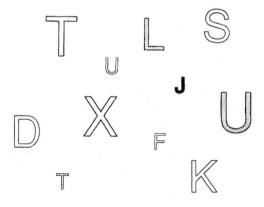

Figure 3.3   Stimuli for a typical experimental search task.

attentional resources) and can be done across the entire visual field, whereas serial search requires attentional resources, and can only be done over a limited portion of the visual field (i.e., the UFOV).

Third, serial search is more likely when the target is difficult to discriminate from distractors (Geisler & Chou, 1995). Nagy and Sanchez (1992) found that search times increased with number of distractors when the luminance or color difference between target and distractor was small, but search times did not increase when the difference was large.

Fourth, exceptions to serial search also occur when the target is defined by having a feature present rather than absent. For example, Treisman and Souther (1985) showed that parallel search occurred when subjects searched for a Q among Os, but serial search occurred when searching for an O among Qs. This is similar to the "target-present" advantage noted in the vigilance situation in Chapter 2 (e.g., Schoenfeld & Scerbo, 1997). Again, this can be interpreted in terms of different discriminabilities of targets in the two situations (Geisler & Chou, 1995).

Fifth, it matters relatively little if the elements are closely spaced, requiring little scanning, or are widely dispersed (Drury & Clement, 1978; Teichner & Mocharnuk, 1979). The increased scanning that is required with wide spacing lengthens the search time slightly. However, the high density of nontarget elements with closely spaced items also lengthens search times slightly. Thus scanning distance and visual clutter trade off with one another as target dispersion is varied.

Sixth, searching for any of *several* different target types is generally slower than searching for only one (Craig, 1981). An example would be to "Search for a P or a Q" in Figure 3.3. The exception occurs when the set of two (or more) targets can be discriminated from all other nontargets by a *single common feature* (e.g., color). Varying levels of training may be necessary for the perceptual system to tune in to this critical discriminating feature. For example, in Figure 3.3, if the instructions were to "search for an X and a K," subjects might learn that given the particular set of nontarget stimuli used, X and K are the only letters that contain diagonal lines, and hence they will be able to search efficiently for this unique shared feature (Neisser, Novick, & Lazar, 1964). Thus, there should be an advantage to training industrial inspectors to focus on the set of unique and defining features common to all faults, distinguishing them from normal items.

Seventh, the role of extensive training in target search can sometimes bring performance to a level of *automaticity*, when search time is unaffected by the number of targets and presumably done in parallel (Fisk, Oransky, & Skedsvold, 1988; Schneider & Shiffrin, 1977). Generally speaking, automaticity results when, over repeated trials, targets never appear as nontarget stimuli, a condition that Schneider and Shiffrin refer to as *consistent mapping*. This is contrasted with *varied mapping* search, when a target may later appear as a nontarget. We will discuss the concept of automaticity further in Chapter 6 in the context of reading, in Chapter 7 in the context of training, and in Chapter 11 in the context of time-sharing.

Although these studies were conducted in the laboratory, they have clear application to a variety of work domains. For example, a vehicle dispatcher might need to scan a computerized city map to locate a vehicle that is not in service and has a large carrying capacity. The military commander must find a particular subset of symbols on an electronic topographic map. Visual search is commonplace in many work domains, and the factors listed above are likely to play a role in the efficiency of those searches.

Application: Symbol Coding In the above examples, a symbol may be used to code multiple dimensions, so that its color represents one dimension, its size another, its shape a third, and so on. Imagine the operator is trying to find a particular target stimulus. When multiple levels of multiple dimensions define the target, serial search results, as noted previously (Treisman & Gelade, 1980). Hence, to determine if each symbol represents the target, the level of each dimension will be examined serially. This serial examination has two implications. First, with more coding dimensions, search times will increase. Second, if operators search the dimensions in a particular order, it implies that the discriminability of two symbols is not just a simple matter of the number of features in common and the number of unique features (e.g., Geiselman, Landee, & Christen, 1982; Tversky, 1977) but is determined by the specific order in which features are examined (Fisher & Tanner, 1992). To develop an optimal symbol set (i.e., to maximize symbol discriminability) the designer must take into account the order of the search through the dimensions. If this is known, the maximally discriminable symbol set can be determined from an algorithm developed by Fisher and Tanner.

Structured Search

Basics The model proposed by Drury (1975) describes a search in which a target could be located anywhere and there is little organization to guide the search (sometimes called *free field* search). Somewhat different is the process of *structured search*, in which information that may help guide the search is available in the display. For example, structured search might occur when a computer user wishes to locate a particular item on a menu or an airline passenger is scanning a TV monitor for information concerning a particular flight. When we perform a structured search, we examine each item in the set in a systematic order, making structured search more amenable to modeling than search in a free field. In the letter-search task developed by Neisser (1963), subjects scan a vertical column of random three- or five-letter sequences until they detect the target letter, as shown at the top of Figure 3.4. The researchers observed a linear relationship between the serial position of the letter in the list and the time needed to detect the target, as shown at the bottom of Figure 3.4. The slope of this function, which represents the time to process each letter in this structured search, is roughly the same as what was observed in free-field search (50–100 milliseconds per item).

Application: Menus One important application of structured search models is in the design of computer-based menu systems, a critical component in human-computer interaction. In the typical menu task, the user must locate a target word, symbol, or command. The user must scan the list until the item is located, and then press a key. Menus may be multilevel, in which case the target term may be reached only after a search through higher-level terms. Thus, a travel agent, searching for a flight from a particular city, may first access a menu of city names and then, after selecting an option within that name level of the menu, scan an embedded menu of all flights departing from that city.

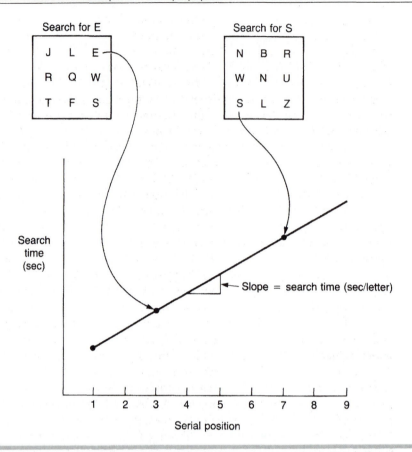

Figure 3.4 Neisser's letter-search paradigm. The top of the figure shows two lists with different targets. The bottom graph shows the search time for letters in each of the two lists as a function of their serial position on the list. Also presented are the data from other serial positions and the resulting linear slope. Across all letters in this list of a, the average search time would be that of the 5th serial position.

Source: U. Neisser, "Decision Time Without Reaction Time," *American Journal of Psychology, 76* (1963), p. 377. Copyright 1963 by the Board of Trustees of the University of Illinois. Reprinted by permission of the University of Illinois Press.

Menu designers would like to structure a menu in such a way that target items are reached in the minimum average time, and the linear visual search model can serve as a useful guide. If menus are organized randomly, given the general tendency to search from the top downward (Somberg, 1987) and the linear search strategy, the target will be located after an average of $NT/2$ seconds, in a self-terminating search where N is the menu size and T is the time to read each item (Lee & MacGregor, 1985). Within each search, the time will be directly proportional to the distance of the item from the top of the menu.

It is possible for designers, capitalizing on this linear search strategy, to reduce the expected search time if they know that some menu items will be searched for more often than others. These items can be positioned toward the top of the menu in proportion to their frequency of use. Using these assumptions, Lee and MacGregor (1985) have developed quantitative models that predict the expected time needed to locate a target item as a function of reading speed and computer response speed when there are embedded (multilevel) menus. Their model guidelines dictate that the optimal number of items per menu is between three and ten, depending on the reading speed and the computer response speed. Their data, consistent with others to be described in Chapter 9, argue against many embedded levels of short menus.

The Lee and MacGregor (1985) model ignores the effects of the similarity of the target item to the correct menu alternative, and the similarity of menu alternatives to each other. Pierce, Parkinson, and Sisson (1992) found that when the target item was highly similar to the correct alternative (e.g., the target item is Ballet, and the correct alternative is Dance), search was faster than when the target word was less similar (i.e., more generic; e.g., target item Ballet, correct alternative Art). When the various menu alternatives were made more similar, search was slower than when alternatives were less similar reflecting the third conclusion in visual search discussed above. A *criterion-based model* developed by Pierce, Sisson, and Parkinson (1992) accounts for the effects of similarity in menu search using a signal detection approach (see Chapter 2) in which the user evaluates a menu alternative in terms of its perceived similarity to the target item. There are two criteria in the model. If the alternative is seen as very different from the target item, then it falls below the lower criterion and is immediately rejected as a response. If the alternative is seen as highly similar to the target item, then it falls above the upper criterion, it is selected as a response, and the search terminates. If the alternative falls between the two criteria, search continues until an alternative falling above the upper criterion is found or the alternative with the highest similarity is selected. When menu alternatives are made more similar, the signal detection distributions representing correct and incorrect alternatives move together, increasing the likelihood of alternatives that fall between the two criteria. The model successfully accounted for the data collected by Pierce, Parkinson, and Sisson.

Such quantitative models are an important first step in understanding structured search with computer menus, and they hold up in a variety of situations. Nonetheless, people perform other tasks with menus than simply finding a target word, and the type of menu organization (e.g., alphabetic, semantic) can affect search effectiveness (Halgren & Cooke, 1993; Hollands & Merikle, 1987; Mehlenbacher, Duffy, & Palmer, 1989; Smelcer & Walker, 1993). A comprehensive model of structured search with computer menus must account for such results.

In conclusion, we note that quantitative models of human visual search and scanning performance are fairly successful. Although they do not succeed in predicting exactly how an operator will accomplish a task or how long it will take for an item to be located, the answers they provide are at a more precise level than those offered by intuition. Visual search is only a small component of human performance, but it offers a success story in the domain of performance models.

Directing Attention

It is sometimes possible to advise an operator in advance where attention should be directed. An air traffic controller's attention, for example, might be directed toward a pending conflict if the symbols for the involved aircraft begin flashing. In the laboratory, this has been investigated by presenting a cue just before the onset of a faint target, at the same location as the target. Detecting the target becomes more accurate as the stimulus-onset asynchrony (SOA) between the warning (or *cue*) and the target increases (e.g., Eriksen & Collins, 1969). That is, if the cue appears 200 milliseconds before the target (SOA = 200 ms), it is more effective than if it appears 50 milliseconds before the target (SOA = 50 ms), allowing the subject more time to redirect attention to the cued location. But cueing helps (relative to no cue) even with a 50-millisecond SOA.

We can distinguish between situations where *peripheral cues* are used (i.e., cues at the pending target location, which is typically out of foveal vision), and where the cue is in some neutral foveal location but indicates the target location in some way (e.g., by using an arrow pointing in the target's direction). This second type is called a *central cue*. Central cues are more effective with longer SOAs (e.g., 400 ms), and their benefits tend to be fairly long lasting; peripheral cues are typically more effective with short SOAs (Muller & Rabbitt, 1989) and have a more transient effect. Egeth and Yantis (1997) refer to peripheral cues as stimulus-driven and central cues as goal-directed, implying different mechanisms for the different types of cueing. The peripheral cues appear to be processed automatically, whereas central cues require controlled interpretation (Muller & Rabbitt, 1989). From a designer's perspective, if a cue (e.g., a warning or prompt) cannot be presented until the last moment, a peripheral cue should be more effective, but a central cue is probably more effective otherwise, since its attention-directing effects are longer lasting.

It appears that cues can direct the spotlight of attention. One might suppose that the spotlight moves in analog fashion. Thus, as you switch attention from the pointer to a particular number on your speedometer, your attentional spotlight would move continuously as you make the switch. However, the evidence suggests otherwise. Eriksen and Webb (1989) failed to find a relation between the time to shift attention and the distance between elements when eye movements were not involved, a relation which one would expect if the attentional shift were continuous. The results are more consistent with attention moving in discrete, "all-or-none" fashion. This implies that intermediate elements in the display would not be attended as the switch was being made.

If cues are not perfectly valid indicators of a target, as may often occur in operational settings, a *cost-benefit* relationship results (Posner, 1986). Assume that the cue is 80 percent reliable in directing attention to the eventual location of the target. The observer can attend to the cue and be faster and make fewer errors on those trials when the cue is accurate but will suffer on the 20 percent of trials when the cue is inaccurate, taking longer and making more errors as a result (Posner, Nissen, & Ogden, 1978). Posner, Nissen, and Ogden found that this was not simply a result of eye fixations—the same results occurred in cases where there was no eye movement.

The question then arises as to whether the fewer errors made in response to an accurate cue are a result of lowering a criterion for detecting a signal at the target location (beta in signal detection theory, discussed in Chapter 2) or an increased sensitivity to the target location (Kinchla, 1992). If the change is in the response criterion only, this means that the observer is responding to the cue (i.e., their attention is directed to the correct part of the display), but this does not increase their accuracy (i.e., sensitivity), since they make more false alarms at that location (i.e., a shift in beta). It appears that the typical result is a change in both d' and beta (e.g., Downing, 1988).

Attention in Depth   We have discussed how certain stimulus cues can be used to direct a person's attention to a particular location on a two-dimensional display. A person's attention might be directed in three-dimensional space analogously. For example, Atchley, Kramer, Andersen, and Theeuwes (1997) used a cue to indicate the approximate depth at which a signal was to occur (they used stereopsis information to produce the sensation of depth). Subjects took longer to respond to the signal when the cue was at a different depth from the signal than when both cue and signal were presented at the same depth. That is, the cue produced a focus of attention at its particular depth. However, this effect may be reduced or eliminated (i.e., the spotlight of attention may be "depth-blind") if the target is difficult to detect or discriminate (Ghiradelli & Folk, 1996).

There are also benefits to showing information at different depths. Chau and Yeh (1995) and Theeuwes, Atchley, and Kramer (1998) had observers detect a target that was separated in depth or not separated in depth from a background containing distractors. When the target was separated in depth from the distractors, search times were shorter.

These results imply that unusual distractor stimuli that typically slow search for a target will not slow search if they are at a different depth from the target. If a target and distractor stimuli are separated in depth, it might be worthwhile to preserve that depth information on a display screen so that an observer can more easily filter out distractors. For example, air and ground objects on a radar screen might be better displayed with a stereo vision facility in order to assist an observer in distinguishing an air target from ground objects.

Applications   The topic of directing attention becomes of greater consequence when we consider that automated systems are being developed to provide *intelligent cueing* in various operational settings. This intelligent cueing directs the user's attention to certain target regions in the display or the world. Yeh, Wickens, and Seagull (1999) investigated the effectiveness of target cueing in the design of see-through helmet-mounted displays. They found that cueing lowered target detection response times for expected targets but made it more difficult to detect unexpected targets—targets of greater potential danger—both in terms of longer response times and more errors (i.e., more missed targets). This result echoes Posner's (1986) cost-benefit result described above. Conejo and Wickens (1997) cued pilots in a simulated air-ground targeting task. When the cue was unreliable, directing attention to an object that was similar to, but was not the designated target, pilots often chose the nontarget, even when the correct target was visible on the display and the pilot knew what the target looked like. This result reflects the role of the response criterion (beta shift) in target cueing (Downing, 1988). Other researchers (e.g., Mosier, Skitka, Heers, & Burdick, 1998; Taylor, Finnie, & Hoy, 1997) have found similar results. In combination, these results suggest that cueing can be effective in directing attention for a variety of tasks, but people sometimes tend to follow and believe the cues indiscriminately—an example of excessive trust in automation, a topic to be discussed in Chapter 13.

In addition to cueing, attention may also be directed implicitly in a complex display by *highlighting* a selected subset of items that some agent infers should be attended (Hammer, 1999). For example, an intelligent filtering system that infers what would be of interest to a reader might highlight a set of document titles within a longer list. Or all aircraft on an air trafic controller display that lie within a certain, relevant, altitude range could be highlighted. Many different physical techniques can be employed to highlight "relevant" items and allow this subset to be easily scanned without distraction from the non-highlighted items (Fisher & Tan, 1989), such as color or intensity coding, boxing, underlining, flashing, or reverse video. The particular technique should be carefully chosen so that the features that may make a set of items stand out (and therefore be easily detected and discriminated from the nonhighlighted options) do not themselves disrupt the ability to read or interpret the items. For example, flashing words may be very difficult to read. Uniquely colored items do not appear to suffer this deficit (Fisher & Tan, 1989).

It is often difficult for the agent driving the highlighting to guarantee that every highlighted item is relevant, and that all "background" items are not relevant. For example, in the case of document search, some documents assumed to be relevant on the basis of keywords (and therefore highlighted) may not, in fact, be of any interest. This defines the issue of *highlighting validity*. Indeed, the exent to which a person uses highlighting to guide search (decreasing the effective number of items to be searched, since the background items can be easily ignored) is based on the user's expectancy that the highlighting is indeed valid; however, even validity that is considerably less than 1.0 will still enable users to search a highlighted subset for a target first, with the result that total search time will be reduced (Fisher, Coury, Tengs, & Duffy, 1989).

PARALLEL PROCESSING AND DIVIDED ATTENTION

The first part of this chapter addressed those aspects of attention and perception that are often serial, as in the search or supervisory/control task. Yet even in this discussion, we alluded to situations where processing is parallel rather than serial. In models of scanning, we discussed the useful field of view, with the assumption that several items within that field might be processed together (in parallel). In reading, there is good evidence that when we fixate on a short word, all letters within that word are processed in parallel (see Chapter 6). We also noted that when a target is defined by one level along one salient dimension or by an automatically processed stimulus, search time did not depend on the number of elements, suggesting that the elements were processed in parallel.

In the last half of this chapter, we will focus on aspects of perceptual processing that operate in parallel. We speak of *divided* rather than *selective* attention in this case. Although divided attention and parallel processing are often good things for human performance—particularly in high-demand environments such as an air traffic control center or a busy office—it is sometimes impossible to narrow the focus of attention when needed and shut out unwanted inputs. This failure occurs when divided attention becomes *mandatory* rather than optional. In this case we speak of a failure of focused attention as being the downside of successful divided attention. In particular, many display principles that facilitate divided attention impair focused attention. For example, in the previous chapter, we saw that integral dimensions help when operators can divide their attention between two redundant dimensions but hurt when they must focus attention on one while ignoring independent changes in the other. Because of this close and sometimes reciprocal relationship between divided and focused attention, our discussion will often treat the two topics in consort. We begin by considering parallel processing at the earliest phases of the visual information-processing sequence; we then consider the role of space, objectness, and color in attention; finally, we shift our discussion to parallel processing and focused and divided attention in the auditory modality.

Preattentive Processing and Perceptual Organization

Many psychologists have argued that the visual processing of a multiple-element world has two main phases: A *preattentive* phase is carried out automatically and organizes the visual world into objects and groups of objects; then we *selectively attend* to certain objects of the preattentive array for further elaboration (Kahneman, 1973; Neisser; 1967). These two processes might be associated with short-term sensory store and perception, respectively, in the model of information processing presented in Figure 1.3. Thus, distinguishing between figure and background is preattentive. So also is the grouping together of similar items on the display shown in Figure 3.5a. Gestalt psychologists (e.g., Wertheimer; see Palmer, 1992) made efforts to identify a number of basic principles that cause items to be preattentively grouped together on the display (e.g., proximity, similarity, common fate, good continuation, closure; see Palmer, 1992) Displays constructed according to these principles have high redundancy (Garner, 1974). That is, knowledge of where one display item is located will allow an accurate guess of the location of other items in a way that is impossible with the less organized display shown in Figure 3.5b. Indeed, Tullis (1988) and Palmiter and Elkerton (1987) have developed a set of information-theory-based measures of display organization that can be used to quantify the organization of alphanumeric and analog displays, respectively. Because all items

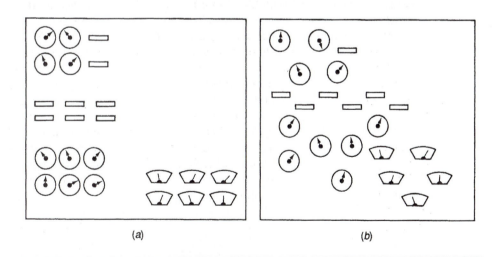

(a)   (b)

Figure 3.5   Gestalt principles of display organization.

of an organized display must be processed together to reveal the organization, such parallel processing is sometimes called *global* or *holistic* processing, in contrast to the *local* processing of a single object within the display.

Two examples illustrate the differences between global and local processing. One example, shown in Figure 3.6, is a stimulus presented to subjects by Navon (1977). Figure 3.6a shows a large F made up of a series of small T's. When subjects are asked to report the name of the large letter, there is a conflict. The small letters perceived by local processing lead one to respond T, whereas the large letter requiring global processing leads one to respond F. This *response conflict* is not present in Figure 3.6b. But this interference is asymmetric. When asked to report the large letters, there is little interference from the incompatibility of the small. Thus, the global aspects of the stimulus appear to be automatically processed in a way that makes them immune to the local aspects, for which more focused attention is required. This phenomenon is known as *global precedence*.

A second example is the texture segregation shown in Figure 3.7. At the top of the figure, the vertical T's appear more different from the slanted T's than from the L's on

```
TTTT            FFFF
T               F
T               F
TTTT            FFFF
T               F
T               F
T               F
T               F
      (a)              (b)
```

Figure 3.6 Global and local perception. (*a*) Global and local letters are incompatible; (*b*) global and local are compatible.

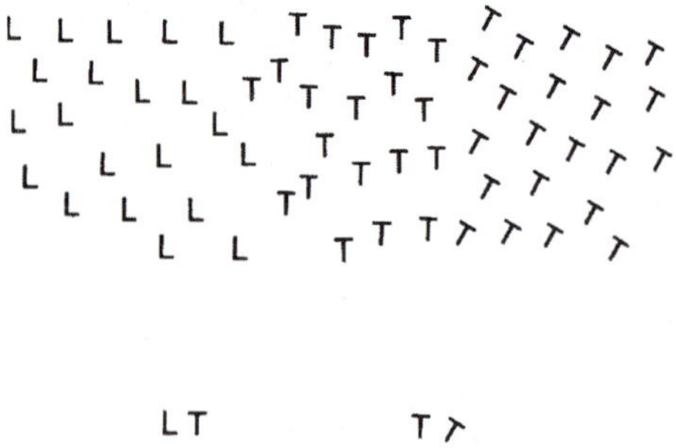

LT   T↗

Figure 3.7 Global versus local perception. On the top (global perception), contrast the L's (left) with the T's (center) with the slanted T's (right). The distinction between the T's and slanted T's is greater. However, in the bottom (local perception), the distinction between the L's and T's is at least as great as between the T's and slanted T's.

the left. This is a discrimination based on global processing (Olson & Attneave, 1970). At the bottom of the figure, however, illustrating local processing, the difference in discriminability between the two pairs is reduced, if not reversed.

The concepts of global and local processing are closely related to the *emergent features* concept discussed in Chapter 2. An emergent feature is a global property of a set of stimuli (or displays) not evident as each is seen in isolation. Consider the two sets of gauges shown in Figure 3.8, in which the normal setting of each gauge is vertical. The vertical alignment of the gauges on the top set allows more rapid detection of the divergent reading because of the emergent feature—a long vertical line—present in the top set but not in the bottom (Dashevsky, 1964).

Because global or holistic processing tends to be preattentive and automatic, it might reduce attentional demands as an operator processes a multielement display. But this savings is only realized under two conditions: First, the Gestalt principles based on information theory (e.g., redundancy) should be used to produce groupings or emergent features. Second, the organization formed by the spatial proximity of different elements on the display panel must be *compatible* with task demands. Thus, for example, in Figure 3.5a, the organization of the displays will not be helpful, and may even be harmful, if the task performed by the operator requires constant comparison of information presented in dials in the top-left with the bottom-right groups. We refer to this as a violation of *compatibility* between the display and task requirements. Some nuclear power consoles were designed with the panels for two reactors lying side by side, one the mirror image of the other. This configuration provided wonderful symmetry, which at a global level provided organization, but it made it difficult for the operator to switch between panels.

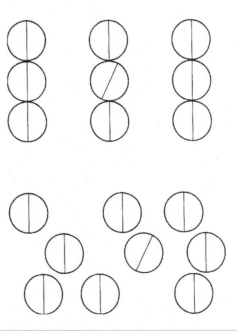

Figure 3.8   Global perception in the detection of misalignment.

Spatial Proximity

Overlapping Views: The Head-Up Display   The previous discussion suggests that spatial proximity, or closeness in space, should also enable parallel processing (and therefore help divided attention). Although one cannot simultaneously look at the speedometer and look out the windshield at the road, a display that could superimpose a view of the speedometer on a view of the road should facilitate divided attention or parallel processing between the two channels (Goesch, 1990, Tufano, 1997).

However, although spatial proximity will allow parallel processing, it certainly will not guarantee it. For example, in an experiment by Neisser and Becklen (1975), subjects watched a video display on which two games were presented simultaneously, one superimposed over the other. One showed distant figures tossing a ball, the other showed two pairs of hands playing a clapping game. One game was designated as relevant, and critical elements were to be monitored and detected. Neisser and Becklen found that while monitoring one game, subjects failed to see events in the other game, even when these were unusual or novel (e.g., the ball tossers paused to shake hands). They also had a difficult time when detecting events in two games at once. These results suggest that separation may be defined not only in terms of differences in visual or retinal location but also in terms of the nature of the perceived activity.

Neisser and Becklen's (1975) display has a counterpart in aviation, the *head-up display* (HUD) (Newman, 1995; Weintraub & Ensing, 1992; Wickens, 1997), which shows critical instrument readings on the glass windscreen superimposed on the forward view, as shown in Figure 3.9. Similar displays are being introduced into the automobile (Goesch, 1990; Tufano, 1997). The HUD was designed to ensure that information inside and outside an aircraft could be processed simultaneously without visual scanning. Neisser and Becklen's results suggest that this may not occur. A pilot may treat the two information sources as different attentional channels and become engrossed in processing instrument information on the HUD while ignoring critical cues from outside the aircraft, a phenomenon observed in experiments by Fischer, Haines, and Price (1980) and Larish and Wickens (1991). In studies using pilots as subjects, Wickens and Long (1995) found that an unexpected obstacle, an airplane crossing the runway, was detected more poorly with the HUD than with the head-down configuration. This airplane may be seen, poised to "move out," in Figure 3.9c. However, the HUD does have its advantages (Fadden, Ververs, & Wickens, 1998). Wickens and Long (1995) showed that a HUD could improve control of position during landing, both when in view and when the runway was obscured by clouds. Sojourner and Antin (1990) compared driver performance with HUDs and head-down displays and found a HUD advantage for detecting cues presented in the road scene. Other studies have also found HUD advantages relative to head-down presentation of the same information (e.g., Martin-Emerson & Wickens, 1997; Ververs & Wickens, 1998).

These apparently contradictory results appear to hinge on the expectations of the observer. The HUD appears to facilitate parallel processing of scene and symbology when the pilot expects the stimulus (e.g., the appearance of a runway during landing, objects that occur repeatedly during driving) and interferes when the stimulus is quite unexpected (e.g., a small airplane crossing the runway). A second factor affecting the costs and benefits of overlapping imagery is the *conformal* nature of the symbology itself, to be discussed below in the context of object displays.

(a)

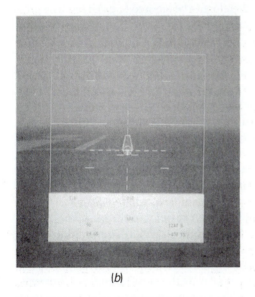

(b)

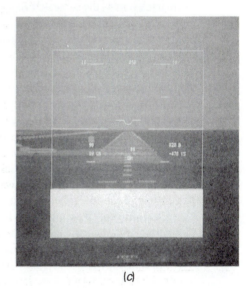

(c)

Figure 3.9   Head-up display used in aviation. (a) Head-up Guidance System (HGS). Courtesy of Flight Dynamics, Inc., Portland, Oregon. (b) Head-up display similar to that used by Wickens and Long (1995) and Martin-Emerson and Wickens (1997) with conformal imagery. Note the runway overlay. (c) Head-up display with nonconformal imagery. Note the airplane on the ground at the far left.

Source: C. D. Wickens & J. Long, "Object Versus Space-Based Models of Visual Attention: Implications for the Design of Head-Up Displays," *Journal of Experimental Psychology: Applied, 1* (1995), pp. 179–193; R. Martin-Emerson & C. D. Wickens, "Superimposition, Symbology, Visual Attention, and the Head-Up Display," *Human Factors, 39* (1997), pp. 581–601

Visual Confusion, Conflict, and Focused Attention   Although close proximity in space may sometimes allow more successful divided attention, it appears that it may increase *confusion* between those items that are momentarily the desired focus of attention and those that are not—that is, a failure to focus attention. Several pieces of evidence support this claim.

First, as we saw earlier in this chapter, in visual scanning, the spatial density of the objects has little effect on visual search time. With a high-density field, any advantages that may be realized in terms of more items per fixation will be negated by the increased clutter. Second, in a study in which subjects monitored several display indicators, Wickens and Andre (1990) found that the most critical variable in predicting performance is the degree of spatial separation of relevant from irrelevant items, not the spatial separation between the relevant items themselves. Third, a study by Holahan, Culler, and Wilcox (1978) found that the ability to locate and respond to a stop sign in a cluttered display is directly inhibited by the proximity of other irrelevant signs in the field of view.

The fourth piece of evidence is found in a classic study by Eriksen and Eriksen (1974), which will be discussed in more detail because it sets the stage for the discussion of object displays. In this experiment, subjects moved a lever to the right if the letter H appeared and to the left if the letter F appeared. Reaction time (RT) was measured in this control condition. In other conditions, the central target was closely flanked by two adjacent letters, which were irrelevant to the subjects' task and were therefore to be ignored (e.g., UHP). The presence of these flanking letters slowed RT relative to the control condition. This is the result of *perceptual competition*, a failure of focused attention caused by the competition for processing resources between close objects in space.

In the particular case in which the flanking letters are mapped to the opposite response (i.e., an H flanked by F's: FHF), RT is slowed still further. There is now an added cost to processing, which Eriksen and Eriksen (1974) describe as *response conflict*, a concept that we introduced in the context of Navon's (1977) experiment on global and local processing. It illustrates more clearly the failure of focused attention. It is as if the navigator sitting next to the automobile driver were saying, "Turn left," while a passenger in the back seat, engaged in a different conversation, says, "Yeah, right." Only when the flanking letters were identical (i.e., an H surrounded by two other H's: HHH) were RTs faster than in the control condition. This is another example of *redundancy gain.*

Response conflict and redundancy gain are thus two sides of the same coin. If two perceptual channels are close together, they will both be processed, even if only one is desired. This processing will inevitably lead to some competition (intrusion or distraction) at a perceptual level. If they have common implications for action, the perceptual competition is overcome because both channels activate the same response. If, however, their implications for action are incompatible, the amount of competition is magnified.

In real-world displays, perceptual competition and redundancy gain effects are more likely to be observed with greater display clutter. Flanking letters interfere most if they are close to the target (e.g., about 1 degree of visual angle), as if there is a minimum diameter of the spotlight of attention that guarantees some parallel processing (Broadbent, 1982). Parallel processing is less if flankers are placed farther from the target (e.g., 2–3 degrees) (Murphy & Eriksen, 1987). However, if the observer cannot be certain about the location of the target, then the interfering effect of flankers can occur at these greater distances (Murphy & Eriksen, 1987). Yantis and Johnston (1990) found that flanker effects could almost be eliminated by cueing subjects about target position. One can account for such results by using the spotlight metaphor. When the target location is uncertain, the observer must broaden the spotlight, which means that the flankers are more likely to be processed. When the target location is certain, the observer can narrow the spotlight so that the flankers have less effect (Kinchla, 1992). This effect is also sometimes described by the metaphor of a "zoom lens." In terms of interface design, there appears to be a penalty for not using a constant location for items of interest (e.g., changing the order of items on a menu in different contexts) in that the broader attentional spotlight produced by target uncertainty will ensure that irrelevant items are processed.

Mori and Hayashi (1995) found evidence for perceptual competition from adjacent windows in a computer display. When Mori and Hayashi had observers perform a visual search task in a main window, they found that increasing the number of peripheral windows increased the interference. When the search task target was nearer to the peripheral windows, performance degraded. Having overlapping windows also increased interference, as did dynamic peripheral windows. Thus, the perceptual competition described by Eriksen and Eriksen (1974) appears to play a part in multiwindow environments common in today's graphical user interfaces.

Object-Based Proximity   In Eriksen and Eriksen's (1974) study, similarity effects were reduced when flanking letters were moved away from the central letter. We might expect that the observed effects of response conflict and redundancy gain would be amplified even further if the different sources of information represented different attributes of a single stimulus object at one spatial location. Indeed several studies have shown that this is the case. Many of these investigations have employed some variation of the *Stroop task* (Stroop, 1935), in which the subject is asked to report the color of a series of stimuli as rapidly as possible. In a typical control condition (e.g., Keele, 1972), the stimuli consist of colored symbols—for example, a row of four X's in the same color. In the critical *conflict* condition, the stimuli are color names that do not match the color of ink in which they are printed (e.g., the word *red* printed in blue ink). We can consider the word as an object having two attributes relevant to the task: its meaning and its ink color. The results are dramatic: Reporting ink color is slow and error prone relative to the control condition, as the semantic attribute of the stimulus (*red*) activates a response incompatible with information the subject must process (the color blue). The mouth cannot say the words *red* and *blue* at the same time, yet both are called for by different attributes of the single stimulus. Redundancy gain effects have also been observed when the color of the ink matches the semantic content of the word (e.g., Keele, 1972).

Similar examples of redundancy gain and response competition have been reported with various kinds of stimuli. Clark and Brownell (1975) observed that judgments of an arrow's direction (up or down) were influenced by the arrow's location within the display. "Up" judgments were made faster when the arrow was higher in the display. "Down" judgments were made faster when it was low. Similarly, Rogers (1979) found that the time it took to decide if a word was *left* or *right* was influenced by whether the word was to the right or left of the display, and Algom, Dekel, and Pansky (1996) found that the time to classify a number as large or small was affected by the size of the numeral used to portray it.

The Stroop effect suggests that multiple dimensions belonging to a single object are likely to be processed in parallel (Logan, 1980; MacLeod, 1991; Kahneman & Treisman, 1984), which will help performance if parallel processing is required but will disrupt performance if one dimension is irrelevant and to be ignored, particularly if it triggers an automatic and incompatible response. Since objects are more likely to define *integral dimensions*, this finding is consistent with results reviewed in Chapter 2. That is, integral dimensions produce a cost for a filtering task and a benefit when dimensions are redundant.

We have discussed an attentional spotlight that allows concurrent processing of elements lying close together in space (a *space-based* model of attention). In contrast, an *object-based* model proposes that concurrent processing occurs when elements lie within a single object, independent of its spatial dimensions. Indeed, several researchers have shown that judgments made about two parts of the same object are faster than judgments made about parts of different objects, even when the distance between parts is held constant (e.g., Behrmann, Zemel, & Mozer, 1998; Egly, Driver, & Rafal, 1994). Other studies have separated objects from their locations using motion (e.g., Kahneman, Treisman, & Gibbs, 1992). In these studies, subjects were shown a pair of simple geometric shapes (e.g., triangle and square) each with a letter inside (a cue). The letters disappeared, and the objects moved to new locations. One of the two letters was presented in either the appropriate or inappropriate object, and the subject's task was to name this target letter. Subjects were faster when the target letter was consistent with the cue letter for that object than when it was not. Here, attention allocated to an object helped the subsequent perception of its properties, even though its location changed.

Object-oriented attention has also been shown in the Eriksen and Eriksen (1974) paradigm described above (identification of a target letter H is impaired when it is flanked with F's). Kramer and Jacobson (1991) showed that the effect of flanking elements was enhanced when lines were drawn connecting the flankers to the target letter (i.e., creating a single object), and reduced when the lines connected the flankers to other display objects. Baylis and Driver (1992) showed that flanking letters matching the target letter in color had greater interference and facilitation effects than did flanking letters of a different color, even when the different-color flankers were closer to the target. When display elements are arranged to form part of an object, they are perceived and attended to differently than when they are not, and in consequence we must give serious consideration to how display elements are combined to form objects in display design. Consider, for example, how menu items for a web site are sometimes placed on various parts of an iconic object.

Applications of Object-Based Processing

It is not a simple thing to define what an object is. In cognitive psychology, an object is typically said to have three features: (1) surrounding contours or connectedness between parts, (2) rigidity of motion of the parts (relative to other elements in the scene), and (3) familiarity. None of these are truly defining features, but the more of these features a stimulus has, the more "object-like" it becomes, and the more it can benefit from object-based attention.

We shall discuss the benefit of objects in two contexts. The first concerns the mapping of display objects to real-world objects using *conformal symbology*. The second involves the construction of *object displays* in which multiple information sources are encoded as the stimulus dimensions of a single object.

Conformal Symbology and Augmented Reality Earlier we mentioned a study by Wickens and Long (1995) that showed that the head-up display could improve control of aircraft position during landing. However, when the runway was in view, this result was true only when the HUD symbology was *conformal*: that is, the position of HUD objects corresponded to the position of objects they represented in the scene (e.g., the HUD runway superimposed on the physical runway as shown in Figure 3.9b). Some have referred to this conformal symbology as a form of *augmented reality* in that the reality of the far domain scene is augmented by computer generated imagery, projected on a near display (e.g., Drascic & Milgram, 1996). The Wickens and Long result is consistent with the object-based theories of attention discussed above: Having two components superimposed (the actual and HUD runways) to form one rigidly moving object using conformal symbology helped the pilot divide attention between the display and the world beyond, align the display object to the real object, and reduce tracking error (Martin-Emerson & Wickens, 1997).

Despite its utility in the aviation context, conformal imagery for automobile HUDs appears problematic. The number of objects a driver must see and keep track of is typically high, and the distances of the various objects from the driver varies considerably (Tufano, 1997). To present all this information at one distance (as HUDs typically do) may both clutter the display and distort the driver's perception of object distances in the scene. Nevertheless, some conformal imagery in vehicles has been considered to enhance visibility of the roadway ahead with synthetic imagery at night or in fog (Bossi, Ward, Parkes, & Howarth, 1997). Furthermore, the fusion of near and far, via augmented reality, has applications in many other domains.

Object Displays Designers have also capitalized on the parallel processing of object features to create multidimensional object displays. In these displays, multiple information sources are encoded as the stimulus dimensions of a single object. Figure 3.10 illustrates four such examples. Figure 3.10a shows an attitude directional indicator, a two-dimensional object display used in aircraft control, which we discussed earlier in this chapter. The vertical location of the aircraft symbol relative to the horizon line indicates aircraft *pitch* (nose up or nose down), and the angle between the symbol and the rotating horizon represents the *bank*, or roll, of the aircraft. In addition to its objectness, this display is configured in a way that represents the aircraft, and is therefore familiar to the pilot. Figure 3.10b shows the safety parameter display for nuclear power reactor operators designed by Westinghouse, in which the values of eight key parameters are indicated by the length of imaginary "spokes" extending from the center of the display and connected by line segments to form a polygon (Woods, Wise, & Hanes, 1981 see Chapter 13). In addition to its objectness, a potential advantage of this display is that each type of system problem produces a unique shape or configuration of the polygon, as seen on the right of the figure, resulting in an *emergent feature*.

The display developed by Cole (1986) for medical applications, in Figure 3.10c, illustrates another example of an emergent feature. The rectangular display represents the oxygen exchange between patient and respirator. The width represents the rate of breathing, and the height represents the depth of breathing. Hence, the *area* of the rectangle—an emergent feature—signals the total amount of oxygen exchanged, a critical variable to be monitored. This correspondence holds true because oxygen amount = rate $\times$ depth, and rectangle area = width $\times$ height.

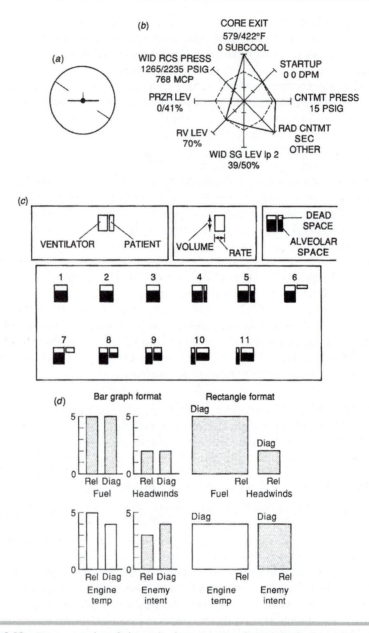

Figure 3.10 Four examples of object displays: (a) aircraft attitude display indicator, (b) safety parameter display, (c) medical display of oxygen exchange, (d) decision aid display.

Source: (c) Adapted from W. G. Cole, "Medical Cognitive Graphics," *Proceedings of CHI '86 Human Factors in Computing Systems.* Copyright 1986 by the Association for Computing Machinery, Inc. Reprinted by permission. (d) Adapted from B. J. Barnett and C. D. Wickens, "Display Proximity in Multicue Information Integration: The Benefits of Boxes," *Human Factors, 30* (1988). Copyright 1988 by the Human Factors Society, Inc. All rights reserved.

One might ask, however, if the critical parameter is oxygen amount, why not display that quantity directly rather than have the operator infer it from the rectangle's area? The reason is that it is sometimes necessary to *focus* attention on one of the variables (rate and depth) contributing to the amount. This raises a question: Will the close proximity created by the object display disrupt the ability to focus attention on one of its dimensions, as when the operator must check one of the values being integrated? We address this question in the next section.

The Proximity Compatibility Principle

In the previous sections, we have discussed three ways in which multiple display channels can be integrated: through configuration to create emergent features, through spatial proximity, and through object integration. The issue of whether different tasks are served differently by more or less integrated displays is represented explicitly in the *proximity compatibility principle* (Barnett & Wickens, 1988; Wickens & Andre, 1990; Wickens & Carswell, 1995). To understand this principle, we must distinguish between display and processing proximity. *Display proximity* defines how close together two display components are. The distance between the components can be defined in spatial terms (i.e., the components are 1 cm apart) or in terms of object-based properties (the components are displayed as part of the same object, as in the display by Cole, 1986). In addition, Wickens and Carswell note that display proximity can be increased by other factors, such as using a common color or coding each variable using a common dimension; e.g., the two variables are both represented by lengths vs. one represented as a length and the other represented by an angle or digit. *Processing proximity* defines the extent to which two information sources are used within the same task (e.g., compared or integrated). A task with high processing proximity might be to estimate whether there is an increasing or decreasing trend in a scatterplot—many information sources (data points) must be considered. A task with low processing proximity might be to estimate the y-axis value of one data point in the scatterplot. The proximity compatibility principle can be summarized as follows:

> If a task requires high processing proximity, there should be high display proximity.

> If a task requires low processing proximity, there should be low display proximity.

Hence, to the extent that information sources must be integrated, there will be a benefit to presenting those sources either close together, in an objectlike format, or by configuring them to create emergent features. To the extent that information sources must be treated separately, the benefit of the high-proximity object display will be reduced, if not sometimes reversed. The advantage of object displays for information integration results from two factors. The first is that object dimensions can be processed in parallel (Treisman & Kahneman, 1984). Hence, the two sources, coded by the two dimensions, will more rapidly gain access to central processing. The second is that an object will be more likely to produce an emergent feature (e g., area or shape) that can directly serve integration task requirements (Bennett & Flach, 1992). This is especially true when the dimensions are of the same type (e.g., all measures of extent, like the height and width of a rectangle) (Carswell, 1990). However, when a task requires focused attention on one dimension, the very emergent feature that helped integration can make the focused attention task more difficult, just as closeness in space can create clutter which disrupts focusing.

The predictions of the proximity compatibility principle have been investigated and generally supported in many different contexts (e.g., Goettl, Wickens, & Kramer, 1991; Haskell & Wickens, 1993; Liu & Wickens, 1992, Mori & Hayashi, 1995; Vincow & Wickens, 1993). The situation illustrated in Figure 3.10d is representative. It shows an intelligent airborne decision aid that advises a pilot about whether to continue the current mission. Each recommendation is based on an information source (e.g., a weather advisory or an engine fuel check). The two dimensions of the display represent the two characteristics of each source: its *reliability* (how much it can be trusted) and its *diagnosticity* (its relevance to the decision at hand). As we will see in Chapter 8, these two features combine to indicate the total information *worth* of the source. Barnett and Wickens (1988) found that tasks requiring the integration of the two dimensions to evaluate total worth were served better by a rectangle display than by a bar graph display. As with Cole's (1986) experiment, the emergent feature of the area directly revealed the quantity (information worth) to be inferred. But when attention had to be focused on one variable to the exclusion of the other (e.g., the question "What was the reliability of weather information?"), the advantage for the rectangle over the bar graph disappeared. The proximity compatibility principle has also been successfully applied to the design of statistical graphs (e.g., Carswell & Wickens, 1988; Hollands & Spence, 1992), to be discussed further in Chapter 4.

Emergent features need not be created exclusively by single objects (Buttigieg & Sanderson, 1991; Sanderson, Flach, Buttigieg, & Casey, 1989). Indeed, we saw the emergent feature created by the vertical array of dials at the top of Figure 3.8. An array of parallel bar graphs representing, for example, four engine parameters, such as that in Figure 3.11, also creates an emergent feature—a horizontal line across the top—when all engines are running at the same level. In this case, display proximity is defined not by belonging to a common object but by the identical form of representation (vertical extent) of all the indicators. Displays that portray higher-order information using emergent features are referred to as *configural displays*. An alternative approach put forth by Elvers and Dolan (1995) proposes that separated displays (e.g., bar graphs) can be *augmented* to

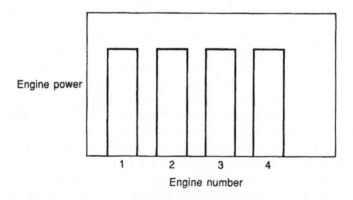

Figure 3.11   Emergent features in engine parameter display.

show directly that information important for an integration task. In either case, it is clear that one can design spatially separated displays that are effective for integrated tasks as long as they use similar attributes to convey information (e.g., spatial extent) and the emergent features are constructed to support the task demands (Bennett & Flach, 1992).

Some researchers have advocated the use of *Chernoff face displays* as a way of integrating information for portraying complex multivariate data (e.g., Jacob, Egeth, & Bevan, 1976). These displays arrange simple geometric symbols in the shape of a face. The size or shape of each symbol varies with the magnitude of the variable it represents. The face may be considered an object in that it is both highly familiar and is enclosed by a single contour, the head. Chernoff face displays tend to be effective for integration tasks (since the expression and appearance of the face change considerably with changes in the data). Suzuki and Cavanagh (1995) had subjects perform integrated and focused search tasks on face displays and a random arrangement of the same features and found that subjects performed better with the face display on the integrated task, but they performed better with the random feature arrangement on the focused task. These results are consistent with the predictions of the proximity compatibility principle.

The identical color of two objects on a display, like the integrality of the dimensions of an object, also creates display proximity that serves processing proximity (Wickens & Andre, 1990). That is, two items on a cluttered display will be more easily integrated or compared if they share the same color (different from the clutter), but the shared identity of color may disrupt the ability to focus attention on one while ignoring the other. A unique color code helps this focusing process, just as it disrupts the integration process. This appears related to the effect of flanker color similarity in the Eriksen and Eriksen (1974) paradigm mentioned earlier (Kramer & Jacobson, 1991).

The proximity compatibility principle also applies to spatial distance in a cluttered display. Two pieces of information that need to be integrated on a cluttered display should be placed in close spatial proximity, as long as this proximity does not also move them too close to irrelevant clutter (Wickens & Andre, 1990). For example, Sweller, Chandler, Tierney, and Cooper (1990) found that visual materials lead to better learning if graphic material and related text (two information sources with close mental proximity because they need to be integrated) are adjacent to one another on the page. Bettman, Payne, and Staelin (1986) discuss the importance of spatial proximity between related items (costs and benefits of a product) in the design of product warning labels. Milroy and Poulton (1978) point to the importance of close proximity between graphed lines and their labels. That is, labels should be set next to the lines, not in a legend below. Weinstein, Gillingham, and Ercoline (1994) found that when a symbol showing vertical velocity was integrated into a circular altimeter, it produced better performance than other arrangements where vertical velocity information was further away from the altimeter. This result supports the proximity compatibility principle because a pilot must often integrate vertical velocity and altitude information.

With computers, an advantage of window-based systems is that they allow simultaneous and adjacent positioning of different information sources that need to be compared (e.g., a version of a document with and without critical comments). This is clearly superior to earlier screen arrangements where comparing two screens meant remembering the information on one while viewing the other. When the windows are placed in adjacent positions, corresponding parts of the documents are located in similar locations and can therefore be compared more easily than otherwise, also helping to reduce attentional demands. By allowing the user to view both windows simultaneously, and by placing the windows adjacently, we are allowing high display proximity when our task requires high processing proximity. The proximity compatibility principle can therefore be used to help reduce attentional demands when comparing information. As noted above, however, closely-spaced irrelevant windows can hurt the focus of attention (Mori & Hayashi, 1995).

An illustration of a violation of the principle is found in the design of the radar display on the *USS Vincennes*. An Iranian passenger airplane was mistaken for an attacking fighter plane by the *Vincennes* and inadvertently shot down in the Persian Gulf (U.S. Navy, 1988; Klein, 1996). In the radar display, the symbol signifying the location of the aircraft was in a separate location from information describing the vertical actions of the approaching aircraft (labeled the "range gate"). It is likely that the lack of close spatial proximity prevented the operators from integrating the two pieces of information correctly. Hence, the aircraft was classified as a descending, attacking fighter rather than a climbing, commercial air carrier.

In conclusion, moving multiple displayed elements close together, providing them with a common representation (e.g., color or format), or integrating them as dimensions of a single object) has the following effects:

1. This close proximity will increase the possibility of parallel processing by moving both dimensions into foveal vision. Parallel processing will be most likely to occur if they are integrated as dimensions of a single object.
2. Both close spatial proximity and objectness can create useful emergent features such as symmetry, shape or order if the display dimensions are the same (e.g., the length of two lines can create an emergent feature; the length of a line and its color cannot). These emergent features can help information integration if they are mapped into key variables of the task. (The mapping calls for creativity and ingenuity by the display designer.) The emergent features can hurt performance if they are not mapped into the task.
3. The close proximity, enhanced by objectness, can create unwanted clutter (sometimes in the form of emergent features) or response conflict. Both response conflict and emergent features will be troublesome to the extent that the task calls for focused attention on one of the variables combined in the display.

Color Coding

Discussions of target search and visual attention must include a brief treatment of the specific effects of color coding in displays, although color coding relates to a number of other topics in this book. For the 97 percent of the population who are not color-blind (roughly 7 percent of males cannot adequately discriminate certain wavelengths of light), differences in color are processed more or less automatically and in parallel with characteristics of shape and motion (Treisman, 1986). Although there are costs, several benefits result from the automatic characteristics of color processing.

1. Color stands out from a monochrome background. Therefore, color-coded targets are rapidly and easily noticed. As suggested in our discussions of visual search, search time for a uniquely color-coded target in a cluttered field is independent of the size of the field. Therefore, color coding of targets or critical elements in a display is quite effective for rapid localization (Christ, 1975). Color is effective as a means of highlighting an important item on a menu, for example (Fisher & Tan, 1989).

2. Certain colors have well established symbolic meaning within a population (e.g., in America, red signals danger, hostility, the order to stop; green signals go, safety), and therefore, color coding can capitalize on these *population stereotypes,* a concept to be discussed further in Chapter 9.

3. Color coding can tie together spatially separated display elements. As noted, this characteristic will be most useful if the commonly colored items also need to be *integrated* as part of the task (Wickens & Andre, 1990). Thus, for example, there will be an advantage to color coding different regions on a weather map according to temperature. Regions having similar temperatures can be perceptually grouped in parallel.

4. The automaticity with which color is coded enhances its value as a *redundant* coding device in combination with shape, size, or location. As noted in Chapter 2, the traffic light is an example of redundant coding of color with location. Both Kopala (1979) and Hughes and Creed (1994) found that redundant use of color improved search times in aircraft displays. Backs and Walrath (1992) found similar results, especially when the task involved identifying a set of multiple targets in the display. Backs and Walrath also found that fewer eye movements were necessary when redundant color coding, suggesting larger UFOVs in this situation. To realize the full benefits of redundant coding was used, however, it may be necessary to cue users as to the existence of the redundancy (Backs & Walrath, 1995).

Because of its aesthetic appeal, color coding has become prevalent in many displays. However, we note several subtle limitations that may be critical for system design.

1. Like other sensory continua, color is subject to the limits of absolute judgment (see Chapter 2). To guarantee that the value (and therefore meaning) of a color will not be misidentified (i.e., no errors), the system designer should use no more than five or six colors in a display (Carter & Cahill, 1979), although maximum information throughput occurs using about ten colors (Flavell & Heath, 1992). Furthermore, if colors are to be perceived under conditions of glare or changing or low illumination (e.g. the dashboard or cockpit), failures of absolute judgment will be even more prevalent, because color perception is affected by ambient light; for example, red may be confused for brown (Stokes, Wickens, & Kite, 1990).

2. Color does not naturally define an ordered continuum. If people are asked, for example, to place five colors in an order from "least" to "most," there will be a great divergence of opinion about the appropriate ordering. Even the rainbow spectrum is far from universally recognized as a continuum. Since color or hue

ordering does not have a strong population stereotype, it is generally ineffective to use color coding to represent an ordered variable like speed or density. Instead quantitative variables should be coded using *saturation* or brightness rather than—or redundantly with—hue (Kaufmann & Glavin, 1990). For example, to code altitude on a map, a single hue (e.g., brown) is used, but greater levels of the variable being coded are shown in more saturated color (e.g., higher altitudes are shown in darker brown, or greater ocean depths are shown in a darker blue) (Tufte, 1990).

3. Population stereotypes can produce poor design if a color-coding scheme associates a color with a conflicting meaning. For example, suppose a temperature-coding scheme is designed in which green represents low temperature, but in the system very low temperatures signal an unsafe operating condition. Hence, the population stereotype of green with "safe" or "go" is not the one that should be inferred by the operator.

4. Given the automaticity with which it is processed, irrelevant color coding can be distracting. When different colors are used to highlight different areas or items, it is important that the distinction made by the colors is compatible with relevant cognitive distinctions that are intended to be interpreted by the viewer. This issue of display-cognitive compatibility was discussed in the context of spatial organization and will emerge again in Chapter 4 in discussions of display motion.

Given the reduced costs of color VDT displays, color has become a more viable option for the display designer. Although operators usually express a preference for color over monochrome displays, caution should be exercised before deciding on its implementation and careful consideration should be given to the limitations and constraints, as described.

ATTENTION IN THE AUDITORY MODALITY

The auditory modality is different from the visual in two respects relevant to attention. First, the auditory sense can take input from any direction, and thus, there is no analog to visual scanning as an index of selective attention. Second, most auditory input is transient. A word or tone is heard and then it ends, in contrast to most visual input, which tends to be more continuously available. For example, the printed word usually remains on the page. Hence, the preattentive characteristics of auditory processing—those required to "hold on" to a stimulus before it is gone—are more critical in audition than in vision. As discussed briefly in Chapter 1, short-term auditory store is longer than short-term visual store.

There is a long history of research in auditory selective attention, which will not be discussed here (see Moray, 1969; Wickens, 1984). Much of this research is based on the *dichotic listening task*, in which the listener hears two independent *channels* of sounds, words, or sentences, one in each ear. Usually the subject attends to only one channel and the other is ignored. Interest has focused on the physical and semantic characteristics of messages that lead to successes and failures in these divided and focused attention tasks (Broadbent, 1958; Cherry, 1953; Moray, 1969; Treisman, 1969).

Auditory Divided Attention

A general model of auditory attention (see Norman, 1968; Keele, 1973) proposes that an unattended channel of auditory input remains in preattentive short-term auditory store for 3–6 seconds (see Chapter 6). The contents of this store can be "examined" if a conscious switch of attention is made. Thus, if your attention wanders while someone is talking to you, it is possible to switch back and "hear" the last few words the person spoke, even if you were not attending to them when they were uttered.

Even in the absence of a conscious attention switch, information in unattended channels may make contact with long-term memory. That is, words in the unattended channel are not just meaningless "blobs" of sound, but their meaning is analyzed at a preattentive level. If the unattended material is sufficiently pertinent, it will often become the focus of attention (i.e., attention will be switched to the unattended channel). For example, a loud sound will almost always grab our attention, as it may signal a sudden environmental change that must be dealt with. Our own name also has a continued pertinence, and so we will sometimes shift attention to it when spoken, even if we are listening to another speaker (Moray, 1959; Wood & Cowan, 1995). So also does material semantically related to the topic that is the current focus of attention (Treisman, 1964a).

What of the fate of the words or sounds that never receive our attention—either because their pertinence is not high enough or because we do not voluntarily choose to listen to them? As Dr. Seuss says, "Oh, their future is dreary" (Seuss, 1971). There is little evidence that this material makes any impact on long-term memory, beyond the brief, transient activation of the semantic unit. Hence, the idea of learning without awareness, whether in one's sleep or through techniques of "subliminal perception," has received little empirical validation (Swets & Druckman, 1988).

Information presented in an unattended channel is temporarily inhibited for several seconds following presentation, demonstrating a phenomenon called *negative priming* (Banks, Roberts, & Ciranni, 1995). On some trials, Banks et al. presented information in the attended channel that had been presented to the unattended channel on the previous trial. When subjects *shadowed* this information, they were slower relative to a control condition in which the information was new, demonstrating negative priming. The negative priming was the same whether both presentations were to the same ear or different ears, suggesting that the inhibition of the unattended information adheres to the content and not the position in space. Negative priming has also been demonstrated in the visual modality (e.g., Fox, 1995).

In our discussion of visual attention, we saw that close proximity, particularly as defined by objectness, was a key to supporting the successful division of attention necessary in an information integration task. We also saw that the same manipulations of proximity that allowed success in divided attention were responsible for the failure of focused attention. These manipulations and observations have analogies in audition.

It is possible to think of an "auditory object" as a sound (or series of sounds) with several dimensions, which seem to enjoy the same benefits of parallel processing as do the dimensions of a visual object. For example, we can attend to both the words and melody of a song and to the meaning and voice inflections of a spoken sentence. Moore and Massaro (1973) found that subjects were able to judge the quality and pitch of a tone simultaneously as well as either dimension could be judged alone. Auditory warning alerts have been designed to capitalize on our parallel processing ability using redundant dimensions like pitch, timbre, and interruption rate in various combinations (Edworthy & Loxley, 1990; Sorkin, 1987).

Focusing Auditory Attention

In vision, we saw that using close proximity to facilitate parallel processing was a double-edged sword because it disrupted the ability to focus attention. In the auditory modality, too, we find that focused attention on one channel is disrupted when two messages have similar spatial locations (e.g., Egan, Carterette, & Thwing, 1954; Treisman, 1964b). For example, in *monaural* listening, two messages are presented by headphones with equal relative intensity to both ears. This is similar to what you would experience when listening to two speakers both directly in front of you. In dichotic listening, the headphones deliver one message to the left ear, and the other to the right, and you hear one voice in each ear. Egan, Carterette, and Thwing (1954) found that there are large benefits of dichotic over monaural listening in terms of the operator's ability to filter out the unwanted channel. However, we become less able to perform this selective filtering task as we age (Barr & Giambra, 1990).

We can also attend selectively to auditory messages even from similar locations. The *cocktail party effect* describes our ability to attend to one speaker at a noisy party and selectively filter out other conversations coming from similar spatial locations (with varying degrees of success). In this case, we must be able to use dimensions other than location to focus attention selectively. One such dimension for selection is defined by pitch. It is easier to attend to one voice in the presence of a second if the second voice is of the opposite sex (and thereby having different pitch) than if the two voices are of the same sex (Treisman, 1964b). Intensity may also serve as a dimension of selection. It is easy to attend to a loud message and tune out a soft one. Semantic properties can also serve as a cue for selection, so that it is easier to focus attention on one auditory message if a concurrent message has a very different semantic content (deals with a different topic) than if the content is similar (Treisman, 1964a)

By moving the eyes to a location, our visual system can selectively attend to the information at that location and ignore other information sources. Although the auditory modality does not have an "earball" that can rotate like an eyeball, it appears that auditory attention can be directed by cueing (e.g., Ward, 1994), just as visual attention can be directed without movement of the eye. Mondor and Zatorre (1995) found that auditory attention can be shifted to a specific location in response to an auditory spatial cue, and that the distance of the shift does not affect the time required for the shift of attention (i.e., the advantage of the cue was no greater when the target was at midline than when fully left or right). As with visual attention (when eye movement is not involved), it appears that the attentional spotlight is moved in discrete fashion rather than continuously as auditory attention is shifted from one spatial position to another.

To summarize, auditory messages differ from one another in terms of many dimensions such as pitch, location, loudness, and semantic content. The greater the difference between two messages along a given dimension and the greater the number of dimensions of difference, the easier it will be to focus on one message and ignore the other. When a message is ignored, its perception is subsequently inhibited for a brief period. Finally, auditory attention can be shifted to a particular location using an auditory cue.

Practical Implications

The characteristics of auditory attention have practical implications for system design, some of which have already been discussed. For example, we noted the concept of an auditory object and that system designers can capitalize on the parallel processing of several dimensions of an object to provide more redundancy or information in a given auditory alert. This will be discussed further when we consider detection of failures in process control (Chapter 13).

The auditory display designer wants to know what features of an alert will grab attention, so that it will be processed (Sorkin, 1987). As described in Chapters 12 and 13, although loud tones call attention to themselves, they can annoy and startle, and their intensity can increase stress, leading to poor information processing. Designers might capitalize on the operator's tendency to switch attention to contextually pertinent material (that is not necessarily loud) to design less noxious alerts. If a pilot is landing an airplane, for example, it may not be necessary to have loud alerts for those operations relevant to landing. However, loud alerts may still be necessary to indicate other changes in the status of the airplane (e.g., a drop in pressure in the passenger cabin). Since one has a low attentional threshold for one's own name, personalized alerts prefaced with the operator's name may also attract attention without high volume. These attention-grabbing but quieter auditory warnings have been called *attensors* (Hawkins & Orlady, 1993).

As noted above, the auditory modality does not have a directional "earball." Hence, greater concern must be given to determining those auditory display features that allow different auditory channels to be distinguished and discriminated. For example, how can the automobile designer ensure that an auditory warning will not be confused with a radio channel, engine noise, or ongoing conversation? The spatial dimension can be employed to some degree. An experiment by Darwin, Turvey, and Crowder (1972) suggests that three "spatial" channels may be processed without distraction if one is presented to each ear and a third is presented with equal intensity to both ears, thereby appearing to originate from the midplane of the head.

In this manner, airplane pilots might have available three distinct audio channels—for example, one for messages from the copilot, one for messages from air traffic control, and a third for messages from other aircraft or for synthesized voice warnings from their own aircraft. They could not process the three in parallel since all would call for common semantic analysis, which we saw was impossible, but they could at least focus on one with less intrusion from the others. The definition of channels in terms of the pitch dimension suggests that additional separation might be obtained by distinguishing the three spatial channels redundantly, through variation in pitch quality. Thus, the center message that is most likely to be confused with the other two could be presented at a substantially different pitch (or with a different speaker's voice) than the others.

The fact that there is no direction-sensitive auditory "earball" has its advantages as well. It can cue the user to locations in space in the full 360° volume of space. Thus, one can use spatial audio to assist a pilot (or potentially, a car driver) to identify targets of interest in the environment (e.g., Begault, 1993; Bronkhorst, Veltman, & van Breda, 1996). Begault (1993) was interested in whether 3D audio information presented redundantly with a visual target would help a pilot locate a target. The 3D audio system (both ears) that auditorially presented the location of the target shortened acquisition times to capture the target relative to an audio signal presented to one ear only. Begault and Pittman (1996) found that 3D audio alone produced shorter target acquisition times than a combined visual-auditory display in which a warning was presented auditorially and the location was presented visually. It is also important to use broadband signals (signals that have a range of different frequencies) in order for pilots to accurately localize signals (King & Oldfield, 1997). This would seem even more necessary if pilots are to distinguish different pitch qualities.

Cross-Modality Attention

The discussion up to this point has focused exclusively on attention within a modality. But we are often confronted with parallel inputs across modalities. Consider our van driver in Chapter 1, who needed to attend to visual information (the map, the stalled car ahead), and auditory (the truck horn) simultaneously. Consider also other everyday situations, as when we drive and our passenger gives us verbal directions, or when the pilot landing an aircraft monitors the visual environment while listening to the copilot's spoken messages regarding key velocities. Advances in multimedia technology make it possible to view text or pictures and hear audio information simultaneously when we visit a web site. The construction of virtual environments, to be discussed in Chapter 5, also requires the proper integration of visual and auditory information.

There are advantages to using multiple modalities. Redundantly coding a target across modalities (e.g., a visual warning is coupled with an auditory beep) speeds processing (Miller, 1991). We saw this in the vigilance situation in Chapter 2. In addition, Miller also found redundancy gain effects depended on how levels of stimuli were paired. High spatial locations were responded to more quickly when they were paired with high-frequency tones than with low, and the opposite was true for low spatial locations, an example of configurable stimulus dimensions as described in Chapter 2, and also similar to the Stroop effects described in this chapter. In Chapter 11, we will discuss some experiments suggesting that dividing attention between modalities may be better than dividing attention within a modality.

It is commonly found that when input from vision and other modalities is put in conflict, the phenomenon of *visual dominance* results. Examples of visual dominance over auditory or proprioceptive modalities are abundant. For example, Colovita (1971) required subjects to respond as fast as possible to either a light (with one hand) or a tone (with the other hand). On infrequent occasions, both stimuli were presented simultaneously. When this occurred, subjects responded to the light and did not notice the tone. Jordan (1972) found that reaction time to a compound stimulus consisting of a light and displacement of a limb was slower than reaction time to the proprioceptive stimulus alone. This result suggests that the light captured attention and slowed down processing of the proprioceptive information. Different examples of visual dominance are observed when vision and proprioception are placed in conflict through prismatically distorted lenses (Rock, 1975). Behavior in these situations suggests that the subject responds to the visual information and disregards that provided by other modalities.

Some time-sharing situations described in Chapter 11 also show a form of visual dominance when auditory and visual tasks are performed concurrently. In these circumstances, the auditory task tends to be hurt more by the division of attention than the visual task (e.g., Massaro & Warner, 1977).

There are circumstances in which visual dominance can lead to nonadaptive behavior. Illusions of movement provide an example. When the visual system gives ambiguous cues concerning the state of motion, the correct information provided by proprioceptive, vestibular, or "seat of the pants" cues is often misinterpreted and distorted. For example, while sitting in a car at an intersection with another car beside, passengers may experience the illusion that their car is moving backward, while in fact their vehicle is stationary and the adjacent car is moving forward. The passengers have discounted the proprioceptive evidence from the seat of the pants that no inertial forces are operating.

Visual dominance can be moderated in some cases. Ward (1994) measured response times for visual or auditory targets (an "x" appearing on the left or right of fixation, or a sound occurring to the left or right, respectively), with no cue, a visual cue, an auditory cue, or both types of cues. He found that when the visual cue conflicted with the auditory cue, visual cues dominated if the target was visual, but auditory cues dominated if the target was auditory. Heller (1992) found that visual dominance was eliminated and haptic dominance was shown when observers identified letter shapes by haptic exploration and vision simultaneously. It may be that in most studies of visual dominance, the fundamental task is visual, but visual dominance is not universal across tasks.

The phenomenon of visual dominance appears to oppose our natural tendency to switch attention to stimuli in the auditory and tactile modalities. These stimuli are intrusive, and the peripheral receptors have no natural way to shut out auditory or tactile information. We cannot close our "earlids," nor can we move our earball away. As a consequence, auditory devices are generally preferred to visual signals as warnings (Simpson & Williams, 1980; Sorkin, 1987). The truck horn effectively warned our van driver of the truck's presence in the Chapter 1 vignette, perhaps saving the driver's life.

In summary, when an abrupt auditory stimulus intrudes on a background of ongoing visual activity, it will probably call attention to itself and alert the operator. However, if visual stimuli are appearing at the same frequency and providing information of the same general type or importance as auditory or proprioceptive stimuli, biases toward the visual source at the expense of the other two is likely if the task is visual in nature.

TRANSITION

In this chapter, we have described attention as a filter to the environment. Sometimes the filter narrows to decrease irrelevant visual or auditory input, and sometimes the filter broadens to take in parallel streams of environmental information. The effective breadth of the filter is dictated by the limits of our senses (e.g., foveal vision), the differences and similarities between stimulus channels, and the strategies and understanding of the human operator. What happens, then, when material passes through the filter of attention? We saw in Chapter 2 that material may be provided with a simple yes-no classification (signal detection) or categorized into a level on a continuum (absolute judgment). More often, however, the material is given a more sophisticated and complex interpretation. This interpretation is the subject of several subsequent chapters.

It is convenient to distinguish between two kinds of perceptual interpretation. The first are *analog-spatial* interpretations, whose relevance is defined by continuous spatial dimensions. Judgments about how far away things are, where they are, how big they are, and how they are oriented involve this type of interpretation. The judgments that a driver makes about the state of a vehicle, or that a pilot makes about the state of an aircraft, are of this form. So also is the reading of a dial, a graph, or the mercury level in a thermometer. The interpretation is directly *analogous* to the physical form. The second class of interpretations consists of those that are *verbal and symbolic*. The meaning of these stimuli is not directly embodied in their physical form (location, shape, or orientation). Rather, this meaning is interpreted by decoding some symbolic representation, a written or spoken word or alphanumeric story or geometric symbol. Hence, this form of perception is heavily language based.

Attention to these stimulus sources, whether analog or symbolic, is necessary but not sufficient to properly interpret the state of the world on which to base future actions. In Chapters 4 and 5, we will discuss the perception and interpretation of analog material; in Chapter 6, we will discuss symbolic verbal material. We will revisit the concept of attention in Chapter 11, in the context of dividing attention among tasks rather than perceptual channels.

REFERENCES

Abernethy, B. (1988). Visual search in sport and ergonomics: Its relationship to selective attention and performer expertise. *Human Performance, 1,* 205–235.

Algom, D., Dekel, A., & Pansky, A. (1996). The perception of number from the separability of the stimulus: The Stroop effect revisited. *Memory and Cognition, 24,* 557–572.

Atchley, P., Kramer, A. F., Andersen, G. J., & Theeuwes, J. (1997). Spatial cuing in a stereoscopic display: Evidence for a "depth-aware" attentional focus. *Psychonomic Bulletin & Review, 4,* 524–529.

Backs, R. W., & Walrath, L. C. (1992). Eye movement and pupillary response indices of mental workload during visual search of symbolic displays. *Applied Ergonomics, 23,* 243–254.

Backs, R. W., & Walrath, L. C. (1995). Ocular measures of redundancy gain during visual search of colour symbolic displays. *Ergonomics, 38,* 1831–1840.

Bacon, W. F., & Egeth, H. E. (1994). Overriding stimulus-driven attentional capture. *Perception & Psychophysics, 55,* 485–496.

Ball, K. K., Beard, B. L., Roenker, D. L., Miller, R. L., & Griggs, D. S. (1988). Age and visual search: Expanding the useful field of view. *Journal of the Optical Society of America A, 5,* 2210–2219.

Banks, W. P., Roberts, D., & Ciranni, M. (1995). Negative priming in auditory attention. *Journal of Experimental Psychology: Human Perception & Performance, 21,* 1354–1361.

Barnett, B. J., & Wickens, C. D. (1988). Display proximity in multicue information integration: The benefit of boxes. *Human Factors, 30,* 15–24.

Barr, R. A., & Giambra, L. M. (1990). Age-related decrement in auditory selective attention. *Psychology & Aging, 5,* 597–599.

Baylis, G. C., & Driver, J. (1992). Visual parsing and response competition: The effect of grouping factors. *Perception & Psychophysics, 51,* 145–162.

Begault, D. R. (1993). Head-up auditory displays for traffic collision avoidance system advisories: A preliminary investigation. *Human Factors, 35,* 707–717.

Begault, D. R., & Pittman, M. T. (1996). Three-dimensional audio versus head-down Traffic Alert and Collision Avoidance System displays. *International Journal of Aviation Psychology, 6,* 79–93.

Behrmann, M., Zemel, R. S., & Mozer, M. C. (1998). Object-based attention and occlusion: Evidence from normal participants and a computational model. *Journal of Experimental Psychology: Human Perception & Performance, 24,* 1011–1036.

Bellenkes, A. H., Wickens, C. D., & Kramer, A. F. (1997). Visual scanning and pilot expertise: The role of attentional flexibility and mental model development. *Aviation, Space, and Environmental Medicine, 68,* 569–579.

Bennett, K. B., & Flach, J. M. (1992). Graphical displays: Implications for divided attention, focused attention, and problem solving. *Human Factors, 34,* 513–533.

Bettman, J. R., Payne, J. W., & Staelin, R. (1986). Cognitive considerations in designing effective labels for presenting risk information. *Journal of Marketing and Public Policy, 5,* 1–28.

Bossi, L. L., Ward, N. J., Parkes, A. M., & Howarth P. A. (1997). The effect of vision enhancement systems on driver peripheral visual performance. In I. Noy (Ed.), *Ergonomics and safety of intelligent driver interfaces.* Mahwah, NJ: Erlbaum.

Broadbent, D. E. (1958). *Perception and communications.* London: Pergamon Press.

Broadbent, D. E. (1982). Task combination and selective intake of information. *Acta Psychologica, 50,* 253–290.

Bronkhorst, A. W., Veltman, J. A., & van Breda, L. (1996). Application of a three-dimensional auditory display in a flight task. *Human Factors, 38,* 23–33.

Buttigieg, M. A., & Sanderson, P. M. (1991). Emergent features in visual display design for two types of failure detection tasks. *Human Factors, 33,* 631–651.

Carbonnell, J. R., Ward, J. L., & Senders, J. W. (1968). A queueing model of visual sampling: Experimental validation. *IEEE Transactions on Man-Machine Systems, MMS–9,* 82–87.

Carswell, C. M. (1990). Graphical information processing: The effects of proximity compatibility. *Proceedings of the 34th annual meeting of the Human Factors Society* (pp. 1494–1498). Santa Monica, CA: Human Factors Society.

Carswell, C. M., & Wickens, C. D. (1988). *Comparative graphics: History and applications of perceptual integrality theory and the proximity compatibility hypothesis.* University of Illinois Technical Report (ARL–88–2–/AHEL–88–1; AHEL Technical Memorandum 8–88). Savoy, IL: Aviation Research Laboratory.

Carter, R. C., & Cahill, M. C. (1979). Regression models of search time for color-coded information displays. *Human Factors, 21,* 293–302.

Chase, R., & Kalil, R. E. (1972). Suppression of visual evoked responses to flashes and pattern shifting during voluntary saccades. *Vision Research, 12,* 215–220.

Chau, A. W., & Yeh, Y. Y. (1995) Segregation by color and stereoscopic depth in three-dimensional visual space. *Perception & Psychophysics, 57,* 1032,1044

Cherry, C. (1953). Some experiments on the reception of speech with one and with two ears. *Journal of the Acoustical Society of America, 25,* 975–979.

Christ, R. E. (1975). Review and analysis of color coding research for visual displays. *Human Factors, 17,* 542–570.

Clark, H. H., & Brownell, H. H. (1975). Judging up and down. *Journal of Experimental Psychology: Human Perception & Performance, 1,* 339–352.

Cole, W. G. (1986). Medical cognitive graphics. *Proceedings of the ACM-SIGCHI: Human factors in computing systems* (pp. 91–95). New York: Association for Computing Machinery, Inc.

Colovita, F. B. (1971). Human sensory dominance. *Perception & Psychophysics, 16,* 409–412.

Conejo, R., & Wickens, C. D. (1997). *The effects of highlighting validity and feature type on air-to-ground target acquisition performance.* University of Illinois Institute of Aviation Technical Report (ARL–97–11/NAWC-ONR–97–1). Savoy, IL: Aviation Research Laboratory.

Craig, A. (1981). Monitoring for one kind of signal in the presence of another. *Human Factors, 23,* 191–198.

Darwin, C., Turvey, M. T., & Crowder, R. G. (1972). An analog of the Sperling partial report procedure. *Cognitive Psychology, 3,* 255–267.

Dashevsky, S. G. (1964). Check-reading accuracy as a function of pointer alignment, patterning and viewing angle. *Journal of Applied Psychology, 48,* 344–347.

Dewar, R. (1993). Warning: Hazardous road signs ahead. *Ergonomics in Design,* July, 26–31.

Donk, M. (1994). Human monitoring behavior in a multiple-instrument setting: Independent sampling, sequential sampling or arrangement-dependent sampling. *Acta Psychologica, 86,* 31–55.

Downing, C. J. (1988). Expectancy and visual-spatial attention: Effects on perceptual quality. *Journal of Experimental Psychology: Human Perception & Performance, 14,* 188–202.

Drascic, D., & Milgram, P. (1996). Perceptual issues in augmented reality. In M. T. Bolas, S. S. Fisher, and J. O. Merritt (Eds.), *Proceedings of the International Society for Optical Engineers (SPIE): Stereoscopic Displays and Virtual Reality Systems III* (pp. 123–134). Bellingham, WA: SPIE.

Drury, C. (1975). Inspection of sheet metal: Model and data. *Human Factors, 17,* 257–265.

Drury, C. (1982). Improving inspection performance. In G. Salvendy (Ed.), *Handbook of industrial engineering.* New York: Wiley.

Drury, C. G., & Clement, M. R. (1978). The effect of area, density, and number of background characters on visual search. *Human Factors, 20,* 597–602.

Edworthy, J., & Loxley, S. (1990). Auditory warning design: The ergonomics of perceived urgency. In E. J. Lovesey (Ed.), *Contemporary ergonomics 1990* (pp. 384–388). London: Francis and Taylor.

Egan, J., Carterette, E., & Thwing, E. (1954). Some factors affecting multichannel listening. *Journal of the Acoustical Society of America, 26,* 774–782.

Egeth, H., & Dagenbach, D. (1991). Parallel versus serial processing in visual search: Further evidence from subadditive effects of visual quality. *Journal of Experimental Psychology: Human Perception & Performance, 17,* 551–560.

Egeth, H. E., & Yantis, S. (1997). Visual attention: control, representation, and time course. *Annual Review of Psychology, 48,* 269–297.

Egly, R., Driver, J., & Rafal, R. D. (1994). Shifting visual attention between objects and locations: evidence from normal and parietal lesion subjects. *Journal of Experimental Psychology: General, 123,* 161–177.

Elkind, J. I., Card, S. K., Hochberg, J., & Huey, B. M. (Eds.). (1990). *Human performance models for computer-aided engineering.* Orlando, FL: Academic Press.

Elvers, G. C., & Dolan, N. J. (1995). A comparison of the augmented bar display and the object display. *Ergonomics, 38,* 777–792.

Eriksen, B. A., & Eriksen, C. W. (1974). Effects of noise letters upon the identification of a target letter in a nonsearch task. *Perception & Psychophysics, 16,* 143–149.

Eriksen, C. W., & Collins, J. F. (1969). Temporal course of selective attention. *Journal of Experimental Psychology, 80,* 254–261.

Eriksen, C. W., & Webb, J. (1989). Shifting of attentional focus within and about a visual display. *Perception & Psychophysics, 42,* 60–68.

Fadden, S., Ververs, P. M., & Wickens, C. D. (1998). Costs and benefits of head-up display use: A meta-analytic approach. *Proceedings of the 42nd annual meeting of the Human Factors and Ergonomics Society* (pp. 16–20). Santa Monica, CA: Human Factors and Ergonomics Society.

Fischer, E., Haines, R., & Price, T. (1980, December). *Cognitive issues in head-up displays* (NASA Technical Paper 1711). Washington, DC: NASA.

Fisher, D. F., Monty, R. A., & Senders, J. W. (Eds.). (1981). *Eye movements: Cognition and visual perception.* Hillsdale, NJ: Erlbaum.

Fisher, D. L., & Tan, K. C. (1989). Visual displays: The highlighting paradox. *Human Factors, 31,* 17–30.

Fisher, D. L., & Tanner, N. S. (1992). Optimal symbol set selection: A semiautomated procedure. *Human Factors, 34,* 79–95.

Fisk, A. D., Oransky, N. A., & Skedsvold, P. R. (1988). Examination of the role of "higher-order" consistency in skill development. *Human Factors, 30,* 567–582.

Fitts, P., Jones, R. E., & Milton, E. (1950). Eye movements of aircraft pilots during instrument landing approaches. *Aeronautical Engineering Review, 9,* 24–29.

Flavell, R., & Heath, A. (1992). Further investigations into the use of colour coding scales. *Interacting With Computers, 4,* 179–199.

Fox, E. (1995). Negative priming from ignored distractors in visual selection: A review. *Psychonomic Bulletin & Review, 2,* 145–173.

Friedman, A., & Liebelt, L. S. (1981). On the time course of viewing pictures with a view towards remembering. In D. F. Fisher, R. A. Monty, & J. W. Senders (Eds.), *Eye movements: Cognition and visual perception* (pp. 137–154). Hillsdale, NJ: Erlbaum.

Garner, W. R. (1974). *The processing of information and structure.* Hillsdale, NJ: Erlbaum.

Geiselman, R. E., Landee, B. M., & Christen, F. G. (1982). Perceptual discriminability as a basis for selecting graphic symbols. *Human Factors, 24,* 329–338.

Geisler, W. S., & Chou, K. (1995). Separation of low-level and high-level factors in complex tasks: visual search. *Psychological Review, 102,* 356–378.

Ghirardelli, T.G., & Folk, C.L. (1996). Spactial cueing in a stereoscopic display: Evidence for a "depth-blind" attentional spotlight. *Psychonomic Bulletin & Review, 3,* 81-86

Goesch, T. (1990). Head-up displays hit the road. *Information Display, 7–8,* 10–13.

Goettl, B. P., Wickens, C. D., & Kramer, A. F. (1991). Integrated displays and the perception of graphical data. *Ergonomics, 34,* 1047–1063.

Halgren, S. L., & Cooke, N. J. (1993). Towards ecological validity in menu research. *International Journal of Man-Machine Studies, 39,* 51–70.

Hammer, J. (1999). Human Factors of Functionality in Avionics. In D. Garland, J. Wise, & V. D. Hopkin (Eds.), *Handbook of Aviation Human Factors.* Mahwah, NJ: Erlbaum.

Harris, R. L., & Christhilf, D. M. (1980). What do pilots see in displays? In G. Corrick, E. Hazeltine, & R. Durst (Eds.), *Proceedings of the 24th annual meeting of the Human Factors Society.* Santa Monica, CA: Human Factors Society.

Haskell, I. D., & Wickens, C. D. (1993). Two- and three-dimensional displays for aviation: A theoretical and empirical comparison. *International Journal of Aviation Psychology, 3,* 87–109.

Hawkins, F., & Orlady, H. W. (1993). *Human factors in flight* (2d. ed.). Brookfield, VT: Gower.

Heller, M. A. (1992). Haptic dominance in form perception: Vision versus proprioception. *Perception, 21,* 655–660.

Holahan, C. J., Culler, R. E., & Wilcox, B. L. (1978). Effects of visual distraction on reaction time in a simulated traffic environment. *Human Factors, 20,* 409–413.

Hollands, J. G., & Merikle, P. M. (1987). Menu organization and user expertise in information search tasks. *Human Factors, 29,* 577–586.

Hollands, J. G., & Spence, I. (1992). Judgments of change and proportion in graphical perception. *Human Factors, 34,* 313–334.

Hughes, P. K., & Creed, D. J. (1994). Eye movement behaviour viewing colour-coded and monochrome avionic displays. *Ergonomics, 37,* 1871–1884.

Jacob, R. J. K., Egeth, H. E., & Bevan, W. (1976). The face as a data display. *Human Factors, 18,* 189–200.

Jordan, T. C. (1972). Characteristics of visual and proprioceptive response times in the learning of a motor skill. *Quarterly Journal of Experimental Psychology, 24,* 536–543.

Kahneman, D. (1973). *Attention and effort.* Englewood Cliffs, NJ: Prentice Hall.

Kahneman, D. & Treisman, A. (1984). Changing views of attention and automaticity. In R. Parasuraman & R. Davies (Eds.), *Varieties of attention.* Orlando, FL: Academic Press.

Kahneman, D., Treisman, A., & Gibbs, B. J. (1992). The reviewing of object files: Object-specific integration of information. *Cognitive Psychology, 24,* 175–219.

Kaufmann, R., & Glavin, S. J. (1990). General guidelines for the use of colour on electronic charts. *International Hydrographic Review, 67,* 87–99.

Keele, S. W. (1972). Attention demands of memory retrieval. *Journal of Experimental Psychology, 93,* 245–248.

Keele, S. W. (1973). *Attention and human performance.* Pacific Palisades, CA: Goodyear.

Kinchla, R. A. (1992). Attention. *Annual Review of Psychology, 43,* 711–742.

King, R. B., & Oldfield, S. R. (1997). The impact of signal bandwidth on auditory localization: Implications for the design of three-dimensional audio displays. *Human Factors, 39,* 287–295.

Klein, G. (1996). The effect of acute stress on decision making. In J.E. Driskell & E. Salas (Eds). *Stress and Human Performance.* Mahwah, NJ: Lawrence Erlbaum.

Kopala, C. (1979). The use of color-coded symbols in a highly dense situation display. *Proceedings of the 23d annual meeting of the Human Factors Society.* Santa Monica, CA: Human Factors Society.

Kramer, A. F. & Jacobson, A. (1991). Perceptual organization and focused attention: The role of objects and proximity in visual processing. *Perception & Psychophysics, 50,* 267–284.

Kundel, H. L., & LaFollette, P. S. (1972). Visual search patterns and experience with radiological images. *Radiology, 103,* 523–528.

Kundel, H. L., & Nodine, C. F. (1978). Studies of eye movements and visual search in radiology. In J. W. Senders, D. F. Fisher, & R. A. Monty (Eds.), *Eye movements and the higher psychological functions* (pp. 317–328). Hillsdale, NJ: Erlbaum.

Larish, I., & Wickens, C. D. (1991). Attention and HUDs: Flying in the dark? *Proceedings of the Society for Information Display*. Playa del Rey, CA: Society of Information Display.

Lee, E., & MacGregor, J. (1985). Minimizing user search time in menu retrieval systems. *Human Factors, 27,* 157–162.

Levy-Schoen, A. (1981). Flexible and/or rigid control of oculomotor scanning behavior. In D. F. Fisher, R. A. Monty, & J. W. Senders (Eds.), *Eye movements: Cognition and visual perception* (pp. 299–314). Hillsdale, NJ: Erlbaum.

Liu, Y., & Wickens, C. D. (1992). Use of computer graphics and cluster analysis in aiding relational judgment. *Human Factors, 34,* 165–178.

Logan, G. D. (1980). Attention and automaticity in Stroop and priming tasks: Theory and data. *Cognitive Psychology, 12,* 523–553.

Mackworth, N. H. (1976). Ways of recording line of sight. In R. A. Monty & J. W. Senders (Eds.), *Eye movements and psychological processing* (pp.173–178). Hillsdale, NJ: Erlbaum.

MacLeod, C. M. (1991). Half a century of research on the Stroop effect: An integrative review. *Psychological Bulletin, 109,* 163–203.

Martin-Emerson, R. & Wickens, C. D. (1997). Superimposition, symbology, visual attention, and the head-up display. *Human Factors, 39,* 581–601.

Massaro, D. W., & Warner, D. S. (1977). Dividing attention between auditory and visual perception. *Perception & Psychophysics, 21,* 569–574.

McConkie, G. W. (1983). Eye movements and perception during resting. In K. Raynor (Ed.), *Eye movements in reading.* New York: Academic Press.

Megaw, E. D., & Richardson, J. (1979). Target uncertainty and visual scanning strategies. *Human Factors, 21,* 303–316.

Mehlenbacher, B., Duffy, T. M., & Palmer, J. (1989). Finding information on a menu: Linking menu organization to the user's goals. *Human-Computer Interaction, 4,* 231–251.

Miller, J. (1991). Channel interaction and the redundant-targets effect in bimodal divided attention. *Journal of Experimental Psychology: Human Perception and Performance, 17,* 160–169.

Milroy, R., & Poulton, E. C. (1978). Labeling graphs for increasing reading speed. *Ergonomics, 21,* 55–61.

Mondor, T. A., & Zatorre, R. J. (1995). Shifting and focusing auditory spatial attention. *Journal of Experimental Psychology: Human Perception and Performance, 21,* 387–409.

Moore, J. J., & Massaro, D. W. (1973). Attention and processing capacity in auditory recognition. *Journal of Experimental Psychology, 99,* 49–54.

Moray, N. (1959). Attention in dichotic listening. *Quarterly Journal of Experimental Psychology, 11,* 56–60.

Moray, N. (1969). *Listening and attention.* Baltimore: Penguin.

Moray, N. (1981). The role of attention in the detection of errors and the diagnosis of errors in man-machine systems. In J. Rasmussen & W. Rouse (Eds.), *Human detection and diagnosis of system failures.* New York: Plenum Press.

Moray, N. (1986). Monitoring behavior and supervising control. In K. R. Boff, L. Kaufman, & J. P. Thomas (Eds.), *Handbook of perception and human performance.* New York: Wiley.

Moray, N., & Rotenberg, I. (1989). Fault management in process control: Eye movements and action. *Ergonomics, 32,* 1319–1342.

Mori, H., & Hayashi, Y. (1995). Visual interference with users' tasks on multiwindow systems. *International Journal of Human-Computer Interaction, 7,* 329–340.

Mosier, K. L., Skitka, L. J., Heers, S., & Burdick, M. (1998). Automation bias: Decision making and performance in high-tech cockpits. *International Journal of Aviation Psychology, 8,* 47–63.

Mourant, R. R., & Rockwell, T. H. (1972). Strategies of visual search by novice and experienced drivers. *Human Factors, 14,* 325–336.

Muller, H. J., & Rabbitt, P. M. (1989). Reflexive and voluntary orienting of visual attention: Time course of activation and resistance to interruption. *Journal of Experimental Psychology: Human Perception & Performance, 15,* 315–330.

Murphy, T. D., & Eriksen, C. W. (1987). Temporal changes in the distribution of attention in the visual field in response to precues. *Perception & Psychophysics, 42,* 576–586.

Nagy, A. L., & Sanchez, R. R. (1992). Chromaticity and luminance as coding dimensions in visual search. *Human Factors, 34,* 601–614.

Navon, D. (1977). Forest before the trees: The precedence of global features in visual processing. *Cognitive Psychology, 9,* 353–383.

Neisser, U. (1963). Decision time without reaction time. *American Journal of Psychology, 76,* 376–385.

Neisser, U. (1967). *Cognitive psychology.* New York: Appleton-Century-Crofts.

Neisser, U., & Becklen, R. (1975). Selective looking: Attention to visually specified events. *Cognitive Psychology, 7,* 480–494.

Neisser, U., Novick, R., & Lazar, R. (1964). Searching for novel targets. *Perceptual and Motor Skills, 19,* 427–432.

Newman, R. L. (1995). *Head up Displays: Designing the Way Ahead.* Brookfield, VT: Ashgate.

Norman, D. (1968). Toward a theory of memory and attention. *Psychological Review, 75,* 522–536.

Olson, R. K., & Attneave, F. (1970). What variables produce stimulus grouping. *American Psychologist, 83,* 1–21.

Palmer, S. E. (1992). Common region: A new principle of perceptual grouping. *Cognitive Psychology, 24,* 436–447.

Palmiter, S., & Elkerton, J. (1987). Evaluation metrics and a tool for control panel design. *Proceedings of 31st annual meeting of the Human Factors Society* (pp. 1123–1127). Santa Monica, CA: Human Factors Society.

Parasuraman, R. (1986). Vigilance, monitoring and search. In K. R. Boff, L. Kaufman, & J. P. Thomas (Eds.), *Handbook of perception and human performance.* New York: Wiley.

Pierce, B. J., Parkinson, S. R., & Sisson, N. (1992). Effects of semantic similarity, omission probability and number of alternatives in computer menu search. *International Journal of Man-Machine Studies, 37,* 653–677.

Pierce, B. J., Sisson, N., & Parkinson, S. R. (1992). Menu search and selection processes: A quantitative performance model. *International Journal of Man-Machine Studies, 37,* 679–702.

Posner, M. I. (1986). *Chronometric explorations of mind.* New York: Oxford University Press.

Posner, M. I., Nissen, M. J., & Ogden, W. C. (1978). Attended and unattended processing modes: The role of set for spatial location. In H. L. Pick & I. J. Saltzman (Eds.), *Modes of perceiving and processing information.* Hillsdale, NJ: Erlbaum.

Remington, R. W., Johnston, J. C., & Yantis, S. (1992). Involuntary attentional capture by abrupt onsets. *Perception & Psychophysics, 51,* 279–290.

Rock, I. (1975). *An introduction to perception.* New York: Macmillan.

Rogers, S. P. (1979). Stimulus-response incompatibility: Extra processing stages versus response competition. *Proceedings of the 23d annual meeting of the Human Factors Society.* Santa Monica, CA: Human Factors Society.

Sanderson, P. M. (1989). The human planning and scheduling role in advanced manufacturing systems: An emerging human factors domain. *Human Factors, 31,* 635–666.

Sanderson, P. M., Flach, J. M., Buttigieg, M. A., & Casey, E. J. (1989). Object displays do not always support better integrated task performance. *Human Factors, 31,* 183–198.

Schneider, W., & Shiffrin, R. (1977). Controlled and automatic human information processing I: Detection, search, and attention. *Psychological Review, 84,* 1–66.

Schoenfeld, V. S., & Scerbo, M. W. (1997). Search differences for the presence and absence of features in sustained attention. *Proceedings of the 41st annual meeting of the Human Factors and Ergonomics Society* (pp. 1288–1292). Santa Monica, CA: Human Factors and Ergonomics Society.

Scialfa, C. T., Kline, D. W., & Lyman, B. J. (1987). Age differences in target identification as a function of retinal location and noise level: Examination of the useful field of view. *Psychology and Aging, 2,* 14–19.

Senders, J. (1964). The human operator as a monitor and controller of multidegree of freedom systems. *IEEE Transactions on Human Factors in Electronics, HFE–5,* 2–6.

Seuss, Dr. (1971). *The lorax.* New York: Random House.

Simpson, C., & Williams, D. H. (1980). Response time effects of alerting tone and semantic context for synthesized voice cockpit warnings. *Human Factors, 22,* 319–330.

Smelcer, J. B., & Walker, N. (1993). Transfer of knowledge across computer command menus. *International Journal of Human-Computer Interaction, 5,* 147–165.

Sojourner, R. J., & Antin, J. F. (1990). The effects of a simulated head-up display speedometer on perceptual task performance. *Human Factors, 32,* 329–339.

Somberg, B. L. (1987). A comparison of rule-based and positionally constant arrangements of computer menu items. *Proceedings of CHI & GI '87 conference on human factors in computing systems.* New York: Association for Computing Machinery.

Sorkin, R. D. (1987). Design of auditory and tactile displays. In G. Salvendy (Ed.), *Handbook of human factors* (pp. 549–576). New York: Wiley.

Stager, P., & Angus, R. (1978). Locating crash sites in simulated air-to-ground visual search. *Human Factors, 20,* 453–466.

Steenblik, J. W. (1989, December). Alaska airlines' HGS. *Air Line Pilot,* pp. 10–14.

Stokes, A. F., Wickens, C. D., & Kite, K. (1990). *Display technology: Human factors concepts.* Warrendale, PA: Society of Automotive Engineers.

Stroop, J. R. (1935). Studies of interference in serial verbal reactions. *Journal of Experimental Psychology, 18,* 643–662.

Suzuki, S., & Cavanagh, P. (1995). Facial organization blocks access to low-level features: An object inferiority effect. *Journal of Experimental Psychology: Human Perception and Performance, 21,* 901–913.

Sweller, O., Chandler, P., Tierney, P., & Cooper, M. (1990). Cognitive load as a factor in the structuring of technical material. *Journal of Experimental Psychology: General, 119,* 176–192.

Swets, J., & Druckman, D. (1988). *Enhancing human performance.* Washington, DC: National Academy Press.

Taylor, R. M., Finnie, S., & Hoy, C. (1997). Cognitive rigidity: The effects of mission planning and automation on cognitive control in dynamic situations. *Proceedings of the 9th international symposium on aviation psychology* (pp. 415–421). Columbus, OH: Dept. of Aviation, Ohio State University.

Teichner, W. H., & Mocharnuk, J. B. (1979). Visual search for complex targets. *Human Factors, 21,* 259–276.

Theeuwes, J. (1992). Perceptual selectivity for color and form. *Perception & Psychophysics, 51,* 599–606.

Theeuwes, J., Atchley, P., & Kramer, A. F. (1998). Attentional control within 3-D space. *Journal of Experimental Psychology: Human Perception & Performance, 24,* 1476–1485.

Theeuwes, J., & Godthelp, H. (1995). Self-explaining roads. *Safety Science, 19,* 217–225.

Treisman, A. (1964a). The effect of irrelevant material on the efficiency of selective listening. *American Journal of Psychology, 77,* 533–546.

Treisman, A. (1964b). Verbal cues, language, and meaning in attention. *American Journal of Psychology, 77,* 206–214.

Treisman, A. (1969). Strategies and models of selective attention. *Psychological Review, 76,* 282–299.

Treisman, A. (1986). Properties, parts, and objects. In K. R. Boff, L. Kaufman, & J. P. Thomas (Eds.), *Handbook of perception and human performance.* New York: Wiley.

Treisman, A. M., & Gelade, G. (1980). A feature-integration theory of attention. *Cognitive Psychology, 12,* 97–136.

Treisman, A., & Souther, J. (1985). Search asymmetry: A diagnostic for preattentive processing of separable features. *Journal of Experimental Psychology: General, 114,* 285–310.

Tufano, D. R. (1997). Automotive HUDs: The overlooked safety issues. *Human Factors, 39,* 303–311.

Tufte, E. R. (1990). *Envisioning information.* Cheshire, CT: Graphics Press.

Tulga, M. K., & Sheridan, T. B. (1980). Dynamic decisions and workload in multitask supervisory control. *IEEE Transactions on Systems, Man, and Cybernetics, SMC–10,* 217–232.

Tullis, T. S. (1988). Screen design. In M. Helander (Ed.), *Handbook of human-computer interaction* (pp. 377–411). Amsterdam: North-Holland.

Tversky, A. (1977). Features of similarity. *Psychological Review, 84,* 327–352.

U.S. Navy. (1988). *Investigating report: Formal investigation into the circumstances surrounding the downing of Iran air flight 655 on 3 July 1988.* Department of Defense Investigation Report.

Ververs, P., & Wickens, C. D. (1998). Head-up displays: Effects of clutter, display intensity, and display location on pilot performance. *International Journal of Aviation Psychology, 8,* 377–403.

Vincow, M., & Wickens, C. D. (1993). Spatial layout and displayed information: Three steps toward developing a quantitative model. *Proceedings of the 37th annual meeting of the Human Factors Society.* Santa Monica, CA: Human Factors Society.

Wachtel, P. L. (1967). Conceptions of broad and narrow attention. *Psychological Bulletin, 68,* 417–419.

Walker, N., & Fisk, A. D. (1995, July) Human factors goes to the Gridiron. *Ergonomics and Design,* 8–13.

Ward, L. M. (1994). Supramodal and modality-specific mechanisms for stimulus-driven shifts of auditory and visual attention. *Canadian Journal of Experimental Psychology, 48,* 242–259.

Weinstein, L. F., Gillingham, K. K., & Ercoline, W. R. (1994). United States Air Force head-up display control and performance symbology evaluations. *Aviation, Space, and Environmental Medicine, 65,* A20–A30.

Weintraub, D., & Ensing, M. (1992). *The book of HUD.* CSERIAC State-of-the-Art Report. Dayton, OH: Wright-Patterson Air Force Base.

Wickens, C. D. (1984). *Engineering psychology and human performance.* New York: Harper Collins.

Wickens, C. D. (1997). Attentional issues in head-up displays. In D. Harris (Ed.), *Engineering psychology and cognitive ergonomics: Vol. 1. Transportation systems.* Aldershot: Ashgate.

Wickens, C. D., & Andre, A. D. (1990). Proximity compatibility and information display: Effects of color, space, and objectness of information integration. *Human Factors, 32,* 61–77.

Wickens, C. D., & Carswell, C. M. (1995). The proximity compatibility principle: Its psychological foundation and relevance to display design. *Human Factors, 37,* 473–494.

Wickens, C. D., Gordon, S. E., & Liu, Y. (1998). *An introduction to human factors engineering.* New York: Addison Wesley Longman.

Wickens, C. D., & Long, J. (1995). Object versus space-based models of visual attention: Implications for the design of head-up displays. *Journal of Experimental Psychology: Applied, 1,* 179–193.

Wickens C. D., Vincow, M. A., Schopper, A. W., & Lincoln, J. E. (1997). *Computational models of human performance in the design and layout of controls and displays.* CSERIAC State of the Art (SOAR) Report. Dayton, OH: Wright-Patterson AFB, Crew Systems Ergonomics Information Analysis Center.

Wiener, E. L. (1977). Controlled flight into terrain accidents: System-induced errors. *Human Factors, 19,* 171.

Wikman, A., Niemeinen, T., & Summala, H. (1998). Driving experience and time-sharing during in-car tasks on roads of different widths. *Ergonomics, 41,* 358–372.

Williams, D. E., Reingold, E. M., Moscovitch, M., & Behrmann, M. (1997). Patterns of eye movements during parallel and serial visual search tasks. *Canadian Journal of Experimental Psychology, 51,* 151–164.

Williams, L. J. (1989). Foveal load affects the functional field of view. *Human Performance, 2,* 1–28.

Wolfe, J. M. (1994). Guided search 2.0: A revised model of visual search. *Psychonomic Bulletin and Review, 1,* 202–238.

Wolfe, J. M., Cave, K. R., & Franzel, S. L. (1989). Guided search: An alternative to the feature integration model for visual search. *Journal of Experimental Psychology: Human Perception & Performance, 15,* 419–433.

Wood, N., & Cowan, N. (1995). The cocktail party phenomenon revisited: How frequent are attention shifts to one's name in an irrelevant auditory channel? *Journal of Experimental Psychology: Learning, Memory, & Cognition, 21,* 255–260.

Woods, D., Wise, J., & Hanes, L. (1981). An evaluation of nuclear power plant safety parameter display systems. In R. C. Sugarman (Ed.), *Proceedings of the 25th annual meeting of the Human Factors Society.* Santa Monica, CA: Human Factors Society.

Yantis, S. (1993). Stimulus-driven attentional capture. *Current Directions in Psychological Science, 2,* 156–161.

Yantis, S., & Hillstrom, A. P. (1994). Stimulus-driven attentional capture: Evidence from equi-luminant visual objects. *Journal of Experimental Psychology: Human Perception & Performance, 20,* 95–107.

Yantis, S., & Johnston, J. C. (1990). On the locus of visual selection: Evidence from focused attention tasks. *Journal of Experimental Psychology: Human Perception & Performance, 16,* 135–149.

Yantis, S., & Jonides, J. (1984). Abrupt visual onsets and selective attention: Evidence from visual search. *Journal of Experimental Psychology: Human Perception & Performance, 10,* 601–621.

Yarbus. A. L. (1967). *Eye movements and vision.* New York: Plenum.

Yeh, M., Wickens, C. D., & Seagull, F. J. (1999). Conformality and target cueing: Presentation of symbology in augmented reality. *Proceedings of the 42nd Annual Meeting of the Human Factors and Ergonomics Society* (pp. 1526–1530). Santa Monica, CA: Human Factors and Ergonomics Society.

Young, L. R., & Stark, L. (1963). Variable feedback experiments testing a sampled data model for eye tracking movements. *IEEE Transactions on Human Factors in Electronics, HFE–4,* 38–51.

Zelinsky, G. J., & Sheinberg, D. L. (1997). Eye movements during parallel-serial visual search. *Journal of Experimental Psychology: Human Perception & Performance, 23,* 244–262.

Spatial Displays

OVERVIEW

When we drive a car, we derive information about the depth and position of other objects in the world from the scene through the windshield. Similarly, when we examine a bar graph or a speedometer, we derive information about the state of the world from a spatial array. The sizes of objects or the distances between them are used to communicate the relevant information. Human performance often depends on accurate judgments of distance, extent, and depth, involving what we call *analog perception*. Our ability to perceive and understand such spatial relations is the focus of this chapter.

In analog perception, large spatial or physical differences are more significant than small ones. Consider reading a graph or an analog meter. A small change in position reflects a small change in the underlying dimension. In contrast, consider reading a digital meter or a word. In a digital meter the spatial difference in the *physical* representation between, say, 79774 and 80000 is substantial—every digit is changed. But the difference in *meaning* between these two values is small. In contrast, the spatial difference between the words *altitude* and *attitude* is small, differing by only the crossbar of one letter, but its significance to a pilot is considerable. The first describes the height of the plane above the ground, the second describes its angle relative to the horizon. (The processing of qualitative, linguistic information will be discussed in Chapter 6).

In this chapter, we first discuss analog perception with respect to statistical graphs. Then we address the role of motion as we consider the design of common displays such as meters and dials. In doing so, we discuss the importance of *compatibility* between the dimension portrayed and display elements. Space, of course, is also *three-dimensional*, and although many displays are only two-dimensional, certain aspects of our perception of depth have implications for displays in two as well as in three dimensions. We close the chapter by discussing the perception of depth and its implication for display design. We will continue our discussion of spatial displays in Chapter 5, where we examine navigation and interaction with real and virtual environments.

GRAPHICAL PERCEPTION

Most of us will, at one time or another, design a graph. In the process, we must make decisions about graph type, assigning variables to axes, coding variables using symbols, and so on. It is important, therefore, to determine what graphical forms are most effective for depicting data. It is also important, as we have already seen when discussing attention in Chapter 3, to consider the task our user will perform with the graph.

We shall define a *graph* as a paper or electronic representation of numeric analog data with multiple data points. A graph is distinguished from an analog *display* in that it is typically static. (However, the distinction between graphs and analog displays is becoming blurred due to developments in dynamic data visualization on computer displays.) A history of the graphic display of data dates back to the pioneering work of Playfair (1786), who first realized the power of using analog symbols, rather than words and digits, to represent quantitative data. Although reading a precise value is generally performed better with tables of digits (Lalomia, Coovert, & Salas, 1992; Meyer, Shinar, & Leiser, 1997), for analog judgments, graphs are typically more effective than tables (e.g., Coll, Thyagarajan, & Chopra, 1991; Miller, Rettig, & Scerbo, 1994). As noted above, for analog judgments, large differences between values are more significant than small ones. It comes as no surprise, therefore, that an analog representation like a graph—where large differences are portrayed with greater length, area, or volume—is more effective for the analog judgment. Although some argue that graphs should be reserved for large data sets (e.g., Tufte, 1983), it is not hard to find empirical evidence suggesting that graphing small data sets is more effective than presenting them in tables (e.g., Carswell & Ramzy, 1997; Spence & Lewandowsky, 1991), and that graphs are more useful under conditions of time stress than tables (Coury & Boulette, 1992). Thus, graphs are an effective method of communicating quantitative analog information.

Graph Guidelines

We list five general guidelines for the construction of graphs here. After the list, we discuss evidence supporting each guideline. Readers wanting further detail should consult Gillan, Wickens, Hollands, and Carswell (1998), Kosslyn (1994) or Lewandowski and Behrens (1999).

1. *Use physical dimensions judged without bias.* Several perceptual illusions adversely influence judgments made with graphs. In addition, some perceptual continua (e.g., area, volume, color saturation) are judged with particular biases (e.g., we tend to underestimate large areas and volumes), whereas other continua are not (e.g., length). The use of volume and depth in graphs also makes scale reading problematic.
2. *Consider the task.* Many judgment tasks are performed with graphs. The relative effectiveness of various graph types depends on the task. The graph designer should choose a graphical form that corresponds to task demands.
3. *Minimize the number of mental operations.* When readers examine a graph to accomplish a task, they perform a sequence of perceptual, attentional, and cognitive operations. The graph designer should try to reduce the number of operations by choosing an appropriate graph type (e.g., bar graph, pie chart) and arranging

information within the graph appropriately. Reducing the number of operations will tend to reduce mental workload and error in judgment and shorten the time to perform the task.

4. *Keep the data-ink ratio high.* Tufte (1983) proposed the principle of the data-ink ratio: Minimize the amount of ink that does not depict actual data points or the relation between those points. Eliminate clutter by graphing only essential information.

5. *Code multiple graphs consistently.* The graph designer should be concerned with the relations among various graphs in a paper or in a presentation. The consistency should allow readers of the graph to perceive related measures across various situations (e.g., sales of various products in different geographical regions).

Biases in Graph Reading

The judgments people make in extracting information from graphs may be *biased* (Gillan, et al. 1998). That is, people tend to systematically overestimate (or underestimate) quantities relative to their true values. Some of these biases are related to optical illusions that distort our sense of perception. For example, when viewing the *Poggendorf illusion* shown in Figure 4.1a, people tend to "flatten" the sloping lines toward the horizontal, giving the impression that the two lines do not connect. Poulton (1985) found that this same illusion was responsible for people's tendency to underestimate the value of points in line graphs, such as that shown in Figure 4.1b. People "bend" the slope of the line to be more horizontal, with the result that points on the line far from a graduated axis are read poorly. Poulton proposed that the solution to this bias is to draw all four sides and place tickmarks on the left and right, as shown in Figure 4.1c.

A second example of graphic bias is provided by Cleveland and McGill (1984) and is illustrated in Figure 4.2: the difficulty in comparing *differences* between two lines of different slope. For example, in the figure, the difference between the two curves is actually smaller in the left than the right regions. Yet perceptually the difference appears smaller in the right because judgments of differences along the *y*-axis are clearly biased

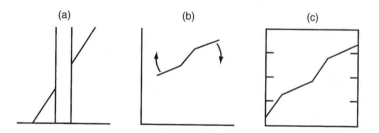

Figure 4.1   (a) The Poggendorf illusion: The two diagonal lines actually connect. (b) A line graph susceptible to "bending" from the Poggendorf illusion. (c) Debiasing of the Poggendorf illusion by marked edges on both sides.

Source: E. C. Poulton, "Geometric Illusions in Reading Graphs," *Perception & Psychophysics, 37* (1985), 543. Reprinted with permission of Psychonomic Society, Inc.

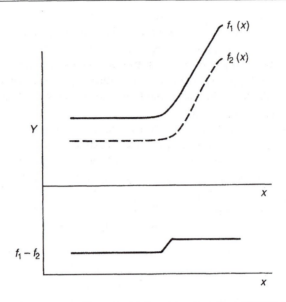

Figure 4.2   Biases in perceiving differences between pairs of lines $f_1(x)$ and $f_2(x)$ with changing slopes. The bottom curve plots the actual difference, $f_1(x) - f_2(x)$, which is larger on the right than on the left.

by the *visual* separation (not the vertical separation) of the two curves, which is in fact less on the right side. Cleveland and McGill suggest that where the difference in differences (a statistical interaction) is an important feature of a set of graphic data, it should be plotted directly, as shown at the bottom of Figure 4.2.

A third example of graphic bias is that we have problems interpreting and remembering linear relationships in data. Bailey (1996) found that when people were asked to fit lines to scatterplots showing a relationship between two variables, they overestimated the steepness of the actual trend, relative to a statistical regression line. This is important because people often use visual inspection of data to determine whether values are outliers. The overestimation of the regression line may lead to inappropriate values being dropped from the analysis. Furthermore, students are often encouraged to visually fit a line to data points to "get a feel" for the relationships in the data; such encouragement—although otherwise beneficial—may be misleading in this case. The scaling of the graph (whether it be more horizontal or vertical) also affects our perception of the data shown within it, affecting both our estimates of trend (Cleveland, 1985; Meyer, Taieb, & Flascher, 1997) and variability (Lawrence & O'Connor, 1993). In addition, we have difficulty accurately remembering the slope of the relationship shown in a graph, remembering it as being closer to 45 degrees than is actually the case (Schiano & Tversky, 1992; Tversky & Schiano, 1989).

Other biases are not a result of an illusion or failure of memory but, rather, result from limitations of our perceptual system in processing areas and volumes. Both area and volume are commonly used to represent quantity in graphs, and volume is becoming especially prevalent given the increased use of 3-D graphical formats (Carswell, Frankenberger, & Bernhard, 1991; Siegrist, 1996; Spence, 1990). Cleveland and McGill (1984, 1985, 1986) proposed that our ability to make comparative judgments of two quantities in a graph falls off directly in the order of the graphic symbology arranged from the top to the bottom in Figure 4.3. The best comparative judgments are made with the evaluation of two linear scales, aligned to the same baseline. The poorest occur when people compare two areas, volumes, or color patches.

This is not surprising, given what we know about biases in judging *perceptual continua* (types of stimuli). When people estimate magnitudes by assigning numbers to various sizes of objects (the *magnitude estimation* procedure developed by Stevens, 1957), they show certain biases. Some continua, such as areas and volumes, produce *response compression*: Each increase in physical magnitude causes less and less increase in perceived magnitude. Other stimuli, such as color saturation, tend to show *response expansion*: Each increase in physical magnitude causes incrementally greater increases in

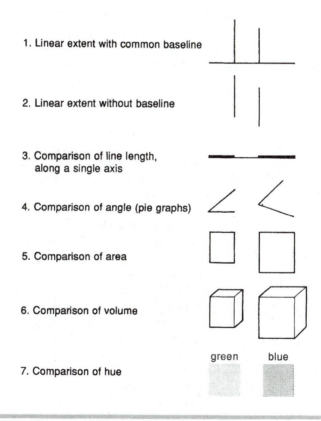

Figure 4.3 Seven graphical methods for presenting quantities to be compared. The graphs are arrayed from most (*top*) to least effective (*bottom*).

Source: W. S. Cleveland and R. McGill, "Graphical Perception and Graphical Methods for Analyzing Scientific Data," *Science, 229* (1985), 828–833. Reprinted by permission of AT&T Bell Labs, Murray Hill, N.J.

perceived magnitude. Lengths tend to be judged with little bias. Stevens (1957, 1975) found that the relation between physical and perceived magnitude could be expressed as an exponential function called *Stevens' law*, with the exponent representing the amount of response compression or expansion (when the exponent is less than one, response compression occurs; when it is greater than one, response expansion occurs; when it is equal to one, no bias occurs). Estimates of the areas and volumes shown in graphs are potentially subject to response compression, so that large areas and volumes will tend to be underestimated. Hence, the use of perceptual continua whose Stevens exponents differ from one should be avoided to code variables shown in graphs.

Moreover, the bias described by Stevens' law appears to affect more complex judgments where multiple quantities are involved, such as judgments of proportion (e.g., what proportion is A of B?) (Hollands & Dyre, in press). Suppose you were asked to divide a horizontal line into two parts corresponding to two slices of a pie, as shown in Figure 4.4a. When judging graphs (e.g., pie charts, stacked bar graphs) depicting proportion, people tend to show cyclical bias patterns (e.g., overestimation from 0 to 0.25, underestimation from 0.25 to 0.75, overestimation from 0.50 to 0.75, and underestimation from 0.75 to 1), as shown in Figure 4.4. Hollands and Dyre showed that the amplitude of the cyclical pattern was determined by the Stevens exponent (for the pie charts shown in the figure, the estimated exponent was less than one), and the frequency of the pattern was determined by the number of available tickmarks (compare the upper panels of Figure 4.4). They proposed that intermediate reference points (correspond-

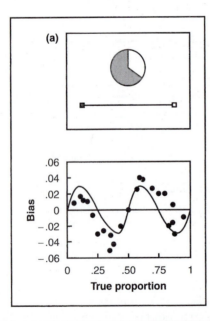
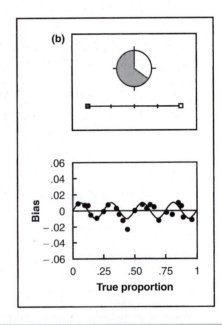

Figure 4.4   Patterns of cyclical bias in judging graphs. (*a*) Bias in proportion judgment as a function of true proportion for pie charts. (*b*) Bias as a function of true proportion when tickmarks are added. Note that the bias pattern changes from two to four cycles and overall error is reduced.

ing to tickmark locations) are used by observers to subdivide the stimulus into components. This has the beneficial side effect that error is reduced, even as the Stevens exponent stays constant, as shown in Figure 4.4. In summary, bias (and therefore error) in making relative judgments with graphs can be reduced by: (1) avoiding continua whose Stevens exponents differ from one, and (2) increasing the frequency of tickmarks in the graph. It is possible to make less effective perceptual continua (e.g., area) more effective if a sufficient number of reference points is available.

Even if only one of two quantities being compared is represented by a stimulus continuum whose Stevens exponent differs from one, bias can result. Consider the box plot shown in Figure 4.5. A box plot shows a distribution of scores (a class's exam scores, for example). The ends of the whiskers are typically the extremes (lowest and highest scores). The ends of the box represent the 25th and 75th percentiles of the distribution, with the median (50th percentile) represented as a line inside the box, as shown in Figure 4.5. Behrens, Stock, and Sedgwick (1990) asked subjects to estimate box length in a box plot using the whisker length as a reference (e.g., "given that the length of the whisker is 20 mm, what is the length of the box?"). They found that the box was overestimated when the box was small relative to the whisker, and underestimated when the box was large. If subjects judged the area of the box rather than its length, it would result in a Stevens exponent less than one, producing the results observed. It would appear that even if subjects are explicitly instructed to judge length, they cannot help but be influenced by area. A better design—that is, a design where this bias would be eliminated—would remove the box and use length to code the values instead. An example—Tufte's (1983) quartile plot—is shown in Figure 4.5. As we discuss below, the quartile plot is an example that minimizes the data-ink ratio.

Task Dependency and the Proximity Compatibility Principle

People can perform a large number of tasks with graphs. The taxonomy developed by Carswell (1992a; Carswell & Wickens, 1988) specifies four basic task categories, each of which is shown in Figure 4.6. In *point reading*, the observer estimates the value of a single graph element. For a *local comparison*, the observer compares two values directly shown in the

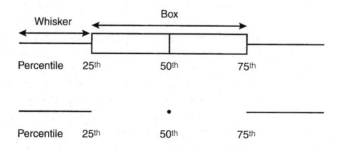

Figure 4.5   A box plot and a quartile plot. The box plot (*top*) is similar to that used by Behrens, Stock, and Sedgwick (1990). The quartile plot (*bottom*) is preferred because length rather than area is used to code values.

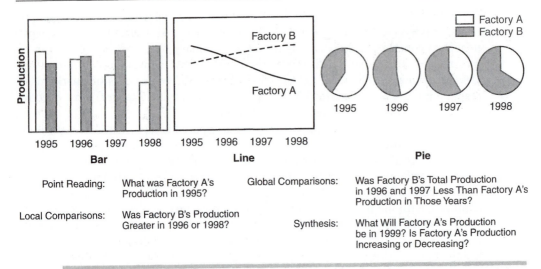

Point Reading: What was Factory A's Production in 1995?

Local Comparisons: Was Factory B's Production Greater in 1996 or 1998?

Global Comparisons: Was Factory B's Total Production in 1996 and 1997 Less Than Factory A's Production in Those Years?

Synthesis: What Will Factory A's Production be in 1999? Is Factory A's Production Increasing or Decreasing?

Figure 4.6 Graph types and reading tasks. (*top*) A bar graph, line graph, and set of pie charts depicting the same data: the production of factories A and B over four years. (*bottom*) Four graph reading tasks that could be performed with each graph.

graph. For a *global comparison,* the observer compares quantities that must be derived from other quantities shown in the graph. For a synthesis judgment, the subject needs to consider all data points and make a general, integrative judgment.

In Chapter 3, we introduced the notion of a compatibility between the arrangement of multiple information sources on a display and their cognitive integration, as defined by the task requirements. We saw that this display-cognitive compatibility could be defined in part by the *proximity compatibility principle* (Wickens & Carswell, 1995). Tasks requiring integration of information are better served by more integral, objectlike displays.

As a specific graphic example of the proximity compatibility principle, using the data in Figure 4.6, consider this question: How is the rate of growth different between the two factories? The separate bar graph (left panel), which contains eight objects, makes this integrative, complex comparison task more difficult than does the integrated line display (middle panel), which contains only two objects. In particular, each object (line) of the line graph offers an emergent feature—its slope—which can be directly perceived, and directly maps to the task (trend estimation). In contrast, judgments requiring focused attention can be made as well or better with the bar graph than with the line graph, a conclusion supported by experimental evidence (Carswell, 1990).

A review of the literature on comparative graphics (studies in which different graphic formats are compared) by Carswell and Wickens (1988; see also Carswell, 1992b) reveals that the proximity compatibility principle applies well to graphs. More integrated forms (e.g., a line graph) were compared with more separable form (e.g., a bar graph or a set of pie charts). Each study was placed into one of the four task categories described above. The task categories can be thought of as a continuum of task proximity, representing the extent to which the integration of all variables is necessary to carry out the task. Figure 4.7 shows the proportion of studies in each category that showed better performance with the more integrated than with separated displays, and those that showed the reverse effect. The figure shows the increasing benefit of integrated graphs as tasks require more integration.

An experiment by Goettl, Wickens, and Kramer (1991) provides a specific example of the application of the proximity compatibility principle to graphic displays. The subjects

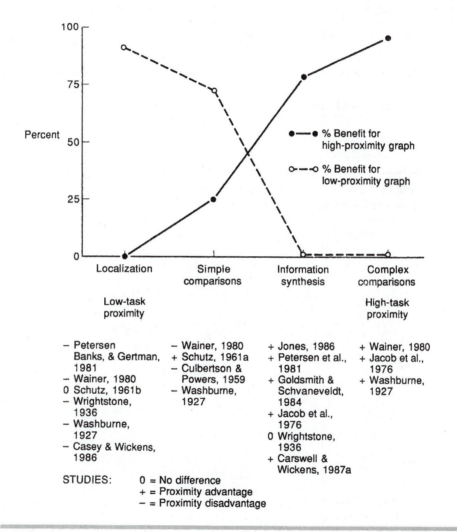

Figure 4.7 Proportion of studies showing an object-display advantage (solid line) or disadvantage (dashed line) as a function of task type (focused, left; integrated, right). The figure illustrates the proximity compatibility principle.

Source: C. M. Carswell and C. D. Wickens, *Comparative graphics: History and applications of perceptual integrality theory and the proximity compatibility hypothesis,* University of Illinois Technical Report ARL–88–2/AHEL–88–1/AHEL Technical Memorandum 8–88 (Savoy, IL: Aviation Research Laboratory, 1988).

were to think of themselves as scientists, examining the data from an experiment in which the speed and accuracy of performance were recorded. In one task, the subjects were asked to make inferences requiring an integration of speed and accuracy data from two hypothetical experimental conditions. Performance in this inference task was better when the data were presented as two points (two objects) in a two-dimensional speed-accuracy space (see Chapter 9) than as four separate bar graphs (four objects) presenting speed and accuracy for each condition separately. In contrast, when subjects were asked to perform a task calling for precise judgment of one particular value, the bar graph display proved superior. The reader will note the similarity of these findings to the predictions made by Garner's theory of integral and separable dimensions, discussed in Chapter 2. The Goettl, Wickens, and Kramer (1991) result is not unique; a large number of graph-reading studies examining the interaction between task and graph show the task-dependent result predicted by the proximity compatibility principle (e.g., Gillie & Berry, 1994; Hollands & Spence, 1992; Liu & Wickens, 1992; Wickens, LaClair, & Sarno, 1995; Wickens, Merwin, & Lin, 1994).

A final example of the proximity compatibility principle in graphic data presentation is often neglected—the attachment of legends to points and lines. When legends refer to lines in a graph, they should, if possible, be placed close to the lines to which they refer (Gillan, et al., 1998; Milroy & Poulton, 1978; Sweller, Chandler, Tierney, & Cooper, 1990). Two pieces of information to be integrated (the line and its label) should be close together in space (as in the line graph of Figure 4.6, but not in the bar graph, where the label is placed in a legend). This guideline becomes progressively more important as the graph contains more lines. If spatial proximity cannot be accomplished, the lines should be distinguished from one another by texture or color (not fine detail differences in point shape), and this texture or color should be a prominent part of the legend.

We have discussed two frameworks for information displays, the Cleveland & McGill hierarchy and the proximity compatibility principle both of which have some empirical support. Based on the Carswell (1992a) meta-analysis, the Cleveland and McGill (1984, 1986) hierarchy is applicable to more focused tasks, and less applicable to integrative tasks, where obtaining specific numerical quantities is not of great importance. Thus, for example, a face (e.g., Apaiwongse, 1995) or polygon (e.g., Beringer & Chrisman, 1991; Green et al., 1996) display might use the low-ranking area cue to encode a variable, and so, focused point reading would tend to be poor, as the Cleveland and McGill hierarchy would predict. However, as discussed in Chapter 3, judging the general arrangements of the parts (the facial expression, the shape of the polygon) is an integrative task, and as such, specific values are not important. Here the Cleveland and McGill hierarchy would not predict graphical effectiveness well. In a direct test of the Cleveland and McGill ranking surveying 39 experimental reports, Carswell (1992b) showed that the ranking (Figure 4.3) was more appropriate for focused tasks, such as local comparison and point reading, but did not predict well for global comparison and synthesis tasks—indeed for synthesis tasks it predicted the wrong way. That is, formats at the bottom of Figure 4.3 are to be preferred for such integrative judgments.

The proximity compatibility principle provides an overarching framework that can account for the effects of task type on graph reading performance. Nonetheless, it is not entirely clear *why* the principle is effective. The next section explores changes in information processing operations that occur when an integrated task is performed with a separated versus an integrated display.

Minimize the Number of Mental Operations

When examining a graph to accomplish a task, we perform a sequence of perceptual and cognitive operations. If operations are performed in series, each with some probability of error, this has two implications: Fewer operations will (1) take less time and (2) produce fewer errors.. How then are cognitive operations affected by the various task-graph combinations? For example, what changes in information processing occur when an integrated task is performed with a separated versus an integrated display? Multiple researchers (e.g., Casner, 1991; Cleveland, 1990; Gillan, 1995; Gillan & LaSalle, 1994; Gillan & Lewis, 1994; Gillan & Neary, 1992; Hollands & Spence, 1992, 1994, 1998; Lohse, 1993; Pinker, 1990; Simkin & Hastie, 1987) have proposed sets of *mental operations* for graph reading. The choice and use of a particular set of operations for a particular task-graph combination underlie some of the predictions of the proximity compatibility principle.

For example, the scanning operations proposed by some researchers (e.g., Lohse, 1993; Simkin & Hastie, 1987) may underlie the general advantage of reducing the distance between graphical elements—shorter distances between elements reduces the time to scan from one element to another. Mental operations can also account for task-dependent results. Hollands and Spence (1992) reported an advantage of line graphs over a set of separated pie charts for an integrated, trend-estimation task, but a cost for the more focused task of judging a single proportion, a result in line with the proximity compatibility principle. However, it seems likely that different operations are used for each task-graph combination (Figure 4.6). Thus, for example, when estimating trend with a line graph, subjects can perform a slope estimation operation; when estimating trend with a set of pie charts, the subject needs to perform multiple size-discrimination operations on various pie slices. In contrast, when estimating proportion with pie charts, the subject can perform a ratio-estimation operation, but with line graphs, the subject must perform multiple summation operations prior to estimating the ratio.

There is significant overlap among the sets of operations proposed by various researchers; nearly all sets include a scanning or visual search component (see Chapter 3), and several researchers (e.g., Cleveland, Hollands & Spence, Gillan) propose summation, ratio estimation, and difference estimation operations. Developing a unified model including a general set of graph reading operations would be a useful advance for understanding graphical perception. Using a mental operations approach, the time and likelihood of error can be predicted in advance for a particular task-graph combination. The graph designer should try to reduce the number of operations by choosing an appropriate graph type and arranging information within the graph appropriately. Reducing the number of operations should reduce error and shorten judgment time.

The Data-Ink Ratio

The principle of the data-ink ratio states that the amount of ink that does not depict data points should be kept to a minimum (Tufte, 1983). In many cases, graph readers will tend to engage in a serial search, and as discussed in Chapter 3, unnecessary visual elements (non-data ink) will slow visual search. Gillan and Richman (1994) found empirical evidence that supports Tufte's principle: The higher the data-ink ratio, the shorter the time to make a variety of judgments, and the greater the accuracy. In addition, integrated tasks (e.g., global comparison, synthesis judgments) are more affected than focused tasks by the data-ink ratio. Gillan and Richman's results also suggest that the use of pictorial backgrounds (e.g., the picture of a bank behind a bar graph depicting financial data) is particularly damaging, resulting in increased response time and decreased accuracy, again especially for more integrated judgments. Thus, there is good evidence to suggest that the use of low data-ink ratios will make a graph more effective, especially for integrated tasks, and that non-data ink should be eliminated from graphs. However, the concept of minimizing data-ink ratios can be carried too far (Carswell, 1992a; Wickens, Gordon, & Liu, 1998). The lines connecting points within a line graph represent ink that conveys no data (data are represented by the points). However, deletion of the redundant lines would impair judgment for some tasks (e.g., trend estimation), because the lines offer the graph reader the emergent feature of the line's slope (see Chapter 3 for a discussion of emergent features).

Multiple Graphs

The previous discussion has focused on the single graphs. An equally important issue lies in the presentation of multiple graphs, which may show related sets of data (e.g., several different dependent variables are plotted as a function of the same independent variables). Here the graph designer should be concerned with the relationship between successively viewed graphs, in addition to the optimization of each graph by itself. Four specific concerns can be identified.

1. *Coding Variables.* If an experiment examines three factorially crossed independent variables (e g., a 2 x 2 x 2 experimental design), how should their effect be displayed? If two panels are created, each presenting the effects of two variables (*A* and *B*) at a different level of the third, as in the upper panels of Figure 4.8, the effects of the third variable (variable *C*) will be hard to perceive because the two levels of this variable are spatially separated in two different panels (Gillan, et al. 1998). This violates the proximity compatibility principle. Indeed, Shah and Carpenter (1995) have found evidence to suggest that our mental representation of coded variables (e.g., *B* and *C* in the upper part of Figure 4.8) is qualitative, whereas our representation of variables placed along the *x*-axis of the graphs (e.g., variable *A*) is in quantitative terms. This has two implications for multiple graph construction: (1) Build the graphs so that quantitative variables are placed on the *x*-axis, and (2) if all variables are qualitative, build the graphs so that the most important differences are encoded as the variables represented by the two points on each line (like *A*), since we seem to be most sensitive to these changes. In this way, the variable's effect is directly represented by an emergent feature—the slope—of the constructed graphs.

2. *Consistency.* When the same data are plotted in different ways, or different data are plotted as a function of the same variables, it is critical to maintain as much consistency as possible between graphs (Gillan, et al., 1998). For example, the

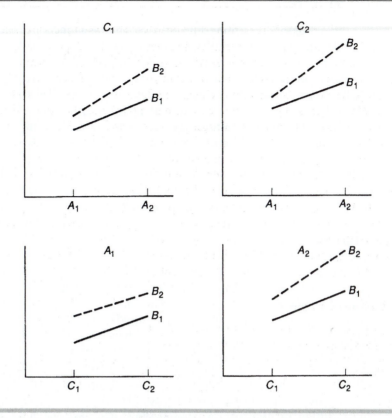

Figure 4.8 Hypothetical graph of three variables. At the top, the differences between the two levels of variable C (C_1 and C_2) will be hardest to perceive accurately because of their greater spatial separation. Between the top and the bottom, the consistency of representing the unchanged B variable has been maintained.

variable coded by line tone (e.g., dashed versus dot) in one graph should be coded by the same physical distinction in all graphs; and of course the association of physical coding to meaning (solid line to one level, dashed line to another) should also be consistent. Thus, notice that in the bottom two panels of Figure 4.8, the coding on B is consistent with the coding in the top panels even though variables A and C have traded places. This is good because it supports easier visualization of the effect of C. If consistency is needlessly violated, the reader will have difficulty in making a transition from one graph to the other. This issue defines poor *visual momentum* (Woods, 1984), a concept we will consider further in Chapter 5.

3. *Highlighting differences.* When related material is presented in different graphs, it becomes critical to highlight the changes or differences from graph to graph, either prominently in the legend or in the symbols themselves. For example, a

series of graphs presenting different *Y* variables as a function of the same *X* variable should highlight the *Y* label. This system allows the same cognitive set to be transferred from graph to graph, while the single mental revision that is necessary is prominently displayed. The time- and effort-consuming visual search necessary to locate the changed element is minimized (Gillan, et al., 1998).

4. *Distinctive legends.* Corresponding to point 3, legends of similar graphs must highlight the distinct features, not bury them as a single word that is nearly hidden in the last line of otherwise identical multi-line legends.

This discussion leads to two further points that have more general relevance. First, some of the failures of consistency, or lack of highlighting (as well as other graphic shortcomings), arise not from short-sightedness on the part of the graph's designer but from reliance on statistical graphics packages that may not have been designed with these perceptual and cognitive principles in mind (Gillan, et al., 1998). This point will be emphasized in Chapter 13. Reliance on automation can have its costs as well as its benefits.

Second, the concern with multiple graphs illustrates that there are different levels of analysis in system design. Each individual system (graph in this case) may be optimized, thereby producing what we might call *local* optimality. Yet the configuration of all systems together, with each one locally optimized, can produce *global* disharmony as certain emergent features (e.g., inconsistency) of the *set* of systems (controls or displays) are revealed that will disrupt their collective use. Optimizing total system design often reflects a compromise between satisfying local compatibility and achieving global harmony (Wickens, Vincow, Schopper, & Lincoln, 1997), and sometimes the latter is more important than the former (Andre & Wickens, 1992).

In conclusion, we note that the graph designer may have one of two general goals: to convey a specific message to the reader or to provide a way of looking at and exploring a data set. In the former case, it is necessary to configure the data in a way that emphasizes the message to be conveyed, as described above. In the latter case, the guidelines are not as clear, and probably the flexibility to produce multiple representations should be the guiding principle—the great advantage to computer-generated graphics. These representations should emphasize different comparisons and contrasts. However, the goal of the graph in most cases is to help people understand subtle relationships in the data that do, by definition, involve integration. Hence, the different formats should highlight different forms of visual proximity and integration (Kolata, 1982). The use of three-dimensional graphs in this regard will be addressed later in this chapter.

DIALS, METERS, AND INDICATORS: DISPLAY COMPATIBILITY

As we noted earlier, graphs are typically *static* representations of quantitative analog data. In contrast, many systems present analog information in the more *dynamic* form of dials, meters, or other changing elements, that represent the momentary state of some part of the system. As with graphs, it is important that dials and meters be compatible with the users information-processing needs and *mental model* of the system. The mental model, a concept we will discuss further in Chapter 7, forms the basis for understanding the system, predicting its future behavior, and controlling its actions (Carroll & Olson, 1987; Gentner & Stevens, 1983; Moray, 1998; Park & Gittelman, 1995). As a consequence, there are three levels of representation that must be considered in designing display interfaces, as shown in Figure 4.9: (1) the physical system itself, (2) the mental model, and (3) the critical interface between these two, the display surface on which changes in the system are presented to update the user's mental model or mental representation, and to form the basis for control action and decision. It is important to maintain a high degree of congruence, or *compatibility*, among these three representations.

In achieving this compatibility, it is important that the user's mental model corresponds accurately to the dynamics of the true physical system, a correspondence that Vicente (1990, 1997, 1999) refers to as *ecological compatibility*. Such correspondence will be attained by good training, as discussed in Chapter 7, and can be reinforced by effective and intuitive displays. *Display compatibility* is achieved by display representations whose structure and organization are compatible with that of the physical system (as well as the mental model). In the following, we discuss static and dynamic aspects of display compatibility.

When considering issues of display compatibility, it is important to distinguish between analog or continuous systems and digital or discrete systems. In general, analog systems are those whose behavior is governed by the laws and constraints of physics, and therefore change continuously over time (e.g., controlling an aircraft, a ground vehicle, or an energy conversion process).

In considering such analog systems, it is important to distinguish two major types of display compatibility: static and dynamic. As we will see, the two interact in terms of their implications for analog display design. However, in terms of processing mechanisms, the research indicates that there are separate sets of perceptual channels to encode static position and dynamic velocity information (e.g., Anstis, 1986; Regan, 1982). The static and dynamic components of display compatibility will now be considered in detail.

The Static Component: Pictorial Realism

The *principle of pictorial realism* dictates that the display representation should look like—be a pictorial representation of—the entity it is representing. For example, if a variable's physical representation is analog, then its display representation should also be analog (Roscoe, 1968). The representation of aircraft altitude is a typical instance.

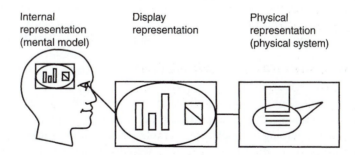

Figure 4.9   Representations of a physical system.

Physically, altitude is an analog quantity. Conceptually, it is also represented to the pilot in analog form, with large changes in altitude more important than small changes. Therefore, to achieve compatibility, a display of altitude (i.e., an altimeter) should also be of analog (moving needle) rather than digital format, a guideline echoing the earlier discussion of graphs. The transformation of symbolic digital information to analog conceptual representation imposes an extra processing step, which will lead to longer visual fixations, longer processing time, or a greater probability of error (Grether, 1949; Tole, Stephens, Harris, & Ephrath, 1982).

Other factors also influence the choice of analog or digital representations of altitude or of other continuously varying quantities. For example, a requirement to read the absolute value of an indicator with high precision would favor the digital format (Simmonds, Galer, & Baines, 1981). On the other hand, the need to perceive rate-of-change information, to estimate the magnitude of the variable when it is rapidly changing, or to estimate at a glance the distance of that variable from some limit favors the analog format (Sanders & McCormick, 1993). In addition to altitude, many variables have analog physical representations (e.g., temperature, pressure speed, power, or direction), as well as conceptual dimensions that have the characteristic of an ordered quantity with multiple levels (e.g., degree of danger or program quality).

Displaying information in analog format that is physically represented in analog fashion is a necessary but not sufficient condition to ensure high display compatibility. Roscoe's (1968) principle of pictorial realism also dictates that the *direction* and *shape* of the display representation be compatible with their physical counterparts (and presumably, the mental representation). Thus, pictorial realism may be violated in direction: for instance, an altimeter might represent altitude so that high altitudes are shown low on the display, or altitude might be represented horizontally. Instead, the altimeter should present high altitudes at the top of the scale and low ones at the bottom. Similarly, high temperatures should be higher, and low temperatures lower.

The principle of pictorial realism may be violated in terms of shape if a circular altimeter (pointer or dial) represents the linear variable of altitude (Grether, 1949). (The main limitation of the linear display is that it must occupy a large physical extent of "real estate" to convey the same level of scale resolution as the more "compact" round dial display.) Finally, pictorial realism may be violated by dissecting and displaying in separate parts a variable that is unitary. This could affect both the direction and shape of the display representation. Grether (1949), for example, reports that operators have a more difficult time extracting altitude information from three concentric pointers of a rotating display (indicating units of 100, 1,000, and 10,000 feet) than from a single pointer. In sum, the direction and shape of displayed quantities should correspond to their physical counterparts and the operator's mental model of them.

The concept of static compatibility may also be applied to systems that are not inherently analog but have some ordered spatial component—for example, an expert system's decision logic, or a circuit diagram. Here, too, the principle of pictorial realism is an important guiding principle. For example, circuit status indicators should be mapped to the topological connections in the real system, as shown in Figure 4.10.

Finally, although our discussion has focused on the role of spatial extent or position to represent analog quantities, color has also been used in this regard (e.g., color coding to indicate temperature). As we have noted previously (in the preceding section on graphical perception and in Chapter 3), it is important to bear in mind that color

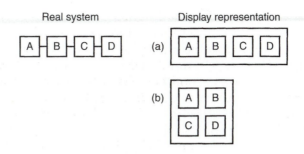

Figure 4.10   Two display representations for a circuit diagram. Representation (*a*) is more compatible than representation (*b*) because it obeys the principle of pictorial realism and makes the topological connections apparent.

(hue) is not effective in depicting continuous amount. Rather, color tends to be perceived categorically rather than continuously and does not generate a natural ordering (e.g., from "most" to "least") in a way that lends itself to analog displays (Merwin, Vincow, & Wickens, 1994). The intensity or saturation of a color better represents a change in analog quantity, as discussed in Chapter 3 (color coding). Color (hue) can be used effectively to show discrete state changes (Smith & Thomas, 1964).

Compatibility of Display Movement

If motion is occurring in the physical system itself, it is best to represent that motion by display motion (rather than by using static displays) to produce an appropriate mental model of the situation (Park & Gittelman, 1995). Beyond that, however, the *compatibility* between motion direction in the display, the physical system, and the mental model is also important. Roscoe (1968) and Roscoe, Corl, and Jensen (1981) propose the *principle of the moving part*—that the direction of movement of an indicator on a display should be compatible with the direction of physical movement and the operator's mental model. There are, however, circumstances in which the principles of the moving part and of pictorial realism conflict in their design implications, and so one or the other must be violated. This occurs in so-called fixed-pointer/moving-scale indicators.

An example of this violation is shown in Figure 4.11, which could represent an altimeter. In the moving-pointer display (Figure 4.11a), both principles—moving part and pictorial realism—are satisfied. High altitude is at the top and an increase in altitude is indicated by an upward movement of the moving element on the display. Unfortunately, this simple arrangement can only show a small range of the displayed variable. One solution to this problem is to have a fixed pointer show only the relevant part of the display scale, and move the scale when necessary (Figures 4.11b and c). If the moving scale is designed to follow the principle of pictorial realism, high altitudes should be at the top of the display (Figure 4.11b). However, this means that the scale must move *downward* to indicate an *increase* in altitude— a violation of the principle of the moving part. If the labeling is reversed to conform to the principle of the moving part (Figure 4.11c), this change will reverse the orientation and display high altitude at the bottom, violating the principle of pictorial realism. (Most modern

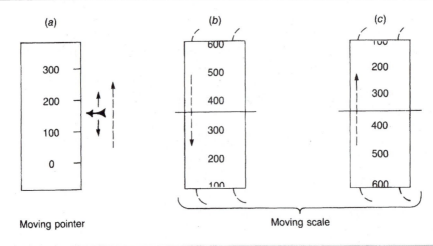

Figure 4.11   Display movement. (*a*) Moving-pointer altimeter; (*b* and *c*) moving-scale or fixed-pointer altimeters. The dashed arrows show the direction of display movement to indicate an increase in altitude.

aircraft have adopted the format of (b) for computer-generated altitude displays.) A disadvantage for both moving-scale displays is that scale values become difficult to read when the variable is changing rapidly since the digits themselves are moving.

The solution here is to employ a hybrid scale. The pointer moves as in Figure 4.11a, but only a small portion of the scale is exposed. When the pointer approaches the top or bottom of the window, the scale shifts more slowly in the opposite direction to bring the pointer back toward the center of the window and expose the newer, more relevant region of the scale. Thus, the pointer moves at higher frequencies in response to the more perceivable motion, and the scale shifts at lower frequencies as needed. This way both principles—pictorial realism and moving part—are satisfied. This concept of *frequency separation* has an important realization in aircraft displays, as we will now describe.

The Frequency-Separated Display

The conventional presentation of an aircraft's attitude on the attitude directional indicator (ADI), discussed in Chapter 3, is given by the *inside-out* moving-horizon display, or pilot's-eye view, shown in Figure 4.12a. This display supports the principle of pictorial realism, since the view from the cockpit appears similar to what is presented on the display (cockpit is level and ground tilts). However, the inside-out display violates the dynamic principle of the moving part. For example, rolling the aircraft to the left generates a counterclockwise rotation of the aircraft but produces a clockwise rotation of the moving element on the display, the artificial horizon bar in a way that disagrees with the pilot's mental model (Johnson & Roscoe, 1972). In most situations, pilots are sufficiently trained with the inside-out display that the violation of the principle of the moving part appears to have little impact.

However, in some situations (e.g., when the real horizon can't be seen and the pilot is stressed or distracted), a pilot may perceive the moving display element (the horizon

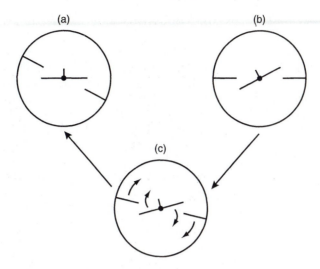

Figure 4.12   Aircraft attitude display. (*a*) Inside-out, (*b*) outside-in, and (*c*) frequency-separated display. All displays show an aircraft banking left. Low-frequency return to steady state is indicated by arrows in *c*.

bar) as being the airplane rather than the horizon and try to control the orientation of the wrong part of the display. The result is a *roll-control reversal*, a phenomenon that has been estimated to lead to about 100 fatalities per year in the United States (Roscoe, 1992). An alternative designed to alleviate the moving horizon display problem is the world-referenced, *outside-in* display, or bird's-eye view, shown in Figure 4.12b.

The outside-in display shows the plane as it would appear to an upright observer looking at the plane from behind. When the plane rolls to the left, the display's aircraft symbol also rotates counterclockwise, and so the principle of the moving part is satisfied. However, the display violates the principle of pictorial realism in that the static picture that is drawn (a horizontal horizon and tilted airplane) is incompatible with what the pilot sees through the cockpit window (a tilted horizon and a horizontal airplane).

To resolve the dilemma between the static and dynamic aspects of aircraft attitude displays, Fogel (1959) proposed the concept of frequency-separation (Johnson & Roscoe, 1972; Roscoe, 1968). In the *frequency-separated* ADI, lateral movement of the controls (changing the bank angle of the aircraft) will produce an immediate outside-in rotation of the aircraft symbol on the display, as in Figure 4.12c, so that display and aircraft motion are compatible when conditions are dynamic. When, however, the pilot enters a turn, which requires the bank angle to be held constant for some period of time and aircraft attitude is static, the horizon and the airplane symbol both rotate slowly to an inside-out format.

For frequency-separated displays, then, the appropriate principle is followed at the appropriate time. For high-frequency responses, when control movement and motion perception are dominant, the principle of the moving part is adhered to. But when aircraft attitude is relatively static, the principle of pictorial realism is restored. This progression is shown by the transition in Figure 4.12 from b to c to a.

Displays based on the frequency-separated concept have been shown to be more effective than either an inside-out or outside-in display in terms of pilot's accuracy of control and the number of inadvertent control reversals that were made when flying. Even skilled pilots who were used to the conventional moving-horizon display showed improved performance (Roscoe & Williges, 1975; Ince, Williges, & Roscoe, 1975; Beringer, Williges, & Roscoe, 1975). These studies were conducted in both airplanes and flight simulators.

In addition, displays incorporating the frequency-separated concept have been integrated into the computer-animated display systems of a primary training simulator, resulting in a large immediate improvement in landing performance by beginning flight students (Lintern, Roscoe, & Sivier, 1990; Roscoe, 1981, 1999). In summary, the frequency-separated display illustrates a more general principle: Sometimes clever design can produce a system that adheres to two apparently contradictory principles with effective results.

Display Integration and Ecological Interface Design

The principle of pictorial realism suggests that an array of displays should be spatially compatible or congruent with the array of physical components that they represent, as illustrated in Figure 4.10. However, as discussed in Chapter 3, there are other ways of integrating information on displays to be compatible with the operator's need to mentally integrate that information. The proximity compatibility principle provides guidance for co-locating, connecting or otherwise making information sources perceptually similar (Wickens & Carswell, 1995), if the cognitive demands of the task require their integration.

In addition, as we discussed in Chapter 3, many creative design solutions can **configure** display elements in a way that is compatible with cognitive processing demands—that is, to produce emergent features, when those elements change in certain critical ways that are relevant to the operator's task. When the display configuration also reflects the constraints of the physical system being represented, it is called an *ecological interface* (Vicente & Rasmussen, 1992). For example, Vicente et al. (1996) compared a single-sensor, single-indicator display with a *Rankine display* (Beltracchi, 1987), which represents several important thermodynamic variables that occur in a water-based nuclear power plant. Deviations in the shape of the display (it resembles a bell-shaped curve) indicate potential problems in the state of the system (e.g., if a line is not perfectly horizontal within the display, it indicates that temperature is not being kept constant as steam is condensing).

The subject's task was to diagnose problems of various kinds (e.g., power loss, instrumentation failures). Vicente et al. found that their subjects, nuclear engineering students who had the necessary thermodynamics background, performed better with the Rankine display than with the single-sensor, single-indicator display. This result is consistent with the proximity compatibility principle if the Rankine display is considered to be an integrated, object display; one would expect better performance for the integrated Rankine format over a set of separated displays for an integrated task like diagnosis which, in complex systems often requires considering the relation between multiple variables. Furthermore, with training, the Rankine display representation may create and shape the user's mental model to more accurately reflect the physical representation. In this sense, the three representations shown in Figure 4.9 are tightly intertwined in a successful system. The issue of display design to support complex systems will be addressed again in Chapter 13.

In summary, the principle of compatibility, which will be discussed again in the context of responses in Chapter 9, is probably one of the most important guidelines in the engineering psychology of display design. Displays that are compatible with the physical system and the user's mental model are read more rapidly and accurately than incompatible ones under normal conditions. More important, their advantages increase under conditions of stress, as discussed in Chapter 12. When the three elements of Figure 4.9 are congruent, the display will equally serve learning and system monitoring.

THREE DIMENSIONS AND DEPTH

Much of our previous discussion has focused on multidimensional displays that are intended to convey information regarding two dimensions at once. However, there are situations in which a third dimension on a display is represented as depth, or as the perceived distance from the observer along an axis perpendicular to the plane of the display. These displays are intended to represent three dimensions of Euclidean space, and they are the focus of this section. Such displays may be developed for one of two general purposes. First, the three dimensions may actually be designed to represent three Euclidean dimensions of space, as when a display is constructed to guide the pilot in a flight path, or to plan the 3D trajectory of a robot arm manipulating hazardous material. Second, the display may use the third (depth) dimension to represent another (nondistance) quantity. Examples of this usage are found in many three-dimensional graphics packages.

To understand the advantages and costs of three-dimensional displays, along with the causes of certain systematic distortions in our ability to use depth in the natural world, it is important to discuss briefly some of the fundamental characteristics of perceiving depth. The reader wishing more detail should refer to Schiffman (1996) or Wickens, Todd, and Seidler (1989).

Depth Judgments

The accurate perception of depth and distance is accomplished through the operation of various perceptual *cues*. Some of these are characteristics of the object or world we are perceiving, and others are properties of our own visual system. We refer to these as *object-centered* and *observer-centered* cues, respectively.

Object-Centered Cues   Object-centered cues are sometimes described as pictorial cues because they are the kinds of cues that an artist could build into a picture to convey a sense of depth. Figure 4.13 is an example of a three-dimensional scene that incorporates eight of the following cues:

1. *Linear perspective.* When we see two converging lines, we assume that they are two parallel lines receding in depth (the road).
2. *Interposition.* When the contours of one object obscure the contours of another, we assume that the obscured object is more distant (the buildings on the right).
3. *Height in the plane.* Because we normally view objects from above, we assume that objects higher in our visual field are farther away (the two trucks).
4. *Light and shadow.* When objects are lighted from one direction, they normally have shadows that offer some clues about the objects' orientation relative to us

Figure 4.13   Contains object-centered cues for depth, as described in the text.

(Ramachandran, 1988) as well as their three-dimensional shapes (the buildings and trucks).

5. *Relative (familiar) size.* If objects are known to be the same true size, those sub-tending a smaller visual image on the retina (the retinal image) are assumed to be farther away (compare the two trucks).

6. *Textural gradients.* Most surfaces are textured, and when the plane of a texture is oriented toward the line of sight, the grain will grow finer at greater distance. This change in grain across the visual field is referred to as a textural gradient (the field on the left and the center line of the road).

7. *Proximity-luminance covariance.* Closely related to textural gradients is the fact that objects and lines are typically brighter as they are closer to us, and so con-tinuous reductions in illumination and intensity are assumed to signal reced-ing distance (the road lines) (Dosher, Sperling, & Wurst, 1986).

8. *Aerial perspective.* More distant objects often tend to be "hazier" and less clearly defined (the mountains).

9. *Motion parallax.* When we move relative to a three-dimensional scene, objects that are closer to us show greater relative motion than those that are more dis-tant. Hence, our perceptual system assumes that distance from us is inversely related to the degree of motion.

Motion, like light and shadow, is also used as a cue to the three-dimensional *shape* of objects themselves, as well as their location. For example, the cloud of points in Figure 4.14 does not appear to be three-dimensional. Yet if these were points of light on a rotating three-dimensional cylinder like a rotating can, they would show a pattern of motion—slow near the edges, fastest at the center—that leads to an unambiguous interpretation of a rotating three-dimensional cylinder (Braunstein & Andersen, 1984). This property is referred to as *structure through motion* (Braunstein, 1990).

Observer-Centered Cues Three sources of information about depth are functions of characteristics of the human visual system.

1. *Binocular disparity.* The images received by the two eyes, located at slightly different points in space, are disparate. Objects at different differences stimulate unique pairs of corresponding points on the retina. The degree of disparity provides a basis for the judgment of distance, the principle employed in some three-dimensional displays, known as *stereoscopic displays*.
2. *Convergence.* The "cross-eyed" pattern of the eyes, required to focus on objects as they are brought close to the observer, is necessary to bring the image onto the detail-sensitive retina of both eyes. Proprioceptive messages from the eye muscles to the perceptual centers of the brain inform the latter of the degree of convergence, and therefore of an object's distance.
3. *Accommodation.* Like convergence, accommodation is a cue provided to the brain by the eye muscles. In this case the muscles adjust the shape of the lens to bring the image into focus on the retina. More adjustment is done for closer objects, and the amount of adjustment can thereby signal the approximate distance of the object from the eye.

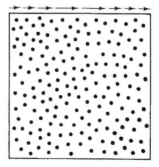

Figure 4.14 Potential stimulus for recovery of structure through motion. If the horizontal motion of the dots were proportional to the velocity vectors at the top of the figure, the flat surface would be perceived as a three-dimensional rotating cylinder.

Effect of Distance on Cue Effectiveness   Not all cues are equally effective at different distances. For example, it is well understood that binocular disparity is not a particularly important cue when the distance between the observer and an object is large (Gibson, 1982). Cutting and Vishton (1995) have summarized the effects of the various depth cues at different distances, and their summary is depicted in Figure 4.15. Cutting and Vishton have separated the continuum of depth into three regions: *personal space, action space,* and *vista space.* Some cues are effective regardless of distance: for example, occlusion and relative size. Other cues tend to be more effective in the different spaces. For example, within personal space (less than 2 meters), binocular disparity is important. However, as distance is increased, the effectiveness of accommodation and binocular disparity decrease, whereas aerial perspective becomes more effective, as illustrated in Figure 4.15. Of course, the range depicted in the figure is based on natural viewing situations and does not necessarily apply when depth is synthesized in displays. For example, stereoscopic displays (discussed below) can be used to represent differences in the distances of objects that are miles away.

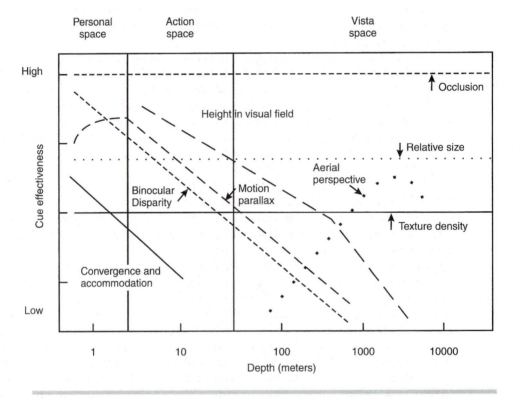

Figure 4.15   Effectiveness of various depth cues as a function of distance from observer.
Source: Adapted from J. E. Cutting and P. M. Vishton, "Perceiving Layout and Knowing Distances: The Integration, Relative Potency, and Contextual Use of Different Information About Depth," in W. Epstein & S. Rogers (Eds.), *Perception of Space and Motion* (San Diego: Academic Press, 1995), p. 80.

Perceptual Hypotheses and Ambiguity

In the description of object-centered cues, the phrase "we assume" was often used to describe the perceiver's interpretation of the world. These interpretations in turn are used by the observer to make inferences about how close and how far away things are. Hence, we often speak of depth and distance perception as governed by perceptual *hypotheses* about the way things are, based on our assumptions. For example, in Figure 4.13, we hypothesize that the two trucks in the visual field are the same true size, and therefore the one with the smaller-sized retinal image is farther away (Gregory, 1980; Rock, 1983). These hypotheses and assumptions reflecting top-down processing are relatively automatic and unconscious. Typically, as we observe the three-dimensional world, our hypotheses are supported by all depth cues working *redundantly* to provide the same information. There is evidence, moreover, that if one depth cue provides incomplete depth information, information from another cue is sometimes used to disambiguate it. For example, when Pong, Kenner, and Otis (1990) showed observers a scene having both motion and binocular disparity, they found that observers could use motion disparity information to clarify inconclusive stereo disparity information. However, there are occasions when the hypotheses we assume do not correspond with reality because the cues are few in number, the assumptions we make about the world are incorrect, or the cues are ambiguous.

Consider, for example, a study by Eberts and MacMillan (1985) of the causes of rear-end collisions. The researchers noted that the frequency with which small cars are rear-ended is considerably greater than that for large cars. They reasoned that drivers' judgments about how far a car is in front, and therefore how soon they must apply the brakes, are based on the cue of relative size. Drivers assume an average size of vehicles and use it as the basis for mentally computing a perceived distance. Smaller-than-average cars are perceived to be relatively farther away than they actually are (just as larger ones are perceived to be relatively closer). So when perceiving small cars, the braking process is initiated later than it should be, with the consequence that closures are too fast. Eberts and MacMillan tested and confirmed this hypothesis in an experiment.

Similar faulty assumptions can occur in aviation. If a pilot is flying over unfamiliar terrain and encounters bushes shaped like trees, the pilot may assume that these are actually trees, believe the plane is further from the ground than it is, and so become dangerously close to colliding with the earth (Hart, 1988). A related example of a false perceptual hypothesis is shown in Figure 4.16a. Flying low over a flat but upward-sloping surface on approach to a runway, the pilot may assume that the surface is not only flat but level (the most probable assumption, since most runways are level). As a consequence of this assumption, the pilot will perceive the plane to be higher than it really is above the runway. The pilot will then erroneously "correct" the altitude by descending, and therefore will be likely to fly an approach that is much closer to the upward-sloping terrain than is advisable, the possible consequence being a "short" landing. Correspondingly, the opposite assumption may be made while approaching over a flat but down-sloping terrain (Figure 4.16b) (Hawkins & Orlady, 1993).

Gregory (1977) has pointed out that perceptual ambiguities of size and distance are particularly likely to occur when the three-dimensional world is represented on a two-dimensional display. Figure 4.17 shows a three-dimensional graphic plot of a set of data. In this case, the data happen to describe the proximity compatibility principle discussed

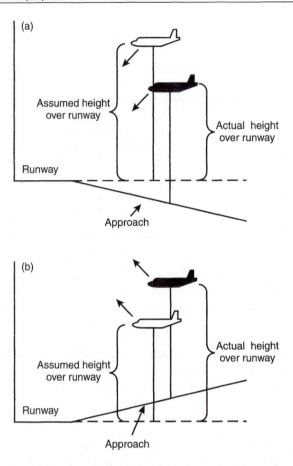

Figure 4.16 Misjudgment of height over a runway. The black airplane is the position of the actual airplane. The white airplane is the pilot's perceived position relative to the ground, based on the (faulty) assumption that the ground beneath is level and not upsloping (as in *a*) or downsloping (as in *b*). The direction of the inappropriate correction is shown by arrows.

earlier in this chapter and in Chapter 3. The graph represents the height of a dependent variable (e.g., data interpretation accuracy) as a function of two independent variables (e.g., whether the task requires focused attention or integration and whether the display is an object or a separated bar graph). The graph depicts the two display types as being equivalent when used for focused attention tasks (the left side), but our perception is that performance with the separated display represented at the back is better because our hypothesis is that the more distant bar must be larger if it is the same retinal size. When the integration task is considered (the right side), performance with the separate display is actually depicted as worse, but our perception is that the two displays provide equivalent accuracy because the bar graphs are perceived to be the same size. The smaller size of the more distant bar is not perceived properly because it is farther away.

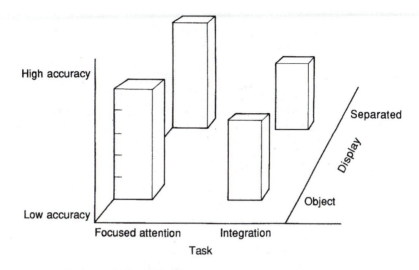

Figure 4.17   Perceptual distortions induced by three-dimensional graphics. The graph presents a hypothetical set of data that might be obtained to demonstrate the proximity compatibility principle. On the left (focused attention task), the two bars are the same height, but the sense of depth makes the more "distant" bar appear larger. On the right (integration task), the rear bar is smaller than the close bar, but perspective makes them appear the same. You may measure the bars to make these comparisons.

It is important to note that these misperceptions are relatively automatic. It is not easy to use our conscious awareness to de-bias the judgments of relative length. Various solutions have been proposed to compensate for these biases. For example, for the misjudgment of aircraft altitude shown in Figure 4.16, Kraft (1978) argued that pilots must pay more attention to their flight instruments, which represents this information unambiguously, even in good visual conditions. For the bias shown in Figure 4.17, we could capitalize on the perceiver's automatic tendency to compensate for the depth dimension, and therefore scale down the more "distant" bar graphs accordingly. However, the problem with this solution is that the amount by which display height should be reduced with greater perceived distance cannot easily be specified because it depends on how "compelling" the impression of distance is, an impression that will vary with the number of depth cues in the display and from person to person. A better solution is to provide scale markings on the blocks themselves so that height can be read by counting the ticks, as shown on the left front bar of the graph.

Three-Dimensional Displays of Three-Dimensional Space

The problems that can arise when making precise, absolute distance judgments in three dimensions suggest that it is not effective to use depth to represent a non-distance dimension. In contrast, there are compelling reasons for using three-dimensional displays to represent three-dimensional worlds, such as the product designed at a computer-aided design (CAD) workstation, the contour map studied by the petroleum geologist, the map of magnetic forces around the human brain, the display of air traffic shown in Figure 4.18a, or the flight path display shown in Figure 4.19a.

In all these cases, a three-dimensional display representation is more compatible with the operator's mental model of the three-dimensional world than a two-dimensional counterpart (Figure 4.18b or 4.19b). Even though the two-dimensional representations provide the necessary information to reconstruct the three-dimensional picture, they require mental effort to integrate and reconstruct the picture. When this picture is used to maintain general spatial awareness or to control flight path guidance, rather than to make precise readings of altitude, orientation and distance, the advantages of the three-dimensional representation should be obvious (Haskell & Wickens, 1993). Indeed, systematic comparisons of 2-D and 3-D representations in flight control and data interpretation domains have found better performance for a 3-D representation on tasks requiring information integration from all three dimensions (e.g., Haskell & Wickens, 1993; Hickox & Wickens, 1999; Liu, Zhang, & Chaffin, 1997; Wickens, Merwin, & Lin, 1994; Wickens & Prevett, 1995). For example, Liu, Zhang, and Chaffin (1997) found that a 3-D human form graphic was more effective than 2-D views when complex, asymmetric postures were

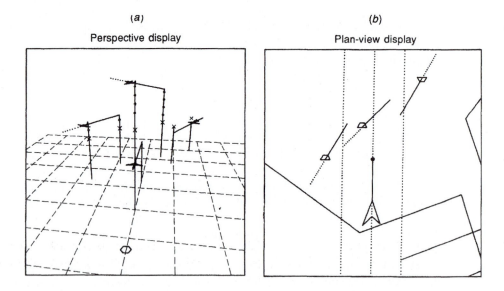

(a)
Perspective display

(b)
Plan-view display

Figure 4.18 A modified air traffic display designed to provide the pilot in the cockpit with greater situation awareness of surrounding air traffic: (*a*) three-dimensional representation; (*b*) two-dimensional representation. The symbols around each aircraft in (*b*) indicate whether they are above or below the altitude of the viewer's own aircraft.

Source: S. R. Ellis, M. W. McGreevy, and R. J. Hitchcock, "Perspective Traffic Display Format and Air Pilot Traffic Avoidance," *Human Factors, 29* (1987). Reprinted with permission. Copyright 1987 by the Human Factors Society, Inc. All rights reserved.

(a)

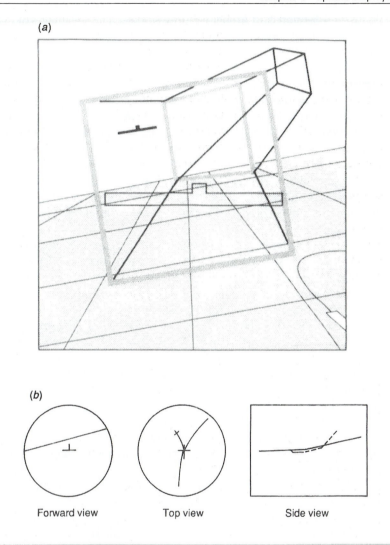

(b)

Forward view   Top view   Side view

Figure 4.19   Flight path displays: (a) three-dimensional perspective display with a future predicted position of the aircraft shown by the smaller black symbol; (b) the same information as it might be represented in two-dimensional plan views.

assessed—postures that would require integration of information from all three spatial dimensions. Wickens, Merwin, and Lin (1994) found that 3-D scatterplot displays were superior to separated 2-D scatterplots for integrated tasks, providing a better visualization of the complex shape of a 3-D surface. These results are consistent with the predictions of the proximity compatibility principle: When information is integrated into three dimensions, performance on tasks requiring such integration should improve.

Focused Attention and Artificial Frameworks   The advantages of three-dimensional displays for flight control and spatial awareness notwithstanding, such displays have two limitations relative to their two-dimensional counterparts. The first limitation, to be discussed in this section, is that three-dimensional displays are not effective displays for focused attention tasks. The second limitation, that three-dimensional displays generate false hypotheses, will be discussed in the next section.

Three-dimensional representations in a two-dimensional display plane are inherently ambiguous in specifying absolute distances and depth. Therefore, such displays will not be useful for the precise reading of values, such as answering the question relative to Figure 4.17: "How much better is performance with object than separate displays?" or to Figure 4.19a: "How far below the flight path is my aircraft predictor symbol?" This deficiency is also consistent with the predictions of the proximity compatibility principle: Focused attention will be disrupted by the object integration of a three-dimensional display.

Many experiments have demonstrated the problem of focused attention for 3-D displays. For example, when Hollands, Pierce, and Magee (1998) had observers estimate the distance between two lines shown in a 3-D display cube or in separate 2-D displays, they found better performance with the 2-D format. The depth information in the 3-D cube interfered with accurate assessment of the distance between the lines. Liu, Zhang, and Chaffin (1997) found that a 3-D graphic of a human form jeopardized their observers' judgments of posture when simple, symmetric postures were analyzed. Haskell and Wickens (1993) found that 2-D displays like those shown in Figure 4.19b were superior to the 3-D display shown in Figure 4.19a when the task specifically focused on a certain variable (e.g., control of airspeed). The problem of focused attention is particularly evident when the axis along which distance must be judged runs parallel to the line of sight into the display (Wickens, Liang, Prevett, & Olmos, 1996). Large changes in distance along this axis may only produce small changes in displayed distances between objects, leading the observer to underestimate the magnitude of the changes.

A potential solution to this limitation, however, may be offered by incorporating *artificial frameworks* into the display. The cockpit display of traffic information (CDTI), developed by Ellis, McGreevy, and Hitchcock (1987) and shown in Figure 4.18a is one example. Each aircraft is "attached" to a post or dropline that protrudes from the ground at its current geographical location, and its altitude is unambiguously specified by the markers on each post. Furthermore, the direction of the predicted flight path of each aircraft can also be unambiguously interpreted through these supports, creating a "wicket" for each aircraft. The posts resolve the ambiguity of position and motion of objects within the space. McGreevy and Ellis (1986), Ellis (1993), and Wickens, Todd, and Seidler (1989) discuss other principles for designing three-dimensional displays to minimize the biases and distortions we experience in resolving three-dimensional ambiguity.

Resolving Ambiguities   A second serious limitation of three-dimensional displays results when ambiguity can allow false hypotheses to be formed about depth and distance because the necessary cues for depth perception are not incorporated into the display. Consider the flight command path display shown in Figure 4.20a, in which the two boxes, like those in Figure 4.19a, represent segments of an imaginary tunnel to be "flown through." Cues of relative size and height in the plane help resolve the ambiguity of which box is closer. Both boxes are assumed to be the same true size, and the higher one is perceived as farther away. But consider the display in Figure 4.20b, in which the pilot is approaching the tunnel from beneath. Here, height in the plane offers information contradictory to relative size, and the perceiver may note perceptual reversals in which the smaller box is sometimes perceived as closer, not more distant.

Errors of display interpretation can be critical in spatial environments when objects must be approached, manipulated, and moved. These environments would include aviation, surgery, and the control of robots and teleoperators in space, under the sea, or in other hostile environments. The logical solution would be to incorporate additional redundant depth cues, such as the cues of interposition (hidden lines) and textural gradient shown in Figure 4.20c. A rough design guideline is provided by the *weighted additive cue model* (Bruno & Cutting, 1988; Ichikawa & Saida, 1996; Sollenberger and Milgram, 1993; Young, Landy, & Maloney, 1993), which proposes that each added cue increases the compellingness of depth, but in weighted fashion, such that some cues are more effective than others. For example, Sollenberger and Milgram (1993) found that stereo and motion parallax cues used as tools for microscopic analysis in neurosurgery had approximately additive effects in several experiments, but that the effects of motion parallax were more pronounced.

From the designer's point of view, the addition of cues, particularly in computer-driven dynamic displays, can be expensive and should be avoided if they are unnecessary. So which cues should be used—which cues have the greatest weights? To determine weights for the different depth cues, studies of *cue dominance* are performed in which ambiguous situations are set up and the "winning" cue is established as the one that governs the final perceived depth (Dosher, Sperling, & Wurst, 1986; Ichikawa & Saida, 1996; Young, Landy, & Maloney, 1993). Thus, for example, the perceived interpretation of Figure 4.20b will establish whether relative size or height in the plane is more dominant. It is clear by looking at Figure 4.20c that interposition is dominant over height in the plane, as it removes ambiguity from the perception. A synthesis of a number of such studies reveals that three cues in particular, *interposition, motion parallax,* and *binocular disparity* (created artificially in stereoscopic displays), are the most dominant (Wickens, Todd, & Seidler, 1989). The last of these will be discussed in more detail because of its special technological requirements.

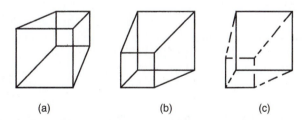

(a)   (b)   (c)

Figure 4.20   Perspective tunnel such as that shown in Figure 4.19. (a) Height in the plane and relative size are redundant cues for depth. (b) With height in the plane and relative size conflicting, a reversal of perception may sometimes be experienced. (c) The conflict is resolved by including interposition and texture gradients on the connecting lines.

Stereoscopic Displays   A relatively accurate sense of three-dimensionality can be created through stereopsis, presenting slightly different images to the two eyes (Patterson, 1997; Patterson & Martin, 1992). As we saw earlier, the amount of disparity can provide a direct, unambiguous cue for depth, and it dominates most other cues with which it is placed in competition. Current display technology allows fairly faithful production of stereoscopic cues in dynamic displays such as those in Figures 4.18 and 4.19. Furthermore, comparative evaluations generally reveal that stereopsis enhances performance (Barfield & Rosenberg, 1995; Brown & Gallimore, 1995; Muhlbach, Bocker, & Prussog, 1995; Sollenberger & Milgram, 1993; Way, 1988; Wickens, Merwin, & Lin, 1994; Zenyuh, Reising, Walchli, & Biers, 1988). For example, Barfield and Rosenberg found an advantage for adding stereo to a perspective display for judgments of azimuth and elevation of computer-generated objects. Sollenberger and Milgram found that stereo displays produced more accurate path-tracing performance, as noted above. Often the advantage is time-based: Brown and Gallimore found a stereo advantage for recognizing previously-seen objects—adding binocular disparity information reduced response times. Wickens, Merwin, and Lin (1994) found a stereo advantage for presenting a 3-D scatterplot, showing that judgments were faster for a large range of task types, and especially when the task required information integration.

Nonetheless, current computer-generated stereoscopic displays require specialized hardware including polarized glasses (which can produce flicker), are somewhat sensitive to disruption from vibration and poor viewing conditions, and are reduced in intensity and spatial resolution. Furthermore, not all people can accurately use stereoscopic cues. A display designer, therefore, may ultimately be asked to balance the added cost of the three-dimensional stereoscopic display against the performance benefits that it provides over its nonstereoscopic rivals (e.g., motion parallax, texture gradient). A study of three-dimensional tracking by Kim, Ellis, Tyler, Hannaford, and Stark (1987) found that the stereoscopic display provided benefits over a two-dimensional perspective display only as long as the cues of the latter were relatively sparse. When a richer set of pictorial cues was added (including texture gradient), the advantages of stereopsis were eliminated. Furthermore, in their review of the literature on three-dimensional displays, Wickens, Todd, and Seidler (1989) concluded that the enhancement of depth perception offered by stereoscopic displays was greatly diminished when the cue of relative motion or of motion parallax was available.

In some situations, such as highly focused tasks, there appears to be little to no advantage to stereo presentation. If stereopsis is the only depth cue, people tend to underestimate the depth of the image and find it difficult to point to the correct 3-D position of the image (Inoue, Kawai, & Noro, 1996). Gallimore and Brown (1993) showed that stereopsis did not improve performance for a task requiring the discrimination of 3-D objects, whereas occlusion did. Hollands, Pierce, and Magee (1998) found little advantage for stereo in their focused attention task requiring estimating the difference between two functions (representing paths of vehicular motion) with 3-D displays.

TRANSITION

This chapter has described issues related to the design of spatial or analog displays. We began with a discussion of graphs, and noted several factors that can make a graph more effective. We then examined analog displays such as meters and dials, and emphasized the concept of compatibility between the display and the cognitive domain. Then, we examined depth perception and discussed how 3-D displays might best be designed to effectively convey information. In Chapter 5, we will focus on interactive displays that are also spatial, and the nature of the navigational tasks that often use such displays (maps); thus, that chapter forms a natural continuation of many of the topics discussed in this chapter. We will address related topics when we discuss spatial working memory in Chapter 7, spatial or analog manual control in Chapter 10, and the compatibility between a display and working memory and response in Chapters 7 and 9, respectively. However, as we are well aware, spatial information plays only a partial role in our interactions with other systems, including people. In Chapter 6, we will discuss the complementary role of verbal and linguistic information in this interaction.

REFERENCES

Andre, A. D., & Wickens, C. D. (1992). Compatibility and consistency in display-control systems: Implications for aircraft decision aid design. *Human Factors, 34,* 639–653.

Anstis, S. (1986). Motion perception in the frontal plane. In K. R. Boff, L. Kaufman, & J. P. Thomas (Eds.), *Handbook of perception and human performance* (vol. 1). New York: Wiley.

Apaiwongse, T. S. (1995). Facial display of environmental policy uncertainty. *Journal of Business and Psychology, 10,* 65–74.

Bailey, C. D. (1996). Empirical statistics: V. Evidence on the extent of the steepness bias in visual estimation of trends. *Perceptual and Motor Skills, 82,* 731–734.

Barfield, W., & Rosenberg, C. (1995). Judgments of azimuth and elevation as a function of monoscopic and binocular depth cues using a perspective display. *Human Factors, 37,* 173–181.

Behrens, J. T., Stock, W. A., & Sedgwick, C. A. (1990). Judgment errors in elementary box-plot displays. *Communications in Statistics, 19,* 245–262.

Beltracchi, L. (1987). A direct manipulation interface for water-based Rankine cycle heat engines. *IEEE Transactions on Systems, Man, and Cybernetics, 17,* 478–487.

Beringer, D. B., & Chrisman, S. E. (1991). Peripheral polar-graphic displays for signal/failure detection. *International Journal of Aviation Psychology, 1,* 133–148.

Beringer, D. B., Williges, R. C., & Roscoe, S. N. (1975). The transition of experienced pilots to a frequency-separated aircraft attitude display. *Human Factors, 17,* 401–414.

Braunstein, M. L. (1990). Structure from motion. In J. I. Elkind, S. K. Card, J. Hochberg, & B. M. Huey (Eds.), *Human performance models for computer-aided engineering* (pp. 89–105). Orlando, FL: Academic Press.

Braunstein, M. L., & Andersen, G. J. (1984). Shape and depth perception from parallel projects of three-dimensional motion. *Journal of Experimental Psychology: Human Perception & Performance, 10,* 749–760.

Brown, M. E., & Gallimore, J. J. (1995). Visualization of three-dimensional structure during computer-aided design. *International Journal of Human-Computer Interaction, 7,* 37–56.

Bruno, N., & Cutting, J. E. (1988). Minimodularity and the perception of layout. *Journal of Experimental Psychology: General, 117,* 161–170.

Carroll, J. M., & Olson, J. R. (1987). *Mental models in human-computer interaction.* Washington, DC: National Academy Press.

Carswell, C. M. (1990). Graphical information processing: The effects of proximity compatibility. *Proceedings of the 34th annual meeting of the Human Factors Society* (pp. 1494–1498). Santa Monica, CA: Human Factors Society.

Carswell, C. M. (1992a). Choosing specifiers: An evaluation of the basic tasks model of graphical perception. *Human Factors, 34,* 535–554.

Carswell, C. M. (1992b). Reading graphs: Interactions of processing requirements and stimulus structure. In B. Burns (Ed.), *Percepts, Concepts and Categories* (pp. 605–645). Amsterdam: Elsevier.

Carswell, C. M., Frankenberger, S., & Bernhard, D. (1991). Graphing in depth: Perspectives on the use of three-dimensional graphs to represent lower-dimensional data. *Behaviour & Information Technology, 10,* 459–474.

Carswell, C. M., & Ramzy, C. (1997). Graphing small data sets: Should we bother? *Behaviour & Information Technology, 16,* 61–71.

Carswell, C. M., & Wickens, C. D. (1988). *Comparative graphics: History and applications of perceptual integrality theory and the proximity compatibility hypothesis* (University of Illinois Technical Report ARL–88–2/AHEL–88–1/AHEL Technical Memorandum 8–88). Savoy, IL: Aviation Research Laboratory.

Carswell, C. M., & Wickens, C. D. (1990). The perceptual interaction of graphical attributes: Configurality, stimulus homogeneity, and object integration. *Perceptions & Psychophysics, 47,* 157–168.

Casner, S. M. (1991). A task-analytic approach to the automated design of graphic presentations. *ACM Transactions on Graphics, 10,* 111–151.

Cleveland, W. S. (1985). *The elements of graphing data.* Monterey, CA: Wadsworth.

Cleveland, W. S. (1990). A model for studying display methods of statistical graphics. In *Proceedings of the Section on Statistical Graphics* (pp. 1–30). Alexandria, VA: American Statistical Association.

Cleveland, W. S., & McGill, R. (1984). Graphical perception: Theory, experimentation, and application to the development of graphic methods. *Journal of the American Statistical Association, 70,* 531–554.

Cleveland, W. S., & McGill, R. (1985). Graphical perception and graphical methods for analyzing scientific data. *Science, 229,* 828–833.

Cleveland, W. S., & McGill, R. (1986). An experiment in graphical perception. *International Journal of Man-Machine Studies, 25,* 491–500.

Coll, R., Thyagarajan, A., & Chopra, S. (1991). An experimental study comparing the effectiveness of computer graphics data versus computer tabular data. *IEEE Transactions on Systems, Man, & Cybernetics, 21,* 897–900.

Coury, B. G., & Boulette, M. D. (1992). Time stress and the processing of visual displays. *Human Factors, 34,* 707–725.

Dosher, B. A., Sperling, G., & Wurst, S. A. (1986). Tradeoffs between stereopsis and proximity luminance covariance as determinants of perceived 3-D structure. *Vision Research, 26,* 973–990.

Eberts, R. E., & MacMillan, A. G. (1985). Misperception of small cars. In R. E. Eberts & C. G. Eberts (Eds.), *Trends in ergonomics/human factors II* (pp. 33–39). Amsterdam: North Holland.

Ellis, S. R. (Ed.). (1993). *Pictorial communication in virtual and real environments.* (2d ed.). London: Taylor & Francis.

Ellis, S. R., McGreevy, M. W., & Hitchcock, R. J. (1987). Perspective traffic display format and air pilot traffic avoidance. *Human Factors, 29,* 371–382.

Fogel, L. J. (1959). A new concept: The kinalog display system. *Human Factors, 1,* 30–37.

Gallimore, J. J., & Brown, M. E. (1993). Visualization of 3-D computer-aided design objects. *International Journal of Human-Computer Interaction, 5,* 361–382.

Gentner, D., & Stevens, A. L. (1983). *Mental models.* Hillsdale, NJ: Erlbaum.

Gibson, J. J. (1982). Perception and judgment of aerial space and distance as potential factors in pilot selection and training. In E. Reed & R. Jones (Eds.), *Reasons for realism: Selected essays of James J. Gibson.* Hillsdale, NJ: Erlbaum.

Gillan, D. J. (1995). Visual arithmetic, computational graphics, and the spatial metaphor. *Human Factors, 37,* 766–780.

Gillan, D. J., & LaSalle, S. M. (1994). A componential model of human interaction with graphs: III. Spatial orientation. *Proceedings of the Human Factors and Ergonomics Society 38th annual meeting* (pp. 285–289). Santa Monica, CA: Human Factors and Ergonomics Society.

Gillan, D. J., & Lewis, R. (1994). A componential model of human interaction with graphs: I. Linear regression modeling. *Human Factors, 36,* 419–440.

Gillan, D. J., & Neary, M. (1992). A componential model of human interaction with graphs: II. Effects of the distances among graphical elements. *Proceedings of the Human Factors Society 36th annual meeting* (pp. 365–368). Santa Monica, CA: Human Factors Society.

Gillan, D. J., & Richman, E. H. (1994). Minimalism and the syntax of graphs. *Human Factors, 36,* 619–644.

Gillan, D. J., Wickens, C. D., Hollands, J. G., & Carswell, C. M. (1998). Guidelines for presenting quantitative data in HFES Publications. *Human Factors, 40,* 28–41.

Gillie, T., & Berry, D. (1994). Object displays and control of dynamic systems. *Ergonomics, 37,* 1885–1903.

Goettl, B. P., Wickens, C. D., & Kramer, A. F. (1991). Integrated displays and the perception of graphical data. *Ergonomics, 34,* 1047–1063.

Green, C. A., Logie, R. H., Gilhooly, K. J., & Ross, D. G. et al. (1996). Aberdeen polygons: Computer displays of physiological profiles for intensive care. *Ergonomics, 39,* 412–428.

Gregory, R. L. (1977). *Eye and brain.* London: Weidenfeld & Nicolson.

Gregory, R. L. (1980). Perceptions as hypotheses. *Philosophical Transactions of the Royal Society of London, 290,* 181–197.

Grether, W. F. (1949). Instrument reading I: The design of long-scale indicators for speed and accuracy of quantitative readings. *Journal of Applied Psychology, 33,* 363–372.

Hart, S. (1988). Helicopter human factors. In E. Wiener & D. Nagel (Eds.), *Human factors in aviation.* San Diego, CA: Academic Press.

Haskell, I. D., & Wickens, C. D. (1993). Two- and three-dimensional displays for aviation: A theoretical and empirical comparison. *The International Journal of Aviation Psychology, 3,* 87–109.

Hawkins, F., & Orlady, H. W. (1993). *Human factors in flight* (2nd ed.). Brookfield, VT: Gower.

Hickox, J. C., & Wickens, C. D. (1999). Effects of elevation angle, complexity and feature type on relating out-of-cockpit field of view to an electronic cartographic map. *Journal of Experimental Psychology: Applied, 5.*

Hollands, J. G., & Dyre, B. P. (in press). Bias in proportion judgments: The cyclical power model. *Psychological Review.*

Hollands, J. G., Pierce, B. J., & Magee, L. (1998). Displaying information in two and three dimensions. *International Journal of Cognitive Ergonomics, 2,* 307–320.

Hollands, J. G., & Spence, I. (1992). Judgments of change and proportion in graphical perception. *Human Factors, 34,* 313–334.

Hollands, J. G., & Spence, I. (1994). Mental operations in graphical perception. *Proceedings of the 12th Triennial Congress of the International Ergonomics Association* (vol. 6, pp. 235–237). Mississauga, Canada: Human Factors Association of Canada.

Hollands, J. G., & Spence, I. (1998). Judging proportion with graphs: The summation model. *Applied Cognitive Psychology, 12,* 173–190.

Ichikawa, M., & Saida, S. (1996). How is motion disparity integrated with binocular disparity in depth perception? *Perception & Psychophysics, 58,* 271–282.

Ince, F., Williges, R. C., & Roscoe, S. N. (1975). Aircraft simulator motion and the order of merit of flight attitude and steering guidance displays. *Human Factors, 17,* 388–400.

Inoue, T., Kawai, T., & Noro, K. (1996). Performance of 3-D digitizing in stereoscopic images. *Ergonomics, 39,* 1357–1363.

Johnson, S. L., & Roscoe, S. N. (1972). What moves, the airplane or the world? *Human Factors, 14,* 107–129.

Kim, W. S., Ellis, S. R., Tyler, M., Hannaford, B., & Stark, L. (1987). A quantitative evaluation of perspective and stereoscopic displays in three-axis manual tracking tasks. *IEEE Transactions on Systems, Man, and Cybernetics, 17,* 61–71.

Kolata, G. (1982). Computer graphics comes to computers. *Science, 217,* 919–920.

Kosslyn, S. M. (1994). *Elements of Graph Design.* San Francisco: Freeman.

Kraft, C. (1978). A psychophysical approach to air safety. Simulator studies of visual illusions in night approaches. In H. L. Pick, H. W. Leibowitz, J. E. Singer, A. Steinschneider, & H. W. Stevenson (Eds.), *Psychology: From research to practice.* New York: Plenum.

Lalomia, M. J., Coovert, M. D., & Salas, E. (1992). Problem-solving performance as a function of problem type, number progression, and memory load. *Behaviour & Information Technology, 11,* 268–280.

Lawrence, M., & O'Connor, M. (1993). Scale, variability, and the calibration of judgmental prediction intervals. *Organizational Behavior and Human Decision Processes, 56,* 441–458.

Lewandowsky, S. and Behrens, J. T. (1999). Statistical Graphs and Maps. In F. Durso (Ed.), *Handbook of Applied Cognition.* W. Sussix, UK: John Wiley & Sons.

Lintern, G., Roscoe, S. N., & Sivier, J. E. (1990). Display principles, control dynamics, and environmental factors in pilot training and transfer. *Human Factors, 32,* 299–317.

Liu, Y., & Wickens, C. D. (1992). Use of computer graphics and cluster analysis in aiding relational judgment. *Human Factors, 34,* 165–178.

Liu, Y., Zhang, X., & Chaffin, D. (1997). Perception and visualization of human posture information for computer-aided ergonomic analysis. *Ergonomics, 40,* 819–833.

Lohse, G. L. (1993). A cognitive model for understanding graphical perception. *Human-Computer Interaction, 8,* 353–388.

McGreevy, M. W., & Ellis, S. R. (1986). The effect of perspective geometry on judged direction in spatial information instruments. *Human Factors, 28,* 439–456.

Merwin, D. H., Vincow, M. A., & Wickens, C. D. (1994). Visual analysis of scientific data: Comparison of 3-D-topographic, color, and gray scale displays in a feature detection task. *Proceedings of the Human Factors and Ergonomics Society 38th annual meeting* (pp. 240–244). Santa Monica, CA: Human Factors and Ergonomics Society.

Meyer, J., Shinar, D., & Leiser, D. (1997). Multiple factors that determine performance with tables and graphs. *Human Factors, 39,* 268–286.

Meyer, J., Taieb, M., & Flascher, I. (1997). Correlation estimates as perceptual judgments. *Journal of Experimental Psychology: Applied, 3,* 3–20.

Miller, R. W., Rettig, K. M., & Scerbo, M. W. (1994). *The "purple haze" of nonsignificant results.* Poster presented at the annual meeting of the Human Factors and Ergonomics Society, Nashville, TN.

Milroy, R., & Poulton, E. C. (1978). Labeling graphs for increasing reading speed. *Ergonomics, 21,* 55–61.

Moray, N. (1998). Mental models in theory and practice. In D. Gopher and A. Koriat (Eds.), *Attention and Performance, 17.* New York: Cambridge University Press.

Muhlbach, L., Bocker, M., & Prussog, A. (1995). Telepresence in videocommunications: A study of stereoscopy and individual eye contact. *Human Factors, 37,* 290–305.

Park, O., & Gittelman, S. S. (1995). Dynamic characteristics of mental models and dynamic visual displays. *Instructional Science, 23,* 303–320.

Patterson, R., & Martin, W. L. (1992). Human stereopsis. *Human Factors, 34,* 669–692.

Patterson, R. (1997). Visual processing of depth information in stereoscopic displays. *Displays, 17,* 69–74.

Pinker, S. (1990). A theory of graph comprehension. In R. Freedle (Ed.), *Artificial intelligence and the future of testing* (pp. 73–126). Hillsdale, NJ: Erlbaum.

Playfair, W. (1786). *Commercial and political atlas.* London: Corry.

Pong, T., Kenner, M. A., & Otis, J. (1990). Stereo and motion cues in preattentive vision processing-some experiments with random-dot stereographic image sequences. *Perception, 19,* 161–170.

Poulton, E. C. (1985). Geometric illusions in reading graphs. *Perception & Psychophysics, 37,* 543–548.

Ramachandran, V. S. (1988). Perceiving shape from shading. *Scientific American, 259,* 76–83.

Regan, D. (1982). Visual information channeling in normal and disordered vision. *Psychological Review, 89,* 407–444.

Rock, I. (1983). *The logic of perception.* Cambridge, MA: MIT Press.

Roscoe, S. N. (1968). Airborne displays for flight and navigation. *Human Factors, 10,* 321–332.

Roscoe, S. N. (1981). *Aviation psychology.* Iowa City: University of Iowa Press.

Roscoe, S. N. (1992). From the roots to the branches of cockpit design: Problems, principles, products. *Human Factors Society Bulletin, 35*(12), 1–2.

Roscoe, S. N. (1999). Forgotten lessons in aviation human factors. In D. O'Hare (Ed.), *Human performance in general aviation* (pp. 11–21). Aldershot, UK: Ashgate.

Roscoe, S. N., Corl, L., & Jensen, R. S. (1981). Flight display dynamics revisited. *Human Factors, 23,* 341–353.

Roscoe, S. N., & Williges, R. C. (1975). Motion relationships in aircraft attitude guidance displays: A flight experiment. *Human Factors, 17,* 374–387.

Sanders, M. S., & McCormick, E. J. (1993). *Human factors in engineering and design* (7th ed.). New York: McGraw-Hill.

Schiano, D. J., & Tversky, B. (1992). Structure and strategy in encoding simplified graphs. *Memory and Cognition, 20,* 12–20.

Schiffman, H. R. (1996). *Sensation and perception: An integrated approach.* New York: Wiley.

Shah, P., & Carpenter, P. A. (1995). Conceptual limitations in comprehending line graphs. *Journal of Experimental Psychology: General, 124,* 43–61.

Shneiderman, B. (1998). *Designing the user interface: Strategies for effective human-computer interaction* (3rd ed.). Addison-Wesley, Reading, MA.

Siegrist, M. (1996). The use or misuse of three-dimensional graphs to represent lower-dimensional data. *Behaviour & Information Technology, 15,* 96–100.

Simkin, D., & Hastie, R. (1987). An information processing analysis of graph perception. *Journal of the American Statistical Association, 82,* 454–465.

Simmonds, G. R. W., Galer, M., & Baines, A. (1981). *Ergonomics of electronic displays.* Society of Automotive Engineers Technical Paper Series 810826, Warrendale, PA: Society of Automotive Engineers.

Smith, S., & Thomas, D. (1964). Color versus shape coding in information displays. *Journal of Applied Psychology, 48,* 137–146.

Sollenberger, R. L., & Milgram, P. (1993). Effects of stereoscopic and rotational displays in a three-dimensional path-tracing task. *Human Factors, 35,* 483–499.

Spence, I. (1990). Visual psychophysics of simple graphical elements. *Journal of Experimental Psychology: Human Perception & Performance, 16,* 683–692.

Spence, I., & Lewandowsky, S. (1991). Displaying proportions and percentages. *Applied Cognitive Psychology, 5,* 61–77.

Stevens, S. S. (1957). On the psychophysical law. *Psychological Review, 64,* 153–181.

Stevens, S. S. (1975). *Psychophysics.* New York: Wiley.

Sweller, O., Chandler, P., Tierney, P., & Cooper, M. (1990). Cognitive load as a factor in the structuring of technical material. *Journal of Experimental Psychology: General, 119,* 176–192.

Tole, J. R., Stephens, A. T., Harris, R. L., Ephrath, A. R. (1982). Visual scanning behavior and mental workload in aircraft pilots. *Aviation, Space, and Environmental Medicine, 53,* 54–61.

Tufte, E. R. (1983). *The visual display of quantitative information.* Cheshire, CT: Graphics Press.

Tversky, B., & Schiano, D. (1989). Perceptual and cognitive factors in distortion in memory for graphs and maps. *Journal of Experimental Psychology: General, 118,* 387–398.

Vicente, K. J. (1990). Coherence- and correspondence-driven work domains: Implications for systems design. *Behaviour & Information Technology, 9,* 493–502.

Vicente, K. J. (1997). Should an interface always match the operator's mental model? *CSERIAC Gateway, 8,* 1–5.

Vicente, K. J., Moray, N., Lee, J. D., & Rasmussen, J., et al. (1996). Evaluation of a Rankine cycle display for nuclear power plant monitoring and diagnosis. *Human Factors, 38,* 506–521.

Vicente, K. J., and Rasmussen, J. (1992). Ecological interface design: Theoretical foundations. *IEEE Transactions on Systems, Man, and Cybernetics, 22,* 589–606.

Way, T. C. (1988). Stereopsis in cockpit display—A part-task test. *Proceedings of the 32nd annual meeting of the Human Factors Society.* (pp. 58–62). Santa Monica, CA: Human Factors Society.

Wickens, C. D., & Carswell, C. M. (1995). The proximity compatibility principle: Its psychological foundation and relevance to display design. *Human Factors, 37,* 473–494.

Wickens, C. D., Gordon, S. E., & Liu, Y. (1998). *An introduction to human factors engineering.* New York: Addison-Wesley.

Wickens, C. D., LaClair, M., & Sarno, K. (1995). Graph-task dependencies in three-dimensional data: Influence of three-dimensionality and color. *Proceedings of the Human Factors and Ergonomics Society annual meeting* (pp. 1420–1424). Santa Monica, CA: Human Factors and Ergonomics Society.

Wickens, C. D., Liang, C. C., Prevett, T. T., & Olmos, O. (1996). Egocentric and exocentric displays for terminal area navigation. *International Journal of Aviation Psychology, 6,* 241–271.

Wickens, C. D., Merwin, D. H., & Lin, E. L. (1994). Implications of graphics enhancements for the visualization of scientific data: Dimensional integrality, stereopsis, motion, and mesh. *Human Factors, 36,* 44–61.

Wickens, C. D., & Prevett, T. T. (1995). Exploring the dimensions of egocentricity in aircraft navigation displays: Influences on local guidance and global situation awareness. *Journal of Experimental Psychology: Applied, 1,* 110–135.

Wickens, C. D., Todd, S., & Seidler, K. (1989). *Three-dimensional displays: Perception, implementation, and applications* (CSERIAC SOAR–89–01). Dayton, OH: Wright-Patterson AFB, Armstrong Aerospace Medical Research Laboratory.

Wickens, C. D., Vincow, M. A., Schopper, A. A., & Lincoln, J. E. (1997). Computational models of human performance in the design and layout of controls and displays. *CSERIAC State of the Art Report (SOAR).* Dayton, OH: Wright Patterson AFB, Crew Systems Information Analysis Center.

Woods, D. D. (1984). Visual momentum: A concept to improve the cognitive coupling of person and computer. *International Journal of Man-Machine Studies, 21,* 229–244.

Young, M. J., Landy, M. S., & Maloney, L. T. (1993). A perturbation analysis of depth perception from combinations of texture and motion cues. *Vision Research, 33,* 2685–2696.

Zenyuh, J. P., Reising, J. M., Walchli, S., & Biers, D. (1988). A comparison of a stereographic 3-D display versus a 2-D display using an advanced air-to-air format. *Proceedings of the 32nd annual meeting of the Human Factors Society* (pp. 53–57). Santa Monica, CA: Human Factors Society.

Navigation and Interaction in Real and Virtual Environments

OVERVIEW

Space is a critical aspect of the environment in which many systems must operate. The van driver described in Chapter 1 navigated his vehicle through space, rotating , pushing, or pulling controls, viewing various in-vehicle displays such as the speedometer, the fuel gauge, and the dynamic map display, which uses on-screen distance to represent physical distance on the ground. In the last chapter, we described how spatial displays are perceived and interpreted. In this chapter, we focus on how we dynamically interact with spatial displays and environments.

An important feature of spatial perception is the role of *motion*. In many situations, we control our motion through space: We can change our direction; we can change our velocity; we can change our acceleration. What information in the environment do we detect that allows us to do so? We can plan and navigate a route through space as we drive. How do we do this, and what display technology might assist us in the process? When designing *virtual environments,* designers must consider the nature of the dynamic spatial information provided to the observer. What information needs to be provided so the observer can navigate accurately and plan a route through a virtual environment? Similar arguments pertain to information visualization systems: How can the designer ensure that the user quickly locates information in a large database (i.e., navigate to the appropriate location), and also give the user a sense of where that location is, relative to other information (get a global contextual, map-like view)? This chapter examines these ideas in general terms and with reference to the World Wide Web. Finally, we discuss the notion of *visual momentum,* a technique used to aid in the transition between different views on a large environment.

NAVIGATION AND SPATIAL COGNITION

An important use of spatial analog displays is to give the traveler through an environment a sense of location, locomotion, and direction: "Where am I and where am I headed?" Naturally, such information does not need to be spatially displayed or represented. Displays can contain directions sych as "pull up," "turn left," or "come to heading 045." These are often referred to as *command displays* (see Chapter 6). Furthermore, our mental representation of space may reside in more categorical terms like "left of" or "farther than" rather than in strict analog form. Indeed, we will discuss some of the issues relating to the verbalization of spatial relations below. However, because the goal of navigation is to achieve movement through space, and because large movements are typically more significant than small ones, it is apparent that the task must be fundamentally anchored in our analog understanding of space.

We begin by considering how people judge their movement through space and how displays may be designed to facilitate this judgment. We then consider how people navigate through a geographical environment, and how navigational performance can be supported through the design of maps and instructions.

Judgments of Egomotion

As we move through an environment, whether in a plane, in an automobile, in a boat, or on foot, our judgments of the direction and speed with which we are moving depend on information distributed across the visual field, not just in the area of foveal vision (Richman, Stanfield, & Dyre, 1998). Thus, good drivers who primarily fixate far down the center of the highway are still making effective use of the flow of texture beside the highway as viewed in peripheral vision (Leibowitz, 1988; Leibowitz & Post, 1982). Correspondingly, performance on a variety of tracking tasks will be degraded to the extent that the amount of peripheral vision is restricted (Wickens, 1986).

As a consequence of the usefulness of peripheral vision, some engineering psychologists have argued that conventional aircraft navigation instruments, such as the attitude directional indicator shown in Figure 4.12 of the last chapter, are not fully effective because they are restricted to foveal vision. This restriction has led to the proposition that the pilot's perception of flight information can be augmented by peripheral displays. Although peripheral vision is not highly effective for recognizing objects, it is proficient at conveying information about motion and orientation (Leibowitz, 1988). One example is the *Malcomb horizon*, which extends a visible horizon all the way across the pilot's field of view, using laser projection (Stokes, Wickens, & Kite, 1990).

A second problem with the conventional instrument panel is that the information necessary for the pilot to obtain a good sense of location and motion is contained in at least four separate instruments—the attitude direction indicator, altimeter, compass, and airspeed indicator—which must then be mentally integrated (Figure 5.1). In addition, the vertical speed indicator, depicting the rate of change of altitude, is often consulted. One solution to this integration problem is achieved through the development of integrated three-dimensional displays, as described in the last chapter. A second solution lies in the design of **ecological displays**, which capitalize on the visual cues people naturally use to perceive their motion through the environment—the cues of direct perception that support *egomotion* (Gibson, 1979; Larish & Flach, 1990; Warren &

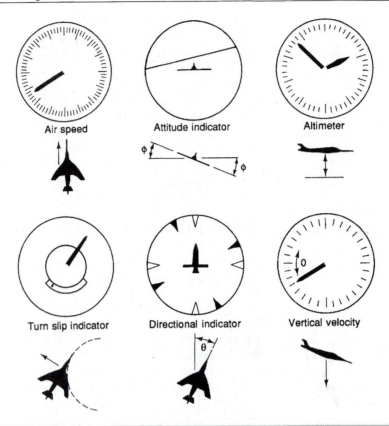

Figure 5.1 A typical aircraft instrument panel.

Source: C. D. Wickens, "The Effects of Control Dynamics on Performance," in K. Boff, L. Kaufman, and J. Thomas (eds.), *Handbook of Perception and Performance,* vol. 2 (New York: Wiley, 1986). Reprinted by permission of John Wiley and Sons, Inc.

Wertheim, 1990; Weinstein, 1990). These cues have sometimes been referred to as *optical invariants* because they represent properties of the light rays that reach the eye (or any display surface) and have an invariant or unchanging relationship to the location and heading of the observer, whether walking, driving, or flying. Gibson (1979) has pointed out a number of such invariants; six of these—compression, splay, optical flow, time-to-contact, global optical flow, and edge rate—are described below.

Compression and Splay   As we saw, textural gradient provides a cue to three-dimensionality. A change in the compression of a textured surface, such as that between the left and the right of Figure 5.2, signals a change in altitude or the angle of slant from which the observer views the surface. Parallel receding lines, providing the depth cue of linear perspective, will signal a change in altitude as given by the angle between the lines—the *splay*. This can be seen by contrasting the two panels of Figure 5.2.

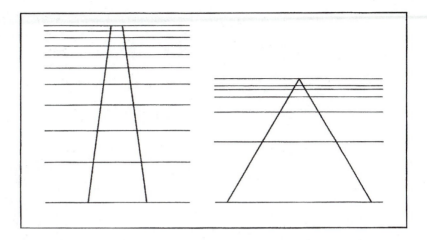

Figure 5.2 Perceptual cues of splay and compression. Splay is defined by the angle of the two receding lines. Compression is defined by the gradient of separation between the horizontal lines frcm the front (bottom) to the back (top) (*left*): the perception is of being high above the field, looking down. Compression (*right*): the observer is at low altitude, looking forward. Note how both splay and compression change with altitude.

Experimental evidence has established the value of both splay and compression in helping the pilot to control altitude (Flach, Hagen, & Larish, 1992; Warren & Riccio, 1985). In particular, splay appears to be the most effective cue for altitude control (Flach et al. 1997). Because these cues present altitude in a more natural, "ecological" fashion, there is some evidence that they are processed more automatically, leaving more attentional resources available for other tasks (Weinstein & Wickens, 1992).

Optical Flow Optical flow refers to the relative velocity of points across the visual field as we move through the world. This velocity is indicated by the arrows in Figure 5.3. Optical flow is an important cue for the perception of heading. Observers can accurately determine heading even if optical flow is the only available cue (Warren & Hannon, 1990).

There are two important sources of information in optical flow to indicate the direction of momentary heading. First, differences in the magnitudes of the motion of objects in the scene let us know what direction we are moving in (Dyre & Andersen, 1997). The second is the *expansion point*, which is that place where there is no flow but from which all flow radiates. For the pilot, the expansion point is critical because if it is below the horizon, its position forecasts an impact with the ground unless corrections are made. Furthermore, the relative rate of flow away from the expansion point, above, below, left, or right, gives a good cue regarding the *slant* of the surface relative to the path of motion. A flow that is of uniform rate on all sides indicates a heading straight into the surface, as a parachutist would see when descending to earth. In Figure 5.3, we see that the aircraft is angling into the surface because the optical flow is greater below than above the expansion point beyond the runway.

Figure 5.3   Optical flow. The arrows indicate the momentary velocity of texture across the visual field that the pilot would perceive on approach to landing.

Since optical flow differs for stationary and moving objects as we move through the world, the human observer can use optical flow information to determine what is stationary and what moves in an environment. This is important because, as we move, stationary objects help in determining our heading, whereas moving objects do not (Berthelon & Mestre, 1993; Cutting, Vishton, & Braren, 1995). This is true whether we are driving a vehicle or on foot. For the van driver in Chapter 1, the different rates of optical flow for the vehicle in front and in the background scene initially let him know that the vehicle was moving. When the vehicle stopped, the rates of optical flow for the vehicle and the background were similar, letting him know that the vehicle had stopped and that he should apply the brakes. Changes in optical flow also let us know whether we are passing in front of or behind a moving object (e.g., imagine a vehicle crossing in front of you as you approach an angled intersection; Cutting, Vishton, & Braren, 1995).

While optical flow provides effective information about heading, some of the depth cues mentioned in Chapter 4 also affect our heading perception. For example, adding binocular disparity information to optical flow information substantially improves judgments of heading (Van den Berg & Brenner, 1994). Motion of the eyes (Royden, Crowell, & Banks, 1994) and of the head (Telford & Howard, 1996) also improves perception of heading.

Time-to-Contact (Tau)   Tau specifies the time remaining until a moving observer makes contact with an object, assuming that the observer's speed and heading remain constant (Grosz et al., 1995; Lee, 1976). It can be thought of as the rate of change of expansion of an object or surface as the observer moves and is clearly specified by information in the visual scene.

Our estimates of time-to-contact are also influenced by other factors besides expansion. Tau is affected by the familiar or relative size of an object—a large far object appears to be nearer than it actually is; the reverse is true for a small near object (DeLucia, 1991). Thus, we underestimate tau for large objects that are far away, and overestimate tau for small objects that are close. Using a simulator, DeLucia and Warren (1994) had observers control their altitude as they approached a floating object, and then jump over the object without colliding with it. They found that observers jumped later for small objects than for large objects, showing the effect of relative size on tau. Tau estimates are also affected by whether the observer or the object is moving. Kruk and Regan (1996) had observers estimate time-to-contact in a helicopter simulator with a helmet-mounted display and showed that egomotion produced an earlier tau estimate than the motion of another object.

Global Optical Flow   The total *rate* of flow of optical texture past the observer (Larish & Flach, 1990) is determined by the observer's velocity and height. Thus, global optical flow will increase as we travel faster and also as we travel closer to the ground.

A potential bias in human perception occurs because our subjective perception of speed is heavily determined by global optical flow. Thus, we feel as if we are traveling faster in a sports car than in a large sedan or bus, in part because the sports car is closer to the ground. This bias caused a problem when the Boeing 747 was first introduced. Pilots taxied the aircraft too fast and, as a result, occasionally damaged the landing gear while turning on or off the runway. The reason for this error, in terms of global optical flow, was simple. The cockpit of the wide-bodied 747 is about twice as high above the runway as cockpits in most other aircraft. For the same true taxiing speed, the global optical flow was half as fast. Pilots therefore perceived themselves to be traveling more slowly than necessary and would unsafely accelerate to obtain a global optical flow to match the taxiing speed established through prior experience. As a result, they achieved a velocity that was unsafe (Owen & Warren, 1987).

Edge Rate   Edge rate can be defined as the number of edges or discontinuities that pass across the observer's visual field per unit time. Edge rate can inform the observer about current speed if the distance between texture elements is known. In most real-world situations, global optical flow and edge rate are correlated. However, edge rate is affected if systematic changes in texture density occur (e.g., if flying and sparse trees change to dense forest), whereas global optical flow is not. Global optical flow and edge rate contribute additively to perception of self-motion (Dyre, 1997; Larish & Flach, 1990).

As edge rate increases (texture is finer), the traveler may perceive a faster velocity. This characteristic of perceptual experience was exploited by Denton (1980) in an ingenious application of perceptual research to highway safety. Denton's concern was with automobile drivers in Great Britain who approached traffic circles at an excessive rate of speed. His solution was to decrease the spacing between road markers gradually and continuously as the distance to the stop point decreased. A driver who might be going too fast (not slowing down appropriately) would see the edge rate as *increasing*. Believing the vehicle to be accelerating, the driver would compensate by braking harder. Denton's solution was imposed on the approach to a particularly dangerous traffic circle in Scotland. Not only was the average approach speed slower following introduction of the markers, but also the rate of fatal accidents was reduced.

Navigation and Understanding of Three-Dimensional Space

When we travel through three-dimensional (3-D) space we generally have one of two goals; to *navigate* through the space, in order to reach a destination without getting lost or colliding with hazards, and to *understand* the structure of the space. Often the two are coupled, as when a traveler first studies a map to understand the space and plan the route, followed by actual travel along the route. In this section, we address the human performance principles that determine the effectiveness of maps or other aids to support navigation and understanding.

Mental Representation of 3-D Space   Following the classic work *The Image of the City* (Lynch, 1960), investigators have used various techniques to understand how well people mentally represent geographical space. For example, people generally tend to distort space in certain ways, imagining it as laid out on more orthogonal (right angle) grid lines than is true. Thus a curved road may be mentally straightened when drawn from memory (Milgram & Jodelet, 1976), and a strange angular intersection may be remembered at right angles (Chase & Chi, 1979). This tendency or bias is referred to as *rectilinear normalization*. Such findings are consistent with observations that people have an easier time making azimuth judgements along or close to the cardinal compass headings of north, south, east, and west than other directions (Maki, Maki, & Marsh, 1977).

People's mental representations of a geographical area are also characterized by what is called a *canonical* or preferred orientation (Franklin & Tversky, 1990). When they have learned about an environment by studying a map, where north is typically represented at the top of the map, the canonical orientation is north-up. On the other hand, when they experience an environment by navigating through it, their canonical orientation is based on other characteristics, such as the direction from which they typically enter a city or campus, or an often-seen view from a building window (Sholl, 1987). Viewing an image of the environment from the same viewpoint as the canonical orientation will improve spatial judgments made about that image.

Finally, mental representation about a geographical area is based on three kinds of knowledge. *Landmark knowledge* is a visual representation of the appearance of prominent landmarks in a region—the house with a funny shape, the tall statue, the skyscraper, or the green park. To the extent that such landmarks are distinct from their surroundings, they provide the traveler with an important aid for navigation (Thorndyke & Hayes-Roth, 1978). The importance of distinctive landmarks is something that should be considered when synthetic environments are designed, as discussed later in the chapter. Landmark knowledge is *egocentric*, or *ego-centered*: gained by direct experience in the environment, and relevant to the individual.

Route knowledge is highly proceduralized verbal knowledge of how to get from one place to another (e.g., turn right at X, three blocks to Y). The importance of landmarks in route knowledge should be evident, since the traveler needs to recognize X in order to turn right at it. Route knowledge is again ego-centered.

Finally, *survey knowledge* is a more abstract and truly spatial knowledge representation that will allow the traveler to draw an accurate map of the environment, containing fewer distortions than one drawn from route knowledge (Thorndyke & Hayes-Roth, 1978; Williams, Hutchinson, & Wickens, 1996). Since survey knowledge represents geographical knowledge generalized across many experiences, it is *exocentric*, or *world-centered*.

As the preceding order suggests, someone who repeatedly visits an area will gradually gain knowledge in the order: landmark, route, survey (Thorndyke & Hayes Roth, 1978). You might recall this order in how you gained knowledge about the layout of your campus, or the city where you live. However, certain "shortcuts" are possible. For example, learning about an environment exclusively through map study will provide very good survey knowledge, but the level of landmark and route knowledge may be relatively primitive (Thorndyke & Hayes-Roth, 1978; Williams, Hutchinson, & Wickens, 1996).

Since users can possess a reasonably accurate mental representation of a familiar environment, they should have little need for additional navigational aids. However, such aids remain of critical importance for two reasons. First, travelers still need navigational aids for those regions with which they are unfamiliar. Second, even in a familiar environment, there may be changing information that is relevant for travel. For example, in a familiar city, a driver could benefit from a dynamic traffic map that depicts particular regions where accidents, construction, or traffic bottlenecks have occurred.

In the following sections, we consider navigational aids within the framework of the two-dimensional matrix of Table 5.1. We begin by comparing verbal and spatial navigational aids, and then discuss the *frame of reference* concept, which describes the extent to which information is presented from the momentary, changing point of view of the traveler (egocentric) or from the more stable point of view of someone outside the environment (exocentric). This is followed by a discussion of task-display dependence and, finally, display augmentations that may compensate for the weaknesses of a particular frame of reference.

Verbal and Spatial Navigational Aids: Route Lists Versus Maps   Words can be used to express ego-referenced navigational terms compatible with route knowledge

TABLE 5.1 Four Representations for Presenting Navigational Guidance Information

Code		*Verbal*	*Spatial*
Frame of Reference	Ego		
	Exo		

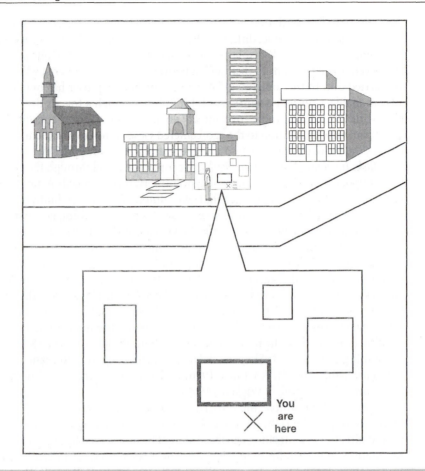

Figure 5.5   A "You-are-here" (YAH) map. Notice that the FFOV corresponds to the orientation of the map. Some YAHs violate this convention, for example, by mounting the map in a different orientation (e.g., a north up positioned to the west of the viewer). Note also that a visually prominent landmark is highlighted.

aspect of the more general concept of situation awareness, discussed in Chapter 7. Here again, we can describe several reasons for this superiority.

First, the egocentric display tends to provide the user with a limited "keyhole view" of the environment (Woods, 1984). Visual scanning cannot provide an overview of what things are where beyond the limited visual angle. Instead, the user must artificially "scan" by rotating the viewpoint in a less natural fashion than using eye movements, piecing together a mental model of the space from a series of successive views (Wickens, Thomas, & Merlo, 1999). This cost can be partially addressed by pulling the viewpoint back from its immersed position to the tethered view of cell B (Wickens & Prevett, 1995). The longer the tether length, the more of the space that can be viewed on a single display, and the greater the ability to integrate spatial information and form a coherent mental map.

Second, fixed, rather than rotating viewpoints (i.e., the right versus the left column of Figure 5.4) provide a consistency of representation, allowing for better spatial learning of where things are (Aretz, 1991; Barfield & Rosenberg, 1995). However, better learning in certain conditions (e.g., learning with a fixed north-up map) does not necessarily lead to better transfer or performance if those conditions are altered (e.g., navigating with a rotating map) (Schmidt & Bjork, 1992; Williams, Hutchinson, & Wickens, 1996).

Third, the three-dimensional properties that characterize the top two rows of Figure 5.4 tend to degrade precise judgments of depth and distance along the line of sight, as discussed in Chapter 4 (Merwin, O'Brien, & Wickens, 1997; Olmos, Wickens, & Chudy, 1999; Wickens, Liang, Prevett, & Olmos, 1996). In addition, a level plane (or objects lying along an inferred plane) is perceived as being rotated toward the observer in an egocentric 3-D display, leading an observer to perceive a level plane as being an uphill surface (the *2-D–3-D effect*, Perrone, 1982). The ambiguity along the line of sight makes egocentric displays problematic for tasks in which such precision is required, like the air traffic controller's task of determining precise 3-D spatial trajectories (May, Campbell, & Wickens, 1996; Merwin, O'Brien, & Wickens, 1997). Thus, such tasks are often performed better with a suite of *co-planar* displays, in which the top-down view captured in the bottom row of Figure 5.4 is coupled with a profile or side view of the same scene, as was shown in Figure 4.19b.

Display Augmentations   The previous discussion has identified strengths and weaknesses with particular viewpoints for particular tasks. Developments of spatial display technology have, fortunately, identified *augmentations* that may compensate for the weakness of a particular frame of reference without necessarily diminishing its strengths (Ellis, 1993; Olmos, Wickens, & Chudy, 1999). For example, including distinct *landmarks* in a real space (i.e., a neighborhood) or a virtual one will help retain user orientation, particularly if the display has an ego-referenced viewpoint. Whitaker and Cuqlock-Knopp (1995) have observed that such landmarks are more useful if they represent artifacts (e.g., buildings or roads) rather than natural objects (e.g. mountains or valleys). In 3-D worlds, orthogonal grids with droplines connecting objects to the grid "walls" can also help the user preserve orientation (Ellis, 1993).

One obvious solution is to provide "dual maps" so that the user can consult an ego-referenced display for navigation, and a more exocentric one for longer range planning or spatial understanding (Ruddle, Payne, & Jones, 1999; Olmos, Wickens, & Chudy, 1999; Vicente et al., 1987; Vincow & Wickens, 1998). In such circumstances, it is important to alert the user to the costs and benefits of using both views, so that a display will not be used for the wrong task. For example, in a hostile-flight scenario, Olmos, Wickens, and Chudy (1999) found that users tended to rely on the egocentric display more than they should, neglecting to monitor the exocentric displays for potential hostile targets to the side and behind (i.e., not seen in the immersed panel). A related technique to the use of dual maps—the fisheye view—is discussed later in the chapter. An overarching technique that addresses the shortcomings of different frames of reference is *visual momentum* (Woods, 1984; Hochberg & Brooks, 1978). We discuss this technique in more detail after we examine virtual environments and information visualization.

VIRTUAL ENVIRONMENTS

A *virtual environment* (VE) can be defined as the multisensory experience of a location or set of locations through artificial, electronic means (Carr, 1995). Key to the concept is that the environment can be interactively experienced and manipulated by the observer (Durlach & Mavor, 1995; Furness & Barfield, 1995).The term *virtual reality* is used to describe similar ideas in the popular press, but VE researchers have noted that "virtual reality" is a contradiction in terms (e.g., Barfield, Zeltzer, Sheridan, & Slater, 1995; Ellis, 1994). Hence, we use "virtual environment" in this section. Virtual environments should realistically depict natural, three-dimensional space, and therefore the ideas discussed in Chapter 4 are relevant. Virtual environments are commonly navigated just as real environments are; therefore, the material in the previous section is also relevant. In this section, we focus on what virtual environments are, the benefits of the technology, and problems for virtual environments.

A discussion of virtual environments requires discussion of the term *presence* (Sheridan, 1996; Slater & Usoh, 1993), defined as the extent to which human participants in a virtual environment allow themselves to be convinced that they are somewhere other than where they physically are. Sometimes the term *immersion* is used to express the same concept. The concept is similar to our experience when we become engrossed in a good movie—momentarily forgetting that we are sitting in a theater and becoming totally engaged in the situation. However, Slater and Usoh note that a person experiencing immersion later reports the sense of having been *in* the virtual environment, but the person watching a movie reports having been in the theater.

A virtual environment is not a single entity; it is a combination of multiple features (Wickens & Baker, 1995). As each feature is added, the experience of a real environment—and therefore the sense of presence—becomes more compelling. We describe six features of a virtual environment below.

1. *Three-dimensional viewing.* Since space is three dimensional, a display representation that preserves that characteristic is more realistic than a two-dimensional representation. Thus, a 3-D model of a house provides a more realistic view than can be obtained through a set of 2-D elevations.

2. *Dynamic.* Perceptually, we experience time as continuous; thus, we perceive a video or movie as more realistic than a set of static images. Hence, a virtual display should allow the user to view (and control) events dynamically in real time.

3. *Closed-loop interaction.* When we act upon objects in the real world, there is typically very little delay from the time the action is initiated until motion occurs. The virtual world should also respond quickly to control inputs (hand, mouse, joystick movements) so that there is little lag.

4. *Ego-centered frame of reference.* As discussed in the previous section, an ego-centered frame of reference presents the image of the world from the FFOV (i.e., cell A in Figure 5.4). For example, rather than viewing a remote representation of ourselves walking on a surface, we view the surface as if we were walking on it (McCormick, Wickens, Banks, & Yeh, 1998; Peterson, Wells, Furness, & Hunt, 1998).

5. *Multimodal interaction.* In real-world interaction, we do not simply view stimuli, but can localize objects by their sound, pick them up, move them, and feel

weight and texture. Therefore, virtual environments may also include auditory feedback using 3-D localized sound techniques, and proprioceptive, kinesthetic, force, and tactile feedback using a dataglove, 3-D mouse, or joystick (e.g., Dede, Salzman, & Loftin, 1996; Werkhoven & Groen, 1998).

6. *Head-mounted display and tracking.* Many VE systems incorporate a head-mounted display (HMD) and motion sensors. These allow changes in head position to control the view on the head-mounted display of the virtual environment in the same way that changes in head position change the visual scene in the real world. The HMD also typically provides a wide field of view, which helps to produce a sense of presence (Barfield, Zeltzer, Sheridan, & Slater, 1995; Snow & Williges, 1997). Some systems also track and update the visual scene based on an observer's eye movements (Kocian & Task, 1995).

To maximize the sense of immersion, all the above features should be used. Although Snow and Williges (1997) suggest that HMD (providing the large field of view) and the presence of multimodal characteristics (especially sound) are particularly important factors for producing presence in virtual environments. However, in many operational systems, it is important to realize that including all features can become expensive and cumbersome. Adding more features increases initial costs, costs of implementation (a more elaborate system is more difficult to construct), and maintenance costs. The additional expense needs to be justified in terms of increased performance on the tasks to be performed in the VE system, and not just the increased sense of presence.

A related technology is called *augmented reality*. Here, virtual objects elements are added to real-world scenes (e.g., Barfield, Rosenberg, & Lotens, 1995; Ellis & Menges, 1997; Ellis et al., 1997; Milgram & Drascic, 1997). Typically, they require the use of a see-through head-mounted display that shows the virtual objects overlaid on the real-world scene. For example, using binocular parallax (see Chapter 4), a symbol could be placed at the point in 3-D space where the operator should move a real-world object, or where a target is expected to be seen. Augmented reality may be useful for controlling remote vehicles, or other teleoperation tasks, such as placing an object in a certain location by controlling a robotic arm.

Benefits of Virtual Environments

Virtual environments appear to have three fundamental benefits. The first is the potential advantage of the ego-centered frame of reference for many guidance tasks, such as remotely controlling a remote vehicle (e.g., McGovern, 1993) or the space shuttle arm (McKinnon & Kruk, 1993). Wickens and Baker (1995) refer to such tasks as *on-line performance.* As we discussed in the previous section, controlling action from a more world-centered, exocentric viewpoint can be difficult, especially if the viewpoint reverses the left-right relationship. Imagine viewing a remote arm such that a control input to the left causes the arm to move to the right (see cell C in Figure 5.4). An ego-centered frame of reference allows the controlled motion to correspond to the natural motion of our limbs.

The second benefit of a virtual environment is its usefulness for *training* because it is often safer or less expensive than training in the real environment. Exploring a virtual environment simulating a large multistory building transfers well to the physical building, for example (e.g., Wilson, Foreman, & Tlauka, 1997; Witmer, Bailey, Knerr,

& Parsons, 1996), which could be useful for navigating in a strange environment (as in military reconnaissance). A virtual environment can be viewed as a tool for rehearsing controlled actions in a benign environment, in preparation for performance in a real environment where the consequences of incorrect actions are more severe (Wickens & Baker, 1995). Some examples include practicing injection for epidural anesthesia (Bostrom et al., 1993), maneuvering a spacecraft (Grunwald & Ellis, 1993), or rehearsing a flight prior to a dangerous mission (Bird, 1993; Williams, Wickens, & Hutchinson, 1994). In addition, training in a virtual environment is often less expensive than training in the real world. For example, training of flight skills in the air includes fuel and manpower costs that are eliminated by training in a virtual environment. (The use of virtual environments for training purposes will be discussed further in Chapter 7.)

The third potential benefit of a virtual environment is in terms of *on-line comprehension* (Wickens & Baker, 1995). The intent here is to assist the user in gaining insight about the structure of an environment. An architect may "walk" through a 3-D virtual building wearing an HMD, gaining insight into the arrangement of rooms. Or the structure of a complex molecule may be understood by an organic chemist or molecular biologist using force feedback in addition to a head-mounted display (Brooks et al., 1990). Typically (although not necessarily), the insight is gained while the interaction is taking place. In sum, it is clear that virtual environments are potentially effective tools for a number of purposes.

Problems for Virtual Environments

Although the increased sense of immersion that occurs with an ego-centered frame of reference and a dynamic, three-dimensional environment can be beneficial, there are associated costs. First, the technology tends to be expensive. One way to deal with the problem of expense is to reduce the number of virtual environment elements, attempting to optimize the remaining elements for the task at hand. For example, the equipment expense may be decreased considerably if the multimodal interaction element is dropped and the number of depth cues is reduced, relying on motion as a primary source of depth information. Sometimes this approach (where the expensive technology of tactile sensors, head trackers, and head-mounted displays is not needed) is called *desktop VR* (Neale, 1996). The smaller view characteristic of most flat panel displays compared to the HMD leads to problems in orientation in navigating a virtual environment (Neale, 1997). With augmented reality, we can specify the depth of a virtual object unambiguously using binocular stereopsis, or more cheaply by having the observer produce head movements while observing (Ellis & Menges, 1997; Ellis et al., 1997).

Second, rendering 3-D graphics in real time is computationally intensive and can lead to serious lag problems, making interactivity impossible. If there is lag, performance can be impaired because observers cannot use feedback from their earlier actions to help execute the current action (making the system open-loop instead of closed-loop; see Chapter 10). In addition, lag reduces presence (Snow & Williges, 1997). Lag can be reduced by reducing the number of virtual environment elements. For example, removing stereopsis and textured surfaces to reduce imagery will reduce the number of graphics computations necessary, reducing lag (Pausch, 1991). An alternative is to use adaptive or progressive imagery where simplified skeleton views are shown when the scene is moving, and texture information is completed when the scene becomes more stationary, as sometimes used for architectural rendering (e.g., Airey et al., 1990).

Some argue that motion be depicted realistically (i.e., without lag), no matter what else suffers (Brooks, 1988). As in real environments, it is important to ensure that optical invariants (e.g., optic flow or splay) are available so that observers have accurate heading, motion, and altitude perception. Regularly spaced, textured, level surfaces are useful, for example, because they improve the perception of optical flow, splay, and tau invariants (Warren & Wertheim, 1990; Wickens & Baker, 1995).

Third, potential biases or distortions occur in virtual environments. One bias, described earlier, is the *2-D–3-D effect,* which makes a level plane appear to be an uphill surface (McGreevy & Ellis, 1986). Another perceptual bias occurring in virtual environments is the *virtual space effect* (McGreevy & Ellis, 1986; Wickens & Baker, 1995), which refers to biases in perceived location of objects resulting from the amount of magnification (or minification) of the view on the virtual environment. High magnification leads to greater estimates of target elevation (McGreevy & Ellis, 1986). That is, targets are perceived as higher than they actually are. Judgments of elevation (up-down) also tend to be poorer than judgments of azimuth (judgments of angle on the horizon) in virtual environments (Barfield, Hendrix, & Bjorneseth, 1995). However, stereo disparity improves estimates of elevation (Barfield & Rosenberg, 1995).

A limited field of view can lead to an underestimation of distances in depth (e.g., Henry & Furness, 1993). However, object-centered, monocular cues (e.g., aerial perspective, occlusion) can be computationally cheap (aerial perspective can be implemented as contrast) and can improve depth perception in virtual spaces (Gallimore & Brown, 1993; O'Shea, Blackburn, & Ono, 1994). Thus these monocular cues can be used to counteract the underestimation of depth problem.

Fourth, if the virtual environment is large, then the user can get lost or disoriented, leading to the need for a world-centered frame of reference of the virtual environment. It is not necessary for the space that is being navigated to be physically "real" to see the effects of disorientation. Some computer games (e.g., Descent, Doom) present a virtual 3-D maze environment through an ego-centered representation (a FFOV), and the user moves through that representation in a manner analogous to physical movement. The designers of these games include a world-centered representation (i.e., a map) of the maze to assist in navigation. The same need for a world-centered representation is evident for general-purpose applications. Reichlen (1993) noted that subjects wearing a tracked, head-mounted display of a map of Boston reported the need to "zoom out" to get a more world-centered view.

Darken and Sibert (1996) compared ego- and world-centered views on a virtual space consisting of a set of several land masses (islands) and open ocean. The ego-centered condition showed the islands and ocean as would be viewed if flying at a low altitude (FFOV only). In the world-centered condition, a map of the entire space took up the lower third of the display and was oriented dynamically to the direction the user was heading. The subject's task was to navigate to several locations in the display and then return to the starting location to end each trial. Darken and Sibert found better performance with the world-centered map displays than when only the immersed view was available, and similar results were reported by Ruddle, Payne, and Jones (1999). Here we see a clear advantage for adding a world-centered frame of reference to the immersed view when navigating virtual space. If a world-centered viewpoint is provided, it is important that the user be able to orient the map appropriately and determine the relationship between the world-centered representation and the FFOV of the virtual space, using the principles of *visual momentum*, described later in this chapter.

Fifth, motion sickness (sometimes referred to as *cybersickness* in VE) is a problem in virtual environments. It is common to have subjects drop out of VE studies due to motion sickness symptoms such as nausea, dizziness, and disorientation (e.g., Ehrlich & Kolasinski, 1998; Ehrlich, Singer, & Allen, 1998), and those subjects who remain often report motion sickness symptoms as well (e.g., Kennedy, Berbaum, Dunlap, & Hettinger, 1996; Stanney & Kennedy, 1998). Cybersickness is reduced if there is a 1:1 relationship between the angle of head motion and the change in display angle; that is, no *gain mismatch* between head movement and display movement (Draper, 1998). Cybersickness also appears to be less likely if the direction of the observer's gaze corresponds to the direction of motion (Ehrlich, Singer, & Allen, 1998).

In sum, virtual environments offer an innovative technological solution to problems for training, on-line performance, and on-line comprehension. The designer must, however, avoid or minimize limitations of the technology (cost, computational demands, perceptual biases, disorientation, cybersickness) to make virtual environments maximally effective.

VISUALIZING INFORMATION

Information and Scientific Visualization

In Chapter 4, we discussed the potential advantages (and disadvantages) of a 3-D representation of a data set. When the designers of powerful computer-driven display processors use three-dimensional graphics, augmented with color, to present complex, sometimes multidimensional data that observers can physically explore and manipulate, it is referred to as *information visualization* (e.g., Shneiderman, 1998). When the observer is a scientist, the technology is often referred to as *scientific visualization* (e.g., Rosenblum et al., 1994; Silver & Wang, 1997; Teylingen, Ribarsky, & van der Mast, 1997). We first consider scientific visualization, and then information visualization more generally.

Scientific Visualization   The biochemist may wish to "take a trip" through the network of a complex molecule; the engineer studying fluid dynamics may wish to examine from different perspectives the three-dimensional patterns of motion and density caused by fluid flowing through a passage; the atmospheric scientist may wish to understand the dynamics of a thunderstorm (see Figure 5.6). Such techniques, although computationally expensive, have proven attractive to scientists and are useful in comprehending their data (e.g., Wilhelmson et al., 1989). A related application is *computer-aided design* (CAD), where the designer is aided by a three-dimensional representation in which objects can be rotated and examined, and design options can be tried and erased. It is clear that many of the virtual environment elements discussed above (e.g., use of three dimensions, motion, and dynamic interaction) apply as well to the design of data visualization and CAD software.

Despite the wide range of scientific visualization techniques available, research investigating the effectiveness of the various techniques in visualization has been scant.

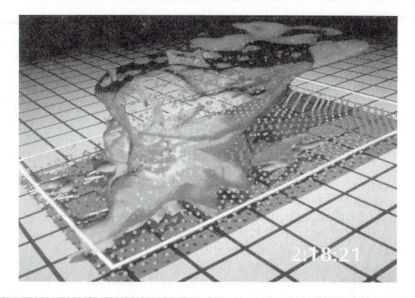

Figure 5.6   Computer-generated visualization of a severe thunderstorm.

Source: Wihelmson et al., "A Study of the Evolution of a Numerically Modeled Severe Storm," *International Journal of Super Computer Applications* 4 (2) (1989), 22–36. Courtesy of National Center for Super Computing Applications.

However, the research on three-dimensional displays of three-dimensional space and navigation in virtual spaces is relevant. As noted above, the integration of information into three dimensions can offer advantages when the judgment task also requires integration. Thus, 3-D visualization techniques would seem to have the greatest benefit for tasks where the entire data set, or a large segment thereof, is being considered. Second, the use of a fully ego-centered frame of reference to show a three-dimensional space can distort our perception of virtual space, as noted above. The appropriate use of stereopsis (e.g., Hollands, Pierce, & Magee, 1998; Wickens, Merwin, & Lin, 1994) or monocular cues (e.g., occlusion) can help reduce these problems, especially for computer-aided design applications (Brown & Gallimore, 1995). The use of a surface or mesh to connect data points in a 3-D space—a technique becoming more common given better surface generation algorithms (von Walsum, Post, Silver, & Post, 1996)—also provides a small accuracy advantage (Liu & Wickens, 1992). In addition, the principle of visual momentum (Woods, 1984) should be followed as the user navigates the information space. These topics are described in the next few sections.

Information Visualization   Given the current predominance of the direct manipulation interface (Shneiderman, 1998), the spatial metaphor is well entrenched in human-computer interaction, and we note several examples where spatial arrays on a display mimic spatial characteristics of real-world scenes and objects. Spatially arranged spreadsheet programs for accounts and record keeping, such as Excel, are one example. Two data points on a spreadsheet may be widely separated or close together. Hierarchical menu structures also have an inherent spatial structure, with menu items being close together in the hierarchy or far apart (Seidler & Wickens, 1992; Wickens & Seidler, 1997). The cursor and the mouse also represent spatial devices that can be used to define areas of interest and operation within a spatial array—an analog to the hand-held pointer (see Chapter 10).

The spatial metaphor has practical impact: For example, greater distances between menu (or spreadsheet) items lead to greater times to navigate a menu (Seidler & Wickens, 1992). Increasing navigational distance in a menu hierarchy also makes it more difficult to perform a second task, an important concern in a number of work environments, such as flying an aircraft (Wickens & Seidler, 1997). The important role of space in database retrieval was also demonstrated in an experiment by Vicente, Hayes, and Williges (1987), in which subjects of varying levels of verbal and spatial ability were required to answer queries about a database. The authors found that spatial ability was the strongest predictor of performance, and in particular, those of low spatial ability were far more likely to get lost in the database.

It is often argued that the spatial organization of a database should be compatible with the user's mental organization (e.g., Durding, Becker, & Gould, 1977; Seidler & Wickens, 1992). Seidler and Wickens used the term *cognitive distance* to refer to how subjectively related two pieces of information are for the user, and the term *organizational distance* as the distance between two items in a menu hierarchy. In effective menu systems, organizational distance should be calibrated with cognitive distance: That is, information that is more subjectively related should be closer together in the hierarchy. Seidler and Wickens showed that if this was the case, menu search times were reduced. Sometimes, however, the user needs to quickly travel between two unrelated menu items. In these cases, search times can be reduced by providing shortcut keys taking the user directly to the top of the hierarchy or to some specified location. One problem with the shortcut key, however, is that users can lose track of their current location, leading to disorientation.

As was the case when we considered visual displays of multidimensional space, there is a need to provide both a specific, ego-centered frame of reference (e.g., one's current location in a screen hierarchy) and a more general, world-centered frame of reference in navigating computer interfaces. Indeed, a repetitive theme in spatial navigation is the need for local, ego-centered and global, world-centered views. In Chapter 3, we also discussed the distinction between global and local processing (Navon, 1977). With large data structures, some indication of current location is typically provided to the user (e.g., the current folder in Windows Explorer, or the DOS or Unix prompt). In contrast, the global view is often absent. Several recent approaches to provide that global view integrated with a local one are discussed next.

Robertson, Card, and Mackinlay (1993) implemented a solution to the problem of "lostness" by graphically representing the data collection as a *data wall* or *cone tree*, shown in Figures 5.7 and 5.8, respectively. One of the problems with conventional 2-D representations of linear time-based data is that the extent of the time domain is usually large relative to the number of projects being tracked, leading to representations that are much wider than they are tall, and so are difficult to contain in a single view (Robertson, Card, & Mackinlay, 1993). Thus, it is difficult to provide detail and allow the user to perceive global context. The data wall displays time-based information on a wall surface (Figure 5.7). Information of interest is shown on the front wall, with two walls shown

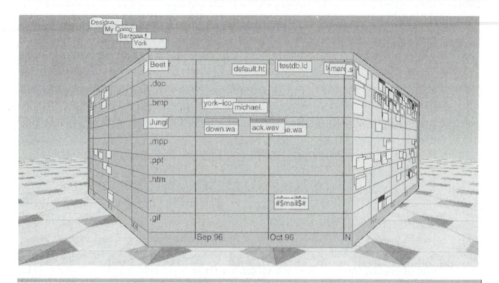

Figure 5.7   The data wall. Time is shown across the screen. The vertical dimension is used here to show files of different types, although it could be used for other purposes.

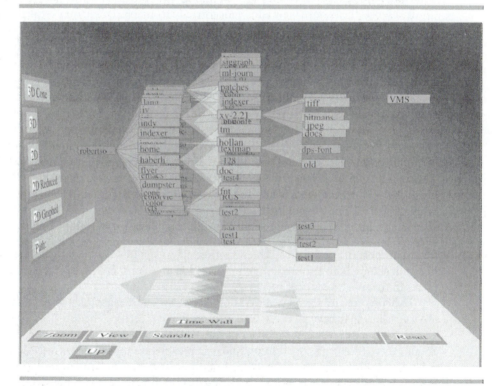

Figure 5.8   The cone tree. The tree depicts a large hierarchical directory structure, with each rectangle representing a directory. The root directory is on the left.

using linear perspective on either side. Mackinlay, Robertson, & Card (1991) report better performance for this 3-D wall representation than for a 2-D representation.

The 3-D perspective wall portrays the time of interest in complete detail, while some global contextual information is provided for other times. The advantage of the data wall representation is that it implicitly provides a *fisheye view* (Furnas, 1986; Sarkar & Brown, 1994). A fisheye view expands and displays in full detail information concerning a specific item of interest, but it provides progressively less information about items as their distance from the item of interest increases. A variant is the *hyperbolic tree browser*, which shows a focal point within a network (a set of directories) at the center of a circle and progressively less detail as one approaches the circumference (Rao et al., 1995). The fisheye view appears to be an effective representation for a variety of tasks, such as estimating best routes in a network (Hollands, Carey, Matthews, & McCann, 1988) or displaying aircraft maintenance data (Mitta & Gunning, 1993). For example, Hollands, Carey, Matthews, and McCann compared performance using a fisheye view of a complex subway network to a scrolling interface where only part of the network could be seen at one time. The subjects' task was to estimate the best route from one subway station to another. Subjects took less time to choose routes with the fisheye view when the destination was not initially visible, probably because there was a greater likelihood that the destination would become visible sooner with the global view provided by the fisheye display.

In a sense, the fisheye view adds egocentricity to an exocentric map-type display. It is as if the exocentric display is redrawn with respect to a particular location in that space, akin to the tethered display shown in Figure 5.4. The typical problem when navigating a large information space is that the user is presented with only the information at the current location (e.g., the contents of a particular directory, a portion of a spreadsheet) and the global context is not displayed. The exocentric display, or combinations of ego- and exocentric such as the fisheye view, appear to be more effective ways to assist in search and navigation tasks in large information spaces (Vincow & Wickens, 1998).

The cone tree shown in Figure 5.8 represents a hierarchical directory structure (as used in DOS or Unix) as a set of boxes connected by lines in three dimensions. The root directory is represented at the left, and subdirectories branching downwards. A user can move from one directory to another by clicking on the directory of choice. The cone tree rotates to move the chosen directory to the front. Hence, the user can move from any given directory to any other one with a single mouse click, reducing search times, but providing a world-centered view to help avoid disorientation. Robertson, Card, and Mackinlay (1993) note that most directory hierarchies are broad and shallow, and a 2-D representation does not allow all the information to be presented on a computer display screen, or it requires the use of size-reduced images that may be unreadable.

The cone tree implemented by Robertson, Card, and Mackinlay (1993) implicitly incorporates the fisheye view because information concerning the directory of interest is displayed in full detail at the front of the 3-D tree, and less information is provided about other directories. In addition, the 3-D perspective makes cognitively distant directories smaller, and nearer directories occlude farther ones. Moreover, the cone tree makes closer directories brighter, and more distant directories are "grayed-out."

Another approach is to allow the user to dynamically control the level of detail that is displayed, using *drill-down* and *roll-up* operations (Roth et al., 1997). Drill-down is the process of segmenting aggregated data to create smaller groups. Roll-up is the opposite process, grouping smaller collections of data into larger aggregates. Roth et al. have implemented these ideas into a working system called Visage, which allows a user to apply dynamic operations to data represented in a table, graph, or map. The user can take data from a table, plot it on a graph, select a subset of the graphically depicted data, and roll it up into an aggregate, showing summary statistics for that aggregate in graphical, tabular, or map form. Here, then, the idea is to allow the user to control the view on the data, allowing global, contextual views and views of specific information.

The World Wide Web

The enormous success of the large public online collection of information known as the World Wide Web is well known. The Web is a large collection of documents (*Web pages*) created by independent authors linked via hypertext and made accessible to anyone with an internet connection (Mayhew, 1998). *Hypertext* is text that when selected (by pointing and clicking with a mouse) allows the user to navigate to a new location. In addition to text information, Web pages include multimedia features such as graphics, animation, and sound. Browsers such as Netscape provide the method for navigating the Web, letting the user select hypertext links and providing a "back" button for returning to pages already seen. Browsers also allow the user to build a library of bookmarks, which the user can select to move to a page directly.

The Web places a great deal of information at our fingertips. However, two concerns are evident, both a result of the huge volume of information on the Web. The first is whether users can find the information they seek. The second is whether users become disoriented when navigating through multiple screens to obtain desired information. We consider each of these problems in turn.

Smith, Newman, and Parks (1997) note that an important usability criterion for the Web is whether the user can obtain task-relevant information in a timely fashion. The typical solution to the problem of search on the Web is to use automated *search engines* that allow a user to type in text information (a *query*) and provide a list of Web pages containing information considered relevant. There are many popular search engines that use various algorithms (sometimes proprietary) to determine best matches to a query. As our discussion of signal detection theory (SDT) in Chapter 2 indicated, a measure such as number of relevant pages (*hits*) is not diagnostic of a search engine's effectiveness, because a search engine can increase its hits by increasing the total number of Web pages returned, which may also increase the number of pages that are not relevant to the user's search (*false alarms*). SDT allows us to distinguish sensitivity to a signal from bias toward saying "yes" or "no." Schlichting and Nilsen (1996) had scientist subjects search for Web pages related to a particular topic of their choice using four common search engines, and then the subjects rated whether each resulting Web page was a hit. Schlichting and Nilsen applied SDT analysis to the results and found low sensitivities (that is, poor ability to distinguish relevant from irrelevant Web pages). Only one search engine—Lycos—had a positive d' value. In addition, the search engines generally had liberal criteria (that is, they were likely to make a lot of false alarms). While search engines certainly reduce the number of potential pages through which a user must sift, there appear to be some limitations to existing search engines in identifying relevant pages.

Given the large number of web pages, and the fact that they are typically accessed one at a time (a local view), disorientation seems inevitable. One solution to the problem of disorientation on the Web is to make important locations distinctive in some way. Whitaker (1998) claims that navigating the Web is analogous to navigating a physical environment and notes two design implications. First, Web pages should contain *landmarks* (e.g., icons or pictures) to make page contents distinctive. Indeed, Merwin et al. (1990) show empirically that icons facilitate recall of database contents relative to text alone. Second, placement of Web page components (menu buttons, icons) should be *consistent* across pages in a set. For example, a "back to main page" button should be placed in the same location across several screens. Just as placing traffic signs or lights in unusual locations will slow their detection, violating expectations, the placement of icons or buttons in unusual locations should also slow performance.

As noted above, popular Web browsers generally show only one Web page at a time (although *frames* allow the user to view a few pages at once). Many researchers note the need to show a broad contextual view on the Web, as was argued above to be appropriate for navigational guidance in real and virtual space (Card, Robertson, & York, 1996; Bederson et al., 1998; Nation, Plaisant, Marchionini, & Komlodi, 1997; Shneiderman, 1997; Smith, Newman, & Parks, 1997; Whitaker, 1998; Wiebe & Howe, 1998). Users comment positively on Web pages that provide overviews of related pages (Shneiderman, 1997). Shneiderman also noted that although Web pages have different importance (e.g., compare Microsoft's home page to a content page in which the most recent fix to the latest release of one of Microsoft's products is described), there is little explicit indication of how important a page is to a site, or how big a site is. Consider, in contrast, how the cover of a book can provide a general overview of its contents, and how its size is perceptually apparent. Shneiderman and Nation et al. both argue that such characteristics need to be made salient to the user browsing the Web.

As in geographic environments and in data visualization, we again see the importance of the global view in navigation of large spaces. It is not surprising, therefore, that multiple techniques have been developed to depict global views of Web pages. For example, Bederson et al. (1998) developed a zooming Web browser called Pad++ that allows the user to select a *focus page*. Once selected, the focus page occupies a larger section of the display. Related pages (pages the user has just visited) are shown at a smaller scale; if one is clicked, it becomes the new focus page, and the other pages are reorganized to reflect the new view. As the distance between the focus page and other pages is increased, the pages become increasingly smaller, providing a fisheye view of the pages. Bederson et al. required users to search a set of about 30 Web pages for information and found faster search times with Pad++ over a conventional browser. The advantage was increased if the entire set of Web pages was "prebuilt" with Pad++ at the beginning of the session, rather than adding pages as the user visited them. This is consistent with Shneiderman's (1998) mantra for information visualization: Provide an overview first, and then details on demand.

An alternative approach to providing an overview is the WebBook browser, developed by Card, Robertson, and York (1996) and depicted in Figure 5.9. The user can construct a book of Web pages, putting related information together in one "place," can ruffle through the pages as through a real book, or choose from various "views" on the book (e.g., a fisheye view). The user examines the book in a 3-D space containing other books (which can be placed on a virtual table or bookshelf, for current and archived work, respectively) or other single pages. Thus, instead of requiring the user to examine each page individually, a global view—subjectively determined by the user—is provided to help in organizing the information and reduce the likelihood of the user getting lost. As noted above in other contexts, adding a world-centered reference frame such as a map or organizational framework to specific, detailed information can help the user avoid disorientation. However, once two views are presented (e.g., ego-referenced and map-view), then an important design issue is how these should be linked. This issue is addressed by the concept of visual momentum, to which we now turn.

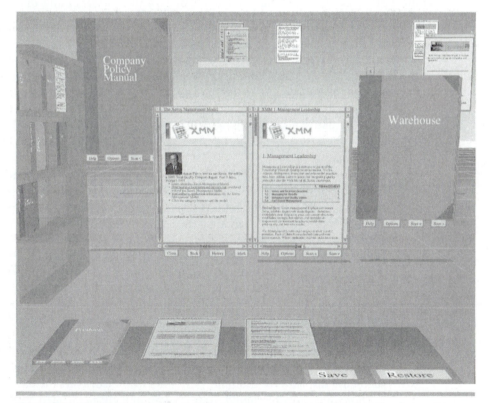

Figure 5.9   The WebBook browser. Web pages can be viewed, placed on the desk surface, or in the bookcase at left. The user has the facility to group Web pages in books, as shown at the center of the display The books can also be stored in the bookcase.

Visual Momentum

As noted in the previous section, people become disoriented as they examine a sequence of Web pages where labels or symbols are used inconsistently from one page to another. We also noted that disorientation is often encountered more generally with large collections of data—in multilevel menu systems, or large databases. One objective of spatially oriented computer systems is to create a familiar spatial world where travel can be accomplished without this disorientation. But as we know, it is possible to get lost in spatial environments as well as in symbolic ones.

The concept of *visual momentum* represents an engineering design solution to the problem of "lostness" when a user traverses multiple displays within a system or database (Wise & Debons, 1987; Woods, 1984; Woods, Roth, Stubler, & Mumaw, 1990). The concept was originally borrowed from film editors as a technique to give the viewer an understanding of how successively viewed film cuts are related (Hochberg & Brooks, 1978). Whether applied to successive views of virtual space (e.g., maps) or conceptual space (e.g., topologically related components in a process control plant, nodes in a menu or database, or graphic representations of data), visual momentum involves four basic guidelines. Some of these integrate good design features discussed in the pages above.

1. *Use consistent representations.* Keep display elements consistent across displays, unless there is an explicit rationale for a change. However, when it is necessary to show new data or a new representation of previously viewed data, display features should highlight the changes and show the relationship of the new data to the old. The next three guidelines indicate how this may be done.

2. *Use graceful transitions.* When changes in representation will be made over time, abrupt discontinuities may be disorienting. For example, on an electronic map, the transition from a small-scale, wide-angle map to a large-scale close-up will be less disorienting if the change is made by a rapid but continuous "zooming in," or at least by the presentation of a few intermediate frames rather than a discrete switch. The Pad++ interface developed by Bederson et al. (1998) used graceful transitions by animating the enlargement of a selected Web page. Similarly, the dynamic rotation of the cone tree with the selection of a node of interest (Robertson, Card, & Mackinlay, 1993) provides a graceful transition. Graceful transitions are also embodied by the drill-down and roll-up techniques developed by Roth et al. (1997).

3. *Highlight anchors.* An anchor may be described as an invariant feature of the displayed "world," whose identity and location is prominently highlighted on successive displays. For example, in aircraft attitude displays the direction of the horizontal horizon should always be prominently highlighted. In dynamic map displays, a salient and consistent color code might highlight both the northerly direction and the heading direction (Andre, Wickens, Moorman, & Boschelli, 1991). Aretz (1991) successfully used an anchor by portraying the

angle subtended by the forward field of view on a top-down, north-up map. Olmos, Liang, and Wickens (1997) and Olmos, Wickens, and Chudy (1999) found similar results. In displays used to examine the components of a complex chemical or electrical process, the direction of causal flow (input-output) should be prominently highlighted. Anchors can be incorporated into the design of you-are-here maps by highlighting a prominent landmark on the map, as shown in Figure 5.5 (Levine, 1982). A corollary principle is to overlap anchors or landmarks in successive display frames. As each new frame is introduced, it should include areas or features that overlap with the previous frame, and these common landmarks should be prominently highlighted (here again, color is an effective highlight).

4. *Display continuous world maps.* Here we refer to a continuously viewable map of the world, always presented from a fixed perspective, as we have discussed several times in the previous pages. Within this map, the current location of the active local display is highlighted. This is a feature of the topographic maps produced by the U.S. Geological Survey, in which a small map of the state is always viewable in the upper left-hand corner, with the currently displayed quadrant highlighted in black.

Recent studies conducted by Olmos, Wickens, and Chudy (1999), and Neale (1996, 1997) show the general effectiveness of visual momentum techniques. In Neale's studies, subjects navigated a virtual building, making distance judgments. Neale augmented the virtual environment with two features that incorporated the visual momentum concept: a continuous world view and salient anchors (landmarks). People performed better with the visual momentum features than they did when those features were absent. Moreover, the advantage of visual momentum was greater when the difficulty of the distance judgment was increased. In sum, visual momentum appears to be a useful engineering concept in system design.

Conclusions

The technology of information representation and display is growing nearly as rapidly as the volume of information itself. Such growth has forced human factors specialists in this area to design visualization tools, some examples of which were discussed above, to aid the human user in navigation and understanding. Unfortunately, these tools are often not systematically evaluated so that their benefits or costs can be identified and linked to fundamental principles of human information processing. Nevertheless the links between the well-crafted tools and the human performance principles is often apparent: between visual momentum and attention switching, between fisheye views and global-local processing, or between consistency of layout and ease of learning. These links provide some confidence that many data visualization tools will be effective and compatible with information processing capabilities. However, it is important that the effectiveness of such tools be determined through careful empirical evaluation.

TRANSITION

This chapter began by describing sources of information that we use to perceive motion in the physical world. We then discussed issues related to spatial cognition—that is, how we mentally represent information about the physical environment, and how that information should be represented on a display. Then we turned to the design of virtual environments and discussed their advantages and disadvantages. Finally, we talked about information visualization—using three-dimensional graphics to present complex multidimensional data that observers can physically explore and manipulate. Many of the same issues in navigating real or virtual environments also were relevant here—especially the need for a global, contextual view on a large data set, and the need to provide visual momentum between successive views.

We will address topics related to spatial cognition again when we examine long-term memory in Chapter 7. We will also discuss spatial working memory in Chapter 7, as well as the use of virtual environments for training purposes. Issues relating to our control of motion and analog perception will be discussed in Chapter 10, and the compatibility between a display and working memory, and display and response in Chapters 6 and 9, respectively. In Chapter 6, we will discuss the role of verbal and linguistic information in communication.

REFERENCES

Airey, J. M., et al. (1990). Towards image realism with interactive update rates in complex virtual building environments. *Computer Graphics, 24,* 41–50.

Andre, A. D., Wickens, C. D., Moorman, L., & Boschelli, M. M. (1991). Display formatting techniques for improving situation awareness in the aircraft cockpit. *International Journal of Aviation Psychology, 1,* 205–218.

Aretz, A. J. (1991). The design of electronic map displays. *Human Factors, 33,* 85–101.

Barfield, W., Hendrix, C., & Bjorneseth, O. (1995). Spatial performance with perspective displays as a function of computer graphics eyepoint elevation and geometric field of view. *Applied Ergonomics, 26,* 307–314.

Barfield, W., & Rosenberg, C. (1995). Judgments of azimuth and elevation as a function of monoscopic and binocular depth cues using a perspective display. *Human Factors, 37,* 173–181.

Barfield, W., Rosenberg, C., & Lotens, W. A. (1995). Augmented-reality displays. In W. Barfield & T. A. Furness III (Eds.), *Virtual environments and advanced interface design* (pp. 542–575). New York: Oxford University Press.

Barfield, W., Zeltzer, D., Sheridan, T., & Slater, M. (1995). Presence and performance within virtual environments. In W. Barfield & T. A. Furness III (Eds.), *Virtual environments and advanced interface design* (pp. 474–513). New York: Oxford University Press.

Bederson, B. B., Hollan, J. D., Stewart, J., Rogers, D., Vick, D., Ring, L., Grose, E., Forsythe, C. (1998). A zooming web browser. In C. Forsythe, E. Grose, & J. Ratner (Eds.), *Human factors and web development* (pp. 255–266). Mahwah, NJ: Erlbaum.

Berthelon, C., & Mestre, D. (1993). Curvilinear approach to an intersection and visual detection of a collision. *Human Factors, 35,* 521–534.

Bird, J. (1993). Sophisticated computer gets new role: System once used only in fighters helping in Bosnia, *Air Force Times,* October 25, p. 8.

Bostrom, M., et al. (1993). Design of an interactive lumbar puncture simulator with tactile feedback. *Proceedings of IEEE Virtual Reality Annual International Symposium (VRAIS)* (pp. 280--286), September 18–21, Seattle, WA.

Brooks, F. P. (1988). Grasping reality through illusion: Interactive graphics serving science. *Proceedings of CHI '88: Human Factors in Computing Systems* (pp. 1–11). New York: Association for Computing Machinery.

Brooks, F. P., et al. (1990). Project GROPE—haptic display for scientific visualization. *Computer Graphics, 24,* 177–185.

Brown, M. E., & Gallimore, J. J. (1995). Visualization of three-dimensional structure during computer-aided design. *International Journal of Human-Computer Interaction, 7,* 37–56.

Card, S. K., Robertson, G. G., & York, W. (1996). The WebBook and WebForager: An information workspace for the World Wide Web. *Proceedings of CHI '96: Human Factors in Computing Systems* (pp. 111–117). New York: Association for Computing Machinery.

Carr, K. (1995). Introduction. In K. Carr & R. England (Eds.), *Simulated and virtual realities: Elements of perception* (pp. 1–9). London: Taylor & Francis.

Chase, W., & Chi, M. (1979). *Cognitive skill: Implications for spatial skill in large-scale environments* (Technical Report No. 1). Pittsburgh: University of Pittsburgh Learning and Development Center.

Cutting, J. E., Vishton, P. M., & Braren, P. A. (1995). How we avoid collisions with stationary and moving obstacles. *Psychological Review, 102,* 627–651.

Darken, R. P., & Sibert, J. L. (1996). Navigating large virtual spaces. *International Journal of Human-Computer Interaction, 8,* 49–71.

Dede, C., Salzman, M., & Loftin, B. (1996). MaxwellWorld: Learning complex scientific concepts via immersion in virtual reality. *Proceedings of the 2nd International Conference on Learning Sciences* (pp. 22–29).

DeLucia, P. R. (1991). Pictorial and motion-based information for depth perception. *Journal of Experimental Psychology: Human Perception & Performance, 17,* 738–748.

DeLucia, P. R., & Warren, R. (1994). Pictorial and motion-based depth information during active control of self-motion: Size-arrival effects on collision avoidance. *Journal of Experimental Psychology: Human Perception & Performance, 20,* 783–798.

Denton, G. G. (1980). The influence of visual pattern on perceived speed. *Perception, 9,* 393–402.

Dingus, T. A., Hulse, M. C., Mollenhauer, M. A., Fleischman, R. N., McGehee, D. V., & Manakkal, N. (1997). Effects of age, system experience, and navigation technique on driving with an advanced traveler information system. *Human Factors, 39,* 177–199.

Draper, M. H. (1998). The effects of image scale factor on vestibulo-ocular reflex adaptation and simulator sickness in head-coupled virtual environments. *Proceedings of the Human Factors and Ergonomics Society 42nd annual meeting* (pp. 1481–1485). Santa Monica, CA: Human Factors and Ergonomics Society.

Durding, B. M., Becker, C. A., & Gould, J. D. (1977). Data organization. *Human Factors, 19,* 1–14.

Durlach, N. I., & Mavor, A. (1995). *Virtual reality: Scientific and technical challenges.* Washington, DC: National Academy of Sciences.

Dyre, B. P. (1997). Perception of accelerating self-motion: Global optical flow rate dominates discontinuity rate. *Proceedings of the Human Factors and Ergonomics Society*

41st annual meeting (pp. 1333–1337). Santa Monica, CA: Human Factors and Ergonomics Society.

Dyre, B. P., & Anderson, G. J. (1997). Image velocity magnitudes and perception of heading. *Journal of Experimental Psychology: Human Perception & Performance, 23,* 546–565.

Ehrlich, J. A., & Kolasinski, E. M. (1998). A comparison of sickness symptoms between dropout and finishing participants in virtual environment studies. *Proceedings of the Human Factors and Ergonomics Society 42d annual meeting* (pp. 1466–1470). Santa Monica, CA: Human Factors and Ergonomics Society.

Ehrlich, J. A., Singer, M. J., & Allen, R. C. (1998). Relationships between head-shoulder divergences and sickness in a virtual environment. *Proceedings of the Human Factors and Ergonomics Society 42d annual meeting* (pp. 1471–1475). Santa Monica, CA: Human Factors and Ergonomics Society.

Ellis, S. R. (Ed.). (1993). *Pictorial communication in virtual and real environments* (2d ed.). London: Taylor & Francis.

Ellis, S. R. (1994). What are virtual environments? *IEEE Computer Graphics & Applications, 14*(1), 17–22.

Ellis, S. R., & Menges, B. M. (1997). Judged distance to virtual objects in the near visual field. *Presence, 6*(4), 452–460.

Ellis, S R., Menges, B. M., Jacoby, R. H, Adelstein, B. D., & McCandless, J. W. (1997). Influence of head motion on the judged distance of monocularly presented virtual objects. *Proceedings of the Human Factors and Ergonomics Society 41st annual meeting* (pp. 1234–1238). Santa Monica, CA: Human Factors and Ergonomics Society.

Flach, J. M., Hagen, B. A., & Larish, J. F. (1992). Active regulation of altitude as a function of optical texture. *Perception & Psychophysics, 51,* 557–568.

Flach, J. M., Warren, R., Garness, S. A., Kelly, L., & Stanard, T. (1997). Perception and control of altitude: Splay and depression angles. *Journal of Experimental Psychology: Human Perception & Performance, 23,* 1–19.

Franklin, N., & Tversky, B. (1990). Searching imagined environments. *Journal of Experimental Psychology: General, 119,* 63–76.

Furnas, G. W. (1986). Generalized fisheye views. *Proceedings of CHI '86: Human Factors in Computing Systems* (pp. 16–23). New York: Association for Computing Machinery.

Furness, T. A., III, & Barfield, W. (1995). Introduction to virtual environments and advanced interface design. In W. Barfield & T. A. Furness III, *Virtual environments and advanced interface design* (pp. 3–13). New York: Oxford University Press.

Gallimore, J. J., & Brown, M. E. (1993). Visualization of 3-D computer-aided design objects. *International Journal of Human-Computer Interaction, 5,* 361–382.

Gibson, J. J. (1979). *The ecological approach to visual perception.* Boston: Houghton Mifflin.

Grosz, J., Rysdyk, R. T., Bootsma, R. J., Mulder, J. A., van der Vaart, J. C., & van Wieringen, P. C. W. (1995). Perceptual support for timing of the flare in the landing of an aircraft. In P. Hancock, J. Flach, J. Caird, & K. Vicente, *Local applications of the ecological approach to human-machine systems* (pp. 104–121). Hillsdale, NJ: Erlbaum.

Grunwald, A. J., & Ellis, S. R. (1993). Visual display aid for orbital maneuvering: Design considerations. *Journal of Guidance, Control, and Dynamics, 16,* 139–150.

Henry, D. & Furness, T. (1993). Spatial perception in virtual environments. *Proceedings of IEEE Virtual Reality Annual International Symposium (VRAIS)* (pp. 33–40), September 18–21, Seattle, WA.

Hickox, J., & Wickens, C. D. (1999). Effects of elevation angle disparity, complexity and feature type on relating out-of-cockpit field of view to an electronic cartographic map. *Journal of Experimental Psychology: Applied, 5.*

Hochberg, J., & Brooks, V. (1978). Film cutting and visual momentum. In J. W. Senders, D. F. Fisher, & R. A. Monty (Eds.), *Eye movements and the higher psychological functions.* Hillsdale, NJ: Erlbaum.

Hofer, E. F., & Wickens, C. D. (1997). Part-mission simulation evaluation of issues associated with electronic approach chart displays. *Proceedings of the 9th International Symposium on Aviation Psychology.* Columbus, OH: Dept. of Aerospace Engineering, Applied Mechanics, and Aviation, Ohio State University.

Hollands, J. G., Carey, T. T., Matthews, M. L., & McCann, C. A. (1989). Presenting a graphical network: A comparison of performance using fisheye and scrolling views. In G. Salvendy & H. Smith (Eds.), *Designing and using human-computer interfaces and knowledge-based systems* (pp. 313–320). Amsterdam: Elsevier.

Hollands, J. G., Pierce, B. J., & Magee, L. (1998). Displaying information in two and three dimensions. *International Journal of Cognitive Ergonomics, 2,* 307–320.

Kennedy, R. S., Berbaum, K. S., Dunlap, W. P., & Hettinger, L. J. (1996). Developing automated methods to quantify the visual stimulus for cybersickness. *Proceedings of the Human Factors and Ergonomics Society 40th annual meeting* (pp. 1126–1130). Santa Monica, CA: Human Factors and Ergonomics Society.

Kocian, D. F., & Task, H. L. (1995). Visually coupled systems hardware and the human interface. In W. Barfield & T. A. Furness III (Eds.), *Virtual environments and advanced interface design* (pp. 175–257). New York: Oxford University Press.

Kruk, R., & Regan, D. (1996). Collision avoidance: A helicopter simulator study. *Aviation, Space, and Environmental Medicine, 67,* 111–114.

Larish, J. F., & Flach, J. M. (1990). Sources of optical information useful for perception of speed of rectilinear self-motion. *Journal of Experimental Psychology: Human Perception & Performance, 16,* 295–302.

Lee, D. N. (1976). A theory of visual control of braking based on information about time-to-collision. *Perception, 5,* 437–459.

Leibowitz, H. (1988). The human senses in flight. In E. Wiener & D. Nagel (Eds.), *Human factors in aviation.* San Diego, CA: Academic Press.

Leibowitz, H., & Post, R. (1982). The two modes of processing concept and some implications. In J. Beck (Ed.), *Organization and representation in perception.* Hillsdale, NJ: Erlbaum.

Levine, M. (1982). You-are-here maps: Psychological considerations. *Environment and Behavior, 14,* 221–237.

Liu, Y., & Wickens, C. D. (1992). Use of computer graphics and cluster analysis in aiding relational judgments. *Human Factors, 34,* 165–178.

Lynch, K. (1960). *The image of the city.* Cambridge, MA: MIT Press.

Mackinlay, J. D., Robertson, G. G., & Card, S, K. (1991). The perspective wall: Detail and context smoothly integrated. In *Proceedings of CHI '91: Human Factors in Computing Systems* (pp. 173–179). New York: Association for Computing Machinery.

Maki, R. H., Maki, W. S., & Marsh, L. G. (1977). Processing locational and orientational information. *Memory & Cognition, 5,* 602–612.

May, P. A., Campbell, M., & Wickens, C. D. (1996). Perspective displays for air traffic control: Display of terrain and weather. *Air Traffic Control Quarterly, 3*(1), 1–17.

Mayhew, D. J. (1998). Introduction. In C. Forsythe, E. Grose, & J. Ratner (Eds.), *Human factors and web development* (pp. 1–13). Mahwah, NJ: Erlbaum.

McCormick, E., Wickens, C.D., Banks, R., & Yeh, M. (1998). Frame of reference effects on scientific visualization subtasks. *Human Factors, 40,* 443–451.

McGreevy, M. W., & Ellis, S. R. (1986). The effect of perspective geometry on judged direction in spatial information instruments. *Human Factors, 28,* 439–456.

McGovern, D. E. (1993). Experience and results in teleoperation of land vehicles. In S. R. Ellis (Ed.), *Pictorial communication in virtual and real environments* (pp. 182–195). London: Taylor & Francis.

McKinnon, G. M., & Kruk, R. V. (1993). Multi-axis control in telemanipulation and vehicle guidance. In S. R. Ellis (Ed.), *Pictorial communication in virtual and real environments* (pp. 247–264). London: Taylor & Francis.

Merwin, D. H., Dyre, B. P., Humphrey, D. G., Grimes, J., & Larish, J. F. (1990). The impact of icons and visual effects on learning computer databases. *Proceedings of the Human Factors Society 34th annual meeting* (pp. 424–428). Santa Monica, CA: Human Factors Society.

Merwin, D., O'Brien J. V., & Wickens, C. D. (1997). Perspective and coplanar representation of air traffic: Implications for conflict and weather avoidance. *Proceedings of the 9th International Symposium on Aviation Psychology.* Columbus, OH: Dept. of Aerospace Engineering, Applied Mechanics, and Aviation, Ohio State University.

Milgram, P., & Drascic, D. (1997). Perceptual effects in aligning virtual and real objects in augmented reality displays. *Proceedings of the Human Factors and Ergonomics Society 41st annual meeting* (pp. 1239–1243). Santa Monica, CA: Human Factors and Ergonomics Society.

Milgram, S., & Jodelet, D. (1976). Psychological maps of Paris. In H. M. Proshansky, W. H. Itelson, & L. G. Revlin (Eds.), *Environmental psychology.* New York: Holt Rinehart & Winston.

Mitta, D., & Gunning, D. (1993). Simplifying graphics-based data: Applying the fisheye lens viewing strategy. *Behaviour & Information Technology, 12,* 1–16.

Mykityshyn, M. G., Kuchar, J. K., & Hansman, R. J. (1994). Experimental study of electronically based instrument approach plates. *International Journal of Aviation Psychology, 4,* 141–166.

Nation, D. A., Plaisant, C., Marchionini, G., & Komlodi, A. (1997). Visualizing web sites using a hierarchical table of contents browser: WebTOC. *Proceedings of the 3rd Conference on Human Factors and the Web,* Denver, CO. Available: http://www.uswest.com/web-conference/.

Navon, (1977). Forest before the trees: The precedence of global features in visual processing. *Cognitive Psychology, 9,* 353–383.

Neale, D. C. (1996). Spatial perception in desktop virtual environments. *Proceedings of the Human Factors and Ergonomics Society 40th annual meeting* (pp. 1117–1121). Santa Monica, CA: Human Factors and Ergonomics Society.

Neale, D. C. (1997). Factors influencing spatial awareness and orientation in desktop virtual environments. *Proceedings of the Human Factors and Ergonomics Society 41st annual meeting* (pp. 1278–1282). Santa Monica, CA: Human Factors and Ergonomics Society.

Olmos, O., Liang, C. C., & Wickens, C. D. (1997). Electronic map evaluation in simulated visual meteorological conditions. *International Journal of Aviation Psychology, 7*, 37–66.

Olmos, O., Wickens, C.D., & Chudy, A. (1999, in press). Tactical displays for combat awareness. *International Journal of Aviation Psychology.*

O'Shea, R. P., Blackburn, S. G., & Ono, H. (1994). Contrast as a depth cue. *Vision Research, 34*, 1595–1604.

Owen, D. H., & Warren, R. (1987). Perception and control of self-motion: Implications for visual simulation of vehicular locomotion. In L. S. Mark, J. S. Warm, & R. L. Huston (Eds.), *Ergonomics and human factors: Recent research* (pp. 40–70). New York: Springer-Verlag.

Pausch, R. (1991). Virtual reality on five dollars a day. *Proceedings of CHI '91: Human Factors in Computing Systems* (pp. 265–269). New York: Association for Computing Machinery.

Perrone, J. A. (1982). Visual slant underestimation: A general model. *Perception, 11*, 641–654.

Peterson, B., Wells, M., Furness, T. A., III, & Hunt, E. (1998). The effects of the interface on navigation in virtual environments. *Proceedings of the Human Factors and Ergonomics Society 42d annual meeting* (pp. 1496–1500). Santa Monica, CA: Human Factors and Ergonomics Society.

Rao, R., Pedersen, J., Hearst, M., Mackinlay, J., Card, S., Masinter, L., Halvorsen, P.-K., & Robertson, G. G. (1995). Rich interaction in the digital library. *Communications of the ACM, 38*(4), 29–39.

Reichlen, B. A. (1993). Sparcchair: A one hundred million pixel display. *Proceedings of the IEEE Virtual Reality Annual International Symposium (VRAIS)* (pp. 300–307), September 18–21, Seattle, WA.

Richman, J. B., Stanfield, J., & Dyre, B. P. (1998). Small fields of view interfere with perception of heading during active control but not passive viewing. *Proceedings of the Human Factors and Ergonomics Society 42d annual meeting* (pp. 1545–1549). Santa Monica, CA: Human Factors and Ergonomics Society.

Robertson, G. G., Card, S. K., & Mackinlay, J. D. (1993). Information visualization using 3-D interactive animation. *Communications of the ACM, 36*, 57–71.

Rosenblum, L., et al. (Eds.) (1994). *Scientific visualization: Advances and challenges.* London: Academic Press.

Roth, S. F., Chuah, M. C., Kerpedjiev, S., Kolojejchick, J., & Lucas, P. (1997). Toward an information visualization workspace: Combining multiple means of expression. *Human-Computer Interaction, 12*, 131–186.

Royden, C. S., Crowell, J. A., & Banks, M. S. (1994). Estimating heading during eye movements. *Vision Research, 34,* 3197–3214.

Ruddle, R., Payne, S. J., & Jones, D. M. (1999). The effects of maps on navigation and search strategies in very large-scale virtual environments. *Journal of Experimental Psychology: Applied, 5,* 54–75.

Sarkar, M., & Brown, M. H. (1994). Graphical fisheye views. *Communications of the ACM, 37*(12), 73–84.

Schlichting, C., and Nilsen, E. (1996). Signal detection analysis of WWW search engines. *Proceedings of the Human Factors and the Web/HTML Conference,* Seattle, WA. Available: http://www.microsoft.com/usability/webconf.htm.

Schmidt, R. A., & Bjork, R. P. (1992). New conceptualizations of practice: Common principles in three paradigms suggest new concepts for training. *Psychological Science, 3,* 207–217.

Schreiber, B., Wickens, C. D., Renner, G., Alton, J., & Hickox, J. (1998). Navigational checking using 3-D maps. *Human Factors, 40,* 209–223.

Seidler, K. S., & Wickens, C. D. (1992). Distance and organization in multifunction displays. *Human Factors, 34,* 555–569.

Shepard, R. N., & Hurwitz, S. (1984). Upward direction, mental rotation and discrimination of left and right turns in maps. *Cognition, 18,* 161–193.

Sheridan, T. B. (1996). Further musings on the psychophysics of presence. *Presence, 5*(2), 241–246.

Shneiderman, B. (1997). Designing information-abundant web sites: Issues and recommendations. *International Journal of Human-Computer Studies, 47,* 5–29. Available: http://ijhcs.open.ac.uk/index.html.

Shneiderman, B. (1998). *Designing the user interface: Strategies for effective human-computer interaction* (3d ed.). Addison-Wesley, Reading, MA.

Sholl, M. J. (1987). Cognitive maps as orienting schemata. *Journal of Experimental Psychology: Learning, Memory and Cognition, 13,* 615–628.

Silver, D., & Wang, X. (1997). Tracking and visualizing turbulent 3-D features. *IEEE Transactions on Visualization and Computer Graphics, 3,* 129–141.

Slater, M. & Usoh, M. (1993) Presence in immersive virtual environments, *IEEE Virtual Reality Int. Symp.,* pp. 90–96.

Smith, P. A., Newman, I. A., and Parks, L. M. (1997). Virtual hierarchies and virtual networks: Some lessons from hypermedia usability research applied to the World Wide Web. *International Journal of Human-Computer Studies, 47,* 67–95. Available: http://ijhcs.open.ac.uk/index.html.

Snow, M. P., & Williges, R. C. (1997). Empirical modeling of perceived presence in virtual environments using sequential exploratory techniques. *Proceedings of the Human Factors and Ergonomics Society 41st annual meeting* (pp. 1224–1228). Santa Monica, CA: Human Factors and Ergonomics Society.

Srinivasan, R., & Jovanis, P. P. (1997). Effect of selected in-vehicle route guidance systems on driver reaction times. *Human Factors, 39,* 200–215.

Stanney, K. M., & Kennedy, R. S. (1998). Aftereffects from virtual environment exposure: How long do they last? *Proceedings of the Human Factors and Ergonomics So-*

ciety 42d annual meeting (pp. 1476–1480). Santa Monica, CA: Human Factors and Ergonomics Society.

Stokes, A. F., Wickens, C. D., & Kite, K. (1990). *Display technology: Human factors concepts.* Warrendale, PA: Society of Automotive Engineers.

Telford, L., & Howard, I. P. (1996). Role of optical flow field asymmetry in the perception of heading during linear motion. *Perception & Psychophysics, 58,* 283–288.

Teylingen, R. V., Ribarsky, W., & van der Mast, C. (1997). Virtual data visualizer. *IEEE Transactions on Visualization and Computer Graphics, 3,* 65–74.

Thorndyke, P. W., & Hayes-Roth, B. (1978, November). *Spatial knowledge acquisition from maps and navigation.* Paper presented at the meetings of the Psychonomic Society, San Antonio, TX.

Van den Berg, A. V., & Brenner, E. (1994). Why two eyes are better than one for judgements of heading. *Nature, 371,* 700–702.

Vicente, K. J., Hayes, B. C., & Williges, R. C. (1987). Assaying and isolating individual differences in searching a hierarchical file system. *Human Factors, 29,* 349–359.

Vincow, M. A., & Wickens, C. D. (1998). Frame of reference and navigation through document visualizations: Flying through information space. *Proceedings of the Human Factors and Ergonomics Society 42d annual meeting* (pp. 511–515). Santa Monica, CA: Human Factors and Ergonomics Society.

Von Walsum, T., Post, F. H., Silver, D., & Post, F. J. (1996). Feature extraction and iconic visualization. *IEEE Transactions on Visualization and Computer Graphics, 2,* 111–119.

Warren, D. H., Rossano, M. J., & Wear, T. D. (1990). Perception of map-environment correspondence: The roles of feature. and alignment. *Ecological Psychology, 2,* 131–150.

Warren, R., & Riccio, G. (1985). *Visual cue dominance hierarchies: Implications for simulator design.* Paper presented at the 1985 SAE Aerospace Technology Conference and Exposition. Long Beach, CA.

Warren, R. & Wertheim, A. H. (1990). (Eds.). *Perception and control of self-motion.* Hillsdale, NJ: Erlbaum.

Warren, W. H., & Hannon, D. J. (1990). Eye movements and optical flow. *Journal of the Optical Society of America A, 7,* 160–169.

Weinstein, L. F. (1990). The reduction of central-visual overload in the cockpit. *Proceedings of the 12th Symposium on Psychology in the Department of Defense.* Colorado Springs, CO: U.S.A.F. Academy.

Weinstein, L. F., & Wickens, C. D. (1992). Use of nontraditional flight displays for the reduction of central visual overload in the cockpit. *International Journal of Aviation Psychology, 2,* 121–142.

Werkhoven, P. J., & Groen, J. (1998). Manipulation performance in interactive virtual environments. *Human Factors, 40,* 432–442.

Whitaker (1998). Human navigation. In C. Forsythe, E. Grose, & J. Ratner (Eds.), *Human factors and web development* (pp. 63–71). Mahwah, NJ: Erlbaum.

Whitaker, L. A., & Cuqlock-Knopp, V. G. (1995). Human exploration and perception in off-road navigation. In P. A. Hancock, J. M. Flach, J. Card, & K. J. Vicente

(Eds.), *Local applications in the ecology of human-machine systems*. Hillsdale, NJ: Erlbaum.

Wickens, C. D. (1986). The effects of control dynamics on performance. In K.R. Boff, L. Kaufman, & J.P. Thomas (Eds.), *Handbook of Human Perception and Performance* (Vol. 2, pp. 39–1–39–60). New York: Wiley & Sons.

Wickens, C. D. (1999). Frames of reference for navigation. In D. Gopher and A. Koriat (Eds.), *Attention and performance* (Vol. 16, pp. 113–144) Orlando, FL: Academic Press.

Wickens, C. D., & Baker, P. (1995). Cognitive issues in virtual reality. In W. Barfield & T. Furness, III (Eds.), *Virtual Environments and Advanced Interface Design* (pp. 514–541). New York: Oxford University Press.

Wickens, C. D., Liang, C. C., Prevett, T. T., & Olmos, O. (1996). Egocentric and exocentric displays for terminal area navigation. *International Journal of Aviation Psychology, 6,* 241–271.

Wickens, C. D., Merwin, D. H., & Lin, E. L. (1994). Implications of graphics enhancements for the visualization of scientific data: Dimensional integrality, stereopsis, motion, and mesh. *Human Factors, 36,* 44–61.

Wickens, C. D., & Prevett, T. T. (1995). Exploring the dimensions of egocentricity in aircraft navigation displays: Influences on local guidance and global situation awareness. *Journal of Experimental Psychology: Applied, 1,* 110–135.

Wickens, C. D., & Seidler, K. S. (1997). Information access in a dual-task context: Testing a model of optimal strategy selection. *Journal of Experimental Psychology: Applied, 3,* 196–215.

Wickens, C. D., Thomas, L., & Merlo, S. (1999). Immersion and battlefield visualization: Effects of frame of reference on navigation tasks and cognitive tunneling. In *Proceeedings, 1999 Annual Meeting of the Human Factors and Ergonomics Society.* Santa Monica, CA: Human Factors Society.

Wickens, C. D., & Todd, S. (1990). Three-dimensional display technology for aerospace and visualization. *Proceedings of the 34th annual meeting of the Human Factors Society.* Santa Monica, CA: Human Factors Society.

Wiebe, E. N., & Howe, J. E. (1998). Graphics design on the Web. In C. Forsythe, E. Grose, & J. Ratner (Eds.), *Human factors and web development* (pp. 225–239). Mahwah, NJ: Erlbaum.

Wilhelmson, R. B., Jewett, B., Shaw, C., Wicker, L., Arrott, M., Bushell, C., Bajuk, M., & Yost, J. (1989). A study of the evolution of a numerically modeled severe storm. *International Journal of Super Computer Applications, 4*(2), 22–36.

Williams, H., Hutchinson, S., & Wickens, C.D. (1996). A comparison of methods for promoting geographic knowledge in simulated aircraft navigation. *Human Factors, 38*(1), 50–64.

Williams, H. P., Wickens, C. D., & Hutchinson, S. (1994). Realism and interactivity in navigational training: A comparison of three methods. *Proceedings of the Human Factors and Ergonomics Society 38th annual meeting* (pp. 1163–1167). Santa Monica, CA: Human Factors and Ergonomics Society.

Wilson, P. N., Foreman, N., & Tlauka, M. (1997). Transfer of spatial information from a virtual to a real environment. *Human Factors, 39,* 526–531.

Wise, J. A., & Debons, A. (1987). Principles of film editing and display system design. *Proceedings of the 31st annual meeting of the Human Factors Society* (pp. 121–124). Santa Monica, CA: Human Factors Society.

Witmer, B. G., Bailey, J. H., Knerr, B. W., & Parsons, K. C. (1996). Virtual spaces and real world places: Transfer of route knowledge. *International Journal of Human-Computer Studies, 45,* 413–428.

Woods, D. D. (1984). Visual momentum: A concept to improve the cognitive coupling of person and computer. *International Journal of Man-Machine Studies, 21,* 229–244.

Woods, D. D., Roth, E. M., Stubler, W. F., & Mumaw, R. J. (1990). Navigating through large display networks in dynamic control applications. *Proceedings of the 34th annual meeting of the Human Factors Society* (pp. 396–399). Santa Monica, CA: Human Factors Society.

Yeh, M., & Wickens, C. D. (1997). Attentional filtering and decluttering techniques in battlefield map interpretation. *Proceedings Advanced Displays and Interactive Displays Federated Laboratory Symposium.* Adelphi, MD. Army Research Lab. pp 2–354/2–47.

Language and Communications

OVERVIEW

The smooth and efficient operation of human-machine systems often depends on the efficient processing of written and spoken language, whether in reading instructions, comprehending labels, or exchanging information with a fellow crew member. Not all communication is language-based—important information can be exchanged through gestures and nonverbal means—and not all instructions need to be verbal—symbols and icons are sometimes helpful. The fundamental tie linking the material in this chapter is the role of language and *symbol* representation. The symbol, whether a letter, word, or icon, stands for something other than itself.

It is easy for all of us to recall instances in which our ability to understand instructions and messages has failed. Sometimes terms or abbreviations are used whose meanings are unclear; in longer instructions, the meaning of each word may be clear, but the way in which they are strung together makes little sense, or imposes a tremendous mental workload to understand.

In this chapter, we first consider the perception of printed language— letters, words, and sentences. We examine how these units are processed hierarchically and automatically, and we consider the role of context and redundancy in their perception. After considering applications to print format and code design, we discuss similar principles in the recognition of pictures and iconic symbols. Next, we address cognitive factors involved in comprehending instructions, procedures, and warnings, and we consider guidelines that should be followed. After a discussion of the perception of speech, we conclude with speech communications in multi-person systems.

THE PERCEPTION OF PRINT

Stages in Word Perception

The perception of printed material is hierarchical in nature. When we read and understand the meaning of a sentence (a categorical response), we must first analyze its words. Each word depends on the perception of letters, and each letter is itself a collection of elementary features (lines, angles, and curves). These hierarchical relations are shown in Figure 6.1, which is based on Neisser (1967). There is good evidence that each level of analysis of the hierarchy (feature, letter, and word) is defined by a set of nodes. The brain carries out a unique, relatively automatic categorical response, characterized by the many-to-one mapping typical of perception. Thus, in describing the perception of words, we may refer to feature units, letter units, or word units. A given unit at any level will become active if the corresponding stimulus is physically available to foveal vision and the perceiver has had repeated experience with the stimulus in question (i.e., its representation is stored in long-term memory).

We consider, first, the evidence provided for the unit at each level of the hierarchy and the role of learning and experience in integrating higher-level units from experience with the repeated combination of lower-level units. Then we consider the manner in which our expectancies guide perceptual processing from the "top down." After we describe the theoretical principles of visual pattern recognition, we address their practical implications for system design.

The Features as a Unit: Visual Search   The features that make up letters are represented as vertical or diagonal lines, angles, and curved segments of different orientations.

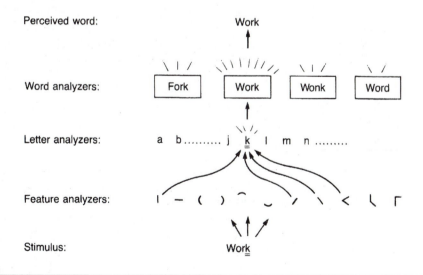

Figure 6.1   Hierarchical process of perception of the visual word *work*.

Examples of these are shown at the bottom of Figure 6.1. Gibson (1969) has demonstrated that the 26 letters of the alphabet can be economically created by the presence or absence of a limited subset of these features. The importance of features in letter recognition is most clearly demonstrated by the visual search task developed by Neisser, Novick, and Lazer (1964) and discussed in Chapter 3. The researchers demonstrated how the search for a target letter (e.g., K) in a list of nontarget "noise" letters was greatly slowed if the latter shared similar features (N, M, X), but it was not slowed if the features were distinct (O, S, U) from those of the target K.

The Letter as a Unit: Automatic Processing   There is strong evidence that a letter is more than simply a bundle of features. That is, the whole letter is greater than the sum of its parts. An experiment by LaBerge (1973) revealed that subjects could process letters like *b* or *d* preattentively, or *automatically*, as their attention was directed elsewhere. In contrast, symbols like K or l, made up of features that were no more complex but not familiarly grouped in past experience, required focal attention in order to be processed. The concept of automaticity—processing that does not require attentional resources—is a key one in understanding human skilled performance. We will encounter it again in our treatment of training in Chapter 7 and again when we discuss attention in Chapter 11. Here we focus on the development of automaticity in language processing.

What produces the automaticity that we use to process letters and other familiar symbols? Familiarity and extensive perceptual experience is necessary; but research summarized by Schneider and Shiffrin (1977) and Schneider, Dumais, and Shiffrin (1984) suggests that experience is not sufficient. In addition, the symbols must be *consistently* mapped to the same response. Inconsistent responding, when a letter (or other symbol) is sometimes relevant and sometimes not, is less likely to develop automaticity.

To illustrate this role of consistent mapping in letter processing, Shiffrin, Schneider, Fisk, and their colleagues have done a series of studies in which subjects search an array of letters, in a version of Neisser's visual search task discussed in Chapter 3 (see Figure 3.4). Some letters are always consistently responded to and categorized as targets (i.e., by pressing a key if they appear), for sometimes thousands of trials. Other letters are sometimes targets but at other times "distractors" to be ignored. After such training, the consistently mapped target letters reach a special status of automaticity, in which they are perceived without attention and even appear to jump out of the printed page in a way that does not occur with the inconsistently mapped letters. As we saw in Chapter 2, this automatic processing can produce signals that are much more resistant to the vigilance decrement (Schneider & Fisk, 1984).

Subsequent research has expanded the list of categorization processes for which automaticity can be developed through consistency. This research suggests that a higher-level automaticity can be developed that is not bound to repeated exposures to the same physical stimuli. For example, Schneider and Fisk (1984) showed how consistently responding to members of a category (like vehicles) can show the features of automatic processing (fast and preattentive) when each category member is presented, even if that member itself has not been seen frequently. Another example of higher-level automaticity is produced when people consistently respond to *rules*, such as "the higher of two digits is the target." With consistent practice, automatic processing of a given digit will occur if it satisfies the rule, even if that digit has not been seen before in the context of the experiment (Fisk, Ackerman, & Schneider, 1987; Kramer, Strayer, & Buckley, 1990).

The Word as a Unit: Word Shape   Usually words are perceived through the analyses of their letters, just as letters are perceived through the analysis of their features. Yet there is also evidence that familiar words can be directly perceived as units, just as LaBerge's (1973) experiment provided evidence that letters were perceived as units because of the familiar co-occurrence of their features. Thus, the pattern of full-line ascending letters (*h, b*), descenders (*p, g*), and half-line letters (*e, r*) in a familiar word such as *the* forms a global shape that can be recognized and categorized as *the,* even if the individual letters are obliterated to such an extent that each is illegible. Broadbent and Broadbent (1977, 1980) propose that the mechanism of spatial frequency analysis is responsible for this crude analysis of word shape.

The analysis based on word shape is more holistic in nature than the detailed feature analysis described above. The role of word shape, particularly with such frequent words as *and* and *the* for which unitization is likely to have occurred, is revealed in the analysis of proofreading errors (Haber & Schindler, 1981; Healy, 1976). Haber and Schindler had subjects read passages for comprehension and proofreading at the same time. They observed that misspellings of short, function words of higher frequency (*the* and *and*) were difficult to detect. The role of word shape contributing to these shortcomings was suggested because errors in these words were concealed most often if the letter change that created the error was one that substituted a letter of the same class (ascender, descender, or half-line) and thereby preserved the same word shape. An example would be *anl* instead of *and.* If all words were only analyzed letter by letter, these confusions should be as hard to detect in long words as in short ones. As Haber and Schindler observe, they are not. Corcoran and Weening (1967) noted that for words that were longer and less frequent (the two variables are, of course, highly correlated), acoustic or phonetic factors (i.e., word sound) play a more prominent role than visual ones in proofreading errors. In this case, misspellings are concealed if the critical letters are not pronounced in the articulation of the word.

Top-Down Processing: Context and Redundancy

In the system shown in Figure 6.1, lower-level units (features and letters) feed into higher-level ones (letters and words). As we saw, sometimes lower-level units may be bypassed if higher-level units are unitized, and automaticity can result. This process then is sometimes described as bottom-up or data-driven processing. There is strong evidence, however, that much of our perception proceeds in a top-down, context-driven manner (Lindsay & Norman, 1972). More specifically, in the case of reading, hypotheses are formed concerning what a particular word should be, given the context of what has appeared before, and this context enables our perceptual mechanism to "guess" the nature of a particular letter within that word, even before its bottom-up feature-to-letter analysis may have been completed. Thus the ambiguous word in the sentence "Move the lever to the rxxxx" can be easily and unambiguously perceived, not because of its shape or its features but because the surrounding context limits the alternatives to only a few (e.g., *right* or *left*) and the apparent features of the first letter eliminate all but the first alternative).

In a corresponding fashion, top-down processing can work on letter recognition. Knowledge of surrounding letters may guide the interpretation of ambiguous features, as in the two words TAE CAT. The middle letters of the two words are physically identical.

The features are ambiguously presented as parallel vertical lines or as converging lines. Yet the hypotheses generated by the context of the surrounding letters quite naturally force the two stimuli into two different perceptual categories. Top-down processing of this sort, normally of great assistance in reading, can actually prove to be a source of considerable frustration in proofreading, in which allowing context to fill in the gaps is exactly what *is not* required. All words must be analyzed to their full-letter level to perform the task properly.

The foundations of top-down processing and its basis on knowledge-based expectancy were established in the discussion of signal detection theory, redundancy, and information in Chapter 2. Top-down processing, in fact, is only possible (or effective) because of the contextual constraints in language that allow certain features, letters, or words to be predicted by surrounding features, letters, words, or sentences. When the redundancy of a language or a code is reduced, the contribution to pattern recognition of top-down, relative to bottom-up, processing is reduced as well. This trade-off of top-down, context-driven processing governed by redundancy and knowledge against bottom-up, data-driven processing governed by sensory quality is nicely illustrated in an investigation by Tulving, Mandler, and Baumal (1964). They presented subjects with sentences of the form "I'll complete my studies at the ____" and displayed the final word for very brief durations, producing a degraded sensory stimulus. The experimenters could adjust both the duration (and therefore the quality) of the stimulus and the amount of prior word context between eight (high), four (medium), and zero (none) letters. The results, shown in Figure 6.2, illustrate the almost perfect trade-off in recognition accuracy between stimulus quality and redundancy. As one of these variables increases, the other may be degraded to maintain a constant level of recognition performance.

In addition to redundancy, there is a second form of top-down or learning-based processing, in which the letters within a word mutually facilitate one another's analysis, so that a letter that appears in a word can sometimes be processed more rapidly than the letter by itself. This *word superiority effect* (Reicher, 1969) has important implications for models of how people read (Rumelhart & McClelland, 1986), and its implications for engineering psychology are straightforward. The letters in a word are processed more accurately under time constraints than a similar number of unrelated letters. Indeed this mutual facilitation of processing units (i.e., letters) within a familiar sequence (words) is certainly one feature that supports automaticity.

The pattern of analysis of word perception described up to this point may be best summarized by observing that top-down and bottom-up processing are continuously ongoing at all levels in a highly interactive fashion (Navon, 1977; Neisser, 1967; Rumelhart, 1977). Sensory data suggest alternatives, which in turn provide a context that helps interpret more sensory data. This interaction is represented schematically in Figure 6.3. The conventional bottom-up processing sequence of features to letters to words is shown by the upward flowing arrows in the middle of the hierarchy. The dashed lines on the left indicate that automatic unitization at the level of the letter and the common word may occur as a consequence of the repeated processing of these units. Thus, unitization may identify a blurred word by word shape alone, even when features, letters, and context aren't available (Broadbent & Broadbent, 1980). Unitization does not necessarily replace or bypass the sequential bottom-up chain but operates in parallel. Represented on the right of Figure 6.3 are the two forms of top-down processing: those that reduce alternatives through context and redundancy (solid lines) and those that actually facilitate the rate of lower-level analysis (dotted lines).

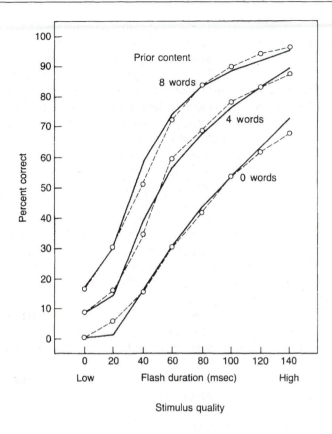

Figure 6.2 Trade-off between bottom-up and top-down processing.

Source: E. Tulving, G. Mandler, and R. Baumal, "Interaction of Two Sources of Information on Tachistoscopic Word Recognition," *Canadian Journal of Psychology, 18* (1964), p. 66. Copyright 1964 by the Canadian Psychological Association. Reproduced by permission.

Although all these factors may be operating simultaneously, two primary dimensions underlie the relative importance of one or the other. The first contrasts sensory quality against context and redundancy, as these trade off in bottom-up versus top-down processing. The second contrasts the relative contribution of higher-level unitization to hierarchical analysis in bottom-up processing. This contribution is determined by the familiarity and consistent mapping of the lower-level units. These two dimensions are important as a framework for later discussion of the applications of pattern recognition.

Reading: From Words to Sentences

The previous analysis focused on the recognition of words. Yet in most applied contexts, other than reading a simple label, word recognition occurs in the context of reading a string of words in a sentence. We have already suggested that sentences must be

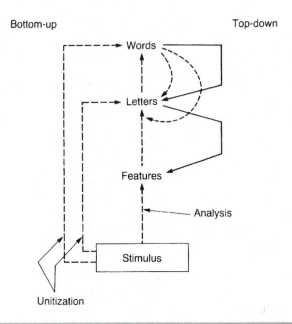

Figure 6.3   Bottom-up processing (analysis and utilization) versus top-down processing.

processed to provide the higher-level context that supports top-down processing for word recognition. In normal reading, sentences are processed by visually scanning across the printed page. Scanning occurs by a series of fixations, joined by the discrete *saccadic* eye movements discussed in Chapter 3. The fixation has a minimum duration of around 200 milliseconds. During each fixation, there is some degree of parallel processing of the letters within the fixated word. Whereas the meaning of an isolated word can normally be determined during fixations as short as the minimum fixation value of 200 milliseconds, fixations made during continuous reading are sometimes considerably longer (Just & Carpenter, 1980; McConkie, 1983). The extra time is required to integrate the meaning of the word into the ongoing sentence context, to process more difficult words, and to extract some information from the words to the right of the fixated words, necessary to define the target destination of the next saccade. Both the absolute duration of fixations and the frequency of fixations along a line of text vary greatly with the difficulty of the text (McConkie, 1983).

Although a given word is fixated, information understood from the preceding words provides context for top-down processing. A series of investigations conducted by McConkie and his colleagues (see McConkie, 1983) addressed how much information is actually processed from different locations along a line of print during fixations when a given letter is in the center of foveal vision. McConkie's research suggests that different kinds of information may be processed at different regions. As far out as 10 to 14 characters to the right of the fixated letter, very global details pertaining to word boundaries may be perceived for the purpose of directing the saccade to the next fixation. Some processing of word shape may occur somewhat closer to the fixated letter. Individual letters, however, are only processed within a fixation span of roughly 10 letters: 4 to the left and 6 to the right. This span itself is not fixed but varies in width according to the size of the word currently fixated and the position of the fixated letter within the word.

In summarizing the results of his research, McConkie (1983) offers a conclusion that is quite consistent with the word superiority effect described previously. It is that the perception of letters within a word are heavily word-driven. When a word lies at the center of fixation, its letters are processed cooperatively and guide the semantic interpretation of the sentence. Letters not in the fixated word may indeed be processed, but the result does not seem to play an active role in comprehension.

Just as important as the visual processes involved in reading are the cognitive processes involved in understanding text. These can be described in terms of the reader integrating, across sentences, the meaning of sets of *propositions* (Kintch & Van Dijk, 1978). For example, the sentence "turn the top switch to on" consists of two propositions: switch → on and switch → top. Because of limitations in working memory, to be described in the next chapter, readers can typically carry only about four propositions from a previous sentence over to the next sentence in order that the former can easily help to interpret the newly encountered information (Kintch & Van Dijk, 1978). This characteristic has important implications for the readability of instructions, as we discuss in the section on comprehension.

APPLICATIONS OF UNITIZATION AND TOP-DOWN PROCESSING

The research on recognition of print is, of course, applicable to system design in contexts in which warning signs are posted or maintenance and instruction manuals are read. These contexts are discussed later in the chapter. It also applies to the acquisition of verbal information from computer terminals and video displays. These displays are designed to present information in such a manner that it can be read rapidly, accurately, and without high cognitive load. In addition, certain critical items of information (one's own identification code, for example, or critical diagnostic or warning information) should be recognized automatically, with a minimal requirement to invest conscious processing. This section examines two broad classes of practical implications of the research that generally align themselves with the two dimensions of pattern recognition described: applications that capitalize on unitization and applications that are related to the trade-off between top-down and bottom-up processing.

Unitization

Training and repetition lead to automatic processing. Some of this training is the consequence of a lifetime's experience (e.g., recognition of letters), but as LaBerge (1973) and Schneider and Shiffrin (1977) clearly demonstrate, the special status of automatic processing of critical key targets can also be developed within a relatively short period of practice. These findings suggest that when a task environment is analyzed, it is important to identify critical signals (and these need not necessarily be verbal) that should always receive immediate priority if they are present. For medical personnel, these might be a pattern of patient symptoms that require immediate response, or for the air traffic controller, they might be the trajectories of two aircraft that define a collision course. As discussed further in the next chapter, part-task training regimes should then develop the automatic processing of those signals. In such training, operators should be presented with a mixture of the critical signals and others and should always make the same consistent responses to the critical signals. A good discussion of applications of automatic processing to training is presented by Schneider (1985) and Rogers, Rousseau, and Fisk (1999).

In this regard, there appears to be a distinct advantage in calling attention to critical information by developing automatic processing rather than by simply increasing the physical intensity of the stimulus. First, as we will describe in the discussion of alarms in Chapter 13, loud or bright stimuli may be distracting and annoying and may not necessarily ensure a response. Second, physically intense stimuli are intense to all who encounter them. Stimuli that are subjectively intense by virtue of automatic processing may be "personalized" to alert only those for whom the alert is relevant.

At any level of perceptual processing, it should be apparent that the accuracy and speed of recognition will be greatest if the displayed stimuli are presented in a physical format that is most compatible with the visual representation of the unit in memory. For example, the prototypal memory units of letters and digits preserve the angular and curved features as well as the horizontal and vertical ones. As a consequence, "natural" letters that are not distorted into an orthographic grid should be recognized more easily than dot matrix letters or letters formed with only horizontal and vertical strokes. These suggestions were confirmed in recognition studies comparing digits constructed in right-angle grids with digits containing angular and curved strokes (e.g., Ellis & Hill, 1978; Plath, 1970). Ellis and Hill, for example, found that five-digit sequences were read more accurately when presented as conventional numerals than in a seven-segment right-angled format. This advantage was enhanced at short exposure durations, as might be typical of time-critical environments.

A similar logic applies to the use of lowercase print in text. Since lowercase letters contain more variety in letter shape, there is more variety in word shape, and so there is a greater opportunity to use this information as a cue for holistic word-shape analysis. Tinker (1955) found that subjects could read text in mixed case BETTER THAN IN ALL CAPITALS. However, the superiority of lowercase over uppercase letters appears to hold only for printed sentences. For the recognition of isolated words, the words appear to be better processed in capitals than in lowercase (Vartabedian, 1972). These findings would seemingly dictate the use of capital letters in display labeling (Grether & Baker, 1972), where only one or two words are required, but lowercase in longer segments of verbal material.

As a result of unitization, words are perceived faster and understood better than are abbreviations or acronyms. This suggests that words should be used instead of abbreviations, except when space is at an absolute premium (Norman, 1981). This guideline is also based on the tremendous variety, across people, in their conception of how a given word should be abbreviated (Landaur, 1995). The cost of a few extra letters is surely compensated for by the benefits of better understanding and fewer blunders. Where abbreviations are used, Norman (1981) suggests that at a minimum relatively uniform abbreviating principles should be employed (i.e., all abbreviations of common length) and that the abbreviated term should be as logical and meaningful to the user as possible. Moses & Ehrenreich (1981) summarized an extended evaluation of abbreviation techniques and conclude that the most important principle is to employ *consistent* rules of abbreviation. In particular, they find that truncated abbreviations, in which the first letters of the word are presented, are understood better than contracted abbreviations, in which letters within the word are deleted. For example, *reinforcement* would be better abbreviated by *reinf* than by *rnfnt*. This finding makes sense in terms of our discussion of reading, since truncation preserves at least part of any unitized letter sequence. Ehrenreich (1982) concludes that whatever rule is used to generate abbreviations, rule-generated abbreviations are always superior to subject-generated ones, in which the operator decides the best abbreviations for a given term. Similar findings of rule-based consistency should apply to the standardization of personal addresses for computer usage; for example, consistently use the first initial and up to seven truncated (not contracted) letters of the last name. The use of middle initials makes little sense, since senders are not likely to know these, and use of hyphen (–) or underscore (_) adds no information but only invites confusion and uncertainty.

A related recommendation derives from the unitizing influence of gaps between words (Wickelgren, 1979). This benefit appears to carry over to the processing of unrelated material such as alphanumeric strings by defining high-order visual "chunks" (see Chapter 7). Klemmer (1969) argues that there is an optimum size of such chunks for encoding unrelated material. In Klemmer's experiment, strings of digits were to be entered as rapidly as possible into a keyboard. In this task, the most rapid entry was achieved when the chunks between spaces were three or four digits long. Speed declined with either smaller or larger groups. These findings have important implications for deciding on formats for various kinds of displayed material—license plates, identification codes, or data to be entered on a keyboard.

Context-Data Trade-offs

The distinction between bottom-up and top-down processing is important for the design of text displays and code systems. An example of the trade-off of design considerations between bottom-up and top-down processing can be seen when a printed message is to be presented in a display in which space is at a premium (e.g., a hand-held display). Given certain conditions of viewing (high stress or vibration), the sensory qualities of the perceived message may be far from optimal. A choice of designs is thereby offered as shown in Figure 6.4: (1) Present large print, thus taking advantage of improving the bottom-up sensory quality but restricting the number of words that can be viewed simultaneously on the screen (and thereby limiting top-down processing). (2) Present more words in smaller print and enhance top-down processing at the expense of bottom-up processing. Naturally the appropriate text size will be determined by an evaluation of the relative contribution of these two factors. For example, if there is more redundancy in the text, smaller text size is indicated. However, if the display contains random strings of alphanumeric symbols, there is no opportunity for top-down processing, and larger presentation of fewer characters is advised. If the display or viewing quality is extremely poor, larger size is again suggested. It is important that the system designer be aware of the factors that influence the trade-off between data-driven and context-driven processing, which determines the optimum point on the trade-off to be selected.

Top-down processing may also be greatly aided through the simple technique of restricting a message vocabulary. With fewer possible alternatives to consider, top-down

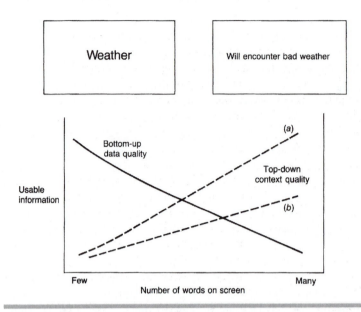

Figure 6.4 The trade-off between top-down and bottom-up processing in display of limited size. The two dashed lines represent different amounts of contextual redundancy: (*a*) high context of printed text; (*b*) low context of isolated word strings.

hypothesis forming (i.e., guessing an unreadable word) becomes far more efficient. This technique is a major factor behind the strict adherence to standard terminology in many message-routing centers or communication systems (Kryter, 1972).

Code Design: Economy Versus Security

The trade-off between top-down and bottom-up processing is demonstrated by the fact that messages of greater probability (and therefore less information content) may be transmitted with less sensory evidence. We have already encountered one example of this tradeoff in the compensatory relation between d' and beta in signal detection theory (Chapter 2). We learned there that as a signal becomes more frequent, thereby offering less information, and beta is lowered, it can be detected at lower sensitivity (i.e., with less evidence and therefore lower d'). It is fortunate that the trade-off in human performance corresponds quite nicely with a formal specification of the optimum design of codes, referred to as the *Shannon-Fano* principle (Sheridan & Ferrell, 1974). In designing any sort of code or message system in which short strings of alphanumeric or symbolic characters are intended to convey longer ideas, the Shannon-Fano principle dictates that the most efficient, or *economic*, code (fewest symbols) will be generated when the length of the physical message is proportional to the information content of the message. The principle is violated if all messages are of the same length. Thus, high-probability, low-information messages should be short, and low-probability ones should be longer. For example, if the four events that make up a code and their associated probabilities are

A (0.4), B (0.4), C (0.1), and D (0.1), a code using binomial symbols that assigns A = 00, B = 01, C = 10, and D = 11 violates the Shannon-Fano principle. One that assigns A = 0, B = 1, C = 01, and D = 10 does not.

It is interesting to observe that all natural languages roughly follow the Shannon-Fano principle. Words that occur frequently (*a*, *of*, or *the*) are short, and ones that occur rarely tend to be longer. This relation is known as Zipf's law (Ellis & Hitchcock, 1986). The relevant finding from the viewpoint of human performance is that adherence to such a code reinforces our natural tendencies to expect frequent signals and therefore require less sensory evidence for those signals to be recognized. For example, in an efficient code designed to represent engine status, the expected normal operation might be represented by N (one unit), whereas *HOT* (three units) should designate a less-expected, lower-probability overheated condition. Violations of the Shannon-Fano principle are observed in a coding system in which all events, independent of their probability, are specified by a message of the same length. Such a violation was evident in the Navy's system of computerized maintenance records. The operator servicing a malfunctioning component was required to enter a nine-digit malfunction code on a computerized form. This code was of uniform length whether the malfunction was highly probable (overheating engine) or was extremely rare.

Several other properties of a useful code design have been summarized by Bailey (1989). For example, a code, like an abbreviation or symbol, should be meaningfully related to its referent. Alphabetic codes, because of the greater richness of the alphabet, generally meet this criterion better than numeric ones. Also, code strings should be relatively short (fewer than 6 characters; the New Jersey driver's license code has 15 digits). It is unwise to make codes two or three digits longer than currently necessary in order to anticipate an expanding population of code vocabulary. For example, a code of the form 00214682, in which the first two 0's anticipate a 100-fold growth in the vocabulary, is not advised. Bailey (1989) points out that the extra cognitive processing required of the two place-holding digits is likely to produce a substantial number of copying, memory, and reading errors over the course of the code's use.

In the context of information theory, there is a second critical factor in addition to efficiency that must be considered when a code or message system is designed. This is security. The security factor illustrates again the trade-offs frequently encountered in human engineering. The Shannon-Fano principle is intended to produce maximum processing efficiency, which is compatible with perceptual processing biases. However, it may often be the case that relatively high-frequency (and therefore short) messages of a low information content are in fact very *important*. It is therefore essential that they be perceived with a high degree of security. In these instances, enhanced data quality should be sought and the principle of economy should be sacrificed by including redundancy, as discussed in Chapter 2. This is particularly true if sensory processing may be degraded. Redundancy is accomplished by allowing a number of separate elements of the code to transmit the same information. For voice communications, the use of a communications-code alphabet in which *alpha*, *bravo*, and *charlie* are substituted for *a*, *b*, and *c* is a clear example of such redundancy for the sake of security. The second syllable in each utterance conveys information that is highly redundant with the first. Yet this redundancy is helpful because of the need for absolute security (communication without information loss) in the contexts in which this alphabet is employed. It is possible to look on the trade-off between efficiency and security in code design as an echo of the trade-off discussed in Chapter 2 between maximizing information transmission and minimizing information loss in absolute judgment. Certain conditions (orthogonal dimensions and adherence to the Shannon-Fano principle) will be more efficient, and other conditions emphasizing redundancy will be more secure.

RECOGNITION OF OBJECTS

Top-Down and Bottom-Up Processing

The combination of bottom-up and top-down processing involved in word perception characterizes the perception of everyday objects as well. For example, just as letters are perceived, in part, through feature analysis, so Biederman (1987) has proposed that humans recognize objects in terms of combinations of a small number of basic features, which consist of simple geometric solids (e.g., straight and curved cylinders and cones). A proposed set of such features, called *geons,* is shown in Figure 6.5. Each geon is discriminable from others in terms of categorical differences shown in the columns of the figure. Biederman's theory suggests that the designers of three-dimensional graphics displays might well capitalize on these basic features, by fabricating objects that can be easily recognized without needing to incorporate excessive detail.

The role of top-down processing in object recognition is as important as it is in word recognition. In a procedure analogous to that described by Tulving, Mandler, and Baumal (1964), Palmer (1975) presented subjects with a context-setting display of a visual scene (e.g., a kitchen). This was followed by a brief presentation of an object that could be appropriate in the context of that scene (a loaf of bread), appropriate in physical form but out of context (a home mailbox, which looks like a loaf of bread but does not belong in the kitchen), or appropriate in neither form nor context (a drum). Palmer found that the visual recognition threshold was predicted directly by the amount of contextual appropriateness from the loaf of bread (highest appropriateness, lowest threshold) to the mailbox to the drum (lowest appropriateness, highest threshold).

In a related study, Biederman et al. (1981) demonstrated top-down processing in rapid photo interpretation of objects. The subjects had to detect objects in a complex visual scene from a rapid 200-millisecond exposure. The objects were in either appropriate or inappropriate contexts, where appropriateness was defined in terms of several expected properties of the objects (e.g., the object must be supported, and it should be of the expected size, given the background). The researchers found that if the object was appropriate, it was detected equally well at visual angles out to 3 degrees of peripheral vision. If it was not, performance declined rapidly with increased visual angle from fixation.

The role of familiarity in object perception demonstrated by these experiments suggests that familiar objects are coded and represented symbolically (in terms of abstract words and ideas) as well as in analog spatial form. We must assume that presentation of familiar objects rapidly activates both visual and symbolic codes in a cooperative manner. Evidence for the speed and efficiency with which the symbolic meaning of objects can be encoded and interpreted is provided by Potter and Faulconer (1975), who found that simple pictures of objects could be understood at least as rapidly as words.

In addition to the distinction defined by level of familiarity, a second distinction between objects, directly related to designing synthetic scenes (for example, 3-D maps)

CROSS SECTION

Geon	Edge Straight S Curved C	Symmetry Rot & Ref ++ Ref + Asymm –	Size Constant ++ Expanded – Exp & Cont ––	Axis Straight + Curved –
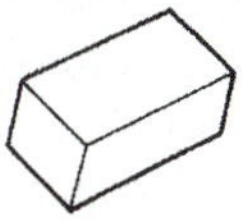	S	++	++	+
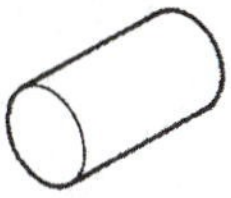	C	++	++	+
	S	+	–	+
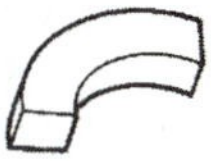	S	++	+	–
	C	++	–	+
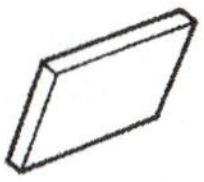	S	+	+	+

Figure 6.5 Proposed set of primitive geometric features, or *geons*, used in object recognition. The attributes or dimensions that distinguish each geon from others in the list are shown to the right.

Source: I. Biederman, "Human Image Understanding," *Computer Vision, Graphics and Image Processing, 32* (1985), pp. 29–73. Copyright 1985 by Academic Press. Reprinted by permission.

is defined, in part, by their three-dimensional structure as discussed in Chapter 4. Three-dimensional objects like roads and buildings typically have an orthogonal right angle structure and are usually represented by straight and parallel lines. Indeed these characteristics often derive from the fact that they are man made, or "cultural features." In contrast, natural features, like rivers, hills, or valleys tend to lack such structure. Two properties of cultural objects and their features give them an advantage in scene recognition (Whitaker & CuQlock-Knopp, 1995; Hickox & Wickens, 1999; Biederman, 1999). First, because of their greater familiarity, they can often be recognized better and therefore used as landmarks. Second, because of their orthogonal structure, they can be recognized equally well from different *viewpoints* in a three-dimensional rendering. For example, thanks to our top-down processing of depth information, the intersection of roads in the three panels of Figure 6.6 is always perceived to be 90 degrees. This property of many cultural features has been labeled that of *viewpoint independence* (Biederman, 1999), and viewpoint-independent features help the processing and recognition of three-dimensional scenes (Hickox & Wickens, 1999). Of course, recognition is not the only important characteristic that is helpful in scene processing. Uniqueness of features will also be critical, so that the cultural feature embedded in a rural or mountainous environment (unique) will be more valuable than one embedded in an urban environment, where there are many other such features.

Pictures and Icons

The fact that pictures can be recognized as rapidly as words leads to the potential application of pictorial symbols or icons to represent familiar concepts. Highway symbols and signs in public buildings are familiar examples of pictures being used to represent or replace words. In a similar way, icons have become a standard feature of computer displays (Figure 6.7), where their value over words in allowing rapid processing has been demonstrated (Camacho, Steiner, & Berson, 1990). In spite of the rapid speed of processing pictures that can be shown in ideal circumstances (Potter & Faulconer, 1975) and their status as an international language, caution must be advised against the use of icons as labels for two reasons: legibility and interpretation.

The *legibility* concern relates to the fact that icons and symbols are not always viewed under ideal conditions (neither, of course, are words). Thus, it becomes important for symbols to be highly discriminable from one another. The key to discriminability under suboptimal viewing conditions lies not in the fine detailed features but rather in the global shape of the symbol as revealed by spatial frequency analysis typical of that used for word shape (Broadbent & Broadbent, 1980). Thus, if "Previous Page" and "Next Page" in Figure 6.7 were differentiated only by the direction of the arrow, confusion would be likely when viewing under degraded conditions. The difference between these icons in the global shape, resulting from the angle of the page, reduces the likelihood of confusion.

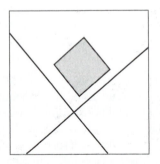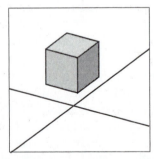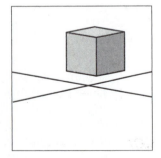

Figure 6.6 Depiction of the viewpoint-independent feature of a right-angle intersection, from three different viewpoints.

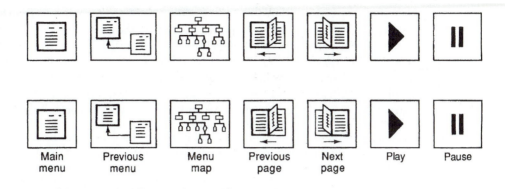

Main menu | Previous menu | Menu map | Previous page | Next page | Play | Pause

Figure 6.7 Typical icons for a computer display.

Source: D. J. Brems & W. B. Whitten, "Learning and Preference for Icon-Based Interface," *Proceedings of the 31st annual meeting of the Human Factors Society* (Santa Monica, CA: Human Factors Society, 1987), pp. 125–129.

The *interpretation* concern relates to the identity of the symbol itself. This concern in turn can be partitioned into two questions: What is depicted on the symbol, and what does that depiction mean? A symbol may clearly depict a recognizable object but remain totally ambiguous concerning the meaning of the object in the context. For example, a clearly defined arrow could be interpreted as pointing to a given region on the display or as commanding an action or movement in a given direction. It is for this reason that Brems and Whitten (1987) caution against the heavy use of icons that are not reinforced by redundant verbal labels. (This theme, the redundancy of verbal with pictorial or spatial material, is repeated later in this chapter as we discuss the presentation of more detailed sequences of information regarding procedures and instructions.) Yet redundancy of presentation itself may have a cost. Redundant labels occupy more space and can result in a more cluttered display. These are the sorts of trade-offs that always confront the human factors engineer.

Just as print has an auditory analogy in the spoken word, so visual icons have an auditory analogy in the sound of familiar objects and events (Gaver, 1986). These have sometimes been referred to as "earcons." Although the number of clearly recognizable sound categories is less than the number of picture categories, and hence the potential for confusion of earcons could be greater, a small vocabulary of such sounds (representing, for example, an unpleasant noise to warn of an illegal operation or a chime to represent an appropriate one) can provide useful feedback for events. These earcons may have particular value when visual processing is engaged by other aspects of the task (see Chapter 11).

COMPREHENSION

Whether presented by voice or by print, words are normally combined into sentences whose primary function is to convey a message to the receiver. So far our discussion has considered how the meaning of the isolated symbols, words, and word combinations is extracted. In this section we consider properties of the word strings themselves, and not just their physical representation, that influence the ease of comprehension (Broadbent, 1977). Instructions and procedures vary dramatically in the ease with which they may be understood. Chapanis (1965), in a delightful article entitled "Words Words Words," provides several examples of instructions that are poorly if not incomprehensibly phrased. Some examples are shown in Figure 6.8.

Wordy phrases that are difficult to understand are often encountered in legal documents and instructions. Consider the following set of instructions issued to a deliberating jury:

> You must not consider as evidence any statement of counsel made during the trial; however, if counsel for both parties have stipulated to any fact, or any fact has been admitted by counsel, you will regard that fact as being conclusively proven as to the party or parties making the stipulation or admission. As to any question to which an objection was sustained, you must not speculate as to what the answer might have been or as to the reason for the objection. You must not consider for any purpose any offer of evidence that was rejected or any evidence that was stricken out by the court; such matter is to be treated as though you have never known of it. (Hastie, 1982)

Now consider a modification that attempts to present the same information in a more understandable format.

> As I mentioned earlier, it is your job to decide from the evidence what the facts are. Here are ... rules that will help you decide what is, and what is not, evidence.
>
> 1. *Lawyer's statement.* Ordinarily, any statement made by the lawyers in this case is not evidence. However, if all the lawyers agree that some particular thing is true, you must accept it as truth.
> 2. *Rejected evidence.* At times during this trial, items or testimony were offered as evidence, but I did not allow them to become evidence. Since they never became evidence, you must not consider them.
> 3. *Stricken evidence.* At times, I ordered some piece of evidence to be stricken, or thrown out. Since that is no longer evidence, you must ignore it, also.

Using this modified text, jurors' comprehension rate was improved by nearly 50 percent.

In writing instructions or procedures that are easy to understand, such as the rewritten set above, it is often sufficient to follow a set of straightforward, commonsense principles similar to those outlined by Bailey (1989; see also Dumas & Redish, 1986):

1. State directly what is desired without adding excess words.
2. Use familiar vocabulary.
3. Ensure that all information is explicitly stated, leaving nothing to be inferred. For example, ambiguous pronouns like "it" or "this" that refer to nouns identified much earlier in the text violate this guideline.
4. Number and physically separate the different points to be made (or procedural steps to be taken), as has been done here, rather than combining them in a single narrative.
5. Highlight key points or words.

The writing of understandable procedures and instructions may be aided by a number of *readability formulas* (Bailey, 1989). These formulas take into account such factors as the average word and sentence length, in order to make quantitative assessments of the likelihood that a passage will be correctly understood by a readership with a given

NOTICE

THIS RADIO USES A LONG LIFE PILOT LAMP THAT MAY STAY ON FOR A SHORT TIME IF RADIO IS TURNED OFF BEFORE RADIO WARMS UP AND STARTS TO PLAY

What it said: (29 words)

NOTICE

DON'T WORRY IF THE PILOT LAMP SHOULD STAY ON FOR A LITTLE WHILE AFTER YOU TURN THE RADIO OFF

What is meant: (19 words)

NOTICE

IF YOU TURN THE RADIO ON, AND THEN OFF RIGHT AWAY. THE PILOT LAMP MAY STAY ON FOR A LITTLE WHILE

This is more accurate: (21 words)

NOTICE

THE PILOT LAMP SOMETIMES STAYS ON FOR A LITTLE WHILE AFTER YOU TURN THE RADIO OFF

But would this do? (16 words)

PLEASE

WALK UP ONE FLOOR

WALK DOWN TWO FLOORS

FOR IMPROVED ELEVATOR SERVICE

What it says: (13 words)

IF YOU ARE ONLY GOING

UP ONE FLOOR

OR

DOWN TWO FLOORS

PLEASE WALK

(IF YOU DO THAT WE'LL ALL HAVE BETTER ELEVATOR SERVICE)

What it means: (24 words)

TO GO UP ONE FLOOR

OR

DOWN TWO FLOORS

PLEASE WALK

Would this do? (11 words)

You can Dial LOCAL and TRUNK CALLS

LOCAL CALLS   cost 3d. for 3 mins (cheap rate 6 mins)

for LONDON exchanges, dial the first three letters of the exchange name followed by the number you want

LONDON exchanges are shown in the DIALLING CODE BOOKLET and Telephone Directory with the first three letters in heavy capitals

For the following exchanges, dial the code shown followed by the number you want

	Code		Code		Code
Byfleet	BY	Hoddesdon	HOD	St. Albans	LN
Crayford	CY	Hornchurch	HX	Slough	SL
Dartford	DA	Ingrebourne	IL	Staines	SW
Erith	FT	Leatherhead	LE7	Uxbridge	UX
Farnborough Kent	FN	Northwood	NL	Waltham Cross	WS
Garston	GR7	Orpington	MM	Walton on Thames	WT
Gerrards Cross	GE4	Potters Bar	PR	Watford	WA
Hatfield	HL6	Romford	RO	Weybridge	WR

You can DIAL other LOCAL CALLS shown in the DIALLING CODE BOOKLET (inside the A–D directory)

TRUNK CALLS

For BIRMINGHAM exchanges Dial 021   Then the first three letters of the
  – EDINBURGH – 031   exchange name
  – GLASGOW – 041   then the number
  – LIVERPOOL – 051   e.g. for Birmingham Midland 7291
  – MANCHESTER – 061   dial 021 MID 7291

You can DIAL other TRUNK CALLS shown in the DIALLING CODE BOOKLET (inside the A–D directory)

To make a call first check the code (see above)

USE 3d bits, 6d or 1/- coins (Not Pennies)

HAVE MONEY READY, but do not try to put it in yet

LIFT RECEIVER, listen for dialling tone and

DIAL — see above — then wait for a tone

Ringing tone (burr-burr) changes, when the number answers, to

Pay tone (rapid pips) — Now PRESS in a coin and speak

(Coins cannot be inserted until first pay tone is heard)

Engaged tone (slow pips) — try again later

N.U. tone (steady note) — check number and redial

INSERT MORE MONEY to prolong the call
at any time during conversation
at once if pay tone returns

Remember—Dial first and when you hear pay tone (rapid pips) press in a coin

For Directory Enquiries dial DIR   For other enquiries dial INF
For OTHER SERVICES and CALL CHARGES
see the DIALLING CODE BOOKLET (inside the A-D directory)

For the Operator – dial 100

Figure 6.8 Three examples of poorly worded instructions.

Source: A. Chapanis, "Words Words Words," *Human Factors,* 7 (1965), pp. 6, 7, 9. Copyright 1965 by the Human Factors Society, Inc. All rights reserved.

educational level. However useful and necessary as these guidelines may be, they do not consider some other important characteristics of comprehension that are directly related to principles in cognitive psychology and information processing. The sections that follow consider five general categories: context, command versus status information, linguistic factors, working memory, and the role of pictures.

Context

The important role of context in comprehension is to influence the perceiver to encode the material in the manner that is intended. This top-down processing influence was considered in two different forms in Chapter 2: the influence of probability on response bias and the influence of context on information. Furthermore, context should provide a framework on which details of the subsequent verbal information may be hung. Bransford and Johnson (1972) demonstrate the dramatic effect that the context of a descriptive picture or even a thematic title can exert on comprehension. In their experiment, the subjects read a series of sentences that describe a particular scene or activity (e.g., the procedures for washing cloths). The subjects were asked to rate the comprehensibility of the sentences and were later asked to recall them. Large improvements in both comprehensibility and recall were found for subjects who had been given a context for understanding the sentences prior to hearing them. This context was in the form of either a picture describing the scene, or a simple title of the activity. For those subjects who received no context, there was little means of organizing or storing the material, and performance was poor.

For context to aid in recall or comprehension, however, it should be made available *before* the presentation of the verbal material and not after (Bower, Clark, Lesgold, & Winzenz, 1969). The important benefits of prior context would account for the results of an investigation by Norcio (1981) of computer program documentation (i.e., commentary on the meaning of the various logical statements). He noted that documentation helped comprehension of the program only if it was given at the beginning and not when it was interspersed throughout. Like a good filing system, context can organize material for comprehension and retrieval if it is set up ahead of time. Even a highly organized filing scheme is of little assistance if it is made available only after the papers are dumped loosely into a drawer.

Command Versus Status

Another issue in the delivery of some classes of time-critical instructions is related to the distinction between status and command information. Should a display simply inform the operator of an existing *status*, such as an icon signalling danger or a verbal statement ("Your speed is too high"), or should a display *command* an action to be carried out ("Lower your speed")?

Arguments can be made on both sides of the issue, and the data are not altogether consistent. For example, in designing flight path displays to help pilots recover from unusual attitudes, Taylor and Selcon (1990) found that a display that told the pilot what direction to fly in order to recover was more effective than one that showed the aircraft's current status. Barnett (1990) observed no difference in performance on a decision-aiding task between status and command (actually recommended procedure) displays. Finally, a study by Crocoll and Coury (1990) obtained results that generally favored status displays. When the information was completely reliable in a decision-aiding task, there were no differences in performance; but when information was not totally reliable (as is often the case with automated decision aids and automated advisors), performance suffered far more when unreliable commands were given than when unreliable status reports were provided. That is, the command display was worse.

What conclusions can be drawn from these studies? First, it is probably true that under conditions of high stress and time pressure, a command display is superior to a status display, as the latter will require an extra cognitive step to go from what is, to what should be done. Second, Crocoll and Coury's (1990) results suggest that these guidelines might be modified if time pressure is relaxed or the source of the status or command information—often automation—is not fully to be trusted, an issue we will revisit in Chapter 13. Finally, as is so often the case in human performance, a strong argument can be made for *redundancy*, presenting both status and command information. This is an approach reflected in the design of the Traffic Alert and Collision Avoidance System (TCAS) in commercial aircraft. A command tells the pilot what to do to avoid a collision ("pull up"), while a status display presents the relative location of the threatening traffic (Wickens, Mavor, Parasuraman, & McGee, 1998). Redundancy of this sort, however, should be introduced only if any possible confusion between what is status and what is command is avoided by making the two sources as different from one another as possible. For example, in the case of the TCAS system, voice command will be easily distinguished from a pictorial status. Otherwise, in the case of information like that involved in spatial directions, a possible user confusion of status ("you are left") with command ("turn left") could lead to disaster. The chance of confusion is reduced if the verb phrase that distinguishes status from command ("you are" versus "turn") is clearly articulated in order to provide redundant discrimination of status and command information, respectively.

Linguistic Factors

Logical Reversals, Negatives, and Falsifications   Whenever a reader or listener is required to logically reverse the meaning of a statement to translate from a physical sequence of words to an understanding of what is intended, comprehension is made more difficult. One example is provided by the use of negatives. We comprehend more rapidly that a particular light should be "on" than that it should be "not off." A second example of logical reversals is falsification. It is faster to understand that a proposition should be true than that it should be untrue or false. Experiments by Clark and Chase (1972) and by Carpenter and Just (1975) suggest that these differences result not simply from the greater number of words or letters that normally occur in reversed statements but from the cognitive difficulties in processing them as well.

The experimental task employed by these investigators was the sentence-picture verification task. It is the experimental analog of an operator who reads a verbal instruction (e.g., "Check to see that disk A is loaded") to verify it either against the physical state or against his or her own mental representation of the state of the system. In the actual experimental task examined by Clark and Chase (1972), the subjects are shown a verbal sentence describing the relationship between two symbols (e.g., "The star is below the plus") along with a picture depicting the two symbols. The symbols are in an orientation that is either true or false relative to the verbal proposition. The subject is to indicate the truth of this statement as rapidly as possible. Sentences vary in their truth value relative to the picture (e.g., whether the correct answer is true or false) and in whether or not they contain a negative ("The star is above the circle" versus "The circle is not above the star"). Four examples of the sentence-picture relationship are shown in Figure 6.9. Beneath each sentence, describing the picture on the left, is the response time that was measured for subjects to verify sentences of that category.

The results of these experiments suggest three important conclusions. First, statements that contain negatives always take longer to verify than those that do not, as shown by the greater response time for the two sentences on the right in Figure 6.9. Therefore, where possible, instructions should contain only positive assertions (i.e., "Check to see that the power is off") rather than negative ones ("Check to see that the power is not on"). An added reason to avoid negatives is that the *not* can sometimes be missed or forgotten if the instructions are read or heard in degraded or hurried circumstances. The conclusion to avoid negatives has also been confirmed in applied environments. Newsome and Hocherlin (1989) observed this advantage in computer operating instructions. In highway traffic-regulation signs, experiments have suggested that prohibitive signs, whether verbal ("no left turn") or symbolic,   , are more difficult to comprehend than permissive signs such as "right turn only" (Dewar, 1976; Whitaker & Stacey, 1981). In designing forms to be filled out, such negative phrases as "Do not delay returning this

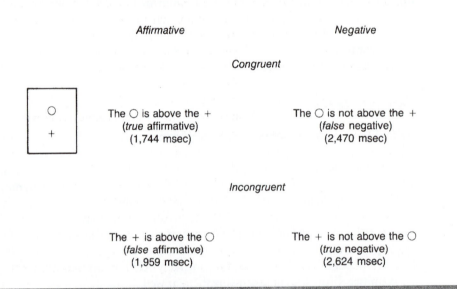

Figure 6.9 The picture-sentence verification task. The four sentences describe the picture on the left. The top two sentences are congruent with the picture relation "circle above plus." The two sentences on the right contain negatives. Response times are shown in parentheses.

Source: H. H. Clark and W. G. Chase, "On the Process of Comparing Sentences Against Pictures," *Cognitive Psychology,* 3 (1972), p. 482. Copyright 1972 by Academic Press. Adapted by permission of the authors.

form even if you do not know your insurance number" are harder to comprehend than positive phrases such as "Return this form at once even if you do not know your insurance number" (Wright & Barnard, 1975).

Second, whether a statement is verified as true or false influences the verification time in a more complex way. If the statement contains no negatives (is positive), true statements are verified faster than false ones (left side of Figure 6.9). However, if statements contain negatives, false statements are verified more rapidly than true ones (right side). The reason for this reversal relates to the principle of *congruence* (described later in this chapter).

Third, Clark and Chase (1972) and Carpenter and Just (1975) find very predictable differences in response time (RT) among the four kinds of picture-sentence relations. In response to this regularity, they have modeled the processes involved as a series of basic *constituent comparisons* (Carpenter & Just, 1975) of constant duration, each performed in sequence and each taking a constant time. These are performed in series until the truth of the relation is verified. Comparisons are made concerning the equality, or "congruence," of the propositional form between picture and sentence, disregarding any negatives. For the two sentences at the top, this form is "circle above plus." For the two at the bottom, it is "plus above circle." This may be roughly thought of as a comparison of the congruence of the word order on the page with the order of representation in memory of the picture. If there is disagreement in this congruence, extra time is added. Since we normally read from top to bottom, the order of the picture in Figure 6.9, circle-plus, is incongruent for the bottom two sentences. A comparison is also made concerning the existence of negatives (the two right sentences). Negatives also add time. As each of these constituent comparisons is made, units of time are added, and the truth value of the comparison is updated. After all comparisons are made, the final response is given with an RT determined by the number of comparisons. The longest response to the true negative sentence occurs because it alone is both incongruent and contains a negative.

When this model is used to help the designer phrase proper instructions or to predict the time that will be required for operators to respond to instructions or checklists, the meaning of true and false must be reconsidered slightly. In Figure 6.9, the relationships are always true or false because the picture never changes. However, in application, a "picture"—the actual state of a system—may take on different values with different probabilities. *True* must thus be defined as the most likely state of a system. Therefore, if a switch is normally in an up position, the instruction should read, "Check to ensure that the switch is up" or "Is the switch up?" Since this position has the greatest frequency, such a statement will normally be verified as a true positive. Furthermore, as long as negatives in wording are avoided, the principle will always hold that affirmations will be processed faster than falsifications.

Absence of Cues   People are generally better at noticing that something unexpected is present than that something expected is missing, just as we learned in Chapter 3 that attention is better captured by the onset of a stimulus than by its offset (Yantis, 1993). The dangers that result when people must extract information from the absence of cues are somewhat related to the recommendation to avoid negatives in instructions. Fowler (1980) states this point in his analysis of an airplane crash near the airport at Palm Springs, California. He notes that the *absence* of an R symbol on the pilot's airport chart in the cockpit was the only indication of the critical information that the airport did *not* have radar. Since terminal radar is something pilots come to depend on and the lack of radar is highly significant, Fowler argues that it is far more logical to call attention to the absence of this information by the *presence* of a visible symbol than it is to indicate the presence of this information with a symbol. In general, the presence of a symbol should be associated with information that an operator *needs to know* rather than with certain expected environmental conditions.

Congruence and Order Reversals   In many cases, instructions are intended to convey a sense of ordered events. This order is often in the time domain (procedure X is followed by procedure Y). When instructions are to convey a sense of order, it is important that the elements in those instructions are *congruent* with the desired order of events. For example, if people are to learn or to verify that the order of elements is A > B > C, it is better to say, (1) "A is greater than B, and B is greater than C," rather than (2) "B is greater than C, and A is greater than B" or (3) "B is less than A, and C is less than B" (DeSota, London, & Handel, 1965). In the first case, the physical ordering of information in the sentence (A,B,B,C) conforms with the intended "true" ordering (A,B,C). In the last two cases, it does not (B,C,A,B or B,A,C,B). Furthermore, in the third case, the word *less* is used to verify an ordering that is specified in terms of *greater*. This represents an additional form of cognitive reversal. This finding would dictate that procedural instructions should read, "Do A, then do B," rather than "Prior to B, do A," since the former preserves a congruence between the actual sequencing of events and the ordering of statements on the page (Bailey, 1989). For example, a procedural instruction should read, "If the light is on, start the component," rather than, "Start the component if the light is on."

Working Memory Load

Characteristics of poor instructions often reflect a structure that imposes unnecessarily on working memory (see Chapter 7) to maintain information until it can be either used or incorporated into the developing meaning of the text. As a simple example, in the incongruent instructions from the previous paragraph ("start the component if the light is on"), the user must hold the proposition "start component" in working memory until after the contingency "light-on" is encountered.

A model of sentence comprehension proposed by Kintch & Van Dijk (1978) characterizes such comprehension in terms of the number of *propositions* that need to be maintained in working memory, or retrieved from long-term memory, in order to integrate new information into the evolving script or schema conveyed by a string of sentences. On the one hand, more propositions lead to greater working memory demand, and hence poorer comprehension. On the other hand, given the assumption of Kintch's model that the capacity of working memory in text comprehension is roughly four propositions, then any new proposition that depends for its interpretation on processing the meaning of a proposition encountered more than four propositions back will require *reinstatement* of information no longer in working memory; either by a time-consuming memory search or (in the case of visual text) by rereading.

Consider as an example the instructions: "Turn on the power, then check the message in Window A; check the message in Window B, determine that the "ready" light is green, comply with the message in Windows A." The propositional structure of this sentence is shown in Table 6.1.

TABLE 6.1 Propositional Structure of a Sentence

1	Power On
2	Check Message
3	Message Window A
4	Check Message
5	Message Window B
6	Light On
7	Comply Message
8	Message Window A

Note that by the time the compliance proposition for Window A has been encountered (Propositions 7 and 8), part of the initial evaluation of Window A (Propositions 2 and 3) will have already dropped from working memory, because of the capacity demands of the intervening propositions 4, 5, and 6. In the instructions shown, it would make far more sense to swap the position of 7 and 8 with 4 and 5.

Finally, the analysis of working-memory demands of text comprehension calls attention to the dangers of the ambiguous pronoun. Working memory is challenged to disambiguate its meaning. As an example, in the sentence you just read, "it" could refer either to working memory or to the ambiguous pronoun. If you were following the "gist" of the paragraph, you probably figured that the "it" referred to the ambiguous pronoun. But the nontrivial problem-solving effort required to figure out what "it" referred to could well have interfered with your ability to understand other parts of the information.

MULTIMEDIA INSTRUCTIONS

We have described the role of text and pictures for presenting instructions and other information. The current technology of voice synthesis (as well as the older technology of tapes and soundtracks) allows voice to be added to the two visual media for presenting instructions. When the strengths and limitations of human information processing are considered, several guidelines emerge for using the three media (text, pictures, and sound) to present instructions. The sections that follow discuss three of these guidelines, relating to the optimal medium, redundancy gain, and realism. (The role of multimedia in presenting more elaborated educational material will be discussed in Chapter 7.)

The Optimal Medium   Text and pictures should logically be tailored to their respective strengths. Pictures or graphics can best convey analog spatial relations and complex spatial patterns. Verbal material (whether print or text) can best convey more abstract information, including action verbs that do not have a strong spatial or iconic component (e.g., "read" or "comply"). If verbal information is lengthy, it should be visual (text) rather than auditory (speech), because of the greater permanence of visual information and the higher working-memory demands of understanding speech. While there is some evidence for advantages of providing different media to individuals with different cognitive strengths (e.g., spatial graphics for those with higher spatial abilities), the strength of this effect does not appear to be great (Yallow, 1980; Landaur, 1995), and it is better to choose the medium as a function of the material and the task, rather than as a function of the learner.

Redundancy Gain   Instead of considering each medium in isolation, better design guidelines usually suggest that pairs of media should be used in combination, to capitalize on redundancy gain and on the particular strengths of each (Mayer, 1997, 1999). Much of the historical evaluation of combined media in instructions has evaluated the use of pictures (graphics) and text.

Three investigations point to the advantage of picture-text redundancy, even as they emphasize the relative strengths of different formats. Booher (1975) evaluated subjects who were mastering a series of procedures required to turn on a piece of equipment. Six different instructional formats were compared: one purely verbal, one purely pictorial, and four combinations of the two codes. Two of these combinations were *redundant*: One code was emphasized and the other provided supplementary cues. Two others were *related*: The nonemphasized mode gave related but not redundant information to the emphasized mode. Booher found the worst performance with the printed instructions and the best with the pictorial emphasis/redundant print format. Although the picture was of primary benefit in this condition, the redundant print clearly provided useful information that was not extracted in the picture-only condition.

Schmidt and Kysor (1987) studied the comprehension of airline passenger safety cards, using samples from 25 of the major air carriers. They found that those cards using mostly words were *least* well understood, those employing mostly diagrams fared better, but the best formats were those in which words were directly integrated with diagrams. The authors describe the value and use of arrows as attention-focusing and attention-directing devices to facilitate this integration.

In the third study, Stone and Gluck (1980) compared subjects' performance in assembling a model using pictorial instruction, text, or a completely redundant presentation of both. Like Booher (1975), Stone and Gluck found the best performance in the redundant condition. The investigators also monitored eye fixation in the redundant condition and found that five times as much time was spent fixating the text as the picture. This finding is consistent with a conclusion drawn by both Booher and by Stone and Gluck: The picture provides an overall context or "frame" within which the words can be used to fill in the details of the procedures or instructions. The importance of context was, of course, emphasized earlier in this chapter.

Reviewing work on multimedia presentation, Wetzel, Radtke, and Stern (1994) and Mayer (1999) also conclude that pictures should proceed text, rather than follow it, if such a sequencing is required. However guidelines derived from the theory of *cognitive load* in instructions, developed by Sweller and his colleagues (Sweller & Chandler, 1994; Sweller, Chandler, Tierney, & Cooper, 1990; Tindall-Ford, Chandler, & Sweller, 1997), suggest the importance of integrating text with pictures as closely as possible (rather than sequencing), in order to reduce the demands on working memory of retaining the textual information until the relevant figures are located, or retaining the graphic information in working memory until the relevant textual information is encountered. As we will learn in the next chapter, even short delays of a second or two can disrupt the quality of information retained in working memory and can impose a high cognitive load that may interfere with comprehension. For example, Tindall-Ford, Chandler, and Sweller found considerably worse comprehension of instructions offered in the separated format of Figure 6.10a than with those in the integrated format of Figure 6.10b (Figures shown on pages 220-221). Such guidelines are fully consistent with the proximity compatibility principle (Wickens & Carswell, 1995), discussed in Chapters 3 and 4: If text is related to pictures or diagrams, the two sources should be placed in as close spatial proximity as possible.

Of course, the verbal information can be presented auditorily as well as in text form, (i.e., the sound track of an instructional video). Here, research suggests an advantage for auditory-pictorial combination over text-pictorial combination (Tindall-Ford, Chandler, & Sweller, 1997; Wetzel, Radtke, & Stern, 1994; Nugent, 1987; Mayer, 1997, 1999), an advantage that can also be related to cognitive load. In this case, as we discuss in more detail in Chapters 7 and 11, the advantage of splitting instruction between the visual and auditory modalities relates to the fact that each channel appears to be supported by separate attentional or cognitive resources. When the cognitive load of the instructional material is high, as it is when the material is complex, and there are a number of interconnections between the material presented in the two channels, some advantage is gained by distributing that load across the two resources (i.e., auditory/speech, and visual/pictures) (Tindall-Ford, Chandler, & Sweller, 1997). That is, the eye can look at the pictures while hearing the text (dual modality), but cannot easily look at the pictures while reading the text (single modality). Naturally, however, any efforts to present verbal material in auditory form must be sensitive to the limits of that modality: nonpermanence implies that long, difficult material should not be presented aurally, and an auditory presentation that is related to pictures or graphics must insure that the linkage to the particular picture (or part thereof) is made clear, in the same manner suggested by the arrows in Figure 6.10b.

Realism of Pictorial Material   If pictures and graphics do indeed contribute to the effectiveness of instructions, how realistic should those graphics be? The consensus of research seems to be that more is not necessarily better (Spencer, 1988; Wetzel, Radtke, & Sterm, 1994). Simple line drawings appear to do just as well if not better than more elaborate artwork, which captures detail that is not necessary for understanding (Dwyer, 1967). In the study evaluating airline safety codes, Schmidt and Kysor (1987) found that photographs, rather than schematic line drawings, led to substantially worse performance. These findings will have some parallels in our discussion of unnecessary simulator fidelity in Chapter 7.

PRODUCT WARNINGS

Nowhere has the study of comprehension had greater importance for the human factors community than in the design of effective product warnings (Ergonomics, 1995). This importance is a result not only of the safety implications for the product user, but also of the litigation costs associated with product liability lawsuits.

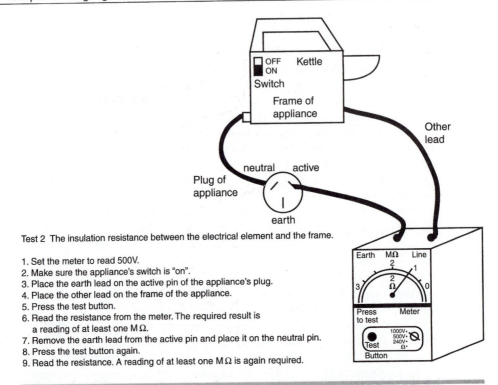

Test 2 The insulation resistance between the electrical element and the frame.

1. Set the meter to read 500V.
2. Make sure the appliance's switch is "on".
3. Place the earth lead on the active pin of the appliance's plug.
4. Place the other lead on the frame of the appliance.
5. Press the test button.
6. Read the resistance from the meter. The required result is
   a reading of at least one MΩ.
7. Remove the earth lead from the active pin and place it on the neutral pin.
8. Press the test button again.
9. Read the resistance. A reading of at least one MΩ is again required.

Figure 6.10 (a) An example of visual-only instructions with text separated. *(Continues)*

Source: S. Tindall-Ford, P. Chandler, & J. Sweller, "When Two Sensory Modes Are Better Than One," *Journal of Experimental Psychology: Applied, 3*(4) (1997), pp. 257–287. Reprinted by permission.

From a human factors perspective, the goal of product warnings is to get the user to comply with the warning and therefore use the product in a safe way, or avoid unsafe behavior. For such compliance to succeed, however, at least four information processing activities must be carried out successfully (Wickens, Gordon, & Liu, 1998).

First, the warning must be *noticed*, an activity that depends on the fundamental properties of human attention, as discussed in Chapter 3. Auditory warnings are more noticeable than visual ones (Wogalter, 1987), and when visual warnings are used, certain design principles should be employed to insure that they are captured by visual attention. Visual warnings should be located so that they will be "encountered" as the user carries out actions that are a necessary part of the equipment use. For example, they might be close to a "power on" switch. Frantz (1994) finds that warnings are more likely to be noticed if they are embedded within the operating instructions, rather than positioned at the end.

Second, warnings must be *read*. Anyone who has ever gazed at the product warnings on the side of a small medicine container realizes that readability is often thwarted by very fine print, just as it is also thwarted by the clutter of an excessive number of multiple warnings. To combat the legibility problem, it is important to prioritize the warnings, insuring that the most important are visible.

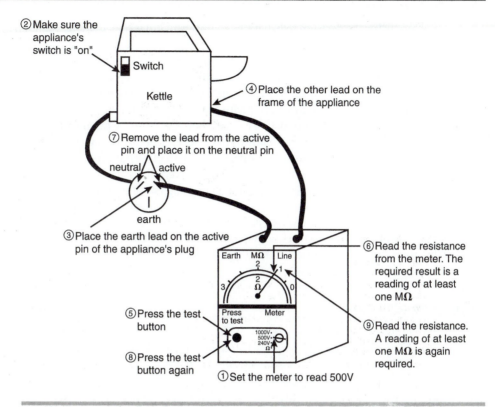

② Make sure the appliance's switch is "on".

Switch

Kettle

④ Place the other lead on the frame of the appliance

⑦ Remove the lead from the active pin and place it on the neutral pin

neutral / active

earth

③ Place the earth lead on the active pin of the appliance's plug

Earth   MΩ   Line

⑥ Read the resistance from the meter. The required result is a reading of at least one MΩ

⑤ Press the test button

Press to test   Meter

⑨ Read the resistance. A reading of at least one MΩ is again required.

⑧ Press the test button again

① Set the meter to read 500V

Figure 6.10   *(Continued)* (*b*) An example of integrated text and picture instructions.

Source: S. Tindall-Ford, P. Chandler, & J. Sweller, "When Two Sensory Modes Are Better Than One," *Journal of Experimental Psychology: Applied, 3*(4) (1997), pp. 257–287. Reprinted by permission.

Third, warnings must be understood. Here all of the material on comprehension discussed in the previous pages is critical. In particular, an effective warning contains four components: a signal word (e.g., caution, warning, danger), a description of the hazard (e.g., "toxic material"), the consequences associated with the hazard (e.g., "could cause death if inhaled"), and a description of the behavior needed to avoid the hazard, or deal with its consequences if encountered. One key issue is the *calibration* of the seriousness, which is fairly accurately conveyed by the three words "danger," "warning," and "caution," each indicating progressively lower risk, in a manner that is generally well understood by the English-speaking population (Wogalter & Silver, 1995). Seriousness can also be redundantly encoded by other properties associated with the signal word, such as color (red-orange-black-blue-green defines a scale of progressively lower risk), or print size (Braun & Silver, 1995). The effective use of readable text, and integrated pictures, can be important in conveying information regarding the seriousness of the consequences, which can influence compliance (Zeitlin, 1994), as well as the behavior to avoid, or deal with the hazard.

Fourth, unfortunately, (and sometimes tragically) even a well understood warning will not guarantee compliance (Zeitlin, 1994). As will be discussed again in Chapter 8, the choice to comply (or the decision to behave in an unsafe manner) can often be analyzed as a decision based on balancing the risks of not complying with the cost of compliance. This cost can include the added time and effort to engage the safety feature in question (e.g., locating and putting on the safety goggles), the possible discomfort associated with compliance (the goggles may be poorly fitting), and in particular, the anticipated loss of productivity that may result from compliance. For our unfortunate driver in the story at the beginning of the book, productivity would have been lost by pulling off the highway to use the dispatcher system. Productivity of drivers is lost by driving at or below the speed limit, if productivity is defined as completing a trip in a timely fashion. Indeed, the high cost of compliance appears to dominate the perceived risks of not complying (Wogalter, Allison, & McKenna, 1989). This imbalance suggests that the design of effective product warnings must be coupled with concern for minimizing both the cognitive and physical effort to comply, as well as any performance costs of compliance. (The important role of cognitive effort in both decision making and multiple task performance will be discussed in Chapters 8 and 11, respectively.)

SPEECH PERCEPTION

In 1977, a tragic event occurred at the Tenerife airport in the Canary Islands: A KLM Royal Dutch Airlines 747 jumbo jet, accelerating for takeoff, crashed into a Pan American 747 taxiing on the same runway. Although poor visibility was partially responsible for the disaster, in which 538 lives were lost, the major responsibility lay with the confusion between the KLM pilot and air traffic control regarding whether clearance had been granted for takeoff. Air traffic control, knowing that the Pan Am plane was still on the runway, was explicit in denying clearance. The KLM pilot misunderstood and, impatient to take off before the deteriorating weather closed the runway, perceived that clearance had been granted. In the terms described earlier, the failure of communications was attributed both to less-than-perfect audio transmission resulting from static and "clipped" messages—poor-quality data or bottom-up processing—and to less-than-adequate message redundancy, so that context and top-down processing could not compensate. The disaster, described in more detail in Hawkins and Orlady (1993) and fully documented by the Spanish Ministry of Transportation and Communications (1978), calls attention to the critical role of speech communications in engineering psychology.

In conventional systems, the human operator's auditory channel has been primarily used for transmitting verbal communication from other operators (e.g., messages to the pilot from air traffic control) and for presenting auditory warning signals (tones, horns, buzzers, etc.). Recently, however, rapid advances in microcomputer technology have produced highly efficient speech-synthesis units generating, for example, telephone menus or simple feedback to users of computer systems (McMillan, Eggleston, & Anderson, 1997). These allow computer-driven displays of auditory verbal messages to be synthesized on-line in a fashion quite analogous to visual information on computer-driven video displays.

Human perception of speech shares some similarities but also a number of pronounced contrasts with the perception of print, described at the beginning of this chapter. In common with reading, the perception of speech involves both bottom-up hierarchical processing and top-down contextual processing. Corresponding to the reading sequence of features to letters to words, the units of speech go from *phonemes* to *syllables* to *words*. In contrast to reading, on the other hand, the physical units of speech are not so nicely segregated from one another as are the physical units of print. Instead, the physical speech signal, like the cursive line but in contrast to print, is continuous, or analog, in format. The perceptual system must undertake some analog to digital conversion to translate the continuous speech waveform into the discrete units of speech perception. To understand the way in which these units are formed and their relationship to the physical stimulus, it is necessary first to understand the representation of speech.

Representation of Speech

Physically, the stimulus of speech is a continuous variation or oscillation of the air pressure reaching the eardrum, represented schematically in Figure 6.11a. As with any time-varying signal, the speech stimulus can be analyzed by using the principle of *Fourier analysis* into a series of separate sine wave components of different frequencies and amplitudes. Figure 6.11b is the Fourier-analyzed version of the signal in Figure 6.11a. We

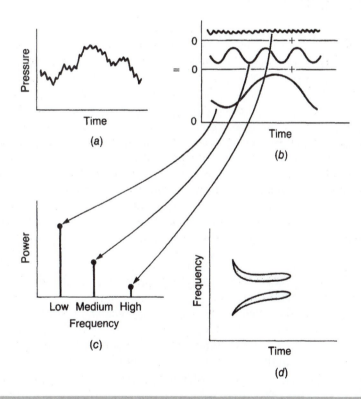

Figure 6.11 Different representations of speech signal: (*a*) time domain, (*b*) frequency components, (*c*) power spectrum, (*d*) speech spectograph.

may think of the three sinusoidal components in Figure 6.11b as three *features* of the initial stimulus. A more economical portrayal of the stimulus is in the *spectral representation* in Figure 6.11c. Here the frequency value (number of cycles per second, or Hertz) is shown on the x-axis; the mean amplitude or power (square of amplitude) of oscillation at that particular frequency is on the y-axis. Thus, the raw continuous wave form of Figure 6.11a is now represented quite economically by only three points in Figure 6.11c.

Because the frequency content of articulated speech does not remain constant but changes very rapidly and systematically over time, the representation of frequency and amplitude shown in Figure 6.11c must also include the third dimension of time. This is done in the *speech spectrograph*, an example of which is shown in Figure 6.11d. Here the added dimension of time is now on the x-axis. Frequency, which was originally on the x-axis of the power spectrum in Figure 6.11c, is now on the y-axis, and the third dimension, amplitude, is represented by the width of the graph. Thus, in the representation of Figure 6.11d, one tone starts out at a high pitch and low intensity and briefly increases in amplitude while it decreases in pitch, reaching a steady-state level. At the same time, a lower-pitched tone increases in both pitch and amplitude to a higher and louder steady level. In fact, this particular stimulus represents the spectrograph that would be produced by the sound *da*. The two separate tones are called *formants*.

Units of Speech Perception

Phonemes   The phoneme, analogous in many respects to the letter unit in reading, represents the basic unit of speech, because changing a phoneme in a word will change its meaning (or change it to a nonword). Thus, the 38 English phonemes roughly correspond to the letters of the alphabet plus distinctions such as those between long and short vowels and representations of sounds such as *th* and *sh*. The letters *s* and soft *c* (as in *ceiling*) are mapped into a single phoneme. Although the phoneme in the linguistic analysis of speech is analogous to the printed letter, there is a sense in which it is quite different from the letter in its actual perception. This is because the physical form of a phoneme is highly dependent on the context in which it appears (the *invariance problem*). The speech spectrograph of the phoneme *k* as in *kid* is quite different from that of *k* as in *lick* (whereas visually the letter *k* has the same physical form in both words). Also, the physical spectrograph of a consonant phoneme differs according to the vowel that follows it.

Syllables   Two or more phonemes generally combine to create the *syllable* as the basic unit of speech perception (Massaro, 1975). This definition is in keeping with the notion that although a following vowel (V) seems to define the physical form of the preceding consonant (C), the syllabic unit (CV) is itself relatively invariant in its physical form. The syllable, in fact, is the smallest unit with such invariance. One line of evidence in support of the syllable unit was provided by Huggins (1964), whose subjects listened to continuous speech that was switched back and forth between the two ears at different rates. Comprehension was somewhat disrupted at all switching rates but was most difficult at a rate of three per second. This is just the rate that would obliterate half of each syllable during the normal rate of speech production (Neisser, 1967). A faster rate obliterating half of each phoneme or a slower one obliterating half of each word was found to be far less disruptive. This finding suggests that people are particularly dependent on the syllable unit in speech perception.

Words Although the word is the smallest cognitive or semantic unit of meaning, like the phoneme it shows a definite lack of correspondence with the physical speech sound. (Actually, the morpheme is a slightly smaller cognitive unit than the word, consisting of word stems along with prefixes and suffixes such as *un-* or *-ing*.) This lack of correspondence defines the *segmentation problem* (Neisser, 1967). In a speech spectrograph of continuous speech, there are identifiable breaks or gaps in the continuous record. However, these physical gaps show relatively little correspondence with the subjective pauses at word boundaries that we seem to hear. For example, the spectrograph of the four-word phrase "She uses st*and*ard oil" would show the two physical pauses marked by *, neither one corresponding to the three word-boundary gaps that are heard subjectively. The segmentation issue then highlights another difficulty encountered by automatic speech-recognition systems that function with purely bottom-up processing. If speech is continuous, it is virtually impossible for the recognition system to know the boundaries that separate the words in order to perform the semantic analysis without knowing what the words are already.

Top-Down Processing of Speech

The description presented so far has emphasized the bottom-up analysis of speech. However, top-down processing in speech recognition is just as essential as it is in reading. The two features that contrast speech perception with reading—the invariance problem and the segmentation problem—make it difficult to analyze the meaning of a physical unit of speech (bottom-up) without having some prior hypothesis concerning what that unit is likely to be. To make matters more difficult, the serial and transient nature of the auditory message prevents a more detailed and leisurely bottom-up processing of the physical stimulus. That is, one cannot reevaluate previous spoken words as easily as one can glance back to an earlier portion of text. This restriction therefore forces a great reliance on top-down processing.

Demonstrations of top-down or context-dependent processing in speech perception are quite robust. In one experiment, Miller and Isard (1963) compared recognition of degraded word strings between (1) random word lists ("loses poetry spots total wasted"), (2) lists that provided some context by virtue only of their syntactic (grammatical) structure but had no semantic content ("sloppy poetry leaves nuclear minutes"), and (3) full semantic and syntactic context ("A witness signed the official document"). The three kinds of lists were presented under varying levels of masking noise. Miller and Isard's data suggest the same trade-off between signal quality and top-down context that was observed by Tulving, Mandler, and Baumal (1964) in the recognition of print. Less context, resulting from the loss of either grammatical or semantic constraints, required greater signal strength to achieve equal performance.

It is apparent that the perception of speech proceeds in a manner similar to the perception of print, through a highly complex, iterative mixture of bottom-up and top-down processing. While lower-level analyzers at the acoustic-feature and syllable level progress in a bottom-up fashion, the context provided at the semantic and syntactic levels generates hypotheses concerning what a particular speech sound should be. The subjective gaps that are heard between word boundaries of continuous speech also give evidence for the dominant role of knowledge-driven top-down processing. Since such gaps are not present in the physical stimulus, they must result from the top-down processes that decide when each word ends and the next begins.

Applications of Voice Recognition Research

Research and theory of speech perception have contributed to two major categories of applications. First, understanding of how humans perceive speech and employ context-driven top-down processing in recognition has aided efforts to design speech-recognition systems that perform the same task. Such systems are becoming increasingly desirable for conveying responses when the hands might be busy and unavailable, or when visual feedback is not available to guide a manual response. They have the potential to replace keyboard typing, as we discuss in Chapter 9.

The second major contribution has been to measure and predict the effects on speech comprehension of various kinds of distortion, which was a source of the Tenerife disaster. Such distortion may be extrinsic to the speech signal—for example, in a noisy environment like an industrial plant. Alternatively, the distortion may be intrinsic to the speech signal when the acoustic wave form is transformed in some fashion, either when synthesized speech is used in computer-generated auditory displays or when a communication channel for human speech is distorted. The following describes how the disruptive effects of speech distortion are represented and identifies some possible corrective techniques.

As discussed earlier, natural speech is conveyed by the differing amplitudes of the various phonemes distributed across a wide range of frequencies. Thus, it is possible to construct a spectrum of the distribution of power at different frequencies generated by "typical" speech. Typical spectra generated by male and female speakers are shown in Figure 6.12. The effects of noise on speech comprehension will clearly depend on the spectrum of the noise involved. A noise that has frequencies identical to the speech spectrum will disrupt understanding more than a noise that has considerably greater power but occupies a narrower frequency range than speech.

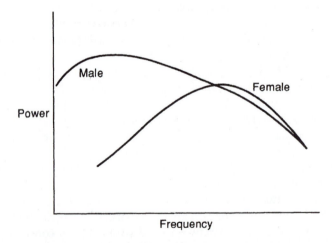

Figure 6.12 Typical power spectra of speech generated by male and female speakers.

Engineers are often interested in predicting the effects of background noise on speech understanding. The *articulation index* (Kryter, 1972) accomplishes this objective by dividing the speech frequency range into bands and computing the ratio of speech power to noise power within each band. These ratios are then weighted according to the relative contribution of a given frequency band to speech, and the weighted ratios are summed to provide the articulation index (AI). A simplified example of this calculation is shown in Figure 6.13. The spectrum of a relatively low-frequency noise is superimposed on a typical speech spectrum. The speech spectrum has been divided into four bands. The ratio of speech to noise power and the logarithm of this ratio are shown

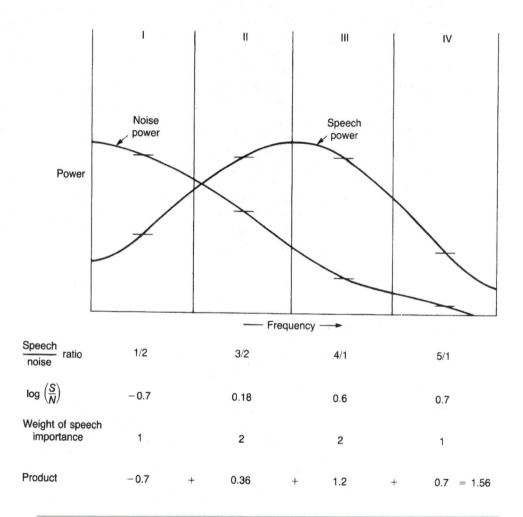

Figure 6.13   Schematic representation of the calculation of an articulation index. The speech spectrum has been divided into four bands weighted in importance by the relative power that each contributes to the speech signal.

below each band, and the contributions (weights) are shown below these. To the right is the sum of the weighted products, the AI, reflecting the extent to which the speech signal can be heard above the noise.

However, *hearing* is not the same as *comprehension*. From our discussions of bottom-up and top-down processing, it is apparent that the AI provides a measure of only bottom-up stimulus quality. A given AI may produce varying levels of comprehension, depending on the information content or redundancy available in the material and the degree of top-down processing used by the listener. To accommodate these factors, measures of *speech intelligibility* are derived by delivering vocal material of a particular level of redundancy over the speech channel in question and computing the percentage of words understood correctly. Naturally, for a given signal-to-noise ratio (defining signal quality and therefore the articulation index) the intelligibility will vary as a function of the redundancy or information content of the stimulus material. A restricted vocabulary produces greater intelligibility than an unrestricted one; words produce greater intelligibility than nonsense syllables; high-frequency words produce greater intelligibility than low-frequency words; and sentence context provides greater intelligibility than no context. Some of these effects on speech understanding are shown in Figure 6.14, which presents data analogous to those in Figure 6.2 concerning print.

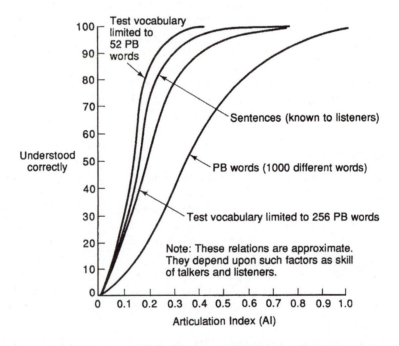

Figure 6.14 The relationship between the articulation index (AI) and the intelligibility of various types of speech test materials made up of phonetically balanced (PB) words and sentences.

Source: K. D. Kryter, "Speech Communications," in *Human Engineering Guide to System Design,* ed. H. P. Van Cott and R. G. Kinkade (Washington, DC: U.S. Government Printing Office).

The important implications of this discussion are twofold: (1) Either the AI or the speech-intelligibility measures by themselves are inherently ambiguous unless the redundancy of the transmitted material is carefully specified. (2) To reiterate a point made earlier in this chapter, data-driven, bottom-up processing may trade off with context-driven, top-down processing. For example, as we saw in the discussion of the KLM and Pan American runway disaster, a high level of expectancy for (or motivation to perceive) one meaning of a message, coupled with an ambiguous signal caused by poor-quality data or imprecise wording, can lead to an incorrect interpretation, sometimes with tragic consequences. Several other compelling examples of ambiguity and misinterpretation in aircraft communications are provided by Hawkins and Orlady (1993), and these are responsible for a large number of pilot errors (Nagel, 1988).

It is important to realize that limitations in signal quality can be compensated for by augmenting top-down processing—creating the ability to "guess" the message without actually (or completely) hearing it. In noisy environments, this may be accomplished by restricting the message set size (i.e., by using standardized vocabulary) or by providing redundant "carrier" sentences to convey a particular message. The latter procedure is analogous to the use of the redundant carrier syllables of the communications-code alphabet (alpha, bravo, charlie, etc.) to convey information concerning a single alphabetic character (a, b, c). A high level of redundancy in the message from air traffic control to the KLM pilot would probably have stopped the premature takeoff attempt and averted the disaster.

An experiment by Simpson (1976) demonstrated the effect of redundant carrier sentences on comprehension. Pilots listened to synthesized speech warnings presented in background noise. The warnings were either the critical words themselves ("fuel low") or the words embedded in a contextual carrier sentence ("Your fuel is low"). Recognition performance was markedly superior in the latter condition. Simpson also found that the beneficial effects of carrier sentences were greater for one-syllable words than for multisyllabic ones. The greater level of redundancy in the multisyllabic words reduces the need for additional redundancy in the carrier sentence.

Communications

Intuition as well as formal experiments tell us that there is more to communications than simply understanding the words and sentences in speech. The difference between the good and bad lecturer is often the difference between the one who uses gestures, pauses, and voice inflection and the one who reads the lecture in a monotone. A demonstration of the advantages of vision in voice communications is shown in Figure 6.15, which portrays data in the same general format as Figure 6.14. As shown in the figure, being able to see the speaker face to face greatly improves communications, particularly when signal quality is low. A similar advantage of face-face over auditory-only communications was observed in a study by Olson, Olson, and Meader (1995), in which participants engaged in generating a design solution.

Nonverbal Communications   There are four possible causes of differences between the two modes of verbal interaction (face-to-face communications and voice-only communications). All of these causes can influence the efficiency of information exchange.

1. *Visualizing the mouth.* Seeing a speaker's mouth move and form words is a useful redundant cue—particularly, one that can fill in the gaps when voice quality

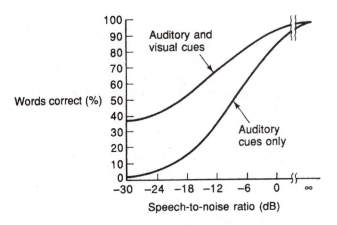

Figure 6.15 Intelligibility of words when perceived with and without visual cues from observing the speaker.

Source: W. Sumby and I. Pollack, "Visual Contribution to Speech Intelligibility in Noise," *Journal of Acoustical Society of America,* 26 (1954), pp. 212–215. Reprinted by permission.

is low. This skill of lipreading is often of critical importance to the hearing impaired. But to understand how important it is to our own speech perception, we need only consider how our understanding of speech in a movie is disrupted when the sound track is poorly dubbed, resulting in desynchronization between sound and mouth movement.

2. *Nonverbal cues.* Being able to see the speaker allows an added range of information conveyance—pointing and gesturing as well as facial cues such as the puzzled look or the nod of acknowledgment that cannot be seen over a conventional auditory channel (e.g., a telephone line). In one study, Chapanis Ochsman, Parrish, and Weeks (1972) compared problem-solving performance between the two modes and concluded that a face-to-face configuration led to a 14 percent reduction in the time required for a pair of subjects to solve geographical-location and equipment-assembly problems. The authors also found that this mode actually *increased* the amount of conversation between the members of a team.

3. *Disambiguity.* Extra nonverbal cues may resolve ambiguous messages by allowing the speaker to follow up on a puzzled look or other cues suggesting that the listener may have misinterpreted the message. Nonverbal cues and disambiguity appear to combine in allowing face-to-face conversation to be more flexible and less formal. This difference is reflected in the greater frequency of formal "turn taking" with audio only dialogues, as well as a greater overall number of words spoken when visual feedback was absent (Boyle et al., 1994; Olson, Olson, & Meader, 1995).

4. *Shared knowledge of action.* In coordinated team performance, such as that typifying the flight crew of an aircraft on a landing approach, a great amount of information is exchanged and shared simply by seeing the actions that a team

member has taken (or failed to take), even if this information is totally unrelated to the contents of oral communications (Segal, 1995). For example, the copilot, seeing that the pilot has turned on the autopilot, will be likely to adopt a different mental set as a consequence. The shared knowledge gained by knowing where each member is looking, reaching, and manipulating potentially contributes a great deal to the smooth functioning of a team (Shaffer, Hendy, & White, 1988).

To the extent that this shared knowledge facilitates communications, changes in the physical configuration of the workspace can affect team performance. For example, the repositioning of flight controls from their position in front of the pilot to the side (the so-called *side-stick controller* used on some modern aircraft) reduces the amount of shared knowledge about control activity between the pilot and copilot, since the control activity of one can no longer be easily seen by the other (Beatson, 1989; Segal, 1995). The advances of modern technology, in which spatially distributed dials and keys may be replaced by centralized CRT displays and chording keyboards, may also inhibit the shared knowledge of action by reducing the amount of head and hand movement that can be seen by the coworker (Wiener, 1989).

Video Mediated Communications The greater advantages of face-to-face over auditory-only communications suggests the advantages to communication that could be achieved by allowing remote video to accompany the voice. While video channels do appear to foster some improvement over audio only (Olson, Olson, & Meador, 1995), investigators have not found it to support the same quality of performance as face-to-face (Doherty-Sneddon et al., 1997; Olson, Olson, & Meador, 1995). Part of the deficiency of remote video can be accounted for by poorer quality (than direct viewing) of both video and auditory information, as well as the problems of synchronizing the two channels (O'Connaill, Whittker, & Wilbur, 1993; O'Malley et al., 1996). But even with highest-quality video and well-synchronized channels, Doherty-Sneddon et al. (1997) found that performance on a collaborative navigation task was less efficient (more words needed) in the remote video condition than with face-to-face dialogue, and the style of remote video communications appeared similar to that of audio only (more formal "turn taking," fewer interruptions).

Crew Resource Management The human factors community has become very much aware of the importance of effective communications in multioperator environments to support team performance. There is also an increasing awareness that characteristics of the social climate between participants in a dialogue can greatly enhance or degrade that communications pattern and thereby have a strong influence on the efficiency of system performance.

The environment in which this issue has been most directly addressed— because it is potentially relevant to the safety of so many—is in the aircraft flight deck, and here the issue is characterized by the label of cockpit resource management (Wiener, Kanki, & Helmreich, 1993; Orlady & Orlady, 1999). The concern for social climate and flight deck communications originates from the analysis of several accidents and near accidents in which the copilot or flight engineer, having seen or suspected that the pilot was in error, either failed to call it to the pilot's attention or did so in such an ambivalent and deferential manner that the error was not corrected (Foushee, 1984, Helmreich, Merritt, & Wilhelm, 1999). Similar incidents are easy to envision in other environments where there is a clear status difference between two operators who must share and exchange information—the surgeon and nurse in the operating room (Helmreich & Merritt, 1998), the pilot and air traffic controller, or the corporate executive and administrative assistant. In these cases the study of group interactions is more generally labeled that of *crew* resource management.

The occurrence of such incidents in aviation has led to the establishment of crew resource management training programs, which have emphasized the importance of two-way information exchanges to flight deck safety (Orlady & Orlady, 1999; Helmreich, Merritt, & Wilhelm, 1999). The impact of these programs on flight safety has been well documented (Diehl, 1991), and there is little doubt that effective cockpit communications has led to less error-prone performance in flight simulator studies (Orasanu & Fischer, 1997). For example, analyzing multicrew simulation studies at NASA Ames Research Center, Foushee and Helmreich (1988) characterized crews that are effective in handling simulated emergencies as sharing more communications, acknowledging communications more frequently, and demonstrating a greater use of commands or assertive statements. It should also be noted that with the effective crews, these assertive statements are directed both up and down the formal chain of command, from pilot to copilot and from copilot to pilot. It is as if each member is aware of a clearly defined responsibility to communicate and is not hesitant to do so. Foushee and Helmreich also observe better performance in flight crews that have flown together for a longer period of time—as if the communications patterns that have been established for a longer duration have had a chance to develop more effectively (Kanki & Foushee, 1989).

An operational example of the successful applications of crew resource management principles is provided by the analysis of communications in the cockpit of the severely crippled United Airlines flight 232 before it crashed near Sioux City, Iowa. The study revealed the strong influence of effective communications patterns, which allowed the plane to be guided into a landing with enough control to avoid a complete disaster. The pilot of the aircraft attributed the success of the landing to the training he received in cockpit resource management (Predmore, 1991).

In summary, the research on communications suggests clearly that the performance of the whole multioperator team is greater than the sum of the parts. This conclusion comes as no surprise to those who have seen a sports team with a collection of superstars fail to meet its expectations because of poor teamwork. The data reemphasize one theme introduced in Chapter 1: The design of effective systems for information display and control with the single operator is a necessary but not sufficient condition for effective human performance.

TRANSITION: PERCEPTION AND MEMORY

Our discussion here and in the previous chapters has been presented under the categories of spatial and verbal processes in perception. Yet it is quite difficult to divorce these processes from those related to memory and learning. There are four reasons for this close association:

1. Perceptual categorizations, as we saw, were guided by expectancy, as manifest in top-down processing. Expectancy was based on recent experience (the active contents of working memory) and the contents of permanent or long-term

memory. Indeed, the rules for perceptual categorization are formed only after repeated exposure to a stimulus. These exposures must be remembered to form the categories.

2. In many tasks when perception is not automatic, such as those related to navigation and comprehension, perceptual categorization must operate hand in hand with activities in working memory.

3. The dichotomy that distinguished codes of perceiving into spatial and verbal categories has a direct analog in terms of two codes of working memory.

4. Perception, comprehension, and understanding are necessary precursors for new information to be permanently stored in long-term memory—the issue of learning and training.

In the following chapter, we discuss these topics of memory and learning in detail.

REFERENCES

Bailey, R. W. (1989). *Human performance engineering using human factors/ergonomics to achieve computer system usability* (2d ed.). Englewood Cliffs, NJ: Prentice Hall.

Barnett, B. J. (1990). Aiding type and format compatibility for decision aid interface design. *Proceedings of the 34th annual meeting of the Human Factors Society* (pp. 1552–1556). Santa Monica, CA: Human Factors Society.

Beatson, S. (1989, April 2). Is America ready to "fly by wire"? *Washington Post*, pp. C3–C4.

Biederman, I. (1987). Recognition-by-components: A theory of human image understanding. *Psychological Review, 94*(2), 115–147.

Biederman, I. (1998). The certainty of viewpoint invarient information in visual recognition tasks. In D. Gopher & A. Koriat (Eds.), *Attention and performance XVII*. Cambridge, MA: MIT Press.

Biederman, I., Mezzanotte, R. J., Rabinowitz, J. C., Francolin, C. M., & Plude, D. (1981). Detecting the unexpected in photo interpretation. *Human Factors, 23*, 153–163.

Booher, H. R. (1975). Relative comprehensibility of pictorial information and printed words in proceduralized instructions. *Human Factors, 17*, 266–277.

Bower, G. H., Clark, M. C., Lesgold, A. M., & Winzenz, D. (1969). Hierarchical retrieval schemes in the recall of categorical word lists. *Journal of Verbal Learning & Verbal Behavior, 8*, 323–343.

Boyle, E. A., Anderson, A. H., & Newlands, A. (1994). The effect of eye contact on dialogue and performance in a cooperative problem-solving task. *Language & Speech, 37*, 1–20.

Bransford, J. D., & Johnson, M. K. (1972). Contextual prerequisites for understanding: Some investigations of comprehension and recall. *Journal of Verbal Learning & Verbal Behavior, 11*, 717–726.

Braun, C. C., & Silver, N. C. (1995). Interaction of signal word and colour on warning labels: Differences in perceived hazard and behavioural compliance. *Ergonomics, 38*(11), 2207–2220.

Brems, D. J., & Whitten, W. B. (1987). Learning and preference for icon-based interface. *Proceedings of the 31st annual meeting of the Human Factors Society* (pp. 125–129). Santa Monica, CA: Human Factors Society.

Broadbent, D. E. (1977). Language and ergonomics. *Applied Ergonomics, 8*, 15–18.

Broadbent, D., & Broadbent, M. H. (1977). General shape and local detail in word perception. In S. Dornic (Ed.), *Attention and performance VI*. Hillsdale, NJ: Erlbaum.

Broadbent, D., & Broadbent, M. H. (1980). Priming and the passive/active model of word recognition. In R. Nickerson (Ed.), *Attention and performance VIII*. New York: Academic Press.

Camacho, M. J., Steiner, B. A., & Berson, B. L. (1990). Icons versus alphanumerics in pilot-vehicle interfaces. *Proceedings of the 34th annual meeting of the Human Factors Society* (pp. 11–15). Santa Monica, CA: Human Factors Society.

Carpenter, P. A., & Just, M. A. (1975). Sentence comprehension: A psycholinguistic processing model of verification. *Psychological Review, 82*(1), 45–73.

Chapanis, A. (1965). Words words words. *Human Factors, 7*, 1–17.

Chapanis, A., Ochsman, R. B., Parrish, R. N., & Weeks, G. D. (1972). Studies in interactive communication: I. The effects of four communication modes on the behavior of teams during cooperative problem-solving. *Human Factors, 14*(6), 487–509.

Clark, H. H., & Chase, W. G. (1972). On the process of comparing sentences against pictures. *Cognitive Psychology, 3*, 472–517.

Corcoran, D. W., & Weening, D. L. (1967). Acoustic factors in proofreading. *Nature, 214*, 851–852.

Crocoll, W. M., & Coury, B. G. (1990). Status or recommendation: Selecting the type of information for decision aiding. *Proceedings of the 34th annual meeting of the Human Factors Society* (pp. 1524–1528). Santa Monica, CA: Human Factors Society.

DeSota, C. B., London, M., & Handel, S. (1965). Social reasoning and spatial paralogic. *Journal of Personal & Social Psychology, 2*, 513–521.

Dewar, R. E. (1976). The slash obscures the symbol on prohibitive traffic signs. *Human Factors, 18*, 253–258.

Diehl, A. E. (1991). The effectiveness of training programs for preventing aircrew error. In R. S. Jensen (Ed.), *Proceedings of the 6th International Symposium on Aviation Psychology* (pp. 640–655). Columbus, OH: Dept. of Aviation, Ohio State University.

Doherty-Sneddon, G., Anderson, A., O'Malley, C., Langton, S., Garrod, S., & Bruce, V. (1997). Face-to-face and video-mediated communication: A comparison of dialogue structure and task performance. *Journal of Experimental Psychology: Applied, 3*(2), 105–125.

Dumas, J. S., & Redish, J. (1986). Using plain English in designing the user interface. *Proceedings of the 30th annual meeting of the Human Factors Society* (pp. 1207–1211). Santa Monica, CA: Human Factors Society.

Dwyer, F. M. (1967). Adapting visual illustrations for effective learning. *Harvard Educational Review, 37*, 250–263.

Ehrenreich, S. (1982). The myth about abbreviations. *Proceedings of the 1982 IEEE International Conference on Cybernetics and Society*. New York: Institute of Electrical and Electronic Engineers.

Ellis, N. C., & Hill, S. E. (1978). A comparison of seven-segment numerics. *Human Factors, 20*, 655–660.

Ellis, S. R., & Hitchcock, R. J. (1986). The emergence of Zipf's law: Spontaneous encoding optimization by users of a command language. *IEEE Transactions on Systems, Man, and Cybernetics, SMC–16*(3), 423–427.

Ergonomics. (1995). Special issue: Warnings in research and practice. *Ergonomics, 38*(11).

Fisk, A. D., Ackerman, P. L., & Schneider, W. (1987). Automatic and controlled processing theory and its applications to human factors problems. In P. A. Hancock (Ed.), *Human factors psychology* (pp. 159–197). North Holland, Netherlands: Elsevier Science Publishers B.V.

Foushee, H. C. (1984). Dyads and triads at 35,000 feet: Factors affecting group process and aircrew performance. *American Psychology, 39*, 885–893.

Foushee, H. C., & Helmreich, R. L. (1988). Group interaction and flightcrew performance. In E. Wiener & D. Nagel (Eds.), *Human factors in aviation*. San Diego, CA: Academic Press.

Fowler, F. D. (1980). Air traffic control problems: A pilot's view. *Human Factors, 22*, 645–654.

Frantz, J. P. (1994). Effect of location and procedural explicitness on user processing of and compliance with product warnings. *Human Factors, 36*(3), 532–546.

Gaver, W. W. (1986). Auditory icons: Using sound in computer interfaces. *Human-Computer Interaction, 33*, 167–177.

Gibson, E. J. (1969). *Principles of perceptual learning and development*. Englewood Cliffs, NJ: Prentice Hall.

Grether, W., & Baker, C. A. (1972). Visual presentation of information. In H. P. Van Cott & R. G. Kinkade (Eds.), *Human engineering guide to system design*. Washington, DC: U.S. Government Printing Office.

Haber, R. N., & Schindler, R. M. (1981). Error in proofreading: Evidence of syntactic control of letter processing? *Journal of Experimental Psychology: Human Perception & Performance, 7*, 573–579.

Hastie, R. (1982). *An empirical evaluation of five methods of instructing the jury* (Final Report Grant 78-NI-AX–0146). Washington, DC: National Institute of Justice.

Hawkins, F. H., & Orlady, H. W. (1993). *Human factors in flight* (2d ed.). Brookfield, VT: Ashgate.

Healy, A. F. (1976). Detection errors on the word "the." *Journal of Experimental Psychology: Human Perception & Performance, 2*, 235–242.

Helmreich, R. L., & Merritt, A. C. (1998). *Culture at work in aviation and medicine*. Brookfield, VT: Ashgate.

Helmreich, R. L., Merritt, A. C., & Wilhelm, J. A. (1999). The evolution of crew resource management training. *International Journal of Aviation Psychology, 9*, 19–32.

Hickox, J. C., & Wickens, C. D. (1999). 3-D electronic maps, design implications for the effects of elevation angle disparity, complexity, and feature type. *Journal of Experimental Psychology: Applied, 5*.

Huggins, A. (1964). Distortion of temporal patterns of speech: Interruptions and alterations. *Journal of the Acoustical Society of America, 36*, 1055–1065.

Just, M. T., & Carpenter, P. A. (1980). Cognitive processes in reading: Models based on reader's eye fixation. In C. A. Prefetti & A. M. Lesgold (Eds.), *Interactive processes and reading*. Hillsdale, NJ: Erlbaum.

Kanki, B. G., & Foushee, H. C. (1989, May). Communication as group process mediator of aircrew performance. *Aviation, Space, and Environmental Medicine*, pp. 402–410.

Kintch, W., & Van Dijk, T. A. (1978). Toward a model of text comprehension and reproduction. *Psychological Review, 85*, 363–394.

Klemmer, E. T. (1969). Grouping of printed digits for manual entry. *Human Factors, 11*, 397–400.

Kramer, A. F., Strayer, D. L., & Buckley, J. (1990). Development and transfer of automatic processing. *Journal of Experimental Psychology: Human Perception & Performance, 16*(3), 505–522.

Kryter, K. D. (1972). Speech communications. In H. P. Van Cott & R. G. Kinkade (Eds.), *Human engineering guide to system design*. Washington, DC: U.S. Government Printing Office.

LaBerge, D. (1973). Attention and the measurement of perceptual learning. *Memory & Cognition, 1*, 268–276.

Landaur, T. (1995). *The trouble with computers*. Cambridge, MA: MIT Press.

Lindsay, P. H., & Norman, D. A. (1972). *Human information processing.* New York: Academic Press.

Massaro, D. W. (1975). *Experimental psychology and information processing.* Chicago: Rand McNally College Publishing.

Mayer, R. (1997). Multimedia instruction: Are we asking the right questions. *Educational Psychologist, 32,* 1–19.

Mayer, R. (1999). Instructional technology. In F. Durso (Ed.) *Handbook of Applied Cognition.* Cambridge University Press.

McConkie, G. W. (1983). Eye movements and perception during reading. In K. Raynor (Ed.), *Eye movements in reading.* New York: Academic Press.

McMillan, G. R., Eggleston, R. G., & Anderson, T. R. (1997). Nonconventional controls. In G. Salvendy (Ed.), *Handbook of human factors and ergonomics* (pp. 729–771). New York: John Wiley & Sons.

Miller, G., & Isard, S. (1963). Some perceptual consequences of linguistic rules. *Journal of Verbal Learning & Verbal Behavior, 2,* 217–228.

Moses, F. L., & Ehrenreich, S. L. (1981). Abbreviations for automated systems. In R. Sugarman (Ed.), *Proceedings of the 25th annual meeting of the Human Factors Society.* Santa Monica, CA: Human Factors Society.

Nagel, D. (1988). Pilot error. In E. Wiener & D. Nagel (Eds.), *Human factors in modern aviation.* Orlando, FL: Academic Press.

Navon, D. (1977). Forest before trees: The presence of global features in visual perception. *Cognitive Psychology, 9,* 353–383.

Neisser, U. (1967). *Cognitive psychology.* Englewood Cliffs, NJ: Prentice Hall.

Neisser, U., Novick, R., & Lazer, R. (1964). Searching for novel targets. *Perceptual and Motor Skills, 19,* 427–432.

Newsome, S. L., & Hocherlin, M. E. (1989). When "not" is not bad: A reevaluation of the use of negatives. *Proceedings of the 33rd annual meeting of the Human Factors Society* (pp. 229–234). Santa Monica, CA: Human Factors Society.

Norcio, A. F. (1981). *Human memory processes for comprehending computer programs* (Technical Report AS–2–81). Annapolis, MD: U.S. Naval Academy, Applied Sciences Department.

Norman, D. A. (1981). The trouble with UNIX. *Datamation, 27*(12), 139–150.

Nugent, W. A. (1987). A comparative assessment of computer-based media for presenting job task instructions. *Proceedings of the 31st annual meeting of the Human Factors Society* (pp. 696–700). Santa Monica, CA: Human Factors Society.

O'Connaill, B., Whittker, S., & Wilbur, S. (1993). Conversations over videoconferences: An evaluation of videomediated interaction. *Human-Computer Interaction, 8,* 389–428.

Olson, J. S., Olson, G. M., & Meader, D. K. (1995). What mix of video and audio is useful for remote real-time work. *Proceedings of the Conference on Human Factors in Computing Systems* (pp. 33–45). Denver, CO: Academic Press.

O'Malley, C., Langton, S., Anderson, A., Doherty-Sneddon, G., & Bruce, V. (1996). Comparison of face-to-face and video-mediated interaction. *Interacting with Computers, 8,* 177–192.

Orasanu, J., & Fischer, U. (1997). Finding decisions in natural environments: The view from the cockpit. In C. E. Zsambok & G. Klein (Eds.), *Naturalistic decision making* (pp. 343–358). Mahwah, NJ: Erlbaum.

Orlady, H. W., & Orlady, L. M. (1999). *Human factors in multi-crew flight operations.* Brookfield, VT: Ashgate.

Palmer, S. E. (1975). The effects of contextual scenes on the identification of objects. *Memory & Cognition, 3*, 519–526.

Plath, D. W. (1970). The readability of segmented and conventional numerals. *Human Factors, 12*, 493–497.

Potter, M. C., & Faulconer, B. A. (1975). Time to understand pictures and words. *Nature, 253*, 437–438.

Predmore, S. C. (1991). Micro-coding of cockpit communications in accident analyses: Crew coordination in the United Airlines flight 232 accident. In R. S. Jensen (Ed.), *Proceedings of the 6th International Symposium on Aviation Psychology*. Columbus, Ohio State University, Department of Aviation.

Reicher, G. M. (1969). Perceptual recognition as a function of meaningfulness of stimulus material. *Journal of Experimental Psychology, 81*, 275–280.

Rogers, W. A, Rosseau, G. K., & Fisk, A. D. (1999). Applications of attention research. In F. Durso (Ed.) *Handbook of Applied Cognition*. West Sussix U.K.: John Wiley & Sons.

Rumelhart, D. (1977). *Human information processing*. New York: Wiley.

Rumelhart, D. E., & McClelland, J. L. (1986). *Parallel distributed processing: Explorations in the microstructure of cognition* (vol. 1). Cambridge, MA: MIT Press.

Schmidt, J. K., & Kysor, K. P. (1987). Designing airline passenger safety cards. *Proceedings of the 31st annual meeting of the Human Factors Society* (pp. 51–55). Santa Monica, CA: Human Factors Society.

Schneider, W. (1985). Training high-performance skills: Fallacies and guidelines. *Human Factors, 27*(3), 285–300.

Schneider, W., Dumais, S. T., & Shiffrin, R. M. (1984). Automatic and control processing and attention. In R. Parasuraman & D. R. Davies (Eds.), *Varieties of attention* (pp. 1–27). Orlando, FL: Academic Press.

Schneider, W., & Fisk, A. D. (1984). Automatic category search and its transfer. *Journal of Experimental Psychology: Learning, Memory, and Cognition, 10*, 1–15.

Schneider, W., & Shiffrin, R. M. (1977). Controlled and automatic human information processing I: Detection, search, and attention. *Psychological Review, 84*, 1–66.

Segal, L. (1995). Designing team workstations: The choreography of teamwork. In P. A. Hancock, J. M. Flach, J. Caird, & K. J. Vicente (Eds.), *Local applications of the ecological approach to human-machine systems* (vol. 2). Hillsdale, NJ: Erlbaum.

Shaffer, M. T., Hendy, K. C., & White, L. R. (1988). An empirically validated task analysis (EVTA) of low level Army helicopter operations. *Proceedings of the 32nd annual meeting of the Human Factors Society* (pp. 178–183). Santa Monica, CA: Human Factors Society.

Sheridan, T. E., & Ferrell, L. (1974). *Man-machine systems*. Cambridge, MA: MIT Press.

Simpson, C. (1976, May). Effects of linguistic redundancy on pilot's comprehension of synthesized speeds. *Proceedings of the 12th Annual Conference on Manual Control* (NASA TM-X-73, 170). Washington, DC: U.S. Government Printing Office.

Spanish Ministry of Transportation and Communications. (1978). Report of collision between PAA B–747 and KLM B–747 at Tenerife. *Aviation Week & Space Technology, 109* (November 20), 113–121; (November 27), 67–74.

Spencer, K. (1988). *The psychology of educational technology and instructional media*. London: Routledge.

Stone, D. E., & Gluck, M. D. (1980). *How do young adults read directions with and without pictures?* (Technical Report). Ithaca, NY: Cornell University, Department of Education.

Sweller, J., & Chandler, P. (1994). Why some material is difficult to learn. *Cognition and Instruction, 12,* 185–233.

Sweller, J., Chandler, P., Tierney, P., & Cooper, M. (1990). Cognitive load as a factor in the structuring of technical material. *Journal of Experimental Psychology: General, 119,* 176–192.

Taylor, R. M., & Selcon, S. J. (1990). Cognitive quality and situational awareness with advanced aircraft attitude displays. *Proceedings of the 34th annual meeting of the Human Factors Society* (pp. 26–30). Santa Monica, CA: Human Factors Society.

Tindall-Ford, S., Chandler, P., & Sweller, J. (1997). When two sensory modes are better than one. *Journal of Experimental Psychology: Applied, 3*(4), 257–287.

Tinker, M. A. (1955). Prolonged reading tasks in visual research. *Journal of Applied Psychology, 39,* 444–446.

Tulving, E., Mandler, G., & Baumal, R. (1964). Interaction of two sources of information in tachistoscopic word recognition. *Canadian Journal of Psychology, 18,* 62–71.

Vartabedian, A. G. (1972). The effects of letter size, case, and generation method on CRT display search time. *Human Factors, 14,* 511–519.

Wetzel, Radtke, & Stern (1994).

Whitaker, L. A., & CuQlock-Knopp, V. G. (1995). Human exploration and perception in off-road navigation. In P. A. Hancock, J. M. Flach, J. Caird, & K. J. Vicente (Eds.), *Local applications of the ecological approach to human-machine systems.* Hillsdale, NJ: Erlbaum.

Whitaker, L. A., & Stacey, S. (1981). Response times to left and right directional signals. *Human Factors, 23,* 447–452.

Wickelgren, W. A. (1979). *Cognitive psychology.* Englewood Cliffs, NJ: Prentice-Hall.

Wickens, C. D., & Carswell, C. M. (1995). The proximity compatibility principle: Its psychological foundation and its relevance to display design. *Human Factors, 37*(3).

Wickens, C. D., Gordon, S., & Liu, Y. (1998). *An introduction to human factors engineering.* New York: Addison Wesley Longman.

Wickens, C. D., Mavor, A. S., Parasuraman, R., & McGee, J. P. (Eds.). (1998). *The future of air traffic control: Human operators and automation.* Washington, DC: National Academy Press.

Wiener, E. L. (1989). Reflections on human error: Matters of life and death. *Proceedings of the 33rd annual meeting of the Human Factors Society* (pp. 1–7). Santa Monica, CA: Human Factors Society.

Wiener, E. L., Kanki, B. G., & Helmreich, R. L. (1993). *Cockpit resource management.* San Diego, CA: Academic Press.

Wogalter, M. S., Allison, S., & McKenna, N. (1989). Effects of cost and social influence on warning compliance. *Human Factors, 3* (2), 133–140.

Wogalter, M. S., & Silver, N. C. (1995). Warning signal words: Connoted strength and understandability by children, elders, and non-native English speakers. *Ergonomics, 38*(11), 2188–2206.

Wogalter, M. S., et al. (1987). Effectiveness of warnings. *Human Factors, 29,* 599–612.

Wright, P., & Barnard, P. (1975). Just fill in this form—A review for designers. *Applied Ergonomics, 6*(4), 213–220.

Yallow, E. (1980). *Individual differences in learning from verbal and figural materials* (Aptitudes Research Project Technical Report No. 13). Palo Alto, CA: Stanford University, School of Education.

Yantis, S. (1993). Stimulus driven attentional capture. *Current Directions in Psychological Science, 2,* 156–161.

Zeitlin, L. R. (1994). Failure to follow safety instructions: Faulty communications or risky decisions? *Human Factors, 36,* 172–181.

Memory and Training

OVERVIEW

Failures of memory often plague the human operator. These may be as trivial as forgetting a phone number or as involved as forgetting the procedures to run a word-processing program. Operators may forget to perform a critical item in a checklist (Degani & Wiener, 1990), or an air traffic controller may forget a "temporary" command issued to a pilot (Danaher, 1980). In 1996, a ramp agent forgot to check the contents of cargo boxes for a ValuJet DC–9. The boxes contained uncapped, full, oxygen generators (mechanics had forgotten to put safety caps on them). One of the generators engaged while the DC–9 was in flight, causing a fire that sent the airplane into the Everglades, killing over a hundred people (Langewiesche, 1998).

When we use a computer system to access information, we may find that information we need while inputting information on one screen can only be found on another. Thus, we have to hold information in memory while we switch between screens, introducing the possibility of error. The van driver discussed in Chapter 1 had to take a second glance down at the screen of his dynamic map display to check his exit number, because he forgot it. The second glance diverted his attention from the road at a critical time, contributing to his accident.

Clearly, then, the success or failure of human memory can have a major impact on the usefulness and safety of a system. As noted in Chapter 1, *memory* may be thought of as the store of information. In this chapter we focus on two different storage systems with different durations: *working memory* and *long-term memory*. Working memory is the temporary, attention-demanding store that we use to retain new information (like a new phone number) until we use it (dial it). We also use working memory as a kind of "workbench" of consciousness where we examine, evaluate, transform, and compare different mental representations. We might use working memory, for example, to carry out mental arithmetic or predict what will happen if we schedule jobs one way instead of another. Finally, working memory is used to hold new information until we give it a more permanent status in memory—that is, encode it into long-term memory. Long-term memory is our storehouse of facts about the world and about how to do things.

Both memory systems may be thought of in the context of a three-stage representation, shown in Figure 7.1. The first stage, *encoding*, describes the process of putting

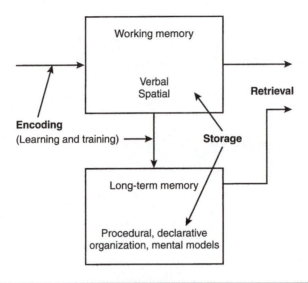

Figure 7.1 A representation of memory functions.

things into a memory system. Encoding can take two forms, shown in the diagram: encoding into working memory, or transferring information from working memory into long-term memory. We use the terms *learning* or *training* to refer to this latter transfer of information. Learning describes how the information transfer occurs, whereas training refers to explicit, intentional techniques used by designers and teachers to maximize learning efficiency. Our concern will be primarily with training.

Storage, the second stage, refers to the *way* in which information is held or represented in the two memory systems. The terms that we use to describe it are different for working memory, where we emphasize spatial versus verbal codes, than for long-term memory, where we emphasize declarative and procedural knowledge and mental models.

The third stage, *retrieval*, refers to our ability to access information in memory. Here we contrast successful retrieval with the various causes of retrieval failure, or *forgetting*. Sometimes material simply cannot be retrieved. At other times it is retrieved incorrectly, as when we mix up the steps in a procedure.

In this chapter, we describe the properties of working memory, its spatial and verbal representations, and its limited capacity. We then discuss the concept of chunking and how it expands working memory's limited capacity. Chunking is tied to expertise in a domain, which leads naturally to a discussion of expertise. We discuss both how expertise interacts with working memory to produce what is called *skilled memory*, and how working memory is involved in planning and problem-solving tasks. Finally, we describe long-term memory, focusing heavily on the issue of encoding through a discussion of training. Particular emphasis is given to *transfer of training*—how skills and knowledge acquired in one domain transfer to another. We then discuss different ways in which knowledge is represented in long-term memory, and we conclude with a discussion of retrieval and forgetting from long-term memory.

WORKING MEMORY

Working memory is typically defined as having three core components, (Baddeley, 1995). The verbal component comprises two subsystems: the phonological store and articulatory loop. The *phonological store* represents information in linguistic form, typically as words and sounds. The information can be rehearsed by articulating those words and sounds, either vocally or subvocally, using an *articulatory loop*. In contrast, the spacial component called the *visuospatial sketchpad* represents information in an analog, spatial form, often typical of visual images (Logie, 1995). Each of these components stores information in a particular form, or *code*. Use of the spatial, dynamic displays discussed in Chapters 4 and 5 would typically involve activity in the visuospatial sketchpad; in contrast, much of the processing of language, the topic of Chapter 6, would involve the phonological store and articulatory loop. The third component of Baddeley's model is the *central executive*, which controls working memory activity and assigns attentional resources to the other subsystems. The topic of executive control in selecting responses will also be discussed in Chapter 9.

The practical implications of different working memory codes are based on three phenomena: (1) The sketchpad and phonological store are susceptible to interference from different sorts of concurrent activities, which has implications for tasks performed concurrently. (2) The control and management activities of the central executive are also susceptible to interference, which again has implications for concurrent task performance. (3) The relationship of codes to display modalities has implications for auditory versus visual displays and verbal versus spatial displays. We discuss each of these implications in turn.

Code Interference

The verbal-phonetic and visual-spatial codes of working memory appear to function more cooperatively than competitively. One implication of this cooperation is that the two codes do not compete for the same limited processing resources or attention. That is, if two tasks employ different working memory codes, they will be time-shared more efficiently than if they share a common code, a theme to be discussed in more detail in Chapter 11.

The research of Baddeley and colleagues (Baddeley, 1986, 1995; Baddeley & Hitch, 1974; Logie, 1995) has contributed substantially to the understanding of this dichotomy, in terms of both the kind of material that is manipulated within working memory (spatial-visual or verbal-phonetic) and the separate processing resources used by each. In an important early experiment, Brooks (1968) required subjects to perform a series of mental operations in spatial working memory (the visuospatial sketchpad). Subjects imagined a capital letter, such as the letter F, as depicted in Figure 7.2. They were then asked to "walk" around the perimeter of the letter, indicating in turn whether each corner was in a designated orientation (e.g., facing the lower right). The yes and no answers were indicated by vocal articulation (verbal response) or by pointing to a column of Y's and N's (spatial response). Brooks found that performance was better in the verbal than in the spatial condition, suggesting that the verbal response code used different resources from those underlying the "walking" operations in spatial working memory. The greater resource competition with spatial working memory in the spatial response condition produced greater interference.

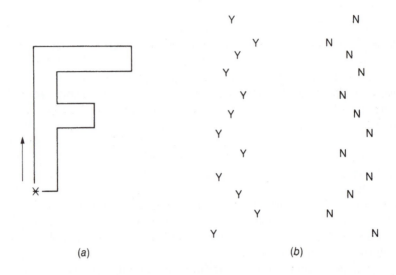

(a)   (b)

Figure 7.2 (a) Example of a stimulus in Brooks's study. (b) Display used in pointing task.
Source: L. R. Brooks, "Spatial and Verbal Components in the Act of Recall," *Canadian Journal of Psychology, 22* (1968), pp. 350–351. Copyright 1968 by the Canadian Psychological Association. Reproduced by permission.

In a second investigation by Brooks (1968), the spatial working memory task was replaced with one relying on verbal working memory (the phonological store). Subjects imagined a familiar sentence (e.g., "The quick brown fox jumped over the lazy dog") and indicated if each word was a particular kind of word (e.g., noun). Once again, responses were indicated by speech or by pointing. Brooks now found the reverse pattern of interference: The verbal task was performed better with the spatial response than with the verbal one. In summary, performance was improved when different working memory codes underlie task and response.

The relevance of such findings may be summarized as follows: We have two forms of working memory. Each processes or retains qualitatively different kinds of information (spatial and visual versus verbal and phonetic), and each can be disrupted by different concurrent activities. *Therefore, tasks should be designed so that this disruption does not occur.* Tasks that impose high loads on spatial working memory (e.g., air traffic control) should not be performed concurrently with other tasks that also use the spatial working memory resources. Spatial tasks are less disrupted by employment of the phonological loop to handle subsidiary information-processing tasks (Liu & Wickens, 1992; Wickens & Liu, 1988). Correspondingly, tasks involving heavy demands on verbal working memory, such as editing texts, computing numbers, and using symbolic-based computers, are more disrupted by concurrent voice input and output than by visuospatial interaction (e.g., control with a mouse).

This guideline does not imply that the primary task display should be in a different format from the working memory code used in the task. As we will see in our discussion of compatibility, a visual-spatial display will be most compatible with the spatial representation in visual working memory. However, there are other circumstances when it is best to display information relevant to the primary task in a code different from that used to process primary task information.

For example, Wetherell (1979) concluded that navigational information for driving was better represented as a phonetic route-list than as a map because the latter interfered more with the spatial characteristics of driving. Wetherell had subjects learn directions between two points in a driving maze. Subjects learned by studying a written list of turns or a map, and then drove the route. Those trained with the map made more errors than those trained with the route-list. With map training, the visuospatial sketchpad is used to maintain the mental map in working memory and meet the spatial-processing demands of driving the route. With route-list training, navigational information could be maintained in the phonological store instead, freeing up the visuospatial sketchpad to meet the spatial processing demands of the driving task.

Similarly, spoken route lists improve performance in a driving task relative to a paper map (Dingus et al., 1997; Srinivasan & Jovanis, 1997), as discussed in Chapter 5. In terms of the working-memory model, spoken route-list information should be maintained in the phonological store, whereas the visuospatial sketchpad would be used for the driving task. As noted by Baddeley (1995), spoken information has obligatory access to the phonological store, so in fact, a spoken route list should be even more effective than a written one. Indeed, there is evidence to support this (Dingus et al., 1997).

If you have worked in a modern open office environment, you know that background noise and speech are commonplace, and you may believe that this interferes with your work. You would be right. When Banbury and Berry (1998) had subjects perform tasks similar to those that would be conducted in a real office (mental arithmetic, memory for text), they found that background noise (e.g., keyboard and printer sounds, a telephone ringing) degraded performance mildly on both tasks (relative to a quiet condition), but a much larger effect was evident when speech was present (with and without the noise). In terms of the working memory model, the obligatory access of the spoken word to the phonological store interfered with the mental arithmetic and text memory tasks that also drew on phonological store resources.

Kinesthetic Working Memory   Some researchers suggest that the model of working memory proposed by Baddeley (1986, 1995) should be amended to include an output, or kinesthetic component. For example, Smyth and Pendleton (1990) and Woodin and Heil (1996) note that although some spatial encoding of action is done in the visuospatial sketchpad, such as the planning of movement to targets external to the body, this activity can be distinguished from working memory for movements made to create specific configurations of body parts. These are referred to as *positional* and *patterned movements*, respectively. Using experienced rowers, Woodin and Heil (1996) found that patterned movements (tapping own body) interfered with memory for rowing positions, but not for positions in a 4 × 4 matrix. In contrast, positional movements (tapping black squares) interfered with memory for matrix positions, but not rowing positions. This result implies that working memory for positional movements appears to be something separate from the kind of information maintained in the visuospatial sketchpad.

Smyth and Waller (1998) found similar results for memory for routes on a climbing wall. One climbing route had greater visibility for hold locations, and the other required a greater range of hand and body configurations. Dynamic visual noise interfered more with recall of the former route; squeezing a pressure switch at a constant rate interfered more with recall of the latter route. Presumably, dynamic visual noise interfered with information in the visuospatial sketchpad, and squeezing the pressure switch interfered more with information in the kinesthetic working-memory component.

This distinction may be important for a large range of occupations involving physical movement. Sports are an obvious example, but others might include performing music or dance, surgery or dentistry, and various crafts or trades, such as carpentry, jewelry making, pottery, or glass blowing. Performance on those components of these tasks involving the visuospatial sketchpad will be affected by the simultaneous performance on tasks demanding sketchpad resources; conversely, performance on components involving the kinesthetic component will be interfered with by tasks also demanding kinesthetic resources. The carpenter making a difficult cut for a cabinet may find that visualizing the final product can be done with ease, but visualizing carrying out the next cut interferes with the current action.

Interference in the Central Executive

Recently, Baddeley and colleagues have turned their attention to the functioning of the central executive component of working memory. Baddeley (1996) described four core functions for the central executive: (1) to coordinate performance on multiple tasks, (2) to temporarily hold and manipulate information stored in long-term memory, (3) to change retrieval strategies from long-term memory, and (4) to attend selectively to stimuli. It is clear that success on many work-related tasks will therefore involve the activity of the central executive. The stockbroker must converse with a client while checking current prices of a volatile stock; the physician may compare the set of symptoms presented by a patient with those of previous patients; the scientist struggling to solve a problem must consider a variety of approaches; the sailor must attend only to the radar display and ignore nearby conversations.

Baddeley (1996) proposed that executive processing is controlled processing; tasks that are automatic are sloughed off to the subsystems (the distinction between controlled and automatic processes was described in Chapter 6). This implies that tasks drawing on the central executive will be interfered with by a task that cannot be performed automatically. One such task studied in detail by Baddeley is a random generation task (e.g., the subject types a random sequence of letters). Even after a lot of practice, this task demands attention; Baddeley has shown that random generation is interfered with by a category generation task such as producing as many items as possible from a particular semantic category (e.g., animals or fruit). However, the random generation task is not interfered with by counting repeatedly from 1 to 6, presumably because the counting task can be performed in verbal working memory (in particular, the articulatory loop).

The central executive coordinates activity in verbal and spatial working memory. For example, Bruyer and Scaulquin (1998) showed that the central executive is involved in the manipulation of information in the visuospatial sketchpad. The act of mentally rotating spatial information portrayed in a map to correspond with the view out the windshield (discussed in Chapter 5) would involve the central executive, although the spatial information itself would be maintained by the visuospatial sketchpad. Bruyer and Scailquin determined this by noting that the random generation task (requiring central executive resources) interfered with subjects' ability to perform a mental rotation task, but did not interfere with a task involving the passive maintenance of an image. Similarly, Awh, Jonides, & Reuter-Lorenz (1998) showed that controlled attentional processes are used to rehearse information in the visuospatial sketchpad; if these processes are interfered with, spatial working memory performance is impaired. These results correspond to the importance of verbal rehearsal (e.g., repeating a phone number over to yourself) in maintaining information in the phonological store. Accessing information in long-term memory also requires attentional resources supplied by the central executive (Anderson, Reder, & Lebiere, 1996).

The limited attentional resource of the central executive implies that a task demanding central executive resources should not be performed concurrently with other tasks drawing on those resources. Writing text serves as an example. McCutchen, Covill, Hoyne, and Mildes (1994) note that the writing task requires repeated long-term memory access for the translation of plans into written text. When a journalist writes a newspaper article or a student writes an essay, central executive resources are necessary, and other tasks requiring those resources cannot be concurrently performed. As writers gain expertise, however, their translation processes become more fluent, helping to reduce memory load during writing (McCutchen, Covill, Hoyne, & Mildes, 1994). The implication is that as writers gain expertise, they can perform other tasks drawing on central executive resources. Gronlund et al. (1998) have similarly implicated central executive resources in air-traffic control.

Matching Display With Working Memory Code

Wickens, Sandry, and Vidulich (1983) described the principle of stimulus/central-processing/response compatibility that prescribes the best association of display formats to codes of working memory. In this principle, S refers to display modality (auditory and visual), C to the two possible central-processing codes (verbal and spatial), and R to the two possible response modalities (manual and vocal). In this section, we discuss the optimum matching between stimulus and central processing codes. The compatibility between stimuli and response (S-R compatibility) will be dealt with in Chapter 9.

Figure 7.3 shows four different formats for information display as defined by code (verbal, spatial) and modality (visual, auditory). Experimental data suggest that the assignment of formats to memory codes should not be arbitrary. The shaded cells in Figure 7.3 indicate the optimum combinations of code and modality.

Visual displays are usually more effective than auditory displays for tasks that demand spatial working memory (Wickens, Vidulich, & Sandry-Garza, 1984). In contrast, tasks that demand verbal working memory are more readily served by speech, especially if the verbal material can only be displayed for a short interval (Wickens, Sandry, & Vidulich, 1983). This is because echoic memory has a slower decay than iconic memory, speech has obligatory access to the phonological store, and speech is more compatible with the vocalization used in rehearsal. This guideline is also supported by laboratory studies showing that verbal material is better retained for short periods when presented by auditory rather than visual means (e.g., Nilsson, Ohlsson, & Ronnberg, 1977).

This observation has considerable practical implication when verbal material is presented for temporary storage (e.g., navigational entries presented to the aircraft pilot;

of one aircraft interferes with information about the altitude of others. The interference can be reduced by using: (1) separate operators, (2) separate attribute labeling, or (3) separate spatial locations. We discuss these potential design solutions and related research next.

Yntema (1963) found better performance when one object varied on a number of attributes than when many objects varied on one attribute, when the total number of variables was the same in both cases. More recently, Venturino (1997) determined that the disadvantage for multiple objects obtained by Yntema stemmed from interference among the objects when the *same attribute* was being retained in running memory. Venturino independently manipulated both the number of objects and whether attributes were different or the same. He found that people could remember the status of attributes for many objects just as well as for one object if the attributes differed between the objects (e.g., keeping track of the temperature of a chemical process in one vessel and the pressure in another). However, performance was worse if attributes remained the same across objects (e.g., keeping track of the temperature of all vessels). The implication is that it is the *similarity* of attributes to other attributes being maintained in working memory that leads to interference. One design implication is that if the attributes being kept track of differ, a single operator can produce good performance; however, when the same attribute must be kept track of for different objects, separate operators should be used to reduce interference. Another technique is to use different scales or scale labels for attributes.

There are other ways to overcome the interference caused by similarity. One of these is using a specific spatial location to display the value of each object-attribute combination. Hess, Detweiler, and Ellis (in press; see also Hess & Detweiler, 1996) used a running-memory task in which subjects had to remember five attributes (e.g., weapons, direction, speed) of five objects (ships). Hess, Detweiler, and Ellis used location in a square grid to code each combination of ship and attribute. For example, information about the direction of Ship 1 was shown in the upper left part of the display; information about Ship 5's weapons was shown in the lower right. This grid arrangement was contrasted with a more conventional "window" arrangement in which all attribute and ship information was shown in one location. Hess, Detweiler, and Ellis showed that the grid arrangement reduced the interference generally found when subjects must keep track of the same attributes for many objects. Hence, the use of consistent (and unique) spatial locations could allow a single operator to keep track of the attributes of multiple objects without penalty.

In sum, a key limiting factor in working memory is confusability. Factors that increase the discriminability of items will help performance in a running memory task. Using different scales or scale labels for attributes is one method for doing this. Another is to use separate and unique spatial locations.

In some real-world systems, recent information is kept available on a display and does not have to be remembered as in the running-memory task. For example, the air traffic controller has aircraft status information continuously visible and so can respond on the basis of perceptual information rather than rely on working memory. However, the principles described above should still apply to these systems. As discussed in Chapter 6, an efficiently updated memory will ease the process of perception through top-down processing and will unburden the operator when perception may be directed away from the display. Furthermore, if a system failure occurs, display information is eliminated. In this case, an accurate working memory becomes essential and not just useful.

EXPERTISE AND MEMORY

In the previous section, we discussed how the capacity and decay limitations of working memory could be reduced by chunking, which makes use of information stored in long-term memory. In this section we first describe expertise, and then relate it to the chunking concept. After that, we describe the concepts of skilled memory and long-term working memory, which provide a theoretical understanding of the relationship between working memory and long-term knowledge.

Expertise

Although it is not entirely clear what is meant by expertise (Fischer, 1991), there is general agreement that expertise is domain specific (Cellier, Eyrolle, & Mariné, 1997): that is, being an expert does not provide general performance advantages but, rather, advantages in a specified domain (e.g., a sport, a game, a particular occupation). Cellier, Eyrolle, and Mariné note the following general characteristics of expertise:

1. It is acquired through practice or training in a domain.
2. It generally provides a measurable performance advantage.
3. It may involve specialized, rather than generic, knowledge.

Being an expert can have corollary benefits. A task that defines the domain of expertise is called *intrinsic* (e.g., playing a chess game); a task that is not central to the domain of expertise, but greater expertise in the domain improves performance nonetheless, is called *contrived* (e.g., better recall of pieces of a chessboard after a game) (Vicente & Wang, 1998). Experts' success on contrived tasks is common in many domains: for example, process control (Vicente, 1992), aviation (Wiggins & O'Hare, 1995), and nursing (Hampton, 1994). Vicente showed that experts had better recall of the state of a simulated thermal–hydraulic process plant when the process variables worked normally and when a fault occurred (intrinsic tasks), but experts also performed better than novices even when process variables were driven in random fashion (a contrived task). Similarly, Wiggins and O'Hare note that aviation experience tends to improve weather-related decision making in pilots, although such decision making is not an intrinsic part of aviation training. Hampton describes a case study of an experienced nurse who immediately surmised that a patient's restlessness and confusion meant poor blood oxygenation—a hypothesis later confirmed by an arterial test. Hampton noted that the successful diagnosis was likely due to good working knowledge of the clinical symptoms that occur with respiratory distress, but not a specific similar experience.

Thus, although expertise tends to be specific to a domain of skill, it is more general than just that information provided at training or that experienced directly. In the next section, we discuss how expertise facilitates the use of chunking. Then we describe a theoretical framework that specifies the mechanism underlying experts' improved performance. In Chapter 8, we describe expertise in decision making.

Expertise and Chunking

Chunking strategies can be acquired through expertise. Chase and Ericsson (1981) examined the memory spans of expert runners and found that they used grouping principles based on running statistics. In fact, a conclusion from studies of expert behavior in domains such as computer programming (Barfield, 1997; Vessey, 1985; Ye & Salvendy, 1994), chess (Chase & Simon, 1973; deGroot, 1965; Gobet, 1998), or planning (Ward & Allport, 1997) is that the expert can perceive and store relevant stimulus material in working memory in terms of chunks rather than lowest-level units (Anderson, 1996).

For example, Barfield (1997) performed a study in which expert and novice programmers viewed a short program organized in executable order, in random chunks, or random lines. The eye movements of the programmers were monitored when they examined the program. Expert programmers encoded more lines of the program per glance than did novices when the program was presented in order or random chunks, but not in random lines. When asked to recall the program later, expert programmers recalled more lines of organized code if it had been in order or in random chunks, but not random lines. That expert programmers could encode more lines of program per glance with organized code suggests that they were encoding chunks into working memory, rather than the individual lines encoded by the novice programmers. Ye and Salvendy (1994) and Vessey (1985) found similar results, both finding increased chunking ability with programming expertise. In addition, Ye and Salvendy found that novices' chunks were smaller than those of experts.

Clearly, then, our ability to chunk information depends on our expertise in the subject domain. In the next section, we discuss *skilled memory*, which involves the use of stored information in long-term memory to aid the perception of domain-relevant material.

Skilled Memory

Consider yourself reading the text on this page. To perform this task well, you must maintain access to large amounts of information. For example, to understand what "this task" refers to in the previous sentence you must retain some knowledge of the first sentence. As you read through this chapter, you retain some information from previous paragraphs in order to properly integrate the current topic with earlier topics. Although we don't think of it as such, text reading is a skilled activity, requiring years of training. Clearly such skilled tasks must involve working memory, but there are two aspects of performance in skilled tasks that are difficult for the traditional view of working memory to account for. The first is that skilled activities can be interrupted, and later resumed, with little effect on performance (Ericsson & Kintsch, 1995). If working memory only stores information temporarily, how can it account for this result? The second is that performance in skilled tasks requires quick access to a large amount of information. However, we know there are limits on the amount of information that can be maintained in working memory, and so, skilled performance defies the concept of a limited capacity. One could argue that such information is retrieved from long-term memory, but access to this information appears to be faster than typical retrieval times for information in long-term memory which is usually several seconds (Ericsson & Kintsch, 1995).

For these reasons, Ericsson and Kintsch (1995) propose that working memory includes another mechanism based on skilled use of storage in long-term memory. They refer to this mechanism as *long-term working memory* (LT-WM). Information in LT-WM is stable, but it is accessed through temporarily active retrieval cues in working memory. Acquiring domain-specific skills allows people to acquire LT-WM, and they can extend their working memory for the skilled activity. Note that LT-WM is acquired for particular skill domains (medical diagnosis, waiting tables, mental arithmetic). There is not an improvement in the general capacity of working memory, and the expert physician, waiter, or calculator is reduced to normal performance in most other situations (Ericsson & Kintsch, 1995).

Expert chess players are better able than novices to reconstruct a chess position after a brief view (Chase & Simon, 1973), showing the advantage of expertise. It has also been shown that this advantage persists even if other tasks are performed between presentation and recall (Charness, 1976), suggesting that the information about the chess pieces was not being maintained in working memory, but rather in long-term memory. How does the expert do this? Ericsson and Kintsch (1995) argue that when experts encode the chess board, they rapidly associate the information on the board with appropriate retrieval cues. The activity must be familiar to the experts so that they can anticipate future demands for later retrieval. Ericsson and Kintsch call a set of retrieval cues a *retrieval structure*, and they propose that experts commonly use retrieval structures stored in working memory to access the information stored in LT-WM.

An example of a retrieval structure is one used by the waiter JC (Ericsson & Polson, 1988). JC would link all items of a food category, such as starches, in a pattern linked to table locations. Going around a table, for example, JC might remember a reversing pattern like rice, fries, fries, rice (Ericsson & Kintsch, 1995). If JC had instead tried to remember each order from multiple tables, interference would result. The advantage of the retrieval structure is that this interference is reduced. The retrieval structure underlies common mnemonic techniques (Wenger & Payne, 1995) and may account for the result that aircraft importance affects air traffic controllers' memory for flight data (Gronlund et al., 1998). Specifically, Gronlund et al. found that as incoming flight information was provided, air traffic controllers classified aircraft in terms of importance and used this classification for later recall.

The biggest practical advantage of a retrieval structure is that information can be provided in scrambled order with little ill effect; for novices, scrambling the order of information typically degrades performance (Ericsson & Kintsch, 1995). Indeed, Stevens provides evidence of this in a real-world setting: She notes that "from the time a waitress takes an order until she serves the dessert and collects payment, her memory is accessing a set of informational items in different ways at different times in the flow of activity" (p. 216). The retrieval structure therefore provides a means for dynamic, adaptive access to information.

The long-term working memory concept described here can incorporate chunking, as described earlier. Chunking can be thought of as a particular kind of retrieval structure. The long-term working memory concept places to-be-remembered information in long-term rather than working memory. There is evidence to support this view. For experts, little interference is produced by performing another task (verbal or spatial) simultaneously with a memory task. Presumably this is because experts store task-related information in the LT-WM retrieval structure; if the information was only stored in the expert's working memory, another task should have interfered with it (Ericsson & Kintsch, 1995).

PLANNING AND PROBLEM SOLVING

The concepts of *planning* and *problem solving* are intertwined, and most research examining one examines the other. A plan can be defined as a strategy for solving a problem. The plan is developed for use in the future to solve the problem. How do planning and problem solving tie in to our earlier discussions of working memory? Generally, planning and problem solving are presumed to occur in the central executive (Baddeley, 1993; see also Allport, 1993). Therefore, we should expect to see working-memory limitations play a role in planning and problem-solving tasks, and we should expect a decrease in planning performance in situations where there is increased working memory load (Ward & Allport, 1997).

It has been said that a person attempting to solve a problem is analogous to an ant working its way across the sand on a beach towards its home (Simon, 1981). The ant's path on the beach is determined as much by the features of the beach (bumps formed by waves, the dryness of the sand) as by the goals of the ant. The analogy is therefore that human planning is determined as much by environmental constraints as by the goals of the operator. The success of a route chosen to avoid traffic at rush hour will partially be determined by the constraints of the environment: the density of traffic, the weather, the routes chosen by other drivers, the likelihood of an accident, and so on. Indeed, in the context of flight planning, Casner (1994) found that nearly half the variability in pilots' problem-solving behavior is due to environmental features.

What makes a planning task difficult? Planning difficulty increases when there are more choices available for action (i.e., fewer constraints) (Ward & Allport, 1997). Ward and Allport had their subjects solve a five-disk "Tower of London" puzzle that requires changing the position of the disks on three vertical poles to a particular goal position in as few moves as possible. The time to prepare a planned solution to this task was affected by the number of competing choices at critical steps. A related factor is whether the choices are equally preferable: Ward and Allport showed that planning becomes more difficult when there are several choices of roughly equal preference, because the problem solver tends to equivocate, leading to longer planning times. This finding was replicated in the context of en-route flight planning by Layton, Smith, and McCoy (1994) (see also Anderson, 1993). In addition, equal-likelihood situations are more likely to occur when there are more alternatives available.

The human problem solver *satisfices*—that is, selects the current best plan with no guarantee that it is the absolute best plan (Anderson, 1991; O'Hara & Payne, 1998; Simon, 1990). The reason is that continued search of problem space takes place at increasing *cost* (Simon, 1978). Thus, potential plans will be generated until the expected improvement over the current plan no longer justifies the cognitive effort to generate further plans. We will discuss the satisficing notion again as it applies to decision making in Chapter 8.

Another type of cost is *implementation cost* (O'Hara & Payne, 1998), the cost associated with performing the actions resulting from a particular plan. It includes factors such as the amount of time required, and the physical or mental effort involved. O'Hara and Payne (1998) describe the example of a computer user entering a command by typing in a string of characters. Typing the string takes time. Longer keystroke sequences take longer time on average. There is physical effort associated with pressing the keys, with longer sequences demanding more physical effort. There is mental effort involved in generating the correct sequence of keystrokes, and longer sequences have greater potential for error. Thus, increasing the problem solver's implementation costs will increase the amount of mental planning required.

To test this, we need a situation in which physical costs can be manipulated but the characteristics of the problem space are kept constant. O'Hara and Payne (1998) note that varying the computer interface used for solving a problem may do just this. In a set of experiments, they compared a command language interface with a direct manipulation interface (discussed in Chapter 4) for a spatial problem-solving task (a puzzle requiring the movement of tiles into a particular configuration) and found that their subjects produced greater planning times and errors with the command language than with the direct manipulation interface, implying greater implementation cost for the command-language interface, even though the core task was the same.

Planning is often done in context of external displays (Casner, 1994; O'Hara & Payne, 1998; Payne, 1991). The displays may be as simple as a piece of paper, or they may be part of a larger complex system (e.g., dynamic graphical map displays for flight planning) (Layton, Smith, & McCoy, 1994). The results obtained by O'Hara and Payne show how the design of a system (a computer interface) imposed constraints that affected the plan chosen by a person in a problem-solving situation. Thus, different display designs affect the environmental constraints, leading to different problem-solving solutions (O'Hara & Payne, 1998; Zhang & Norman, 1994).

In many display-based contexts, people act on the world as soon as the first actions are decided, and plan further actions as they act, similar to the satisficing notion described above. The problem solving occurs by following the most promising leads at any point in time, like the art of navigating the beach. This strategy has been called *opportunistic planning*. Vinze, Sen, and Liou (1993) studied the problem solving of managers performing real-world planning tasks (e.g., auditing, production planning) and found clear evidence of opportunistic planning. The problem is that opportunistic planning can lead to solutions that are not optimal. For example, Layton, Smith, and McCoy (1994) described a case in which a pilot engaged in flight planning solved each step in route selection accurately—following the apparently best strategy at any given stage—but produced a route that was not globally optimal. Thus, opportunistic planning tends to lead to locally optimal but globally suboptimal solutions.

Opportunistic planning also tends to lead to an interleaving of planning and action. This interleaving is evident in the use of programming languages, where expertise also plays a role. Expertise in one programming language helps a person learn another programming language but hinders acquisition of information specific to the new language. The result is that programmers tend to want to program immediately in the new language, rather than learn it. An inefficient program (essentially, a bad plan) is the result (Scholtz & Wiedenbeck, 1993).

Human planning and problem solving can be improved by incorporating an artificial automated planning system into the planning process (Robertson, Zachery, & Black, 1990). Layton, Smith, and McCoy (1994) examined the utility of an automated planning system for assisting the commercial airline pilot with the task of inflight planning regarding weather, mechanical problems, and so on. They found that pilots using the automated system were more likely to find the most efficient route when there were a high number of possible solutions than were pilots using a manual, route-sketching interface. We noted earlier that too many alternatives for action impair human problem solving. Automated systems may provide a solution to this problem.

However, Layton, Smith, and McCoy (1994) also found that pilots using an automated system were less likely to explore as many alternatives than those using a manual route-sketching interface. Pilots using the automatic version were also less likely to consider the uncertainty of the forecast information they were given than were those with the manual sketching interface. Therefore, the automated planning system studied by Layton, Smith, and McCoy had its pros and cons: It was useful when there were multiple solutions, but the pilot's exploratory search of the problem space tended to decrease, and consideration of uncertainty in the decision decreased. In situations where a plan must be generated quickly, however, these may not be entirely negative characteristics. The costs and benefits of a variety of different automation systems will be discussed further in Chapter 13.

In summary, we note that the difficulty of planning is affected by the number of choices for action, and that people tend to satisfice, choosing a problem solution that seems good enough at the time. Both these constraints can be attributed to the heavy demands that planning places on working memory. Better solutions may be obtained by using visual displays or automated systems to present choices, but there are problems. In particular, the availability of display information appears to lead to opportunistic planning, which can produce a generally optimal solution, but may not. Automated systems are useful to the human planner when there are multiple solutions, but they appear to decrease exploratory behavior and lead to a deterministic interpretation of presented information.

SITUATION AWARENESS

In order to plan or problem solve effectively in dynamic, changing environments, people must have a relatively accurate awareness of the current and evolving situation. For example, in planning an efficient driving route across town at rush hour, it helps to know about the current traffic situation. In planning a course of treatment for a critically ill patient, the physician needs to be aware of the patient's current and projected future status. This concept of *situation awareness* has received considerable attention from engineering psychologists over the past decade (Durso & Gronlund, 1999; Endsley, 1995; Endsley & Garland, 1999; *Human Factors*, 1995) because of its relevance for designing displays to support situation awareness, and because of its relevance for understanding the causes of disasters and accidents in which situation awareness has been lost. For example, the tragic case of a transport airline that ran into a mountainside in Columbia, South America, occurred because pilots lost awareness of their geographic location relative to the terrain (Strauch, 1997).

The link between situation awareness and working memory is direct. Our awareness of an evolving situation mostly resides in working memory and therefore degrades as resources are reallocated to competing tasks. However, as we learned above, experts in a particular field can maintain information about an evolving situation in long-term working memory (Ericsson & Kintsch, 1995) such that the information can be rapidly retrieved if needed, even if it is not actively maintained in the limited-capacity working-memory system.

To understand situation awareness, it is important to stress its relation to, but distinctiveness from, other information-processing components discussed in the book. Thus, while accurate situation awareness depends on the deployment of selective attention (discussed in Chapter 3), situation awareness is not the same as attention. Correspondingly, while experts having retrieval structures in long-term memory are better able to incorporate new, dynamic information, the retrieval structures are not situation awareness, since they are relatively enduring properties of memory. Thus, we may distinguish between the *process* of maintaining situation awareness, supported by attention, working memory, and long-term memory, and the awareness itself (Adams, Tenney, & Pew, 1995). Finally, while situation awareness may support effective responding, it does not itself incorporate response selection and execution. Indeed, responding can be done effectively when situation awareness is lacking. Consider, for example, how well we can drive on an uncrowded highway even as our mind drifts away from awareness of the road conditions. Our driving responses are good, but our situation awareness is low.

Situation awareness is also relatively *domain specific*. It is not true to say that a person "has good situation awareness." Instead, one must specify "awareness of what" (Wickens, 1999): for example, awareness of surrounding traffic, of the approaching weather, of the state of automation in a vehicle, of the momentary responsibility for tasks, or of a stress-related decrease in one's physical or cognitive capabilities. The domain-specific nature of situation awareness affects the way it is measured (Endsley, 1995; Endsley & Garland, 1999). Thus, asking people to rate their level of awareness on a scale of 1 to 10 will not provide a terribly valid measure. This is because people are not aware of those things of which they are not aware. On the other hand, probing awareness with more specific questions ("Where is the nearest traffic to you?" or "What is the state of automation in your aircraft?") provides a more valid assessment (Endsley, 1995; Durso & Gronlund, 1999).

Finally, the concept of situation awareness has important application for design. First, it has implications for display design. As discussed in Chapters 4 and 5, displays designed to support specific routine tasks in dynamic systems are often not well suited for supporting broader situation awareness—which is particularly important when failures or unexpected circumstances develop (Wickens, 1999). Second, as we will learn in Chapter 13, situation awareness has implications for automation. Higher levels of automation may improve performance and reduce workload, but may decrease situation awareness (Sarter & Woods, 1995).

LEARNING AND TRAINING

Although limitations of working memory represent a major bottleneck in the operation of many systems, equally important sources of potential failures are the actions people take incorrectly or fail to take because they have forgotten to do them or have forgotten how to do them. For example, the fatal crash of Northwest Airlines flight 255 near Detroit in 1988 was believed to have occurred in part because the pilot forgot to lower the flaps on takeoff (National Transportation Safety Board, 1988; see also Chapter 10). Hours of wasted time result when naive computer users use simpler but less efficient commands rather than the more powerful but complex ones they were taught but have forgotten.

Development of Expertise: Learning

Before we examine training, it would be good if we had some idea of how people learn. To do so, we describe two general cognitive models proposed to explain learning: ACT-R (Anderson, 1996) and Soar (Newell, 1990). After we describe each one, we will summarize their similarities and applications for training.

ACT-R (Anderson, 1996) is a *production system* model. In a production system, currently active information (such as that in working memory) is compared to a set of *production rules*. Production rules are IF-THEN statements like those found in computer programming languages. A production is said to fire (i.e., is carried out) when the IF condition is met. The IF condition typically contains a goal (e.g., add two numbers) and some declarative knowledge (e.g., the fact that 3 + 4 = 7). For example, in an addition problem, IF the goal is to add 3 and 4, AND 3 + 4 = 7, THEN write 7 at the bottom of the column.

Procedural knowledge is knowledge of how to do things (knowing how); *declarative knowledge* is knowledge of facts (knowing what). Thus, declarative knowledge might describe the safety rules and regulations of a particular company or organization; procedural knowledge might describe the steps you need to take to operate a lathe, ride a bicycle, or tie your shoe. Declarative and procedural knowledge are intertwined in ACT-R (Anderson, 1996). Production rules embody procedural knowledge, but their conditions and actions are defined in terms of declarative knowledge, as the example above shows. Declarative knowledge is represented in terms of chunks (an addition fact is that 3 + 4 = 7).

Anderson (1996) proposes that the chunks of declarative knowledge in the production rule are strengthened through exposure to particular examples. This is part of the learning process. Chunks therefore have particular levels of activation that determine the likelihood they will be retrieved (Anderson, Reder, & Lebiere, 1996). Production rules are developed by attempting to map various sources of information in a problem to each other. For example, the student shown the problem

$$2x + 4 = 8$$

$$2x = 4$$

and knowing that the equations are related must find some mapping from one equation to the other. ACT-R will look for a chunk of declarative knowledge to determine the mapping. If it finds a chunk that 4 + 4 = 8, then ACT-R will form a generic production rule to map one equation to the other, as illustrated in Figure 7.6. This production rule could then be applied to other similar equations. Formation of these production rules is a key part of learning. The implication is that one learns to solve problems by imitating examples of solutions (Anderson, 1996). Hence, there is an emphasis on practice on *specific examples* to improve learning in the ACT-R framework. This has important implications for training, which we discuss later in the "Training Techniques" section.

Suppose a mathematics student is shown the equations:

2x + 4 = 8   (Equation 1)

2x = 4   (Equation 2)

and must determine how they are related.

The student knows that **4 + 4 = 8** (a declarative knowledge "Chunk"). The student can use the chunk to map Equation 1 onto Equation 2. This is done using a production rule:

> **IF the goal is to solve arg + n1 = n3**
> **And n1 + n2 = n3**
> **THEN make a goal to solve an equation arg = n2**

In terms of our example, the rule would be specified as:

> **IF the goal is to solve 2x + 4 = 8**
> **AND 4 + 4 = 8**
> **THEN make the goal to solve an equation 2x = 4**

The production rule therefore links one equation to the other. Since the production rule is generic, it can be used to solve other similar problems, e.g., **3x + 4 = 10** reduces to **3x = 6.**

Figure 7.6   An example illustrating how a generic production rule is formed.

Anderson, Reder, and Lebiere (1996) obtained a decrement in performance in solving equations when a concurrent digit span task was introduced. Their experiments were similar to those discussed earlier in the context of working memory. They also found that the majority of errors were misretrievals of declarative knowledge. As tasks increase in complexity there is less activation for retrieval of chunks of declarative information. Working memory (in particular the central executive) may be the source of the capacity limitation. That is, performing tasks simultaneously may draw on working memory resources, but since these resources are the source of activation for chunks of declarative knowledge, a greater number of misretrievals should occur, leading to poorer performance (Anderson, Reder, & Lebiere, 1996).

Like ACT-R, *Soar* (Laird & Rosenbloom, 1996; Newell, 1990) is a general *cognitive architecture* relying on production rules. Unlike ACT-R, Soar does not distinguish between declarative and procedural knowledge (Howes & Young, 1997). Soar might best be thought of as a programming language, weakly constraining the way in which a mental activity (such as learning) is modeled. Howes and Young showed how Soar predicts an advantage for learning graphical user interfaces (incorporating display-based reminders of available commands) over command languages (where the user must remember the command and type it in). This is because determining how to elicit a computer command depends on generating suitable candidate names. Once a candidate is generated, it can be recognized by a Soar model. It is easier to generate suitable names when they are presented on the external display than when they must be recalled from long-term memory. Eventually, given enough instances, Soar learns the particular response that must be made (e.g., choosing "file" from the File menu), and stores that as a chunk (similar to ACT-R).

The common characteristics of ACT-R and Soar suggest five pervasive characteristics of how cognitive learning occurs. First, note that there is an emphasis on *instances*. That is, people learn about specific situations and generalize from them rather than learn abstract rules and derive specific implications. Second, the way that people deal with those instances changes with experience from an algorithm to recall of the instance through *chunking*. Initially, an algorithmic solution or formula is used. Consider this example.

1) Determine the sum of 4 + 3 +2 + 1.

2) Do it again.

Notice how the second time you did not go through the computation. You recalled your last answer instead. As we become experts in a domain, we rely more on the strategy of recall of specific instances and less on explicit addition (an algorithmic approach). There is therefore a reduction in working memory load, potentially freeing up resources for other tasks.

Third, note that any display characteristic that facilitates the recall strategy will be effective both for training and for people who are experienced. Howes and Young (1996) noted that multiple studies show that expert users of computer systems are often not able to remember how to perform a task away from the computer, even though they are highly practiced at it. Models such as Soar account for this by proposing that the chunks can be triggered directly by information on a computer display.

Fourth, note that as proposed by Soar, novices often engage in open-ended strategies such as *means-end analysis* when confronted with a problem. This involves performing an action—any action—and seeing if it reduces the distance between the current state and the goal state. This strategy is cognitively demanding, impeding training effectiveness; when other tasks are performed simultaneously, training is impaired. Reducing cognitive load (Sweller, 1993) in this way has been shown to be an effective training technique and is discussed in more detail later, in the "Training Techniques" section.

Finally, there are *intelligent tutors* based on ACT-R that teach cognitive skills (Anderson, 1996). The instruction provided by the tutors is based on the production rules used by the ACT-R model. The learning of each production rule improves gradually with practice, with error rates decreasing most quickly early. Anderson notes that the tutors speed up students' learning by a factor of 3 relative to conventional instruction. Thus, if the production rules can be identified for a specific set of cognitive skills, the rules can then be taught to students of the task, producing a training system that speeds up learning.

Transfer of Training

Information can be learned in many ways—formal classroom teaching, practice, on-the job training, focus on principles, theory, and so on. The engineering psychologist developing a new training procedure or device is concerned with three issues: What procedure (or device) (1) provides the best learning in the shortest time, (2) leads to the longest retention, and (3) is cheapest? Together these criteria define the issue of *training efficiency*.

A critical factor in skill acquisition is the extent to which learning a new skill, or a skill in a new environment, capitalizes on what has been learned before. This is called *transfer of training* (Holding, 1987; Singley & Andersen, 1989). How well, for example, do lessons learned in a driving simulator transfer to performance on the highway? Or how much does learning one word-processing program help (or hinder) learning another? Measures of transfer of training are normally used to evaluate the effectiveness of different training strategies (Fabiani et al., 1989).

Measuring Transfer Although there are many ways to measure transfer, the most typical is illustrated in Figure 7.7. The top row represents a *control group*, who learns the target task in its normal setting. This group achieves some satisfactory performance criterion after a certain time—in this example, ten hours. Suppose you propose a new training technique with the purpose of shortening the time needed to learn the target task. To evaluate the technique a *transfer group* is given some practice with the new technique and then is transferred to the target task. In the second row, we see that the transfer group trains with the new technique for four hours and then learns the target task faster than the control group, a *savings* of two hours. Hence, the technique provided some information that

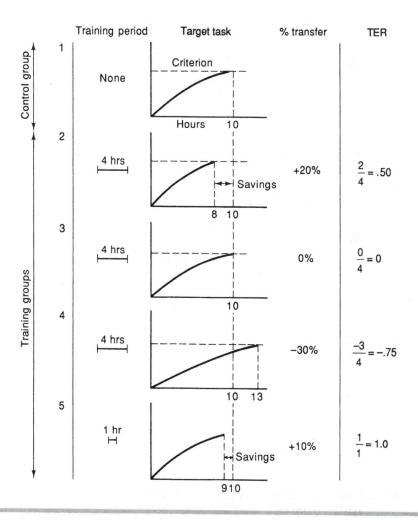

Figure 7.7 The measurement of transfer performance.

carried over to the effective performance (or learning) of the target task. Because there were savings, we say that transfer was *positive*. In row 3, we see that a second training technique had no relevance to the target task (no savings, zero transfer). In row 4, a third technique was employed, and we see that this training *inhibited* learning the target task. That is, people would have learned the target task faster without the training! We say here that transfer was *negative*.

A common formula for expressing transfer presents the amount of savings as a percentage of the control-group learning time:

$$\% \text{ transfer} = \frac{(\text{control time - transfer time})}{\text{control time}} \times 100 = \frac{\text{savings}}{\text{control time}} \times 100$$

The results of these calculations are shown in Figure 7.7 for the three training conditions.

Positive transfer is generally desirable, but it is not always clear how *much* positive transfer is necessary to be effective. Consider the following example, which might have produced the hypothetical data shown in row 2 of Figure 7.7. A driving simulator is developed that produces 20 percent positive transfer to training on the road. That is, trainees who use the simulator can reach satisfactory performance on the road in 20 percent fewer road lessons than trainees who do all their training on the road. This sounds good, but notice that to get the 20 percent transfer (the 2-hour savings) the simulator group had to spend 4 hours in the simulator. Therefore, they spent 12 total hours, compared to the 10 hours spent by the control group. Hence the simulator, while transferring positively, is less *efficient* in terms of training time than the actual vehicle.

A measure called the *transfer effectiveness ratio* (TER) expresses this relative efficiency (Povenmire & Roscoe, 1973):

$$TER = \frac{\text{amount of savings}}{\text{transfer group time in training program}}$$

Examining this formula, we see that if the amount of time spent in the training program (the denominator) is equal to the amount of savings (the numerator), TER = 1. If the total training for the transfer group (training and practice on the target task) is less efficient than for the control group, as is the case with all three groups in Figure 7.7 (right column), the TER will be less than 1. If training is more efficient, the TER is greater than 1. A TER less than 1 does not mean that the experimental training program is worthless. Two factors may make such programs advantageous: (1) They may be safer (it is clearly safer to train a driver in the simulator than on the road), and (2) they may be cheaper. In fact, a major determinant of whether a company will invest in a particular training program or device depends on the *training cost ratio* (TCR):

$$TCR = \frac{\text{training cost in target environment (per unit time)}}{\text{training cost in the training program (per unit time)}}$$

In short, the cheaper the training device, the lower the TER can be. The cost-effectiveness of a training program may be assessed by multiplying TER by TCR. IF TER × TCR > 1, the program is cost effective. If their product is less than one, the program is not cost effective. Even if a program is not cost effective, however, safety considerations may be important to consider.

There is often a diminishing efficiency of training devices with increased training time. In the example in row 2 of Figure 7.7, four hours of training were given, and a TER of 0.5 was obtained. But now consider row 5, in which the same device was used for only one hour. Although the savings is now only one hour (half of what it was before), the training time was reduced by 75 percent, and so the TER is 1.0. The general result is shown in Figure 7.8. TERs typically decrease as more training is given, although for very short amounts of training, TERs are typically greater than 1 (Povenmire & Roscoe, 1973). The point at which training should stop and transfer to the target task should begin will depend, in part, on the training cost ratio (TCR). In fact, the amount of training at which TER $\times$ TCR = 1 is the point beyond which the training program is no longer cost effective. As noted, however, the training program may still be useful for longer amounts of training if it is safer than performing the task in the real situation.

What causes transfer to be positive, negative, or zero? Generally, positive transfer occurs when a training program and target task are similar (in fact, if they are identical, transfer is usually about as positive as it can be, although there are some exceptions). Extreme differences between training and target task typically produce zero transfer. Learning to type, for example, does not help learning to swim or drive an automobile. Negative transfer occurs from a unique set of circumstances relating to perceptual and response aspects of the task, to be described later. We first consider the similarity between training device and target task: the issue of training system fidelity. Then we examine the special case of virtual environments as used for training. Last, we consider negative transfer between old and new tasks.

Training System Fidelity   We stated that maximum positive transfer would generally occur if all elements of a task were identical to the target task. Does this mean that training simulators should resemble the real world as closely as possible? The answer to this question is no for a number of reasons (Schneider, 1985). First, highly realistic simulators tend to be expensive, but their added realism does not necessarily add to their TER (Hawkins & Orlady, 1993; Moroney & Moroney, 1999). Druckman and Bjork (1994) note that multiple studies show no training advantage for real equipment or realistic simulators over cheap cardboard mockups or drawings. Second, in some cases, high similarity, if it does not achieve complete identity with the target environment, may be detrimental by leading to incompatible response tendencies or strategies. For example, there is little evidence

Figure 7.8   Relationship between time in training and transfer effectiveness ratio, CTER.

that motion in flight simulators, which cannot approach the actual motion of an air-craft, offers positive transfer benefits (Hawkins & Orlady, 1993). Finally, if high realism increases complexity, it may increase workload and divert attention from the skill to be learned so that learning is inhibited (Druckman & Bjork, 1994).

Instead of total fidelity in training, researchers have emphasized understanding *which* components of training should be made similar to the target task (Druckman & Bjork, 1994; Holding, 1987; Singley & Andersen, 1989). For example, training simula-tors for a sequence of procedures may be of low fidelity yet effective as long as the sequences of steps are compatible (Hawkins & Orlady, 1993). Sometimes an effective training situation need not even be superficially similar to the transfer situation. Go-pher, Weil, and Bareket (1994) trained two different groups of air force cadets on the Space Fortress game, a complex video-game task that demands working-memory re-sources and controlled attention. Gopher, Weil, and Bareket were interested in transfer from this game to actual flight performance. While playing the game, one group received specific training on each component of the game task; the other received more general training to cope with the game's high processing demands. Although the specific train-ing group performed better on the game, both groups showed good transfer to test flights, and both performed better than a control group (matched on ability) who re-ceived no training. The implication is that a general improvement in attentional con-trol gained by playing the Space Fortress game is important in improving eventual flight performance rather than specific game skills.

A major portion of learning complex skills may be tied to the recognition and use of perceptual consistencies, or *invariants*, in the environment (Lintern, Roscoe, & Sivier, 1990; Schneider, 1985), a concept discussed in Chapter 5. Hence, simulators should be designed to preserve these invariants, and the learner should be made aware of them in the training environment (Lintern, Thomley-Yates, Nelson, & Roscoe, 1987). For example, beginning drivers should recognize the heading of a vehicle rel-ative to the vanishing point and use this information to steer the vehicle, rather than the momentary deviation.

In summary, some departures from full fidelity do not have the detrimental impact on transfer that would be predicted from the view that maximum similarity produces maximum transfer. Furthermore, departures from full fidelity can actually enhance transfer if they focus the attention of trainees on critical task components, processing demands, or task-relevant perceptual consistencies in the environment.

Virtual Environments   Training is expensive, especially when it involves the use of real systems. For example, training ship-handling skills on real ships involves all the expenses necessary to put a ship to sea (e.g., fuel, manpower). In contrast, building a virtual en-vironment of the situation is less expensive (Kozak, Hancock, Arthur, & Chrysler, 1993). For similar reasons, virtual environments discussed in Chapter 5 are becoming a cost-effective method for training in many domains.

Although virtual environments can be used for training a variety of tasks, the naviga-tion of three-dimensional spaces (e.g., the rooms in a building) has received the most de-tailed study. For example, Witmer, Bailey, Knerr, and Parsons (1996) had people learn about an office building environment in one of three ways: by exploring the actual building, by exploring a virtual environment simulation, or by verbal directions and photographs. Route learning was found to be better for the virtual environment than for verbal directions, but was worse than learning in the real environment. Wilson, Foreman, and Tlauka (1997) performed a similar study on a desktop virtual reality system. They found that the error in pointing to not-visible objects in the building was less for those subjects trained in the virtual environment than for controls, but the virtual environment group produced greater pointing error than the group trained in the actual environment. Clawson, Miller, Knott, & Sebrechts (1998) and Kozak, Hancock, Arthur, & Chrysler (1993) obtained similar results.

In sum, these results provide a nice illustration of the tradeoff between TER and TCR (transfer effectiveness ratio and training cost ratio). Although training in the virtual environment is less effective than training in the actual physical one (lower TER for the virtual environment), virtual environments cost less to build than a physical environment (increasing the TCR), and so the virtual environment may become a more effective training technique for navigation of space than building a physical mockup or relocating trainees to an existing physical environment.

In addition, virtual environments have certain advantages over the physical environments they mimic. Occluding walls may be a source of difficulty in learning a spatial layout (Thorndyke & Hayes-Roth, 1982). For example, Clawson, Miller, Knott, and Sebrechts (1998) note that transparent (rather than opaque) walls may aid in acquiring information about a spatial layout. To test this, Clawson, Miller, Knott, and Sebrechts compared transparent to opaque walls in a virtual environment and found beneficial training effects for the transparent walls.

Given the rapidly declining cost of virtual environment technology, it is likely that we will see many more proposed applications for training, particularly in environments that are expensive or risky (e.g., fire fighting). The transfer methodology described above provides a useful yardstick for establishing the cost-benefit tradeoffs of such technology.

Negative Transfer   Negative transfer is an important concern, as the continued emergence of new technology and different system designs require operators to switch systems. What causes skills acquired in one setting to inhibit performance in another? A history of research in this area (see Holding, 1976) reveals that the critical conditions for negative transfer are related to stages of processing. When two situations have similar (or identical) stimulus elements but different response mapping or strategic components, transfer will be negative, particularly if new and old responses are incompatible with one another (i.e., they cannot easily be performed at the same time). The relationship between the similarity of stimulus and response elements and transfer is shown in Table 7.1. For example, consider two word-processing systems that present identical screen layouts but require a different set of key presses to accomplish the same editing commands. A high level of skill acquired through extensive training on the first system will inhibit transfer to the second, even though overall transfer will be positive.

Negative transfer is also a concern for an operator who switches back and forth between two systems. Consider two control panels in different parts of a plant that both require a lever movement to accomplish the same function. In one panel the lever must be pushed up, and in the other it must be pushed down to accomplish the same function. Negative transfer is inevitable as the operator moves from one panel to the other. In commercial aviation, a concern relates to the number of different types of aircraft a pilot may be allowed to fly (transfer between) without undergoing an entirely new

TABLE 7.1 Relationship between Old and New Task

Stimulus Elements	Response Elements	Transfer
Same	Same	++
Same	Different	−
	(incompatible)	− −
Different	Same	+
Different	Different	0

training program (Braune, 1989). The lack of standardization in the control arrangements for light aircraft can also lead to serious problems of negative transfer.

The designer should therefore be concerned about negative transfer in many contexts: when a company installs a new word-processing system, when it changes an operating procedure, or when equipment controls are modified.

Sometimes different systems can yield positive transfer. As shown in Table 7.1, two systems may differ in their display characteristics, but positive transfer may be observed if there is identity in the response elements. For example, there will be high positive transfer between two automobiles with identical control layouts and movements, even with different dashboard displays. Furthermore, if the responses for two systems are different and incompatible, Table 7.1 suggests that the amount of negative transfer may be reduced by actually *increasing* the display differences. For example, the operator confronting two control levers with incompatible motion directions will have fewer problems if each lever has a distinct appearance.

In summary, many real-world tasks involve the transfer of many different components, most of them producing positive transfer. Hence, given similar tasks, most transfer is positive. However, the designer should focus on the differences between training and transfer (or between an old and new system) that *do* involve incompatible responses or inappropriate strategies.

Training Techniques

Many principles, strategies, and considerations can be employed to enhance training. We discuss eight factors that the engineering psychologist should be aware of when devising a training program.

Practice and Overlearning   We are all familiar with the expression "practice makes perfect," but the issue of *how much* practice is not always obvious. Generally, skills continue to improve after days, months, and even years of practice (Proctor & Dutta, 1995). For many skills, such as typing or using a piece of equipment, errorless performance can be obtained after a relatively small number of practice trials. However, two other characteristics of performance continue to develop long after performance errors have been eliminated: The speed of performance will continue to increase at a rate proportional to the logarithm of the number of trials (Anderson, 1981), and the attention or resource demand will continue to decline, allowing the skill to be performed in an *automated* fashion (Fisk, Ackerman, & Schneider, 1987; Rogers, Rousseau, & Fisk, 1999; Schneider 1985). (Overlearning will also decrease the *rate of forgetting* of the skill, as discussed later in this chapter.) Thus, when training stops after the first or second errorless trial, it shortchanges the automaticity of skill development.

Giving the learner control over the amount of practice can produce beneficial results. Shute, Gawlick, and Gluck (1998) compared four groups of subjects studying statistics problems. Each group was assigned a different number of problems to solve per topic area. Not surprisingly Shute, Gawlick, and Gluck found that the more problems solved per topic, the better the results on testing six months later. However, they also examined a *learner-control group* who were allowed to choose the number of problems they solved for each set. This group performed better than any other in the experiment, even though the learner-control group solved fewer statistics problems than the group who solved the maximum number of problems per topic.

The advantage for learner control may lie in learners monitoring their knowledge, leading away from a rote memorization strategy and toward elaboration of the information, discussed in the next section. The design of computer-based instruction that lets individuals set the amount of practice should therefore be beneficial.

Elaborative Rehearsal As noted, rehearsal is an active process, necessary to maintain chunks of information in working memory. In fact, there are two types of rehearsal. *Maintenance rehearsal*, in which you simply repeat to-be-remembered information (such as repeating the digits in a phone number), is a good way to maintain information in working memory, but is not very effective for transferring material to long-term memory (Craik & Lockhart, 1972). In contrast, *elaborative rehearsal* involves a greater focus on the meaning of the material, thereby relating the material's elements to each other and to information stored in long-term memory. Thus, elaborative rehearsal may involve chunking.

Elaborative rehearsal can result from an active learning situation. For example, your knowledge of nearby cars is affected by whether you are the passenger or the driver. Gugerty (1997) found that drivers who had active control of the driving task could remember the locations of potentially hazardous cars better than could passengers viewing the same driving scenes. Presumably, the more active driving task led to more elaborative encoding of the information, which led to better recall. We revisit this issue in our discussion of automation in Chapter 13, where we see that when people actively control a large-scale system (e.g., nuclear process control), they derive a better understanding of the current system state.

However, elaborative rehearsal demands working-memory resources, which means that other mental activity demanding the same resources will interfere with learning. In the next section, we consider training approaches that strive to minimize working-memory demands as learning takes place.

Reducing Cognitive Load Many training and instructional techniques impose high demands on working memory, impeding the learning process. Sweller and coworkers (Sweller, 1993; Sweller, van Merrienboer, & Paas, 1998) proposed *cognitive load theory* to account for the effects of such demands on training effectiveness. The theory proposes that many instructional procedures not effective because they ignore the capacity limits of working memory. Sweller and coworkers propose several techniques for reducing cognitive load, based on a large numbers of empirical studies. We review some of these next.

Marcus, Cooper, and Sweller (1996) gave trainees several electronics resistor problems with instructions in diagram or text form. The same information was presented in both formats. With text instructions, learners had more difficulty with a task in which they wired resistors in parallel than in which they wired resistors in series. With diagrammed instructions, however, there was no difference between serial and parallel situations. Further, with text presentation, performance on a concurrent task was poorer for the parallel than the series task; but with the diagram presentation there was no difference. The results can be interpreted in terms of chunking: The diagram allowed the learner to chunk groups of interacting elements (resistors) to form a general organizational schema for the arrangement of elements. Without the diagram, more working-memory "slots" are needed to maintain information about the resistors, imposing a greater working-memory load and leaving less working memory for learning.

When the designer of instructional material adds graphics to text, the two kinds of information need to be integrated so that related information in the two formats is placed close together. Otherwise, the trainee is forced to divide attention across multiple information sources, which imposes an excessive cognitive load that interferes with learning. For example, as discussed in Chapter 6, Sweller, Chandler, Tierney, and Cooper (1990) noted that separation of text from graphics in a textbook description of technical material impedes learning. These effects are consistent with the proximity compatibility principle discussed in Chapter 3.

We noted earlier in this chapter that spoken information has obligatory access to verbal working memory. In contrast, printed text may require the use of central executive or visuospatial sketchpad resources. There is growing evidence that we can take advantage of the obligatory access of speech to working memory for learning and training purposes. Tindall-Ford, Chandler, and Sweller (1997; also discussed in Chapter 6) compared two instructional formats for electronic technicians. The first presented spoken text with visual diagrams, and the second presented the text visually in printed form with the same diagrams. They found better performance with the dual-mode presentation than with the visual-only format when the instructional content was difficult. A study by Mousavi, Low, and Sweller (1995) showed a similar advantage to dual-modality presentation for learning geometry problems.

These results can be interpreted in terms of cognitive load. By using different modalities, different working-memory components (phonological store and visuospatial sketchpad) are accessed, reducing interference within working memory. When the visual modality is used to present both text and diagrams, text information must be processed by the visuospatial sketchpad, which is also processing information contained in the diagram, leading to interference. Thus, dual-modality presentation effectively enlarges working-memory capacity, reducing cognitive load and improving learning.

Cognitive load also applies to the presentation of examples in training problem-solving skills. Suppose you are asked to derive a single quantity from a set of given values and equations that you already know. If you are a novice at solving that type of problem, you will probably engage in *means-end analysis* (discussed earlier) to arrive at a solution. That is, you will probably start with those values you have, and try to change the equation so that you obtain the desired answer. Sweller (1993) argues that performing this type of means-end analysis produces a high cognitive load. Determining differences between the current state and goal state, considering potential actions, and keeping track of subgoals impose cognitive overhead. In contrast, Sweller argues that if you are given a set of *worked examples* instead, you obtain a reduction in working-memory load. Sweller has compared equation-solving performance for means-end analysis and worked examples, and found that worked examples resulted in better learning.

In summary, reducing working-memory load enhances training, and there are multiple ways to reduce it (using a diagram format, integration of material in different formats, using different sensory modalities, or using worked examples). Two other techniques that reduce working-memory load—part-task training and error prevention—are covered in the next two sections.

Part-Task Training   In *part-task training*, the elements of a complex task are learned separately. We can distinguish between two forms of part-task training, shown schematically in Figure 7.9 (Wightman & Lintern, 1985). In *segmentation*, each sequential phase of a task is practiced extensively in isolation before being integrated into the whole. An example is extensive practice on a particularly difficult arpeggio of a piano piece, with relatively little practice on a simpler phrase. Afterwards, the two musical sections would be played in sequence. Segmentation is a useful strategy when different segments of the skill vary greatly in their difficulty (Wightman & Lintern, 1985).

In contrast to segmentation, *fractionization* involves separate practice on two or more components (or two or more tasks) that must eventually be performed together. Some examples are practicing each hand of a piano piece alone, or practicing shifting gears without driving. The merits of fractionization are not clear-cut due to two conflicting factors. On one hand, fractionization allows attention to be focused on each component, reducing cognitive load and allowing automatic processing to develop (Schneider & Detweiler, 1988; Whaley & Fisk, 1993). On the other hand, separating task components prevents the development of *time-sharing skills* for linking and coordinating components (see Chapter 10; Lintern & Wickens, 1991; Wickens, 1989). Time-sharing skills are crucial when there are dependencies between task components—for example, working the gear shift, clutch, and accelerator in a car having manual transmission.

The competition between these two factors helps to explain the ambiguity of experimental results regarding the effectiveness of fractionization (Wightman & Lintern, 1985). Nonetheless, there are three successful approaches to making fractionization successful. The first is to identify task components that have little dependence on other components. The second is to identify components that are most important, and the third is to de-emphasize (rather than eliminate) certain components as one performs the whole task. We will discuss each of these approaches in turn.

Part-task training may be effective if the whole-task skill is carefully analyzed to identify components that can be independently broken off (i.e., are not correlated or integrated with the rest of the components) and those that may contain learnable consistencies that can be automated. This approach was successfully taken with the Space Fortress game described earlier, using task analysis to identify task components (Mane, Adams, & Donchin, 1989). Fractionization is also effective if task components draw on different working memory subsystems (Detweiler & Lundy, 1995).

Identifying important task components also improves fractionization. One approach to identifying important components is the *backward transfer technique*. In this technique, one group is trained on the whole task, another is trained on task components.

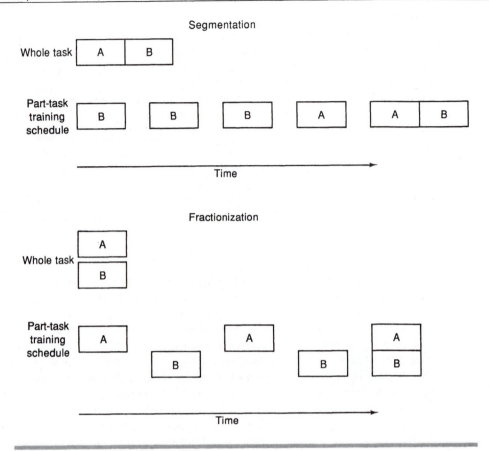

Figure 7.9 Two types of part-task training schedules.

Source: D. C. Wightman and G. Lintern, "Part-task Training for Tracking and Manual Control," *Human Factors,* *27*(3), pp. 267–283.

During the transfer phase, both groups are tested on the component tasks. Backward transfer can be estimated by comparing the transfer performance of the whole-task group to the initial performance of the task-component group. The result gives an indication of task components that are important for performance on the whole task (Goettl & Shute, 1996). Goettl and Shute used the backward transfer technique to identify critical components of an airborne slalom task in which trainees used a simulator to travel through a sequence of "gates" in the sky. They then trained one group of subjects on the critical components and found that this training was as effective as whole-task training. In summary, backward transfer is a promising development for improving the effectiveness of fractionization.

A final method for making fractionization effective is called *varied-priority training* (Gopher, Weil, & Siegel, 1989). In this technique, one task component is emphasized to the trainee and others are de-emphasized, even as all are performed concurrently. Hence the integrality of the whole task is not destroyed, and yet attention can be focused to some degree on particular task components. Varied-priority training has been applied to various tasks with some success (Fabiani et al., 1989; Kramer, Larish, & Strayer, 1995). For example, Kramer, Larish, and Strayer showed that varied-priority training produced more effective learning than equal-priority training for monitoring and mental arithmetic tasks performed simultaneously. They also found that varied-priority training led to faster development of automatic processing than did equal-priority training.

Guided Training   Training that allows errors to be repeated trial after trial is detrimental because the errors become learned. In addition to creating high workload, complex learning environments may be confusing so that unwanted errors occur, leading to further confusion (Carroll & Carrithers, 1984). Error prevention is often accomplished by *guided training*, which ensures that the learner's performance never strays far from what the task requires.

One guided training technique developed for word-processing systems is called *training wheels* (Carroll & Carrithers, 1984; Catrombone & Carroll, 1987). The training-wheels concept was developed to prevent users from making typical mistakes that would affect system performance. In systems without guided training, the mistakes would result in wasted time. Instead of allowing the error to affect the system, the training-wheels approach offers explicit and immediate feedback about the error. Compared with a conventional training approach, Catrombone and Carroll found both faster learning and better transfer to the full word-processing system, noting that a substantial training advantage was gained when subjects did not become confused while recovering from errors.

Of course, errors should not be eliminated completely. When performance is maximized by eliminating error during training, long-term learning can be impaired. That is, making errors during training improves long-term transfer to some degree (Schmidt & Bjork, 1992). Schmidt and Bjork note that difficulty in acquisition may produce a different strategy than when training is simplified, and the strategy acquired in the difficult learning conditions ultimately leads to better performance. This does not negate what we have said above regarding the training-wheels approach; rather, it appears that a happy medium is necessary, eliminating sources of error that change the task or increase wasted training time, but ensuring that those sources of error that are intrinsic to the task are kept. In addition, when errors are made, feedback about those errors can be provided to the trainee, and this feedback can be a valuable means for the trainee to improve performance, the topic of the next section.

Knowledge of Results   Providing the learner with knowledge of results (KR), or feedback about the quality of performance, is useful for motivation and for improving performance (Holding, 1987). Two factors are important in determining the effectiveness of KR: (1) If KR is delayed and the interval is filled with other activity, memory for the performance declines through retroactive interference and KR becomes less effective. This is a particular problem for decision-making tasks (see Chapter 8). (2) KR offered during performance is processed less well than immediately after completion because attention must be divided in the former case. For example, Schmidt and Wulf (1997) showed that continuous feedback during the acquisition of a motor task interfered with the rate of learning.

Learning by Example   All of us have had the experience of wanting to see an example of something we are asked to produce—an example of a good essay, a good C++ program, or a good basketball layup. In many professions (e.g., law, business, medicine), training is done through the use of *case studies*, example scenarios that illustrate certain principles. We noted earlier that current learning theories (e.g., ACT-R, Soar) emphasize the importance of specific situations and examples in learning. Indeed, many studies show the effectiveness of learning through the provision of examples (e.g., Catrombone, 1994, 1995; Lee & Hutchison, 1998; Reed & Bolstad, 1991). For example, Catrombone (1995) showed that providing an example for a word-processing concept led to better initial performance and did not penalize transfer performance later.

However, it is important for learning to specify what features of the example are particularly important for the concept to be learned—providing annotations within a problem solution are one means for doing this and are easily implemented in software form (Lee & Hutchison, 1998). It is also valuable to provide the student or trainee with questions to be answered after reviewing an example. In answering the questions, the student elaborates on task-relevant concepts. Lee and Hutchison compared these two techniques (annotation and elaboration) to a situation in which the example was provided alone and found that the addition of either made the example more effective, with elaboration providing the biggest advantage. Finally, as noted above, it is important that the cognitive load of processing examples (e.g., sample problems) not be excessive, or it will result in poorer training (Sweller, 1993).

Consistency of Mapping   For training to be most effective, there should be a *consistent mapping* between target information and the trainee's response. For example, a target word or symbol should remain the same across trials in a search task. In a visual search experiment, Rogers, Lee, and Fisk (1995) found that if there was consistent mapping between target information and the trainee's response, the rate of learning was faster than with *varied mapping* (when the distractor on one trial was a target on the previous trial). Varied mapping also impairs performance that is well learned and highly automatized (see Chapter 6). For example, Lee and Fisk (1993) found that even after 6,000 consistent mapping trials, overlearned performance is disrupted by inconsistency on the 6,001st trial.

The advantage for consistent mapping is seen even if the general context changes trial to trial. In the Rogers, Lee, and Fisk (1995) experiment, they periodically changed the general context (e.g., instead of looking for weapons, I look for vehicles). They found that there was an advantage for consistent mapping (that is, whenever the context is weapons, I look for cannons) over varied mapping in visual search—even if the context changed every trial.

However, there are many real-world work situations in which the mapping between target information and the observer's response is not consistent (Lee & Fisk, 1993). In this case, is it better to train with consistent mapping, or to train with varied mapping? Varied mapping might provide an advantage if the trainee must eventually deal with a varied mapping situation on the job: one day searching for bolts among screws, the next day searching for screws among bolts. In addition, although consistent mapping produces a greater rate of learning, as noted above, varied mapping does produce some improvement in performance during training (e.g., Rogers, Lee, & Fisk, 1995). More importantly, Rogers, Lee, and Fisk found that a reversal of targets and distractors impaired performance after consistently mapped training, but a change in target had little effect on performance after training with varied mapping.

Finally, if an operator must search for various targets in various contexts, the *feature learning* procedure developed by Rogers, Lee, and Fisk (1995) may serve as a compromise between consistent and varied mapping. Here, a set of training trials uses targets from a particular category (e.g., weapons) and distractors from another category (e.g., vehicles). In later trials, the categories are switched, so that targets are from the vehicles category, and distractors are from the weapons category. Training in this situation leads to faster learning rates than varied mapping, but slower learning rates than consistent mapping. Rogers, Lee, and Fisk also demonstrated less disruption by a reversal of targets and distractors than was the case with consistent mapping.

Thus, if I am a radar operator required to detect a particular type of target, and that is the only type of target I am searching for, consistent mapping will be more effective than varied mapping. In contrast, if targets and distractors vary in the real-world situation, my training will be more effective with varied mapping, although the learning rate during training will be poorer. Feature learning offers a compromise between these two extremes and may represent a viable training strategy when targets can be grouped into types.

Conclusions   In summary, the research on training strategies and transfer has produced results suggesting that a particular training strategy cannot be blindly applied to all tasks. However, a careful analysis of the information-processing requirements of a given task can reveal the conditions under which a given strategy may be more or less effective (Druckman & Bjork, 1994; Frederiksen & White, 1989; Mane, Adams, & Donchin, 1989; Schmidt & Bjork, 1992). The results of various training strategies discussed above should give the reader an understanding of what factors make training more or less effective. Learning—the storage of new information in long-term memory—is an information-processing task like any other discussed in this book. Thus the successful application of principles of training depends in part on an understanding of these information-processing components.

LONG-TERM MEMORY: REPRESENTATION, ORGANIZATION, AND RETRIEVAL
Knowledge Representation

Once information is encoded into long-term memory through learning and training, its long-term representation can take on a variety of forms. Some knowledge is procedural (how to do things), and other knowledge is declarative (knowledge of facts). Another distinction is drawn between general knowledge of things, like word meaning (semantic memory), and memory for specific events (episodic memory). Engineering psychologists have concerned themselves with the organization of the knowledge in memory, with methods for representing long-term knowledge, and with the concept of a mental model. We shall describe each of these in turn.

Knowledge Organization   We have long known that information is not stored in long-term memory as a random collection of facts. Rather, information has specific structure and organization, defining the ways in which items of knowledge are associated with one another. Systems designed to allow the operator to use knowledge from a domain will be well served if their features are congruent with the operator's organization of that knowledge. Consider the index for a book on engineering psychology. The author may index information relevant to display design under the heading "Perception, visual," whereas the engineer who is using the book would want to look under "Visual displays." To support a variety of users, indexes should be relatively broad and redundant, with entries accessible under different categories (Bailey, 1989; Roske-Hofstrand & Paap, 1986).

Or consider an index or a menu system for retrieving information from a database. If the categories and the structures defined by the system do not correspond to the user's mental organization of them, the user's search for a particular item may be time-consuming and frustrating, requiring slow serial search. That is, the user starts at the first list item and scans down until the target is reached. Thus, it is important to understand the mental representation of the typical user. Seidler and Wickens (1992) showed that if subjectively related information was closer together in a menu system, faster menu search resulted than if menu items were structured randomly (this study is described in more detail in Chapter 5). Similar results were obtained by Durding, Becker, and Gould (1977) and Roske-Hofstrand and Paap (1986).

However, as users gain knowledge about the information stored in the database (domain knowledge), they also become more flexible in how they can access information. Studies that have compared alphabetic and semantic organizations have shown that domain experts are generally effective with either kind of organization, but for novices the best organization depends on the task. For example, Hollands and Merikle (1987) found that novices were better with an alphabetic menu when the task required subjects to find a particular term, but were better with a semantically organized menu when the term was described but not actually provided. In contrast, experts were equally good with either organization for either task. That is, experts were more flexible than novices for menu search.

The results found by Hollands and Merikle (1987) have been replicated in different ways and in different domains. Smelcer and Walker (1993) found the same pattern of results with command menus. At the beginning of the study, their subjects were novices. When their novice users knew the exact names of commands, they were better with an alphabetic organization, and when they did not know the exact name, they were better off with semantically organized menus. After having acquired knowledge of the domain, the now expert subjects could perform well with either menu organization, demonstrating the flexibility of expertise. Salterio (1996) examined auditors at a large public accounting firm and found that after they had gained domain experience, the auditors were better able to perform command searches and used more flexible and complex search strategies. In sum, these results show that for domain novices, the task will determine the best way to organize the information; but for domain experts, various organizational approaches can be effective.

Methods for Representing Long-Term Knowledge   The engineering psychologist sometimes wants to gain access to the organization of an expert user's knowledge. This information may be useful for training programs, improving the design of an interface, or building a menu/indexing structure. Multiple *knowledge acquisition* techniques allow the engineering psychologist to do this (Gordon, 1994). One method is to use a *scaling technique* (see Kraiger, Salas, & Cannon-Bowers, 1995, or Rowe, Cooke, Hall, & Halgren, 1996, for examples), which gives one a sense of how domain concepts are related to each other, usually by having experts rate pairs of concepts. Another method is called *protocol analysis*, in which people perform typical tasks with a system and "think aloud" as they do so. *Interviews*, *observation*, and *document analysis* (i.e., deriving information about the task from manuals) are three other common techniques.

Once user's knowledge is acquired, how is it best represented? One technique that has been especially successful with respect to training is *conceptual graph analysis* (CGA) (Gordon, Schmierer, & Gill, 1993). A conceptual graph is a representation of a user's knowledge of a system. An example depicting a user's knowledge about a hi-fi VCR system is shown in Figure 7.10.

A specific syntax is used to constrain the types of nodes and links available, and which nodes can be connected to which links (Gordon, Schmierer, & Gill, 1993). Gordon,

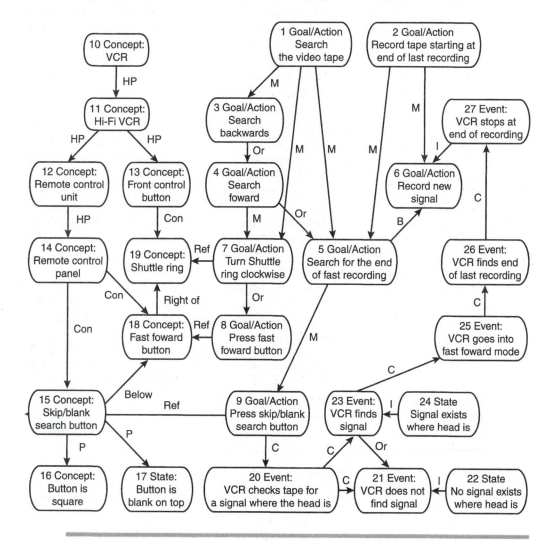

Figure 7.10 Partial conceptual graph for knowledge about a hi-fi VCR. The abbreviations for arc categories are B = Before; C = Has Consequence; Con = Contains; HP = Has Part; I = Initiates; M = Means; P = Has Property; Ref = Refers to.

Source: S. E. Gordon, K. A. Schmierer, & R. T. Gill, "Conceptual Graph Analysis: Knowledge Acquisition for Instructional System Design," *Human Factors, 35* (1993), p. 464.

Schmierer, and Gill used CGA to develop an instructional text for a topic in engineering dynamics. First, a document written by an expert was constructed as a conceptual graph. After construction, the graph was translated into a standard text format. Students using this knowledge-engineered text successfully solved more dynamics problems than students who used the original text.

Mental Models The concept of a mental model was discussed briefly in the context of display compatibility in Chapter 4. Here we consider the concept in a bit more depth. Carroll and Olson (1987) define a *mental model* as a mental structure that reflects the user's understanding of a system. In particular, they note that it can be conceived as knowledge about the system sufficient to permit the user to mentally try out actions before choosing one. A mental model may be created spontaneously by the user or carefully formed and structured through training.

An accurate mental model of a system can be advantageous because it provides the user with knowledge that is useful when other learned procedures fail. Yet mental models may be inaccurate, and when they are, breakdowns in performance occur and errors are committed (Doane, Pellegrino, & Klatzky, 1990). It would be advantageous, therefore, to create a correct mental model by explicit training on the underlying causal structure and principles operating in a system—the principles that lurk behind the procedures used to operate the system and its visible controls and displays. Incorporating a mental model into a training program can be effective. For instance, Halasz and Moran (1983) taught two groups of students how to use a calculator. One was taught procedures and the other given a mental model of the calculator's operations. Although both groups fared equally well in performing standard tasks, those trained with the mental model did better on novel tasks.

Although a training program may be the most effective method for providing a user with a mental model of a system, this approach is generally not taken for the design of consumer products and everyday household devices. As a result, people often have erroneous mental models for everyday devices; Norman (1988) offers some compelling examples and notes that an aid to the formation of a correct mental model of a system is the concept of *visibility*. A device is said to have visibility if by looking at it one can immediately tell the state of the device and possibilities for action. The relation between operator actions and state changes can be immediately seen (and thereby more easily learned). The concept of visibility also refers to the ability of a system to display intervening variables between user action and system response. For example, a thermostatic system that shows the state of the system that is generating or removing heat, as well as the momentary temperature, has visibility. Visibility is often reduced by high levels of automation (Chapter 13).

In sum, if the correct mental model for the operation of a device is provided to the user, either through training or by design, better performance should result. The main advantage to a correct mental model is that it allows the user to make correct predictions about untested situations, a useful characteristic for large and small systems alike.

Memory Retrieval and Forgetting

Knowing that information is stored in long-term memory does not guarantee that it will be retrieved when needed. Hence engineering psychologists must be concerned with the sources of memory failure. To do so, we distinguish between two forms of retrieval: recall and recognition.

Recall and Recognition   *Recall* describes the situation in which you must produce information stored in memory. For example, recall your telephone number. In *recognition*, you are provided with information and must indicate whether that information corresponds with what is stored in memory. For example, is your telephone number 555–6367, yes or no? Or can the eyewitness who is shown a suspect recognize that person as the perpetrator of a crime (see Chapter 2)? Recognition is typically indicated with a yes–no response or a choice response (as in recognizing the correct answer on a multiple-choice test), although these responses may be augmented by a "strength" estimate or confidence statement. To use Norman's (1988) terms, recall requires "knowledge in the head"; recognition places some "knowledge in the world." The long history of research on recognition versus recall shows that recognition is typically a more sensitive measure. That is, even though we may not be able to recall things, we can often recognize them as familiar once we see or hear them.

The contrast between recognition and recall is evident in the design of computer software. Recall failures are often a source of frustration for novices with older-style command-based interfaces (Mandler, 1980). Novices tend to prefer menus of commands, because they can scroll through the list until a particular command is recognized, a point captured nicely by the Soar model discussed earlier in the chapter (Newell, 1990). In contrast, for experts, using command menus can be frustrating because the expert must scroll through multiple menus to make selections. To deal with these problems, command menus found at the top of the display window in most current software also allow the user to press a sequence of keystrokes to accomplish the same functions. Once a command sequence can be recalled (e.g., File, Print, All), the user can press a sequence of keystrokes rather than scan the menus. Well-designed software allows both techniques to be used so that experts can use recall, and recognition can be used when recall fails.

What causes the failures of recognition and recall that lead to human performance errors? As with working memory, retroactive and proactive interference play a role. Also the similarity of to-be-remembered information to other information stored in long-term memory is a factor. As we saw in the discussion of negative transfer, a set of procedures learned for one word-processing system can become confused in memory with a set of procedures for a different system, particularly if many other aspects of the two systems are identical.

Another source of forgetting is the absence of *retrieval cues*, information in the external world that serves to help activate information stored in long-term memory. For example, I may need to remember the sequence of activities for operating a gasoline pump. Without retrieval cues, I may err in the performance sequence (e.g., by removing the nozzle before pushing the *on* button). In contrast, if the numbers 1, 2, 3 . . . are printed next to the controls to be activated, they provide a sequence of retrieval cues and I am less likely to err. In commercial aviation, the checklist has become the predominant method for reducing error in flight activities. The checklist provides retrieval cues for the sequence of activities the pilot must perform (Degani & Wiener, 1990; Reason, 1990).

Finally, the mere *passage of time* causes forgetting. We remember best those things that have happened most recently, a phenomenon known as *recency* that is relevant to our discussion of information integration in decision making in Chapter 8.

One particular kind of recall is that related to remembering to do something—like bring a book to class, or turn off the oven at a particular time. This type of memory is sometimes called *prospective memory* (Harris & Wilkins, 1982) and can be improved both by checklists, as discussed in Chapter 6, and by computer assistance such as the personal data assistant (Herrmann, Brubaker Yoder, Sheets, & Tio, 1999).

Event Memory   In Chapter 2, we described biases that affect the recognition memory of eyewitness testimony. In many other real-world situations, people must also remember events accurately; for example, the witness in a judicial proceeding (Neisser, 1982), or the system operator questioned in an investigation of a large-scale industrial or transportation accident. Two sources of bias emerge: the loss of knowledge about the event (forgetting), and the tendency to include new information that did not occur at the time of the event. Thus, witnesses are likely to "fill in" plausible details of an event even though those details were not explicitly observed (Neisser, 1982). This is especially characteristic of the expert (Arkes & Freedman, 1984), who has a large amount of domain-relevant knowledge. Put another way, top-down processing (Chapter 6) operates on one's memory for events.

Of equal concern is the way post-event information can be absorbed into one's memory of an event (Loftus, 1979; Wells & Loftus, 1984). For example, Brown, Deffenbacher, and Sturgill (1982) had subjects witness staged crimes in poor viewing conditions. Much later, the witnesses were asked to pick the perpetrator from a lineup. Witnesses were likely to pick an innocent person from the lineup if they had seen a picture of that person in the time between the crime and the lineup viewing. What is most disturbing is that witnesses tend to be unaware of their occurrence. As a result, witnesses are overconfident about their memory's accuracy, and this overconfidence is passed on to the jury or inquiry board (Lindsay, Wells, & Rumpel, 1981). We will deal with this form of overconfidence in Chapter 8.

Furthermore, there is good evidence that false memories can be created, or planted. That is, rather than post-event information changing an existing memory, memory for an event can be produced when there was no actual event! Loftus, Coan, and Pickrell (1996) presented stories to subjects that described events that had occurred in the subjects' childhoods. The stories were supplied by close relatives. However, one false story described getting lost in a shopping mall, a plausible childhood experience. Subjects read each story and then were asked to write what they remembered about each event. For the false story, they remembered about 25 percent of the events (for the true stories, they remembered 68 percent). None of the subjects had actually been lost in a mall.

Would the same results occur for more unusual events? The answer is yes: People will falsely remember events from the first year of life (Spanos, 1996), even though adults are unlikely to have such memories. These results are germane to *repressed memory syndrome*, in which people in therapy remember horrific events about their childhood. It is quite possible that many of these individuals never experienced such events, but rather they were planted by therapists' suggestions. Clearly, eyewitness testimony can be deceptive.

Since human testimony remains a necessary source of information in judicial proceedings or accident investigations, a jury or board of investigation should be made aware of the following empirically demonstrated facts: (1) information occurring after the event can be incorporated into the memory for an event, (2) confidence is not calibrated with accuracy, and (3) individuals can recall events that did not occur.

Skill Retention

In many work situations, operators are called upon to perform a particular learned skill. This *procedural memory* is different from the recall (or recognition) of specific episodes. Very often, the recall of procedures is accurate and effortless. For example, we do not forget how to drive a car, even though we might not have done so for a few days, weeks, or even years. But sometimes the problem of skill forgetting is a substantial one, in particular when the skill was not thoroughly learned in the first place. The commercial airline industry is sufficiently concerned with pilots forgetting skills not often practiced (e.g., recovery from emergencies) that recurrency training is required every six months.

It is important for the engineering psychologist to have some way to predict what skills will be forgotten at what rate in order to know how often operators should be required to participate in recurrency training. Generally, skilled performance declines with the retention interval, although the rate of forgetting can be slow, sometimes nonexistent. For example, Cooke, Durso, and Schvaneveldt (1994) showed that for skilled visual search, there is no loss in the search rate even after a nine-year interval. The following three factors are important in determining how well skilled performance is remembered (Rose, 1989).

Degree of Overlearning   Overlearning involves additional trials of practice after performance reaches some criterion or is error free. These additional practice trials help to automate the task and reduce the forgetting rate. This critical factor is sometimes neglected in training programs in which the operator is assumed to be sufficiently practiced once a criterion level of skill is first reached. Of course, in training for skills that are subsequently used on a daily basis (like driving or word processing), such overlearning will occur in the subsequent performance. But because learning skills related to emergency response procedures, for example, will not receive this same level of on-the-job training, their retention will greatly benefit from overlearning. Note, however, that the first few trials of additional practice will give the greatest retention benefits and subsequent trials have less benefit (Rose, 1989).

Skill Type   Different skill types have different lengths of skill retention (Rose, 1989). *Perceptual-motor skills*, such as driving, flight control, and most sports skills, show very little forgetting over long periods of time. In contrast, *procedural skills*, which require a sequence of steps, such as how to use a text processor or how to run through a checklist for turning on a piece of equipment, are more rapidly forgotten. Procedural skills may be particularly vulnerable if they cannot be associated with perceptual motor activity but are cognitive in nature, like some problem-solving procedures.

Individual Differences   Faster learners tend to show better retention than slower learners. Rose (1989) suggests that this difference may be related to chunking skills. As we have seen, better chunking will lead to faster acquisition as well as more effective and efficient storage in long-term memory.

TRANSITION

In this chapter, we discussed the separate components of verbal and spatial working memory and long-term memory. Each has different properties and different codes of representation, yet all are characterized by stages of encoding, storage, and retrieval.

Failures of each of these processes result in forgetting, which is a critical problem in human-system interaction. Techniques of system and task design and procedures to facilitate memory storage (training) were discussed.

In the next chapter, we discuss decision making, coupling the memory box in Figure 1.3 with the forward flow of information processing to include the selection of decision choices. Our treatment of decision making, however, depends on an understanding of memory and learning in three respects. First, many decisions place heavy loads on working memory. The costs imposed by these loads often lead to mental shortcuts, or *heuristics*, which produce systematic biases in decision performance. Second, other decisions are affected by long-term memory and experience. We decide on an action because the circumstances correspond to a memory of a situation in which we made the same decision and its outcome was successful. Finally, we will learn that the decision-making task has unique features, which cause learning and expertise in decision making to be somewhat different from that in other skills.

REFERENCES

Adams, M. J., Tenney, Y. J., & Pew, R. W. (1995). Situation awareness and the cognitive management of complex systems. *Human Factors, 37*, 85–104.

Allport, D. A. (1993). Attention and control: Have we been asking the wrong questions? A critical review of the last 25 years. In D. E. Meyer & S. Kornblum (Eds.), *Attention and performance XIV: A silver jubilee*. Cambridge, MA: MIT Press.

Anderson, J. R. (1981). *Cognitive skills and their acquisition*. Hillsdale, NJ: Erlbaum.

Anderson, J. R. (1991). Is human cognition adaptive? *Behavioral and Brain Sciences, 14*, 471–484

Anderson, J. R. (1993). *Rules of the mind*. Hillsdale, NJ: Erlbaum.

Anderson, J. R. (1996). ACT: A simple theory of complex cognition. *American Psychologist, 51*, 355–365.

Anderson, J. R., Reder, L. M., & Lebiere, C. (1996). Working memory: Activation limitations on retrieval. *Cognitive Psychology, 30*, 221–256.

Anderson, M. C., & Neely, J. H. (1996). Inference and inhibition in memory retrieval. In *Memory* (pp. 237–313). New York: Academic Press.

Arkes, H., & Freedman, M. R. (1984). A demonstration of the costs and benefits of expertise in recognition memory. *Memory & Cognition, 12*, 84–89.

Awh, E., Jonides, J., & Reuter-Lorenz, P. A. (1998). Rehearsal in spatial working memory. *Journal of Experimental Psychology: Human Perception & Performance, 24*, 780–790.

Baddeley, A. D. (1986). *Working memory*. Oxford: Clarendon.

Baddeley, A. D. (1990). *Human memory: Theory and practice*. Boston: Allyn and Bacon.

Baddeley, A. D. (1993). Working memory or working attention? In A. Baddeley & L. Weiskrantz (Eds.), *Attention: Selection, awareness and control. A tribute to Donald Broadent* (pp. 152–170). Oxford: Oxford University Press.

Baddeley, A. D. (1995). Working memory. In M. S. Gazzaniga et al. (Eds.), *The cognitive neurosciences* (pp. 755–784). Cambridge, MA: MIT Press.

Baddeley, A. D. (1996). Exploring the central executive. *Quarterly Journal of Experimental Psychology, 49A*, 5–28.

Baddeley, A. D., & Hitch, G. (1974). Working memory. In G. Bower (Ed.), *Recent advances in learning and motivation* (vol. 8). New York: Academic Press.

Bailey, R. W. (1989). *Human performance engineering using human factors/ergonomics to achieve computer system usability* (2d ed.). Englewood Cliffs, NJ: Prentice Hall.

Banbury, S., & Berry, D. C. (1998). Disruption of office-related tasks by speech and office noise. *British Journal of Psychology, 89,* 499–517.

Barfield, W. (1997). Skilled performance on software as a function of domain expertise and program organization. *Perceptual and Motor Skills, 85,* 1471–1480.

Bower, G. H., & Springston, F. (1970). Pauses as recoding points in letter series. *Journal of Experimental Psychology, 83,* 421–430.

Braune, R. J. (1989). *The common/same type rating: Human factors and other issues.* Anaheim, CA: SAE.

Brooks, L. R. (1968). Spatial and verbal components in the act of recall. *Canadian Journal of Psychology, 22,* 349–368.

Brown, E., Deffenbacher, K., & Sturgill, W. (1982). Memory for faces and the circumstances of encounter. In U. Neisser (Ed.), *Memory observed: Remembering in natural contexts* (pp. 130–138). San Francisco: W. H. Freeman.

Brown, J. (1959). Some tests of the decay theory of immediate memory. *Quarterly Journal of Experimental Psychology, 10,* 12–21.

Bruyer, R., & Scailquin, J.-C. (1998). The visuospatial sketchpad for mental images: Testing the multicomponent model of working memory. *Acta Psychologica, 98,* 17–36.

Card, S., Moran, T., & Newell, A. (1986). The model human processor. In K. Boff, L. Kaufman, & J. Thomas (Eds.), *Handbook of perception and human performance* (vol. 2). New York: Wiley.

Carroll, J. M., & Carrithers, C. (1984). Blocking learner error states in a training-wheels system. *Human Factors, 26,* 377–389.

Carroll, J. M., & Olson, J. (Eds.). (1987). *Mental models in human-computer interaction: Research issues about what the user of software knows.* Washington, DC: National Academy Press.

Casner, S. M. (1994). Understanding the determinants of problem-solving behavior in a complex environment. *Human Factors, 36,* 580–596.

Catrambone, R. (1994). Improving examples to improve transfer to novel problems. *Memory & Cognition, 22,* 606–615.

Catrambone, R. (1995). Following instructions: Effects of principles and examples. *Journal of Experimental Psychology: Applied, 1,* 227–244.

Catrambone, R., & Carroll, J. M. (1987). Learning a word processing system with training wheels and guided exploration. *Proceedings of CHI & GI human-factors in computing systems and graphics conference.* New York: Association for Computing Machinery, 169–174.

Cellier, J. M., Eyrolle, H., & Mariné, C. (1997). Expertise in dynamic environments. *Ergonomics, 40,* 28–50.

Chapanis, A., & Moulden, J. V. (1990). Short-term memory for numbers. *Human Factors, 32,* 123–137.

Charness, N. (1976). Memory for chess positions: Resistance to interference. *Journal of Experimental Psychology: Human learning and Memory, 2,* 641–653.

Chase, W. G., & Ericsson, A. (1981). Skilled memory. In S. A. Anderson (Ed.), *Cognitive skills and their acquisition.* Hillsdale, NJ: Erlbaum.

Chase, W. G., & Simon, H. A. (1973). The mind's eye in chess. In W. G. Chase (Ed.), *Visual information processing*. New York: Academic Press.

Clawson, D. M., Miller, M. S., Knott, B. A., & Sebrechts, M. M. (1998). Navigational training in virtual and real buildings. *Proceedings of the 42nd annual meeting of the Human Factors and Ergonomics Society* (pp. 1427–1431). Santa Monica, CA: Human Factors and Ergonomics Society.

Cooke, N. J., Durso, F. T., & Schvaneveldt, R. W. (1994). Retention of skilled search after nine years. *Human Factors, 36*, 597–605.

Craik, F. I. M., & Lockhart, R. S. (1972). Levels of processing: A framework for memory research. *Journal of Verbal Learning and Verbal Behavior, 11*, 671–684.

Danaher, J. W. (1980). Human error in ATC systems. *Human Factors, 22*, 535–546.

Degani, A., & Wiener, E. L. (1990). *Human factors of flight deck checklists: The normal checklist* (NASA Contractor Report 177549). Moffett Field, CA: NASA Ames Research Center.

deGroot, A. D. (1965). *Thought and choice in chess*. The Hague: Mouton.

Detweiler, M. C., & Lundy, D. H. (1995). Effects of single- and dual-task practice on acquiring dual-task skill. *Human Factors, 37*, 193–211.

Dingus, T. A., Hulse, M. C., & Barfield, W. (1998). Human-system interface issues in the design and use of advanced traveler information systems. In W. Barfield & T. A. Dingus (Eds.), *Human factors in intelligent transportation systems* (pp. 359–395). Mahwah, NJ: Erlbaum.

Dingus, T. A., Hulse, M. C., Mollenhauer, M. A., Fleischman, R. N., McGehee, D. V., & Manakkal, N. (1997). Effects of age, system experience, and navigation technique on driving with an advanced traveler information system. *Human Factors, 39*, 177–199.

Doane, S. M., Pellegrino, J. W., & Klatzky, R. L. (1990). Expertise in a computer operating system: Conceptualization and performance. *Human-Computer Interaction, 5*, 267–304.

Druckman, D., & Bjork, R. A. (1994). Transfer: Training for performance. In *Learning, remembering, believing* (pp. 25–56). Washington, DC: National Academy Press.

Durding, B. M., Becker, C. A., & Gould, J. D. (1977). Data organization. *Human Factors, 19*, 1–14.

Durso, F., & Gronlund, S. (1999). Situation awareness. In F. T. Durso (Ed.), *Handbook of Applied Cognition* (pp. 283–314). New York: John Wiley & Sons.

Endsley, M. R. (1995) Toward a theory of situation awareness in dynamic systems. *Human Factors, 37*, pp. 85–104.

Endsley, M. R., & Garland, D. J. (1999) *Situation awareness analysis and measurement*. Mahwah, NJ: Erlbaum.

Ericsson, K. A., & Kintsch, W. (1995). Long-term working memory. *Psychological Review, 102*, 211–245.

Ericsson, K. A., & Polson, P.G. (1988a). An experimental analysis of a memory skill for dinner orders. *Journal of Experimental Psychology: Learning, Memory, and Cognition, 14*, 303–316.

Fabiani, M., Buckley, J., Gratton, G., Coles, M. G. H., Donchin, E., & Logie, R. (1989). The training of complex task performance. *Acta Psychologica, 71*, 259–299.

Fischer, J., (1991). Defining the novice user. *Behaviour & Information Technology, 10*, 437–441.

Fisk, A. D., Ackerman, P. L., & Schneider, W. (1987). Automatic and controlled processing theory and its applications to human factors problems. In P. A. Hancock (Ed.), *Human factors psychology* (pp. 159–197). Amsterdam: Elsevier.

Fowler, F. D. (1980). Air traffic control problem: A pilot's view. *Human Factors, 22,* 645–654.

Frederiksen, J. R., & White, B. Y. (1989). An approach to training based upon principled task decomposition. *Acta Psychologica, 71,* 89–146.

Gobet, F. (1998). Expert memory: A comparison of four theories. *Cognition, 66,* 115–152.

Goettl, B. P., & Shute, V. J. (1996). Analysis of part-task training using the backward-transfer technique. *Journal of Experimental Psychology: Applied, 2,* 227–249.

Gopher, D., Weil, M., & Bareket, T. (1994). Transfer of skill from a computer game trainer to flight. *Human Factors, 36,* 387–405.

Gopher, D., Weil, M., & Siegel, D. (1989). Practice under changing priorities: An approach to the training of complex skills. *Acta Psychologica, 71,* 147–177.

Gordon, S. E. (1994). *Systematic training program design: Maximizing effectiveness and minimizing liability.* Englewood Cliffs, NJ: Prentice-Hall.

Gordon, S. E., Schmierer, K. A., & Gill, R. T. (1993). Conceptual graph analysis: Knowledge acquisition for instructional system design. *Human Factors, 35,* 459–481.

Gronlund, S. D., Ohrt, D. D., Dougherty, M. R. P., Perry, J. L., & Manning, C. A. (1998). Role of memory in air traffic control. *Journal of Experimental Psychology: Applied, 4,* 263–280.

Gugerty, L. J. (1997). Situation awareness during driving: Explicit and implicit knowledge in dynamic spatial memory. *Journal of Experimental Psychology: Applied, 3,* 42–66.

Haelbig, T. D., Mecklinger, A., Schriefers, H., & Friederici, A. D. (1998). Double dissociation of processing temporal and spatial information in working memory. *Neuropsychologia, 36,* 305–311.

Halasz, F. G., & Moran, T. P. (1983). Mental models and problem solving in using a calculator. In A. Janda (Ed.), *Human factors in computing systems: Proceedings of CHI 1983 Conference* (pp. 212–216). New York: Association for Computing Machinery.

Hampton, D. C. (1994). Expertise: The true essence of nursing art. *Advances in Nursing Science, 17,* 15–24.

Harris, J. E., & Wilkins, A. J. (1982). Remembering to do things: A theoretical framework and an illustrative experiment. *Human Learning 1,* 123–136.

Hart, S. G., & Loomis, L. L. (1980). Evaluation of the potential format and content of a cockpit display of traffic information. *Human Factors, 22,* 591–604.

Hawkins, F. H., & Orlady, H. W. (1993). *Human factors in flight* (2d ed.). Brookfield, VT: Gower.

Herrmann, D., Brubaker, B., Yoder, C., Sheets, V., & Tio, A. (1999). Devices that remind. In F. T. Durso (Ed.), *Handbook of Applied Cognition* (pp. 377–408). New York: John Wiley & Sons.

Hess, S. M., & Detweiler, M. C. (1996). The value of display space at encoding and retrieval in keeping track. In *Proceedings of the 40th annual meeting of the Human Factors and Ergonomics Society* (pp. 1232–1236). Santa Monica, CA: Human Factors and Ergonomics Society.

Hess, S. M., Detweiler, M. C., & Ellis, R. D. (in press). The utility of display space in keeping track of rapidly changing information. *Human Factors.*

Holding, D. H. (1976). An approximate transfer surface. *Journal of Motor Behavior, 8,* 1–9.

Holding, D. H. (1987). In G. Salvendy (Ed.), *Handbook of human factors.* New York: Wiley.

Hole, G. J. (1996). Decay and interference effects in visuospatial short-term memory. *Perception, 25,* 53–64.

Hollands, J. G., & Merikle, P. M. (1987). Menu organization and user expertise in information search tasks. *Human Factors, 29,* 577–586.

Hopkin, V. S. (1980). The measurement of the air traffic controller. *Human Factors, 22,* 347–360.

Howes, A., & Young, R. M. (1997). The role of cognitive architecture in modeling the user: Soar's learning mechanism. *Human-Computer Interaction, 12,* 331–343.

Human Factors Journal (1995). Special Issue on Situation Awareness, *37*(1).

Keppel, G., & Underwood, B. J. (1962). Proactive inhibition in short-term retention of single items. *Journal of Verbal Learning and Verbal Behavior, 1,* 153–161.

Kozak, J. J., Hancock, P. A., Arthur E. J., & Chrysler, S. T. (1993). Transfer of training from virtual reality. *Ergonomics, 36,* 777–784.

Kraiger, K., Salas, E., & Cannon-Bowers, J. A. (1995). Measuring knowledge organization as a method of assessing learning during training. *Human Factors, 37,* 804–816.

Kramer, A. F., Larish, J. F., & Strayer, D. L. (1995). Training for attentional control in dual task settings: A comparison of young and old adults. *Journal of Experimental Psychology: Applied, 1,* 50–76.

Labiale, G. (1990). In-car road information: Comparison of auditory and visual presentation. In *Proceedings of the 34th annual meeting of the Human Factors Society* (pp. 623–627). Santa Monica, CA: Human Factors Society.

Laird, J. E., & Rosenbloom, P. S. (1996). The evolution of the Soar cognitive architecture. In D. Steier & T. M. Mitchell (Eds.), *Mind matters: A tribute to Allen Newell* (pp. 1–50). Mahwah, NJ: Erlbaum.

Langewiesche, W. (1998). The lessons of ValuJet 592. *Atlantic Monthly*, March, 81–98.

Layton, C., Smith, P. J., & McCoy, C. E. (1994). Design of a cooperative problem-solving system for en-route flight planning: An empirical evaluation. *Human Factors, 36,* 94–119.

Lee, A. Y., & Hutchison, L. (1998). Improving learning from examples through reflection. *Journal of Experimental Psychology: Applied, 4,* 187–210.

Lee, M. D., & Fisk, A. D. (1993). Disruption and maintenance of skilled visual search as a function of degree of consistency. *Human Factors, 35,* 205–220.

Lindsay, R. C., Wells, G. L., & Rumpel, C. M. (1981). Can people detect eyewitness identification accuracy within and across situations? *Journal of Applied Psychology, 67,* 79–89.

Lintern, G., & Wickens, C. D. (1987). *Attention theory as a basis for training research* (Technical Report ARL–87–2/NASA–87–3). Savoy, IL: University of Illinois, Institute of Aviation.

Lintern, G., Roscoe, S. N., & Sivier, J. (1990). Display principles, control dynamics, and environmental factors in pilot performance and transfer of training. *Human Factors, 32,* 299–317.

Lintern, G., Thomley-Yates, K. E., Nelson, B. E., & Roscoe, S. N. (1987). Content, variety, and augmentation of simulated visual scenes for teaching air-to-ground attack. *Human Factors, 29,* 45–59.

Liu, Y., & Wickens, C. D. (1992). Visual scanning with or without spatial uncertainty and divided and selective attention. *Acta Psychologica, 79,* 131–153.

Loftus, E. F. (1979). *Eyewitness testimony.* Cambridge, MA: Harvard University Press.

Loftus, E. F., Coan, J. A., & Pickrell, J. E. (1996). Manufacturing false memories using bits of reality. In L. Reder (Ed.), *Implicit memory and metacognition* (pp. 195–220). Mahwah, NJ: Erlbaum.

Loftus, G. R., Dark, V. J., & Williams, D. (1979). Short-term memory factors in ground controller/pilot communications. *Human Factors, 21,* 169–181.

Logie, R. H. (1995). *Visuo-spatial working memory.* Hove, UK: Erlbaum.

Mandler, G. (1980). Recognizing: The judgment of previous occurrence. *Psychological Review, 87,* 252–271.

Mane, A. M., Adams, J. A., & Donchin, E. (1989). Adaptive and part-whole training in the acquisition of a complex perceptual-motor skill. *Acta Psychologica, 71,* 179–196.

Marcus, N., Cooper, M., & Sweller, J. (1996). Understanding instructions. *Journal of Educational Psychology, 88,* 49–63.

Mayhew, D. J. (1992). *Principles and guidelines in software user interface design.* Englewood Cliffs, NJ: Prentice-Hall.

McCutchen, D., Covill, A., Hoyne, S. H., & Mildes, K. (1994). Individual differences in writing: Implications of translating fluency. *Journal of Educational Psychology, 86,* 256–266.

McGeoch, J. A. (1936). Studies in retroactive inhibition: VII. Retroactive inhibition as a function of the length and frequency of presentation of the interpolated lists. *Journal of Experimental Psychology, 19,* 674–693.

Melton, A. W. (1963). Implications of short-term memory for a general theory of memory. *Journal of Verbal Learning and Verbal Behavior, 2,* 1–21.

Miller, G. A. (1956). The magical number seven plus or minus two: Some limits on our capacity for processing information. *Psychological Review, 63,* 81–97.

Moray, N. (1980, May). *Human information processing and supervisory control* (Technical Report). Cambridge, MA: MIT, Man-Machine System Laboratory.

Moray, N. (1986). Monitoring behavior and supervising control. In K. R. Boff, L. Kaufman, & J. P. Thomas (Eds.), *Handbook of perception and human performance.* New York: Wiley.

Moroney, W. F., & Moroney, B. W. (1999). Flight simulation. In D. Garlond, J. Wise, and V. D. Hopkin (Eds.), *Handbook of Aviation Human Factors.* Mahwah, NJ: Lawrence Erlbaum.

Mousavi, S. Y., Low, R., & Sweller, J. (1995). Reducing cognitive load by mixing auditory and visual presentation modes. *Journal of Educational Psychology, 87,* 319–334.

National Transportation Safety Board (1988). *Northwest Airlines, Inc. McDonnell Douglas DC–9–82 N312RC, Detroit Metropolitan Wayne County Airport, Romulus, Michigan, August 16, 1987* (Report No. NTSB-AAR–88–05). Washington, DC: National Transportation Safety Board.

Neisser, U. (1982). *Memory observed: Remembering in natural contexts.* San Francisco: W. H. Freeman.

Newell, A. (1990). *Unified theories of cognition,* Cambridge, MA: Harvard University Press.

Nilsson, L. G., Ohlsson, K., & Ronnberg, J. (1977). Capacity differences in processing and storage of auditory and visual input. In S. Dornick (Ed.), *Attention and Performance VI.* Hillsdale, NJ: Erlbaum.

Norman, D. A. (1988). *The psychology of everyday things.* New York: Harper & Row.

O'Hara, K. P., & Payne, S. J. (1998). The effects of operator implementation cost on planfulness of problem solving and learning. *Cognitive Psychology, 35,* 34–70.

Payne, S. J. (1991). Display-based action at the user interface. *International Journal of Man-Machine Studies, 35,* 275–289.

Peterson, L. R., & Peterson, M. J. (1959). Short-term retention of individual verbal items. *Journal of Experimental Psychology, 58,* 193–198.

Povenmire, H. K., & Roscoe, S. N. (1973). Incremental transfer effectiveness of a ground-based general aviation trainer. *Human Factors, 15,* 534–542.

Proctor, R. W., & Dutta, A. (1995). *Skill acquisition and human performance.* Thousand Oaks, CA: Sage.

Reason, J. (1990). *Human error.* Cambridge, England: Cambridge University Press.

Reed S. K., & Bolstad, C. A. (1991). Use of examples and procedures in problem solving. *Journal of Experimental Psychology: Learning, Memory, and Cognition, 17*, 753–766.

Robertson, S., Zachery, W., & Black, J. (Eds.). (1990). *Cognition, computing, and cooperation.* Norwood, NJ: Ablex.

Rogers, W. A., Lee, M. D., & Fisk, A. D. (1995). Contextual effects on general learning, feature learning, and attention strengthening in visual search. *Human Factors, 37*, 158–172.

Rogers, W. A., Rousseau, G. K., & Fisk, A. D. (1999). Applications of attention research. In F. T. Durso (Ed.), *Handbook of Applied Cognition* (pp. 33–56). New York: John Wiley & Sons.

Rose, A. M. (1989). Acquisition and retention of skills. In G. MacMillan (Ed.), *Applications of human performance models to system design.* New York: Plenum.

Roske-Hofstrand, R. J., & Paap, K. R. (1986). Cognitive networks as a guide to menu organization: An application in the automated cockpit. *Ergonomics, 29*, 1301–1311.

Rowe, A. L., Cooke, N. J., Hall, E. P., & Halgren, T. L. (1996). Toward an on-line knowledge assessment methodology: Building on the relationship between knowing and doing. *Journal of Experimental Psychology: Applied, 2*, 31–47.

Salterio, S. (1996). Decision support and information search in a complex environment: Evidence from archival data in auditing. *Human Factors, 38*, 495–505.

Sarter, N., & Woods, D. (1995). How in the world did we ever get into that mode? *Human Factors, 37*, 5–19.

Schmidt, R. A., & Bjork, R. A. (1992). New conceptualizations of practice: Common principles in three paradigms suggest new concepts for training. *Psychological Science, 3*, 207–217.

Schmidt, R. A., & Wulf, G. (1997). Continuous concurrent feedback degrades skill learning: Implications for training and simulation. *Human Factors, 39*, 509–525.

Schneider, W. (1985). Training high-performance skills: Fallacies and guidelines. *Human Factors, 27*, 285–300.

Schneider, W., & Detweiler, M. (1988). The role of practice in dual-task performance: Toward workload modeling in a connectionist/control architecture. *Human Factors, 30*, 539–566.

Scholtz, J., & Wiedenbeck, S. (1993). Using unfamiliar programming languages: The effects of expertise. *Interacting with Computers, 5*, 13–30.

Seidler, K. S., & Wickens, C. D. (1992). Distance and organization in multifunction displays. *Human Factors, 34*, 555–569.

Shulman, H. G. (1972). Semantic confusion errors in short-term memory. *Journal of Verbal Learning and Verbal Behavior, 11*, 221–227.

Shute, V. J., Gawlick, L. A., & Gluck, K. A. (1998). Effects of practice and learner control on short- and long-term gain and efficiency. *Human Factors, 40*, 296–310

Simon, H. A. (1978). Rationality as process and product of thought. *Journal of the American Economic Association, 68*, 1–16.

Simon, H. A. (1981). *The sciences of the artificial* (2d ed.). Cambridge, MA: MIT Press

Simon, H. A. (1990). Invariants of human behaviour. *Annual Review of Psychology, 41*, 1–19.

Singley, M. K., & Andersen, J. R. (1989). *The transfer of cognitive skill.* Cambridge, MA: Harvard University Press.

Smelcer, J. B., & Walker, N. (1993). Transfer of knowledge across computer command menus. *International Journal of Human-Computer Interaction, 5*, 147–165.

Smyth, M. M., & Pendleton, L. R. (1990). Space and movement in working memory. *Quarterly Journal of Experimental Psychology, 42A*, 291–304.

Smyth, M. M., & Waller, A. (1998). Movement imagery in rock climbing: Patterns of interference from visual, spatial and kinaesthetic secondary tasks. *Applied Cognitive Psychology, 12*, 145–157.

Spanos, N. P. (1996). *Multiple identities and false memories.* Washington, DC: American Psychological Association.

Srinivasan, R., & Jovanis, P. P. (1997). Effect of selected in-vehicle route guidance systems on driver reaction times. *Human Factors, 39*, 200–215.

Stevens, J. (1993). An observational study of skilled memory in waitresses. *Applied Cognitive Psychology, 7*, 205–217.

Strauch, B. (1997). Automation and decision making—Lessons from the Cali accident. In *Proceedings of the annual meeting of the Human Factors and Ergonomics Society* (pp. 195–199). Santa Monica, CA: Human Factors and Ergonomics Society.

Sweller, J. (1993). Some cognitive processes and their consequences for the organisation and presentation of information. *Australian Journal of Psychology, 45*, 1–8.

Sweller, J., Chandler, P., Tierney, P., & Cooper, M. (1990). Cognitive load as a factor in the structuring of technical material. *Journal of Experimental Psychology: General, 119*, 176–192.

Sweller, J., van Merrienboer, J. J. G., & Paas, F. G. W. C. (1998). Cognitive architecture and instructional design. *Educational Psychology Review, 10*, 251–296.

Thorndyke, P. W., & Hayes-Roth, B. (1982). Differences in spatial knowledge acquired from maps and navigation. *Cognitive Psychology, 14*, 560–589.

Tindall-Ford, S., Chandler, P., & Sweller, J. (1997). When two sensory modes are better than one. *Journal of Experimental Psychology: Applied, 3*, 257–287.

Venturino, M. (1997). Interference and information organization in keeping track of continually changing information. *Human Factors, 39*, 532–539.

Vessey, I. (1985). Expertise in debugging computer programs: A process analysis. *International Journal of Man-Machine Studies, 23*, 459–494.

Vicente, K. J. (1992). Memory recall in a process control system: A measure of expertise and display effectiveness. *Memory & Cognition, 20*, 356–373.

Vicente, K. J. & Wang, J. H. (1998). An ecological theory of expertise effects in memory recall. *Psychological Review, 105*, 33–57.

Vinze, A. S., Sen, A., & Liou, S. F. T. (1993). Operationalizing the opportunistic behavior in model formulation. *International Journal of Man-Machine Studies, 38*, 509–540.

Ward, G., & Allport, A. (1997). Planning and problem-solving using the five-disc Tower of London task. *Quarterly Journal of Experimental Psychology, 50A*, 49–78.

Wells, G. L., & Loftus, E. F. (1984). *Eyewitness testimony: Psychological perspective.* New York: Cambridge University Press.

Wenger, M. J., & Payne, D. G. (1995). On the acquisition of mnemonic skill: Application of skilled memory theory. *Journal of Experimental Psychology: Applied, 1*, 194–215.

Wetherell, A. (1979). Short-term memory for verbal and graphic route information. *Proceedings of the 23d annual meeting of the Human Factors Society.* Santa Monica, CA: Human Factors Society.

Whaley, C. J., & Fisk, A. D. (1993). Effects of part-task training on memory set unitization and retention of memory-dependent skilled search. *Human Factors, 35*, 639–652.

Wickelgren, W. A. (1964). Size of rehearsal group in short-term memory. *Journal of Experimental Psychology, 68,* 413–419.

Wickens, C. D. (1989). Attention and skilled performance. In D. Holding (Ed.), *Human skills* (2d ed.) (pp. 71–105). New York: Wiley.

Wickens, C. D. (1999). The tradeoff in the design for routine and unexpected performance: implications for situation awareness. In M. R. Endsley, & D. J. Garland (Eds.), *Situation awareness analysis and measurement.* Mahwah, NJ: Erlbaum.

Wickens, C. D., & Liu, Y. (1988). Codes and modalities in multiple resources: A success and a qualification. *Human Factors, 30,* 599–616.

Wickens, C. D., Sandry, D., & Vidulich, M. (1983). Compatibility and resource competition between modalities of input, central processing, and output: Testing a model of complex task performance. *Human Factors, 25,* 227–248.

Wickens, C. D., Vidulich, M., & Sandry-Garza, D. (1984). Principles of S-C-R compatibility with spatial and verbal tasks: The role of display-control location and voice-interactive display-control interfacing. *Human Factors, 26,* 533–543.

Wiener, E., & Nagel, D. (1988). *Human factors in aviation.* San Diego, CA: Academic Press.

Wiggins, M., & O'Hare, D. (1995). Expertise in aeronautical weather-related decision making: A cross-sectional analysis of general aviation pilots. *Journal of Experimental Psychology: Applied, 1,* 305–320.

Wightman, D. C., & Lintern, G. (1985). Part-task training for tracking and manual control. *Human Factors, 27,* 267–283.

Wilson, P. N., Foreman, N., & Tlauka, M. (1997). Transfer of spatial information from a virtual to a real environment. *Human Factors, 39,* 526–531.

Winstein, C. J., & Schmidt, R. A. (1989). Sensorimotor Feedback. In D. H. Holding (Ed.) *Human Skills* (2nd ed.). Chichester, UK: Wiley.

Witmer, B. G., Bailey, J. H., Knerr, B. W., & Parsons, K. C. (1996). Virtual spaces and real world places: transfer of route knowledge. *International Journal of Human-Computer Studies, 45,* 413–428.

Woodin, M. E., & Heil, J. (1996). Skilled motor performance and working memory in rowers: Body patterns and spatial positions. *The Quarterly Journal of Experimental Psychology, 49A,* 357–378.

Ye, N., & Salvendy, G. (1994). Quantitative and qualitative differences between experts and novices in Chunking computer software knowledge. *International Journal of Human-Computer Interaction, 6,* 105–118.

Yntema, D. (1963). Keeping track of several things at once. *Human Factors, 6,* 7–17.

Zhang, J., & Norman, D. A. (1994). Representations in distributed cognitive tasks. *Cognitive Science, 18,* 87–122.

Decision Making

OVERVIEW

The driver described at the beginning of this book made several decisions prior to his unfortunate accident. Just before the accident, he decided to steer left, and then right again. These were rapid decisions, with little conscious thought or cognitive processing before them. On the other hand, his decision to look downward and use the dispatching device without stopping the car was preceded by a little more "conscious" deliberation; even more conscious were the various decisions he would make en route, regarding which destination to travel to next. Decisions typical of the steering choices, the rapid choices in response to clearly visible or audible stimuli or events, are the topic of Chapter 9. In this chapter, we consider choices of a more deliberative nature, in which the risks and benefits of different outcomes are considered.

Many serious accidents in which human error has been involved can be attributed to faulty operator decision making: The decision to launch the *Challenger* space shuttle, which later exploded because cold temperature at launch time destroyed the seals, is one example; another is the decision of personnel on board the *USS Vincennes* to fire on an unknown aircraft, which turned out to be a civilian transport rather than a hostile fighter (U.S. Navy, 1988; Klein, 1996). A contrasting tragic decision was made by those on board the *USS Stark,* cruising in the Mediterranean, not to fire on an approaching target that turned out to be hostile, which cost several lives on board the *Stark.* Of course, these and other decisions gain notoriety because they generated unfortunate or tragic outcomes. In the same manner, we may recall most strongly our own personal decisions that went awry: the class we chose to take that we failed, or the poor investment we made. However, in terms of frequency, our lives are far more dominated by the less salient decisions that went right. In this chapter, we consider the processes that underlie decisions of both kinds, and the characteristics of the information and choice that can either improve the likelihood of the favorable outcome, or can make the decision more difficult and increase the likelihood of an unwanted result.

FEATURES AND CLASSES OF DECISION MAKING

From an information processing perspective, decisions typically represent a many-to-one mapping of information to responses. That is, a lot of information is typically perceived and evaluated in order to produce a single choice. However the *complexity* of that choice can vary greatly. Perhaps the simplest sort of decision is the *go–no go* choice, such as the decision to proceed at a traffic light, or the decision to continue on with any activity or halt it (Orasanu & Fischer, 1997). More complex is the multiple-choice task, in which several possible options are available—the student deciding which course to take for example, or our driver deciding which destination to pursue next.

Uncertainty   An important feature of any decision is the degree of *uncertainty* of the consequences. Such uncertainty is generally a result of the probabilistic nature of the world in which we live, in which a given choice may lead to one sort of outcome if certain characteristics of the world are in effect, and a different outcome otherwise. If some of the possible but uncertain outcomes are unpleasant or costly ones, we usually consider the uncertainty decision as involving *risk*. The decision to purchase one of two possible vehicles is generally low risk, if you have done advanced research on product quality, since the probable outcomes of one purchase or the other are known. However, the pilot's decision to proceed with a flight in uncertain weather may have a high amount of risk, since it is difficult to predict in advance what impact the weather will have on the safety of the flight.

Familiarity and Expertise   All of us have made decisions in circumstances and about options that are highly familiar. Those choices are often made rapidly and with little deliberation (Zsambok & Klein, 1997). At the same time, we are sometimes confronted by choices in which the outcomes are uncertain, in which the cues are unfamiliar, and the deliberation is difficult. In Chapter 7, we considered the differences between novices and experts in the way in which information is processed, and such differences indeed play an important role in decision making. We note, however, that just because experts make decisions more rapidly and with less effort than novices, this does not imply that they are always more accurate (Camerer & Johnson, 1997; Shanteau, 1992; Ebbeson & Konecni, 1980).

Time   Time plays at least two important roles in influencing the decision process. First, we may contrast "one shot" decisions like the choice of a purchase, with evolving decisions like those involved in treating an uncertain disease, in which tests are followed by medication, which may be followed by further tests and then a choice of further treatment. Second, *time pressure* has a critical influence on the nature of the decision process (Svenson & Maule, 1993); we discuss this in detail in Chapter 12.

Classes of Decision-Making Research   Certain features described above have played a prominent role in distinguishing three important classes of decision-making research. The study of *rational* or *normative* decision making (e.g., Edwards, 1987; Lehto, 1997) has focused its efforts on how people *should* make decisions according to some optimal framework or "gold standard": for example, one that will maximize the expected profit, or minimize the expected loss. Efforts here are often focused on the departures of human decision making from these optimal prescriptions. We considered a simple example of this in the context of setting the "optimal beta" for signal-detection decisions in Chapter 2, and we discuss it in more detail below. The *cognitive* or *information processing* approach to decision making focuses more directly on the sorts of biases and processes used in decision making that can be related to limitations in human attention, working memory, or strategy choice, as well as on familiar decision routines—known as *heuristics*—that work well most of the time but occasionally lead to undesirable outcomes (Kahneman, Slovic, & Tversky, 1982; Hogarth, 1987; Wallsten, 1981). Less emphasis here is placed on departures from optimal choice, and more is placed on understanding the *causes* of such biases and strategies in terms of the structure of the human information processing system. Finally, the most recent approach, *naturalistic decision making* (Zsambok & Klein, 1997), places its greatest emphasis on how people make decisions in real environments (i.e., outside of the laboratory), where they possess expertise in the domain, and where the decisions have many of the aspects of complexity (evolving time, time pressure, multiple cues) that may be absent in laboratory studies of decision making. In the model and discussion below, features of all three approaches are discussed as they are relevant.

AN INFORMATION PROCESSING MODEL OF DECISION MAKING

Figure 8.1 presents a model of the information processing components that are involved in decision making. To provide context, the full model of information processing presented in Chapter 1 is displayed within the box in the upper corner. The decision-making model here highlights and elaborates some components of the full model, while de-emphasizing others (e.g., sensory processing, response execution).

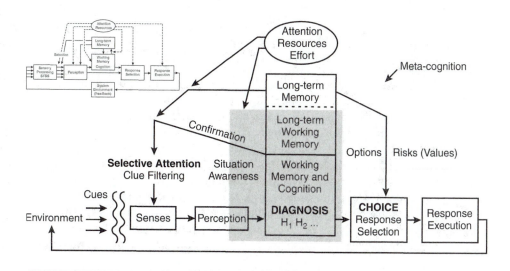

Figure 8.1   Key processes and components involved in an information processing model of decision making. These components may be easily mapped onto the components of the general model from Chapter 1 (shown in the inset), but this model highlights concepts, operations, and terms more typically associated with decision making.

Beginning at the left, the decision maker must seek *cues* or sensory information from the environment. However, we note that in decision making (unlike much of pattern recognition), these cues are often processed through the "fuzzy haze" of uncertainty, and hence, may be ambiguous or interpreted incorrectly. Our driver in Chapter 1, for example, decided to gaze downward toward his display, assuming, incorrectly, that the environment did not present a stalled vehicle in his forward path. *Selective attention* plays a critical role in decision making, in choosing which cues to process and which to filter out. Such selection is based on past experiences (long-term memory) and requires effort or attentional resources.

The cues that are then selected and perceived now form the basis of an understanding, assessment, or awareness of "the situation" confronting the decision maker (Prince & Salas, 1997), a process that is sometimes labeled *diagnosis* (Rasmussen & Rouse, 1981). Recently the term *situation awareness* (Endsley, 1995; Garland & Endsley, 1995), shown in the shaded box of Figure 8.1 and discussed in Chapter 7, has been used to connote the combined operations in perception, working memory, and long-term working memory (Kintsch & Ericsson, 1995), that enable the decision maker to entertain hypotheses about the current and future state of the world. This is also sometimes referred to as *situation assessment*. For example, the physician must diagnose a patient's status before deciding on a treatment, the battlefield commander should become aware of the enemy's intent before choosing a course of action, and the student may wish to become aware of an instructor's quality prior to choosing a course. This diagnosis is based on information from two sources: the external cues filtered by selective attention (bottom-up processing), and long-term memory. The latter can provide the decision maker with various possible hypotheses of system state (e.g., the physician's knowledge of possible diseases and their associated symptoms or cures), as well as estimates of the likelihood or expectancy that each might be true (top-down processing). What makes decision making distinct from many other aspects of information processing is that diagnosis or situation assessment on which a choice is based, is often incorrect, either because of the uncertain nature of the cues, their ambiguous mapping to hypotheses, or because of vulnerabilities in the cognitive processing of the decision maker related to selective attention (Chapter 3) and working memory (Chapter 7).

Many diagnoses are *iterative* in the sense that initial hypotheses will trigger the search for further information to either confirm or refute them. Troubleshooting a system failure, like that in the driver's automated scheduler, will often trigger repeated tests to confirm or refute possible hypotheses (Rouse, 1981). This characteristic defines the important feedback loop to cue filtering, labeled "confirmation" in Figure 8.1.

Following from the stages of cue seeking and situation awareness (or diagnosis), the third principle stage in decision making is the *choice* of an action. From long-term memory, the decision maker can generate a set of possible courses of action or decision options; but if the diagnosis of the state of the world is uncertain (as it is in much decision making), then the consequence of the different choices define their *risks*. Consideration of risk requires the estimation of *values*, just as we saw in Chapter 2, that the decisions made in signal detection theory depended on the values (costs and benefits) of different outcomes (hits, false alarms, misses, correct rejections). Thus, the physician will consider the values and costs of various outcomes before she decides which treatment (do nothing, drugs, surgery) to recommend for a patient's abnormality of uncertain identity.

The major feedback loop shown at the bottom of Figure 8.1 remains as important as it was in the information processing model in Chapter 1. First, feedback of decision outcomes is sometimes used to assist in diagnosis. This is clearly the case for an operator who is *troubleshooting* a piece of equipment; decisions to make tests will provide information to confirm or refute a diagnosis. Second, feedback *may* be employed in a learning sense, to improve the quality of future decisions (i.e., learning from one's mistakes); this feedback (although often delayed) may eventually be processed in long-term memory in order for the decision maker to revise his or her internal rules of decision making or the estimates of risks. (Improving decision making is discussed in more detail later in this chapter.)

Finally, the figure depicts the role of *meta-cognition* (Reder, 1998). This process—awareness of one's own knowledge, effort, and thought processes—is closely linked with situation awareness (in this case, the "situation" of which one is aware involves the evolving decision process) and turns out to have an important influence on the overall quality of decision making: Is one aware of the limitations in one's own decision process? Does the decision-maker know that he or she does not possess all the information necessary to make a good decision and, hence, seeks more?

WHAT IS "GOOD" DECISION MAKING?

The previous section emphasized several information processing components involved in decision making (e.g., cue perception, selective attention, working memory). In previous chapters, we discussed many of these components in detail and outlined strengths and limitations of each one, such as the limited capacity of working memory. Hence, it is not surprising that the decision process may fall short of "perfect" or "optimal" performance and mistakes are made. Yet at the same time, the concept of what really is "good" decision-making has proven to be elusive (Brehmer, 1981; Lipshitz, 1997; Shanteau, 1992;), in contrast to other aspects of human performance, where speed and accuracy have a clearly defined status of quality. In fact, at least three different characterizations of "good" decision making have been offered, which are not in perfect agreement with each other.

First, early decision research of the normative school offered the *expected value* of a decision as the "gold standard." That is, the optimum decision would produce the maximum value if repeated numerous times (Edwards, 1961, 1987). However, it turned out that defining expected value depends on assigning universally agreed on values to the various possible outcomes of a choice; but values are often personal, making this a difficult undertaking. Even if values could be agreed on, the optimal choice if the decision was repeated time and again, with plenty of time for weighing all the cues, will not necessarily be optimal for a single choice. This will be particularly true if the decision is made under time pressure, with little time to fully diagnose the situation and consider all possible outcomes (Zsambok & Klein, 1997). Furthermore, for a single decision, the decision maker may be more concerned about minimizing the maximum possible loss (worst case), rather than maximizing expected long-term gain, which after all can only be realized following a long-term average of the outcome of several decisions (Lehto, 1997). Choices to purchase insurance are often based, rationally, upon avoiding the "worst case".

Second, one may say that "good" decisions are those that produce "good" outcomes, and bad decisions conversely produce bad outcomes, such as the decision to launch the *Challenger* or to fire on the Iranian airliner from the *USS Vincennes,* or the decision of a jury to convict a suspect who subsequently is found innocent. Yet we also know that in a probabilistic, uncertain world, where cues are uncertain, it may only be with 20–20 hindsight that the decision can be labeled "bad." After all, the decision makers on board the *USS Vincennes* must have considered that the decision made a year earlier on board the *USS Stark,* not to fire on an approaching contact, had turned out to be "bad," leading to the loss of life on the *Stark* (Klein, 1996).

A third approach to decision quality has been based on the concept of *expertise* (Zsambok & Klein, 1997; Brehmer, 1981; Shanteau, 1992; see Chapter 7). Since other fields (e.g., chess, physics) are known to produce "good" and sometimes exceptional performance, perhaps expert decision makers do the same. The problem is that analyses of decision making in different domains have shown that experts do not necessarily make better decisions than novices (Dawes, 1979; Brehmer, 1981; Eddy, 1982; Shanteau, 1992; Serfaty, MacMillan, Entin, & Entin, 1997); indeed, several "bad" decisions, according to our second criterion, have been made by highly trained experts. However, it is possible to identify some domain characteristics that help determine when experts will excel or be deficient in their decision quality (Shanteau, 1992), an issue we discuss later in this chapter.

We adopt the approach here that, when all three characteristics converge, it becomes increasingly easy to discriminate good from bad decision making. But when they do not, it is more appropriate to look at the ways that different environmental and informational characteristics influence the processing operations and outcomes of the decision process. This is the framework shown in Figure 8.1, and is how we treat the material below, first considering how people accumulate and assess evidence bearing on a diagnosis, and then how they use that assessment to choose an action.

DIAGNOSIS AND SITUATION AWARENESS IN DECISION MAKING

As we have noted, *understanding* the situation, often in terms of diagnosing which possible states of the world might be in effect (or predicted), must form the foundation for effective choice (Swets & Pickett, 1982). Indeed, recent research suggests that situation awareness is one of the most important components of effective decision making. Pilots who are good decision makers (by the various criteria above) take *longer* in understanding a situation or decision problem, even as they select and execute the choice more rapidly (Orasanu & Fischer, 1997). As shown in Figure 8.1, we can distinguish four information processing components whose limitations influence the quality of diagnosis: the role of *perception* in estimating a cue, the role of *attention* in selecting and integrating the information provided by the cues, the role of *long-term memory* in providing background knowledge to establish possible hypotheses or beliefs, and, most importantly, the role of *working memory* as the "workbench" for updating and revising beliefs or hypotheses on the basis of newly arriving information. Given the iterative nature of these four components in the decision process, there is no single appropriate starting point; however, consistent with the ordering of chapters above, we consider the more peripheral processes of perception and attention in cue processing first, before addressing the role of working memory and long-term memory in diagnosis.

Estimating Cues: Perception

Previous chapters in this book have discussed many of the issues in perception. However, many of the cues that are relevant to a decision problem are probabilistic in nature and require some inference to be drawn regarding the state of the world that generated the cue. Thus, we can examine the way in which the human performs as an "intuitive statistician" (Peterson & Beach, 1967), estimating the state of the world from some sampling of multiple observations, and we can evaluate the kind of biases and shortcomings that human performance demonstrates, when compared to the computer or calculator in evaluating descriptive statistics from a set of observations.

Humans appear to estimate the mean value of a set of observations relatively well (Sniezek, 1980). Correspondingly, when perceiving a set of dichotomous observations (e.g., faulty versus normal parts on an inspection line; see Chapter 2), they do a reasonably accurate job of estimating the *proportion*, so long as proportion values fall within the midrange of the scale (e.g., between around 0.05 and 0.95); however, with more extreme proportions, their estimates tend to be "conservative," biased away from the extremes of 0 and 1.0 (Varey, Mellers, & Birnbaum, 1990). Such biases may result from an inherent conservative tendency ("never say never"), or alternatively they may result from the greater *salience*, noticeability, or impact of the single outlying observation (which is, by definition, the infrequent event) in the sea of more frequent events. For example, if I have seen 99 normal parts, then detecting the one abnormal part will make more of an impact on my consciousness than detecting a 100th normal one. Its greater impact could well lead me to overestimate its *relative* frequency in hindsight. (However, note that, as discussed in Chapter 2, the rarity of the abnormal part will make me less likely to *detect* it in the first place, if its abnormality is not salient.) For whatever reason it is that we overestimate the frequency of very rare events, it does appear to have important implications for choice behavior. In Chapter 2, we saw how this tendency could affect the setting of the response criterion. Later in this chapter, we see how it affects risky decision making.

Humans' estimation of the *variance* or variability of a set of observations, as might be done by the quality control inspector who judges the health of a manufacturing process by the regularity of its output, is influenced by two factors, neither of which formally enters into the calculation of variance. People tend to estimate the variability as less if the *mean* of the values is greater, a reflection of Weber's Law of psychophysics. Thus, in Figure 8.2a, one sees greater variability in the length of line segments on the left than on the right (Lathrop, 1967). Second, estimates of variability are disproportionately influenced by the extreme values in a distribution, causing greater estimates on the left than the right side of Figure 8.2b (Pitz, 1980). Humans' intuitive estimation of the *correlation* between two variables expressed in a scatter plot is also somewhat biased, based on the geometric orthogonal deviation of points away from the regression line, rather than the actual measure of shared variance, which is based on deviation parallel to the *y*-axis (Meyer, Taieb, & Flascher, 1997); this bias leads to an underestimation of high correlations, and an overestimation of low correlations.

Finally, humans are not always effective in *extrapolating* nonlinear trends, often biasing their estimates toward a more linear extrapolation of the tangent where the data end, as shown in Figure 8.3 (Waganaar & Sagaria, 1975; Wickens, 1992). Thus, for example, in predicting the future temperature of a process whose history shows exponential growth, people would be likely to underestimate its future values. Like the bias

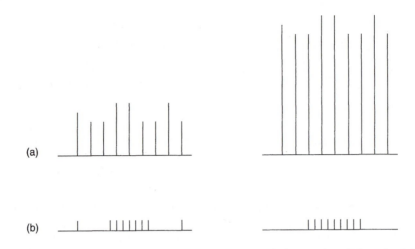

Figure 8.2 (a) The variance in line length on the left is estimated to be greater than the variance on the right. (b) The variance in position of entries along the line on the left is perceived to be greater than on the right.

in estimating proportions, this can be thought of as a "conservative" one, inferring the quantity to be less extreme than the statistical data would suggest. However, such prediction is, by definition, an inference, and so the conservative bias in extrapolation can possibly be explained on the basis that most exponentially increasing quantities do eventually encounter self-correcting mechanisms that slow the rate of growth. For example, exponential population increases will encounter natural (through disease) or artificial means (i.e., birth control) to lower the rate of growth. Exponentially increasing temperatures will often trigger fire-extinguishing efforts, or pressure relief that will reduce the rate of pressure growth. So the long-term memory of experience will lead the decision maker—accurately—to *infer* that the rapidly growing quantity will eventually slow its rate of growth.

The previous discussion of biases in the perceptual estimation of quantities spawns an important design message. When possible, systems should display the parameters estimated from separate observations, rather than allowing the human to estimate or infer those quantities. The format in which these parameters should be displayed (e.g., digital, graphical) was an issue discussed in earlier chapters and has important implications for decision-making displays, as will be discussed toward the end of this chapter.

Evidence Accumulation: Cue Seeking and Hypothesis Formation

As shown in Figure 8.4, we can represent the diagnostic stage of decision making as a process by which the decision maker is confronted by a series of cues or sources of information, as shown near the bottom, bearing on the true state of the world. The decision maker attends to some or all of these with the goal of using those cues to

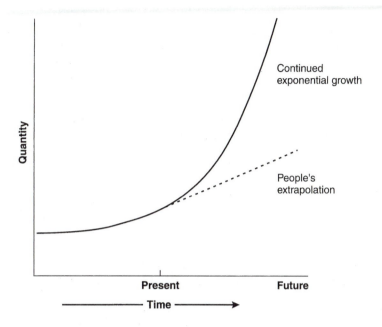

Figure 8.3   Conservatism in extrapolation.

influence *belief* in one of several alternative hypotheses, shown at the top right. Conveniently, we can represent this as a "belief scale" between two alternative hypotheses, H_1 and H_2 as shown in the figure. Thus, we may think of the physician diagnosing a tumor as benign or malignant, the planner (for a flight, a parade, a picnic) diagnosing or forecasting that the weather will be either clear or rainy; or the investment broker forecasting that the stock value in a company will either climb or dive.

Each cue that potentially bears on the hypothesis can also be characterized analytically by three important properties:

1. *Cue diagnosticity* formally refers to how much evidence a cue should offer regarding one or the other hypothesis. If one sees rain drops falling, this is a 100 percent diagnostic cue that it is raining. On the other hand, a forecast of "a 50 percent chance of showers" is totally undiagnostic of precipitation. Dark clouds on the horizon are relatively diagnostic, but not perfectly so. The diagnosticity of any cue can be expressed in terms of its value (high or low), as well as its polarity (i.e., which hypothesis the cue favors).
2. *Cue reliability* or *credibility* refers to the likelihood that the physical cue can be believed. This feature is independent of diagnosticity. An eyewitness to a crime may state categorically that "the suspect did it" (high diagnosticity), but if the witness is a notorious liar, his or her reliability is low. Collectively, diagnosticity and reliability can be expressed on scales of 0 to 1.0 (e.g., as correlations), and then their *product* can reflect the *information value* of a cue. If the decision maker

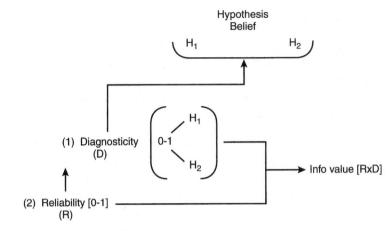

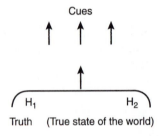

Figure 8.4 Representation of the process of information integration (from bottom to top) to form a belief or diagnosis related to one of two hypotheses.

attends to a cue with an information value = 1.0 ($d = 1.0 \times r = 1.0$), then that single cue is all that needs to be processed to make an error-free diagnosis. However, most diagnostic problems encountered have an information value less than 1.0 and, hence, can produce circumstances in which cues may *conflict*. (Consider opposing witnesses for the defense and prosecution in a legal trial.)

3. The *physical features* of the cue that make it conspicuous or *salient* have an important bearing on the attention and subsequent processing that it receives.

How should the multiple cues be processed to form a belief that correlates with the true state of the world? Here we can consider four information processing operations, three of them having parallels with our discussion of perception in earlier chapters. First, *selective attention* must be deployed to *process* the different cues, ideally giving different weight according to their information value. Second, the cues—raw perceptual information—must be *integrated*, analogous to the *bottom-up processing* of perceptual features in pattern recognition (Chapter 6) or the integration of dimensions in an object display (Chapter 3). Third, *expectancies* or prior beliefs may play a role in biasing one hypothesis to be favored over the other, analogous to the way that expectancies stored in long-term memory influence the *top-down processing* in perceptual pattern recognition and signal detection. Fourth, an operation that is not paralleled by those in perceptual pattern recognition is iterative *testing* and *retesting* of a belief, to attain the final belief that is a basis for choice.

Having established the role of reliability and diagnosticity in determining the information value of a cue, we are then in a position to establish the optimal degree of belief in one hypothesis or another on the basis of multiple cues. One perspective is that this belief should simply be the sum of the information values for the original cues (considering, of course, their polarity). Another perspective, sometimes called a "Bayesian" perspective, is that this sum should be weighted by the *prior* beliefs, an issue we address below (Edwards, Lindman, & Savage, 1963; Edwards, 1961). For our discussion here, we consider some of the reasons why the integration of evidence to form beliefs appears to depart from the optimal integration process.

Attention and Cue Integration

The process of attending to and integrating multiple cues, typically located at different places, and or delivered at different times along various sensory channels, presents a major challenge to human attention, and hence can be a source of four major vulnerabilities, as we discuss below.

Information Cues Are Missing   Often a decision maker will simply not have all the information at hand to make an accurate diagnosis. An operator's judgment to turn on a faulty piece of equipment cannot be blamed if the operator was not informed by maintenance personnel of the failure in the equipment. At the same time, however, one quality of good decision makers is that they will often be aware of what they do *not* know (i.e., missing cues), and may proceed to seek these cues before making a firm diagnosis (Orasanu & Fischer, 1997). Thus, the planner of a mission will attempt to obtain and rely on only the most recent weather data and, if the available forecast is outdated, may postpone a decision till a diagnosis can be made only on the most recent data.

Cues Are Numerous: Information Overload   As we have noted, when the information value of any cue is known to be 1.0 (*both* reliability and diagnosticity = 1.0), then other information need not be sought. But this is rarely the case, and so, effective diagnosis will rely on the integration of multiple cues. However, this can present a selective attention problem, as we discussed in Chapter 3. In the face of a major failure, the operators monitoring any nuclear plant may be confronted with literally hundreds of indicators, illuminated or otherwise flashing (Rubenstein & Mason, 1979; see Chapter 13). Which of these should be attended first as the operator tries to form a diagnosis as to the nature of the fault?

When several different information sources are available, each with less than perfect information value, the likelihood of a correct diagnosis can increase as more cues are considered. In practice, however, as the number of sources grows much beyond two, people generally do not use the greater information to make better, more accurate decisions (Allen, 1982; Dawes, 1979; Dawes & Corrigan, 1974; Malhotra, 1982; Schroeder & Benbassat, 1975). Oskamp (1965), for example, observed that when more information was provided to psychiatrists, their confidence in their clinical judgments increased but the accuracy of their judgments did not. Allen (1982) observed the same finding with weather forecasters. The limitations of human attention and working memory seem to be so great that an operator cannot easily integrate simultaneously the diagnostic impact of more than a few sources of information. In fact, Wright (1974) found that under time stress, decision-making performance deteriorated when more rather than less information was provided. Despite these limitations, people have an unfortunate tendency to seek far more information than they can absorb adequately. The admiral or executive, for example, will demand "all the facts" (Samet, Weltman, & Davis, 1976).

To account for the finding that more information may not improve decision making, we must assume that the human operator employs a selective filtering strategy to process informational cues. When few cues are initially presented, this filtering is unnecessary. When several sources are present, however, the filtering process is required, and it competes for the time (or other resources) available for the integration of information. Thus, more information leads to more time-consuming filtering at the expense of decision quality.

Cues Are Differentially Salient   The *salience* of a cue, its attention-attracting properties or ease of processing, can influence the extent to which it will be attended and weighted in information integration (Payne, 1980). For example, loud sounds, bright lights, underlined or highlighted information, abrupt onsets of intensity or motion, and spatial positions in the front or top of a visual display are all examples of salient stimulus features, discussed in Chapter 3 in the context of selective attention. Thus, Wallsten and Barton (1982) showed that subjects under time pressure in decision making selectively processed those cues that were presented at the top of an information display. Top locations presumably were more salient to the subjects (as we read from top to bottom), despite the fact that the information presented there was of no greater diagnostic value than that at lower locations.

These findings lead us to expect that in any diagnostic situation, the brightest flashing light or the meter that is largest, is located most centrally, or changes most rapidly will cause the operator to process its diagnostic information content over others. It is important for a system designer to realize, therefore, that the goals of alerting (high signal salience) are not necessarily compatible with those of diagnosis, in which salience should be directly related to the information value of the cue in making a diagnosis, not just in detecting a fault. These will not always be the same, as when a loud alarm has relatively little diagnostic value.

In contrast to salience, which may lead to "overprocessing," research also suggests that information that is difficult to interpret or integrate, because it requires arithmetic calculations or contains confusing language, will tend to be underweighted (Bettman, Johnson, & Payne, 1990; Johnson, Payne, & Bettman, 1988). For example, Stone, Yates, and Parker (1997) found that presenting risk information in digital form led to less appropriate processing than presenting it in the analog form of stick figures with the number of figures representing the magnitude of risk.

A special case of differences in cue salience relates to the absence of a cue. There are circumstances in which a hypothesis can gain credibility on the basis of what is *not* seen. For example, the computer or automotive troubleshooter may be able to eliminate one potential cause of failure on the basis of a symptom that is *not* observed. Yet people tend to be relatively poor in using the absence of cues to assist in diagnosis in fields such as medicine (Balla, 1980), or logical troubleshooting (Hunt & Rouse, 1981).

The observation that cue salience influences cue processing is a part of the more general observation that the physical format or array of information relevant to a decision problem can influence the nature of the decision processes, an issue we discuss later in the chapter.

Processed Cues Are Not Differentially Weighted   People do not effectively *modulate* the amount of weight given to a cue based on its value, as determined by it's diagnosticity or reliability. Instead, they tend to treat all cues *as if* they were of equal value (Johnson, Cavenaugh, Spooner, & Samet, 1973; Schum, 1975), thereby reducing the cognitive effort required to consider differential weights. It is a heuristic that, like others we discuss below, will not generally do damage to the diagnosis (Dawes, 1979); but under certain circumstances, particularly when a low value cue happens to be quite salient, its use can invite a wrong diagnosis.

Kahneman and Tversky (1973) have demonstrated that even those well trained in statistical theory do not give proportionally more weight to more reliable cues, when making predictions. In Figure 8.5, the optimal diagnostic weighting of a predictive cue is contrasted with the weights as indicated by subjects' predictive performance. Optimally, the information extracted, or how much weight is given to a cue, should vary as a linear function of the variable's correlation with the criterion. In fact, the weighting varies in more of an "all or none" fashion, as shown in the figure.

Numerous examples of the "as if" heuristic can be identified. As one example, Griffin and Tversky (1992) found that evaluators, forming impressions of an applicant on

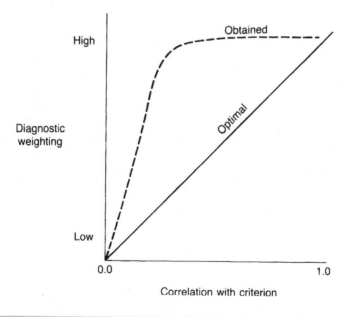

Figure 8.5   Demonstration of the "as if" heuristic. The function shows the relationship of the validity of cues to the optimal and obtained weighting of cues in prediction.

the basis of letters of recommendations, tended to give more weight to the tone or enthusiasm of the letter (a *salient* feature) than to the credibility or reliability of the evidence. Kanarick, Huntington, and Peterson (1969) observed that subjects preferred to purchase cheap, unreliable information over more expensive but reliable information when performing a simulated military diagnostic task. This "cheapskate mentality" was exhibited despite the fact that a greater amount of total information per dollar spent could be attained by purchasing the reliable information. Rossi and Madden (1979) found that trained nurses were uninfluenced by the degree of diagnosticity of symptoms in their decision to call a physician. This decision was based only on the total number of symptoms observed.

A particularly dangerous situation occurs when less than perfectly informative information is passed from observer to observer. The lack of perfect reliability or diagnosticity may become lost as the information is transmitted, and what originated with uncertainty might end with conviction. For example, in the *USS Vincennes* incident described at the beginning of this chapter, the uncertain status of the identity of the radar contact may have become lost as the fact of its presence was relayed up the chain of command (U.S. Navy, 1988).

Another potential cause of unreliable data results when the sample size of data used to draw an inference is limited. A political poll based on 10 people is a far less reliable indicator of voter preferences than one based on 100. Yet these differences tend to be ignored by people when contrasting the evidence for a hypothesis provided by the two polls (Fischhoff & Bar-Hillel, 1984; Tversky & Kahneman, 1971, 1974).

The insensitivity to differences in predictive validity or cue reliability should make people ill suited for performing tasks in which diagnosis or prediction involves multiple cues of different information value. In fact, a large body of evidence (e.g., Dawes & Corrigan, 1974; Dawes, Faust, & Meehl, 1989; Kahneman & Tversky, 1973; Kleinmuntz, 1990; Meehl, 1954) does indeed suggest that humans, compared to machines, make relatively poor intuitive or clinical predictors. In these studies, subjects are given information about a number of attributes of a particular case. The attributes vary in their weights, and the subjects are asked to predict some criterion variable for the case at hand (e.g., the likelihood of applicant success in a program to which they have applied or the diagnosis of a patient). Compared with even a crude statistical system that knows only the polarity of cue diagnosticity (e.g., higher tests scores will predict higher criterion scores) and assumes equal weights for all variables, the human predicts relatively poorly. This observation has led Dawes, Faust, and Meehl (1989) to propose that the optimum role of the human in prediction should be to identify relevant predictor variables, determine how they should be measured and coded, and identify the direction of their relationship to the criterion. At this point, a computer-based statistical analysis should take over and be given the exclusive power to integrate information and derive the criterion value.

Why do people demonstrate the "as if" heuristic in prediction and diagnosis? The heuristic seems to be an example of cognitive simplification, in which the decision maker reduces the load imposed on working memory by treating all data sources as if they were of equal reliability. Thus, a person avoids the differential weighting or mental multiplication across cue values that would be necessary to implement the most accurate diagnosis. When people are asked to estimate differences in reliability of a cue directly, they can often do so. However, when this estimate must be used as part of a larger aggregation, the values become distorted. Of course, as we see with other heuristics, the "as if" heuristic usually works adequately. But the occasions when it leads to biases can be serious.

Expertise and Cue Correlation

In the previous section, we described two important distortions from optimal diagnosis: a salience bias, which can never be good (unless a display designer has explicitly designed the more valuable cues to be more salient), and the as-if heuristic. It is important to realize that there are many diagnostic judgments or situation assessments in which neither of these distortions present major concerns for the accuracy of the assessment (Zsambok & Klein, 1997; Hammond, Hamm, Grassia, & Pearson, 1987; Medin, Alton, Edelson, & Freko, 1982; Shanteau, 1992). In particular, these are situations in which there are multiple cues, they are highly *correlated* with each other, and are relatively equally weighted, as in Figure 8.6a, and so may invite what Hammond, Hamm, Grassia, and Pearson (1987) refer to as a relatively *intuitive* form of information integration, which has many aspects in common with the perceptual pattern recognition discussed in Chapter 6. Of course, it takes a certain amount of experience for the decision maker to *learn* the pattern of correlation between cue values and, hence, take advantage of them in classification, just as it takes familiarity with the consistent correlation or co-occurrence of features in perceptual patterns to be able to recognize them rapidly and automatically (Chapters 6 and 7). Hence, this intuitive form of diagnosis is closely associated with expertise.

Klein (1989) has explicitly labeled this pattern of diagnosis as *recognition-primed decision making* (RPD), and has noted that it is characteristic of decision makers in a number of domains. The decision maker in essence "recognizes" the pattern of cues in a problem as one that matches a template of typical cues in prior experience, and thereby rapidly categorizes (diagnoses) the situation, without going through the time- and effort-consuming processes of cue weighting and integration. An expert fire fighter, for example, can rapidly and automatically classify the nature of a fire from the collection of symptoms observed. Indeed, because the RPD process is rapid and relatively automatic, it may be the *only* diagnostic option available to some expert decision makers under conditions of high time stress: the fire fighter (Klein, Calderwood, & Clinton-Cirocco, 1996), the military commander under attack, or the operator of a complex chemical process facing a sudden emergency failure and possible need to evacuate.

It is important to realize, however, that just because experts can make such diagnoses well, under time stress, in their domains of expertise, does not imply that all expert decisions are good, nor that all effective experts will necessarily employ RPD. Indeed, there may be other circumstances that directly invite a more analytic strategy of diagnosis (Hammond, Hamm, Grassia, & Pearson, 1987). For example, if a correlation between cues does not exist (Figure 8.6b) or is not known by the expert, if time pressure is removed, or if a single cue value departs from the expected correlation (Figure 8.6c), then even the expert *should* abandon an RPD style and consider a slower, more analytical one; just as the careful perceiver should note when the bottom-up pattern of sensory evidence departs from the top-down expectation. A longer delay in perceptual classification is warranted here, in order to prevent the misclassification that would result if perceptual classification were made on the basis of top-down expectations.

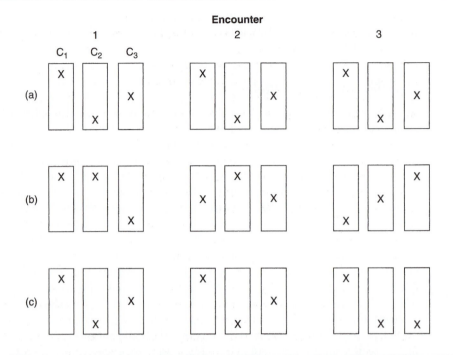

Figure 8.6   The correlation of cues over time. Each of the 9 cells represents a pattern of three cue values (C_1, C_2, C_3) relevant to a diagnosis. The level of *x* within each cue represents cue value (e.g., pressure, temperature). Multiple encounters (1–3) with these cue sets will define a correlation between cue values. Row (*a*) This correlation is high, since particular values tend to be repeated over time. Here, expertise can develop if the user can learn the co-occurrence of cue values. Row (*b*) Such correlation is absent. Row (*c*) The correlation is present, but not in occasion 3, where the third cue violates the expected pattern, inviting misclassification based on expectancy.

Expectations in Diagnosis: The Role of Long-term Memory

In the previous section, we described two qualitatively different aspects of long-term memory in diagnosis, which reflected two features of perception and pattern recognition: (1) the correlation of cues (co-occurrence of features in perception) that support recognition-primed decision making, and (2) the expectancies of different hypotheses or states of the world (top-down processing in perception) that bias classification toward the most expected, most frequent diagnostic category. Decision-making research reveals that these two influences of memory—cue correlation and hypothesis frequency—have a sort of complimentary relationship with each other in terms of two decision heuristics related to *representativeness* and *availability,* respectively. We describe each of these below, along with the trade-off between them.

Representativeness   In the *representativeness heuristic* (Tversky & Kahneman, 1974), people are assumed to diagnose a situation, or chose a hypothesis, by evaluating the extent to which a set of cues, symptoms, or perceptual evidence matches or corresponds with the set that is representative of the hypothesis, which is stored, on the basis of experience, in long-term memory. For example, the troubleshooter will observe a set of cues (a certain warning message goes on, another light is off, one part of the system receives intermittent power) and match this against one of a number of possible patterns of symptoms from past experience stored in long-term memory, each corresponding to a particular hypothesis or diagnostic state. If a match is made, that state is chosen. As we saw earlier in the chapter, this is behavior typical of recognition-primed decision making, or visual pattern recognition.

There is nothing really wrong with following this heuristic, *except* that people tend to use representativeness when the cues are somewhat ambiguous without adequately considering the base rate, probability, or likelihood that a given hypothesis might actually be observed. For example, following the representativeness heuristic, a physician, observing a patient who matches 4 out of 5 symptoms typical of disease X, and 3 out of 5 typical of disease Y, will be likely to diagnose disease X as being most representative of the patient's symptoms, following the representativeness heuristic, the physician would do so even if X occurs very rarely in the population, compared to disease Y.

Christenssen-Szalanski and Bushyhead (1981) observed that physicians are insufficiently aware of disease prevalence rates (base rate) in making diagnostic decisions. Balla (1980, 1982) confirmed the limited use of prior probability information by both medical students and senior physicians in a series of elicited diagnoses of hypothetical patients. Furthermore, the sluggish beta adjustment in response to signal probability, described in Chapter 2, in which decision-making criteria are not adjusted sufficiently on the basis of signal frequency information, is another example of this failure to account for base-rate information. Perrin, Barnett, and Walrath (1993) found that experienced naval tactical operations officers failed to take base rate into account, focusing instead on perceptual features as they classified flight tracks as civilian or hostile.

Representativeness may be thought to reflect another example of the distorting effects of salience in decision making. Symptoms are salient and visible; probability is abstract and mental and, hence, seems to be "discounted" when placed in competition with a pattern of perceivable symptoms. Does the representativeness heuristic mean that people ignore probability or base rates altogether in reaching diagnoses? No; it only means that physical similarity to a prototype hypothesis *dominates* probability consideration when the two are integrated to determine the most likely hypothesis on the basis of past experience and the physical evidence. If, on the other hand, the physical evidence is itself ambiguous (or missing), then people will use probability. They will be quite likely to diagnose the hypothesis which, *in their mind*, has the greatest probability of being true (Fischhoff & Bar-Hillel, 1984). However, this mental representation of probability leads us to consider the second important heuristic in evidence consideration, the *availability* heuristic.

The Availability Heuristic   Availability refers to "the ease with which instances or occurrences [of a hypothesis] can be brought to mind" (Tversky & Kahneman, 1974, p.1127). This heuristic can be employed as a convenient means of approximating prior probability, in that more frequent events or conditions in the world generally *are* recalled more easily. Therefore, people typically entertain more available hypotheses. Unfortunately, other factors strongly influence the availability of a hypothesis that may be quite unrelated to their absolute frequency or prior probability. As we noted in our discussion of memory, recency is one such factor. An operator trying to diagnose a malfunction may have encountered a possible cause recently, either in a true situation, in training, or in a description just studied in an operating manual. This recency factor makes the particular hypothesis or cause more available to memory retrieval, and thus it may be the first one to be considered. Availability also may be influenced by hypothesis *simplicity*. For example, a hypothesis that is easy to represent in memory (e.g., a single failure rather than a compounded double failure) will be entertained more easily than one that places greater demands on working memory. Another factor influencing availability is the elaboration in memory of the past experience of the event. For example, in an experiment simulating the job of an emergency service dispatcher, Fontenelle (1983) found that those emergencies that were described in greater detail to the dispatcher were recalled as having occurred with greater frequency.

Belief Changes Over Time: Anchoring, Overconfidence, and the Confirmation Bias

As we have noted, many diagnoses are not the short, "one shot" pattern classifications characterized by RPD, but rather take place over time, as an initial tentative hypothesis may be formed, and more evidence is sought (or arrives) to confirm or refute it. Most troubleshooting seems to work this way, in which various tests are performed, specifically designed to provide new cues or evidence in an effort to identify the "true" state. Jurors in a criminal trial also may form an initial hypothesis or degree of belief in the guilt or innocence of the suspect but find these beliefs altered as further evidence is presented. In this process of refining beliefs over time, we can identify three further characteristics that can sometimes work against the most accurate estimate of the "truth": overconfidence, anchoring, and the confirmation bias.

Overconfidence Bias   The decision to seek more evidence before reaching a final diagnosis can be thought of as a "decision within a decision." More evidence will be sought if the decision maker remains uncertain of the state of the world (and has time available for such seeking). However, a considerable amount of experimental data suggest that people in general are *overconfident* in their state of knowledge or beliefs (Bremmer, Koehler, Liberman, & Tversky, 1996; Fischhoff & MacGregor, 1982; Fischhoff, Slovic, & Lichtenstein, 1977; Bjork, 1998; Henry & Sniezek, 1993; Bornstein & Zickafoose, 1999). If one is more confident than is warranted in the correctness of one's hypothesis, then one will not be likely to seek additional information (which may refute the hypothesis), even when it is appropriate to do so.

The evidence for overconfidence is strong and pervasive (although there are several exceptions). For example the average driver believes that he or she is within the top 25 percent of safe drivers (Svenson, 1981). Yet if all people were correctly *calibrated* in their assessment of their own driving safety, only 50 percent would report themselves to be above average in safety. Fischhoff and MacGregor (1982) provided a compelling demonstration of overconfidence in prediction by having people make predictions about various upcoming events (e.g., who would win a particular sports contest or election), and then offer their confidence ratings on the likelihood that their prediction would be correct. After the events occurred, the average accuracy of prediction could be scored and compared with the mean confidence rating. Consistently, confidence exceeded accuracy, sometimes by as high as 20 to 30 percentage points. Several investigators found similar expressions of overconfidence in the accuracy of our own memory, for facts of general knowledge (Fischhoff, Slovic, & Lichtenstein, 1977) and recall or recognition of specific events, such as those offered in eye-witness testimony (Bornstein & Zickafoose, 1999; Wells, Lindsay, & Ferguson, 1979). Bjork (1999) has summarized studies documenting the extent to which learners are overconfident of the knowledge acquired while studying and practicing (e.g., Glenberg & Epstein, 1987).

As we discuss later in the chapter, overconfidence has implications that range beyond diagnosis and hypothesis formation. Its relevance to diagnosis is simply the likelihood that people will *prematurely* close off the search for evidence, feeling more confident than is warranted that they "know the truth."

Anchoring Heuristic Even when additional evidence is actively sought (in the case of troubleshooting), or simply arrives (in the case, for example, of forming an impression of a new employer or employee), research suggests that not all hypotheses are treated equally. Instead, we sometimes have a tendency to bias our belief revisions in favor of the initially chosen hypothesis, as if we have attached a "mental *anchor*" to that hypothesis, and we do not easily shift it away to the alternative (Tversky & Kahneman, 1974; Einhorn & Hogarth, 1982). Such a tendency is consistent with the general observation that "first impressions are lasting."

One clear implication of this *anchoring heuristic* is that the strength of belief in one hypothesis over another will be different, and may even reverse, depending on the *order* in which evidence is perceived (Hogarth & Einhorn, 1992). Allen (1982) observed such reversals as weather forecasters study meteorological data on the probability of precipitation, and Einhorn and Hogarth (1982) considered similar reversals as people hear evidence that is either supporting or damaging to a particular hypothesis about an event, for example, jurors hearing different pieces of evidence for the guilt or innocence of a suspect.

A study by Tolcott, Marvin, and Bresoick (1989) of professional Army intelligence analysts clearly demonstrates anchoring. The analysts were given varying pieces of information regarding the intent of an enemy force. After establishing an initial hypotheses, the analysts gave considerably more weight to evidence consistent with that initial hypothesis than to evidence that was contrary.

It should be noted that while anchoring represents a sort of *primacy* in memory (see Chapter 7), there is also sometimes a recency effect in cue integration, in that the most recently encountered of a set of cues may, temporarily, have a strong weighting on the diagnosis (Perrin, Barnett, & Walrath, 1993). The lawyer who "goes second" in presenting closing arguments to a jury may well leave the jury with a bias toward that side, in making their judgment of guilt or innocence (Davis, 1984).

Indeed, a careful review of studies and a program of experiments carried out by Hogarth and Einhorn (1992) revealed that a number of factors tend to moderate the extent to which primacy (anchoring) vs. recency is observed when integrating information for a diagnosis. For example, primacy is dominant when information sources are fairly simple (e.g., a numerical cue, rather than a page of an intelligence report), and the integration procedure is one that calls for a single judgment of belief at the end of all evidence, rather than a revision of belief after each piece of evidence. However, if the sources are more complex and, hence, often require an explicit updating of belief after each source is considered, then recency tends to be more likely. In some circumstances recency may be considered more optimal than primacy, when the validity or reliability of information declines over time. Recent information will thus be more valid than earlier information.

right, people would soon abandon them. Secondly, using the shortcuts offered by heuristics often is a necessity, given the time constraints of a decision environment. As we have noted, the fire captain *must* depend on the speed of recognition-primed decision making in certain time-critical situations, when a delay in selecting an action can result in loss of life (Klein, 1996; Orasann & Fisher, 1997; Zsambok & Klein, 1997). The confirmation bias can at times provide a very useful and adaptive way of gathering information (Klayman & Ha, 1987).

Finally, for all of the biases and heuristics described above, decision research has examined certain conditions under which they may be modulated or eliminated entirely. For example, anchoring may be reduced or eliminated by properties of the cues (Hogarth & Einhorn, 1992). Overconfidence in forecasting appears to be eliminated from the forecasts offered by meteorologists (Murphy & Winkler, 1984), but not by experts in many other professions (Shanteau, 1992). Moreover, there are great differences between circumstances and people in the amount of overconfidence in diagnostic estimates (Paese & Sniezek, 1991). The interested reader should consult books by Kahneman, Slovic, and Tversky (1982), and Goldstein and Hogarth (1997), to learn more about many of these modulating factors.

Most critical from the perspective of this book is that analysis of these sorts of biases can lead to suggested training, procedural, and design remediations, which can lessen their degrading impact on diagnosis in the circumstances when those impacts may be severe or safety compromising. We discuss these remediations in the final section of this chapter.

CHOICE OF ACTION

Up to this point, our discussion of decision making has focused on a collection of processes involved with assessing or estimating the state of the world and diagnosing or maintaining situation awareness. These processes are necessary to sustain effective decision making, but they are not sufficient. As represented in Figure 8.1, the output of decision making must also include a choice of some action, which we discuss in this section. In this regard, the dichotomy of situation assessment and action choice is analogous to that in signal detection theory discussed in Chapter 2, between the evidence variable (representing the likelihood of a signal), and the response criterion (by which the evidence variable was transformed into a dichotomous choice). The analogy with signal detection theory is apt in another way. In decision making, a diagnosis can be easily "scored" as more or less accurate (better or worse, respectively), just as the sensitivity of evidence accumulation can be scored as better (high d') or worse (low d'). But as we shall see, it is harder to place an evaluative scale on the outcome of choice, just as this process was hard in the setting of the signal detection response criterion beta.

One key feature of choice that did not enter into our discussion of diagnosis but was clearly represented by signal detection theory is the *value* that the decision maker places on different outcomes. We consider, below, how people "should" and do combine information on value and probability to make decisions, just as, in our discussion of signal detection theory, we saw how they combined information on values and probabilities in setting beta for the decision of whether a signal was present or not. We discuss, first, the nature of decisions that consider values only; then we consider the added complexity of combining probability with value when examining decision making *under uncertainty*.

Certain Choice

When choosing which product to buy, the consumer's decision can often be conceptualized as in Figure 8.7, in which an array of possible *objects* (products) are compared, each with varying *attributes*. For example, the set of personal computers to purchase may vary in attributes such as price, usability, maintainability, and warranty. In making a choice that will maximize the consumer's overall satisfaction, the decision maker should carry out the following steps:

1. Rank order the *importance* of each attribute (highest number, greatest importance). In Figure 8.7, the left attribute (price) is least important (1), the next attribute across (warranty) is much more important at number 4, and so forth.
2. Assess the *value* of each object on each attribute (highest number, greatest value). For example, the highest number would be for the least expensive product, the best warranty, etc.
3. For each object, assess the sum of the products of (value × importance), as is shown in the bottom of the figure.
4. Chose to purchase the object with the highest sum of products. As the calculation shows, in the example of Figure 8.7, this turns out to be object A.

This decision process is known as a *compensatory* one, in that a product which may be low on the most important attribute (for example, an expensive computer, when cost is most important) can still be chosen if this deficiency is *compensated* for by high values on many other attributes of lesser importance. For example, the most expensive computer may have far and away the best user interface, the most reliable maintenance record, and the best warranty, allowing these strengths to *compensate* for the weakness in price.

While people may, in the long run, best satisfy their own expressed values by following the prescriptions of the compensatory method, many choices in everyday life are

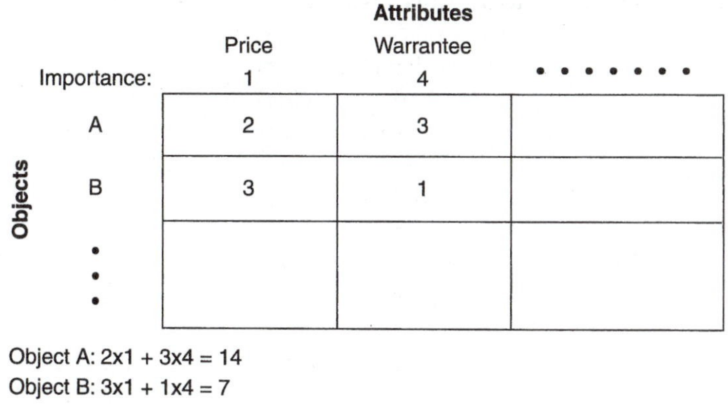

Object A: 2x1 + 3x4 = 14
Object B: 3x1 + 1x4 = 7

Figure 8.7   Choice under certainty. The calculations at the bottom are based on a choice between only two objects, although the extended rows and columns suggest that the procedure could generalize to many more objects and attributes.

made with much less systematic analysis, following heuristics or other shortcuts. The rule of *satisficing* (Simon, 1955) is one in which the decision maker does not go through the mental work to chose the best option, but rather one that is "good enough" (Lehto, 1997). A more systematic heuristic that people sometimes employ when the number of attributes and objects is quite large is known as *elimination by aspects* (Tversky, 1972). Here, for example, the most important attribute is first chosen, then any product that does not lie within the top few along this attribute (aspect) is eliminated from consideration, and then the remaining products are evaluated by comparing more of the aspects on the remaining few objects. As a heuristic, this technique will easily reduce the cognitive effort of needing to compare all attributes across all objects. Furthermore, it will usually prove satisfactory, only failing to pick a satisfactory choice if an object that is low on the most important attribute (and hence eliminated) happens to be near the top on all others.

Choice Under Uncertainty: The Expected Value Model

Unlike those choices discussed in the previous section in which the consequences of the choice were relatively well known, many decisions are made in the face of uncertainty regarding their future consequences. Such uncertainty may result because we do not know the current state of the world; for example, a physician may choose a particular treatment but be uncertain about the diagnosis. Sometimes it may result because the future cannot be foretold with certainty. Our driver at the beginning of the chapter chose to look downward at his automated device, not predicting that the future roadway would place a stopped vehicle in his path.

We can often represent decision making under uncertainty as shown in Figure 8.8, by providing the possible states of the world (A, B, C, . . .) across the top of a matrix.

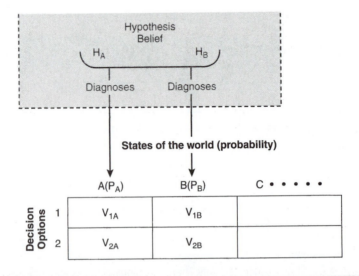

Figure 8.8 Decision making under uncertainty. The decision option with the highest expected value will be that which maximizes sigma ($V \times P$).

Each possible diagnostic state is associated with its estimated probability or likelihood, and the possible decision options (1, 2, ...) are listed down the rows of Figure 8.8. The representation in Figure 8.8 echoes three other analyses considered earlier. First, the estimated probabilities of states of the world can be thought of as being "passed on" from the degree of belief in one of two or more hypotheses, as represented in Figure 8.4 and shown at the top of Figure 8.8. Second, the matrix of decision option choice shares an analogous form with the object choice matrix shown in Figure 8.7, and indeed, the computations for the optimal choice are similar between the two matrices. Third, the matrix is in fact a direct analog to the signal detection theory decision matrix discussed in Chapter 2, with its two states of the world and two choices. However, in the context of the present chapter, there may be more than two states of the world and more than two decision options. As you will recall, a key aspect of the discussion of signal detection theory was the setting of the optimal beta, in a formula that was determined by the probability of the two states of the world, and by the *outcome costs and values* of the different states of the world that would be forecast from the four joint events. In Figure 8.8, these costs and values are represented by a value (V), of the outcome associated with the consequence of each decision option made in each state of the world. V can be either positive or negative. One might consider, for example, the costs and benefits to shutting down a large power generating plant, under the alternative states that either nothing is wrong, or that the plant is failing and will suffer major damage if it continues in operation.

In the analysis of decision making under uncertainty, the exact same procedures as in signal detection theory can be applied for maximizing the *expected value* of a choice, as long as the probabilities of the different states of the world can be estimated, and as long as values can be placed within the different cells of the matrix (there will be more than 4 cells if there are more than 2 states or 2 outcomes). The process by which the optimum choice can be proposed involves following calculations analogous to those discussed in the context of Figure 8.7:

1. The probability of each state of the world (P_S) is multiplied by the outcome value (V_{XY}) in each cell, assigning positive values to "good" outcomes, and negative values to "bad" ones.
2. These "probability × value" products are summed across decision options within each row, to produce the expected value of each option.
3. The decision option with the greatest expected values is chosen.

To the extent that this option is chosen repeatedly over multiple opportunities to exercise the choice, and that values are objective and known, then the algorithm will, over the long run, provide the greatest payoff. Such an algorithm, for example, is directly suited to apply to a gambling scenario, in which these conditions are met; it is indeed such an algorithm that is used by gambling casinos or lotteries to guarantee that they receive a profit (and therefore guarantee that the long-term expected value for the gambling consumer is for a loss).

While expected value maximization is clear, simple, and objective, several factors complicate the picture when it is applied to most human decisions under uncertainty. First, it is not necessarily the case that people want to maximize their winnings (or minimize their expected losses) over the long run. For example, they may wish to minimize the maximum loss (i.e., avoid picking the option which has the most negative outcome value even if this occurs rarely). This is, of course, one reason people purchase fire insurance and avoid the decision option of "no purchase," even though the expected value of the purchase option is negative (if it were not negative for the consumer, the insurance company would soon be out of business). Second, in many decisions it is difficult to assign objective values like money to the different outcomes. A case in point are decisions regarding safety, in which consequences may be human injury, suffering, or the loss of life. Third, as we discuss in the following section, it does not appear that humans treat their subjective estimates of costs and values as linearly related to objective values (i.e., of money). Finally, people's estimates of probability do not always follow the objective probabilities that will establish long-term costs and benefits.

In spite of those many departures from the maximum expected value choices in Figure 8.8, departures which we discuss in more detail below, it remains important that we understand the optimal prescription of expected value choices. This is because, like the optimal beta, this prescription establishes a benchmark against which the causes of different human departures can be evaluated (Kahneman, 1991), and given the great frequency with which humans make decisions under uncertainty or risk. A few examples are:

Does the operator shut down a nuclear reactor following an uncertain diagnosis of failure, given the high cost to the utilities company of a shutdown; or does he keep running, given the much greater cost of a meltdown if the failure is real?

Does the company institute a costly safety program, or does it take a gamble that its factory will not be inspected and that an accident will not occur at the workplace?

Do you purchase the expensive expanded warranty option for your new computer system, given the likely possibility that it may never fail?

Does the pilot continue flying through bad weather, or turn back?

Does the student decide *not* to read the chapter, gambling that its material will not be covered on the exam?

All of these are examples of risky decision making for which, if probabilities and values are known, the procedures in Figure 8.8 could be applied. We now explore some of the departures and why people make choices that do not agree with the expected value model.

Biases and Heuristics in Uncertain Choice

Whether a choice is between two risky outcomes, or between a risk and a "sure thing" (i.e., an option for which the outcome is known with certainty), decision-making research has revealed a number of ways in which choices depart from the optimum payoff prescribed by expected value theory. These departures in subjective costs and probability estimation are not necessarily "bad," and as with diagnosis heuristics, some can be shown to be optimal under certain circumstances. Insight into their nature can help to understand the fundamental cognitive processes involved in human decision making (Kahneman, 1991). Furthermore, it is important to note that the phenomena described below are not invariably shown by all decision makers under all circumstances; understanding the variables that can moderate the strength of influences on subjective values and probability perception can provide important guidance in improving decision making. We consider, first, a shortcut related to direct retrieval that totally bypasses the explicit considerations of risk, and then the forms of influences of human perception of value and of probability, which have been incorporated into a theory of choice known as *prospect theory* (Kahneman & Tversky, 1984).

Direct Retrieval   As we have noted above, many skilled decisions are made without much conscious thought given to risks (probabilities and values). Choices of action may sometimes be implemented simply on the basis of past experience. If the conditions are similar to those confronted in a previous experience, and an action worked in that previous case, it may now be selected in the present case with confidence that it will produce a satisfactory outcome (Zsambok & Klein, 1997). Studies of decision makers in high-stress realistic environments such as fire fighting (Klein, 1996, 1997) reveal the frequency of such decision-making strategies. So long as the domain is familiar to the decision maker, and the diagnosis of the state of the world is clear and unambiguous, the comparative risks of alternatives need not be explicitly considered. Indeed, in many environments, like aviation, the establishment of formal *procedures* to be learned and followed represents such an approach to direct retrieval. Sometimes the direct retrieval approach may be coupled with a *mental simulation* (Klein & Crandall, 1995), in which the anticipated consequences of the choice are simulated in the mind, to assure that they produce a satisfactory outcome. Good arguments can be made that a direct retrieval strategy like recognition-primed decision making is in fact a highly adaptive one in a familiar domain if time pressure is high (Svenson & Maule, 1993), and it appears to be frequently used.

Distortions of Values and Costs   As we have noted, expected value theory is based on optimizing some function that, in the economic framework used to analyze much of human decision making, uses money or objective value as its fundamental currency. But the way that people actually make decisions suggests that they do not view money as a linear function of worth. Instead, much human decision making can be better understood if it is assumed that humans are trying to maximize an expected *utility* (Edwards, 1987), in which *utility* is the subjective value of different expected outcomes. As one important component of their *prospect theory* of decision making, Kahneman and Tversky (1984) propose an explicit function, as shown in Figure 8.9, relating objective value on the x-axis to subjective utility on the y-axis. To the right, the figure addresses the functions for utility gains (receiving money or other valuable items). To the left, it addresses the functions for losses. Certain features of this curve nicely account for some general tendencies in human decision making.

The prominent difference in the slope of the positive (gains) and negative (losses) segments of the function implies that a potential loss of a given amount is perceived as having greater subjective consequences, and therefore exerts a greater influence over decision-making behavior than does a gain of the same amount. As an example to illustrate this difference, suppose you are given a choice between refusing or accepting a gamble that offers a 50 percent chance to win or lose $1. Most people would typically decline the offer because the potential $1 loss is viewed as more negative than the $1 gain is viewed as positive. As a result, the expected utility of the gamble (as shown in Figure 8.8, the sum of the probability of outcomes times their utilities) is a loss. Kahneman and Tversky (1984) refer to this characteristic—that losses are perceived as "more bad" than gains are perceived as good—as "loss aversion."

Another characteristic of the function in Figure 8.9 is that both positive and negative limbs are curved toward the horizontal as they diverge away from zero, each showing that equal changes in value produce progressively smaller changes in utility the farther one is from the zero point. This property makes intuitive sense. The gain of $10 if we have noth-

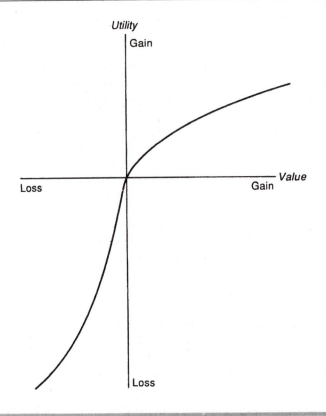

Figure 8.9 The hypothetical relationship between value and utility.

Source: A. Tversky and D. Kahneman, "The Framing of Decisions and the Psychology of Choice," *Science, 211* (1981), pp. 453–458. Copyright 1981 by the American Association for the Advancement of Science.

ing at all is more valued than the gain of the same $10 if we already have $100. Similarly, we notice the first $10 we lose, more than an added $10 penalty to a loss that is already $100. Thus, this property captures Weber's Law of Psychophysics as applied to perceived value.

The utility concept is important in psychology, not only because of its nonlinear relationship with value, shown in Figure 8.9, but also because it can account for influences on choice and decision making that cannot easily be expressed as values. In addition to commodities such as pain or happiness, an important concept in many decision models is the utility to a decision maker of expending or conserving cognitive *effort* (Shugan, 1980). We noted earlier that applying decision-making heuristics like availability and representativeness could be viewed as "optimal" if the reduced effort achieved by their use is taken into account. Similarly, Bettman, Johnson, and Payne (1990), Johnson and Payne (1985), and Payne, Bettman, and Johnson (1993) propose a model of decision making (discussed in more detail below) in which the negative utility of expending effort is combined with the expected utility of decision accuracy to predict the kind of decision strategy that will be employed to tackle a particular problem. When considered as an aspect of choice, we may refer to the utility of the *anticipated* effort associated with a particular option (Fennema & Kleinmuntz, 1995).

Perception of Probability   We have noted at least three times previously that people's perception of probability is not always accurately calibrated. The "sluggish Beta" phenomenon discussed in Chapter 2, and the representativeness heuristic discussed in this chapter, illustrated a tendency to downweight the influences of probability in detection and diagnosis, respectively, and we introduced the biases in judging proportions, above. Consistent with these biases, Kahneman and Tversky (1984) suggest a function relating true (objective) probability to subjective probability (as the latter is found to guide risky decision making) that is shown in Figure 8.10. Three different aspects of this function are critical for understanding risky choice. The first is the way in which the probability of very rare events is overestimated, which accounts for two important departures from decision-making strategies that maximize expected value: (1) Why people purchase insurance (choosing a sure loss of money— the cost of the policy—over the risky loss of an accident or disaster, which probably won't happen), and (2) why people gamble (sacrificing the sure gain of holding onto money for the risky gain of winning). In both cases the risky events are quite rare (the disaster covered by insurance or the winning ticket in the lottery), and hence as shown in Figure 8.10, their probability is subjectively overestimated: The image of winning a gamble looms large, as does the possibility of the disaster for which insurance is purchased. With a an overestimated probability value being applied to the subjective decision making function, the decision option which anticipates the improbable outcome is more likely to be made.

The second feature is the relatively lower (than 1.0) slope of the function at its low probability end. This "flat slope" characterizes the reduced sensitivity to probability changes underlying the "sluggish Beta" as well as the representativeness heuristic and ignorance of base rates discussed earlier in this chapter.

The third feature of the function in Figure 8.10 is that for most of its range (i.e., except for the very infrequent events discussed above), the function shows perceived probability as less than actual probability. If the perceived probability that influences one's decision is

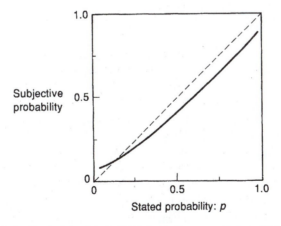

Figure 8.10   A hypothetical weighting function. The solid line represents estimates of subjective probability compared to the perfect calibration of the dashed line.

Source: A. Tversky and D. Kahneman, "The Framing of Decisions and the Psychology of Choice," *Science, 211* (1981), pp. 453–458. Copyright 1981 by the American Association for the Advancement of Science.

less than the true probability, then when choosing between two positive outcomes, one risky and one certain, the probability of gain associated with the positive risky outcome will be underestimated, and this will also cause the expected gain of the risky option to be underestimated; therefore, the bias will be to choose the sure thing. When choosing between negative outcomes, the probability of the risky negative outcome will also seem less, the expected *loss* of this option will be *under*estimated, and it will now be *more* likely to be chosen over the certain loss. This third feature can be used to account for a very important effect or "bias" in choice that is referred to as the *framing effect* (Kahneman & Tversky, 1984; Mellers, Schwartz, & Cooke, 1998; Kuhberger, 1998), which we now discuss in detail.

The Framing Effect   The framing effect accounts for people's preferences when faced with a choice between a risk and a sure thing. A classic example, faced by most of us at some time or another, is when we chose between adhering to some time (or cost) consuming safety procedure (a sure loss of time, efficiency, or money), or adopting the risk of avoiding the procedure (driving too fast, running the red light, failing to wear safety glasses) because the cost of compliance outweighs the expected benefits of enhanced safety (avoiding the unexpected accident which the safety procedure is designed to prevent). The framing effect, as derived from Figure 8.10, accounts for the risk-seeking bias when the choice is between negatives, as in the example above, but a risk-aversion bias when the choice is between positives (risk and sure thing) (Kahneman & Tversky, 1984).

As a simpler example, if given the choice between winning $1 for sure (no risk) and taking a gamble with a 50–50 chance of winning $2 or nothing at all (risky)—people typically choose the certain option. They tend to "take the money and run." However, suppose the word "winning" was replaced by "losing," so that the choice is between losses. This choice produces a so-called avoidance–avoidance conflict, characteristic of the safety decision described in the previous paragraph, and people here tend to choose the risky option. They are risk seeking when choosing between losses.

The importance of these differences between perceived losses and gains is that a given change in value (or expected value) may often be viewed *either* as a change in loss or a change in gain, depending on what is considered to be the neutral point or *frame* of reference for the decision making: hence, the title of *the framing effect*. For example, a tax cut may be perceived as a reduction in loss if the neutral point is "paying no taxes," or as a positive gain if the neutral point is "paying last year's taxes" (Tversky & Kahneman, 1981). A meat product may be considered healthy if labeled 75 percent lean, or unhealthy if labeled 25 percent fat. As a consequence, different *frames of reference* used to pose the same decision problem may produce fairly pronounced changes in decision-making behavior (Carroll, 1980; Tversky & Kahneman, 1981). Framing effects have been observed outside the laboratory in professional buyers (Puto, Patton, & King, 1985; Schurr, 1987), physicians (McNiel, Pauker, Sox, & Tversky 1982), health care financing (Schwetzer, 1995), and other endeavors (Kuhberger, 1998).

The effects of framing in an engineering context can be illustrated by considering a process control operator choosing between two courses of action after diagnosing a possibly damaging failure in a large industrial process: continue to run while further diagnostic tests are performed, or shut down the operation immediately. The first action is perceived to lead to a very large financial cost (serious damage to the equipment) with some probability less than 1.0. The second action will produce a substantial cost that is almost certain but of lesser magnitude (lost production time and start-up costs). According to the framing effect, when the choice is framed in this fashion, as the choice between losses, the operator would tend to select the higher-risk alternative (continue to run) over the low-risk alternative (shut down) as long as the expected values of the two actions are seen to be similar. On the other hand, if the operator's perceptions were based on a framework of profits to the company (i.e., gains), the first, risky alternative would be perceived as a probability mix of a full profit if nothing is wrong and a substantially diminished profit if the disastrous event occurs. The second alternative would be perceived as a certain large (but not maximum) profit. In this case, the choice would be biased toward the second, low-risk alternative.

The framing effect can also be used to account for the "sunk cost" bias (Arkes & Blumer, 1985; Bazerman, 1998). Here, if we have made a bad decision, perhaps a poor investment, and have already lost a great deal, then when confronted with the choice of whether to "get out" and cut the losses, rather than continue with the investment, people will be more likely to continue (throw good money after bad), even when it is in their economic interest to withdraw (a lower expected loss). Rationally, the previous history of investment should not enter into the decision for the future. Yet it does. People faced with the exact same choice but *not* responsible for the initial investment decision (that had lost utility) will be far more inclined to cut their losses and terminate the investment (a sure loss). The interpretation of the sunk-cost bias within the framing context is straightforward. For the investor whose previous decision was poor, the choice is between a sure loss (get out now) and a risky loss (the bad investment may turn good in the future and the lost funds will be recovered). For the newcomer encountering the same situation, but whose own utility had not been diminished by the bad decision, the "sure thing" option is neither loss nor gain. Hence, the choice is between 0 utility and an expected loss; a circumstance that fairly easily leads to bias the choice to terminate the investment.

Risky Choices in Daily Life

The preceding analysis of decision making under uncertainty does not just apply to workers on the job, but also applies to a wide variety of risky choices made by people in society. As we have noted, a common choice is whether or not to adhere to a particular safety regulation; wearing a seatbelt, a protective helmet or harness, or some other protective behavior. The sure "cost of compliance" is always explicity or implicitly compared against the expected negative utility of the more risky behavior. In making such choices, it is important to bear in mind the influence of the framing effect—to the extent that outcomes are viewed as negatives, the risky behavior may be more likely—as well as two other heuristics that influence diagnosing the state of the world: availability and representativeness.

The *availability* heuristic indicates that the perceived frequency of different negative consequences of unsafe behavior will be based not on their actual frequency (objective risk), but on their salience in memory. Where these do not correspond, risks can be seriously misestimated. Second, the *representativeness* heuristic and its implication that we ignore base rates suggests that we may not be very sensitive to the probability of disastrous consequences at all; indeed, a study by Young, Wogalter, and Brelsford (1992) found that the perceived *severity* of a hazard has a greater impact on risk estimation than does the probability of the hazard. Finally, it is the case that both perceived severity and probability are *abstract* experiences in making the choice, only possibly envisioned in the future, whereas the cost of compliance imposes a direct tangible and "here and now" experience (e.g., the discomfort of wearing a safety device or the inconvenience of adhering to safety procedure). As discussed also in Chapter 6, this analysis suggests that risk mitigation efforts should be directed heavily to reducing the cost of compliance more than on increasing the perceived negative consequences of the accident.

In addition to the "sure-thing risk" choice to behave safely, people also allow risks to enter into their everyday decisions by balancing risks, for example in their choice of transportation modes, in foods to eat, and in choices of political candidates or propositions to support or oppose. In analyzing such behavior, it is important to realize that people's perception of relative risks substantially depart from the true measures of risk, as defined, for example, by probability of death (Slovic, 1987). For example, the probability of death from a fall in the home is far more likely than the probability of death from an airplane crash, but people's perceptions of these risks are sometimes reversed.

At least three factors appear to be responsible for the fact that people elevate their estimate of risk above the true "objective" values associated with, for example, probability of death. The first, of course, is the fact that publicity, for example from the news media, tends to make certain risks more *available* to memory than others. Hence, we observe the high perceived risks of well-publicized events like a major plane crash or a terrorist bombing (Combs & Slovic, 1979). Second, people's perception of risk is driven upward by what is described as a "dread factor" (uncontrollable, catastrophic consequences, unavoidable), and third, perceived risk is inflated by an "unknown" factor, which characterizes the risk of new technology, such as genetic manipulations and many aspects of automation (Slovic, 1987).

It is important for policy makers to consider these influences on the risk perceived by the public, but it is equally important for all people who make choices based on risk to consider the consequences of those choices on scarce resource allocation (Keeney, 1988). For example, the choice to allocate a large amount of money to reduce a particular risk whose objective risk is small (but perceived riskiness is large) may be made at a cost of pulling those resources away from reducing a much larger objective risk.

Strategies in Choice: The Decision Within the Decision

In the previous pages, we have described many decision-making options: to seek more information for diagnosis or to stop; to emphasize early (primacy) or late (recency) evidence; to follow pattern matching, compensatory, or EBA strategies in processing cues; to use expected utility maximization, satisficing, mental simulation, or direct retrieval strategies in choosing a course of action. Thus we may think of the *strategy* of decision making in terms of the choice among these varying options—the "decision within the decision" (Beach & Mitchell, 1978; Payne, Bettman, & Johnson, 1993; Gopher & Koriat, 1999). Cognitive psychologists have argued that it is the role of *metacognition*, as shown in Figure 8.1, to help make such choices, on the basis of awareness of one's own decision-making strengths and limitations, knowledge about what is known about a problem, what kinds of decision outcomes are acceptable, and what effort cost will be anticipated to implement a strategy. We see elsewhere in this book other references to metacognitive processes in memory (Chapter 7) and workload management (Chapter 11).

One aspect of decision strategy is whether to continue to monitor the consequence of a decision. The fact that people tend to be overconfident in the correctness of their choice (as in the correctness of their diagnosis) suggests that people may be *less* likely than they should be to monitor decision consequences (and be ready to reverse, or modify their choice, if need be). An important approach to these metacognitive processes in decision making has been taken by Payne, Bettman, and Johnson (1993), whose research and modeling address two critical components that people use in deciding which strategy to employ when tackling a particular decision problem: the *anticipated effort* of the strategy, and the *anticipated accuracy* of the decision outcome with that strategy. Thus, in contemplating a decision approach, one decides, implicitly or explicitly, if the added effort which is anticipated to be needed for a particular strategy, produces enough of a gain in *anticipated accuracy* to be worth adopting. If so, the strategy is chosen. If not, the easier "quick and dirty" method may be used. Such an implicit choice is involved every time someone chooses to use a heuristic (like elimination by aspects) rather than a more accurate, but effort-consuming optimization algorithm (like a full compensatory expected utility computation). The heuristics that have evolved in human judgment are typically those that do yield a substantial amount of anticipated accuracy, given a relative economy of cognitive effort.

Another important example of this *contingency* of decision-strategy choice on effort and accuracy requirements, is in the choice of whether to terminate a diagnosis or seek further (often confirmatory) evidence, given the effort required for further information access. For example, in deciding whether or not a particular set of findings warrants inclusion as a general principle in this text, I make decisions on whether it is worth the effort and time to go back to the library and do further information search regarding the findings in question. What will be the perceived gain in seeking more information (MacGregor, Fischhoff, & Blackshaw, 1987)? How much time will it take me to do so? How confident am I now that I have made an appropriate diagnosis of the state of human performance knowledge already to include the principle in question as part of a chapter?

As the above example illustrates, such decisions depend on *metacognition*: one's knowledge of one's own abilities knowledge and effort expenditures, and of the nature of the outcomes produced by different choice strategies. Hence, a critical issue in evaluating the effectiveness of such contingent decisions is the accuracy or calibration with which people are able to estimate such things as anticipated decision accuracy, effort, and the current state of knowledge. In this regard, our previous discussions concerning diagnosis and situation awareness in decision making suggest a need for caution. For example, people appear to be inherently overconfident about the state of their own knowledge. How much people know about the distorting effects of heuristics and other biases in decision making presumably depends in part on their familiarity with issues covered in this chapter. The findings of one study by Fennema and Kleinmuntz (1995) examining performance of subjects who in turn were judging the advisability of student loans based on loan applications, suggest that neither anticipated accuracy nor anticipated effort of different evaluation strategies were closely calibrated with the actual perceived accuracy and effort. Extensive training improved this calibration to some extent but did not eliminate the discrepancies.

The discussion of strategy choice, calibration, and metacognitive processes in decision making highlights the importance of two critical issues: training in the awareness of the impact of different strategies, and feedback to provide better calibration between anticipation and actual experience. These two issues are directly relevant to the more general discussion of how the limitations of human decision making can be addressed by interventions recommended by the engineering psychologist, and implemented by the human factors engineer. We consider these in the final section of this chapter, summarizing what is known about improving decision making.

IMPROVING HUMAN DECISION MAKING

In reviewing the material we have covered in this chapter, one may either characterize human decision making as either generally "good" (by focusing on its many successes), or "faulty" (by focusing on its failures). While we have no interest in taking a stand on this scale of evaluating human decision making, we believe that as long is there is evidence that some decision making can be improved in some circumstances, it is the responsibility of engineering psychology to recommend possible ways of supporting that improvement. This section considers three such techniques related to training, proceduralization, and automation.

Training Decision Making: Practice and Debiasing

In most skills, extensive experience or practice is sufficient to guarantee improved performance. If decision making is faulty, then simply let the decision maker have a few years of experience, and performance will get better. We have seen, however, that practice in decision making does not necessarily make perfect. Furthermore, expertise in some decision-making tasks does not guarantee immunity to certain biases and heuristics (Camerer & Johnson, 1997; Hinds, 1999). Some assistance in solving the puzzle as to why experienced decision makers are neither perfect, nor sometimes better than novices, is provided by Shanteau's (1992) careful classification of the domains and properties of those domains that distinguish when expertise does develop from practice, and when it does not (Table 8.1).

Einhorn and Hogarth (1978) have added insight to understanding the problems of learning in decision making, characteristic of the right side of Table 8.1, by addressing the role of feedback in the typical decision-making problem. As we noted in Chapter 7, feedback is critical for nearly any form of learning or skill acquisition. Yet several characteristics of decision making prevent it from offering its usual assistance.

1. *Feedback is often ambiguous*, in a probabilistic or uncertain world. That is, sometimes a decision process will clearly be poorly executed but, because of good luck, will produce a positive outcome; at other times, a decision process can follow all of the best procedures, but bad luck produces a negative outcome. In the first case, the positive reinforcement will increase reliance on the bad process, whereas in the second case, the punishment, realized by the bad outcome, will extinguish the effective processing that went into the decision.

2. *Feedback is often delayed*. In many decisions, such as those made in investment, or even prescribing treatment in medicine, the outcome may not be realized for some time. As we discussed in Chapter 7, added delay in feedback beyond a few minutes is rarely of benefit. When the feedback finally arrives, the decision maker may have forgotten the processes and strategies used to make the decision in the first place, and therefore may fail to either reinforce those processes (if the feedback was good), or correct them (if the feedback was bad). Furthermore, because feedback is delayed, decision makers may well have turned their attention to other problems and provide less attention to processing it than they would if feedback arrived immediately after. Finally, in a phenomenon that we know as "Monday morning quarterbacking" or "hindsight bias," Fischhoff (1977) documented the extent to which, after an outcome is known, we revise our memory of what we knew before the decision was made, in such a way as to downplay our "surprise" at its outcome ("I knew it all along"). If we do not consider ourselves surprised by the outcome (in hindsight), we will foresee less reason to revise our decision process (i.e., learn from the outcome).

3. *Feedback is processed selectively.* Einhorn and Hogarth (1987) considered the learning of a decision maker who is classifying applicants as either acceptable to or rejected from a program and is learning from feedback regarding the out-

TABLE 8.1 Domains of Decision Making

Domains of "Good" Decision Making	Domains of "Poor" Decision Making
Weather Forecasting	Clinical Psychologists
Chess Masters	Personnel Selectors
Physicians	Parole Officers
Photointelligence Analysts	Stock Brokers
Accountants	Court Judges

Characteristics of the Domains:

Dynamic	Static
Decisions about Things	Decisions about People
Repetitive	Less Predictable
Feedback Available	Less Feedback
Decomposable Decision Problems	Not Decomposable

come of those who were selected (see Figure 8.11). As the decision maker may process feedback from this process, we note that he or she will typically only have available feedback from those who were admitted (and succeeded or failed), rarely learning if the people excluded by the decision-making rule would have succeeded had they been admitted. Furthermore, the confirmation bias will tend to lead people to focus more attention on those who were admitted and succeeded (therefore confirming that the decision rule was correct) than those who were admitted and failed (therefore disconfirming the validity of the decision rule). As shown in Figure 8.11b, they may provide extra assistance to those admitted by their rule—influencing the outcome of the decision to provide further confirmation of the correctness of the rule.

Collectively, then, these three features of decision-making feedback help explain why *general* practice in making decisions does not always lead to improved performance. However, somewhat more success has been fostered by tailoring more specific training to target certain aspects of decision-making flaws. This approach has been referred to as *debiasing* (Fischhoff, 1982). Koriat, Lichtenstein, and Fischhoff (1980) and Cohen, Freeman, and Thompson (1997) found that forcing forecasters to entertain reasons why their forecasts might *not* be correct reduced their biases toward overconfidence in the accuracy of the forecast. Hunt and Rouse (1981) succeeded in training operators to extract diagnostic information from the absence of cues. Lopes (1982) achieved some success at training subjects away from nonoptimal anchoring biases when processing multiple information sources over time. She called subjects' attention to their tendency to anchor on initial stimuli that may not be informative and had them anchor instead on the most informative sources. When this was done, the biases were reduced. The study of intelligence analysts by Tolcott, Marvin, and Bresoick (1989), described earlier, included an experimental treatment designed to reduce the influence of anchoring and the confirmation bias by administering a brief training program regarding their effects. This training was partially successful.

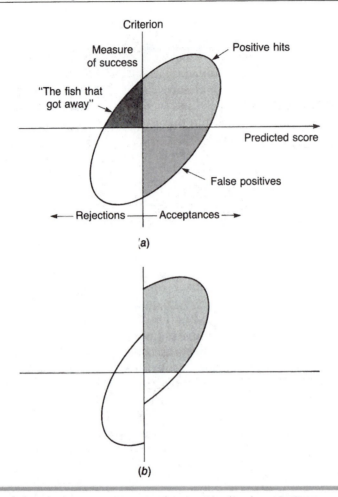

Figure 8.11   Source of unwarranted confidence in prediction. A predicted score of applicants, reflecting the decision maker's rule, is shown on the *x*-axis. The actual measure of success is shown on the *y*-axis.

Source: H. J. Einhorn and R. M. Hogarth, "Confidence in Judgment: Persistence of the Illusion of Validity," *Psychological Review, 85* (1978), p. 397. Copyright 1978 by the American Psychological Association. Adapted by permission of the authors.

A second kind of training aid is to provide more comprehensive and immediate feedback in predictive and diagnostic tasks, so that operators are forced to attend to the degree of success or failure of their rules. We noted that the feedback given to weather forecasters is successful in reducing the tendency for overconfidence in forecasting (Murphy & Winkler, 1984); but in other domains such as eye witness testimony, it is not fully effective in restoring confidence callibration (Bornstein & Zickafoose, 1999). Jenkins and Ward (1965) demonstrated that providing decision makers simultaneously with data in all four outcomes of a decision like that represented in Figure 8.11, instead of simply the hit probability, improves their appreciation of predictive relations. Where selection tasks or diagnostic treatments are prescribed, box scores should be maintained to integrate data in as many cells of the matrix as possible (Einhorn & Hogarth, 1978). Tversky and Kahneman (1974) suggest that decision makers should be taught to encode events in terms of probability rather than frequency, since probabilities intrinsically account for events that did not occur (negative evidence) as well as those that did.

Proceduralization

While debiasing is a form of training that often focuses people's awareness directly on understanding the sources of their cognitive limitations, proceduralization is simply a technique for outlining prescriptions of techniques that should be followed to improve the quality of decision making (Bazerman, 1998). This may include, for example, prescriptions of following the decision decomposition steps of multiattribute utility theory, as shown in Figures 8.7 and 8.8. Such a technique has been employed successfully in certain real-world decisions that are easily decomposable into attributes and values, such as selecting the location of the Mexico City airport (Kenney, 1973), or assisting land developers and environmentalists reach a compromise on coastal development policy (Gardner & Edwards, 1975). The formal representation of fault tree and failure modes analysis (Kirwan & Ainsworth, 1992; Wickens, Gordon, & Liu, 1998) is a procedure that can assist the decision maker in diagnosing the possibility of different kinds of system failures. A study of auditors by Ricchiute (1998) recommends a procedure by which evidence, accumulated by a junior auditor, is compiled and presented to a senior auditor who makes decisions, in such a way as to avoid the sequential biases often encountered in processing information. As we noted earlier in this chapter, several researchers have advocated procedures whereby humans estimate weights and cue values for diagnostic problems, but computers perform the integration of those values (e.g., Dawes, Faust, & Meehl, 1989).

Automation: Displays and Decision Aids

As we will learn further in Chapter 13, computer automation has the power to substantially improve different aspects of decision making. Using the representation in Figure 8.1, one can classify three different categories of assistance that automation can offer, based on the three major stages of processing involved in decision making: attention and cue perception, diagnosis, and choice. First, computers can offer considerable assistance in information aggregation by rendering the appropriate *display* of multiple sources. Several studies document the extent to which features of the display can influence the quality and the process of information integration. For example, Stone, Yates, and Parker (1997) observed that pictorial representations of risk data provided more calibrated risk decisions than did numerical or verbal statements; Schkade and Kleinmuntz (1994), studying the decision processes of loan officers, found that the format in which information regarding the attributes of different loan applicants was structured influenced the nature of the judgments in a way suggesting that people minimized the amount of attentional effort required for information integration. Clearly, the proximity compatibility principle (Wickens & Carswell, 1995), described in Chapter 3, is relevant to effective decision making, prescribing that sources of information that need to be integrated in diagnosis should be made available simultaneously and in close display proximity, so that all can be accessed with minimal effort. Emergent features of object displays can sometimes facilitate the integration process (Barnett & Wickens, 1988).

Automation can also benefit the diagnosis stage of decision making, and may work in one of two ways. First, as a relatively passive support, automation can be used to offload those aspects of working memory that are particularly vulnerable to overload and to concurrent cognitive demands (see Chapters 7 and 11). It can, for example, keep track of and aggregate evidence for different hypotheses in diagnosis, or remind the decision maker of what those diagnoses are. When information is encountered in sequence, automation aiding can provide a permanent record of that information. Second, automation also can exert a more active role in making inferences about the current (diagnosis) or future (prediction) situation. Such is the role of many *expert systems* (Chignell & Peterson, 1988) to offer assistance in areas such as disease diagnosis (Shortliffe, 1983).

Finally, automation can use the output of diagnosis to provide the user with different recommendations as to the *choice* of action. As we will learn in Chapter 13, automation of diagnosis and choice does not always offer an ideal support, in particular when the decisions made are risky ones under uncertainty, with a reasonable probability of failure (bad outcomes) or costs when such failures do occur (Wickens, Mavor, Parasuraman, & McGee, 1998). The reasons for such concerns will be dealt with in Chapter 13.

TRANSITION

In this chapter, we discussed decisons that were, generally, made slowly and with conscious deliberation. However, we noted features of the expert decision maker, under time pressure, that could allow decisions to be made rapidly. Furthermore, when there is little uncertainty in the state of the world, these decisions are usually correct and accurate. In the following chapter then, we consider such rapid decisions or action selections in detail, when the time to repond is often the critical measure of performance.

REFERENCES

Allen, G. (1982). Probability judgment in weather forecasting. *Ninth Conference in Weather Forecasting and Analysis*. Boston: American Meteorological Society.

Arkes, H. R., & Blumer, C. (1985). The psychology of sunk cost. *Organizational Behavior and Human Performance, 35*, 129–140.

Arkes, H., & Harkness, R. R. (1980). The effect of making a diagnosis on subsequent recognition of symptoms. *Journal of Experimental Psychology: Human Learning and Memory, 6*, 568–575.

Balla, J. (1980). Logical thinking and the diagnostic process. *Methodology and Information in Medicine, 19*, 88–92.

Balla, J. (1982). The use of critical cues and prior probability in concept identification. *Methodology and Information in Medicine, 21*, 9–14.

Barnett, B. J., & Wickens, C. D. (1988). Display proximity in multicue information integration: The benefit of boxes. *Human Factors, 30*, 15–24.

Bazerman, M. (1998). *Judgment in managerial decision making* (4th ed.). New York: Wiley.

Beach, L. R., & Mitchell, T. R. (1978). A contingency model for the selection of decision strategies. *Academy of Management Review, 3*, 439–449.

Bettman, J. R., Johnson, E. J., & Payne, J. (1990). A componental analysis of cognitive effort and choice. *Organizational Behavior and Human Performance, 45*, 111–139.

Bettman, J. R., Payne, J. W., & Staelin, R. (1986). Cognitive considerations in designing effective labels for presenting risk information. *Journal of Marketing and Public Policy, 5*, 1–28.

Bjork, R. A. (1999). Assessing our own competence: Heuristics and illusions. In D. Gopher & A. Koriat (Eds.), *Attention and performance XVII: Cognitive regulation of performance: Interaction of theory and application*. New York: Academic Press.

Bornstein, B. H., & Zickafoose, D. J. (1999). "I know I know it, I know I saw it": The stability of confidence-accuracy relationships. *Journal of Experimental Psychology: Applied 5* (1), 76–88.

Brehmer, B. (1981). Models of diagnostic judgment. In J. Rasmussen & W. Rouse (eds.), *Human detection and diagnosis of system failures.* New York: Plenum.

Bremmer, L.A., Koehler, D. J., Liberman, V., & Tversky, A. (1996). Overconfidence in probability and frequency judgments: A critical examination. *Organizational Behavior and Human Decision Processes, 65,* 212–219.

Camerer, C. F., & Johnson, E. J. (1997). The process-performance paradox in expert judgment: How can experts know so much and predict so badly? In W M. Goldstein & R. M. Hogarth (Eds.), *Research on judgment and decision making: Currents, connections, and controversies* (pp. 342–364). New York: Cambridge University Press.

Carroll, J. S. (1980). Analyzing behavior: The magician's audience. In T. S. Wallsten (Ed.), *Cognitive processes in choice and decision making.* Hillsdale, NJ: Erlbaum.

Chignell, M. H., & Peterson, J. G. (1988). Strategic issues in knowledge engineering. *Human Factors, 30,* 381–394.

Christenssen-Szalanski, J. J., & Bushyhead, J. B. (1981). Physicians' use of probabilistic information in a real clinical setting. *Journal of Experimental Psychology: Human Perception & Performance, 7,* 928–936.

Clark, H. H., & Chase, W. G. (1972). On the process of comparing sentences against pictures. *Cognitive Psychology, 3,* 472–517.

Cohen, M. S., Freeman, J. T., & Thompson, B. B. (1997). Training the naturalistic decision maker. In C. E. Zsambok & G. Klein (Eds.), *Naturalistic decision making* (pp. 257–268). Mahwah, NJ: Erlbaum.

Combs, B., & Slovic, P. (1979). Newspaper coverage of causes of death. *Journalism Quarterly, 56*(4), 837–843; 849.

Davis, J. H. (1984). Order in the courtroom. In D. J. Miller, D. G. Blackman, & A. J. Chapman (Eds.), *Perspectives in psychology and law.* New York: Wiley.

Dawes, R. M. (1979). The robust beauty of improper linear models in decision making. *American Psychologist, 34,* 571–582.

Dawes, R. M., & Corrigan, B. (1974). Linear models in decision making. *Psychological Bulletin, 81,* 95–106.

Dawes, R. M., Faust, D., & Meehl, P. E. (1989). Clinical versus statistical judgment. *Science, 243,* 1668–1673.

Ebbeson, E. D., & Konecni, V. (1980). On external validity in decision-making research. In T. Wallsten (Ed.), *Cognitive processes in choice and decision making.* Hillsdale, NJ: Erlbaum.

Eddy, D. M. (1982). Probabilistic reasoning in clinical medicine: Problems and opportunities. In D. Kahneman, P. Slovic, & A. Tversky (Eds.), *Judgment under uncertainty: Heuristics and biases.* New York: Cambridge University Press.

Edwards, W. (1961). Behavioral decision theory. *Annual Review of Psychology, 12,* 473–489.

Edwards, W. (1987). Decision making. In G. Salvendy (Ed.), *Handbook of human factors* (pp. 1061–1104). New York: Wiley.

Edwards, W., Lindman, H., & Savage, L. J. (1963). Bayesian statistical inference for psychological research. *Psychological Review, 70,* 193–242.

Einhorn, H. J., & Hogarth, R. M. (1978). Confidence in judgment: Persistence of the illusion of validity. *Psychological Review, 85,* 395–416.

Einhorn, H. J., & Hogarth, R. M. (1981). Behavioral decision theory. *Annual Review of Psychology, 32,* 53–88.

Einhorn, H. J., & Hogarth, R. M. (1982). *Theory of diagnostic interference 1: Imagination and the psychophysics of evidence* (Technical Report no. 2). Chicago: University of Chicago, School of Business.

Endsley, M. (1995). Toward a theory of situation awareness in dynamic systems. *Human Factors, 37*(4), 32–64.

Fennema, M. G., & Kleinmuntz, D. N. (1995). Anticipations of effort and accuracy in multiattribute choice. *Organizational Behavior and Human Decision Processes, 63*(1), 21–32.

Fischhoff, B. (1977). Perceived informativeness of facts. *Journal of Experimental Psychology: Human Perception & Performance, 3,* 349–358.

Fischhoff, B. (1982). Debiasing. In D. Kahneman, P. Slovic, & A. Tversky (Eds.), *Judgment under uncertainty: Heuristics and biases* (pp. 422–444). New York: Cambridge University Press.

Fischhoff, B., & Bar-Hillel, M. (1984). Diagnosticity and the base-rate effect. *Memory and Cognition, 12*(4), 402–410.

Fischhoff, B., & MacGregor, D. (1982). Subjective confidence in forecasts. *Journal of Forecasting, 1,* 155–172.

Fischhoff, B., Slovic, P., & Lichtenstein, S. (1977). Knowing with certainty: The appropriateness of extreme confidence. *Journal of Experimental Psychology: Human Perception & Performance, 3,* 552–564.

Fontenelle, G. A. (1983). *The effect of task characteristics on the availability heuristic or judgments of uncertainty* (Report No. 83–1). Office of Naval Research, Rice University.

Gardner, P. C., & Edwards, W. (1975). Public values: Multiattribute ability measurement for social decision making. In M. F. Kaplan & B. Schwarts (Eds.), *Human judgment and decision processes.* New York: Academic Press.

Garland, D., & Endsley, M. (1995). *Proceedings of international conference: Experimental analysis and measurement of situation awareness.* Daytona Beach, FL: Embrey Riddle Press.

Glenberg, A. M., & Epstein, W. (1987). Inexpert calibration of comprehension. *Memory & Cognition, 15,* 84–93.

Goldstein, W. M., & Hogarth, R. M. (1997). *Research on judgment and decision making: Currents, connections, and controversies.* New York: Cambridge University Press.

Goodstein, L. P. (1981). Discriminative display support for process operators. In J. Rasmussen & W. B. Rouse (Eds.), *Human detection and diagnosis of system failures.* New York: Plenum.

Gopher, D. & Koriat, A. (Eds.) (1998). *Attention and performance XVII: Cognitive regulation of performance: Interaction of theory and application.* New York: Academic Press.

Griffin, D., & Tversky, A. (1992). The weighting of evidence and the determinants of confidence. *Cognitive Psychology, 24,* 411–435.

Hammond, K. R., Hamm, R. M., Grassia, J., & Pearson, T. (1987). Direct comparison of the efficacy of intuitive and analytical cognition in expert judgment. *IEEE Transactions on Systems, Man, and Cybernetics, SMC–17*(5), 753–770.

Henry, R. A., & Sniezek, J. A. (1993). Situational factors affecting judgments of future performance. *Organizational Behavior and Human Decision Processes, 54,* 104–132.

Hinds, P. (1999). The curse of expertise. *Journal of Experimental Psychology: Applied, 5,* 205–221.

Hogarth, A. (1987). *Judgment and choice* (2d ed.). Chichester: Wiley.

Hogarth, R. M., & Einhorn, H. J. (1992). Order effects in belief updating: The belief-adjustment model. *Cognitive Psychology, 24,* 1–55.

Hunt, R., & Rouse, W. (1981). Problem-solving skills of maintenance trainees in diagnosing faults in simulated power plants. *Human Factors, 23,* 317–328.

Jenkins, H. M., & Ward, W. C. (1965). Judgment of contingency between responses and outcomes. *Psychological Monographs: General and Applied, 79* (no. 594).

Johnson, E. J., & Payne, J. W. (1985). Effort and accuracy in choice. *Management Science, 31*, 395–414.

Johnson, E. J., Payne, J. W., & Bettman, J. R. (1988). Information displays and preference reversals. *Organizational Behavior and Human Decision Processes, 42*, 1–21.

Johnson, E. M., Cavenaugh, R. C., Spooner, R. L., & Samet, M. G. (1973). Utilization of reliability estimates in Bayesian inference. *IEEE Transactions on Reliability, 22,* 176–183.

Kahneman, D. (1991). Judgment and decision making: A personal view. *Psychological Science, 2*(3), 142–145.

Kahneman, D., Slovic, P., & Tversky, A. (Eds.). (1982). *Judgment under uncertainty: Heuristics and biases.* New York: Cambridge University Press.

Kahneman, D., & Tversky, A. (1973). On the psychology of prediction. *Psychological Review, 80,* 251–273.

Kahneman, D., & Tversky, A. (1984). Choices, values, and frames. *American Psychologist, 39,* 341–350.

Kanarick, A. F., Huntington, A., & Peterson, R. C. (1969). Multisource information acquisition with optimal stopping. *Human Factors, 11,* 379–386.

Keeney, R. L. (1988). Facts to guide thinking about life threatening risks. *Proceedings 1988 IEEE Conference on Systems, Man, and Cybernetics.* Beijing, China: Pergamon-CNPIEC.

Kenney, R. L. (1973). A decision analysis with multiple objectives: The Mexico City airport. *Bell Telephone Economic Management Science, 4,* 101–117.

Kintsch, W., & Ericcson, K. A. (1995). Long-term working memory. *Psychological Review 102,* 211–245.

Kirwan, B., & Ainsworth, L. K. (1992). *A guide to task analysis.* London: Taylor & Francis.

Klayman, J., & Ha, Y. W. (1987). Confirmation, disconfirmation, and information in hypothesis testing. *Journal of Experimental Psychology: Human Learning and Memory,* 211–228.

Klein, G. (1989). Recognition primed decision making. *Advances in Man-Machine Systems Research, 5,* 47–92.

Klein, G. (1996). The effect of acute stressors on decision making. In J. E. Driskell & E. Salas (Eds.), *Stress and human performance.* Mahwah, NJ: Erlbaum.

Klein, G. (1997). The recognition-primed decision (RPD) model: Looking back, looking forward. In C. E. Zsambok & G. Klein (Eds.), *Naturalistic decision making* (pp. 285–292). Mahwah, NJ: Erlbaum.

Klein, G., Calderwood, R., & Clinton-Cirocco, A. (1996). Rapid decision making on the fire ground. *Proceedings of the 30th annual meeting of the Human Factors and Ergonomics Society* (vol. 1, pp. 576–580). Santa Monica, CA: Human Factors and Ergonomics.

Klein, G., & Crandall, B. W. (1995). The role of mental simulation in problem solving and decision making. In P. Hancock, J. Flach, J. Caird, & K. Vicente (Eds.), *Local applications of the ecological approach to human-machine systems* (vol., 2, pp. 324–358). Hillsdale, NJ: Erlbaum.

Kleinmuntz, B. (1990). Why we still use our heads instead of formulas: Toward an integrative approach. *Psychological Bulletin, 107*(3), 296–310.

Koriat, A., Lichtenstein, S., & Fischhoff, B. (1980). Reasons for confidence. *Journal of Experimental Psychology: Human Learning and Memory, 6,* 107–118.

Kuhberger, A. (1998). The influence of framing on risky decision: A meta analysis. *Organizational Behavior and Human Decision Processes. 75,* 23–54.

Lathrop, R. G. (1967). Perceived variability. *Journal of Experimental Psychology, 23,* 498–502.

Lehto, M. R. (1997). Decision making. In G. Salvendy (Ed.), *Handbook of human factors and ergonomics* (pp. 1201–1248). New York: Wiley.

Lipshitz, R. (1997). Naturalistic decision making perspectives on decision errors. In C. E. Zsambok & G. Klein (Eds.), *Naturalistic decision making* (pp. 151–162). Mahwah, NJ: Erlbaum.

Lopes, L. L. (1982, October). *Procedural debiasing* (Technical Report WHIPP 15). Madison: Wisconsin Human Information Processing Program.

MacGregor, D., Fischhoff, B., & Blackshaw, L. (1987). Search success and expectations with a computer interface. *Information Processing and Management, 23,* 419–432.

MacGregor, D., & Slovic, P. (1986). Graphic representation of judgmental information. *Human-Computer Interaction, 2,* 179–200.

Malhotra, N. K. (1982). Information load and consumer decision making. *Journal of Consumer Research, 8,* 419–430.

McNeil, B. J., Pauker, S. G., Sox, H. C., Jr., & Tversky, A. (1982). On the elicitation of preferences for alternative therapies. *New England Journal of Medicine, 306,* 1259–1262.

Medin, D. L., Alton, M. W., Edelson, S. M., & Freko, D. (1982). Correlated symptoms and simulated medical classification. *Journal of Experimental Psychology: Learning, Memory, and Cognition, 8,* 37–50.

Meehl, P. C. (1954). *Clinical versus statistical prediction.* Minneapolis: University of Minnesota Press.

Mellers, B. A., Schwartz, A., & Cooke, A. D. J. (1998). Judgment and decision making. *Annual Review of Psychology, 49,* 447–477.

Meyer, J., Taieb, M., & Flascher, I. (1997). Correlation estimates as perceptual judgments. *Journal of Experimental Psychology: Applied, 3* (1), 3–20.

Moray, N. (1981). The role of attention in the detection of errors and the diagnosis of errors in man-machine systems. In J. Rasmussen & W. Rouse (Eds.), *Human detection and diagnosis of system failures.* New York: Plenum.

Mosier, K. L., Skitka, L. J., Heers, S., & Burdick, M. (1998). Automation bias: Decision making and performance in high-tech cockpits. *The International Journal of Aviation Psychology, 8,* 47–63.

Murphy, A. H., & Winkler, R. L., (1984). Probability of precipitation forecasts. *Journal of the Association Study of Perception, 79,* 391–400.

Mynatt, C. R., Doherty, M. E., & Tweney, R. D. (1977). Confirmation bias in a simulated research environment: An experimental study of scientific inference. *Quarterly Journal of Experimental Psychology, 29,* 85–95.

Orasanu, J., & Fischer, U. (1997). Finding decisions in natural environments: The view from the cockpit. In C. E. Zsambok & G. Klein (Eds.), *Naturalistic decision making* (pp. 343–358). Mahwah, NJ: Erlbaum.

Oskamp, S. (1965). Overconfidence in case-study judgments. *Journal of Consulting Psychology, 29,* 261–265.

Paese, P. W., & Sniezek, J. A. (1991). Influences on the appropriateness of confidence in judgment: Practice, effort, information, and decision making. *Organizational Behavior and Human Decision Processes, 48,* 100–130.

Payne, J. W. (1980). Information processing theory: Some concepts and methods applied to decision research. In T. S. Wallsten (Ed.), *Cognitive processes in choice and decision behavior.* Hillsdale, NJ: Erlbaum.

Payne, J. W., Bettman, J. R., & Johnson, E. J. (1993). *The adaptive decision maker.* Cambridge, UK: Cambridge University Press.

Perrin, B. M., Barnett, B. J., & Walrath, L. C. C. (1993). Decision making bias in complex task environments. *Proceedings of the Human Factors Society 37th annual meeting* (Vol. 2, pp. 1117–1121). Santa Monica, CA: Human Factors.

Peterson, C. R., & Beach, L. R. (1967). Man as an intuitive statistician. *Psychological Bulletin, 68,* 29–46.

Pitz, G. F. (1980). The very guide of life: The use of probabilistic information for making decisions. In T. S. Wallsten (Ed.), *Cognitive processes in choice and decision behavior.* Hillsdale, NJ: Erlbaum.

Prince, C., & Salas, E. (1997). Situation assessment for routine flight and decision making. *International Journal of Cognitive Ergonomics, 1* (4), 315–324.

Puto, C. P., Patton, W. E., III, & King, R. H. (1985). Risk handling strategies in industrial vendor selection decisions. *Journal of Marketing, 49,* 89–98.

Rasmussen, J. (1981). Models of mental strategies in process control. In J. Rasmussen & W. Rouse (Eds.), *Human detection and diagnosis of system failures.* New York: Plenum.

Rasmussen, J., & Rouse, W. B. (1981). *Human detection and diagnosis of system failures.* New York: Plenum.

Reder, L. (1998). *Implicit memory and meta cognitive processes.* Mahway, NJ: Lawrence Erlbaum.

Ricchiute, D. N. (1998). Evidence, memory, and causal order in a complex audit decision task. *Journal of Experimental Psychology: Applied, 4*(1), 3–15.

Rossi, A. L., & Madden, J. M. (1979). Clinical judgment of nurses. *Bulletin of the Psychonomic Society, 14,* 281–284.

Rouse, W. B. (1981). Experimental studies and mathematical models of human problem solving performance in fault diagnosis tasks. In J. Rasmussen & W. Rouse (Eds.), *Human detection and diagnosis of system failures.* New York: Plenum.

Rubenstein, T., & Mason, A. F. (1979, November). The accident that shouldn't have happened: An analysis of Three Mile Island. *IEEE Spectrum,* pp. 33–57.

Russo, J. E. (1977). The value of unit price information. *Journal of Marketing Research, 14,* 193–201.

Samet, M. G., Weltman, G., & Davis, K. B. (1976, December). *Application of adaptive models to information selection in C3 systems* (Technical Report PTR–1033–76–12). Woodland Hills, CA: Perceptronics.

Schkade, D. A., & Kleinmuntz, D. N. (1994). Information displays and choice processes: Differential effects of organization, form, and sequence. *Organizational Behavior and Human Decision Processes, 57,* 319–337.

Schroeder, R. G., & Benbassat, D. (1975). An experimental evaluation of the relationship of uncertainty to information used by decision makers. *Decision Sciences, 6,* 556–567.

Schum, D. (1975). The weighing of testimony of judicial proceedings from sources having reduced credibility. *Human Factors, 17,* 172–203.

Schurr, P. H. (1987). Effects of gain and loss decision frames on risky purchase negotiations. *Journal of Applied Psychology, 72* (3), 351–358.

Schustack, M. W., & Sternberg, R. J. (1981). Evaluation of evidence in causal inference. *Journal of Experimental Psychology: General, 110,* 101–120.

Serfaty, D., MacMillan, J., Entin, E. E., & Entin, E. B. (1997). The decision-making expertise of battle commanders. In C. E. Zsambok & G. Klein (Eds.), *Naturalistic decision making* (pp. 233–246). Mahwah, NJ: Erlbaum.

Shanteau, J. (1992). Competence in experts: The role of task characteristics. *Organizational Behavior and Human Decision Processes, 53,* 252–266.

Shortliffe, E. H. (1983). Medical consultation systems. In M. E. Sime and M. J. Coombs (Eds.), *Designing for human-computer communications* (pp. 209–238). New York: Academic Press.

Shugan, S. M. (1980). The cost of thinking. *Journal of Consumer Research, 7,* 99–111.

Simon, H. A. (1955). A behavioral model of rational choice. *Quarterly Journal of Economics, 69,* 99–118.

Slovic, P. (1987). Perception of risk. *Science, 236,* 280–285.

Sniezek, J. A. (1980). Judgments of probabilistic events: Remembering the past and predicting the future. *Journal of Experimental Psychology: Human Perception & Performance, 6,* 695–706.

Stone, E. R., Yates, J. F., & Parker, A. M. (1997). Effects of numerical and graphical displays on professed risk-taking behavior. *Journal of Experimental Psychology: Applied, 3*(4), 243–256.

Svenson, O. (1981). Are we less risky and more skillful than our fellow drivers? *Acta Psychologica, 47*, 143–148.

Svenson, S., & Maule, A. (1993). *Time pressure and stress in human judgment and decision making.* New York: Plenum.

Swets, J. A., & Pickett, R. M. (1982). *The evaluation of diagnostic systems.* New York: Academic Press.

Tolcott, M. A., Marvin, F. F., & Bresoick, T. A. (1989). *The confirmation bias in military situation assessment.* Reston, VA: Decision Science Consortium.

Tversky, A. (1972). Elimination by aspects: A theory of choice. *Psychological Review 79*, 281–299.

Tversky, A., & Kahneman, D. (1971). The law of small numbers. *Psychological Bulletin, 76*, 105–110.

Tversky, A., & Kahneman, D. (1974). Judgment under uncertainty: Heuristics and biases. *Science, 185*, 1124–1131.

Tversky, A., & Kahneman, D. (1981). The framing of decisions and the psychology of choice. *Science, 211*, 453–458.

U.S. Navy. (1988). *Investigation report: Formal investigation into the circumstances surrounding the downing of Iran airflight 655 on 3 July 1988.* Washington, DC: Department of Defense Investigation Report.

Varey, C. A., Mellers, B. A., & Birnbaum, M. H. (1990). Judgments of proportions. *Journal of Experimental Psychology: Human Perception & Performance, 16*(3), 613–625.

Waganaar, W. A., & Sagaria, S. D. (1975). Misperception of exponential growth. *Perception & Psychophysics, 18*, 416–422.

Wallsten, T. S. (Ed.). (1981). *Cognitive processes in decision and choice behavior.* Hillsdale, NJ: Erlbaum.

Wallsten, T. S., & Barton, C. (1982). Processing probabilistic multidimensional information for decisions. *Journal of Experimental Psychology: Learning, Memory, and Cognition, 8*, 361–384.

Wason, P. C., & Johnson-Laird, P. N. (1972). *Psychology of reasoning: Structure and content.* London: Batsford.

Wells, G. L., Lindsay, R. C., & Ferguson, T. I. (1979). Accuracy, confidence, and juror perceptions in eyewitness testimony. *Journal of Applied Psychology, 64*, 440–448.

Wickens, C. D. (1992). *Engineering psychology and human performance* (2d ed.). New York: HarperCollins.

Wickens, C. D., & Carswell, C. M. (1995). The proximity compatibility principle: Its psychological foundation and relevance to display design. *Human Factors, 37*(3), 473–494.

Wickens, C. D., Gordon, S., & Liu, Y. (1998). *An introduction to human factors engineering.* New York: Addison Wesley Longman.

Wickens, C. D., Mavor, A. S., Parasuraman, R., & McGee, J. P. (Eds.). (1998). *The future of air traffic control: Human operators and automation.* Washington, DC: National Academy Press.

Woods, S. D., & Cook, R. (1999). Perspectives on human error. In F. Durso (Ed.), *Handbook of Applied Cognition.* West Sussix UK: Cambridge University Press.

Woods, D., Johannesen, L. J., Cook, R. I., & Sarter, N. B. (1994). *Behind human error: Cognitive systems, computers, and hindsight* (CSERIAC State-of-the-Art Report 94–01). Dayton, OH: Wright Patterson AFB, CSERIAC.

Woods, D. D., O'Brien, J. F., & Hanes, L. F. (1987). Human factors challenges in process control: The case of nuclear power plants. In G. Salvendy (Ed.), *Handbook of human factors* (pp. 1724–1770). New York: Wiley.

Wright, P. (1974). The harassed decision maker: Time pressures, distractions, and the use of evidence. *Journal of Applied Psychology, 59*, 555–561.

Young, S. L., Wogalter, M. S., & Brelsford, J. W. (1992). Relative contribution of likelihood and severity of injury to risk perceptions. *Proceedings of the 36th annual meeting of the Human Factors and Ergonomics Society* (pp. 1014–1018). Santa Monica, CA: Human Factors and Ergonomics Society.

Zsambok, C. E., & Klein, G. (1997). *Naturalistic decision making.* Mahwah, NJ: Erlbaum.

Selection of Action

OVERVIEW

In many systems, the human operator must translate the information that is perceived about the environment into an action. Sometimes the action is an immediate response to a perceived event: We slam on the brake when a car unexpectedly pulls into the intersection ahead; the robot operator must press a button rapidly when the robot arm moves beyond safety limits (Helander, Karwan, & Etherton, 1987); or the monitor in an intensive care unit must make an immediate corrective action to the patient's cardiac arrest. At other times, the action is based more on a thorough, time-consuming evaluation of the current state of the world, integrating information from a large number of sources over a longer period of time. Many examples of this latter process were considered in Chapter 8, including the medical diagnosis and selection of treatment by a physician.

The two types of action selection represent end points on a continuum related to the degree of *automaticity* with which the action is chosen. This automaticity in turn is often determined by the amount of practice that operators have had in applying the rules of action selection. Rasmussen (1980, 1986) distinguishes three distinct categories on this continuum: skill-based, rule-based, and knowledge-based behavior. At the most automated level, *skill-based* behavior assigns stimuli to responses in a rapid automatic mode with a minimum investment of resources (see Chapter 11). Applying the brake on a car in response to the appearance of a red light is skill-based behavior. The signals for skill-based behavior need not be simple. For example, certain combinations of correlated features—a syndrome—may be rapidly classified into a category that triggers an automatic action. This is an example of skill-based action with high stimulus complexity. However, when such complexity exists, the rapid action will occur only after the operator has received extensive training and experience. The skilled emergency room physician, for example, may immediately detect the pattern of symptoms indicating a certain patient condition and identify the appropriate treatment at once. The medical school student or intern with far less medical training will evaluate the same symptoms in a much more time-consuming fashion to reach the same conclusion.

The level typified by the medical student illustrates *rule-based* behavior. Here, an action is selected by bringing into working memory a hierarchy of rules: "If X occurs, then do Y." After mentally scanning these rules and comparing them with the stimulus conditions, the decision maker will initiate the appropriate action. The situation may be familiar, but the processing is considerably less automatic and timely. The final category of action, *knowledge-based* behavior, is invoked when entirely new problems are encountered. Neither rules nor automatic mappings exist, and more general knowledge concerning the behavior of the system, the characteristics of the environment, and the goals to be obtained must be integrated to formulate a novel plan of action. This level is often typical of the kinds of diagnoses, decisions, and troubleshooting behavior discussed in Chapter 8, and the problem solving behavior discussed in Chapter 7.

In decision making and diagnosis, more characteristic of rule- and knowledge-based behavior, accuracy is the most important measure of performance. This chapter will focus more on the *speed* of selection of skill-based actions. Although accuracy is still important, it is usually quite high in these tasks, and so response time is usually considered to be the critical measure of the performance quality of a person (interacting with a system).

In the laboratory, the selection of skill-based actions is understood through the study of *reaction time*, or RT. What are the factors that determine the speed with which an operator can perceive a stimulus and translate that perception into a well-learned action? The trade-off between speed and errors will be considered in this chapter, and the nature of errors will be considered in Chapter 12. Note that in many real-world tasks, speed is important, but response times are in the order of seconds, rather than the tenth of a second range found in the lab in which the subject is literally "reacting" to a stimulus. Hence, for many real-world tasks, the term "response time" is more appropriate than "reaction time." In the following, we will use the term "RT" to represent both.

Many different variables influence RT inside and outside of the laboratory. One of the most important is the degree of uncertainty about what stimulus event will occur, and therefore, the degree of choice in the action to make. For the sprinter at the starting line of a race, there is no uncertainty about the stimulus—the sound of the starting gun—nor is there a choice of what response to make: to get off the blocks as fast as possible. On the other hand, for the driver of an automobile, wary of potential obstacles in the road, there is both stimulus uncertainty and response choice. An obstacle could be encountered on the left, requiring a swerve to the right; on the right, requiring a swerve to the left; or perhaps at dead center, requiring that the brakes be applied. The situation of the sprinter illustrates the *simple reaction time* task, the vehicle driver the task of *choice reaction time*.

Examples of simple reaction time rarely occur outside of the laboratory— the sprinter's start is a rare exception. Yet the simple RT task is nevertheless important for the following reason: All of the variables that influence reaction time can be dichotomized into those that depend in some way on the choice of a response and those that do not, that is, those that influence only choice RT and those that affect all reaction times. When the simple RT task is examined in the laboratory, it is possible to study the second class of variables more precisely because the measurement of response speed cannot be contaminated by factors related to the degree of choice. We will see that the influences of the latter are considerable. Hence, in the following treatment, we consider the variables that influence both choice and simple RT before discussing those variables unique to the choice task.

After both sets of variables are discussed, and a stage model of speeded information processing is presented, we consider what happens when several reaction times are strung together in a series—the *serial reaction time* task and its manifestations beyond the laboratory.

VARIABLES INFLUENCING BOTH SIMPLE AND CHOICE REACTION TIME

In the laboratory, simple reaction time is investigated by providing the subject with one response to make as soon as a stimulus occurs. The subject may or may not be warned prior to the appearance of the stimulus. Four major variables—stimulus modality, stimulus intensity, temporal uncertainty, and expectancy—appear to influence response speed in this paradigm.

Stimulus Modality

Several investigators have reported that simple RT to auditory stimuli is about 30 to 50 milliseconds faster than to visual stimuli: roughly 130 milliseconds and 170 milliseconds, respectively (Woodworth & Schlossberg, 1965). This difference has been attributed to differences in the speed of sensory processing between the two modalities. It should be noted that in most real-world designs, the choice of presenting information in the auditory or visual modality should be based on factors other than simple RT (e.g., resource competition, as discussed in Chapter 11).

Stimulus Intensity

Simple RT decreases with increases in intensity of the stimulus to an asymptotic value, following a function as shown in Figure 9.1. Simple RT reflects the latency of a *decision* process that something has happened (Fitts & Posner, 1967; Teichner & Krebs, 1972).

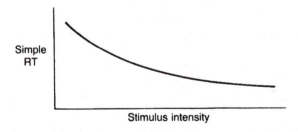

Figure 9.1   Relationship between stimulus intensity and simple reaction time.

This decision is based on the aggregation over time of evidence in the sensory channel until a criterion is exceeded.

In this sense, the simple RT is conceived as a two-stage process, as in signal detection theory, discussed in Chapter 2. Aggregation of stimulus evidence may be fast or slow, depending on the intensity of the stimulus, and the criterion can be lowered or raised, depending on the "set" of the person to repond. In the example of the sprinter, a lowered criterion might well induce a false start if a random noise from the crowd exceeded the criterion. After one false start, the runner will raise the criterion and be slower to start on the second gun in order to guard against the possibility of being disqualified. This model then attributes the only source of uncertainty in simple RT to be *time* or *temporal* uncertainty.

Temporal Uncertainty

The degree of predictability of when the stimulus will occur is called temporal uncertainty. This factor can be manipulated by varying the *warning interval* (WI) occurring between a *warning signal* and the *imperative stimulus* to which the person must respond. In the case of the sprinter, two warning signals are provided: "Take your mark" and "Set." The gunshot then represents the imperative stimulus. If the warning interval (WI) is short and remains constant over a block of trials, then the imperative stimulus is highly predictable in time, temporal uncertainty is low, and the RT will be short. In fact, if the WI is always constant at around 0.5 seconds, the simple RT can be shortened to nearly 0 seconds by synchronizing the response with the predictable imperative stimulus. On the other hand, if the warning intervals are long *or* variable, temporal uncertainty is higher and RT will be long (Klemmer, 1957). Warrick, Kibler, Topmiller, and Bates (1964) investigated variable warning intervals as long as two and a half days! The subjects were secretaries engaged in routine typing. Occasionally they had to respond with a key press when a red light on the typewriter was illuminated. Even with this extreme degree of variability, simple RT was prolonged only to around 700 milliseconds.

Temporal uncertainty thus results from increases in the variability and the length of the WI. When the variability of the WI is increased, this uncertainty is in the environment. When the mean length of the WI is greater, the uncertainty is localized in the person's internal timing mechanism, since the variability of their estimates of time intervals increases linearly with the mean duration of those intervals (Fitts & Posner, 1967).

Although warning intervals should not be too long, neither should they be so short that there is not enough time for preparation. This characteristic is illustrated in a real-world example: the duration of the yellow light on a traffic signal, the time that a driver has to prepare to make a decision of whether or not to stop when the red signal occurs. In a study of traffic behavior at a number of intersections in the Netherlands, Van Der Horst (1988) concluded that the existing warning interval (yellow light duration) was too short to allow adequate preparation. When the duration was lengthened by one second at two selected intersections, over a period of one year the frequency of red-light violations was reduced by half, with the obvious implications for traffic safety. At the same time, Van Der Horst warns against excessively long warning intervals because of the temporal uncertainty that results. This uncertainty, he notes, is a contributing cause to the many warning-signal violations at drawbridges, where a 30-second warning signal precedes the lowering of the gate.

Expectancy

Whereas basic research reveals that the RT increases as the *average WI* of a block of trials becomes longer (the effect of temporal uncertainty), an opposite effect is observed when RTs for long and short WIs are examined *within* a block having randomly varied WIs. In an illustration of this effect, Drazin (1961) examined individual RTs within a block of variable WIs and found that responses that follow long WIs tend to be faster than those following short WIs. This shortened reaction time with longer warning intervals is explained by the concept of *expectancy*. The longer the time since the warning signal has passed, the more the subject *expects* the imperative stimulus to occur. As a consequence, the response criterion is progressively lowered with the passing of time and produces fast RTs when the imperative stimulus finally does appear after a long wait. In terms of the sprinting example, if the delay of the starter's gun is variable from one sprint to the next, those sprinters who must wait an exceptionally long time between "Set" and the gun will produce fast RTs and fast times. On the other hand, if the gun is delayed too long, there will be an increased number of false starts.

The role of expectancy and warning intervals in reaction time is critical in many real-world situations. Helander, Karwan, and Etherton (1987), for example, model the RT to respond to an unexpected (and potentially dangerous) move of a robot arm, in terms of an expectancy-driven criterion. As we have noted, yellow traffic lights provide warnings for the red light to come, and many cautionary road signs ("STOP AHEAD") provide the same function. In his study of traffic behavior, Van Der Horst (1988) compared constant timed lights to lights with vehicle-controlled timing. The latter lights tend to remain green when an approaching driver is sensed, and hence, they maintain a more continuous flow of traffic. However, they also increase the oncoming driver's *expectancy* that the light will remain green. Consistent with the predictions of the underlying expectancy principle, Van Der Horst found that such lights increase by a full second the time at which the driver will stop when a yellow light appears at any point prior to the intersection. That is, lower expectancy of yellow seems to add a full second to the stop-response RT.

In all of the circumstances described above, RT was measured under human operator expectancy that the imperative stimulus (red light, starting gun) *could* indeed occur, even if its time of arrival was not expected. However, in the real world, there is another class of events that appear to be so unexpected that the operator simply does not envision their occurrence, and here response times are extremely long, in the order of several seconds (Wickens, 1998). One example of the response to such a "truly surprising" event might be the "emergency stop RT"—the time required for a driver to press the brake following the sudden appearance of a totally unexpected roadway obstacle. Such RTs are estimated in the range of 2–4 seconds, with slower RTs by some individuals considerably longer (Summala, 1981; Dewar, 1993). In Chapter 13, we examine how such unexpected RTs can describe the response to truly surprising automation failures.

VARIABLES INFLUENCING ONLY CHOICE REACTION TIME

When actions are chosen in the face of environmental uncertainty, additional factors related to the choice process itself influence the speed of action. In the terms described in Chapter 2, the operator is *transmitting information* from stimulus to response. This characteristic has led several investigators to use information theory to describe the effects of many of the variables on choice reaction time.

The Information Theory Model: The Hick-Hyman Law

It is intuitive that the more complex decisions or choices require longer to initiate. A straightforward example is the difference between simple RT, and choice RT in which there is uncertainty about which stimulus will occur and therefore about which action to take. More than a century ago, Donders (1869/1969) demonstrated that choice RT was longer than simple RT. The actual function that related the amount of uncertainty or degree of choice to RT was first presented by Merkel (1885). He found that RT was a negatively accelerating function of the number of stimulus-response alternatives. Each added alternative increases RT, but by a smaller amount than the previous alternative.

The theoretical importance of this function remained relatively dormant until the early 1950s, when in parallel developments Hick (1952) and Hyman (1953) applied information theory to quantify the uncertainty of stimulus events. Recall from Chapter 2 that three variables influence the information conveyed by a stimulus: the number of possible stimuli, the probability of a stimulus, and its context or sequential constraints. These variables were also found by Hick and Hyman to affect RT in a predictable manner. First, both investigators found that choice RT increased linearly with stimulus information —$\log_2 N$, where N is the number of alternatives—in the manner shown in Figure 9.2a. Reaction time increases by a constant amount each time N is doubled or, alternatively, each time the information in the stimulus is increased by one bit. When a linear equation is fitted to the data in Figure 9.2a, RT can be expressed by the equation $RT = a + bH_s$, a relation often referred to as the Hick-Hyman law. The constant b reflects the slope of the function—the amount of added processing time that results from each added bit of stimulus information to be processed. The constant a describes the sum of those processing latencies that are unrelated to the reduction of uncertainty. These would include, for example, the time taken to encode the stimulus and to execute the

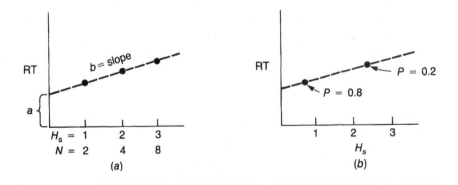

Figure 9.2   The Hick-Hyman law of choice reaction time: $RT = a + bH_s = a + bH_i$. (a) RT as a function of the number of alternatives. (b) RT for two alternatives of different probabilities.

response. The issue of whether stimulus-response uncertainty affects perception, response selection, or both will be considered later in the chapter.

If the Hick-Hyman law is valid in a general sense, a function similar to that in Figure 9.2 should be obtained when information is manipulated by various means, as described in Chapter 2. Both Hick (1952) and Hyman (1953) varied the number of stimulus-response alternatives, N. Thus, the points representing 1, 2, and 3 bits of information on the x-axis of Figure 9.2a could be replaced by the values $\log_2 2$, $\log_2 4$, and $\log_2 8$, respectively. Hyman further demonstrated that the function was still linear when the average information transmitted by stimuli during a block of trials was manipulated by varying the probability of stimuli and their sequential expectancy. If probability is varied, then when N alternatives are equally likely, as described in Chapter 2, information is maximum (i.e., four alternatives yield two bits). When the probabilities are imbalanced, the average information is reduced. Hyman observed that the mean RT for a block of trials is shortened by this reduction of information in such a way that the new, faster data point (averaging RTs to the rare and frequent stimuli) still lies along the linear function of the Hick-Hyman law. When sequential constraints were imposed on the series of stimuli, thus also increasing redundancy and reducing the information conveyed, Hyman found a similar reduction in RT so that the faster point still lies along the function in Figure 9.2a.

Hyman's data measured the average reaction time for trial blocks. Fitts, Peterson, and Wolpe (1963) examined the RT to rare and frequent stimuli *within* a block of trials. They found that frequent stimuli, highly expected and conveying little information, produced faster RTs than rare, surprising, high-information stimuli. Adding further generality to the Hick-Hyman Law, Fitts, Peterson, and Wolpe demonstrated that individual stimuli of low (or high) probability, and therefore high (or low) information content, produced RTs that also fall along the linear function describing the average RTs. Figure 9.2b presents these results for two stimuli randomly occurring in a series, one with a probability of 0.2 (high information) and the other with a probability of 0.8 (low information). Note that the response time to the low-probability, unexpected stimulus is slower, but it is slowed just enough to fall along the function at the point predicted by its higher information value, $\log_2 (0.2) = 2.2$ bits. It is important to note, however, that the response time to truly surprising events like the roadway obstacle, or the automation failure, as discussed in the previous section on simple RT, may produce RTs considerably larger than that predicted from the linear function of the Hick-Hyman Law.

Thus, the Hick-Hyman Law seems to capture the fact that, in many circumstances, the human has a relatively constant rate of processing information, defined by the inverse slope ($1/b$) of Figure 9.2: a constant number of bits/second.

The Speed-Accuracy Trade-off

In RT tasks, and in speeded performance in general, people often make errors. Furthermore, they tend to make more errors as they try to respond more rapidly. This reciprocity between time and errors is referred to as the *speed-accuracy trade-off*. According to the analysis of information transmission in Chapter 2, errors of response will reduce the information transmitted (H_t). We described the concept of a *bandwidth* as H_t/RT expressed as bits/seconds. If a person actually has a constant bandwidth for transmitting information as seems to characterize the inverse slope ($1/b$) of the Hick-Hyman

Law, then shifting the speed-accuracy trade-off from accurate to fast performance by changing the relative emphasis on these two dimensions of performance should decrease H_t by the same proportion that RT is decreased, keeping the bandwidth constant.

It turns out however, that the constant bandwidth model of human performance is not quite accurate. Rather, there is one level of the speed-accuracy trade-off that produces optimal performance in terms of processing bandwidth. For example, Howell and Kreidler (1963, 1964) compared performance on easy and complex choice RT tasks as the set for speed versus accuracy was varied by different instructions. Different subjects were told to be fast, to be accurate, or to be fast *and* accurate, and finally they were given instructions that explicitly induced them to maximize the information transmission rate in bits per second. With both simple and complex tasks, Howell and Kreidler found that instructions changed RT and error rate in the expected directions, with the speed instructions having the largest effect on both variables. However, performance efficiency was not constant across the different sets for either task. When the choice task was easy, maximum information transmission rate was obtained by subjects instructed to maximize this quantity. When the task was complex, the highest level of performance efficiency (bits per second) was obtained with the speed set instructions.

Other investigations by Fitts (1966) and Rabbitt (1981, 1989), using reaction time, and by Seibel (1972), employing typing, also conclude that performance efficiency reaches a maximum value at some intermediate level of speed-accuracy set. These investigators conclude furthermore that operators left to their own devices will seek out and select the level of set that achieves the maximum performance efficiency. This searching and maximizing behavior may be viewed as a nice example of the optimality of human performance.

The Speed-Accuracy Operating Characteristic   Reaction time and error rate represent two dimensions of the efficiency of processing information. These dimensions are analogous in some respects to the dimensions of hit and false-alarm rate in signal detection (Chapter 2). Furthermore, just as operators can adjust their response criterion in signal detection, so they can also adjust their set for speed versus accuracy to various levels defining "optimal" performance under different occasions, as the preceding experiments demonstrated. The *speed-accuracy operating characteristic*, or SAOC, is a function that represents RT performance in a manner analogous to the receiver operating characteristic (ROC) representation of detection performance.

Conventionally, the SAOC may be shown in one of two forms. In Figure 9.3, the RT is plotted on the *x*-axis and some measure of accuracy (the inverse of error rate) on the *y*-axis (Pachella, 1974). The four different points in the figure represent mean accuracy and RT data collected on four different blocks of trials when the speed-accuracy set is shifted. From the figure, it is easy to see why information transmission is optimal at intermediate speed-accuracy sets. When too much speed stress is given, accuracy will be at chance, and no information will be transmitted. When too much accuracy stress is given, performance will be greatly prolonged with little gain in accuracy. This characteristic has an important practical implication concerning the kind of accuracy instructions that should be given to operators in speeded tasks such as typing or keypunching. Performance efficiency will be greatest at intermediate levels of speed-accuracy set. It is reasonable to tolerate a small percentage of errors in order to obtain efficient performance, and it is probably not reasonable to demand zero defects, or perfect performance.

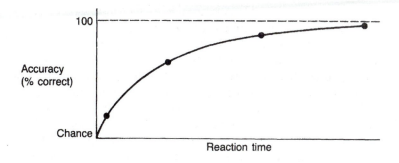

Figure 9.3   The speed-accuracy trade-off.

We can see why this is so by examining the speed-accuracy trade-off plotted in Figure 9.3. Forcing the operator to commit no errors could induce impossibly long RTs.

An important warning to experimenters emphasized by Pachella (1974) and Wickelgren (1977) is also implied by the form of Figure 9.3. If experimenters instruct their subjects to make no errors, they are forcing them to operate at a region along the SAOC in which very small changes in accuracy generate very large differences in latency, since the slope of the right-hand portion of Figure 9.3 is almost flat at that level. Hence, reaction time will be highly variable, and the reliable assessment of its true value will be a difficult undertaking.

Pew (1969) has shown that when accuracy is expressed in terms of the measure log [P(correct)/P(errors)], the SAOC is typically *linear*. This relationship, shown in Figure 9.4, indicates that a constant increase in time buys the operator a constant increase in the logarithm odds of being correct. In terms of the SAOC space, one should think of movement from lower right to upper left as changing performance effectiveness, efficiency, or bandwidth (bits per second). Movement *along* an SAOC, on the other hand, represents different cognitive sets for speed versus accuracy (i.e., qualitative shifts to different styles of performance). Two such SAOCs are shown in Figure 9.4. An excellent discussion of the speed-accuracy trade-off in reaction time may be found in Pachella (1974) and Wickelgren (1977).

From a human factors one important aspect of the speed-accuracy trade-off is its usefulness in deciding what is "best." Suppose, for example, that SAOC lines A and B in Figure 9.4 described the performance of operators on two data entry devices. From the graph, there is no doubt that A supports better performance than B. But suppose the evaluation had only compared one level on the SAOC of each device and produced the data of point 1 (for system B) and point 2 (for system A). If the evaluator examined only response time (or data-entry speed), he or she would conclude that B is the better device because it has shorter RT. Even if the evaluator looked at both speed and accuracy, any conclusion about which is the superior device would be difficult because there is no way of knowing how much of a trade-off there is between speed and accuracy, unless the trade-offs are actually manipulated. If SAOCs are not actually created, it is critical to try to keep the error rate or the latency of the two systems at

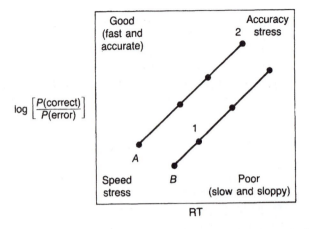

Figure 9.4 The speed-accuracy operating characteristic (SAOC). Lines *A* and *B* represent two different SAOCs. Points 1 and 2 are different "styles" of responding along the SAOCs.

Source: R. W. Pew, "The Speed-Accuracy Operating Characteristic," *Acta Psychological, 30* (1969), p. 18. Copyright 1969 by the North Holland Publishing Company. Reproduced by permission.

equivalent levels to one another and to the real-world conditions in which the systems (and their operators) are expected to operate.

System designers should also be aware that certain design features seem automatically to shift performance *along* the SAOC. For example, auditory rather than visual presentation often leads to more rapid but more error-prone processing, a fact that in part leads aircraft designers to use auditory displays only for the most critical alerts, where speed of response is vital. Presenting more information, of greater precision, on a visual display will often lead to more accurate performance (assuming that information is used by the operator) but at a greater cost of time. For example, magnifying the displayed error in a target aiming task will prolong the aiming response, as we discuss in Chapter 10. Using SAOC analysis, Strayer, Wickens, and Braune (1987) showed that older adults were less efficient in responding than younger ones, but they also operated at a more conservative, accuracy-emphasis portion of the SAOC. As we will discuss in more detail in Chapter 12, the stress induced by emergency conditions sometimes leads to a speed-accuracy trade-off such that operators are disposed to take rapid but not always appropriate actions. It is for this reason that regulations in some nuclear power industries require controllers to stop and take no action at all for a specified time following a fault, thereby encouraging an accuracy set on the speed-accuracy trade-off. Orasanu and Strauch (1994) note that pilots who are good decision makers are more effective than poor decision makers in moderating their speed-accuracy set based on external conditions and time availability.

The Speed-Accuracy Micro-Trade-off   The general picture presented suggests that conditions or sets in which speed is emphasized tend to produce more errors. A different way of looking at the speed-accuracy relationship is to compare the accuracy of fast and slow responses *within* a block of trials, using the same system (or experimental condition). (Alternatively, one can compare the mean RT of correct and error responses.) This comparison describes the speed-accuracy *micro-trade-off*. Although the details of the micro-trade-off and its relationship to the models of human information processing are beyond the scope of this book (see Coles, 1988; Gratton et al., 1988; Pachella, 1974; Rabbitt, 1989; Wickens, 1984; Meyer & Kieras, 1997a,b), the most important general point that can be made is that whether errors are faster or slower than correct responses seems to depend on the particular nature of the RT task, which in turn determines what varies from trial to trial, thereby causing some trials to be correct and others to be in error.

If the RT task is viewed as a decision task, with a criterion for how much perceptual evidence is required to respond, then it is easy to see that variability in the setting of the response criterion will cause the micro-trade-off to have the same form as the macro-trade-off: When the criterion is conservative, full information will be processed, taking a longer time, and accuracy will be high. When the criterion is risky, a response will be initiated rapidly, on the basis of little evidence, and errors will be likely to occur. In the extreme, the subject may emit "fast guesses," in which a random response is initiated as soon as the stimulus is detected (Gratton et al., 1988; Pachella, 1974). The nature of this fast guess is usually that of the most probable response. This positive micro-trade-off between reaction time and accuracy in which error RTs are faster than correct RTs seems to be characteristic of most speeded tasks when RTs are generally short and stimulus quality is good.

In contrast, Wickens (1984) concludes that when stimulus evidence is relatively poor (as in many signal detection tasks) or processing is long and imposes a working-memory load (as in many decision tasks), the opposite form of the micro-trade-off is more likely to be observed. Fast responses are no longer more error prone and may even be more likely to be correct. When there is generally poor signal quality, the responses on some trials will be longer because more processing is required to identify the signal; but this poor quality also makes an error more likely. When decision tasks impose memory load, anything that delays processing imposes a greater (longer) memory load, which yields poorer decision quality. Hence, the "inverted," or negative, form of the speed-accuracy micro trade-off is observed: Error responses tend to be slower than correct ones.

DEPARTURES FROM INFORMATION THEORY

The Hick-Hyman law has proven to be quite successful in accounting for the changes in RT with informational variables. The linear relationship between reaction time and information, in fact, led a number of investigators to conclude that people have a relatively constant bandwidth of information processing, provided by the inverse slope of the Hick-Hyman Law function (bits/sec). Yet it soon became evident that information theory was not entirely adequate to describe RT data. We have noted already that bandwidth is not constant across wide ranges of speed and accuracy set. More crucially, six additional variables will be discussed that influence RT but are not easily quantified by information theory. These relate to stimulus discriminability, the repetition effect, response factors, practice, executive control, and compatibility. The existence of these variables does not invalidate the Hick-Hyman Law but merely restricts its generality.

Stimulus Discriminability

RT is lengthened as a set of stimuli are made less discriminable from one another (Vickers, 1970). This "noninformation" factor has some important implications. Tversky (1977) argues that we judge the similarity or difference between two stimuli on the basis of the ratio of shared features to total features within a stimulus, and not simply on the basis of the absolute number of shared (or different) features. Thus, the numbers 4 and 7 are quite distinct, but the numbers 721834 and 721837 are quite similar, although in each case only one digit differentiates the pair. Discriminability difficulties in RT, like confusions in memory (see Chapter 7), can be reduced by deleting shared and redundant features where possible. In the context of nuclear power plant design, Kirkpatrick and Mallory (1981) emphasize the importance of avoiding confusability between display items by minimizing the feature similarity between separate labels. Similarity is also, of course, a cause of errors, as we discuss in Chapter 12.

The Repetition Effect

In a random stimulus series, the repetition of a stimulus-response (S-R) pair yields a faster RT to the second stimulus than does an alternation. For example, if the stimuli were designated A and B, the response to A following A will be faster than to A following B (e.g., Hyman, 1953; Kirby, 1976). Thus, we may see the mail sorter in a post office becoming progressively faster as each letter encountered has the same zip code. The advantage of repetitions over alternations, referred to as the *repetition effect* is enhanced by increasing N (the number of S-R alternatives), by decreasing S-R compatibility (see below), and by shortening the interval between each response and the subsequent stimulus (Kornblum, 1973). Research by Bertelson (1965) and others (see Kornblum, 1973, for a summary) suggests that the response to repeated stimuli is speeded by the repetition of the stimulus and by the repetition of the response.

In two important circumstances, the repetition effect is *not* observed. (1) As summarized by Kornblum (1973), the repetition effect declines with long intervals between stimuli and may sometimes be replaced by an alternation effect (faster RTs to a stimulus change). In this case, it appears that the "gambler's fallacy" takes over. Subjects do not expect a continued run of stimuli of the same sort, just as gamblers believe that they are "due for a win" after a string of losses. (2) In some tasks, such as typing, rapid repetition of the same finger or even fingers on the same hand will be slower than alternations (Sternberg, Kroll, & Wright, 1978). The nature of this reversal of the repetition effect in fast-responding (transcription) tasks will be discussed more fully at the end of this chapter.

Response Factors

Two characteristics of the response appear to influence RT. (1) RT is lengthened as the *confusability* between the responses is increased. Thus, for example, Shulman and McConkie (1973) found that two choice RTs executed by two fingers on the same hand were longer than those executed by the fingers on opposite hands, the former pair being less discriminable from one another. Similarly, distinct shape and feel of a pair of controls reduces the likelihood of their being confused (Bradley, 1971). (2) RT is lengthened by the *complexity* of the response. For example, Klapp and Irwin (1976) showed that the time to select a vocal or manual response is directly related to the duration of the response. Sternberg, Kroll, and Wright (1978) found that it takes progressively longer to *initiate* the response of typing a string of characters as the number of characters in the string is increased.

Practice

Consistent results suggest that practice, a noninformational variable, decreases the slope of the Hick-Hyman Law function relating RT to information (i.e., increases the information transmission rate). In fact, compatibility (to be discussed below) and practice appear to trade off reciprocally in their effect on this slope. This trade-off is nicely illustrated by comparing three studies. Leonard (1959) found that no practice was needed to obtain a flat slope with the highly compatible mapping of finger presses to tactile stimulation of the fingertips. Davis, Moray, and Treisman (1961) required a few hundred trials to obtain a flat slope with the slightly lower compatibility task of naming a heard word. Finally, Mowbray and Rhoades (1959) examined a RT mapping of slightly lower (but still high) compatibility. The subject depressed keys adjacent to lights. For one unusually stoic subject, 42,000 trials were required to produce a flat slope.

Executive Control

Any speeded response task must be characterized by a rule, by which responses or actions are associated with stimuli or events. It appears to take some time to "load" or activate these rules when they are first used, much as it takes time to load a program on a computer, or shift from one program to another. Such rule loading in human performance is assumed to be the function of central *executive control* (Rogers & Monsell, 1995; Allport, Styles, & Hsieh, 1994; Jersild, 1927), which also accomplishes functions like shifting the speed-accuracy trade-off and, as discussed in Chapter 7, managing operations in working memory. An experiment that nicely illustrates the time costs of executive control is one in which speeded responses are made following one rule discriminating between high and low digits, and then abruptly shift to follow a different rule, like discriminating between odd and even digits (Rogers & Monsell, 1995; Jersild, 1927). Here, the first RT following the switch is longer than the following ones, reflecting the switch cost of executive control. While such costs will be greater when the switch is not expected (Allport, Styles, & Hsieh, 1994), some time is still required even when the new task is anticipated (Rogers & Monsell, 1995). We will discuss the role of switching further when we discuss task switching in dual task performance in Chapter 11.

Stimulus-Response Compatibility

In June 1989, the pilots of a commercial aircraft flying over the United Kingdom detected a burning engine but mistakenly shut down the good engine instead. When the remaining engine (the burning one) eventually lost power, leaving the plane with no engines, the plane crashed, with a large loss of life. Why? Analysis suggests that a violation of *stimulus-response compatibility* in the display-control relation may have been a contributing factor (Flight International, 1990). We have already encountered the concept of compatibility in earlier chapters—in Chapter 3, the compatibility of *proximity* between display elements and information processing; in Chapter 4, compatibility between a display and the static or dynamic properties of the operator's mental model of the displayed elements. We also discussed in Chapter 4 the direct manipulation interface, whose advantages, in part, relate to the compatibility between actions and display changes. Now we discuss compatibility between a display location or movement and the location or movement of the associated operator response. We devote a fair amount of space to this topic because of its historic prominence in engineering psychology research and because of its tremendous importance in system design.

As suggested, S-R compatibility has static elements (where response devices should be located to control their respective displays) and dynamic elements (how response devices should move to control their displays). We refer to these as *locational* and *movement* compatibility, respectively. Much of compatibility describes spatially oriented actions (e.g., the location of switches in space or the movement of switches and continuous controls in space), but it can also characterize other mappings between displays and responses. More compatible mappings require fewer mental transformations from display to response. We will also examine compatibility in terms of *modalities* of control and display. What is common about all of these different types of S-R compatibility, however, is the importance of *mapping*. There is no single best display configuration or control configuration. Rather, each display configuration will be compatible only when it is appropriately mapped to certain control configurations.

Location Compatibility   The foundations of location compatibility are provided in part by the human's intrinsic tendency to move or orient toward the source of stimulation (Simon, 1969). Given the predominance of this effect, it is not surprising that compatible relations are those in which controls are located next to the relevant displays, a characteristic that defines the *colocation principle*. Touch-screen CRT displays are an example of designs that maximize S-R compatibility through colocation (but see Chapter 10 for some limitations of this concept). Point-and-click cursor controls achieve colocation somewhat indirectly, to the extent that a mouse-driven cursor is viewed as a direct extension of the hand. However, many systems in the real world often fail to adhere to the colocation principle, for example, the location of stove burner controls (Chapanis & Lindenbaum, 1959; Payne, 1995). Controls colocated beside their respective burners (Figure 9.5a) are compatible and will eliminate the possible confusions caused by less compatible arrays shown in Figure 9.5 (b and c), which are more typical.

Unfortunately the principle of colocation is not always possible to achieve. Operators of some systems may need to remain seated, with controls at their fingertips that activate a more distant array of displays. In combat aircraft, the high gravitational forces encountered in some maneuvers may make it impossible to move the hands far to reach colocated controls. Even the colocation of Figure 9.5a may require the cook to reach across an active (hot) burner to adjust a control. Where colocation cannot be obtained, two important compatibility principles are *congruence* and *rules*.

The general principle of *congruence* is based on the idea that the spatial array of controls should be congruent with the spatial array of displays. This principle is illustrated

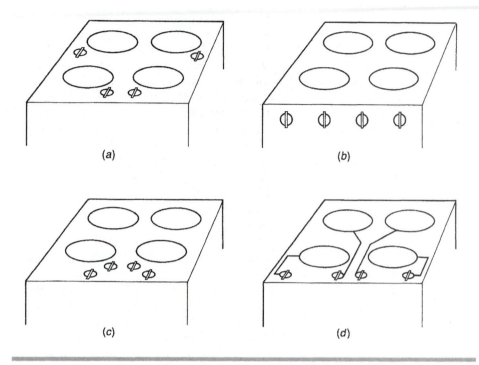

Figure 9.5 Possible arrangements of stove burner controls. (a) Controls adhere to colocation principle. (b) and (c) Controls exhibit less compatible mapping. (d) Controls solve the compatibility problem by the visual linkages.

in a study by Fitts and Seeger (1953), who evaluated RT performance when each of the three patterns of light stimuli on the left in Figure 9.6 was assigned to one of the three response mappings (moving a lever) indicated across the top. In each case an eight-choice RT task was imposed. In stimulus array S_a, any one of the eight lights could illuminate (and for R_a the eight lever positions could be occupied). In S_b, the same eight angular positions could be defined by the four single lights and the four combinations of adjacent lights. In R_b, the eight shaded lever positions could be occupied. In S_c, the eight stimuli were defined by the four single lights and four pairwise combinations of one light from each panel. In R_c, each or both levers could be moved to either side. Fitts and Seeger found that the best performance for each stimulus array was obtained from the spatially congruent response array: S_a to R_a, S_b to R_b, and S_c to R_c. This advantage is indicated by faster responses as well as greater accuracy.

A stove-top array such as that shown in Figure 9.5c would also achieve this congruence. Notice in Figure 9.5b and d that there is no possible congruent mapping of the linear array of controls to the square array of burners (displays). The only way to bypass this lack of compatibility is through the drawn links as shown in Figure 9.5d (Osborne & Ellingstad, 1987).

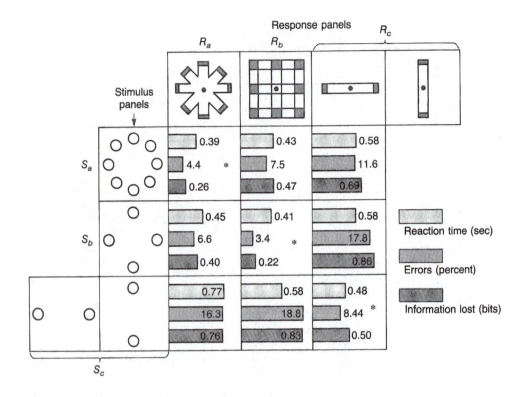

Figure 9.6 Each of the three stimulus panels on the left was assigned to one of the three response panels across the top. The natural compatibility assignments are seen down the negative diagonal and indicated by an asterisk (*).

Source: P. M. Fitts and C. M. Seeger, "S-R Compatibility: Spatial Characteristics of Stimulus and Response Codes," *Journal of Experimental Psychology*, 46 (1953), p. 203.

Congruence is often defined in terms of an ordered array (e.g., left-right or top-down). An analysis by Hartzell, Dunbar, Beveridge, and Cortilla (1983) revealed a marked departure of left-right congruence in the design of the military helicopter, which is configured in such a way that altitude information is presented to the right of the instrument display and controlled with the left hand, whereas airspeed information, presented to the left, is controlled with the right hand. In a simulation experiment, this configuration produced considerably worse performance in adjusting the two variables than a more congruent design in which the two display elements are reversed. In the 1989 airplane crash over England discussed above, a violation of location compatibility resulted because the relevant indicator of malfunction of the burning engine, which was the left engine, was located on the right side of the cockpit midline.

Why are incongruent systems difficult to map? In an analysis of S-R compatibility effects, Kornblum, Hasbroucq, and Osman (1990) argue that if the response dimension can be physically mapped to any dimension along which the stimuli are ordered (e.g., both are linear arrays), the onset of a stimulus in an array automatically activates a tendency to respond at the associated location. If this is not the correct location, then a time-consuming process is required to suppress this response tendency and activate the rule for the correct response mapping. This discussion brings us to the second feature of location compatibility—the importance of *rules* when congruence is not obtained (Payne, 1995). Simple rules should be available to map the set of stimuli to the set of responses (Kornblum, Hasbroucq, & Osman, 1990). This feature is illustrated in a study by Fitts and Deininger (1954), who compared three mappings between a linear array of displays and a linear array of controls. One mapping was congruent; the second was reversed, so that the leftmost display was associated with the rightmost control and so forth; the third mapping involved a random assignment of controls to displays. Fitts and Deininger found, as expected, that performance was best in the first array, but also was considerably better in the reversed than in the random array. In the reversed array, a single rule can provide the mapping. A study by Haskell, Wickens, and Sarno (1990) revealed that the number of rules necessary to specify a mapping between linear arrays of four displays and four controls was a strong predictor of RT. Payne (1995), however, notes that the contribution of such rules to RT is often underestimated by users if they are simply allowed to *rate* the estimated S-R compatibility of different mappings that are shown to them. People are not always good at estimating the effects on their own performance.

At times, even congruence is difficult to achieve. Consider a linear array of switches that must be positioned along an armrest to control (or respond to) a vertical array of displays. Since a congruent, vertical array of switches on the armrest would be difficult to implement (and an anthropometrically poor design), the axis of switch orientation must be incongruent with the display axis. However, there are rules to guide the designer. These rules describe a mapping of ordered quantities from least to most in space, which specifies that *increases* move from left to right, aft to forward, clockwise (for a circular array), and (to a lesser extent) from bottom to top. Hence, a far-right control should be mapped to a top display when a left-right array is mapped to a vertically oriented display (Weeks & Proctor, 1990). It is unfortunate, however, that the top-down ordering is not strong. On the one hand, high values are compatible with top locations (as noted in Chapter 4; see also the typical calculator keyboard). On the other hand, the order of counting (1, 2, 3, . . .), following the order of reading in English, is from top to bottom (see the push-button telephone). These conflicting stereotypes suggest that vertical display (or control) arrays that are not congruent with control (display) arrays should only be used with caution. An important design solution that can resolve any potential mapping ambiguity is to put a slight cant, or angling, of one array in a direction that is congruent with the other, as shown in Figure 9.7. If this cant is as great as 45 degrees, then reaction time can be as fast as if the control and display axes are parallel (Andre, Haskell, & Wickens, 1991).

Movement Compatibility   When an operator moves a position switch, rotary, or sliding control (e.g., a mouse), it often changes the state of a displayed variable. *Movement compatibility* defines the set of expectancies that an operator has about how the display will respond to the control activity. Technically we may define this as cognitive-response-stimulus (C-R-S) compatibility because a cognitive intention to change a variable leads to a response on the control, which in turn produces a stimulus change in the display.

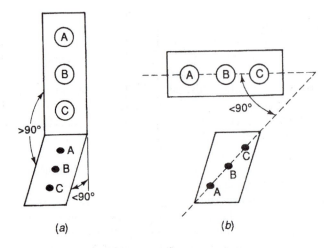

Figure 9.7 Solutions of location compatibility problems by using cant. (*a*) The control panel slopes downward slightly (an angle greater than 90 degrees), so that control A is clearly above B, and B is above C, just as they are in the display array. (*b*) The controls are slightly angled from left to right across the panel, creating a left-right ordering that is congruent with the display array.

When C-R-S compatibility is violated, an operator may move the control, then perceive the system responding in what he or she thinks is the opposite direction, triggering a further unnecessary and possibly disastrous control action.

The congruence principle of location compatibility discussed above, can also be applied to the compatibility of movement. Thus, linear controls should move in an axis and direction parallel to display movement (and as discussed in Chapter 4, this movement should also be parallel to the operator's mental model of the displayed variable). Dial displays are more compatible or congruent with rotary controls and linear displays with sliding controls. When congruence must be violated, a common mapping of *increase* (up, right, forward, and clockwise) should be used to identify how the display responds to the control. Thus in Figure 9.8a, the operator would expect a clockwise rotation to move the linear pointer upward over the fixed scale.

Movement compatibility, however, is also governed by a principle of *movement proximity*, which is not related to congruence. This principle, also known as the Warrick principle (Warrick, 1947), asserts that the closest part of the moving element of a control should move in the same direction as the closest part of the moving element of a display, as if the operator has a mental model of a mechanical linkage between the two. To illustrate, consider Figure 9.8b, in which the clockwise-to-move-upward dial has been placed to the left of the linear display. Here the clockwise stereotype conflicts with the movement proximity stereotype, since the movement proximity principle would say that a clockwise rotation should move the pointer downward. In these circumstances, Loveless (1963) concludes that the movement proximity stereotype is dominant. That is, counterclockwise rotation would be expected to increase. However, as shown in Figure 9.8c, a simple

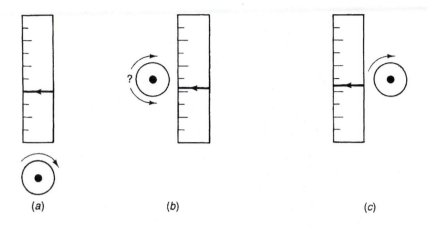

Figure 9.8   Three control-display layout configurations illustrating movement compatibility principles. The arrow indicates the expected control rotation direction to *increase* the indicator. (b) The display is ambiguous because the clockwise-to-increase and proximity of movement principles are in opposition. In (c) these two principles are congruent.

relocation of the rotary control to the right of the linear scale is the sort of engineering psychology solution that is so gratifying because it captures both principles at once.

A study by Hoffmann (1990) examined how these (and other) principles of compatibility interact in different control-display layouts. He finds that the overall compatibility of a given layout can be modeled as the sum of the forces exerted by the different components of compatability as they either work together (Figure 9.8c) or in opposition (Figure 9.8b).

Compatibility Ambiguities   Applying compatibility principles to control-display movement relations is not always straightforward because the operator's *mental model* of what a control is doing may sometimes make the relation ambiguous, as seen in two examples. First, Hoffmann (1990) found that the movement proximity principle was far less pronounced for students of psychology than students of mechanical engineering, suggesting that only the latter had the strong mental model of the mechanical linkage. Second, Figure 9.9a is a control design for the vertical speed of an aircraft. Immediately, an incompatibility appears evident: Move the control up to set the speed downward? However, if as in Figure 9.9b the operator (in this case the pilot) conceives of the control motion not as a linear slide but as a rotating wheel whose front surface is exposed, and the pilot has a mental model that this rotation is directly coupled to the rotation of the aircraft around the axis of its wings (upward rotation for increased vertical speed), the relation now is quite compatible.

A third form of compatibility ambiguity, discussed in Chapter 5, relates to the distinction between ego-referenced and world-referenced displays. When you move a control in one direction, do you see your cursor move in the same direction, as if you were outside looking in (exocentric viewpoint), or do you see the "world" within which the

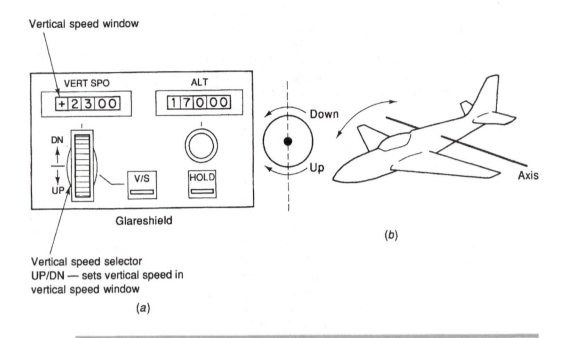

Vertical speed window

VERT SPO

ALT

+2300

17000

DN

V/S

HOLD

UP

Glareshield

Down

Up

Axis

(b)

Vertical speed selector
UP/DN — sets vertical speed in
vertical speed window

(a)

Figure 9.9 Example of the role of the mental model in compatibility of a vertical speed control. (a) Vertical speed selector control, suggesting an apparent incompatibility. (Courtesy of Boeing Commercial Airplane Co., Seattle.) (b) Mental model of the aircraft, rotating around the axis parallel to its wings. Here the rotary control is quite compatible with the desired change of state.

cursor resides moving in the opposite direction, as you would see if you were positioned "inside" the cursor (or vehicle represented by the cursor) and were looking out: the egocentric view. In the exocentric case, there is compatible S-R movement. In the egocentric case, there is not. But as we discuss in Chapter 5, the "incompatible" egocentric view is sometimes appropriate, to the extent that the display can present a realistic portrayal that the user is "immersed" in the environment. What is important here is that the nature of the frame of reference is made clear, and consistent to the user.

A final compatibility ambiguity example relates to the distinction between status and command displays. In Chapter 6, we saw that a status display presents the current status of a variable (e.g., "Your power setting is too high"). A command display tells you what to do to correct the situation ("Lower your power setting"). From the strict viewpoint of S-R compatibility, it is apparent that a command display satisfies the principle that movement of the display is compatible with the required action (i.e., the display would signal a commanded lowering of the power variable). But this mapping bypasses the display of a representation of the state for which the command is required; and as we discuss in Chapter 13, it is not always good design to tell the operator what should be done without displaying the reasons why. A status display achieves this requirement; but now, if the display is S-C compatible, it requires a movement that is S-R incompatible (e.g., the upward display movement "too high" triggers the downward control movement "reduce").

In most circumstances, it would appear that the need for status information would override a command configuration that is more S-R compatible, and indeed when operators have a good mental model of the system under control, they perform as well if not better with status than with command displays (Andre, Wickens, & Goldwasser, 1990). As noted in Chapter 6, however, high levels of time pressure may favor command displays. Presentation of both status and command information, but insuring that they can be easily discriminated and not confused, is probably the most effective format.

Transformations and Population Stereotypes   Not all compatibility relationships are spatially defined. Any S-R mapping that requires some *transformation*, even if it is not spatial, will be reduced in its compatibility. Hence, a mapping between stimulus and response digits of 1–1, 2–2, and 3–3 is more compatible than 1–2, 2–3, and 3–4, which imposes the transformation "add one." Similarly, the relationship between stimulus digits and response letters (1-A, 2-B, 3-C, etc.) is less compatible than digits-digits or letters-letters mappings. Also, any S-R mapping that is many-to-one will be less compatible than a one-to-one mapping (Norman, 1988; Posner, 1964). Consider, for example, the added cognitive difficulty of dialing alphabetic phone numbers, like 437-HELP, resulting from the 3–1 mapping of letters (stimuli) to buttons (responses). Ironically, in Chapter 7 we identified this form of phone number as better from the standpoint of memory load. As we continuously see, human engineering is always encountering such trade-offs.

Population stereotypes define mappings that are more directly related to *experience*. For example, consider the relationship between the desired lighting of a room and the movement of a light switch. In North America, the compatible relation is to flip the switch up to turn the light on. In Europe, the compatible relation is the opposite (up is off). This difference is clearly unrelated to any difference in the psychological hardware between Americans and Europeans but rather is a function of experience. S. Smith (1981) evaluated population stereotypes in a number of verbal-pictorial relations. For example, he asks whether the "inside lane" of a four-lane highway refers to the centermost lane on each side or to the driving lane. Smith finds that the population is equally divided on this categorization. Any mapping that bases order on reading patterns (left-right and top-bottom) will also be stereotypic, and thereby not applicable, say, to Hebrew or Chinese readers. Finally, as noted in Chapter 3, color coding is strongly governed by population stereotypes (e.g., red for danger or stop).

Modality S-R Compatibility   Stimulus-response compatibility appears to be defined by stimulus and response modality as well as by spatial correspondence. Brainard, Irby, Fitts, and Alluisi (1962) found that if a stimulus was a light, choice RT was faster for a pointing (manual) than a voice response, but if the stimulus was an auditorily presented digit, RT was more rapid with a vocal naming response than with a manual pointing one. In a thorough review of the factors influencing choice RT, Teichner and Krebs (1974) summarized a number of studies and concluded that the four S-R combinations defined by visual and auditory input and manual and vocal response produced reaction times in the following order: A voice response to a light is slowest, a key-press response to a digit is of intermediate latency, and a manual key-press response to a light and naming of a digit are fastest. Wang and Proctor (1996) observe that modality compatibility linkages (e.g., manual to lights) amplify the effects of mapping of elements. That is, the benefits of left-left and right-right (relative to the costs of left-right and right-left) are amplified in modality-compatible mappings.

Greenwald (1970) discusses the related concept of *ideomotor compatibility*, which will occur if a stimulus matches the sensory feedback produced by the response. Under these conditions, RT will be fast and relatively automatic (Greenwald, 1979). Thus, Greenwald observes fast RTs in the ideomotor compatible conditions when a written response is given to a seen letter and when a spoken response is given to a heard letter. Incompatible mappings in which a written response is made to a heard letter and a spoken response to a seen letter are slower. Ideomotor compatible mappings not only are fast but also appear to be influenced neither by the information content of the RT task (N) nor by dual-task loading (Greenwald & Shulman, 1973).

Wickens, Sandry, and Vidulich (1983) and Wickens, Vidulich, and Sandry-Garza (1984) proposed that these modality-based S-R compatibility relations may partially depend on the central working-memory processing code (verbal or spatial) used in the task, as discussed in Chapter 7. In both the laboratory environment and in an aircraft simulator, they demonstrated that tasks that use verbal working memory are served best by auditory inputs and vocal outputs, whereas spatial tasks are better served by visual inputs and manual outputs. In the aircraft simulation, Wickens, Sandry, and Vidulich found that these compatibility effects were enhanced when the flight task became more difficult.

As noted in Chapter 6, however, these guidelines would hold only when the material is short, since a long auditory input of verbal material can lead to forgetting. Furthermore, for the voice control, the guidelines would hold only when the vocal response does not disrupt rehearsal of the retained information (Wickens & Liu, 1988). The particular advantages of voice control in multitask environments such as the aircraft cockpit (Henderson, 1989) or the computer design station (Martin, 1989) will be further discussed in Chapters 10 and 11.

Consistency and Training Compatibility is normally considered to be an asset in system design. However, to reiterate a point made in Chapter 4, the designer should always be wary of any possible violation of *consistency* across a set of control-display relations that may result from trying to optimize the compatibility of each. For example, Duncan (1984) found that subjects actually had a more difficult time responding to two RT tasks if one was compatibly mapped and one incompatible than responding when both were incompatible. In other words, the consistency of having identical (but incompatible) mappings in both tasks outweighed the advantages of compatibility in one. Correspondingly, a designer who needs to add another function to a system that already contains a lot of control-display mappings should be wary of whether the compatible addition proposed (e.g., status display) is in disharmony with the existing set (e.g., several command displays) (Andre & Wickens, 1992).

We have seen how training and experience form the basis for population stereotypes. Training can also be used to formulate correct mental models or enhance the agreement between the mental model and the correct dynamics, as in Figure 9.9. It is also evident that training will improve performance on both compatible and incompatible mappings. In fact, the rate of improvement with practice is actually faster with the incompatible mappings because they have more room to improve (Fitts & Seeger, 1953). However, the data are also clear that extensive training of an incompatible mapping will never fully catch up to a compatible one. Moreover, when the operator is placed under stress, performance with the incompatible mapping will regress further than with the compatible one (Fuchs, 1962; Loveless, 1963). Hence, the system user should be wary of a designer who excuses an incompatible design with the argument that the problem can be "trained away."

Knowledge in the World   Most of our discussion of compatibility has focused on the mapping of stimuli to responses, or displays to controls. In this context, it can be argued that good S-R compatibility provides the user with direct visual knowledge of what action to take. Norman (1991) refers to this as "knowledge in the world," which can be contrasted with "knowledge in the head," when the appropriate response must be derived from learning and experience (the stovetops in Figures 9.5a and 9.5d provide examples of knowledge in the world, while those in Figures 9.5c and particularly 9.5b require knowledge in the head).

The concept of knowledge in the world, however, applies to a broader range of actions than merely those triggered by, or in response to, an event. When approaching a piece of equipment to turn it on (or otherwise use it), one is not responding to an "event" in a way described by the RT paradigm. Yet the importance of knowledge in the world of what action to take remains critical, particularly for the novice user. Good design should provide easily discriminable sets of options for allowable actions (such as a set of menu options always available on a computer screen; see Figure 9.10a); or it should provide an invitation to the appropriate actions, referred to as an *affordance*, or forcing function (Figures 9.10b and 9.10c), as well as a "lockout" of the inappropriate actions (Figure 9.10d) (Norman, 1988).

STAGES IN REACTION TIME

A number of variables have been discussed that influence or prolong RT. The model of information processing presented in Chapter 1 also assumes that total reaction time equals the sum of the duration of a number of component processing stages (e.g., perceptual encoding, and response selection). In a series of experiments and theoretical papers, psychologists have attempted to establish where these variables have their effects and, in fact, if processing really does proceed by discrete stages or sequential mental operations. Pachella (1974) has contrasted two approaches used to justify the existence of processing stages and to examine the influences of stage duration on total RT latency. These are the *subtractive method* and the *additive factors* technique. A third approach is based on the *event-related brain potential*.

The Subtractive Method

In the subtractive method, an experimental manipulation is used to delete a mental operation entirely from the RT task. The decrease in RT that results is then assumed to reflect the time required to perform the absent operation. More than a century ago, Donders (1869/1969) first used the subtractive method in RT to provide evidence for a response selection stage. He compared reaction time in which several stimuli were assigned to several responses (conventional choice RT) with reaction time in which there were several possible stimuli but only one demanded a response. This is known as the disjunctive or "go–no-go" RT. The difference between these two conditions was assumed by Donders to be the time taken to select a response, since response selection is not necessary when only one response is required. By similar logic, when disjunctive RT was compared with simple RT, Donders assumed that the difference reflected the latency of a

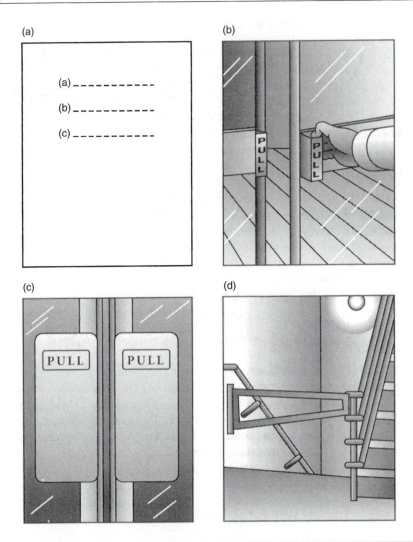

Figure 9.10 (*a*) Illustrates the availability of action options (knowledge in the world) through a menu. (*b*) Illustrates the invitation or affordance to open a door handle, which affords grabbing and pulling. (*c*) A violation of knowledge in the world, because it is not obvious that one should open the door by pushing on its surface. The verbal label should not be required. (*d*) A lockout, to prevent people from descending the stairs beyond the ground-floor, fire-exit level.

Source: D. Norman, *The Psychology of Everyday Things* (New York: HarperCollins, 1990).

stimulus discrimination stage, since only in disjunctive RT is it necessary to discriminate the stimuli. In simple RT, detection, not recognition, is sufficient to initiate the response.

Additive Factors Technique

The subtractive method is intuitive, and its application leads to a number of plausible findings, although some of its assumptions have been criticized (Pachella, 1974). Fortunately, confirming evidence for the existence and identity of processing stages has been provided by the *additive factors* method (Sternberg, 1969, 1975). Although all of the specific assumptions underlying the applications will not be described here, the intent of additive factors is to define the existence and distinctiveness of different stages by manipulating variables that are known to lengthen reaction time.

In a typical application, two variables are manipulated independently. It assumed that if the two influence a common stage of processing, their effects on reaction time will interact; that is, the extent to which one variable lengthens RT will be amplified at the more difficult level of the other. This situation, shown in Figure 9.11a and 9.11 b, is

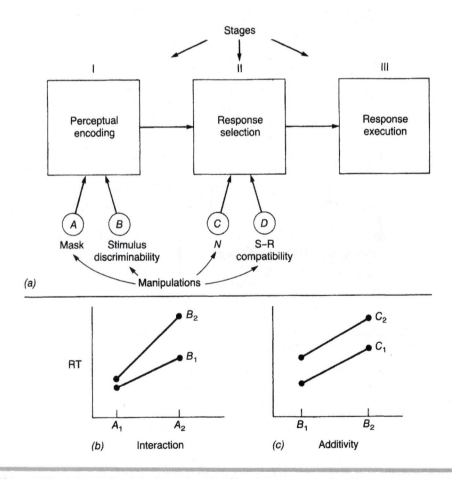

Figure 9.11 (a) Hypothetical relationship between independent manipulation of four variables interpreted in the framework of additive factors. (b) Variables A and B interact, affecting a common stage. (c) Variables B and C are additive, affecting different stages.

similar to one in real life, when troubles from one source disrupt our ability to deal with troubles from another source, particularly if both sources affect the same general aspect of our life (e.g., both relate to trouble with classwork). If, however, the two manipulated variables influence different stages of processing (e.g., variables A and C in Figure 9.11a), their effects will be additive, as shown in Figure 9.11c. That is, the influence of one variable will not be affected by the level of the other.

Experimental Techniques A specific example using the additive factors method is represented in Figure 9.11. The experimenter wishes to make inferences about what manipulations influence what stages of processing, as shown in Figure 9.11a. The experimenter first identifies four experimental variables to manipulate, each identified by a letter and each examined at an easy and difficult level. In our examples, these variables are the absence or presence of a mask over the stimulus (A_1 and A_2, respectively), which degrades stimulus quality; the discriminability of the stimuli in a set (B_1: high; B_2: low); the number of S-R pairs N(C_1: small; C_2: large); and stimulus-response compatibility (D_1: high; D_2: low). (Notice that the subscript 1 always designates the easy level of the variable.) The experimenter then measures reaction time as each pair of variables is manipulated independently. For example, RT is measured when stimuli of high and low discriminability are presented both with and without a mask. The RT measures from the resulting four conditions are shown in Figure 9.11, indicating an interaction. The effect of the mask (A_1 versus A_2) is more pronounced when discriminability is low (B_2) than when it is high (B_1) (figure 9.11b). Hence the experimenter concludes that discriminability and stimulus quality must influence the same processing stage—perception—as shown in Figure 9.11a.

Next, the experimenter manipulates discriminability and set (N) size together by presenting stimuli of high and low discriminability in, for example, a two- and four-choice RT task. Here the results are shown in Figure 9.11c. The two variables are additive. The set-size effect is not influenced by the ease of discriminating the stimuli. The experimenter concludes that the two variables influence different processing stages. Since, therefore, N cannot affect perceptual encoding, it is likely instead to influence response selection. This finding would be confirmed if the experimenter manipulated N and S-R compatibility together. These variables would be found to interact like those in Figure 9.11b.

As experimenters have performed a large number of these independent manipulations of RT difficulty, the additive factors data have provided a fairly consistent picture of processing stages. Certain pairs of variables consistently interact, and others are consistently additive. The experimenters use a certain amount of intuition to infer the stage affected by a cluster of interacting variables. For example, it is clear intuitively that S-R compatibility must influence response selection and that stimulus quality must influence perceptual processing. These anchors help interpret the locus of effect of other factors.

Figure 9.12 presents the pattern of additivity and interactions that have been collectively aggregated from a number of RT investigations. Four processing stages are portrayed across the bottom. Experimental manipulations are circled, and additive or interactive relations obtained between these manipulations are indicated by narrow or thick lines, respectively. Each line is coded by the investigation in which the manipulation was performed, and the codes are identified by the list below the figure. The dashed arrows point to the stages inferred to be affected by the manipulation in question.

Generally, the relationships that are shown in Figure 9.12 are consistent. For example, clusters of variables, such as S-R compatibility, N, and the repetition effect, are consistently found to interact with one another by a number of investigators and to be additive with variables that logically should affect other stages.

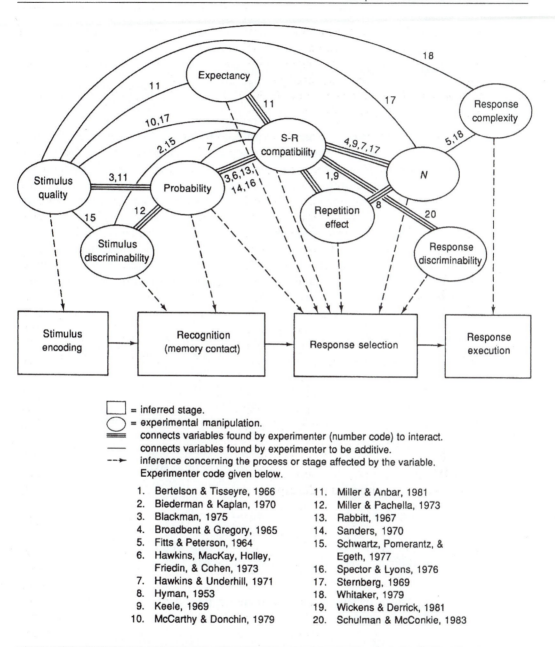

Figure 9.12   Patterns of additive factors results.

In addition to the pattern of interactions and additivity, the picture of results shown in Figure 9.12 allows two general conclusions to be drawn. First, the seat of the "action" of most of the variables seems to be in response selection, emphasizing a point that is addressed again later in this chapter: the response selection process is a major bottleneck in speeded information processing (Pashler, 1998). Second, stimulus probability appears to affect two stages: Improbable stimuli require longer to be recognized, and their associated responses take longer to be selected.

Applications of Additive Factors Methodology   The additive factors methodology has served as a useful applied tool for establishing how the speed of information processing is influenced by different environmental and individual factors, such as aging (Strayer, Wickens, & Braune, 1987), poisoning (Smith & Langolf, 1981), and mental workload, as discussed in Chapter 11 (Crosby & Parkinson, 1979; Wickens et al., 1986).

When the technique is applied for these purposes, latency in the RT task is measured as the demands of different processing stages are manipulated, in both the low and high level of the factor (e.g., aging) to be investigated. This factor is then treated just like any other manipulation. If it interacts with a variable that influences a known stage, the environmental variable is assumed to affect the stage in question. For example, Smith and Langolf (1981) used a Sternberg memory search task—in which a stimulus is judged to be the same or different from one held in working memory—in order to measure the information processing deficits of workers who had been exposed to different amounts of mercury in industrial environments. They found an interaction between memory load and the amount of mercury poisoning in the bloodstream. Therefore, the behavioral effects of such toxins were localized at the stage of working-term memory retrieval.

Problems With Additive Factors   The additive factors technique has had a remarkable history of success in accounting for RT data, and it has been employed in a number of applied contexts. One primary criticism, however, is directed at the assumption that stages proceed strictly in series—like a factory assembly line—and that the effects that either slow down or speed up an earlier stage have no effect on the speed of processing at a later stage. By now there is convincing evidence that information processing does not strictly proceed in a serial fashion (Coles, Gratton, & Donchin, 1988; McClelland, 1979; Meyer & Kieras, 1997a,b). For example, the process of preparation based on expectancy may overlap different stages in time, so that an increase in preparation that is made for a particular, frequent response (hence, reducing response selection time) can proceed while perceptual recognition is still taking place (Coles, Gratton, & Donchin, 1988). This overlap in time can occasionally do strange things to the RT relationship shown in Figure 9.11, such as producing an *underadditive* relationship, where the delay caused by increasing the difficulty at one stage of processing is actually smaller at the more difficult level of the other stage (Schwartz, Pomerantz, & Egeth, 1977).

The Event-Related Brain Potential as an Index of Mental Chronometry

Despite some shortcomings, Sternberg's additive factors approach provides a reasonably good approximation of the processing mechanisms involved in reaction time. In fact, the inferences concerning the influence of manipulations on stages that are made from additive and interaction data are still sound in many instances, even when processes do overlap in time (McClelland, 1979). However, no matter what theory is adopted, all RT investigations must make inferences about the processes between stimulus and response by looking at the final product of the response and not examining directly those intervening processes. To augment this mental chronometry, the event-related brain potential (ERP) has been used to provide a direct estimate of the timing of processes up to the intermediate stage of stimulus categorization (Donchin, 1981; Gratton et al., 1988; McCarthy & Donchin, 1979). The ERP is a series of voltage oscillations or components that are recorded from the surface of the scalp to indicate the brain's electrical response to discrete environmental events.

An investigation by McCarthy and Donchin (1979) suggests that the late positive, or P300, component of the ERP covaries with the duration of perceptual processing but not with the duration of response selection. Their subjects performed the RT task in which the displayed words *left* and *right* were responded to by pressing left and right keys. The difficulty of stimulus encoding was varied by increasing noise on the display. Response selection difficulty was manipulated by changing S-R compatibility (i.e., responding "right" to the word "left"). As shown in Figure 9.13, when RT was examined, an additive effect of both variables was observed, as would be expected by the data shown in Figure 9.12. The latency of the P300 component elicited by the stimuli was also delayed by the display mask but was *unaffected* by S-R compatibility. This finding suggested that compatibility influenced a stage *after* perceptual categorization, a conclusion perfectly consistent with that derived from additive factors logic. An interesting observation from their data was that the delay produced by the display noise was greater for RT than for P300. This finding also provides support for a model of information processing, which assumes that the effects of degrading an earlier stage (perception) can carry through to prolong processing at a subsequent stage (response selection). Longer processing at encoding will delay P300 somewhat. The final manual response will be delayed even more because it includes slower response selection as well as slower encoding.

The Value of Stages

Collectively, the data from the subtractive method and additive factors and from the event-related potential (ERP) are quite consistent with the model of information processing described in Chapter 1. However, these data also suggest that the separation of processing stages should not be taken too literally. In speeded reactions to external events there undoubtedly is some overlap in time between processing in successive stages, just as the brain in general is capable of a good deal of parallel processing (Meyer & Kieras, 1997a,b; see Chapters 3 and 11). However, as with other models and conceptions discussed in this book, the stage concept is a useful one that is consistent with dichotomies made elsewhere between sensitivity and response bias in detection, and between early and late processing resources in time sharing (see Chapter 11). The integrating value of the stage concept more than compensates for any limitations in its complete accuracy.

SERIAL RESPONSES

So far we have discussed primarily the selection of a single discrete action in the RT task. Many tasks in the real world, however, call for not just one but for a series of repetitive actions. Typing and assembly-line work are two examples. The factors that influence single reaction time are just as important in influencing the speed of repetitive performance. However, the fact that several stimuli must be processed in sequence brings into play a set of additional influences that relate to the timing and pacing of sequential stimuli and responses.

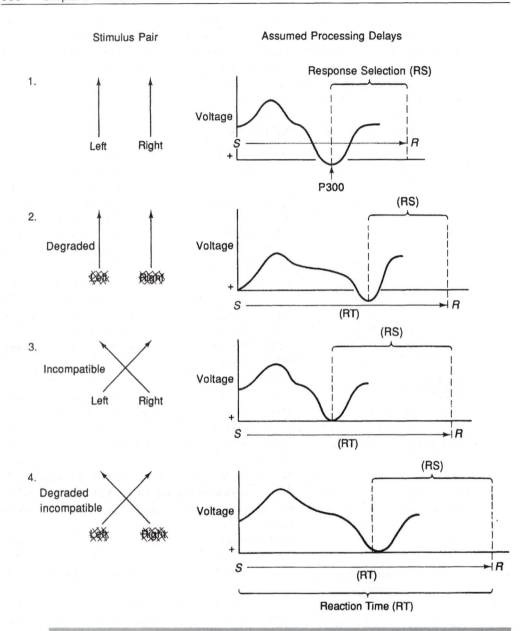

Figure 9.13 Schematic representation of McCarthy and Donchin's experiment. The left of each row shows the stimulus pair presented in a condition, along with the mapping to the response (arrows). To the right is the time line of the event-related potential (ERP) and response for a particular experimental condition. The ERP is conventionally plotted with positive voltages at the bottom. Changes in encoding delay are reflected in P300 latency and reaction time (compare row 1 to 2 and 3 to 4). Changes in response selection delay are reflected in the difference between RT and P300 latency (compare conditions 1 to 3 and 2 to 4). The effects of masking and S-R compatibility in this experiment show an additive relationship.

In the discussion of serial or repeated responses, we focus initially on the simplest case: only two stimuli presented in rapid succession. This is the paradigm of the *psychological refractory period*. Next we examine response times to several stimuli in rapid succession, the serial RT task. This discussion leads us to an analysis of transcription skills, such as typing.

The Psychological Refractory Period

The psychological refractory period, or PRP (Telford, 1931; Pashler, 1998; Kantowitz, 1974; Meyer & Kieras, 1997b), describes a situation in which two RT tasks are presented close together in time. The separation in time between the two stimuli is called the *interstimulus interval*, or ISI. (This separation is sometimes referred to as the stimulus onset asynchrony, or SOA). The general finding is that the response to the second stimulus is delayed by the processing of the first when the ISI is short. Suppose, for example, a subject is to press a key (R_1) as soon as a tone (S_1) is heard, and is to speak (R_2) as soon as a light (S_2) is seen. If the light is presented a fifth of a second or so after the tone, the subject will be slowed in responding to the light (RT_2) because of processing the tone. However, reaction time to the tone (RT_1) will be unaffected by the presence of the light response task. The PRP delay in RT_2 is typically measured with respect to a single-task control condition, in which S_2 is responded to without any requirement to process S_1.

The most plausible account of the PRP is a model that proposes the human being to be a *single-channel processor* of information. The single-channel theory of the PRP was originally proposed by Craik (1947) and has subsequently been expressed and elaborated on by Bertelson (1966), Davis (1965), Kantowitz (1974), Meyer and Kieras (1997a,b), Pashler (1989, 1998), and Welford (1967). It is compatible with Broadbent's (1958) conception of attention as an information-processing bottleneck that can only process one stimulus or piece of information at a time (see Chapter 3). In explaining the PRP effect, single-channel theory assumes that the processing of S_1 temporarily "captures" the single-channel bottleneck of the decision-making/response-selection stage. Thus, until R_1 has been released (the single channel has finished processing S_1), the processor cannot begin to deal with S_2. The second stimulus S_2 must therefore wait at the "gates" of this single-channel bottleneck until they open. This waiting time is what prolongs RT_2. The sooner S_2 arrives, the longer it must wait. According to this view, anything that prolongs the processing of S_1 will increase the PRP delay of RT_2. Reynolds' (1966), for example, found that the PRP delay in RT_2 was lengthened if the RT task of RT involved a choice rather than a simple response.

This bottleneck in the sequence of information-processing activities does not appear to be located at the peripheral sensory end of the processing sequence (like blinders over the eyes that are not removed until R_1 has occurred). If this were the case, no processing of S_2 whatsoever could begin until RT_1 is complete. However, as described in Chapter 6, much of perception is relatively automatic. Therefore, the basic *perceptual* analysis of S_2 can proceed even as the processor is fully occupied with selecting the response to S_1 (Karlin & Kestinbaum, 1968; Keele, 1973; Pashler, 1989, 1998). Only after its perceptual processing is completed does S_2 have to wait for the bottleneck to dispense with R_1. These relations are shown in Figure 9.14.

Imagine as an analogy a kindergarten teacher (who is the bottleneck) who must get two children (S_1 and S_2) ready for recess. Both are able to put on their coats by themselves

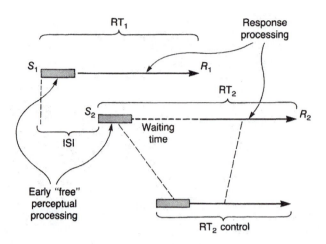

Figure 9.14 Single-channel theory explanation of the psychological refractory period. The figure shows the delay (waiting time; the dashed line) imposed on RT_2 by the processing involved in RT_1. This waiting time makes RT_2 in the dual-task setting (*top*) longer than in the single-task control (*bottom*).

(this is the automatic "early" processing that does not require the teacher—the single channel—to function), but both need the teacher to button the coats (select and execute a response). Therefore, how long child$_2$ will have to wait is a joint function of how soon she arrives after child$_1$ (the ISI) and how long it takes the teacher to button the coat. But the waiting time will not include the time it takes child$_2$ to put on the coat, since this can be done in parallel with the buttoning of child$_1$. Only once child$_2$'s coat is on must she wait. Therefore, the total time required for child$_2$ to get the coat on and buttoned (analogous to RT_2) is equal to the time it normally takes to put the coat on and have the teacher button it, plus the waiting time. The latter may be predicted by the ISI and by the time to button the first child's coat.

Returning to the PRP paradigm, we see that the *delay* in RT_2 beyond its single-task baseline will increase linearly (on a one-to-one basis) with a decrease in ISI and with an increase in the complexity of response selection of RT_1, since both increase the waiting time. This relationship is shown in Figure 9.15. Assuming that the single-channel bottleneck is perfect (i.e., post-perceptual processing of S_2 will not start at all until R1 is released), the relationship between ISI and RT_2 will look like that shown in Figure 9.15. When ISI is long (much greater than RT_1), RT_2 is not delayed at all. When ISI is shortened to about the length of RT_1, some temporal overlap will occur and RT_2 will be prolonged because of a waiting period. This waiting time will then increase linearly as ISI is shortened further.

The relationship between ISI and RT_2 as shown in Figure 9.15 describes rather successfully a large amount of the PRP data (Bertelson, 1966; Kantowitz, 1974; Meyer & Kieras, 1997a,b; Pashler, 1989, 1998; M. Smith, 1967). There are, however, two important qualifications to the general single-channel model as it has been presented so far.

1. When the ISI is quite short (less than about 100 msec), a qualitatively different processing sequence occurs; both responses are emitted *together* (grouping) and

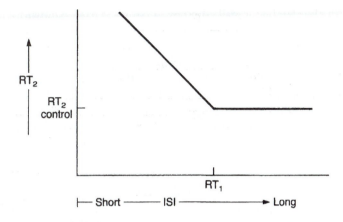

Figure 9.15   Relationship between ISI and RT_2 predicted by single-channel theory.

both are delayed (Kantowitz, 1974). It is as if the two stimuli are occurring so close together in time that S_2 gets through the single-channel gate while it is still accepting S_1 (Kantowitz, 1974; Welford, 1952).

2. Sometimes RT_2 suffers a PRP delay even when the ISI is greater than RT_1. That is, S_2 is presented after R_1 has been completed. This delay occurs when the subject is monitoring the feedback from the response of RT_1 as it is executed (Welford, 1967).

In the real world, operators are more likely to encounter a *series* of stimuli that must be rapidly processed than a simple pair. In the laboratory the former situation is realized in the *serial RT paradigm*. Here, a series of RT trials occurs sufficiently close to one another in time that each RT is affected by the processing of the previous stimulus in the manner described by the single-channel theory. A large number of factors influence performance in this paradigm, typical of tasks ranging from quality control inspection to keyboard transcription to assembly-line manufacturing. Many of these variables were considered earlier in this chapter. For example, S-R compatibility, stimulus discriminability, and practice influence serial RT just as they do single-trial-choice RT. However, some of these variables interact in important ways with the variables that describe the sequential timing of the successive stimuli. Other variables describe that timing itself. Four of these factors will be considered: decision complexity, pacing, response factors, and preview in transcription.

The Decision Complexity Advantage

Earlier, we described how the linear relationship between choice RT and the amount of information transmitted—the Hick-Hyman Law—was seen to reflect a capacity limit of the human operator. The slope of this function expressed as seconds per bit could be inverted and expressed as bits per second. Early interpretations of the Hick-Hyman Law assumed that the latter figure provided an estimate of the fixed bandwidth of the human processing system. As decisions become more complex, decision rate slows proportionately.

If the human being really did have a constant fixed bandwidth for processing information, in terms of bits per second, this limit should be the same whether we make a small number of high-bit decisions per unit time or a large number of low-bit decisions. For example, if one 6-bit decision/sec was our maximum performance, we should also be able to make two 3-bit decisions/sec, three 2-bit decisions/sec, or six 1-bit decisions/sec. In fact, however, this trade-off does not appear to hold. The most restricting limit in human performance appears to relate to the absolute number of decisions that can be made per second rather than the number of bits that can be processed per second. For example, people are better able to process information delivered in the format of one 6-bit decision per second than in the format of six 1-bit decisions per second (Alluisi, Muller, & Fitts, 1957; Broadbent, 1971). Thus, the frequency of decisions and their complexity do *not* trade off reciprocally. The advantage of a few complex decisions over several simple ones may be defined as a *decision complexity advantage*. This finding suggests that there is some fundamental limit to the central-processing or decision-making rate, independent of decision complexity, that limits the speed of other stages of processing. This limit appears to be about 2.5 decisions/sec for decisions of the simplest possible kind (Debecker & Desmedt, 1970). Such a limit might well explain why our motor output often outruns our decision-making competence. The *uhs* or *uhms* that we sometimes interject into rapid speech are examples of how our motor system fills in the noninformative responses while the decision system is slowed by its limits in selecting the appropriate response (Welford, 1976).

The most general implication of the decision complexity advantage is that greater gains in information transmission may be achieved by calling for a few complex decisions than by calling for many simple decisions. Several investigations suggest that this is a reasonable guideline. For example, Deininger, Billington, and Riesz (1966) evaluated push-button dialing. A sequence of 5, 6, 8, or 11 letters to be dialed was drawn from a vocabulary of 22, 13, 7, and 4 alternatives, respectively (22.5 bits each). The total dialing time was lowest with the shortest number of units (5 letters), each delivering the greatest information content per letter.

A general guideline in computer menu design is that people work better with broad-shallow menus—each choice is among a fairly large number of alternatives (more information/decisions), but there are only a few layers (fewer decisions)—than with narrow-deep menus—choices are simple, but several choices must be made to get to the bottom of the menu (Shneiderman, 1998).

The decision complexity advantage also has implications for any data-entry task, such as typewriting. For example, Seibel (1972) concluded that making text more redundant (less information per keystroke) will increase somewhat the rate at which key responses can be made (decisions per second) but will decrease the overall information transmission rate (bits per second). It follows from these data that processing efficiency could be *increased* by allowing each key press to convey more information than the 1.5 bits provided on the average by each letter (see Chapter 2). One possibility is to allow separate keys to indicate certain words or common sequences such as *and*, *ing*, or *th*. This "rapid type" technique has indeed proven to be more efficient than conventional typing, given that the operator receives a minimal level of training (Seibel, 1963). However, if there are too many of these high-information units, the keyboard itself will become overly large, like the keyboard of a Chinese-character typewriter. In this case, efficiency may decrease because the sheer size of the keyboard will increase the time it takes to locate keys and to move the fingers from one key to another (see Chapter 10).

One obvious solution to this motor limitation is to allow *chording*, in which simultaneous rather than sequential key presses are required (Baber, 1997). This approach would increase the number of possible strokes without imposing a proportional increase in the number of keys. Thus, with only a five-finger keyboard, it is possible to produce $2^5 - 1$, or 31, possible chords without requiring any finger movement to different keys. With ten fingers resting on ten keys the possibilities are $2^{10} - 1$, or 1,023.

A number of studies suggest that the greater information available per keystroke in chording provides a more efficient means of transmitting information. For example, Seibel (1963) found that increasing the number of possible chords beyond five had little effect on processing speed (chords per minute) but increased overall information transmission. Another study by Seibel (1964) examined skilled court typists using a chording "court writer," or stenotype. Although these operators responded at a third of the rate of skilled typists in the number of keys per unit time, they also succeeded in transmitting twice as much information (bits per second), again consistent with the decision complexity advantage. Lockhead and Klemmer (1959) observed successful performance with a chord typewriter, and Conrad and Longman (1965) found that chording was better than conventional typing as a means of sorting letters in automatic mail-sorting consoles. A ten-key chording board was selected by the British post office for foreign-mail sorting, having demonstrated faster performance than a sequential keying device (Bartram, 1986).

Besides capitalizing on the decision complexity advantage, chording keyboards are also useful because they can be easily operated while vision is fixated elsewhere. A major problem with chording keyboards, however, is that the sometimes arbitrary finger assignments take a long time to learn (Richardson, Telson, Koch, & Chrysler, 1987). One solution is to capitalize on visual imagery, assigning the chording fingers in a way that "looks" like the image of the letters. Such a chording keyboard was designed by Sidorsky (1974), following the scheme in Figure 9.16. Using three fingers, the operator presses twice for each letter, "painting" it from the top row to the bottom. In the figure, the dots are keys that are not pressed. Once the operator remembers the particular idiosyncratic shapes of the letters, little learning is required, and Sidorsky found that subjects were able to type from 60 to 110 percent as fast with this as they could with the conventional keyboard (see also Gopher & Raij, 1988). Because only one hand is required, the chording keyboard can work in harmony with a mouse, controlled by the other hand.

Pacing

The pacing factor defines the circumstances under which the operator proceeds from one stimulus to the next. Pacing can be characterized in terms of two dimensions, one dichotomous and one continuous, both of which generally describe the degree of time constraints placed on the human operator. The dichotomous dimension contrasts a *force-paced* with a *self-paced* stimulus rate. In the force-paced schedule, each stimulus follows the preceding stimulus at a constant interval. The critical variable is the inter-stimulus interval, or ISI. The frequency of stimulus presentation in the force-paced schedule is thus independent of the operator's responses. Work on an assembly line in

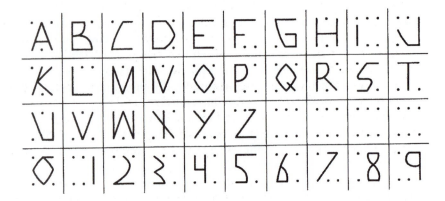

Figure 9.16 The letter-shape keyboard devised by Sidorsky uses visual imagery to specify the form of the key press for an alphanumeric character. There are three keys, and one to three of them must be pressed twice. The small dots indicate the keys that are not pressed. The top row of each letter represents the first key press; the bottom row represents the second. The keys that are successively pressed have a movement pattern that approximates the visual pattern of the letter.

Source: C. Sidorsky, *Alpha-dot: A New Approach to Direct Computer Entry of Battlefield Data* (Arlington, VA: U.S. Army Research Institute for the Behavioral and Social Sciences, 1974), Figure 1.

which the items continuously move past the operator on a conveyor belt is force paced. The speed of the belt defines the ISI. This schedule is typical of semiautomated letter-sorting consoles in the post office. In the self-paced schedule each stimulus follows the previous *response* by a controlled interval known as the *response-stimulus interval,* or RSI. In this case, the frequency with which stimuli appear depends on the latency of the operator's response. This schedule characterizes manual letter sorting, in which letters are tossed into the appropriate bins, and after each toss the operator will initiate the next response.

The continuous dimension in pacing defines the value of the timing parameters. Either self-paced or force-paced schedules may be perceived as leisurely if the RSI or ISI, respectively, is long, so that a long time passes between a response and a subsequent stimulus. However, if the self-paced RSI is reduced to near zero or the force-paced ISI is reduced to a value near the average RT, then the speed stress can be quite intense indeed. In fact, the self-paced schedule with a zero RSI can seem just as forced as the force-paced schedule if the operator is responding rapidly. No matter how short the response, the subsequent stimulus will always be waiting.

The differences between these two schedules and the ease with which one or the other may be implemented in such systems as automatic postal sorting, assembly-line work, or industrial inspection have led investigators repeatedly to ask which is better. Welford (1968, 1976) argues on intuitive grounds in favor of the self-paced schedule: As long as there is any variability in the RT response (because of fluctuations in decision complexity, stimulus quality, or operator efficiency), then the self-paced schedule will allow long responses at one time to be compensated for by shorter responses at another to keep average productivity high. Welford argues that the force-paced schedule allows no such flexibility: either the ISI must be set longer than the longest expected RT to avoid temporal overlap, in which case the number of stimuli processed will be fewer than in the self-paced rate, or the ISI can be set shorter (e.g., at the mean response rate of the self-paced condition). In this case, a long RT to one stimulus will cause processing to overlap in time with the subsequent stimulus, and a "psychological refractory period" effect will then result. This effect would not be damaging if the subsequent stimulus was permanently displayed and required a short latency response. However, if the stimulus was transient and disappeared before the processing of S_1 was dispensed with, an error might result. If the processing of S_2 was also lengthy, the PRP effect would propagate to S_3, and so on.

Unfortunately, the empirical data appear to be so ambiguous that firm conclusions are difficult to draw concerning which schedule is better (e.g., Drury & Coury, 1981; Knight & Salvendy, 1981; Waganaar & Stakenberg, 1975; Wickens, 1984). One reason is that differences between schedules depend so much on the timing parameters, the RSI and ISI, that are chosen. If these are short, then with long-duration tasks, subjects in a force-paced schedule will be unable to rest, unless these rest intervals too are built into the system. With long RSIs, however, rest will occur often. It seems safe to assert that as the variability of processing latency increases, for whatever reasons (human or stimulus variability), then the relative merits of self-paced as opposed to force-paced schedules will improve. The exact level of variability at which a superiority of self- over force-paced schedules will be observed cannot be stated with confidence.

Response Factors

Response Complexity   As shown in Figure 9.12, more complex responses require longer to initiate. In the serial RT task, one important consequence of increased response complexity is the requirement for more monitoring of the response. As noted in the discussion of the psychological refractory period, monitoring the execution of and feedback from a response will sometimes delay the start of processing a subsequent stimulus (Welford, 1976).

Response Feedback   The feedback from a response can have two effects on performance, depending on the sensory modality in which it is received. Consider, first, the case in which the feedback is an *intrinsic* part of the response—the perceived sound of one's voice or the visualization of one's moving hand. These are linkages described earlier in the chapter as ideomotor compatible (Greenwald, 1970). Delays, distortions, or elimination of the intrinsic feedback can produce substantial deficits in performance (K. U. Smith, 1962). For example, consider the difficulty one has in speaking in a controlled voice when listening to loud music over headphones so that one's voice cannot be perceived, or in speaking when a delayed echo of the voice is heard.

Less serious are distortions of extrinsic feedback, such as the click of a depressed key or the appearance of a visual letter on a screen after the keystroke. Delays or degradation of this feedback can be harmful (Miller, 1968), particularly for novice operators. However, as expertise on the skill develops, and the operator becomes less reliant on the feedback to ensure that the right response has been executed, such feedback can be ignored; by appropriate use of focused attention, the harmful effects of its delays (or elimination) are themselves reduced (Long, 1976).

Response Repetition   Earlier in this chapter, we saw that a response that repeated itself was more rapid than if it followed a different response (Kornblum, 1973). However, there is a trend in many serial response skills such as typewriting for the opposite effect to occur, in which a response is slowed by its repetition.

The differing effects of response repetition between the single-trial RT paradigm (in which repetition is good) and the typing task described here (in which it is harmful) is worthy of note. In the single-trial RT, the repetition effect is considered to be a kind of shortcut, which eliminates the repeated engagement of the response selection stage. If a stimulus repeats, the same response is activated as before, and time is saved. However, reaction times in this case are relatively long (around 200–300 msec), compared to the interresponse times in typing, which may be less than half that amount. This faster responding produces a typing speed of five to eight responses per second. In light of Debecker and Desmedt's (1970) data, which showed a limit to serial response speed of two to three decisions per second, the high speeds in typing indicate that the separate responses may be selected without engaging a higher-level decision process. As a consequence, there is no longer any benefit to repetitions by bypassing this process, since the process is not involved. In fact, with the shorter interresponse times, processing instead begins to impose on the refractoriness of the motor system when repeated commands are issued to the same muscles (Fitts & Posner, 1967). In this case, it becomes advantageous to employ separate muscle groups for successive responses—hence, the advantage for alternations.

The slowing of repeated responses is greatest when a single finger is repeated, particularly when the repeated finger must strike two different keys because movement time is now required (see Chapter 10). However, slowing is also evident when two different digits on the same hand are repeated (Rumelhart & Norman, 1982). For example, Sternberg, Kroll, and Wright (1978) observed that words that needed keystrokes of alternate hands were typed faster than those in which all letters were typed with one hand. One characteristic of the keyboard layout on the conventional Sholes, or QWERTY, keyboard is that keys are placed so that common sequences of letters will be struck with keys that are far apart and therefore, on the average, are likely to be struck with different hands.

Unfortunately, the QWERTY design fails to include some other characteristics that would lead to more rapid performance. For example, more letters are typed on the row above than on the home keys, thus adding extra movement. Also the amount of effort between the two hands is not balanced. Dvorak (1943) designed a keyboard that reflects these two considerations and that attempts as well to maximize between-hand alternations. There is some consensus that with proper training, the Dvorak keyboard could lead to improved typing performance. However, the Dvorak board will probably never prove to be practical because the 5 to 10 percent estimated improvement (Alden, Daniels, & Kanarick, 1972; Norman & Fisher, 1982) is small relative to the familiarity that users have with the conventional keyboard, which in turn produces the great inertia against change.

Preview and Transcription

We have noted that the limits of serial RT performance are around 2.5 decisions per second. Yet skilled typists can execute keystrokes at a rate of more than 15 per second for short bursts (Rumelhart & Norman, 1982). The major difference here is in the way in which typing and, more generally, the class of *transcription tasks* (e.g., typing, reading aloud, and musical sight reading) are structured to allow the operator to make use of *preview*, *lag*, and *parallel processing*. These are characteristics that allow more than one stimulus to be displayed at a time (preview is available) and therefore allow the operator to lag the response behind perception. Thus, at any time, the response executed is not necessarily relevant to the stimulus that was most recently encoded but is more likely to be related to a stimulus encoded earlier in the sequence. Therefore, perception and response are occurring in parallel. Whether one speaks of this as *preview* (seeing into the future) or *lag* (responding behind the present) obviously depends on the somewhat arbitrary frame of reference one chooses to define the "present."

Preview and lag are both possible in either self-paced or force-paced tasks. Thus, in typing (a self-paced activity), the typist typically encodes letters (as judged from visual fixation) approximately one second before they are entered into the keyboard. Similarly, in reading aloud, the voice will lag well behind the eye fixations. Oral translation is a force-paced task because the auditory speech flows at a rate that is not determined by the translator. There is a lag of a few words between when a word is heard and when it is spoken. In general, this lag in transcription is beneficial to performance for reasons explained below. Yet the physical constraints of the task determine the extent to which a lag is possible. In a self-paced task, a lag can be created only if a preview of two or more stimuli is provided (e.g., two or more stimuli are displayed simultaneously). This typifies the cases of typing or reading aloud, in which preview is essentially unlimited and is subject only to the constraints of visual fixation (see Chapters 3 and 6). In a force-paced task, in which a stimulus does not wait for a response to occur—for example, taking oral dictation or translating spoken languages—the operator need only build up a slight lag or queue before responding.

When operators use preview and lag, they must maintain a running "buffer" memory of encoded stimuli that have not yet been executed as responses. It is therefore interesting to consider why the lag is beneficial in transcription, in light of the fact that task-induced lags between input and response were shown to be harmful in the running memory tasks discussed in Chapter 7. A major difference between the two cases concerns the size of the lag involved. The lag typically observed in transcription is short—around one second—relative to the decay of echoic memory; so the contents of memory are still fresh at the time that output is called for. Resource-demanding rehearsal processes are not needed. The problems of running memory are typically observed when the delay is greater.

Since the costs encountered in running-memory tasks are not present in the lags of transcription, it is possible for the transcriber to realize the two important benefits of these lags: (1) allowance for variability and (2) allowance for chunking (Salthouse & Saults, 1987; Shaffer, 1973; Shaffer & Hardwick, 1970).

Allowance for Variability   In a nonlagged system, if an input is encountered that is particularly difficult to encode, the resulting delay will be shown at the response as well. Correspondingly, a particularly difficult response will slow down processing of the subsequent input in a PRP-like fashion. However, if there is a lag between input and output, accounted for by a buffer of three or four items, a steady stream of output at a constant rate can proceed (for at least a short while) even if input encoding is temporarily slowed.

The buffer is just "emptied" at a constant rate. A prolonged input delay will, of course, temporarily reduce the size of the buffer until it may be "refilled" with a more rapidly encoded input. If easily encoded stimuli do not appear, the operator may eventually be forced to adopt a less efficient nonlagged mode of processing, which is what occurs when the text on a page being typed becomes degraded.

Allowance for Chunking   There is good evidence in typing that inputs are encoded in chunks (i.e., a word), so that the letters within each chunk are processed more or less in parallel (Rumelhart & McClelland, 1986; Reicher, 1969). The output, however, must be serial (assuming that a "rapidtype" keyboard is not employed). The creation of a lag, therefore, allows the steady flow of serial output to proceed even as the buffer is suddenly increased in the number of required output units (key presses stored) as a result of the parallel perception of a chunk. Furthermore, factors affecting the speed of individual responses (i.e., the reach time for letters on a keyboard) are totally unrelated to encoding difficulty. A buffer will prevent slow responses from disrupting subsequent encoding. Figure 9.17 provides a schematic example in which a relatively constant output stream (response per unit time) is maintained in spite of variations in encoding speed and buffer contents caused by variations in input chunks and input quality. These variations will cause the size of the buffer to vary yet allow an even, rhythmic flow of responses.

One remarkable characteristic of all of these activities—encoding, buffer storage, and response—is that they appear to proceed more or less in parallel, with little mutual interference, and are even time shared with a fourth mental activity, the monitoring of errors in response (Rabbitt, 1981). This success stands in general contrast to the failures that are often observed in multiple-task performance, a topic that will be addressed in Chapter 11. It suggests that parallel processing of mental operations within a task is easier than parallel processing between tasks.

Use of Preview   The availability of preview in transcription tasks does not, of course, mean that preview will necessarily be used. The unskilled typist will still type one letter at a time and will go no faster if preview is available than it if it is not. The skilled typist depends heavily on preview for efficient transcription. Investigations by Hershon and Hillix (1965), Shaffer (1973), and Shaffer and Hardwick (1970) suggest that preview helps performance. These data make clear that there are two benefits of preview: making available more advance information and giving the operator an opportunity to perceive chunks (see Chapter 7). Hershon and Hillix had subjects type a written message, of which various numbers of letters could be displayed in advance. They increased the number of preview letters from one to two, then to three, then to six, and finally to an unlimited number. Greater preview provided some benefits to typing random-letter strings but provided much greater benefits to typing random words. The greater benefit in the latter condition, of course, resulted because of the chunkability of words.

Shaffer (1973) conducted a systematic investigation of preview effects using one highly skilled typist. Shaffer examined the differences in interresponse times (IRT) as the subject typed varying kinds of text with different amounts of preview. The slowest typing was obtained while typing random letters with no preview, a condition equivalent to a self-paced serial RT task with negligible response-stimulus interval. Here the IRT was 500 milliseconds. Progressively shorter IRTs (faster typing) were obtained while typing random letters with unlimited preview (IRT = 200 msec) and typing random words with preview

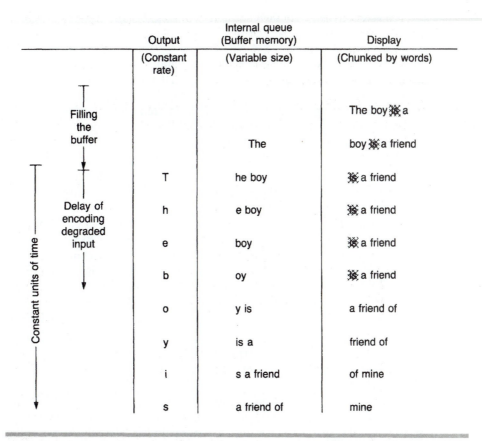

	Output	Internal queue (Buffer memory)	Display
	(Constant rate)	(Variable size)	(Chunked by words)
Filling the buffer			The boy ※ a
		The	boy ※ a friend
	T	he boy	※ a friend
Delay of encoding degraded input	h	e boy	※ a friend
	e	boy	※ a friend
	b	oy	※ a friend
	o	y is	a friend of
	y	is a	friend of
	i	s a friend	of mine
	s	a friend of	mine

(left axis: Constant units of time)

Figure 9.17 Schematic representation of transcription, following a time-line running down the page. The figure shows that variable input rate (caused by chunking and stimulus quality) provides constant output rate. Note the long delay when encoding the degraded word *is*.

(IRT = 100 msec). In a fourth condition, words in coherent text were typed with unlimited preview. The results of this condition were interesting because no further gain in typing speed was observed over the random-word condition. This finding suggests that the benefits of preview are *not* related to the semantic level of processing but rather to the fact that preview allows the letters within chunk-sized units (i.e., words) to be processed in parallel (see Chapter 6).

Further support for the conclusion that word chunks and not semantic content is the critical factor in preview is provided by another of Shaffer's findings. In typing either coherent prose or random words, eight letters of preview are sufficient to accomplish all necessary gains in performance. Eight letters would be sufficient to encompass the great majority of words but generally not enough to extract coherent semantic meaning from word strings. The absence of heavy semantic involvement in transcription would thereby explain how skilled typists may be able to carry on a conversation or perform other verbal activity while typing (Shaffer, 1975; see also Chapter 11).

A second conclusion of Shaffer's (1975) research is that the benefits of chunking are primarily perceptual and may be seen in storage but not in response. Groups of letters are perceived as a unit, perhaps are stored in the buffer memory as a unit, but are rarely output to the keyboard as an integrated motor program; that is, they are not a highly overlearned response pattern, such as one's signature, that is executed as an open-loop motor chunk or motor program (Keele, 1973; Summers, 1981; see Chapter 10). Shaffer's arguments are based primarily on an analysis of the interresponse times between letters within a word. If these are, in fact, parts of a motor chunk or motor program, the sum of the IRTs within a chunked word should be less than a similar sum of mean IRTs derived from all words. For example, since the IRT averaged across typing words with preview is 100 milliseconds, to be typed as a chunk the total IRT in the word *cat* should be *less* than 200 milliseconds (i.e., less than two 100-msec IRTs). Shaffer observes that this motor-packaging effect holds true for only a few extremely common sequences (*and*, *the*, and *-ing*) but not for the general class of common words. This conclusion is supported by investigations of typing by Gentner (1982) and Sternberg, Kroll, and Wright (1978). Gentner, for example, performed a detailed analysis of finger movements in typing and concluded that they were determined entirely by constraints of the hands and keyboard interacting with the letter sequence. Higher-level word units played no role in response timing.

In summary, people are remarkably efficient at performing transcription tasks, overcoming many of the limits of reaction time. Only relatively small margins for improvement are probably feasible in the redesign of the typewriter or data-entry keyboard (Norman & Fisher, 1982). Furthermore, it is possible that future developments in automatic speech recognition devices may eventually make a person's manual function in typing obsolete. The read or created message may simply be spoken to the computer and a printed text prepared from the automatically recognized speech. The major benefit of research on typing would not then appear to be on issues of keyboard redesign. Instead, its value seems to be in terms of how models of optimal text-typing performance such as those of Card, Moran, and Newell (1983; Card, Newell, & Moran, 1986; see Chapter 1), Gentner (1982), Rumelhart and Norman (1982), and Shaffer and Hardwick (1970) can be applied to design interfaces for other transcription and data-entry tasks such as those involved in more complex human-computer interactions.

TRANSITION

This chapter discussed the selection or choice of actions in which time is at a premium. We also briefly introduced the concept of response factors and feedback. In Chapter 10, we consider in more detail the execution of those actions, thereby completing the visit of the various processing stages depicted in Figure 1.3. In our discussion of response execution, the role of muscular coordination becomes more prominent, but so too does the role of continuous visual feedback to guide the execution of motor control in tasks such as pointing, steering, or flying, thereby highlighting the closed loop properties in Figure 1.3, and revisiting some of the issues discussed in Chapters 3, 4, and 5.

REFERENCES

Alden, D. G., Daniels, R. W., & Kanarick, A. F. (1972). Keyboard design and operations: A review of the major issues. *Human Factors, 14,* 275–293.

Allport, D. A., Styles, E. A., & Hsieh, S. (1994). Shifting intentional set: Exploring the dynamic control of tasks. In C. Umilta & M. Moscovitch (Eds.), *Attention and performance XV* (pp. 421–452). Cambridge, MA: MIT Press.

Alluisi, E., Muller, P. I., & Fitts, P. M. (1957). An information analysis of verbal and motor response in a force-paced serial task. *Journal of Experimental Psychology, 53*, 153–158.

Andre, A. D., Haskell, I. D., & Wickens, C. D. (1991). S-R compatibility effects with orthogonal stimulus and response dimensions. *Proceedings of the 35th annual meeting of the Human Factors Society* (pp. 1546–1550). Santa Monica, CA: Human Factors Society.

Andre, A. D., & Wickens, C. D. (1992). Compatibility and consistency in display-control systems: Implications for aircraft decision aid design. *Human Factors, 34* (6), 639–653.

Andre, A. D., Wickens, C. D., & Goldwasser, J. B. (1990). *Compatibility and consistency in display-control systems: Implications for decision aid design.* University of Illinois Institute of Aviation Technical Report (ARL–90–13/NASA-A3I–90–2). Savoy, IL: Aviation Research Laboratory.

Baber, C. (1997). *Beyond the desktop.* San Diego, CA: Academic Press.

Bartram, D. (1986). The development of a new keyboard for outward sorting foreign mail. *IMechE*, 57–63.

Bertelson, P. (1965). Serial choice reaction-time as a function of response versus signal-and-response repetition. *Nature, 206*, 217–218.

Bertelson, P. (1966). Central intermittency twenty years later. *Quarterly Journal of Experimental Psychology, 18*, 153–163.

Bradley, J. V. (1971).Tactual coding of cylindrical knobs. In W. C. Howell & I. L. Goldstein (Eds.), *Engineering psychology: Current perspectives in research* (pp. 276–287). New York: Appleton-Century-Crofts.

Brainard, R. W., Irby, T. S., Fitts, P. M., & Alluisi, E. (1962). Some variable influencing the rate of gain of information. *Journal of Experimental Psychology, 63*, 105–110.

Broadbent, D. (1958). *Perception and communications.* New York: Permagon.

Broadbent, D. E. (1971). *Decision and stress.* London: Academic Press.

Card, S., Moran, T. P., & Newell, A. (1983). *The psychology of human-computer interactions.* Hillsdale, NJ: Erlbaum.

Card, S., Newell, A., & Moran, T. (1986). The model human processor. In K. Boff, L. Kaufman, & J. Thomas (Eds)., *Handbook of perception and performance* (vol. 2, ch. 45). New York: Wiley.

Chapanis, A., & Lindenbaum, L. E. (1959). A reaction time study of four control-display linkages. *Human Factors, 1*, 1–14.

Coles, M. G. H. (1988). Modern mind-brain reading: Psychophysiology, physiology, and cognition. *Psychophysiology, 26* (3), 251–269.

Coles, M. G. H., Gratton, G., & Donchin, E. (1988). Detecting early communication: Using measures of movement-related potentials to illuminate human information processing. *Biological Psychology, 26*, 69–89.

Conrad, R., & Longman, D. S. A. (1965). Standard typewriter vs. chord keyboard: An experimental comparison. *Ergonomics, 8*, 77–88.

Craik, K. W. J. (1947). Theory of the human operator in control systems I: The operator as an engineering system. *British Journal of Psychology, 38*, 56–61.

Crosby, J. V., & Parkinson, S. R. (1979). A dual task investigation of pilot's skill level. *Ergonomics, 22*, 1301–1313.

Davis, R. (1965). Expectancy and intermittency. *Quarterly Journal of Experimental Psychology, 17*, 75–78.

Davis, R., Moray, N., & Treisman, A. (1961). Imitation responses and the rate of gain of information. *Quarterly Journal of Experimental Psychology, 13*, 78–89.

Debecker, J., & Desmedt, R. (1970). Maximum capacity for sequential one-bit auditory decisions. *Journal of Experimental Psychology, 83*, 366–373.

Deininger, R. L., Billington, M. J., & Riesz, R. R. (1966). The display mode and the combination of sequence length and alphabet size as factors of speed and accuracy. *IEEE Transactions on Human Factors in Electronics, 7*, 110–115.

Dewar, R. (1993, July). Warning: Hazardous road signs ahead. *Ergonomics in Design*, 26–31.

Donchin, E. (1981). Surprise! . . . Surprise? *Psychophysiology, 18*, 493–513.

Donders, F. C. (1869, trans. 1969). On the speed of mental processes (trans. W. G. Koster). *Acta Psychologica, 30*, 412–431.

Drazin, D. (1961). Effects of fore-period, fore-period variability and probability of stimulus occurrence on simple reaction time. *Journal of Experimental Psychology, 62*, 43–50.

Drury, C., & Coury, B. G. (1981). Stress, pacing, and inspection. In G. Salvendy & M. J. Smith (Eds.), *Machine pacing and operational stress*. London: Taylor & Francis.

Duncan, J. (1984). Selective attention and the organization of visual information. *Journal of Experimental Psychology: General, 113*, 501–517.

Dvorak, A. (1943). There is a better typewriter keyboard. *National Business Education Quarterly, 12*, 51–58.

Fitts, P. M. (1966). Cognitive aspects of information processing III: Set for speed versus accuracy. *Journal of Experimental Psychology, 71*, 849–857.

Fitts, P. M., & Deininger, R. L. (1954). S-R compatibility: Correspondence among paired elements within stimulus and response codes. *Journal of Experimental Psychology, 48*, 483–492.

Fitts, P. M., Peterson, J. R., & Wolpe, G. (1963). Cognitive aspects of information processing II: Adjustments to stimulus redundancy. *Journal of Experimental Psychology, 65*, 423–432.

Fitts, P. M., & Posner, M. A. (1967). *Human performance*. Pacific Palisades, CA: Brooks Cole.

Fitts, P. M., & Seeger, C. M. (1953). S-R compatibility: Spatial characteristics of stimulus and response codes. *Journal of Experimental Psychology, 46*, 199–210.

Flight International. (1990, October 31). *Lessons to be learned*, pp. 24–26.

Fuchs, (1962). The progression regression hypothesis in perceptual-motor skill learning. *Journal of Experimental Psychology, 63*, 177–192.

Gentner, C. R. (1982). Evidence against a central control model of timing in typing. *Journal of Experimental Psychology: Human Perception & Performance, 9*, 793–810.

Gopher, D., & Raij, D. (1988). Typing with a two-hand chord keyboard—will the QWERTY become obsolete? *IEEE Transactions in System, Man, and Cybernetics, 18*, 601–609.

Gratton, G., Coles, M. G. H., Sirevaag, E., Eriksen, C. W., & Donchin, E. (1988). Pre- and post-stimulus activation of response channels: A psychophysiological analysis. *Journal of Experimental Psychology: Human Perception & Performance, 14*, 331–344.

Greenwald, A. (1970). A double stimulation test of ideomotor theory with implications for selective attention. *Journal of Experimental Psychology, 84*, 392–398.

Greenwald, A. G., (1979). Time-sharing, ideomotor compatibility and automaticity. In C. Bensel (Ed.), *Proceedings of the 23rd annual meeting of the Human Factors Society*. Santa Monica, CA: Human Factors Society.

Greenwald, H., & Shulman, H. (1973). On doing two things at once: Eliminating the psychological refractory period affect. *Journal of Experimental Psychology, 101*, 70–76.

Hartzell, E. J., Dunbar, S., Beveridge, R., & Cortilla, R. (1983). Helicopter pilot response latency as a function of the spatial arrangement of instruments and controls. *Proceedings of the 18th annual Conference on Manual Control* (pp. 345–364). Dayton, OH: Wright Patterson AFB.

Haskell, I., Wickens, C. D. & Sarno, K. (1990). Quantifying stimulus-response compatibility for the Army/NASA A³I display layout analysis tool. *Proceedings of the 5th mid-central Human Factors/Ergonomics Conference.* Dayton, OH.

Helander, M. G., Karwan, M. H., & Etherton, J. (1987). A model of human reaction time to dangerous robot arm movements. *Proceedings of the 31st annual meeting of the Human Factors Society* (pp. 191–195). Santa Monica, CA: Human Factors Society.

Henderson, B. W. (1989, May 22). Army pursues voice-controlled avionics to improve helicopter pilot performance. *Aviation Week & Space Technology*, p. 43.

Hershon, R. L., & Hillix, W. A. (1965). Data processing in typing: Typing rate as a function of kind of material and amount exposed. *Human Factors, 7*, 483–492.

Hick, W. E. (1952). On the rate of gain of information. *Quarterly Journal of Experimental Psychology, 4*, 11–26.

Hoffmann, E. R. (1990). Strength of component principles determining direction-of-turn stereotypes for horizontally moving displays. *Proceedings of the 34th annual meeting of the Human Factors Society* (pp. 457–461). Santa Monica, CA: Human Factors Society.

Howell, W. C., & Kreidler, D. L. (1963). Information processing under contradictory instructional sets. *Journal of Experimental Psychology, 65*, 39–46.

Howell, W. C., & Kreidler, D. L. (1964). Instructional sets and subjective criterion levels in a complex information processing task. *Journal of Experimental Psychology, 68*, 612–614.

Hyman, R. (1953). Stimulus information as a determinant of reaction time. *Journal of Experimental Psychology, 45*, 423–432.

Jersild, A. T. (1927). Mental set and shift. *Archives of Psychology*, no. 89.

Kantowitz, B. H. (1974). Double stimulation. In B. H. Kantowitz (Ed.), *Human information processing.* Hillsdale, NJ: Erlbaum.

Karlin, L., & Kestinbaum, R. (1968). Effects of number of alternatives on the psychological refractory period. *Quarterly Journal of Experimental Psychology, 20*, 160–178.

Keele, S. W. (1973). *Attention and human performance.* Pacific Palisades, CA: Goodyear.

Kirby, P. H. (1976). Sequential affects in two choice reaction time: Automatic facilitation or subjective expectation. *Journal of Experimental Psychology: Human Perception & Performance, 2*, 567–577.

Kirkpatrick, M., & Mallory, K. (1981). Substitution error potential in nuclear power plant control rooms. In R. C. Sugarman (ed.), *Proceedings of the 25th annual meeting of the Human Factors Society* (pp. 163–167). Santa Monica, CA: Human Factors Society.

Klapp, S. T., & Irwin, C. I. (1976). Relation between programming time and duration of response being programmed. *Journal of Experimental Psychology: Human Perception & Performance, 2*, 591–598.

Klemmer, E. T. (1957). Simple reaction time as a function of time uncertainty. *Journal of Experimental Psychology, 54*, 195–200.

Knight, J., & Salvendy, G. (1981). Effects of task stringency of external pacing on mental load and work performance. *Ergonomics, 24*, 757–764.

Kornblum, S. (1973). Sequential effects in choice reaction time. A tutorial review. I Kornblum (Ed.), *Attention and performance IV.* New York: Academic Press

Kornblum, S., Hasbroucq, T., & Osman, A. (1990). Dimensional overlap: Cognitive basis for stimulus-response compatibility—A model and taxonomy. *Psychological Review, 97,* 253–270.

Leonard, J. A. (1959). Tactile choice reactions I. *Quarterly Journal of Experimental Psychology, 11,* 76–83.

Lockhead, G. R., & Klemmer, E. T. (1959, November). *An evaluation of an 8-k wordwriting typewriter* (IBM Research Report RC–180). Yorktown Heights, NY: IBM Research Center.

Long, J. (1976). Effects of delayed irregular feedback on unskilled and skilled keying performance. *Ergonomics, 19,* 183–202.

Loveless, N. E (1963). Direction of motion stereotypes: A review. *Ergonomics, 5,* 357–383.

McCarthy, G., & Donchin, E. (1979). Event-related potentials: Manifestation of cognitive activity. In F. Hoffmeister & C. Muller (Eds.), *Bayer Symposium VIII: Brain function in old age.* New York: Springer.

McClelland, J. L. (1979). On the time-relations of mental processes: An examination of processes in cascade. *Psychological Review, 86,* 287–330.

Martin, G. (1989). The utility of speech input in user-computer interfaces. *International Journal of Man-Machine System Study, 18,* 355–376.

Merkel, J. (1885). Die zeitlichen Verhaltnisse der Willensthatigkeit. *Philosophische Studien, 2,* 73–127.

Meyer, D. E., & Kieras, D. E. (1997a). A computational theory of executive cognitive processes and multiple-task performance: Part 1. Basic mechanisms. *Psychological Review, 104,* 3–65.

Meyer, D. E., & Kieras, D. E. (1997b). A computational theory of executive cognitive processes and multiple-task performance: Part 2. Accounts of psychological refractory-period phenomena. *Psychological Review, 104,* 749–791.

Miller, R. B. (1968). Response time in non-computer conversational transactions. In *Proceedings of 1968 Fall Joint Computer Conference.* Arlington, VA: AFIPS Press.

Mowbray, G. H., & Rhoades, M. V. (1959). On the reduction of choice reaction time with practice. *Quarterly Journal of Experimental Psychology, 11,* 16–23.

Norman, D. (1988). *The psychology of everyday things.* New York: Harper & Row.

Norman, D. A., & Fisher, D. (1982). Why alphabetic keyboards are not easy to use: Keyboard layout doesn't matter much. *Human Factors, 24,* 509–520.

Norman, K. (1991). *The psychology of menu selection.* Hillsdale, NJ: Erlbaum.

Orasanu, J., & Strauch, B. (1994). Temporal factors in aviation decision making. *Proceedings of the 38th annual meeting of the Human Factors and Ergonomics Society.* Santa Monica, CA: Human Factors and Ergonomics Society.

Osborne, D. W., & Ellingstad, V. S. (1987). Using sensor lines to show control-display linkages on a four burner stove. *Proceedings of the 31st annual meeting of the Human Factors Society* (pp. 581–584). Santa Monica, CA: Human Factors Society.

Pachella, R. (1974). The use of reaction time measures in information processing research. In B. H. Kantowitz (Ed.), *Human information processing.* Hillsdale, NJ: Erlbaum.

Pashler, H. (1989). Dissociations and contingencies between speed and accuracy: Evidence for a two-component theory of divided attention in simple tasks. *Cognitive Psychology, 21,* 469–514.

Pashler, H. E. (1998). *The psychology of attention.* Cambridge, MA: MIT Press.

Payne, S. J. (1995). Naive judgments of stimulus-response compatibility. *Human Factors, 37*(3), 495–506.

Pew, R. W. (1969). The speed-accuracy operating characteristic. *Acta Psychologica, 30,* 16–26.

Posner, M. I. (1964). Information reduction in the analysis of sequential tasks. *Psychological Review, 71,* 491–504.

Rabbitt, P. M. A. (1981). Sequential reactions. In D. Holding (Ed.), *Human skills.* New York: Wiley & Sons.

Rabbitt, P. M. A. (1989). Sequential reactions. In D. H. Holding (Ed.), *Human skills* (2d ed.). New York: Wiley.

Rasmussen, J. (1980). The human as a system's component. In H. T. Smith & T. R. Green (Eds.), *Human interaction with computers.* London: Academic Press.

Rasmussen, J. (1986). *Information processing and human-machine interaction: An approach to cognitive engineering.* New York: North Holland.

Reicher, G. M. (1969). Perceptual recognition as a function of meaningfulness of stimulus material. *Journal of Experimental Psychology, 81,* 275–280.

Reynolds, D. (1966). Time and event uncertainty in unisensory reaction time. *Journal of Experimental Psychology, 71,* 286–293.

Richardson, R. M. M., Telson, R. U., Koch, C. G., & Chrysler, S. T. (1987). Evaluation of conventional, serial, and chord keyboard options for mail encoding. *Proceedings of the 31st annual meeting of the Human Factors Society* (pp. 911–915). Santa Monica, CA: Human Factors Society.

Rogers, D., & Monsell, S. (1995). Costs of a predictable switch between simple cognitive tasks. *Journal of Experimental Psychology: General, 124,* 207–231.

Rumelhart, D. E., McClelland, J. L., & The PDP Research Group (1986). *Parallel distributed processing, I: Foundations.* Cambridge, MA: MIT Press.

Rumelhart, D., & Norman, D. (1982). Simulating a skilled typist: A study of skilled cognitive-motor performance. *Cognitive Science, 6,* 1–36.

Salthouse, T. A., & Saults, J. S. (1987). Multiple spans in transcript typing. *Journal of Applied Psychology, 72,* 187–196.

Schwartz, S. P., Pomerantz, S. R., & Egeth, H. E. (1977). State and process limitations in information processing. *Journal of Experimental Psychology: Human Perception & Performance, 3,* 402–422.

Seibel, R. (1963). Discrimination reaction time for a 1,023-alternative task. *Journal of Experimental Psychology, 66,* 215–226.

Seibel, R. (1964). Data entry through chord, parallel entry devices. *Human Factors, 6,* 189–192.

Seibel, R. (1972). Data entry devices and procedures. In R. G. Kinkade & H. S. Van Cott (Eds.), *Human engineering guide to equipment design.* Washington, DC: U.S. Government Printing Office.

Shaffer, L. H. (1973). Latency mechanisms in transcription. In S. Kornblum (Ed.), *Attention and performance IV.* New York: Academic Press.

Shaffer, L. H. (1975). Multiple attention in continuous verbal tasks. In S. Dornic (Ed.), *Attention and performance V.* New York: Academic Press.

Shaffer, L. H., & Hardwick, J. (1970). The basis of transcription skill. *Journal of Experimental Psychology, 84,* 424–440.

Shneiderman, B. (1998). *Designing the user interface: Strategies for effective human-computer interaction.* (3rd Ed.) Reading, MA: Addison-Wesley.

Shulman, H. G., & McConkie, A. (1973). S-R compatibility, response discriminability and response codes in choice reaction time. *Journal of Experimental Psychology, 98,* 375–378.

Sidorsky, R. C. (1974, January). *Alpha-dot: A new approach to direct computer entry of battlefield data* (Technical Paper 249). Arlington, VA: U.S. Army Research Institute for the Behavioral and Social Sciences.

Simon, J. R. (1969). Reaction toward the source of stimulus. *Journal of Experimental Psychology, 81,* 174–176.

Smith, K. U. (1962). *Delayed sensory feedback and balance.* Philadelphia: Saunders.

Smith, M. (1967). Theories of the psychological refractory period. *Psychological Bulletin, 19,* 352–359.

Smith, P., & Langolf, G. D. (1981). The use of Sternberg's memory-scanning paradigm in assessing effects of chemical exposure. *Human Factors, 23,* 701–708.

Smith, S. (1981). Exploring compatibility with words and pictures. *Human Factors, 23,* 305–316.

Sternberg, S. (1969). The discovery of processing stages: Extension of Donders' method. *Acta Psychologica, 30,* 276–315.

Sternberg, S. (1975). Memory scanning: New findings and current controversies. *Quarterly Journal of Experimental Psychology, 27,* 1–32.

Sternberg, S., Kroll, R. L., & Wright, C. E. (1978). Experiments on temporal aspects of keyboard entry. In J. P. Duncanson (Ed.), *Getting it together: Research and application in human factors.* Santa Monica, CA: Human Factors Society.

Strayer, D. L., Wickens, C. D., & Braune, R. (1987). Adult age differences in the speed and capacity of information processing. II. An electrophysiological approach. *Psychology and Aging, 2,* 99–110.

Summala, H. (1981). Driver/vehicle steering response latencies. *Human Factors, 23,* 683–692.

Summers, J. J. (1981). Motor programs. In D. H. Holding (Ed.), *Human skills.* New York: Wiley.

Teichner, W., & Krebs, M. (1972). The laws of simple visual reaction time. *Psychological Review, 79,* 344–358.

Teichner, W., & Krebs, M. (1974). Laws of visual choice reaction time. *Psychological Review, 81,* 75–98.

Telford, C. W. (1931). Refractory phase of voluntary and associate response. *Journal of Experimental Psychology, 14,* 1–35.

Tversky, A. (1977). Features of similarity. *Psychological Review, 84,* 327–352.

Van Der Horst, R. (1988). Driver decision making at traffic signals. In *Traffic accident analysis and roadway visibility* (pp. 93–97). Washington, DC: National Research Council.

Vickers, D. (1970). Evidence for an accumulator model of psychophysical discrimination. *Ergonomics, 13,* 37–58.

Waganaar, W. A., & Stakenberg, H. (1975). Paced and self-paced continuous reaction time. *Quarterly Journal of Experimental Psychology, 27*, 559–563.

Wang, H., & Proctor, R. W. (1996). Stimulus-response compatibility as a function of stimulus code and response modality. *Journal of Experimental Psychology: Human Perception & Performance, 22*, 1207–1217.

Warrick, M. J. (1947). *Direction of movement in the use of control knobs to position visual indicators* (USAF AMC Report no. 694–4C). Dayton, OH: Wright AFB, U.S. Air Force.

Warrick, M. S., Kibler, A., Topmiller, D. H., & Bates, C. (1964). Response time to unexpected stimuli. *American Psychologist, 19*, 528.

Weeks, D. J., & Proctor, R. W. (1990). Salient features coding in the translation between orthogonal stimulus and response dimensions. *Journal of Experimental Psychology: General, 119*, 355–366.

Welford, A. T. (1952). The psychological refractory period and the timing of high speed performance. *British Journal of Psychology, 43*, 2–19.

Welford, A. T. (1967). Single channel operation in the brain. *Acta Psychologica, 27*, 5–21.

Welford, A. T. (1968). *Fundamentals of skill*. London: Methuen.

Welford, A. T. (1976). *Skilled performance: Perceptual and motor skills*. Glenview, IL: Scott, Foresman.

Wickelgren, W. (1977). Speed accuracy trade-off end information processing dynamics. *Acta Psychologica, 41*, 67–85.

Wickens, C. D. (1984). Processing resources in attention. In R. Parasuraman & R. Davies (Eds.), *Varieties of attention* (pp. 63–101). New York: Academic Press.

Wickens, C. D. (1999). Automation in air traffic control: The human performance issues. In M. W. Scerbo & M. Mouloua (Eds.), *Automation technology and human performance*. Mahwah, NJ: Erlbaum.

Wickens, C. D., Hyman, F., Dellinger, J., Taylor, H., & Meador, M. (1986). The Sternberg memory search task as an index of pilot workload. *Ergonomics, 29*, 1371–1383.

Wickens, C. D., & Liu, Y. (1988). Codes and modalities in multiple resources: A success and a qualification. *Human Factors, 30*, 599–616.

Wickens, C. D., Sandry, D., & Vidulich, M. (1983). Compatibility and resource competition between modalities of input, central processing, and output: Testing a model of complex task performance. *Human Factors, 25*, 227–248.

Wickens, C. D., Vidulich, M., & Sandry-Garza, D. (1984). Principles of S-C-R compatibility with spatial and verbal tasks: The role of display-control location and voice-interactive display-control interfacing. *Human Factors, 26*, 533–543.

Woodworth, R. S., & Schlossberg, H. (1965). *Experimental psychology*. New York: Holt, Rinehart & Winston.

Yntema, D. (1963). Keeping track of several things at once. *Human Factors, 6*, 7–17.

CHAPTER

10

Manual Control

OVERVIEW

In the previous chapter, our focus was on the choice of which action to take, rather than the coordination and execution of the action that is chosen. In the context of our driver, we were interested in how (and how fast) he *decided* to swerve left or right, rather than the cause of the improper execution of that choice, which led to the crash. In the present chapter, we are interested in the analog form or the time-space trajectory of the response. We consider the class of tasks in which this trajectory is critical—the domain of continuous control. In most applications, this control is exerted manually. Hence, we focus our discussion on manual control but also briefly consider voice control.

Human performance in manual control has been considered from two quite different perspectives: skills and dynamic systems. Each has used different experimental paradigms and different analytical tasks, and each has been generalized to different applied environments. The skills approach primarily involves analog motor behavior, in which the operator must produce or reproduce a movement pattern from memory when there is little environmental uncertainty. The gymnast performs such a skill when executing a complex maneuver; so too does the assembly-line worker who coordinates a smooth, integrated series of actions around a set of environmental stimuli—the products to be assembled—that are highly predictable from one instance to the next. Because there is little environmental uncertainty, such skills in theory may be performed perfectly and identically from trial to trial. In Figure 1.3 the behavior is described as open loop because, once the skill has developed there is little need to process the visual feedback from the response. The emphasis of experiments on skills has focused heavily on the time course of skill acquisition and the optimal conditions of practice.

In contrast to the skills approach, the dynamic systems approach examines human abilities in controlling or *tracking* dynamic systems to make them conform with certain time-space trajectories in the face of environmental uncertainty (Poulton, 1974, Hess, 1997; Wickens, 1986). Most forms of vehicle control fall into this category, as does the control of many complex energy processes (Moray, 1997). Because of the need to process error signals, in the context of Figure 1.3, this has been described as "closed loop" control. The research on tracking has been oriented primarily toward engineering, focusing on mathematical representations of the human's analog response when processing uncertainty. Unlike the skills approach, which focuses on learning and practice, the tracking approach generally addresses the behavior of the well-trained operator.

The general treatment of manual control that follows reflects this dichotomy but acknowledges that as is so often the case in psychology, the dichotomy is really more of a continuum. Basketball players who execute a skilled, highly practiced maneuver by themselves may be engaging in a pure open-loop skill, but when they do so in the middle of a game, with a defender providing some degree of environmental uncertainty, the response becomes more of a compromise between open-loop skills and tracking. Many forms of human computer interaction based on direct manipulation, whether positioning a cursor with a mouse, or "flying" through information space or virtual reality, also involve forms of manual control that may span the range between open and closed loop control.

We will begin by considering the simplest form of analog response—the minimum time taken to move from a starting point to a target with constrained accuracy. The data describing this skill, it turns out, are quite well captured by a basic "law" of motor control, whose principles seem to underlie both open-loop skills and the tracking of dynamic systems. More complex forms of open-loop skills are then discussed before turning to an extensive treatment of manual control in tracking, manipulation, and vehicle control. We then address the strengths and weaknesses of different devices for discrete control in computer-based tasks. Finally, the chapter supplement considers in some detail the efforts that have been made to model the human operator in tracking. The supplement provides an introduction to the mathematical language of frequency-domain analysis, which has been used in these modeling efforts.

OPEN-LOOP MOTOR SKILLS

Discrete Movement Time

Pioneering investigations by Woodworth (1899) and Brown and Slater-Hammel (1949) found that the time required to move the hand or stylus from a starting point to a target obeys the basic principles of the speed-accuracy trade-off, discussed in Chapter 9. Quite intuitively, faster movements terminate less accurately in a target, whereas targets of small area, requiring increased accuracy, are reached with slower movements. The amplitude of a movement also influences this speed-accuracy relationship. It takes a longer time to move a greater distance into a target of fixed area. However, if precision is allowed to decline with longer movements, movement time is essentially unchanged with length.

Fitts (1954) investigated the relationship among the three variables of time, accuracy, and distance in the paradigm shown in Figure 10.1. Here, the subject is to move the stylus as rapidly as possible from the start to the target area. Fitts found that when movement amplitude (A) and target width (W) were varied, their joint effects were summarized by a simple equation that has subsequently become known as Fitts's Law:

$$MT = a + b\left[\log_2\left(\frac{2A}{W}\right)\right] \tag{10.1}$$

where a and b are constants. This equation describes formally the speed-accuracy trade-off in movement: Movement time and accuracy (target width W) are reciprocally related.

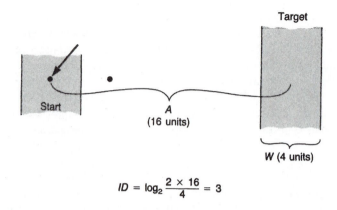

$$ID = \log_2 \frac{2 \times 16}{4} = 3$$

Figure 10.1   The Fitts movement-time paradigm. The movement may be either a single discrete movement from start to target or a series of alternating taps between the two targets. Computation of the idex of difficulty (ID) of the movement at the top is shown by the formula at the bottom.

Longer movements can be made (increasing A), but if their time is to be kept constant, accuracy must suffer proportionately. That is, the target into which the movement will terminate, W, must be widened proportionally.

Fitts described the specific quantity $\log 2$ $(2A/W)$ as the *index of difficulty* (*ID*) of the movement. In Figure 10.1, $ID = 3$. Movements of the same index of difficulty can be created from different combinations of A and W but will require the same time to complete. Figure 10.2 shows the linear relationship between MT and ID obtained by Fitts when different combinations of amplitude and target width were manipulated. Each ID value shows the similar movement time created by two or three different amplitude/width combinations. The slope of this relation is reflected by the constant "*b*" in the equation, steeper slopes (higher *b*) indicate less efficient movements. The constant "*a*" is the intercept, which reflects the start-up time for a movement. The high degree of linearity is evident in Figure 10.2 for all but the lowest condition, in which the linear relationship slightly underpredicts MT.

Several investigations have demonstrated the generality of Fitts's Law (Jagacinski, 1989). For example, Fitts and Peterson (1964) found that the law is equally accurate for describing single, discrete movements, or reciprocal tapping between two targets. Langolf, Chaffin, and Foulke (1976) observed that the relationship accurately describes data for manipulating parts under a microscope. Drury (1975) found that the law accurately describes movement of the foot to pedals of varying diameter and distance, and Card (1981) employed the law as a basic predictive element of key-reaching time in keyboard tasks (Card, Newell, & Moran, 1986). Jagacinski, Repperger, Ward, and Moran (1980) extended the model to predict performance in a dynamic target-acquisition task.

Other investigators have examined more theoretical properties of the basic relationship. For example, Fitts and Peterson (1964) studied the relationship between movement

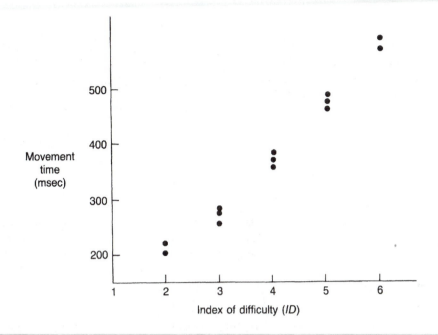

Figure 10.2   Data on movement time as a function of the index of difficulty.

Source: P. M. Fitts, "The Information Capacity of the Human Motor System in Controlling the Amplitude of Movement," *Journal of Experimental Psychology, 47* (1954), p. 385.

time and the time to initiate the movement and found that they were relatively independent of one another. Increasing the index of difficulty, which made movement time longer, did not affect the reaction time to initiate the movement. Conditions that varied reaction time (i.e., single versus choice) had no effect on subsequent movement time. Such relative interdependence provides justification for assuming the separation of stages of response selection and execution in the information processing model of Figure 1.3. In contrast to this independence of stages, the two hands appear to be *inter*dependent. Thus, Kelso, Southard, and Goodman (1979) examined movement times for simultaneous two-handed movements to two targets of varying index of difficulty. They observed that the two movements were *not* independent of one another, but that movement time of the easier (lower *ID*) hand was slowed down to be in synchrony with the time taken for the more difficult and therefore slower movement.

Models of Discrete Movement   Figure 10.3a shows a typical trajectory or time history recorded as the stylus approaches the target in the paradigm of Figure 10.1. Two important characteristics of this pattern are apparent: (1) The general form of the movement is that of an exponential approach to the target with an initial high-velocity approach followed by a smooth, final, "homing" phase. In the earliest research in this area, Woodworth (1899) distinguished between these two phases, labeling the first the *initial*

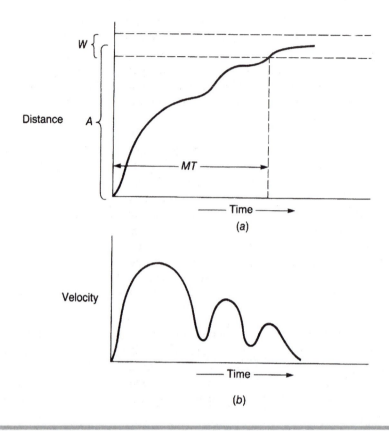

Figure 10.3   Typical position (*a*) and velocity (*b*) profile of Fitts's Law movement.

ballistic and the second *current control.* (2) The velocity profile of the movement shown in Figure 10.3b reveals that control is not continuous but appears to consist of a number of discrete corrections, each involving an acceleration and a deceleration.

The pattern of data shown in Figure 10.3 can be explained by a feedback processing assumption (Pew, 1974). As operators approach the target, the remaining error to the target is sampled, either continuously or intermittently, and corrections that are proportional to the error are implemented to nullify the error. This sample-and-correct process is continued until the target boundary is crossed (Pew, 1974). Such closed-loop behavior will produce the generally exponential approach shown in Figure 10.3, in which stylus velocity is roughly proportional to momentary error. This characteristic of target-aiming responses is important in describing continuous tracking skill, as well as discrete control.

Motor Schema

Visually guided responses such as those described by Fitts's Law are critical components in a wide variety of real-world skills, such as those required in assembly-line work, computer-screen cursor control, or performance on complex or unfamiliar keyboards. Yet with highly learned skills performed under conditions of minimal environmental uncertainty, it is evident that visual feedback is not necessary. We say that these skills may be performed in *open-loop* fashion. In fact, sometimes this visual feedback may actually be harmful. Shoe tying, touch typing, or the performance of a skilled pianist are good examples of skilled performance that does not require visual feedback.

Psychologists and motor-learning theorists have identified two general characteristics of such well-learned motor skills: (1) They may well depend on feedback, but the feedback is *proprioceptive*. Information from the joints and muscles is relayed back to central movement-control centers to guide the execution of the movement in accordance with centrally stored goals or "templates" of the ideal time-space trajectory (Adams, 1971, 1976). (2) The pattern of desired muscular innervation may be stored centrally in long-term memory and executed as an open-loop *motor program* without benefit of visual feedback correction and guidance (Schmidt, 1975; Summers, 1989).

The terms *motor program* and *motor schema* have been used to label highly overlearned skills that, as a consequence of this learning, do not depend on guidance from visual feedback (Keele, 1968; Schmidt, 1975; Shapiro & Schmidt, 1982; Summers, 1989). In addition to its high level of practice, the motor program or schema has three additional characteristics: low attention demand, single-response selection, and consistency of outcome.

Low Attention Demand The motor program tends to be *automated* in the terms described in Chapters 6, 7, and 11. Task practice is assumed to have a major influence on resource demand. Here the limited resource demand is a major criterion for defining the motor program. A well-learned complex sequence of responses may be executed while disrupting only slightly the performance of a concurrent task (Bahrick & Shelly, 1958).

Single-Response Selection Within the framework of the information-processing model in Chapter 1, it is assumed that a single-response selection is required to activate or "load" a single motor program, even though the program itself may contain a number of separate, discrete responses. Thus, resources are demanded only once, at the point of initiation, when the program is selected.

Programs may vary in their complexity. Investigators such as Klapp and Erwin (1976); Martenuik and MacKenzie (1980); and Shulman, Jagacinski, and Burke (1978) have argued that motor programs of greater complexity will take longer to "load." Therefore, choice reaction times will be longer when responses of greater complexity are chosen. For example, Shulman, Jagacinski, and Burke found that reaction time to initiate a double key press was longer than for a single press. The relationship between program complexity and reaction time only appears to hold, however, as long as the program cannot be loaded in advance. In a simple RT task, for example, it is possible to load or activate the entire response sequence in advance of the imperative signal, since that response is the only one possible. In this case, the relationship between program complexity and response latency is no longer observed (Klapp & Erwin, 1976; Martenuik & MacKenzie, 1980).

Consistency of Outcome: Programs Versus Schemata A motor program is assumed to generate very consistent space-time trajectories from one replication to another. Investigators have pointed out that what is consistent is not the *process* of muscular innervation (and therefore the specific pattern of neural commands) but the *product* of the response (Pew, 1974; Schmidt, 1975, 1988; Shapiro & Schmidt, 1982; Summers, 1989). The signature of one's name meets the criteria of a motor program. Yet the signature may vary drastically in the actual muscular commands used (or even total muscle groups), depending on the context in which one's name is signed—whether, for example, on a small horizontal piece of paper or on a large vertical blackboard. MacNielage (1970) argues that the articulation of familiar words is an example of motor programs. The product of an articulation is roughly the same whether the speaker speaks normally or through clenched teeth. Yet the *process* of muscular innervation is totally changed between these two conditions.

In these examples, large changes in motor patterns have occurred. Yet certain characteristics of the time-space trajectory have remained invariant across the modification. Thus, whatever is learned and stored in long-term memory cannot be a specific set of muscle commands but must represent a more generic or general set of specifications of how to reach the desired goal. These specifications were labeled by Bartlett (1932) and Schmidt (1975) as a *motor schema*. Once a schema is selected, the process of loading requires the specific instance parameters to be specified to meet the immediate goals at hand (e.g., the size of the signature) (Pew, 1974). Two major characteristics of performance are preserved in the final output: (1) the *relative* timing of highlights (directional changes) in the movement, which may be slowed down or speeded up in this absolute value, and (2) the *relative* positioning of these highlights in *x, y,* and *z* coordinates of space, even as the absolute extent of the movement may be expanded or shrunk along any of these three dimensions.

TRACKING OF DYNAMIC SYSTEMS

In performing manual skills, we often guide our hands through a coordinated time-space trajectory. Yet at other times, we use our hands to guide the position of some other analog system or device. At the simplest level, the hand may merely guide a pointer on a blackboard, a light pen on a video display, or a hose on a garden. The hand may also be used to control the steering wheel and thereby guide a vehicle on the highway, or it may be used to adjust the temperature of a heater or the closure of a valve to guide the parameters of a chemical process through a carefully defined trajectory of values over time. When describing human operator control of physical systems, research moves from the domain of perceptual motor skills and motor behavior to the more engineering domain of tracking. This shift in domain results primarily from the great influence of three nonhuman elements on the performance of the operator who must make a system state correspond to a desired goal or trajectory: (1) the *dynamics* of the system itself: how it responds in time to the guidance forces applied; (2) the *input* to the operator (the desired trajectory of the system); and (3) the *display*, the means by which the operator perceives the information concerning the desired and actual state of the system. These three elements interact with many of the human operator's limitations to impose difficulties on tracking in the real world.

Real-world tracking is demonstrated in almost all aspects of vehicle control ranging from bicycles to cars, aircraft, ships, and space vehicles. It also characterizes many of the tasks performed in complex chemical and energy process control industries, when flow, pressure, and temperature must be controlled and regulated. It is common in direct manipulation computer systems when continuous analog movement of a mouse or joystick is used to position cursors on display screens, or to change the viewpoint of more immersive "virtual reality" systems (Chapter 5). In the experimental laboratory, the tracking paradigm is typically one in which the subject controls a system whose dynamics are simulated by a computer, by manipulating a control device and observing the response as a moving symbol on a visual display.

The Tracking Loop: Basic Elements

Figure 10.4 presents the basic elements of a tracking task. These elements will be described within the context of automobile driving, although the reader should realize that they may generalize to any number of different tracking tasks. Each element produces a time-varying output, which is expressed as a function of time, $x(t)$, where "x" is the element in question.

When driving an automobile, the *human operator* may perceive a discrepancy or error between the desired state of the vehicle and its actual state. The car may have deviated from the center of the lane or may be pointing in a direction away from the road. The driver wishes to reduce this error, which changes as a function of time, $e(t)$. To do so, a force (in this case a torque), $f(t)$, is applied to the steering wheel, or control. This force in turn produces a rotation, $u(t)$, of the steering wheel itself. The relationship between the force applied and the steering wheel movement is defined as the *control dynamics*. For example, the steering wheel may be stiff or very sensitive. Movement of the wheel or control by a given time function, $u(t)$, in turn causes the vehicle's actual position to move laterally on the highway. This movement is the *system output*, $o(t)$. The relationship between control *position*, $u(t)$, and system response, $o(t)$, is defined as the *system dynamics*. When presented on a display, the representation of this output position is called the *cursor*. If the operator is successful in the correction, it will reduce the discrepancy between vehicle position on the highway, $o(t)$, and the desired, or "commanded," position at

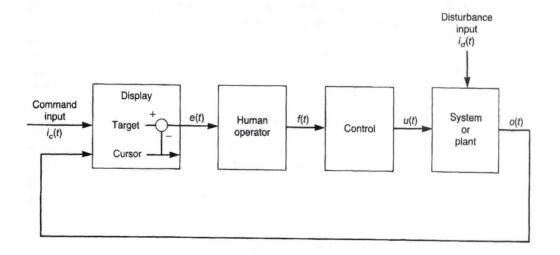

Figure 10.4 The tracking loop.

the center of the lane, $i(t)$. On a display, the symbol representing the commanded input is called the *target*. The difference between the output (cursor) and input (target) signals is the error, $e(t)$, the starting point of our discussion. The good driver will respond in such a way as to keep $o(t) = i(t)$ or $e(t) = 0$. It should be clear from the course of this discussion, which has taken us around the loop, and from the form of Figure 10.4, why tracking is often called closed-loop behavior: an output becomes an input.

Because errors in tracking stimulate the need for corrective responses, the operator need never respond as long as there is no error. However, errors typically arise from one of two sources, represented in Figure 10.4. *Command inputs*, $i_c(t)$, are changes in the *target* that must be tracked. For example, if the road curves, it will generate an error for a vehicle traveling in a straight line and so will require a response. *Disturbance inputs*, $i_d(t)$, are those applied directly to the system. For example, a wind gust that pushes the car off the center of the lane is a disturbance input. So also is an accidental movement of the steering wheel by the driver. As shown in Figure 10.5, either kind of input may be *transient*, such as a step displacement or a gradual ramp shift. As an example of the first case, called a *step*, imagine that the disturbance effect of a crosswind on a highway suddenly shifts. In the second case, called a *ramp*, imagine that the crosswind gradually increases as a car goes around a curve. Alternatively, the input may be *continuous*, in which case it may be described as either predictable and periodic, or random. As described in Chapter 6, either random or periodic inputs may be represented in the frequency domain as spectra. The representation of tracking signals in the frequency domain is discussed more fully in the supplement to this chapter.

The source of all information necessary to implement the corrective response is the *display*. For the automobile driver, the display is simply the field of view through the windshield, but for the aircraft pilot making an instrument landing, the display is represented by the instruments depicting pitch, roll, altitude, and course information. An important distinction may be drawn between *pursuit* and *compensatory* displays (Roscoe, Corl, & Jensen, 1981). A pursuit display presents independent movement of both the target and the cursor. Thus, the driver of a vehicle views a pursuit display because movement of the automobile can be distinguished and viewed independently from the curvature of the road (the command input). A compensatory display presents only movement of the error relative to a fixed 0-error reference on the display. The display

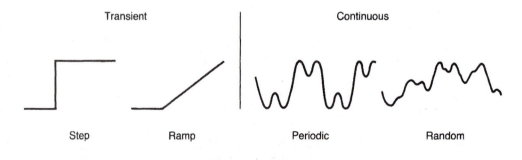

Figure 10.5 Tracking inputs.

provides no indication of whether this error arose from a change in system output or command input. Many flight navigation instruments are compensatory displays. Most compensatory displays are artificial means of depicting real-world conditions, and these are discussed in some detail later in the chapter.

Finally, tracking performance is typically measured in terms of error. It is calculated at each point in time and then cumulated and averaged over the duration of the tracking trial. Kelley (1968) discusses different means of calculating tracking performance.

Transfer Functions

Figure 10.4 presented three examples in which a time-varying input to a system produces a time-varying response: The operator's force, $f(t)$, applied to the control produced control displacement, $u(t)$. The displacement, $u(t)$, produced a change in system position, $o(t)$. Finally, in the same terms, we may think of the error, $e(t)$, "applied to," or viewed by, the human as generating the force, $f(t)$. In all cases, the *transfer-function* represents the mathematical relationship between the input and output of a system. When describing human behavior in terms of transfer functions, the output of the human is usually considered to be the control position $u(t)$, rather than the force, $f(t)$. It is assumed that the human "intends" to produce a given position. The force, $f(t)$, used to achieve this position is usually applied fairly automatically.

The transfer function may be expressed either by a mathematical equation in calculus (change over time) or graphically by showing the time-varying output produced by a given time-varying input. When systems are said to be *linear*, their transfer functions may be thought of as built from the combinations of a number of fundamental, atomistic dynamic elements. Because the limits of human tracking performance depend in important ways on the transfer function of the system being controlled, and because many of the models of tracking behavior have used transfer functions to describe human performance, it is important to describe these fundamental dynamic elements.

Figure 10.6 shows the dynamic response of six of these basic elements to the step input in Figure 10.5; this response is sometimes called the *step response*. In addition, the mathematical equation that relates output to input is presented in two different formats: differential equations in the time domain and the Laplace transform in the frequency domain. The reader should not be concerned with the Laplace function at this point, as it is covered in more detail in the chapter supplement.

Pure Gain   Pure gain is a feature that describes the ratio of the amplitude of the output to that of the input: O/I. The element in Figure 10.6a has a gain of 2, since the output is twice the size of the input. High-gain systems, like the steering mechanism of a sports car, are highly responsive to inputs. However, they may sometimes lead to instability, a characteristic described below. Low-gain systems tend to be described as "sluggish," since large inputs produce only small outputs. Output and input do not need to be measured in the same units to describe gain. Thus one can speak of the gain of a radio volume control as the ratio of loudness change to angle of knob rotation. Such a measure of gain has meaning when the relative gains of two different systems are compared.

Pure Time Delay   The pure time delay, or transmission lag, delays the input but reproduces it in identical form T seconds later (Figure 10.6b). This would describe the response

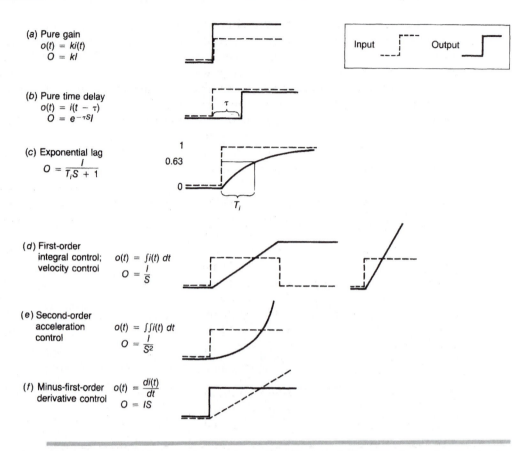

(a) Pure gain
$o(t) = ki(t)$
$O = kI$

(b) Pure time delay
$o(t) = i(t - \tau)$
$O = e^{-\tau S} I$

(c) Exponential lag
$O = \dfrac{I}{T_i S + 1}$

(d) First-order integral control; velocity control
$o(t) = \int i(t)\, dt$
$O = \dfrac{I}{S}$

(e) Second-order acceleration control
$o(t) = \int\int i(t)\, dt$
$O = \dfrac{I}{S^2}$

(f) Minus-first-order derivative control
$o(t) = \dfrac{di(t)}{dt}$
$O = IS$

Input Output

Figure 10.6   Basic dynamic elements in tracking. The transfer functions for most elements are presented in both the time domain (lowercase letters) and, underneath, in the Laplace domain (capital letters).

of a remotely located robot equipped with a television camera (Sheridan, 1997). It also describes the display from many computer imaging systems when complex imagery must be recalculated as the operator changes viewpoint location. A pure time delay has no effect on gain, nor does gain have any effect on time delay.

Exponential Lag   Some lags do not reproduce the input identically but instead gradually "home in," or stabilize, on the target input. The *exponential lag*, shown in Figure 10.6c, is defined by its *time constant*, T_i, which is the time that the output takes to reach 63 percent of its final value. The response bears considerable resemblance to the human target-acquisition response described by Fitts's Law shown in Figure 10.3a. In a more general sense, it describes the response of many systems with a built-in negative feedback loop to ensure that an output is reached. A similar response would be shown by the tires on a car with a hydraulic power-steering system following the command indicated by steering-wheel step position change or by the hydraulic response of many airplane control surfaces to inputs applied by the pilot.

Velocity-Control, Integrator, or First-Order System   The step response shown in Figure 10.6d is a constant velocity (change in position per unit time) with a magnitude that is proportional to the step size. In calculus, this response is defined by the *time integral* of the input. Notice that if the input is withdrawn, the velocity returns to zero but the output is at a new location. Such systems are frequently encountered in manual control. An example is the relationship between the angle of steering-wheel deflection and the heading of a vehicle. A constantly held steering-wheel position off the center will produce a constant rate of change of heading (i.e., constant rate of turn) as the vehicle travels in an arc. Many cursor keys are also velocity controls, such that constant depression of the key will lead to a constant rate movement of the cursor across the screen. In an aircraft, a constant bank will also lead to a constant rate of turn. Any first-order or velocity-control system must also be defined by its gain. A low-gain system is shown on the left of Figure 10.6d; a high-gain system is on the right. The term *order* refers to the number of time integrations in the transfer function. Therefore, since it contains one integration, the system shown in Figure 10.6d is a first-order system. (The systems portrayed in Figure 10.6a and Figure 10.6b are zero order, since they contain no integrations.) The first-order dynamic response is closely related to the exponential lag shown in Figures 10.3 and 10.6c. If a system makes a first-order response to the *error* rather than to the command input, the result will be an exponential lag. Since the response velocity to correct the error is proportional to the size of the error, as the error is reduced, response velocity is reduced proportionately. Thus, in Figure 10.6c the velocity approaches zero, on the right side, as the error approaches zero.

Acceleration-Control, Double-Integrator, or Second-Order System   A second-order system combines two integrators in series. The step response shown in Figure 10.6e is therefore the constant acceleration that would be obtained if the velocity response in Figure 10.6d were integrated: that is, each time sample, the velocity increases by a constant amount. The pure second-order system is typical of any physical system with large mass and therefore great inertia when a constant force is applied. It is *sluggish*, in that it will not respond immediately, particularly if the gain is low. Thus, its response has a lag. When tracked, second-order systems also tend to be *unstable*, or difficult to control, because once the system does begin to respond, its high inertia will tend to keep it going in the same direction and cause it to overshoot its destination. The operator will have to make a series of reverse corrections, which often produces oscillatory behavior, as happened to the van driver trying to control his vehicle in the incident discussed at the beginning of the book. As an intuitive example of a pure second-order system, imagine rolling an orange or bowling ball from one end of a flat board to the other by suddenly tilting the board (step input). The relationship between the board angle and the position of the orange on the board is a second-order one. Second-order systems are very prevalent in aviation, seagoing vehicles, and chemical processes.

Differentiator   The minus-first-order, or differentiator, control system, shown in Figure 10.6f, will produce an output position of a value equal to the rate of change of the input. The step response of the differentiator is theoretically a "spike" of infinite height and zero width, since the "step" is an instantaneous change in position (and so has infinite velocity). As a result, the step response is not shown in Figure 10.6f. Instead, the *ramp response* is shown (i.e., the response to a ramp input). The system response is therefore just the opposite of the first-order system shown in Figure 10.6d. In the calculus representation, these two are also opposite. If a time function is differentiated and then integrated, the original function will be recovered. In isolation, differential control systems are not frequently observed. An example might be an electrical generator in which the output (current) is proportional to the rate of turn of the input coils. However, differentiator control systems are of critical importance when they are placed in series with systems of higher order. They can reduce the order of the system by "canceling" one of the integrators and so make it easier to control. For example, a differentiator placed in series with the second-order system of Figure 10.6e will produce a first-order system. This point is considered later, when we see how humans should track second-order systems.

Frequency-Domain Response   The transient step or ramp response of the elements shown in Figure 10.6 is in the time domain. Yet engineers are often more concerned about the response of these elements to continuous periodic or random inputs. Indeed, most tracking studies involve continuous inputs. For some of the dynamic elements of Figure 10.6, the response to random or periodic inputs is intuitively, as well as formally, quite predictable from the step response. A pure gain element with a 0 order system, for example, will reproduce a periodic signal perfectly but at a higher or lower amplitude, given by the value of the gain. For other elements, however, the response to continuous inputs is considerably more complex. In the chapter supplement, we consider the frequency-domain response of different elements as they are used in human operator modeling.

Human Operator Limits in Tracking

The previous chapters of this book identified a number of limitations in human information processing. Five of these limits in particular influence the operator's ability to track: processing time, information transmission rate, predictive capabilities, processing resources, and compatibility. Each of these is described here briefly in the context of manual control and then considered in more detail as they influence specific aspects of the manual-control task.

Processing Time   The discussion of reaction time in Chapter 9 suggested that humans do not process information instantaneously. In tracking, a perceived error will be translated by the human to a control response only after a lag, referred to as the *effective time delay* (McRuer & Jex, 1967). Its absolute magnitude seems to depend somewhat on the order of the system being controlled. Zero and first-order systems are tracked with time delays from 150 to 300 milliseconds. For a second-order system, the delay is longer, about 400 to 500 milliseconds, reflecting the more complex error-correction decisions that need to be made (McRuer & Jex, 1967).

   Time delays, whether the result of human processing or system lag, are harmful to tracking for two reasons: (1) Obviously, any lag will cause output to no longer line up with input. The error thus resulting, shown as the shaded region in Figure 10.7, will grow with the increasing magnitude of the delay from panel (a) to panel (b). (2) Often more seriously, when periodic or random inputs are tracked, delays will induce problems of *instability*, producing oscillatory behavior. These problems are discussed later in the chapter.

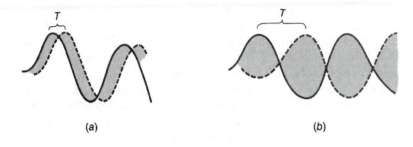

Figure 10.7 Error resulting from time delay: (a) small, (b) large.

Bandwidth Tracking involves the transmission of information, whether displayed as a command or as a disturbance-induced error. Time-varying input and output signals may be quantified by information theory, and it is not surprising that the same limitations of information transmission in discrete tasks discussed in Chapter 9 are evident in continuous tracking as well. Thus, Baty (1971), Crossman (1960), and Elkind and Sprague (1961) found that the limit of information transmission in tracking is between 4 and 10 bits per second, depending on the particular conditions of display. Elkind and Sprague observed that the transmission rate increases if a preview of the input is available before it is tracked, much as automobile drivers preview segments of the road ahead before the vehicle actually reaches them.

In Chapter 9, it was argued that the limits of serial reaction time were defined by the frequency of decisions, not by their complexity. In tracking, too, there appears to be an upper limit in the frequency with which corrective decisions can be made that is more restrictive than the limit imposed by their complexity. This frequency limit in turn determines the maximum *bandwidth* of random inputs that can be tracked successfully; it is normally found to be between 0.5 and 1.0 Hz (Elkind & Sprague, 1961). This value corresponds quite closely with estimates that the maximum frequency with which corrections are exerted in tracking is roughly two times per second (Craik, 1948; Fitts & Posner, 1967). Because two corrections are required for each cycle, this limit corresponds to a bandwidth of one cycle per second. This limit appears to be a central one, related to processing uncertainty in the tracking signal, rather than a motor one, because operators have no difficulty in tracking *predictable* signals as high as 2 to 3 Hz (Pew, 1974; Pew, Duffenback, & Fensch, 1967). The limit of two corrections per second in continuous tracking is close to the maximum decision-making speed in the serial RT paradigm of 2.5 decisions per second (Debecker & Desmedt, 1970; see Chapter 9).

Prediction and Anticipation Fortunately, human operators are rarely placed in real-world environments in which they must track inputs at bandwidths so high that the limits on processing rate become restrictive. The more serious limits instead appear to be imposed when operators track systems like ships and aircraft that have lags. Here the operator must *anticipate* future errors on the basis of present values to make control corrections that will be realized by the system output only after a considerable lag. Consider the pilot of a supertanker in a channel who realizes the vessel is off course and wishes to correct this error. Because of the high inertia of the ship and its higher-order control characteristics, a correction delivered to the rudder will not substantially alter the ship's course for a matter of tens of seconds, or even minutes. Therefore, to stay within the limits of the channel effectively, the operator must base corrections issued now on estimates of future error and not on perception of present error. Corrections based on present error will be implemented too late to be effective, as the captain of the ship Titanic tragically discovered (Scerbo, 1999).

Future error, of course, equals the difference between future input and future output. In the case of ship control, future command input can easily be *previewed* (this is the view ahead of the channel or path to be negotiated). But future output must be derived and anticipated, a function, as we have noted in Chapter 8, that humans do not perform effectively. In tracking, we estimate future position by perceiving the present velocity and acceleration of the error signal. That is, where a signal *will be* in the future is best indicated by its present velocity and acceleration. However, ample data are available to suggest that humans perceive position changes more precisely than velocity changes, and perceive both velocity and position changes more precisely than acceleration changes (Fuchs, 1962; Gottsdanker, 1952; Kelley, 1968; McRuer et al., 1968; Runeson, 1975). Thus, when tracking slow, sluggish systems, the operator's perceptual mechanisms are called on to perform predictive functions for which they are relatively ill equipped.

Processing Resources   Another source of difficulty in anticipation relates to the resource demands of spatial working memory, as discussed in Chapter 7. When anticipating where a sluggish, higher-order system like a supertanker will be in the future, it helps to be able to perceive its acceleration, but it is also important to be able to perform calculations and estimations of where that system will be in the future, given a *mental model* of the system's dynamics (Eberts & Schneider, 1985; Pew & Baron, 1978). For the operator who is not highly trained, the operations based on this mental model demand the processing of working memory. Tracking thus is often disrupted by concurrent tasks. The limits of human resources also account for tracking limitations when the operator must perform more than one tracking task at once, that is, in multi-axis tracking (discussed later in this chapter).

Compatibility   The discussion of S-R compatibility in Chapter 9 emphasized that certain spatial compatibility relationships were relatively "natural." Because tracking is primarily a spatial task, it is apparent that these relationships should affect tracking performance. The research on control and display relationships in tracking suggests that indeed they do. Incompatibility is seen in compensatory displays, as when a left-moving error cursor requires a right-moving response (Roscoe, Corl, & Jensen, 1981). It is also seen whenever the axis of control motion is not aligned with the axis of display motion. The disruption of tracking performance becomes particularly bad when the misalignment is greater than 45 degrees (Kim et al., 1987; Macedo et al., 1998; Wickens, 1999).

Effect of System Dynamics on Tracking Performance

The interaction between human limitations and the dynamic properties of the system to be controlled determines the level of tracking performance. In this section, we consider the effects on performance of three important characteristics of those system dynamics: gain, time delay, and order. In certain combinations, these variables produce problems of *stability*, a factor that is considered separately.

Gain Both tracking error and subjective ratings of effort appear to follow a U-shaped function of system gain (system output/control input) (Gibbs, 1962; Hess, 1973; Wickens, 1986). Whether tracking steps or compensating for random disturbances, systems with intermediate levels of gain have the lowest error and are easiest to track. The advantage of middle-gain systems results from the trade-off between the benefits and costs of more extreme gains. When gain is high, minimal control effort is required to produce large corrections. For example, the steering wheel on a sports car has to be turned only slightly to round a curve. Thus, in a sense, high gain is economical of effort, and this economy is quite valuable when continuous corrections are required to track random input. On the other hand, gain that is too high can lead to overcorrections and oscillations. For example, such problems will be encountered if the user of a high-gain mouse system tries to position a display cursor in a very small target. Furthermore, high-gain problems of instability will result if there are also lags in the system. Undesirable instability and overcorrections can be eliminated by reducing gain, but at the cost of imposing more effort. The crossover point of the two functions describing instability at high gain and effort at low gain determines the optimal level of gain. This level cannot be precisely specified in a general sense because it is determined by the extent to which effort at low gain and instability at high gain is the more important concern to be avoided.

Time Delay Pure time delays are universally harmful in tracking, and tracking performance gets progressively worse with greater delays. The reason for this cost is apparent from the discussion of processing time limits. If a control input will not be reflected by a system change until some point in the future (the consequences of the delay), the corrective input generated by the human operator must be based on the *future* value of error rather than on its present value. Such anticipation, as noted, is imperfectly done and demands cognitive resources.

System Order The effects of system order on all aspects of performance may be best described in the following terms: Zero-order and first-order systems are roughly equivalent, each having its costs and benefits. However, with orders above first, both error and subjective workload increase dramatically (Wickens, 1986). The reason that zero- and first-order systems are nearly equivalent may be appreciated by realizing that successful tracking requires both position and velocity to be matched. Under some circumstances, matching one of these quantities might be more important than matching the other. Compare the two functions in Figure 10.8. In Figure 10.8a, position error is quite frequently reduced to zero, but the velocities of input and output are rarely matched. In Figure 10.8b, although velocity is fairly closely matched, the positions of input and output rarely agree. Which form of tracking is superior? Clearly the answer to this question depends on the circumstances. If one were a passenger in an aircraft, the response in Figure 10.8a would not suggest a very comfortable ride compared to that of Figure 10.8b, but if the aircraft were flying at a low level, needing to follow a precise course with a minimum tolerance for error, the performance in Figure 10.8b might be disastrous.

If we view tracking performance as a mixture of position matching and velocity matching, the fact that the human control input to a zero-order (position control) system directly accomplishes the former and that input to a first-order (velocity control) system accomplishes the latter indicates why neither is unequivocally preferable to the other. The intermediate level between zero- and first-order control can be created either

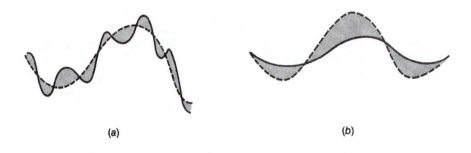

(a)   (b)

Figure 10.8 Styles of control: (a) minimized position error but high velocity error, (b) minimized velocity error but high position error.

---

by linearly combining the outputs of the two pure orders (called a rate-aided system) or by varying the time constant of the exponential lag shown in Figure 10.6c (Wickens, 1986). These systems generate performance that is also equivalent to either pure first- or pure zero-order control, depending on the relative importance of making a position or velocity match (Chernikoff & Taylor, 1957).

Another contrast between systems of 0 and first order is economy of movement and space. In a velocity control system, any change in output position can eventually be accomplished by displacing the control only a small amount (how rapidly this change occurs, of course, depends on the gain). On the other hand, in a position control system, larger position changes must be accomplished by moving a linear control through a larger physical space. When the amount of area available for control space is limited, as in the cockpit of a high-performance aircraft, this feature imposes constraints on the use of linear position controls unless their gain is extremely high, which we saw is unwise. (Rotary position controls, such as radio tuning dials, can avoid this space constraint.)

Control systems of second order and higher are unequivocally worse than either zero- or first-order systems (Kelley, 1968). The problems with second-order control are many. As noted, to control any higher-order system effectively, because of its lag one must *anticipate* its future state from its present. To do so requires that higher-error derivatives (velocity and acceleration) be perceived as a basis for correction, a process known as *generating lead*. This is requiring humans to act like a differentiator, as shown in Figure 10.6f. Humans, as we have discussed, do not perform this function well. As McRuer and Jex (1967) observed, the operator's effective time delay is also longer when higher derivatives must be perceived under second-order control because of the congitive complexity of generating lead. This increased lag contributes an additional penalty to performance.

Second-order systems may be controlled by two strategies. The strategy described above requires the operator to perceive the higher-error derivatives continuously and respond smoothly on the basis of this information. An alternative strategy of second-order control is sometimes referred to as "bang-bang," double-impulse, or time-optimal control (Hess, 1979; Wickens & Goettl, 1985; Young & Meiry, 1965). The operator perceives an error and reduces it in the minimum time possible with an open-loop "bang-bang" correction. As shown in Figure 10.9, this is accomplished by throwing the

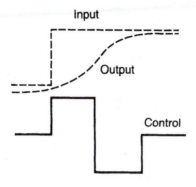

Figure 10.9   Required bang-bang response to reduce an error with a second-order system in minimum time.

stick hard over ("bang") in one direction to generate maximum acceleration for half the interval and then quickly reversing the stick ("bang" again) to produce maximum deceleration for the other half, monitoring and checking the result at the end. Because the double-impulse strategy reduces large errors in the shortest possible time, it is referred to as a form of *optimal control* (Young, 1969). Imagine using a bang-bang control strategy to roll an orange from one end of a board to the other.

Although the double-impulse control strategy eliminates the need for continuous perception of error derivatives of smooth analog control, it does not necessarily reduce the total processing burden (Wickens & Goettl, 1985). More precise timing of the responses is now required, and an accurate mental model of the state of the system must be maintained in working memory, in order to apply the midcourse reversal at the appropriate moment (Jagacinski & Miller, 1978). Also, as suggested by Figure 10.9, the bang-bang strategy will produce high velocities. As in the response shown in Figure 10.8a, there are circumstances (like riding as a passenger in a vehicle) when a lower-velocity "smooth ride" is preferable. The *optimal control model* of tracking behavior discussed in the chapter supplement dictates the appropriate strategy, given the importance of a smooth ride versus low error.

Instability   A major concern in the control of real-world dynamic systems is whether or not control will be *stable*—that is, whether the output will follow the input and eventually stabilize without diverging or producing excessive oscillations. Oscillatory and unstable behavior can result from two very different causes: positive and negative feedback.

To illustrate *positive feedback systems*, imagine two people sleeping under an electric blanket with dual temperature controls, one for each side. Suppose that the controls inadvertently become switched. If A now feels cold, A will turn the heat up. This action will lead to an increase in heat on the other side causing B to turn the heat down, and thereby leading A to feel still colder. Person A will then adjust the heat still higher, and the resulting chain of events is evident. This is an example of a positive feedback system: Once an error is in existence, feedback in the system works to add to the error in the same direction; hence the term "positive."

Whereas this example is unlikely to occur in real-world systems, unless switches are inadvertently misconnected, a second kind of positive feedback is not unusual in aviation systems. An intuitive example occurs when one must balance a stick on the end of one's finger. Once a small error (offset from vertical) exists, it will work to magnify itself (the stick will fall faster), unless corrected. A computer analog of this task was built as the *critical instability tracking task* (Allen & Jex, 1968; Jex, McDonnel, & Phatak, 1966).

Positive feedback loops characterize a number of complex dynamic vehicles, for example, a booster rocket, controlled by swiveling, tail-mounted engines. Another example is the control task of wheeling a bicycle backward or backing up a trailer. Positive feedback loops may also be found in certain aspects of the control of helicopters and other complex aircraft. Like second-order systems, those with positive feedback are universally harmful for the obvious reason that they cannot be left unattended. Unless error is perfectly at zero, they will eventually diverge if control is not exercised, just as the stick almost balanced on the fingertip must eventually fall unless the finger is moved back under the top of the stick.

Negative feedback systems are more typical. Humans and most well-designed systems function in such a way as to reduce (negate) rather than increase detected errors. This is the property of a negative feedback system, described clearly by Jagacinski (1977) and Toats (1975). As we see in Figure 10.4, the human responds in a direction opposite (negative) the direction of the existing error, in order to reduce that error. Such "purposeful" control action normally results in good stability. However, there are certain occasions when even a negative feedback loop with the best error-correcting intentions produces oscillatory or even unstable behavior. Such was the case with our unfortunate van driver as he tried to swerve off the road. A potentially disastrous example in aircraft control occurs when *pilot-induced oscillations* are produced. The vertical path of the aircraft swings violently up and down with growing amplitude as a consequence of the pilot's well-intentioned but inappropriately executed corrections (Hess, 1981, 1997).

Instability caused by negative feedback results from high gain coupled with large lags or with any delay around the closed tracking loop, shown in Figure 10.4. For example, because the second-order system is sluggish with a long lag in its response, control of the system tends to be unstable. However, instability may also occur with lower-order systems when there are long delays in system response. Examples may include the delay in image updating with complex computer graphics in a virtual reality environment, or the delay due to communications bandwidth limitations in remote manipulation systems (Sheridan, 1997).

The reason high gain and long phase lag collectively produce instability may be appreciated by the following example taken from Jagacinski (1977). Imagine that you are adjusting the temperature of shower water to your ideal comfort value (a command input). You are controlling to reduce the error and so acting as a negative feedback system. However, because of the plumbing, there is a lag between your adjustment of the faucet and the change in water temperature—the source of the perceived error used to guide correction. If your gain is high, then when you feel initially cold, you increase the hot water by a large amount and will continue to increase it as long as you feel cold. As a consequence, you will probably overshoot and scald yourself once the hot water reaches the faucet, and the error will now be on the "hot" side. If your gain remains high, your compensatory cooling correction (turning the handle to "cold") will also be overapplied, and the water will, after a lag, become too cold. The eventual temperature-time history will be a series of growing oscillations (and discomfort). Clearly in these circumstances, you must reduce your gain to avoid the unstable behavior resulting from the time lag. A gain reduction involves applying a smaller corrective turn of the faucet in response to the detected error—tolerating a mild discomfort now in anticipation of an eventual stable response.

The difference between high- and low-gain systems and their association with unstable and sluggish behavior, respectively, is an important one in human performance because gain may be thought of as a "strategic parameter," like the response criterion in signal detection or the speed-accuracy set in reaction time. It is a parameter, then, that can be strategically adjusted to different values according to different environmental conditions or strategic goals. The difference in the tracking performance of the two systems shown in Figure 10.8, for example, could be attributed in part to a difference in the gain of the feedback system that is tracking the error: high and oscillatory in panel (a), low and sluggish in panel (b).

The role of stability and its dependence on gain and lag is, of course, critically important in the design and testing of piloted vehicles and represents a major application of manual-control research. However, engineering-oriented research on stability normally uses the language of the *frequency* domain, described briefly in Chapter 6. The supplement to the present chapter covers the frequency-domain analysis of tracking in more detail, with the goal of making the sometimes mystical language of this area more understandable to the psychologist.

In addition to reducing gain, there is an alternative control strategy for making corrections when the lag is long: to base control correction on the *trend* of the error rather than its absolute level. Thus, in the shower, if you feel that the water is *getting* warmer even if you are still too cold in an absolute sense, this trend can serve as a signal to stop increasing the heat. This control strategy, based on error rate rather than error value, should by now be familiar. Earlier in this chapter, we suggested that it formed the basis of anticipation when controlling systems with long lags. Here we see that this strategy is essential because it is often necessary to avoid instability. Also, when describing the control elements in Figure 10.6, we suggested that a differentiator could cancel an integration in controlling higher-order systems. When humans respond predictively on the basis of trends, they are effectively becoming differentiators and so are canceling one of the integrators of second-order dynamics. In the next section, we see how certain tracking displays have been modified to make this prediction easier and induce humans to control as differentiators do.

Tracking Displays

Preview   The problems associated with prediction and anticipation in tracking can be divided into those of predicting the command input and those of predicting the future trajectory of the system output, since both of these together determine the future error.

Clearly, the future input will be most accurately available when there is *preview*. The automobile driver, for example, has preview of the course of the road ahead, except when driving in the fog. Figure 10.10 shows preview as it might be presented on a typical tracking display, the future course shown by the curvy line on the top. The large benefits of

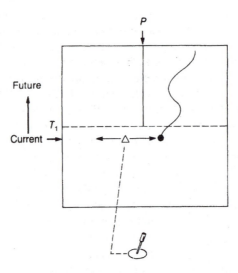

Figure 10.10 Tracking with preview. The role of T_1 and P are descibed in the text.

preview (Crossman, 1960; Elkind & Sprague, 1961, Grunwald, Robertson, & Hatfield, 1981; Reid & Drewell, 1972) occur in part because it enables the operator to compensate for processing lags in the tracking loop. Thus, when there are long system lags, preview is beneficial farther into the future (Wickens, 1986). The supertanker pilot must track, or attend to, the channel several hundred yards ahead of the bow of the ship because of the extremely long lags in ship control. This is a command input signal that will not be traversed by the ship until minutes later. For aircraft pilots, flight path preview that is tens of seconds into the future will be useful.

In the absence of preview, the human operator must use whatever information and mental computational facilities are available to *predict* the future course of the input. To some extent, this prediction may be based on the statistical properties of the input. For example, if the bandwidth of a random input is low, the present position and velocity provide some constraints on future position. Even if we had no preview of the input function shown in Figure 10.10, we would consider it unlikely that the input would be to the left of point P at time T_1. Our past experience with this input tells us that it just doesn't change that rapidly.

To the extent that the input is nonrandom or contains periodicities, the knowledge of future input is increased considerably and prediction becomes easier. When this occurs, the operator can track by using what Krendel and McRuer (1968) describe as a *precognitive mode*.

Output Prediction and Quickening   As described previously, the future trajectory of the command input may be predicted with some confidence, given its current position, velocity, and acceleration. Correspondingly, as we have also described, the best estimate of where a higher-order system with some mass and inertia will be in the future (output prediction) is provided by a combination of its present position and its higher derivatives. This kind of prediction, as we have seen, is not easily done and extracts a heavy toll on operator resources. In trying to reduce this burden, engineering psychologists have developed displays in which a computer estimates error (or output) derivatives and explicitly presents them as predicted symbols of future position (Gallagher, Hunt, & Williges, 1977; Kelley, 1968; Lintern, Roscoe, & Sivier, 1990). This format is called a *predictive display*. A typical one-dimensional predictive display for aircraft control is that used in a modern commercial aircraft, shown in Figure 10.11. Figure 10.12 shows a three-dimensional flight path predictor (Wickens, Haskell, & Harte, 1989; Haskell & Wickens, 1993). Note that the future aircraft predictor symbol (the black aircraft) is accompanied by *preview*, represented as a desired flight path tunnel.

Any number of different computation techniques can be used to estimate where a vehicle will likely be in the future (Grunwald, 1985). For example, the predictive elements may be driven by directly computing the position, velocity, and acceleration of the present system state and adding these values together with appropriate weights. Alternatively, these values may be inferred by directly measuring different internal states of the system (Gallagher, Hunt, & Williges, 1977). To provide an example of these two computational procedures, a predictive display of a car's future lateral position on the highway could be driven by summing the present values of its lateral position, velocity, and acceleration. Alternatively, since these three values are roughly equivalent to the current position of the car, the heading of the car, and the deflection of the steering wheel,

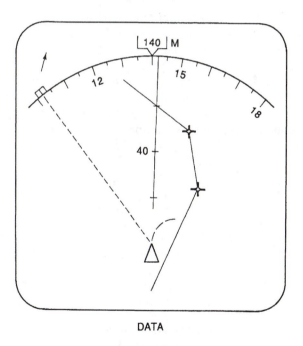

DATA

Figure 10.11 Predictor element on map display for a modern aircraft. The curved arc from the triangular aircraft symbol is the predicted flight path.

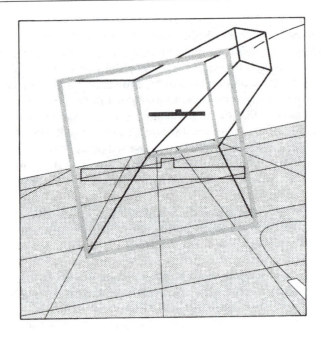

Figure 10.12 Three-dimensional predictor of flight path information. The small black bar is the aircraft predictor. The 3-D tunnel is preview.

respectively, the three variables could be directly measured, weighted, and summed to provide an accurate predictive display.

Prediction of the future is of course an inference, and every predictive display must make some assumptions about the future forces acting on the system (either from operator control inputs or from disturbances) in order to make this inference. For example, is it assumed in predicting the future trajectory of the system that the operator will apply an optimal correction, a suboptimal correction, or no correction at all? The nature of these assumptions may differ somewhat from display to display and will determine the accuracy and therefore the effectiveness of the display. It is also apparent that the accuracy of any prediction will decline into the future. Just how far into the future a prediction is valid depends on such factors as the sluggishness (inertia) of the system and the frequency of control or disturbance inputs. Prediction will be more accurate longer into the future if systems are more sluggish and disturbance inputs are of lower frequency. Thus, a supertanker (which is sluggish) can have a longer predictive accuracy than an aircraft, and so can a spacecraft traveling in a wind-free environment (no turbulence). For a light aircraft traveling in turbulence, however, the predictive interval will be short. The amount of time into the future, represented by a predictive symbol, is called the *predictive span*.

No matter how the predictive information is derived, predictive displays have proven to be of great assistance in the tracking of higher-order systems. Wickens, Haskell, and

Harte (1989); Lintern, Roscoe, and Sivier (1990); and Morphew and Wickens (1998) have demonstrated the value of prediction in the cockpit displays like that shown in Figure 10.12 and Figure 9.18a. Kelley (1968) described the tremendous benefit of predictive displays for submarine depth control, an example of very sluggish high-order dynamics. We will discuss the value of predictors in the context of process control, in Chapter 13.

As we have noted, prediction involves an automation-based computational inference about the future. Such inference can be incorrect. If the user trusts this inferential display of the future, as the base for control, and it turns out to be in error, then problems will result (Wickens, Gempler, & Conejo, 1999). For this reason, predictive display designers should be careful that displayed prediction spans do not exceed the competence of reliable inference.

In 1954, Birmingham and Taylor proposed a technique known as *quickening* that was closely related to the predictive display. A quickened display presents only a single indicator of quickened tracking error, which is calculated by combining the present error position, velocity, and acceleration. Like the prediction element in a predictive display, the quickened element indicates where the system error is likely to be in the future if it is not controlled. Unlike the predictive display, a quickened display has no indication of the current error. The justification for this absence is that the current error provides no information that is useful for correction. This absence, of course, has a disadvantage: There are certainly times when you want to know where you are and not just where you will be. Quickened displays are used in the *flight director* of many modern commercial airliners.

Pursuit Versus Compensatory Displays   The goal of tracking is to match the output to the input, or to minimize the error. These two seemingly equivalent statements define the *pursuit* and *compensatory* display formats, respectively. The operator with a pursuit display views the command input and the system output moving separately with respect to the display frame. The flight path display shown in Figure 10.12 is a pursuit display, since the pilot can view changes in the command input (the tunnel) independently of changes in the aircraft's position. In the compensatory display, only the difference between these two—the error—is portrayed. Pursuit displays generally provide superior performance to compensatory ones (Poulton, 1974) for two major reasons: the ambiguity of compensatory information and the compatibility of pursuit displays.

On the compensatory display, the operator cannot distinguish among the three potential causes of error: command input, disturbance input, and the operator's own incorrect control actions. As a result, error is ambiguous and control is more difficult than in the pursuit display, in which command and disturbance inputs can be distinguished. If, however, there is only one source of input, then the advantage of the pursuit display decreases, since errors on the compensatory display are now less ambiguous. Flying an aircraft toward a fixed runway, for example, is a tracking task in which there is information only in the disturbance input. The runway, representing the command input, does not move. In contrast, flying an aircraft along a curved approach in the sky, or toward the runway on a moving, rolling aircraft carrier now has a time-varying command input added.

Whenever there is a changing command input, the pursuit display will also provide some advantage because its stimulus-response compatibility is greater (see Chapter 9). If the command input suddenly moves to the left, it will require a leftward correction on the pursuit display. A left-moving stimulus therefore is corrected with a leftward response. This is an inherent motion compatibility that is consistent with the operator's tendency to move toward the source of stimulation (Roscoe, 1968; Roscoe, Corl, & Jensen, 1981; Simon, 1969). In contrast, in the compensatory display, the left-moving command input will be displayed as a right-moving error. In this case, a right-moving stimulus requires an incompatible leftward response. Whenever some portion of tracking input is command, this compatibility factor will benefit the pursuit display.

MULTIAXIS CONTROL

People must often perform more than one tracking task simultaneously. As the computer user navigates through a virtual environment (see Chapter 5), she may change her viewpoint orientation while traveling, both laterally and vertically. A vehicle driver may steer, while simultaneously controlling speed, to execute a passing maneuver. Even the simple computer mouse allows the user to simultaneously move a cursor vertically and laterally across the screen. There is often a cost to multiaxis tracking that results from the division of processing resources between axes, a concept that will be discussed further in Chapter 11. However, the severity of this cost may be influenced by the nature of the relationship between the two (or more) variables that are controlled and the way in which they are physically configured.

Cross-Coupled and Hierarchical Systems

A major distinction can be drawn between multiaxis systems in which the two variables to be controlled as well as their inputs are essentially independent of one another and those in which there is cross-coupling, so that the state of the system or variable on one axis partially constrains or determines the state of the other. An example of two basically independent axes is provided by the control of lateral lane position and car radio frequency while driving. In contrast, there is a small degree of cross-coupling between the pitch and roll axes of aircraft control. What the pilot does to control the roll (rotation around the longitudinal axis of the aircraft fuselage) has a small effect on the pitch (nose down). Similarly, when the car driver controls speed, it has a minor effect on the lateral (steering) handling characteristics of the vehicle. At the far extreme of cross-coupling, control of the heading and lateral position of an automobile on the highway are highly cross-coupled axes. This is because control of vehicle heading directly affects lateral position. In this case, the two cross-coupled tasks are considered to be *hierarchical*. That is, lateral position cannot be changed independently of a control of heading. The steering wheel, which directly controls headings, is *used* to obtain a change in lateral position.

Many higher-order control systems in fact possess similar hierarchical relationships (Kelley, 1968; Wickens, 1986). Lower-order variables must be controlled to regulate or track higher-order variables. Figure 10.13 shows analogous representations of three such hierarchically organized control systems: automobile control, aircraft heading control, and submarine depth control. In each case the operator controls the variable on the far left, with the final goal of tracking the variable on the far right. For driving, this is a second-order task, since there are two integrals in the control loop between the change in

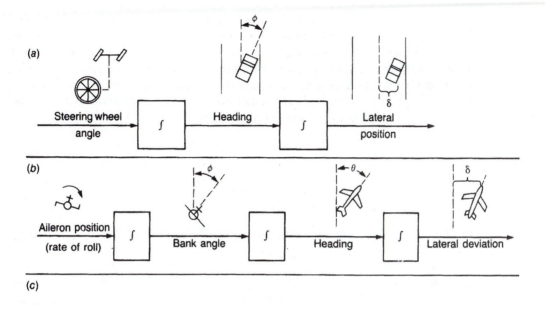

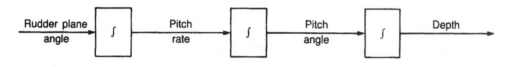

Figure 10.13 Three examples of hierarchical control systems: (*a*) automobile driving, (*b*) aircraft heading control (*c*) submarine depth control.

steering wheel position and the lateral position on the highway. For flying and submarine control, it is a third-order task. Variables on the left are said to be inner-loop, and those on the right define outer-loop variables.

Whereas hierarchical systems often have a number of *displayed* elements (e.g., steering wheel angle, vehicle heading, and lateral position can all be seen), normally a smaller number of control elements (or sometimes only one) give control over the inner-loop variable (e.g., the steering wheel). Kelley (1968) and Roscoe (1968) argue that it is important to organize the displayed elements coherently in a manner that is congruent with the operator's mental model of the system being controlled. Thus, if three variables have an ordered causal relation to one another by virtue of three increases in system order, as in Figure 10.13c, displays of the three variables should be presented in such a format that the coherent ordering is preserved.

The strategy of hierarchical loop control is one in which the operator typically sets goals for the highest-order, or outer-loop, variable (e.g., a change in the aircraft lateral position from a desired path). To accomplish this, the operator must, in turn, control the variable of the next lower level (a change in aircraft heading, which changes lateral velocity). This, in turn, places constraints on the variables of the next inner loop (bank angle equal to rate of change of heading), whose rate of change must then be controlled by the innermost loop, aileron control (directly controlled by rotating the yoke or stick left or right). Hierarchical control thus involves the parallel efforts to control outer loops through the regulation of inner loops. At any given time, the operator may be focusing attention on errors of inner-loop variables, outer-loop variables, or both. Because the inner-loop control is often rapid and is somewhat "mindless" in slavish pursuit of the more purposeful cognitive outer-loop goals, systems are being designed with automation of the inner-loop control so that the operator has a direct means of controlling outer-loop variables. For example, the automated cockpit allows the pilot to dial in a desired heading on the autopilot, and the automated control system will accomplish the necessary tracking of inner-loop variables (ailerons or bank angle) to attain the goal. Automated tracking control will be discussed further in Chapter 13.

Factors That Influence the Efficiency of Multiaxis Control

Display Separation   Whether hierarchical, cross-coupled, or independent, multiaxis control will obviously be harmed if the error or output indicators are more separated across the visual field. When the separation is so great that the indicators are not simultaneously in foveal vision, then, as discussed in Chapter 3, operator scan patterns may provide a useful index of the sequence of information extraction from the display. In some of the earliest classic work on formatting of aviation displays, Fitts, Jones, and Milton (1950) provided fundamental data on the importance of various sources of information in flight control derived from instrument scan patterns. The principles of display formatting derived from scan information were summarized in Chapter 3.

The problems associated with visual scanning and sampling strategies were also discussed in some detail in Chapter 3. The resulting loss of performance was caused by peripheral interference. That is, when the eye is fixated on one display, the other display will be in peripheral vision and therefore generate data of lower quality. In tracking, this does not mean that a display can be tracked only if it is fixated on. There is good evidence that a considerable amount of peripheral information concerning both position and velocity may be used for effective control (Allen, Clement, & Jex, 1970; Levison, Elkind, & Ward, 1971; Wickens, 1986), although tracking is still poorer in the periphery than in the fovea (Weinstein & Wickens, 1992).

The obvious solution to the problems of degraded performance with the separation of tracking displays is the same as with the discrete tasks discussed in Chapter 3: Minimize display separation by bringing the displayed axes closer together. In the extreme, two control dimensions may be represented by the motion of a single variable in the x- and y-axes of space—an integrated object display such as the aircraft attitude directional indicator (see Chapter 3) or the computer screen cursor. In these cases, peripheral interference no longer contributes a cost to multiaxis tracking, and other sources of diminished efficiency may be identified. Three such sources, related to resource demand, control similarity, and proximity compatibility, are considered below.

Resource Demand   When people must transmit information along two axes at once—dual-axis tracking—there will typically be some cost to tracking performance along one axis or the other (or both), since as we discuss in the next chapter, performing two tasks is typically harder (imposes more on attention resources) than performing a single task.

In this light, it is not surprising to find that the cost of dual-axis control increases as the resource demands of a single axis are increased. For example, Baty (1971) had subjects time-share the tracking of two zero-order, two first-order, and two second-order systems. He found little evidence for a difference in interference between zero- and first-order control—the two were described earlier in this chapter as substantially similar in their demands when performed singly. However, the magnitude of interference imposed by time-shared second-order control was considerably greater. Similar results have been obtained by Fracker and Wickens (1989).

Similarity of Control Dynamics   An experiment performed by Chernikoff, Duey, and Taylor (1960) indicates that the increasing resource demand of higher-order control may under certain circumstances be lessened by making the control dynamics more similar between the two axes. Different orders of control require the operator to adopt different control strategies. It is apparently more difficult for the operator to time-share control with two different strategies than to maintain a single strategy for both axes. In their experiment, the subjects were asked to perform dual-axis tracking with all three control orders (zero, first, and second) in all pairwise combinations. It was therefore possible to evaluate error on a given axis as a function of the order of control on the time-shared axis. The data are shown in Figure 10.14. For zero-order tracking, error increases when

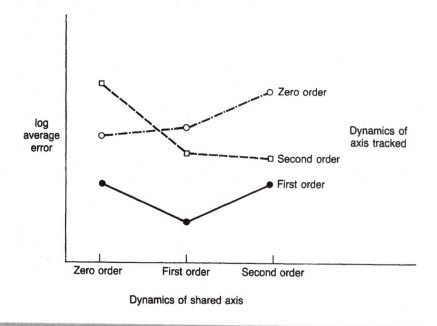

Figure 10.14   Effect of time-shared control order on tracking performance at different orders. Note that the absolute height of the three curves is arbitrary. What is important is the change in error within each curve.

Source: R. Chernikoff, J. W. Duey, and F. V. Taylor, "Two-Dimensional Tracking with Identical and Different Control Dynamics in Each Coordinate," *Journal of Experimental Psychology, 60* (1960), p. 320. Copyright 1960 by the American Psychological Association. Adapted by permission of the authors.

there is higher order on the paired axis. However, for first-order tracking, error is lower when the time-shared axis is also of first order than it is when time-shared with the lower but different zero-order system. Likewise, for second-order tracking, performance is no worse when the shared axis is also the more difficult second-order than when shared with the easier but different first- and zero-order controls. In fact, error is a good bit higher when second order is shared with zero order. In this case the advantage of the lower resource demands of zero- and first-order tracking is nullified by the greater interference resulting from the fact that separate dynamics must be controlled. It is apparently beneficial to have a single mental model that can be employed for both axes of control.

Display and Control Integration   When two axes are tracked, the degree of display or control integration may be varied independently. The four quadrants in Figure 10.15 show the four different display-control combinations that can be generated by integrating or separating the axes on both displays and controls. Further options are available when the separate-separate display is employed (quadrant IV), for here it is possible to present the two axes either in parallel or at right angles to one another.

A general finding that emerges from the literature is that the integrated displays, seen in the top row of the figure, support better performance than the separated displays in the bottom row (Chernikoff & Lemay, 1963; Baty, 1971; Fracker & Wickens, 1989). Such an advantage of display integration to flight path tracking was also found by Haskell and Wickens (1993) when the integrated and separated flight displays, shown in Figure 4.19, were compared. It is reasonable to assume that the general advantage for integrated displays results, in part, from the advantages granted by single object perception, discussed in Chapter 3 (Kahneman & Treisman, 1984).

Control integration (the left column of Figure 10.15) appears to be somewhat less beneficial than does display integration (Fracker & Wickens, 1989; Chernikoff & LeMay,

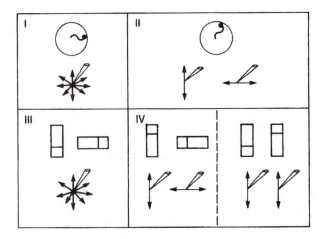

Figure 10.15   Different configurations of display and control integration. Within each quadrant, the display is above and the control is below.

1963). That is, the advantage of one hand performing a single coordinated action appears to be offset by the "crosstalk" resulting when movement of the single hand in one axis spills over to the other axis. As discussed in the next chapter, such crosstalk can act as a source of task interference. Within the two cells in quadrant IV, Levison, Elkind, and Ward (1971) found that the configuration with parallel axes produced the poorest performance, apparently because such crosstalk is amplified when the two hands engage in parallel movements (Kelso, Southard, & Goodman, 1979).

Interactions

Research also shows that the advantages of display or control integration are modulated by each other, and by the similarity of tracking dynamics, in a way that is reminiscent of the proximity compatibility principle, discussed in Chapter 3 (Wickens & Carswell, 1995). That is, the benefits of similarity (or integration) at one stage are enhanced by similarity at other stages. For example, Fracker and Wickens (1989) found that the benefits of display integrality were enhanced if controls were also integrated. Both Chernikoff and LeMay (1963) and Fracker and Wickens (1989) examined tracking with similar versus different dynamics, establishing, as noted above, a cost for different dynamics. However, Chernikoff and LeMay also observed that such costs could be reduced to the extent that separate, rather than integrated displays and controls were employed, as in quadrant IV. Fracker and Wickens found that the benefits of integrated displays only emerged when similar dynamics were employed. Thus, both investigations revealed the sort of "harmony" between similarity (or separation) across different stages that underlies prediction of the proximity compatiblity principle.

Increasing Complexity

An important issue is how these results scale up, to account for multiaxis tracking with considerably greater complexity. For example, Zhai, Milgram, and Rastogi (1997) examined multiaxis tracking of six simultaneous axes, the sort of task that might be confronted by an astronaut trying to capture a tumbling moving object in space, and therefore needing to align a robot arm with three axes of rotation and three axes of translation. In support of the benefits of display and control integration, Zhai, Milgram, and Rastogi found that, with practice, such a task was quite feasible for subjects to perform when subjects used an integrated display and control.

However, Zhai, Milgram, and Rastogi did not compare integrated control with one in which axes were separated. It is easy to imagine that such a task with six separated axes would have been quite difficult indeed; but a possible separation of the axes of rotation (controlled by one hand) and the axes of translation (controlled by the other) is feasible. Indeed, two studies that compared such configurations observed conflicting results (Rice, Yorchak, & Hartely, 1986; O'Hara, 1987), a pattern that is consistent with the ambivalence of separate versus single-handed controls found in the simpler tracking tasks.

Zhai, Milgram, and Rastogi also examined more closely differences between the integrated axes tracked. Although all axes were of the same dynamics, there were still important differences between them, reflecting both perceptual factors and strategic differences. Thus "z-axis" or in-depth tracking was consistently more difficult than tracking in the x- and y-axis, an effect attributable, in part, to the lack of resolution along the depth axis, as discussed in Chapter 4. Furthermore, subjects showed distinct patterns of resource allocation, initially giving priority to the *x*-axis over the *y*-axis, and consistently giving priority to translational over rotational tracking. The importance of priority shifts such as these in multiple-task performance will be addressed in Chapter 11.

Auditory Displays

As noted, a major difficulty with multiaxis control occurs when the operator must scan between displays. We have seen that this difficulty may be reduced by display integration, but this procedure can also impose some cost if the dynamics differ. Furthermore, there are clearly limits to how tightly information can be condensed in the visual field without encountering problems of display clutter (see Chapter 3). One potential solution is to present some tracking-error information through the auditory modality, thus leaving vision able to concentrate on fewer axes. The auditory modality is indeed quite capable of processing spatial information (Begault & Pittman, 1996; Nelson et al., 1998). After all, we do this whenever we turn our head to the source of sound. It is important to realize, however, that audition is less intrinsically compatible with spatial localization than is vision (Wickens, Vidulich, & Sandry-Garza, 1984; see Chapter 9). These properties suggest that single-task auditory tracking will never be superior and will probably be inferior to single-axis visual tracking, but it may provide benefits in environments with a heavy concurrent visual load.

Generally speaking, these hypotheses have been confirmed by the experimental data (Wickens, 1986). The earliest investigation of auditory tracking, carried out in World War II, concerned whether the auditory modality could be used to convey turn, bank angle, and airspeed information in an aircraft simulator (Forbes, 1946). The display, known as "flybar," indicated turn by a sweeping tone, from one ear to the other, whose sweep rate was proportional to the turn rate. Bank angle was indicated by pitch changes in one ear or the other, and airspeed by the frequency of interruption of a single pitch. With sufficient training on this display, Forbes found that pilots and nonpilots could fly the simulator as well as with the visual display.

Subsequently, with more precise performance measurement, Vinge (1971) found that auditory tracking is nearly but not quite equivalent to visual tracking. In the single-axis display used by Vinge, error was represented by the apparent spatial location of a tone, which was adjusted by playing tones of different relative intensity through stereo headphones. In addition, the absolute value of the error was represented redundantly by tone pitch. Low error was indicated by a low pitch. Vinge (1971) found that control over two independent tracking axes was superior when one was presented auditorily and the other visually, as compared to a visual-visual condition. These results replicate the findings of within-modality resource competition discussed in the dual-task literature (to be discussed in Chapter 11). Although Isreal (1980) subsequently found that single-task auditory and visual tracking was nearly equivalent, he also found that auditory tracking was more disrupted by a secondary task displayed in *either* modality. These results suggest that auditory tracking is intrinsically more difficult than visual tracking, a characteristic that probably reflects the fact that we rarely use our sense of hearing to make fine manual adjustments in space. Thus, as discussed in Chapter 9, the auditory modality is less compatible with spatial tasks than is the visual modality.

In spite of its early success in the flybar experiment and subsequent studies showing near equivalence with vision, auditory displays in tracking have received only minimal investigation over the past four decades. This neglect results in part from the fact that the auditory channel is more intrinsically tuned to the processing of verbal (speech) information. Hence, the feeling is that the auditory channel should be dedicated to speech processing. Also, the auditory modality is hampered somewhat because it does not have spatial reference points that are precisely defined, as vision does. Nevertheless, it does appear that under certain conditions auditory spatial displays could provide valuable supplementary and redundant information (Flanagan et al., 1998), particularly if this information were presented along channels that do not peripherally mask the comprehension of speech input. Such redundancy can be of considerable use in environments that are visually loading.

CONTROL DEVICES

At the beginning of the chapter, we discussed Fitts's Law, and its ubiquitous relevance to human performance, because so much of human interaction with systems involves simple pointing (e.g., reaching for keys, controls, and other elements). Computer-based "pointing" (e.g., cursor movement) can also be accomplished through a myriad of different control devices, such as the light pen, touch screen, trackball, mouse, cursor keys, or joysticks (Baber, 1997). In this section, we consider the implication of these different control devices for simple positioning tasks, characterized by those modeled by Fitts's Law. In the following section, we examine the explicit use of voice control for this and other tracking tasks.

Manual Control

The costs and benefits of different sorts of manual control devices for cursor positioning depend, in part, on a large number of anthropometric and biomechanical factors that are beyond the scope of this chapter (see Baber, 1997; Wickens, Gordon, & Liu, 1998). As brief examples, the space constraints required by a mouse pad make the mouse a poor choice for use in a limited-area work space such as a vehicle cab. The fatigue associated with hand pointing makes the touch screen or light pen a poor choice for interaction on a vertical screen, and these devices may sometimes obscure the view of the screen. High vibration environments also limit the effectiveness of many input devices (Baber, 1997). There are, however, two important factors in the choice of devices that derive directly from the human performance implications discussed earlier in this chapter.

The Speed-Accuracy Trade-off   Research indicates that direct pointing devices, such as the light pen or touch screen, tend to provide very rapid but less accurate positioning than do indirect devices such as the mouse (Baber, 1997). Since, as we noted earlier, Fitts's Law accounts for the trade-off between speed and accuracy, it is appropriate to consider the *slope* of the Fitts's Law function, as an index of the overall effectiveness of a control device, when both variables are taken into account (lower slopes, more effective pointing). In this regard, a study by Card, English, and Burr (1978) revealed that the Fitts's Law slope generated by the mouse was lower than that of other control devices, suggesting that the mouse is the best control device when both speed and accuracy are taken into consideration.

Control Order Compatibility Most control devices can be configured such that their displacement will produce either a constant displacement (zero order) or constant rate of movement (first order) of the cursor across the screen. (Only the light pen and touch screen must, by definition, be zero-order controllers, since the end of the pen or finger *is* the cursor.) However, it turns out that there are certain natural "affinities" or "compatibilities"· between other control devices and either zero- or first-order system dynamics: Mice are best served by zero-order control dynamics, and joysticks are best served by first-order control dynamics.

For the mouse, a zero-order control best captures the natural eye-hand coordination that is developed as a result of a lifetime of experience of pointing and reaching. The fact that the location of control movement (the mouse pad) is displaced from the location of visual (cursor) movement does not disrupt the naturalness of this link. For a zero-order mouse, it appears that the optimal gain is between one and three (Baber, 1997). That is, the cursor should travel between one and three times the distance traveled by the hand.

In contrast, if a mouse were to generate first-order control, this not only abandons the natural eye-hand coordination, but would create a second problem, relating to the zero-velocity resting place. In pointing tasks, a zero-velocity (i.e., stationary) state is often the target point of a movement. Hence, it is a desirable feature for the control system to automatically "seek" that stationary state. A mouse with first-order dynamics will not do that. The user must consciously move the mouse to the precise position on the pad where no motion occurs; and if there is a slight offset, the cursor will "drift."

Quite a different circumstance describes the spring-loaded joystick. (Spring loading maximizes proprioceptive and kinesthetic feedback.) Such a system indeed *has* a natural resting state. The stick will "snap back" to center if left unattended and the zero-velocity resting state will be automatically recovered. While the spring-loaded joystick thus has the natural affinity for or compatibility with first-order control, so it also has an inherent problem as a zero-order control device: the lack of precision with which any position off of the center can be maintained. The human must exert a constant and unvarying force against the spring, in order to maintain the cursor at the desired position, a task of substantial resource cost (Wickens, 1976). A further problem with the joystick as a zero-order controller is the lack of available movement range. The hand moving a joystick cannot move as far—at most perhaps 2–3 inches—as it can on a mouse surface. With a 2-inch maximum movement, then, a screen size of 6–9 inches is the largest that can be accommodated if the gain is to be maintained within the desirable range of one to three.

Thus, certain features make the mouse desirable for zero-order control, and undesirable for first-order control, just as these and other features make the spring-loaded joystick better suited for first-order than for zero-order control. The compatibility is established.

Voice Control

Given the prevalence of voice control in many systems (e.g., voice menus) as discussed in the previous chapter, it is reasonable to consider the strengths and weaknesses of this medium as a position-control device. As noted in the previous chapter in the context of modality compatibility, voice control can be advantageous when one or particularly both hands are otherwise busy. However, the human voice evolved primarily (and compatibly) to convey linguistic, symbolic, and categorical information (e.g., "acquire the red square"), rather than analog information ("a little to the left; now up a bit"), a task that is far better and more naturally accomplished by the hand (Fitts & Deinniger, 1954; Wickens, Sandry, & Vidulich, 1983; Wickens, Vidulich, & Sandry-Garza, 1984). Thus, the voice's use as a position controller will only be an asset (a) when the voice is not used for other vocal tasks (unlike the hands, the voice cannot produce two outputs at once), and (b) when the nature of the desired target destination can be *unambiguously* signaled (for example, if you were electronically editing this text, "position the cursor on the subheading: *voice control*").

Even in these circumstances, the possible advantages of voice over manual control for spatial cursor movement are questionable. Two sorts of problems can eliminate any advantages that voice control might have for designating targets symbolically or by spatial directions: (1) Computer-based voice recognition technology may fail to correctly categorize an utterance; (2) such control may categorize it correctly, but interpret it incorrectly. In either case, a time-consuming dialogue will be encountered as the user and system together try to address a situation in which the system moved the cursor to a target that was not intended by the user. Alternatively, if the user does not recognize the system's mistake in target designation, the problem could become still more serious as the incorrect destination is chosen. Thus, the inherent compatibility of each modality (voice, hands) for conveying its favored information (symbolic, spatial) suggests that every effort should be made to remove the voice from the obligation of conveying analog spatial material (Wickens, Zenyuh, Culp, & Marshak, 1985).

MODELING THE HUMAN OPERATOR IN MANUAL CONTROL

There are many circumstances in vehicle control in which the need to keep error low but also to maintain stability greatly constrains the controller's freedom of action to engage in different strategies of control. These constraints have one great advantage. They allow human performance in manual control to be modeled and predicted with a far greater degree of precision than is possible in many other tasks. In fact, the mathematical models of tracking performance that have been derived have been some of the most accurate, successful, and useful of any of the models of human performance that we have examined. As discussed in Chapter 1, if systems designers know before it is built whether an aircraft with a given set of dynamics is flyable, by combining the model of vehicle dynamics with the transfer function of a pilot, they can realize a tremendous savings in engineering cost. The supplement to this chapter describes two such models—the crossover model (McRuer & Krendel, 1959) and the optimal control model (Baron, 1988; Kleinman, Baron, & Levison, 1971) along with the frequency-domain language of manual control. Both models share certain characteristics with previous models discussed in the book. They specify optimal behavior and can represent some trade-off of operator strategies.

TRANSITION

Motor and manual control is often difficult, time-consuming, and heavily loading. In Chapter 11, we consider how the nature of the workload in manual control, along with other tasks, disrupts the ability to perform these tasks concurrently. At the same time, as noted previously, many aspects of manual control reflect lower-level, noncognitive processes that might readily be assigned to machines in a systems analysis. This approach is clearly being adopted to some extent. As robots in industrial assembly tasks are performing tracking, and so also are autopilots and stability augmentation devices in aircraft control. Unfortunately, however, the trend toward automation is not without a number of problems Chapter 13 will consider automation of control in the broader context of other decision-making and cognitive tasks that have been discussed in previous chapters. The chapter also will examine process control as a broader extension of manual control and other aspects of control related to supervisory control and air traffic control.

SUPPLEMENT

Engineering Models of Manual Control

As noted previously, it is possible to think of the human operator as perceiving an error and translating it to a response in the same conceptual terms used for any other dynamic element responding to an input to produce an output. Figure 10.6 showed examples of several such elements. The objective of human operator models in tracking is to describe the human in terms similar to these dynamic elements.

FREQUENCY-DOMAIN REPRESENTATION

Figure 10.6 shows the step response of the different dynamic elements as functions of time—that is, the response in the *time domain*. The mathematical expression of these elements—a differential or integral equation—is also a function of time. Each different element is uniquely described by its step response and its time-domain transfer function.

In manual-control research in engineering psychology, it is sometimes preferable to represent transfer functions in the *frequency domain* in terms of spectra. This procedure was described briefly in our discussion of the speech signal in Chapter 6. In tracking, we assume that the human operator tracks an error, which is a continuous signal varying in time (see Figure 10.5), to produce a response, also a continuous time-varying signal. Spectral analysis breaks down each of the signals into its component frequencies of oscillation, as was shown in Figure 6.11. Then the transfer function between the two signals, input and output, can be specified by two fundamental relationships that exist between two signals specified at each frequency of oscillation: the *gain*, or *amplitude ratio*, and the *lag*. The gain, as we have seen, is the ratio of output to input amplitude. The lag is the amount by which the output trails the input. Lag is normally expressed in degrees of a cycle rather than in units of time. Thus, a half-second time delay will be a half-cycle lag at a frequency of one cycle per second (1 Hz) but will be a quarter-cycle lag at a 0.5-Hz frequency (1 cycle/2 seconds).

These two properties are shown at the top of Figure 10.16. On the left, at a frequency of oscillation of 1 Hz, the output amplitude is twice the magnitude of the input. Hence, the amplitude ratio, or gain, is 2/1, or 2. The output also lags behind the input by one-fourth of a cycle: That is, the output reaches its peak when the input is already halfway to its trough. Hence, the phase lag is said to be 90 degrees, since 360 degrees is a full cycle. To the right is a higher frequency of 10 Hz. Here the gain is less than 1, since the input amplitude is larger

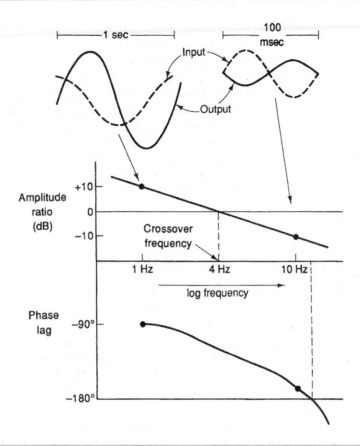

Figure 10.16   Bode plot of system $O(t) = kfi(t - \tau)dt$.

than the output, and the phase lag is near 180 degrees: Peaks of the inputs occur at troughs of the output, and vice versa. The two signals are completely out of phase.

Typically, the frequency-domain representation of a transfer function is depicted in a *Bode plot* (pronounced *Bodey*), an example of which is shown in Figure 10.16. Each Bode plot actually consists of two functions, plotting gain and phase on the same frequency axis. Therefore, at the top of the Bode plot, the amplitude ratio expressed in *decibels* (log of the ratio) is shown as a function of the logarithm (base 10) of the frequency. Across the bottom, phase lag in degrees is expressed again as a function of log frequency. The particular gain and phase relationships of the 1 Hz and 10 Hz frequencies at the top of the figure are shown as four points in the Bode plot. In fact, these points have been connected with solid lines to show the gain and phase values that would have been observed if the dynamic system whose input and output we were measuring had the time-domain transfer function of the form

$$Y = Kfe(t - \tau_e)dt$$

and was measured continuously at all frequencies. This function is a first-order system with gain K and time delay τ_e, a combination of the dynamic elements shown in

Figure 10.6b and d. The importance of this particular function is that it represents a model of human performance, as discussed below.

In the Bode plot, the value of K determines the intercept of the gain function. Changes in K will shift the curve up and down but will leave its slope unchanged. The constant time delay causes a greater phase lag at higher frequencies. Hence, there is an exponential drop-off with the increase in log frequency. (The phase lag would increase linearly if frequency were plotted on a linear rather than a logarithm scale.) Finally, on a Bode plot, the single integral in the transfer function, characteristic of the first-order system, contributes an amplitude ratio that becomes linearly smaller at high lag frequencies and is reduced at a rate of − 20 dB for each decade increase of frequency. The phase lag produced by a first-order system is always a constant 90 degrees at all frequencies. In Figure 10.16, the constant lag caused by the integrator and the exponentially increasing lag caused by the time delay are simply added together. At very low frequencies, the time delay lag is negligible, and so the constant integrator lag of 90 degrees is the only one seen.

Often, two transfer functions are placed in series. For example, in the tracking loop shown in Figure 10.4, the transfer function of the human operator, the control, and the plant are all in series. In this case, the components of the combined Bode plot are simply added. Thus, since a second-order system (Figure 10.6e) is just two first-order systems in series (Figure 10.6d), the second-order Bode plot would correspond to the added components of two first-order Bode plots. The result would be a plot with phase lag of 180 degrees and an amplitude ratio slope of − 40 dB/decade (gains are multiplied, so their logarithmic values in decibels are added). This is why it is convenient to express the amplitude ratio on a log scale.

At this point, it is possible to see why higher-order systems lead to instability in some closed-loop negative-feedback systems. Recall from our earlier discussion that instability was caused by a combination of high phase lag and high gain. The long phase lag in responding to periodic signals with higher-order systems (180 degrees for second order) is present at every frequency. The other element that leads to instability—high gain—is present only at lower frequencies. These two characteristics jointly lead to a critical principle in the analysis of system stability: *If the gain is greater than 1.0 (O dB) at frequencies at which the phase lag is also greater than 180 degrees, the system will be unstable when responding to frequencies of that value.* The reason is that when the phase lag is 180 degrees, a correction intended to reduce an error at that frequency will, by the time it is realized by the system response (one-half cycle, or 180 degrees, later), be *added to* rather than subtracted from the error, since the error will now have reversed in polarity. If the gain is greater than 1, this counterproductive correction will increase the error, leading to the kinds of oscillations described earlier.

According to this principle of closed-loop stability, the system shown in Figure 10.16 is stable. The frequency at which the phase lag becomes greater than 180 degrees (about 12 Hz) is higher than the frequency at which the gain curve becomes less than 1 (above 4 Hz). This latter frequency measure—critical for stability analysis—is called the *crossover frequency*. Figure 10.17 shows a Bode plot of the same system in Figure 10.16, responding with higher gain, thereby raising the amplitude ratio curve. This change moves the crossover frequency to a higher value, which is now greater than the critical frequency at which the phase lag becomes greater than 180 degrees. The system in Figure 10.17 will therefore be unstable.

First- and Second-Order Lags in the Frequency Domain

Figure 10.18 shows Bode plots for pure zero-, first-, and second-order systems (no time delay). Each order adds a phase lag of 90 degrees and increases the slope of the gain

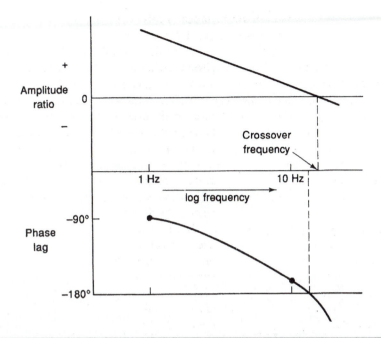

Figure 10.17   Bode plot of the system in Figure 10.16, now unstable because of a higher value of *K*.

function by − 20 dB/decade. Earlier we suggested that the first-order or exponential lag shown in Figure 10.6c represents something of a compromise between a zero- and first-order system. Examination of the Bode plot of the first-order lag, in Figure 10.19, shows how this compromise is realized in the frequency domain. When a first-order lag is driven by low-frequency inputs, the system responds as a zero-order system. There is no

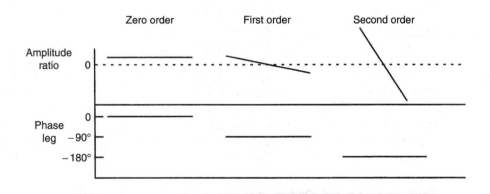

Figure 10.18   Bode plot of zero-, first-, and second-order system.

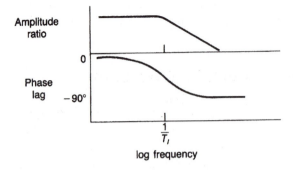

Figure 10.19 Bode plot of a first-order lag, showing zero-order behavior at low frequency and first-order behavior at high frequency.

phase lag, and the gain is constant at all frequencies. When driven by high frequencies, in contrast, the system responds as the first-order system of Figure 10.18: a 90-degree phase lag and decreasing amplitude ratio. The break-point transitioning from zero to first order is given by the frequency $1/T_1$. T_1 is referred to as the *time constant* of the lag.

Operations in the Frequency and Laplace Domain

In Figure 10.6, the dynamic elements are described by differential equations in the time domain. The functions are of the form $f(t)$. When dealing with systems in the frequency domain, dynamic elements can be expressed in the form $F(j\omega)$, where $j\omega$ represents a particular frequency characteristic. Alternatively, they may be represented in the *Laplace domain* in the form $F(S)$. The Laplace operator S is one that accounts for both frequency-domain *and* time-domain characteristics, and so it is the most general way of describing dynamic systems and their associated inputs and outputs. A description of the mathematical nature of the frequency-domain and Laplace-domain operations is beyond the scope of this chapter, and the reader is referred to treatments by Toats (1975) and Wickens (1986) for intuitive discussions of their derivations.

We will focus on one major benefit of the Laplace representation, the reason for its attractiveness to engineering analysis: both signals *and* the dynamic elements of the tracking loop can be represented by Laplace transforms. To determine the output of a dynamic element from its input, all that needs to be done is to multiply the Laplace transform of the input by the transform of the dynamic element, and the product will be the transform of the output. If we know the Laplace transform of the input and the output, we can compute the transfer function of the dynamic element simply by dividing output by input. This calculation turns out to be a lot simpler than performing differential and integral calculus in the time domain. The Laplace-domain transfer functions of some of the dynamic elements are shown on the left side of Figure 10.6. Here the simplicity is evident. The Laplace representation of an integrator is K_1/S, and that of a differentiator is K_2S (K_1 and K_2 are simply gains). Hence placing the two transfer functions in series produces $K_1/S \times K_2S = K_{12}$, that is, a pure gain. In the discussion of models of human-operator tracking below, both the time-domain and the Laplace-domain transfer functions will be considered—the time domain because it is perhaps slightly more intuitive, the frequency domain or Laplace domain because it provides a bridge to the engineering literature, in which these models are often used.

MODELS OF HUMAN OPERATOR TRACKING

The initial efforts to model human tracking behavior in the late 1940s and the 1950s were described as *quasi-linear* models (McRuer, 1980; McRuer & Jex 1967; McRuer & Krendel, 1959). The term *quasi-linear* derives from the engineer's assumption that the human operator's control behavior in perceiving an error and translating it to a response can be modeled as a linear transfer function such as those dynamic elements shown in Figure 10.6. However, they acknowledge that this representation is indeed only an approximation to linear behavior, which is why the modifier *quasi* is attached. Because the human response is not truly linear, it is referred to as a *describing function* rather than a transfer function. Quasi-linear models have been applied with greatest success to describing tracking behavior in the frequency domain.

The Crossover Model

Early efforts to discover the invariant characteristics of the human operator as a transfer function relating perceived error, $e(t)$, to control response, $u(t)$, encountered considerable frustration (see Licklider, 1960, for an excellent discussion of these models). The most successful of these early approaches, the crossover model developed by McRuer and Krendel (1959; McRuer & Jex, 1967), was successful because it departed from previous efforts in one important respect, which may be appreciated by reviewing Figure 10.4. Rather than looking for an invariant relationship between error $e(t)$ and operator control, $u(t)$, McRuer and Jex examined that between error and system response, $o(t)$. That is, how the human responds to the perceived error to make the system output respond in a certain way. In this form, their model allows the operator's describing function to be flexible or adaptable and to change with the plant transfer function in order to achieve the characteristics of a "good" control system, described below. Humans seem to behave in this way.

As described earlier, the two primary characteristics of good control are low error and a high degree of system stability. To meet these criteria, the crossover model asserts that the human responds in such a way as to make the total open-loop transfer function—the function that relates perceived error to system output—behave as a first-order system with gain and effective time delay. That is,

$$o(t) = Kfe(t - \tau_e)dt$$

or, in the Laplace domain,

$$O(S) = (KE^{-\tau_e S})/S$$

$$(KE - \tau_e S)/S$$

This transfer function is the simple crossover model, and its frequency-domain representation was in fact that shown in Figure 10.16. The way in which the crossover model describes the human and the plant together is shown in Figure 10.20. (The control dynamics box of the tracking loop is conventionally deleted, since it is assumed that the fundamental human output for analysis is the position of the control, not the force required to obtain that position.) As noted, in the Laplace domain the transfer function of two components in series can simply be "multiplied" together (adding phase lags and multiplying gains), which is why the combined Laplace domain function is expressed as *HG*.

The crossover model is described by two parameters: the gain and the effective time delay. The gain is of course the ratio of output velocity to perceived error. (Output is expressed as velocity rather than amplitude because the transfer function is a first-order system or integrator that produces velocity output from position input.) Humans adjust their own gain to compensate for increases or decreases in plant gain, in order to maintain the total open-loop gain, the ratio *O/E*, at a constant value (McRuer & Jex, 1967). The variable τ_e is the effective time delay, described as the continuous analog of the human operator's discrete reaction time. Unlike gain, for which there are advantages and disadvantages at both high and low levels, long time delays are invariably harmful. There is not much that the human operator can do to shorten this parameter unless prediction and preview are available.

The third element of the model is its first-order characteristics—the single time integration. It is important in understanding the crossover model to consider why the operator chooses to behave in a way that makes the operator-plant "team" respond as a first-order system. The answer may be expressed in terms of either of two compromises—one expressed intuitively, one formally. At an intuitive level, it is possible to view a first-order response as a compromise between the costs and benefits of zero- and higher-order controls. Zero-order controls are tight and, as shown in Figure 10.6a, instantly correct detected errors. However, if the errors are sudden steps, as in Figure 10.6, an instant response of this kind might be quite unpleasant if, for example, one were riding in a vehicle corrected in this manner. Greater smoothness of correction is thereby obtained by a control of higher order. However, second-order control, as we have noted, is so sluggish that it becomes unstable. Hence, first-order

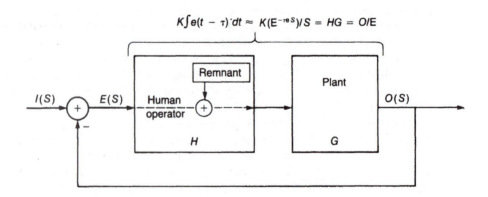

Figure 10.20 The crossover model of McRuer and Krendel (1959).

Source: D. T. McRuer and H. R. Jex, "A Review of Quasi-linear Pilot Models," *IEEE Transactions on Human Factors in Electronics, 8* (1967), p. 240. Copyright 1967 by the Institute of Electrical and Electronics Engineers. Adapted by permission.

control makes an appropriate compromise between the jerkiness of zero-order control and the sluggish instability of second order.

The formal compromise expresses the rationale for adopting a first-order control system in terms of an attempt to meet the two criteria of a good control system: low error and stability (McRuer & Jex, 1967). Considering the system depicted in Figure 10.20, it is evident that low error (at least as spatially defined) will be accomplished by a system in which the gain of the entire *closed-loop* transfer function (relating command input, I, to system output, O) is equal to 1. In this case, inputs will be directly matched in amplitude by outputs, and barring any phase lags, the error will be zero. However, to accomplish a unity gain of the closed-loop transfer function, the *open-loop* function describing the relationship of error to output must have an infinite (or very high) gain (i.e., small errors should be corrected with large corrective responses in the opposite direction). This property can be shown formally (see Jagacinski, 1977, and Wickens, 1986).

Whereas "tight" closed-loop control and low error can therefore be obtained by making the open-loop gain very high, as we have seen, a high-gain response strategy will generate instability problems whenever system phase lags are greater than 180 degrees of the frequencies being corrected. These problems could occur any time an operator with effective time delay enters the control loop or whenever the plant itself has phase lags. As a consequence, at high frequencies, good control *must* keep the open-loop gain to a value of less than 1 at a frequency, the crossover frequency, below that where the phase lag is greater than 180 degrees (compare Figures 10.16 and 10.17). The first-order system, with its downsloping amplitude ratio in the frequency domain, shown in Figure 10.16, nicely accomplishes this function.

The human operator, the "flexible" element of the open-loop function, HG, insures that these two criteria are met by responding in such a way as to make HG behave like a first-order system, with the unavoidable time delay. Thus the form of the crossover model, $o(t) = Kfe(t - \tau_e)dt$, is adopted. Referring to Figure 10.16, we see that such a function will produce high gain at low frequencies and low gain at high frequencies, thereby jointly meeting the criteria of minimizing low-frequency error and maintaining high-frequency stability. The human can always adjust gain downward to keep the crossover frequency just below the critical instability phase lag, and thereby avoid the unfortunate circumstances shown in Figure 10.17.

To achieve this first-order form of the open-loop transfer function, $O/E = GH$, the ideal human operator must adapt to changes in the system transfer function. This adaptation is accomplished in two ways. First, human gain will be adjusted upward or downward to compensate for decreases or increases in control gain respectively, to keep the crossover frequency just below the -180-degree phase lag. Second, the operator changes the form of H (the operator's transfer function or control response to an error) to first-order when the system is zero-order, to zero-order when the system is first-order, and to a minus-first-order, or derivative control, system when the system is second-order. In the Laplace domain, the reason for this adaptation is very easy to see. The total transfer function, HG, must be first-order, K/S. Thus when the plant is zero-order (K), the human is $1/S$ and $K \times 1/S = K/S$. When the plant is first-order $(1/S)$, the human is zero-order (K) and $1/S \times K = K/S$. When the plant is second-order $(1/S^2)$, the human is a derivative controller, KS, and $KS \times 1/S^2 = K/S$. With the second-order control dynamics, the fact that the human becomes a derivative controller agrees with our earlier discussion of second-order control. We said that perceiving the derivative of the error signal (behaving as a KS controller) is an aid to anticipation and prediction. Here we see that this perception is not only desirable but also may be *essential* to maintain stability. If third-order dynamics are to be controlled, the crossover model is less applicable because it requires the human operator to adopt a minus-second-order, KS^2, or double-derivative control function to maintain stability, responding directly to error acceleration. The human's ability to perceive acceleration of visual signals is limited (Fuchs, 1962; McRuer, 1980).

In a series of validation studies, McRuer and his colleagues (McRuer, 1980; McRuer & Jex, 1967; McRuer & Krendel, 1959; McRuer et al., 1968) found that the human behaves similarly to the crossover model when performing compensatory tracking tasks with random input. When Bode plots of the human transfer function between error and output are constructed in a compensatory task, more than 90 percent of the variance of well-trained operators can be accounted for by the simple two-parameter model. The model, therefore, compares favorably with other models of human behavior that we have discussed. Figure 10.21, taken from McRuer and Jex, shows the unchanging form of the crossover model Bode plot *HG* as humans track zero-, first-, and second-order systems. The figure then indicates how the human operator adapts to compensate for the changing dynamics of the system. Only when the system becomes second-order does the fit of data to the model begin to deteriorate somewhat.

The mathematical equation of the crossover model describing functions cannot predict all the output that will be observed when the human tracks a given error signal. The remaining variance in system response that is not accounted for by the linear describing function is referred to as the *remnant*. Some of the remnant results from nonlinear forms of behavior such as the bang-bang impulse control shown in second-order tracking. In addition, a remnant is also caused by such factors as time variations in the describing function parameters or random "noise" in human behavior. It is often depicted as a quantity injected into the human processing signal, as shown in Figure 10.20 (Levison, Baron, & Kleinman, 1969; McRuer & Jex, 1967).

The crossover model has proven to be quite successful in accounting for human behavior in dynamic systems. It has allowed design engineers to predict the closed-loop stability of piloted aircraft by combining the transfer function of the aircraft provided by aeronautical engineers with the crossover model of its pilot. It has also provided a useful means of predicting the mental workload encountered by aircraft pilots from the amount of lead or derivative control that the pilot must generate to compensate for higher-order control lags (Hess, 1977, 1997). Finally, the time delay, gain, and remnant measures of the model provide a convenient means of capturing the changes in the frequency domain that occur as a result of such factors as stress, fatigue, dual-task loading, practice, or supplemental display cues (Fracker & Wickens, 1989, Wickens & Gopher, 1977). To the extent that these three parameters capture fundamental changes in human processing mechanisms, their expression forms a more economical means of representation than does the raw Bode plot.

The Optimal Control Model

Despite the great degree of success that the crossover model has had in accounting for tracking behavior, it is not without some limitations (McRuer, 1980; Pew & Baron 1978). (1) It is essentially a frequency-domain model and so does not readily account for time-domain behavior. (2) The form of the model and its parameters are based purely on fits of the equations to the input-output relations of tracking; they are not derived from consideration of the processing mechanisms or stages actually used by the human operator. (3) Unlike models of reaction time, signal detection, or dual-task performance, the crossover model does not readily account for different operator strategies of performance.

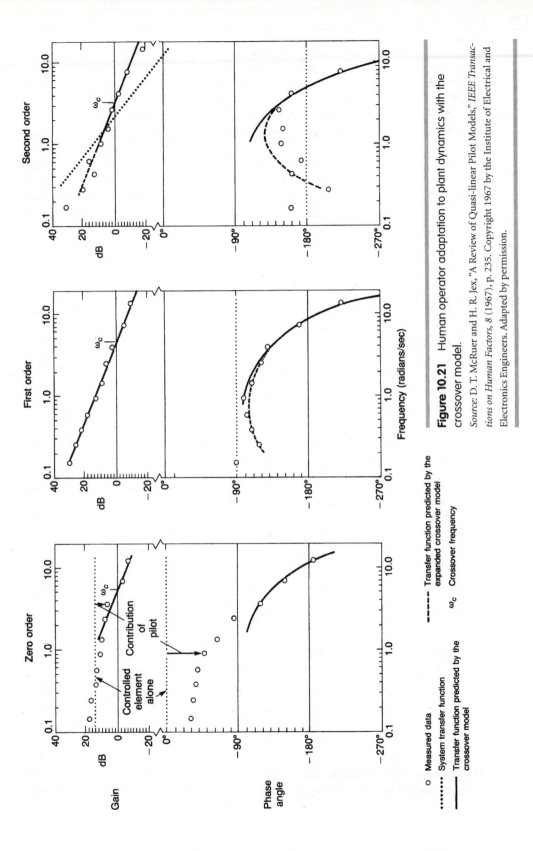

Figure 10.21 Human operator adaptation to plant dynamics with the crossover model.

Source: D. T. McKuer and H. R. Jex, "A Review of Quasi-linear Pilot Models," *IEEE Transactions on Human Factors, 8* (1967), p. 235. Copyright 1967 by the Institute of Electrical and Electronics Engineers. Adapted by permission.

Although the operator is assumed to be flexible—adapting the order of the describing function or compensatorily adjusting gain to the form of the plant—these adjustments are dictated by characteristics of the system. They are not chosen according to "styles" of tracking or instructional sets in the same way that beta was adjusted in signal detection theory. In contrast, the *optimal control model* incorporates an explicit mechanism to account for this sort of strategic adjustment (Baron, 1988; Levison, 1989; Pew & Baron, 1978; Hess, 1997).

The basic components of the Optimal Control Model are shown in Figure 10.22. The human operator perceives a set of displayed quantities and must exercise control to minimize a quantity, *J*, known as the quadratic *cost functional* and shown in the middle of the figure. This quantity, a critical component of the optimal control model, is often expressed in the form

$$J = f\,(Au^2 + Be^2)\,dt$$

The integrated quantity within parentheses that is to be minimized is a weighted combination of squared control velocity and squared error. The relative constants of the two

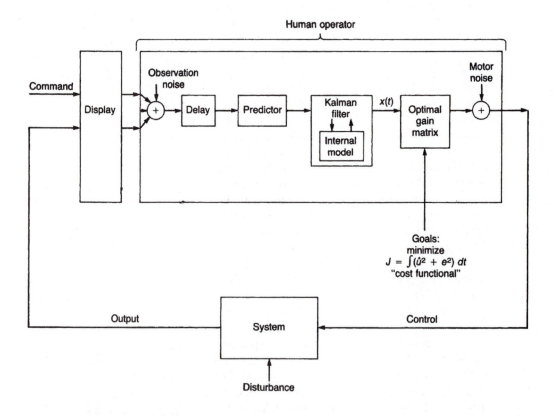

Figure 10.22 The optimal control model.

terms A and B will depend on the relative importance which the operator places on control precision, e or e^2, as opposed to control effort, u or u^2 (the square of control velocity turns out to be a very good measure of control effort). This importance may vary from occasion to occasion or from operator to operator. Thus, as shown in the comparison of the two signals in Figure 10.8, attempts to minimize error at all costs may require fairly rapid control, but attempts to make a ride comfortable, or to save fuel if controlling a space vehicle require less control action and therefore will increase error. Thus, as the operator trades off between tracking with low error and tracking with smooth control, the quantities u^2 and e^2 will also trade off accordingly.

The assumption that the operator attempts to minimize the cost function represents one aspect of the optimal characteristic of the optimal control model. To minimize this quantity, the operator adjusts the gains that are used to translate the various perceived quantities (i.e., error and error velocity) into control. These gains are represented by the *optimal gain matrix* in Figure 10.22, a set of rules whose formulations are beyond the scope of the present treatment (see Baron, Kleinman, & Levison, 1970).

Optimal control is not perfect control. The human operator suffers two kinds of limitations: time delay and disturbance. Typically, all of the time delays in operator response are lumped into one delay, shown in the left side of the box in Figure 10.22. The sources of disturbance are attributable either to external forces or to the remnant of the operator. In Figure 10.22, these are shown as a noise in perceiving (observation noise) and a noise in responding (motor noise). To provide the most precise and current estimate of the current state of the system on which to base the optimal control, the operator must engage in two further processing operations: (1) *Optimal prediction* is done to compensate for the time delay, taking into account the manner in which future states may be predicted from past states. (2) *Estimation* of the true state of the system from the noisy state perturbed by the remnant is accomplished by applying a *Kalman filter*. The Kalman filter is an optimization technique similar in some respects to the Bayesian decision-making procedures described in Chapter 8. It combines estimates of system noise, operator remnant, and an internal model of the system to make a "best guess" of true system state. Application of the Kalman filter represents a second way in which the human is assumed to behave optimally, since the estimation of system state is based on an optimal weighting of system noise and operator remnant. The final, current, best guess of the system state, $x(t)$, is then used as the input to the control gains that were selected by the cost function, J, and from this process the appropriate motor response is generated, although perturbed by motor noise.

Like the crossover model, the optimal control model has also proven quite successful in accounting for much of the variance of human performance in tracking (Baron, 1988; Levison, 1989; Hess, 1997). A key feature is the derived reciprocal relationship between the observation noise and the *fraction of attention* that is allocated to a tracking axis. This relationship allows the designer to predict in quantitative terms the degree of degradation of the perceived input signal and, hence, by applying the model, the amount of loss of control accuracy when attention is diverted to other aspects of information processing (Baron, 1988; Levison, 1989; Wewerinke, 1989). However, the computational complexities of the optimal control model, as well as the greater number of parameters in the model that must be specified to fit the data, make it somewhat more difficult to apply than the crossover model. Nevertheless, the ability of the model to account for shifts in operator strategies gives it a desirable degree of flexibility that the crossover model does not have. Discussions by Baron, (1988); Baron and Levison (1977); Curry, Kleinman, and Hoffman (1977); Hess (1977,

1997); Levison (1989); and Levison, Elkind, and Ward (1971) provide examples of the manner in which the model has been applied to optimize the design of aviation systems and to assess operator workload and attention allocation in a quantitative model of attention.

SUMMARY

Models of human tracking have come about as close as any to providing useful predictive information that can assist in system design. As we have pointed out, however, these models are accurate precisely because they describe behavior that is fairly tightly constrained. The pilot of certain aircraft simply cannot depart from the error and stability prescriptions of the crossover model or else the plane will crash. Yet, ironically, these very constraints on flexibility have made manual controls some of the easiest functions to replace by automation, thereby potentially making the models obsolete. However, the extent to which humans will be replaced by automatic controllers is determined by a host of other factors above and beyond the simple ability of automatic controllers to perform as well as humans. These issues will be addressed in the final chapter of the book.

REFERENCES

Adams, J. A. (1971). A closed loop theory of motor learning. *Journal of Motor Behavior, 3,* 111–150.

Adams, J. A. (1976). Issues for a closed loop theory of motor learning. In G. E. Stelmach (Ed.), *Motor control: Issues and trends.* New York: Academic Press.

Allen, R. W., Clement, W. F., & Jex, H. R. (1970, July). *Research on display scanning, sampling, and reconstruction using separate main and secondary tracking tasks* (NASA CR–1569). Washington, DC: NASA.

Allen, R. W., & Jex, H. R. (1968, June). *An experimental investigation of compensatory and pursuit tracking displays with rate and acceleration control dynamics and a disturbance input* (NASA CR–1082). Washington, DC: NASA.

Baber, C. (1997). *Beyond the desktop.* San Diego, CA: Academic Press.

Bahrick, H. P., & Shelly, C. (1958). Time-sharing as an index of automatization. *Journal of Experimental Psychology, 56,* 288–293.

Baron, S. (1988). Pilot control. In E. Wiener & D. Nagel (Eds.), *Human factors in aviation.* New York: Academic Press.

Baron, S., Kleinman, D., & Levison, W. (1970). An optimal control model of human response. *Automatica, 5,* 337–369.

Baron, S., & Levison, W. H. (1977). Display analysis with the optimal control model of the human operator. *Human Factors, 19,* 437–457.

Bartlett, F. C. (1932). *Remembering: A study in experimental social psychology.* London: Cambridge University Press.

Baty, D. L. (1971). Human transinformation rates during one-to-four axis tracking. *Proceedings of the 7th Annual Conference on Manual Control* (NASA SP–281). Washington, DC: U.S. Government Printing Office.

Begault, D. R., & Pittman, M T. (1996). Three-dimensional audio versus head-down traffic alert and collision avoidance system displays. *International Journal of Aviation Psychology, 6*, 79–93.

Birmingham, H. P., & Taylor, F. V. (1954). *A human engineering approach to the design of man-operated continuous control systems* (Report no. 433). Washington, DC: U.S. Naval Research Laboratory.

Brown, J. S., & Slater-Hammel, A. T. (1949). Discrete movements in a horizontal plane as a function of their length and direction. *Journal of Experimental Psychology, 10*, 12–21.

Card, S. K. (1981). The model human processor: A model for making engineering calculations of human performance. In R. Sugarman (Ed.), *Proceedings of the 25th annual meeting of the Human Factors Society*. Santa Monica, CA: Human Factors Society.

Card, S. K., English, W. K., & Burr, B. J. (1978). Evaluation of mouse, rate-controlled isometric joystick, step keys, and task keys for text selection on a CRT. *Ergonomics, 21*(8), 601–613.

Card, S., Newell, A., & Moran, T. (1986). The model human processor. In K. Boff, L. Kaufman, & J. Thomas (Eds), *Handbook of perception and performance* (vol. 2, chpt. 45). New York: Wiley.

Chernikoff, R., Duey, J. W., & Taylor, F. V. (1960). Two-dimensional tracking with identical and different control dynamics in each coordinate. *Journal of Experimental Psychology, 60*, 318–322.

Chernikoff, R., & Lemay, M. (1963). Effect on various display-control configurations on tracking with identical and different coordinate dynamics. *Journal of Experimental Psychology, 66*, 95–99.

Chernikoff, R., & Taylor, F. V. (1957). Effects of course frequency and aided time constant on pursuit and compensatory tracking. *Journal of Experimental Psychology, 53*, 285–292.

Craik, K. W. J. (1948). Theory of the human operator in control systems II: Man as an element in a control system. *British Journal of Psychology, 38*, 142–148.

Crossman, E. R. F. W. (1960). The information capacity of the human motor system in pursuit tracking. *Quarterly Journal of Experimental Psychology, 12*, 1–16.

Curry, R. E., Kleinman, D. L., & Hoffman, W. C. (1977). A design procedure for control/display systems. *Human Factors, 19*, 421–436.

Debecker, J., & Desmedt, R. (1970). Maximum capacity for sequential one-bit auditory decisions. *Journal of Experimental Psychology, 83*, 366–373.

Drury, C. (1975). Application to Fitts' law to foot pedal design. *Human Factors, 17*, 368–373.

Eberts, R., & Schneider, W. (1985). Internalizing the system dynamics for a second-order system. *Human Factors, 27*(4), 371–393.

Elkind, J. I., & Sprague, L. T. (1961). Transmission of information in simple manual control systems. *IRE Transactions on Human Factors in Electronics, HFE–2*, 58–60.

Fitts, P. M. (1954). The information capacity of the human motor system in controlling the amplitude of movement. *Journal of Experimental Psychology, 47*, 381391.

Fitts, P. M., & Deinninger, R. L. (1954). S-R compatibiity: Correspondence among paired elements within stimulus and response codes. *Journal of Experimental Psychology, 48*, 483–491.

Fitts, P. M., Jones, R. E., & Milton, J. L. (1950). Eye movements of aircraft pilots during instrument-landing approaches. *Aeronautical Engineering Review, 9*(2), 24–29.

Fitts, P. M., & Peterson, J. R. (1964). Information capacity of discrete motor responses. *Journal of Experimental Psychology, 67,* 103–112.

Fitts, P. M., & Posner, M. A. (1967). *Human performance.* Pacific Palisades, CA: Brooks/Cole.

Flanagan, P., McAnally, K. I., Martin, R. L., Meehan, J. W., & Oldfield, S. R. (1998). Aurally and visually guided visual search in a virtual environment. *Human Factors, 40*(3), 461–468.

Forbes, T. W. (1946). Auditory signals for instrument flying. *Journal of Aeronautical Science, 13,* 255–258.

Fracker, M. L., & Wickens, C. D. (1989). Resources, confusions, and compatibility in dual axis tracking: Displays, controls, and dynamics. *Journal of Experimental Psychology: Human Perception and Performance, 15,* 80–96.

Fuchs, A. (1962). The progression regression hypothesis in perceptual-motor skill learning. *Journal of Experimental Psychology, 63,* 177–192.

Gallagher, P. D., Hunt, R. A., & Williges, R. C. (1977). A regression approach to generate aircraft predictive information. *Human Factors, 19,* 549–566.

Gibbs, C. B. (1962). Controller design: Interactions of controlling limbs, time-lags, and gains in positional and velocity systems. *Ergonomics, 5,* 385–402.

Gottsdanker, R. M. (1952). Prediction-motion with and without vision. *American Journal of Psychology, 65,* 533–543.

Grunwald A. J. (1985, September/October). Predictor laws for pictorial flight displays. *Journal of Guidance, Control, and Dynamics, 8*(5).

Grunwald, A. J., Robertson, J. B., & Hatfield, J. J. (1981). Experimental evaluation of a perspective tunnel display for three-dimensional helicopter approaches. *Journal of Guidance and Control, 4*(6), 623–631.

Haskell, I. D., & Wickens, C. D. (1993). Two-and three-dimensional displays for aviation: A theoretical and empirical comparison. *International Journal of Aviation Psychology, 3*(2), 87–109.

Hess, R. A. (1973). Nonadjectival rating scales in human response experiments. *Human Factors, 15,* 275–280.

Hess, R. A. (1977). Prediction of pilot opinion ratings using an optimal pilot model. *Human Factors, 19,* 459–475.

Hess, R. A. (1979). A rationale for human operator pulsive control behavior. *Journal of Guidance and Control, 2,* 221–227.

Hess, R. A. (1981). An analytical approach to predicting pilot-induced oscillations. *Proceedings of the 17th Annual Conference on Manual Control.* Pasadena, CA: Jet Propulsion Laboratory.

Hess, R. A. (1997). Feedback control models–Manual control and tracking. In G. Salvendy (2d ed.), *Handbook of human factors and ergonomics* (pp. 1249–1294). New York: Wiley, Inc.

Isreal, J. (1980). Structural interference in dual task performance: Behavioral and electrophysiological data. Unpublished Ph.D. dissertation, University of Illinois, Champaign.

Jagacinski, R. J. (1977). A qualitative look at feedback control theory as a style of describing behavior. *Human Factors, 19,* 331–347.

Jagacinski, R. J. (1989). Target acquisition: Performance measures, process models, and design implications. In G. R. McMillan, D. Beevis, E. Salas, M. H. Strub, R. Sutton, & L. Van Breda (Eds.), *Applications of human performance models to system design* (pp. 135–150). New York: Plenum.

Jagacinski, R. J., & Miller, D. (1978). Describing the human operator's internal model of a dynamic system. *Human Factors, 20*, 425–434.

Jagacinski, R. J., Repperger, D. W., Ward, S. L., & Moran, M. S. (1980). A test of Fitts's law with moving targets. *Human Factors, 22*, 225–233.

Jex, H. R., McDonnel, J. P., & Phatak, A. V. (1966). A "critical" tracking task for manual control research. *IEEE Transactions on Human Factors in Electronics, HFE–7*, 138–144.

Kahneman, D., & Treisman, A. (1984). Changing views of attention and automaticity. In R. Parasuraman & R. Davies (Eds.), *Varieties of attention.* (pp. 29–61). New York: Academic Press.

Keele, S. W. (1968). Movement control in skilled motor performance. *Psychological Bulletin, 70*, 387–403.

Kelley, C. R. (1968). *Manual and automatic control.* New York: Wiley,

Kelso, J. A., Southard, D. L., & Goodman, D. (1979). On the coordination of two-handed movements. *Journal of Experimental Psychology: Human Perception and Performance, 5*, 229–259.

Kim, W. S., Ellis, S. R., Tyler, M., Hannaford, B., & Stark, L. (1987). A quantitative evaluation of perspective and stereoscopic displays in three-axis manual tracking tasks. *IEEE Transactions on Systems, Man, and Cybernetics, SMC–17*, 61–71.

Klapp, S. T., & Erwin, C. I. (1976). Relation between programming time and duration of response being programmed. *Journal of Experimental Psychology: Human Perception and Performance, 2*, 591–598.

Kleinman, D. L., Baron, S., & Levison, W. H. (1971). A control theoretic approach to manned-vehicle systems analysis. *IEEE Transactions in Automatic Control, AC–16*, 824–832.

Krendel, E. S., & McRuer, D. T. (1968). Psychological and physiological skill development. *Proceedings of the 4th Annual NASA Conference on Manual Control* (NASA SP–182). Washington, DC: U.S. Government Printing Office.

Langolf, C. D., Chaffin, D. B., & Foulke, S. A. (1976). An investigation of Fitts' law using a wide range of movement amplitudes. *Journal of Motor Behavior, 8*, 113–128.

Levison, W. H. (1989). The optimal control model for manually controlled systems. In G. R. McMillan, D. Beevis, E. Salas, M. H. Strub, R. Sutton, & L. Van Breda (Eds.), *Application of human performance models to systems design* (pp. 185–198). New York: Plenum.

Levison, W. H., Baron, S., & Kleinman, D. L. (1969). A model for human controller remnant. *IEEE Transactions in Man-Machine Systems, MMS-IO*, 101–108.

Levison, W. H., Elkind, J. I., & Ward, J. L. (1971, May). *Studies of multivariable manual control systems: A model for task interference* (NASA CR–1746). Washington, DC: NASA.

Licklider, J. C.R. (1960). Quasi-linear operator models in the study of manual tracking. In R. D. Luce (Ed.), *Mathematical psychology.* Glencoe, IL: Free Press.

Lintern, G., Roscoe, S. N., & Sivier, J. L. (1990). Display principles, control dynamics, and environmental factors in pilot training and transfer. *Human Factors, 32*, 299–318.

Macedo, J. E., Kaber, D. E., Endsley, M. R., Powanusorn, P., & Myurg, S. (1998). The effects of automated compensation for incongruent axes on teleoperator performance. *Human Factors, 40*, 541–553.

MacNielage, P. F. (1970). Motor control of serial ordering of speech. *Psychological Review, 77*, 182–196.

Martenuik, R. G., & MacKenzie, C. L. (1980). Information processing in movement organization and execution. In R. S. Nickerson (Ed.), *Attention and performance VIII.* Hillsdale, NJ: Erlbaum.

McRuer, D. T. (1980). Human dynamics in man-machine systems. *Automatica, 16,* 237–253.

McRuer, D. T., Hoffmann, L. G., Jex, H. R., Moore, G. P., Phatak, A. V., Weir, D. H., & Wolkovitch, J. (1968). *New approaches to human-pilot/vehicle dynamic analysis* (AFFDL-TR–67–150). Dayton, OH: Wright Patterson AFB.

McRuer, D. T., & Jex, H. R. (1967). A review of quasi-linear pilot models. *IEEE Transactions on Human Factors in Electronics, 8,* 231.

McRuer, D. T., & Krendel, E. S. (1959). The human operator as a servo system element. *Journal of the Franklin Institute, 267,* 381–403, 511–536.

Moray, N. (1997). Human factors in process control. In G. Salvendy (Ed.), *Handbook of human factors and ergonomics* (2d ed.). New York: Wiley, Inc.

Morphew, E. & Wickens, C. D., (1998). Pilot performance and workload using traffic displays to support free flight. *Proceedings 42nd annual meeting of the Human Factors and Ergonomics Society.* Santa Monica, CA: Human Factors.

Nelson, W. T., Hettinger, L. J., Cunningham, J. A., Brickman, B. J., Haas, M. W., & McKinley, R. L. (1998). Effects of localized auditory information on visual target detection performance using a helmet-mounted display. *Human Factors, 40*(3), 452–460.

O'Hara, J. O. (1987). Telorobotic control of a dexterous manipulator using master and six DOF hand controllers. *Proceedings of the 31st annual meeting of the Human Factors Society.* Santa Monica, CA: Human Factors.

Pew, R. W. (1974). Human perceptual-motor performance. In B. Kantowitz (Ed.), *Human information processing.* Hillsdale, NJ: Erlbaum.

Pew, R. W., & Baron, S. (1978). The components of an information processing theory of skilled performance based on an optimal control perspective. In G. E. Stelmach (Ed.), *Information processing in motor control and learning.* New York: Academic Press.

Pew, R. W., Duffenback, J. C., & Fensch, L. K.(1967). Sine-wave tracking revisited. *IEEE Transactions on Human Factors in Electronics, HFE–8,* 130–134.

Poulton, E. C. (1974). *Tracking skills and manual control.* New York: Academic Press.

Reid, D., & Drewell, N. (1972). A pilot model for tracking with preview. *Proceedings of the 8th Annual Conference on Manual Control* (Wright Patterson AFB, Ohio Flight Dynamics Laboratory Technical Report AFFDL-TR–72, 92). Washington, DC: U.S. Government Printing Office.

Rice, J. R., Yorchak, J. P., & Hartely, C. S. (1986). Capture of satellites having rotational motion. *Proceedings of the 30th annual meeting of the Human Factors Society.* Santa Monica, CA: Human Factors.

Roscoe, S. N. (1968). Airborne displays for flight and navigation. *Human Factors, 10,* 321–322.

Roscoe, S. N., Corl, L., & Jensen, R. S. (1981). Flight display dynamics revisited. *Human Factors, 23,* 341–353.

Runeson, D. (1975). Visual predictions of collisions with natural and nonnatural motion functions. *Perception & Psychophysics, 18,* 261–266.

Scerbo, M. (1999). The R.M.S. Titanic: A siren of technology. In M. W. Scerbo and M. Mouloun (Eds.), *Automation technology and human performance.* Mahway, NJ: Lawrence Erlbaum.

Schmidt, R. A. (1975). A schema theory of discrete motor skill learning. *Psychological Review, 82,* 225–260.

Schmidt, R. A. (1988). *Motor control and learning: A behavioral emphasis* (2d ed.). Champaign, IL: Human Kinetics.

Shapiro, D. C., & Schmidt, R. A. (1982). The schema theory: Recent evidence and development of implications. In J. A. S. Kelso & J. E. Clark (Eds.), *The development of movement control and coordination*. Norwich, Eng.: Wiley.

Sheridan, T. (1997). Supervising control. In G. Salvendy (Ed.), *Handbook of human factors and ergonomics* (2d ed.). New York: Wiley.

Shulman, H. G., Jagacinski, R. J., & Burke, M. W. (1978). *The time course of motor preparation*. Paper presented at the 19th annual meeting of the Psychonomics Society, San Antonio, TX.

Simon, J. R. (1969). Reactions toward the source of stimulation. *Journal of Experimental Psychology, 81*, 174–176.

Summers, J. J. (1989). Motor programs. In D. H. Holding (Ed.), *Human skills* (2d ed.) New York: Wiley.

Toats, F. (1975). *Control theory in biology and experimental psychology*. London: Hutchinson Education.

Vinge, E. (1971). Human operator for aural compensatory tracking. *Proceedings of the 7th Annual Conference on Manual Control* (NASA SP–281). Washington, DC: U.S. Government Printing Office.

Weinstein, L. F., & Wickens, C. D. (1992). Use of nontraditional flight displays for the reduction of central visual overload in the cockpit. *International Journal of Aviation Psychology, 2*, 121–142.

Wewerinke, P. H. (1989). *Models of the human observer and controller of a dynamic system*. Twerte, Neth.: University of Twente.

Wickens, C. D. (1976). The effects of divided attention on information processing in tracking. *Journal of Experimental Psychology: Human Perception and Performance, 2*, 1–13.

Wickens, C. D. (1986). The effects of control dynamics on performance. In K. Boff, L. Kaufman, & J. Thomas (Eds.), *Handbook of perception and performance* (vol. II, pp. 39–1–39–60). New York: Wiley.

Wickens, C. D. (1999). Frames of reference for navigation. In D. Gopher & A. Koriat (Eds.), *Attention and performance, Vol. 16* (pp. 113–144). Orlando, FL: Academic Press.

Wickens, C. D., & Carswell, C. M. (1995). The proximity compatibility principle: Its psychological foundation and relevance to display design. *Human Factors, 37*(3), 473–494.

Wickens, C. D., Gempler, K., & Conejo, R. (1999). Unreliable automated attention cueing for air-ground targeting and traffic maneuvering. *Proceedings 43rd annual conference of the HumanFactors and Ergonomics Society*. Santa Monica, CA: Human Factors.

Wickens, C. D., & Goettl, B. (1985). The effect of strategy on the resource demands of second order manual control. In R. Eberts & C. Eberts (Eds.), *Trends in ergonomics and human factors*. North Holland, Neth.: North Holland.

Wickens, C. D., & Gopher, D. (1977). Control theory measures of tracking as indices of attention allocation strategies. *Human Factors, 19*, 349–365.

Wickens, C.D., Gordon, S., & Liu, Y. (1998). *An introduction to human factors engineering*. New York: Addison Wesley Longman.

Wickens, C. D., Haskell, I., & Harte, K. (1989). Ergonomic design for perspective flight-path displays. *IEEE Control Systems Magazine, 9*(4), 3–8.

Wickens, C. D., Sandry, D., & Vidulich, M. (1983). Compatibility and resource competition between modalities of input, output, and central processing. *Human Factors, 25*, 227–248.

switch soon enough from head-down diagnostics to head-up lane monitoring. Some literature in aviation psychology reveals the failures in task management and timely switching to high-priority tasks (Schutte & Trujillo, 1996), sometimes in ways that can lead to aircraft incidents and accidents (Chou, Madhavan, & Funk, 1996).

2. The concept of switching attention suggests a "movement metaphor" such that it should take longer to shift attention between more distant tasks than more proximate ones. This is, of course, true when attention is shifted between widely spaced visual sources (greater scanning distance imposes greater time requirements), but it does not necessarily apply for "cognitive distance" (i.e., switching between dissimilar tasks is not necessarily longer than switching between more related ones). In fact, a high degree of relatedness or similarity between old (pre-switch) and new (post-switch) activity may actually lead to interference as the new activity is undertaken.

3. Different physical or salient sensory annunciators or reminders to perform a task will be more likely to trigger a switch to that task than will less salient properties, or purely memorial representations (Wickens & Seidler, 1997). For example, when the physical nature of a stimulus uniquely defines the nature of the cognitive processing required of that stimulus, switching to that task is more rapid than if the stimulus signals ambiguously (Allport, Styles, & Hsieh, 1994).

4. In contrast to computer optimization models, people do not tend to maintain elaborate and highly optimal planning strategies for task management (Liao & Moray, 1993; Laudeman & Palmer, 1995; Raby & Wickens, 1994), such as carefully calculating the appropriate optimal sequence in which to perform tasks of differing priority. This simplification apparently results because applying such strategies themselves are a source of high cognitive workload or resource demand (Tulga & Sheridan, 1980) and, hence, would be self-defeating at the very time they might be most necessary.

5. As a correlate of item 4, people tend to be more proactive in task management when workload is modest (i.e., establishing various contingency plans for future uncertain events), and more reactive when workload becomes high (Hart & Wickens, 1990).

6. There is a good possibility that well-designed automation can provide support for people's task management skills, by monitoring their performance and providing reminders if high priority tasks are "dropped" (Funk & McCoy, 1996; Wiener & Curry, 1980; Hammer, 1999).

Summary   It is important to place the first two characteristics accounting for variance in time-sharing efficiency in contrast. The characteristics of automaticity and resource demand were properties of a *single task*, just as relevant to single- as to dual-task performance. They could be delivered either by characteristics (difficulty) of the task itself or by the skill level (practice) of the operator. In contrast, resource allocation is and must be an *emergent property* of the combining of two or more tasks (or channels). One cannot speak of allocating resources or switching between a single task. Furthermore, while the first characteristic, resource demand, may sometimes be related to the skill level of the operator, but often is an intrinsic property of the task, it appears that the second characteristic, resource allocation policy, is nearly totally related to operator skills. This distinction is important for training. As we discussed in Chapter 7, limited training time can be devoted to single-task components (part-task training) *or* dual-task skills (whole-task training). Only automaticity will develop in the former condition, but both automaticity *and* resource allocation skills may have the opportunity to develop in the latter, if care is taken to follow good training guidelines. Hence, whole-task training tends to be more effective than fractionized part-task training.

Up to now, we have not distinguished our discussion of resource allocation between a graded allocation (e.g., providing 80 percent of one's resource to task *A* and 20 percent to *B*) and a discrete or attention switching allocation (e.g., switching attention exclusively to task or channel *B* for two seconds out of every 10, and remaining focused exclusively on *A* for the remaining time). With respect to the importance of training, these two mechanisms (graded or discrete) are probably equivalent. Furthermore, if the time base of switching becomes sufficiently fine (e.g., switching 2–3 times/second), then the two are probably functionally equivalent insofar as prediction of performance is concerned. However, it is important to recognize that certain *structural constraints* limit the ability of the operator to engage in concurrent processing and, therefore, are more likely to force a sequential switching policy. The most obvious of these constraints is the access to foveal vision, and it is for this reason that the visual scanning measure represents such a nice index of attention allocation policy, as discussed in Chapter 3. It appears however that other structural properties in the body or brain physiology also modulate the ease of concurrent processing, and these are discussed in the following section.

Structural Factors in Time-Sharing Efficiently

In the previous two sections, we portrayed a model of resource demand and allocation that implicitly suggested that these resources were fairly well *undifferentiated*—that it did not matter much whether tasks were visual, auditory, spatial, or linguistic, perceptual, action-oriented. The key feature in predicting time-sharing interference was the demand for resources and the allocation policy. Yet some obvious observations inform us that other factors are at play in dictating time-sharing efficiency. As one obvious example, it is harder (and thus more dangerous) to read a book while driving than to listen to the same book on tape. The time-sharing efficiency of the two activities is drastically changed by using visual rather than auditory input channels for language processing. In this section, we consider two somewhat different but complimentary approaches to these structural effects on resource allocation: bottleneck theory and multiple resource theory.

Bottleneck Theory　An understanding of the structural constraints on time sharing has emerged from the work that has been carried out in the dual stimulation or psychological refractory period paradigm discussed in Chapter 9 (Welford, 1952, 1967; Pashler, 1998; Kantowitz, 1974). Here, time sharing is challenged to its utmost as people are asked to perform two reaction-time tasks at the same time. As discussed in Chapter 9, the challenge for perfect time-sharing is essentially impossible to meet, and one RT task or the other (usually RT to the second stimulus arriving) suffers a decrement. Sometimes both RTs will be prolonged beyond their single-task baseline.

Through careful manipulation of perceptual and response demands, and the timing of the various stimulus arrivals, Pashler (1998) carefully modeled the process to confirm earlier data that the primary bottleneck in this process is at the stage of response selection (Pashler refers to this as "central processing"). That is, two independent responses, based on unpredictable stimulus input, cannot be selected at the same time; one or the other must be postponed. In contrast, however, his analysis reveals that selection of the response for one stimulus can proceed concurrently with perceptual processing of the other stimulus (Pashler, 1989) or with the execution (but not selection) of the other response. Thus, the bottleneck model suggests that the resource available for response selection must be allocated in an all or none fashion to one task or the other.

While concurrent response selection for two tasks is prohibited according to bottleneck theory, there is also ample evidence, some of it discussed in Chapter 3, that concurrent perceptual activity for two tasks can also compete. This, of course, meets with our intuition even when the structured constraints of foveal vision are not encountered: Reading and listening—two perceptual activities—cannot be perfectly time shared. Thus a more elaborated model of resources within the information processing system, shown in Figure 11.4, suggests that the resources available for perception are limited (and must sometimes be shared between channels), just as are the resources available for response selection (although Pashler's model suggests that the latter might be even more limited and allocated on an all or none basis, rather than a graded one). But the use of separate—limited—resources for the two processes, perception and response, should avail more efficient concurrent processing when both are required, compared to the use of a single resource for two activities.

Multiple Resources The distinction, shown in Figure 11.4. between resources underlying perception (and working memory) and those underlying the selection of actions turns out to be only one of at least three important structural dichotomies within the human brain that can help to account for variations in time-sharing efficiency. These variations can be modeled in terms of the differences in resources supplying the two sides of the three dichotomies that are represented as a cube in Figure 11.5. In addition to the

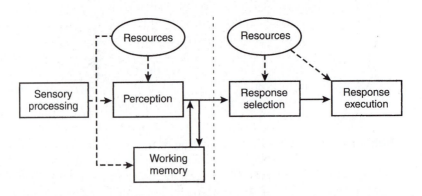

Figure 11.4 The distinction between resources underlying perception and resources underlying the selection of actions.

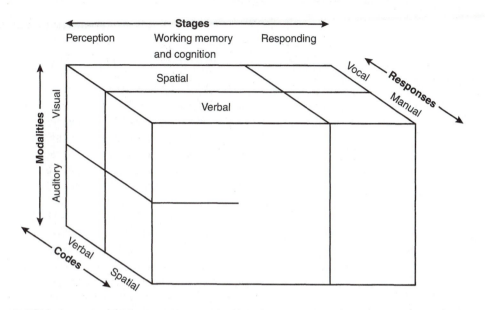

Figure 11.5 The proposed structure of processing resources. Operations on either side of a solid line use different resources.

Source: From C. D. Wickens, "Processing Resources in Attention," in *Varieties of Attention,* ed. R. Parasuraman and R. Davies (New York: Academic Press, 1984). Reproduced by permission.

stages dichotomy shown in Figure 11.4, there is evidence for differences due to auditory and visual perceptual modalities, and to spatial (analog) and verbal (linguistic) processing. Collectively, all three dimensions have been incorporated into the multiple resource model shown in Figure 11.5, which is an elaboration by Wickens (1980, 1984, 1991) of the more general concept of multiple processing resources proposed by Kantowitz and Knight (1976) and Navon and Gopher (1979). The cubelike graphical depiction in Figure 11.5 is meant to suggest that the three dimensions are somewhat independent of each other, that the vertical modality dichotomy between auditory and visual resources can only be defined for perception, but that the code distinction between verbal and spatial processes is relevant to all stages of processing. The left-right placement of the code dichotomy is intentional, suggesting that the dichotomy is often (although not invariably) associated with the left (verbal) and right (spatial) cerebral hemisphere. Finally, the stage of processing dimension is represented with only two resources rather than three, suggesting, as shown also in Figure 11.4, that perceptual and cognitive (i.e., working memory) processes demand the same resources, different from those involved in action selection and execution. As noted in Chapter 7, sensory store is relatively resource-free. In the following, we discuss evidence for each dimension in turn (in terms of evidence for better time-sharing between two levels of the dichotomy than within levels).

Stages   The resources used for perceptual and working memory or cognitive activities appear to be the same, and they are functionally separate from those underlying the selection and execution of responses. Evidence for this dichotomy is provided when the difficulty of responding in a task is varied and this manipulation does not affect performance of a concurrent task whose demands are more perceptual in nature. We have noted already how this view is consistent with bottleneck theory, and the research of Pashler and his colleagues (Pashler, 1998) has elegantly demonstrated the relative independence of perceptual demand and response selection processes in concurrent RT tasks. The stage dichotomy can be further supported by physiological evidence. In a series of experiments by Isreal, Chesney, Wickens and Donchin (1980) and Isreal, Wickens, Chesney, and Donchin (1980), the amplitude of the P300 component of an event-related brain potential (see Chapter 9) elicited by a series of counted tones is assumed to reflect the investment of perceptual and cognitive processing resources, since the P300 can be elicited without requiring any overt responses. The experiments revealed that the P300 is not sensitive to response-related manipulations of tracking difficulty but is influenced by manipulations of display load. Shallice, McLeod, and Lewis (1985) examined dual-task performance on a series of tasks involving speech recognition (perception) and production (response) and concluded that the resources underlying these two processes are separate. It is also important to note as well that the stage dichotomy can be associated with different brain structures. That is, speech and motor activity tend to be controlled by frontal regions in the brain (forward of the central sulcus), while perceptual and language comprehension activity tends to be posterior of the central sulcus.

As an operational example of separate stage-defined resources, we would predict that the added requirement for an air traffic controller to acknowledge vocally or manually each change in aircraft state (a response demand) would not alter his or her ability to maintain an accurate mental model of the airspace (a perceptual-cognitive demand).

Perceptual Modalities   It is apparent that we can sometimes divide attention between the eye and ear better than between two auditory channels or two visual channels. That is, cross-modal time-sharing is better than intramodal. Wickens, Sandry, and Vidulich (1983) found advantages to cross-modal over intramodal displays in both a laboratory tracking experiment and a fairly complex flight simulation. Parkes and Coleman (1990) found that discrete route guidance was better presented auditorily than visually while subjects were concurrently driving a simulated vehicle (visual input). Wickens (1980) reviews several other studies that report similar advantages.

However, the relative advantage of cross-modal (auditory-visual or AV) over intramodal (VV and AA) time-sharing may not really be the result of separate perceptual resources within the brain but rather the result of the peripheral factors that place the two intramodal conditions at a disadvantage, as we discussed above. Thus, two competing visual channels, if they are far enough apart, will require visual scanning between them—an added cost, discussed in Chapter 3. If too close together, they may impose confusion and masking, just as two auditory messages may mask one another. The degree to which peripheral rather than central factors are responsible for the examples of better cross-modal time-sharing remains uncertain, and when visual scanning is carefully controlled, cross-modal displays do not always produce better time-sharing (Wickens & Liu, 1988). However, in most real-world settings, visual scanning is enough of a factor that dual-task interference can be reduced by off-loading some information channels from the visual to the auditory modality. Simultaneous auditory messages are difficult enough to process that an advantage can usually be gained by displaying one of them visually (Rollins & Hendricks, 1980).

Focal-Ambient Vision   In addition to the distinction between auditory and visual modalities of processing, there is good evidence that two aspects of visual processing, referred to as *focal* and *ambient* vision, appear to define separate resources in the sense of (a) supporting efficient time-sharing, (b) being characterized by qualitatively different brain structures, and (c) being associated with qualitatively different types of information processing (Leibowitz & Post, 1982; Weinstein & Wickens, 1992). Focal vision, which is nearly always *foveal,* is required for fine detail and pattern recognition. In contrast, ambient vision heavily (but not exclusively) involves peripheral vision and is used for sensing orientation and ego motion (see Chapter 4). When we successfully walk down a corridor while reading a book, we are effectively exploiting the parallel processing capabilities of focal and ambient vision, just as we are when keeping the car moving forward in the center of the lane (ambient vision) while reading a road sign (focal vision). The former heavily uses peripheral vision. Aircraft designers have considered several ways of exploiting ambient vision to provide guidance and alerting information to pilots while their focal vision is heavily loaded by perceiving specific channels of displayed instrument information (Stokes, Wickens, & Kite, 1990).

Although the focal-ambient distinction is not explicitly represented as a separate dimension within the multiple resource model in Figure 11.5, it may conveniently be represented within the processing *codes* dimension, which we discuss next.

Processing Codes   The role that the spatial and verbal codes play in defining separate processing resources has been discussed in some detail in previous sections and chapters: ambient (exclusively spatial) and focal (often verbal or symbolic) vision in the previous section, spatial and verbal perceptual processes in Chapters 4, 5, and 6, the degree of interference within and between spatial and verbal working memory in Chapter 7, and the compatibility of these two codes with information display in Chapter 9. Data from multiple-task studies indicate that spatial and verbal processes, or *codes,* whether functioning in perception, working memory, or response, depend on separate resources and that this separation can often be associated with the two cerebral hemispheres (Polson & Friedman, 1988).

The separation of spatial and verbal resources seemingly accounts for the high degree of efficiency with which manual and vocal outputs can be time-shared, assuming that manual responses are usually spatial in nature and vocal ones are verbal. In this regard, investigations by Martin (1989); McLeod (1977); Tsang and Wickens (1988); Vidulich (1988); Wickens (1980); Wickens and Liu (1988); and Wickens, Sandry, and Vidulich (1983) have shown that tracking and a discrete verbal task are time-shared more efficiently when the latter employs vocal as opposed to manual response mechanisms. Discrete manual responses using the nontracking hand appear to interrupt the continuous flow of the tracking response, whereas discrete vocal responses leave this flow untouched (Wickens & Liu, 1988).

Finally, consider the near perfect time-sharing efficiency with which auditory shadowing (see Chapter 3) and visual-manual transcription tasks (typing from text and sight-reading piano music, see Chapter 6) can be carried out by skilled operators, as demonstrated by Shaffer (1975) and by Allport, Antonis, and Reynolds (1972), respectively. This success is clearly due in large part to the separation of codes and modalities of processing of the two tasks. If the auditory shadowing and piano sight-reading task pair investigated by Allport, Antonis, and Reynolds is examined within the framework of Figure 11.5, we see that auditory shadowing is clearly auditory, verbal, and vocal. Piano sight-reading is visual and manual. If the further assumption is made that music involves right-hemispheric processing (Nebes, 1977), the two tasks may be considered to require predominately separate resources.

An important practical implication of the processing codes distinction is the ability to predict when it might or might not be advantageous to employ voice versus manual control. As noted by Brooks (1968) and confirmed in a more applied context by Wickens and Liu (1988), manual control may disrupt performance in a task environment imposing heavy demands on spatial working memory (e.g., driving), whereas voice control may disrupt performance of tasks with heavy verbal demands (or be disrupted by those tasks, depending on resource allocation policy). Thus, for example, the model predicts the potential dangers of manual dialing of cellular phones, given the visual, spatial, and manual demands of vehicle driving, and it suggests the considerable benefits to be gained from voice dialing (Goodman, Tijerna, Bents, & Wierwille, 1999).

When considering different resource modalities, it is important to recall that verbal tasks may be most *compatibly* responded to with voice control, and spatial tasks with manual control, as discussed in Chapter 9. Occasionally, then, the choice between control types may be dictated by a consideration of trade-offs between compatibility and resource competition, addressed explicitly by Wickens, Vidulich, and Sandry-Garza (1984; Wickens, Sandry, & Vidulich, 1983). Research generally indicates, however, that resource conflict, rather than compatibility, is the more dominant of the two forces in dual-task situations (Goettl & Wickens, 1989).

Application   In applying the multiple resource model to understanding multiple-task interference, there are a few key points to keep in mind. First, the model predicts that the amount of interference will depend on the number of shared levels on all three dimensions. Thus, the mold does *not* imply that two tasks using separate levels on any one dimension (e.g., an auditory and visual task) will foster perfect time-sharing. Indeed, in this case both the auditory and visual task *must* involve some perceptual processing, which will be a source of resource competition, and therefore potential interference, unless one or both tasks are automated.

Second, the model is complimentary to, rather than competitive with, the single-resource demand mechanism described earlier in the chapter, and indeed, many task-interference situations can be easily understood by assuming a single-resource model (Liao & Moray, 1993). This is true whenever conditions or designs being compared do not differ in the qualitative makeup of their resource structure. Within a multiple-resource perspective, the degree of demand (task difficulty) within a resource will modulate the amount of competition with other tasks demanding the same resource, and this demand level could dominate the benefits of resource separation. Suppose, for example, we compare two different modality interfaces for displaying instructions to an automobile driver. The auditory display will create low perceptual interference with the visual demands of driving; but if that display is coupled with a greater working-memory load, for example, to remember the implications of the instructions, this greater resource demand could overwhelm the benefits for the separate perceptual modalities. The precise mechanisms by which demand and resource differences are coupled to predict dual-task interference are beyond the scope of the current chapter but may be found in Navon and Gopher (1979) and Wickens (1991, 1992; Sarno & Wickens, 1995).

Confusion and Similarity

A hallmark of the mechanisms we have demonstrated so far is that they are associated with resource demand and strategic allocation, and with three relatively gross and anatomically defined dichotomies within the brain. Yet there appear to be several other sources of variance in time-sharing efficiency that cannot be described by the above mechanisms but, instead, are related to more continuous characteristics of the nature of the information processing activities, similar to the role of proximity discussed in Chapter 3. In this role, processing proximity is like a two-edged sword, having its benefits (to cooperation) as well as its costs (to confusion).

Cooperation   The improvement of time-sharing efficiency by increasing similarity results from circumstances in which a common display property, mental set, processing routine, or timing mechanism can be cooperatively shared in the service of two tasks that are performed concurrently. We have noted in Chapter 3 how the close proximity fostered by a single object can improve parallel perceptual processing. Such object-based proximity, as well as other attributes of similarity between two display sources, has been found to improve performance of concurrent tracking tasks (Fracker & Wickens, 1989), such as the lateral and vertical dimensions of aircraft control (Haskell & Wickens, 1993). Levy, Foyle, and McCann (1998) found that the proximity of representation of tracking axes in three-dimensional space improved time-sharing between control of the flight axes.

With regard to central processing operations, there is some evidence that the performance of two tracking tasks is better if the dynamics on both axes are the same than if they are different, even if like dynamics are produced by combining two more difficult tasks (Chernikoff, Duey, & Taylor, 1960) (see Chapter 10). Even when the performance of two identical but difficult tasks is not actually better than the performance of a difficult-easy pair, performance of the difficult pair is less degraded than would be predicted by a pure resource model (Braune & Wickens, 1986; Fracker & Wickens, 1989). That is, there is an advantage for the identity of two difficult dynamics, which compensates for the cost of their difficulty.

A similar phenomenon has been observed in the domain of choice reaction time by Duncan (1979). He observed better time-sharing performance between two incompatibly mapped RT tasks than between a compatible and an incompatible one, in spite of the fact that the average difficulty of the incompatible pair was greater. Here again, the common rules of mapping helped performance. A series of investigations point to the superior time-sharing performance of two rhythmic activities when the rhythms are the same rather than different (Klapp, 1979, 1981; Peters, 1981), and investigators have noted that when a manual and vocal response are simultaneously mapped to a single stimulus (i.e., in a coordinated redundant fashion), then the bottleneck normally associated with simultaneous response selection is eliminated (Fagot & Pashler, 1992; Schvaneveldt, 1969).

These examples illustrate that similarity in information-processing routines leads to cooperation and facilitation of task performance, whereas differences lead to interference, confusion, and conflict, an issue we address in more detail shortly. Other aspects of identity and cooperation are also reflected in a kind of resonance or compatibility *between* similarity at one stage of processing and similarity at another. This resonance is described by the proximity compatibility principle (Wickens & Carswell, 1995), discussed in the context of object displays in Chapter 3, graphs in Chapter 4, and multiaxis tracking in Chapter 10. Thus, for example, Fracker and Wickens (1989) and Chernikoff and Lemay (1963) found that two tracking tasks benefited from an integrated display if they shared similar dynamics, but not if the dynamics were different.

Confusion   We have discussed ways in which increasing similarity of processing *routines* can bring about improved dual-task performance. A contradictory trend, in which the increasing similarity of processing *material* may reduce rather than increase time-sharing efficiency, is a result of *confusion*. For example, Hirst and Kalmar (1987) found that time-sharing between a spelling and mental arithmetic task is easier than time-sharing between two spelling or two mental arithmetic tasks. Hirst (1986) showed how distinctive acoustic features of two dichotic messages, by avoiding confusion, can improve the operator's ability to deal with each separately. Many of these confusion effects may be closely related to interference effects in memory, discussed in Chapter 7. Indeed, Venturino (1991) showed similar effects when tasks are performed successively, so that the memory trace of one interferes with the processing of the other.

Although these findings are similar in one sense to the concepts underlying multiple-resources theory (greater similarity producing greater interference), it is probably not appropriate to label these elements as "resources" in the same sense as the stages, codes, and modalities of Figure 11.5, since such items as a spelling routine or distinctive acoustic features hardly share the gross anatomically based dichotomous characteristics of the dimensions of the multiple-resources model (Wickens 1986, 1991). Instead, it appears that interference of this sort is more likely based on confusion, or a mechanism that Navon (1984; Navon & Miller, 1987) labeled *outcome conflict*. Responses (or processes) relevant for one task are activated by stimuli or cognitive activity for a different task, producing confusion or crosstalk between the two. The most notorious example of this phenomenon is in the Stroop task, discussed in Chapter 3, in which the semantic characteristics of a color word *(white or blue)* interfere with the subjects' ability to report the color of ink in which the word is printed. The necessary condition for confusion and crosstalk to occur is similarity. In the Stroop task, there is similarity both in the common location of the two stimulus properties and in their common reference to color. As a result, Stroop interference may be lessened either by reducing the physical similarity (increased distance) between the two attributes or by increasing the "semantic distance" between the color and semantic properties of the word (Klein, 1964). Thus, in manipulating physical distance, Stroop interference is reduced when the color word is placed next to a color patch rather than printed in the color ink (Kahneman & Chajczyk, 1983).

In semantic distance, color-related words like *sky* or *grass* produce some but reduced Stroop interference, whereas color-neutral words like *but* or *office* produce very little interference at all.

However, the Stroop task is a focused, not a divided-attention, task. Are confusion and crosstalk also mechanisms that cause dual-task interference? Experiments by Fracker and Wickens (1989) and by Navon and Miller (1987) suggest that they have at least some role. Navon and Miller studied subjects' abilities to categorize simultaneously words in two visually displayed word sequences. They found that items on one sequence that were similar to those on the other slowed down the response to the other, as if producing an outcome conflict. Fracker and Wickens asked subjects to perform two tracking tasks at the same time. By looking at the time-series analysis between input and output signals of the two tasks, they could measure the degree of crosstalk, in which the error of one task was compensated for by an unwanted control response of the hand controlling the other task. Generally this crosstalk was small, but when the displays and controls of the two axes were made more similar by integrating them, the crosstalk increased. However, this increase was not the source of increased tracking error, nor was there an increase in crosstalk when the resource demands of one of the tasks was increased, producing greater interference.

In summary, although confusion due to similarity certainly contributes to task interference in some circumstances, it is not always present nor always an important source of task interference (Pashler, 1998; Fracker & Wickens, 1989). Its greatest impact probably occurs when an operator must deal with two verbal tasks requiring concurrently working memory for one and active processing (comprehension, rehearsal, or speech) for the other, or with two manual tasks with spatially incompatible motions. In the former case, as discussed in Chapter 7, similarity-based confusions in working memory probably play an important role.

PRACTICAL IMPLICATIONS

The practical implications of research and theory on attention and time-sharing are as numerous as the cases in which a human operator is called on to perform two activities concurrently, and his or her limitations in doing so represent a bottleneck in performance. These instances include the pilot of the high-performance aircraft who may have a variety of component tasks simultaneously imposed; the process control or nuclear power plant monitor who is trying to diagnose a fault and is simultaneously deciding, remembering, and scanning to acquire new information; the musical performer who is attending to notes, rhythm, accompanist, and the quality of his or her own performance; the learner of any skill who must concurrently perceive different stimuli associated with a task, make responses, and process feedback; or the vehicle driver who must drive safely while operating a navigational device or cellular phone. The safety implications of breakdowns in multiple-task performance are graphically revealed in the analysis of cellular phone use while driving by Violanti and Marshall (1996), who report accident rates five times those of driving without cellular phone use (see also Goodman, et al., 1999).

As with any domain of human performance, there are three broad categories of applications of attention theory: to system and task design, to operator training, and to operator selection. The applications to the last two areas will be described only briefly. When operators must be trained for time-sharing in complex environments, such as the aircraft cockpit, as we noted earlier in this chapter, attention must be given both to the development of automaticity and to the training of time-sharing skills, issues that are discussed in considerable detail by Damos and Wickens (1980), Gopher (1991), Rogers, Rousseau and Fisk (1999), Schneider (1985), and Schneider and Detweiler (1988). Considerably more is known about training for automaticity than about the training of time-sharing skills (Gopher, 1991; Gopher, Weil, & Bareket, 1994). If operators are to be *selected* for task environments in which they will be required to engage in time-sharing activity, at issue is the extent to which tests can be derived that will predict success in time-sharing.

The third applications category, which will concern us most, is that of predicting multiple-task performance imposed by different task environments or system design features. This issue is also closely tied to the issues of predicting and measuring the mental workload imposed by these design features, to be discussed at the end of this chapter.

Predicting Multiple-Task Performance

Using the structural and demand characteristics of models like the multiple-resources model, system designers may be concerned with either relative or absolute predictions of task interference (Hart & Wickens, 1990). *Relative predictions* allow the designer to know ahead of time which of two or more configurations will provide better multiple-task performance. (This is closely related to the issue of which configuration will provide lower workload, a distinction to be made in the next section.) If the computer user wishes to move a cursor while reading a screen, will the two activities interfere least with keyboard, voice, or mouse control (Martin, 1989)? Should automated navigational commands be presented to the automobile driver auditorily or visually (Parkes & Coleman, 1990)? Should the in-vehicle cellular phone be "dialed" with voice or hands (Goodman, Tijerina, Bents, & Wierwille, 1999)?

To these sorts of questions, multiple-resource theory can provide some answers (Sarno & Wickens, 1995). For example, the adoption of voice recognition and synthesis technology (a talking, listening computer) may not provide many advantages—and may even be worse than a visual/manual interface—if the information exchange is to be carried out in an environment in which the operator must rehearse other verbal material. As we have seen before, voice technology will offer its greatest benefits for reducing task interference if the concurrent task demands are heavily spatial, as in computer-based design (Martin, 1989), or flying (Wickens, Sandry, & Vidulich, 1983).

The role of confusion in dual-task performance is also relevant to performance prediction. Where concurrent activity may be required, designers should not impose two different tasks using similar material. For example, the entering or transcription of digital data will be disrupted if others in the surrounding environment are currently speaking digits, but less so if others are engaged in normal conversations.

An interesting application here concerns the presence of music as background or entertainment for operators engaged in various tasks. Multiple-resource theory would predict relative independence between the perception of music (more associated with spatial/analog processing) and the involvement with tasks that are manual or verbal. This prediction seems to be consistent with the results of a study by Tayyari and Smith (1987), who found no interference between "light orchestral" music listening (at up to 85 decibels) and visual-manual data entry (and in fact a slight improvement in the speed of data entry). Similarly, Martin, Wogalter, and Forlano (1988) found no interference between instrumental music and reading comprehension, but did find that comprehension suffered when lyrics were added, thus imposing a dual load on the verbal code.

Relative predictions may also be based on any quantifiable variables that are predicted to increase mental workload. Often these are "count" variables such as the number of aircraft "handed" by an air traffic controller at any one time, the arrival rate of customers to a store clerk, or the traffic density encountered by a driver on the highway. It is straightforward (but important) to say that higher levels along these "count" scales often produce lower time-sharing performance than lower levels (relative prediction). However, where possible, human factors practitioners would also like to be able to define *absolute* performance predictions along the scales defined by such variables. For example, *at what level* of traffic density is workload "excessive"? Of course, the lower ranges of such scales do not place operators in a region in which they must engage in multiple-task performance. However, maximum advisable levels often serve as warnings, in that exceeding such levels will impose time-sharing or divided attention requirements, which would be considered an "overload" condition.

The goal of *absolute predictions* of task interference and task performance calls to mind the kind of question asked by the Federal Aviation Administration before certifying new aircraft: Are the demands imposed on the pilot excessive? If *excessive* is to be defined relative to some absolute standard, such as "80 percent of maximal capacity," an absolute question is being asked. A common approach to absolute workload and performance prediction is *time-line analysis,* which will enable the system designer to "profile" the workload that operators encounter during a typical mission, such as landing an aircraft or starting up a power-generating plant (Kirwan & Ainsworth, 1992). In a simplified but readily usable version, it assumes that workload is proportional to the ratio of the time occupied performing tasks to total time available. If one is busy with some measurable task or tasks for 100 percent of a time interval, workload is 100 percent during that interval. Thus, the workload of a mission would be computed by drawing lines representing different activities, of length proportional to their duration. The total length of the lines would be summed and then divided by the total time (Parks & Boucek, 1989), as shown in Figure 11.6. In this way, the workload encountered by or predicted for different members of a team (e.g., pilot, copilot, and flight engineer) may be compared and tasks reallocated if there is a great imbalance. Furthermore, epochs of peak workload or work overload, in which load is calculated as greater than 100 percent, can be identified as potential bottlenecks.

The straightforward assumption of time as the key component for performance prediction appears adequate in many circumstances (Hendy, Liao, & Milgram, 1997), particularly with multiple visual tasks that cannot share access to foveal vision (Liao & Moray, 1993). However, when these conditions do not apply, the basic research in multiple-task performance suggests at least four directions in which the time-line analysis described in Figure 11.6 needs to be extended to accurately predict performance. First,

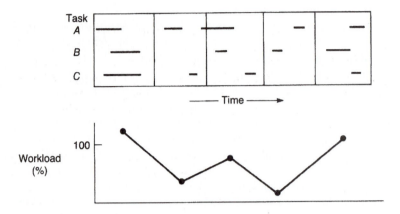

Figure 11.6 Time-line analysis. The percentage of workload at each point is computed as the average number of tasks per unit time within each time window.

it is clear that operators may not necessarily choose to time-share two tasks (as dictated by a particular time line) if they have an opportunity to reschedule (i.e., postpone) one or the other. Hence, effective time-line analysis should be coupled with models of task selection based on the kind of logic presented in Chapter 3 and discussed earlier in this chapter. These kinds of advancement have been made in a number of predictive models reviewed by Wickens (1990). Second, any time-line analysis must incorporate activities that are covert, such as planning or rehearsal. Covert actions are a much greater challenge to include than overt actions because their time duration cannot be as easily estimated, nor can they be easily "seen" by an analyst observing an operator performing a task. Yet it is clear that intense cognitive activity does compete with other perceptual and cognitive tasks, in a way that should be predicted. Ask any driver who has been distracted from careful driving by thinking about serious problems. Thus, such an extension requires the adoption of specialized techniques for cognitive task analysis (Seamster, Redding, & Kaempf, 1997; Gordon & Gill, 1997).

Third, as discussed earlier, the analysis must be sensitive to the differences in resource demands of different tasks. Two time-shared tasks will not impose a 100 percent workload if they are easy and automated but may very well exceed that value if they are difficult (Parks & Boucek, 1989). However, because more difficult tasks generally occupy more space on the time line (and hence will predict greater interference), the requirement for demand coding appears to be somewhat less critical for predicting multiple-task performance (Sarno & Wickens, 1995). Finally, an accurate time-line analysis model should incorporate the multiple-resources concept, recognizing that two tasks overlapping on the time line could provide either very efficient performance or very disruptive performance, depending on their degree of resource conflict. This issue has been addressed in time-line models proposed by North and Riley (1989), Sarno and Wickens (1995), and Plott (1995).

Assessing Mental Workload

Within the last three decades, the applied community has demonstrated considerable interest in the concept of *mental workload:* How busy is the operator? How complex are the tasks? Can any additional tasks be handled above and beyond those that are already performed? Will the operator be able to respond to unexpected events? How does the operator feel about the difficulty of the tasks being performed? The substantial number of articles, books, and symposia in the field (O'Donnell & Eggemeier, 1986; Gopher & Donchin, 1986; Tsang & Wilson, 1997; Hancock & Meshkati,1988; Leplat & Welford, 1978; Moray, 1979, 1988; Smith, 1979; Williges & Wierwille, 1979; Hendy, Liao, & Milgram, 1997) is testimony to the fact that system designers and company managers realize that workload is an important concern. Organizational decisions to downsize or eliminate a position of employment must be made on the basis of whether the capacity of the remaining workers is adequate to still perform the remaining tasks (i.e., workload is not excessive). This was an issue in the late 1970s when a landmark decision was made to reduce the crew size of medium-range jet aircraft by eliminating the flight engineer's position (Lerner, 1983); the decision was the result of a presidential commission formed to address the question. The Federal Aviation Administration requires certification of aircraft in terms of workload measures, and the Air Force and Army also impose workload criteria on newly designed systems. All of these concerns lead to a very relevant question: What is mental workload and how is it measured?

Importance of Workload   Designers and operators realize that performance is not all that matters in the design of a good system. It is just as important to consider what demand a task imposes on the operator's limited resources. As shown in Figure 11.1, demand may or may not correspond with performance. More specifically, the importance of research on mental workload may be viewed in three different contexts: workload prediction (discussed in the previous section in the context of multitask performance prediction), the assessment of workload imposed by equipment, and the assessment of workload experienced by the human operator. The difference between the second and third is their implications for action. When the workload of systems is assessed or compared, the purpose of such a comparison is to optimize the system. When the workload experienced by an operator is assessed, it is for the purpose of choosing between operators or providing an operator with further training. Workload in all three contexts may be initially represented by a simplified single-resource model of human processing resources. (We consider the added complexities of multiple-resource theory later.) The supply-demand function in Figure 11.7 shows the relationship between the important variables in this model. The resources demanded by a task are shown on the horizontal axis. The resources supplied are shown on the vertical axis, along with the level of performance. If adequate performance of a task demands more resources from the operator than are available, performance will break down, as shown to the right. If, however, the available supply exceeds the demand, as shown to the left, then the amount of the excess expresses the amount of reserve capacity.

We make the assumption in this chapter that the concept of workload is fundamentally defined by this relationship between resource supply and task demand. In the region to the left of the break point of Figure 11.7, which we might call the "underload" region, workload is inversely related to reserve capacity. In the region to the right, it is inversely related to the level of task performance, as discussed in the previous

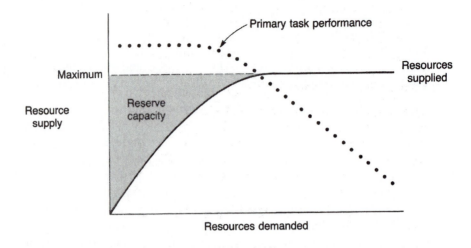

Figure 11.7   Schematic relationship among primary-task resource demand, resources supplied, and performance.

section. These two quantities are primarily what system designers should wish to predict. Note that changes in workload according to this conception may result either from fluctuations of *operator* capacity or from changes in *task resource* demands.

Equipment Assessment   Although workload and performance prediction before a system is designed is desirable, it is often essential to measure the workload of a system already existing at some stage of production. This assessment may be made to identify those bottlenecks in system or mission performance in which resource demands momentarily exceed supply and performance breaks down. Alternatively, workload may be assessed to compare two alternate pieces of equipment that may achieve similar performance but differ in their resource demands because they possess differently shaped performance resource functions (see, e.g., Figure 11.1). Sometimes the criterion of workload may offer the only satisfactory means of choosing between alternatives. As we have noted, an even greater challenge to workload assessment techniques is posed by the requirement to determine if the *absolute level* of workload imposed by a system is above or below a given absolute criterion level. The goal of developing workload certification criteria for complex systems has spawned the need for such absolute scales.

Assessing Operator Differences   Workload measures may also assess differences in the residual resources available to reflect changes and differences in operator capacity, rather than system demand. This may be done in one of two contexts: (1) The level of skill or automaticity achieved by different operators who may be equivalent in their primary-task performance may be compared. For example, Crosby and Parkinson (1979) and Damos (1978) showed that flight instructors differed from student pilots in their level of residual attention. Damos furthermore found that applied to students, this measure was a good predictor of subsequent success in pilot training. (2) Operators may be monitored on-line in real task performance. In this case, intelligent computer-based systems could decide to assume responsibility for the performance of certain tasks from the human operator when momentary demands were measured to exceed capacity (Scerbo, 1996; Wickens & Gopher, 1977), although this form of on-line human-computer interaction, known as *adaptive automation,* requires a certain level of cooperation from the human operator (see Chapter 13).

Criteria for Workload Indexes   O'Donnell and Eggemeier (1986) propose a number of criteria that should ideally be met by any technique to assess workload. Of course it is true that some of these criteria may trade off with one another, and so rarely if ever will one technique be found that satisfies all criteria. The following list of five criteria of a workload index is similar to the list proposed by O'Donnell and Eggemeier.

>   *Sensitivity.* The index should be sensitive to changes in task difficulty or resource demand.

>   *Diagnosticity.* An index should indicate not only when workload varies but also the cause of such variation. In multiple-resource theory, it should indicate *which* of the capacities or resources are varied by demand changes in the system. This information makes it possible to implement better solutions.

>   *Selectivity.* The index should be selectively sensitive only to differences in resource demand and not to changes in such factors as physical load or emotional stress, which may be unrelated to mental workload or information-processing ability.

>   *Obtrusiveness.* The index should not interfere with, contaminate, or disrupt performance of the primary task whose workload is being assessed. This is particularly true if workload is being assessed while operators are performing real (nonlaboratory) tasks, especially in safety critical environments (e.g., vehicle driving).

>   *Bandwidth and Reliability.* As with any measure of behavior, a workload index should be reliable. However, if workload is assessed in a time-varying environment (e.g., if it is necessary to track workload changes over the course of a mission), it is important that the index offer a reliable estimate of workload rapidly enough so that the transient changes may be estimated (Humphrey & Kramer, 1994).

A myriad of workload assessment techniques have been proposed, some meeting many of these criteria, but few satisfying all of them. These may be classified into four broad categories related to primary-task measures, secondary-task measures of spare capacity, physiological measures, and subjective rating techniques.

Primary-Task Measures   In evaluating any system or operator, one should always examine first the performance on the system of interest, like computer data-entry speed, driving deviations from the center of the lane, or learning comprehension with a particular method of instruction. Because this is the target of evaluation, we refer to the task performed with this system as the *primary task.* Yet there are four important reasons that primary-task performance may be insufficient to reveal clearly the merits of the primary task. First, in Figure 11.7, two primary tasks may lie in the "underload" region of the supply-demand space (see the two tasks represented by the PRFs in Figure 11.1). Since both have sufficient reserve capacity to reach perfect performance, the latter measure cannot discriminate between them. Second, two primary tasks to be compared may differ in how they are measured or what those measures mean. A designer of prosthetic devices to enable the blind to read may find that the two kinds of devices produce qualitatively different forms of errors (e.g., semantic confusions versus letter confusions) or that they differ greatly in the speed-accuracy trade-off. As we saw in Chapter 10, comparisons of systems at different levels of speed and accuracy are possible but much less certain than if either accuracy or speed comparisons are identical.

Third, sometimes it is simply impossible to obtain good measures of primary-task performance. As noted in Chapter 8, decision making may impose tremendous cognitive demands on the operator, yet the performance outcome (right or wrong) is a very poor measure of all of the mental operations that were involved in reaching the final outcome. As discussed in Chapter 2, vigilance tasks may impose very high levels of workload (Hancock & Warm, 1989), but by their very nature, the performance data of vigilance can be very sparse.

Finally, two primary tasks may differ in their performance, not by the resources demanded to achieve that performance, but by differences in data limits. In decision making, for example, if a heuristic yields lower performance than a computational algorithm, this may be important information for the system or job designer, but this difference does not mean that the heuristic imposes greater workload. In fact, as suggested by the two PRFs in Figure 11.3, the difference may well be the result of the *lower* resource demands of the heuristic. Similarly, automated voice-recognition systems often yield poorer performance than manual data-entry systems for simple data strings. Yet this difference may be attributable to machine limits in the voice-recognition algorithm rather than to operator difference in the speed and resource demands of response production. In short, primary-task performances may differ for a lot of reasons that are not related to workload, as the latter is defined in the context of Figure 11.7.

For these reasons, system designers have often turned to the three other workload assessment techniques—secondary-task performance, physiological measures, and subjective measures—which may assess more directly either the effort invested into primary-task performance or the level of residual capacity available during that performance.

The Secondary-Task Technique   Imposing a secondary task as a measure of residual resources or capacity not utilized in the primary task (Ogden, Levine, & Eisner, 1979; Rolfe, 1973) is a technique that has a long history in the field of workload research. Secondary-task performance is assumed to be inversely proportional to the primary-task resource demands. In this way, secondary tasks may reflect differences in task resource demand, automaticity, or practice that are not reflected in primary-task performance. The logic behind the secondary task in the PRF space is shown in Figure 11.8. The operator is requested to perform as well as possible on the primary task and then allocate any left over resources to the secondary task. Thus, as we see in Figure 11.8a, three increasing levels of primary task difficulty will yield three successively smaller margins of available resources, and therefore three diminishing levels of secondary-task performance. As just one example, Bahrick and Shelly (1958) found that the secondary task was sensitive to differences in automaticity. Performance of their subjects on a serial RT task (the primary task) did not differ between a random and a predictable sequence of

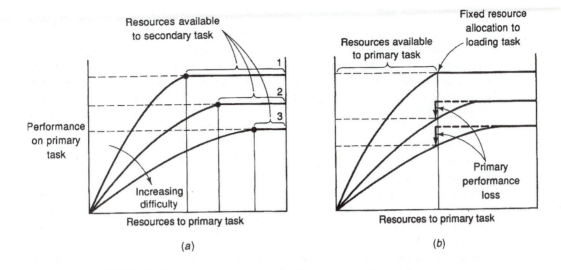

Figure 11.8 Relationships among the performance-resource function, resource allocation, and primary-task difficulty. (*a*) Secondary-task technique, (*b*) loading-task technique.

stimuli. However, performance on a secondary task did discriminate between them. With practice, the repeated sequence required fewer resources.

As we have noted, when using the secondary-task technique, the investigator is interested in variation in the secondary-task decrement (from a single secondary-task control condition) to infer differences in primary-task demand. The primary task is thus both the task of interest and the task whose priority is emphasized, as shown in Figure 11.8a. In contrast, a variant of the secondary-task technique is the use of a *loading task* (Ogden, Levine, & Eisner, 1979; Rolfe, 1973), shown in Figure 11.8b, in which different allocation instructions are provided. The subject is now asked to devote all necessary resources to the loading task, and the degree of intrusion of this task on performance of the primary task is examined to compare differences between primary tasks.

Secondary Task Examples   A multitude of secondary tasks have been proposed and employed at one time or another to assess the residual capacity of primary tasks. Although the reader is referred to reviews by Ogden, Levine, and Eisner (1979), O'Donnell and Eggemeier (1986), and Tsang and Wilson (1997) for a more exhaustive listing of these tasks, a few prominent candidates are described here.

In the *rhythmic tapping* task, the operator must produce finger or foot taps at a constant rate (Michon, 1966; Michon & Van Doorne, 1967). Tapping variability increases as primary-task workload increases. *Random number generation* requires the operator to generate a series of random numbers (Baddeley, 1966; Logie et al., 1989; Wetherell, 1981). As workload increases, the degree of randomness declines and the operator begins to generate more repetitive sequences (e.g., 456, 456, 456). *Probe reaction time* tasks are commonly used as workload measurement techniques, as it is assumed that greater primary-task workload will prolong the reaction time to a secondary-task stimulus (Kantowitz, Bortolussi, & Hart, 1987; Lansman & Hunt, 1982; Wetherell, 1981). Such tasks may involve lesser or greater degrees of processing complexity. For example, the Sternberg memory-search RT task described in Chapter 9 can provide a diagnosis of the primary tasks that impose greater load on working memory (Crosby & Parkinson, 1979; Wetherell, 1981; Wickens et al., 1986).

Time production and *time estimation* are two related techniques with somewhat different underlying assumptions (Zakay, Block, & Tsal, 1999). If the operator is asked to *produce* time intervals of a constant duration (e.g., 10 seconds), the intervals will tend to be overestimated when there are higher demands (Hart, 1975), as if the higher levels of workload interfere with (and postpone) whatever internal mechanism is responsible for mental time counting. (As suggested by the tapping task of Michon, 1966, high workload will also make these intervals more variable.) In contrast, if the operator is asked to *estimate* (retrospectively) durations of time that have passed ("how long has it been since you started the task"), two somewhat different and opposing phenomena appear to operate. On the one hand, to the extent that we estimate the average passage of time by a certain amount of work accomplished, then high workload can lead to overestimation ("to accomplish all I have done, I *must* have been working more than 10 minutes"). On the other hand, there are circumstances when time "drags," when we are bored (very low workload), and this too will increase estimates ("I've been waiting for *hours*"). These two contradictory trends suggest that retrospective estimates may be increased at both lower and higher workload levels, but may also offset each other, rendering retrospective technique a less than fully reliable technique, in contrast to time production (Hart, 1975).

Benefits and Costs of Secondary Tasks   The secondary-task technique has two very distinct benefits. First, it has a high degree of face validity. It is designed to predict the amount of residual attention an operator will have available if an unexpected failure or environmental event occurs. This validity places the technique in contrast with the physiological and subjective measures described below. Second, the same secondary task can be applied to two very different primary tasks and will give workload measures in the same units (which can therefore be compared). As we have seen, this is not the case with primary-task performance measures.

One difficulty is that the secondary-task technique must account for the fact that there are different kinds of resources (O'Donnell & Eggemeier, 1986). Workload differences that result from changes in a primary-task variable can be greatly underestimated if the resource demands of the primary-task variation do not match those of most importance for secondary-task performance. Thus, the secondary-task index is not always *sensitive*. For example, the secondary task of vocally responding to heard digits (auditory verbal speech) would mismatch the resource demands of driving (a visual-spatial manual task) and, hence, might underestimate driving workload.

Kahneman (1973) proposes that the ideal secondary-task technique is one that employs a battery of secondary-task measures sensitive to different resources in the system. Schlegel, Gilliland, and Schlegel (1986) propose a structured set of tasks, known as the *criterion task set*, that are mapped onto different resource dimensions. When it is clear that one level of a dimension does not contribute to primary-task performance, the dimensionality of the battery may be reduced accordingly. For example, a verbal processing task with no spatial components need not be assessed by a spatial secondary task. However, in cases in which an activity is performed that potentially engages all "cells" of processing resources, as depicted in Figure 11.5, a secure secondary task workload estimate should involve a battery that also incorporates those cells, or at least taps early and late processing of a verbal and spatial nature.

A second problem often encountered with the secondary-task technique is that it may interfere with and disrupt performance of the primary task; that is, the technique suffers on the *obtrusiveness* criterion (Wierwille, Rahimi, & Casali, 1985). On the one hand, this may be inconvenient or even dangerous if the primary task is one like flying or driving; a diversion of resources to the secondary task at the wrong time could lead to an accident. On the other hand, disruption of the primary task could present problems of interpretation if the amount of disruption suffered by two primary tasks to be compared is not the same. That is, the measurement technique differentially disrupts that which is being measured.

Problems with obtrusiveness often affect the operator's attitude toward and willingness to perform the secondary task. In response, some researchers have advocated *embedded secondary tasks.* Here the "secondary task" is actually a legitimate component of the operator's total task responsibilities, but it is a component of lower priority in the task hierarchy than the primary task of interest (Raby & Wickens, 1994). For example, the latency of responding to a verbal request from air traffic control would be a good embedded task for assessing the pilot's workload demands of keeping the aircraft stable, since the latter is of higher priority. In driving, one might consider the frequency of glances to the rearview mirror as an embedded secondary task to assess the workload of vehicle control.

Physiological Measures One solution to performance obtrusiveness is to record, unobtrusively, the manifestations of workload or increased resource mobilization through appropriately chosen physiological measures of autonomic or central nervous system activity (Kramer, 1987). Three such techniques are briefly described here, and a further review is provided by O'Donnell and Eggemeier (1986), and Tsang and Wilson (1997).

Heart-Rate Variability A number of investigators have examined different measures associated with the variability or regularity of heart rate as a measure of mental load. Variability is generally found to decrease as the load increases, particularly that variability which cycles with a period of around 10 seconds (0.1 Hz) (Mulder & Mulder, 1981). When this variability is associated specifically with the periodicities resulting from respiration, the measure is termed sinus arrhythmia (Mulder & Mulder, 1981; Tattersal & Hockey, 1995; Sirevaag et al., 1993; Vicente, Thornton, & Moray, 1987). Heart-rate variability is sensitive to a number of different difficulty manipulations and therefore appears to be more sensitive than diagnostic. Derrick (1988) investigated this measure with four quite different tasks performed in different combinations within the framework of the multiple-resource model. His data suggest that the variability measure reflected the total demand imposed on all resources within the processing system more than the amount of resource competition (and therefore dual-task decrement) between tasks.

Pupil Diameter Several investigators have observed that the diameter of the pupil correlates quite closely with the resource demands of a large number of diverse cognitive activities (Beatty, 1982) These include mental arithmetic (Kahneman, Beatty, & Pollack, 1967), short-term memory load (Beatty & Kahneman, 1966; Peavler, 1974), air traffic control monitoring load (Jorna, 1997), and logical problem solving (Bradshaw, 1968, see Beatty, 1982, for an integrative summary). This diversity of responsiveness suggests that the pupilometric measure may be highly sensitive, although as a result it is undiagnostic. It will reflect demands imposed anywhere within the system. Its disadvantage, of course, is that relevant pupil changes are in the order of tenths of a millimeter, which means that accurate measurement requires considerable head constraint and precise measuring equipment. Additionally, changes in ambient illumination must be monitored, since these also affect the pupil. Because of its association with the autonomic nervous system, the measure will also be susceptible to variations in emotional arousal.

Visual Scanning   While discussed as a measure of attention allocation in Chapter 3, visual scanning—the direction of pupil gaze—can also contribute extensively to workload modeling in two different ways. First, as we have noted, dwell time can serve as an index of the resources required for information extraction from a single source. In an aircraft simulation, Bellenkes, Wickens, and Kramer (1997) found that dwells were largest on the most information-rich flight instrument (the attitude directional indicator or ADI; see Chapter 3), and that dwells were much longer for novice than expert pilots, reflecting the novice's greater workload in extracting the information. Second, scanning can be a diagnostic index of the *source* of workload within a multi-element display environment. For example, Bellenkes, et al. found that long novice dwells on the ADI were coupled with more frequent visits and, hence, served as a major "sink" for visual attention. Little time was left for novices to monitor other instruments, and as a consequence, their performance declined on tasks using those other instruments. Dinges, Orne, Whitehouse, and Orne (1987) and Wikman, Nieminen, and Summala (1998) used scanning as a critical measure of the in-vehicle head-down time caused by the workload associated with different in-vehicle systems such as maps, radio buttons, etc. Thus, scanning measures can contribute to modeling the strategic aspects of resource allocation, as discussed earlier in this chapter.

Costs and Benefits   Physiological indexes have two great advantages: (1) They provide a relatively continuous record of data over time. (2) They are not obtrusive into primary-task performance. On the other hand, they often require that electrodes be attached (heart measures) or some degree of physical constraints be imposed (pupilometric measures, eye fixations), and therefore they are not really unobtrusive in a physical sense. These constraints will influence user acceptance. Many physiological measures have a further potential cost in that they are, generally, one conceptual step removed from the inference that the system designers would like to make. That is, workload differences measured by physiological means must be used to *infer* that performance breakdowns would result or to *infer* how the operator would feel about the task. Secondary- or primary-task measures assess the former directly, whereas subjective measures, which we now discuss, assess the latter.

Subjective Measures   A variety of techniques have been proposed to assess the subjective effort required to perform a task. Some of them use a structured rating scale to elicit a single dimensional rating (Wierwille & Casali, 1983), whereas others have adopted the view that subjective workload, like the resource concept itself, has several dimensions (Derrick, 1988; O'Donnell & Eggemeier, 1986). Two common multidimensional assessment techniques are the NASA Task Load Index (TLX) scale (Hart & Staveland, 1988), which assesses workload on each of five 7-point scales, and the subjective workload assessment (SWAT) technique (Reid & Nygren, 1988), which measures workload on three 3-point scales (see Table 11.1). Each of these techniques has formal prescriptions for how the multiple scales may be combined to obtain a single measure. Although both scales tend to yield similar outcomes when they are applied to the same set of data (Vidulich & Tsang, 1986), the TLX technique, having a greater number of scales and greater resolution per scale, allows it to convey more information, and appears to provide a more reliable measure (Hill et al., 1992).

Costs and Benefits The benefits of subjective techniques are apparent. They do not disrupt primary-task performance, and they are relatively easy to derive. Their costs relate to the uncertainty with which an operator's verbal statement diagnostically reflects the investment of or demand for processing resources and is not influenced by other biases (e.g., dislike or unfamiliarity of the task, or rater's reluctance to report that things are difficult).

TABLE 11.1 Two Multi-Dimensional Workload Rating Scales

SWAT Scale

Time Load	*Mental Effort Load*	*Stress Load*
1. Often have spare time. Interruptions or overlap among activities occur infrequently or not at all.	1. Very little conscious mental effort or concentration required. Activity is almost automatic, requiring little or no attention.	1. Little confusion, risk, frustration, or anxiety exists and can be easily accomodated.
2. Occasionally have spare time. Interruptions or overlap among activities occur frequently.	2. Moderate conscious mental effort or concentration required. Complexity of activity is moderately high due to uncertainty, unpredictability, or unfamiliarty. Considerable attention required.	2. Moderate stress due to confusion, frustration, or anxiety noticeably adds to the workload. Significant compensation is required to maintain adequate performance.
3. Almost never have spare time. Interruptions or overlap among activities are very frequent, or occur all the time.	3. Extensive mental effort and concentration neccessary. Very complex activity requiring total attention.	3. High to very intense stress due to confusion, frustration or anxiety. High to extreme determination and self-control required.

(continues)

TABLE 11.1 (continued)

NASA TLX Scale

Title	Endpoints	Descriptions
MENTAL DEMAND	Low/High	How much mental and perceptual activity was required (e.g., thinking, deciding, calculating, remembering, looking, searching, etc.)? Was the task easy or demanding, simple or complex, exacting or forgiving?
PHYSICAL DEMAND	Low/High	How much physical activity was required (e.g., pushing, pulling, turning, controlling, activating, etc.)? Was the task easy or demanding, slow or brisk, slack or strenuous, restful or laborious?
TEMPORAL DEMAND	Low/High	How much time pressure did you feel due to the rate or pace at which the tasks or task elements occured? Was the pace slow and leisurely or rapid and frantic?
PERFORMANCE	Perfect/Failure	How successful do you think you were in accomplishing the goals of the task set by the experimenter (or yourself)? How satisfied were you with your performance in accomplishing these goals?
EFFORT	Low/High	How hard did you have to work (mentally and physically) to accomplish your level of performance?
FRUSTRATION LEVEL	Low/High	How insecure, discouraged, irritated, stressed, and annoyed versus secure, gratified, content, relaxed, and complacent did you feel during your task?

Relationship Between Workload Measures

If all measures of workload demonstrated high correlation with one another and the residual disagreement was due to random error, there would be little need for further validation research in the area. The practitioner could adopt whichever technique was methodologically simplest and most reliable for the workload measurement problem at hand. Generally, high correlations between measures will be found if the measures are assessed across tasks of similar structure and widely varying degrees of difficulty. For example, Jex and Clement's (1979) found a high correlation between subjective and secondary task measures of flight-control difficulty (e.g., tracking order as discussed in Chapter 10). However, the correlations may not be high and may even be negative when quite different tasks are contrasted. For example, consider an experiment conducted by Herron (1980) in which an innovation designed to assist in a target-aiming task was subjectively preferred by users over the original prototype but generated reliably poorer performance than the original. Similar dissociations have been observed by Childress, Hart, and Bortalussi (1982) and Murphy et al. (1978), who measured pilot workload associated with cockpit-display innovations.

We use the term *dissociation* to describe these circumstances in which conditions that are compared have different effects on different workload measures. The understanding of attention and resource theory can be quite useful in interpreting why these dissociations occur. Yeh and Wickens (1988) paid particular attention to the dissociation between primary task and subjective measures. Their assumption is that subjective measures directly reflect two factors: the effort that must be invested into performance of a task and the number of tasks that must be performed concurrently. These two factors, however, do not always influence performance in the same way. To illustrate, consider the following situations:

1. If two different tasks are in the underload region on the left of Figure 11.7, the greater resources invested on the more difficult task (and therefore the higher subjective workload) will not yield better performance.
2. If the operator performs the three tasks shown in Figure 11.8b while investing full resources, performance will differ, but the resources invested (and therefore the subjective workload experienced) will not differ. Subjective measures often fail to reflect differences due to data limits, particularly if the lower level of performance caused by the lower level of the data limit is not immediately evident to the performer who is giving the rating. (Note in Table 11.1, however, that this is an advantage of NASA TLX measure, which allows the operator to separately rate "performance" and "mental effort".)
3. If two systems are compared, one of which induces a greater investment of effort, the latter will probably show higher subjective workload, even as its performance is improved (through the added effort investment). This dissociation is shown when effort investment is induced through monetary incentives (Vidulich & Wickens, 1986). However, it also appears that greater effort is invested when better (e.g., higher resolution) display information is available to achieve better performance. Thus, in tracking tasks, features like an amplified error signal (achieved through magnification or prediction—see Chapter 10) will increase tracking performance but at the expense of higher subjective ratings of workload (Yeh & Wickens, 1988).
4. Yeh and Wickens (1988) have concluded that a very strong influence on subjective workload is exerted by the number of tasks that must be performed at once. The subjective workload from time-sharing two (or more) tasks is almost always greater than that from a single task. We can see here the source of another dissociation with performance because a single task might be quite difficult (and result in poor performance as a result), whereas a dual-task combination, if the

tasks are not difficult and use separate resources, may indeed produce a very good performance in spite of its higher level of subjective load.

The presence of dissociations often leaves the system designer in a quandary. Which system should be chosen when performance and workload measures do not agree on the relative merits between them? The previous discussion, and the chapter as a whole, do not provide a firm answer to this question. However, the explanation for the causes of dissociation and its basis on a theory of resources should at least help the designer to understand why the dissociation occurs, and thus why one measure or the other may offer a less reliable indicator of the true workload of the system in specific circumstances.

Consequences of Workload

Increases on workload do not inherently have "bad" consequences. In many environments, it is the low levels of workload that, when coupled with boredom, fatigue, or sleep loss, can have negative implications for human performance (Chapter 2; Huey & Wickens, 1993). Given some flexibility, operators usually work homeostatically to achieve an "optimal level" of workload by seeking tasks when workload is low, and shedding them when workload is excessive (Hart & Wickens, 1990). This basis for strategic task management was discussed earlier in the chapter.

In revisiting these task management issues, we must highlight the importance of understanding the strategy of task management that operators adapt when workload becomes excessive (i.e., crosses from the underload to the overload region of Figure 11.7 as measured by the techniques described above). At a most general level, four types of adaptation are possible. (1) People may allow performance of tasks to *degrade*, as a vehicle driver might allow lane position to wander as the workload of dealing with an in-vehicle automation system increases. (2) People may perform the tasks in a more efficient, less resource-consuming way. For example, in decision making, they may shift from optimal algorithms to satisfactory heuristics. (3) People may shed tasks altogether, in an "optimal" fashion, eliminating performance of those of lower priority. For example, under high workload, the air traffic controller may cease to offer pilots weather information unless requested, while turning full attention to traffic separation. (4) People may shed tasks in a nonoptimal fashion, abandoning those that should be performed. As an example here, we end the chapter as we began both the chapter and the book, with the unfortunate driver who chose to shed that most critical task of roadway monitoring to address the high workload of failure diagnosis. Unfortunately, beyond the material covered earlier in this chapter on resource allocation, very little is known about general principles that can account for when people adopt one strategy or the other. Perhaps the one principle that can be stated with most certainty is that training and expertise play a strong role in successful workload management (Orasanu & Fischer, 1997), and so it is no surprise that such training has been a formalized component of many training programs in high-risk multi-task environments like aviation (Wiener, Kanki, & Helmreich, 1993).

TRANSITION

In this chapter we have outlined the potential causes of multiple-task interference, discussing the role of switching, confusion, and cooperation but emphasizing most heavily the role of resource competition. The consideration of resources led to the discussion of the theory and measurement of mental workload and the fundamental importance of the resource concept to this theory.

Stress is often a consequence of high levels of mental workload, particularly if such workload is sustained for some time. Stress in turn will often produce changes in functioning of all of the information processing components that we have discussed, and so will produce effects on performance. Of course, stress may be experienced from other sources than high workload—sleep loss, noise, and anxiety, to name a few. In the following chapter, we will examine some of these sources of stress and determine whether and how their effects might be predicted.

A second consequence of high workload is the occurrence of errors. However, as with stress, errors may be caused by other factors as well. In the following chapter, we will see that one of the prominent effects of stress is a shift in the speed-accuracy trade-off to error-prone performance. Furthermore, errors may be caused by the characteristics of the task and by differences in the skill level of the operator. Thus, in the next chapter we will describe the causes and models of human error and show how human factors engineers have tried to use this information to predict human reliability and to design error-tolerant systems. Because of the close linkage between stress and errors and because both may be related to all stages of processing, they are included together in a single chapter.

REFERENCES

Allport, D. A., Antonis, B., & Reynolds, P. (1972). On the division of attention: A disproof of the single channel hypothesis. *Quarterly Journal of Experimental Psychology, 24,* 255–265.

Allport, D. A., Styles, E. A., & Hsieh, S. (1994). Shifting intentional set: Exploring the dynamic control of tasks. In C. Umilta & M. Moscovitch (Eds.), *Attention and performance XV* (pp. 421–452). Cambridge, MA: MIT Press.

Baddeley, A. (1966). The capacity for generating information by randomization. *Quarterly Journal of Experimental Psychology, 18,* 119–130.

Bahrick, H. P., Noble, M., & Fitts, P. M. (1954). Extra task performance as a measure of learning a primary task. *Journal of Experimental Psychology, 48,* 298–302.

Bahrick, H. P., & Shelly, C. (1958). Time-sharing as an index of automization. *Journal of Experimental Psychology, 56,* 288–293.

Beatty, J. (1982). Task-evoked pupillary responses, processing load, and the structure of processing resources. *Psychological Bulletin, 91,* 276–292.

Beatty, J., & Kahneman, D. (1966). Pupillary changes in two memory tasks. *Psychonomic Science, 5,* 371–372.

Bellenkes, A. H., Wickens, C. D., & Kramer, A. F. (1997). Visual scanning and pilot expertise: The role of attentional flexibility and mental model development. *Aviation, Space, and Environmental Medicine, 68*(7), 569–579.

Bettman, J. R., Johnson, E. J., & Payne, J. W. (1990). A componential analysis of cognitive effort and choice. *Organizational Behavior and Human Decision Processes, 45,* 111–139.

Bradshaw, J. L. (1968). Pupil size and problem-solving. *Quarterly Journal of Experimental Psychology, 20,* 116–122.

Braune, R., & Wickens, C. D. (1986). Time-sharing revisited: Test of a componential model for the assessment of individual differences. *Ergonomics, 29*(11), 1399–1414.

Brooks, L. (1968). Spatial and verbal components of the act of recall. *Canadian Journal of Psychology, 22*, 349–368.

Chernikoff, R., Duey, J. W., & Taylor, F. V. (1960). Effect of various display-control configurations on tracking with identical and different coordinate dynamics. *Journal of Experimental Psychology, 60*, 318–322.

Chernikoff R., & Lemay, M. (1963). Effect of various display-control configurations on tracking with identical and different coordinate dynamics. *Journal of Experimental Psychology, 66*, 95–99.

Childress, M. E., Hart, S. G., & Bortalussi, M. R. (1982). The reliability and validity of flight task workload ratings. In R. Edwards (Ed.), *Proceedings of the 26th annual meeting of the Human Factors Society*. Santa Monica, CA: Human Factors Society.

Chou, C., Madhavan, D., & Funk, K. (1996). Studies of cockpit task management errors. *The International Journal of Aviation Psychology, 6*(4), 307–320.

Crosby, J. V., & Parkinson, S. (1979). A dual task investigation of pilot's skill level. *Ergonomics, 22*, 1301–1313.

Damos, D. (1978). Residual attention as a predictor of pilot performance. *Human Factors, 20*, 435–440.

Damos, D., & Wickens, C. D. (1980). The acquisition and transfer of time-sharing skills. *Acta Psychologica, 6*, 569–577.

Derrick, W. L. (1988). Dimensions of operator workload. *Human Factors, 30*(1), 95–110.

Dinges, D. F., Orne, K. T., Whitehouse, W. G., & Orne, E. C. (1987). Temporal placement of a nap for alertness: Contributions of circadian phase and prior wakefulness. *Sleep, 10*, 313–329.

Dornic, S. S. (1980). Language dominance, spare capacity, and perceived effort in bilinguals. *Ergonomics, 23*, 369–378.

Duncan, J. (1979). Divided attention: The whole is more than the sum of its parts. *Journal of Experimental Psychology: Human Perception & Performance, 5*, 216–228.

Fagot, C., & Pashler, H. (1992). Making two responses to a single object: Exploring the central bottleneck. *Journal of Experimental Psychology: Human Perception & Performance, 18*, 1058–1079.

Fennema, M. G., & Kleinmuntz, D. N. (1995). Anticipations of effort and accuracy in multiattribute choice. *Organizational Behavior and Human Decision Processes, 63*(1), 21–32.

Fracker, M. L., & Wickens, C. D. (1989). Resources, confusions, and compatibility in dual axis tracking: Display, controls, and dynamics. *Journal of Experimental Psychology: Human Perception & Performance, 15*, 80–96.

Funk, K. H., II, & McCoy, B. (1996). A functional model of flight deck agenda management. In *Proceedings of the 40th annual meeting of the Human Factors and Ergonomics Society* (pp. 254–258). Santa Monica, CA: Human Factors and Ergonomics Society.

Goettl, B. P. & Wickens, C. D. (1989). Multiple resources vs. information integration. *Proceedings of the 33d annual meeting of the Human Factors Society*. Santa Monica, CA: Human Factors Society.

Goodman, M. J., Tijerina, L., Bents, F. D., & Wierwille, W. W. (1999). Using cellular telephones in vehicles: Safe or Unsafe? *Transportation Human Factors, 3*.

Gopher, D. (1991). The skill of attention control: Acquisition and execution of attention strategies. In D. Meyer & S. Kornblum (Eds.), *Attention and performance IVX*. Hillsdale, NJ: Erlbaum.

Gopher, D., & Donchin, E. (1986). Workload: An experimentation of the concept. In K. Boff, L. Kauffman, & J. Thomas (Eds.), *Handbook of perception and performance* (vol. 2). New York: Wiley.

Gopher, D., Weil, M., & Bareket, T. (1994). Transfer of skill from a computer game trainer to flight. *Human Factors, 36*(4), 387–405.

Gopher, D., Weil, M., & Siegel, D. (1989). Practice under changing priorities: An approach to training of complex skills. *Acta Psychologica, 71*, 147–179.

Gordon, S. E., & Gill, R. T. (1997). Cognitive task analysis. In C. Zsambok & G. Klein (Eds.), *Naturalistic decision making*. Hillsdale, NJ: Erlbaum.

Hancock, P. A., & Meshkati, N. (1988). *Human mental workload*. Amsterdam: North Holland.

Hancock, P., & Warm, J. (1989). A dynamic model of stress and sustained attention. *Human Factors, 31*, 519–537.

Hart, S. G. (1975, May). Time estimation as a secondary task to measure workload. *Proceedings of the 11th Annual Conference on Manual Control* (NASA TMX–62, N75–33679, 53; pp. 64–77). Washington, DC: U.S. Government Printing Office.

Hart, S. G., & Staveland, L. E. (1988). Development of NASA-TLS (Task Load Index): Results of empirical and theoretical research. In P. A. Hancock & N. Meshkati (Eds.), *Human mental workload*. Amsterdam: North Holland.

Hart, S. G., & Wickens, C. D. (1990). Workload assessment and prediction. In H. R. Booher (Ed.), *MANPRINT: An emerging technology. Advanced concepts for integrating people, machines and organizations* (pp. 257–300). New York: Van Nostrand Reinhold.

Haskell, I. D., & Wickens, C. D. (1993). Two- and three-dimensional displays for aviation: A theoretical and empirical comparison. *The International Journal of Aviation Psychology, 3*(2), 87–109.

Hendy, K. C., Liao, J., & Milgram, P. (1997). Combining time and intensity effects in assessing operator information-processing load. *Human Factors, 39*, 30–47.

Herron, S. (1980). A case for early objective evaluation of candidate displays. In G. Corrick, M. Hazeltine, & R. Durst (Eds.), *Proceedings of the 24th annual meeting of the Human Factors Society*. Santa Monica, CA: Human Factors Society.

Hill, S. G., Iavecchia, H. P., Byers, J. C., Bittner, A. C., Jr., Zaklad, A. L., & Christ, R. E. (1992). Comparison of four subjective workload rating scales. *Human Factors, 34*, 429–440.

Hirst, W. (1986). Aspects of divided and selected attention. In J. LeDoux & W. Hirst (Eds.), *Mind and brain* (pp. 105–141). New York: Cambridge University Press.

Hirst, W., & Kalmar, D. (1987). Characterizing attentional resources. *Journal of Experimental Psychology: General, 116*(1), 68–81.

Huey, M. B., & Wickens, C. D. (Eds.). (1993). *Workload transition: Implications for individual and team performance*. Washington, DC: National Academy Press.

Humphrey, D., & Kramer, A. (1994). Towards a psychophysiological assessment of dynamic changes in mental workload. *Human Factors, 36*, 3–26.

Isreal, J., Chesney, G., Wickens, C. D., & Donchin, E. (1980). P300 and tracking difficulty: Evidence for a multiple capacity view of attention. *Psychophysiology, 17*, 259–273.

Isreal, J., Wickens, C. D., Chesney, G., & Donchin E. (1980). The event-related brain potential as a selective index of display monitoring load. *Human Factors, 22*, 211–224.

Jersild, A. T. (1927). Mental set and shift. *Archives of Psychology*, Whole no. 89.

Jex, H. R., & Clement, W. F. (1979). Defining and measuring perceptual-motor workload in manual control tasks. In N. Moray (Ed.), *Mental workload: Its theory and measurement*. New York: Plenum.

Jorna, P. (1997). Human machine interactions with future flight deck and air traffic control systems. In D. Harris (Ed.), *Engineering psychology and cognitive ergonomics: Vol 1*. Brookfield, VT: Ashgate.

Kahneman, D. (1973). *Attention and effort*. Englewood Cliffs, NJ: Prentice Hall.

Kahneman, D., Beatty, J., & Pollack, I. (1967). Perceptual deficits during a mental task. *Science, 157*, 218–219.

Kahneman, D., & Chajczyk, D. (1983). Tests of the automaticity of reading: Dilution of Stroop effects by color-irrelevant stimuli. *Journal of Experimental Psychology Human Perception & Performance, 9*, 497–501.

Kantowitz, B. H. (1974). Double stimulation. In B. H. Kantowitz (Ed.), *Human information processing*. Hillsdale, NJ: Erlbaum.

Kantowitz, B. H., Bortalussi, M. R., & Hart, S. G. (1987). Measuring pilot workload in a motion base simulator: III. Synchronous secondary task. *Proceedings of the 31st annual meeting of the Human Factors Society* (pp. 834–837). Santa Monica, CA: Human Factors Society.

Kantowitz, B. H., & Knight, J. L. (1976). Testing tapping timesharing: I. Auditory secondary task. *Acta Psychologica, 40*, 343–362.

Keele, S. W. (1973). *Attention and human performance*. Pacific Palisades, CA: Goodyear.

Kirwan, B., & Ainsworth, L. (1992). *A guide to task analysis*. London: Taylor & Francis.

Klapp, S. T. (1979). Doing two things at once: The role of temporal compatibility. *Memory & Cognition, 7*, 375–381.

Klapp, S. T. (1981). Temporal compatibility in dual motor tasks II: Simultaneous articulation and hand movements. *Memory & Cognition, 9*, 398–401.

Klein, G. S. (1964). Semantic power measured through the interference of words with color naming. *American Journal of Psychology, 77*, 576–588.

Kramer, A. F. (Ed.). (1987). Special issue on cognitive psychophysiology. *Human Factors, 29*, Whole no. 2.

Kramer, A. F., Larish, J. F., & Strayer, D. L. (1995). Training for attentional control in dual task settings: A comparison of young and old adults. *Journal of Applied Psychology: Applied, 1*(1), 50–76.

LaBerge, D. (1973). Attention and the measurement of perceptual learning. *Memory & Cognition, 1*, 268–276.

Lansman, M., & Hunt, E. (1982). Individual differences in secondary task performance. *Memory & Cognition, 10*, 10–24.

Laudeman, I. V., & Palmer, E. A. (1995). Quantitative measurement of observed workload in the analysis of aircrew performance. *The International Journal of Aviation Psychology, 5*(2), 187–198.

Leibowitz, H. W., & Post, R. B. (1982). The two modes of processing concept and some implications. In J. Beck (Ed.), *Organization and representation in perception* (pp. 343–363). Hillsdale, NJ: Erlbaum.

Leplat, J., & Welford, A. T. (Eds.). (1978). Whole issue on workload. *Ergonomics, 21*(3).

Lerner, E. J. (1983). The automated cockpit. *IEEE Spectrum, 20*, 57–62.

Levy, J. L., Foyle, D. C., & McCann, R. S. (1998). Performance benefits with scene-linked HUD symbology: An attentional phenomenon? *Proceedings of the 42d annual meeting of the Human Factors and Ergonomics Society*. Santa Monica, CA: Human Factors and Ergonomics Society.

Liao, J., & Moray, N. (1993). A simulation study of human performance deterioration and mental workload. *Le Travail humain, 56*(4), 321–344.

Logie, R., Baddeley, A., Mane, A., Donchin, E., & Sheptak, R. (1989). Working memory in the acquisition of complex cognitive skills. *Acta Psychologica, 71*, 53–87.

Martin, G. (1989). The utility of speech input in user-computer interfaces. International *Journal of Man-Machine System Study, 18*, 355–376.

Martin, R. C., Wogalter, M. S., & Forlano, J. G. (1988). Reading comprehension in the presence of unattended speech and music. *Journal of Memory and Language, 27*, 382–398.

McLeod, P. (1977). A dual task response modality effect: Support for multiprocessor models of attention. *Quarterly Journal of Experimental Psychology, 29*, 651–667.

Michon, J. A. (1966). Tapping regularity as a measure of perceptual motor load. *Ergonomics, 9*, 401–412.

Michon, J. A., & Van Doorne, H. (1967). A semi-portable apparatus for measuring perceptual motor load. *Ergonomics, 10*, 67–72.

Moray, N. (Ed.). (1979). *Mental workload: Its theory and measurement.* New York: Plenum.

Moray, N. (1986). Monitoring behavior and supervisory control. In K. R. Boff, L. Kaufman, & J. P. Thomas (Eds.), *Handbook of perception and performance* (vol. 2, pp. 40–1–40–51). New York: Wiley.

Moray, N. (1988). Mental workload since 1979. *International Reviews of Ergonomics, 2*, 123–150.

Mulder, G., & Mulder, L. J. (1981). Information processing and cardiovascular control. *Psychophysiology, 18*, 392–401.

Murphy, M. R., McGee, L. A., Palmer, E. A., Paulk, C. H., & Wempe, T. E. (1978). Simulator evaluation of three situation and guidance displays for V/STOL aircraft zero-zero landing approaches. *Proceedings of the IEEE International Conference on Cybernetics and Society* (pp. 563–471). New York: IEEE.

Navon, D. (1984). Resources: A theoretical soupstone. *Psychological Review, 91*, 216–334.

Navon, D., & Gopher, D. (1979). On the economy of the human processing systems. *Psychological Review, 86*, 254–255.

Navon, D., & Miller, J. (1987). The role of outcome conflict in dual-task interference. *Journal of Experimental Psychology: Human Perception & Performance, 13*, 435–448.

Nebes, R. D. (1977). Man's so-called minor hemisphere. In M. C. Wittrock (Ed.), *The human brain.* Englewood Cliffs, NJ: Prentice Hall.

Norman, D., & Bobrow, D. (1975). On data-limited and resource-limited processing. *Journal of Cognitive Psychology, 7*, 44–60.

North, R. A. & Riley, V. A. (1989). A predictive model of operator workload. In G. R. McMillan, D. Beevis, E. Salas, M. H. Strub, R. Sutton, & L. Van Breda (Eds.), *Applications of human performance models to system design* (pp. 81–90). New York: Plenum.

O'Donnell, R. D., & Eggemeier, F. T. (1986). Workload assessment methodology. In K. Boff, L. Kaufman, & J. Thomas (Eds.), *Handbook of perception and performance* (vol. 2). New York: Wiley.

Ogden, G. D., Levine, J. M., & Eisner, E. J. (1979). Measurement of workload by secondary tasks. *Human Factors, 21*, 529–548.

Orasanu, J., & Fischer, U. (1997). Finding decisions in natural environments: The view from the cockpit. In C. E. Zsambok & G. Klein (Eds.), *Naturalistic decision making* (pp. 343–358). Mahwah, NJ: Erlbaum.

Parkes, A. M., & Coleman, N. (1990). Route guidance systems: A comparison of methods of presenting directional information to the driver. In E. J. Lovesey (Ed.), *Contemporary ergonomics 1990* (pp. 480–485). London: Taylor & Francis.

Parks, D. L., & Boucek, G. P., Jr. (1989). Workload prediction, diagnosis, and continuing challenges. In G. R. McMillan, D. Beevis, E. Salas, M. H. Strub, R. Sutton, & L Van Breda (Eds.), *Applications of human performance models to system design* (pp. 47–64). New York: Plenum Press.

Pashler, H. (1989). Dissociations and contingencies between speed and accuracy: Evidence for a two-component theory of divided attention in simple tasks. *Cognitive Psychology, 21,* 469–514.

Pashler, H. E. (1998). *The psychology of attention.* Cambridge, MA: MIT Press.

Payne, J. W., Bettman, J. R., & Johnson, E. J. (1993). *The adaptive decision maker.* New York: Cambridge University Press.

Peavler, W. S. (1974). Individual differences in pupil size and performance. In M. Janissee (Ed.), *Pupillary dynamics and behavior.* New York: Plenum.

Peters, M. (1981). Attentional asymmetries during concurrent bimanual performance. *Quarterly Journal of Experimental Psychology, 33A,* 95–103.

Plott, B. (1995). *Software user's manual for WinCrew, the windows-based workload and task analysis tool.* Aberdeen Proving Ground, MD: U.S. Army Research Laboratory.

Polson, M. C., & Friedman A. (1988). Task-sharing within and between hemispheres: A multiple-resources approach. *Human Factors, 30,* 633–643.

Raby, M., & Wickens, C. D. (1994). Strategic workload management and decision biases in aviation. *The International Journal of Aviation Psychology, 4*(3), 211–240.

Reid, G. B., & Nygren, T. E. (1988). The subjective workload assessment technique: A scaling procedure for measuring mental workload. In P. A. Hancock & N. Meshkati (Eds.), *Human mental workload* (pp. 185–213). Amsterdam: North Holland.

Rogers, W., Rousseau, G. K., & Fisk, A. D. (1999). *Applications of attention research.* In F. Durso (Ed.), *Handbook of applied cognition.* West Sussix, UK: John Wiley & Sons.

Rogers, R. D., & Monsell, S. (1995). Costs of a predictable switch between simple cognitive tasks. *Journal of Experimental Psychology: General, 124*(2), 207–231.

Rolfe, J. M. (1973). The secondary task as a measure of mental load. In W. T. Singleton J. G. Fox, & D. Whitfield (Eds.), *Measurement of man at work* (pp. 135–148). London: Taylor & Francis.

Rollins, R. A., & Hendricks, R. (1980). Processing of words presented simultaneously to eye and ear. *Journal of Experimental Psychology: Human Perception & Performance, 6,* 99–109.

Sarno, K. J., & Wickens, C. D. (1995). Role of multiple resources in predicting time-sharing efficiency: Evaluation of three workload models in a multiple-task setting. *International Journal of Aviation Psychology, 5*(1), 107–130.

Scerbo, M. (1996). Theoretical perspectives on adaptive automation. In R. Parasuraman & M. Mouloua (Eds.), *Automation and human performance: Theory and applications.* Mahwah, NJ: Erlbaum.

Schlegel, R. E., Gilliland, K., & Schlegel, B. (1986). Development of the criterion task set performance data base. *Proceedings of the 30th annual meeting of the Human Factors Society* (pp. 58–62). Santa Monica, CA: Human Factors Society.

Schneider, W. (1985). Training high-performance skills: Fallacies and guidelines. *Human Factors, 27*(3), 285–300.

Schneider, W., & Detweiler, M. (1988). The role of practice in dual-task performance: Toward workload modeling in a connectionist/control architecture. *Human Factors, 30*(5), 539–566.

Schneider, W., & Fisk, A. D. (1982). Concurrent automatic and controlled visual search: Can processing occur without cost? *Journal of Experimental Psychology: Learning, Memory, and Cognition, 8,* 261–278.

Schneider, W., & Shiffrin, R. M., (1977). Controlled and automatic human information processing I: Detection, search, and attention. *Psychological Review, 84*, 1–66.

Schutte, P. C., & Trujillo, A. C. (1996). Flight crew task management in non-normal situations. *Proceedings of the 40th annual meeting of the Human Factors and Ergonomics Society* (pp. 244–248). Santa Monica, CA: Human Factors and Ergonomics Society.

Schvaneveldt, R. W. (1969). Effects of complexity in simultaneous reaction time tasks. *Journal of Experimental Psychology, 81*, 289–296.

Seamster, T. L., Redding, R. E., & Kaempf, G. L. (1997). *Applied cognitive task analysis in aviation*. Brookfield, VT: Ashgate.

Senders, J. (1964). The human operator as a monitor and controller of multidegree freedom systems. *IEEE Transactions on Human Factors in Electronics, HFE–5*, 2–6.

Shaffer, L. H. (1975). Multiple attention in continuous verbal tasks. In S. Dornic (Ed.), *Attention and performance V*. New York: Academic Press.

Shallice, T., McLeod P., & Lewis, K. (1985). Isolating cognition modules with the dual-task paradigm: Are speech perception and production modules separate? *Quarterly Journal of Experimental Psychology, 37*, 507–532.

Sheridan, T. (1972). On how often the supervisor should sample. *IEEE Transactions on Systems, Science, and Cybernetics, SSC–6*, 140–145.

Shingledecker, C. A. (1989). Handicap and human skill. In D. H. Holding (Ed.), *Human skills* (2d ed., pp. 249–279). New York: Wiley.

Sirevaag, E. J., Kramer, A. F., Wickens, C. D., Reisweber, M., Strayer, D. L., & Grenell, J. F. (1993). Assessment of pilot performance and mental workload in rotary wing aircraft. *Ergonomics, 36*, 1121–1140.

Smith, G. (Ed.). (1979). *Human Factors, 21* (5).

Soede, M. (1980). *On the mental load of arm prosthesis control*. Leiden, Neth.: TNO.

Stokes, A. F., Wickens, C. D., & Kite, K. (1990). *Display technology: Human factors concepts*. Warrendale, PA: Society of Automotive Engineers.

Summers, J. J. (1989). Motor programs. In D. H. Holding (Ed.), *Human skills* (2d ed., pp. 49–69). New York: Wiley.

Tattersal, A. J., & Hockey, G. R. J. (1995). Level of operator control and changes in heart rate variability during simulated flight maintenance. *Human Factors, 37*(4), 682–698.

Tayyari, F., & Smith, J. L. (1987). Effect of music on performance in human-computer interface. *Proceedings of the 31st annual meeting of the Human Factors Society* (pp. 1321–1325). Santa Monica, CA: Human Factors Society.

Tsang, P. S., & Wickens, C. D. (1988). The structural constraints and strategic control of resource allocation. *Human Performance, 1*, 45–72.

Tsang, P., & Wilson, G. (1997). Mental workload. In G. Salvendy (Ed.), *Handbook of human factors and ergonomics* (2d ed.). New York: Wiley.

Tulga, M. K., & Sheridan, T. B. (1980). Dynamic decisions and workload in multitask supervisory control. *IEEE Transactions on Systems, Man, and Cybernetics, SMC–10*, 217–232.

Venturino, M. (1991). Automatic processing, code dissimilarity, and the efficiency of successive memory searches. *Journal of Experimental Psychology: Human Perception & Performance, 17*, 677–695.

Vicente, K. J., Thornton, D. C., & Moray, N. (1987). Spectral analysis of sinus arrhythmia: A measure of mental effort. *Human Factors, 29*(2), 171–182.

Vidulich, M. A. (1988). Speech responses and dual task performance: Better time-sharing or asymmetric transfer. *Human Factors, 30*, 517–534.

Vidulich, M. A., & Tsang, P. S. (1986). Techniques of subjective workload assessment: A comparison of SWAT and the NASA-bipolar methods. *Ergonomics, 29,* 1385–1398.

Vidulich, M. A., & Wickens, C. D. (1986). Causes of dissociation between subjective workload measures and performance. *Applied Ergonomics, 17,* 291–296.

Violanti, J. M., & Marshall, J. R. (1996). Cellular phones and traffic accidents: An epidemiological approach. *Accident Analysis and Prevention, 28*(2), 265–270.

Walker, N., & Fisk, A. D. (1995). Human Factors goes to the gridiron: Developing a quarterback training program. *Ergonomics in Design, 3,* July, 8–13.

Weinstein, L. F., & Wickens, C. D. (1992). Use of nontraditional flight displays for the reduction of central visual overload in the cockpit. *International Journal of Aviation Psychology, 2*(2), 121–142.

Welford, A. T. (1952). The psychological refractory period and the timing of high speed performance. *British Journal of Psychology, 43,* 2–19.

Welford, A. T. (1967). Single channel operation in the brain. *Acta Psychologica, 27,* 5–21.

Wetherell, A. (1981). The efficacy of some auditory-vocal subsidiary tasks as measures of the mental load on male and female drivers. *Ergonomics, 24,* 197–214.

Wickens, C. D. (1980). The structure of attentional resources. In R. Nickerson (Ed.), *Attention and performance VIII* (pp. 239–257). Hillsdale, NJ: Erlbaum.

Wickens, C. D. (1984). Processing resources in attention. In R. Parasuraman & R. Davies (Eds.), *Varieties of attention* (pp. 63–101). New York: Academic Press.

Wickens, C. D. (1986). Gain and energetics in information processing. In R. Hockey, A. Gaillard, & M. Coles (Eds.), *Energetics and human information processing* (pp. 373–390). Dordrecht, Neth.: Martinus Nijhoff.

Wickens, C. D. (1990). Resource management and time-sharing. In J. I. Elkind, S. K. Card, J. Hochberg, & B. M. Huey (Eds.), *Human performance models for computer-aided engineering* (pp. 181–202). Orlando, FL: Academic Press.

Wickens, C. D. (1991). Processing resources and attention. In D. Damos (Ed.), *Multiple task performance.* London: Taylor & Francis.

Wickens, C. D. (1992). *Engineering psychology and human performance* (2d ed.). New York: Harper Collins.

Wickens, C. D., & Carswell, C. M. (1995). The proximity compatibility principle: Its psychological foundation and relevance to display design. *Human Factors, 37*(3), 473–494.

Wickens, C. D., & Gopher, D. (1977). Control theory measures of tracking as indices of attention allocation strategies. *Human Factors, 19,* 54–366.

Wickens, C. D., Hyman, F., Dellinger, J., Taylor, H., & Meador, M. (1986). The Sternberg Memory Search task as an index of pilot workload. *Ergonomics, 29,* 1371–1383.

Wickens, C. D., & Liu, Y. (1988). Codes and modalities in multiple resources: A success and a qualification. *Human Factors, 30,* 599–616.

Wickens, C. D., Sandry, D., & Vidulich, M. (1983). Compatibility and resource competition between modalities of input, output, and central processing. *Human Factors, 25,* 227–248.

Wickens, C. D., & Seidler, K. S. (1997). Information access in a dual-task context: Testing a model of optimal strategy selection. *Journal of Experimental Psychology: Applied, 3*(3), 196–215.

Wickens, C. D., Vidulich, M., & Sandry-Garza, D. (1984). Principles of S-C-R compatibility with spatial and verbal tasks. *Human Factors, 26,* 533–543.

Wiener, E. L., & Curry, R. E. (1980). Flight deck automation: Promises and problems. *Ergonomics, 23*(1), 995–1011.

Wiener, E. L., Kanki, B. G., & Helmreich, R. L. (1993). *Cockpit resource management.* San Diego, CA: Academic Press.

Wierwille, W. W., & Casali, J. G. (1983). A validated rating scale for global mental workload measurement applications. *Proceedings of the 27th annual meeting of the Human Factors Society.* Santa Monica, CA: Human Factors Society.

Wierwille, W. W., Rahimi, M., & Casali, J. G. (1985). Evaluation of 16 measures of mental workload using a simulated flight task emphasizing mediational activity. *Human Factors, 25,* 1–16.

Wikman, A. S., Nieminen, T., & Summala, H. (1998). Driving experience and time-sharing during in-car tasks on roads of different width. *Ergonomics, 41*(3), 358–372.

Williges, R. C., & Wierwille, W. W. (1979). Behavioral measures of aircrew mental workload. *Human Factors, 21,* 549–5

Yeh, Y.-Y., & Wickens, C. D. (1988). The dissociation of subjective measures of mental workload and performance. *Human Factors, 30,* 111–120.

Zakay, D., Block, R. A., & Tsal, Y. (1999). Prospective time judgments and workload. In D. Gopher & A. Koriat (Eds.), *Attention and performance XVII.* Cambridge, MA: MIT Press.

Stress and Human Error

OVERVIEW

There is little doubt that the van driver whose plight was discussed in Chapter 1 was under stress: The weather was poor, the driving conditions were unsafe, and the equipment was failing. This stress escalated to near panic when the driver saw the stalled car and heard the truck horn, and it could well have caused the inappropriate overcorrection that overturned the vehicle. Going beyond this fictional case, disasters such as the *USS Vincennes* incident (Klein, 1996; see Chapter 8) or the Three Mile Island nuclear power plant accident have led people to ask the extent to which high levels of stress, either existing before the disaster (as in the case of the combat threat environment in the *USS Vincennes*) or caused by the first few seconds of crisis (Three Mile Island), will degrade human information processing. This degradation may compound the effects of any initial error or failure that led to the crisis in the first place. Indeed, it often seems that stress and errors are tightly linked in a closed-loop combination: When errors are made (and we become aware of them), they cause stress; and when high levels of stress exist, errors are more likely to occur. Hence, it is appropriate that we discuss in the same chapter these two important dimensions of human performance, each of which is relevant to all of the stages of processing and mental operations that we have discussed in the previous chapters. We begin by discussing stress, its definition, its measurement, and most important, its effects.

STRESS

The concept of stress is most easily understood in the context of Figure 12.1. On the left of the figure is a set of *stressors*, typically degrading, influences on information processing and cognition that are not inherent in the content of that information itself, nor in the skills of the human. Stressors may include such influences as noise, vibration, heat, dim lighting, and high acceleration, as well as such psychological factors as anxiety,

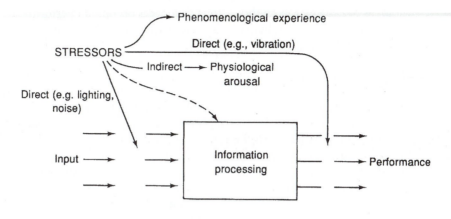

Figure 12.1 A representation of stress effects.

fatigue, frustration, and anger. As discussed in Chapter 8, they may also include time pressure (Svenson & Maule, 1993). Such forces typically have three manifestations: (1) They produce a phenomenological experience and often an emotional or "affective" one. For example, we are usually (but not always) able to report a feeling of frustration or arousal as a consequence of a stressor. (2) Closely linked, a change in physiology is often observable. This might be a short-term change—such as the increase in heart rate associated with flying an aircraft (Hart & Hauser, 1987) or the stress of air traffic controllers in high-load situations (Romhert, 1979)—or it might be a more sustained effect, such as the change in the output of catecholamines, measured in the urine, after periods of flying simulated combat maneuvers in an F16 (Burton, Storm, Johnson, & Leverett, 1977) or actual battlefield events (Bourne, 1971). The phenomenological and physiological characteristics are often, but not invariantly, linked. (3) Stressors affect characteristics of information processing, although this effect need not always degrade performance.

As Figure 12.1 shows, these effects may be characterized as having either external or internal influences on human performance. External stressors influence the quality of information received by the receptors, or the precision of the motor or vocal response, and hence, their influences and effects are more easily predictable. For example, vibration will reduce the quality of visual input for fine detail and the precision of motor control, and noise will do the same for auditory input (see Chapter 6). Time stress may simply curtail the amount of information that can be perceived in a way that will quite naturally degrade performance. Sleep loss can have an external influence on sustained visual tasks, by increasing the frequency of eye closures.

Some of these stressors, however—like noise or sleep loss—as well as others for which no external effect can be observed—like anxiety, fear, or incentives—also appear to influence the efficiency of information processing through internal mechanisms that have not yet been described. Because of our emphasis on engineering psychology and human performance, rather than on the nonpsychological aspects of human factors, we will focus our discussion on those stress influences on human performance that have internal influences, rather than those such as lighting, cold, or vibration that have physically measurable external effects.

Stress Effects on Performance

The engineering psychologist wishes to predict stress effects on human performance because many environments in which people work can be stressful: the store clerk under pressure from impatient customers, the student making her first oral presentation to the class, or the operator of complex equipment that has suddenly failed. Knowing how human performance degrades can help to support the design of more stress-tolerant interfaces, or to develop stress-reducing training techniques. But developing models that will accurately predict stress effects is challenging for two reasons. First, ethical considerations make it difficult to carry out controlled experiments that place human subjects under the same levels of stress that might be characteristic of environments or conditions for which that prediction is desired: for example combat or other life- or health-threatening circumstances. Hence, relatively little empirical data exist, compared to the available human performance data in many other domains of engineering psychology. Second, for reasons that are described below, human performance response to stressors appears to be inconsistent and unpredictable, modulated by a great number of cognitive, skill, and personality variables, which makes derivation of general predictions quite challenging. Before we describe the pattern of effects that have been observed by different stressors, we consider some of the possible sources of data from which the pattern of human stress response can be inferred.

First, it is possible to examine many situations like the *USS Vincennes* incident, or Three Mile Island, in which errors were made, and stress was undoubtedly high (Orasanu, 1997). One might draw inferences that stress was a causal factor in the errors made in the events, yet the causal inferences will always be ambiguous. Did stress cause the error? Or was stress a consequence of an error that might have occurred just as well under unstressed conditions? How many similar stressful circumstances have people confronted *without* making the errors of the incident in question? A careful analysis of the *USS Vincennes* incident carried out by Klein (1996) revealed relatively little evidence that stress was responsible for the unfortunate decision to fire on the commercial aircraft.

Second, there have been a series of efforts to capitalize on stress imposed for other reasons, to gain insights into performance changes. Ursin, Baade, and Levine (1978) and Simonov, Frolov, Evtushenko, and Suiridov (1977) examined performance of parachutists awaiting their first jump. In a classic study, Berkun (1964) examined performance of army soldiers in combat exercises when high stress conditions were imposed. Berkun employed three different experimental manipulations to induce a very realistic experience of stress. In one manipulation, the subjects were led to believe—as they attempted to fill out an insurance form—that the aircraft in which they were flying was in danger of crashing. In a second manipulation, the subjects were led to believe that artillery shells were exploding around them, the result of a confusion in their location by the artillery, as they tried to follow procedures to initiate a radio call to redirect the fire. In the third manipulation, the subjects believed that a demolition had seriously injured one of their fellow soldiers, and they needed to follow procedures in calling for help. Thus, in all cases, the subjects believed that they or someone they felt responsible for was at serious mortal risk. All of these studies revealed substantial effects of stress on different aspects of performance (form filling, equipment repair, procedures following).

Third, a number of studies have examined the effects of stressors such as the threat of shock, temperature, noise, sleep loss, or time pressure in more controlled laboratory environments. Such studies have been important in confirming some of the patterns of effects that will be discussed below (Hockey, 1986). However, most have the inevitable shortcoming that the laboratory conditions can never fully replicate the true experienced stress of the danger in emergency conditions, a pattern whose prediction is so important for system design.

Stress Component Effect

One of the best ways of integrating the effects of stress on performance of tasks, observed from the different classes of data discussed above, is to consider their influence on the different *information processing components* or mechanisms that have been discussed in the previous chapters of this book (Hockey, 1986). Thus, given the nature of a stressor effect on processing components, like selective attention, working memory, or response choice, and given the dependence of a task on particular components, a framework is established for predicting task performance changes. For example, if stressor A affects working memory and task B uses working memory but task C does not, we can predict that stressor A will affect task B but not task C. In the following pages, we first describe these component effects and then discuss how a large amount of variance in stress response is related to the *adaptation strategies* invoked by a particular human operator. We then describe the way in which stress response can be mediated by other nonstress factors, and finally consider some of the ways in which the negative effects of stress on performance have been remediated.

Arousal   One of the easiest ways to measure the quantitative levels of many stressors is through physiological measures of arousal, many mediated by activities of the sympathetic nervous system. These include measures such as heart rate, pupil diameter, or the output of catacholomines in the bloodstream or urine. Many of these measures reflect the increased arousal or effort associated with the motivational variable of "trying harder," either as tasks impose increasing difficulty or as goals are imposed for better performance, as discussed in our treatment of resource theory in the previous chapter (Kahneman, 1973; Maule & Hockey, 1993; Hockey, 1997). The concept of arousal has itself been differentiated into different components (Gopher & Sanders, 1985) related to input, central processing, and output, but it can generally be associated with improving the level of performance (as shown on the performance-resource function in Figure 11.1). While most stressors such as anxiety and noise are thought to increase the level of arousal, others like sleep loss or fatigue will decrease arousal.

Selective Attention: Narrowing   Changes in human selective and focused attention, as discussed in Chapter 3, mediate many stress effects. One of the most important and robust of these appears to be an increased selectivity or *attentional narrowing* that results from a wide variety of different stressors (Stokes and Kite, 1994). For example,

Weltman, Smith, and Egstrom (1971) compared the performance of two groups of subjects on a central and peripheral detection task. One group was led to believe it was experiencing the conditions of a 60-foot dive in a pressure chamber, and the other was not. In fact, there was no change in pressure for either group. Both groups showed similar performance on the central task, but performance on the peripheral task was significantly degraded for the stressed group. Similar perceptual-narrowing effects have also been found by other investigators (e.g., Bacon, 1974; Baddeley, 1972; Hockey, 1970). Although stress-produced perceptual tunneling will usually degrade performance, it is also possible to envision circumstances in which it may actually facilitate performance, that is, when focused attention is desired. Indeed, this positive effect was observed in a study by Houston (1969) in which the presence of noise stress improved rather than hurt performance on the Stroop task, described in Chapter 3. In this task, it will be recalled, one's ability to report the color ink in which a word is printed is disrupted if the word spells a color name. The failure to focus attention normally activates the competing but irrelevant color name in place of the ink color. However, the presence of noise apparently leads to greater focus on the relevant (ink color) aspect of the task and to improved Stroop performance.

Houston's (1969) data suggest that the stress effect on tunneling is not simply defined by a reduction of the spatial area of the attention spotlight, so that peripheral stimuli are automatically filtered. Rather, the filtering effect seems to be defined by subjective importance, or priority. Performance of those tasks of greatest subjective importance remain unaffected—or perhaps enhanced (through arousal)—in their processing, whereas those of lower priority are filtered (Bacon, 1974; Broadbent, 1971). In one sense, this kind of tunneling is adaptive, but it will produce undesirable effects if the high subjective importance of the attended channel proves to be unwarranted. Such was the case, for example, in the Three Mile Island incident. Operators, under the high stress following the initial failure appeared to fixate their attention on the one indicator supporting their belief that the water level was too high, thereby filtering attention from more reliable indicators that supported the opposite hypothesis. Stress-induced tunneling should have less of an effect if the task requires the processing of few information channels than if it requires the processing of many (Edland, 1989), since there is more information filtered in the latter use.

Selective Attention: Distraction Many stressors simply impose a distraction and thus divert selective attention away from task-relevant processing. Loud or intermittent noises, or even the conversation at a nearby table at the library, will serve as a source of such distraction. The documented influence of life stress events (like family or financial problems) at the workplace (Wine, 1971; Alkov, Borowsky, & Gaynor, 1982) is characterized by the distraction or diversion of attention to thinking about these issues, at the expense of processing job-related information.

Working-Memory Loss Davies and Parasuraman (1982) and Wachtel (1968) directly identified the negative effects of anxiety stress on working memory. Many of the difficulties in cognitive aspects of problem solving that Berkun (1964) observed when his army subjects were placed under the stress of perceived danger can also be attributed to reduced working-memory capacity. Noise, as well as danger and anxiety, will also degrade working memory (Hockey, 1986). The stress effects of noise on working memory can be seen to result from either of two causes. First, it is clear that noise will disrupt the "inner speech" necessary to carry out rehearsal of verbal information in the phonetic loop, as discussed in Chapter 7 (Poulton, 1976), because rehearsal is a resource-limited process. Second, both noise and non-noise stressors can distract or divert attention away from rehearsal of material that is either phonetic or spatial, in a way that will allow the representation of that information to be degraded. This second effect can account for the influence of non-noise stressors such as anxiety on working memory (Berkun, 1964), as well as the effects of either noise *or* non-noise stressors on spatial working memory (Stokes & Raby, 1989). As an example, in a simulation study of pilot decision making, Wickens, Stokes, Barnett, and Hyman (1993) observed that the negative effects of noise were quite pronounced on decision problems that relied on spatial visualization for their successful resolution. Examining aviation accident reports that might be attributed to stress effects, Orasanu (1997) noted the greater frequency of stress effects on situation awareness, a process that (as discussed in Chapter 8) is closely tied to working memory. Given the important role of working memory as well as broad selective attention in encoding new information into long-term memory, it would appear that stress would not lead to efficient learning (Keinan & Friedland, 1984). This reasoning is certainly one of the important factors behind the advocacy of simulators as useful training devices for dangerous activities such as flying or deep-sea diving (Flexman & Stark, 1987; O'Hare & Roscoe, 1990; see also Chapter 7). That is, simulators can support the complexity of the real task, without imposing its stressful dangers. It is also justification for avoiding a highly negative climate for instruction given for example the stressful implications of punishment and threats (O'Hare & Roscoe, 1990).

The Yerkes Dodson Law It is important to note that the stress effects described to this point, on arousal, attention, and working memory, may be considered collectively to define an inverted U-shaped pattern relating stress to human performance that is characterized by the *Yerkes Dodson* Law (Yerkes & Dodson, 1908). The pattern of performance effects predicted by the law are shown in Figure 12.2, and suggest that at the lower end of the arousal scale (low stress), increasing stress by increasing arousal and effort mobilization will increase performance. Higher levels of arousal, however, however, stress begins to produce the attentional and memory difficulties that cause performance to decrease. In addition to the inverted U, a second characteristic of the Yerkes Dodson Law is that the "knee" in the curve, or the optimum level of arousal, is at a lower level for the more complex task (or the less skilled operator) than for the simpler task (or expert operator). This prediction is consistent with the assumption that more complex tasks usually involve greater demands for attentional selectivity (more possible cues to sample), as well as greater working-memory load, and hence will be more vulnerable to the breakdowns of these processes at higher arousal levels.

Perseveration There is evidence that high levels of stress will cause people to "perseverate" or continue with a given action or plan of action that they have used in the past (Zakay, 1993). For example, in problem solving (Luchins, 1942) under stress, people are more likely to continue trying the same unsuccessful solution (the very failure of which might be a cause of increasing stress). Cowen (1952) found that people perseverated longer with an inappropriate problem-solving solution under the threat of shock. The concept of perseveration with previous action patterns is also consistent with the view that, under stress, familiar behavior is little hampered, but more novel behavior becomes disrupted, an effect that has profound implications for the design of procedures to be

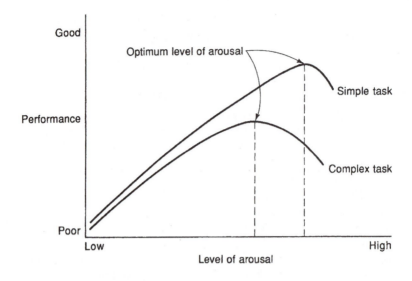

Figure 12.2 The Yerkes Dodson Law.

used under the stressful conditions of emergency. The greater disruptive effect of stress on novel or creative behavior is consistent with an effect that was observed by Shanteau and Dino (1993), who observed a selective decrease in performance on tests of creativity, caused by the combined stress of heat, crowding, and distraction.

It is apparent that the combined effects of stress on attentional narrowing and perseveration can contribute to a pattern of convergent thinking or "cognitive narrowing or tunneling" that can be dangerous in crisis decision making (Woods, Johannesen, Cook, & Sarter, 1994; see Chapter 8): Stress will initially narrow the set of cues processed to those that are perceived to be most important; as these cues are viewed to support one hypothesis, the decision maker will perseverate to consider only that hypothesis and will process the (restricted) range of cues consistent with that set. That is, stress will enhance the confirmation bias discussed in Chapter 8, causing the decision maker to be even less likely to consider the information (process cues) that might support an alternative hypothesis. This pattern can be used to describe the behavior of the operators at Three Mile Island, or the dangerous pattern of behavior in which unqualified pilots may continue to fly into bad weather (Jensen, 1982; Simmel, Cerkovnik, & McGarthy, 1987; Griffin & Rockwell, 1987).

Strategic Control Perhaps the most important processing changes that occur under stress can be characterized by the general label of *strategic control,* that is, the characterization of a set of strategies that the human will consciously adapt to cope with the perceived stress effects. These strategies are incorporated in a feedback control model, presented in Figure 12.3, which is based on similar concepts proposed by Lazarus and Folkman (1984) and Hockey (1997; Hockey, Wastell, & Sauer, 1998; Maule & Hockey, 1993). The form of the model can be seen to have important similarities with the closed-loop

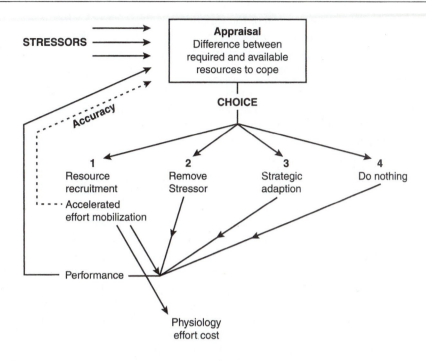

Figure 12.3   An adaptive closed-loop model of stress, based on concepts proposed by Hockey. The ability to cope with stressors is appraised at the top. A choice of one of four categories of strategies is made as a consequence of this appraisal. These choices will affect performance to varying degrees (and hence lead to a reappraisal). The choice to mobilize effort for long durations may have physiological costs. The choice to accelerate will have a selected effect of lowering accuracy.

Source: Adapted from G. R. J. Hockey, "Compensatory Control in the Regulation of Human Performance Under Stress and High Workload," *Biological Psychology, 45,* 1997, pp. 73–93; A. J. Maule and G. R. J. Hockey, "State, Stress, and Time Pressure," in *Time Pressure and Stress in Human Judgment and Decision Making,* ed. O. Svenson and A. J. Maule (New York: Plenum, 1993), pp. 83–102.

tracking feedback model described in Chapter 10 and has two key components: appraisal and strategic choice. One important concept of the model is that the operator does not respond to the stressor per se, but to the *perceived* or understood level of stress. Lazarus and Folkman label this the process of *cognitive appraisal*. Thus, two people could be in identical circumstances (i.e., under the same physical stress or dangerous conditions), but have very different appreciations of how much danger they were in, or the extent to which they had resources available to cope with the stressor. Stress would increase as the perceived disparity between necessary and available resources increases.

Having then appraised the level of stress, the human has the option of choosing a variety of different information processing strategies to cope with the stressor (Maule &Hockey, 1993; Hockey, 1997). It is in the selection of the appropriate or inappropriate strategies that a great deal of the variability of stress response between people is found. Adapting the framework proposed by Hockey (1997; Maule & Hockey, 1993), four major categories of adaptive responses may be proposed, each with somewhat different implications for performance.

1. Recruitment of More Resources   Here the response is simply to "try harder," or mobilize more resources in the face of the stressor. If the source of stress is time pressure (Svenson & Maule, 1993), then this strategy may be labeled as "acceleration" (Stiensmeier-Pelster & Schürmann, 1993): doing more in less time. Such a strategy can be adaptive, but it has risks. In the first place, the sustained mobilization of increased effort may impose long-term costs of fatigue and possible health risks (Hockey, 1997), which may leave the human vulnerable after the stressor is removed (Huey & Wickens, 1993). Furthermore, in some cases, acceleration may eliminate redundancies. As discussed in Chapter 6, removing redundancies in communications systems can invite confusions and errors.

Finally, the strategy of acceleration is one that invites a shift in the speed-accuracy trade-off, toward faster but more error-prone performance, an effect that has been observed under a variety of stressors (Hockey, 1986). For example, Villoldo and Tarno (1984) report that bomb-disposal experts worked more rapidly but made more procedural errors under stress. Keinan and Friedland (1987) found that subjects prematurely terminated problem-solving activities under the stress of a potential shock. The tendency of the stress of emergency to cause a shift in performance from accurate to fast (but error-prone) responding has been cited as a concern in operator response to complex failure in nuclear power control rooms. As discussed in Chapter 9, the operator has a desire to "do something" rapidly, when in fact, this impatience is often counterproductive until the nature of the failure is well understood. The hasty action of the control-room operators in response to the Three Mile Island incident was to shut down an automated device that had in fact been properly doing its job. To combat this tendency for a nonoptimal speed-accuracy shift in an emergency, as we noted in Chapter 9, nuclear power plant regulations in some countries explicitly require operators to perform no physical actions for a fixed time following an alarm while they gain an accurate mental picture of the nature of the malfunction.

2. Remove the Stressor   The human may sometimes adapt successfully by simply trying to eliminate the source of stress. At times this is easy, such as turning off (or removing oneself from) a stressful source of noise, postponing performance of a task till a time in which one is no longer sleep deprived, or postponing a deadline to remove time pressure. At other times, removal may be more difficult, such as putting a source of anxiety out of mind, and may depend on the availability of trained stress-coping skills, to be described below.

3. Change the Goals of the Task   Within the last two decades, stress researchers have revealed a variety of ways in which people *adaptively* invoke qualitatively different performance strategies under higher stress conditions. (Ford et al., 1989; Klein, 1996; Driskell, Salas, & Hall, 1994; Johnson, Payne, & Bettman, 1993). What makes these strategies adaptive is that they are chosen to be ones that are more immune to the known degrading effects of stress on information processing, as discussed above. Hence, a simpler, less effortful strategy is often chosen. Many of these changes have been observed in decision-making tasks under time pressure (Svenson & Maule, 1993; Flin, Salas, Strub, & Martin, 1997), as discussed in Chapter 8. In these circumstances, it has been consistently found that such pressure leads people to abandon *compensatory* strategies (in which multiple attributes of multiple options are compared) in favor of simpler noncompensatory ones, like elimination by aspects, or holistic pattern matching (Klein, 1996). The latter are simpler, quicker, and require less working memory, and hence are more stress resistant.

The skilled operator will often have available a repertoire of such strategies from which to chose the one most immune from stress effects. It is for this reason, in part, that stressors sometimes fail to produce performance decrements: Humans adapt by choosing a simpler and more efficient strategy. Indeed, sometimes stressors even produce performance *improvements* (Driskell, Salas, & Hall, 1994). For example, Lusk (1993) studied professional weather forecasters and found that, under the time pressure imposed by busier forecast (more meteorological information to be processed per unit time), forecasting discriminability actually improved.

However, it is also the case that strategy choice can degrade performance if the task is not well served by the simpler strategy. For example, a robust finding that we discussed above is that people chose to process fewer cues in decision tasks carried out under time pressure. If a decision task contains few cues, this strategy will produce no penalty, but for multiple-cue tasks, it will (Edland, 1989). Furthermore, the effects of processing fewer cues will depend on the extent to which those cues that are filtered out are less important (little cost to performance), or simply less salient. In the latter case, there *will* be a cost if the less salient cues that were filtered are also more important. Wallsten (1993) notes that both importance *and* salience are used as cue filtering attributes by people under time pressure.

4. Do Nothing   The final strategy identified by Maule and Hockey (1993) is for people to simply do nothing to adjust their processing under stress, allowing the stress effects to influence performance in a more predictable way.

In considering these four categories of choice of strategic response shown in Figure 12.3, it should be apparent that different people can respond quite differently to the same stressors in terms of when (or whether) each of the three different adjustment strategies (1–3) are invoked. Further differences will result if strategy 1 is chosen, depending on the extent to which more effort will be mobilized (a motivational issue), and if strategy 3 is chosen, depending on the extent to which the selected way of performing the task is optimal or not. It is, in part, these large degrees of choice that make accurate stress predictions hard to attain. However, some insight in stress prediction may be gained by considering some of the additional factors that *moderate* stress effects (Bowers, Weaver, & Morgan, 1996), an issue to which we now turn.

Moderating Effects

An excellent review of the influences that moderate the effects of stress is provided by Bowers, Weaver, and Morgan (1996). Here we only provide a brief overview of three such mediating variables.

Other Stressors   As we have noted, a given stress may have multiple effects. Sometimes these effects may offset each other in unexpected ways if stressors are coupled; one stressor may reduce rather than amplify the effect of another. A fairly robust example is the combined effects of sleep loss and noise (Wilkinson, 1963). Each stressor in isolation will contribute to a loss of performance. However, both together will produce a loss that is *less* than each in isolation. This effect can be understood by considering the stress effects described above in the context of Figure 12.2. The loss of performance with sleep loss results from a loss of arousal. That from noise results from increased selectivity. However, in combination, noise can often impose an increased arousal that will at least partially offset the effects of sleep deprivation.

Personality   Several investigators have examined the influence of stable measures of personality on difference in the response to stressors. Locus of control describes the extent to which individuals believe that they, rather than other forces, have control over things that influence their lives, including stressful conditions in the environment (Kanfer & Seidner, 1973). These two beliefs (self vs. other) describe an internal versus external locus of control, respectively. Given the importance of cognitive appraisal in modifying stress effects, it is not surprising that those with an internal locus of control are less stressed by an anxiety-provoking situation because of their belief that they can exert some control over it (Driskell et al., 1991). A second personality variable, identified by Kuhl (1985), is the distinction between action-oriented and state-oriented people. The action-oriented tend to be more proactive in responding to increases in time pressure and effectively *filter* less relevant material. State-oriented people tend to be more reactive and are more inclined to *accelerate* performance (Stiensmeier-Pelster & Schürmann, 1993). This contrast illustrates a difference in the strategic adaptation characteristic between the first and third mode shown in Figure 12.3.

Training and Expertise   A well-validated effect in stress research is that highly skilled operators are generally more immune or "buffered" from the negative effects of stress than are novices. The effect, for example, has been shown both for Army combat personnel in Berkun's (1964) experiment and for pilot decision making under stress (Stokes, Kemper, & Kite, 1997, Stokes & Kite, 1994). The general effect can be associated with three more specific causes. First, as we noted in previous chapters, skill leads to automaticity of tasks and to replacement of knowledge-based behavior by rule and skill-based behavior. In the context of our discussion of multiple-task performance in Chapter 11, such performance is less resource limited. Hence, the expert is less likely to be placed in circumstances in which performance will fail (a source of stress), and any reallocation of resources away from the task at hand to address the stressor will be less likely to degrade performance. However, it should be noted here that many of the *emergency* circumstances that cause stress may also be those for which the well-trained and automated routines of the expert are no longer well suited, and the expert may be nearly as unfamiliar or unpracticed with emergency response behavior as is the novice. Hence, pure expertise in routine performance is not sufficient to provide an effective stress response to failure (Keinan & Friedland, 1996).

Second, the expert will be more likely to have a greater repertoire of strategies available to perform a given task, to monitor and know the effectiveness of those strategies, through meta cognition and hence be better able to carry out an adaptive shift, as reflected in Figure 12.3. Third, high levels of experience may themselves lead to greater familiarity with the stressors, or with knowledge of the effects of stressors on performance and, hence, better ways of coping with those effects. Successful experience in a stressful situation can greatly reduce the anticipated anxiety of repeated performance (Mandler, 1984), and this effect can actually exert itself fairly early in practice. For example, Ursin, Baade, and Levine (1978) assessed the physiological measures of stress before the first and second parachute jumps of a group of trainees. The investigators observed a large drop in those measures between the two jumps, signaling the relief, as it were, that successful performance was possible. The notion that people can be explicitly trained to understand the effects of stress on their performance is embodied in a set of techniques for Stress Exposure Training (Johnston & Cannon-Bowers, 1996; Meichenbaum, 1985), which we discuss below.

Stress Remediation

A variety of techniques may be adopted in the effort to minimize the degrading effects of stress on human performance. Roughly these may be categorized as environmental solutions, design solutions that address the task, and personal solutions that address the operator, either through task training or through training of stress management strategies.

Environmental Solutions   Clearly, where possible, stressors should be removed from the environment, a solution that is more feasible in the case of external stressors, such as noise or temperature, than for internal stressors such as those related to anxiety.

Design Solutions   Design solutions may focus on the human factors of displays (Wickens, 1996). If perceptual narrowing among information sources or unsystematic scanning does occur, then reducing the amount of unnecessary information (visual clutter) and increasing its organization as discussed in Chapter 3 will somewhat buffer the degrading effects of stress. Schwartz and Howell (1985) found that the degrading effects of time pressure on a simulated decision task were reduced by using a graphic rather than a digital display. Similarly, it is clear that any design efforts that minimize the need for operators to maintain or transform information in working memory should be effective. Also, high display compatibility, either with responses or with the mental model of the task, is important. The manner in which this is achieved through the design of ecological interfaces was briefly discussed in Chapter 3 and 4 and will be discussed again in the final chapter.

Particular attention should be given to the design of support for emergency procedures, since these will probably be less familiar than routine procedures (to the extent that emergencies happen rarely), and will likely be needed under the high-stress conditions that are, by definition, the properties of an emergency. Hence, these procedures must be clear and simply phrased (see Chapter 6) and should be as consistent as possible with routine operations. Ideally, procedural instructions of what to do should be redundantly coded with speech as well as with print or pictures, should avoid arbitrary symbolic coding (abbreviations or tones, other than general alerting alarms), and should be phrased in direct statements of what action to take rather than as statements of what *not* to do (avoid negatives). As discussed in Chapter 6, commanded actions or procedures should augment any information that only describes the current state of the system and should not be confusable with that status information. This is the policy inherent in voice alerts for aircraft in air traffic emergencies, in which commands are directed to the pilot of what to do to avoid collision ("Climb, climb, climb") (Avionics, 1990).

Training   We have noted before the beneficial effects of training, particularly extensive training of key emergency procedures so that they become the dominant and easily retrieved habits from long-term memory when stress imposes that bias. A case can possibly be made that training for emergency procedures should be given greater priority than training for routine operations, particularly when emergency procedures (or those to be followed in high-stress situations) are in some way inconsistent with normal operations. As an example of this inconsistency, the procedure to be followed in an automobile when losing control on ice (an emergency) is to turn in the direction *toward* the skid, precisely the opposite of our conventional turning habits in normal driving. Clearly, where possible, systems should be designed so that procedures followed under emergencies are as consistent as possible with those followed under normal operations.

Programs of *stress inoculation training* or *stress exposure training* have been designed to introduce humans to the consequences of stress on their performance (Meichenbaum, 1985, 1993; Keinan & Friedland, 1996; Johnston & Cannon-Bowers, 1996). Such programs provide a mixture of explanation of anticipated stress effects, teaching of stress coping strategies, and actual experience of stressors on performance, an experience that is gradually introduced and *adaptively* increased (see Chapter 7). A review of studies that have evaluated such techniques, applied to such stressful circumstances as test taking, rock descending, public speaking, or volleyball performance, reveals that many of them have been successful (Johnston & Cannon-Bowers, 1996). However, positive benefits to trainee attitude (greater confidence) seems to be more consistently observed across these studies than benefits to actual performance, although some of the latter have been observed.

Conclusion

In conclusion, it is apparent that prediction of the effects of stressors on performance remains one of the greatest challenges for human performance theory, a consequence of the multidimensional effects of stress, and the multiple compensatory or coping strategies available. These must be revealed by looking beyond the final output of task performance to consider the behavior and cognitive processes involved in that performance, as well as physiological reflections of coping strategies. However, the very availability of those strategies, which can make performance prediction difficult for engineering psychology, serves as a real benefit for human factors, by making available several options for effective remediation, through training and design.

Finally, as we have noted, stress and error are integrally related. Increased errors are likely to occur as a consequence of an accelerated coping strategy, and errors themselves represent sources of stress. Hence, we turn now to an in-depth discussion of errors—both those resulting from stress and those resulting from other causes.

HUMAN ERROR

In all phases of human performance, errors seem to be a frequent occurrence. It has been estimated in various surveys that human error is the primary cause of 60 to 90 percent of major accidents and incidents in complex systems such as nuclear power, process control, and aviation (Rouse & Rouse, 1983; Reason, 1997). Card, Moran, and Newell (1983) estimate that operators engaged in word processing make mistakes or choose inefficient commands on 30 percent of their choices. In one study of a well-run intensive care unit, doctors and nurses were estimated to make an average of 1.7 errors per patient per day (Gopher et al., 1989); and although the overall accident rate in commercial and business aviation is extremely low, the proportion of accidents attributable to human error is considerably greater than that due to machine failure (Nagel, 1988; Wiegmann & Shappell, 1997). In the face of these statistics, it is important to reiterate a point made in Chapter 1—that many of the errors people commit in operating systems are the result of bad system design or bad organizational structure rather than irresponsible action (Norman, 1988; Reason, 1990, 1997; Woods & Cook, 1999). Furthermore, although human error in accident analysis may be statistically defined as a contributing cause to an accident, usually the error was only one of a lengthy and complex chain of breakdowns—many of them mechanical or organizational—that affected the system and weakened its defenses (Perrow, 1984; Reason, 1997).

We have already discussed human error in various guises and forms, as we have discussed the different ways in which human performance can fall short. Examples include misses and false alarms in signal detection, failures of absolute judgment or discrimination leading to misclassification, failures of working memory leading to forgetting, a variety of "decision errors" resulting from biases and heuristics, or tracking errors resulting from high bandwidth or instability.

We have also considered human error directly in the context of the speed-accuracy trade-off and reaction time in Chapter 9. Cognitive sets for fast performance produce more errors; some design or environmental factors (e.g., stress or voice display) lead to faster but more error-prone responding. When processing is easy, faster responses are more likely to be in error; but when processing is more difficult, because of low perceptual quality or high memory load, slow responses are more likely to be in error.

Why focus, then, explicitly on the product of human error, having covered the processes by which that error is generated? One reason is that the study of human error has emerged as an important and well-defined discipline (Norman, 1981; Park, 1997; Reason, 1990, 1997; Senders & Moray, 1991; Woods, Johannesen, Cook, & Sarter, 1994; Woods & Cook, 1999). Many human factors practitioners have realized that errors made in operating systems are far more important and costly than delays of the 10 to 500 millisecond magnitude typically observed in laboratory RT studies. This realization has forced human performance theorists to consider the extent to which design guidelines based on RT generalize to error prediction; it has also led researchers to consider classes of errors that do not necessarily result from the speed stress typical of the RT paradigm—for example, forgetting to change a mode switch on a computer or pouring orange juice rather than syrup on your waffles. A second reason is that a number of important human factors concerns in the treatment of human error cannot be isolated only in errors of a certain kind (e.g., nonoptimal beta settings or fast guesses in reaction time). Rather, these concerns, related to the statistics of error description and prediction and the approaches to error remediation, address errors of all kinds, no matter from which stage of processing they originate. Hence, it is appropriate to treat them together in a single chapter.

We first consider how human error is categorized within a framework that is consistent with the information processing model presented in this book. We next turn to efforts to predict human errors statistically through the applications of reliability analyses. We then place human error in the context of larger organizational factors, and finally, we consider its remediation. How should training, system design, or task design be brought to bear to reduce its likelihood or impact.

Categories of Human Error: An Information Processing Approach

A variety of taxonomies or classification schemes have been proposed for characterizing human error (Park, 1997; Wiegmann & Shappell, 1997). One example is the simple dichotomy between errors of commission (doing the wrong thing), and errors of omission (not doing anything when something should have been done). A more elaborate classification scheme, consistent with the information processing representation in this book, is presented in Figure 12.4 and is based on schemes developed by Norman (1981, 1988) and Reason (1984, 1990, 1997). The human operator, confronting a state of the world represented by stimulus evidence, may or may not interpret that evidence correctly; then, given an interpretation, the operator may or may not *intend* to carry out the right action

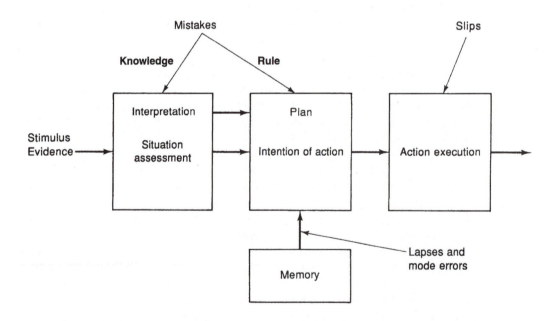

Figure 12.4 Information processing context for representing human error.

to deal with the situation; finally, the operator may or may not execute that intention correctly. Errors of interpretation or of the choice of intentions are called *mistakes*. Thus, the misdiagnosis of the status of the nuclear power plant at Three Mile Island is a clear example of a mistake. So, too, would be the misunderstanding of the meaning of a button on a push-button phone—a misunderstanding that would lead to its incorrect use.

Quite different from mistakes are *slips,* in which the understanding of the situation is correct and the correct intention is formulated, but the wrong action is accidentally triggered. Common examples are the typist who presses the wrong key or the driver who turns on the wipers instead of the headlights.

As shown in Figure 12.4, it is possible for either or both kinds of errors to occur in a given operation. In fact, it may even be possible for both kinds of errors to cancel one another out in various ways. For example, you mistakenly formulate the intention to push the wrong button, but you slip and push what actually turns out to be the right one. Mistakes and slips have a number of interesting characteristics and discriminating features, but a full understanding of error in human information processing requires the categorization of error types to be somewhat expanded to include those related to memory failures. Following are five categories that have been synthesized from the more detailed schemes (and excellent readings) of Norman (1981, 1988) and Reason (1990, 1997), all presented within the context of Figure 12.4.

Mistakes Mistakes—failing to formulate the right intentions—can actually result from the shortcomings of perception, memory, and cognition. Reason (1990) has discriminated between knowledge-based and rule-based mistakes. *Knowledge-based-mistakes* are like the kinds of errors made in decision making, in which incorrect plans of actions are arrived at because of a failure to understand the situation (i.e., incorrect knowledge). Such failures result, in part, from the influences of many of the biases and cognitive limits described in Chapters 6, 7, and 8. Operators misinterpret communications, their working memory limits are overloaded, they fail to consider all the alternatives, they may succumb to a confirmation bias, and so forth. Knowledge-based mistakes may also result from insufficient knowledge or expertise to interpret complex information. Finally, knowledge-based mistakes can often be blamed on poor displays that either present inadequate information or present it in a poor format, for example a table of digital readouts rather than clear graphical readouts.

Rule-based mistakes, in contrast, occur when operators are somewhat more sure of their ground. They know (or believe they know) the situation, and they invoke a rule or plan of action to deal with it. The choice of a rule typically follows an "if-then" logic. When understanding the environmental conditions (diagnosis) matches the "if" part of the rule or when the rule has been used successfully in the past, the "then" part is activated. The latter may be an action—"If my computer fails to read the disk, I'll reload and try again"—or simply a diagnosis or situation assessment—"If the patient shows a set of symptoms, then the patient has a certain disease."

Why might rules fail and thereby cause mistakes? Reason notes that a good rule might be misapplied when the "if" conditions that trigger it are not actually met by the environment. This mistake often occurs as exceptions to rules are encountered. The rule has worked well in most cases, but subtle distinctions in the environment or context now indicate that it is no longer appropriate. These distinctions or qualifications might be overlooked, or their importance might not be realized. For example, although it is usually appropriate to turn a vehicle in the direction in which you wish to go, an exception occurs when skidding on ice. The correct rule then is to turn first *toward* the direction of the skid to regain control of the vehicle. Alternatively, rule-based mistakes can result when a "bad rule" is learned and applied.

Reason (1990) argues that the choice of a rule is guided very much by frequency and reinforcement. That is, rules will be chosen that have frequently been employed in the past if they have been successful and therefore reinforced. Rule-based mistakes tend to be made with a fair degree of certainty, as the operator believes that the triggering conditions are in effect and that the rule is appropriate and correct. Thus, Reason describes rule-based mistakes as "strong but wrong."

While both rule-based and knowledge-based mistakes characterize intentions that are not appropriate for the situation, there are some important differences between the two. Rule-based mistakes will be performed with confidence, whereas in a situation in which rules do not apply and where knowledge-based mistakes are more likely, the operator will be less certain. The latter situation will also involve far more conscious effort, and the likelihood of making a mistake while functioning at a knowledge-based level is higher than it is at a rule-based level (Reason, 1990) because there are so many more ways in which information acquisition and integration can fail—through shortcomings of attention, working memory, logical reasoning, and decision making.

Slips   In contrast to mistakes, in which the intended action is wrong (either because the diagnosis is wrong or the rule for action selection is incorrect), slips are errors in which the right intention is incorrectly carried out. A common class of slips are capture errors, which result when the intended stream of behavior is "captured" by a similar, well-practiced behavior pattern. Such a capture is allowed to take place for three reasons: (1) The intended action (or action sequence) involves a slight departure from the routine, frequently performed action, (2) some characteristics of either the stimulus environment or the action sequence itself are closely related to the now inappropriate (but more frequent) action; and (3) the action sequence is relatively automated and therefore not monitored closely by attention. As Reason (1990) says, "When an attentional check is omitted, the reins of action or perception are likely to be snatched by some contextually appropriate strong habit (action schema), or expected pattern (recognition schema)."

Pouring orange juice rather than syrup on the waffles while reading the newspaper is a perfect example of a slip. Clearly, the act was not intended, nor was it attended, since attention was focused on the paper. Finally, both the stimulus (the tactile feel of the pitcher) and the response (pouring) of the intended and the committed action were sufficiently similar that capture was likely to occur. A more serious type of slip—related to the same underlying cause—occurs when the incorrect one of two similarly configured and closely placed controls is activated, for example, flaps and landing gear on some classes of small aircraft. Both controls have similar appearance, feel, and direction; they are located close together; both are relevant during the same phases of flight (takeoff and landing); and both are to be operated when there are often large attention demands in a different direction (outside the cockpit). One might also imagine slips occurring in a lengthy procedure of checks and switch setting that is operated in one particular way when a system is in its usual state but involves a change midway through the sequence when the system is in a different state. In the absence of close attention, the standard action sequence could easily capture the stream of behavior.

Lapses   Whereas slips represent the commission of an incorrect action different from the intended one, lapses represent the failure to carry out any action at all. As such, they can be directly tied to failures of memory, but they are quite distinct from the knowledge-based mistakes associated with working-memory overload typical of poor decision making. Instead, the typical lapse is what is colloquially referred to as forgetfulness, like forgetting to remove the last page from the photocopier when you have finished (Reason, 1997). Important lapses may involve the omission of steps in a procedural sequence. In this case, an interruption is what often causes the sequence to be stopped, then started again a step or two later than it should have been, with the preceding step now missing. The analysis of the crash of a Northwest Airlines MD–80 outside of the Detroit airport revealed that the pilots, progressing through a routine taxi checklist, were interrupted midway by air traffic control, who requested a runway change. When the checklist was resumed, a critical step of setting the flaps had been skipped, a major cause of the subsequent failure of the aircraft to take off safely (National Transportation Safety Board, 1988).

Unfortunately, lapses occur all too frequently in maintenance or installation procedures when a series of steps must be completed but the omission of a single step can be critical (Reason, 1997). Such a step might be the tightening of a nut, closing a fastener, or removing a tool that had been used in the maintenance procedure. One survey of the causes of 276 in-flight aircraft engine shutdowns revealed that incomplete installation (i.e., a step was missed) was by far the largest cause, occurring over twice as frequently as the second largest (Boeing, 1994).

Mode Errors   Mode errors are closely related to slips but also have the memory failure characteristic of lapses. They result when a particular action that is highly appropriate in one mode of operation is performed in a different, inappropriate mode because the operator has not correctly remembered the appropriate context (Norman, 1988). An example would be pressing the accelerator of a car to start at an intersection when the transmission is in the "reverse" mode. Mode errors are becoming of increasing concern in more automated cockpits, which have various modes of autopilot control (Sarter & Woods, 1995; Wiener, 1988). Mode errors are also of major concern in human-computer interactions if the operator must deal with keys that serve very different functions, depending on the setting of another part of the system. Even on the simple word processor, a typist who intends to type a string of digits (e.g., 1965) may mistakenly leave the case setting in the uppercase mode and so produce !(^%. Mode errors may occur in computer text editing, in which a command that is intended to delete a line of text may instead delete an entire page (or data file) because the command was executed in the wrong mode.

Mode errors are a joint consequence of relatively automated performance or of high workload—when the operator fails to be aware of which mode is in operation—and of improperly conceived system design, in which such mode confusions can have major consequences. The reason, of course, that mode errors can occur is that a single action may be made in both appropriate and inappropriate circumstances.

Distinctions Between Error Categories   The various categories of error can be distinguished in a number of respects. For example, as already noted, knowledge-based mistakes tend to be characteristic of a relatively low level of experience with the situation and a high attention demand focused on the task, whereas rule-based mistakes, and particularly slips, are associated with higher skill levels. Slips are also more likely to occur when attention is directed away from rather than to the problem in question (a redirection that is only possible and likely when the task *is* well learned and somewhat automated).

One of the most important contrasts between slips on the one hand, and mistakes and lapses on the other, is in the ease of detectability. The detection of slips appears to be relatively easy because people typically monitor, consciously or unconsciously, their motor output, and when the feedback of this output fails to match the expected feedback (based on the correctly formulated intentions), the discrepancy is often detected. Thus, as noted in Chapter 9, typing errors (usually slips) are very easily detected (Rabbitt & Vyas, 1970). In contrast, when the intentions themselves are wrong (mistakes) or a step is omitted (lapse), any feedback about the error arrives much later, if at all, and errors cannot easily be detected on-line. This distinction in error correction is clearly backed up with data. In an analysis of simulated nuclear power plant incidents, Woods (1984) found that half of the slips were detected by the operators themselves, whereas none of the mistakes were noted. Sarter and Alexander (1999) note the easier detectability of slips than mistakes and lapses in aviation incidents. Reason (1990) summarized data from other empirical studies to conclude that the ease of error correction, as well as error detection, also favors slips over mistakes. This factor is in part related to the easier cognitive process of revising an action rather than reformulating an intention, rule, or diagnosis. However, system design principles related to the visibility of feedback and the reversibility of action, to be discussed below, can have a large impact on how easy it is to *recover* from a slip after its detection.

Given the many differences between slips and mistakes, it is logical to assume that the two major categories should have somewhat different prescriptions for their remediation: heaviest emphasis on preventing slips should focus on system and task design, addressing issues like S-R compatibility and the similarity and confusability between stimuli and between controls. For the prevention of mistakes, in contrast, it is necessary to focus relatively more on design features related to effective displays (supporting accurate updating of a mental model) and on training (Rouse & Morris, 1987).

Human Reliability Analysis

In the wake of the public's concern for the possibility of a nuclear accident and, therefore, the reliability of nuclear power systems, within which the human operator represents a vital link, a number of efforts have been directed toward applying engineering reliability analysis to the human operator (Park, 1997; Kirwan & Ainsworth, 1992; Miller & Swain, 1987). The objective of this analysis is to predict human error.

A fairly precise analytic technique can predict the reliability (probability of failure or mean time between failures) of a complex mechanical or electrical system consisting of components of known reliabilities that are configured in series or in parallel (Figure 12.5). For example, consider a system consisting of two components, each with a reliability of 0.9 (i.e., a 10 percent chance of failure during a specified time period). Suppose the components are arranged in series, so that if either fails, the total system fails (Figure 12.5a). This describes "the chain is only as strong as its weak-

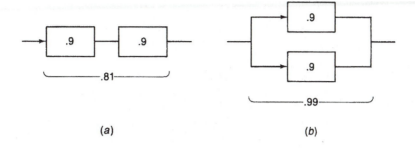

Figure 12.5 (a) Two components in series; (b) two components in parallel. The numbers in the boxes indicate the component reliabilities. The numbers below indicate the system reliabilities. Probability of error = 1.0 − reliability.

est link" situation. The probability that the system will *not* fail (the probability that both components will work successfully) is $0.9 \times 0.9 = 0.81$. This is the system reliability. Therefore, the probability of system failure is precisely $1 − (0.9 \times 0.9) = 1 − 0.81 = 0.19$. In contrast, if the two components are arranged in parallel (redundantly), as in Figure 12.5b, so that the system will fail only if *both* of them fail, the probability of system failure is $0.1 \times 0.1 = 0.1$. Its reliability is 0.99.

The work of Swain and his colleagues on the technique for human error rate prediction (THERP) attempts to bridge the gap between machine and human reliability in the prediction of human error (Miller & Swain, 1987; Swain, 1990; Swain & Weston, 1988). THERP has three important components.

1. Human error probability (HEP) is expressed as the ratio of the number of errors made on a particular task to the number of opportunities for errors. For example, for the task of routine keyboard data entry, a HEP = 1/100. These values are obtained, where possible, from databases of actual human performance (Park, 1997). When such data are lacking, they are instead estimated by experts, although such estimates can be heavily biased and are not always terribly reliable (Reason, 1990).
2. When a task analysis is performed on a series of procedures, it is possible to work forward through an event tree, or fault tree, such as that shown in Figure 12.6. In the figure, the two events (or actions) performed are A and B, and each can be performed either correctly (lower case) or in error (capital). An example might be an operator who must read a value from a table (event A) and then enter it into a keyboard (event B). Following the logic of parallel and serial components, and if the reliability of the components can be accurately determined, it is then possible to deduce the probability of successfully (5) completing the combined procedure or, alternatively, the probability that the procedure will fail (F) and be in error, as shown at the bottom of the figure.
3. The HEPs that make up the event tree can be modified by performance-shaping factors, multipliers that predict how a given HEP will increase or decrease as a function of expertise or the stress of an emergency (Miller & Swain, 1987). Table 12.1 is an example of the predicted effects of these two variables.

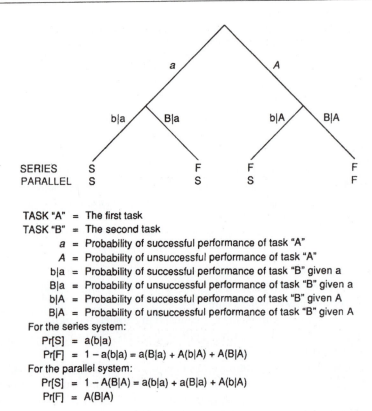

SERIES	S	F	F	F
PARALLEL	S	S	S	F

TASK "A" = The first task
TASK "B" = The second task
        a = Probability of successful performance of task "A"
        A = Probability of unsuccessful performance of task "A"
      $b|a$ = Probability of successful performance of task "B" given a
      $B|a$ = Probability of unsuccessful performance of task "B" given a
      $b|A$ = Probability of successful performance of task "B" given A
      $B|A$ = Probability of unsuccessful performance of task "B" given A
For the series system:
    $\Pr[S] = a(b|a)$
    $\Pr[F] = 1 - a(b|a) = a(B|a) + A(b|A) + A(B|A)$
For the parallel system:
    $\Pr[S] = 1 - A(B|A) = a(b|a) + a(B|a) + A(b|A)$
    $\Pr[F] = A(B|A)$

Figure 12.6   Fault tree. S and F represent success and failure of the combined operation.
Source: D. Miller and A. Swain, "Human Reliability Analysis," in *Handbook of Human Factors*, ed. G. Salvendy (New York: Wiley, 1987). Copyright 1987 by Wiley. Reprinted by permission.

Further advances of human reliability analysis have focused specifically on speed stress, by modeling the probability that specific events will be diagnosed and acted on correctly within a given period of time, subsequent to a system failure (Wreathall, 1982). This and other techniques for estimating human reliability are described in some detail by Reason (1990), Kirwan and Ainsworth (1992), and Park (1997).

Human reliability analysis represents an admirable beginning to the development of predictive models of human error. Its advocates argue that it can be a useful tool for identifying critical human factors deficiencies. Furthermore, as noted in Chapter 1, providing hard HEP numbers, the output from the model, which document poor human factors in the form of increased predicted errors, can be an effective tool for lobbying designers to incorporate human factors concerns (Swain, 1990). In spite of its potential value, however, human reliability analysis has a number of major shortcomings, which have been carefully articulated by

TABLE 12.1 Model Accounting for Stress and Experience in Performing Routine Tasks

	Increase in error probability	
Stress Level	*Skilled*	*Novice*
Very low	× 2	× 2
Optimum	× 1	× 1
Moderately high	× 2	× 4
Extremely high	× 5	× 10

Source: D. Miller & A. Swain, "Human Reliability Analysis," in G. Salvendy (ed.), *Handbook of Human Factors*. New York: John Willey & Sons, Inc. Reprinted by permission.

Adams (1982), Reason (1990), Dougherty (1990), and Apostolakis (1990). Briefly, these are as follows.

Lack of Database   Empirically based data exist for HEP in simple acts, such as dial reading or keyboard entry under nonstressed conditions (Park, 1997). However, the data on the frequency of cognitive errors related to diagnosis and problem solving, along with data concerning stress effects, are scanty at best and estimates rely much more heavily on expert opinion. These opinions may be faulty, and so it may sometimes be dangerously misleading to assign precise numerical values to HEPs or performance-shaping factors.

Error Monitoring   When machine components fail, they require outside repair or replacement. Yet as we have seen, humans normally have the capability to monitor their own performance, even when operating at a relatively automated level. As a result, humans often correct errors before those errors ultimately affect system performance, particularly capture errors or action slips (Rabbitt, 1978). The operator who accidentally activates the wrong switch may be able to shut it off quickly and activate the right one before any damage is done. Thus, it is difficult to associate the probability of a human error with the probability that it will be cascaded onward to induce a system error.

Nonindependence of Human Errors   The assumption is sometimes made in analyzing machine errors that the probability of the failure of one component is independent of that of another. Although this assumption is questionable when dealing with equipment (Perrow, 1984), with humans it is particularly untenable. Such dependence may work in two opposing directions. On the one hand, if we make one error and notice it, our resulting frustrations and stress may sometimes increase the likelihood of a subsequent error. On the other hand, the first error may increase our care and caution in subsequent operations and make future errors less likely. Whichever the case, it is impossible to claim that the probability of making an error at one time is independent of whether an error was made at an earlier time, a critical assumption normally made in reliability analysis. The actuarial database on human error probability, which is used to predict reliability, will not easily capture these dependencies because they are determined by mood, caution, personality, and other uniquely human properties (Adams, 1982).

A similar lack of independence can characterize the parallel operation of two human "components." When machine reliability is analyzed, the operation of two parallel (or redundant) components is assumed to be independent. For example, three redundant autopilots are often used on an aircraft so that if one fails, the two remaining in agreement will still give the true guidance input. None of the autopilots will influence the others' operation (unless they are all affected by a superordinate factor such as a total loss of power). This independence, however, cannot be said to hold true of multiple human operators. In the control room of a power station, for example, it is unlikely that the diagnosis made by one operator in the face of a malfunction will be independent of that made by another. Thus, it is unlikely that there will be independent probabilities of error shown by the two operators. Social factors may make the two operators relatively more likely to agree than had they been processing independently, particularly if one is in a position of greater authority (see also Chapter 6). Their overall effect may be to make correct performance either more or less likely, depending on a host of influences that are beyond the scope of this book.

Integrating Human and Machine Reliabilities   Adams (1982) argues that it is difficult to justify mathematically combining human-error data with machine-reliability data, derived independently, to come up with joint reliability measures of the total system. Here again, a nonindependence issue is encountered. When a machine component fails (or is perceived as being more likely to fail), it will probably alter the probability of human failure in ways that cannot be precisely specified. It is likely, for example, that the operator will become far more cautious, trustworthy, and reliable when interacting with a system that has a higher likelihood of failure or with a component that itself has just failed than when interacting with a system that is assumed to be infallible. This is a point that will be considered again in the discussion of automation mistrust in Chapter 13.

The important message here, as stated succinctly by both Reason (1990) and Adams (1982), is that a considerable challenge is imposed to integrate actuarial data of human error with machine data to estimate system reliability. Unlike some other domains of human performance (see particularly manual control in Chapter 11), even if the precise mathematical modeling of human performance were achieved, it would not appear to allow accurate prediction of total system performance. Although the potential benefits of accurate human reliability analysis and error prediction are great, it seems likely that the most immediate human factors benefits will be realized if effort is focused on case studies of individual errors in performance (Woods, Johannesen, Cook, & Sarter, 1994). These case studies can be used to diagnose the resulting causes of errors and to recommend the corrective system modification.

Errors in the Organizational Context

The greatest focus of public awareness on human error has resulted from major accidents and disasters, such as the nuclear meltdown at Chernobyl; the disaster at Three Mile Island; the explosion of the *Challenger* space shuttle; the chemical plant accident at Bhopal, India, in which over 1,000 lives were lost; or the sinking of the ferry boat *Herald of Free Enterprise* in 1987 (188 lives lost). In all of these cases, human error has been singled out as a contributing cause. But Reason (1990, 1997) carefully analyzed these and other accidents and identified human operator error as only one small component in a set of more serious organizational deficiencies.

Reason draws the important distinction between *local triggers* or active failures on the one hand, and *resident pathogens* or latent conditions on the other. He argues that the "local trigger" of human error that caused each of the five accidents listed above, along with numerous others, is only the final event in a series of poor design, management, and maintenance decisions, many of which existed long before the local trigger. The local trigger is, we might imagine, the tip of the iceberg, whereas the faulty design and management decisions—the base of the iceberg—are a collection of factors that represent an accident waiting to happen. Like a silent virus in the human body, these latter factors are resident pathogens or latent conditions. The Three Mile Island incident is certainly consistent with this analysis. Poor instrument-panel design, the poor valve design, and poor procedures (the fact that plant status had been changed because of maintenance, a change of which the operators on duty were unaware) contributed to the operators' mistake in dealing with the local trigger, a temporary clog in the feedwater lines providing cooler to the reactor.

Figure 12.7 presents Reason's (1990) representation of the relationship between decision errors, made at various points in a complex system, which can create the conditions for a local trigger, and the final unsafe acts committed by the system operator. All of the factors in the boxes may be thought of as the different dimensions of resident pathogens. Together they promote the conduct of unsafe acts and also lower the defenses of the system against the potentially disastrous consequences. Full descriptions of each box are well beyond the scope of this book, and the reader is referred to Reason (1990, 1997) and Perrow (1984) for highly readable details. However, the top and bottom boxes are worth some further discussion. Hardware defects refer to all of the human factors problems of displays and controls. But also important here is the design of the system itself, rather than the human interface. Perrow argues that complex, multicomponent systems, because of their very complexity, are guaranteed (1) to fail and (2) to fail in ways that are beyond the capacity of human cognition to readily understand, a point that will be expanded in Chapter 13.

The bottom box in Figure 12.7 draws the important distinction between errors and violations. In preceding discussions, we have assumed that errors are unintentional. Reason (1990) distinguishes errors from violations, which are intentional departures from specified operating procedures but are not intended to create accidents or to cause harm. Driving 60 in a 55 mph speed zone is a violation, and so is riding without a seat belt. The incident at Chernobyl was the direct result of a violation, in which operators intentionally "experimented" with the plant at unsafe operating conditions (Nature, 1986). Furthermore, violations of procedures appear to make up a majority of pilot errors responsible for major aircraft accidents (Nagel, 1988). Violations, then, are caused by operating conditions in which safety is not stressed or by management goals that run contrary to safety. Usually the latter involve an emphasis on production and profit.

In addressing the conditions in many large organizations that lead to errors and violations, Reason (1997) points to the choices that are often faced by industrial managers who must allocate scarce resources either to production (a sure gain) or to safety (avoiding a risky loss). Using the analysis of decision framing described in Chapter 8, it is easy to see why the choice is so often biased toward the more certain gain (enhance production) over the risky alternative (avoid the low-probability accident by implementing safety programs and procedures). Reason notes also that the reinforcement to managers from

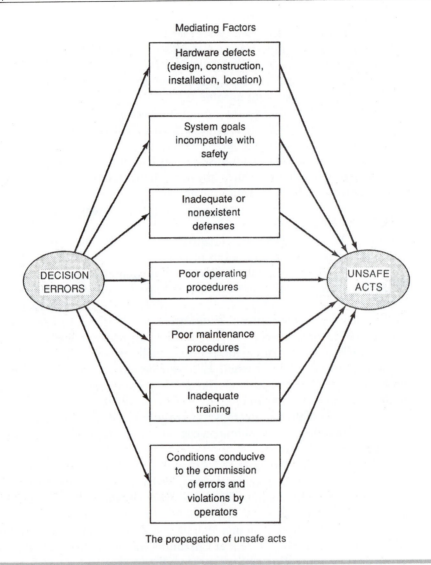

Mediating Factors

The propagation of unsafe acts

Figure 12.7 Framework for understanding resident pathogens.

Source: J. Reason, *Human Error* (New York: Cambridge University Press, 1990). This draft version reproduced with permission of the author.

emphasizing production is generally frequent, immediate, and represented by the presence of positive evidence (profit). The reinforcement for emphasizing safety, in contrast, is less salient and tangible and is usually characterized by the *absence* of evidence (the accident that does not happen). We noted in Chapter 8 how such absent evidence is not easily perceived. This unfortunate asymmetry all too often leads to the operating conditions in which unsafe behavior is tolerated, violations will occur, and resident pathogens will thrive.

Error Remediation

We now discuss the solutions offered to minimize the likelihood of errors or the potential damage that they might cause. Clearly many of the ways to eliminate resident pathogens, as suggested by Figure 12.7, lie in organizational climate and effectiveness—topics that lie beyond the domain of this book. However, implicit in our discussions and in those of Norman (1988), Senders and Moray (1991), and Reason (1990, 1997) are several specific remediations.

Task Design Designers should try to minimize operator requirements to perform tasks that impose heavy working-memory load under conditions of stress or other tasks for which human cognitive mechanisms are poorly suited. Such efforts will generally decrease the frequency of mistakes.

Equipment Design A number of equipment design remedies can reduce the invitation for errors:

1. Minimize perceptual confusions. Norman (1988) describes the care that is taken in the automobile to ensure that fluid containers and apertures look distinct from one another, so that oil will not be poured into the antifreeze opening, for example, nor antifreeze into the battery. Such a design stands in stark contrast to the identical appearance of different fluid tubes and fluid containers supporting the patient in an intensive care unit, a situation that describes an error waiting to happen (Bogner, 1994; Gopher et al., 1989, see also Figure 12.7). There are, of course, a series of design solutions that can ensure discriminability between controls and between displays, which have been described earlier in the book: distinct color and shape, spatial separation, distinct feel, and different control motions.

2. Make the execution of action and the response of the system *visible* to the operator (Norman, 1988). When slips occur, they cannot easily be detected (and hence corrected) if the consequences of actions cannot be seen. Hence, feedback from switches and controls that change a state should be clearly and immediately visible. If it is not too complex, the way a system carries out its operations should be revealed. Unfortunately, extreme simplicity, economy, and aesthetics in engineering design can often mask the visibility of response feedback and system operation, a visibility useful in noticing and thereby preventing errors.

3. Use constraints to "lock out" the possibility of errors (Norman, 1988; see Figure 9.10d). Sometimes these can be cumbersome and cause more trouble than they are worth. For example, interlock systems that prevent a car from starting before the seat belts are fastened have proven to be so frustrating that people disconnect the systems. On the other hand, an effective constraint is that seen in the car doors that cannot be locked unless the key is inserted and turned on the outside. This slight inconvenience will prevent the key from being locked in the car. Other constraints may force a sequence of actions in the computer that will prevent the commission of major errors—like erasing important files.

4. Offer reminders. Given the prevalence of lapses, care can be taken to remind users of steps that are known to be particularly likely to be omitted. An example is a

prominent note on the photocopier reading: "Take the last page" (Reason, 1997), which addresses the common lapse of leaving the final page in the copier.

5. Avoiding multimode systems. Systems in which identical actions accomplish different functions in different contexts, like the multimode digital watch, are a sure invitation for mode errors. When they cannot be avoided, the designer should make the discrimination of modes as visible as possible by employing salient visual cues. A continuous flashing light on a computer system, for example, is a salient visual reminder that an unusual mode is in effect. Designers should resist the temptation to create a great number of modes.

Training   Because lack of knowledge is an important source of mistakes, it is not surprising that increased training will reduce their frequency (although, as we have seen, training may have little effect on slips). As we have noted in Chapter 7, however, it is appropriate that *some* errors *do* occur during training. If operators are not practiced at correcting errors that occur during training, they will not know how to deal with the errors that might occur in real system operation.

Assists and Rules   Both assists and rules can represent designer solutions to error-likely situations, and some of these make very obvious sense. For example, such assists as memory aids or procedures checklists can be extremely valuable (Rouse, Rouse, & Hammer, 1982), whether for operators of equipment following a start-up procedure or for maintenance personnel carrying out a complex sequence of lapse-prone steps. If rules are properly explained, are logical, and are enforced, they can reduce the likelihood of safety violations. However, if the implications of rules adopted for complex systems, like nuclear and chemical process control plants, are not thought through, they can create unforeseen problems of their own. As Reason (1990) describes it, the "band-aid" approach to human error may only make the situation worse. Rules may unexpectedly prohibit necessary behavior in times of crisis in a way that the rule designer had not anticipated.

Error-Tolerant Systems   Although human error is typically thought of as undesirable, it is possible to see its positive side (Senders & Moray, 1991). In discussing both signal detection theory (Chapter 2) and decision theory (Chapter 8), we saw that in a probabilistic world, certain kinds of errors will be inevitable, and engineering psychologists are concerned as much with controlling the different kinds of errors (e.g., misses versus false alarms) as with eliminating them. In Chapter 9, we saw that the optimal setting of the speed-accuracy trade-off was usually at some intermediate level, where from the perspective of efficiency, at least a small number of errors was better than none at all. In Chapter 7, we saw that error is often necessary for learning to occur (so long as the error is not repeated).

Finally, error may be viewed as the inevitable downside of the valuable flexibility and creativity of the human operator. Rasmussen (1989) addresses this issue explicitly in the context of many large complex systems, such as the nuclear power plants we will be discussing in Chapter 13. There are so many possible strategies for accomplishing plant goals, that the specification of a single "correct" precise sequence of step-by-step procedures is not possible. The human operator must be opportunistic, responding differently according to the conditions of the moment. Under such circumstances, it becomes nearly essential for the operator to be able to explore the limits of the system, particularly when the operator is learning the system characteristics and developing a good mental model. This exploration makes a certain amount of error inevitable, if not desirable.

Understanding the inevitable and sometimes even desirable properties of human error has forced a rethinking of conventional design philosophies, in which all errors were to be irradicated (Rasmussen, 1989). Instead, researchers and human factors practitioners have advocated the design of error-tolerant systems (Rouse & Morris, 1987; Norman, 1988). An error-tolerant design, for example, would not allow the user to carry out irreversible actions. A file-delete command on a computer might not irreversibly delete the file but simply remove it and "hold" it in another place for some period of time (e.g., until the computer is turned off). Then the operator would have the chance to recover from the slip—in this case, an incorrect deletion command (Norman, 1988).

In describing their conceptual approach to error-tolerant design, Rouse and Morris (1987) and Hammer (1999) propose a fairly sophisticated intelligent monitoring system that continuously makes inferences about human intentions. If such a system then infers, on the basis of human output and system status, that those intentions are in danger of violating safety, or if human actions have been committed that are inconsistent with the inferred intentions, a graded series of interventions can be implemented. These run from increased vigilance of human performance monitoring by the system, to feedback of the nature of the error (which allows the operator to disregard it if he or she chooses), to the final level of direct intervention and control. Here the system will step in and take over if it infers that the consequences of error are severe.

The philosophy of error-tolerant systems has a great deal of appeal and has been echoed in Wiener's (1989) recommendation of an "electronic cocoon" surrounding the pilot of advanced aircraft. In such a concept, computer-based recommendations and controls will intervene only if the pilot "flies" the aircraft beyond this cocoon in a way that is deemed unsafe. The design of modern commercial airplanes such as the Airbus A–320 are adapting this philosophy in many respects. It is apparent that effective error-tolerant systems of the sort envisioned by Rouse and Morris (1987) impose greatly increased responsibility on the intelligence of the computer-based monitoring system (Wiener, 1989) and, hence, the wisdom of the designer and the reliability of the software code. The extent to which computer intelligence is ready for this challenge and the way in which the human operator will respond to imperfect levels of machine intelligence are issues that will be addressed in Chapter 13.

TRANSITION

This chapter has shown how the understanding of two important and related facets of human performance, stress and human error, depends on an understanding of all of the performance components and stages discussed in previous chapters. These components mediate the effects of stressors and the causes and classification of human error.

As incidents such as Three Mile Island have shown, stress and particularly human error are critical features in the performance of the human operator of complex high-risk systems like air traffic control or nuclear power generation, where errors coupled with resident pathogens can have catastrophic costs for human safety and welfare. Because of this complexity, many such systems are also characterized by high levels of *automation*: computers replacing tasks previously carried out by the human. These two themes—complex systems and automation—provide the focus of the final chapter, which, like the present one, integrates many of the processing components addressed in the previous chapters.

REFERENCES

Adams, J. J. (1982). *Simulator study of a pictorial display for instrument flight* (NASA Technical Paper no. 1963). Hampton, VA: NASA Langley Research Center.

Alkov, R. A., Borowsky, M. S., & Gaynor, M. S. (1982). Stress coping and U.S. Navy aircrew factor mishap. *Aviation, Space, and Environmental Medicine, 53,* 1112–1115.

Apostolakis, G. E. (1990). *Reliability engineering and system safety.* Elsevier Science Publishers, Amsterdam, the Netherlands.

Avionics (December, 1990). TCAS for Transports: Part III (pp. 22–45).

Bacon, S. J. (1974). Arousal and the range of cue utilization. *Journal of Experimental Psychology, 102,* 81–87.

Baddeley, A. D. (1972). Selective attention and performance in dangerous environments. *British Journal of Psychology, 63,* 537–546.

Berkun, M. M. (1964). Performance decrement under psychological stress. *Human Factors, 6,* 21–30.

Boeing. (1994). *Maintenance error decision aid.* Seattle: Boeing Commercial Airplane Group.

Bogner, M. S. (1994). *Human error in medicine.* Mahwah, NJ: Erlbaum.

Bourne, P. G. (1971). Altered adrenal function in two combat situations in Vietnam. In B. E. Eleftheriou and J. P. Scott (Eds.), *The physiology of aggression and defeat.* New York: Plenum.

Bowers, C. A., Weaver, J. L., & Morgan, B. B., Jr. (1996). Moderating the performance effects of stressors. In J. E. Driskell & E. Salas (Eds.), *Stress and human performance* (pp. 163–192). Mahwah, NJ: Erlbaum.

Broadbent, D. E. (1971). *Decision and stress.* New York: Academic Press.

Burton, R. R., Storm, W. F., Johnson, L. W., & Leverett, S. D., Jr. (1977). Stress responses of pilots flying high-performance aircraft during aerial combat maneuvers. *Aviation, Space, and Environmental Medicine, 48* (4), 301–307.

Card, S., Moran, T., & Newell, A. (1983). *The psychology of human-computer interaction.* Hillsdale, NJ: Erlbaum.

Cowen, E. L. (1952). The influence of varying degrees of psychosocial stress on problem-solving rigidity. *Journal of Abnormal and Social Psychology, 47,* 512–519

Davies, D. R., & Parasuraman, R. (1982). *The psychology of vigilance.* London: Academic Press.

Dougherty, E. M. (1990). Human reliability analysis—Where shouldst thou turn? *Reliability Engineering and System Safety, 29,* 283–299.

Driskell, J. E., Hughes, S. C., Guy, W., Willis, R. C., Cannon-Bowers, J., & Salas, E. (1991). *Stress, stressors, and decision-making* (Technical Report). Orlando, FL: Naval Training Systems Center.

Driskell, J. E., Salas, E., & Hall, J. K. (1994). *The effect of vigilant and hypervigilant decision training on performance.* Paper presented at the Annual Meeting of the Society of Industrial and Organizational Psychology, Nashville, TN.

Edland, A. (1989). On cognitive processes under time stress: A selective review of the literature on time stress and related stress. *Reports from the Department of Psychology.* Stockholm: University of Stockholm.

Flexman, R., & Stark, E. (1987). Training simulators. In G. Salvendy (Ed.), *Handbook of human factors.* New York: Wiley.

Flin, R., Salas, E., Strub, M., & Martin, L. (1997). *Decision making under stress: Emerging themes and applications.* Brookfield, VT: Ashgate.

Ford, J. K., Schmitt, N., Scheitman, S. L., Hults, B. M., & Doherty, M. L. (1989). Process tracing methods: Contributions, problems, and neglected research questions. *Organizational Behavior & Human Decision Processes, 43,* 75–117.

Gopher, D., Olin, M., Badhih, Y., Cohen, G., Donchin, Y., Bieski, M., & Cotev, S. (1989). The nature and causes of human errors in a medical intensive care unit. *Proceedings of the 32nd annual meeting of the Human Factors Society*. Santa Monica, CA: Human Factors Society.

Gopher, D., & Sanders, A. F. (1985). S-Oh-R: Oh stages! Oh resources! In W. Prinz & A. F Sanders (Eds.), *Cognition and motor processes* (pp. 231–253). Amsterdam: North Holland.

Griffin, W. C., & Rockwell, T. H. (1987). A methodology for research on VFR flight into IMC. In R Jensen (Ed.), *Proceedings of the Fourth International Symposium on Aviation Psychology*. Columbus: Ohio State University.

Hammer, J. (1999). Human factors of functionality and intelligent avionics. In D. Garland, J. Wise, and V. D. Hopkin (Eds.), *Handbook of Aviation Human Factors*. Mahwah, NJ: Lawrence Erlbaum.

Hart, S. G., & Hauser, J. R. (1987). In-flight application of three pilot workload measurement techniques. *Aviation, Space, and Environmental Medicine, 58*, 402–410.

Hockey, G. R. J. (1970). Effect of loud noise on attentional selectivity. *Quarterly Journal of Experimental Psychology, 22*, 28–36.

Hockey, G. R. J. (1986). Changes in operator efficiency as a function of environmental stress, fatigue, and circadian rhythms. In K. R. Boff, L. Kaufman, & J. P. Thomas (Eds.), *Handbook of perception and human performance* (vol. 2). New York: Wiley.

Hockey, G. R. J. (1997). Compensatory control in the regulation of human performance under stress and high workload. *Biological Psychology, 45*, 73–93.

Hockey, G. R. J., Wastell, D. G., & Sauer, J. (1998). Effects of sleep deprivation and user interface on complex performance: A multilevel analysis of compensatory control. *Human Factors, 40* (2), 233–253.

Houston, B. K. (1969). Noise, task difficulty, and Stroop color-word performance. *Journal of Experimental Psychology, 82*, 403–404.

Huey, M. B., & Wickens, C. D. (Eds.). (1993). *Workload transition: Implications for individual and team performance*. Washington, DC: National Academy Press.

Jensen, R. S. (1982). Pilot judgment: Training and evaluation. *Human Factors, 24*, 61–74.

Johnson, E. J., Payne, J. W., & Bettman, J. R. (1993). Adapting to time constraints. In O. Svenson & A. J. Maule (Eds.), *Time pressure and stress in human judgment and decision making* (pp. 103–116). New York: Plenum.

Johnston, J. H., & Cannon-Bowers, J. A. (1996). Training for stress exposure. In J. E. Driskell & E. Salas (Eds.), *Stress and human performance* (pp. 223–256). Mahwah, NJ: Erlbaum.

Kahneman, D. (1973). *Attention and effort*. Englewood Cliffs, NJ: Prentice Hall.

Kanfer, F. H., & Seidner, M. L. (1973). Self-control: Factors enhancing tolerance of noxious stimulation. *Journal of Personality and Social Psychology, 25*, 381–389.

Keinan, G., & Freidland, N. (1984). Dilemmas concerning the training of individuals for task performance under stress. *Journal of Human Stress, 10*, 185–190.

Keinan, G., & Friedland, N. (1987). Decision making under stress: Scanning of alternatives under physical threat. *Acta Psychologica, 64*, 219–228.

Keinan, G., & Friedland, N. (1996). Training effective performance under stress: Queries, dilemmas, and possible solutions. In J. E. Driskell & E. Salas (Eds.), *Stress and human performance* (pp. 257–278). Mahwah, NJ: Erlbaum.

Kirwan, B., & Ainsworth, L. K. (1992). *A guide to task analysis*. London: Taylor & Francis.

Klein, G. (1996). The effects of acute stressors on decision making. In J. E. Driskell & E. Salas (Eds.), *Stress and human performance* (pp. 49–88). Mahwah, NJ: Erlbaum.

Kuhl, J. (1985). Volitional mediators of cognition-behavior consistency: Self-regulatory processes and action versus state orientation. In J. Kuhl & J. Beckmann (Eds.), *Action control: From cognition to behavior* (pp. 101–128). Berlin: Springer.

Lazarus, R., & Folkman, S. (1984). *Stress, appraisal and coping*. New York: Springer.

Luchins, A. S. (1942). Mechanizations in problem solving: The effect of Einstellung. *Psychological Monographs, 54* (Whole no. 248).

Lusk, C. M. (1993). Assessing components of judgment in an operational setting: The effects of time pressure on aviation weather forecasting. In O. Svenson & A. J. Maule (Eds.), *Time pressure and stress in human judgment and decision making* (pp. 309–322). New York: Plenum.

Mandler, G. (1984). Thought processes, consciousness, and stress. In V. Hamilton & D. M. Warburton (Eds.), *Human stress and cognition: An information processing approach*. Chichester, UK: Wiley.

Maule, A. J., & Hockey, G. R. J. (1993). State, stress, and time pressure. In O. Svenson & A. J. Maule (Eds.), *Time pressure and stress in human judgment and decision making* (pp. 83–102). New York: Plenum.

Meichenbaum, D. (1985). *Stress inoculation training*. New York: Pergamon.

Meichenbaum, D. (1993). Stress inoculation training: A twenty year update. In R. L. Woolfolk & P. M. Lehrer (Eds.), *Principles and practice of stress management* (2d ed., pp. 373–406). New York: Guilford.

Miller, D., & Swain, A. (1987). Human reliability analysis. In G. Salvendy (Ed.), *Handbook of human factors*. New York: Wiley.

Nagel, D. C. (1988). Human error in aviation operations. In E. Wiener & D. Nagel (Eds.), *Human factors in aviation* (pp. 263–303). New York: Academic Press.

National Transportation Safety Board. (1988). *Northwest Airlines, Inc. McDonnell Douglas DC–9–82 N312RC. Detroit Metropolitan Wayne County Airport, Romulus, Michigan, August 16, 1987* (Report No. NTSB-AAR–88–05). Washington, DC: Author.

Nature. (1986). Whole issue on Chernobyl (vol. 323), p. 36.

Norman, D. A. (1981). Categorization of action slips. *Psychological Review, 88*, 1–15.

Norman, D. (1988). *The psychology of everyday things*. New York: Harper & Row.

O'Hare, D., & Roscoe, S. N. (1990). *Flightdeck performance: The human factor*. Ames: Iowa State University Press.

Orasanu, J. (1997). Stress and naturalistic decision making: Strengthening the weak links. In R. Flin, E. Salas, M. Strub, & L. Martin (Eds.), *Decision making under stress: Emerging themes and applications* (pp. 43–66). Brookfield, VT: Ashgate.

Park, K. D. (1997). Human error. In G. Salvendy (Ed.), *Handbook of human factors and ergonomics* (2d ed., pp. 150–173). New York: Wiley.

Perrow, C. (1984). *Normal accidents: Living with high-risk technology*. New York: Basic Books.

Poulton, E. C. (1976). Continuous noise interferes with work by masking auditory feedback and inner speech. *Applied Ergonomics, 7*, 79–84.

Rabbitt, P. M. A. (1978). Detection of errors by skilled typists. *Ergonomics, 21*, 945–958.

Rabbitt, P. M. A., & Vyas, S. M. (1970). An elementary taxonomy for some errors in laboratory choice RT tasks. *Acta Psychologica, 33*, 56–76.

Rasmussen, J. (1989). Human error and the problem of causality in analysis of accidents. Invited paper for Royal Society meeting on human factors in high risk situations, London.

Reason, J. T. (1984). Lapses of attention. In R. Parasuraman & R. Davies (Eds.), *Varieties of attention*. New York: Academic Press.

Reason, J. (1990). *Human error.* New York: Cambridge University Press.

Reason, J. (1997). *Managing the risks of organizational accidents.* Brookfield, VT: Ashgate.

Romhert, W. (1979). Determination of stress and strain at real work places: Methods and results of field studies with air traffic control officers. In N. Moray (Ed.) *Mental workload.* New York: Plenum.

Rouse, S. H., Rouse, W. B., & Hammer, J. M. (1982). Design and evaluation of an onboard computer-based information system for aircraft. *IEEE Transactions on Systems, Man, and Cybernetics, SMC–12,* 451–463.

Rouse, W. B., & Morris, N. M. (1987). Conceptual design of a human error tolerant interface for complex engineering systems. *Automatica, 23* (2), 231–235.

Rouse, W. B., & Rouse, S. H. (1983). Analysis and classification of human error. *IEEE Transactions on Systems, Man, and Cybernetics, SMC–13,* 539–549.

Sarter, N. B., & Alexander, H. M. (1999). Error types and related error detection processes in the aviation domain. *International Journal of Aviation Psychology, 9,* xxx-xxx.

Sarter, N., & Woods, D. (1995). How in the world did we ever get into that mode? Mode error in supervisory control. *Human Factors, 37,* 5–19.

Schwartz, D. R., & Howell, W. C. (1985). Optional stopping performance under graphic and numeric CRT formatting. *Human Factors, 27,* 433–444.

Senders, J., & Moray, N. (1991). *Human error: Cause, prediction and reduction.* Hillsdale, NJ: Erlbaum.

Shanteau, J., & Dino, G. A. (1993). Environmental stressor effects on creativity and decision making. In O. Svenson & A. J. Maule (Eds.), *Time pressure and stress in human judgment and decision making* (pp. 293–308). New York: Plenum.

Simmel, E. C., Cerkovnik, M., & McGarthy, J. E. (1987). Sources of stress affecting pilot judgment. In R. Jensen (Ed.), *Proceedings, 4th Symposium on Aviation Psychology.* Columbus: Ohio State University.

Simonov, P. V., Frolov, M. V., Evtushenko, V. F., & Suiridov, E. P. (1977). *Aviation, Space, and Environmental Medicine, 48,* 856–858.

Stiensmeier-Pelster, J., & Schürmann, M. (1993). Information processing in decision making under time pressure: The influence of action versus state orientation. In O. Svenson & A. J. Maule (Eds.), *Time pressure and stress in human judgment and decision making* (pp. 241–254). New York: Plenum.

Stokes, A., & Kite, K. (1994). *Flight Stress.* Brookfield, VT: Ashgate.

Stokes, A. F., & Raby, M. (1989). Stress and cognitive performance in trainee pilots. *Proceedings of the 33rd annual meeting of the Human Factors Society.* Santa Monica, CA: Human Factors Society.

Stokes, A. F., Kemper, K., & Kite, K. (1997). Aeronautical decision making, cue recognition, and expertise under time pressure. In C. E. Zsambok & G. Klein (Eds.), *Naturalistic decision making* (pp. 183–196). Mahwah, NJ: Erlbaum.

Svenson, O., & Maule, A. J. (Eds.). (1993). *Time pressure and stress in human judgment and decision making.* New York: Plenum.

Swain, A. D. (1990). Human reliability analysis: Need, status, trends and limitations. *Reliability engineering and system safety, 29,* 301–313.

Swain, A. D., & Weston, L. M. (1988). An approach to the diagnosis and misdiagnosis of abnormal conditions in post-accident sequences in complex man-machine systems. In L. Goodstein, H. Anderson, & S. Olsen (Eds.). *Tasks, errors, and mental models.* London: Taylor & Francis.

Ursin, H., Baade, E., & Levine, S. (Eds.). (1978). *Psychobiology of stress: A study of coping men.* New York: Academic Press.

Villoldo, A., & Tarno, R. L. (1984). *Measuring the performance of EOD equipment and operators under stress* (DTIC Technical Report AD-B083–850). Indian Head, MD: Naval Explosive and Ordnance Disposal Technology Center.

Wachtel, P. L. (1968). Anxiety, attention and coping with threat. *Journal of Abnormal Psychology, 73*, 137–143.

Wallsten, T. S. (1993). Time pressure and payoff effects on multidimensional probabilistic inference. In O. Svenson & A. J. Maule (Eds.), *Time pressure and stress in human judgment and decision making* (pp. 167–180). New York: Plenum.

Weltman, G., Smith, J. E., & Egstrom, G. H. (1971). Perceptual narrowing during simulated pressure-chamber exposure. *Human Factors, 13* (2), 99–107.

Wickens, C. D. (1996). Designing for stress. In J. E. Driskell & E. Salas (Eds.), *Stress and human performance* (pp. 279–296). Mahwah, NJ: Erlbaum.

Wickens, C. D., Stokes, A. F., Barnett, B., & Hyman, F. (1993). The effects of stress on pilot judgment in a MIDIS simulator. In O. Svenson & A. J. Maule (Eds.), *Time pressure and stress in human judgment and decision making* (pp. 271–292). New York: Plenum.

Wiegmann, D. A., & Shappell, S. A. (1997). Human factors of post-accident data: Applying theoretical taxonomies of human error. *International Journal of Aviation Psychology, 7*, 67–81.

Wiener, E. L. (1988). Cockpit automation. In E. L. Wiener & D. C. Nagel (Eds.), *Human factors in aviation* (pp. 433–461). San Diego: Academic Press.

Wiener, E. L. (1989). Reflections on human error: Matters of life and death. *Proceedings of the 33d annual meeting of the Human Factors Society* (pp. 1–7). Santa Monica, CA: Human Factors Society.

Wilkinson, R. T. (1963). Interaction of noise with knowledge of results and sleep deprivation. *Journal of Experimental Psychology, 66*, 332–337.

Wine, J. (1971). Test anxiety and direction of attention. *Psychological Bulletin, 76*, 92–104.

Woods, D. D. (1984). Some results on operator performance in emergency events. *Institute of Chemical Engineers Symposium Series, 90*, 21–31.

Woods, D. D. & Cook, R. (1999). Perspectives on human error: Hindsight binges and local rationality. In F. Durso (Ed.), *Handbook of Appied Cognition*. West Sussix, UK: John Wiley & Sons.

Woods, D. D., Johannesen, L. J., Cook, R. I., & Sarter, N. B. (1994). *Behind human error: Cognitive systems, computers, and hindsight* (State of the Art Report CSERIAC 94–01). Dayton, OH: Wright-Patterson AFB, CSERIAC Program Office.

Wreathall, J. (1982). *Operator action trees: An approach to quantifying operator error probability during accident sequences* (Report no. NUS–4159). Gaithersburg, MD: NUS Corporation.

Yerkes, R. M., & Dodson, J. D. (1908). The relation of strength of stimulus to rapidity of habit formation. *Journal of Comparative Neurological Psychology, 18*, 459–482.

Zakay, D. (1993). The impact of time perception processes on decision making under time stress. In O. Svenson & A. J. Maule (Eds.), *Time pressure and stress in human judgment and decision making* (pp. 59–72). New York: Plenum.

Complex Systems, Process Control, and Automation

OVERVIEW

The final chapter of this book addresses complex systems, process control, and automation. We present these topics at the end because, like the topics of stress and human error discussed in the previous chapter, they are relevant to all stages of processing and mental operations discussed in the earlier chapters. The supervision of such complex processes as steel making, energy production, human physiology (by the anesthesiologist), or air traffic (by the air traffic controller) requires detection, perception, attention deployment, diagnosis, communications, memory, decision making, and action selection. Many of these processes are continuous and analog in nature, so their control bears some resemblance to tracking. However, four important differences from the tracking task discussed in Chapter 10 are prominent. (1) These processes are generally more complex than vehicle dynamics, with a greater number of interacting variables. (2) The system responses are often so slow that human manual control is more discrete and open loop than analog and closed loop. (3) As a consequence of this slower control, it is an area that is less constrained by human motor limitations but that makes issues of decision making, attention allocation, perception, and memory, discussed in Chapters 2 through 7, much more relevant. (4) Finally, the process control task is closely tied to concepts of automation, discussed at the end of this chapter.

Process control is certainly not synonymous with automation, as much of the control can be carried out manually. However, because of the tremendous complexities of the processes involved and because hazardous environments and toxic materials are often employed, the process control environment is one in which automation is an inevitable companion. Regulating and controlling large chemical, energy, or thermal processes impose many demands that are simply beyond the capabilities of the human operator. Some of these limitations result from obvious physical constraints. Humans, for example, cannot readily manipulate the chemicals that are involved in many industrial processes, they cannot handle the radioactive fuel in nuclear processes, nor can they come in physical contact with elements at the extreme temperatures of many energy-conversion systems. Other constraints are directly related to the complexity of the process variables involved, which impose limits on human cognitive processes. Thus, many components of process control have been automated, and increasing computer technology makes it inevitable that automation will proceed a good bit further. It is essential, therefore, that the nature of human involvement in process control be clearly specified so that the automation that is implemented will be appropriate and functional (Bainbridge, 1983).

PROCESS CONTROL

In our discussion of complex process control, we first focus on process control during normal operations, describing its cognitive aspects and the human factors design implications. We then consider issues of problem solving and fault diagnosis under the critical and dangerous conditions of abnormal operation, and some of the solutions to these issues provided by the application of cognitive engineering (Rasmussen, Pjetersoen, & Goodstein 1995). Much of this discussion revolves around nuclear process control because of its high risk, complexity, and public visibility. However, we integrate examples from other process industries, recognizing that nuclear power plant control is, in some respects, quite unique (Moray, 1997).

Characteristics of Process Control

The specific kinds of processes of concern to the human operator in this domain are diverse. They include the management of cake-baking ovens (Beishon, 1969) and the control of blast furnaces (Bainbridge, 1974), paper mills (Beishon, 1966), steel rolling (Moray, 1997), distribution of electric power (Umbers, 1976; Williams, Seidenstein, & Goddard, 1980), anesthesiology (Cook, 1996; Gaba, Howard, & Small, 1995), air traffic control (Wickens, Mavor, & McGee 1997; Wickens, Mavor, Parasuraman, & McGee, 1998; Hopkin, 1994), and of course, nuclear power (Hollnagel, Mancini, & Woods, 1988; Moray & Huey, 1988; Rasmussen, 1983; Sheridan, 1981; Woods, O'Brien, & Hanes, 1987). These diverse examples have four general characteristics that allow them to be classified together.

First, the process variables that are controlled and regulated are slow. They have long time constants, relative to the controlled or tracked systems discussed in Chapter 10. Thus, the control delivered by an operator in process control may not produce a visible system response for seconds and sometimes even minutes. Using the terminology introduced in Chapter 10, we say that the operator is more often controlling outer-loop variables, whereas automated adjustment and feedback loops handle the inner-loop control. Thus, the operator of a blast furnace may choose a set point of desired temperature, and automated inner-loop control will provide the amount of fuel and energy to the furnace necessary to achieve that temperature some minutes later.

Second, although controls are often adjusted in discrete fashion, the variables that are being controlled are essentially analog, continuous processes. Thus, in terms of the concepts discussed in Chapters 4, 5, and 6, the operator's ideal mental model of the processes should also be analog and continuous rather than discrete and symbolic.

Third, the processes typically consist of a large number of interrelated variables. Some are hierarchically organized, as in Figure 10.13; others are cross-coupled, so that changes in one variable will influence several other variables simultaneously. The staggering magnitude of this complexity is demonstrated by the display confronting the typical supervisor of a nuclear power plant control room (Figure 13.1). Grimm (1976), for example, notes that the complexity of power station control rooms, as measured by the number of controls and displays, grew geometrically from under 500 in 1950 to around 1,500 in 1970 to more than 3,000 in 1975. This complexity of interactions can severely tax the operator's mental model of the status of the plant, a model whose level of accuracy is important for normal control and critical for the response to malfunctions or failures. It also taxes the capability of analytic models to describe the process accurately.

Fourth, many of these processes are characterized by high risk. As incidents at Chernobyl, Three Mile Island, and Bhopal have demonstrated (Reason, 1997), as well as breakdowns in air traffic control leading to mid-air collisions, the consequences of human error in terms of costs to society and to human life can be severe. Yet operators must often function under conflicting goals, balancing productivity and profit against safety. This difficult trade-off, affected by management attitudes (as discussed in the previous chapter), will influence many aspects of the operator's decisions and actions (Roth & Woods, 1988; Reason, 1997).

To illustrate the characteristics of one of these processes, a conceptual overview of the nuclear power plant environment is seen in Figure 13.2. At the left is a reactor, and

Figure 13.1 Typical nuclear power plant control room. Controls are placed on the benchboard or just above, quantitative displays are placed on the vertical segment of the boards, and qualitative annunciator displays are placed in the uppermost segments of the boards.
Source: Common Wealth Edison..

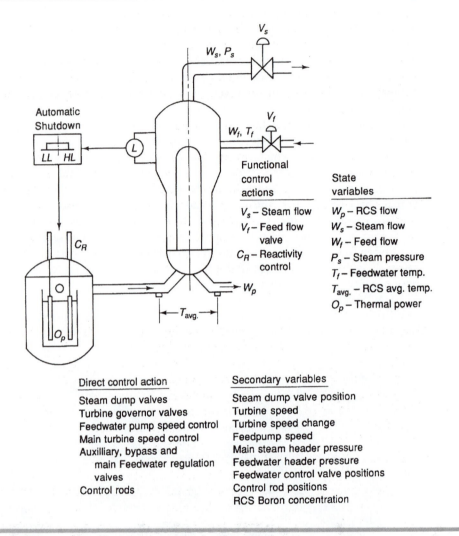

Figure 13.2 Schematic diagram of the processes that affect indicated level in a steam generator of a steam supply system in a nuclear reactor.

Source: E. M. Roth and D. D. Woods, "Aiding Human Performance: I. Cognitive Analysis," *Le Travail Humain, 51,* 1988, p. 46. Copyright 1986 by Westinghouse Electric Corp.

when the control rods (CR) are withdrawn, the fission reaction of the uranium atoms produces heat. This heat is removed from the reactor by a primary steam loop (bottom right), in which the water is somewhat radioactive. In a pressurized water reactor, the water circulates through a heat exchanger (center of the figure). Here the heat is transferred to a secondary cooling loop that contains pure water and makes steam, which passes at high pressure to the turbines to drive them to generate electricity (top right). The steam in the primary loop is condensed back to water, preheated, and returned to the core by powerful pumps. An automatic shutdown device (top left) shuts down, or scrams, the reactor if the delicate balance between heat and mass is disrupted so that pressure becomes either too high or too low within the reactor. The reactor scram is a major event that has substantial financial costs within the plant. Even when no damage occurs, it can cost up to $250,000 a day to buy electricity from other utilities to replace the lost power, and restarting the reactor, as we describe below, is a time-consuming and hazardous process in itself.

In the following pages, two contrasts are emphasized. One is the contrast between normal routine operation and abnormal operation that may characterize either start-up operations or fault management. The other is the contrast between the efforts to model the cognitive and information processing requirements of the operator's task and the actual human factors efforts to improve control room design. The latter efforts, in turn, belong to two categories: the standard human factors principles of control-display design and anthropometry (Seminara, Pack, Seidenstein, & Eckert, 1980; Moray, 1997), and more sophisticated efforts to optimize design on the basis of cognitive models of the human operator—the field of cognitive engineering (Woods & Roth, 1988; Rasmussen et al., 1995; Vicente, 1999).

Control Versus Diagnosis

In many process control environments, the operator's task has typically been described as hours of intolerable boredom punctuated by a few minutes of pure hell. This dichotomy is perhaps somewhat overstated. For example, in some process industries (e.g., steel rolling, air traffic control), there is quite a bit to do at all times (Moray, 1997). Nevertheless, the dichotomy serves nicely to discriminate between the two major functions of the process controller: the normal control and regulation of the process which is well handled by standard procedures, and timely detection, diagnosis, and corrective action in the face of the very infrequent malfunctions that may occur. As the incident at Three Mile Island indicates, the low frequency at which these failures occur must not diminish concern for their accurate detection and diagnosis.

The duties of the process controller normally begin with the start-up of the process—for example, bringing a nuclear reactor on-line. Although a fairly standardized set of procedures is followed during start-up, the task is nonroutine, since shutdowns and start-ups occur rarely. The cognitive demands of this phase of operation are heavy, and the task is complex. As described later, a large number of warning signals, designed to be appropriate for steady-state operation, may be flashing during the transient conditions of start-up.

In nuclear power control during start-up, a very delicate balance must be maintained between energy and mass flow among the various reactor elements, and in spite of the standardization of procedures, there is a high degree of uncertainty in the precise display readings an operator will perceive, and in the actions that must be taken (Roth & Woods, 1988). Once most process control systems are in a steady state, the operator typically engages in periodic adjustments, or "trimming," of process variables, to keep certain critical process parameters within designated bounds and meet changing production criteria. In the framework of the tracking paradigm, these adjustments may be made because of disturbances (e.g., a reduction in water quality will require more purification) or because of command inputs. For example, in a power generating plant, the need for electric power will increase at peak times, requiring the production of more high-pressure, high-temperature steam to drive the turbines.

Although the control aspects of process control are thus somewhat allied with the discussion of manual control in Chapter 10, the detection and diagnosis aspects (along with many of those related to start-up) are more closely related to the discussion of those topics in Chapters 2 and 8, as well as to the treatment of mental representations in Chapter 7. In addition to the obvious differences in the quantitative workload associated with the two phases, there are a number of other ways in which routine control and abnormal diagnosis and problem solving differ from one another. Routine control primarily involves following well-learned procedures (rule-based behavior); while fault management may involve the need for innovation (knowledge-based behavior). Landeweerd (1979) notes that the controller in normal circumstances must focus on the forward flow of events: what causes what. The diagnostician in times of failure, in contrast, must often reverse the entire pattern and think about what was caused by what. People generally have greater difficulty with diagnostic than with causal reasoning (Eddy, 1982; Wickens, 1992). Moray (1981) suggests that visual scan patterns and information-seeking strategies will also differ between these phases (Moray & Rotenberg, 1989). Scanning strategies appropriate for normal operation may be inappropriate if there is a failure. If these normal strategies are continued in the presence of a failure, they may prevent the operator from realizing that the failure is there.

If the two phases are truly independent, then those who are good controllers may not necessarily be effective at detection and diagnosis; conversely, good diagnosticians may not necessarily be good controllers. A study by Landeweerd (1979) suggests that individual differences in ability of these two components are indeed independent. Drawing a similar conclusion in the realm of training, rather than individual differences, Kessel and Wickens (1982) found that operators who had prior training in the detection of dynamic system failures were not helped by this training in the ability to control these systems.

We have emphasized that control versus detection and diagnosis, both integral aspects of the overall process control task, may be independent in terms of operator abilities. Because this distinction is seen in a number of different ways, the two aspects of the process controller's task are considered separately in the sections that follow.

Control

Two characteristics of routine process control have received special attention by engineering psychologists and human factors engineers. These relate, first, to some of the fundamental principles of good human factors applied to control-room design and, second, to a careful analysis and modeling of the human control process itself.

Human Factors Design Process   Since the time of the Three Mile Island incident, human factors specialists have taken a critical look at several features of current control-room design and found substantial violations of several design principles (Electrical Power Research Institute, 1977; Hopkins et al., 1982; Seminara, Pack, Seidenstein, & Eckert, 1980).

1. Lack of consistency. Two side-by-side control panels had been designed with mirror-image symmetry, so that identical controls to the right side as the operator faced one panel were to the left as he or she faced the other panel. Or as shown in Figure 13.3a and b, two identical (and important) functional switches

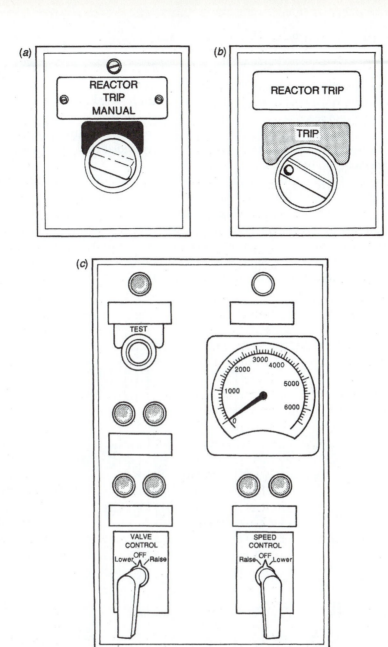

Figure 13.3 Inconsistent labeling and coding on critical controls (the control on the left is coded with a black background; the one on the right with a lightly shaded background). (*a*) Control located in reactor control area. (*b*) Control located on turbine panel. (*c*) Inconsistent direction-of-movement relationships.

Source: D. D. Woods, J. F. O'Brien, and L. F. Hanes, "Human Factors Challenges in Process Control: The Case of Nuclear Power Plants," in *Handbook of Human Factors,* ed. G. Salvendy (New York: Wiley, 1987). Figures copyrighted 1979 by Electric Power Research Institute, EPRI NP–1118, *Human Factors Method for Nuclear Power Control Room Design,* vol. 1. Reproduced by permission.

for a reactor shutdown had different characteristics, or two dials rotated in opposite directions to achieve the same goal (Figure 13.3c).

2. Violations of basic anthropometry. Many controls were hard to reach and displays hard to see.

3. Violations of S-R compatibility. Displays were not necessarily positioned in close proximity to the controls that they reflected, violating the colocation principle discussed in Chapter 9.

4. Absence of organization and functional grouping. Sets of controls and displays, like those in Figure 13.4a, were not clearly delineated into meaningful clusters, a feature of importance discussed in Chapter 3.

5. Perceptual and response confusion. Numerous control devices, often affecting different actions, were identically structured, as shown in Figure 13.1. If these appear the same— are perceptually identical except for their location—they invite an "action slip," as discussed in Chapter 12.

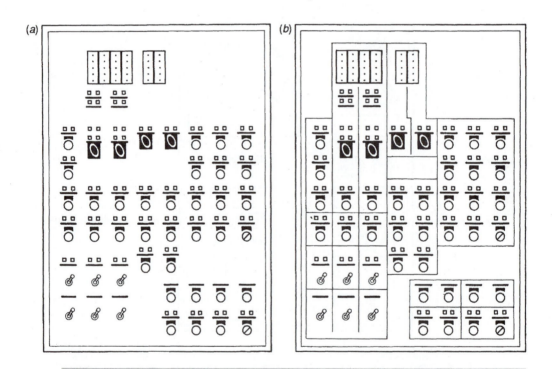

Figure 13.4   (a) Control panel before enhancements. (b) Same control panel after enhancements.

Source: D. D. Woods, J. F. O'Brien, and L. F. Hanes, "Human Factors Challenges in Process Control: The Case of Nuclear Power Plants," in *Handbook of Human Factors,* ed. G. Salvendy (New York: Wiley, 1987). Figures copyrighted 1979 by Electric Power Research Institute, EPRI NP–1118, *Human Factors Method for Nuclear Power Control Room Design,* vol. 1. Reproduced by permission.

Many of these deficiencies can be and have been addressed with relative ease (Moray, 1997). For example, Figure 13.3b shows how simple paint can emphasize important features of the structural grouping. Ivergard (1989) has written a comprehensive textbook describing the appropriate application of many fundamental human factors design principles to control-room layout and anthropometry. Naturally, many of these design principles are as important to abnormal operations as they are to the normal ones involved in control.

Performance Strategies　The operator's primary responsibilities during normal process control is to monitor system instruments and periodically adjust control settings to maintain production quantities within certain bounds. Although the task bears some similarity to tracking, the difference is that tracking normally involves continuous closed-loop behavior, whereas much of the responding in process control uses the discrete open-loop strategy typical of the highly skilled operator (see Chapter 10). In a simulated process control task, Crossman and Cooke (1962) and McLeod (1976) found that subjects employed both modes of control but performed better on the open-loop mode. Beishon (1966) reports that skilled paper mill operators would initiate their adjustments with open-loop control action, followed later by discrete closed-loop adjustment. The open-loop strategy, however, becomes available only after the process is well learned. Moray, Lootsteen, and Pajak (1986) found that operators' performance evolved from closed- to open-loop strategies when they received training in a simulated process control task. Roth and Woods (1988) observed that the expert controller of a feed-water reactor tended to use more open-loop control than did the nonexpert.

Open-loop is superior to closed-loop behavior in process control because the long time constants typically involved cause a closed-loop strategy to be inefficient and potentially unstable (see Chapter 10). Process variables often change so slowly that operators cannot readily perceive their rate and acceleration of change in a manner that makes for stable closed-loop control (McLeod, 1976). In many nuclear reactor tasks, the difficulties imposed by the lag are amplified by the presence of counterintuitive "shrink-swell" dynamics, as shown in Figure 13.5. The initial response of a variable produced by a step-control input designed to increase its value is a decrease in value (shrink), followed only later by an appropriate increase (swell) (Roth & Woods, 1988). It is easy to imagine how a closed-loop strategy in this case could invite instability, as the operator, detecting a decrease in the quantity, would then impose a further compensatory increase on the control, leading to overcontrol.

When the task of the process controller is carefully analyzed, successful control, like successful tracking, requires three important components: (1) a clear specification and understanding of the future goals of production, that is, a command input; (2) an accurate mental representation of the current state of the process, which, because of the sluggish nature of the variables involved, must be used to predict future state; and (3) an accurate mental model of the dynamics of the process. This third element is important in guiding visual attention, as discussed in Chapter 3, and is also essential if open-loop control is to be employed, since it represents the means by which a plan of control action is formulated to bring the process to a future state (Moray, Lootsteen, & Pajak, 1986; Moray, 1997). If there is no mental model, the operator must respond, wait to see what happens, and then respond again. That is, in this case, the operator must engage in slow and inefficient closed-loop control.

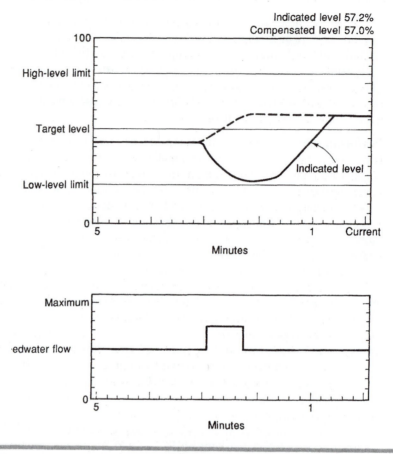

Figure 13.5 Illustration of shrink/swell dynamics. Following an increase in feedwater flow (*bottom graph*), the indicated water level first decreases, then approaches its longer-term asymptotic value. The dotted line illustrates what level the behavior would be, given an increase in feedwater flow, if the system dynamics were minimum phase.

Source: E. M. Roth and D. D. Woods, "Aiding Human Performance: I. Cognitive Analysis," *Le Travail Humain, 51,* 1988, p. 52. Copyright 1986 by Westinghouse Electric Corp.

These three components—goals, a mental representation of the current and future state, and a mental model of the process dynamics—along with the inherently sluggish nature of these processes, highlight the great importance of the future in process control. In Chapter 10, we showed how the planning of future activities in control may be partitioned into two components: planning and anticipating future goals (these may be command inputs or internally specified goals, and are referred to as *preview*) and anticipating or *predicting* the future system responses. Since the system in process control responds slowly and sometimes, initially, in a backward direction, actions implemented now must be based on future, not present, states. Further evidence of the importance of both future goals and future states comes from verbal protocols taken from process and industrial control operators, which indicate that a significant portion of their time is spent in planning operations (Bainbridge, 1974), anticipating future demands or slacks in the process. Roth and Woods (1988) found substantial improvements from novice to expert controllers in the extent to which operators anticipated future states in their control activity and mentally kept track of controls they had issued that were "in the pipe line," that is, controls whose effects had not yet been realized by display changes.

Display Implications Given the importance of future information, the use of computer aiding can be of considerable value when a prediction of the system response is displayed, having the same advantages as those described in Chapter 10; however, these advantages are typically even greater in process control because of the longer time constants involved. Long time constants usually mean that little motion is observable in display indicators (McLeod, 1976). As a consequence, status indicators that are based only on present time do not provide adequate trend information. Trend information may be derived from one of three sources.

1. Historical displays, typically presented by strip charts, give some estimate of future trends to the extent that the future may be mentally extrapolated from the past. An example of a historical display used in nuclear power plants is shown in Figure 13.6.
2. Predictive displays, as described in Chapter 10, generate predicted outputs based on computer models of the plant, or anticipated demand (preview). West and Clark (1974) found that considerable assistance was provided by the predictive

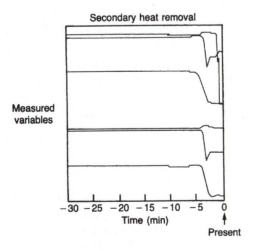

Figure 13.6 Historical strip-chart display.

Source: D. D. Woods, J. Wise, and L. Hanes, "An Evaluation of Nuclear Power Plant Safety Parameter Display Systems," *Proceedings of the 25th Annual Meeting of the Human Factors Society* (Santa Monica, CA: Human Factors, 1981), p. 111. Copyright 1981 by the Human Factors Society. Reproduced by permission.

display but little by the historical strip chart. Liaos (1978) demonstrated the value of preview displays in a steel-rolling process. In the very different domain of air traffic control (the "process" controlled is the movement of a collection of aircraft across the skies), the value of predictive displays is well realized (Wickens, Mavor, & McGee, 1997; Wickens, Mavor, Parasuraman, & McGee, 1998). Woods and Roth (1988) developed a two-element predictor display to aid in controlling the flow of feedwater to a steam generator, as shown in Figure 13.7. Recall that this is a cognitively difficult task because of the shrink-swell phenomenon: corrections to increase level produce an initial response in the opposite direction. To address these difficulties, the display portrays both the actual level of steam generation and a predictor of the future minimum (or maximum) level that will be reached with the present control input. This display gives the operator an estimate of how a given control will affect future values and how close those values will come to critical limits that may shut down the plant. The compensated level, shown in the figure, is another form of prediction and indicates where the steam-generation level will eventually stabilize after the cognitively difficult shrink-swell effects have been computationally removed.

3. The third source of predictive information, found to be of use by Brigham and Liaos (1975), is derived from the display of intervening process variables between the control manipulations and the actual output changes. In the terms described in Chapter 10 and shown in Figure 10.13, this is analogous to the information that the controller of higher-order hierarchical systems may derive

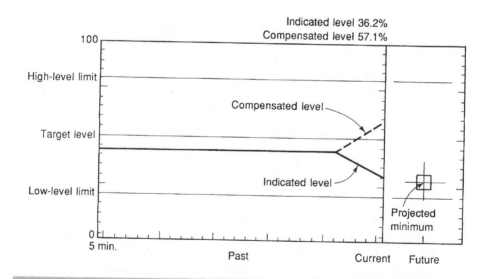

Figure 13.7 Predictive display for assisting in setting the water level in a nuclear reactor.

Source: E. M. Roth and D. D. Woods, "Aiding Human Performance: I. Cognitive Analysis," *Le Travail Humain, 51,* 1988, p. 149. Copyright 1986 by Westinghouse Electric Corp.

from a display of lower-order variables—the information, for example, that the automobile driver controlling lateral position derives from vehicle heading and steering-wheel angle, both derivative predictors of future lateral position. In process control, the heat applied (e.g., by a furnace) is an intervening variable that predicts the actual temperature.

Abnormal Operations

When discussing abnormal operation, fault detection, and fault diagnosis in process control, our treatment comes full circle, touching base again with the concepts discussed in Chapter 2 (vigilance and detection) and Chapter 8 (decision making and diagnosis). However, we now address these concepts distinctly from the point of view of the process monitor's task. In spite of the formal equivalence between failure detection in the process control environment and the concepts of detection and vigilance discussed in Chapter 2, there are three characteristics of process control that emphasize its differences from the simulated environment that is most often employed in laboratory vigilance studies.

1. In process control, the operator is not typically waiting passively between failures but is intermittently engaged in moderate levels of control adjustments, parameter checking, log keeping, and communications necessary to maintain a current mental representation of the system and to ensure productivity. These are the sort of intervening activities that maintain at least a modest level of arousal and reduce this source of vigilance decrement. Indeed, in some process environments like steel making or air traffic control, those activities may be quite high.

2. When a failure does occur, it is normally indicated by a visual and/or auditory alarm. The latter will be sufficiently salient to call attention to itself so that the probability of a miss (in the vigilance sense) is quite low. Nevertheless, the consequences of a miss may still be drastic.

3. More than in most vigilance situations, the process control environment is characterized by an excessive number of machine false alarms, that is, alarms that sound (or warning lights that illuminate) when there is in fact nothing abnormal with the plant. These machine false alarms, discussed in detail later in this chapter, occur either because the set points of the alarms are too sensitive or because an abnormal level of a variable in one context (appropriately triggering an alarm) may in fact be quite normal in a different context.

These three qualifications do not eliminate the concern about failure detection in process control. In the design of any discrete warning device, it is necessary to assume a threshold for the indicated variable that is sufficiently tolerant that random variations in the process variables do not trigger false alarms. To attain this level of tolerance, it is likely that information regarding true failures that occur gradually rather than catastrophically will be available in trends in the variables that are visible before the activation of the warning. A sensitive, alert operator with a well-formulated mental representation will be able to use this advance information to prepare for the upcoming event and possibly take corrective action before the alarm sounds. In this regard, historical displays (e.g., stripcharts, Figure 13.7), can provide valuable information, particularly if these are coupled with clear indications of the threshold values that trigger alarms or representation of the range of expected values.

Alarms may be triggered because what is normal in one context is abnormal in another. This state is represented in Figure 13.8, which illustrates the complexity of power plant design (Woods, O'Brien, & Hanes, 1987). The indicators in the middle represent a series of parameters set to trigger alarms when their value exceeds or falls below a certain level. The circles above represent various root-cause failures. Each failure may affect different (but overlapping) sets of indicators, and each indicator may be triggered by a number of possible failures. Pictured below are a series of nonfailure states, such as those that might occur during maintenance or start-up. These states may also produce some of the same parameter values and alarms associated with failure states. Hence, many alarms are ambiguous both with regard to what a failure might be and whether a failure exists at all. Woods, O'Brien, and Hanes note that some operators relate to certain alarms as "old friends" because their appearance is assumed to signal no danger or simply because, if there are several hundred or more visual alarm annunciators, some of these themselves will probably be faulty. Similar problems with alarms are observed at the work station of the anesthesiologist (Gaba, Howard, & Small, 1995).

In summary, either a vigilant operator with a current mental representation or one equipped with well-configured displays will be likely to suspect or detect a malfunction prior to the activation of annunciator systems (De Keyser, 1988). However, even if this is not the case, detection will nevertheless be fairly well guaranteed by the alarms and lights of the annunciation system. Then diagnosis becomes the next phase of operator

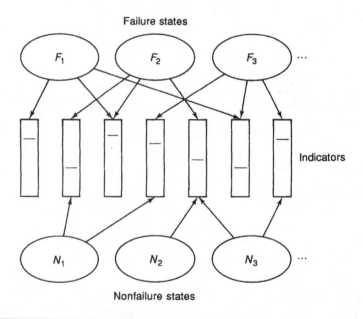

Figure 13.8 Complexity of nuclear power plant operations.

response. However, there is a certain paradoxical relationship between detection and diagnosis: The very characteristics of annunciators that may guarantee timely detection—salience and prominence—can greatly inhibit their effective use in diagnosis.

Fault Diagnosis

Once a failure or abnormality is detected, the operator is faced with a choice of what actions to take in order to meet three criteria. In most process environments, these criteria, in decreasing order of importance, are (1) actions that will ensure plant or system safety, (2) actions that will not jeopardize system economy and efficiency, and (3) diagnostic actions that will localize and correct the fault. Unfortunately, these criteria are not always compatible with one another, and operators who must function in a probabilistic world, in which outcomes of actions cannot be predicted with certainty, should at least be certain about the relative importance of each. This importance must be emphasized, for example in the nuclear power industry, when a choice must be made to take a turbine or plant off the line, thereby ensuring safety (criterion 1) but potentially sacrificing economy (criterion 2). This will be particularly true given that costly (and risky) start-ups are required following a shutdown. The status of the third criterion, diagnosis, is also somewhat ambivalent. In the nuclear industry, written procedures emphasize that control actions that will restore critical system variables to their normal range must take priority over diagnosis of a fault (Zach, 1980). The intent of this prioritization is to emphasize that the operator need not worry about what caused the failure until the system has been stabilized. However, diagnosis is often a necessary precursor to restoring or maintaining system safety. As the incident at Three Mile Island revealed (see Chapter 1), misdiagnosis can lead to disastrous circumstances. Hence, the overall ordering of priorities remains somewhat ambiguous for the operator.

Concerns for problem solving and diagnosis under abnormal conditions have generally taken two complementary approaches. One is to try to model and understand the cognitive difficulties that operators have in this problem-solving environment (Roth & Woods, 1988), and the other is to examine possible remedial solutions through applications of cognitive engineering (Woods & Roth, 1988; Rasmussen, 1986; Rasmussen, Pjetersoen, & Goodstein, 1995; Vicente, 1999; Vicente & Rasmussen, 1992). The nature of the problems encountered in fault diagnosis and in control under abnormal states, such as plant start-up, have been revealed by four different methods.

Case Studies   The case study of Three Mile Island provides a clear example of how cognitive performance can break down. In this case, the analysis highlights the role of cognitive tunnel vision or the confirmation bias, discussed more fully in Chapter 8. Following each nuclear power incident, a fairly detailed failure analysis is carried out (by the Nuclear Regulatory Commission in the United States) that focuses both on human as well as equipment limitations.

Error Analysis   Woods (1984; Woods, O'Brien, & Hanes, 1987) has made a more systematic effort to collect and categorize sources of error committed by power-plant operators. A critical source of difficulty was found in the operator's ability to modify the adherence to prespecified procedures if this modification was necessary in changing and uncertain environmental conditions (Woods, Johannesen, Cook, & Sarter, 1994). Reactor designers have carefully documented numerous procedures that should be followed in abnormal circumstances. But these procedures should not be followed in a rigidly open-loop fashion, without carefully monitoring the effect of each action on the state of the plant and adjusting the procedures if necessary when that effect is not what was intended or does not occur precisely when it was intended.

Novice-Expert Differences   Roth and Woods (1988) carried out a systematic analysis of the differences between novices and experts performing a steam generator start-up procedure. Although this is not truly a failure or fault situation, it is, as we have noted above, a highly unstable, dynamic, and abnormal condition, taxing operator problem-solving capabilities extensively. Characteristics that distinguish the performance of experts from that of novices were found in (1) the ability to anticipate the future; (2) a superior mental model of the process, its time constants, and interconnections (as we saw, this mental model provides a partial basis for anticipation); (3) a conscious setting of the speed-accuracy trade-off to go slow (see Chapters 9 and 12), indicating that experts know that rapid actions carried out with sluggish and complex systems can be an invitation to error and instability; (4) a broader spotlight of attention, guarding against cognitive tunneling; and (5) a better ability to communicate and coordinate with other operators in the complex, multitask environment of the control room.   .

Cognitive Task Analysis   Major research efforts by Rasmussen (e.g., Goodstein & Rasmussen, 1988; Rasmussen, 1983, 1986; Rasmussen et al., 1995; Vicente & Rasmussen, 1992) and Woods (1988; Roth & Woods, 1988; Vicente, 1999) focused on analysis of the task requirements in problem solving and diagnoses, revealing two key concepts. First, Woods highlighted the *brittleness* of preprogrammed procedures designed to deal with unusual events. As noted, such lists of procedures do not easily accommodate the dynamic and uncertain characteristics of the plant environment. These characteristics dictate that procedures must often be bent or modified on the fly to deal with an unexpected plant response (or with the consequences of operator error in carrying out the procedures). Such procedures may be written as a series of actions or rules, and each action may be conditional on a particular state of the plant ("if *x*, do *y*"). But too often the "if *x*" part is just assumed by the operator, and *y* is done, foregoing careful evaluation of whether condition *x* actually exists and producing a rule-based mistake as a consequence (Reason, 1997, see Chapter 12). Another way of looking at this problem is in terms of Rasmussen's (1983) trichotomy between skill-based behavior, rule-based behavior, and knowledge-based behavior (discussed in Chapter 9). Operators must be sensitive to when skill- and rule-based behavior is no longer appropriate and they must, therefore, move into a knowledge-based problem-solving domain.

Second, Rasmussen and his colleagues focused attention on the need for operators to problem solve flexibly by moving up and down to different *levels of abstraction*. In the failure of a power generating plant, sometimes operators must think at very concrete levels in terms of variables like steam or water flow, heat measurement, and valve settings; at other times they must conceptualize at more abstract levels related to the thermodynamics of the energy conversion process under their supervision—thinking, for example, about the appropriate balance between mass and energy. At other times, the required level of thinking may be still more abstract, defined in terms of concepts like plant safety, human risk, and company profits. Similar distinctions between abstraction levels can be made in other process environments. For example, in solving an unexpected air traffic control problem, the controller may need to move between thinking about the actual flight parameters of one particular aircraft (concrete), and the anticipated overall flow and congestion of all traffic in the area (abstract). These different levels of the abstraction hierarchy all interact, such as the multiloop control systems in Figure 10.13, and a major hurdle for effective problem solving during fault management is to provide the operator with the necessary tools to think conceptually at these different abstraction levels and rapidly make transitions between them (Vicente & Rasmussen, 1990, 1992; Vicente, 1999).

Collectively, the problems confronted by the operator in the fault diagnosis problem-solving phase are formidable; they have been summarized in Table 13.1, along with some fairly abstract requirements necessary to remediate the problems. One goal of cognitive engineering is to use this problem analysis to define a series of more concrete remediation recommendations (Rasmussen, Pjetersoen, & Goodstein, 1995, Vicente & Rasmussen, 1992).

Remedies to Address Abnormality Problems

Researchers have identified a number of approaches that can be taken to improve the accuracy and efficiency of complex system fault diagnosis. Globally, these can be categorized into system design issues (including error tolerance and several display issues), training issues, and organizational factors.

Error Tolerance and Prediction The concept of error-tolerant systems, discussed in Chapter 12 (Rouse & Morris, 1986), is nowhere of greater potential importance than in the complex process control environment, where reversible operator actions should be considered. A related option is to allow the operator the opportunity to experiment with the control of variables and predict their influence in a computer-simulated off-line mode (Sheridan, 1992). Ideally, this mode should have a fast-time model of the plant, so that potential solutions can be tried out to establish their effectiveness (or reveal their disastrous consequences) before they are finally put into the system. Such an approach is challenged because of the high complexity of many processes which makes accurate modeling a difficult process.

TABLE 13.1 Human Operator Problems and System Requirements in Fault Diagnosis

Problem	Requirements
Cognitive tunnel vision	Need for fresh perspective
Sluggish process	Need for anticipation, good predictive displays
Complexity of system connections	Need for good mental model, communications, good displays
Brittleness of rigid procedures	Need for flexible adaptation of procedures (pay attention to "if" part of "if-then" rule)
Pressure to go fast	Need to slow down
Multilevel problem solving	Need to move up and down in level of abstraction

Display Issues Researchers in the nuclear power control field have continually called attention to the difficulties operators have in maintaining a mental representation of the evolving situation (Bainbridge, 1983; De Keyser, 1988; Goodstein & Rasmussen, 1988; Woods, 1988; Vicente et al., 1996; Vicente & Rasmussen, 1992). This problem can be most directly remediated by considering improvements in display design over the simple "one variable, one indicator" (1V–1I) mapping shown in Figure 13.1. As we have seen in Figure 13.8, such displays are problematic because the meaning of a given reading on any single indicator depends on the context of the other indicators. Also problematic is the replacement of the wide-panel display in Figure 13.1 with a centralized CRT display, in which information must be called up to the CRT screen by keyboard data entry. This means of information retrieval denies the operator the continuously available readings that can be accessed by a mere scan of the eyes or a turn of the head producing a sort of "keyhole view" on the state of the plant (Moray, 1997). Instead of 1V–1I designs or centralized CRT displays, a number of more sophisticated display innovations are available, eight of which are described below.

1. Predictive Displays The value of predictive displays has already been discussed in several contexts (see Figure 13.7). The information they provide is as valuable in diagnosis as it is in control. Yet it should be emphasized that the value of predictive information is only as great as the reliability of that information, a reliability that must decline with longer predictive spans.

2. Feedback Woods (1988) has noted that one of the greatest problems in the process control environment is the absence (or poor quality) of feedback on the effects and implications of a control action, illustrating the principle of visibility (discussed in Chapter 12).

3. Annunciator and Alarm Information A good deal of preliminary information concerning the nature of a failure is potentially available in the alarms and annunciators that first indicate its existence (these annunciators are shown in the panels at the top of the workstations depicted in Figure 13.1). The word "potentially" is emphasized, however, because from the operator's point of view, the information is often essentially uninterpretable. This unfortunate state of affairs occurs because the vast interconnectedness of the modern process control or nuclear power plant often means that one primal failure will drive conditions at other parts of the plant out of their normal operating range so rapidly that, within minutes or even seconds, scores of annunciator lights or buzzers will create a buzzing-flashing confusion. At one loss-of-coolant incident at a nuclear reactor, more than 500 annunciators changed status within the first minute, and more than 800 within the first two minutes (Sheridan, 1981). Operators on the scene at Three Mile Island complained that this rapid growth prevented them from obtaining good information concerning the initial, primal conditions that led to the other, secondary failures (Goodstein, 1981). The problem can be exacerbated by a central master alarm (usually auditory), which will sound whenever a fault appears anywhere in the system. Difficulties can occur when this alarm, often very annoying, is turned off. When this happens, some systems are configured to turn off the causal alarms, or to freeze their state, so that even if the variables return to normal conditions, this information is not registered (Goodstein, 1981; Sheridan, 1981). Thus, the very annoyance of the master alarm that guarantees failure detection induces a form of behavior that may be counterproductive to effective diagnosis.

Investigators have concluded that the confusing nature of annunciator systems could be greatly reduced by implementing certain basic principles, which would also increase the diagnostic value of the annunciators. The next three categories of innovations appear to be particularly useful: sequencing, color, and informativeness.

4. Sequencing This procedure allows the operator to recover an accurate picture of a progressive series of annunciators and, therefore, be better able to deduce the primal fault. A simple variant of sequencing is the concept of a "first-out panel," in which the first alarm to appear in a series is somehow distinctively identified for a prolonged period, for example, by a flashing light (Benel, McCafferty, Neal, & Mallory, 1981). The more complex form of sequencing, depending on computer services, requires a buffer memory that could replay on a schematized display—at a speed chosen by the operator—the sequence of annunciator appearances. Computer automation itself could analyze the alarm sequence and use its own logic to help identify the primal fault. Sequencing is thus another example of how smart displays can assist the fallible records of human memory. This intelligence could also alleviate the problem (illustrated in Figure 13.8) in which the deeper meaning of any given alarm indicator is influenced by the context of other variables.

5. Color As discussed in Chapters 2 and 3, color, if properly and consistently used, can aid greatly in interpreting the diagnostic information available from alarms. Yet, as we also discussed in Chapter 3, it is extremely important for display colors to agree with population stereotypes (e.g., red = danger; yellow = caution; green = normal) and for these stereotypes to be consistently adhered to (Osborne, Barsam, & Burgy, 1981). A classic example of the lack of consistency has been pointed out by Osborne, Barsam, and Burgy in process plants, where green indicates the status of an open, flowing valve, and red the status of a closed one. On the one hand, this coding runs contrary to stereotypes in the electronics industry, in which green means "circuit not live" and red means "circuit hot, do not touch." This convention would place alternate coding interpretations side by side where electrical and hydraulic systems are mixed. Furthermore, under normal plant operations, some valves will be open and some will be closed. The resulting "Christmas tree" depiction of normal operation may be indistinguishable at a glance from the appearance of a failure. The writers contrast this coding with a higher conceptual level of coding in which green indicates the normal valve position (whether open or closed) and red the abnormal. In this "greenboard" display, abnormalities will thereby show up with great salience as any red indicator in a sea of green.

The complex issues involved in good display design are revealed, however, when it is seen that even this concept has certain limitations: The same valve positions that are normal during one phase of operation—the steady running of a nuclear plant—may be abnormal during alternate phases such as start-up and shutdown. Thus the Christmas-tree pattern will reappear during these transient phases and provide an uninterpretable array that cannot readily distinguish normal from abnormal conditions. This situation is particularly dangerous because start-up and shutdown are periods of the highest cognitive load. The only solution is to incorporate computer logic to make the assignment of color code to valve position defined not only by the criterion of normality but also by that of the operational phase. With complex systems such as those found in the nuclear industry, this automation is an extremely challenging undertaking.

6. Informativeness Thompson (1981) suggests that annunciators should be made to supply a fair degree of information, in the formal sense of the word discussed in Chapter 2. We concluded in Chapter 9 that humans can process a small number of information-rich stimuli more efficiently than a large number of stimuli of small information content: the decision complexity advantage. This characteristic reinforces the value of more informative, higher-level annunciator systems that can provide a single piece of evidence for a *set* of symptoms that covary, rather than one annunciator for each. Further economy is gained if the single physical annunciator may be configured to provide more than one bit of information (i.e., present 2 or 3 state information on the likelihood that a variable is abnormal) (Sorkin & Woods, 1985; Sorkin, Kantowitz, & Kantowitz, 1988).

7. Compatibility We have discussed compatibility extensively in previous chapters, and here, our focus will be on compatibility of two kinds: proximity (Chapter 3) and display (Chapter 4). In applying the proximity compatibility principle (Wickens & Carswell, 1995) to the design of complex system displays, task analysis must be employed to identify sources of information that may need to be compared and integrated. Efforts should be made to colocate these sources (or otherwise render them similar). Such efforts may include configuring these as object displays, such as the safety parameters "polygon" display shown in Figure 13.9. By clustering these together such that the normal values are of equal extent, then the normal state is indicated by symmetry, an emergent feature (Figure 13.9a), and a departure from symmetry is easy to detect. Furthermore, the

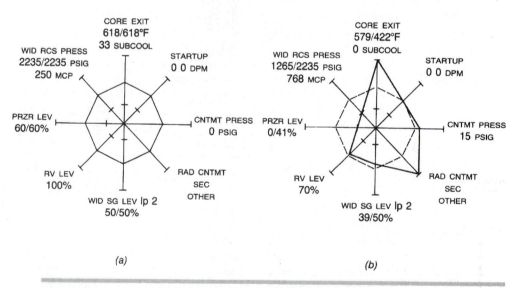

(a)   (b)

Figure 13.9 Integrated spoke or polar display for monitoring critical safety parameters in nuclear power. (*a*) Normal operation. (*b*) Wide-range iconic display during loss-of-coolant accident.

Source: D. D. Woods, J. Wise, and L. Hanes, "An Evaluation of Nuclear Power Plant Safety Parameter Display Systems," *Proceedings of the 25th Annual Meeting of the Human Factors Society* (Santa Monica, CA: Human Factors, 1981), p. 111. Copyright 1981 by the Human Factors Society. Reproduced by permission.

nature of the departure (i.e., identity of the failure) could be signaled by a unique shape (Figure 13.9b). However, the challenges to creating such displays in a way that serves both detection and diagnosis are substantial. Some evidence suggests that they are more satisfactory for the former than the latter task (Moray, 1997).

Proximity compatibility can be achieved after a task/information analysis has revealed the information integration requirements. In contrast, display compatibility principles such as the principle of pictorial realism (Roscoe, 1968; see Chapter 4) depend on presenting the configuration of display elements in a way that is compatible both with the configuration of elements in a real system and with the operator's mental model of that configuration (for a well-trained operator, the two should agree). One way to accomplish this is through the "mimic diagram" shown in Figure 13.10. Such diagrams have been shown to be superior to the standard 1 variable–1 indicator display (Vicente et al., 1996). However, simply depicting the spatial or topological relations between system variables is not always adequate in many complex systems, and for such systems, cognitive engineers have proposed the concept of the "ecological interface display," discussed next.

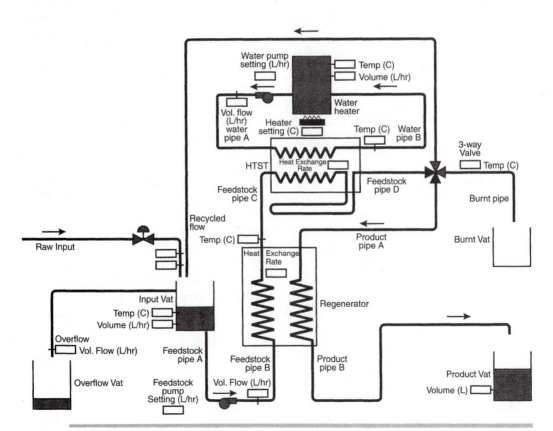

Figure 13.10   Example of a functional mimic display. Courtesy of Dal Vernon Reising.

8. Ecological Interface Displays   Rasmussen (1986; Vicente & Rasmussen, 1992; Reising & Sanderson, 1998) offers a philosophy of display design for complex systems that provides the viewer with two critical components: making *constraints* in the system dynamics easily visible, and displaying different *levels of abstraction*. Both of these features are considered to be particularly valuable for diagnosis and fault management if there is a system failure. System failures are often signaled by a breakdown in the constraints that characterize a normally operating system. Examples of such constraints are the relationship between pressure and temperature for a process plant, the relationship between respiration and blood oxygen for the human body (monitored in surgery by the anesthesiologist), or the relationship between aircraft departures and downstream traffic flow (monitored by the air traffic manager). An ecological interface should make these constraints easily and intuitively visible. For example, in Figure 13.11a, the expected relation (constraints) between pressure and temperature is shown by the line. A departure, triggered for example by a leak in the pipes or pumps, would be immediately evident by a break in the structure of the line.

For very complex systems, constraints may be displayed, consistent with the correct mental model, by more sophisticated displays such as the Rankine cycle display shown in Figure 13.11b. Here the constraints are those imposed by the laws of thermodynamics, as water is converted to steam, releasing mechanical energy (turning the turbine), and is converted back to water again (the Rankine cycle). Because this display characterizes the thermodynamic laws of the natural environment, it may be called "ecological" and has been shown to be more effective in fault management than either the mimic display or the 1V–1I display suite shown in Figure 13.1 (Vicente et al., 1996).

The second concept underlying the ecological interface is the abstraction hierarchy. As we noted above, particularly during fault management, but also during routine monitoring, operators must think at varying levels of abstraction: ranging from the more abstract goals to the highly concrete knowledge about the "physical state." In process control, high, medium, and low levels of abstraction might be, respectively, information about profit and risk, information about mass and energy, and information about specific pumps and pipes in operation. In air traffic control, these might be, respectively, information about traffic flow of a stream of aircraft, information about the achievable trajectory of a single aircraft, and information about the momentary controls of that aircraft. These variables are "hierarchically" organized as shown in Figure 13.12 such that the processes in lower level variables generally influence those above them. If one examines *what* a variable is doing at a given level, then variables below that level in the abstraction hierarchy serve to express *how* the "what" variable is being influenced, or how its change is accomplished; in contrast, variables above that level serve to indicate *why* the "what" variable is being changed (i.e., the purpose of its change) or the higher level consequences of the change. Note that if the operator's focus of attention shifts, as reflected by moving from the left to the right of the figure (e.g., attention to the "how" variable in Figure 13.12, moving to a lower level of abstraction), then new variables address the "why" and "how."

While there are no clear guidelines as to how different levels of the abstraction hierarchy should be displayed, the philosophy of ecological interface design dictates that the display interface allow the operator to rapidly and easily "visit" or transition between different levels. Because different levels are related to each other, as shown in Figure 13.12, it is important that techniques of *visual momentum* be employed (Woods, 1984; see also Chapter 5), in order to support rapid shifts of attention between levels, without cognitive

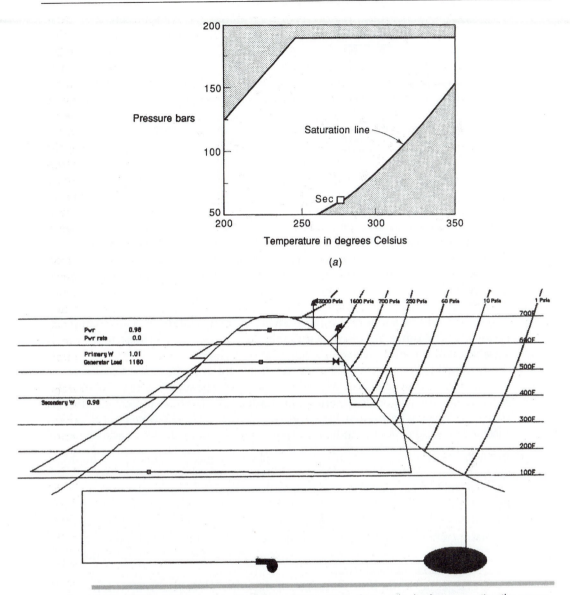

Figure 13.11 (*a*) Pressure temperature display. (*b*) Rankine cycle display supporting the operator's mental model of the thermodynamic process of energy-mass conversion.

Source: (*a*) L. P. Goodstein and J. Rasmussen, "Representation of Process, State, Structure, and Control," *Le Travail Humain, 51,* 1988, pp. 19–37. (*b*) K. Vincente et al., "Evaluation of a Rankine Cycle Display for Nuclear Power Plant Monitoring and Diagnosis," *Human Factors, 38* (1996), pp. 506–522. Reproduced by permission.

disorientation. Thus, the supervisor of an energy process who detects a breakdown in the constraints between mass and energy (mid-level in the hierarchy) should rapidly be able to ascertain the implications of this breakdown on plant safety and economy (top level) as well as to examine possible physical sources of the breakdown (lower level). Visual

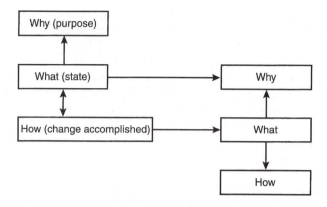

Figure 13.12   Schematic representation of abstraction hierarchy. The column on the right represents a shift of attention to a lower level in the hierarchy.

momentum will be supported by consistency of representation at different levels (Goodstein & Rasmussen, 1988), as well as by careful use of visual links, to show how variables at one level are related to changes at other levels.

It should be apparent that the effective guide for ecological interface design involves a great deal of analysis and creativity that cannot be simply prescribed; such design also involves a good deal more sophistication than has been presented here. The reader is referred to Rasmussen, Pjetersoen, and Goodstein (1995), Vicente et al. (1996), Vicente (1999), and Vicente and Rasmussen (1992) for more detailed discussions.

Training   Successful performance in a control room depends on knowledge of procedures and on a good mental model of the system—a model both of its normal operating state and of its failure states, although these two will not be identical (Kragt & Landeweerd, 1974). In the case of normal operations, the model is a set of expectancies of what control actions lead to what changes in variables, and when. In the case of abnormal operations, the necessary diagnostic model will be more complex and must consider the variety of ways in which the system could fail. At issue, then, is how knowledge of system relations should be trained.

De Keyser (1988) argues that this knowledge is best acquired through the actual experience of incidents (either real or simulated), which form kernels of knowledge that eventually constitute knowledge of the plant. In contrast to this on-the-job training, research in this area has often focused on whether explicit training should involve fundamental theory or more specific control heuristics.

Crossman and Cooke (1962) and Kragt and Landeweerd (1974) report that an understanding of the general scientific principles underlying the process provides no assistance in the operator's ability to control it. This finding also suggests that an internal model is not a highly general concept. Other studies support the conclusion that instruction in general theory does not help performance in these operational process control contexts

(Patrick, Haines, Munley, & Wallace, 1989). In contrast, understanding the specific principles underlying the given system to be controlled does assist the operator in process control (Attwood, 1970; Brigham & Liaos, 1975). Landeweerd, Seegers, and Praageman (1981), for example, found that operators with two hours of instruction on the dynamics of a complex chemical process learned to control the process more rapidly than those who received information on the input/output relations for the same duration of study. These findings reinforce the validity of the mental model. They suggest that effective control not only is learned by acquiring a series of stimulus-response mappings but also is based on an understanding of the structure of causal sequencing in the plant.

The importance of learning a causal sequence, based on an internal model for a particular system, suggests that training should not be focused only on following rote procedures. As discussed, Woods (1988) points out the brittleness of such procedures and the dangers inherent in following them rigidly without paying attention to whether or not each step is effective. If a given step is not effective, a well-trained troubleshooter should know why the procedure was intended to be carried out in that context, allowing for the necessary flexibility (Roth & Woods, 1988; Woods, 1988).

Organizational Structure   The nuclear power plant typifies the complex, multi-operator system that serves as a breeding ground for resident pathogens as described in Chapter 12 (Reason, 1990). These pathogens are latent error opportunities, which are embedded in system complexity, procedures, training inadequacies, organizational structure or management policies, and attitudes (e.g., attitudes toward safety versus economy and production). A review of human factors in nuclear process control rooms highlights the importance of organizational factors over specific human factors in influencing overall plant safety (Moray & Huey, 1988). Two specific examples are briefly mentioned here.

1. Communications. In Chapter 6, we discussed briefly the human factors of communications, focusing heavily on aviation systems. The coordination of process control plants is also very much of a team operation, and smooth team performance and communications can be critical for success in normal operations as well as in fault management (Moray, 1997). Roth and Woods (1988) highlight this feature in their analysis of expert performance in the steam generator start-up phase. Similarly, it is easy to understand how the confirmation bias, identified as a contributing cause to the Three Mile Island disaster, might have been reduced by better communications between operators. A pair of "fresh eyes" might have interpreted the symptoms differently (and correctly), thereby alleviating the chain of incorrect actions, which was based on the mistaken belief that reactor pressure was too high.

2. Conflicting goals. As noted, most process industries operate under somewhat conflicting goals of production and profits versus safety (Reason, 1997; Woods & Cook, 1999). The relative priorities between these two objectives can be clearly stated by the management of a company (or the policy of a regulatory agency), or they may remain ambiguous. But their impact, whether established from above or chosen by the control-room operators, will directly influence performance. Heavy emphasis on production in a steam generating plant, for

example, may lead to strategies that will proceed through the costly and time-consuming process of bringing a reactor on-line in the most rapid fashion possible, thereby ignoring the go-slow strategy and shortcutting safety (Roth & Woods, 1988). Within the framework of signal detection theory (Chapter 2) and risky decision making (Chapter 8), these attitudes may also influence the detection criterion an operator adopts in categorizing a warning signal as a true system failure rather than as a machine false alarm. General attitudes toward safety will of course dictate the extent to which allowable procedures are followed or violated, the Chernobyl accident in the Soviet Union illustrating a case in which such procedures were intentionally violated (Reason, 1997).

Finally, a critical organization issue—and one that is sometimes advocated as a solution to many of the human performance problems in process control—is the continued development and deployment of higher and higher levels of control-room automation (Bainbridge, 1983). Because the issues of automation extend well beyond the process control environment, we address them in this broader context shortly.

Conclusion

Human factors research on complex processes, both their control and their fault management and diagnosis, remains an immature domain. Many of the recommendations concerning display layout, anthropometry, control location, lighting and legibility, and clearly written procedures translate directly from the general practice of good human factors (Bailey, 1989; Ivergard, 1989; Sanders & McCormick, 1993; Moray, 1997; Wickens, Gordon, & Liu, 1998), and this approach has been implemented with some degree of success. Yet it is equally clear that great improvements are possible by combining theories of cognitive psychology with increasingly available computer and display technology. This area of cognitive engineering is one in which relatively little engineering psychology research has been conducted to assess the utility of the recommendations made by such researchers as Rasmussen, Vicente, and Woods. The potential payoffs of this research appear to be quite high, in light of the fact that systems are evolving toward greater complexity with increasing levels of automation.

AUTOMATION

We define automation here to refer to the mechanical or electrical accomplishment of work. In many cases, this involves the substitution of automation components for tasks that humans are capable of performing (e.g., using automobiles to transport, rather than walking or cycling), although it may also describe those for which humans are incapable (e.g., robots lifting heavy loads, or handling toxic material). Automation may be described in terms of its *purposes*, the *human performance functions* it replaces, and the *strengths* and *weaknesses* it shows as humans interact with automated devices ranging from the electrical can opener to the sophisticated autopilot, financial investment advisor, or process control regulator. We consider these below.

Examples and Purposes of Automation

Automation varies from that which totally replaces the human operator by computer or machine to computer-driven aids that help an overloaded operator. The different purposes of automation may be assigned to four general categories.

1. Performing functions that the human cannot perform because of inherent limitations. This category describes many of the complex mathematical operations performed by computers (e.g., those involved in statistical analysis). In the realm of dynamic systems, examples include control guidance in a manned booster rocket, in which the time delay of a human operator would cause instability (see Chapter 10); aspects of control in complex nuclear reactions, in which the dynamic processes are too complex for the human operator to respond to on-line; or robots for the manipulation of materials in hazardous or toxic environments. In these and similar circumstances, automation appears to be essential and unavoidable, whatever its costs.

2. Performing functions that the human can do but performs poorly or at the cost of high workload. Examples include the autopilots that control many aspects of flight on commercial aircraft (Sarter & Woods, 1995, 1997) and the automation of certain complex monitoring functions, such as the ground proximity warning system (GPWS) or traffic alert and collision advisory system (TCAS) alerting pilots to the possibility of collision with the terrain or with other aircraft respectively (Wickens, Mavor, Parasuraman, & McGee, 1998). Recent efforts in automation have been directed toward automating diagnosis and decision processes in such areas as medicine (Klatzky & Ayoub, 1995), or nuclear process control (Woods & Roth, 1988). These approaches generally involve the implementation of computer-based artificial intelligence or expert systems (Madni, 1988).

3. Augmenting or assisting performance in areas in which humans show limitations. This category is similar to the preceding one, but automation is intended not as a replacement for integral aspects of the task but as an aid to peripheral or supporting tasks necessary to accomplish the main task. As we have seen, there are major bottlenecks in performance, because of limitations in human working memory and prediction/anticipation, for which automation would be useful. An automated display, or visual echo of auditory messages, is one such example, as discussed in Chapter 7. Examples of this might be the phone number retrieved from operator information which appears on a small telephone display; or digitized instructions from air traffic control "uplinked" to the aircraft that can appear as a text message on the pilot's console (Kerns, 1991, 1999; Wickens, Mavor, Parasuraman, & McGee, 1998).

   Another example is a computer-displayed "scratch pad" of the output of diagnostic tests in fault diagnosis of the chemical, nuclear, or process control industries. As suggested in Chapter 8, this procedure would greatly reduce working memory load. Computer-displayed checklists of required procedures, coupled with a voice-recognition system, would allow operators to indicate orally when each procedure had been completed. The automated display could then check off each step accordingly (Palmer & Degani, 1991). As noted several times throughout this book, any sort of predictive display that would off-load the human's cognitive burden of making predictions would be of great use. Yet another example of an automated aid is the display "decluttering" option, which can remove unnecessary detail from an electronic display when it is not needed, thereby facilitating the process of focused and selective attention (Stokes, Wickens, & Kite, 1990).

4. Economic reasons. Finally, automation is often introduced because it is less expensive than paying people to do equivalent jobs or to be trained for those jobs. Thus, we see robots replacing workers in many manufacturing plants, or automated phone menus replacing the human voice on the other end of the line. As the latter example suggests, the economy achieved by such automation does not necessarily make the service "user friendly" to the human who must interact with it (Landauer, 1995).

Human Functions Replaced by Automation

This book has been structured within a framework emphasizing different stages of information processing, and automation too can be conceptualized in terms of how it augments or assists those different processing stages. Furthermore, adopting an approach suggested by Sheridan (1992, 1997; see also Endsley & Kiris, 1995), automation at each stage can be characterized by different *levels*, as shown in Figure 13.13 (Wickens, Mavor, Parasuraman, & McGee, 1998; Wickens, 1999). Here, automation of information acquisition and analysis (stage 1) can be characterized by the amount of "work" that automation (usually computers) does to acquire, interpret, and integrate information, hence replacing (or assisting) early human components such as selective attention (e.g., by automatic highlighting), perception (e.g., by automation target recognition), or cognition (e.g., the inference involved in prediction, or the integration accomplished by many graphic displays, such as the electronic map discussed in Chapter 5, or the ecological interface shown in Figure 13.11). Thus, the *level* of automation at stage 1 can be characterized by the amount of "work" that computer intelligence carries out to assemble information in a usable form that can support subsequent decisions, the second stage of Figure 13.13.

Higher levels of automation at the second stage—decision making—can also be described by the amount of computer work, but more specifically by the degree of constraints that automation imposes on choices by the human operator (Sheridan, 1992). Thus, at lowest levels, the human must be entirely responsible for this choice. At level 2, a "decision aid" may recommend a small number of options, as discussed in Chapter 8. At level 3, only a single "best" choice may be offered. We discussed such level 3 decision automation in the context of "command displays" in Chapter 6. An example is the airborne traffic warning system, which provides a *resolution advisory* that "advises" the pilot to fly one particular maneuver (e.g., "climb, climb") to avoid a collision. At level 4, the automation itself will act if the human approves; at level 5, it will act *unless* the human vetoes within some time; at the highest level, the action will be taken regardless of human intentions.

Finally, at the third stage, automation may *execute* various forms of action, such as when it sharpens a pencil, opens a can, or rolls down a car window. Automation of

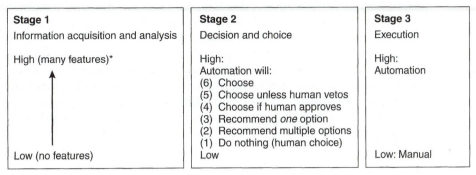

Stage 1	Stage 2	Stage 3
Information acquisition and analysis	Decision and choice	Execution
High (many features)*	High: Automation will:	High: Automation
↑	(6) Choose	
	(5) Choose unless human vetos	
	(4) Choose if human approves	
	(3) Recommend *one* option	
	(2) Recommend multiple options	
	(1) Do nothing (human choice)	
Low (no features)	Low	Low: Manual

* Features of computer automation:
  Selection, Filtering, Highlighting and cueing,
  Configuration, Prediction, Interpolation, Inference

Figure 13.13   Stages and levels of automation

C. D. Wickens, M. Mavor, R. Parasuraman, & J. McGee, *The Future of Air Traffic Control* (Washington, DC: National Academy of Sciences, 1998).

response execution may occur regardless of whether the decision was made at higher or lower automation levels at stage 2, although logically the highest levels of stage 2 automation must assume stage 3 automation.

It is clear that high levels of automation at all stages *can* be useful, if such automation works as the designer intends (and as the user expects), and hence is perceived to be reliable. Furthermore, high automation levels will certainly be valuable if they exceed the capability of the human to do the tasks accurately and in the time available. Troubles occur when automation does not function in this way, as we discuss in detail in the following section. A review of automation research suggests that, if automation is less than fully reliable, there is a greater concern if high levels are pursued in decision (stage 2) than in information acquisition and analysis (stage 1) (Wickens, Mavor, Parasuraman, & McGee, 1998; Crocoll & Coury, 1990). Briefly, this difference results because incorrect acquisition and analysis by automation can usually be verified by alternative means by a vigilant operator before a choice is taken, but an incorrect automation *choice* (high levels of stage 2) can only be recovered and corrected under some circumstances. Moreover, if the choice is one involving high risk—like the administration of medicine to a critically ill patient—the consequences of automation error can be severe, and may be irreversible.

Automation Advantages

There is little doubt that automation offers a number of advantages, in addition to those of cost savings that were mentioned above. In many instances, automation improves efficiency. The pilot who uses the autopilot, for example, can fly more fuel- and time-efficient routes. Automation can expand the frontiers of performance and, hence, increase overall system productivity. For example, the "autoland" function on an aircraft can bring the automated aircraft into an airport that is otherwise "fogged out" and hence unavailable to the airplane without autoland capabilities. Furthermore, automation, if well crafted, can reduce workload: in response execution and muscular exertion (consider the automated can opener, screw driver, or pencil sharpener), in decision choice (recall the mental effort involved in making high-risk decisions in unfamiliar domains, as discussed in Chapter 8), and in information acquisition and analysis (recall the cost of scanning a cluttered display, or mentally multiplying two numbers). More than anything else, this workload reduction feature of automation makes it attractive to the human operator in many environments in which time stress is high or in which cognitive effort needs to be reduced. Yet, as we see in the following sections, this workload-reducing feature *can* invite problems with automation.

Potential Costs of Automation

In this section, we deal much more extensively with the potential human factors problems with automation than we did in addressing their advantages above. This disparity does not signify that problems are more numerous than advantageous. Indeed, in many areas, automation has had well-documented benefits on both safety and user comfort (Wickens, Mavor, Parasuraman, & McGee, 1998; Landauer, 1995). Instead, our cost emphasis is based, simply, on the fact that benefits can be preserved and need no further work, whereas the costs of automation should be addressed by human factors remediations, and to do so, they must be clearly understood by the engineering psychologist. We identify four major categories of such costs below. It should be noted, first, that several problems with automation simply result from the absence of human factors concerns for the *interfaces* with automation devices—that is, problems discussed in Chapters 3–5 and 9. We will not repeat these here; instead, we discuss human performance issues more directly related to the automated functionality itself.

Complexity   Automation replaces functions that were originally performed by humans with mechanical or computer components. Thus, while eliminating human error, discussed in the previous chapter, the increased number of nonhuman components will increase the probability of a system error or fault, according to the reliability calculations discussed in Chapter 12. Furthermore, the greater the levels or complexity of an automation function, the more components it will contain, and, by virtue of the reliability equations, the greater is the possibility that something, somewhere, will fail, a failure that has human performance implications addressed in the following section. Since automation increasingly relies on software, then increasing sophistication leads to more lines of software code, in which insidious "bugs" have a tendency to hide (Landauer, 1995).

Increased automation complexity brings with it a second concern. If algorithms are so complex as to do things a different way from how humans normally (or previously) accomplished the same task, then the human operator may become surprised by and sometimes suspicious of automated functioning. An example is the flight management system, a collection of sophisticated autopilots that guide an aircraft through flight-efficient routes, using algorithms and logic considerably more sophisticated than a pilot would use to fly the same routes (Sarter & Woods, 1995, 1996, 1997; Dagani, Shafto, & Kirlick, 1999). Because of these complex, nonhuman (and therefore nonintuitive) algorithms, such systems will on occasion do things (legitimately) that pilots do not expect, and hence lead them to ask "Why is it doing this?"—a concept in aviation described as "automation induced surprises" (Sarter & Woods, 1997). In general, such surprises do not have major implications *unless* they lead the human to assume that the automation has failed and, hence, intervene, perhaps inappropriately. This issue leads directly to our discussion of the second major human performance issue with automation, its reliability, which in turn generates concerns about trust calibration, addressed in the next two sections.

Reliability: Undertrust   Even when automation is perfectly reliable, its operation can produce the perception that it is unreliable if its complexity leads to automation surprises, as discussed above. As it turns out, the perceived reliability (or unreliability) whether accurately related to true reliability or not has important implications regarding *trust* issues we discuss here.

When an operator distrusts automation either because of its complexity or because of its true level of unreliability, there is a possibility that the system may be trusted less than is warranted, a failure of *trust calibration*. As a consequence, such automation may be abandoned (Parasuraman & Riley, 1997), even when it is generally accurate (after all, 10 percent unreliable automation will still be accurate 90 percent of the time). Nowhere is the phenomenon better illustrated than in the "alarm false alarm" problem, in which an alarm (a form of automated advice) will sound even if no actual failure condition exists (Sorkin, 1989; Stanton, 1994; Parasuraman, Mouloua, & Hilburn, 1999). Such circumstances invite the operator to mistrust the alarm system—that is, to be "undercalibrated" as to the true value that the alarm can offer. With similar consequences, automation that is perfectly reliable but confusing because of its complexity can also lead to operator distrust, and hence disuse. Whether because of true unreliability or complexity (leading to perceived unreliability), disuse can have consequences that range from relatively minor—sometimes we are less efficient when we turn off automation than we would be with its assistance—to catastrophic. Such catastrophic incidents may occur because a true (valid) alarm was ignored, or because a critical condition was never announced in the first place because the "annoying" unreliable alarm system had been turned off previously.

Many solutions can be offered to address the problems of mistrust of alarms and other automation functions. First, automation design can be simplified. For example, computer systems often contain far more features than necessary, purchasing what the designer believes to be "flexibility" but at the cost of complexity (Landauer, 1995). Second, whatever automation algorithms *are* adapted (preferably simpler ones) can be made to be better understood, with a combination of effective training and good (cognitively compatible) display design (Norman, 1988). Third, regarding the "alarm false alarm" problem, both training and display design possibilities again suggest themselves. With regard to training, it is necessary for users of alarm systems to realize that, in conditions in which system failures may be subtle yet catastrophic and early warnings are thus desirable, and in which the *base rate* of failures is quite low; then alarm false alarms *must* be an inevitable consequence to be tolerated (Parasuraman et al., 1997). Fortunately, a design remediation is also available in the form of the "likelihood alarm" (Sorkin, Kantowitz, & Kantowitz, 1988), which can offer two or more graded levels of certainty that the critical condition exists. In essence, such a concept allows the system to say "I'm not sure" rather than just blurting out a full alarm or nothing at all, while setting a risky criterion to avoid misses. As we learned in Chapter 2, allowing human signal detectors to express their confidence in "signal-present" at more than one level improves human sensitivity performance. Allowing the alarm system a corresponding resolution in confidence provides a corresponding improvement in the sensitivity of the human and system together (Sorkin, Kantowitz, & Kantowitz, 1988; Sorkin & Woods, 1985).

Reliability: Overtrust The previous section dealt with the consequences of too little trust in automation; here, we consider the opposite case: overtrust or *complacency* (Funk, et al., 1999; Parasuraman, Molloy, & Singh, 1993). As an example in the context of Figure 13.13, consider stage 1 automation guidance, in which a cue directs the user's attention to an inferred target. Overtrust is manifest if the user follows the cue, even if the target is not there (Conejo & Wickens, 1997). As another example at stage 1, suppose that an automation-based inference as to the diagnostic state of a system is believed, even if it is incorrect (Mosier, Skitka, Heers, & Burdick, 1998). As an example at stage 2, an automation-based decision will be trusted, and its consequences not carefully monitored, because the human supervisor does not believe that the decision might be wrong (Endsley & Kiris, 1995; Kaber, Onal, & Endsley, 1999).

Thus, complacency does not create a problem *until* automation fails, and such a failure, although often unlikely, is never impossible. One of the ironies of automation is that the more reliable it is, the more it is trusted, and the more complacent the operator becomes (Bainbridge, 1983; Parasuraman, Molloy, & Singh, 1993).

Complacency, which is cognitive state (Parasuraman, Molloy, & Singh, 1993), breeds at least two behavioral consequences. On the one hand, the infrequent and therefore unexpected automation failures, when they do occur, will be quite hard to detect (Beringer & Harris, 1999), as we learned in Chapter 2 (expectancy effects on signal detection) and Chapter 9 (expectancy effects on RT). On the other hand, an operator who is complacent that automation is doing its job will be less likely to monitor the job it *is* doing, therefore losing siutation awareness of the evolving state of, or surrounding, the automated system (Endsley & Kiris, 1995; Kaber, Onal, & Endsley, 1999). Hence, if the failure *does* occur and is detected, the monitor will be less able to deal with it appropriately—for example, a pilot jumping back into the control loop to fly the aircraft manually, should the autopilot unexpectedly fail. Furthermore, research findings reveal that it is easier to remember an action if you have chosen it yourself than if you have witnessed another agent (another person, or automation) choose that action (Hopkin, 1994; Slameca, & Graf, 1978). Thus, automation leaves an operator less aware of the chosen actions in the system.

To these two consequences of complacency (detection and situation awareness) may sometimes be added a third. If the operator trusts automation excessively, it may be used so frequently that operator skills at performing the same task may degrade (Lee & Moray, 1994). But such skills may be called upon if the automation fails. Collectively then, the three phenomena of degraded detection, awareness/diagnosis, and manual skills may be referred to as the syndrome of "out of the loop unfamiliarity" or "OOTLUF."

In many automated systems, OOTLUF concerns are pitted against the very real automation benefit of reduced workload. For the busy vehicle driver who is navigating in an unfamiliar freeway environment, reliable guidance automation will likely be preferred, and a true benefit to safety. By offloading some aspects of the inner-loop driving control (e.g., lane keeping and headway monitoring) to an intelligent and reliable autopilot, the driver can consult navigational information and make decisions without diversion of resources. However, the implications of this trade-off should be considered carefully, so that the OOTLUF syndrome does not occur.

Some evidence indicates there might be optimum levels of stage 2 automation on the trade-off that do not produce OOTLUF, yet still provide automation at a high enough level so that workload is tempered. In an experiment by Endsley and Kiris (1995), different subjects were supported by any of five levels of automation choice supports (stage 2 automation) in a driving navigation task, ranging from full manual decisions to fully automated decisions. Their interest, and operational assessment of OOTLUF, was in how effectively the drivers intervened when the automation failed. The investigators found that performance (measured by manual intervention time following the failure) suffered at the highest automation level, but was no different across the three mid levels; levels which also showed equivalent measures of subjectively rated system understanding. In this case then, higher (but not full) levels of automation (and therefore reduced workload) could be pursued without leading to a major increase in OOTLUF. Similar findings were revealed in a study of robot supervision carried out by Kaber, Onal, and Endsley (1999).

In conclusion, the key issues with regard to operator trust in automation is that of *calibration* of the user's trust (and corresponding system oversight) to the actual reliability of a system. To the extent that automated guidance (attention cueing) or inference may be incorrect (stage 1 automation), humans should broaden their attention to consider other locations, evidence, or hypotheses, even as the guidance of generally (but not perfectly) reliable automation *should* usually be followed. To the extent that automated choice may be incorrect (stage 2 automation), humans should be somewhat prepared for the consequences of the incorrect choice.

Communications   If automation is not carefully introduced, it can have the characteristics that Sarter and Woods (1996) label "not a team player." Much of this deficiency may result from the absence of effective feedback to the human monitor of the automation's work, regarding what it is doing and why, an issue that has long concerned pilots as they supervise their powerful but complex and often uncommunicative flight management system (Sarter & Woods, 1995, 1997). Additional communication deficiencies result from the inherent inflexibility in the *dialogue* with most automated systems. Such systems must, after all, be preprogrammed with a fixed set of rules, which limits their "conversational flexibility." The increasingly prevalent phone menu is the perfect example of such inflexibility, where a simple question that does not meet the prespecified set of menu categories cannot be easily handled. Often, one must wait till the final option: "if you need to speak to an operator, press eight." Finally, as we noted in Chapter 6, a number of nonlinguistic features of human-human communications cannot be readily captured by computer-mediated (i.e., automated) communications.

Human Centered Automation

In the previous pages, we identified a number of problems with automation. Addressing these problems, several solutions may be suggested, many of which can be loosely grouped under the rubric of "human-centered automation" (Billings, 1996). These solutions will not necessarily provide the optimal use of automation from the point of productivity or system performance, but should, if followed, provide the greatest satisfaction for the human user, and the least disruptive episodes of "manual recovery" in the instance of system failure. Five of these solutions or "prescriptions" for human-centered automation are briefly described as follows.

1. *Implement automation with good human factors.* Here we simply refer to the application of good design of displays and controls at the automation interface, as has been described in previous chapters of the book.

2. *Keep the operator informed.* This addresses many of the issues of OOTLUF described above. Human-centered design of automation should make efforts to display critical information regarding the current state of automation, changes in those states (e.g., a switch in automation levels or modes), and the status of the process being monitored or controlled by the automation e.g., the continuous variable that is sensed by the automated alarm. (This is sometimes referred to as the "raw data".) Furthermore, as in prescription 1, such information should be offered in intuitive *compatible* displays, as discussed in Chapter 4.

3. *Keep the operator trained.* Training can be carried out on three important components. First, recurrent training should be implemented for whatever skills *might* be required should manual intervention be necessary following a system failure with which automation cannot cope. For example, pilots who fly highly automated aircraft should be required, periodically, to "hand fly" the aircraft, just as the student should periodically practice mental arithmetic in case the calculator battery fails in mid test. Second, operators should be trained in the algorithms and logic that automation employs, so that they will not be "surprised" by their operations (Irving, Polson, & Irving, 1994; Casner, 1995). Third, in the interest of trust calibration, operators should receive some training on the expected failure rates of automation (and the reason for those failures). This is particularly true of alarm systems with low baseline rates of true events (Parasuraman & Hancock, 1999).

4. *Introduce automation gracefully.* Automation will be more likely to be accepted by humans if it is introduced "gracefully" into the workplace. This includes not only attention to training as above, but also to a management policy that advocates computer support or automation as an assistant to human performance, rather than as a replacement. In the case of introduction of a new system to the workplace, a management process should be in place to monitor the introduction for unanticipated problems, and be prepared to intervene with remediation (training, or perhaps redesign) should such problems appear serious (Wickens, Mavor, Parasuraman, & McGee, 1998).

5. *Make automation flexible.* There are at least two forms of this prescription. The first, which we describe only briefly, is that different *users* should have the flexibility of whether to deploy automation or not (or the level at which it should be deployed). In most environments, this flexible policy makes sense; however, in some situations, safety policy might override total discretionary use. For example, there are certain safety-critical tasks for which the human's capabilities are clearly inferior to automation. A case in point is airborne navigation in bad weather. More complex and uncertain in its implementation is a second form of flexibility in which different *occasions* may call for different levels of automation assistance for a given user. This technique is sometimes referred to as

adaptive automation (Scerbo, 1996), which is dealt with in some detail in the following section.

Adaptive Automation

Adaptive automation, represented schematically in Figure 13.14, involves invoking some form of automation—typically task aiding—as a function of the human's momentary needs for such automation because of a transient increase in workload for example, or loss of capacity from sleep deprivation or fatigue (Scerbo, 1996; Hancock & Chignell, 1989; Hammer, 1999). Although the concept has considerable intuitive appeal, few studies have examined its benefits in comparison to appropriate nonadaptive control conditions. The small number of such studies that do exist, however, demonstrate its advantages (Parasuraman, Mouloua, & Hilburn, 1999; Hilburn, Jorna, Byrne, & Parasuraman, 1997; Inagaki, 1999), and a comparative analysis of human and machine abilities can sometimes make a very compelling argument for the concept (Inagaki, 1999).

Indeed, the basis for the adaptive automation argument is the inherent trade-off between workload and situation awareness that results as level of automation is varied, as discussed in the earlier pages of this chapter. Given an assumption that automation should be kept at lower levels (to prevent OOTLUF and preserve situation awareness) *unless* high workload precludes effective human performance, then adaptive automation will optimize the contribution of both human and machine in a workload varying environment. There are, however, three important issues in implementing adaptive automation: what to adapt, how to infer, and who decides.

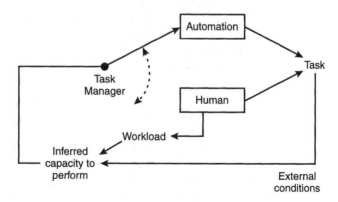

Figure 13.14   Adaptive automation. Workload or the capacity of the human to perform is inferred and used by a "task manager" to assign more of a task to automation (if workload is high) or to the human (if workload is reduced). The task manager itself could be automation, human, or a cooperative enterprise.

What to Adapt   The first issue concerns what aspect of a task (or task complex) should be adapted. Parasuraman, Mouloua, and Hilburn (1999) distinguish between *adaptive aiding*, in which a certain component of a task is made simpler (by automation), and *adaptive task allocation*, in which an entire task (from a larger multitask context) is shifted to automation.

Figure 13.15 provides a context for understanding what task(s) are best to adapt. A reasonable argument can be made that the appropriate choice should be one that reduces workload to the greatest extent, even as it also reduces situation awareness (i.e., moves from point A to point B in Figure 13. 15). The rationale for such an argument is that if the adaptive automation moves from C to B, there is no workload savings and hence no reason to invoke automation in the first place; and if it moves from D to B, the task component might as well be fully and inflexibly automated, since this would produce no loss of situation awareness. Such a choice of what to adapt could be applied independently of whether adaptive aiding or adaptive task allocation is implemented.

How to Infer   A second issue concerns the bases of the inference that workload is excessive (or performance capacity is otherwise degraded), compelling the need for increased automation. Here, as shown in Figure 13.14, any of three philosophies could be employed in isolation or jointly. First, most easily, this inference could be driven by *external task conditions*, that is, easily measurable operating conditions known to demand increased resources. For example, Parasuraman, Mouloua, & Hilburn (1999) demonstrate the success of adaptive automation in aviation that was invoked in takeoff and landing phases (known to be most demanding), but removed during the low-workload midflight cruise portion. In this case, the external conditions were the known phase of flight. Inagaki (1999) suggests that different time periods during the acceleration of an airplane for takeoff make it more or less important for automation to assume responsibility for a rejected takeoff decision, should such a decision be required following an engine failure. Here, the passage of time and speed of the aircraft are the external conditions. The design of an automatic ground collision avoidance system (GCAS) in aircraft uses

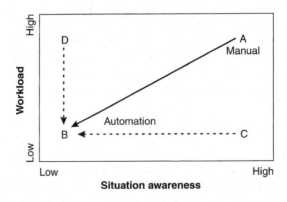

Figure 13.15   Three possible strategies of adaptive automation. It is assumed that point B is at a higher level of automation than points A, C, and D.

the projected time till impact as an external condition to infer that the pilot's attention is incapacitated and perform an automated "fly up" evasive maneuver (Scott, 1999). In driving, one might consider an automation aid that uses the darkness of night (an external condition) to infer that a driver might be more fatigued and less vigilant, hence adapting an automated alerting device, sensitive to lane deviations.

Second, the inference of diminished capacity could be derived from measures of performance itself, particularly to the extent that good performance modeling has revealed clear "leading indicators" that preview subsequent breakdowns. Kaber and Riley (1999), for example, demonstrate the benefits of adaptive aiding on a primary task (a dynamic cognitive monitoring and control task) that is based on degradation of an automation-monitored secondary task.

Third, mental workload or cognitive state could be monitored directly as assessed by physiological measures, inferring, for example, that arousal has dropped via EEG measures, or eye-blink recording, or that workload is excessive via heart rate (Kramer & Weber, 1999; Humphrey & Kramer, 1994; Makeig & Inlow, 1993) (see Chapter 11).

The prominent concern with leading indicators and assessments of physiological state is that both of these sources require some time to integrate a sufficient amount of data so that a reliable inference can be made that the capacity to perform is diminishing (or restored). If adequate time (and data) is not allowed, an inference of capacity change might be incorrect, and this could lead to increasing workload when a decrease is desired, or vice versa. On the other hand, if sufficient time to attain a *reliable* estimate is used and dynamic changes in environmental workload are present, then, given the negative feedback loop properties shown in Figure 13.14, the resulting lag in inference could produce closed-loop instability, in the sense described in Chapter 10. That is, an inference of high (or low) workload could be drawn after a sufficient delay, and adaptive aiding implemented (or removed) at the very time that workload has now diminished (or increased). In this regard, it is important that advocates of closed-loop adaptive automation systems try to establish the time required to make reliable estimates of workload, as Humphrey and Kramer (1994) have done using a measure of EEG.

Who Decides The third issue regarding adaptive automation, and perhaps the most controversial, is the issue of "who decides" whether to implement or remove automation. That is, in the context of Figure 13.14, who is the "task manager"? In the previous section, it was implicitly assumed that the machine itself was responsible for invoking automation, following the signal of one or more of the three inference sources: external conditions, leading indicators, or workload. In contrast, an argument could be made that humans are capable of monitoring their own workload (or capacity to perform) and making the appropriate choice to invoke or remove higher automation levels.

Existing data remain ambiguous as to where the choice should lie. One relevant issue is the accuracy of the human's own assessment of his or her capability to perform. To the extent that humans tend to be overconfident in this ability (Svenson, 1981; see Chapter 8), particularly in relation to machine performance at equivalent tasks (Liu, Fuld, & Wickens, 1993), some caution should be exercised concerning the wisdom of human choice. Reinforcing this preference for machine over human choice is the results of the adaptive aiding study by Kaber and Riley (1999). Using secondary task performance to implement adaptive aiding on a video game task, Kaber and Riley compared two strategies: A *mandating* strategy directly implemented the aiding when it was assumed, by automation, to be desirable, whereas an *advising* strategy only provided the corresponding suggestion. The authors observed a cost for the less automated advising strategy, a cost that they attributed to the added workload demands when the operator must monitor own performance and then decide whether or not automation is required. In the design of the GCAS solution for terrain collision avoidance, designers considered but rejected an advising solution which allowed the pilot to override the system, because their simulations revealed that the added time to do so would cause the maneuver to be too late (Scott, 1999).

To these formal, data-driven arguments for assigning computer authority as task manager can be added consideration of some compelling hypothetical scenarios. For example, most people would probably agree that automation should be responsible for adapting automated steering and slowing (along with alerting) should a *reliable* inference be drawn that the driver has fallen asleep or is otherwise incapacitated. The key factor here is reliability, and it would seem that the less reliable the inference, the lower level that the automation decision should be, on the stage 2 scale of Figure 13.13 in any adaptive automation. By adapting mid levels of this scale, the designer is thus endorsing a collaborative and cooperative human-machine concept; one well within the spirit of human-centered automation.

Conclusion The concept of adaptive automation is a conceptually attractive approach to human-machine system design, capitalizing on the strengths of human and machine in a dynamic and cooperative fashion. The concept certainly remains in the forefront of the thinking of designers of many highly automated complex systems (Scerbo & Mouloua, 1999; Hammer, 1999). Yet as we have discussed, a large number of issues must be addressed before viable systems can become effective or even feasible. Most important, these will depend on a continued and better understanding of the fundamentals of human attention, along with fascinating areas of human performance theory that have only recently received interest in the human factors domain—communication, cooperation, and trust.

SUMMARY

The discussion of process control and automation in this final chapter has alluded to every previous chapter in the book. This global characteristic emphasizes an important general point: The best design of the system must take into account human limitations and strengths, but these are not isolated components, as the somewhat arbitrary division of chapters might suggest. The human brain is complex. Perception, memory, attention, and action all interact. A well-designed system must consider the way in which these processes interrelate, as well as their limitations. A system that is so designed will never eliminate the possibility of human error, but it can at least remove the system designer as a contributing factor, and that will be a major step.

REFERENCES

Attwood, D. D. (1970). The interaction between human and automatic control. In F. Bolam (Ed.), *Paper making systems and their control*. London: British Paper and Board Makers Association.

Bailey, R. W. (1989). *Human performance engineering* (2d ed.). Englewood Cliffs, NJ: Prentice Hall.

Bainbridge, L. (1974). Analysis of verbal protocols from a process-control task. In E. Edwards & F. P. Lees (Eds.), *The human operator in process control*. London: Taylor & Francis.

Bainbridge, L. (1983). Ironies of automation. *Automatica, 19*(6), 775–779.

Beishon, R. J. (1966). *A study of some aspects of laboratory and industrial tasks*. Unpublished D.Phil. thesis, University of Oxford, Oxford, Eng.

Beishon, R. J. (1969). An analysis and simulation of an operator's behavior in controlling continuous baking ovens. In F. Bressen & M. deMontmollen (Eds.), *The simulation of human behavior*. Paris: Durod.

Benel, D. C. R., McCafferty, D. B., Neal, V., & Mallory, K. M. (1981). Issues in the design of annunciator systems. In R. C. Sugarman (Ed.), *Proceedings of the 25th annual meeting of the Human Factors Society*. Santa Monica, CA: Human Factors Society.

Beringer, D. & Harris, H. C. (1999). Automation in general aviation: *International Journal of Aviation Psychology, 9,* 155–174.

Billings, C. (1996). *Toward a human centered approach to automation*. Englewood Cliffs, NJ: Erlbaum.

Brigham, F. R., & Liaos, L. (1975). Operator performance in the control of a laboratory process plant. *Ergonomics, 29,* 181–201.

Casner, S. (1995). A personal laptop CBT for the 737–300 autoflight system. In R. Jensen & L. Rakavan (Eds.), *Proceedings of the 8th International Symposium on Aviation Psychology*. Columbus: Ohio State University, Department of Aviation.

Cook, R. (1996). Adapting new technology in the operating room. *Human Factors, 38,* 593–613.

Conejo, R., & Wickens, C. D. (1997). *The effects of highlighting validity and feature type on air-to-ground target acquisition performance* (Technical Report ARL–97–11/NAWC-ONR–97–1). Savoy: University of Illinois, Institute of Aviation, Aviation Research Lab.

Crocoll, W. M., & Coury, B. G. (1990). Status or recommendation: Selecting the type of information for decision aiding. *Proceedings of the 34th annual meeting of the Human Factors Society* (pp. 1524–1528). Santa Monica, CA: Human Factors.

Crossman, E. R. F. W., & Cooke, J. E. (1962). *Manual control of slow response systems*. Paper presented at the International Congress on Human Factors in Electronics, Long Beach, CA.

Dagani, A., Shafto, M., & Kirlick, A. (1999). Modes in human-machine interaction. *International Journal of Aviation Psychology, 9,* 155–174.

De Keyser, V. (1988). How can computer-based visual displays aid operators? In E. Hollnagel, G. Mancini, & D. D. Woods (Eds.), *Cognitive engineering in complex dynamic worlds* (pp. 15–22). London: Academic Press.

Funk, K., Lyall, B., Wilson, J., Vint, R., Niemczyk, M., Suroteguh, C., & Owen, G. (1999). Flight Deck Automation Issues. *International Journal of Aviation Psychology, 9,* 109–124.

Eddy, D. M. (1982). Probabilistic reasoning in clinical medicine: Problems and opportunities. In D. Kahneman, P. Slovic, & A. Tversky (Eds.), *Judgment under uncertainty: Heuristics and biases*. New York: Cambridge University Press.

Electrical Power Research Institute (1977, March). *Human factors review of nuclear plant design* (Project 501, NP–309-SY). Sunnyvale, CA: Lockheed Missiles and Space Co.

Endsley, M. R., & Kiris, E. O. (1995). The out-of-the-loop performance problem and level of control in automation. *Human Factors, 37(2),* 381–394.

Gaba, D. M., Howard, S. K., & Small, S. D. (1995). Situation awareness in anesthesiology. *Human Factors, 37,* 20–31.

Goodstein, L. P. (1981). Discriminative display support for process operators. In J. Rasmussen & W. B. Rouse (Eds.), *Human detection and diagnosis of system failures*. New York: Plenum.

Goodstein, L. P., & Rasmussen, J. (1988). Representation of process state, structure, and control. *Le Travail Humain, 51*, 19–37.

Grimm, R. (1976). Autonomous I/O-colour-screen-system for process-control with virtual keyboards adapted to the actual task. In T. B. Sheridan & G. Johannsen (Eds.), *Monitoring behavior and supervisory control*. New York: Plenum.

Hancock, P. A., & Chignell, M. H. (Eds.). (1989). *Intelligent interfaces: Theory, research and design*. North Holland: Elsevier Science Publishers.

Hilburn, B., Jorna, P. G. A. M., Byrne, E. A., & Parasuraman, R. (1997). The effects of adaptive air traffic control (ATC) decision aiding on controller mental workload. In M. Mouloua & J. Koonce (Eds.), *Human-automation interaction: Research and practice* (pp. 84–91). Mahwah, NJ: Erlbaum.

Hollnagel, E., Mancini, G., & Woods, D. D. (Eds.). (1988). *Cognitive engineering in complex dynamic worlds*. London: Academic Press.

Hopkin, D. V. (1994). Human performance implications of air traffic control automation. In M. Mouloua & R. Parasuraman (Eds.), *Proceedings of the First Automation Technology and Human Performance Conference: Human performance in automated systems: Current research and trends*. (pp. 314–319). Hillsdale, NJ: Erlbaum.

Hopkins, C. D., Snyder, H., Price, H. E., Hornick, R., Mackie, R., Smillie, R., & Sugarman, R. C. (1982). *Critical human factor issues in nuclear power regulation and a recommended comprehensive human factors long-range plan* (vols. 1–3, NUREG/CR–2833). Washington, DC: U.S. Nuclear Regulatory Commission.

Humphrey, D., & Kramer, A. (1994). Towards a psychophysiological assessment of dynamic changes in mental workload. *Human Factors, 36*, 3–26.

Inagaki, T. (1999). Situation-adaptive autonomy: Trading control of authority in human-machine systems. In M. W. Scerbo & M. Mouloua (Eds.), *Automation technology and human performance: Current research and trends* (pp. 154–159). Mahwah, NJ: Erlbaum.

Irving, S., Polson, P., & Irving, J. E. (1994). A GOMS analysis of the advanced automated cockpit. *Proceedings of CHI*. New York: Association of Computing Machinery.

Ivergard, T. (1989). *Handbook of control room design and ergonomics*. London: Taylor & Francis.

Kaber, D. B., Onal, E., & Endsley, M. R. (1999). Level of automation effects on telerobot performance and human operator situation awareness and subjective workload. In M. W. Scerbo & M. Mouloua (Eds.), *Automation technology and human performance: Current research and trends* (pp. 165–170). Mahwah, NJ: Erlbaum.

Kaber, D. B., & Riley, J. M. (1999). Adaptive automation of a dynamic control task based on workload assessment through a secondary monitoring task. In M. W. Scerbo & M. Mouloua (Eds.), *Automation technology and human performance: Current research and trends* (pp. 129–133). Mahwah, NJ: Erlbaum.

Kerns, K. (1991). Data link communications between controllers and pilots. *International Journal of Aviation Psychology, 1*, 181–204.

Kerns, K., (1999). Human factors in air traffic control/flight deck integration. In D. J. Garland, J. A. Wise, & V. D. Hopkin (Eds.), *Handbook of Aviation Human Factors*. Mahway, NJ: Lawrence Erlbaum.

Kessel, C. J., & Wickens, C. D. (1982). The transfer of failure-detection skills between monitoring and controlling dynamic systems. *Human Factors, 24*, 49–60.

Klatzky, R. L., & Ayoub, M. M. (1995). Health care. In R. S. Nickerson (Ed.), *Emerging needs and opportunities for human factors research.* (pp. 131–157). Washington, DC: National Academy Press.

Kragt, H., & Landeweerd, J. A. (1974). Mental skills in process control. In E. Edwards & F. P. Lees (Eds.), *The human operator in process control.* London: Taylor & Francis.

Kramer, A. F., & Weber, T. (1999). Application of psychophysiology to human factors. In J. Cacioppo, L. Tassinary & G. Bertson (Eds.), *Handbook of psychophysiology.* New York: Cambridge University Press.

Landauer, T. (1995). *The trouble with computers.* Cambridge, MA: MIT Press.

Landeweerd, J. A. (1979). Internal representation of a process fault diagnosis and fault correction. *Ergonomics, 22*, 1343–1351.

Landeweerd, J. A., Seegers, J. J., & Praageman, J. (1981). Effects of instruction, visual imagery, and educational background on process control performance. *Ergonomics, 24*, 133–141.

Lee, J. D., & Moray, N. (1994). Trust, self-confidence, and operators' adaptation to automation. *International Journal of Human-Computer Studies, 40*, 153–184.

Liaos, L. (1978). Predictive aids for discrete decision tasks with input uncertainty. *IEEE Transactions on Systems, Man, and Cybernetics, SMC–8*(1), 19–29.

Liu, Y., Fuld, R., & Wickens, C. D. (1993). Monitoring behavior in manual and automated scheduling systems. *International Journal of Man-Machine Studies, 39*, 1015–1029.

Madni, A. M. (1988). The role of human factors in expert systems design and acceptance. *Human Factors, 30*, 395–414.

Makeig, S., & Inlow, M. (1993). Lapses in alertness: coherence of fluctuations in performance and EEG spectrum. *Electroencephalography and Clinical Neurophysiology, 86*, 23–35.

McLeod, P. (1976). Control strategies of novice and experienced controllers with a slow response system (a zero-energy nuclear reactor). In T. B. Sheridan & G. Johannsen (Eds.), *Monitoring behavior and supervisory control.* New York: Plenum.

Moray, N. (1981). The role of attention in the detection of errors and the diagnosis of errors in man-machine systems. In J. Rasmussen & W. Rouse (Eds.), *Human detection and diagnosis of system failures.* New York: Plenum.

Moray, N. (1997). Human factors in process control. In G. Salvendy (Ed.), *Handbook of ergonomics and human factors* (pp. 1944–1971). New York: Wiley.

Moray, N. P., & Huey, B. M. (Eds.). (1988). *Human factors research and nuclear safety.* Washington, DC: National Academy Press.

Moray, N., Lootsteen, P., & Pajak, J. (1986). Acquisition of process control skills. *IEEE Transactions on Systems, Man, and Cybernetics, SMC–16*, 497–504.

Moray, N., & Rotenberg, I. (1989). Fault management in process control: Eye movements and action. *Ergonomics, 32*(11), 1319–1342.

Mosier, K. L., Skitka, L., Heers, S., & Burdick, M. (1998). Automation bias: Decision making and performance in high-tech cockpits. *International Journal of Aviation Psychology, 8*, 47–63.

Norman, D. A. (1988). *The psychology of everyday things.* New York: Basic Books.

Osborne, P. D., Barsam, H. F., & Burgy, D. C. (1981). Human factors considerations for implementation of a "green board" concept in an existing "red/green" power plant control room. In R. C. Sugarman (Ed.), *Proceedings of the 25th annual meeting of the Human Factors Society*. Santa Monica, CA: Human Factors Society.

Palmer, E., & Degani, A. (1991). Electronic checklists: Evaluation of two levels of automation. In R. Jensen (Ed.), *Proceedings of the 6th International Symposium on Aviation Psychology*. Columbus: Ohio State University Department of Aviation.

Parasuraman, R., & Hancock, P. A. (1999). Using signal detection theory and Bayesian analysis to design parameters for automated warning systems. In M. W. Scerbo & M. Mouloua (Eds.), *Automation technology and human performance: Current research and trends* (pp. 63–67). Mahwah, NJ: Erlbaum.

Parasuraman, R. M., Molloy, R., & Singh, I. L. (1993). Performance consequences of automation induced "complacency." *International Journal of Aviation Psychology, 3*, 1–23.

Parasuraman, R., Mouloua, M., & Hilburn, B. (1999). Adaptive aiding and adaptive task allocation enhance human-machine interaction. In M. W. Scerbo & M. Mouloua (Eds.), *Automation technology and human performance: Current research and trends* (pp. 119–123). Mahwah, NJ: Erlbaum.

Parasuraman, R., & Riley, V. (1997). Humans and automation: Use, misuse, disuse, abuse. *Human Factors, 39*(2), 230–253.

Patrick, J., Haines, B., Munley, G., & Wallace, A. (1989). Transfer of fault-finding between simulated chemical plants. *Human Factors, 31*, 503–518.

Queinnec, Y., DeTerssac, G., & Thon, P. (1981). Field study of the activities of process controllers. In H. G. Stassen (Ed.), *First European Annual Conference on Human Decision Making and Manual Control*. New York: Plenum.

Rasmussen, J. (1983). Skills, rules, and knowledge: Signals, signs and symbols, and other distinctions in human performance models. *IEEE Transactions on Systems, Man, and Cybernetics, SMC–13*, 257–266.

Rasmussen, J. (1986). *Information processing and human-machine interaction: An approach to cognitive engineering*. New York: North Holland.

Rasmussen, J., Pjetersoen, A., & Goodstein, L. (1995). *Cognitive engineering concepts and applications*. New York: Wiley.

Reason, J. (1990). *Human error*. Cambridge University Press.

Reason, J. (1997). *Managing the risks of organizational accidents*. Brookfield, VT: Ashgate.

Reising, D. V. & Sanderson, P. (1998). Designing displays under ecological interface design. In *Proceedings 42nd annual meeting of the Human Factors Society*. Santa Monica, CA: Human Factors.

Roscoe, S. N. (1968). Airborne displays for flight and navigation. *Human Factors, 10*, 321–332.

Roth, E. M., & Woods, D. D. (1988). Aiding human performance: I. Cognitive analysis. *Le Travail Humain, 51*, 39–64.

Rouse, W. B., & Morris, N. M. (1986). Understanding and enhancing user acceptance of computer technology. *IEEE Transactions on Systems, Man, and Cybernetics, SMC–16*, 539–549.

Sanders, M. S., & McCormick, E. J. (1993). *Human factors in engineering and design*. (7th ed.). New York: McGraw Hill.

Sarter, N., & Woods, D. D. (1995). How in the world did we ever get into that mode? Mode error and awareness in supervisory control. *Human Factors, 37*, 5–19.

Sarter, N., & Woods, D. D. (1997). Teamplay with a powerful and independent agent: A corpus of operational experiences and automation surprises on the Airbus A–320. *Human Factors, 39*, 553–569.

Scerbo, M. (1996). Theoretical perspectives on adaptive automation. In R. Parasuraman & M. Mouloua (Eds.), *Automation and human performance: Theory and applications*. Mahwah, NJ: Erlbaum.

Scerbo, M., & Mouloua, M. (1999). Automation technology and human performance. Mahwah, NJ: Erlbaum.

Scott, W. B. (1999). Automatic GCAS: You can't fly any lower. *Aviation Week and Space Technology*, February 1, 76–79.

Seminara, J. L., Pack, R. W., Seidenstein, S., & Eckert, S. K. (1980). Human factors engineering enhancement of nuclear power-plant control rooms. *Nuclear Safety, 21*(3), 351–363.

Sheridan, T. B. (1981). Understanding human error and aiding human diagnostic behavior in nuclear power plants. In J. Rasmussen & W. B. Rouse (Eds.), *Human detection and diagnosis of system failures*. New York: Plenum.

Sheridan, T. (1992). *Telerobotics: Automation and supervisory control*. Cambridge, MA: MIT Press.

Sheridan, T. (1997). Supervisory control. In G. Salvendy (Ed.), *Handbook of human factors and ergonomics*. New York: Wiley.

Slameca, N. J., & Graf, P. (1978). The generation effect: Delineation of a phenomenon. *Journal of Experimental Psychology: Human Learning and Memory, 4*, 592–604.

Sorkin, R. (1989). Why are people turning off our alarms? *Human Factors Bulletin, 32*, 3–4.

Sorkin, R. D., Kantowitz, B. H., & Kantowitz, S. C. (1988). Likelihood alarm displays. *Human Factors, 30*, 445–460.

Sorkin, R. D., & Woods, D. D. (1985). Systems with human monitors: A signal detection analysis. *Human-Computer Interaction, 1*, 49–75.

Stanton, N. (Ed.). (1994). *Human factors in alarm design*. London: Taylor & Francis.

Stokes, A. F., Wickens, C. D., & Kite, K. (1990). *Display technology: Human factors concepts*. Warrendale, PA: Society of Automotive Engineers.

Svenson, O. (1981). Are we less risky and more skillful than our fellow drivers? *Acta Psychologica, 47*, 143–148.

Thompson, D. A. (1981). Commercial aircrew detection of system failures: State of the art and future trends. In J. Rasmussen & W. B. Rouse (Eds.), *Human detection and diagnosis of system failures*. New York: Plenum.

Umbers, I. G. (1976). *A study of cognitive skills in complex systems*. Unpublished Ph.D. dissertation, University of Aston, Aston, England.

Vicente, K. J. (1999). *Cognitive Work Analysis*. Mahwah, NJ: Lawrence Erlbaum.

Vicente, K. J., Moray, N., Lee, J. D., Rasmussen, J., Jones, B. G., Brock, R., & Toufsk, D. (1996). Evaluation of a Rankine cycle display for nuclear power plant monitoring and diagnosis. *Human Factors, 38*, 506–522.

Vicente, K. J., & Rasmussen, J. (1990). The ecology of human-machine systems II: Mediating "direct perception" in complex work domains. *Ecological Psychology, 2*(3), 207–249.

Vicente, K., & Rasmussen, J. (1992). Ecological interface design: Theoretical foundations. *IEEE Transactions on Systems, Man, & Cybernetics, 22(4)*, 589–606.

West, B., & Clark, J. A. (1974). Operator interaction with a computer controlled distillation column. In E. Edwards & F. P. Lees (Eds.), *The human operator in process control*. London: Taylor & Francis.

Wickens, C. D. (1992). *Engineering psychology and human performance* (2d ed.). New York: HarperCollins.

Wickens, C. D. (1999) Automation in air traffic control: The human performance issues. In Scerbo, M. W. and Moulova, M. (Eds.), *Automated technology and human performance.* Mahwa, NJ: Lawrence Erlbaum Associates.

Wickens, C. D., & Carswell, C. M. (1995). The proximity compatibility principle: Its psychological foundation and relevance to display design. *Human Factors, 37*(3), 473–494.

Wickens, C. D., Gordon, S., & Liu, Y. (1998). *An introduction to human factors engineering.* New York: Addison Wesley Longman.

Wickens, C. D., & Kramer, A. (1985). Engineering psychology. *Annual Review of Psychology, 36,* 307–348.

Wickens, C. D., Mavor, M., & McGee, J. (1997). *Flight to the future: Human factors of air traffic control.* Washington, DC: National Academy of Science.

Wickens, C. D., Mavor, M., Parasuraman, R., & McGee, J. (1998). *The future of air traffic control.* Washington, DC: National Academy of Science.

Wiener, E. L., & Curry, R. E. (1980). Flight deck automation: Promises and problems. *Ergonomics, 23,* 995–1012.

Williams, A. R., Seidenstein, S., & Goddard, C. J. (1980). Human factors survey of electrical power control centers. In G. Corrick, E. Haseltine, & R. Durst (Eds.), *Proceedings of the 24th annual meeting of the Human Factors Society.* Santa Monica, CA: Human Factors Society.

Woods, D. D. (1984). Visual momentum: A concept to improve the coupling of person and computer. *International Journal of Man-Machine Studies, 21,* 229–244.

Woods, D. D. (1988). Commentary: Cognitive engineering in complex and dynamic worlds. In E. Hollnagel, G. Mancini, & D. D. Woods (Eds.), *Cognitive engineering in complex dynamic worlds* (pp. 115–129). London: Academic Press.

Woods, D. D., Johannesen, L. J., Cook, R. I., & Sarter, N. B. (1994). *Behind human error: Cognitive systems, computers, and hindsight* (State-of-the Art Report CSERIAC 94–01). Dayton, OH: Wright-Patterson AFB, CSERIAC Program Office.

Woods, D. D., O'Brien, J. F., & Hanes, L. F. (1987). Human factors challenges in process control: The case of nuclear power plants. In G. Salvendy (Ed.), *Handbook of human factors* (pp. 1724–1770). New York: Wiley.

Woods, D. D., & Roth, E. (1988). Aiding human performance: II. From cognitive analysis to support systems. *Le Travail Humain, 51,* 139–172.

Zach, S. E. (1980). Control room operating procedures: Content and format. In G. E. Corrick, E. C. Haseltine, & R. T. Durst, Jr. (Eds.), *Proceedings of the 24th annual meeting of the Human Factors Society.* Santa Monica, CA: Human Factors Society.

SUBJECT INDEX

A

Abbreviations 204–205
Absolute judgment 50–61
  applications of 52–53, 60–61
  multidimensional 53–61
  theory of 58–60
Abstraction hierarchy 528, 534–536
ACT-R 262–264
Additive factors 363–364
Aging 346, 364, 445
Air traffic control 250–251, 529, 534
Alarms 104,105, 107, 525, 526,
  530–532, 539, 543
Anthropometry 2, 520
Arousal
  and stress 481, 483, 488
  in vigilance 39–40
  in workload 465–466
Articulation Index 229–231
Artificial intelligence. See Expert systems
Attensors 105
Attention. See Divided attention;
  Directing attention; Single channel
  theory; Focused attention; Selective
  attention, Timesharing; Workload
Attention Skills. See Training, attention
Attentional cueing 83–86, 544
Attentional narrowing 74, 90,
  483–484, 486, 527
Attentional switching 107, 445–446
Auditory processing. See also Alarms,
  compatibility
  attention in 102–107, 450–451
  cocktail party effect 104
  dichotic listening task 102
  in instructions 220–221, 272
  of icons (earcons) 209
  in reaction time 339, 357–358
  of speech 226–231
  warnings 105, 107
Augmented reality 95, 173
Automatic processing (automaticity)
  of color 101, 102
  and errors 496
  in motor programs 391
  in reading 198–199, 203–204
  in timesharing 442, 444–445, 462
  in training 196, 276–277, 490

  in vigilance 41–42
  in visual search 80
  in working memory 246
Automation 538–550
  adaptive 451, 547–550
  in aviation, 215, 259–260, 541–542,
  544–545
  in decision support 260, 306, 329,
  330
  flexible automation 546
  intelligent agents 86
  and planning 260
  problems with 132, 409, 542–545
  in process control 513, 531
  purpose of 446, 539–540
  trust in 85–86, 215, 502, 543–546
Automobiles
  accidents in 143, 163
  automation in 250, 545
  control dynamics of 393–394,
  410–411
  head-up displays 90, 95
  memory in 271
  navigation in 166, 245
  traffic lights 340, 341
  timesharing in 245, 248, 445, 452,
  455, 456
  visual scanning in 76, 77, 268
Aviation
  accidents in 137, 163, 217, 224, 234,
  260, 262, 349, 446, 497
  automation in 215, 259–260, 507,
  540–541, 544–545, 548
  cockpit display of traffic information (CDTI) 106, 146, 148,
  249–250
  crew resource management 233–234
  communications in 233–234, 250
  controls. See also Aviation, flight dynamics; Tracking 269–270, 352,
  356, 496
  decision making 255, 485
  displays 90–91, 95, 99, 105–106,
  134–138, 146–149, 159–161, 215,
  249–250, 352, 407–409
  flight dynamics 404–405, 428
  perceptual biases in 143–144
  training and transfer 268, 445
  visual scanning 77, 85
  workload in 446, 481, 485

B

Bandwidth 50, 399
Behavior level (skill, rule, knowledge)
  335–336, 496, 518, 528
Binocular disparity 141–142, 149
Bode plot 420–425, 427–428
Bottleneck theory. See Single channel
  theory
Box plot 125
Brain waves 43, 364–365, 450, 549
Business applications 278, 323, 325,
  329

C

Cellular phones 452, 455
Checklists 217, 282, 497, 539
Chernobyl 503, 538
Chording 371–372
Chunking 205, 250–252, 256, 262,
  376–378
Code design 206–208
Cognitive appraisal 487–489
Cognitive load 221, 271–273, 276. See
  also Workload
Cognitive tunneling. See Attentional
  narrowing
Color coding 53, 100–102, 134–135,
  185, 531
Communications 231–233, 250, 537,
  545
Compatibility
  control 418–419
  display 89, 126, 132–136, 138–139,
  247–248, 416, 532–533, 546
  modality 357–358, 416
  population stereotypes 101–102,
  357, 531
  of proximity. See Proximity compatibility
  S-R 349–359, 365, 400, 410, 452, 453,
  520
Complacency 544
Computer-aided design 176
Computers. See Human-computer interaction
Confidence 27, 42, 282, 543. See also
  Overconfidence
Configural dimensions 58
Confirmation bias. See Decision making
Confusion 104, 131–132, 520

WRIGHT STATE
UNIVERSITY

For **Dr. Nagy**

Date **1/31/11**

Time **3:45 pm**

From **John Houston (formerly in San Diego)**

Phone _____

(646)	- 918-	6120
AREA CODE	NUMBER	EXTENSION

In NYC now — Called to say

"hello."

☐ Please call   ☐ Came to see you
☐ Will call later   ☐ Will come again
☐ Returned your call   ☐ Wants to see you

Signed _____

NAME INDEX